EDUCATIONAL PSYCHOLOGY
DEVELOPING LEARNERS

JEANNE ELLIS ORMROD
University of Northern Colorado (Emerita)

ERIC M. ANDERMAN
The Ohio State University

LYNLEY ANDERMAN
The Ohio State University

NINTH EDITION

PEARSON

Boston   Columbus   Indianapolis   New York   San Francisco
Amsterdam   Cape Town   Dubai   London   Madrid   Milan   Munich   Paris   Montreal   Toronto
Delhi   Mexico City   São Paulo   Sydney   Hong Kong   Seoul   Singapore   Taipei   Tokyo

Vice President and Editorial Director: *Jeffery W. Johnston*

Vice President and Publisher: *Kevin M. Davis*

Editorial Assistant: *Marisia Styles*

Executive Field Marketing Manager: *Krista Clark*

Senior Product Marketing Manager: *Christopher Barry*

Project Manager: *Pamela D. Bennett*

Program Manager: *Janelle Criner*

Operations Specialist: *Carol Melville*

Text Designer: *Cenveo Publisher Services*

Cover Design Director: *Diane Lorenzo*

Cover Art: *Monkey Business Images/Shutterstock*

Media Project Manager: *Lauren Carlson*

Full-Service Project Management: *Norine Strang, Cenveo Publisher Services*

Composition: *Cenveo Publisher Services*

Printer/Binder: *RR Donnelley/Harrisonburg South*

Cover Printer: *Phoenix Color/Hagerstown*

Text Font: *Garamond 3 LT Pro*

Library of Congress Cataloging-in-Publication Data is available upon request.

5   18

PEARSON

ISBN 10:   0-13-402243-2
ISBN 13: 978-0-13-402243-7

About the Authors

JEANNE ELLIS ORMROD received her A.B. in psychology from Brown University and her M.S. and Ph.D. in educational psychology from The Pennsylvania State University. She earned licensure in school psychology through postdoctoral work at Temple University and the University of Colorado at Boulder and has worked as a middle school geography teacher and school psychologist. She was Professor of Educational Psychology at the University of Northern Colorado until 1998, when she moved east to return to her native New England. She has published and presented extensively on cognition and memory, cognitive development, instruction, and related topics but is probably best known for this book and four others: *Human Learning* (currently in its seventh edition); *Essentials of Educational Psychology* (currently in its fourth edition); *Child Development and Education* (co-authored with Teresa McDevitt, currently in its sixth edition); and *Practical Research* (co-authored with Paul Leedy, currently in its eleventh edition). She has also published a non-textbook for a broad audience: *Our Minds, Our Memories: Enhancing Thinking and Learning at All Ages*. She and her husband Richard live in New Hampshire, where (she is happy to report) she is within a 90-minute drive of her three young grandchildren.

ERIC M. ANDERMAN received his B.S. in Psychology and Spanish from Tufts University, his Ed.M. from Harvard University, and his Ph.D. in Educational Psychology from The University of Michigan. He earned licensure as a social studies and foreign language teacher, and taught at the middle school and high school levels before attending graduate school. He is currently Professor of Educational Psychology and Chair of the Department of Educational Studies at The Ohio State University. He has published extensively on academic motivation, with emphases on (a) school transitions, (b) school effects on motivation, (c) motivation and risky behavior during adolescence, and (d) academic cheating. He is the editor of *Theory Into Practice*, and former associate editor of the *Journal of Educational Psychology*. He has co-edited several books, including the third edition of the *Handbook of Educational Psychology* (with Lyn Corno); the *International Guide to Student Achievement* (with John Hattie); *Psychology of Academic Cheating* (with Tamera Murdock); and *Psychology of Classroom Learning* (with Lynley Anderman). He also co-authored the book *Classroom Motivation* (currently in its second edition) with Lynley Anderman.

LYNLEY H. ANDERMAN received her B.A. and M.A. (Hons.) in Education from the University of Auckland, New Zealand, and her Ph.D. in Educational Psychology from The University of Michigan. A graduate of North Shore Teachers College (Auckland, New Zealand) she taught for several years in primary and intermediate schools in Auckland. Currently, she is Professor of Educational Psychology at The Ohio State University. She has published and presented extensively on academic motivation, particularly in relation to the roles of instructional and social-relational characteristics of classrooms that support students' motivation and engagement, and on the role of Educational Psychology in Teacher Education. She is the former editor of the *Journal of Experimental Education* and former associate editor of *Theory into Practice*. She has co-edited *Psychology of Classroom Learning* and co-authored the book *Classroom Motivation* with Eric Anderman.

Preface

New to this Edition

In this ninth edition of *Educational Psychology: Developing Learners,* I'm pleased to welcome my fellow educational psychologists Eric and Lynley Anderman as coauthors. More specifically, Eric and Lynley have overhauled Chapter 11 and also brought their perspectives to Chapters 4, 5, 10, and 13.

Many features that have made previous editions of the book so popular with instructors and students remain in this edition, including a conversational writing style, Experiencing Firsthand features, organizational tables and diagrams, and an ongoing emphasis on classroom applications. Yet there are also significant changes. As always, all 15 chapters have been updated to reflect recent advances in research, theory, and classroom practices. Perhaps even more importantly, the greatly enhanced etext format has enabled us to make the book a truly interactive one in which—with quick clicks on hotlinks within each chapter—readers can regularly apply what they're learning to actual and hypothetical classroom scenarios and problems. Interactive features include Self-Check Quizzes, Application Exercises, and case study analyses in the Licensure Exam activities; all of these features ask readers to respond to either open-ended or multiple-choice questions, and then give readers immediate feedback about their responses. Such features, along with many hotlinked Video Examples and Video Explanations—the latter of which target concepts and principles that students in educational psychology classes sometimes struggle to understand and apply—make the book a truly multimedia learning experience.

More specific additions and changes to this edition include the following:

- **Chapter 1**: New heading to give greater visibility to mixed-methods research; new discussion of *principles* (in addition to *theories*) in the section "From Research to Practice."
- **Chapter 2**: Expanded discussion of Bronfenbrenner's bioecological systems theory, with a new Figure 2.1 depicting the various layers of environmental influence proposed by Bronfenbrenner; updated discussion of physical development (in a hotlinked Content Extension feature); hotlinked Video Explanation showing various basic brain structures and their key roles; two hotlinked Video Explanations illustrating certain concepts in Vygotsky's theory (e.g., *cognitive tools, zone of proximal development*).
- **Chapter 3**: Addition of a fourth important role of peers in children's development (i.e., to teach new skills, such as computer programming or skateboarding techniques); replacement of the term *peer pressure* with the broader term *peer contagion,* in line with current thinking about the nature of peer influences; expanded discussion of popularity and social isolation; broadened discussion of diversity in moral development to include six different dimensions that moral reasoning and behavior might encompass.
- **Chapter 4**: Expanded discussion of distinctions between ethnic and racial groups; expanded discussions of students who speak languages other than English at home and of cultural differences in conceptions of time; discussion of increasing expectations for students to use technology at home and the challenges that such expectations impose on children in low-income families; expanded discussion of possible strategies for assisting homeless students.
- **Chapter 5**: New Experiencing Firsthand exercise related to fluid versus crystallized intelligence; updated critical examination of different theoretical conceptions of intelligence and measurement of intelligence; discussion of noncognitive contributors to intelligence; expanded discussions of how certain widely advocated strategies have little or no research support and thus are questionable practices at best (see the sections "Do Students Have Distinct Learning Styles?" and "Does It Make Sense to Teach to Students' 'Right Brains' or 'Left Brains'?"); expanded discussion of advantages versus drawbacks of inclusion as a general approach to working with students who have special educational needs.

- **Chapter 6:** Two hotlinked Video Explanations regarding the nature of human memory; addition of *executive function* as a key term (because this term has increasingly been appearing in practitioner-oriented literature); new discussion of the brain's need for some mental downtime during the school day; discussion of *reconsolidation* as a possible reason for forgetting or, more accurately, misremembering.

- **Chapter 7:** New discussion of self-reflection as a strategy for enhancing metacognitive awareness; new section "Metacognitive Strategies in the Digital Age"; expanded discussion of epistemic beliefs; expanded discussion of critical thinking.

- **Chapter 8:** Revision of the discussion of *situated learning* and *situation cognition* to encompass two somewhat different meanings that various theorists have ascribed to these terms; greater visibility given to Vygotsky's and Bronfenbrenner's theories as foundations for the contextual perspectives described in the chapter (with a new hotlinked Video Explanation regarding Vygotsky's theory); new example of culturally relevant practice in teaching math; greater attention to how literacy and various content domains are interdependent, especially as reflected in a new hotlinked Application Exercise.

- **Chapter 9:** Five hotlinked Video Explanations that explain and illustrate certain behaviorist ideas and applications (e.g., negative reinforcement versus punishment, use of functional analysis to address chronic behavior problems); content of the previous edition's section "Strengths and Potential Limitations of Behaviorist Approaches" now integrated into the section "Strategies for Encouraging Productive Behaviors"; revision of section on classical conditioning to encompass the idea that the association between the unconditioned stimulus (UCS) and unconditioned response (UCR) might have been acquired at an earlier time (a footnote introduces the concept of *higher-order conditioning* for readers who might want to pursue this idea further); revision of discussion of *time-out* to be more in line with current practices; new bullet on using technology to reinforce desirable behaviors and achievements.

- **Chapter 10:** Expanded discussion of teacher efficacy; addition of *proximal goal* as a key term in this chapter, with discussion of the benefits of setting proximal goals, within the contexts of self-efficacy and self-regulation; new table comparing various self-related concepts.

- **Chapter 11:** Reorganization of sections, with distinctions among different perspectives on the roles of "needs" in motivation; discussion of self-determination theory as both a cognitively and needs-based theory of motivation; addition of the distinction between *mastery-approach goals* and *mastery-avoidance goals;* new section on *mindsets;* new concluding section on motivating students in any environment.

- **Chapter 12:** Revision of opening case study to incorporate uses of digital technology and the Internet; more extensive coverage of Common Core, with an effort to address some common misconceptions (and help alleviate widespread concerns) about these standards; addition of Next Generation Science Standards to the discussion of standards; new Figure 12.3 to illustrate how content-area standards can be integrated into a backward-design approach to instructional planning; new hotlinked Application Exercises in which readers apply what they have learned about Common Core and backward design; new discussion of *My Science Tutor* (including two screenshots) as an example of an instructional website in which students interact with a virtual tutor via spoken language; expanded discussion of discovery and inquiry activities.

- **Chapter 13:** Expanded discussion of planning activities that keep students on task as a means of preventing misbehavior; updated use of terminology in discussions of schoolwide positive behavioral supports and interventions; inclusion of additional strategies for communicating with parents; expanded discussion of dealing with misbehaviors; modification of the previous edition's discussion of gang-related problems.

- **Chapter 14:** Two new hotlinked Video Explanations regarding formative versus summative assessments and rubric design; new rubric in the text that better illustrates good rubric design (Figure 14.5); discussion of backward design as an essential tool in planning assessments (with Figure 12.3 being repeated as Figure 14.6); integration of discussions of digital technologies (which were previously in a separate section near the end of the chapter) into discussions of formative assessment and formal paper–pencil assessments; new discussion of how students might cheat via digital technologies.

- **Chapter 15:** Expansion of section on criterion-referenced scores, with a new discussion of problems associated with combining multiple criterion-referenced scores (e.g., obtained with a rubric) into a single overall score; expanded discussion of the pros and cons of value-added assessment as a means of evaluating teacher effectiveness.

General Rationale for the Book

As teachers, we play critical roles in the lives of children and adolescents. Some of us help them learn to read and write. Some of us help them understand their physical and social worlds through explorations of science, mathematics, geography, history, or literature. Some of us help them express themselves through physical movement, the visual arts, or music. And some of us teach them specific skills they will need as adult professionals in, say, auto mechanics, cooking, or computer technology. But regardless of the subject matter we teach, we help those in the generations that follow us to become knowledgeable, self-confident, and productive citizens.

In my mind, teaching is the most rewarding profession we could possibly choose. Yet it's often a challenging profession as well. Students don't always come to us ready or eager to learn classroom subject matter. How can we help them develop the knowledge and skills they need to become productive adults? What strategies can we use to motivate them? What tasks and instructional materials are appropriate for students at different developmental levels? Over the years, researchers and practitioners have worked together to answer such questions. Collectively, we're in the fortunate position of being able to benefit from the many insights that such experts offer.

I've been teaching educational psychology since 1974, and I've loved every minute of it. How children and adolescents learn and think, how they change as they grow and develop, why they do the things they do, how they're often very different from one another—our understandings of all of these things have innumerable implications for classroom practice and, ultimately, for the lives of young people.

In this and the previous eight editions, I've written this textbook in much the same way that I've taught my college classes. Because I want the field of educational psychology to captivate you the way it has captivated me, I've tried to make the book interesting, meaningful, and thought-provoking as well as informative. I have a definite philosophy about how future teachers can best learn and apply educational psychology, and this philosophy has guided me as I've written every edition. In particular, I believe that human learners of all ages actively *construct* their own understandings of what they read in textbooks—an idea reflected in the puzzle-piece motif you'll see throughout the book.

Helping Our Readers Learn and Apply Educational Psychology

You can gain much more from your study of educational psychology when you:

- Focus on core concepts and principles of the discipline
- See these principles in action in your own learning and behavior
- Use the principles to understand the learning and behavior of children and adolescents
- Consistently apply the principles to classroom practice

You'll find numerous features throughout the book to help you do all of these things. We authors hope you'll learn a great deal from what educational psychology has to offer, not only about the students you may be teaching but also about yourself.

FOCUSING ON CORE CONCEPTS AND PRINCIPLES

Rather than superficially explore every aspect of educational psychology, this book zeroes in on fundamental concepts and principles that have broad applicability to classroom practice. Throughout the book, core concepts appear in boldfaced blue font. Core principles are clearly identified in sections labeled "Basic Principles" or "Basic Assumptions" and then often summarized in *Principles/Assumptions* tables. Each table includes educational implications and concrete examples. See the following pages for some examples: 22, 175, and 250.

SEEING CONCEPTS AND PRINCIPLES IN ACTION IN YOUR OWN LEARNING

A central goal of this book has always been to help our readers discover more about themselves as thinkers and learners. Thus we include *Experiencing Firsthand* exercises throughout the book—exercises that illustrate such diverse concepts as constructive processes, working memory, sense of self, social cognition, ethnic stereotyping, and confidentiality in assessment. All of these exercises are designed to do exactly what their name implies: help our readers observe principles of educational psychology *in themselves.* See the following pages for some examples: 112, 174, and 179.

UNDERSTANDING CHILDREN'S AND ADOLESCENTS' LEARNING AND BEHAVIOR

Throughout the book we continually urge our readers to look closely at and try to make sense of what children and adolescents do and say. Each chapter begins with a *Case Study* that situates chapter content in a real-life scenario; for instance, see page 171. We also make frequent use of *real artifacts* from children's journals and school assignments to illustrate concepts and principles in action. For examples, see pages 34, 183, and 336.

EXAMINING DEVELOPMENTAL TRENDS

Unique to this book is a focus on children's and adolescents' development in every chapter. For example, Chapters 2 through 4 and 6 through 15 all have one or more *Developmental Trends* tables that summarize age-typical characteristics at four grade levels (K–2, 3–5, 6–8, and 9–12), present concrete examples, and offer suggested classroom strategies for each level. You can find three of these tables on pages 190, 269, and 471.

APPLYING CORE IDEAS OF EDUCATIONAL PSYCHOLOGY TO CLASSROOM PRACTICE

Throughout this text, psychological concepts and principles are consistently applied to classroom practice. We also provide *Into the Classroom* and *Creating a Productive Classroom Environment* boxes that suggest and illustrate strategies related to particular areas of concern for teachers. You can find three such features on pages 111, 222, and 396.

This book is consistently praised for its emphasis on application. Throughout the book we identify suggested strategies—within the text, in tables, and in the margins—with apple icons; for instance, see pages 27 and 30.

HELPING YOU PREPARE FOR LICENSURE

All chapters end with *Practice for Your Licensure Exam* exercises. These exercises provide readers with opportunities to use the content they've learned in a particular chapter to answer multiple-choice and constructed-response questions similar to those that appear on many teacher licensure tests. Three of these exercises are on pages 93, 168, and 321.

New Digital Features in the Pearson Etext with MyEducationLab®

The most visible change in the ninth edition (and certainly one of the most significant changes) is the expansion of the digital learning and assessment resources embedded in the etext. Designed to bring you more directly into the world of K–12 classrooms and to help you see the very real impact that educational psychology concepts and principles have on learning and development, these digital learning and assessment resources also

- Provide you with practice using educational psychology concepts in teaching situations;
- Help you and your instructor see how well you understand the concepts presented in the book and the media resources; and
- Help you think about, and process more deeply, educational psychology and how to use it both as a teacher and as a learner.

The online resources in the Pearson Etext with MyEducationLab include:

Video Examples   Several times per chapter, an embedded video provides an illustration of an educational psychology principle or concept in action. These video examples most often show students and teachers working in classrooms. Sometime they show students or teachers describing their thinking or experiences. See pages 23 and 35 for examples.

Video Explanations   Throughout the text, I (Jeanne Ormrod) have provided video explanations of essential concepts. Excerpted from my series of longer educational psychology modules, these brief lectures include animated slides and worked examples. See pages 176 and 299 for examples.

Self-Checks   Throughout the chapters you will find MyEducationLab: Self-check quizzes. There are three to six of these quizzes in each chapter at the ends of major text sections. They are meant to help you assess how well you have mastered the learning outcome addressed in the section you just read. These self-checks are made up of self-grading multiple-choice items that not only provide feedback on whether questions are answered correctly or incorrectly, but also provide rationales for both correct and incorrect answers. See pages 256 and 284 for examples.

Application Exercises   Also at the ends of major sections and tied to specific chapter learning outcomes, these scaffolded analysis exercises challenge you to use chapter content to reflect on teaching and learning in real classrooms. The questions you answer in these exercises are usually open-ended, constructed-response questions. Once you provide your own answers to the questions, you receive feedback in the form of model answers written by experts. See pages 181 and 474 for examples.

Ancillary Materials

The following resources are available for instructors to download on www.pearsonhighered.com/educators. Instructors can enter the author or title of this book, select this particular edition of the book, and then click on the "Resources" tab to log in and download textbook supplements.

INSTRUCTOR'S RESOURCE MANUAL (ISBN 0-13-402394-3)

An Instructor's Resource Manual includes suggestions for learning activities, additional Experiencing Firsthand exercises, supplementary lectures, case study analyses, discussion topics, group activities, and additional media resources.

POWERPOINT® SLIDES (ISBN 0-13-402393-5)

The PowerPoint slides include key concept summarizations, diagrams, and other graphic aids to enhance learning. They are designed to help students understand, organize, and remember core concepts and theories.

TEST BANK (ISBN 0-13-402239-4)

I (Jeanne Ormrod) have personally written many of the test questions in the Test Bank that accompanies the book; Test Bank coauthors have added new ones to reflect the updates to the eighth and ninth editions. Some items (lower-level questions) simply ask students to identify or explain concepts and principles they have learned. But many others (higher-level questions) ask students to apply those same concepts and principles to specific classroom situations—that is, to actual student behaviors and teaching strategies. Ultimately it is these higher-level questions that assess students' ability to use principles of educational psychology in their own teaching practice.

TESTGEN (ISBN 0-13-402240-8)

TestGen is a powerful test generator that you install on your computer and use in conjunction with the TestGen test bank file for your text. Assessments, including equations, graphs, and scientific notation, may be created for both print and online testing.

TestGen is available exclusively from Pearson Education publishers. You install TestGen on your personal computer (Windows or Macintosh) and create your own tests for classroom testing and for other specialized delivery options, such as over a local area network or on the web. A test bank, which is also called a Test Item File (TIF), typically contains a large set of test items, organized by chapter and ready for your use in creating a test, based on the associated textbook material.

The tests can be downloaded in the following formats:

TestGen Test bank file—MAC

TestGen Test bank file—PC

Angel TestGen Conversion

Test Bank for Blackboard Learning System

Desire to Learn TestGen Conversion

Moodle TestGen Conversion

Sakai TestGen Conversion

Test Bank for Blackboard CE/Vista

CASE STUDIES: APPLYING EDUCATIONAL PSYCHOLOGY (2ND ED.)

Many instructors use Ormrod and McGuire's *Case Studies* book (0-13-198046-7) as a supplement to this book. It includes 48 real cases involving students and classrooms ranging from preschool to high school. It illustrates concepts and principles in many areas of educational psychology, including child and adolescent development, learning and cognition, motivation, classroom management, instructional practices, and assessment.

ARTIFACT CASE STUDIES: INTERPRETING CHILDREN'S WORK AND TEACHERS' CLASSROOM STRATEGIES

Another possible supplement to the book is Ormrod's *Artifact Case Studies* book (0-13-114671-8). The artifact cases in this supplement offer work samples and instructional materials that cover a broad range of topics, including literacy, mathematics, science, social studies, and art. Every artifact case includes background information and questions to consider as readers examine the artifact. Instructors should contact their local Pearson sales representative to order a copy of this book.

Acknowledgments

I've been fortunate to have had a great deal of help in writing the many editions of this book. First and foremost, the book wouldn't be what it is today without long-term partnerships with my editor and publisher, Kevin Davis. Kevin first came on board as developmental editor for the book in 1989 and, except for a 2-year hiatus while he served in other roles at Pearson, has continued to guide the book through its multiple iterations, first only in paper and now in the ever-changing digital world. Although Kevin hasn't penned the words, his influence permeates every page of text and every hotlinked activity. His ideas, suggestions, and occasional gentle demands have consistently pushed and stretched me to new heights in my efforts to create the best possible pedagogical experience for readers.

My coauthors and I are also deeply indebted to developmental editor Gail Gottfried, who has kept all three of us on course, reminding us of our long-term targets and nudging us ever closer to those targets. Whereas authors can sometimes get lost in the nitpicky details of a monumental writing task such as this one, Gail has an amazing ability to direct our attention simultaneously to both the specific trees and the overall forest of which each one is a part. Especially with two new authors coming on board, Gail has gone way, way, *way* beyond the call of duty this time around. I hope that she is finally finding the time to sit back and relax with a big glass of wine as she celebrates the book's final arrival on the scene.

Three other critical players have been project managers Lauren Carlson, Pam Bennett, and Norine Strang, who have expertly organized and overseen the countless steps involved in transforming our word-processed manuscripts and rough sketches into the finished product you see before you. In this high-tech day and age, publishing a book is a very complicated process that I'm grateful they know how to complete. Many thanks, too, to Raye Lakey, who has created all of the Self-Check Quizzes and some of the new Application Exercises in MyEducationLab. In fact, she took charge of the overall media plan for Chapters 4, 5, 10, 11, and 13 and created all of the Application Exercises for those chapters.

In addition, numerous colleagues across the nation have strengthened the book itself by reviewing one or more of its previous versions. Reviewers for the first eight editions were Jane Abraham, Virginia Tech University; Joyce Alexander, Indiana University; Eric M. Anderman, then at University of Kentucky; Linda M. Anderson, Michigan State University; Margaret D. Anderson, SUNY–Cortland; Cindy Ballantyne, Northern Arizona University; J. C. Barton, Tennessee Technical University; Timothy A. Bender, Southwest Missouri State University; Angela Bloomquist, California University of Pennsylvania; Phyllis Blumenfeld, University of Michigan; Gregory Braswell, Illinois State University; Kathy Brown, University of Central Oklahoma; Randy L. Brown, University of Central Oklahoma; Stephen L. Benton, Kansas State University; Karen L. Block, University of Pittsburgh; Kathryn J. Biacindo, California State University–Fresno; Barbara Bishop, Eastern New Mexico University; Robert Braswell, Winthrop College; Kay S. Bull, Oklahoma State University; Margaret W. Cohen, University of Missouri–St. Louis; Theodore Coladarci, University of Maine; Sharon Cordell, Roane State Community College; Roberta Corrigan, University of Wisconsin–Milwaukee; Richard D. Craig, Towson State University; José Cruz, Jr., The Ohio State University; David Yun Dai, SUNY–University at Albany; Peggy Dettmer, Kansas State University; Joan Dixon, Gonzaga University; Leland K. Doebler, University of Montevallo; Kellah Edens, University of South Carolina; Catherine Emilhovich, SUNY–Buffalo; Joanne B. Engel, Oregon State University; Kathy Farber, Bowling Green State University; William R. Fisk, Clemson University; Victoria Fleming, Miami University of Ohio; M. Arthur Garmon, Western Michigan University; Roberta J. Garza, Pan American University–Brownsville; Mary Gauvain, University of California–Riverside; Sister Nancy Gilchriest, St. Joseph's College; Nathan Gonyea, SUNY–Oneonta; Cheryl Greenberg, University of North Carolina–Greensboro; Richard Hamilton, University of Houston; Jennifer Mistretta Hampston, Youngstown State University; Ken Hay, Indiana University; Arthur Hernandez, University of Texas–San Antonio; Lynley Hicks, University of Missouri-Kansas City; Heather Higgins, University of North Carolina—Greensboro; Frederick C. Howe, Buffalo State College; Peggy Hsieh, University of Texas–San Antonio; Dinah Jackson, University of Northern Colorado; Janina M. Jolley, Clarion University of Pennsylvania; Caroline Kaczala, Cleveland State University; CarolAnne M. Kardash, University of Missouri–Columbia; Pamela Kidder-Ashley, Appalachian State University; Kenneth Kiewra, University of Nebraska–Lincoln; Nancy F. Knapp, University of Georgia; Mary Lou Koran, University of Florida; Randy Lennon, University of Northern Colorado; Howard Lloyd, University of Kentucky; Susan C. Losh, Florida State University; Pamela Manners, Troy State University; Hermine H. Marshall, San Francisco State University; Teresa McDevitt, University of Northern Colorado; Sharon McNeely, Northeastern Illinois University; Michael Meloth, University of Colorado–Boulder; Kelly S. Mix, Michigan State University; Bruce P. Mortenson, Louisiana State University; Janet Moursund, University of Oregon; P. Karen Murphy, The Pennsylvania State University; Gary A. Negin, California State University; Joe Olmi, The University of Southern Mississippi; Helena Osana, Concordia University; James Persinger, Emporia State University; Judy Pierce, Western Kentucky University; James R. Pullen, Central Missouri State University; Gary F. Render, University of Wyoming; Robert S. Ristow, Western Illinois University; Jeff Sandoz, University of Louisiana—Lafayette; Rolando Santos, California State University—Los Angeles; Gregg Schraw, University of Nebraska–Lincoln; Dale H. Schunk, University of North Carolina—Greensboro; Mark Seng, University of Texas; Glenn E. Snelbecker, Temple University; Johnna Shapiro, University of California–Davis; Kenneth Springer, Southern Methodist University; Harry L. Steger, Boise State University; Bruce Torff, Hofstra University; Ann Turnbull, University of Kansas; Julianne C. Turner, University of Notre Dame; Tina Van Prooyen, Heartland Community College; Enedina Vazquez, New Mexico State University; Courtney Vorell, Minnesota School of Business; Alice A. Walker, SUNY–Cortland; Mary Wellman, Rhode Island College; Jane A. Wolfle, Bowling Green State University; Ya-Shu Yang, University of Nebraska–Lincoln; and Karen Zabrucky, Georgia State University.

Coming on board for the ninth edition were these reviewers, who offered helpful suggestions now reflected in the book: E. Namisi Chilungu, Georgia State University; Darlene DeMarie, University of South Florida; Beverly K. McIntyre, University of North Carolina–Charlotte; Joseph Pizzillo, Rowan University; Thomas R. Scheira, SUNY–Buffalo; and Julia Yoo, Lamar University.

Some of our own students and teacher interns—especially Jenny Bressler, Kathryn Broadhead, Ryan Francoeur, Gerry Holly, Michele Minichiello, Shelly Lamb, Kim Sandman, Melissa Tillman, Nick Valente, and Brian Zottoli—have at one time or another agreed to let us use their interviews, essays, and experiences as examples. Teachers and administrators at schools both home and abroad (including two of my own children, now teachers themselves) have allowed us to share their strategies with our readers; we thank Liz Birnam, Berneen Bratt, Tom Carroll, Barbara Dee, Jackie Filion, Tina Ormrod Fox, Sarah Gagnon, Dinah Jackson, Sheila Johnson, Don Lafferty, Gary MacDonald, Sharon McManus, Linda Mengers, Mark Nichols, Jeff Ormrod, Ann Reilly, and Gwen Ross. The Andermans are particularly grateful to two of their graduate students, Megan Sanders and Alyssa Emery, who assisted them with several administrative tasks in the preparation of their chapters.

Many young people, too, deserve thanks for letting us use their work. In particular, I want to acknowledge the contributions of the following present and former elementary and secondary school students: Andrew and Katie Belcher; Noah and Shea Davis; Zachary Derr; Amaryth, Andrew, and Anthony Gass; Ben and Darcy Geraud; Dana Gogolin; Colin Hedges; Erin Islo; Charlotte Jeppsen; Laura Linton; Michael McShane; Frederik Meissner; Alex, Jeff, and Tina Ormrod; Patrick Paddock; Isabelle Peters; Cooper Remignanti; Ian Rhoads; David and Laura Riordan; Corey and Trisha Ross; Ashton and Haley Russo; Alex and Connor Sheehan; Matt and Melinda Shump; Andrew Teplitz; Emma Thompson; Grace Tober; Grant Valentine; Caroline and Hannah Wilson; and Geoff Wuehrmann.

Last but certainly not least, the Andermans and I must thank our families, who have forgiven our countless hours spent either buried in our books and journals or else glued to our computers. Without their continuing understanding and support, this ninth edition would never have seen the light of day.

J. E. O.

Brief Contents

Contents

PART II

LEARNING AND MOTIVATION

10 Social Cognitive Views of Learning 322

11 Motivation and Affect 358

PART III

CLASSROOM STRATEGIES

12 Instructional Strategies 412

Moodboard Premium/Glow Images

1

Teaching and Educational Psychology

CASE STUDY: THE "NO D" POLICY

Anne Smith is a ninth-grade English teacher with 10 years of teaching experience, and by all accounts she is an excellent teacher. Even so, in previous years many of her students haven't invested much time or energy in their writing assignments and seemingly haven't been bothered by the Cs and Ds they've eventually earned in her classes. In an effort to more fully engage this year's students in their schoolwork, Ms. Smith begins fall semester by initiating two new policies. First, to pass her course, students must earn at least a C; she won't give anyone a final grade of D. Second, students will have multiple opportunities to revise and resubmit assignments; she'll give whatever feedback students need—and, if necessary, one-on-one instruction—to help them improve their work. She solicits students' questions and concerns about the new policies, gains their agreement to "try something new," and engages them in a discussion of specific, concrete characteristics of A-quality, B-quality, and C-quality work. Then, as the semester progresses, she regularly administers brief surveys to get students' feedback about her innovations, asking such questions as "How is the 'no D' working for you?" "Do you think your grade is an accurate reflection of your learning?" and "Any suggestions?"

Students' responses on the surveys are overwhelmingly positive. Students mention noticeable improvements in the quality of their writing and increasingly report that they believe themselves to be in control of both their learning and their grades. Furthermore, they begin to see their teacher in a new light—"as one who will help them achieve their best work, not as one who just gives out grades . . . as a coach encouraging them along the long race of learning." Final course grades also confirm the value of the new policies: A much higher percentage of students earn grades of C or better than has been true in past years. (Action research project described in A. K. Smith, 2009.)

- Effective teachers don't simply transmit new information and skills to students; they also work hard to help students *master* the information and skills. In the case study just presented, what various strategies does Ms. Smith use to foster her students' writing development?

Teaching other people—especially teaching the generation that will follow you into the adult world—can be one of the most rewarding professions on the planet. It can also be a very challenging profession. Certainly effective teaching involves presenting a topic or skill in such a way that students can understand and master it. Yet it involves many other things as well. For instance, teachers must motivate students to *want* to learn the subject matter, must help students recognize what true mastery involves, and—in order to appropriately individualize instruction—must assess each student's progress in his or her learning and development. And, in general, effective teachers create an environment in which students believe that if they work hard and have reasonable support, they can achieve at high levels. In the opening case study, Anne Smith does all of these things.

Mastering the multifaceted nature of teaching takes time and practice, of course. But it also takes knowledge about human learning and motivation, developmental trends, individual and group differences, and effective classroom practices. Such topics are the domain of educational psychology. This book will help you understand children and adolescents—how they learn and develop, how they're likely to be similar to but also different from one another, what topics and activities are apt to engage them in the classroom, and so on. It will also give you a toolbox of strategies for planning and carrying out instruction, creating an environment that keeps students motivated and on task, and assessing students' progress and achievement.

Teaching as Evidence-Based Practice

You yourself have been a student for many years now, and in the process you've undoubtedly learned a great deal about how children change over time and about how teachers can foster their learning and development. But exactly how much *do* you know? To help you find out, we authors offer a short pretest, Ormrod's Own Psychological Survey (OOPS).

EXPERIENCING FIRSTHAND
ORMROD'S OWN PSYCHOLOGICAL SURVEY (OOPS)

Decide whether each of the following statements is *true* or *false*.

True False   1. Some children are predominantly left-brain thinkers, whereas others are predominantly right-brain thinkers.

True False   2. Children's personalities are largely the results of their home environments.

True False   3. Instruction is most effective when it is tailored to students' individual learning styles.

True False   4. The best way to learn and remember a new fact is to repeat it over and over.

True False   5. Students often misjudge how much they know about a topic.

True False   6. Anxiety sometimes helps students learn and perform more successfully in the classroom.

True False   7. Playing video games can enhance children's cognitive development and school achievement.

True False   8. The ways in which teachers assess students' learning influence what and how students actually learn.

Following are the correct answers to each item, along with an explanation regarding *why* it is true or false.

The brain's structure, functioning, and development are discussed in Chapter 2 and in Applying Brain Research features throughout the book.

1. *Some children are predominantly left-brain thinkers, whereas others are predominantly right-brain thinkers.* FALSE. With the development of new medical technologies in recent years, researchers have learned a great deal about how the human brain works and which parts of it specialize in which aspects of human thinking. The two halves, or *hemispheres,* of the brain do seem to have somewhat different specialties, but they continually communicate and collaborate in tackling even the simplest of daily tasks. For all intents and purposes, there's no such thing as left-brain or right-brain thinking (Bressler, 2002; M. I. Posner & Rothbart, 2007).

2. *Children's personalities are largely the results of their home environments.* FALSE. Certainly children's home environments mold their behaviors to some extent, but so, too, can teachers and other people outside the family have some influence (e.g., Morelli & Rothbaum, 2007).

Furthermore, inherited characteristics have a significant impact on children's personalities. From day 1 infants are noticeably different in the extent to which they're calm or fussy, shy or outgoing, fearful or adventurous, and attentive or easily distractible. Such differences in *temperament* appear to have their roots in biology and genetics, and they persist throughout the childhood years and into adulthood (Kagan & Snidman, 2007; Keogh, 2003; Rothbart, 2011).

> Chapter 3 discusses temperament and personality development.

3. *Instruction is most effective when it is tailored to students' individual learning styles.* FALSE. Contrary to a popular belief, most measures of supposed "learning styles" merely reflect students' self-reported *preferences*, and tailoring instruction to such preferences doesn't noticeably enhance students' learning or academic achievement (Kirschner & van Merriënboer, 2013; Kozhevnikov, Evans, & Kosslyn, 2014; Krätzig & Arbuthnott, 2006; Mayer & Massa, 2003). It is far more important that teachers base their instructional practices on knowledge of the cognitive processes that underlie how virtually *all* students think and learn.

> Chapter 5 describes individual differences in cognitive abilities and dispositions that can significantly impact students' learning and academic achievement. Chapter 6 describes general mental processes that underlie effective thinking, learning, and memory.

4. *The best way to learn and remember a new fact is to repeat it over and over.* FALSE. Although repeating information several times is better than doing nothing at all, repetition of specific facts is a relatively *ineffective* way to learn. Students learn information more easily and remember it longer when they connect it with things they already know. One especially effective strategy is elaboration: using prior knowledge to expand or embellish on a new idea in some way, perhaps by drawing inferences from a historical fact, identifying new examples of a scientific concept, or thinking of situations in which a mathematical procedure might be helpful (J. R. Anderson, 2005; Graesser & Bower, 1990).

> Chapter 6 discusses elaboration and its implications for instructional practice.

5. *Students often misjudge how much they know about a topic.* TRUE. Most adults and children are *not* the best judges of what they do and don't know. For example, many students think that if they've spent a long time studying a textbook chapter, they must know its contents very well. Yet if they've spent most of their time studying ineffectively—perhaps by "reading" while thinking about something else altogether or by mindlessly copying definitions—they may know far less than they think they do (N. J. Stone, 2000; Thiede, Griffin, Wiley, & Redford, 2009).

> Chapter 7 describes this *illusion of knowing* in more detail.

6. *Anxiety sometimes helps students learn and perform more successfully in the classroom.* TRUE. Many people think that anxiety is always a bad thing. In fact, a *little bit* of anxiety can actually *improve* learning and performance, especially when students perceive a task to be something they can accomplish with reasonable effort. For instance, a small, manageable amount of anxiety can spur students to complete their work carefully and to study for tests (Cassady, 2010b; N. E. Perry, Turner, & Meyer, 2006; Shipman & Shipman, 1985).

> Chapter 11 explores anxiety's effects in different situations.

7. *Playing video games can enhance children's cognitive development.* TRUE—or more accurately, SOMETIMES TRUE. A great deal of time spent playing video games *instead of* reading, doing homework, and engaging in other school-related activities can definitely interfere with children's long-term academic success. But some video games can be powerful tools for promoting important cognitive abilities, such as sustained attention and spatial reasoning (Gentile, 2011; Rothbart, 2011; Tobias & Fletcher, 2011). And increasingly, educational technologists have been designing highly motivating video games that simulate real-world problems and foster complex problem-solving skills (Barab, Gresalfi, & Ingram-Goble, 2010; Gee, 2010; Squire, 2011).

> Chapter 3 describes potential adverse effects of violent video games on children's aggression. Chapter 12 explores potential benefits of appropriately designed video games.

8. *The ways in which teachers assess students' learning influence what and how students actually learn.* TRUE. We see this principle in action in the opening case study: When Anne Smith's "No D" and multiple-submission policies convey the message that students can't get by with marginal work, students are more likely to seek feedback about their work, benefit from their mistakes, and enhance their writing skills. *Good* assessments encourage cognitive processes essential for high-quality learning. For example, students are more likely to pull class material into an integrated, meaningful whole if they expect assessment activities to require such synthesis, and they're more likely to focus on applying what they learn to new situations if they think that assessments will involve application tasks (Carpenter, 2012; N. Frederiksen, 1984b; Lundeberg & Fox, 1991).

> Chapter 14 and Chapter 15 explore numerous ways in which assessment practices affect students' learning.

How many of the OOPS items did you answer correctly? Did some of the false items seem convincing enough that you marked them true? Did one or more of the true items contradict certain beliefs you had? If either of these was the case, you're hardly alone. College students often agree with statements that seem to be obviously "true" but are, in fact, partially or completely incorrect (Gage, 1991; L. S. Goldstein & Lake, 2000; Woolfolk Hoy, Davis, & Pape, 2006).

It's easy to be persuaded by "common sense" and to assume that what seems logical must be true. Yet common sense and logic don't always give us the real scoop about how people actually learn and develop, nor do they always give us appropriate guidance about how best to help students succeed in classrooms. Instead, our knowledge about learning and instruction must come from a more objective source of information—that is, from systematic research.

As professionals, teachers are *decision makers* who must choose among many, many possible strategies for helping students learn and develop. Certainly teaching is an art to some degree: Good teachers are creative and innovative, and they add many imaginative touches to classroom lessons and activities. But that art must be based on a firm foundation of research findings both about how human beings learn and about how teachers can help them learn effectively; in other words, it must be based on the *science of learning* and the *science of instruction*. Ultimately, good teaching involves evidence-based practices—the use of instructional methods and other classroom strategies that research has consistently shown to bring about significant gains in students' development and academic achievement.

> MyEdLab **Self-Check 1.1**

Understanding and Interpreting Research Findings

Many research studies involve quantitative research: They yield numbers that reflect percentages, frequencies, or averages related to certain characteristics or phenomena. For example, a quantitative study might provide information about students' scores on achievement tests, students' responses to rating-scale questionnaires, or school district records of students' attendance and dropout rates.

Other studies involve qualitative research: They yield nonnumerical data—perhaps in the form of verbal reports, written documents, pictures, videos, or maps—that capture many aspects of a complex situation. For example, a qualitative study might involve one-on-one interviews in which students describe their hopes for the future, a detailed case study of interpersonal relationships within a tight-knit clique of adolescent girls, or in-depth observations of several teachers who create distinctly different psychological atmospheres in their classrooms.

To a considerable degree, the research study described at the beginning of the chapter is a quantitative one: Anne Smith tabulates students' responses to various survey questions and computes the percentages of various final class grades. But when she collects the completed surveys, she also looks closely at students' specific comments and suggestions—qualitative information.

Not all research on learning and instruction is *good* research, of course. Furthermore, people sometimes draw inappropriate conclusions from even the best of research studies. It's important, therefore, that teachers understand what various kinds of research studies can and cannot tell us about learning and instruction.

QUANTITATIVE RESEARCH

Quantitative research studies vary widely in nature, but you might think of them as falling into four general categories: descriptive, correlational, experimental, and quasi-experimental. These categories yield different kinds of information and warrant different kinds of conclusions.

DESCRIPTIVE STUDIES

A descriptive study does exactly what its name implies: It *describes* a situation. Descriptive studies might give us information about the characteristics of students, teachers, or schools. They might also provide information about how often certain events or behaviors occur. In general, descriptive studies enable us to draw conclusions about the way things are—the current state of affairs.

CORRELATIONAL STUDIES

A correlational study explores possible associations among two or more variables. For instance, it might tell us how closely various human characteristics are associated with one another, or it might give us information about the consistency with which certain human behaviors occur in conjunction with certain environmental conditions. In general, correlational studies enable us to draw conclusions about correlation: the extent to which two characteristics or phenomena tend to be found together or to change together. Two variables are correlated when one tends to increase as the other increases (a *positive correlation*) or when one tends to *decrease* as the other increases (a *negative correlation*). Correlations are often described numerically with a statistic known as a *correlation coefficient*.

You can learn about correlation coefficients in Appendix A.

Sometimes correlational studies involve comparing two or more groups that differ with respect to a particular characteristic, such as age, gender, or background.[1] For example, a correlational study might compare the average achievement test scores of boys and girls, or it might investigate whether young children who have had considerable exposure to reading materials at home learn to read more quickly at school than children without such exposure.

Any correlation between two variables allows us to make *predictions* about one variable when we know the status of the other. For example, if we find that, on average, 15-year-olds are more capable of abstract thought than 10-year-olds—in other words, if age and abstract thinking ability are correlated—we can predict that high school students will benefit more from an abstract discussion of democratic government than fourth graders will. And if we find that children learn to read more easily if they've had many previous experiences with books at home, we might take proactive steps to enhance the early literacy skills of children without such experiences. Yet our predictions will be imprecise ones at best, with exceptions to the general rule. For example, even if, *on average,* 15-year-olds have considerable ability to think about abstract ideas, some 15-year-olds will often struggle with abstract subject matter.

A more significant limitation of correlational studies is that although they may demonstrate that a relationship exists, they never tell us for certain *why* it exists. They don't tell us what specific factors—previous experiences, personality, motivation, or perhaps other things we haven't thought of—are the cause of the association we see. In other words, *correlation does not necessarily indicate causation.*

EXPERIMENTAL AND QUASI-EXPERIMENTAL STUDIES

Descriptive and correlational studies describe things as they exist or have previously existed naturally in the environment. In contrast, an experimental study, or experiment, is a study in which the researcher intentionally changes, or *manipulates,* one or more aspects of the environment (often called *independent variables*) and then measures the effects of such changes on something else. In educational research the "something else" being affected (a *dependent variable*) is typically some aspect of student behavior—perhaps end-of-semester grades, persistence in trying to solve difficult math problems, or ability to interact appropriately with peers. In a good experiment, a researcher *separates and controls variables,* testing the possible effects of one independent variable while holding all other potentially influential variables constant.

Some experimental studies involve simultaneously giving a single group of individuals two or more distinct treatments and comparing the specific effects of each treatment. Other experimental studies involve two or more groups that are treated differently. The following three examples illustrate the multiple-group approach:

- A researcher uses two different instructional methods to teach reading comprehension skills to two different groups of students. (Instructional method is the independent variable.) The researcher then assesses students' reading ability (the dependent variable) and compares the average reading-ability scores of the two groups.
- A researcher gives three different groups of students varying amounts of practice with woodworking skills. (Amount of practice is the independent variable.) The researcher

---

[1]Such group-comparison studies are sometimes called *causal-comparative studies.* However, as B. Johnson (2001) has pointed out, this label may mislead us to believe that such studies reveal cause-and-effect relationships, when in fact they do not.

subsequently scores the quality of each student's woodworking project (the dependent variable) and compares the average scores of the three groups.

- A researcher gives one group of students an intensive instructional program designed to improve their study skills. The researcher gives another group either no instruction or, better still, instruction in subject matter unrelated to study skills. (Presence or absence of instruction in study skills is the independent variable.) The researcher later (a) assesses the quality of students' study skills and (b) obtains their grade point averages—thus, there are two dependent variables—to see whether the program had an effect.

Each of these examples includes one or more **treatment groups** that are recipients of a planned intervention. The third example also includes a **control group** that receives either no intervention or a *placebo* intervention that's unlikely to affect the dependent variable(s) in question. In many experimental studies, participants are assigned to groups *randomly*—for instance, by drawing names out of a hat. Such random assignment is apt to yield groups that are, on average, roughly equivalent on other variables (e.g., pre-existing ability levels, personality characteristics, motivation) that might affect the dependent variable(s).

Random assignment to groups isn't always possible or practical, however, especially in research studies conducted in actual schools and classrooms. For example, when studying the potential benefits of a new teaching technique or therapeutic intervention, a researcher may not be able to completely control which students receive the experimental treatment and which do not, *or* a particular treatment or intervention may have important benefits for *all* students. In such situations, researchers often conduct a **quasi-experimental study**, in which they take into account but don't completely control other influential factors. Following are two examples:

- A researcher implements a new after-school homework program at one high school and identifies a comparable high school without such a program to serve as a control group. The researcher obtains achievement test data for students at both schools both before and after the program's implementation. Ideally, to document the homework program's effectiveness, the average test scores for the two high schools should be the same *before* program begins but different *after* its implementation. (Such an approach is known as a *pretest–posttest study*.)
- Three researchers want to study the effects of safety instructions on children's behaviors on the playground. The researchers present the instructional intervention to first graders one week, second graders the following week, and kindergartners and third graders the week after that. The researchers monitor students' playground behavior before, during, and after the intervention to determine whether each grade-level group's risky playground behavior decreases immediately following the intervention. (Such an approach is known as a *multiple-baselines study;* study described here was conducted by Heck, Collins, & Peterson, 2001.)

When researchers conduct quasi-experimental studies, they don't control for all potentially influential variables and so can't completely rule out alternative explanations for the results they obtain. For instance, in the preceding after-school homework program example, possibly the school getting the new homework program—but *only* that school—has simultaneously begun to use more effective instructional methods, and those methods are the reason for any increase in achievement scores. And in the playground safety example, perhaps certain other things coincidentally happened in the four classrooms during their respective safety-instructions weeks, and those things were the true causes of children's behavior changes.

When carefully designed and conducted, experimental studies and, to a lesser degree, quasi-experimental studies enable us to draw conclusions about *causation*—about *why* behaviors occur. Yet for practical or ethical reasons, many important questions in education don't easily lend themselves to experimental manipulation and tight control of other potentially influential variables. For instance, although we might reasonably hypothesize that children can better master difficult math concepts if they receive individual tutoring, most public school systems can't afford such a luxury, and it would be unfair to provide tutoring for some students and deny it to a control group of other, equally needy students. And, of course, it would be highly unethical to study the effects of aggression by intentionally placing some children in a violent environment. Some important educational questions, then, can be addressed only with descriptive or correlational studies, even though such studies can't help us pin down precise cause-and-effect relationships.

Columns 2, 3, and 4 of Table 1.1 contrast descriptive, correlational, experimental, and quasi-experimental studies and give examples of the kinds of questions each type of study might address.

QUALITATIVE RESEARCH

Rather than address questions related to quantity—questions regarding *how much, how many,* or *how often*—researchers sometimes want to look in depth at the nature of certain characteristics or behaviors. Imagine, for example, that a researcher wants to find out what kinds of study strategies high-achieving students tend to use. One approach would be simply to ask the students questions such as "What things do you do to help you remember what you read in your

COMPARE/CONTRAST

TABLE 1.1 • Contrasting Various Types of Research				
	QUANTITATIVE RESEARCH STUDIES			
	DESCRIPTIVE STUDIES	**CORRELATIONAL STUDIES**	**EXPERIMENTAL AND QUASI-EXPERIMENTAL STUDIES**	**QUALITATIVE RESEARCH STUDIES (DESCRIPTIVE)**
General Nature and Purposes	• Capture the current state of affairs regarding a real-world issue or problem	• Identify associations among characteristics, behaviors, and/or environmental conditions • Enable predictions about one variable, given knowledge of the degree or quantity of another variable • Provide an alternative when experimental manipulations are unethical or impossible	• Manipulate one (independent) variable in order to observe its possible effect on another (dependent) variable • Eliminate other plausible explanations for observed outcomes (especially in carefully controlled experimental studies) • Enable conclusions about cause-and-effect relationships	• Portray the complex, multifaceted nature of human behavior, especially in real-world social settings
Limitations	• Don't enable either (a) predictions about one variable based on another variable or (b) conclusions about cause-and-effect relationships	• Enable only imprecise predictions, with many exceptions to the general relationships observed • Don't enable conclusions about cause-and-effect relationships	• May not completely eliminate alternative explanations for observed outcomes (especially true for quasi-experimental studies) • In some cases, involve artificial laboratory conditions that don't resemble real-life learning environments (true for many tightly controlled experimental studies)	• Don't enable either predictions or conclusions about cause-and-effect relationships
Examples of Questions That Might Be Addressed	• How pervasive are gender stereotypes in popular children's literature? • What kinds of aggressive behaviors occur in schools, and with what frequencies? • How well have students performed on a recent national achievement test?	• Are better readers also better spellers? • Are students more likely to be aggressive at school if they often see violence at home or in their neighborhoods? • To what extent are students' class grades correlated with their scores on achievement tests?	• Which of two reading programs produces greater gains in reading comprehension? • Which method is most effective in reducing aggressive behavior—reinforcing appropriate behavior, punishing aggressive behavior, or a combination of both? • Do different kinds of tests (e.g., multiple-choice vs. essay tests) encourage students to study in different ways?	• What things do high-achieving students say they do "in their heads" when they read and study their textbooks? • What distinct qualities characterize high schools in which members of various adolescent gangs interact congenially and respectfully? • In what ways do teachers' instructional practices change when their jobs and salaries depend on their students' scores on statewide or national achievement tests?

textbooks?" and "How do you prepare for tests in your classes?" Students' responses to such open-ended questions are apt to go in many different directions, sometimes focusing on various behaviors (e.g., taking notes, working on practice problems) and at other times focusing on various mental processes (e.g., trying to make sense of a passage, generating new examples of concepts). Although it might be possible to categorize students' responses and count those falling into each category (thereby obtaining some quantitative data), the researcher may also want to preserve the multifaceted qualities of students' responses by reporting word-for-word excerpts from the interviews.

Qualitative research is often used to explore the complex nature of human behavior in social settings—perhaps in particular social groups, classrooms, schools, or cultures. For example, in-depth qualitative studies have contributed in important ways to our knowledge of school characteristics that affect the academic and social success of students from diverse backgrounds (e.g., Hemmings, 2004; Ladson-Billings, 1995b; Ogbu, 2003).

Like descriptive quantitative studies, qualitative studies *describe* the current state of affairs; they're inappropriate for drawing hard-and-fast conclusions about correlation or cause–and–effect. The rightmost column of Table 1.1 presents examples of questions that might best be answered by qualitative research.

MIXED-METHODS RESEARCH

You shouldn't think of quantitative and qualitative research as an either–or situation. Like Anne Smith in the opening case study, many educational researchers can best address their research questions by combining elements of both quantitative and qualitative research in what is known as a mixed-methods study. For example, in a study described in the *American Educational Research Journal* in 1999, researchers Melissa Roderick and Eric Camburn tracked more than 27,000 students' academic progress as they made the transition from small elementary or middle schools to much larger high schools in the Chicago public school system. Many students showed a sharp decline in academic achievement in ninth grade, their first year of high school. More than 40% of first-semester ninth graders (males especially) failed at least one course, and students who achieved at low levels early in their high school careers were more likely to drop out before graduation.

Such troubling findings are examples of quantitative data, but the researchers also obtained qualitative information that can help us understand the numbers. For instance, they described a student named Anna, who had done well in her neighborhood K–8 school and seemingly had the basic skills she needed to successfully tackle a high school curriculum. Unfortunately, Anna was overwhelmed by the new demands that her ninth-grade classes placed on her, and her first-semester final grades included several Ds and an F. In an interview with one of the researchers, she gave the following explanation:

> In geography, "he said the reason why I got a lower grade is 'cause I missed one assignment and I had to do a report, and I forgot that one." In English, "I got a C . . . 'cause we were supposed to keep a journal, and I keep on forgetting it 'cause I don't have a locker. Well I do, but my locker partner she lets her cousins use it, and I lost my two books there. . . . I would forget to buy a notebook, and then I would have them on separate pieces of paper, and I would lose them." And, in biology, "the reason I failed was because I lost my folder . . . it had everything I needed, and I had to do it again, and, by the time I had to turn in the new folder, I did, but he said it was too late. . . ." (Roderick & Camburn, 1999, p. 305)

Additionally, the interview revealed Anna's perception of most school faculty members as being uncaring, inattentive to students' difficulties, and inflexible in evaluating students' achievement.

If Anna's behaviors, experiences, and perceptions are common ones—and apparently they are—they point to the need for greater faculty support as students make the transition from a close-knit elementary or K–8 school to a more impersonal high school environment. This support might be not only emotional but also *academic*—for instance, it should probably include instruction and guidance in organizational skills and effective study habits. We must be careful in drawing such inferences, however. Remember, qualitative data are essentially *descriptive* data: They tell us *how things are* rather than *what causes what.* Any hypotheses about cause-and-effect relationships drawn from qualitative data are only that—hypotheses—that ideally should be tested with experimental, quantitative studies.

INTERPRETING RESEARCH RESULTS: A CAUTIONARY NOTE

Whenever we look at the results of a research study, we can determine that a particular condition or intervention has led to a particular outcome—that is, there is a cause-and-effect relationship between the two—only if we've eliminated all other possible explanations for the results we've observed. As an example, imagine that Hometown School District wants to find out which of two reading programs, *Reading Is Great* (RIG) or *Reading and You* (RAY), leads to better reading in third grade. The district asks each of its third-grade teachers to choose one of these two reading programs and use it throughout the school year. The district then compares the end-of-year achievement test scores of students in the RIG and RAY classrooms and finds that RIG students have substantially higher reading comprehension scores than RAY students. We might quickly jump to the conclusion that RIG promotes better reading comprehension than RAY—in other words, that a cause-and-effect relationship exists between the instructional method and reading comprehension. But is this really so?

Not necessarily. The fact is, the school district hasn't eliminated all other possible explanations for the difference in students' reading comprehension scores. Remember, the third-grade teachers personally *chose* the instructional program they used. Were the teachers who chose RIG different in some way from those who chose RAY? For instance, were RIG teachers more open-minded and enthusiastic about using innovative methods, did they have higher expectations for their students, or did they devote more class time to reading? Or, perhaps, did the RIG teachers have students who were, on average, better readers to begin with? If the RIG and RAY classrooms were different from each other in any of these ways—or perhaps different in some other way we haven't thought of—then the district hasn't eliminated alternative explanations for why the RIG students have outperformed the RAY students. A better way to study the causal influence of a reading program on reading comprehension would be to *randomly assign* third-grade classes to the RIG and RAY programs, thereby making the two groups similar (on average) in terms of student abilities and teacher characteristics.

Whenever you read descriptions of research findings—whether they be in professional journals, in popular print media, on television, or on Internet websites—be careful that you don't jump too quickly to conclusions about what factors are affecting students' learning, development, and behavior in particular situations. Scrutinize the reports carefully, always with these questions in mind: *Have the researchers separated and controlled variables that might have an influence on the outcome? Have they ruled out other possible explanations for their results?* Only when the answers to these questions are undeniably *yes* and *yes* should you draw a conclusion about a cause-and-effect relationship.

Draw conclusions about cause-and-effect relationships only when other possible explanations for an outcome have been eliminated.

FROM RESEARCH TO PRACTICE: THE IMPORTANCE OF PRINCIPLES AND THEORIES

Consistent patterns in research findings have led psychologists to make many generalizations about students' learning and development, along with many generalizations about classroom strategies that can effectively enhance students' academic achievement and personal and social well-being. Some of these generalizations take the form of **principles**, which identify certain factors that affect learning or development and describe the specific effects these factors have. For example, consider this principle:

> A behavior that is followed by a satisfying state of affairs—a reward—is more likely to occur again than a behavior not followed by a reward.

In this principle, a particular factor (a rewarding consequence) is identified as having a particular effect (an increase in the behavior's frequency). The principle can be observed in many situations; following are two examples:

- A student's interpersonal skills improve after we begin praising the student for interacting with peers respectfully and cooperatively. (Here the reward is *praise.*)

• A student becomes more diligent in completing math assignments once we've begun to tailor assignments to the student's current ability level, such that the student more often achieves success in the assignments. (Here the reward is a *success experience.*)

Principles are most useful when they can be applied to many different situations. The "reward" principle—many psychologists instead use the term *reinforcement*—is an example of such broad applicability: It holds true for many different types of learning and a wide variety of pleasant consequences.

Whereas principles tell us *what* factors are important for human learning and development, **theories** tell us *why* certain factors might be important. More specifically, theories provide possible explanations about the underlying mechanisms involved in learning or development. By giving us ideas about why we are consistently observing certain cause-and-effect relationships, theories can ultimately help us create learning environments that facilitate students' learning, development, and achievement to the greatest extent possible.

Let's consider an example. One prominent theory of how people learn—information processing theory—proposes that attention is an essential ingredient in the learning process. More specifically, if a learner pays attention to new information, the information moves from one component of the human memory system (the sensory register) to another, longer-lasting component (working memory). If the learner *doesn't* pay attention, the information quickly disappears from the memory system; in the words of a common expression, the information "goes in one ear and out the other." The importance of attention in information processing theory suggests that strategies that capture and maintain students' attention—perhaps assigning interesting reading materials or presenting intriguing real-world problems—are apt to enhance students' learning and achievement. It also alerts us to the fact that a concrete reward for learning something new might be detrimental (rather than helpful) if it subsequently *distracts* a student's attention from a learning activity.

You might think of principles as reflecting relatively enduring conclusions about cause-and-effect relationships related to people's learning and development. Principles tend to be fairly stable over time: Researchers observe many of the same factors having an influence over and over again. In contrast, psychological theories are rarely, if ever, set in stone. Instead, they're continually expanded and modified as additional data come to light, and in some cases one theory may be abandoned in favor of another that better explains a particular phenomenon. Furthermore, different theories focus on different aspects of human functioning, and psychologists haven't yet pulled them together into a single mega-theory that adequately accounts for all the diverse phenomena and experiences that comprise human existence.

Although psychological theories will inevitably change in the future, they can be quite valuable even in their unfinished forms. They help us integrate thousands of research studies into concise understandings of human learning and development, and they enable us to draw inferences and make predictions about how students are apt to perform and achieve in particular classroom situations. In general, theories help us to both *explain* and *predict* human behavior, thereby giving us countless ideas about how best to promote students' academic and social success at school.

In this book, you'll encounter a variety of theories related to different aspects of human functioning, and they don't always lead to the same conclusions about human beings' thinking and behavior. Yet we authors firmly believe that each theory we introduce offers unique insights and thus has important things to say about students' classroom learning and performance. We hope that our readers will take an equally open-minded approach. It's probably most helpful to think of psychological theories in terms of their *usefulness* in classroom decision making, rather than in terms of their *this-is-the-ultimate-truth* completeness and accuracy.

Chapter 6 describes information processing theory in depth.

MyEdLab **Self-Check 1.2**

MyEdLab **Application Exercise 1.1.** In this exercise, you can practice distinguishing among various kinds of research studies and determining reasonable conclusions from each one.

Collecting Data and Drawing Conclusions about Your Own Students

Certainly the collection and interpretation of quantitative and qualitative data aren't restricted only to highly trained researchers who work in universities and research laboratories. In fact, practicing teachers continually collect and interpret data about their own students through formal and informal assessments of students' written work and classroom behaviors. Furthermore, many teachers plan and conduct their own research to help them better understand their students and schools—a process known as *action research*.

ASSESSING STUDENTS' ACHIEVEMENTS AND INTERPRETING THEIR CLASSROOM BEHAVIORS

Most teachers regularly assess what their students know and can do, perhaps by examining students' performance in assignments, projects, oral or technology-based presentations, and quizzes. But effective teachers don't limit themselves only to such formal, planned evaluations. They continually observe their students in a variety of contexts—not only in the classroom but also in the hallways and cafeteria, on the playground, during parent–teacher conferences, and so on—for clues about what students might be thinking, believing, feeling, and learning. Students' comments, questions, body language, work habits, and interactions with friends and classmates can provide valuable insights into their learning, development, and motivation.

Use assessment results to form hypotheses—but *not* to draw hard-and-fast conclusions—about students' current characteristics and abilities and about effective instructional strategies.

To get your feet wet in the process of assessment, read 7-year-old Justin's short story "The Pet Who Came to Dinner," presented in Figure 1.1. As you read it, consider what you might conclude about Justin's progress in writing. Consider, too, what inferences you might make about Justin's family and home life.

As you can see, Justin has learned how to spell some words (e.g., *dinner, came*) but not others (e.g., he spells *once* as "owans" and *started* as "stor did"). Overall, he knows which alphabet letters represent which sounds in speech, but he sometimes reverses the letter *d* so that it looks like a *b,* and he occasionally leaves out sounds in his word spellings (e.g., his spelling of *drink* begins with *b* and omits the *n* sound). Justin has made some progress in common spelling patterns (e.g., the *-ing* suffix for verbs) and in the use of periods and apostrophes. He has learned to tell a simple story, but he does so merely by listing a series of seemingly unrelated events, and he hasn't yet learned that the title of a story should appear on a line by itself, centered at the top of the page.

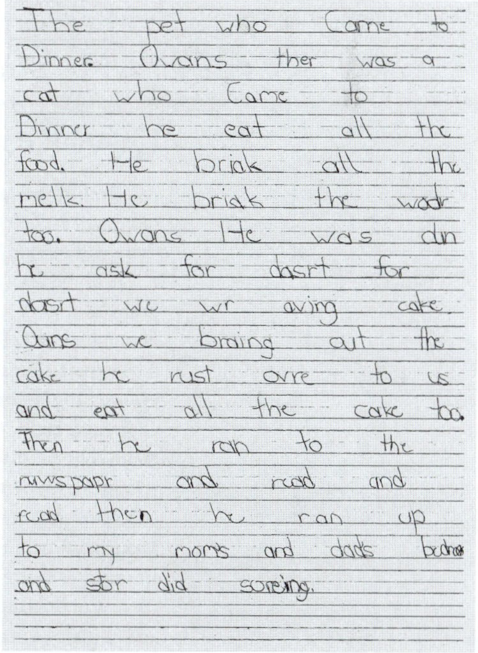

Justin's story offers a few hints about home life as well. For instance, it appears that Justin lives with two parents, and he talks about the pet reading the newspaper ("nuwspapr"), suggesting that reading is a familiar activity at home. Are such inferences about Justin accurate? Not necessarily. The conclusions we reach about our students are—like the theories that researchers formulate about learning and development—only reasonable guesses based on the evidence at hand. We must think of such conclusions as tentative *hypotheses* to be tested further, rather than as indisputable *facts*.

CONDUCTING ACTION RESEARCH

Like Anne Smith in the opening case study, teachers sometimes have questions that existing research findings don't fully answer. In **action research**, teachers conduct systematic studies of issues and problems in their own schools, with the goal of seeking more effective strategies for working with students. For example, an action research project might involve examining the effectiveness of a new teaching technique, seeking students' opinions on a new classroom policy (as Ms. Smith does), or ascertaining reasons why many students rarely complete homework assignments.

FIGURE 1.1 Seven-year-old Justin's story "The Pet Who Came to Dinner."

Any action research study typically involves the following steps (described in greater depth in Mills, 2011):

1. *Identify an area of focus.* The teacher–researcher begins with a problem and gathers preliminary information that might shed light on the problem, perhaps by reading relevant books or journal articles, surfing the Internet, or discussing the issue with colleagues or students. The teacher–researcher then identifies one or more specific questions to address and develops a research plan (data-collection techniques, necessary resources, schedule, etc.) for answering those questions. At this point, the teacher also seeks permission to conduct the study from school administrators and any other appropriate authorities. Depending on the nature of the study, parents' permission may be necessary as well.

2. *Collect data.* The teacher–researcher collects data relevant to the research questions. Such data might, for example, be obtained from questionnaires, interviews, achievement tests, students' journals or portfolios, existing school records (e.g., attendance patterns, school suspension rates), observations, or any combination of these.

3. *Analyze and interpret the data.* The teacher–researcher looks for patterns in the data. Sometimes the analysis involves computing particular statistics (e.g., percentages, averages, correlation coefficients)—this would be a quantitative study. At other times the analysis involves an in-depth, nonnumerical inspection of the data—this would be a qualitative study. In either case, the teacher–researcher relates the findings to the original research questions.

4. *Develop an action plan.* The final step distinguishes action research from the more traditional research studies described earlier in the chapter. In particular, the teacher–researcher uses the information collected to *take action*—for instance, to change instructional strategies, school policies, or the classroom environment.

Many colleges and universities now offer courses in action research. You can also find many inexpensive paperback books on the topic.

MyEdLab **Self-Check 1.3**

MyEdLab **Application Exercise 1.2.** In this interactive activity, you can gain practice in identifying useful information from students' behaviors by watching and analyzing actual classroom examples.

Developing as a Teacher

As a beginning teacher, you may initially find your role a bit overwhelming. Virtually any classroom will be one of nonstop action requiring you to be constantly attentive and on your toes, and there will always be a great deal to think about.

If you are currently enrolled in a teacher education program, you should think of your program as a very good start on the road to becoming a skillful teacher (Bransford, Darling-Hammond, & LePage, 2005; Brouwer & Korthagen, 2005). However, it is *only* a start. Developing true expertise in any profession, including teaching, takes many years of experience, although even a single year of teaching experience can make a significant difference (Berliner, 2001; Clotfelter, Ladd, & Vigdor, 2007; Henry, Bastian, & Fortner, 2011). So be patient with yourself, and recognize that occasionally feeling a bit unsure and making mistakes is par for the course. As you gain experience, you'll gradually become able to make decisions about routine situations and problems quickly and efficiently, giving you the time and energy to think creatively and flexibly about how best to teach classroom subject matter (Borko & Putnam, 1996; Bransford, Derry, Berliner, & Hammerness, 2005; Feldon, 2007).

Conducting action research is obviously one possible way of developing your knowledge and skills as a teacher. But in addition, we offer the following strategies—all of them based on research on teacher effectiveness. It's important to note here that most public and private schools *require* teachers to document their ongoing professional growth through such strategies.

* *Keep up to date on research findings and innovations in education.* Additional university coursework and in-service training sessions at your school are two good ways to increase your teaching effectiveness (Desimone, 2009; Hattie, 2009; McDonald, Robles-Piña, & Polnick, 2011). In addition, effective teachers typically subscribe to one or more professional journals, and, as time allows, they occasionally attend professional conferences in their area.

* *Learn as much as you can about the subject matter you teach.* When we look at effective teachers—for example, those who are flexible in their approaches to instruction, help students develop a thorough understanding of classroom topics, and convey obvious enthusiasm for whatever they're teaching—we typically find teachers who know their subject matter extremely well (Borko & Putnam, 1996; Cochran & Jones, 1998; H. C. Hill et al., 2008).

* *Learn as much as you can about specific strategies for teaching your particular subject matter.* In addition to knowing general teaching strategies, it's helpful to acquire strategies specific to the topic you're teaching—strategies that are collectively known as pedagogical content knowledge. Effective teachers typically have a large number of strategies for teaching particular topics and skills. Furthermore, they can usually anticipate—and so can also address—the difficulties students will have and the kinds of errors students will make in the process of mastering a skill or body of knowledge (Baumert et al., 2010; Krauss et al., 2008; P. M. Sadler, Sonnert, Coyle, Cook-Smith, & Miller, 2013; L. S. Shulman, 1986).

* *Learn as much as you can about the culture(s) of the community in which you are working.* Students are more likely to do well in school when the school curriculum and classroom environment take their cultural backgrounds into account (Brayboy & Searle, 2007; Moje & Hinchman, 2004; Tyler, Uqdah, et al., 2008). Reading about various cultures can certainly be helpful. But ideally, you can best inform yourself about students' cultural beliefs and practices if you participate in local community activities and converse regularly with community members (Castagno & Brayboy, 2008; McIntyre, 2010).

> You can find discussions of cultural differences in many chapters of this book, and especially in Chapter 4.

* *Continually reflect on and critically examine your assumptions, inferences, and teaching practices.* In the opening case study, Anne Smith reflects on her students' performance in previous years and then institutes new assessment policies that she thinks might be more motivating and productive. Like Ms. Smith, effective teachers engage in reflective teaching: They continually examine and critique their assumptions, inferences, and instructional practices, and they regularly adjust their beliefs and strategies in the face of new evidence (Hammerness, Darling-Hammond, & Bransford, 2005; T. Hogan, Rabinowitz, & Craven, 2003; Larrivee, 2006).

* *Communicate and collaborate with colleagues.* Effective teachers rarely work in isolation. Instead, they frequently communicate with colleagues in their own school district, across the nation, and, often, in other countries. Furthermore, they regularly coordinate their efforts to enhance students' learning and personal well-being at a schoolwide level (Bransford, Darling-Hammond, et al., 2005; Raudenbush, 2009). Teacher lounges, email, Internet websites, and blogs—all of these can potentially offer ideas for lesson plans and instructional activities on a wide range of topics. For example, you might look at Smithsonian Education (smithsonianeducation.org), Khan Academy (khanacademy.org), or Open Educational Resources (oercommons.org). You should also look at the websites of professional organizations related to your field; the websites for the National Council of Teachers of Mathematics (nctm.org) and the National Council for the Social Studies (socialstudies.org) are just two of the many possibilities.

* Keep in mind, too, that even the most masterful of teachers had to begin their teaching careers as novices, and they probably entered their first classroom with the same concerns and uncertainties that you may initially have. Most experienced teachers are happy to offer you advice and support during challenging times; in fact, they're apt to be flattered that you're asking them! Ideally, teachers and administrators at a single school create a professional learning community, in which they share a common vision for students' learning and achievement, work collaboratively to achieve desired outcomes for all students,

and regularly communicate with one another about their strategies and progress (DuFour, DuFour, & Eaker, 2008; P. Graham & Ferriter, 2009; Raudenbush, 2009).

🍎 *Believe that you can make a difference in students' lives.* In general, human beings achieve at higher levels in their endeavors when they have high self-efficacy—that is, when they believe they are capable of executing certain behaviors or reaching certain goals. Students are more likely to try to learn something if they believe they *can* learn it—in other words, if they have high self-efficacy. But as a teacher, you, too, must have high self-efficacy. Believing that you can be a good teacher will give you confidence to try new strategies and help you persist in the face of occasional setbacks. Students who achieve at high levels are apt to be those whose teachers have confidence that, *as teachers*, they can make a genuine difference as they work both individually in their classrooms and collectively with their colleagues (Holzberger, Philipp, & Kunter, 2013; J. A. Langer, 2000; Skaalvik & Skaalvik, 2008). Ultimately, what teachers do in the classroom *matters* for students, not only in the short term but for years to come (Hattie, 2009; Konstantopoulos & Chung, 2011).

You can learn more about the nature and effects of self-efficacy in Chapter 10.

> MyEdLab **Self-Check 1.4**
>
> MyEdLab **Application Exercise 1.3.** In this exercise, you can apply what you have learned about research, theories, and teacher development to a classroom scenario.

Strategies for Studying and Learning Effectively

You'll learn much more about effective learning and study strategies in upcoming chapters, especially in Chapter 6 and Chapter 7.

As you learn more about educational psychology—and especially as you learn about the nature of human thinking and learning—you'll gain many insights into how you can help students more effectively master classroom subject matter. We authors hope that you'll also gain insights into how *you yourself* can better learn and remember course material. For now, we suggest five general strategies.

🍎 *Relate what you read to your existing knowledge and prior experiences.* For example, connect new concepts and principles with memorable childhood events, previous coursework, or your general knowledge about human beings and their behavior. In general, people learn and remember things more easily and effectively when they engage in *meaningful learning*—that is, when they connect new information and ideas to things they've previously learned.

🍎 *Actively consider how some new information might contradict your existing beliefs.* As the earlier OOPS test may have shown you, some of what you currently "know" and believe may be sort-of-but-not-quite accurate or even out-and-out *in*accurate. People's existing beliefs can occasionally wreak havoc with new learning. For example, many students in teacher education classes reject research findings that appear to be inconsistent with their personal beliefs and experiences (Fives & Gill, 2015; Gregoire, 2003; Richardson, 2003).

Chapter 6 explores meaningful learning and conceptual change in greater depth.

Chapter 2 discusses the development of abstract thinking and other significant cognitive advancements during the school years.

As you read about and study educational psychology, then, think about how some ideas and research findings might actually contradict and discredit your prior "knowledge." When you encounter puzzling or seemingly "wrong" ideas and findings, we hope you'll keep an open mind and, in particular, consider how and why they might have some validity and worth. Ideally, effective learners undergo *conceptual change*: They revise their existing notions to accommodate new and discrepant information.

🍎 *Tie abstract concepts and principles to concrete examples.* Children become increasingly able to think about abstract ideas as they get older, but people of *all* ages can more readily understand and remember abstract information when they tie it to concrete objects and events. Short examples and lengthier case studies that involve real children and teachers, videos that depict classrooms in action, Experiencing Firsthand exercises such as the OOPS test—all of these can enhance your understanding and memory of new concepts and help you recognize them when you see them in your own work with children and adolescents.

🍎 *Elaborate on what you read, going beyond it and adding to it.* Earlier in the chapter we mentioned that the process of *elaboration*—embellishing on new information in some way—enhances learning and memory of the information. So try to think *beyond* the information you read. Draw inferences from the ideas presented. Generate new examples of concepts. Identify your own educational applications of various principles of learning, development, and motivation.

🍎 *Periodically check yourself to make sure you remember and understand what you have read.* There are times when even the most diligent students don't concentrate on what they're reading—when they're actually thinking about something else as their eyes go down the page. So stop once in a while (perhaps once every two or three pages) to make sure you've really learned and understood the things you've been reading. Try to summarize the material. Ask yourself questions about it, and make sure everything makes sense to you. Check your mastery of various concepts by doing activities and taking self-check quizzes sprinkled throughout a chapter in the Pearson etext. And tackle the Practice for Your Licensure Exam exercise that appears after each chapter summary.

MyEdLab **Content Extension 1.1.** For additional strategies, read "Study Tips."

When all is said and done, your goal in studying educational psychology isn't to memorize enough facts that you can get good grades on tests and quizzes. Instead, your goal is to become the best teacher—and also the best *learner*—you can possibly be. As you look forward to your entry into the teaching profession, we urge you to be confident that with time, practice, a solid understanding of how children and adolescents learn and develop, a large toolkit of instructional strategies, and every student's best interests at heart, you can truly make a significant difference in young people's lives.

MyEdLab **Self-Check 1.5**

1   What Have You Learned?

The beginning of the chapter lists five *learning outcomes*—five general things you should accomplish—while reading and studying this chapter. Let's return now to these outcomes and identify key points related to each one.

■ **1.1: Explain the importance of research in classroom decision making.** As teachers, we must make countless daily decisions about how to interact with, instruct, and guide students in our classrooms. Although we can sometimes use simple common sense in making these decisions, such "sense" may occasionally lead us to draw unwarranted, even inaccurate conclusions. We are most likely to make good decisions—those that maximize students' learning and development over the long run—when we base them on contemporary research findings and on general principles and theories that synthesize those findings.

■ **1.2: Draw appropriate conclusions from different types of research studies.** Knowledge of findings from both quantitative and qualitative research can greatly enhance our teaching effectiveness, but different kinds of studies are appropriate for different kinds of issues and conclusions. Qualitative studies and descriptive quantitative studies can yield a great deal of information about *how things are* at the present time.

Correlational quantitative studies enable conclusions about *what variables are associated with what other variables*. But only carefully controlled experimental studies—and, to a lesser extent, quasi-experimental studies—yield dependable conclusions about *what causes what*. In some cases, researchers effectively combine both quantitative and qualitative research methods to more fully address their research questions.

■ **1.3: Describe several strategies for collecting information about your own students.** To be effective teachers, we must regularly collect data about our students, sometimes by giving them preplanned assessments and sometimes by observing them "on the fly" as they act and interact in class, on the playground, and elsewhere. In addition, we may often find it helpful to conduct action research in order to address questions about our own particular students or about local issues and concerns.

■ **1.4: Plan long-term strategies for gaining expertise as a teacher.** Truly effective teachers are also life-long learners. To maximize our development as teachers, we must think critically and reflectively about our assumptions, beliefs, and classroom strategies. We must also continue to modify what we think and do as we acquire new information related to our profession. Such information can come from a variety of sources, including formal coursework, in-service training sessions, professional journals and conferences, Internet websites, consultation with colleagues and community members, and our own action research.

■ **1.5: Use effective strategies when you read and study.** Successful learning is active, *strategic* learning. A few simple strategies can greatly enhance your learning and memory of what you read and study. In particular, we authors urge you

to: (1) connect new concepts and principles to things you already know; (2) reconsider your existing beliefs when new information might potentially discredit them; (3) tie abstract ideas to concrete examples; (4) embellish (elaborate) on the concepts and principles you learn, perhaps by drawing inferences or thinking of possible applications; and (5) regularly check yourself to make sure you understand and can remember what you've read—for instance, by summarizing it or asking yourself questions about it.

Practice For Your Licensure Exam

New Software

High school math teacher Mr. Gualtieri begins his class one Monday with an important announcement: "Our school has just purchased a new instructional software program that we can use on our classroom computer tablets. This program, called Problem-Excel, will give you practice in applying the mathematical concepts and procedures we'll be studying this year. I strongly encourage you to use it whenever you have free time so that you can get extra instruction and practice with things you might be having trouble with."

Mr. Gualtieri is firmly convinced that the new software will help his students better understand and apply certain concepts in his math curriculum this year. To test his hypothesis, he keeps a record of which students use the software and which students do not. He then looks at how well the two groups of students perform on his next classroom test. Much to his surprise, he discovers that, on average, the students who have used the software have earned *lower* scores than those who have not used it. "How can this be?" he puzzles. "Is the software actually doing more harm than good?"

1. **Constructed-response question:**

   Mr. Gualtieri wonders whether the instructional software is actually hurting, rather than helping, his students. Assume that the software has been carefully designed by an experienced educator. Assume, too, that Mr. Gualtieri's classroom test is a good measure of how well his students have learned the material they've been studying.

   A. Explain why Mr. Gualtieri cannot draw a conclusion about a cause-and-effect relationship from the evidence he has. Base your response on principles of educational research.

   B. Identify another plausible explanation for the results Mr. Gualtieri has obtained.

2. **Multiple-choice question:**

   Which one of the following results would provide the most convincing evidence that the Problem-Excel software enhances students' mathematics achievement?

   a. Ten high schools in New York City purchase Problem-Excel and make it available to their students. Students at these high schools get higher mathematics achievement test scores than students at 10 other high schools that have *not* purchased the software.

   b. A high school purchases Problem-Excel, but only four of the eight math teachers at the school decide to have their students use it. The students of these four teachers score at higher levels on a mathematics achievement test than the students of the other four teachers.

   c. All 10th graders at a large high school take a mathematics achievement test in September. At some point during the next 2 months, each student spends 20 hours working with Problem-Excel. The students all take the same math achievement test again in December and, on average, get substantially higher scores than they did in September.

   d. Students at a high school are randomly assigned to two groups. One group works with Problem-Excel, and the other group works with a software program called Write-Away, designed to teach better writing skills. The Problem-Excel group scores higher than the Write-Away group on a subsequent mathematics achievement test.

MyEdLab **Licensure Exam 1.1**

PRAXIS Go to Appendix C, "Matching Book Content and Ebook Activities to the Praxis Principles of Learning and Teaching Tests," to discover sections of this chapter that may be especially applicable to the Praxis tests.

Losevsky Photo and Video/Shutterstock

2

Cognitive and Linguistic Development

2.1 Describe four principles portraying the general nature of child development and the interactive roles of heredity and environment in guiding it.

2.2 Explain how the brain and its development influence children's thinking and learning.

2.3 Apply Piaget's theory of cognitive development to classroom practice.

2.4 Apply Vygotsky's theory of cognitive development to classroom practice.

2.5 Describe developmental changes in language during the school years, and explain how you might adapt instruction to children with diverse linguistic abilities and needs.

CASE STUDY: APPLE TARTS

Ms. Lombard's fourth-grade class has learned how to add and subtract fractions but not yet studied how to divide by fractions. Nevertheless, students are working in small groups to tackle the following problem, which requires dividing 20 by $^3/_4$:

> Mom makes small apple tarts, using three-quarters of an apple for each small tart. She has 20 apples. How many small apple tarts can she make? (J. Hiebert et al., 1997, p. 118)[1]

One group has already agreed that Mom can use three-fourths of each apple to make 20 tarts, with one-fourth of each apple being left to make additional tarts.

Liz:	So you've got twenty quarters *left*.
Jeanette:	Yes, . . . and twenty quarters is equal to five apples, . . . so five apples divided by—
Liz:	Six, seven, eight.
Jeanette:	But three-quarters equals three.
Kerri:	But she can't make only three apple tarts!
Jeanette:	No, you've still got twenty.
Liz:	But you've got twenty quarters, if you've got twenty quarters you might be right.
Jeanette:	I'll show you.
Liz:	No, I've drawn them all here.
Kerri:	How many quarters have you got? Twenty?
Liz:	Yes, one quarter makes five apples and out of five apples she can make five tarts which will make that twenty-five tarts and then she will have, wait, one, two, three, four, five quarters, she'll have one, two, three, four, five quarters. . . . (J. Hiebert et al., 1997, p. 121)

Eventually the group arrives at the correct answer: Mom can make 26 tarts and will have half an apple left over.

- Is the apple-tarts problem developmentally appropriate for Ms. Lombard's students? Why or why not?
- What advantages might there be for making this task a group activity?

———————————————

As you undoubtedly know from your own experiences as a student, fractions are more difficult to understand and work with than are whole numbers. But Liz, Jeanette, and Kerri rise to the challenge of the apple-tarts problem and, in the process, possibly acquire new mathematical understandings and problem-solving skills. In other words, the task is *developmentally appropriate* for them.

———————————————

[1]In case your memory of how to divide by a fraction is rusty, you can approach the problem $20 \div ^3/_4$ by inverting the fraction and multiplying, like so: $20 \times ^4/_3 = ^{80}/_3 = 26^2/_3$. In the problem Ms. Lombard presents, Mom can make 26 tarts and have enough apple to make two-thirds of another tart. If Mom has two-thirds of the three-fourths of an apple she needs to make another whole tart, then she has half an apple left over ($^2/_3 \times ^3/_4 = ^1/_2$).

Classroom instruction must take into account the physical, cognitive, personal, and social characteristics and abilities that students at a particular age are likely to have. In this chapter we'll look at general principles of development and then zero in on children's cognitive development—that is, developmental changes in thinking, reasoning, and language. As we look at these topics in the pages ahead, we'll be better able to answer the preceding questions about Ms. Lombard's apple-tarts activity.

General Principles of Human Development

Four general principles characterize children's physical, cognitive, personal, and social development.

- *The sequence of development is somewhat predictable.* Researchers have observed many universals in development; that is, they've seen similar patterns in how children change over time despite considerable differences in the environments in which the children grow up. Some of this universality is marked by the acquisition of developmental milestones—new, developmentally more advanced behaviors—in predictable sequences. For example, children must be able to walk before they can run and jump, and they must be able to count and work with whole numbers before they become capable of using fractions in mathematical problem solving.

- *Children develop at different rates.* Not all children reach particular milestones at the same age: Some reach them earlier, some later. Accordingly, we're apt to see considerable *diversity* in students' developmental accomplishments at any single grade level. As teachers, we should never jump to conclusions about what individual students can and cannot do based on age alone. For example, although Ms. Lombard's apple-tarts problem appears to be developmentally appropriate for some of her students, it might be too advanced for others.

Keep in mind that students of any single age show considerable diversity in what they can and cannot do.

- *Development is often marked by periods of relatively rapid growth (spurts) between periods of slower growth (plateaus).* Development doesn't necessarily proceed at a constant rate. For example, toddlers may speak with a limited vocabulary and one-word "sentences" for several months, yet sometime around their second birthday their vocabulary expands rapidly and their sentences become longer and longer within just a few weeks. And after seemingly stalling out height-wise, many young adolescents undergo an adolescent growth spurt, shooting up several inches within a year or so. Occasionally children even take a temporary step *backward,* apparently because they're in the process of overhauling a particular physical or cognitive skill and are about to make a major leap forward (Gershkoff-Stowe & Thelen, 2004; Morra, Gobbo, Marini, & Sheese, 2008).

    Some developmental theorists have suggested that such patterns of uneven growth reflect distinctly different periods, or *stages,* in development; you'll see an example in the discussion of Piaget's theory later in this chapter. Other theorists instead believe that most aspects of development can best be characterized as reflecting general *trends* that can't really be broken into discrete stages. Either way, early developmental advancements almost certainly provide a foundation on which later advancements can build—hence the predictable *this-before-that* nature of many developmental progressions.

Chapter 3 examines temperamental differences in greater depth.

- *Heredity and environment interact in their effects on development.* Virtually all aspects of development are influenced either directly or indirectly by a child's genetic makeup. For example, soon after birth children begin to show genetic inclinations, or *temperaments,* that predispose them to respond to physical and social events in certain ways—perhaps to be calm or irritable, outgoing or shy, cheerful or fearful. Not all inherited characteristics appear so early, however. Heredity continues to guide a child's growth through maturation—a gradual, genetically driven acquisition of more advanced physical and neurological capabilities over the course of childhood and adolescence. For example, motor skills such as walking, running, and jumping develop primarily as a result of neurological development, increased strength, and increased muscular control—changes that are largely determined by inherited biological "instructions." And genetically driven maturational changes in the brain have a significant impact on children's increasing ability to think and behave effectively and efficiently (more about this point shortly).

Yet environmental factors also make substantial contributions to development. For example, although height and body build are primarily inherited characteristics, good nutrition and regular physical exercise also make a difference. And although children's behaviors are partly the result of inherited temperaments, the ways in which their environment encourages them to behave are just as influential, sometimes even more so.

Historically, many researchers have sought to determine the degree to which various human characteristics are the result of heredity versus environment—an issue often referred to as *nature versus nurture.* But increasingly psychologists have come to realize that heredity and environment interact in ways we can probably never disentangle (e.g., S. W. Cole, 2009; W. Johnson, 2010; Spencer et al., 2009). First and foremost, genes need environmental support in order to do their work. For instance, a child with "tall" genes can grow tall only if good nutrition supports such growth. Furthermore, some genetically driven maturational processes seem to be characterized by sensitive periods—age-related time periods during which certain environmental conditions are especially important for normal development (we'll see examples in the upcoming sections on the brain and language development). In addition, children's inherited characteristics may lead other people to treat them in particular ways. For instance, a physically attractive child will be accepted more readily by peers than a less attractive one, and a temperamentally hyperactive child might be disciplined more harshly than a quieter one. Finally, children can *choose* their environments to some extent, especially as they get older, and they're apt to seek out situations that match their inherited temperaments and abilities.

The last point in the preceding paragraph is important enough to repeat: *Children can choose their environments to some extent.* Children are hardly passive recipients of their environmental legacies. Instead, they actively and intentionally *think about* and *act on* their environments, and in doing so they alter their environments—and the effects of those environments—in significant ways (Mareschal et al., 2007; Nettles, Caughy, & O'Campo, 2008; Nuemi, 2008).

THE MULTIPLE LAYERS OF ENVIRONMENTAL INFLUENCE: BIOECOLOGICAL SYSTEMS AND THE IMPORTANCE OF CULTURE

As we consider the various ways in which the environment might influence children's development, we must be careful that we don't limit our thinking only to children's immediate surroundings. In fact, as developmental theorist Urie Bronfenbrenner has pointed out in his bioecological systems theory, any large society encompasses several "layers" of environment that all have significant impacts on children's development and are, in turn, either directly or indirectly influenced by the other layers and by the children themselves (Bronfenbrenner, 2005; Bronfenbrenner & Ceci, 1994; Bronfenbrenner & Morris, 1998).

Figure 2.1 depicts the various layers of influence that Bronfenbrenner has proposed. More specifically:

1. The *child* brings certain individual characteristics (e.g., unique temperaments and physiological features) and age-related developmental acquisitions (e.g., cognitive abilities and interpersonal skills) that influence the child's behaviors in any given situation.

2. The child is regularly immersed in certain *microsystems*—certain everyday contexts (e.g., family, school, friendships) that both influence and are influenced by the child's characteristics and behaviors.

3. The microsystems in which a child lives and grows *influence one another* in what Bronfenbrenner has called a *mesosystem.* For example, a temperamentally hyperactive child might initially elicit stringent disciplinary actions at school (one microsystem), but concerned parents (another microsystem) might actively seek out the child's teachers and suggest alternative strategies that can channel the child's behaviors into productive activities.

4. Encompassing the day-to-day contexts in which a child lives, works, and plays is a broader *exosystem,* which includes people and institutions that indirectly affect the child's development through their influences on various microsystems. For example, the nature of parents' employment can affect their ability to provide adequate living quarters, nutrition, and health care for their family, and a good social support network can give parents advice,

MyEdLab
Content Extension 2.1.

Learn more about children's physical development in "Physical Development Across Childhood and Adolescence."

MyEdLab
Video Example 2.1.

In this video, 16-year-old Josh describes how his early growth spurt and voice change affected his peer relationships in high school. In what specific ways did his maturational changes influence his social environment?

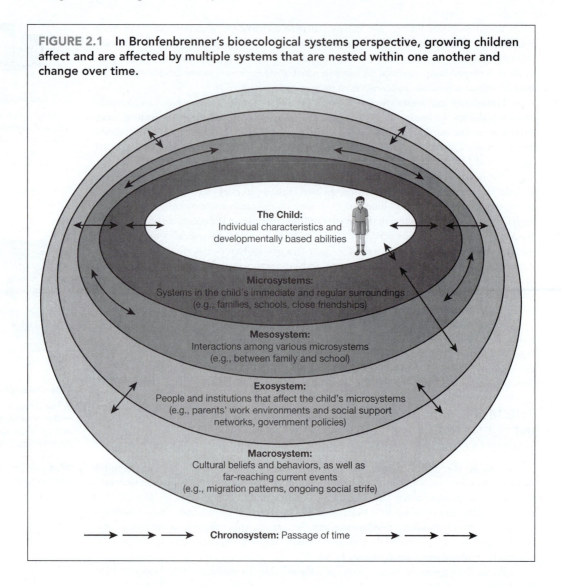

FIGURE 2.1 In Bronfenbrenner's bioecological systems perspective, growing children affect and are affected by multiple systems that are nested within one another and change over time.

The Child:
Individual characteristics and developmentally based abilities

Microsystems:
Systems in the child's immediate and regular surroundings
(e.g., families, schools, close friendships)

Mesosystem:
Interactions among various microsystems
(e.g., between family and school)

Exosystem:
People and institutions that affect the child's microsystems
(e.g., parents' work environments and social support
networks, government policies)

Macrosystem:
Cultural beliefs and behaviors, as well as
far-reaching current events
(e.g., migration patterns, ongoing social strife)

Chronosystem: Passage of time

assistance, and emotional support in challenging circumstances. Meanwhile, local and federal agencies and policies may or may not support teachers and schools in their efforts to nurture children's cognitive development and social well-being.

5. A child's exosystem is enmeshed within an even broader *macrosystem,* which includes a society's general beliefs, ideological perspectives, and behavior patterns, as well as far-reaching current events (e.g., war, migration patterns, ongoing social or political strife).

6. Children and the systems in which they grow up are by no means static entities. Instead, they all change over time—in part because they influence one another—in what Bronfenbrenner has called a *chronosystem* (see the bottom set of arrows in Figure 2.1). For example, teachers' instructional practices might change as academic researchers report new research findings, government agencies might provide websites that help parents and teachers more effectively foster children's cognitive development, and society's general beliefs and practices can change as two or more subgroups regularly interact. In general, children's environments are *dynamic systems* encompassing mutually influencing variables that are in constant flux (also see C. D. Lee, 2010; Thelen & Smith, 1998).

It has become increasingly clear that a key factor impacting *all* of these systems is a child's **culture**—the behaviors and belief systems that characterize any long-standing social group of which the child is a member. Culture is pervasive in many aspects of a child's home environment—for instance, in the behaviors parents and other family members encourage, the disciplinary practices parents use, the books children have access to, the television shows they watch, and so on. Culture influences the broader environmental contexts as well—for instance, by offering certain outlets for leisure time (e.g., basketball courts, Cinco de Mayo festivals) and by advocating or discouraging certain activities (e.g., seeking a college degree, playing video games). Ultimately, culture is an inside-the-head thing as well as an out-there-in-the-world thing: It provides an overall framework by which a child comes to determine what things are normal and abnormal, true and not true, rational and irrational, good and bad (M. Cole, 2006; Shweder et al., 1998).

MyEdLab **Self-Check 2.1**

Role of the Brain in Learning and Development

One key player in children's development is, of course, the brain. The human brain is an incredibly complicated organ that includes several *trillion* cells. About 100 billion of them are nerve cells, or **neurons**, that are microscopic in size and interconnected in countless ways. Some neurons receive information from the rest of the body, others synthesize and interpret that information, and still others send messages that tell the body how to respond to its present circumstances. Accompanying neurons are perhaps 1 to 5 trillion **glial cells**, which serve a variety of specialized functions that enhance the functioning of neurons or in other ways keep the brain going.

Every neuron has numerous branchlike structures, called *dendrites,* that receive messages from other neurons (see Figure 2.2). Every neuron also has an *axon,* a long, armlike structure that transmits information on to still other neurons. The axon may branch out many times, and the ends of its branches have *terminal buttons* that contain certain chemical substances (more about these substances in a moment). For some (but not all) neurons, much of the axon has a white, fatty coating called a *myelin sheath.*

When a neuron's dendrites are stimulated by other neurons—which might also be in the brain or, instead, might extend from other parts of the body—the dendrites become electrically charged. If the total charge reaches a certain level, the neuron fires, sending an electrical impulse along its axon to the terminal buttons. If the axon has a myelin sheath, the impulse travels quite rapidly because it leaps from one gap in the myelin to the next, almost as if it were playing leapfrog. If the axon doesn't have a myelin sheath, the impulse travels more slowly.

Curiously, neurons don't actually touch one another. Instead, they send chemical messages to their neighbors across tiny spaces known as **synapses**. When an electrical impulse moves along a neuron's axon, it signals the terminal buttons to release chemicals known as **neurotransmitters** that travel across the synapses and stimulate neighboring neurons. Any single neuron may have synaptic connections with hundreds or even thousands of other neurons (Goodman & Tessier-Lavigne, 1997; Lichtman, 2001).

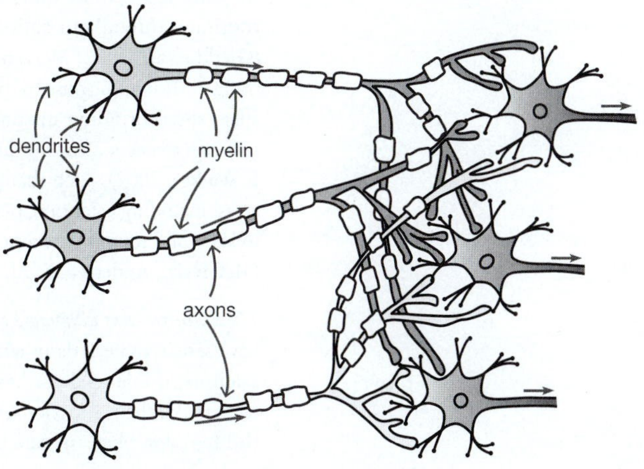

With these basics in mind, let's consider four key points about the brain and its role in cognitive development.

- *Different parts of the brain have different specialties, but they all work closely with one another.* Brain structures in the lower and middle parts of the brain specialize in essential physiological processes (e.g., breathing), habitual body movements (e.g., riding a bicycle), and basic perceptual skills (e.g., diverting attention to potentially life-threatening stimuli). Complex, conscious thinking takes place primarily in the **cortex**, which rests on the top and sides of the brain like a thick, lumpy toupee. The part of the cortex located just behind the forehead, known as the *prefrontal cortex,* is largely responsible for a wide variety of

FIGURE 2.2   Neurons and their interconnections.

dendrites   myelin

axons

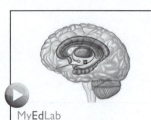

MyEdLab
Video Explanation 2.1.
In this short video, you can learn a little more about basic structures in the brain.

very human activities, including sustained attention, planning, reasoning, decision making, coordination of complex activities, and inhibition of nonproductive thoughts and behaviors. Other areas of the cortex are actively involved in interpreting visual and auditory information, identifying the spatial characteristics of objects and events, and retaining general knowledge about the world.

To some degree, the left and right halves of the cortex—its two *hemispheres*—also have somewhat distinct specialties. For most people, the left hemisphere takes primary responsibility for language and logical thinking, whereas the right hemisphere is more dominant in visual and spatial tasks (Byrnes, 2001; Ornstein, 1997; Siegel, 2012). Yet contrary to a popular belief, people rarely, if ever, think exclusively in one hemisphere. There's really no such thing as "left-brain" or "right-brain" thinking: The two hemispheres constantly collaborate in day-to-day tasks. In fact, learning or thinking about virtually anything, even a fairly simple idea, tends to be *distributed* across many parts of the brain (Bressler, 2002; Gonsalves & Cohen, 2010; Haxby et al., 2001).

- *Learning and cognitive development involve changes in synapses, neurons, and glial cells.* Much of human learning involves strengthening existing synapses between neurons or else forming new ones. Sometimes, however, making progress actually involves *eliminating* synapses. Effective learning requires not only that people think and do certain things but also that they *not* think and do other things—in other words, that they inhibit tendencies to think or behave in particular ways (C. N. Davidson, 2011; Lichtman, 2001; Merzenich, 2001). In addition, a good deal of learning seems to involve the formation of new neurons or glial cells (Koob, 2009; Spalding et al., 2013).

- *Developmental changes in the brain enable increasingly complex and efficient thought.* Neurons begin to form synapses long before a child is born. But shortly after birth, the rate of synapse formation increases dramatically. Neurons sprout new dendrites in many directions, and so they come into contact with a lot of their neighbors, especially in the first 2 or 3 years of life. Much of this early synaptogenesis appears to be driven primarily by genetic programming rather than by learning experiences. Thanks to synaptogenesis, children in the elementary grades have many more synapses than adults do (Bruer, 1999; C. A. Nelson, Thomas, & de Haan, 2006).

  As children encounter different stimuli and experiences in their daily lives, some synapses come in quite handy and are used repeatedly. Others are largely useless, and these gradually fade away through another genetically driven process known as synaptic pruning, a process that continues throughout the elementary and secondary school years and into adulthood. Most synaptic pruning is a *good* thing—not a bad one—because it eliminates "nuisance" synapses that are inconsistent with typical environmental events and appropriate responses. Synaptic pruning, then, may be Mother Nature's way of making the brain more efficient (Bruer & Greenough, 2001; Bryck & Fisher, 2012; Huttenlocher & Dabholkar, 1997).

  Another important developmental process in the brain is myelination. When neurons first develop, their axons have no myelin sheath. As they acquire this myelin over time, they fire much more quickly, greatly enhancing the brain's overall efficiency. Myelination continues throughout childhood, adolescence, and early adulthood, especially in the cortex (Giedd et al., 2012; Merzenich, 2001; Paus et al., 1999).

  In addition, the onset of puberty is marked by significant changes in hormone levels, which affect the continuing maturation of brain structures and possibly also affect the production and effectiveness of neurotransmitters (Kolb, Gibb, & Robinson, 2003; Shen et al., 2010; E. F. Walker, 2002). Such changes can have an impact on adolescents' functioning in a variety of areas, including attention, planning, and impulse control. To some degree, adolescents' abilities to learn and respond appropriately may temporarily *decrease* until brain functioning restabilizes (McGivern, Andersen, Byrd, Mutter, & Reilly, 2002; Shen et al., 2010; Steinberg, 2009).

- *The brain remains adaptable throughout life.* Some aspects of cognitive development appear to have sensitive periods in which certain kinds of environmental stimulation are crucial. For example, if infants don't have normal exposure to patterns of light (e.g., if congenital cataracts make them functionally blind), they may soon lose the ability to see normally. And if children don't hear spoken language in the first few years of life, they're apt to have trouble mastering some of its complexities once they *do* begin to hear it (more about this point later

Applying Brain Research

Taking Developmental Changes in the Brain into Account

Be careful—many recently published books and articles about "using brain research" and "brain-based learning" either misrepresent or misapply researchers' findings about brain development. The following three recommendations are consistent with current knowledge about the brain and how it changes with age.

- **Provide reasonable stimulation for young children; don't overload them with new information and activities for fear of their "losing synapses."** Some well-meaning educators have proposed that the proliferation of new synapses in the preschool and early elementary years points to a sensitive period in brain development. Accordingly, they urge us to maximize children's educational experiences—providing reading instruction, violin lessons, art classes, and the like—during this time period. Before you, too, jump to such a conclusion, consider this point: Although adequate nutrition and everyday forms of stimulation are critical for normal brain development, there is *no* evidence that jam-packed, information- and skills-intensive experiences in the early years enhance brain power over the long run (Bruer, 1999; R. A. Thompson & Nelson, 2001).

- **Keep in mind that adolescents' brains have not yet fully matured.** Synaptic pruning and myelination—two developmental processes that enhance the brain's efficiency—continue throughout adolescence and beyond. Adolescents' brains are *not* adult brains, especially in the prefrontal cortex—that part of the brain that controls sustained attention, planning, reasoning, impulse control, and other abilities so important for independent learning and responsible behavior (Reyna, Chapman, Dougherty, & Confrey, 2012; Steinberg, 2009). Thus, many middle school and high school students need considerable structure and guidance in order to get and keep them on the road to academic success.

- **Be optimistic that students of all ages can acquire a wide variety of new topics and skills.** For some content areas—for instance, in music and foreign languages—instruction in the preschool or early elementary years appears to mold the brain somewhat differently than does instruction in the later school years (K. L. Hyde et al., 2009; P. K. Kuhl et al., 2005). Furthermore, children of differing ages have differing levels of prior knowledge and experience on which to draw as they work to acquire new information and skills. But ultimately we must keep in mind the *plasticity* of the human brain: With reasonable effort, practice, and support, human learners of any age can master a great many things.

in the chapter). However, seeing patterned light and hearing spoken language are *normal* experiences, not exceptional ones. There is *no* evidence to indicate that sensitive periods exist for traditional academic subjects such as reading and mathematics.

From a physiological standpoint, the brain's ability to reorganize itself in order to adapt to changing circumstances—that is, its plasticity—persists throughout the life span (Chein & Schneider, 2012; Kolb et al., 2003; C. A. Nelson et al., 2006). The early years are important for development, to be sure, but so are the later years. For most topics and skills, there isn't a single "best" or "only" time to learn (Bruer, 1999; Byrnes & Fox, 1998; Geary, 1998, 2008). The human brain never goes into lockdown mode.

As researchers gradually pin down how the brain works and develops, they're also beginning to get clues about how we can best foster children's and adolescents' cognitive development; three research-based recommendations are presented in the Applying Brain Research feature "Taking Developmental Changes in the Brain into Account." Even so, current knowledge of brain physiology doesn't yield many specifics about how best to foster students' learning and cognitive development (Byrnes, 2007; G. A. Miller, 2010; Varma, McCandliss, & Schwartz, 2008). By and large, if we want to understand the nature of human learning and cognitive development, we must look primarily at what psychologists, rather than neurologists, have discovered. Two early theories—those of Jean Piaget and Lev Vygotsky—have been especially influential in molding contemporary views of how children learn and develop.

> MyEdLab **Self-Check 2.2**
>
> MyEdLab **Application Exercise 2.1.** In this exercise, see if you can detect common teacher and parent misconceptions about how the brain develops.

Piaget's Theory of Cognitive Development

Do you think of yourself as a logical person? Just how logical *are* you? Try out your logical reasoning abilities in the following exercise.

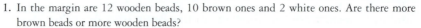

EXPERIENCING FIRSTHAND
BEADS, BEINGS, AND BASKETBALLS

Take a moment to solve the following three problems:

1. In the margin are 12 wooden beads, 10 brown ones and 2 white ones. Are there more brown beads or more wooden beads?

2. If all children are human beings,
   And if all human beings are mammals,
   Then must all children be mammals?

3. If all children are basketballs,
   And if all basketballs are jellybeans,
   Then must all children be jellybeans?

You undoubtedly found the first problem quite easy; there are, of course, more wooden beads than brown beads. And when you read the second problem, you probably concluded fairly quickly that, yes, all children must be mammals. The third problem is a bit tricky: It follows the same line of reasoning as the second, but the logical conclusion—all children must be jellybeans—contradicts what is true in reality.

In the early 1920s the Swiss biologist Jean Piaget began studying children's responses to problems of this nature. He used an approach he called the **clinical method**, in which an adult presents a task or problem and asks a child a series of questions about it, tailoring later questions to the child's responses to previous ones. For example, let's look at what happened when a researcher in Piaget's laboratory presented the wooden beads problem to a 6-year-old, whom we'll call Brian:[2]

> *Adult:* Are there more wooden beads or more brown beads?
>
> *Brian:* More brown ones, because there are two white ones.
>
> *Adult:* Are the white ones made of wood?
>
> *Brian:* Yes.
>
> *Adult:* And the brown ones?
>
> *Brian:* Yes.
>
> *Adult:* Then are there more brown ones or more wooden ones?
>
> *Brian:* More brown ones. (dialogue from Piaget, 1952a, pp. 163–164)

During further questioning, Brian continued to assert that the brown beads outnumbered the wooden beads. In an effort to help him see otherwise, the adult asked him to draw two necklaces, one made of the brown beads and another made of the wooden beads. Brian drew a series of black rings for the brown-beads necklace; he drew a series of black rings plus two white rings for the wooden-beads necklace.

> *Adult:* Good. Now which will be longer, the one with the brown beads or the one with the wooden beads?
>
> *Brian:* The one with the brown beads. (dialogue from Piaget, 1952a, p. 164)

Piaget suggested that young children such as Brian have trouble with **class inclusion** tasks in which they must think of an object as simultaneously belonging to a category and to one of its subcategories—in this case, thinking of a bead as being both *brown* and *wooden* at the same time. Piaget found that many 4- and 5-year-olds have difficulty with class inclusion tasks such as the beads problem but that 7- and 8-year-olds almost always respond to such tasks correctly. He found, too, that 10-year-olds have an easier time with logic problems that involve real-world

---

[2]Piaget used abbreviations to identify specific children in his studies. In this case he used the letters *BRI*, but we've given the child a name to allow for easier discussion.

phenomena (such as categories and subcategories of living creatures) than with problems involving hypothetical and contrary-to-fact ideas (such as jellybean children), whereas many adolescents can effectively deal with both kinds of problems.

Through a wide variety of thought-provoking questions and tasks, Piaget and his research colleagues discovered a great deal about what and how children think about the world around them (e.g., Inhelder & Piaget, 1958; Piaget, 1929, 1952b, 1959, 1970, 1980). Piaget integrated his findings into a theory of cognitive development that has made major contributions to contemporary understandings of children's learning and development.

PIAGET'S BASIC ASSUMPTIONS

Piaget introduced a number of ideas and concepts to describe and explain the changes in logical thinking he observed in children and adolescents.

- *Children are active and motivated learners.* Piaget believed that children are naturally curious about their world and actively seek out information to help them make sense of it. They continually experiment with the objects they encounter, manipulating them and observing the effects of their actions.

- *Children construct rather than absorb knowledge.* In their day-to-day experiences, children don't just passively soak up a collection of isolated facts. Instead, they pull their experiences together into an integrated view of how the world operates. For example, by observing that objects always fall down (never up) when released, children begin to construct a basic understanding of gravity. As they interact with family pets, visit farms and zoos, and look at picture books, they develop more complex understandings of animals. Because Piaget proposed that children construct their own beliefs and understandings from their experiences, his theory is sometimes called a *constructivist* theory or, more generally, constructivism.

MyEdLab
Video Example 2.2.
Young children are naturally curious about things in their environment. In what ways does 2-year-old Maddie explore the properties of her new toy?

In Piaget's terminology, the things children do and know are organized as schemes— groups of similar actions or thoughts that are used repeatedly in response to the environment. Initially, children's schemes are largely behavioral in nature, but over time they become increasingly mental and, eventually, abstract. For example, an infant may have a putting-things-in-mouth scheme that she applies to a variety of objects, including her thumb, cookies, and toys. A 7-year-old may have a scheme for identifying snakes that includes their long, thin bodies, lack of legs, and slithery nature. A 13-year-old may have a scheme for what constitutes *fashion,* allowing him to classify certain peers as being either really cool or "total losers."

Over time, children's schemes are modified with experience, and many become integrated with one another. For instance, children begin to take hierarchical interrelationships into account: They learn that poodles, cocker spaniels, and German shepherds are all dogs; that dogs, snakes, and birds are all animals; and that both animals and plants are living creatures. A progressively more organized body of knowledge and thought processes allows children to think in increasingly complex and logical ways.

- *Children continually learn new things through two complementary processes: assimilation and accommodation.* Assimilation involves responding to or thinking about an object or event in a way that's consistent with an existing scheme. For example, an infant may assimilate a new teddy bear into her putting-things-in-mouth scheme. A 7-year-old may quickly identify a new slithery creature in the garden as a snake. A 13-year-old may readily label a classmate's apparel or hairstyle as being either quite fashionable or "soooo yesterday."

But sometimes children can't easily interpret and respond to a new object or event using existing schemes. In these situations one of two forms of accommodation occurs: Children either (1) modify an existing scheme to account for the new object or event or (2) form a new scheme to deal with it. For example, an infant may have to open her mouth wider than usual to accommodate a teddy bear's fat paw. A 13-year-old may have to revise his existing scheme of fashion according to changes in what's hot and what's not. A 7-year-old who encounters a long, slithery creature with four legs can't apply the *snake* scheme (snakes don't have legs) and thus, after some research, may acquire a new scheme—*salamander.*

Assimilation and accommodation typically work hand in hand as children develop their knowledge and understanding of the world. Children interpret each new event within the

When introducing a new concept or procedure, show students how it relates to something they already know.

context of their existing knowledge (assimilation) but at the same time may modify their knowledge as a result of the new event (accommodation). Accommodation rarely happens without assimilation: Children can benefit from, or accommodate to, new experiences only when they can relate those experiences to their current knowledge and beliefs.

• *Interactions with one's physical and social environments are essential for cognitive development.* According to Piaget, active experimentation with the physical world is critical for cognitive growth. By exploring and manipulating physical objects—for instance, fiddling with sand and water, playing games with balls and bats, and conducting science experiments—children see the effects of erosion, discover principles related to force and gravity, and so on.

In Piaget's view, interaction with other people is equally important. Frequent social interactions—both pleasant (e.g., conversations) and unpleasant (e.g., conflicts about sharing and fair play)—help young children come to realize that different people see things differently and that their own view of the world isn't necessarily completely accurate or logical. And as children get older, discussions and disagreements about complex issues and problems—for instance, the apple-tarts problem in the opening case study—can help them recognize and reexamine inconsistencies in their own reasoning.

Occasionally induce disequilibrium by presenting puzzling phenomena that students cannot easily explain using their existing understandings.

• *A process of equilibration promotes progression toward increasingly complex thought.* Piaget suggested that children are often in a state of equilibrium: They can comfortably interpret and respond to new events using existing schemes. But as children grow older and expand their horizons, they sometimes encounter situations for which their current knowledge and skills are inadequate. Such situations create disequilibrium, a sort of mental discomfort that spurs them to try to make sense of what they're observing. By replacing, reorganizing, or better integrating certain schemes (i.e., through accommodation), children can better understand and address previously puzzling events. The process of moving from equilibrium to disequilibrium and back to equilibrium again is known as equilibration. In Piaget's view, equilibration and children's intrinsic desire to achieve equilibrium promote the development of more complex levels of thought and knowledge.

As an example, let's return to Brian's responses to the beads problem. Recall that the adult asked Brian to draw two necklaces, one made with the brown beads and one made with the wooden beads. The adult presumably hoped that after Brian drew a brown-and-white necklace that was longer than an all-brown necklace, he would notice that his drawings were inconsistent with his statement that there were more brown beads. The inconsistency might have led Brian to experience disequilibrium, perhaps to the point where he would revise his conclusion. In this case, however, Brian was apparently oblivious to the inconsistency, remained in equilibrium, and thus had no need to revise his thinking.

• *In part as a result of maturational changes in the brain, children think in qualitatively different ways at different ages.* Long before researchers knew much about how the brain changes with age, Piaget speculated that it *does* change in significant ways and that such changes enable more complex thought processes. He suggested that major neurological changes take place when children are about 2 years old, again when they're 6 or 7, and yet again around puberty. Changes at each of these times allow new abilities to emerge, such that children progress through a sequence of stages that reflect increasingly sophisticated thought. As you've already learned, the brain does, in fact, continue to develop throughout childhood and adolescence, but whether some of its changes enable the cognitive advancements Piaget described is still an open question.

PIAGET'S PROPOSED STAGES OF COGNITIVE DEVELOPMENT

Piaget proposed that as a result of brain maturation, innumerable experiences in children's physical and social environments, and children's natural desire to make sense of and adapt to their world, cognitive development proceeds through four distinct stages, with the last three being constructed from children's accomplishments in preceding stages (e.g., Piaget, 1971). Thus, the stages are

Ta-daa!!

An event that contradicts what we currently know and believe about the world creates *disequilibrium*—a feeling of discomfort that motivates us to try to resolve the contradiction in some way.

hierarchical—each stage provides a foundation for any subsequent ones—and so children progress through them in a particular order.

Table 2.1 summarizes Piaget's proposed stages and presents examples of abilities acquired during each one. As you look at the table, please keep three things in mind. First, some children are apt to be in *transition* from one stage to the next, displaying characteristics of two adjacent stages at the same time. Second, as children gain abilities associated with more advanced stages, they don't necessarily leave behind the characteristics they acquired in previous stages. Finally, many developmental theorists suggest—and Piaget himself acknowledged—that the four stages better describe how children and adolescents *can* think, rather than how they always *do* think, at any particular age (Flavell, 1994; Halford & Andrews, 2006; Klaczynski, 2001; Tanner & Inhelder, 1960).

COMPARE/CONTRAST

TABLE 2.1 • Piaget's Proposed Stages of Cognitive Development			
STAGE	**PROPOSED AGE RANGE**[a]	**GENERAL DESCRIPTION**	**EXAMPLES OF ABILITIES ACQUIRED**
Sensorimotor Stage	Begins at birth	Schemes are based largely on behaviors and perceptions. Especially in the early part of this stage, children cannot think about things that are not immediately in front of them, and so they focus on what they are doing and seeing at the moment.	• **Trial-and-error experimentation with physical objects:** Exploration and manipulation of objects to determine their properties • **Object permanence:** Realization that objects continue to exist even when removed from view • **Symbolic thought:** Representation of physical objects and events as mental entities (*symbols*)
Preoperational Stage	Emerges at about age 2	Thanks in part to their rapidly developing symbolic thinking abilities, children can now think and talk about things beyond their immediate experience. However, they do not yet reason in logical, adultlike ways.	• **Language:** Rapid expansion of vocabulary and grammatical structures • **Extensive pretend play:** Enactment of imaginary scenarios with plots and assigned roles (e.g., mommy, doctor, Superman) • **Intuitive thought:** Some logical thinking (especially after age 4), but based primarily on hunches and intuition rather than on conscious awareness of logical principles
Concrete Operations Stage	Emerges at about age 6 or 7	Adultlike logic appears but is limited to reasoning about concrete, real-life situations.	• **Distinction between one's own and others' perspectives:** Recognition that one's own thoughts and feelings may be different from those of others and do not necessarily reflect reality • **Class inclusion:** Ability to classify objects as belonging to two or more categories simultaneously • **Conservation:** Realization that amount stays the same if nothing is added or taken away, regardless of alterations in shape or arrangement
Formal Operations Stage	Emerges at about age 11 or 12[b]	Logical reasoning processes are applied to abstract ideas as well as to concrete objects and situations. Many capabilities essential for advanced reasoning in science and mathematics appear.	• **Logical reasoning about abstract, hypothetical, and contrary-to-fact ideas:** Ability to draw logical deductions about situations that have no basis in physical reality • **Proportional reasoning:** Conceptual understanding of fractions, percentages, decimals, and ratios • **Formulation of multiple hypotheses:** Ability to identify two or more competing hypotheses about possible cause-and-effect relationships • **Separation and control of variables:** Ability to test hypotheses by manipulating one variable while holding other relevant variables constant • **Idealism:** Ability to envision alternatives to current social and political practices, sometimes with little regard for what is realistically possible under existing circumstances

[a]The age ranges presented in the table are *averages*; some children reach more advanced stages a bit earlier, others a bit later. Also, some children may be in *transition* from one stage to the next, displaying characteristics of two adjacent stages at the same time.
[b]Researchers have found considerable variability in when adolescents begin to show reasoning processes consistent with Piaget's formal operations stage. Furthermore, not all cultures value or nurture formal operational logic, perhaps because it is largely irrelevant to people's daily lives and tasks in those cultural groups.

The preoperational, concrete operations, and formal operations stages all occur during the school years, and so we'll look at these three stages more closely.

PREOPERATIONAL STAGE (AGE 2 THROUGH AGE 6 OR 7)

In the early part of the preoperational stage, children's language skills virtually explode, and the many words in their rapidly increasing vocabularies serve as *symbols* that enable them to mentally represent and think about a wide variety of objects and events. However, preoperational thought has some definite limitations, especially when compared to the concrete operational thinking that emerges later. For example, Piaget described young children as exhibiting preoperational egocentrism: They don't yet have sufficient reasoning abilities to look at a situation as someone else might look at it. Thus, preschoolers might play games together without checking to be sure they're all playing by the same rules, and they may tell stories in which they leave out details that are critical for listeners' understanding.

Young children's thinking also tends to be somewhat illogical at times, at least from an adult's point of view. We've already seen how young children have difficulty with class inclusion problems (recall Brian's insistence that the brown beads outnumber the wooden ones). In addition, they're apt to have trouble with conservation: They fail to realize that if nothing is added or taken away, the amount of a substance or set of objects must stay the same regardless of changes in the shape or arrangement of items. As illustrations, consider what happens when we present two conservation tasks to 5-year-old Nathan:

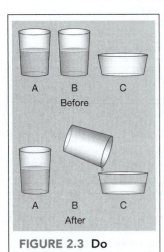

FIGURE 2.3 Do Glasses A and C contain the same amount of water?

Conservation of liquid: We show Nathan the three glasses in Figure 2.3. We ask him whether Glasses A and B contain the same amount of water, and he replies confidently that they do. We then pour the water from Glass B into Glass C and ask him whether A and C have the same amount. Nathan replies, "No, that glass [pointing to Glass A] has more because it's taller."

Conservation of number: We next show Nathan two rows of seven pennies each, like so:

Nathan counts the pennies in each row and agrees that the two rows have the same amount. We spread the second row out, and the pennies now look like this:

When we ask Nathan whether the two rows still have the same number, he replies, "No, this one [pointing to the bottom row] has more because it's longer."

As children approach the later part of the preoperational stage, perhaps at around age 4 or 5, they show early signs of adultlike logic. For example, they sometimes draw correct conclusions about class inclusion and conservation problems. But they base their reasoning on hunches and intuition rather than on any conscious awareness of underlying logical principles, and thus they can't yet explain *why* their conclusions are correct.

CONCRETE OPERATIONS STAGE (AGE 6 OR 7 THROUGH AGE 11 OR 12)

Piaget proposed that as children enter the concrete operations stage, their thought processes become organized into larger systems of mental processes—*operations*—that allow them to think more logically than they have previously. They now realize that their own perspectives and feelings aren't necessarily shared by others and may reflect personal opinions rather than reality. They also exhibit such logical reasoning abilities as class inclusion and conservation. For example, they should readily conclude, as you presumably did in an earlier Experiencing Firsthand exercise, that in a group of brown and white wooden beads, there obviously must be more wooden beads than brown ones.

FIGURE 2.4 Conservation of weight: Ball A and Ball B initially weigh the same. When Ball B is flattened into a pancake shape, how does its weight now compare with that of Ball A?

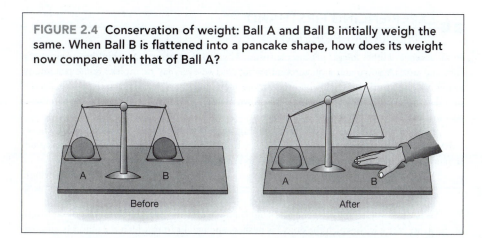

Children continue to refine their newly acquired logical thinking capabilities for several years. For instance, some forms of conservation, such as conservation of liquid and conservation of number, appear at age 6 or 7, whereas other forms emerge later. Consider the problem in Figure 2.4. Using a balance scale, an adult shows a child that two balls of clay have the same weight. One ball is removed from the scale and smashed into a pancake shape. Does the pancake weigh the same as the unsmashed ball, or are the weights different? Children typically don't achieve conservation of weight—they don't realize that the flattened pancake weighs the same as the round ball it was earlier—until about age 9 (Morra et al., 2008).

Although students displaying concrete operational thought show many signs of logical thinking, their cognitive development isn't yet complete. For example, they have trouble understanding abstract ideas, and they may struggle with problems involving fractions and other proportions, as Liz, Jeanette, and Kerri do in the opening case study.

FORMAL OPERATIONS STAGE (AGE 11 OR 12 THROUGH ADULTHOOD)

Once children acquire abilities characterizing Piaget's formal operations stage, they can think about concepts that have little or no basis in concrete reality—for instance, abstract concepts, hypothetical ideas, and contrary-to-fact statements. Thus, they begin to find underlying meanings in proverbs such as *A rolling stone gathers no moss* and *Don't put the cart before the horse.* They can also recognize that what is logically valid might be different from what is true in the real world. For example, recall the earlier children-basketballs-jellybeans problem: *If* all children are basketballs and *if* all basketballs are jellybeans, then formal operational thinkers can logically conclude that all children must be jellybeans, even though in the real world children *aren't* jellybeans.

From Piaget's perspective, students' mathematical abilities are likely to improve when formal operational thinking develops. Abstract math problems, such as word problems, should become easier to solve. And students should become capable of understanding such concepts as *negative number, pi* (π), and *infinity*—for instance, they should now comprehend how temperature can be below zero and how two parallel lines will never touch even if they go on forever. In addition, because students can now understand proportions (see Table 2.1), they can more easily use fractions, decimals, and ratios when solving problems.

Scientific reasoning is also likely to improve when students are capable of formal operational thought. Three of the formal operational abilities listed in Table 2.1—reasoning logically about hypothetical ideas, formulating multiple hypotheses, and separating and controlling variables—together allow many adolescents to use the *scientific method,* in which they test several possible explanations for an observed phenomenon in a systematic manner. As an example, consider the pendulum problem in the following exercise.

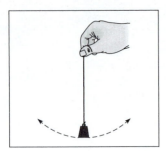

In the absence of other forces, an object suspended by a rope or string—a pendulum—swings at a constant rate. (A yo-yo and a playground swing are two everyday examples.) Some pendulums swing back and forth rather slowly; others move more quickly. What characteristics of a pendulum determine how quickly it swings? Jot down at least three hypotheses about the variable(s) that might affect a pendulum's oscillation rate.

Now gather several small objects of varying weights (e.g., a paper clip, a house key, a heavy bolt) and a piece of string. Tie one of the objects to one end of the string, and set your pendulum in motion. Conduct one or more experiments to test each of your hypotheses.

What can you conclude? What variable or variables affect the rate at which a pendulum swings?

What hypotheses did you generate? Four common ones involve weight of the object, length of the string, force with which the object is pushed, and height from which the object is released. Did you test each of your hypotheses in a systematic fashion? That is, did you *separate and control variables,* testing one at a time while holding all others constant? For example, if you were testing the hypothesis that weight makes a difference, you might have tried objects of different weights while keeping constant the length of the string, the force with which you pushed each object, and the height from which you released or pushed each one. Similarly, if you hypothesized that length was a critical factor, you might have varied the string length while continuing to use the same object and setting the pendulum in motion in a consistent manner. If you carefully separated and controlled each variable, you should have come to the correct conclusion: Only *length* affects a pendulum's oscillation rate.

An additional outcome of abstract and hypothetical thinking is the ability to envision how the world might be different from the way it actually is (e.g., see Figure 2.5). In some cases

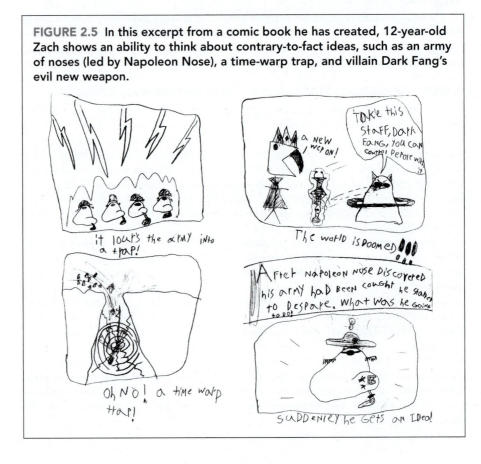

FIGURE 2.5 In this excerpt from a comic book he has created, 12-year-old Zach shows an ability to think about contrary-to-fact ideas, such as an army of noses (led by Napoleon Nose), a time-warp trap, and villain Dark Fang's evil new weapon.

adolescents envision a world that is *better* than the one they live in, and they exhibit considerable concern and idealism about social and political issues. Some secondary school students devote a great deal of energy to local or global problems, such as water pollution and animal rights. However, they may offer recommendations for change that seem logical but aren't practical in today's world. For example, a teenager might argue that racism could disappear overnight if people would just begin to "love one another," or that their country should eliminate its armed forces and weaponry as a way of moving toward world peace. Piaget proposed that adolescent idealism reflects formal operational egocentrism, an inability to separate one's own logical abstractions from the perspectives of others and from practical considerations. Only through experience do adolescents eventually begin to temper their optimism with some realism about what is possible in a given time frame and with limited resources.

Encourage adolescents to discuss their visions for a better world, but point out instances when their ideals are unrealistic.

CRITIQUING PIAGET'S THEORY

Perhaps Piaget's greatest contribution to our understanding of cognitive development was the nature of the *questions* he asked and tried to answer about how children think and reason. In addition, some of his key ideas have stood the test of time, including his ideas that children construct their own knowledge about the world, that they must relate new experiences to what they already know, and that encountering puzzling phenomena can sometimes spur them to revise their understandings.

Piaget's descriptions of processes that *propel* development—especially assimilation, accommodation, and equilibration—can be frustratingly vague, however (M. Chapman, 1988; diSessa, 2006; Klahr, 2001). And interaction with one's physical environment, although certainly valuable, may be less critical than Piaget believed. For instance, children with significant physical disabilities, who can't actively experiment with physical objects, learn a great deal about the world simply by observing what happens around them (Bebko, Burke, Craven, & Sarlo, 1992; Brainerd, 2003).

A SECOND LOOK AT PIAGET'S STAGES

Piaget's proposal that cognitive development progresses in stages has sparked a great deal of follow-up research. In general, this research supports Piaget's proposed *sequence* in which different abilities emerge but not necessarily the *ages* at which they emerge. Piaget probably underestimated the thinking capabilities of preschoolers and elementary school students. For example, under some circumstances preschoolers are capable of class inclusion and conservation, and they have some ability to comprehend abstract and contrary-to-fact ideas (S. R. Beck, Robinson, Carroll, & Apperly, 2006; Goswami & Pauen, 2005; McNeil & Uttal, 2009; Rosser, 1994). Many first and second graders can understand and use simple proportions (e.g., $\frac{1}{2}$, $\frac{1}{3}$, $\frac{1}{4}$) if they can relate the proportions to everyday objects and situations (Empson, 1999; Van Dooren, De Bock, Hessels, Janssens, & Verschaffel, 2005). And some older elementary school children can separate and control variables if a task is simplified in some way (Lorch et al., 2010; Metz, 1995; Ruffman, Perner, Olson, & Doherty, 1993).

Yet Piaget seems to have *over*estimated what adolescents can do. Formal operational thinking processes emerge more gradually than he suggested, and even high school students and adults don't necessarily use them regularly (Flieller, 1999; Kuhn & Franklin, 2006; Morra et al., 2008; Tourniaire & Pulos, 1985). Many adolescents seem to better understand abstract ideas when those ideas are accompanied by concrete examples and materials (Blair & Schwartz, 2012; Kaminski & Sloutsky, 2012). Furthermore, students may demonstrate formal operational thought in one content domain while thinking concretely in another (Lovell, 1979; Tamburrini, 1982).

Even in the high school grades, accompany abstract ideas with concrete examples and experiences.

Explicit training and other structured experiences can sometimes help children acquire reasoning abilities sooner than Piaget thought was possible (Brainerd, 2003; Kuhn, 2006). For example, children as young as age 4 or 5 begin to show conservation after having experience with conservation tasks, especially if they can actively manipulate the task materials and discuss their reasoning with someone who already exhibits conservation (Halford & Andrews, 2006; Siegler & Chen, 2008; Siegler & Lin, 2010). Similarly, instruction with concrete or graphic materials can help children and adolescents better understand how to work with fractions and other proportions (Fujimura, 2001; Jitendra, Star, Rodrigues, Lindell, & Someki, 2011; Sarama & Clements, 2009). And in the upper elementary grades, children become increasingly able to separate and control variables when they have many experiences that require them to do so, and they can more easily solve logical problems involving hypothetical ideas if they're taught

MyEdLab
Video Example 2.3.

In what specific ways does this fourth-grade teacher use concrete materials to help his students understand how to add fractions with different denominators?

relevant problem-solving strategies (Kuhn & Pease, 2008; S. Lee, 1985; Lorch et al., 2014; Schauble, 1990).

In light of such evidence, most researchers believe that the logical thinking abilities Piaget described emerge in gradual, trend-like ways rather than in discrete stages. Nevertheless, as you'll see shortly, some theorists have offered stage-based theories that might account for children's logical reasoning in specific skill areas or content domains.

CONSIDERING DIVERSITY FROM THE PERSPECTIVE OF PIAGET'S THEORY

As a researcher working in Switzerland, Piaget conducted his studies with a particular population: Swiss children. However, the course of cognitive development appears to vary somewhat from one cultural group to another, probably because different cultures provide somewhat different experiences. For example, Mexican children who have had considerable experience in hand-weaving complex flower, animal, and geometric designs show preoperational and concrete operational abilities in new weaving problems sooner than do their same-age counterparts in the United States; the difference remains even if the U.S. children are given explicit training in the Mexican weaving techniques (Maynard & Greenfield, 2003). And Mexican children whose families make pottery for a living acquire conservation skills earlier than their peers in other Mexican families, probably because making pottery requires children to make frequent judgments about needed quantities of clay regardless of the clay's shape (Price-Williams, Gordon, & Ramirez, 1969).

Formal operational reasoning skills—for example, reasoning about hypothetical ideas and separating and controlling variables—also vary from culture to culture (Flieller, 1999; Norenzayan, Choi, & Peng, 2007; Rogoff, 2003). Mainstream Western culture actively nurtures these skills through formal instruction in such academic content domains as science, mathematics, literature, and social studies. In some other cultures, however, such skills may have little relevance to people's daily lives (M. Cole, 1990; J. G. Miller, 1997; Norenzayan et al., 2007).

Even within a single cultural group, logical reasoning abilities vary considerably from one individual to another, in part as a result of differences in background knowledge about particular topics. For example, adolescents (adults, too) often apply formal operational thought to topics about which they know a great deal yet think concretely about topics with which they're unfamiliar (Girotto & Light, 1993; M. C. Linn, Clement, Pulos, & Sullivan, 1989; Schliemann & Carraher, 1993). As an illustration, in a study by Pulos and Linn (1981), 13-year-olds were shown a picture similar to the one in Figure 2.6 and told, "These four children go fishing every week, and one child, Herb, always catches the most fish. The other children wonder why." If you look at the picture, you can see that Herb differs from the other children in several ways, including his location, the bait he uses, and the length of his fishing rod. Students who had fished a great deal more effectively separated and controlled variables for this situation than they did for the pendulum problem presented earlier, whereas the reverse was true for students with little or no fishing experience.

CONTEMPORARY EXTENSIONS AND APPLICATIONS OF PIAGET'S THEORY

Despite its shortcomings, Piaget's theory has had considerable influence on present-day thinking about cognitive development and classroom practice. A few contemporary *neo-Piagetian* theories integrate elements of Piaget's theory with current theories of thinking and learning. Furthermore,

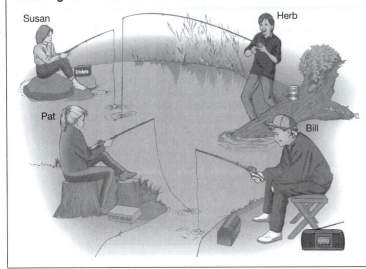

FIGURE 2.6 What are some possible reasons that Herb is catching more fish than the others?

Susan
Herb
Pat
Bill

Source: Based on image created by Steven Pulos. Adapted with permission.

MyEdLab
Video Example 2.4.

Knowledge about a particular content domain enhances children's ability to separate and control variables in that domain. For example, notice how a child with fishing experience (10-year-old Kent) identifies more variables in the fishing problem than does an older child who has never fished (14-year-old Alicia).

Into The Classroom

Applying Piaget's Theory

🍎 **Use Piaget's stages as a rough guide to what students at different grade levels can do, but don't take them too literally.**

Knowing from both research and her own experience that 6- and 7-year-olds can understand simple proportions in familiar situations, a first-grade teacher asks her students to tackle this problem: "Two children want to share five cupcakes so that each child gets the same amount. Show how much each child can have." When some of the students decide that each child can have two cupcakes, she points to the fifth cupcake and says, "They want to share this one too. How can they do that?"

🍎 **When young children show signs of egocentric thinking, express confusion or explain that others think differently.**

A kindergartner asks, "What's this?" about an object that is out of the teacher's view. The teacher responds, "What's *what*? I can't see the thing you're looking for."

🍎 **Relate abstract and hypothetical ideas to concrete objects and observable events.**

To help students understand that even seemingly weightless substances such as air have mass and weight, an eighth-grade teacher blows up a balloon and places it on one side of a balance scale. She then places an uninflated balloon on the other side of the scale. The inflated balloon tips the scale downward, showing that it weighs more than the uninflated one.

🍎 **Ask students to explain their reasoning about physical phenomena, and challenge illogical explanations.**

Sources: Empson, 1999, p. 295 (cupcake example); C. L. Smith, 2007 (balloon example).

When learning about pendulums, cooperative groups in a middle school science class conduct experiments with three variables (weight, length, and angle at which the pendulum is dropped) to see which variable or variables determine the rate at which a pendulum swings. After three of four students in one group assert that weight affects the oscillation rate, the teacher asks a series of questions that eventually lead the group to realize it has simultaneously varied both weight and length in its experiments.

MyEdLab
Video Example 2.5.
This video shows the pendulum example.

🍎 **Draw on adolescents' idealism to engage them in public service projects and other charitable endeavors.**

In a unit on Africa, several students in a ninth-grade social studies class express their horror about the extreme poverty in which some Africans live. The teacher mentions that a friend is traveling to Rwanda the following month and wants to take several large suitcases full of used children's clothing to give to an especially poor Rwandan village. Over the next few days the students ask their parents and neighbors for donations and gather many usable items for the teacher's friend to take.

---

educators have found many of Piaget's ideas quite useful in instructional settings. We'll examine three of his ideas—his clinical method, his emphasis on the importance of hands-on experiences, and his concept of disequilibrium—in upcoming sections. The Into the Classroom feature "Applying Piaget's Theory" offers additional suggestions for translating Piaget's ideas into classroom practice.

NEO-PIAGETIAN THEORIES

Neo-Piagetian theories echo Piaget's belief that cognitive development depends somewhat on brain maturation. For instance, some neo-Piagetian theorists suggest that a component of the human memory system known as *working memory* is especially important for cognitive development. In particular, working memory is a brain-based mechanism that enables people to temporarily hold and think about a small amount of new information. Children's working memory capacity increases with age, and thus their ability to think about several things at the same time also increases (Case & Mueller, 2001; Fischer & Bidell, 2006; Lautrey, 1993).

Neo-Piagetian theorists reject Piaget's notion that a single series of stages characterizes children's overall cognitive development. However, they speculate that cognitive development in specific content domains—for example, in understanding numbers or spatial relationships—often has a stage-like nature (e.g., Case, 1985; Case & Okamoto, 1996; Fischer & Immordino-Yang, 2002). Children's entry into a particular stage is marked by the acquisition of new abilities, which children practice and gradually master over time. Eventually they integrate these abilities into more complex structures that mark their transition into a subsequent stage. Thus, as is true in Piaget's theory, the stages are *hierarchical,* with each one being constructed out of abilities acquired in the preceding stage.

You will learn more about working memory in Chapter 6.

Even in a particular subject area, however, cognitive development isn't necessarily a single series of stages through which children progress as if they were climbing rungs on a ladder. In some cases development might be better characterized as progression along "multiple strands" of skills that occasionally interconnect, consolidate, or separate in a weblike fashion (Fischer & Daley, 2007; Fischer & Immordino-Yang, 2002). From this perspective, children may acquire more advanced levels of competence in a particular area through any one of several pathways. For instance, as they become increasingly proficient in reading, children may gradually develop various word decoding and reading comprehension skills, and they draw on all of these skills when reading a book. However, the rate at which each skill is mastered varies from one child to the next.

PIAGET'S CLINICAL METHOD AS AN ASSESSMENT TOOL

Earlier in the chapter we considered Piaget's clinical method, in which an adult probes children's thoughts about a particular task or problem through a sequence of individually tailored questions (recall the dialogue with Brian about the wooden beads). By presenting a variety of Piagetian tasks involving either concrete or formal operational thinking skills (e.g., conservation or separation and control of variables) and asking students to explain what they're thinking, we can gain valuable insights into their logical reasoning abilities (e.g., diSessa, 2007). We need not stick to traditional Piagetian reasoning tasks, however. To illustrate, a teacher might present various kinds of maps (e.g., a road map of Ireland, an aerial map of Chicago, a three-dimensional relief map of a mountainous area) and ask students to interpret what they see. Children in the early elementary grades are apt to interpret maps very concretely, perhaps thinking that lines separating states and countries are actually painted on the earth or that an airport symbolized by a small airplane has only one plane. They might also have difficulty with the scale of a map, perhaps thinking that a line can't be a road because "it's not fat enough for two cars to go on" or that a mountain depicted by a bump on a relief map isn't really a mountain because "it's not high enough" (Liben & Myers, 2007, p. 202). Understanding the concept of *scale* in a map requires proportional reasoning—an ability that doesn't fully emerge until after puberty—and thus it's hardly surprising that young children will be confused by it.

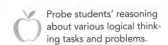
Probe students' reasoning about various logical thinking tasks and problems.

HANDS-ON EXPERIENCES

Piaget suggested that exploration of the physical environment should be largely a child-initiated and child-directed effort. Young children can certainly learn a great deal from their informal interactions with sand, water, and other natural substances (Hutt, Tyler, Hutt, & Christopherson, 1989). And in the elementary and secondary school grades, opportunities to manipulate physical objects—or their virtual equivalents on a computer screen—can enhance students' understanding of basic mathematical and scientific concepts (M. C. Brown, McNeil, & Glenberg, 2009; Lorch et al., 2010; Sarama & Clements, 2009; Sherman & Bisanz, 2009).

Researchers are finding, however, that hands-on experiences are typically more effective *when combined with instruction* that helps students draw appropriate conclusions from what they observe (Fujimura, 2001; Hardy, Jonen, Möller, & Stern, 2006; R. E. Mayer, 2004). In the absence of teacher guidance and directive questions, students may draw inferences based solely on what they see and feel—for instance, erroneously concluding that a very small piece of Styrofoam must have no weight whatsoever—and they may fail to separate and control variables in their experimentation (M. C. Brown et al., 2009; Lorch et al., 2014; C. L. Smith, 2007).

Combine hands-on experiences with age-appropriate instruction that enables students to draw appropriate conclusions from their observations.

CREATING DISEQUILIBRIUM: THE VALUE OF SOCIOCOGNITIVE CONFLICT

In the opening case study, the girls argue about various ways to solve a problem involving the use of a fraction (³/₄) in making apple tarts. When Jeanette offers a seemingly nonproductive idea ("But three-quarters equals three"), Kerri points out her illogical thinking ("But she can't make only three apple tarts!"). As noted earlier, interaction with peers helps children realize that others often view the world differently than they do and that their own ideas aren't always completely logical or accurate. Furthermore, interactions with age-mates that involve wrestling with contradictory viewpoints—interactions that involve sociocognitive conflict—create disequilibrium that may spur children to reevaluate and possibly revise their current understandings. Whereas children may accept an adult's ideas without argument, some may be quite willing to disagree with and challenge the ideas of their peers (D. W. Johnson & Johnson, 2009b; Lampert, Rittenhouse, & Crumbaugh, 1996; M. C. Linn, 2008).

Ultimately, social interaction—not only with peers but also with adults—is probably even more important for children's cognitive development than Piaget realized. Lev Vygotsky's theory, which we turn to now, describes additional ways in which interactions with fellow human beings promote cognitive growth.

> MyEdLab **Self-Check 2.3**
>
> MyEdLab **Application Exercise 2.2.** As you watch children in this exercise, look for certain reasoning skills that Piaget described.

Have students wrestle with complex issues and problems in small groups, where they can hear opinions and arguments that might conflict with their own ways of thinking. Monitor such interactions to be sure that they are mutually respectful and socially appropriate.

Vygotsky's Theory of Cognitive Development

In Piaget's view, children are largely in control of their own cognitive development; for example, they initiate interactions with objects in their environment and develop self-constructed understandings of what they observe. In contrast, an early Russian developmentalist, Lev Vygotsky, believed that the adults in any society intentionally *foster* children's cognitive development in a somewhat systematic manner. Because Vygotsky emphasized the importance of adult instruction and guidance for promoting cognitive development—and more generally because he emphasized the influence of social and cultural factors on children's cognitive growth—his perspective is known as a sociocultural theory.

Vygotsky and his students conducted many studies of children's thinking from the 1920s until Vygotsky's early death from tuberculosis in 1934. Instead of determining the kinds of tasks children could successfully perform *on their own* (as Piaget did), Vygotsky often examined the kinds of tasks children could complete *only with adult assistance*. For example, he described two hypothetical children who could, without help, do things that a typical 8-year-old might be able to do. He would give each of the children progressively more difficult tasks and offer a little bit of assistance, perhaps by asking a leading question or suggesting a reasonable first step. With such help, both children could almost invariably tackle more difficult tasks than they could handle on their own. However, the *range* of tasks that the two children could complete with assistance might be quite different, with one child stretching his or her abilities to succeed at typical 12-year-old-level tasks and the other succeeding only with typical 9-year-old-level tasks (Vygotsky, 1934/1986, p. 187).

Western psychologists were largely unfamiliar with Vygotsky's work until the last few decades of the 20th century, when his major writings were translated from Russian into English (e.g., Vygotsky, 1978, 1934/1986, 1997). Although Vygotsky never had the chance to develop his theory fully, his views are clearly evident in many contemporary theorists' discussions of learning and development and have become increasingly influential in guiding teachers' classroom practices.

VYGOTSKY'S BASIC ASSUMPTIONS

Vygotsky acknowledged that biological factors—such as maturational processes in the brain—play a role in cognitive development. Children bring certain characteristics and dispositions to the situations they encounter, and their responses vary accordingly. Furthermore, children's behaviors, which are influenced in part by inherited traits, affect the particular experiences children have (Vygotsky, 1997). However, Vygotsky's primary focus was on the role of children's social and cultural environments in fostering cognitive growth—and especially in fostering those complex mental abilities that are unique to human beings as a species. Following are central ideas and concepts in Vygotsky's theory.

- *Through both informal conversations and formal schooling, adults convey to children the ways in which their culture interprets and responds to the world.* Vygotsky proposed that as adults interact with children, they share the *meanings* they attach to objects, events, and, more generally, human experience. In the process they transform, or *mediate,* the situations children encounter. Meanings can be conveyed through a variety of mechanisms, including language (spoken words, writing, etc.), mathematical symbols, graphic displays, fine arts, and music.

Informal conversations are one common mechanism through which adults pass along culturally relevant ways of interpreting situations. But even more important is formal education, through which teachers systematically impart the ideas, concepts, and terminology used in various academic disciplines (Vygotsky, 1934/1986). Although Vygotsky, like Piaget, saw value in allowing children to make some discoveries themselves, he also saw value in having adults pass along the discoveries of previous generations (Vygotsky, 1934/1986).

- *Every culture passes along physical and cognitive tools that make daily living more productive and efficient.* Not only do adults teach children specific ways of interpreting experiences but they also pass along specific tools that can help children tackle the various tasks and problems they're apt to face. Some tools, such as scissors, sewing machines, and computers, are physical objects. Others, such as writing systems, maps, and spreadsheets, are partly physical and partly symbolic. Still others, such as the concept of *fraction* and the process of division (recall the opening case study involving fractions of apples), may have little physical basis at all. In Vygotsky's view, acquiring tools that are at least partly symbolic or mental in nature—cognitive tools—greatly enhances growing children's thinking and functioning.

- *Thought and language become increasingly interdependent in the first few years of life.* One very important cognitive tool is language. For us as adults, thought and language are closely interconnected. We often think by using specific words that our language provides. For example, when we think about household pets, our thoughts may contain such words as *dog* and *cat*. In addition, we usually express our thoughts when we converse with others. In other words, we "speak our minds."

    Vygotsky proposed that thought and language are separate functions for infants and young toddlers. In these early years, thinking occurs independently of language, and when language appears, it's first used primarily as a means of communication rather than as a mechanism of thought. But sometime around age 2, thought and language become intertwined: Children begin to express their thoughts when they speak, and they begin to think in words.

    When thought and language first merge, children often talk to themselves—a phenomenon known as self-talk (you may also see the term *private speech*). Vygotsky suggested that self-talk serves an important function in cognitive development. By talking to themselves, children learn to guide and direct their own behaviors through difficult tasks and complex maneuvers in much the same way that adults have previously guided them. Self-talk eventually evolves into inner speech, in which children talk to themselves mentally rather than aloud. They continue to direct themselves verbally through tasks and activities, but others can no longer see and hear them do it (Vygotsky, 1934/1986). In other words, both self-talk and inner speech help children engage in *self-regulation*.

- *Complex mental processes begin as social activities and gradually evolve into internal mental activities that children can use independently.* Vygotsky proposed that many complex thought processes have their roots in social interactions. As children discuss objects, events, tasks, and problems with adults and other knowledgeable individuals, they gradually incorporate into their own thinking the ways in which the people around them talk about and interpret the world, and they begin to use the words, concepts, symbols, and strategies—in essence, the cognitive tools—that are commonly used in their culture.

    The process through which social activities evolve into internal mental activities is called internalization. The progression from self-talk to inner speech just described illustrates this process: Over time, children gradually internalize adults' directions so that they are eventually giving *themselves* the directions.

    Not all mental processes emerge as children interact with adults; some instead develop as children interact with peers. For example, children frequently argue with one another

---

Help students understand how different academic disciplines can enhance their ability to make sense of various physical and social events and phenomena in their lives.

MyEdLab
Video Explanation 2.2.
This video illustrates the use of cognitive tools in a high school physics class.

Chapter 10 more fully describes the nature and development of children's ability to regulate their own behavior and thinking processes.

about a variety of matters—how best to carry out an activity, what games to play, who did what to whom, and so on. According to Vygotsky, having arguments helps children discover that there are often several ways to view the same situation. Eventually, he suggested, children internalize the arguing process, developing the ability to look at a situation from a variety of angles *on their own.*

- *Children appropriate their culture's tools in their own idiosyncratic manner.* Children don't necessarily internalize *exactly* what they see and hear in a social context. Rather, they often transform ideas, strategies, and other cognitive tools to suit their own needs and purposes—thus, Vygotsky's theory has a constructivist element to it. The term appropriation is often used to refer to this process of internalizing but also adapting the ideas and strategies of one's culture for one's own use.

- *Children can accomplish more difficult tasks when assisted by more advanced and competent individuals.* Vygotsky distinguished between two kinds of abilities that characterize children's skills at any particular point in development. A child's actual developmental level is the upper limit of tasks that he or she can perform independently, without help from anyone else. A child's level of potential development is the upper limit of tasks that he or she can perform with the assistance of a more competent individual. To get a true sense of children's cognitive development, Vygotsky suggested, we should assess their capabilities not only when performing alone but also when performing with assistance—a strategy that contemporary educators call *dynamic assessment.*

  As mentioned earlier, Vygotsky found that children can typically do more difficult things in collaboration with adults than they can do on their own. For example, they can play more challenging piano pieces when an adult helps them locate some of the notes on the keyboard or provides suggestions about which fingers to use where. They can solve more difficult math problems when their teacher helps them identify critical problem components and potentially fruitful problem-solving strategies. And they can often read more complex prose in a reading group at school than they're likely to read independently at home.

- *Challenging tasks promote maximum cognitive growth.* The range of tasks that children cannot yet perform independently but *can* perform with the help and guidance of others is, in Vygotsky's terminology, the zone of proximal development (ZPD) (see Figure 2.7). A child's zone of proximal development includes learning and problem-solving abilities that are just beginning to emerge and develop.

  Vygotsky proposed that children learn very little from performing tasks they can already do independently. Instead, they gain new skills primarily by attempting tasks they can accomplish only with assistance and support—that is, when they attempt tasks within their zone of proximal development. Thus, it's the challenges in life, *not* the easy successes, that

Chapter 14 provides more details about dynamic assessment.

Give students sufficient guidance to enable them to successfully accomplish difficult tasks.

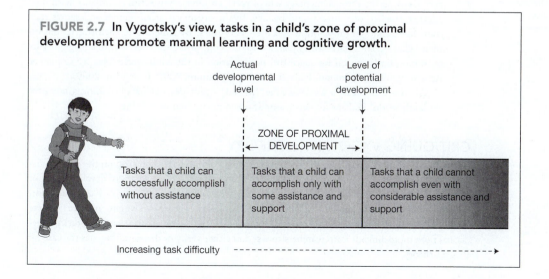

FIGURE 2.7 In Vygotsky's view, tasks in a child's zone of proximal development promote maximal learning and cognitive growth.

promote cognitive development. But whereas challenging tasks are beneficial, impossible tasks, which children can't do even with considerable structure and guidance, are of no benefit whatsoever (Vygotsky, 1987). For example, it would be pointless to ask most 5-year-olds to solve for *x* in an algebraic equation. In general, a child's ZPD sets a limit on what he or she is cognitively capable of learning.

As teachers, then, we should assign some tasks that students can accomplish successfully *only* with some support. In some instances, this support must come from us or other, more skillful individuals. In other situations, students of equal ability might work together to jointly accomplish difficult assignments—such as the apple-tarts problem in the opening case study—with each student bringing unique strengths to contribute to the overall effort.

Regardless of the nature of the support we provide, we must remember that every student's ZPD will change over time. As some tasks are mastered, other, more complex ones will appear on the horizon to take their place. In addition, students' ZPDs may vary considerably in "width." Some students may, with assistance, be able to stretch several years above their actual (independent) developmental level; others may be able to handle tasks that are only slightly more difficult than what they can currently do on their own. In some instances, students with different zones of proximal development will need individualized tasks and assignments so that they all have challenges that optimally promote their personal cognitive growth.

- *Play allows children to cognitively "stretch" themselves.* One of us authors recalls how, as 5-year-olds, her son Jeff and his friend Scott sometimes played "restaurant." In a corner of Jeff's basement, the boys created a dining area from several child-sized tables and chairs, as well as a restaurant "kitchen" with a toy sink, stove, and supply of plastic dishes and food items. They also created menus, sometimes asking how to spell a word but more often guessing about a word's spelling. On one occasion they invited both sets of parents to "dine," and when the parents arrived, the boys wrote everyone's meal orders on paper tablets and scurried to the kitchen to assemble the requested items. Eventually they returned with the meals (hamburgers, French fries, and cookies—all of them plastic—plus glasses of imaginary milk), which the parents "ate" and "drank" with gusto.

In their restaurant play, the two boys took on several adult roles (restaurant manager, waiter, cook) and practiced a variety of adultlike behaviors. In real life such a scenario would be virtually impossible: Very few 5-year-olds have the cooking, reading, writing, mathematical, or organizational skills necessary to run a restaurant. Yet the element of make-believe brought these tasks within the boys' reach. In Vygotsky's words, "In play a child always behaves beyond his average age, above his daily behavior; in play it is as though he were a head taller than himself" (Vygotsky, 1978, p. 102).

Furthermore, as children play, their behaviors must conform to certain standards or expectations. In the early elementary school years, children often act in accordance with how a father, teacher, or waiter would behave. In the organized group games and sports that come later, children must follow specific sets of rules. By adhering to such restrictions on their behavior, children learn to plan ahead, to think before they act, and to engage in self-restraint—skills critical for successful participation in the adult world (also see Coplan & Arbeau, 2009; A. Diamond, Barnett, Thomas, & Munro, 2007; Pellegrini, 2009).

Play, then, is hardly a waste of time. Instead, it provides a valuable training ground for the adult world. Perhaps for this reason it's seen in children worldwide.

CRITIQUING VYGOTSKY'S THEORY

Vygotsky focused more on the processes through which children develop than on the characteristics that children of particular ages are likely to exhibit. He described stages of development but portrayed them in only the most general terms (e.g., see Vygotsky, 1997, pp. 214–216). In addition, Vygotsky's descriptions of developmental processes were often vague and speculative (Gauvain, 2001; Haenan, 1996; Moran & John-Steiner, 2003). For such reasons, Vygotsky's theory has been more difficult for researchers to test and either verify or disprove than has the case for Piaget's theory.

MyEdLab
Video Explanation 2.3.
This video illustrates the zone of proximal development and its change over time.

Give students time to explore new activities and roles through play.

Nevertheless, contemporary theorists and educators have found Vygotsky's ideas insightful and helpful. Most significantly, his theory points out the many ways in which *culture* influences cognitive development. A society's culture ensures that each new generation benefits from the accumulating wisdom of preceding generations. Any culture guides children in certain directions by encouraging them to pay attention to particular stimuli (and not to others) and to engage in particular activities (and not in others). In addition, it provides a lens through which children come to view and interpret their experiences in culturally appropriate ways. We see obvious effects of culture in many of children's everyday activities—in the books they read, the roles they enact in pretend play, the extracurricular activities they pursue—but we must remember that culture permeates their unobservable thinking processes as well.

Furthermore, some research has supported Vygotsky's views regarding the progression and role of self-talk and inner speech. The frequency of children's audible self-talk decreases during the preschool and early elementary years, but this decrease is at first accompanied by an increase in whispered mumbling and silent lip movements, presumably reflecting a transition to inner speech (Bivens & Berk, 1990; Winsler & Naglieri, 2003). Self-talk increases when children are performing more challenging tasks, at which they must exert considerable effort to be successful (Berk, 1994; Schimmoeller, 1998). As you undoubtedly know from your own experience, even adults occasionally talk to themselves when they face new challenges!

CONSIDERING DIVERSITY FROM THE PERSPECTIVE OF VYGOTSKY'S THEORY

Vygotsky's theory leads us to expect greater diversity among children—at least in cognitive development—than Piaget's theory does. As we've seen, children in any single age-group are apt to have different zones of proximal development: Tasks that are easy for some children may be quite challenging or virtually impossible for others. In addition, to the extent that specific cultural groups pass along unique concepts, ideas, and beliefs, children from different cultural backgrounds will acquire somewhat different knowledge, skills, and ways of thinking. For instance, children are more likely to acquire map-reading skills if they regularly encounter maps (e.g., of roads, subway systems, and shopping malls) in their community and family life (Liben & Myers, 2007). And children are more apt to have a keen sense of time if cultural activities are tightly regulated by clocks and calendars (K. Nelson, 1996).

CONTEMPORARY EXTENSIONS AND APPLICATIONS OF VYGOTSKY'S THEORY

The Into the Classroom feature "Applying Vygotsky's Theory" presents concrete examples of how teachers might make use of Vygotsky's ideas. In the upcoming sections, we'll consider several ways in which contemporary theorists and educators have built on the foundations that Vygotsky laid.

SOCIAL CONSTRUCTION OF MEANING

Contemporary psychologists have elaborated on Vygotsky's proposal that adults help children attach meanings to the objects and events around them. Often an adult will help a child make sense of the world through a joint discussion of a phenomenon or event they are both experiencing (Feuerstein, Feuerstein, & Falik, 2010; P. K. Murphy, Wilkinson, & Soter, 2011). Such an interaction, sometimes called a mediated learning experience, encourages the child to think about the phenomenon or event in particular ways—to attach labels to it, recognize principles that underlie it, draw certain conclusions from it, and so on. As an example, consider the following exchange, in which a 5-year-old boy and his mother are talking about a prehistoric animal exhibit at a natural history museum.

> *Boy:* Cool. Wow, look. Look giant teeth. Mom, look at his giant teeth.
>
> *Mom:* He looks like a saber tooth. Do you think he eats meat or plants?
>
> *Boy:* Mom, look at his giant little tooth, look at his teeth in his mouth, so big.
>
> *Mom:* He looks like a saber tooth, doesn't he. Do you think he eats plants or meat?
>
> *Boy:* Ouch, ouch, ouch, ouch. (referring to sharp tooth)

Into the Classroom

Applying Vygotsky's Theory

🍎 **Provide cognitive tools that students can use in thinking about and tackling new tasks.**
A high school chemistry teacher places three equal-size inflated balloons into three beakers of water, one heated to almost 100°C, one kept at room temperature, and one containing recently melted ice. The students all agree that the balloon placed in the warmest water expands the most. The teacher then introduces Charles's Law as a means of determining how much the volume of a gaseous substance such as air will change as its temperature changes.

MyEdLab
Video Example 2.6.

This video shows the Charles's Law example.

🍎 **Encourage students to talk themselves through difficult tasks.**
As his students work on complex mathematical equations such as this one

$$x = \frac{2(4 \times 9)^2}{6} + 3$$

a junior high school mathematics teacher gives students a mnemonic (**P**lease **e**xcuse **m**y **d**ear **A**unt **S**ally) they might repeat to themselves to help them remember the order in which they should perform various operations (**p**arentheses, **e**xponents, **m**ultiplication and **d**ivision, **a**ddition and **s**ubtraction).

🍎 **Present some tasks that students can perform successfully only with assistance.**

When a fifth-grade teacher assigns students their first research paper, he breaks the process into several discrete steps and provides a great deal of structure and guidance.

🍎 **Provide sufficient support, or scaffolding, to enable students to perform challenging tasks successfully; gradually withdraw the support as they become more proficient.**
An elementary physical education teacher begins a lesson on tumbling by demonstrating forward and backward rolls in slow motion and physically guiding her students through the correct movements. As the students become more skillful, the teacher stands back from the mat and gives verbal feedback about how to improve.

🍎 **Have students work in small groups to accomplish complex, multifaceted tasks.**
A middle school art teacher asks his students to work in groups of four or five to design large murals that depict various ecosystems—rainforest, freshwater wetland, prairie, desert, and tundra—and the kinds of plant and animal species that live in each one. The groups then paint their murals on the walls of the school corridors.

🍎 **Engage students in adult activities that are common in their culture.**
A high school publishes a monthly school newspaper with news articles, editorials, cartoons, announcements of upcoming events, advertisements for local businesses, and classified ads. Students assume various roles, including reporters, cartoonists, editors, proofreaders, photocopiers, marketers, and distributors.

🍎 **Give young children time to practice adult roles and behaviors through play.**
A kindergarten teacher equips his classroom with many household items (e.g., dress-up clothes, cooking utensils, a toy cell phone) so that students can play house during free-play time.

Mom: Do you think he eats plants or meat?

Boy: Meat.

Mom: How come?

Boy: Because he has sharp teeth. (growling noises) (Ash, 2002, p. 378)

Even without his mother's assistance, the boy would almost certainly have learned something about saber-toothed tigers from his museum visit. Yet Mom helps him make better sense of what he is looking at than he might have done on his own—for instance by using the label *saber tooth* and helping him connect tooth characteristics to eating preferences. Notice how persistent Mom is in asking her son to make the tooth–food connection: She continues to ask him about meat versus plants until the boy finally correctly infers that the tigers must have been meat eaters.

In addition to co-constructing meanings with adults, children and adolescents often talk among themselves to make sense of their experiences. School provides an ideal setting in which young people can toss around ideas and perhaps reach consensus about how best to interpret and understand a complex issue or problem—perhaps about a challenging math problem involving apple tarts, perhaps about troubling interpersonal dynamics with peers, or perhaps about moral dilemmas with no easy right and wrong answers.

Interacting with adults and interacting with peers possibly play somewhat different roles in children's development. Adults usually have more experience and expertise than age-mates do, and they tend to be more skillful teachers. Accordingly, adults are often the partners of choice when children are trying to master complex new tasks and procedures (Gauvain, 2001; Radziszewska & Rogoff, 1988). Working with peers has a different set of advantages. First, as mentioned in the earlier discussion of Piaget's theory, children who hear age-mates express perspectives quite different from their own may experience sociocognitive conflict that motivates them to overhaul their own understandings. Second, as Vygotsky suggested, peer interactions provide a social context in which children practice and eventually internalize complex cognitive processes, such as effective reading comprehension and argumentation skills (Andriessen, 2006; Chinn, Anderson, & Waggoner, 2001; P. K. Murphy et al., 2011). A third benefit is that children learn valuable social behaviors—including how to plan a joint enterprise and how to coordinate differing roles—when they work on cognitive tasks with their peers (Gauvain, 2001).

SCAFFOLDING

Recall Vygotsky's suggestion that children are most likely to benefit from tasks and activities they can successfully accomplish only with the assistance and support of more competent individuals—that is, tasks within their zone of proximal development. Contemporary theorists have identified a variety of techniques—collectively known as scaffolding—that can help students accomplish challenging tasks in instructional contexts. The following are examples:

- Demonstrate correct performance in a manner that students can easily imitate.
- Divide a complex task into several smaller, simpler activities.
- Provide a structure or set of guidelines for accomplishing the task (e.g., see Figure 2.8).
- Provide a calculator, computer software (word processing program, spreadsheet, etc.), or other technology that makes some aspects of the task easier.
- Keep students' attention focused on critical aspects of the task.
- Ask questions or give hints that encourage students to think about the task in productive ways.
- Give frequent feedback about how students are progressing. (A. Collins, 2006; Gallimore & Tharp, 1990; Rogoff, 1990; van de Pol, Volman, & Beishuizen, 2010; D. Wood, Bruner, & Ross, 1976)

MyEdLab
Video Explanation 2.4.

See examples of teacher scaffolding as children assemble picture puzzles.

FIGURE 2.8 **High school language arts teacher Jeff Ormrod uses this checklist to scaffold ninth graders' efforts to write a five-paragraph essay.**

Essay Checklist

Use the following checklist each time you write an essay to make sure that you have completed the steps and have every part you need.

Introduction

- My first sentence is a Hook sentence.
- I have a clear Thesis sentence that answers the question of the assignment.
- I have a List sentence that introduces my three main body paragraphs.
- I have a Transition sentence at the end.

Main Body Paragraphs

- Each of my main body paragraphs talks about one main idea or point.
- Each of my main body paragraphs gives information that supports this point.

Conclusion

- My conclusion paragraph restates my List sentence in a different way.
- My conclusion paragraph restates my Thesis sentence.
- My conclusion paragraph connects my essay to me or to the world.

Source: Excerpt by Jeffrey Ormrod. Copyright © by Jeffrey Ormrod. Reprinted with permission of the author.

Depending on their particular knowledge and ability levels, different students in any single grade may need different kinds of scaffolding to support their success in a task. As students become more adept at performing a new task, scaffolding is ideally modified to nurture newly emerging skills. And over time the scaffolding is gradually phased out—a process known as *fading*—until students can complete the task entirely on their own. In fact, providing *too much* scaffolding—more than students need—can overwhelm and distract them (van Merriënboer & Sweller, 2005).

GUIDED PARTICIPATION IN CHALLENGING NEW ACTIVITIES

A concept very similar to *guided participation* is *legitimate peripheral participation*, discussed in Chapter 8.

When you were a young child, did you sometimes help a parent or older sibling bake cookies or other goodies? Did the cook let you pour, measure, and mix ingredients when you were old enough to do so? Did the cook also give you directions or suggestions as you performed these tasks? Such experiences are examples of guided participation, in which children gain new skills by working on complex, meaningful tasks in close, scaffolded collaboration with an adult or more experienced peer. As children acquire greater competence, they gradually take a more central role in an activity until, eventually, they're full-fledged participants (Rogoff, 2003; Rogoff et al., 2007). From a Vygotskian perspective, guided participation enables children to engage in behaviors and thinking skills within their zone of proximal development. It also helps children tie newly acquired skills and thinking abilities to the specific contexts in which they're likely to be useful later on.

Guided participation can take many forms in instructional settings. For instance, we might get students involved in scientific investigations, creation of museum displays, or focused Internet searches, while always providing the guidance and support students need to accomplish such tasks successfully. As we engage students in these activities, we might also use some of the language that adults frequently use in such contexts. For example, when conducting scientific investigations with students, we should use such words as *hypothesis, evidence,* and *theory* as we go along (Perkins, 1992).

APPRENTICESHIPS

An especially intensive form of guided participation is an apprenticeship, in which a novice works with an expert mentor for a lengthy period to learn how to perform many complex tasks within a particular domain. The expert provides considerable structure and guidance throughout the process, gradually removing scaffolding and giving the novice more independence and responsibility as competence increases (A. Collins, 2006; Rogoff, 1990, 1991). Many cultures use apprenticeships as a means of gradually introducing children to particular skills and trades in the adult community—perhaps weaving, tailoring, or playing a musical instrument (D. J. Elliott, 1995; Lave & Wenger, 1991; Rogoff, 1990).

In a good apprenticeship, a student learns not only how to perform a task but also how to productively *think about* the task—a situation known as a cognitive apprenticeship (J. S. Brown, Collins, & Duguid, 1989; A. Collins, 2006; Dennen & Burner, 2008). For instance, a student might work with a biologist to collect samples of various plants in a certain ecosystem, or a student might work with an experienced carpenter to design and build a kitchen cabinet. In the process of talking about various aspects of the task, the expert and student together analyze the problem at hand and develop the best approach to take, and the expert models effective ways of thinking about and mentally processing the situation.

Apprenticeships differ widely from one context to another, but they typically have some or all of these features (A. Collins, 2006; A. Collins, Brown, & Newman, 1989):

- *Modeling:* The mentor carries out the task, simultaneously thinking aloud about the process, while the learner observes and listens.
- *Coaching:* As the learner performs the task, the mentor gives frequent suggestions, hints, and feedback.
- *Scaffolding:* The mentor provides various forms of support for the learner, perhaps by simplifying the task, breaking it into smaller and more manageable components, or providing less complicated equipment.
- *Articulation:* The learner explains what he or she is doing and why, allowing the mentor to examine the student's knowledge, reasoning, and problem-solving strategies.
- *Reflection:* The mentor asks the learner to compare his or her performance with that of experts, or perhaps with an ideal model of how the task should be done.

- *Increasing complexity and diversity of tasks:* As the learner gains greater proficiency, the mentor presents more complex, challenging, and varied tasks to complete.
- *Exploration:* The mentor encourages the learner to frame questions and problems on his or her own, and in doing so to expand and refine acquired skills.

Because apprenticeships are clearly labor intensive, their use in the classroom isn't always practical or logistically feasible. Even so, we can certainly use elements of an apprenticeship to help students develop more complex skills. For example, we might help students think about writing tasks in the same ways that expert writers do by providing such prompts as "To liven this up, I'll . . ." and "I can tie this together by . . . ." Prompts like these provide the same sort of scaffolding that an expert writer might provide, and they help students develop more sophisticated writing strategies (S. L. Benton, 1997; Scardamalia & Bereiter, 1985; Wong, Hoskyn, Jai, Ellis, & Watson, 2008).

CONTRASTING PIAGET'S AND VYGOTSKY'S THEORIES

Both Piaget and Vygotsky have had a profound influence on contemporary views of learning, thinking, and cognitive development. If we look beyond their differing terminologies, we can see some common themes in the two perspectives. First, both theorists suggested that children acquire increasingly complex thinking processes with age and experience. Second, both argued for the importance of challenge, perhaps in the form of puzzling new information (Piaget's *disequilibrium*) or perhaps in the form of tasks that can be completed only with another person's support (Vygotsky's *zone of proximal development*). And third, at any given point in development children are cognitively ready for some experiences but not for others. In Piaget's view, a child can accommodate to new objects and events only when the child can, to some degree, also assimilate them into existing schemes—that is, there must be some overlap between the "new" and the "old." From Vygotsky's perspective, some challenging new tasks may fall within a child's ZPD—and thus be accomplishable with guidance and support—but other tasks are likely to be out of reach for the time being.

Nevertheless, Piaget's and Vygotsky's theories differ in significant ways. For one thing, Piaget maintained that children's cognitive development is largely the result of their own efforts—for instance, their informal experiments with physical objects and their attempts to restore equilibrium in the face of puzzling events. In contrast, Vygotsky placed considerable emphasis on the role of adults and other, more advanced individuals, who can mediate new experiences and provide needed support during challenging activities. The difference, then, is one of self-exploration and discovery (Piaget) versus guided exploration and instruction (Vygotsky).

A second key difference lies in the potential influence of the culture in which children grow up. Piaget recognized that cultural differences might have an impact, but he didn't systematically explore them in children's thinking processes. In Vygotsky's theory, however, culture is of paramount importance in molding the specific thinking skills children acquire—a perspective that Bronfenbrenner echoed in describing the multiple layers of environmental influence on children's development. Increasingly, contemporary researchers have come to the same conclusion: Children's cultural environments can have a *huge* influence on what children learn and how they develop.

Finally, the two theorists offer differing perspectives on how language enters into the picture. For Piaget, language certainly enhances cognitive development: It provides many labels (*symbols*) that help children mentally represent their world, and it's the primary means through which children gain knowledge of other people's diverse perspectives on various situations and topics. For Vygotsky, on the other hand, language is absolutely essential for cognitive growth. Children's thought processes are internalized versions of social interactions that are largely verbal in nature. Furthermore, in their conversations with adults, children learn the meanings their culture ascribes to particular events and gradually begin to interpret the world in culture-specific ways. In addition, through two language-based phenomena—self-talk and inner speech—children begin to guide their own behaviors in ways that others have previously guided them.

With such benefits in mind, many contemporary theorists share Piaget's and Vygotsky's belief that acquiring language is an important—perhaps the *most* important—factor in cognitive development (e.g., Pinker, 2007; Premack, 2004; Spelke, 2003). We can better understand cognitive development, then, when we also know something about language development.

Give prompts that get students thinking about a complex task as an expert might.

Chapter 4 describes a variety of cultural and ethnic differences that can shape children's behaviors and development.

MyEdLab **Self-Check 2.4**

MyEdLab **Application Exercise 2.3.** This short exercise can give you practice in determining whether or not students are working within their ZPDs.

MyEdLab **Application Exercise 2.4.** In this exercise, you can apply your knowledge of Vygotsky's concepts to a variety of classroom scenarios.

Language Development

Acquiring the language of one's culture is an extremely complex and challenging undertaking. To understand and use a language effectively, children must master four basic components of the language. First, they must master their language's *phonology:* They must know how words sound and be able to produce the sequence of sounds that make up any given word. Second, they must master *semantics,* the meanings of many thousands of words. Third, they must have a good command of *syntax,* knowing how words can legitimately be combined to form understandable phrases and sentences. And finally, children must master the *pragmatics* of their language—the social conventions and speaking strategies that enable effective communication with others.

Mastering these four components of language is a remarkable achievement for any child, yet before children reach kindergarten, most of them have acquired sufficient proficiency in language to carry on productive conversations with the people around them. Their language development continues throughout childhood and adolescence, in part as a result of informal social interactions and in part as a result of formal instruction (see Table 2.2).

Some aspects of language development during the school years reflect an increasing ability to think abstractly about physical and social phenomena. For example, abstract thought enables children to reflect, deliberately and consciously, on the general nature and functions of language—an acquisition known as **metalinguistic awareness** (Owens, 2008; Yaden & Templeton, 1986). With such awareness comes an ability to recognize the figurative nature of words—the nonliteral meanings of proverbs, the symbolism in poems and literature, and so on. At the same time, children's ever-expanding language capabilities probably also *help* them think abstractly (K. Nelson, 1996; Pinker, 2007).

THEORETICAL ISSUES REGARDING LANGUAGE DEVELOPMENT

Without doubt, children's immediate environments play a significant role in their language development. The richer the language that children hear—that is, the greater the variety of words and the greater the complexity of syntactic structures to which other people expose them—the faster their vocabulary develops (Hoff, 2003; Raikes et al., 2006; Risley & Hart, 2006). Yet children don't simply absorb the language spoken around them. Instead, they appear to use what they hear to construct their own understandings of the language, including knowledge about word meanings, rules governing how words can be combined into sentences, and so on (Cairns, 1996; Cromer, 1987; Karmiloff-Smith, 1993). Thus, we see in language development some of the knowledge *construction* of which Piaget spoke.

Most developmental theorists agree that heredity is also involved in language development to some degree. Human beings have the capacity to acquire a far more complex language than any other species on the planet. Exactly *what* human beings inherit that enables them to learn language is a matter of considerable controversy, however. At a minimum, infants inherit a few key predispositions—for instance, a preference for human voices over other sounds and an ability to hear very subtle differences among speech sounds—that make language learning possible (DeCasper & Fifer, 1980; Jusczyk, 1995; P. K. Kuhl, 2004; J. L. Locke, 1993). In addition, some theorists believe that part of our genetic heritage is a *language acquisition device,* a language-specific learning mechanism that enables infants and toddlers to acquire many intricacies of language in an amazingly short amount of time (Chomsky,

Children in the early and middle elementary grades have only limited ability to make sense of figurative language. Here 8-year-old Jeff takes a common expression at face value, rather than recognizing its underlying meaning: that someone has ordered more food than can possibly be eaten.

DEVELOPMENTAL TRENDS

TABLE 2.2 • Examples of Linguistic Characteristics and Abilities at Different Grade Levels			
GRADE LEVEL	**AGE-TYPICAL CHARACTERISTICS**	**EXAMPLE**	**SUGGESTED STRATEGIES**
K–2	• Knowledge of 8,000–14,000 words by age 6; understandings of some words only partially correct (e.g., use of the word *animal* may be restricted largely to four-legged mammals) • Difficulty understanding lengthy, complex sentences (e.g., those with multiple clauses) • Superficial understanding of being a "good listener" (e.g., just sitting quietly) • Literal interpretations of messages and requests (e.g., not realizing that "Goodness, this class is noisy" means "Be quiet") • Increasing ability to tell a story, both orally and in writing • Mastery of most sounds; some difficulty pronouncing *r, th, dr, sl,* and *str* • Occasional use of regular word endings (-s, -ed, -er) with irregular words (*sheeps, goed, gooder*) • Basic etiquette in conversations (e.g., taking turns, answering questions) • Reluctance to initiate conversations with adults (for many students from Asian and Mexican American backgrounds)	When two police officers visit a first-grade class to talk about how to go to and from school safely each day, the students listen quietly and respectfully. After the visit, however, the students can recall very little about what the officers have told them.	• Read age-appropriate storybooks as a way of enhancing vocabulary. • Give gentle corrective feedback when students' use of words indicates inaccurate understanding. • Work on listening skills (e.g., sitting quietly, paying attention, trying to understand and remember). • Ask follow-up questions to make sure students accurately understand important messages. • Ask students to construct narratives about recent events (e.g., "Tell me about your camping trip last weekend").
3–5	• Incomplete knowledge of irregular word forms • Correct pronunciation of all sounds in one's language (by age 9 for typically developing children) • Sustained conversations about concrete topics • Increasing ability to take listeners' prior knowledge into account during explanations • Construction of stories with plots and cause-and-effect relationships • Linguistic creativity and word play (e.g., rhymes, word games)	Students in a third-grade class love corny jokes and riddles that involve a play on words. For example, many are amused by "Why did the cookie go to the doctor?" ("He felt crumby") and "Why couldn't the sailors play cards?" ("Because the captain was standing on the deck").	• Teach irregular word forms (e.g., the past tense of *ring* is *rang*, the past tense of *bring* is *brought*). • Consult with a speech-language specialist if articulation problems persist in the upper elementary grades. • Use group discussions as a way to explore academic subject matter. • Have students create short stories that they present orally or in writing. • Encourage jokes and rhymes that capitalize on double meanings and homonyms (i.e., sound-alike words).
6–8	• Knowledge of about 50,000 words at age 12 • Increasing knowledge of words used in particular academic disciplines (e.g., *ecosystem* in science, *hypotenuse* in mathematics) • Emerging ability to carry on lengthy conversations about abstract topics • Emerging ability to look beyond literal interpretations; comprehension of simple proverbs and increasing ability to detect sarcasm • Increasing metalinguistic awareness; that is, increasing ability to reflect on the underlying nature of language • Increasing proficiency in expository (nonfiction) writing, especially with teacher scaffolding	Students in a sixth-grade class write better persuasive essays when their teacher gives them explicit guidance about elements to include, including (1) an introductory statement expressing one's opinion, (2) supporting evidence for that opinion, (3) reasons why other people might disagree, and (4) explanations of why those reasons are invalid.	• Assign reading materials that introduce new vocabulary. • Introduce some of the terminology used by experts in various content areas (e.g., *simile* in language arts, *molecule* in science). • Conduct structured debates to explore controversial issues. • Ask students to consider the underlying meanings of common proverbs. • Explore the nature of words and language as entities in and of themselves. • Frequently ask students to write about topics; provide guidance about effective writing and frequent feedback about what students have written.

(continued)

TABLE 2.2 *(Continued)*

GRADE LEVEL	AGE-TYPICAL CHARACTERISTICS	EXAMPLE	SUGGESTED STRATEGIES
9–12	• Knowledge of about 80,000 words • Acquisition of many vocabulary words related to particular academic disciplines • Subtle refinements in syntax, mostly as a result of formal instruction • General ability to understand figurative language (e.g., metaphors, proverbs, hyperbole) • Significant improvements in expository writing, especially with experience and constructive feedback	When a ninth-grade class reads Robert Frost's poem "The Road Not Taken," most students realize that the poem is only superficially about choosing one of two paths through the woods—that at a deeper level it's about choosing among various paths in life.	▪ Regularly use the terminologies associated with various academic disciplines. ▪ Distinguish between similar abstract words (e.g., *weather* vs. *climate, velocity* vs. *acceleration*). ▪ Explore complex syntactic structures (e.g., multiple embedded clauses). ▪ Consider the underlying meanings and messages in poetry and fiction. ▪ When students have a native dialect other than Standard English, encourage them to use it in informal conversations and creative writing; encourage Standard English for more formal situations.

Sources: Adger, Wolfram, & Christian, 2007; Byrnes, 1996; Capelli, Nakagawa, & Madden, 1990; S. Carey, 1978, 1985; Ferretti, MacArthur, & Dowdy, 2000; C. A. Grant & Gomez, 2001; K. R. Harris, Graham, & Mason, 2006; K. R. Harris, Santangelo, & Graham, 2010; Karmiloff-Smith, 1979; Maratsos, 1998; T. M. McDevitt & Ford, 1987; T. M. McDevitt, Spivey, Sheehan, Lennon, & Story, 1990; Nippold, 1988; O'Grady, 1997; Owens, 2008; Reich, 1986; Stanovich, 2000; Thelen & Smith, 1998.

1972, 2006; M. Gopnik, 1997; Karmiloff-Smith, 1993). Other theorists believe instead that children learn language in much the same way they learn other things about their environment and culture: through detecting and making use of regular patterns of input from their social environment (Gentner & Namy, 2006; Pelucchi, Hay, & Saffran, 2009; Saffran, 2003).

Research evidence does point to a language-specific developmental mechanism for at least *some* aspects of language learning (Lai, Fisher, Hurst, Vargha-Khadem, & Monaco, 2001; Maratsos, 1998; Trout, 2003). Children of all cultures learn language very quickly and acquire complex syntactic structures even when those structures aren't necessary for effective communication. In addition, brain research reveals that certain parts of the left hemisphere seem to be biologically predisposed to specialize in either understanding or producing speech (Aitchison, 1996; J. L. Locke, 1993).

Additional evidence for heredity's influence comes from research findings suggesting that there may be *sensitive periods* in some aspects of language development. Children who have little or no exposure to *any* language in the early years often have trouble acquiring complex language later on, even with intensive language instruction (Curtiss, 1977; Newport, 1990). Furthermore, when learning a *second* language, people have an easier time mastering correct pronunciations, various verb tenses, and complex grammatical structures if they're immersed in the language during childhood or early adolescence (Bialystok, 1994; Bortfeld & Whitehurst, 2001; Bruer, 1999; M. S. C. Thomas & Johnson, 2008). Possibly such sensitive periods reflect biologically built-in time frames for learning language. Alternatively, perhaps what appear to be predetermined "best" times for learning particular aspects of language are simply the result of the brain's tendency to adapt fairly quickly to whatever forms its early auditory environment takes (P. K. Kuhl, 2004; P. K. Kuhl, Conboy, Padden, Nelson, & Pruitt, 2005).

DIVERSITY IN LANGUAGE DEVELOPMENT

Some diversity in language development seems to be the result of biology. For instance, children with a specific language impairment develop normally in all respects except for language. These children have trouble perceiving and mentally processing particular aspects of spoken language—perhaps the quality, pitch, duration, or intensity of specific speech sounds. Often, although not always, the source of the impairment can be traced to heredity or a specific brain abnormality (Bishop, 2006; Bishop, McDonald, Bird, & Hayiou-Thomas, 2009; Corriveau, Pasquini, & Goswami, 2007; Spinath, Price, Dale, & Plomin, 2004).

Chapter 4 looks more closely at the nature and implications of children's dialects.

Cultural factors play a role in linguistic diversity as well. For example, different cultural groups may nurture different *dialects*—distinct forms of a language that characterize particular ethnic groups or geographic regions—and different social conventions for human conversation (i.e., different pragmatic skills) (Adger et al., 2007; Kitayama & Cohen, 2007; Tyler, Uqdah, et al., 2008). Occasionally a cultural or ethnic group specifically nurtures certain aspects of language development. For example, many inner-city African American communities make heavy use of figurative language—such as similes, metaphors, and hyperbole (intentional exaggeration)—in their day-to-day conversations, jokes, and stories (C. D. Lee, 2005; H. L. Smith, 1998; Smitherman, 2007). The following anecdote illustrates this point:

> I once asked my mother, upon her arrival from church, "Mom, was it a good sermon?" To which she replied, "Son, by the time the minister finished preaching, the men were crying and the women had passed out on the floor." (H. L. Smith, 1998, p. 202)

With such a rich oral tradition, it isn't surprising that many inner-city African American youth are especially advanced in their use and understanding of figurative language (Ortony, Turner, & Larson-Shapiro, 1985; H. L. Smith, 1998; Smitherman, 2007).

SECOND-LANGUAGE LEARNING AND ENGLISH LANGUAGE LEARNERS

As mentioned earlier, exposure to a second language in childhood or early adolescence may be especially important for acquiring flawless pronunciation and certain aspects of syntax. Early exposure to a second language seems to be most advantageous if the second language is very different from the first. For example, a native English speaker benefits more from an early start in Arabic or Navajo than from an early start in, say, Spanish or German (Bialystok, 1994; Strozer, 1994). Aside from such caveats, there appears to be no definitive "best" time to begin studying a second language (e.g., P. K. Kuhl et al., 2005; G. Stevens, 2004).

Yet beginning second-language instruction in the early years has other noteworthy advantages. For one thing, it appears that learning a second language facilitates achievement in such other academic areas as reading, vocabulary, and grammar (Diaz, 1983; Reich, 1986). Instruction in a foreign language also sensitizes young children to the international and multicultural nature of the world. Students who learn a second language during the elementary school years express more positive attitudes toward people who speak that language and are more likely to enroll in foreign language classes in high school (Reich, 1986).

Make it possible for students of all ages to learn one or more foreign languages.

BILINGUALISM

At least half of the world's children are *bilingual*—that is, they speak at least two languages fluently (Hoff-Ginsberg, 1997). Although children who grow up in bilingual environments may initially have more limited vocabularies in each language, research reveals clear long-term advantages of bilingualism. Bilingual children appear to have a head start in their development of metalinguistic awareness (Adesope, Lavin, Thompson, & Ungerleider, 2010; Bialystok, 2001). For instance, in the early elementary grades, bilingual children have greater phonological awareness—awareness of the individual sounds, or *phonemes,* that make up spoken words—and this awareness can get them off to an especially good start in learning to read (X. Chen et al., 2004; Rayner, Foorman, Perfetti, Pesetsky, & Seidenberg, 2001). Furthermore, when children are truly fluent in both languages, they tend to perform better on tasks requiring focused attention and on tasks requiring flexible, creativity thinking (Adesope et al., 2010; Bialystok, Craik, Green, & Gollan, 2009). Their superior performance on such tasks may be partly the result of enhanced development in certain areas of the brain (Espinosa, 2008; Mechelli et al., 2004).

Being bilingual can have cultural and social advantages as well. In any English-speaking country, mastery of spoken and written English is, of course, essential for long-term educational and professional success. But when a resident of that country belongs to a cultural group that speaks a different language, maintaining social relationships within the culture requires knowledge of its language (McBrien, 2005b). For instance, in many Native American groups, the ancestral language is important for communicating oral history and cultural heritage and for conducting local business (McCarty & Watahomigie, 1998). And Puerto Rican children in the United States often speak Spanish at home as a way of showing respect to their elders (Torres-Guzmán, 1998). Finally, at school, when different students in a single classroom each speak only one of two different languages (perhaps some speaking only English and others speaking only Spanish), teaching students both languages increases student interaction and cross-cultural understanding (A. Doyle, 1982; Padilla, 2006).

MyEdLab
Video Example 2.7.

Sometimes bilingualism involves knowing one spoken language and one manual language (e.g., American Sign Language). In the classroom shown in this video, what evidence do you see that such bilingualism enables productive interactions among hearing children and children who have profound hearing loss?

TEACHING A SECOND LANGUAGE

Most children in Western, English-speaking countries are exposed to only one language before they reach school age. That single language may or may not be English. School-age children who are fluent in their native language but not in English are often referred to as **English language learners (ELLs)**. To the extent that elementary and secondary school students have limited knowledge of English, they're apt to have trouble with schoolwork in an English-based classroom (Kieffer, 2008; Padilla, 2006; Slavin & Cheung, 2005; Valdés, Bunch, Snow, & Lee, 2005).

Just as very young children typically learn their native language through informal daily exposure, so, too, can they learn two languages simultaneously if they have frequent, ongoing exposure to both languages. However, when children begin to learn a second language at an older age, perhaps in the elementary grades or even later, they often learn it more quickly if their language-learning experiences are fairly structured (Dixon et al., 2012; Strozer, 1994).

Yet teaching a second language for one 45-minute period a day—as is typically done in high schools—hardly promotes mastery. Two more intensive approaches, immersion and bilingual education, can be quite effective, with each being useful in somewhat different situations. To keep our discussion simple, let's assume that students are living in an English-speaking country. If these students are native English speakers, total **immersion** in the second language—hearing and speaking it almost exclusively in the classroom during the school day—appears to be the more effective approach. A variation of this approach is a *dual-immersion* program, in which some topics are taught exclusively in English and others are taught exclusively in the second language. For native English speakers living in an English-speaking country, immersion in the second language for part or all of the school day helps students acquire proficiency in the language fairly quickly, and any adverse effects on achievement in other academic areas appear to be short lived (Bialystok et al., 2009; Collier, 1992; Genesee, 1985; Padilla, 2006).

In contrast, English language learners living in an English-speaking country typically fare better in **bilingual education**, in which they receive intensive instruction in English while studying other academic subject areas in their native language. Not only is their academic achievement at least as good or better in bilingual education, but they also have greater self-esteem and better attitudes toward school (Dixon et al., 2012; Garcia & Jensen, 2009; Marsh, Hau, & Kong, 2002; Tong, Lara-Alecio, Irby, Mathes, & Kwok, 2008; Wright, Taylor, & Macarthur, 2000). The optimal bilingual education program proceeds through a gradual phase-in of English in instruction, perhaps in a sequence such as the following:

1. Students join native-English speakers for classes in subject areas that don't depend too heavily on language skills (e.g., art, music, physical education). They study other subject areas in their native language and also begin classes in English as a second language (ESL).

2. After students have acquired some English proficiency, instruction in English begins for one or two additional subject areas (perhaps math and science).

3. When it's clear that students can learn successfully in English in the subject areas identified in Step 2, they join their English-speaking classmates in regular classes in these subjects.

4. Eventually students are sufficiently proficient in English to join the mainstream in all subject areas, and they may no longer require their ESL classes (Krashen, 1996; Padilla, 2006; Valdés et al., 2005).

Ideally, the transition from instruction in a student's native language to instruction in English occurs very gradually over a period of several years. Simple knowledge of basic conversational English—knowledge collectively known as **basic interpersonal communication skills (BICS)**—isn't enough for academic success in an English-only curriculum. Ultimately, students must have sufficient mastery of English vocabulary and syntax that they can easily understand and learn from English-based textbooks and lectures; in other words, they must have **cognitive academic language proficiency (CALP)**. Such mastery of English takes considerable time to achieve—often 5 to 7 years (Carhill, Suárez-Orozco, & Páez, 2008; Cummins, 2000, 2008; Dixon et al., 2012; Padilla, 2006).

Why is immersion better for some students whereas bilingual education is better for others? As we've learned, language is an important foundation for cognitive development: Among other things, it provides symbols for mentally representing the world, enables children to exchange ideas with others, and helps them internalize sophisticated cognitive strategies. Students in an English-speaking country who are immersed in a different language at school still have many opportunities—not only at home but also with their friends and in the local community—to continue using and developing their English. In contrast, nonnative English speakers may have few opportunities outside their homes to use their native language. If they're taught exclusively in English, they may

To maximize second-language learning for native English speakers who live in an English-speaking country, completely immerse them in the second language for part or all of the school day.

very well lose proficiency in their native language before developing adequate proficiency in English—a phenomenon known as subtractive bilingualism—and their cognitive development suffers as a result. Because bilingual education is designed to foster growth in *both* English and a child's native language, it's apt to promote cognitive development as well as English proficiency (Pérez, 1998; Tse, 2001; Winsler, Díaz, Espinosa, & Rodriguez, 1999).

We must remember that students' native languages are very much a part of their sense of identity—their sense of who they are as people (Nieto, 1995; Tatum, 1997). A high school student named Marisol made the point this way:

> I'm proud of [being Puerto Rican]. I guess I speak Spanish whenever I can. . . . I used to have a lot of problems with one of my teachers 'cause she didn't want us to talk Spanish in class and I thought that was like an insult to us, you know? (Nieto, 1995, p. 127)

Incorporating children's cultural backgrounds as well as their native language into the classroom curriculum can further promote their academic success (Igoa, 1995, 2007; U.S. Department of

Into the Classroom

Working with English Language Learners

🍎 **Teach early reading skills in students' native languages.**
When working with students whose families recently immigrated from Mexico, a first-grade teacher teaches basic letter–sound relationships and word decoding skills in Spanish (e.g., showing how the printed word *dos*, meaning "two," can be broken up into the sounds "duh," "oh," and "sss").

🍎 **If you don't speak a student's native language yourself, recruit and train parents, community volunteers, or other students to assist in providing instruction in that language.**
A boy in a kindergarten class has grown up speaking Hmong, a language spoken in some Asian immigrant communities in the United States. His teacher recruits a fourth grader who can read an English picture book to the boy and translate it into Hmong. At one point the teacher points to a lily pad on a page of the book and asks the fourth grader to describe a lily pad in Hmong, as the boy has never encountered lily pads in his own life.

🍎 **Use bilingual software.**
Conducting a quick Google search using the key terms *bilingual*, *educational*, and *software*, a teacher finds many educational software programs with both English and Spanish options, including some free programs he can easily download to his classroom computers.

🍎 **When using English to communicate, speak more slowly than you might otherwise, and clearly enunciate each word.**
A third-grade teacher is careful that he always says "going to" rather than "gonna" and "want to" rather than "wanna."

🍎 **Use visual aids to supplement verbal explanations.**
A high school history teacher uses photographs she has downloaded from the Internet to illustrate her verbal description of ancient Egypt. She also gives students a one-page outline that identifies the main ideas in her lesson.

🍎 **During small-group learning activities, encourage same-language students to communicate with one another in their native language.**
When a high school science teacher breaks students into cooperative groups to study the effects of weight, length, and amount of push on a pendulum's oscillation rate, she puts three native Chinese speakers in a single group. She suggests that they can talk in either English or Chinese as they conduct their experiments.

🍎 **Encourage—but don't force—students to contribute to class discussions in English; be understanding of students who are initially reluctant to participate.**
A high school social studies teacher often breaks his class into small groups to discuss controversial social and political issues. He intentionally places two recent immigrants with peers who are likely to be supportive as these English language learners struggle in their efforts to communicate.

🍎 **Have students work in pairs to make sense of textbook material.**
As two middle school students read a section of their geography textbook, one reads aloud while the other listens and takes notes. They frequently stop to talk about what they've just read or to switch roles.

🍎 **Have students read, write, and report about their native countries; also have them create art that depicts aspects of their countries and cultures.**
A middle school social studies teacher has students conduct research on a country from which they or their ancestors emigrated. The students create posters to display what they've learned, and they proudly talk about their posters at a class-sponsored International Day that students from other classes attend.

Sources: Strategies are based on research and recommendations by Carhill et al., 2008; Comeau, Cormier, Grandmaison, & Lacroix, 1999; Duff, 2001; Egbert, 2009; Espinosa, 2007; García, 1995; Herrell & Jordan, 2004; Igoa, 1995, 2007; Janzen, 2008; Krashen, 1996; McClelland, 2001; McClelland, Fiez, & McCandliss, 2002; Padilla, 2006; Slavin & Cheung, 2005; Solórzano, 2008; Tong et al., 2008; Valdés et al., 2005; Walshaw & Anthony, 2008.

Education, 1993). The strategies in the Into the Classroom feature "Working with English Language Learners" take language, sense of identity, and culture into account.

MyEdLab **Self-Check 2.5**

MyEdLab **Application Exercise 2.5.** In this exercise you will identify some of the challenges that English language learners face, as well as the many strengths on which they might build.

2 What Have You Learned?

As a way of summing up our discussion of development in this chapter, we now return to the learning outcomes identified at the beginning of the chapter.

■ **2.1: Describe four principles portraying the general nature of child development and the interactive roles of heredity and environment in guiding it.** Children develop skills and abilities in a somewhat predictable sequence, but they don't all develop at the same rate, and their development in any particular domain is apt to show occasional spurts within periods of slower growth. To some degree, children's developing physical, cognitive, personal, and social characteristics depend on maturation—that is, on a genetically driven unfolding of physiological advancements. But equally critical is an environment that nurtures and supports the acquisition of new knowledge and skills. As is evident in Urie Bronfenbrenner's bioecological systems theory, children grow up within the context of several layers of environmental influence, some of which impact them directly (as is true for family and school environments) and others of which have indirect effects on their development (as is true for parents' employment circumstances and general government policies); each of these layers reflects the particular practices and beliefs of one or more cultural groups. At the same time, children also *change* their environment—and thus also change how their environment affects them—in part by eliciting certain kinds of behaviors from others and in part by choosing among the various opportunities and activities that come their way.

■ **2.2: Explain how the brain and its development influence children's thinking and learning.** The human brain changes in significant ways throughout childhood, adolescence, and early adulthood, partly as a result of environmental experiences and partly as a result of such genetically driven processes as synaptogenesis, synaptic pruning, and myelination. Although different parts of the brain have different specialties, they are closely interconnected and all work together to support complex human activities. The brain has considerable *plasticity*—that is, it can learn a great many new things at virtually any age. As teachers, we should be optimistic that students can acquire a wide variety of knowledge and skills in both the elementary and secondary grades. Yet we must keep in mind that even at the high school level, many students' brains haven't sufficiently matured to support planning, reasoning,

impulse control, and other abilities important for independent learning and responsible behavior.

■ **2.3: Apply Piaget's theory of cognitive development to classroom practice.** Swiss psychologist Jean Piaget proposed that children are intrinsically motivated to make sense of their world and self-construct increasingly complex understandings of it through the two complementary processes of assimilation and accommodation. His four stages of cognitive development give us a rough idea of when various logical thinking capabilities are likely to emerge; however, most contemporary developmental theorists believe that children's developmental progress can probably be better characterized as gradual trends that depend at least partly on children's specific informal experiences and formal instruction.

Piaget's theory has numerous implications for classroom practice. For example, his clinical method offers a way of exploring children's reasoning processes in depth. His proposal that abstract thinking doesn't appear until adolescence encourages us to make heavy use of concrete, hands-on experiences in the elementary and middle school grades. And his concept of disequilibrium suggests that by challenging students' illogical reasoning, we can sometimes spur them to revise incomplete understandings and think in more sophisticated ways.

■ **2.4: Apply Vygotsky's theory of cognitive development to classroom practice.** In contrast to Piaget, who portrayed children as being largely in control of their own cognitive development, Russian psychologist Lev Vygotsky proposed that children's cognitive development is a very social enterprise. In particular, adults and other more advanced individuals communicate the meanings their culture assigns to objects and events, pass along physical and cognitive tools that make everyday tasks and problems easier, and assist children with tasks within each child's zone of proximal development. In Vygotsky's view, social activities are often precursors to and form the basis for complex mental processes: Children initially use new skills in the course of interacting with adults or peers and slowly internalize and adapt these skills for their own, independent use.

Vygotsky's theory suggests that, as teachers, we should help students make sense of their experiences (e.g., by tying their observations to particular scientific concepts and principles), assign activities that require them to stretch their existing abilities, scaffold their efforts on challenging new tasks, and have them occasionally work in small groups to tackle multifaceted issues and problems.

■ **2.5: Describe developmental changes in language during the school years, and explain how you might adapt instruction to children with diverse linguistic abilities and needs.** By the time they reach kindergarten, most children have considerable proficiency in their native language. Nevertheless, their language development continues throughout the school years. For example, in addition to acquiring an ever-expanding vocabulary, children become increasingly able to listen effectively, conduct sustained conversations about particular topics, and comprehend the underlying meanings of figurative speech.

Both hereditary and environmental factors contribute to language development. One important environmental variable is, of course, the particular language—or languages—that children speak at home and in their communities. Researchers have identified many advantages to knowing two or more languages, including more advanced metalinguistic awareness, more creative thinking, and greater cross-cultural understanding. Different approaches to promoting bilingualism are recommended in different situations. In an English-speaking community, native English speakers can gain fluency in a second language through complete or partial immersion in that language at school, but students who speak a language other than English at home typically achieve at higher levels in bilingual education programs.

Practice For Your Licensure Exam

A Floating Stone

After lunch one day, first-grade teacher Mr. Fox calls his students to the carpet area so that he can show them a "curious thing." Once the children are all seated and attentive, he puts a large fishbowl in front of them and fills it with water. Then, out of his jacket pocket, he pulls a piece of granite a little smaller than a golf ball and holds the stone over the bowl.

"What's going to happen when I drop this stone into the water?" he asks the children. "Do you think it will float like a boat does?"

Several of the children shout, "No, it's gonna sink!" Mr. Fox drops the stone into the water, and, sure enough, it sinks.

"You were right," Mr. Fox says. "Hmm, I have another stone in my pocket." He pulls out a much larger one—in this case, a piece of pumice (cooled lava) that is filled with tiny air pockets. "When I was traveling last summer, I found this at the bottom of an old volcano. Do you think this one will sink like the other one did?"

The children declare that it will definitely sink. Mr. Fox drops it into the fishbowl, where it momentarily submerges and then floats to the surface. "Hmm, what just happened?" he says as he looks inquisitively at his class.

Many of the children gasp with surprise. When a girl named Cora insists, "You didn't do it right!" Mr. Fox retrieves the pumice and drops it in the water again, with the same result. "No, no, that's impossible!" Cora yells. "Stones always sink—*always!*" She rubs and shakes her head, almost as if she's a bit upset. (Case based on similar lesson described by Hennessey & Beeth, 1993.)

1. Constructed-response question:

Cora is noticeably surprised and possibly upset when she sees the pumice float.

A. Use one or more concepts from Jean Piaget's theory of cognitive development to explain why Cora reacts as strongly as she does to the floating pumice.

B. Again drawing on Piaget's theory, explain why Mr. Fox intentionally presents a phenomenon that will surprise the children.

2. Multiple-choice question:

Imagine that you perform the same demonstration with high school students rather than first graders. If you were to make use of Vygotsky's theory of cognitive development, which one of the following approaches would you be most likely to take in helping the students understand the floating pumice?

a. Before performing the demonstration, ask students to draw a picture of the fishbowl and two stones.

b. Drop several light objects (e.g., a feather, a piece of paper, a small sponge) into the fishbowl before dropping either stone into it.

c. Teach the concept of *density,* and explain that an object's average density relative to water determines whether it floats or sinks.

d. Praise students who correctly predict that the larger stone will float, even if they initially give an incorrect explanation about why it will float.

MyEdLab **Licensure Exam 2.1**

PRAXIS Go to Appendix C, "Matching Book Content and Ebook Activities to the Praxis Principles of Learning and Teaching Tests," to discover sections of this chapter that may be especially applicable to the Praxis tests.

3

Personal and Social Development

Learning Outcomes

3.1 Describe the nature and origins of children's temperaments and personality characteristics, and explain how you might adapt your classroom practices to students' diverse personalities.

3.2 Explain how students' sense of self is apt to influence their behavior and how you can help students develop healthy self-perceptions.

3.3 Apply your knowledge of peer relationships and social cognition as you identify strategies for promoting productive social skills and addressing student aggression.

3.4 Describe typical advancements in moral and prosocial development over the course of childhood and adolescence, and identify strategies for promoting moral and prosocial development at school.

CASE STUDY: HIDDEN TREASURE

Six-year-old Lupita has spent most of her life in Mexico with her grandmother, but she recently joined her migrant-worker parents in the United States and is now a quiet, well-behaved student in Ms. Padilla's kindergarten class. Ms. Padilla rarely calls on her because of her apparent lack of academic skills and is thinking about holding her back for a second year of kindergarten. Yet a researcher's video camera captures a side of Lupita her teacher hasn't noticed. On one occasion Lupita is quick to finish her Spanish assignment and starts to work on a puzzle during her free time. A classmate approaches, and he and Lupita begin playing with a box of toys. A teacher aide asks the boy whether he has finished his Spanish assignment, implying that he should return to his seat to complete it, but the boy doesn't understand the aide's subtle message. Lupita gently persuades the boy to finish his schoolwork and then returns to her puzzle. Two classmates having trouble with their own puzzles request Lupita's assistance, and she patiently shows them how to work cooperatively to assemble the pieces.

Ms. Padilla is amazed when she views the video. She readily admits, "I had written her off—her and three others. They had met my expectations [for low achievement] and I just wasn't looking for anything else." Ms. Padilla and her aides begin working closely with Lupita on academic skills and often allow her to take a leadership role in group activities. At the end of the school year, Lupita earns achievement test scores indicating exceptional competence in language and math, and she is promoted to first grade. (Based on case described by Carrasco, 1981)

- What distinctive personality characteristics and social skills does Lupita exhibit? Which of them are likely to enhance her classroom success? Which of them might potentially interfere with her classroom success?
- What might have happened to Lupita if her many strengths had gone unnoticed?

Lupita's behaviors during free time reveal a conscientious, socially astute child with strong teaching and leadership skills. However, perhaps because of Lupita's quiet, restrained nature—or perhaps because of her family background—Ms. Padilla initially concludes that Lupita hasn't mastered the knowledge and skills she'll need in first grade. If the researcher's video hadn't captured Lupita's social skills and proficiency and persistence with puzzles, Lupita might very well have remained on the sidelines throughout much of the school year, getting little assistance on academic skills and few opportunities to capitalize on her many positive personal qualities. Thus, Ms. Padilla's low expectations for Lupita may have ensured that Lupita *wouldn't* gain the knowledge and skills she would need in first grade—a self-fulfilling prophecy.

School isn't just a place for acquiring cognitive and linguistic skills. It's also a place for **personal development**, whereby children and adolescents continue to develop their emerging personality traits and gain an increasing understanding of who they are as individuals. Furthermore, the very social nature of school makes it an ideal context for **social development**, in which young people come to better understand their fellow human beings, develop productive social skills and interpersonal relationships, and gradually internalize their society's standards for behavior.

Personality Development

All of us have unique qualities that make us different from the people around us. Our distinctive ways of behaving, thinking, and feeling comprise our **personalities**. For example, whereas Lupita tends to be quiet and well behaved in class, some of her peers are probably noisy and rambunctious. And whereas Lupita is conscientious about completing her work, we might reasonably guess that some of her classmates are easily distracted and must be prodded to stay on task.

Children's personalities are the result of both heredity—especially in the form of inherited temperaments—and environmental factors. As you will see, heredity and environment often interact in their influences.

TEMPERAMENT

A child's **temperament** is his or her general tendency to respond to and deal with environmental stimuli and events in particular ways. Children seem to have distinct temperaments almost from birth. Researchers have identified many temperamental styles that emerge early in life and are relatively enduring, including general activity level, adaptability, self-control, persistence, adventurousness, outgoingness, shyness, fearfulness, irritability, and distractibility. Most psychologists agree that such temperamental differences are biologically based and have genetic origins, and to some degree the differences persist into adolescence and adulthood (Else-Quest, Hyde, Goldsmith, & Van Hulle, 2006; Keogh, 2003; Rothbart, 2011; A. Thomas & Chess, 1977).

By influencing children's behaviors, inherited temperaments also influence the specific environmental circumstances they experience and so indirectly affect other aspects of personal and social development (N. A. Fox, Henderson, Rubin, Calkins, & Schmidt, 2001; Rothbart, 2011; Strelau, 2008). For example, children who are energetic and adventuresome seek out a wider variety of experiences than those who are quiet and restrained. And children who are naturally vivacious and outgoing typically have more opportunities to learn social skills and establish rewarding interpersonal relationships—including good relationships with their teachers—than do children who are subdued and shy.

MyEdLab

Video Example 3.1.

Even when all students are productively engaged in a classroom activity, they show temperamental differences in such traits as general energy level and assertiveness. For example, notice how some boys dominate this small-group activity in which several students experiment with a small water wheel.

Furthermore, many temperamental characteristics affect how students engage in and respond to classroom activities and thus indirectly affect their academic achievement (Keogh, 2003; A. J. Martin, Nejad, Colmar, & Liem, 2013; Saudino & Plomin, 2007). For instance, students are more likely to achieve at high levels if they are persistent, reasonably (but not overly) energetic, and able to ignore minor distractions. They can also achieve greater academic success if their behaviors lead to friendly, productive relationships with teachers and peers—people who can bolster their self-confidence and support their efforts to learn. Underlying some of their academic and social success is an aspect of temperament known as **effortful control**—their general ability to inhibit immediate impulses in order to think and act productively (Rothbart, 2011; Valiente, Lemery-Chalfant, & Swanson, 2010).

ENVIRONMENTAL INFLUENCES ON PERSONALITY DEVELOPMENT

Genetic differences in temperament are only *predispositions* to behave in certain ways, and environmental conditions and experiences point different children with the same predispositions in somewhat different directions. Two key environmental factors influencing personality development are family dynamics and cultural expectations for behavior.

FAMILY DYNAMICS

Many parents and other family caregivers (e.g., grandparents, older siblings) lovingly interact with a new infant and consistently and dependably provide for the infant's physical and psychological needs. When they do such things, a strong, affectionate caregiver–child bond known as **attachment** typically forms (Ainsworth, Blehar, Waters, & Wall, 1978). Infants who become closely attached to parents or other caregivers early in life are apt to develop into amiable, independent, self-confident children and adolescents who adjust easily to new classroom environments, establish productive relationships with teachers and peers, and have an inner conscience that guides their behavior. In contrast, children who don't become closely attached to a parent or some other individual early in life can be immature, dependent, unpopular, and prone to disruptive and aggressive behaviors later on (J. P. Allen, Porter, McFarland, McElhaney, & Marsh, 2007; Kochanska, Aksan, Knaack, & Rhines, 2004; Mikulincer & Shaver, 2005; S. Shulman, Elicker, & Sroufe, 1994; Sroufe, Carlson, & Shulman, 1993).

In addition to forming emotional attachments with children, parents and other family caregivers tend to adopt fairly consistent *parenting styles* they use in raising the children. In mainstream Western culture, the best situation for most children seems to be authoritative parenting, which combines affection and respect for children with reasonable restrictions on behavior. Authoritative parents provide a loving and supportive home, hold high expectations and standards for performance, explain why behaviors are or are not acceptable, enforce household rules consistently, include children in decision making, and provide age-appropriate opportunities for autonomy. Children from authoritative homes tend to be happy, energetic, self-confident, and likeable. They make friends easily and show self-control and concern for the rights and needs of others. Children of authoritative parents appear well adjusted, in part, because their behavior fits well with the values espoused by mainstream Western culture. They listen respectfully to others, follow reasonable rules for behavior, work well independently, and strive for academic achievement (Barber, Stolz, & Olsen, 2005; Baumrind, 1989, 1991; Bradley, 2010; M. R. Gray & Steinberg, 1999; J. M. T. Walker & Hoover-Dempsey, 2006). Given such benefits, authoritative parenting can provide a good model for how we, as teachers, should generally conduct our classrooms.

Authoritative parenting isn't universally "best," however. Certain other parenting styles may be better suited to particular cultures and environments. For instance, in authoritarian parenting, parents expect complete and immediate compliance; they neither negotiate expectations nor provide reasons for their requests. In many Asian American and Hispanic families, high demands for obedience are made within the context of close, supportive parent–child relationships. Underlying the message of control is a more important message: "I love you and want you to do well, but it's equally important that you act for the good of the family and community" (X. Chen & Wang, 2010; Halgunseth, Ispa, & Rudy, 2006; Rothbaum & Trommsdorff, 2007). Authoritarian parenting is also more common in impoverished economic environments. When families live in low-income, inner-city neighborhoods where danger potentially lurks around every corner, parents may better serve their children by being strict and directive about activities (Hale-Benson, 1986; McLoyd, 1998).

Some degree of parental guidance and discipline seems to be important for optimal personal and social development. Parents who are overly permissive—for instance, those who let their children come and go as they please and impose few consequences for inappropriate actions—tend to have children who are immature and impulsive, do poorly in school, and act aggressively toward peers (Aunola & Nurmi, 2005; Joussemet et al., 2008; Lamborn, Mounts, Steinberg, & Dornbusch, 1991). Yet we must be careful that we don't point accusatory fingers or in other ways be judgmental about how parents are bringing up their children. Some parents may have learned ineffective parenting strategies from their own parents. Others may have challenges in their lives—perhaps mental illness, marital conflict, or serious financial problems—that hamper their ability to nurture and support their children.

It's important to note, too, that most research on parenting involves correlational studies that reveal associations between parents' behaviors and children's characteristics but don't necessarily demonstrate cause-and-effect relationships. A few experimental studies have documented that specific parenting styles probably *do* influence children's personalities to some degree (Bakermans-Kranenburg, van IJzendoorn, Pijlman, Mesman, & Juffer, 2008; W. A. Collins, Maccoby, Steinberg, Hetherington, & Bornstein, 2000). In some cases, however, parents' disciplinary strategies seem to be the *result,* rather than the cause, of how children behave. For instance, temperamentally lively or adventuresome children typically require more parental control than quieter, restrained ones (J. R. Harris, 1998; Rothbart, 2011; Stice & Barrera, 1995).

As teachers, we can certainly serve as sources of information about effective disciplinary strategies. But we should keep in mind that parenting styles have, at most, only a *moderate* influence on children's personalities. Many children and adolescents thrive despite their caregivers' diverse parenting styles, provided that those caregivers aren't severely neglectful or abusive. Children with certain temperaments—for instance, those who tend to be adaptable, self-disciplined, and

In the classroom, convey reasonably high expectations and standards for behavior, but always within the context of affectionate and respectful relationships with students.

Serve as a resource regarding effective parenting strategies, perhaps through newsletters or parent discussion groups.

outgoing—seem to be especially resilient in the face of difficult family circumstances (Bates & Pettit, 2007; Belsky & Pluess, 2009; D. Hart, Atkins, & Fegley, 2003; Rothbart, 2011).

Child maltreatment. In a few unfortunate instances, parents' behaviors toward their children constitute child maltreatment. One form of child maltreatment is child *neglect:* Parents fail to provide nutritious meals, adequate clothing, and other basic necessities of life. In other cases parents or other family members *abuse* children physically, sexually, or emotionally. Possible indicators of neglect or abuse are chronic hunger, lack of warm clothing in cold weather, untreated medical needs, frequent or serious physical injuries (e.g., bruises, burns, broken bones), and exceptional knowledge about sexual matters.

Parental neglect and abuse can have significant adverse effects on children's personal and social development. On average, children who have been routinely neglected or abused have low self-esteem, poorly developed social skills, and low school achievement. Many are angry, aggressive, and defiant. Others can be depressed, anxious, socially withdrawn, and possibly suicidal (Crosson-Tower, 2010; J. Kim & Cicchetti, 2006; Maughan & Cicchetti, 2002; R. A. Thompson & Wyatt, 1999).

Teachers are both legally and morally obligated to report any cases of suspected child abuse or neglect to the proper authorities (e.g., the school principal or child protective services). Two helpful resources are the National Child Abuse Hotline at 1-800-4-A-CHILD (1-800-422-4453) and the website for Childhelp at www.childhelp.org.

CULTURAL EXPECTATIONS AND SOCIALIZATION

As we've seen, various cultural groups influence children's personalities indirectly through the parenting styles they encourage. Culture also has a more direct influence on children's personal and social development through a process known as socialization. That is, members of a cultural group work hard to help growing children adopt the behaviors and beliefs that the group holds dear. Children typically learn their earliest lessons about their culture's expectations for behavior from parents and other family members, who teach them simple manners (e.g., saying please and thank you), encourage them to do well in school, and so on (W.-B. Chen & Gregory, 2008; Eccles, 2007). Once children reach school age, teachers become equally important socialization agents. For example, in mainstream Western society, teachers typically expect and encourage such behaviors as showing respect for authority figures, following rules and directions, controlling impulses, working independently, and asking for help when it's needed (Manning & Baruth, 2009; Wentzel & Looney, 2007). Cultures around the globe encourage many of these behaviors, but they don't necessarily endorse *all* of them. For instance, many children of Mexican heritage are more accustomed to observing events quietly and unobtrusively—as Lupita does in the opening case study—than to asking adults for explanations and help (Correa-Chávez, Rogoff, & Mejía Arauz, 2005; Gutiérrez & Rogoff, 2003).

Researchers have observed other cultural differences in socialization practices as well. For example, many European American families encourage children to think for themselves and be assertive in expressing their needs and opinions, but families from many other countries (e.g., Mexico, China, India) are more likely to encourage restraint, obedience, and deference to elders (Goodnow, 1992; Joshi & MacLean, 1994; Morelli & Rothbaum, 2007). And whereas many American children are encouraged to be outgoing and emotionally expressive, children in many Asian cultures are encouraged to be shy and emotionally reserved (X. Chen, Chung, & Hsiao, 2009; Huntsinger & Jose, 2006; Morelli & Rothbaum, 2007). However, considerable diversity exists *within* any culture, with different parents, teachers, and other adults encouraging somewhat different behaviors and beliefs.

When behaviors expected of students at school differ from those expected at home or when belief systems presented by teachers are inconsistent with those of children's parents, children may initially experience some culture shock. At a minimum, these children are apt to be confused and distracted, at least in the first few days or weeks of school. Some children with less adaptable or more irritable temperaments may even become angry or resistant (Rothbart, 2011; C. Ward, Bochner, & Furnham, 2001).

As teachers, we must certainly encourage behaviors essential for students' long-term success, such as obeying rules, following instructions, and working independently. At the same time, students will need our guidance, support, and patience when our expectations differ from those of their family or cultural group.

Chapter 5 describes possible warning signs that a student is contemplating suicide.

 Report suspected cases of child maltreatment *immediately.*

Chapter 4 examines cultural differences such as these in greater depth.

Teach students behaviors they will need for long-term success in Western society, but be patient when such behaviors are very different from those learned at home.

THE "BIG FIVE" PERSONALITY TRAITS

As children grow older, the many interactions among their inherited temperaments and environmental circumstances lead to unique and somewhat stable personality profiles. Research with both children and adults has yielded five general personality traits that are relatively independent of one another and appear to involve somewhat different areas of the brain. You can remember them using the mnemonic *OCEAN:*

- *Openness:* The extent to which one is curious about the world and receptive to new experiences and ideas

- *Conscientiousness:* The extent to which one is careful, organized, self-disciplined, and likely to follow through on plans and commitments

- *Extraversion:* The extent to which one is socially outgoing and seeks excitement

- *Agreeableness:* The extent to which one is pleasant, kind, and cooperative in social situations

- *Neuroticism:* The extent to which one is prone to negative emotions (e.g., anxiety, anger, depression) (Caspi, 1998; DeYoung et al., 2010; A. J. Martin et al., 2013; G. Matthews, Zeidner, & Roberts, 2006)

Creating a Productive Classroom Environment

Accommodating Students' Diverse Temperaments and Personality Traits

Minimize downtime for students with high energy levels.
As a way of letting a chronically restless third grader release pent-up energy throughout the school day, his teacher gives him small chores to do (e.g., erasing the board, sharpening pencils, cleaning art supplies) and shows him how to complete the chores quietly so as not to disturb his classmates.

Provide many opportunities for highly sociable students to interact with classmates.
In a unit on colonial America, a fifth-grade teacher assigns a project in which students must depict a typical colonial village in some way (e.g., by writing a research paper, drawing a map on poster board, or creating a miniature three-dimensional model). The students can choose to work on the project alone or with one or two classmates, with the stipulation that students who work with peers must undertake more complex projects than students who work alone.

Be especially warm and attentive with very shy students, and identify contexts in which they feel comfortable interacting with peers and openly expressing their ideas.
A ninth-grade teacher has a new student join one of his classes midway through the school year. The student comes to class alone each day and doesn't join in conversations with peers before or after class. When the teacher sees her eating lunch by herself in the cafeteria one day, he sits beside her and engages her in conversation about her previous school and community. The following day in class, he assigns a small-group, cooperative learning project that students will work on periodically over the next 2 weeks. He forms cooperative groups of three or four students each, making sure to place the new girl with two students who he knows will be friendly and helpful to her.

When students have trouble adapting to new circumstances, give them advance notice of unusual activities and provide extra structure and reassurance.
A kindergarten teacher has discovered that two children in his class do well when the school day is orderly and predictable but often become anxious or upset when the class departs from its usual routine. To prepare the children for a field trip to the fire station on Friday, the teacher begins to talk about the trip at the beginning of the week, explaining what the class will do and see during the visit. He also recruits the father of one of the anxiety-prone children to serve as a parent assistant that day.

If students seem overwhelmed by noisy or chaotic situations, locate or create a more calm and peaceful environment for them.
Several middle school students find the school cafeteria loud and unsettling. Their math teacher offers her classroom as a place where they can occasionally eat instead. On some days she eats with them. At other times she sits at her desk and grades papers, but the students know she will gladly stop to talk if they have a question or concern.

Teach self-control strategies to students who act impulsively.
A high school student often shouts out comments and opinions in her history class. One day the student's teacher takes her aside after school and gently explains that her lack of restraint is interfering with classmates' ability to participate in discussions. To sensitize the student to the extent of the problem, the teacher asks her to keep a daily tally of how many times she talks without first raising her hand. A week later the two meet again, and the teacher suggests a quiet self-talk strategy that can help the student participate actively without dominating a discussion.

Sources: Some strategies based on suggestions by M.-L. Chang & Davis, 2009; Keogh, 2003.

Remember that despite some consistency in students' personalities, their behaviors are likely to vary somewhat in different contexts.

Personality traits such as the "Big Five" lead to some consistency—but not *total* consistency—in children's behaviors across situations (Hampson, 2008; Mendoza-Denton & Mischel, 2007). Variability is particularly common when circumstances change considerably. For instance, a student might be very outgoing and sociable with his close friends but shy and withdrawn with people he doesn't know very well. And a student is more likely to be conscientious about completing homework if she is given some guidance about how to organize her assignments in a "to-do" list.

TEMPERAMENT, PERSONALITY, AND GOODNESS OF FIT

On average, students who are conscientious about their work and open to new experiences achieve at higher levels at school (Hattie, 2009; A. J. Martin et al., 2013; M. C. O'Connor & Paunonen, 2007). Yet there is no single best temperament or personality that maximizes students' adjustment and achievement in the classroom. Instead, children are more likely to succeed at school when there is a goodness of fit—rather than a mismatch—between their natural inclinations and typical behaviors, on the one hand, and classroom activities and expectations, on the other (A. Thomas & Chess, 1977). For example, when teachers want students to participate actively in whole-class discussions, highly energetic, outgoing children are apt to shine, but quieter students (like Lupita) might feel anxious or intimidated. When teachers require a lot of independent seatwork, quieter children often do well, but some energetic children may be viewed as disruptive (Keogh, 2003; Rothbart, 2011).

As teachers, we must keep in mind that students' distinctive ways of behaving in the classroom—their energy levels, sociability, impulsiveness, and the like—aren't entirely within their control. The Creating a Productive Classroom Environment feature "Accommodating Students' Diverse Temperaments and Personality Traits" offers several suggestions for adapting instruction and classroom management strategies to accommodate students' individual behavioral styles.

> MyEdLab **Self-Check 3.1**
>
> MyEdLab **Application Exercise 3.1.** In this interactive exercise, you can practice applying what you have learned about temperament and goodness of fit.

Development of a Sense of Self

With their increasing capacity for symbolic thinking and (eventually) abstract reasoning, growing children begin to draw conclusions about who they are as people. As an example, try the following exercise.

EXPERIENCING FIRSTHAND
DESCRIBING YOURSELF

List at least 10 words or phrases that describe you as a person.

How did you describe yourself? Are you smart? Friendly? Open-minded? Physically attractive? Moody? Your answers provide a window into a key component of your personality known as sense of self—your perceptions, beliefs, judgments, and feelings about who you are as a person. Many psychologists distinguish between two aspects of the sense of self: *self-concept*—assessments of one's own characteristics, strengths, and weaknesses—and *self-esteem*—judgments and feelings about one's own value and worth. These two aspects closely overlap, however, and thus the two terms are often used interchangeably (Bracken, 2009; Byrne, 2002; McInerney, Marsh, & Craven, 2008).

In overall self-assessments, young children tend to make distinctions between two general domains: how competent they are at day-to-day tasks (including schoolwork) and how much their family and friends like them. As they grow older, children make finer and finer distinctions—for instance, they realize that they may be more or less competent or "good" in various academic subjects, athletic activities, peer relationships, and physical attractiveness (Arens, Yeung, Craven, & Hasselhorn, 2011; Davis-Kean & Sandler, 2001; Harter, 1999). Each of these domains may have a greater or lesser influence on students' overall sense of self. For some students, academic achievement may be the overriding factor, whereas for others, physical attractiveness or popularity with peers may be more important (Crocker & Knight, 2005; D. Hart, 1988; Harter, 1999).

Children and adolescents tend to behave in ways that mirror their beliefs about themselves (M. S. Caldwell, Rudolph, Troop-Gordon, & Kim, 2004; Marsh & O'Mara, 2008; Valentine, DuBois, & Cooper, 2004). For instance, if they see themselves as good students, they're more likely to pay attention, follow directions, persist at difficult problems, and enroll in challenging courses. If they see themselves as friendly and socially desirable, they're more likely to seek the company of their classmates and perhaps run for student council. If they see themselves as physically skillful, they'll more eagerly pursue extracurricular athletics.

Students' beliefs about themselves are, like their beliefs about the world around them, largely self-constructed. Accordingly, their self-assessments may or may not be accurate. When students evaluate themselves fairly accurately, they're in a good position to choose age-appropriate tasks and activities (Baumeister, Campbell, Krueger, & Vohs, 2003; Harter, 1999). A slightly inflated self-assessment can be beneficial as well, because it encourages students to work toward challenging yet potentially reachable goals (Bjorklund & Green, 1992; Pajares, 2009). However, a sense of self that is *too* inflated can give some students an unwarranted sense of superiority over classmates and lead them to bully or in other ways act aggressively toward peers (Baumeister et al., 2003; Baumeister, Smart, & Boden, 1996; Menon et al., 2007). And as you might guess, students who significantly *under*estimate their abilities are apt to avoid the many challenges that would enhance their cognitive and social growth (Schunk & Pajares, 2004; Zimmerman & Moylan, 2009).

FACTORS INFLUENCING SENSE OF SELF

Students often gain initial insights about their general competence in a certain domain from their *own successes and failures* in that domain (Chiu, 2012; Marsh & O'Mara, 2008). For instance, they may discover that they can easily solve—or, instead, consistently struggle with—simple math problems. Or they may find that they can run faster—or more slowly—than most of their peers. Through such experiences, students acquire a sense of **self-efficacy** about the degree to which they can succeed in certain activities and accomplish certain goals. Over time, students' specific self-efficacies for various tasks and activities contribute to their more general sense of self (Bong & Skaalvik, 2003; McInerney et al., 2008).

Unfortunately, an interplay between self-perceptions and behaviors can create a vicious cycle: A poor sense of self leads to less productive behaviors, which leads to fewer successes, which perpetuates the poor sense of self. However, simply telling students that they're good or smart or in some other way "special" is unlikely to break the cycle (Brummelman, Thomaes, Orobio de Castro, Overbeek, & Bushman, 2014; McMillan, Singh, & Simonetta, 1994; Pajares, 2009). Instead, we must make sure that students have many opportunities to improve and eventually succeed at academic, social, and physical tasks—not obviously easy tasks (which presumably anyone could do) but challenging ones that reflect a genuine sense of accomplishment. When we present such challenges, we must, of course, be sure that students have the prerequisite knowledge and scaffolding they need to be successful (Bouchey & Harter, 2005; Dunning, Heath, & Suls, 2004; Leary, 1999).

Yet students' personal successes and failures aren't the only things affecting their sense of self. A second important factor is students' social context—and more specifically, *other people's behaviors*—which influences their self-perceptions in at least two ways. For one thing, how students evaluate themselves depends to some extent on how their own performance compares to that of their peers. For example, students who see themselves achieving at higher levels than classmates are apt to develop a more positive sense of self than those who consistently find themselves falling short (R. Butler, 2008; Liem, Marsh, Martin, McInerney, & Yeung, 2013; Trautwein, Gerlach, & Lüdtke, 2008). Thus, peer comparisons can dampen high-ability students' sense of self when they attend classes made up largely of students with similarly high ability (Chiu, 2012; Seaton, Marsh, & Craven, 2010).

In addition, students' self-perceptions are affected by how others behave *toward* them. Peers often communicate information about children's social and athletic competence, perhaps by seeking out a child's companionship or ridiculing a child in front of others (M. S. Caldwell et al., 2004; Crosnoe, 2011; Rudolph, Caldwell, & Conley, 2005). Adults, too, influence children's sense

Enhance students' sense of self indirectly by supporting their efforts to meet new challenges.

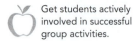

Minimize competitive situations in which students might compare themselves unfavorably with peers, and present any negative feedback within the context of an optimistic message about future performance.

Chapter 11 describes more specific effects of teacher expectations.

Get students actively involved in successful group activities.

Remember that a student's sense of self becomes increasingly stable with age. Especially in the upper elementary and secondary grades, then, enhancing a student's low self-esteem may take time and persistence.

of self, in part by the kinds of expectations they hold for children's performance and in part by drawing attention to various things children do well or poorly (M. J. Harris & Rosenthal, 1985; O'Mara, Marsh, Craven, & Debus, 2006; Pajares, 2009). As teachers, we should, of course, communicate realistically high expectations for achievement and give positive feedback about the specific things students do well. And when we find that we must give students negative feedback—and occasionally we must—we should do so while also communicating optimism about their future performance. For instance, we might point out that mistakes are a natural part of the learning process, and we should offer concrete suggestions about how to improve.

A third general factor that can impact students' sense of self is *membership in a successful group* (Harter, 1999; Thorkildsen, Golant, & Cambray-Engstrom, 2008; Wigfield, Eccles, & Pintrich, 1996). If you think back to your own school years, perhaps you can recall taking pride in something your entire class accomplished or feeling good about a community service project completed through an extracurricular club. School groups aren't the only groups affecting students' sense of self. For instance, some cultures encourage children to take pride in the accomplishments of their families as well as—or perhaps instead of—their own accomplishments (Banks & Banks, 1995; P. M. Cole & Tan, 2007). And as we'll see a bit later in the chapter, students' membership in certain ethnic groups can also be a source of pride.

DEVELOPMENTAL CHANGES IN SENSE OF SELF

We've already seen one way in which self-perceptions change with age: Children increasingly differentiate among the many aspects of who they are as people—their academic abilities, physical qualities, social relationships, and so on. But children's and adolescents' beliefs and feelings about themselves change in other ways as well. One early personality theorist, Erik Erikson, proposed that people's personalities and sense of self continue to evolve throughout the life span in a predictable sequence of *psychosocial stages,* described in Figure 3.1. However, our focus in the upcoming sections will be on what more contemporary researchers have learned about developmental changes in children's and adolescents' sense of self.

Childhood Elementary school children tend to think of themselves in terms of concrete, easily observable characteristics and behaviors, such as their age, sex, and favorite activities (D. Hart, 1988; Harter, 1983). In racially and culturally diverse communities, where different skin colors, languages, and customs are obvious, children may also classify themselves as belonging to one or another racial or ethnic group (Phinney, 1990; Sheets, 1999). For instance, when she was in second grade, 7-year-old Tina drew the self-portrait shown in Figure 3.2. As a girl with a Native American and Hispanic genetic heritage, she was clearly aware that her hair and skin tone were darker than those of most of her classmates.

Most young children have a generally positive sense of self. Sometimes they believe they're more capable than they really *are* and that they can easily overcome initial failures (R. Butler, 2008; Lockhart, Chang, & Story, 2002; Robins & Trzesniewski, 2005). As children have more opportunities to compare themselves with peers during the elementary grades and as they become cognitively more able to *make* such comparisons, their self-assessments become increasingly realistic (R. Butler, 2008; J. W. Chapman, Tunmer, & Prochnow, 2000; Davis-Kean et al., 2008). They also begin to pull together their many self-observations into generalizations about the kinds of people they are—perhaps friendly, good at sports, smart, or dumb—and such generalizations lead to the development of increasingly stable self-concepts (D. A. Cole et al., 2001; Harter, 1999).

Early adolescence As students reach adolescence and gain greater capability for abstract thought, they increasingly think of themselves in terms of general, fairly stable traits. Consider 12-year-old Tina's self-description in sixth grade:

> I'm cool. I'm awesome. I'm way cool. I'm 12. I'm boy crazy. I go to Brentwood Middle School. I'm popular with my fans. I play viola. My best friend is Lindsay. I have a gerbil named Taj. I'm adopted. I'm beautiful.

Although Tina listed a few concrete features, she had clearly developed a fairly abstract self-perception. Her focus on coolness, popularity, and beauty, rather than on intelligence or academic

---

FIGURE 3.1 Erikson's eight stages of psychosocial development

Overview of Erikson's Stages

Erik Erikson (1963, 1972) proposed that people proceed through eight distinct stages over the course of their lives. Each stage presents a unique developmental task, and how a person addresses it influences her or his general mental health and progress through later stages.

Trust versus mistrust (infancy). According to Erikson, the major developmental task in infancy is to learn whether other people, especially primary caregivers, regularly satisfy basic needs. If caregivers are consistent sources of food and comfort, an infant learns *trust*—that others are dependable and reliable. If caregivers are neglectful or abusive, the infant learns *mistrust*—that the world is an undependable, unpredictable, and possibly dangerous place.

Autonomy versus shame and doubt (toddler years). As toddlers gain increasing muscular control, they begin to satisfy some of their own needs—for example, by feeding and dressing themselves. If caregivers encourage self-sufficient behavior, toddlers develop a sense of *autonomy*—a sense of being able to handle many problems on their own. but if caregivers demand too much too soon or, in contrast, restrict or ridicule early attempts at self-sufficiency, children may instead develop *shame and doubt* about their abilities.

Initiative versus guilt (preschool years). With their growing independence, preschoolers have many choices about the activities they pursue. If parents and preschool teachers encourage and support children's efforts while also helping them make realistic and appropriate choices, children develop *initiative*—independence in planning and undertaking activities. but if, instead, adults discourage the pursuit of independent activities or else dismiss them as silly and bothersome, children develop *guilt* about their needs and desires.

Industry versus inferiority (elementary school years). Elementary school provides many opportunities for children to achieve the recognition of teachers, parents, and peers by producing things—drawing pictures, writing short stories, and so on. If children are encouraged to make and do things and then praised for their accomplishments, they begin to demonstrate *industry* in that they diligently pursue and persist at certain tasks and often put work before pleasure. If they are instead punished for their efforts or if they find they are incapable of meeting others' expectations, they develop a sense of *inferiority* about their capabilities.

Identity versus role confusion (adolescence). Adolescents begin to ponder the roles they might play in the adult world. Initially, they're apt to experience some *role confusion*—mixed ideas and feelings about the specific ways in which they will fit into society—and may experiment with a variety of behaviors and activities (e.g., tinkering with cars, babysitting for neighbors, affiliating with certain religious groups). Erikson proposed that eventually most adolescents achieve a sense of *identity* regarding who they are and where their lives are headed.

Intimacy versus isolation (young adulthood). In Erikson's view, once young people have established their identities, they're ready to make long-term social commitments. Many become capable of *intimacy*, forming one or more reciprocal relationships that involve compromise and self-sacrifice. People who can't form intimate relationships—perhaps because they have trouble putting aside their own needs—develop a sense of *isolation*.

Generativity versus stagnation (middle age). During middle age the primary developmental task is one of contributing to society and helping to guide future generations. When a person makes a contribution during this period, he or she feels a sense of *generativity*—a sense of productivity and accomplishment. In contrast, a person who is self-centered and unable or unwilling to help society move forward develops a feeling of *stagnation*—a dissatisfaction with his or her relative lack of productivity.

Integrity versus despair (retirement years). As people reach retirement, they look back on their lives and accomplishments. If they believe that they've led a happy, productive life, they gain feelings of contentment and *integrity*. But if they look back on a life of disappointments and unachieved goals, they may develop a sense of *despair*.

Critiquing Erikson's Theory

Erikson's theory reminds us that development is a life-long process: Children and adults alike have new things to learn and new challenges to meet. At the same time, his theory has shortcomings. First, Erikson drew his ideas largely from personal anecdotes rather than systematic research (Crain, 2005). Second, he based his stages primarily on work with men; for many women, a focus on intimacy emerges either before or in conjunction with a focus on identity (Josselson, 1988). And third, Erikson didn't take into account the important role that culture plays in development. Many cultures intentionally discourage autonomy, initiative, and self-assertiveness in young children, sometimes as a way of protecting children from the very real dangers of their environments (X. Chen et al., 2009; Harwood, Miller, & Irizarry, 1995; G. J. Powell, 1983).

As teachers, we should keep in mind that the age ranges for accomplishing Erikson's eight developmental tasks are probably broader than Erikson proposed. For instance, most people probably don't achieve a sense of identity as early or as easily as Erikson suggested (see the discussion of identity in the section "Late Adolescence"). Nevertheless, the first five stages have implications for us as teachers, who must work hard to do the following:

- Help students overcome early difficulties with trust, autonomy, or initiative—in particular, by being reliable sources of affection and support (trust) and by giving students age-appropriate opportunities to work independently (autonomy) and undertake self-chosen activities (initiative).

- Promote a sense of industry by engaging students in meaningful tasks and completing worthwhile projects.

- Help adolescents in their search for identity by providing opportunities to explore various roles they might play in adult society.

---

achievement (or, we might add, modesty), is fairly typical: Social acceptance and physical appearance are far more important to many young adolescents than academic competence (D. Hart, 1988; Harter, 1999).

Students' self-concepts and self-esteem often drop as they make the transition from elementary school to middle school or junior high, with the drop being more pronounced for girls (D. A. Cole et al., 2001; Harter, 1999; Robins & Trzesniewski, 2005). The physiological changes accompanying puberty may be a factor: Many boys and girls think of themselves as being somewhat less attractive once they reach adolescence (S. Moore & Rosenthal, 2006; Stice, 2003). Changes in the

FIGURE 3.2 As early as the primary grades, students in racially diverse communities have some awareness of their membership in a particular racial group. Notice how 7-year-old Tina portrays herself as having darker hair and skin than the classmates behind her.

school environment—including disrupted friendships, more superficial teacher–student relationships, and more rigorous academic standards—probably also have a negative impact.

Also with early adolescence come two new phenomena with implications for sense of self. First, students become more cognitively able to reflect on how others might see them (Harter, 1999). They may initially go to extremes, thinking that in any social situation everyone else's attention is focused squarely on them—a phenomenon known as the imaginary audience (Elkind, 1981; R. M. Ryan & Kuczkowski, 1994; Somerville, 2013). Because they believe themselves to be the center of attention, young teenagers (especially girls) are often preoccupied with their physical appearance and can be quite self-critical. To some degree, this heightened concern about what other people might think of them appears to be linked to maturational changes in certain areas of the brain, including areas that underlie self-focused emotions such as shame and embarrassment (Somerville et al., 2013).

A second noteworthy phenomenon in early adolescence is emergence of the personal fable: Young teenagers often believe they are completely unlike anyone else (Elkind, 1981; Lapsley, 1993). For instance, they may think that no one else—and certainly not a parent and teacher—has ever experienced the intensity of emotions they feel about thwarted goals or unhappy love affairs. Furthermore, some have a sense of invulnerability and immortality, believing themselves immune to the normal dangers of life. Thus they may take foolish risks, such as experimenting with drugs and alcohol, having unprotected sexual intercourse, and driving at high speeds (DeRidder, 1993; Dodge et al., 2009; Galván, 2012; Nell, 2002). It's important to note, however, that adolescents are apt to take risks even when they *don't* believe themselves to be invulnerable, for reasons you can discover in the Applying Brain Research feature "Understanding and Addressing Adolescent Risk Taking."

Late adolescence The majority of older adolescents recover sufficiently from the double whammy of puberty and a changing school social environment to enjoy positive self-concepts and overall mental health (Harter, 1999; S. I. Powers, Hauser, & Kilner, 1989). The imaginary audience and personal fable phenomena slowly decline, although remnants remain throughout the high school years.

Older teenagers increasingly reflect on their own characteristics and abilities and begin to struggle with seeming inconsistencies in their self-perceptions, as one ninth grader explained:

> I really don't understand how I can switch so fast from being cheerful with my friends, then coming home and feeling anxious, and then getting frustrated and sarcastic with my parents. Which one is the *real* me? (Harter, 1999, p. 67)

Eventually, perhaps around 11th grade, most students integrate their various self-perceptions into a complex, multifaceted sense of self that reconciles apparent contradictions—for instance, recognizing that their inconsistent behaviors on different occasions mean that they're "flexible" (Harter, 1999).

As older adolescents pull the numerous parts of themselves together, many of them begin to form a general sense of identity: a self-constructed definition of who they are, what things they find important, and what goals they want to accomplish in life. In their ongoing search for a long-term identity, adolescents may initially take on temporary identities, aligning themselves with a particular peer group, insisting on a certain mode of dress, or continually changing self-descriptions and photos on Facebook, Instagram, and other social media (Alemán & Vartman, 2009; Greenhow, Robelia, & Hughes, 2009; Seaton, Scottham, & Sellers, 2006). Adolescents may also have somewhat different identities in different contexts, depending on the traditional roles they have played in each context (Eccles, 2009; Greeno, 2006; Vadeboncoeur, Vellos, & Goessling, 2011). For example, a student might be a "loser" at school but a "star" in an out-of-school activity or a "leader" in a neighborhood gang.

Erik Erikson proposed that most people achieve an overall sense of identity by the end of adolescence (see Figure 3.1). In contrast, many contemporary developmental theorists believe that identity formation continues to be a work-in-progress well into adulthood, especially as people move into new and different life circumstances (Bandura, 2008; Sinai, Kaplan, & Flum, 2012; Vadeboncoeur et al., 2011). Marcia (1980, 1991) has described four distinct patterns of behavior that may characterize the status of a young person's search for identity:

MyEdLab
Video Example 3.2.

Especially in the teenage years, an obsession with physical appearance can sometimes lead to eating disorders, as 16-year-old Josh explains.

Applying Brain Research

Understanding and Addressing Adolescent Risk Taking

The human brain continues to mature in important ways throughout adolescence and early adulthood. With puberty come significant changes in brain regions that play a role in pleasure seeking, potentially heightening the desire for enjoyable activities and immediate rewards. Only later, perhaps in the late teens or early 20s, do regions of the prefrontal cortex that support rational decision making and self-restraint fully mature (V. F. Reyna, Chapman, Dougherty, & Confrey, 2012; Somerville, Jones, & Casey, 2010; Steinberg, 2009). Furthermore, young people show significant individual differences in brain activity levels in these important regions—differences that are correlated with their predisposition to seek out exciting but potentially dangerous activities, on the one hand, or to be cautious and prudent, on the other (Gianotti et al., 2009; Hollenstein & Lougheed, 2013; Joseph, Liu, Jiang, Lynam, & Kelly, 2009).

For such reasons, many adolescents have trouble planning ahead and controlling their impulses (Spear, 2007; Steinberg, Cauffman, Woolard, Graham, & Banich, 2009). In addition, they tend to make choices based on emotions ("This will be fun") rather than on logic ("There's a high probability of a bad outcome") (Casey & Caudle, 2013; Luna, Paulsen, Padmanabhan, & Geier, 2013; V. F. Reyna et al., 2012). Thus, adolescent risk taking is most common in social contexts, where having fun is typically a high priority and it's easy to get swept away by what peers are doing or suggesting.

With such research findings in mind, we offer two recommendations.

- **Channel adolescents' risk-taking tendencies into safe activities.** Many adolescents enjoy trying things that are new, different, and perhaps a bit risky; such activities are reasonable if appropriate safeguards are in place. Team sports provide one outlet for both risk taking and social camaraderie. Preplanned, organized activities during traditionally high-risk periods are also beneficial; for example, many high schools offer all-night after-prom parties to keep students sober and safe when they might otherwise be drinking and driving.

- **Provide avenues through which students can safely and productively gain status with their peers.** Sometimes adolescents engage in risky behaviors—such as drinking, drug use, and sexual intercourse—in an attempt to project an adultlike image, to be "cool" and "with it" (J. P. Allen & Antonishak, 2008; Blanton & Burkley, 2008; Crosnoe, 2011). There are much healthier ways to show one's coolness and withitness, some of which we can support at school. Gaining competence and prominence in rock music, student government, and community service are just a few of the many possibilities.

- *Identity diffusion.* The individual has made no commitment to a particular career path or ideological belief system. Some haphazard experimentation with particular roles or beliefs may have taken place, but the individual hasn't yet embarked on a serious exploration of issues related to self-definition.

- *Foreclosure.* The individual has made a firm commitment to an occupation, a particular set of beliefs, or both. The choices have been based largely on what others (especially parents) have prescribed, without an earnest exploration of other possibilities.

- *Moratorium.* The individual has no strong commitment to a particular career or set of beliefs but is actively exploring and considering a variety of professions and ideologies. In essence, the individual is undergoing an identity crisis.

- *Identity achievement.* After going through a period of moratorium, the individual has emerged with a clear choice of occupation, a commitment to particular political or religious beliefs, or both.

For most young people, the ideal situation seems to be to proceed through a period of moratorium and exploration—a period that may continue well into adulthood—and to eventually settle on a clear identity that can flexibly evolve as life circumstances change (A. Kaplan & Flum, 2012; Luyckx et al., 2008; Sinai et al., 2012).

Table 3.1 presents developmental changes in children's and adolescents' sense of self and offers suggestions for how, as teachers, we can enhance their self-perceptions at different grade levels.

DIVERSITY IN SENSE OF SELF

As you undoubtedly know from your own experiences, students differ considerably in their self-esteem and overall sense of self. Sometimes such differences are indirectly the result of biology. For instance, students who are physically attractive tend to have more positive self-concepts than students with less appealing physical features (Harter, Whitesell, & Junkin, 1998). And on average, students with cognitive, social, or physical disabilities have lower self-esteem than their classmates (T. Bryan, 1991; Marsh & Craven, 1997; Martinez & Huberty, 2010).

DEVELOPMENTAL TRENDS

TABLE 3.1 • Sense of Self at Different Grade Levels

GRADE LEVEL	AGE-TYPICAL CHARACTERISTICS	EXAMPLE	SUGGESTED STRATEGIES
K–2	• Self-descriptions largely limited to concrete, easily observable characteristics • Some tendency to overestimate abilities and chances of future success, especially in domains in which one has little or no prior experience	When 6-year-old Jeff is asked to describe himself, he says, "I like animals. I like making things. I do good in school. I'm happy. Blue eyes, yellow hair, light skin." He mentions nothing about his shyness, sense of humor, and ability to work and play independently—characteristics that would require considerable self-reflection and abstract thought to identify.	● Encourage students to stretch their abilities by tackling the challenging tasks they think they can accomplish. ● Provide sufficient scaffolding to make success possible in various domains. ● Praise students for the things they do well; be specific about the behaviors you're praising.
3–5	• Increasing awareness of and differentiation among particular strengths and weaknesses • Association of such emotions as pride and shame with various self-perceptions	When Kellen begins fifth grade at his neighborhood middle school, his classwork rapidly deteriorates, despite individualized instruction in reading and spelling. At home one day, his mother finds him curled in a ball under his desk, crying and saying, "I can't do this anymore!" Alarmed, Mom takes him to a series of specialists, who diagnose severe dyslexia. Kellen's parents eventually find a school that provides considerable structure and scaffolding for students with learning disabilities. There Kellen shows dramatic improvement in virtually every area of the curriculum, and his self-esteem skyrockets.	● Focus students' attention on their improvement over time. ● Encourage pride in individual and group achievements, but be aware that students from some ethnic groups may prefer that recognition be given only for group achievements. ● Provide opportunities for students to look at one another's work only when *everyone* has something to be proud of.
6–8	• Increasingly abstract self-conceptions • For many, a decline in self-esteem after the transition to middle or junior high school (especially for girls) • Heightened concern about others' perceptions and judgments of oneself (imaginary audience) • Excessive belief in one's own uniqueness, sometimes accompanied by risk taking and a sense of invulnerability to normal dangers (personal fable)	Meghan describes a recent event in her eighth-grade algebra class: "I had to cough but I knew if I did everyone would stare at me and think I was stupid, hacking away. So I held my breath until I turned red and tears ran down my face and finally I coughed anyway and everyone *really* noticed then. It was horrible."	● After students make the transition to middle school or junior high, be especially supportive and optimistic about their abilities and potential for success. ● Minimize opportunities for students to compare their own performance unfavorably with that of others. ● Be patient when students show exceptional self-consciousness; give them strategies for presenting themselves well to others.
9–12	• Search for the "real me" and an adult identity; experimentation with a variety of possible identities • Increasing integration of diverse self-perceptions into an overall, multifaceted sense of self • Gradual increase in self-esteem • Continuing risk-taking behavior (especially for boys)	Sixteen-year-old Kayla often revises her profile on Facebook—for instance, modifying the "Details About You" section—and regularly changes the photo that appears at the top of her profile. Sometimes she displays a happy Kayla, at other times a more sullen one; an early photo shows her in her basketball uniform, but a later one shows her in a skimpy party dress.	● Give students opportunities to examine and try out a variety of adultlike roles. ● Encourage students to explore and take pride in their cultural and ethnic heritages. ● When discussing the potential consequences of risky behaviors, present the facts but don't make students so anxious or upset that they can't effectively learn and remember the information (e.g., avoid scare tactics).

Sources: Bracken, 2009; R. Butler, 2008; Davis-Kean et al., 2008; Dweck, 2000; Elkind, 1981; Figner & Weber, 2011; Greenhow, Robelia, & Hughes, 2009; Harter, 1999; Liem, Marsh, Martin, McInerney, & Yeung, 2013; Lockhart et al., 2002; Marcia, 1980, 1991; T. M. McDevitt & Ormrod, 2007 (Kellen example); Nell, 2002; Nuemi, 2008; O'Mara et al., 2006; Orenstein, 1994, p. 47 (Meghan example); Pajares, 2009; Robins & Trzesniewski, 2005; Seaton et al., 2006; Sinai, Kaplan, & Flum, 2012; Somerville et al., 2013; Spear, 2007; Tatum, 1997; Whitesell et al., 2006.

Gender differences.   For most young people, their gender is a core ingredient in their sense of self and can become increasingly prominent during puberty. Thus, many children and adolescents prefer to engage in behaviors and activities that are stereotypically "appropriate" for their gender. For example, to the extent that boys believe that getting good grades at school is something that "girls do," they may have little interest in classroom activities and assignments (Elmore & Oyserman, 2012).

Some researchers have found gender differences in overall self-esteem, with boys rating themselves more highly than girls, especially in adolescence. Many students' self-perceptions tend to be consistent with stereotypes about what males and females are supposedly "good at." For instance, even when actual ability levels are the same, boys tend to rate themselves more highly in math and sports, and girls tend to rate themselves more highly in language and literacy (Bracken, 2009; D. A. Cole et al., 2001; Herbert & Stipek, 2005; Joët, Usher, & Bressoux, 2011).

Cultural and ethnic differences.   In many Native American communities and many Middle Eastern and Far Eastern countries, children and adolescents see their group membership and connections with other individuals as central parts of who they are as human beings (Kağitçibaşi, 2007; M. Ross & Wang, 2010; Whitesell, Mitchell, Kaufman, Spicer, & the Voices of Indian Teens Project Team, 2006). In addition, many young people have a strong **ethnic identity**: They're both aware and proud of their ethnic group and willingly adopt some of the group's behaviors. Occasionally students' ethnic identities can lead them to reject mainstream Western values. In some ethnic minority groups, peers may accuse high-achieving students of "acting White," a label that essentially means "You're not one of us" (Bergin & Cooks, 2008; Cross, Strauss, & Fhagen-Smith, 1999; Ogbu, 2008a). For the most part, however, students with a strong and positive ethnic identity do *well* in school both academically and socially (Altschul, Oyserman, & Bybee, 2006; Hamm, Hoffman, & Farmer, 2012; Smokowski, Buchanan, & Bacalleo, 2009). Furthermore, pride in one's ethnic heritage and high academic achievement can serve as an emotional buffer against other people's prejudicial insults and discrimination (L. Allen & Aber, 2006; P. J. Cook & Ludwig, 2008; DuBois, Burk-Braxton, Swenson, Tevendale, & Hardesty, 2002).

 Encourage students to take pride in their cultural heritage.

Not all students from minority groups affiliate strongly with their cultural and ethnic groups. Some students—especially those with multiple racial or cultural heritages—fluctuate in the strength of their ethnic identity depending on the context and situation (Hitlin, Brown, & Elder, 2006; Y.-Y. Hong, Wan, No, & Chiu, 2007; Yip & Fuligni, 2002). In addition, older adolescents may experiment with varying forms of an ethnic identity. Some teens, for instance, may initially adopt a fairly intense, inflexible, and perhaps hostile ethnic identify before eventually retreating to a more relaxed, open-minded, and productive one (Cross et al., 1999; Nasir, McLaughlin, & Jones, 2009; Seaton et al., 2006).

MyEdLab **Self-Check 3.2**

MyEdLab **Application Exercise 3.2.** In this exercise, you can examine two student artifacts and form a few hypotheses about each student's sense of self.

Development of Peer Relationships and Interpersonal Understandings

For many students, interacting with and gaining the acceptance of peers—in some way *fitting in*— are more important than classroom learning and achievement (Crosnoe, 2011; Dowson & McInerney, 2001; LaFontana & Cillessen, 2010). Yet social success and academic success aren't an either-or situation. In fact, students who enjoy good relationships with their peers at school are *more* likely to achieve at high levels (Gest, Domitrovich, & Welsh, 2005; Patrick, Anderman, & Ryan, 2002; Pellegrini & Bohn, 2005).

ROLES OF PEERS IN CHILDREN'S DEVELOPMENT

Peer relationships, especially friendships, serve at least four functions in children's and adolescents' personal and social development. First, they provide an arena for learning and practicing a

FIGURE 3.3 In this writing sample, 7-year-old Andrew describes the many benefits of having friends.

frens our for you when you are lonley and sad. they play with you, they are nice, they are mean, they tell stores And the thing they Do. they walk youto the nurse,

variety of social skills, including cooperation, negotiation, emotional control, and conflict resolution (J. P. Allen & Antonishak, 2008; Granic, Lobel, & Engels, 2014; Larson & Brown, 2007). Second, young people can help one another with schoolwork and teach one another valued physical and cognitive skills—say, in skateboarding or computer programming—in which parents and other local adults have little or no expertise (Barron, 2006; Hickey, 2011; Ladd, Kochenderger-Ladd, Visconti, & Ettekal, 2012).

In addition, peers provide companionship, safety, and emotional support, as illustrated in Figure 3.3. They become a group with whom to eat lunch, a safe haven from playground bullies, and shoulders to cry on in times of trouble or confusion (Jordan, 2006; Laursen, Bukowski, Aunola, & Nurmi, 2007; Wentzel, 2009). Many adolescents (especially girls) reveal their innermost thoughts and feelings to their friends (Levitt, Guacci-Franco, & Levitt, 1993; Patrick et al., 2002; A. J. Rose et al., 2012). Friends often understand a teenager's perspectives—for instance, a preoccupation with physical appearance and concerns about the opposite sex—when others are seemingly clueless.

Peers play a fourth important role in personal and social development as well: They serve as socialization agents who both directly and indirectly encourage certain ways of behaving (M. H. Jones, Audley-Piotrowski, & Kiefer, 2012; A. M. Ryan, 2000; Wentzel & Watkins, 2011). Peers define options for leisure time, perhaps forming study groups, playing video games, or smoking cigarettes behind the school building. They serve as role models and provide standards for acceptable behavior, showing what's possible, what's admirable, what's cool. And they sanction one another for stepping beyond acceptable bounds, perhaps through ridicule, gossip, or ostracism. Traditionally such influences have been known as *peer pressure,* but many of them are better described as **peer contagion**, in which certain behaviors "spread" from one child or adolescent to another through a variety of means (B. B. Brown, Bakken, Ameringer, & Mahon, 2008; Sandstrom, 2011).

Much of the pressure to conform to other people's standards and expectations actually comes from within rather than from outside. In particular, most children and adolescents engage in **self-socialization**, putting pressure on *themselves* to adopt the behaviors they think others will find acceptable (B. B. Brown, 1990; Bukowski, Velasquez, & Brendgen, 2008; Crosnoe, 2011; Juvonen, 2006). Such self-pressure tends to be strongest in early adolescence; as an example, 12-year-old Mariel explains what happened when, in fifth grade, students from two different elementary schools transitioned to the same middle school:

> When you get to middle school the other school comes in, you're like, "Oh no, what if they don't like me?" So you try to be cool and stuff. But you never seem to get there. They're always one step ahead of you.

A common misconception is that peer influences are invariably a bad thing, but in fact they're a mixed bag. Many peers encourage such desirable qualities as working hard in school, treating people kindly, and engaging in community service. Others, however, encourage cutting class, bullying certain students, consuming alcohol or drugs, or in other ways behaving in counterproductive ways (Altermatt, 2012; Mayeux, Houser, & Dyches, 2011; Prinstein & Dodge, 2008; Spinrad & Eisenberg, 2009; Wentzel & Watkins, 2011).

Although peers' behaviors and values certainly have an impact, their effects have probably been overrated. Most children and adolescents acquire a strong set of values and behavioral standards from their families, and they don't necessarily abandon these values and standards in the company of peers (B. B. Brown, 1990; W. A. Collins et al., 2000; Galambos, Barker, & Almeida, 2003). Furthermore, they tend to choose friends who are similar to themselves in academic achievement, leisure-time activities, and long-term goals (Kindermann, 2007; Prinstein & Dodge, 2008; A. M. Ryan, 2001). In some cases, they may lead "double lives" that enable them to attain academic success while maintaining peer acceptance (Grimes, 2002; Hemmings, 2004; Juvonen, 2006; Mac Iver, Reuman, & Main, 1995). For example, although they attend class and faithfully do homework, they may feign disinterest in scholarly activities, disrupt class with jokes or goofy behaviors, and express surprise at receiving high grades. In addition, they may act tough when they're in public, saving their softer sides for more private circumstances, as one sixth grader's reflection reveals:

You'd still have to have your bad attitude. You have to act—it's just like a movie. You have to act. And then at home you're a regular kind of guy, you don't act mean or nothing. But when you're around your friends you have to be sharp and stuff like that, like push everybody around. (Juvonen & Cadigan, 2002, p. 282)

It's important to keep in mind that self-socialization involves adopting behaviors that a child or adolescent *believes* to be critical for gaining favor with important peers. For example, many students think that their peers will look down on them for working hard at school, achieving at high levels, and in other ways being "smart," when in fact their peers may secretly admire such behaviors (Hamm et al., 2012). And in any case, as the brain continues to mature in late adolescence, especially in the relatively "rational" prefrontal cortex, the concern about pleasing peers seems to dissipate a bit (Albert, Chein, & Steinberg, 2013).

As teachers, we can help students maintain a good public image in a variety of ways. For instance, we can help them acquire skills for presenting themselves in a favorable light—perhaps by teaching public-speaking techniques, nurturing artistic talents, or tactfully suggesting personal hygiene strategies. We can assign small-group projects in which every student has a unique talent to contribute. And when valued classmates ridicule academic achievement, we can allow students to demonstrate their accomplishments privately (e.g., through written assignments or one-on-one conversations) instead of in front of classmates.

Young adolescents often work hard to look cool in the eyes of their peers, as this drawing by 11-year-old Marci illustrates.

 Help students look good in the eyes of their peers.

COMMON SOCIAL GROUPS IN CHILDHOOD AND ADOLESCENCE

Researchers have distinguished among a variety of social groups in young people's lives, including friendships, cliques, crowds, subcultures, gangs, and romantic relations.

FRIENDSHIPS

Close friends find activities that are mutually meaningful and enjoyable, and over time they acquire a common set of experiences that enable them to share certain perspectives on life (Gottman, 1986; Suttles, 1970). Because friends typically have an emotional investment in their relationship, they work hard to look at situations from one another's point of view and to resolve disputes that threaten to separate them. As a result, they develop increased perspective-taking and conflict resolution skills. Close, supportive friendships also foster self-esteem and a general sense of well-being (Basinger, Gibbs, & Fuller, 1995; Berndt, 1992; Bukowski, Motzoi, & Meyer, 2009; Newcomb & Bagwell, 1995).

CLIQUES, CROWDS, AND SUBCULTURES

With age and experience, many students form larger social groups that frequently get together. In early adolescence, cliques—moderately stable friendship groups of perhaps 3 to 10 individuals—provide the setting for most voluntary social interactions. Clique boundaries tend to be fairly rigid and exclusive—some people are "in," whereas others are "out"—and memberships in various cliques often affect students' social status (B. B. Brown, 2011; Crockett, Losoff, & Peterson, 1984; Goodwin, 2006; Kindermann, McCollam, & Gibson, 1996). Here is 14-year-old Courtney's description of an especially exclusive "popular" clique in her eighth-grade class:

MyEdLab
Video Example 3.3.
Good friendships can offer many benefits. What benefits does 13-year-old Ryan describe?

There are table groups at lunch. My group gave them all names. The popular ones, we call them the Sardines. They are in their little box, they don't let anyone into their box, they're so close together. You'll never see one of them by themselves. Like one of them's a TV and the other ones are like little remotes following her.

Crowds are considerably larger than cliques and don't have the tight-knit cohesiveness and carefully drawn boundaries of cliques. Their members tend to share certain characteristics and behaviors (e.g., "brains" study a lot, "jocks" are active in sports), attitudes about academic achievement, and (occasionally) ethnic background (B. B. Brown, 2011; Steinberg, 1996). Crowd membership may or may not be a voluntary thing; for instance, membership in a so-called "popular" crowd is apt to be based as much on a student's reputation as on his or her actual efforts to affiliate with certain peers (B. B. Brown et al., 2008; Juvonen & Galván, 2008).

Occasionally a crowd takes the form of a subculture—a group that resists a powerful dominant culture by adopting a significantly different lifestyle (J. S. Epstein, 1998). Some subcultures are relatively benign; for example, as one of us authors knows well, some young teens may consistently wear baggy pants, address peers as "dude," and spend a good deal of their time mastering new tricks on their skateboards. Other subcultures are worrisome, such as those that endorse racist and anti-Semitic behaviors (e.g., skinheads) and those that practice Satanic worship and rituals. Adolescents are more likely to affiliate with troublesome subcultures when they feel alienated from the dominant culture—perhaps that of their school or that of society more generally—and want to distinguish themselves from it in some way (Crosnoe, 2011; J. R. Harris, 1998).

In the upper high school grades, a greater capacity for abstract thought allows many adolescents to think of other people more as unique individuals and less as members of stereotypical categories. They may also discover characteristics they have in common with peers from diverse backgrounds. Perhaps as a result of such changes, ties to specific social groups tend to dissipate, hostilities between groups soften, and students become more open-minded in their friendship choices (B. B. Brown, Eicher, & Petrie, 1986; Gavin & Fuhrman, 1989; Shrum & Cheek, 1987).

GANGS

A gang is a cohesive social group characterized by initiation rites, distinctive colors and symbols, "ownership" of a specific territory, and feuds with one or more rival groups. Typically, gangs are governed by strict rules for behavior and stiff penalties for violations. Young people affiliate with gangs for a variety of reasons. Some do so as a way of demonstrating loyalty to their family, friends, or neighborhood. Some seek the status and prestige that gang membership brings. Some have poor academic records and perceive gang activity as an alternative means of gaining recognition for accomplishments. Many members of gangs have troubled relationships with their families or have been consistently rejected by peers, and so they turn to gangs to get the emotional support they can find nowhere else (Dishion, Piehler, & Myers, 2008; Kodluboy, 2004; Petersen, 2004; Simons, Whitbeck, Conger, & Conger, 1991).

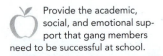
Provide the academic, social, and emotional support that gang members need to be successful at school.

Chapter 13 offers specific strategies for minimizing—and ideally eliminating—gang-related aggression and violence at school.

As teachers, we can definitely make a difference in the lives of any gang members in our classes (S. G. Freedman, 1990; Parks, 1995). We must, first and foremost, show these students that we truly care about them and their well-being. For instance, we can be willing listeners in times of trouble and can provide the support that gang members need to achieve both academic and social success. We must also have some knowledge of students' backgrounds—such as their family dynamics, economic circumstances, and cultural upbringings—so that we can better understand the issues with which they may be dealing. And we must certainly work cooperatively and proactively with our colleagues to minimize violent gang activity at school.

ROMANTIC RELATIONSHIPS

As early as the primary grades, children talk of having boyfriends or girlfriends, and the opposite sex is a subject of interest throughout the elementary school years. With the onset of adolescence, the biological changes of puberty bring on new and sometimes unsettling feelings and sexual desires. Not surprisingly, then, romance is a frequent topic of conversation in the middle and high school grades. Middle school students' romances tend to exist more in their minds than in reality; for example, two students might be identified as "going out" even if they never actually date. Young adolescents' romantic thoughts may also involve crushes on people who are out of reach—perhaps favorite teachers or movie stars (B. B. Brown, 1999; Eckert, 1989; B. C. Miller & Benson, 1999).

Eventually many adolescents begin to date, especially if their friends are dating. Early choices in dating partners are often based on physical attractiveness or social status, and dates may involve only limited and superficial interaction (B. B. Brown, 2011; Furman, Brown, & Feiring, 1999; Pellegrini, 2002). As adolescents move into the high school grades, some form more intense, affectionate, and long-term relationships with

For many children, thoughts of romance emerge early, as 5-year-old Isabelle's artwork illustrates.

members of the opposite sex, and these relationships often (but by no means always) lead to sexual intimacy (J. Connolly & McIsaac, 2009; Furman & Collins, 2009).

From a developmental standpoint, romantic relationships have definite benefits: They can address young people's needs for companionship, affection, and security, and they provide an opportunity to experiment with new social skills and interpersonal behaviors (Davila, 2008; Furman & Simon, 2008; B. C. Miller & Benson, 1999). At the same time, romance can wreak havoc with adolescents' emotions. Adolescents have more extreme mood swings than younger children or adults, and for many this instability may be partly due to the excitement and frustration of being romantically involved or *not* involved (Davila, 2008; Furman & Collins, 2009; Larson, Clore, & Wood, 1999).

As students reach high school (occasionally earlier), a significant minority of them find themselves attracted to their own sex either instead of or in addition to the opposite sex. Adolescence can be a particularly confusing time for gay, lesbian, and bisexual individuals. Some struggle to make sense of their sexual orientation and may experience considerable depression. Yet many others enjoy good mental health, especially if their home and school environments communicate acceptance of diverse sexual orientations (Darwich, Hymel, & Waterhouse, 2012; Espelage, Aragon, Birkett, & Koenig, 2008; Savin-Williams, 2008).

The extent to which we, as teachers, talk about sexuality with our students must be dictated, in part, by school policies and the values of the community in which we work. At the same time, especially if we're teaching at the middle school or high school level, we must be aware that romantic and sexual relationships—whether real or imagined—are a considerable source of excitement, frustration, confusion, and distraction for students, and we must lend a sympathetic ear and an open mind to those students who seek our counsel and support.

Offer emotional support when valued romantic relationships fizzle or don't materialize.

POPULARITY AND SOCIAL ISOLATION

When the daughter of one of us authors was in junior high school, she sometimes said, "No one likes the popular kids." As self-contradictory as her remark might have been—and Mom always told her that it was—it's consistent with research findings. When students are asked to identify their most "popular" classmates, they identify peers who have dominant social status at school (perhaps those who belong to a prestigious social group) but in many cases are aggressive or stuck-up (Cillessen, Schwartz, & Mayeux, 2011; W. E. Ellis & Zarbatany, 2007; Hawley, 2014). For example, when 14-year-old Courtney was asked what the popular kids were like, she had this to say:

> Nobody likes the popular kids. We all think they're bratty, they're mean. The only reason they're popular is because they'll make out with guys at the back of the bus. . . . They don't include anyone. They have their own parties that consist only of themselves. They can't branch out.

Yet contrary to Courtney's description, *truly popular students*—those whom many classmates select as people they'd like to do things with—may or may not hold high-status positions, but they're kind, trustworthy, and socially skillful, as Lupita is in the opening case study. They also tend to show genuine concern for others—for instance, by sharing, cooperating, and empathizing with peers (Asher & McDonald, 2009; Cillessen & van den Berg, 2012; Mayeux et al., 2011).

In contrast to popular students, rejected students are those whom classmates select as being the *least* preferred social companions. Students with few social skills—for example, those who are impulsive or aggressive—typically experience peer rejection (Asher & McDonald, 2009; Pedersen, Vitaro, Barker, & Borge, 2007; Rubin, Cheah, & Menzer, 2010). Students who are noticeably overweight and those who appear to be gay or lesbian are also frequent targets of ridicule, harassment, and rejection, as are some members of racial and ethnic minority groups (Graham & Hudley, 2005; Swearer, Espelage, Vaillancourt, & Hymel, 2010). Peer rejection over a lengthy period—psychologists call it *social marginalization*—can cause students considerable psychological distress and shame. To cope with such feelings and try to preserve a positive sense of self, these students may psychologically disengage from school life, jeopardizing their academic achievement as well as their social development and emotional well-being. Some of them begin to associate with other marginalized peers, who may or may not encourage attitudes and behaviors that will be productive over the long run (Bellmore, 2011; Ladd et al., 2012; Loose, Régner, Morin, & Dumas, 2012).

In this self-portrait, 10-year-old Sarah characterizes herself as a nerd ("neard")—that is, as someone who isn't as "cool" as she might be within her peer group.

Members of a third group, **controversial students**, elicit diverse reactions, in that some peers really like them and others really *dis*like them. These students can, like some rejected students, be quite aggressive, but they also have good social skills that make them popular with at least some of their peers (Asher & McDonald, 2009; Cillessen & van den Berg, 2012; Mayeux et al., 2011). Many students whom classmates refer to as "popular" actually fall into this category.

Researchers have described a fourth category as well. **Neglected students** are those whom peers rarely choose as someone they would either most like or least like to do something with (Asher & Renshaw, 1981). Some of these seemingly overlooked students prefer to be alone, others are quite shy or don't know how to go about initiating interaction, and still others are content with having only one or two close friends (Gazelle & Ladd, 2003; Guay, Boivin, & Hodges, 1999; McElhaney, Antonishak, & Allen, 2008). Occasionally "neglected" status is a temporary situation, but some students are friendless and socially marginalized for extended periods—such is often the case for recent immigrants and for students with disabilities—and these students are at higher-than-average risk for depression (Gazelle & Ladd, 2003; Igoa, 2007; Yuker, 1988).

Especially in the middle school and high school grades, most students are well aware of which peers do and don't have high social status, and some of them do things that aren't in their own or others' best interests—for instance, engaging in substance abuse or casual sexual intimacy—in an effort to gain or maintain membership in an allegedly "popular" group (Cillessen et al., 2011; Crosnoe, 2011). For example, they may ridicule and bully peers whom they perceive to be odd or nerdy. And they may abruptly abandon friendships that could undermine their image of "coolness," as 14-year-old Courtney revealed when describing something that happened in a close-knit group of five girls:

> The five of us would hang out, sit at the same lunch table. Then Jamie became good friends with another group. They had parties, became the popular group, so Jamie left us. She had been Maggie's best friend, so Maggie was devastated. Jamie wouldn't talk to us, wouldn't even wave at us in the hallway.

Not all status-seeking students successfully climb to the top of the social hierarchy, of course, and their failure to do so can leave them feeling isolated, depressed, and uninterested in school achievement (Cillessen et al., 2011; Crosnoe, 2011; Somerville, 2013).

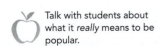

Talk with students about what it *really* means to be popular.

One way that, as teachers, we might discourage counterproductive status-seeking behaviors is to act as *myth busters,* explicitly opening up conversations about what true popularity involves. For example, we might begin by having students think of a few peers they genuinely like and then of a few peers they really *don't* like. These mental lists must remain only in students' own heads—*no names should be mentioned*—but by asking students to reflect on such questions as "What characteristics do people on your first list have in common?" and "Why don't you like the people on your second list?," qualities such as "kind" and "trustworthy" (for the first list) and "stuck-up" and "mean" (for the second list) might come to light.

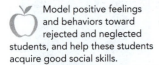

Model positive feelings and behaviors toward rejected and neglected students, and help these students acquire good social skills.

We can also help offset the hard feelings that peer rejection or neglect may engender by being especially warm and attentive with socially isolated students (Crosnoe, 2011; Wentzel, 1999). In fact, when *we* show that we like particular students, their classmates are more likely to accept and act positively toward them as well (L. Chang, 2003; L. Chang et al., 2004). We can also assist with interpersonal skills. Because of their social isolation, rejected and neglected students have fewer opportunities to develop the social skills that many of them desperately need (Coie & Cillessen, 1993; McElhaney et al., 2008; Vitaro, Boivin, Brendgen, Girard, & Dionne, 2012).

SOCIAL COGNITION

To be effective in interpersonal relationships, students must engage in **social cognition:** They must consider how people around them are likely to think about, behave in, and react to various situations. Those who think regularly about other people's thoughts and feelings tend to be socially skillful and make friends easily (Bosacki, 2000; P. L. Harris, 2006; Izard et al., 2001). Some psychologists propose that social cognition is a distinct human ability—which they call *emotional intelligence*—whereas others believe that it's simply an integral part of people's general intellectual and social functioning (J. D. Mayer, Salovey, & Caruso, 2008; Waterhouse, 2006; Zeidner,

Roberts, & Matthews, 2002). In any case, certain structures in the brain do seem to be dedicated to it (Spunt & Lieberman, 2013).

PERSPECTIVE TAKING

One important element of social cognition is **perspective taking**, looking at the world from other people's viewpoints. The following situation provides an example.

■■ EXPERIENCING FIRSTHAND
LAST PICKED

Consider this scenario:

> Kenny and Mark are co-captains of the soccer team. They have one person left to choose for the team. Without saying anything, Mark winks at Kenny and looks at Tom, who is one of the remaining children left to be chosen for the team. Mark looks back at Kenny and smiles. Kenny nods and chooses Tom to be on their team. Tom sees Mark and Kenny winking and smiling at each other. Tom, who is usually one of the last to be picked for team sports, wonders why Kenny wants him to be on his team. . . .

- Why did Mark smile at Kenny?
- Why did Kenny nod?
- Why did Kenny choose Tom to be on the team? How do you know this?
- Do you think that Tom has any idea of why Kenny chose him to be on the team? How do you know this? . . .
- How do you think Tom feels? (Bosacki, 2000, p. 711)

To answer these questions, you must look at the situation from the perspectives of the three boys involved. For instance, if you put yourself in Tom's shoes, you might suspect that he has mixed feelings. If he enjoys soccer, he may be happy to have a chance to play, but he may also be wondering whether the other boys' nonverbal signals indicate a malicious intention to make him look foolish on the soccer field. And, of course, Tom may feel embarrassed or demoralized at consistently being one of the last children picked for a team. (Accordingly, asking some students to select classmates for team games is generally *not* recommended.)

Recent brain research indicates that, to some degree, human beings may be "prewired" to look at situations from other people's perspectives as well as their own. In particular, certain neurons in the brain, known as **mirror neurons**, fire either when a person is performing a particular behavior *or* when the person watches *someone else* perform that behavior. Some of these mirror neurons are involved both in feeling certain emotions—perhaps disgust or anguish—and in observing such emotions in others' facial expressions (Gallese, Gernsbacher, Heyes, Hickok, & Iacoboni, 2011; Rizzolatti & Sinigaglia, 2008).

Yet truly effective perspective taking also involves active, conscious thinking and learning about human beings' general mental and psychological states. As children grow older, most develop and increasingly refine a **theory of mind**—a self-constructed understanding of their own and others' thoughts, beliefs, feelings, and motives. The development of a theory of mind appears to involve the prefrontal cortex of the brain—a part of the brain that continues to mature over the course of childhood and adolescence (Liu, Sabbagh, Gehring, & Wellman, 2009; Steinberg, 2009).

Probably as a result of both experience and brain maturation, children gain an increasingly complex understanding of human thought processes and feelings as they grow older, enabling them to become increasingly effective in interacting with others.

Childhood. Consistent with what we know about cognitive development, young children tend to focus on other people's concrete, observable characteristics and behaviors (e.g., look once again at Andrew's essay in Figure 3.3). However, they do have some awareness of other people's inner worlds. As early as age 4 or 5, they realize that what *they* know may be different from what *other people* know (Wellman, Cross, & Watson, 2001; Wimmer & Perner, 1983). They also have some ability to make inferences about other people's mental and emotional states—for instance, to deduce that people who behave in certain ways have certain intentions or feelings (P. L. Harris,

MyEdLab
Video Example 3.4.
What examples of perspective taking can you identify in this interview with 13-year-old Crystal?

2006; Schult, 2002; Wellman, Phillips, & Rodriguez, 2000). As children progress through the elementary grades, they also begin to understand that people's actions don't always reflect their thoughts and feelings—for instance, that someone who appears to be happy may actually feel sad (Flavell, Miller, & Miller, 2002; Gnepp, 1989; Selman, 1980).

Early adolescence. Most young adolescents realize that people can have mixed feelings about events and other individuals (Donaldson & Westerman, 1986; Flavell & Miller, 1998; Harter & Whitesell, 1989). And courtesy of their expanding cognitive abilities, memory capacity, and social awareness, young adolescents become capable of recursive thinking (Oppenheimer, 1986; Perner & Wimmer, 1985). That is, they can think about what other people might be thinking about them and eventually can reflect on other people's thoughts about them through multiple iterations (e.g., "You think that I think that you think . . ."). This isn't to say that adolescents (or adults, for that matter) always use this capacity, however. Consistent with our earlier discussion of the *imaginary audience,* focusing primarily about one's *own* perspective is a common phenomenon in the early adolescent years (Tsethlikai & Greenhoot, 2006; Tsethlikai, Guthrie-Fulbright, & Loera, 2007).

Late adolescence. In the high school years, teenagers can draw on a rich body of knowledge derived from numerous social experiences. Consequently, most of them become ever more skillful at drawing inferences about people's psychological characteristics, intentions, and needs (Eisenberg, Carlo, Murphy, & Van Court, 1995; Paget, Kritt, & Bergemann, 1984). In addition, they're more attuned to the complex dynamics that influence behavior—not only thoughts, feelings, and present circumstances but also past experiences (C. A. Flanagan & Tucker, 1999; Selman, 1980). What we see emerging in the high school years, then, are budding psychologists: individuals who can be quite astute in deciphering and explaining the motives and actions of others.

Promoting perspective taking. Virtually any classroom offers many opportunities for perspective taking. One strategy is to talk frequently about people's thoughts, feelings, and motives (Ruffman, Slade, & Crowe, 2002; Wittmer & Honig, 1994; Woolfe, Want, & Siegal, 2002). In the process, we must, of course, use age-appropriate language. With first graders we might use such words as *think, want,* and *sadness.* With fifth graders we might talk about *misunderstanding, frustration,* and *mixed feelings.* Most high school students have the cognitive and social reasoning capabilities to understand fairly abstract and complex psychological terms, such as *being passive-aggressive* and *having an inner moral compass.*

Another important strategy is to take advantage of situations in which people have diverse perspectives and beliefs about a situation. For example, in times of disagreement or conflict, students and teachers alike benefit from putting themselves in the other party's shoes (Adalbjarnardottir & Selman, 1997; Gehlbach, Brinkworth, & Harris, 2012). And when two or more students clash in the classroom or elsewhere on school grounds, an effective approach is *peer mediation,* in which specially trained peers elicit their differing points of view and help them reach an equitable solution (Deutsch, 1993; D. W. Johnson & Johnson, 1996, 2006).

Opportunities for perspective taking also arise in lessons about academic subject matter. For example, in discussions of current events, teachers might have different students—or, using the Internet, same-age classes at different schools—take various countries' perspectives as they explore significant world problems, such as climate change or arms control (Gehlbach et al., 2008).

SOCIAL INFORMATION PROCESSING

Children and adolescents have a lot to think about when they consider what other people are thinking, feeling, and doing. The mental processes involved in understanding and responding to social events are collectively known as social information processing (e.g., Burgess, Wojslawowicz, Rubin, Rose-Krasnor, & Booth-LaForce, 2006; Fontaine, Yang, Dodge, Bates, & Pettit, 2008; E. R. Smith & Semin, 2007). Among other things, social information processing involves paying *attention* to certain behaviors in a social situation and trying to *interpret* and make sense of those behaviors. For example, when students interact with classmates, they might focus on certain remarks, facial expressions, and body language and try to figure out what a classmate really means by, say, a thoughtless comment or sheepish grin. Students also consider one or more *goals* they hope to achieve during an interaction—perhaps preserving a friendship, on the one hand, or teaching

---

When students seem focused only on their own points of view, encourage them to consider why others might reasonably think and behave as they do.

Regularly ask students to reflect on other people's thoughts, feelings, and motives.

Chapter 10 describes peer mediation in more detail.

Chapter 6 discusses *information processing theory,* on which this concept of social information processing is based.

somebody a "lesson," on the other. Then, taking into account both their interpretations and their goals, students draw on their previous knowledge and experiences to identify a number of possible responses and choose what is, in their eyes, a productive course of action. As you'll see in the next section, an understanding of social information processing is especially helpful in explaining why some students are unusually aggressive toward their peers.

AGGRESSION

Aggression is an action intentionally taken to hurt another person either physically or psychologically. The word typically brings to mind some form of physical aggression (e.g., hitting, shoving), which can potentially cause bodily injury. But it may instead involve psychological aggression—an action intended to cause mental anguish or reduce self-esteem. In some cases, psychological aggression is specifically aimed at undermining friendships and other interpersonal relationships—perhaps by spreading unkind rumors or ostracizing someone from a valued social group—in which case it's also called relational aggression. As a general rule, aggression declines over the course of childhood and adolescence, but it increases for a short time after students make the transition from elementary school to middle school or junior high (Bradshaw, Waasdorp, & O'Brennan, 2013; Pellegrini, 2002).

Researchers have identified two distinct groups of aggressive students (Crick & Dodge, 1996; Poulin & Boivin, 1999; Vitaro, Gendreau, Tremblay, & Oligny, 1998). Those who engage in proactive aggression deliberately initiate aggressive behaviors as a means of obtaining desired goals. Those who engage in reactive aggression act aggressively primarily in response to frustration or provocation. Of the two groups, students who exhibit proactive aggression are more likely to have trouble maintaining productive friendships (Hanish, Kochenderfer-Ladd, Fabes, Martin, & Denning, 2004; Poulin & Boivin, 1999). Those who direct considerable aggression toward particular peers—whether it be physical or psychological aggression—are known as bullies. Students who are immature, anxious, and socially isolated are frequent victims of bullies, as are students with nontraditional sexual orientations and students with disabilities (Hamovitch, 2007; J. P. Robinson & Espelage, 2012; M. W. Watson, Andreas, Fischer, & Smith, 2005).

Some children and adolescents are genetically more predisposed to aggression than their peers, and others may exhibit heightened aggression as a result of neurological abnormalities (Brendgen et al., 2008; Raine, 2008; van Goozen, Fairchild, & Harold, 2008). But environmental factors can foster aggressive behavior as well. Many aggressive students live in dysfunctional conditions at home, perhaps including frequent conflicts and displays of anger, harsh punishment or child maltreatment, and a general lack of affection and appropriate social behavior (Christenson, 2004; Maikovich, Jaffee, Odgers, & Gallop, 2008; Pettit, 2004). In addition, regular exposure to violence in the community or through various media (e.g., television, music, video games) seems to increase aggressive behavior in young people (C. A. Anderson et al., 2003; Guerra, Huesmann, & Spindler, 2003; Huesmann, Moise-Titus, Podolski, & Eron, 2003; Prot et al., 2014).

It's important to note here that many children and adolescents who are routinely exposed to violence at home or elsewhere are *not* especially aggressive (Margolin & Gordis, 2004; M. J. Pearce, Jones, Schwab-Stone, & Ruchkin, 2003). Certain cognitive and motivational factors seem to underlie aggressive behavior, including the following:

- *Poor perspective-taking ability.* Students who are highly aggressive tend to have limited ability to look at situations from other people's perspectives or to empathize with their victims (Coie & Dodge, 1998; Damon & Hart, 1988; Marcus, 1980).

- *Misinterpretation of social cues.* Students who are aggressive toward peers tend to interpret others' behaviors as reflecting hostile intentions, especially when those behaviors have ambiguous meanings. This hostile attributional bias is especially prevalent in children who are prone to *reactive* aggression (Bukowski, Brendgen, & Vitaro, 2007; Crick, Grotpeter, & Bigbee, 2002; Dodge et al., 2003).

- *Prevalence of self-serving goals.* For most students, establishing and maintaining interpersonal relationships is a high priority. For aggressive students, however, achieving more self-serving goals—perhaps maintaining an inflated self-image, seeking revenge, or gaining power and dominance—often takes precedence (Baumeister et al., 1996; Cillessen & Rose, 2005; Menon et al., 2007; Pellegrini, Roseth, Van Ryzin, & Solberg, 2011).

- *Ineffective social problem-solving strategies.* Aggressive students often have little knowledge of how to persuade, negotiate, or compromise. Instead, they're apt to resort to hitting, shoving, barging into play activities, and other ineffective strategies (Neel, Jenkins, & Meadows, 1990; D. Schwartz et al., 1998; Troop-Gordon & Asher, 2005).

- *Belief in the appropriateness and effectiveness of aggression.* Many aggressive students believe that violence and other forms of aggression are acceptable ways of resolving conflicts and retaliating against others' misdeeds (Paciello, Fida, Tramontano, Lupinetti, & Caprara, 2008; M. W. Watson et al., 2005; Zelli, Dodge, Lochman, & Laird, 1999). Those who display high rates of *proactive* aggression are also apt to believe that aggressive action will yield positive results—for instance, that it will enhance social status at school or restore "honor" to one's family or social group (R. P. Brown, Osterman, & Barnes, 2009; Mayeux et al., 2011; Pellegrini & Bartini, 2000). Not surprisingly, aggressive children tend to associate with one another, thereby confirming one another's beliefs that aggression is appropriate (Crick, Murray-Close, Marks, & Mohajeri-Nelson, 2009; Espelage & Swearer, 2004).

Both initiators and recipients of aggression often have problems later on. Unless adults actively intervene, many aggressive students (especially those who exhibit proactive aggression) show a continuing pattern of aggression and violence as they grow older, and such a pattern almost guarantees long-term maladjustment and difficulties with peers (Dodge et al., 2003; Ladd & Troop-Gordon, 2003; Swearer et al., 2010). Meanwhile, children who are frequent targets of bullying can become anxious and depressed—sometimes suicidal—and may frequently skip school or even drop out altogether (Cornell, Gregory, Huang, & Fan, 2013; Hoglund, 2007; Ladd et al., 2012). Often the psychological aggression involved in bullying—taunts, name-calling, blatant exclusion from social activities, and the like—causes more long-term harm than any physical aggression that accompanies it (Bradshaw et al., 2013; Doll, Song, & Siemers, 2004; Goodwin, 2006).

Even innocent bystanders tend to suffer from the aggression they witness at school. For example, when they observe one classmate bullying another, their own sense of safety at school diminishes (M. J. Mayer & Furlong, 2010; Rivers, Poteat, Noret, & Ashurst, 2009). Furthermore, if they see bullying and other aggressive behaviors going unpunished, they may come to believe that such actions are perfectly acceptable (E. J. Meyer, 2009; D. T. Miller & Prentice, 1994).

As teachers, we *must* intervene when some students victimize others, and we must keep a watchful eye for additional incidents of physical or psychological aggression down the road. Regular victims of aggression need social and emotional support from us and from their classmates. Some may also need one or more sessions with a school counselor, perhaps to address feelings of vulnerability and depression or perhaps to learn skills that will minimize future victimization incidents (Espelage & Swearer, 2004; R. S. Newman, 2008; Yeung & Leadbeater, 2007).

The perpetrators of aggression require intervention as well. They must be given appropriate consequences for their actions, of course, but they should also be helped to behave more appropriately. Specific strategies should be tailored to the thoughts and motives that underlie their aggression. Such strategies as encouraging perspective taking, helping students interpret social situations more accurately, and teaching effective social problem-solving skills are potentially useful in reducing aggression and other disruptive behaviors (Cunningham & Cunningham, 2006; Frey, Hirschstein, Edstrom, & Snell, 2009; Guerra & Slaby, 1990; Horne, Orpinas, Newman-Carlson, & Bartolomucci, 2004; Hudley & Graham, 1993). Putting students in situations where they must explicitly *help,* rather than harm, others—for instance, asking them to tutor younger children—can also be beneficial (J. R. Sullivan & Conoley, 2004). Ultimately, interventions with aggressive students are most likely to be effective if schools communicate the importance of acting kindly and respectfully toward all members of the school community, teachers and students alike (Espelage & Swearer, 2004; E. J. Meyer, 2009; Parada, Craven, & Marsh, 2008; S. W. Ross & Horner, 2009).

TECHNOLOGY AND PEER RELATIONSHIPS

Thanks to wireless technologies (e.g., cell phones) and the Internet, many students now communicate quite frequently—daily, sometimes almost hourly—with some of their peers (Crosnoe, 2011; Greenhow et al., 2009; Valkenburg & Peter, 2009). For example, email and instant messaging (i.e., "texting") allow quick and easy ways of asking classmates about homework assignments,

Be on the lookout for bullying and other forms of aggression, and take appropriate actions with both the victims and the perpetrators.

MyEdLab
Interactive Case 3.1.

Teachers must intervene whenever students are either the perpetrators or victims of aggression. In this activity, you can gain practice with potentially effective intervention strategies.

making plans for weekend social activities, and seeking friends' advice and emotional support. Social networking sites (e.g., Facebook, Instagram) provide means of sharing personal information and potentially finding like-minded age-mates. Internet chat rooms allow group discussions about virtually any topic. Judicious use of such mechanisms can enhance students' self-esteem, connectedness with peers, social problem solving, and general psychological well-being (Ellison, Steinfield, & Lampe, 2007; Greenhow et al., 2009; Gross, Juvonen, & Gable, 2002; Valkenburg & Peter, 2009).

Unfortunately, wireless technologies and the Internet also provide vehicles for cyberbullying—electronically transmitting hostile messages, broadcasting personally embarrassing information, or in other ways causing someone significant psychological distress. For example, a student might upload humiliating video footage on YouTube, post malicious (and possibly false) gossip on Facebook, or set up a website on which classmates can "vote" for their class's "biggest loser" or "easiest slut" (Shariff, 2008; Valkenburg & Peter, 2009; Willard, 2007). Cyberbullying can be more harmful than face-to-face bullying, in part because the perpetrators often remain anonymous (and so can't be confronted) and in part because highly defamatory material can spread like wildfire through a large peer group (Kowalski & Limber, 2007; Rivers, Chesney, & Coyne, 2011). Unfortunately, cyberbullying is one form of aggression that *doesn't* seem to decline over the course of adolescence (Bradshaw et al., 2013).

As teachers, we must join with other faculty members and school administrators to talk with students about wise and socially appropriate uses of modern technology, and we must explain in no uncertain terms that cyberbullying in any form—whether it involves taunts, threats, unkind rumors, or any other material that can cause psychological harm to others—is *totally unacceptable.* And, of course, we must monitor students' in-class use of the Internet.

Explain what cyberbullying is and why it is unacceptable.

DIVERSITY IN PEER RELATIONSHIPS AND SOCIAL COGNITION

Some students with disabilities have delays in the development of social cognition and, as a result, often have trouble in interpersonal relationships. For example, students with significant delays in their overall cognitive development (i.e., children with intellectual disabilities) typically have limited understanding of appropriate behaviors in social situations (S. Greenspan & Granfield, 1992; Leffert, Siperstein, & Millikan, 2000). Also, some students with seemingly normal cognitive abilities have specific deficits in social cognition. In a mild form of autism known as *Asperger syndrome,* students may show average or above-average academic achievement but have great difficulty drawing accurate inferences from others' behaviors and body language, apparently as a result of a brain abnormality (G. Dawson & Bernier, 2007; Hobson, 2004; Tager-Flusberg, 2007). In addition, many students with chronic emotional and behavioral disabilities have poor perspective-taking and social problem-solving abilities and thus may have few, if any, friends (Espelage, Mebane, & Adams, 2004; Harter et al., 1998; Webber & Plotts, 2008).

Gender differences.   Gender differences have been observed in interpersonal behaviors. Boys tend to hang out in large groups, whereas girls tend to favor smaller, more intimate gatherings with close friends (Maccoby, 2002). Also, girls seem to be more astute at reading other people's body language, and they work harder to maintain group harmony (Benenson et al., 2002; Bosacki, 2000; Rudolph et al., 2005). Furthermore, aggression tends to take different forms in boys (who are prone to physical aggression) and in girls (who are more apt to engage in relational aggression, such as disrupting friendships and tarnishing others' reputations) (Card, Stucky, Sawalani, & Little, 2008; Crick et al., 2002; Pellegrini, 2011; Pellegrini & Archer, 2005).

Cultural and ethnic differences.   Interpersonal behaviors vary from culture to culture as well. For instance, some cultural groups (e.g., some groups in northern Canada and in the South Pacific) regularly use seemingly antisocial behaviors—especially teasing and ridicule—to teach children to remain calm and handle criticism (Rogoff, 2003). In contrast, many Native Americans, many people of Hispanic heritage, and certain African American communities place particular emphasis on interpersonal relationships and group harmony, and many Asian groups strongly discourage aggression. Children from these backgrounds may be especially adept at negotiation and peace making (Gardiner & Kosmitzki, 2008; P. Guthrie, 2001; Halgunseth et al., 2006; Leonard & Martin, 2013; Rubin et al., 2010; Witmer, 1996).

PROMOTING HEALTHY PEER RELATIONSHIPS

As teachers, we're in an excellent position to assess how students think about and behave in social situations and to help them interact more effectively with others. Following are several strategies that research has shown to be effective.

Extracurricular activities can promote productive peer relationships and a general "team spirit." They can also be a source of success for students who struggle with academic tasks. Here 7-year-old Danny, who has a learning disability, expresses his love of baseball.

- *Provide regular opportunities for social interaction and cooperation.* By their very nature, some instructional strategies require considerable student interaction. Assignments and activities that require students to work cooperatively to achieve a common goal can foster leadership skills and a willingness to both help and get help from peers (Certo, 2011; Ladd et al., 2014; Y. Li et al., 2007). And activities in which students communicate with one another online—for instance, by posting their ideas and questions about classroom topics on a class website—can be especially valuable for students who are shy or otherwise feel uncomfortable communicating with peers in a more public fashion (Hewitt & Scardamalia, 1998).

  A typical school day also includes many occasions in which students can interact in less structured ways. For example, during recess, students' play activities—whether the fantasy play of preschoolers and kindergartners or the rule-based games of older children and adolescents—can promote cooperation, sharing, perspective taking, and conflict resolution skills (Coplan & Arbeau, 2009; Creasey, Jarvis, & Berk, 1998; Jarrett, 2002). And before and during class, students often talk and joke with peers who are seated nearby. Accordingly, we might frequently change assigned seating arrangements so that students can get to know certain classmates better and perhaps discover common interests or similar senses of humor (van den Berg, Seters, & Cillessen, 2012).

- *Help students interpret social situations accurately and productively.* When students consistently have trouble getting along with peers, explicit training in social cognition can make a difference. Effective interventions are likely to involve a series of training sessions—sometimes over a lengthy time period—in which, through role-playing and similar activities, students practice making inferences about other people's intentions and identifying appropriate courses of action. Students also learn strategies for reminding themselves of how to behave in various situations—for example, "When I don't have the information to tell what he meant, I should act as if it were an accident" (Hudley & Graham, 1993, p. 128). Such interventions can significantly reduce the degree to which students perceive hostile intentions in others or endorse aggressive retaliation in response to peers' behaviors (Dodge, Godwin, & The Conduct Problems Prevention Research Group, 2013; Hudley & Graham, 1993).

- *Teach specific social skills, provide opportunities for students to practice them, and give feedback.* The vast majority of children and adolescents want to have positive interactions with their agemates and, better still, make friends with peers who can offer regular companionship and support (Ladd et al., 2012; A. M. Ryan & Shim, 2008). Because we teachers spend so much time with growing children, we're in an excellent position to teach them important social skills that they haven't acquired on their own—for instance, how to cooperate with others, say "no" in tactful ways, and amicably resolve conflicts. We can teach students appropriate ways of interacting with others both through explicit verbal instructions and through modeling desired behaviors. Such instruction is especially effective when we also ask students to practice their newly learned social skills (perhaps through role-playing) and give them concrete feedback about how they're doing (Bierman & Powers, 2009; Leaf et al., 2012; S. Vaughn, 1991; Watkins & Wentzel, 2008).

- *Promote understanding, communication, and interaction among diverse groups.* Even when students have good social skills, many of them interact almost exclusively within small, close-knit groups, and a few others remain socially isolated. For example, students often divide themselves along ethnic lines when they eat lunch and interact in the school yard. In fact, ethnic segregation *increases* once students reach the middle school grades. As young adolescents

MyEdLab
Video Example 3.5.

Some students need explicit instruction in social skills. What strategies does this special education teacher use to teach her students how to give compliments?

from ethnic minority groups begin to look closely and introspectively at issues of racism and ethnic identity, they often find it helpful to compare experiences and perspectives with other group members. Ethnic stereotypes and prejudices can also contribute to this self-imposed segregation (B. B. Brown et al., 2008; G. L. Cohen & Garcia, 2008; Ogbu, 2008b; Tatum, 1997).

Yet when students from diverse groups interact regularly—and especially when they come together as equals, work toward a common goal, and see themselves as members of the same team—they're more likely to accept and value one another's differences (Hodson, 2011; Oskamp, 2000; Pfeifer, Brown, & Juvonen, 2007). The Creating a Productive Classroom Environment box "Encouraging Positive Interactions Among Diverse Individuals and Groups" offers several strategies for expanding students' friendship networks.

Explain what bullying is and why it cannot be tolerated. Students and teachers alike often have misconceptions about bullying. For instance, they may think it always involves physical aggression, even though psychological forms of aggression—such as name calling, sexual harassment, deliberate social exclusion, and defamatory Internet postings—constitute bullying as well. Another common misconception is that the victims of bullies somehow deserve what they get, perhaps because they display immature behaviors or need to "toughen up" and learn to defend themselves. Thus, many students condone bullying and act as a supportive audience for the perpetrators (Salmivalli & Peets, 2009; Swearer et al., 2010). And teachers who refuse to intervene when they see or hear about bullying and harassment indirectly communicate the message that such behaviors are acceptable

Creating a Productive Classroom Environment

Encouraging Positive Interactions Among Diverse Individuals and Groups

Set up situations in which students can form cross-group friendships.
To help her students get to know a greater number of their peers, a junior high school science teacher gives them assigned seats in her classroom and changes the seating chart once a month. She also decides how students will be paired for weekly lab activities.

Minimize or eliminate barriers to social interaction.
Students in a third-grade class learn basic words and phrases in American Sign Language so that they can work and play with a classmate who is deaf.

Encourage and facilitate participation in extracurricular activities, and take steps to ensure that no single group dominates in membership or leadership in any particular activity.
When recruiting members for the scenery committee for the eighth grade's annual class play, the committee's teacher–adviser encourages both "popular" and "unpopular" students to participate. Later he divides the workload in such a way that students who don't know one another well must work closely and cooperatively.

As a class, discuss the undesirable consequences of intergroup hostilities.
A high school English teacher in a low-income, inner-city school district uses a lesson on Shakespeare's *Romeo and Juliet* to initiate a discussion about an ongoing conflict between two rival ethnic-group gangs in the community. "Don't you think this family feud is stupid?" she asks her students, referring to Shakespeare's play. When they agree, she continues, "The Capulets are like the Latino gang, and the Montagues are like the Asian gang. . . . Don't you think it's stupid that the Latino gang and the Asian gang are killing each other?" The students immediately protest, but when she presses them to justify their thinking, they gradually begin to acknowledge the pointlessness of a long-standing rivalry whose origins they can't even recall.

Develop nondisabled students' understanding of students with disabilities, *provided that* the students and their parents give permission to share what might otherwise be confidential information.
In a widely publicized case, Ryan White, a boy who had contracted AIDS from a blood transfusion, met considerable resistance against his return to his neighborhood school because parents and students thought he might infect others. After Ryan's family moved to a different school district, school personnel actively educated the community about the fact that AIDS doesn't spread through casual day-to-day contact. Ryan's reception at his new school was overwhelmingly positive. Later Ryan described his first day at school: "When I walked into classrooms or the cafeteria, several kids called out at once, 'Hey, Ryan! Sit with me!'"

Sources: Certo, Cauley, & Chafin, 2003; D. J. Connor & Baglieri, 2009; Dilg, 2010; Feddes, Noack, & Rutland, 2009; Feldman & Matjasko, 2005; Freedom Writers, 1999, p. 33 (Shakespeare example); Mahoney, Cairns, & Farmer, 2003; A. J. Martin & Dowson, 2009; Schofield, 1995; K. Schultz, Buck, & Niesz, 2000; Sleeter & Grant, 1999; Tatum, 1997; M. Thompson & Grace, 2001 (school play example); van den Berg et al., 2012; R. White & Cunningham, 1991, p. 149 (Ryan White example).

(Buston & Hart, 2001; Juvonen & Galván, 2008; Veenstra, Lindenberg, Huitsing, Sainio, & Salmivalli, 2014).

Earlier in the chapter we authors urged you to be on the lookout for incidents of bullying. This is easier said than done, because many incidents of bullying occur beyond the watchful eyes of school faculty members (K. Carter & Doyle, 2006; Swearer et al., 2010). It's important, then, that *students* learn about the many forms bullying can take and the truly harmful effects it can have on its victims. One simple strategy is to use the mnemonic *PIC* to describe what bullying involves:

- **P**urposeful behavior—"He meant to do it."
- **I**mbalanced—"That's not fair, he's bigger."
- **C**ontinual—"I'm afraid to enter the classroom because she's always picking on me." (Horne et al., 2004, pp. 298–299)

Teach students effective strategies for responding to bullies.

We can also teach students strategies to use when they're being bullied (e.g., they might walk away or respond with a humorous come-back) or when they observe others being victimized (e.g., they might say "Stop, you're being disrespectful" and escort the victim from the scene) (Juvonen & Galván, 2008; S. W. Ross & Horner, 2009). In general, through our school policies and day-to-day actions, all students must learn that bullying is *never acceptable* and that there will be serious consequences for engaging in or encouraging it (Ansary, Elias, Greene, & Green, 2015; Thapa, Cohen, Guffey, & Higgins-D'Alessandro, 2013).

 Help change the reputations of formerly antisocial students. Unfortunately, students' bad reputations often live on long after their behavior has changed for the better, and thus their classmates may continue to dislike and reject them (Bierman, Miller, & Stabb, 1987; Caprara, Dodge, Pastorelli, & Zelli, 2007; Juvonen & Weiner, 1993). So when we work to improve the behaviors of aggressive and other antisocial students, we must work to improve their reputations as well. For example, we might encourage their active involvement in extracurricular activities or place them in structured cooperative learning groups where they can use their newly developed social skills. We should also demonstrate through our words and actions that *we* like and appreciate them, as our attitudes are apt to be contagious (L. Chang, 2003; L. Chang et al., 2004).

Underlying our behaviors as teachers should be the message that *anyone can change for the better*. For instance, students can more easily forgive a former bully if they learn that the classmate's behaviors did *not* reflect innate nastiness or some other permanent personality flaw—that, instead, those behaviors were due to temporary factors that have now been resolved (Yeager & Dweck, 2012). In one way or another we must help students discover that previously antisocial classmates have changed and are worth getting to know better.

 Create a general climate of respect for others. Teachers who effectively cultivate productive student interactions and friendships also communicate a more general message: We must all have compassion for and respect one another as human beings. Fernando Arias, a high school vocational education teacher, once put it this way:

> In our school, our philosophy is that we treat everybody the way we'd like to be treated. . . . Our school is a unique situation where we have pregnant young ladies who go to our school. We have special education children. We have the regular kids, and we have the drop-out recovery program . . . we're all equal. We all have an equal chance. And we have members of every gang at our school, and we hardly have any fights, and there are close to about 300 gangs in our city. We all get along. It's one big family unit it seems like. (Turnbull, Pereira, & Blue-Banning, 2000, p. 67)

Compassion and respect for one another's rights and needs are aspects of students' moral and prosocial development, a domain to which we turn now.

MyEdLab **Self-Check 3.3**

MyEdLab **Application Exercise 3.3.** In this activity, you can apply what you have learned about children's social development to a second-grade writing activity.

Moral and Prosocial Development

In the opening case study Lupita helps a classmate interpret a teacher aide's subtle message and assists two others with their puzzles. Such actions are examples of prosocial behavior, behavior aimed at benefiting others more than oneself. Prosocial behaviors—plus such traits as honesty, fairness, and concern about other people's rights and welfare—fall into the domain of morality. By and large, students who think and behave in moral and prosocial ways gain more support from their teachers and peers and, as a result, achieve greater academic and social success over the long run (Caprara, Barbaranelli, Pastorelli, Bandura, & Zimbardo, 2000; Spinrad & Eisenberg, 2009).

Morality and prosocial behavior are complex entities that appear to involve multiple parts of the brain. Certainly the mirror neurons mentioned earlier are involved, as they partially underlie people's ability to look at situations from someone else's perspective. But ultimately moral and prosocial actions also have components that involve distinctly different brain regions, including (a) *emotions* (e.g., affection and concern for others); (b) *complex reasoning abilities* (e.g., logically determining what actions are morally right and wrong); and (c) *implicit values and beliefs* (e.g., immediately "knowing" that an action is morally wrong but without having a good explanation as to why) (Dinh & Lord, 2013; Gallese et al., 2011; Moll et al., 2007; Young & Saxe, 2009).

DEVELOPMENTAL TRENDS IN MORALITY AND PROSOCIAL BEHAVIOR

Most children behave more morally and prosocially as they grow older. Table 3.2 describes the forms that morality and prosocial behavior are apt to take at various grade levels. Some entries in the table reflect the following developmental trends.

- *Even very young children use internal standards to evaluate behavior.* Well before their first birthday, children show that they value prosocial behavior over antisocial behavior, and by age 3 they have some understanding that behaviors causing physical or psychological harm are inappropriate (Hamlin & Wynn, 2011; Helwig, Zelazo, & Wilson, 2001). By age 4 most children understand that causing harm to another person is wrong regardless of what authority figures might tell them and regardless of what consequences certain behaviors may or may not bring (Laupa & Turiel, 1995; Smetana, 1981; Tisak, 1993).

- *Children's capacity to respond emotionally to others' harm and distress increases over the school years.* Within the first 2 or 3 years of life, two emotions important for moral development emerge (Kochanska, Gross, Lin, & Nichols, 2002; M. Lewis & Sullivan, 2005). First, children occasionally show guilt—a feeling of discomfort when they know they've inflicted damage or caused someone else pain or distress. They also feel shame—a feeling of embarrassment or humiliation when they fail to meet their own or other people's standards for moral behavior. Both guilt and shame, although unpleasant emotions, are good signs that children are developing a sense of right and wrong and will work hard to correct their misdeeds (Eisenberg, 1995; Harter, 1999; Narváez & Rest, 1995).

  Guilt and shame are the result of doing something wrong. In contrast, empathy—experiencing the same feelings as someone in unfortunate circumstances—appears in the absence of wrongdoing. Although the mirror neurons mentioned earlier may to some degree underlie human beings' ability to empathize, this ability continues to develop throughout childhood and adolescence (Eisenberg et al., 1995; Rizzolatti & Sinigaglia, 2008; Spinrad & Eisenberg, 2009). When empathy also evokes sympathy—whereby children not only assume another person's feelings but also have concerns for the individual's well-being—it tends to spur prosocial behavior (Batson, 1991; Eisenberg & Fabes, 1998; Malti, Gummerum, Keller, & Buchman, 2009).

- *Children increasingly distinguish between moral and conventional transgressions.* Virtually every culture discourages some behaviors—moral transgressions—because they cause damage or harm, violate human rights, or run counter to basic principles of equality, freedom, or justice. A cultural group typically also discourages certain other behaviors—conventional transgressions—that, although not unethical, violate widely held understandings about how one

hopes
goals
dreams
happiness
 broken
  destroyed
   eliminated
    exterminated
no steps forward
no evolution
no prosperity
no hope
But
maybe
perhaps
except
if we
help
together
we stand
a chance.

In this poem, Matt, a middle school student, shows empathy for victims of the Holocaust.

DEVELOPMENTAL TRENDS

TABLE 3.2 • Moral Reasoning and Prosocial Behavior at Different Grade Levels			
GRADE LEVEL	**AGE-TYPICAL CHARACTERISTICS**	**EXAMPLE**	**SUGGESTED STRATEGIES**
K–2	• Some awareness that behaviors causing physical or psychological harm are morally wrong • Ability to distinguish between behaviors that violate human rights and dignity versus those that violate social conventions • Guilt and shame about misbehaviors that cause obvious harm or damage • Some empathy for, as well as attempts to comfort, people in distress • Appreciation for the need to be fair; fairness seen as strict equality in how a desired commodity is divided	When Jake pushes Otis off the ladder of a playground slide, several classmates are horrified. One child shouts, "That's wrong!" and three others rush to Otis's side to make sure he's not hurt.	• Make standards for behavior very clear. • When students misbehave, give reasons that such behaviors are unacceptable, focusing on the harm and distress they have caused others (i.e., use *induction*, a strategy described later in the chapter). • Encourage students to comfort others in times of distress. • Model sympathetic responses; explain what you're doing and why you're doing it. • Keep in mind that some selfish behavior is typical for the age-group; when it occurs, encourage perspective taking and prosocial behavior.
3–5	• Knowledge of social conventions for appropriate behavior • Increasing empathy for unknown individuals who are suffering or needy • Recognition that one should strive to meet others' needs as well as one's own; growing appreciation for cooperation and compromise • Growing realization that fairness doesn't necessarily mean equality—that some people (e.g., peers with disabilities) may need more of a desired commodity than others • Increased desire to help others as an objective in and of itself	At the suggestion of his third-grade teacher, 8-year-old Jeff acts as a "special friend" to Evan, a boy with severe physical and cognitive disabilities who joins the class for 2 or 3 days a week. Evan can't speak, but Jeff gives him things to feel and manipulate and talks to him whenever class activities allow conversation. And the two boys regularly sit together at lunch. Jeff comments, "Doing things that make Evan happy makes me happy, too."	• Make prosocial behaviors (e.g., sharing, helping others) a high priority in the classroom. • Explain how students can often meet their own needs while helping others (e.g., when asking students to be "reading buddies" for younger children, explain that doing so will help them become better readers themselves). • Use prosocial adjectives (e.g., *kind*, *helpful*) when praising altruistic behaviors.
6–8	• Growing awareness that some rules and conventions are arbitrary; in some cases accompanied by resistance to these rules and conventions • Interest in pleasing and helping others, but with a tendency to oversimplify what "helping" requires • Tendency to believe that people in dire circumstances (e.g., homeless people) are entirely responsible for their own fate	After the midwinter break, 13-year-old Brooke returns to school with several large nose rings and her hair styled into long, vertical spikes above her head. The school principal tells her that her appearance is inappropriate and insists that she go home to make herself more presentable. Brooke resists, claiming, "I have a right to express myself however I want!"	• Talk about how rules enable classrooms and other groups to run more smoothly. • Involve students in group projects that will benefit their school or community. • When imposing discipline for moral transgressions, accompany it with explanations about the harm that has been caused (i.e., use *induction*), especially when working with students who appear to have deficits in empathy and moral reasoning.
9–12	• Increasing concern about doing one's duty and abiding by the rules of society as a whole, rather than simply pleasing certain authority figures • Realization that most rules and conventions serve useful purposes • Genuine empathy for people in distress • Belief that society has an obligation to help people in need	Several high school students propose and establish a school chapter of Amnesty International, an organization dedicated to the preservation of human rights around the world. The group invites knowledgeable guest speakers from various countries and conducts several fundraisers to help combat abusive practices against women.	• Explore moral issues in social studies, science, and literature. • Encourage community service as a way of engendering a sense of commitment to helping others. Ask students to reflect on their experiences through group discussions or written essays. • Have students read autobiographies and other forms of literature that depict heroic figures who have actively worked to help people in need.

Sources: Eisenberg, 1982; Eisenberg & Fabes, 1998; Farver & Branstetter, 1994; C. A. Flanagan & Faison, 2001; Gibbs, 1995; Gummerum, Keller, Takezawa, & Mata, 2008; D. Hart & Fegley, 1995; Hastings et al., 2007; Helwig & Jasiobedzka, 2001; Helwig et al., 2001; Hoffman, 2000; Kohlberg, 1984; Krebs & Van Hesteren, 1994; Kurtines, Berman, Ittel, & Williamson, 1995; Laupa & Turiel, 1995; M. Lewis & Sullivan, 2005; Nucci, 2009; Nucci & Weber, 1995; Rothbart, 2011; Rushton, 1980; Smetana & Braeges, 1990; Spinrad & Eisenberg, 2009; Turiel, 1983, 1998; Wainryb, Brehl, & Matwin, 2005; Yates & Youniss, 1996; Yau & Smetana, 2003; Youniss & Yates, 1999; Zahn-Waxler, Radke-Yarrow, Wagner, & Chapman, 1992.

should act (e.g., children shouldn't talk back to adults or burp at meals). Conventional transgressions are usually specific to a particular culture; in contrast, many moral transgressions are universal across cultures (Nucci, 2009; Smetana, 2006; Turiel, 2002).

Children's awareness of social conventions increases throughout the elementary school years (Helwig & Jasiobedzka, 2001; Laupa & Turiel, 1995; Nucci & Nucci, 1982). But especially as children reach adolescence, they don't always agree with adults about which behaviors constitute moral transgressions, which ones fall into the conventional domain, and which ones are simply a matter of personal choice. Hence, many adolescents resist rules they think are infringements on their personal freedoms—for instance, rules about clothing, hair style, and talking in class (Nucci, 2009; Smetana, 2005).

- *With age, reasoning about moral issues becomes increasingly abstract and flexible.* To probe children's thinking about moral issues, researchers sometimes present moral dilemmas, situations in which two or more people's rights or needs may be at odds and for which there are no clear-cut right or wrong responses. The scenario in the following exercise is an example.

EXPERIENCING FIRSTHAND
MARTIN'S PLIGHT

Imagine that you're a student in the ninth grade. You're walking quickly down the school corridor on your way to your math class when you see three boys from the so-called "popular" crowd cornering a small, socially awkward boy named Martin. The boys first make fun of Martin's thick glasses and unfashionable clothing, then they start taunting him with names such as "fag" and "retard." What do you do?

   a. You look the other way, pretending you haven't heard anything, and hurry on to class. If you were to stop to help, the boys might taunt you as well, and that will only make the situation worse.

   b. You shoot Martin a sympathetic look and then head to class so that you won't be late. Afterward, you anonymously report the incident to the principal's office, because you know that the boys' behaviors have violated your school's antibullying policy.

   c. You stop and say, "Hey, you jerks, cut it out! Martin's a really nice guy and doesn't deserve your insulting labels. Come on, Martin, let's go. We might be late for math class, so we need to hurry."

Looking for the moral high ground in this situation, you might very well have chosen Alternative *c.* But if you were a ninth grader—someone who might still be working hard to fit in with your peer group—is that *really* what you would do?

In his groundbreaking early research on moral development, Lawrence Kohlberg gave children and adults a variety of moral dilemmas and asked them both what they would do and why they would do it. Based on the hundreds of responses he obtained, Kohlberg proposed that as children grow older, they construct increasingly complex views of morality. In Kohlberg's view, development of moral reasoning is characterized by a sequence of six stages grouped into three general *levels* of morality: preconventional, conventional, and postconventional (see Table 3.3). Children with preconventional morality haven't yet adopted or internalized society's conventions regarding what things are right and wrong but instead focus largely on external consequences that certain actions might bring to themselves, as illustrated in Alternative *a* in the exercise. Kohlberg's second level, conventional morality, is characterized by general, often unquestioning obedience either to an authority figure's dictates or to established rules and norms, even when there are no consequences for disobedience. Alternative *b* in the exercise is an example: You report a violation of school rules to school authorities, but you don't want to be late to class—that would violate another school rule—and through your actions you don't jeopardize any good relationships you might have with the supposedly "popular" boys.

In contrast to the somewhat rigid nature of conventional morality, people at Kohlberg's third level, postconventional morality, view rules as useful but changeable mechanisms

COMPARE/CONTRAST

TABLE 3.3 • The Three Levels and Six Stages of Moral Reasoning in Kohlberg's Theory of Moral Development

LEVEL	AGE RANGE	STAGE	NATURE OF MORAL REASONING
Level I: Preconventional morality	Seen in preschool children, most elementary school students, some junior high school students, and a few high school students	Stage 1: Punishment-avoidance and obedience	People make decisions based on what is best for themselves, without regard for others' needs or feelings. They obey rules only if established by more powerful individuals; they may disobey if they aren't likely to get caught. "Wrong" behaviors are those that will be punished.
		Stage 2: Exchange of favors	People recognize that others also have needs. They may try to satisfy others' needs if they can satisfy their own needs at the same time (e.g., "You scratch my back; I'll scratch yours"). They continue to define right and wrong primarily in terms of consequences to themselves.
Level II: Conventional morality	Seen in a few older elementary school students, some junior high school students, and many high school students (Stage 4 typically does not appear before high school)	Stage 3: Good boy/good girl	People make decisions based on what actions will please others, especially authority figures (e.g., teachers, popular peers). They are concerned about maintaining relationships through sharing, trust, and loyalty, and they consider other people's perspectives and intentions when making decisions.
		Stage 4: Law and order	People look to society as a whole for guidelines about right and wrong. They know that rules are necessary for keeping society running smoothly and believe that it's their duty to obey the rules. However, they perceive rules to be inflexible; they don't necessarily recognize that as society's needs change, rules should change as well.
Level III: Postconventional morality	Rarely seen before college (Stage 6 is extremely rare even in adulthood)	Stage 5: Social contract	People recognize that rules represent agreements among many individuals about appropriate behavior. Rules are seen as useful mechanisms that maintain the general social order and protect individual rights, rather than as absolute dictates that must be obeyed simply because they are the law. People also recognize the flexibility of rules; rules that no longer serve society's best interests can and should be changed.
		Stage 6: Universal ethical principles	Stage 6 is a hypothetical, ideal stage that few people ever reach. People in this stage adhere to a few abstract, universal principles (e.g., equality of all people, respect for human dignity, commitment to justice) that transcend specific norms and rules. They answer to a strong inner conscience and willingly disobey laws that violate their own ethical principles.

Sources: Colby & Kohlberg, 1984; Colby, Kohlberg, Gibbs, & Lieberman, 1983; Kohlberg, 1976, 1984, 1986; Reimer, Paolitto, & Hersh, 1983; Snarey, 1995.

that ideally can maintain the general social order and protect human rights and safety; rules aren't absolute dictates that must be obeyed without question. These people live by their own abstract principles about right and wrong and may disobey rules inconsistent with these principles. Alternative *c* has an element of postconventional reasoning: You're more concerned about protecting Martin's physical and psychological safety than you are about getting to class on time.

Considerable research on moral development has followed on the heels of Kohlberg's work. Some of it supports Kohlberg's proposed sequence: Generally speaking, people seem to make advancements in the order Kohlberg proposed (Boom, Brugman, & van der Heijden, 2001; Colby & Kohlberg, 1984; Snarey, 1995; Stewart & Pascual-Leone, 1992). And as Kohlberg suggested, moral development emerges out of children's own, self-constructed beliefs—beliefs they often revisit and revise over time. Nevertheless, his theory has several weaknesses. For one thing, Kohlberg underestimated young children, who, as you discovered earlier, acquire some internal standards of right and wrong long before they reach school age. Also, Kohlberg's stages encompassed a mixture of moral issues (e.g., causing harm) and social conventions (e.g., having rules to help society run smoothly), but as we've seen, children distinguish between these two domains, and their views about each domain may change at different times and in different ways (Nucci, 2001, 2009). Furthermore, Kohlberg's theory pays little attention to a second important aspect of morality—*showing compassion for and helping* other people—and its focus is largely on *reasoning*, with little consideration of people's moral *behaviors* (Gilligan, 1982, 1987; P. L. Hill & Roberts, 2010; J. G. Miller, 2007). Finally, Kohlberg largely overlooked situational factors that young people take into account when deciding what's morally right and wrong in specific contexts (more about these factors in a moment).

Many contemporary developmental psychologists believe that moral reasoning involves general *trends* rather than distinct stages. It appears that children and adolescents gradually construct several different standards that guide their moral reasoning and decision making in various situations. Such standards include the need to address one's own personal interests, consideration of other people's needs and motives, a desire to abide by society's rules and conventions, and, perhaps eventually, an appreciation for abstract ideals regarding human rights and society's overall needs (Killen & Smetana, 2008; Krebs, 2008; Rest, Narvaez, Bebeau, & Thoma, 1999). With age, youngsters increasingly apply more advanced standards, but even a fairly primitive one—satisfying one's own needs without regard for others—may occasionally take priority (Rest et al., 1999; Turiel, 1998).

- *As children get older, they increasingly behave in accordance with their self-constructed moral standards, but other factors come into play as well.* On average, children and adolescents with more advanced moral reasoning behave in more moral and prosocial ways (e.g., Blasi, 1980; P. A. Miller, Eisenberg, Fabes, & Shell, 1996; Paciello et al., 2008). However, the correlation between moral reasoning and moral behavior isn't an especially strong one. Youngsters' perspective-taking ability and emotions (shame, guilt, empathy, sympathy) also influence their decisions to behave morally or otherwise (Batson, 1991; Damon, 1988; Eisenberg, Zhou, & Koller, 2001). And although young people may truly want to do the right thing, they may also be concerned about the consequences for themselves in specific situations—for instance, how much personal sacrifice will be involved and how much various actions will gain other people's approval or respect (Batson & Thompson, 2001; Cillessen et al., 2011; Hawley, 2014; Narváez & Rest, 1995; Wentzel, Filisetti, & Looney, 2007).

Finally, sense of self seems to be an important factor affecting one's inclinations to act morally and prosocially. Young people must believe they're actually capable of helping other people—in other words, they must have high self-efficacy about their ability to "make a difference" (Narváez & Rest, 1995). Furthermore, in adolescence, some of them begin to integrate a commitment to moral values into their overall sense of identity: They think of themselves as moral, caring individuals who make other people's rights and well-being a high priority (Blasi, 1995; Hastings, Utendale, & Sullivan, 2007; Thorkildsen et al., 2008).

MyEdLab
Video Example 3.6.

In this video, four students give varying reasons why it's wrong for a boy to cheat on a history test. What important difference do you notice between the two younger students' reasons and those of the two older students?

FACTORS INFLUENCING MORAL AND PROSOCIAL DEVELOPMENT

To some degree, advanced moral reasoning depends on *cognitive development*. In particular, it depends on the ability to think simultaneously about multiple issues (e.g., about various people's motives and intentions in a situation) and also on the ability to comprehend such abstract ideals as justice and basic human rights. However, cognitive development doesn't *guarantee* moral development. It's quite possible to think abstractly about academic subject matter and yet reason in a self-centered, preconventional manner (Kohlberg, 1976; Nucci, 2006, 2009; Turiel, 2002).

Children's social and cultural environments have a significant influence on their moral and prosocial development. For example, when children see adults or peers being generous and showing concern for others, they tend to do likewise (Hoffman, 2000; Rushton, 1980; Spinrad & Eisenberg, 2009). And when they watch television shows that emphasize perspective taking and prosocial actions, they're more inclined to exhibit such behaviors themselves (Dubow, Huesmann, & Greenwood, 2007; Hearold, 1986; Rushton, 1980; Singer & Singer, 1994). Prosocial video games, too, seem to have a positive impact (Greitemeyer, 2011; Prot et al., 2014). Ideally, society's prosocial messages must be consistently conveyed through other people's behaviors. Children do *not* make advancements in moral reasoning and behavior simply by hearing adults advocate certain moral values—say, through a short "character education" program (Higgins, 1995; N. Park & Peterson, 2009; Turiel, 1998).

Children also tend to make gains in moral and prosocial development when adults consistently use **induction**, asking children to think about the harm and distress that some of their behaviors have caused others (Hoffman, 2000; Rothbart, 2011). Induction is victim-centered: It helps youngsters focus on others' distress and recognize that they themselves have been the cause. Consistent use of induction in disciplining children, especially when accompanied by *mild* punishment for misbehavior—for instance, insisting that children make amends for their wrongdoings—appears to promote compliance with rules and foster the development of empathy, compassion, and altruism (G. H. Brody & Shaffer, 1982; Hoffman, 1975; Nucci, 2001; Rushton, 1980).

Yet another factor that appears to promote moral and prosocial advancements is *disequilibrium*—in particular, encountering moral dilemmas and arguments that children can't adequately address with their current moral standards and viewpoints. For instance, classroom discussions of controversial topics and moral issues can promote increased perspective taking and a gradual transition to more advanced reasoning (DeVries & Zan, 1996; Power, Higgins, & Kohlberg, 1989; Schlaefli, Rest, & Thoma, 1985). As Kohlberg suggested, children *construct* (rather than absorb) their moral beliefs; disequilibrium can spur them to revise their beliefs in ways that allow them to consider increasingly complex moral issues.

DIVERSITY IN MORAL AND PROSOCIAL DEVELOPMENT

Some diversity in moral and prosocial development is, of course the result of differences in children's environments. But biology seems to be involved as well. For example, other things being equal, children who have a somewhat fearful, anxious temperament in infancy tend to show more guilt and empathy in the early elementary grades than their less anxious classmates. And as children grow older, the degree to which they show effortful control—an ability to inhibit selfish and other unproductive impulses—appears to be a factor in their acquisition of a moral conscience (Eisenberg, Spinrad, & Sadovsky, 2006; Kochanska, Tjebkes, & Forman, 1998; Rothbart, 2011).

Genetically based disabilities, too, come into the picture. For example, certain human genes seem to give rise to the development of brain abnormalities that, in turn, predispose their owners to antisocial behavior (Raine, 2008; Viding & McCrory, 2012).

Gender differences. Researchers have observed minor gender differences in moral and prosocial development. For instance, on average, girls are more likely than boys to feel guilt and shame—in part because they're more willing to take personal responsibility for their misdeeds. Girls are also more likely to feel empathy for people in distress (Alessandri & Lewis, 1993; Lippa, 2002; A. J. Rose, 2002; Zahn-Waxler & Robinson, 1995).

Historically, researchers have disagreed about the extent to which girls and boys *reason* differently about situations involving moral issues. In his work with college students, Kohlberg found that males reasoned at a slightly more advanced level than females (Kohlberg & Kramer, 1969). In response, psychologist Carol Gilligan argued that Kohlberg's stages don't adequately describe female moral development (Gilligan, 1982, 1987; Gilligan & Attanucci, 1988). She suggested that Kohlberg's stages reflect a *justice orientation*—an emphasis on fairness and equal rights—that characterizes males' moral reasoning. In contrast, females are socialized to take a *care orientation* toward moral issues—that is, to focus on interpersonal relationships and take responsibility for others' well-being. To see how these two orientations might play out differently, try the following exercise.

EXPERIENCING FIRSTHAND
THE PORCUPINE DILEMMA

Consider the following scenario:

> A group of industrious, prudent moles have spent the summer digging a burrow where they will spend the winter. A lazy, improvident porcupine who has not prepared a winter shelter approaches the moles and pleads to share their burrow. The moles take pity on the porcupine and agree to let him in. Unfortunately, the moles did not anticipate the problem the porcupine's sharp quills would pose in close quarters. Once the porcupine has moved in, the moles are constantly being stabbed. (Meyers, 1987, p. 141, adapted from Gilligan, 1985)

What do you think the moles should do? Why?

According to Gilligan, males are apt to view the problem as involving a violation of someone's rights: The moles own the burrow and so can legitimately evict the porcupine. In contrast, females are more likely to show compassion, perhaps suggesting that the moles cover the porcupine with a blanket so that his quills won't annoy anyone (Meyers, 1987).

Gilligan raised a good point: Males and females are often socialized quite differently. Furthermore, by including compassion for other human beings as well as consideration for their rights, Gilligan broadened our conception of what morality *is* (L. J. Walker, 1995). But in fact, most research studies *don't* find major gender differences in moral reasoning (Eisenberg, Martin, & Fabes, 1996; Nunner-Winkler, 1984; L. J. Walker, 1991). And as Gilligan herself has acknowledged, males and females alike typically reveal concern for both justice and compassion in their reasoning (L. M. Brown, Tappan, & Gilligan, 1995; Gilligan & Attanucci, 1988; Turiel, 1998).

Cultural and ethnic differences.   Virtually all cultures worldwide acknowledge the importance of individual rights and fairness (reflecting a *justice* orientation) and of compassion for others (reflecting a *care* orientation). Yet until recently researchers have largely overlooked certain other values that may be key components of morality in certain cultures:

- *Loyalty to one's own group,* with a sense of "all for one, and one for all," possibly accompanied by feelings of animosity toward other groups
- *Respect for and obedience to authority figures,* with willing acceptance of a subordinate position in a social decision-making hierarchy
- *Sacredness of certain beings, objects, or life in general,* with unswerving reverence and devotion to these things
- *Liberty,* with preservation of everyone's individual choices and decision making taking precedence over any needs of the larger group (Haidt, 2012)

People can't simultaneously be "moral" in all six ways; for instance, obedience to authority figures conflicts with personal liberties, and loyalty to one's own group can sometimes diminish one's respect for the rights of *other* groups. Accordingly, different cultural groups prioritize these various elements somewhat differently (Haidt, 2012; J. G. Miller, 2007). For example, in much of North America, helping others (or not) is considered to be a voluntary choice—reflecting respect for individual liberties—but in some societies (e.g., in many Asian and Arab countries) it is one's moral *duty* to help people in need. Such a sense of duty, which is often coupled with a strong sense of loyalty to family and the community, can lead to considerable prosocial behavior (X. Chen et al., 2009; Markus & Kitayama, 1991; Rubin et al., 2010).

Some diversity is also seen in the behaviors that cultural groups view as moral transgressions versus those they see as conventional transgressions (Haidt, 2012; Nucci, 2001, 2009). For example, in mainstream Western culture, how one dresses is largely a matter of convention and personal choice. In some deeply religious groups, however, certain forms of dress (e.g., head coverings) are seen as moral imperatives. As another example, in mainstream Western culture, telling lies to avoid punishment for inappropriate behavior is considered morally wrong, but it's a legitimate way of saving face in certain other cultures (Triandis, 1995). As teachers, then, we must remember that our students' notions of morally appropriate and inappropriate behaviors may sometimes be quite different from our own. At the same time, we must *never* accept behaviors that violate such basic principles as equality and respect for other people's rights and well-being.

ENCOURAGING MORAL AND PROSOCIAL DEVELOPMENT AT SCHOOL

As teachers, we play an important role in helping children and adolescents acquire the beliefs, values, and behaviors critical to their effective participation in a democratic and compassionate society—a society in which everyone's rights are respected and everyone's needs are taken into consideration. Following are several general suggestions based on research findings.

🍎 *Encourage perspective taking, empathy, and prosocial behaviors.* Systematic efforts to promote perspective taking, empathy, and such prosocial skills as sharing and helping others do seem to enhance students' moral and prosocial development (Chernyak & Kushnir, 2013; Nucci, 2009; Spinrad & Eisenberg, 2009). Perspective taking and empathy can and should be encouraged in the study of academic subject matter as well (Brophy, Alleman, & Knighton, 2009; Davison, 2011). For example, Figure 3.4 shows two writing samples created during history lessons about slavery in the pre–Civil War United States. The reaction paper on the left was written by 10-year-old Charmaine, whose fifth-grade class had been watching

Chapter 4 describes many gender differences and their possible origins, including socialization practices.

Keep in mind that students from diverse cultures may have different ideas about behaviors that are morally desirable (and in some cases mandatory) versus behaviors that are morally wrong. If necessary, explain to a student in private that some behaviors considered appropriate in his or her culture are unacceptable in your classroom because they infringe on other people's rights and well-being.

FIGURE 3.4 Two examples of perspective taking related to slavery in the pre–Civil War United States.

> Roots II ON THE BOAT TO AMERICA
>
> I could feel the pain Kunta-Kinte was having. Once I had a paper cut and when in the ocean it hurt more than a wasp sting, and that was just paper cut! I can't even imagine the pain or fright that Kunta-Kinte had being taken from his family and home. Or his parents hurt finding out that their first son was being taken to be a slave, their son that had just become a man. I also am horrified about how they treated women. Beely-warmers! The makes angre!

My Diary

July 1, 1700
Dear Diary - Today was a scorcher. I could not stand it and I was not even working. The slaves looked so hot. I even felt for them. and it is affecting my tobacco. It's too hot too early in the season. The tobacco plants are not growing quickly enough. I can only hope that it rains. Also today Robert Smith invited me to a ball at his house in two days. In 5 days I am going to have my masked ball. We mailed out the invitations two days ago. My wife, Beth, and I thought of a great idea of a masked ball. We will hire our own band.

July 2, 1700
Dear Diary - It was another scorcher. I wish it would cool down. I don't think the salves can handle it. It looked like some of them would faint. I had them drink more water. Later in the day a nice breeze came up. Then I gave them the rest of the day off. Also today we planned a trip to Richmond. . . .

July 5, 1700
Dear Diary - Today we had to wake up before the sun had risen. After a breakfast of hot cakes, eggs, and sausage, we headed back home. We got there at the end of the morning. When I got back it was very, very hot. One of the slaves fainted so I gave him the rest of the day off, fearing revolt. I also gave them extra food and water. It makes me think that they are only people too. I know that this is unheard of but it really makes me think.

Roots, a miniseries about a young African man (Kunta Kinte) who is captured and brought to America as a slave. Charmaine acknowledges that she can't fully grasp Kunta Kinte's physical pain. Even so, she talks about his "pain" and "fright" and about his parents' "hurt" at losing their firstborn son, and she is incensed by some colonists' view of African women as little more than "beeby [baby] warmers." The diary entries on the right were written by 14-year-old Craig, whose ninth-grade history teacher asked his class to write journal entries that might capture the life of a Southern plantation owner. Notice that Craig tries to imagine someone else (a plantation owner) taking *other people's* perspectives (those of slaves). Such two-tiered perspective taking is similar to recursive thinking but in this case involves thinking "I think that you think that someone else thinks. . . ."

◉ *Give reasons for why some behaviors are unacceptable.* Although it's important to impose consequences for immoral and antisocial behaviors, punishment by itself often focuses children's attention primarily on their own hurt and distress. To promote moral and prosocial development, we must accompany punishment with induction, focusing students' attention on the hurt and distress their behaviors have caused *others* (Hoffman, 2000; Nucci, 2009; M. Watson, 2008). For example, we might describe how a behavior harms someone else either physically ("Having your hair pulled the way you just pulled Mai's can really be painful") or emotionally ("You hurt John's feelings when you call him names like that"). We might also show students how they have caused someone else inconvenience ("Because you ruined Marie's jacket, her parents are making her work around the house to earn the money for a new one"). Still another approach is to explain someone else's perspective, intention, or motive ("This science project you've just ridiculed may not be as fancy as yours, but I know that Jake spent many hours working on it and is quite proud of what he's done").

One behavior we must explicitly and consistently discourage is *cheating* in its various forms, whether it be submitting a research paper downloaded from the Internet (i.e., plagiarism), copying other students' responses to quizzes or homework, or giving friends unfair advance notice of test questions. Sadly, students don't always see cheating as being a violation of moral standards (L. H. Anderman, Freeman, & Mueller, 2007; Honz, Kiewra, & Yang, 2010). Perhaps they're trying to help a friend, they say, or perhaps they see an assignment as being a waste of time or hopelessly beyond their ability levels. Not only does cheating hinder students' classroom learning—students gain very little from copying other people's work—but it is also dishonest and therefore immoral. Several strategies can potentially discourage cheating:

- Explain in clear, concrete terms what cheating is—for example, that it includes not only representing another person's work as one's own but also giving certain classmates an unfair advantage over others.

- Contrast cheating with legitimate collaboration, in which everyone learns something and the submitted work is honestly represented as a joint effort.

- Independently verify suspected instances of cheating (e.g., by searching the Internet for a document that you think a student might have copied word for word).

- Provide enough guidance and support that students can reasonably accomplish assigned tasks on their own. (L. H. Anderman et al., 2007; Bellanca & Stirling, 2011; Honz et al., 2010; Lenski, Husemann, Trautwein, & Lüdtke, 2010)

- *Expose students to numerous models of moral and prosocial behavior.* Children and adolescents are more likely to exhibit moral and prosocial behavior when they see other people (including their teachers!) behaving in moral rather than immoral ways. Powerful models of moral behavior can be found in literature as well—for instance, in some age-appropriate children's books and in such classics as Harper Lee's *To Kill a Mockingbird* and Nathaniel Hawthorne's *The Scarlet Letter.* Works of fiction are especially likely to have this beneficial effect when they give readers a good sense of what various characters are thinking and feeling, thus enhancing readers' *theory of mind* (Ellenwood & Ryan, 1991; Kidd & Castano, 2013; Nucci, 2001).

- *Engage students in discussions of moral issues related to academic subject matter.* Social and moral dilemmas often arise within the school curriculum. Consider the following questions that might emerge in discussions about academic topics:

- Is military retaliation for acts of terrorism justified if it involves killing innocent people?

- Should laboratory rats be used to study the effects of cancer-producing agents?

- Was Hamlet justified in killing Claudius to avenge the murder of his father?

Such dilemmas don't always have clear-cut right or wrong answers. As teachers, we can encourage student discussions of such issues in several ways:

- Create a trusting and nonthreatening classroom atmosphere in which students can express their beliefs without fear of censure or embarrassment.

- Help students identify all aspects of a dilemma, including the needs and perspectives of the various individuals involved.

- Encourage students to explore their reasons for thinking as they do—that is, to clarify and reflect on the moral principles on which they're basing their judgments. (Reimer, Paolitto, & Hersh, 1983)

- *Get students actively involved in community service.* As we've seen, students are more likely to adhere to strong moral principles when they have high self-efficacy for helping others and when they have integrated a commitment to moral ideals into their overall sense of identity. Such self-perceptions don't appear out of the blue, of course. Children are more likely to have high self-efficacy for prosocial activities when they have the guidance and support they need to carry out the activities successfully. And they're more likely to integrate moral and prosocial values into their overall sense of self when they become actively involved in service to others, ideally even before they reach puberty (Hastings et al., 2007; Nucci, 2001; Youniss & Yates, 1999). Through ongoing community service activities—sometimes collectively referred to as **service learning**—elementary and secondary students alike learn that they have the skills and the responsibility for helping people in dire straits and in other ways making the world a better place in which to live. In the process, they also begin to think of themselves as concerned, compassionate, and moral citizens who have an obligation to help those less fortunate than themselves (J. P. Allen & Antonishak, 2008; Kahne & Sporte, 2008; Thorkildsen et al., 2008).

MyEdLab **Self-Check 3.4**

MyEdLab **Application Exercise 3.4.** In this exercise, you can apply what you have learned to identify age-appropriate strategies for enhancing students' moral and prosocial development.

3   What Have You Learned?

We now return to the learning outcomes listed at the beginning of the chapter and identify key ideas related to each one.

■ **3.1: Describe the nature and origins of children's temperaments and personality characteristics, and explain how you might adapt your classroom practices to students' diverse personalities.** Children exhibit distinct personalities—consistent ways of behaving across a wide range of situations—long before they begin school. To some degree their personalities reflect their temperaments—their genetic predispositions to be active or subdued, outgoing or shy, adventurous or fearful, and so on. Yet environmental factors affect personality as well: The quality of parent–child emotional bonds (reflecting attachment), the nature of caregivers' parenting styles, and general cultural norms and expectations all play roles in molding children's characteristic ways of behaving.

Students are most likely to thrive and succeed when there is a *goodness of fit* between students' temperaments and personality traits, on the one hand, and classroom activities and assignments, on the other. For example, temperamentally quiet and self-controlled students may do well with independent paper-and-pencil tasks, more energetic students may be more productive during hands-on activities, and students with poor impulse control may require greater-than-average guidance and supervision.

■ **3.2: Explain how students' sense of self is apt to influence their behavior and how you can help students develop healthy self-perceptions.** As young people progress through childhood and adolescence, they construct and continually revise their *sense of self*—their perceptions, beliefs, judgments, and feelings about themselves. Children derive their self-views not only from their own experiences (e.g., their successes and failures) but also from other people's behaviors and from the achievements of social and ethnic groups to which they belong. As children reach adolescence, their sense of self increasingly incorporates abstract qualities and, eventually, a general sense of identity regarding who they are as people, what things they find important, and what goals they hope to accomplish.

With adolescence, too, come heightened concern about other people's opinions of oneself (the imaginary audience phenomenon) and an exaggerated belief in one's uniqueness relative to others (the personal fable phenomenon). Perhaps partly as a result of the personal fable—but also as a result of incomplete brain maturation—many adolescents take foolish risks and engage in dangerous activities.

As teachers, we must provide the support students need to be successful and give them feedback that engenders optimism about future accomplishments. And working as either individuals or a team, we can offer and advocate for activities that channel teenagers' desires for risk and social status into safe, productive behaviors.

■ **3.3: Apply your knowledge of peer relationships and social cognition as you identify strategies for promoting productive social skills and addressing student aggression.** Productive peer relationships (especially friendships) serve several important functions: They (a) provide a testing ground for emerging social skills, (b) introduce children to new physical and cognitive skills, (c) offer emotional support in times of trouble or uncertainty, and, ideally, (d) promote socially and culturally appropriate behaviors. In the middle school and high school years, many students become members of larger social groups (e.g., cliques, subcultures, or gangs) and form romantic relationships. Yet some students are consistently rejected or neglected by their classmates, and these students may especially need teachers' friendship and support.

Most children and adolescents actively try to make sense of their social world. With age, such social cognition becomes increasingly complex and insightful, allowing young people to interact effectively with adults and peers alike. But some students have trouble interpreting social cues correctly and may have few effective social skills. Furthermore, some students engage in either physical or psychological aggression toward certain peers, perhaps as a way of gaining prestige and status within their social group. As teachers, then, we may sometimes need to monitor and guide students' interpersonal interactions; for example, we must explain that psychological bullying (e.g., posting defamatory material on the Internet) is as harmful and inappropriate as physical aggression. We should also take active steps to promote communication and interaction across individuals and groups with diverse backgrounds and abilities.

■ **3.4: Describe typical advancements in moral and prosocial development over the course of childhood and adolescence, and identify strategies for promoting moral and prosocial development at school.** As children move through the grade levels, most acquire an increasingly sophisticated sense of right and wrong. This developmental progression is the result of many things, including increasing capacities

for abstract thought and empathy, an evolving appreciation for human rights and other people's welfare, and ongoing encounters with moral dilemmas and problems. Even at the high school level, however, students don't always take the moral high road, as personal needs and self-interests almost invariably enter into their moral decision making to some degree. As teachers, we can help students develop more advanced moral reasoning and increasingly prosocial behavior by giving them reasons why certain behaviors are unacceptable, encouraging them to recognize how others feel in various situations, exposing them to models of moral behavior, challenging their thinking with moral dilemmas, and providing opportunities for community service and other prosocial activities.

Practice For Your Licensure Exam

The Scarlet Letter

MyEdLab
Video Example 3.7.
You can observe Ms. Southam's class discussion here.

Ms. Southam's 11th-grade English class has been reading Nathaniel Hawthorne's *The Scarlet Letter.* Set in 17th-century Boston, the novel focuses largely on two characters who have been carrying on an illicit love affair: Hester Prynne, a young woman who has not seen or heard from her husband for the past 2 years, and the Reverend Arthur Dimmesdale, a pious and well-respected local preacher. When Hester becomes pregnant, she is imprisoned for adultery and soon bears a child. The class is currently discussing Chapter 3, in which the governor and town leaders, including Dimmesdale, are urging Hester to name the baby's father.

> *Ms. Southam:* The father of the baby . . . How do you know it's Dimmesdale . . . the Reverend Arthur Dimmesdale? . . . What are the clues in the text in Chapter 3? . . . Nicole?
>
> *Nicole:* He acts very withdrawn. He doesn't even want to be involved with the situation. He wants the other guy to question her, because he doesn't want to look her in the face and ask her to name him.
>
> *Ms. Southam:* OK. Anything else? . . .
>
> *Student:* The baby.
>
> *Ms. Southam:* What about the baby?
>
> *Student:* She starts to cry, and her eyes follow him.
>
> *Ms. Southam:* That is one of my absolutely favorite little Hawthornisms.

Ms. Southam reads a paragraph about Dimmesdale and then asks students to jot down their thoughts about him. She walks around the room, monitoring what students are doing until they appear to have finished writing.

> *Ms. Southam:* What pictures do you have in your minds of this man . . . if you were directing a film of *The Scarlet Letter?*
>
> *Mike:* I don't have a person in mind, just characteristics. About five-foot-ten, short, well-groomed hair, well dressed. He looks really nervous and inexperienced. Guilty look on his face. Always nervous, shaking a lot.
>
> *Ms. Southam:* He's got a guilty look on his face. His lips always trembling, always shaking.
>
> *Mike:* He's very unsure about himself.
>
> *Matt:* Sweating really bad. Always going like this. [He shows how Dimmesdale might be wiping his forehead.] He does . . . he has his hanky . . .
>
> *Ms. Southam:* Actually, we don't see him mopping his brow, but we do see him doing what? What's the action? Do you remember? If you go to the text, he's holding his hand over his heart, as though he's somehow suffering some pain.
>
> *Student:* Wire-framed glasses . . . I don't know why. He's like. . . .
>
> *Mike:* He's kind of like a nerd-type guy . . . short pants.
>
> *Ms. Southam:* But at the same time . . . I don't know if it was somebody in this class or somebody in another class . . . He said, "Well, she was sure *worth* it." Worth risking your immortal soul for, you know? . . . Obviously she's sinned, but so has he, right? And if she

was worth it, don't we also have to see him as somehow having been worthy of her risking *her* soul for this?

Student: Maybe he's got a good personality . . .

Ms. Southam: He apparently is, you know, a spellbinding preacher. He really can grab the crowd.

Student: It's his eyes. Yeah, the eyes.

Ms. Southam: Those brown, melancholy eyes. Yeah, those brown, melancholy eyes. Absolutely.

1. **Constructed-response question:**

In this classroom dialogue Ms. Southam and her students speculate about what the characters in the novel, especially Arthur Dimmesdale, might be thinking and feeling. In other words, they are engaging in social cognition.

A. Identify two examples of student statements that show social cognition.

B. For each example you identify, explain what it reveals about the speaker's social cognition.

2. **Multiple-choice question:**

Ms. Southam does several things that are apt to enhance students' perspective-taking ability. Which one of the following is the best example?

a. She models enthusiasm for the novel ("That is one of my absolutely favorite little Hawthornisms").

b. She walks around the room as the students write down their thoughts about Dimmesdale.

c. She points out that Dimmesdale is "holding his hand over his heart, as though he's somehow suffering some pain."

d. She agrees with Mike's description of Dimmesdale as having a guilty look on his face.

MyEdLab **Licensure Exam 3.1**

PRAXIS Go to Appendix C, "Matching Book Content and Ebook Activities to the Praxis Principles of Learning and Teaching Tests," to discover sections of this chapter that may be especially applicable to the Praxis tests.

iofoto/Fotolia

4

Group Differences

Learning Outcomes

4.1 Describe frequently observed between-group differences and within-group variability for various cultural and ethnic groups; also describe the teacher attitudes and strategies that underlie culturally responsive teaching.

4.2 Describe the nature and origins of typical gender differences in school-age children and adolescents, and explain how you might best accommodate such differences in your classroom.

4.3 Identify challenges that students from low-income families often face; also identify several strategies through which you can foster their resilience and help them be successful at school.

4.4 Explain how you might recognize students who are at risk for academic failure and dropping out of school, and identify strategies for helping these students stay in school and get on the path to academic and social success.

CASE STUDY: WHY JACK WASN'T IN SCHOOL

Jack was a Native American seventh grader who lived in the Navajo Nation in the American Southwest. Although he enjoyed school, worked hard in his studies, and got along well with his classmates, he had been absent from school all week. In fact, he had been absent from home as well, and his family (who didn't have a telephone) wasn't sure exactly where he was.

Jack's English teacher described the situation to Donna Deyhle, an educator who had known Jack for many years:

> That seventh grader was away from home for 5 days, and his parents don't care! . . . Almost one-third of my Navajo students were absent this week. Their parents just don't support their education. How can I teach when they are not in my classes? (Deyhle & LeCompte, 1999, p. 127)

A few days later, Jack's sister explained why her parents had eventually begun to look for Jack:

> He went to see [the film] *Rambo II* with friends and never came home. If he was in trouble we would know. But now the family needs him to herd sheep tomorrow. (Deyhle & LeCompte, 1999, p. 127)

It was spring—time for the family to plant crops and shear the sheep—and all family members needed to help out. Jack's whereabouts were soon discovered, and the family stopped by Donna's house to share the news:

> Jack's dad said, "We found him." His mother turned in his direction and said teasingly, "Now maybe school will look easy!" Jack stayed at home for several days, helping with the irrigation of the cornfield, before he decided to return to school. (Deyhle & LeCompte, 1999, p. 128)

- Did you interpret Jack's absence from school in the same way his English teacher did, concluding that "his parents don't care" about his education? If so, how might your own cultural background have influenced your conclusion?
- Like most parents, Jack's mother and father cared deeply about his school achievement and general well-being. What alternative explanations might account for their behaviors in this situation?

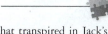

To fully understand what transpired in Jack's family, we need to know a couple of facts about Navajo culture. First, Navajo people place high value on individual autonomy: Even children must be self-sufficient and make their own decisions (Deyhle & LeCompte, 1999). From this perspective, good parenting doesn't mean demanding that children do certain things or behave in certain ways; instead, Navajo parents offer suggestions and guidance, perhaps in the form of gentle teasing ("Now maybe school will look easy!"), that nudge children toward productive choices. But in addition to individual autonomy, Navajos value cooperation and interdependence, believing that community members should work together for the common good; hence Jack's highest priority was helping his family. Such respect for both individual decision making and cooperative interdependence is seen in many other Native American communities as well (Frankland, Turnbull, Wehmeyer, & Blackmountain, 2004; Rogoff, 2003; Tyler et al., 2008).

The attitude of Jack's English teacher may seem somewhat troubling. Her belief that the Navajo students' parents "just don't support their education" seems to be based on assumptions, rather than knowledge of their parents' actual values. As we will see in this chapter, if teachers hold such beliefs, they can begin to treat some students differently from others, which could lead to subsequent psychological and behavioral problems for Navajo students (and other students as well) (Galliher, Jones, & Dahl, 2011).

In this chapter we'll look in depth at group differences—differences we're apt to see *on average* among students of diverse cultural and ethnic groups, different genders, and different socioeconomic backgrounds. As we do so, we must keep in mind three very important points. First, *a great deal of individual variability exists within any group.* We'll be examining research regarding how students of different groups behave *on average,* even though many students within each group are not at all like those averages. Second, *a great deal of overlap typically exists between two groups.* Consider gender differences in verbal ability as an example. Many research studies have found girls to have slightly higher verbal ability than boys (Halpern & LaMay, 2000). The difference is often statistically significant—that is, it probably wasn't a one-time-in-a-hundred fluke that happened simply by chance. Yet the average difference between girls and boys in overall verbal ability is quite small, with a great deal of overlap between the sexes. Figure 4.1 shows the typical overlap between girls and boys on general measures of verbal ability. Notice that some boys (those whose scores fall in the rightmost part of their curve) have higher verbal ability than most of their female peers despite the average advantage for girls.

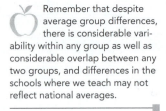 Remember that despite average group differences, there is considerable variability within any group as well as considerable overlap between any two groups, and differences in the schools where we teach may not reflect national averages.

We also need to be aware that group differences shouldn't always be taken at face value. Some of the differences often reported by the media actually are somewhat more complex when examined more critically. For example, let's consider the achievement gap between Hispanic and European American students in the United States. Whereas European American students, overall, tend to achieve at higher levels in both math and reading than do Hispanic students, there actually is much variation in the achievement gap across U.S. states. For example, achievement gaps are lower than the national average in some states (e.g., Florida, Georgia, and Kentucky), and larger than the national average gap in other states (e.g., California, Connecticut, and Rhode Island) (Hemphill, Vanneman, & Rhaman, 2011).

Keep in mind that there are many forms of diversity, not just the ones covered in this chapter. Throughout our careers, we will will encounter many types of diversity in our classrooms. We need to be aware of these possibilities, and use the presence of uniquely diverse students as an opportunity for learning, respect, and appreciation of diversity for all students. Examples could include students whose parents are of the same gender, students who have been adopted either domestically or internationally, students who are HIV or hepatitis positive, or students who have a particularly unique cultural background (e.g., a student who has recently moved here from Iceland).

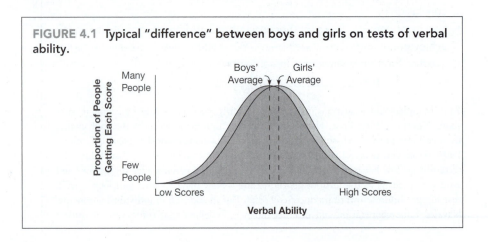

FIGURE 4.1 Typical "difference" between boys and girls on tests of verbal ability.

If we are to maximize the learning and development of all of our students, we must be aware of group differences that may influence their classroom performance. Our challenge is to keep these differences in mind *without* either (1) imposing our own culturally based assumptions on what behaviors are "right" and "wrong" or (2) assuming that all members of a particular group fit typical group patterns. Our erroneous preconceptions about how various students will perform may actually *increase* differences among those students (de Boer, Bosker, & van der Werf, 2010; Rubie-Davies, Hattie, & Hamilton, 2006; Sirin & Ryce, 2010; van den Bergh, Denessen, Hornstra, Voeten, & Holland, 2010).

Chapter 11 describes and explains potential effects of teachers' expectations on students' achievement.

Cultural and Ethnic Differences

The concept of **culture** encompasses the behaviors and belief systems that characterize a long-standing social group. Our cultures affect virtually every aspect of our lives. The culture in which we live influences the perspectives and values we acquire, the skills we find important and master, and the adult roles to which we aspire. It also guides the development of our language and communication skills, our expression and regulation of emotions, and our formation of a sense of self. Sometimes we use the word *culture* to refer to behaviors and beliefs that are widely shared over a large geographic area. For example, *mainstream Western culture* encompasses behaviors, beliefs, and values shared by many people in North America and western Europe. Members of this culture generally value self-reliance, academic achievement, democratic decision making, and respect for other individuals' rights and possessions, among other things. However, any single country in North America or western Europe—in fact, almost every country on the planet—encompasses considerable cultural diversity within its borders. Some of this within-country diversity is the result of growing up in particular geographic regions, religious groups, or socioeconomic circumstances (A. B. Cohen, 2009; Payne, 2005; Rasmussen & Lavish, 2014).

In addition, most countries include citizens from a variety of ethnic groups. In general, an **ethnic group** is a group of individuals with a common culture and the following characteristics:

- Its roots either precede the creation of or are external to the country in which it resides. It may be comprised of people of the same race, national origin, or religious background.

- Its members share a sense of interdependence—a sense that their lives are intertwined. (NCSS Task Force on Ethnic Studies Curriculum Guidelines, 1992)

Holiday Family Traditions

Ever year I do a gringer bread makeing party with all of my friends at and with my cousins too.

Considerable diversity exists in any culture. For example, 7-year-old Emma's family makes gingerbread houses during the holiday season, but many others in her culture do not.

Ethnic groups are often confused with racial groups. Definitions and conceptualizations of race vary greatly (Spencer et al., 2012), and, as teachers, we need to be aware that many students and parents will have diverse attitudes toward race. Racial groups generally are based on physical differences between groups of people; those physical differences are usually genetic in origin. Thus a student might belong to the Caucasian racial group, but the student may also belong to several ethnic groups (e.g., the student might identify as being Catholic and Italian).

Cultures aren't static entities. Instead, they continue to change over time as people incorporate new ideas, innovations, and ways of thinking, and as they interact with other cultures (Kitayama, Duffy, & Uchida, 2007; O. Lee, 1999; Rogoff, 2003). Furthermore, there's considerable variation in attitudes and behaviors within a particular culture; individual members may adopt some cultural values and practices but reject others (Goodnow, 2010; Markus & Hamedani, 2007). For example, you might encounter a student who comes from a culture that prohibits eating certain foods and does not afford equal rights to males and females. You may notice, however, that your student accepts cultural norms for diet but also rejects the notion of gender inequality.

When people come into contact with a culture very different from their own (e.g., through immigration to a new country), many of them—especially children—gradually undergo **acculturation**, adopting some of the new culture's values and customs. Some acculturation is critical for success in the new cultural environment, but *rapid* acculturation can be detrimental to children's social and emotional well-being. In most instances, children's own cultural groups give them a support network and stable set of values that enable them to do well in school and maintain their self-esteem in the face of discrimination and other challenges (Deyhle, 2008; Matute-Bianchi, 2008; Sam & Berry, 2010).

In general, we can get the best sense of students' cultural backgrounds and ethnic-group memberships by learning the extent to which they have participated and continue to participate in various cultural and ethnic-group activities (Gutiérrez & Rogoff, 2003). For example, some Mexican American students live in small, close-knit communities where Spanish is spoken and traditional Mexican practices and beliefs permeate everyday life, but others live in more culturally heterogeneous communities in which Mexican traditions may be cast aside to make time for mainstream American activities. And in some instances students may participate actively in two or more cultures, perhaps because they have emigrated from one country to another or perhaps because their parents come from distinctly different ethnic or racial backgrounds (Herman, 2004; A. M. Lopez, 2003; Mohan, 2009). In general, *membership in a particular cultural or ethnic group is a more-or-less phenomenon rather than an either-or situation.* In this age of increasing cross-cultural interaction, many students cannot easily be pigeonholed.

Keep in mind that some students may have multiple cultural affiliations.

NAVIGATING DIFFERENT CULTURES AT HOME AND AT SCHOOL

When they first begin school, many children experience some *culture shock*—confusion about the behaviors expected of them in this new setting. Culture shock is more intense for some students than for others. Most schools in North America and western Europe embrace the norms and values of mainstream Western culture, and so students with this cultural background often adjust quickly to classroom practices. In contrast, students who come from cultural groups with radically different norms and values may experience a **cultural mismatch** between home and school. In particular, they may find school an unsettling place in which they don't know what to expect from others or what behaviors other people expect of *them*. Significant differences between home and school cultures can interfere with students' adjustment to the school setting and ultimately with their academic achievement as well (Phelan, Yu, & Davidson, 1994; Turner, 2015; Tyler et al., 2008; Ward, Bochner, & Furnham, 2001).

Cultural mismatch is compounded when teachers misinterpret the behaviors of students from cultural and ethnic minority groups. The following exercise provides an example.

EXPERIENCING FIRSTHAND
ARGUMENT

Imagine that, as a new teacher, you're approaching the school building on the first day of school. You see seven or eight boys standing in a cluster just outside the front door. Two of them are engaged in a heated argument, and the others are watching and listening with apparent delight. Here are just a few of the many insults you hear being hurled back and forth:

> "Your momma so fat her driver's license says, 'Picture continued on other side'!"
> "Yeah? Well, your momma so fat she got to iron her pants on the driveway!"
> "That ain't nothin'. Your momma so fat her cereal bowl comes with a lifeguard!"
> "Hey, man, your momma so fat she got smaller fat women orbitin' around her!"

The argument seems to be escalating, with the insults about the two boys' mothers becoming more and more outrageous. Should you intervene?

The incident you've just witnessed is probably an example of "sounding" or "playing the dozens," a friendly exchange of insults common among male youth in some African American communities. Some boys engage in such exchanges to achieve status among their peers—those who concoct the biggest, most creative insults are the winners—whereas others do it simply for amusement. But people unfamiliar with African American culture might misinterpret them as being potentially serious and worrisome (Adger, Wolfram, & Christian, 2007; R. E. Reynolds, Taylor, Steffensen, Shirey, & Anderson, 1982; Smitherman, 1998).

As students gain experience with the culture of their school, they become increasingly aware of their teachers' and peers' expectations for behavior and ways of thinking, and many eventually become adept at switching their cultural vantage point as they move from home to school and back again (Y. Hong, Morris, Chiu, & Benet-Martínez, 2000; LaFromboise, Coleman, & Gerton, 1993; Matute-Bianchi, 2008). One Mexican American student's recollection provides an example:

> At home with my parents and grandparents the only acceptable language was Spanish; actually that's all they really understood. Everything was really Mexican, but at the same time they wanted me to speak good English. . . . But at school, I felt really different because everyone was American, including me. Then I would go home in the afternoon and be Mexican again. (Padilla, 1994, p. 30)

Not all students make an easy adjustment, however. Some students actively resist adapting to the school culture, perhaps because they view it as conflicting with their own cultural background and identity (Cross, Strauss, & Fhagen-Smith, 1999; Gay, 2010; Irving & Hudley, 2008; Phelan et al., 1994). Still others try desperately to fit in at school yet find the inconsistencies between home and school difficult to resolve, as illustrated by this report from a teacher whose students included immigrant Muslim children from Pakistan and Afghanistan:

> During the days of preparation for Ramadan Feast, the children fasted with the adults. . . . They had breakfast [before dawn] and then went back to sleep until it was time to get themselves ready for school. In school they refrained from food or drink—even a drop of water—until sunset. By noon, especially on warm days, they were a bit listless. . . . They spoke about their obligation to pray five times daily. In their writing they expressed the conflict within:
>
> > *I always think about my country. I think about going there one day, seeing it and practicing my religion with no problems. . . . Before sunrise, I can pray with my family. But at school we can't say to my teacher, "Please, teacher, I need to pray."* (Igoa, 1995, p. 135)

As teachers, we must learn as much as we can about the ways in which students from various cultural and ethnic groups are apt to be different from one another and from ourselves. Equipped with such knowledge, we can make reasonable accommodations to help students from all backgrounds adjust to and thrive in our classrooms.

EXAMPLES OF CULTURAL AND ETHNIC DIVERSITY

Tremendous cultural variation exists within African American, Hispanic, Asian American, Native American, European American, and numerous other groups. Thus, we must be careful not to form stereotypes about *any* group. At the same time, knowledge of frequently observed cultural differences, such as those described in the following sections, can sometimes help us better understand why students behave as they do.

LANGUAGE AND DIALECT

One obvious cultural difference is language. Although most students speak English at school, our students may experience different language environments outside of school. In the United States, 21.8% of children between the ages of 5 through 14 speak a language other than English at home (U.S. Census Bureau, 2013). There can also be much variation within individual students' homes regarding how much English or another language is used (Branum-Martin, Mehta, Carlson, Francis, & Goldenberg, 2014). Whereas the entire family may speak another language almost all of the time in some homes, in other homes, one parent may speak English much of the time. But even if children speak English at home, they may use a form of English different from the **Standard English** typically used at school. More specifically, they may speak in a different **dialect**, a form of a particular language that includes some unique pronunciations, idioms, and grammatical structures. Dialects tend to be associated either with particular geographical regions or with particular ethnic and cultural groups.

Perhaps the most widely studied ethnic dialect is **African American English** (you may also see the terms *Black English Vernacular* and *Ebonics*). This dialect—which is illustrated in the earlier "Argument" exercise and is actually a group of dialects that vary somewhat from place to place

—is characterized by certain ways of speaking that are distinctly different from those of Standard English (e.g., "He got ten dollar," "Momma she mad," "He be talkin' ") (Hulit & Howard, 2006, p. 346; Owens, 1995, p. A-8). At one time, many researchers believed that an African American dialect represented a less complex form of speech than Standard English and thus urged educators to teach students to speak "properly" as quickly as possible. But most researchers now realize that African American dialects are, in fact, very complex languages with predictable sentence structures and that these dialects promote communication and sophisticated thinking processes as readily as Standard English (Alim & Baugh, 2007; Fairchild & Edwards-Evans, 1990; Hulit & Howard, 2006; Spears, 2007).

Many children and adolescents view their native dialect as an integral part of their ethnic identity. Furthermore, when a particular dialect is the language preferred by local community members, it's often the means through which people can most effectively connect with one another in face-to-face interactions and text messaging (Godley & Escher, 2011; Ogbu, 2003; D. Paris & Kirkland, 2011).

Nevertheless, lack of proficiency in Standard English can impede children's reading and writing development, and in later years, their use of a distinct regional or cultural dialect may lead other people to underestimate or discredit their abilities. For such reasons, many experts recommend that all students in English-speaking countries develop proficiency in Standard English. Ultimately, children and adolescents function most effectively when they can use both their local dialect and Standard English in appropriate settings. For example, although we may wish to encourage Standard English in most written work or in formal oral presentations, we might find other dialects quite appropriate in creative writing or informal classroom discussions (Adger et al., 2007; DeBose, 2007; Ogbu, 1999, 2003; Smitherman, 1994). In general, being aware of and accommodating students' cultural differences in language use can enhance our ability to educate students from diverse linguistic backgrounds (Bailey, Osipova, & Reynolds-Kelly, 2015).

> Encourage students to use both Standard English and their local dialect, each in appropriate settings.

TALKATIVENESS AND VERBAL ASSERTIVENESS

Relatively speaking, mainstream Western culture is a chatty one. People often say things to one another even when they have little to communicate, making small talk a way of maintaining interpersonal relationships (Gay, 2010; Trawick-Smith, 2003). In some African American communities as well, people talk a lot, often with a great deal of energy and enthusiasm (Gay, 2006; Tyler et al., 2008). In certain other cultures, however, silence is golden (Norenzayan, Choi, & Peng, 2007; Trawick-Smith, 2003). For example, many people from Southeast Asian countries believe that effective learning is best accomplished through attentive listening rather than through speaking (J. Li, 2005; J. Li & Fischer, 2004; Volet, 1999).

> Chapter 11 looks more closely at cultural differences in emotional expressiveness.

Some talkative cultures are also assertive ones, in that people readily voice their opinions, perhaps interrupting those who are speaking; for example, this is the case for many African Americans, European Americans, and Hawaiians. People from quieter cultures, such as many Asian Americans, tend to be more subtle and tentative in expressing their opinions—for instance, they might begin a sentence by saying "I'm not sure, but perhaps . . . "—and they aren't as likely to reveal their emotions during conversations (Gay, 2010; Morelli & Rothbaum, 2007; Tyler et al., 2008; Ward et al., 2001).

In addition, different cultural and ethnic groups have diverse views about how assertive children should be with adults. In mainstream Western culture a common expectation is that children will speak up whenever they have comments or questions. Yet in many parts of the world, children are expected to learn primarily by close, quiet observation of adults, rather than by asking questions or otherwise interrupting what adults are doing (Correa-Chávez, Rogoff, & Mejía Arauz, 2005; Gutiérrez & Rogoff, 2003; Kağıtçıbaşı, 2007). And in some cultures—for instance, in many Mexican American and Southeast Asian communities and in some African American communities—children learn very early that they should engage in conversation with adults only when their participation has been directly solicited (Delgado-Gaitan, 1994; C. A. Grant & Gomez, 2001; Ochs, 1982).

As teachers, we need to be sensitive to such differences in talkativeness, particularly when students have recently arrived from another country. A student who has recently moved from a culture where children and adolescents are socialized to be quiet in classrooms may find the linguistic environments in Western classrooms disruptive and disrespectful. Parents of such students may be particularly concerned that their children will be ignored and not receive sufficient attention from teachers (Mizuochi & Dolan, 1994).

EYE CONTACT

For many of us, looking someone in the eye is a way to show that we're trying to communicate or are listening intently to what the person is saying. But in many Native American, African American, Mexican American, Puerto Rican, and Polynesian communities, a child who looks an adult in the eye is showing disrespect. In these communities children are taught to look down in the presence of adults (Jiang, 2010; McCarthy, Lee, Itakura, & Muir, 2006; Tyler et al., 2008).

The following anecdote shows how a teacher's recognition of children's beliefs about eye contact can make a difference:

> A teacher [described a Native American] student who would never say a word, nor even answer when she greeted him. Then one day when he came in she looked in the other direction and said, "Hello, Jimmy." He answered enthusiastically, "Why hello Miss Jacobs." She found that he would always talk if she looked at a book or at the wall, but when she looked at him, he appeared frightened. (Gilliland, 1988, p. 26)

PERSONAL SPACE

In some cultures, such as those of some African American and Hispanic communities, people stand close together when they talk, and they may touch one another frequently. In contrast, European Americans and East Asians tend to keep a fair distance from one another, maintaining some **personal space**, especially if they don't know each other very well (Slonim, 1991; Trawick-Smith, 2003; Ward et al., 2001). As teachers, we must be sensitive to the personal space that students from various cultural backgrounds need in order to feel comfortable in interactions with us and with classmates.

In some cultures, including many Native American communities, children are taught to look down as a sign of respect for an adult who speaks to them.

Keep in mind that some students have been taught that initiating a conversation with an adult is disrespectful.

Don't rely on eye contact as the only indicator that students are paying attention.

RESPONDING TO QUESTIONS

A common interaction pattern in many Western classrooms is the IRE cycle: A teacher *initiates* an interaction by asking a question, a student *responds* to the question, and the teacher *evaluates* the response (Mehan, 1979). Similar interactions are often found in parent–child interactions in middle-income European American homes. For instance, when our own children were toddlers and preschoolers, the authors often asked them questions such as "How old are you?" and "What does a cow say?" and praised them when they answered correctly. But children reared in other cultural groups aren't necessarily familiar with such question-and-answer sessions when they first come to school. Furthermore, some children may be quite puzzled when a teacher asks questions to which he or she already knows the answer (Adger et al., 2007; Crago, Annahatak, & Ningiuruvik, 1993; Heath, 1989; Rogoff, 2003, 2007). And children in some communities are specifically taught *not* to answer questions from strangers about personal and home life—questions such as "What's your name?" and "Where do you live?" (Heath, 1982, 1989).

The issue, then, isn't that children are unaccustomed to questions; rather, it's that they have little experience with certain *kinds* of questions, as one child's mother explains:

> Miss Davis, she complain 'bout Ned not answerin' back. He says she asks dumb questions she already know about. (Heath, 1982, p. 107)

Meanwhile, teachers may misinterpret the children's silence, as this teacher does:

> The simplest questions are the ones they can't answer in the classroom; yet on the playground, they can explain a rule for a ballgame or describe a particular kind of bait with no problem. Therefore, I know they can't be as dumb as they seem in my class. (Heath, 1983, p. 269)

Be aware that some children are unaccustomed to answering certain kinds of questions.

Teachers often ask students questions for which they themselves already know the answers, but not all children are familiar with this strategy—known as an *IRE cycle*—for assessing students' knowledge.

Cultural differences have also been observed in how long people wait before answering another person's question. People from some cultures use lengthy pauses before responding as a way of indicating respect, as this statement by a Northern Cheyenne individual illustrates:

Even if I had a quick answer to your question, I would never answer immediately. That would be saying that your question was not worth thinking about. (Gilliland, 1988, p. 27)

When teachers expect immediate answers to their questions—with a delay of, say, a second or less—students from these cultures may not have the time they need to show respect as they respond. Be wary of interpreting such delays as lack of ability or engagement. Such students are more likely to participate in class and answer questions when their teachers provide a more extended **wait time**—that is, when several seconds of silence can elapse after the teacher's question or another student's comment (Castagno & Brayboy, 2008; Mohatt & Erickson, 1981; Tharp, 1989).

Increase wait time as a means of encouraging students from diverse backgrounds to participate in discussions.

Increasing teacher wait time also enhances thinking and learning, as you'll discover in Chapter 6.

Remember that some students feel more comfortable practicing new skills in private.

PUBLIC VERSUS PRIVATE PERFORMANCE

In many classrooms learning is a very public enterprise. Individual students are often expected to answer questions or demonstrate skills in full view of their classmates, and they're encouraged to ask questions themselves when they don't understand. Such practices, which many teachers take for granted, may confuse or even alienate the students of some ethnic groups (Eriks-Brophy & Crago, 1994; García, 1994; Lomawaima, 1995). For example, many Native American children are accustomed to practicing a skill privately at first, performing in front of a group only after they've attained a reasonable level of mastery (Castagno & Brayboy, 2008; Suina & Smolkin, 1994). And children in some Native American and Hawaiian communities may feel more comfortable responding to questions as a group rather than interacting with adults one on one (K. H. Au, 1980; L. S. Miller, 1995).

VIEWS ABOUT TEASING

Although people in some cultures think of teasing as mean spirited, it's a common form of social interaction in certain other cultures. For example, in the earlier "Argument" exercise, two African American boys engaged in playful one-upmanship, flinging increasingly outlandish insults at each other. And in the opening case study, Jack's mother teased him by suggesting that "Now maybe school will look easy!" When taken in the right spirit, teasing serves a variety of functions for particular cultural groups—perhaps providing a source of amusement and an outlet for verbal creativity, exerting gentle pressure to engage in more productive behavior, or helping children learn how to take criticism in stride (Adger et al., 2007; P. M. Cole, Tamang, & Shrestha, 2006; Rogoff, 2003). As teachers, we need to pay particular attention to instances when students from different cultural backgrounds tease one another. Whereas it may be acceptable for students from within a specific cultural group to tease each other, boundaries may be crossed when students from outside of that cultural group engage in the teasing.

COOPERATION VERSUS COMPETITION

In a traditional Western classroom, students are rewarded when, as individuals, they achieve at high levels. In some cases—for example, when teachers grade on a curve or post "best" papers on a bulletin board—students must actually compete with one another in order to be successful.

Yet in some cultures—including many Native American, Mexican American, African, Southeast Asian, and Pacific Island communities—*group* achievement is valued over individual success. Students from these cultures are often more accustomed to working cooperatively and for the benefit of the community, rather than for themselves, and value humility about their personal accomplishments (X. Chen, Chung, & Hsiao, 2009; Lomawaima, 1995; Mejía-Arauz, Rogoff, Dexter, & Najafi, 2007; Tyler et al., 2008). Such a cooperative spirit is epitomized by the Zulu word *ubuntu,* which reflects the belief that people become fully human largely through caring relationships with others and regular contributions to the common good.

Students from cooperative cultures may resist when asked to compete against their classmates, as 16-year-old Maria explains:

> I love sports, but not competitive sports. [My brother is] the same way. I think we learned that from our folks. They both try to set things up so that everyone wins in our family and no one is competing for anything. (Pipher, 1994, p. 280)

Students may also be confused when teachers reprimand them for helping one another on assignments or for sharing answers, and they may feel uncomfortable when their individual achievements are publicly acknowledged. Group work, with an emphasis on cooperation rather than competition, often facilitates the school achievement of these students (Deyhle & Margonis, 1995; Lipka, 1998; L. S. Miller, 1995; Rogoff, 2003).

FAMILY RELATIONSHIPS AND EXPECTATIONS

In many groups—for example, in many Hispanic, Native American, Arab American, Polynesian, and Asian groups, as well as in some rural European American communities—family bonds and relationships are especially important, and extended family members often live nearby. Students growing up in these cultures are likely to feel responsibility for their family's well-being, to have a strong sense of loyalty to other family members, and to go to great lengths to please their elders. It isn't unusual for students in such communities to leave school when their help is needed at home, as Jack does in the opening case study (Banks & Banks, 1995; Fuligni, 1998; Kağitçibaşi, 2007; McIntyre, 2010).

In most cultures school achievement is highly valued, and parents encourage their children to do well in school (Monzó, 2010; R. R. Pearce, 2006; Spera, 2005). But some cultural groups place even higher priority on other accomplishments. For example, when preparing young children for school, many Hispanic families place particular emphasis on instilling appropriate social behaviors—for instance, showing respect for adults and cooperating with peers (Greenfield et al., 2006; Tyler et al., 2008). And in some cultural groups, an early pregnancy is a cause for joy even if the mother-to-be is young or hasn't yet completed high school (Deyhle & Margonis, 1995; McMichael, 2013; Stack & Burton, 1993).

We must certainly be sensitive to situations in which the achievements that *we* think are important are seemingly not valued by students' families. Whenever possible, we must show our students how the school curriculum and classroom activities relate to their cultural environment and their own life goals (Brayboy & Searle, 2007; Lipman, 1995; Moje & Hinchman, 2004). We must also maintain open lines of communication with students' parents. Because some parents of minority-group children feel intimidated by school personnel, teachers often need to take the first step in establishing productive parent–teacher relationships. When teachers and parents realize that both groups want students to succeed in the classroom, they're more apt to work cooperatively to promote student achievement (Anderman & Anderman, 2014; Edwards & Turner, 2010; Reschly & Christenson, 2009).

CONCEPTIONS OF TIME

Many people regulate their lives by the clock: Being on time to appointments, social engagements, and the dinner table is important. This emphasis on punctuality isn't characteristic of all cultures, however. For example, many Hispanic and Native American groups don't observe strict schedules and timelines (Tyler et al., 2008; Ward et al., 2001). Not surprisingly, children from these communities may sometimes be late for school and may have trouble understanding the need to complete school tasks within a certain time frame.

Make frequent use of cooperative activities, especially when students' cultures place high value on cooperation.

Relate the school curriculum to students' home environments and cultures. Establish and maintain open lines of communication with parents, and work with them to identify ways in which home and school can collaborate in helping students be successful at school.

Chapter 13 identifies many strategies for working effectively with parents.

In most Western cultures, we tend to emphasize thinking about future time—what we will do tomorrow, our plans for next summer, or our goals for the next 10 years. Nevertheless, not all cultures emphasize future time; we need to be aware that some of our students may be less focused on the future than are others. For example, results of studies of individuals who speak Arabic indicate that an orientation toward the past is more prominent than an orientation toward the future (de la Fuente, Santiago, Román, Dumitrache, & Casasanto, 2014). Thus students from some cultural or linguistic backgrounds may tend to talk about and value the past more than do other students.

To succeed in mainstream Western society, students eventually need to learn punctuality. At the same time we must recognize that not all students will be especially concerned about clock time when they first enter our classrooms. Certainly we should expect students to come to class on time and to turn in assignments when they're due. But we must be patient and understanding when, for cultural reasons, students don't develop such habits immediately.

WORLDVIEWS

The cultural and ethnic differences identified so far reveal themselves, in one way or another, in students' behaviors. Yet the definition of culture presented early in the chapter includes the behaviors *and belief systems* that characterize a social group. Our general beliefs and assumptions about the world—collectively known as our worldview—are often so integral to our everyday thinking that we take them for granted and aren't consciously aware of them (Koltko-Rivera, 2004; Losh, 2003). Some beliefs that permeate the curriculum in traditional Western schools aren't universally shared, however. Consider the following examples:

- After a major hurricane ripped through their community, many fourth and fifth graders attributed the hurricane to natural causes, but some children from minority-group backgrounds had heard explanations elsewhere that led them to believe that people's actions or supernatural forces also played a role in the hurricane's origins and destructiveness (O. Lee, 1999).

- Fourth graders from the Menominee culture (a Native American group) often show exceptionally high achievement scores in science, but by eighth grade their scores may decline considerably. Menominee culture encourages children to think about the many ways in which they are a *part* of nature, rather than taking care of or dominating it, and children increasingly find the school science curriculum at odds with this view (Atran, Medin, & Ross, 2005; Medin, 2005).

- When American high school students read newspaper articles about the appropriateness or inappropriateness of prayer in public schools, some view the trend away from prayer as a sign of progress toward greater religious freedom. But others—those from deeply religious Christian families, for instance—view the same trend as a decline that reflects abandonment of the country's religious heritage (Mosborg, 2002).

As you can see, then, students' worldviews are likely to influence their interpretations of current events and classroom subject matter (Kağitçibaşi, 2007; Keil & Newman, 2008).

CREATING A CULTURALLY INCLUSIVE CLASSROOM ENVIRONMENT

Clearly, we must be aware of and responsive to the different ways in which students of various cultural and ethnic groups are likely to think and act. It's equally important that we help our *students* develop such awareness and responsiveness, enabling them to become productive members both of the school community and of our increasingly multicultural society. Following are several suggestions.

Come to grips with your own cultural lens and biases. In the opening case study Jack's English teacher complained that "his parents don't care" and that, in general, the parents of Navajo students "just don't support their [children's] education" (Deyhle & LeCompte, 1999, p. 127). This teacher was looking at parents' behaviors from the perspective of a non-Navajo. The assumptions and worldviews we've acquired in our own culture—for instance, the assumption that good parents actively direct and control their children's behaviors—are often

---

Sidebar notes (left margin):

Encourage punctuality, but be patient if students' cultural backgrounds have placed little emphasis on clock time.

Consider how students' diverse worldviews might influence their interpretations of classroom subject matter.

so pervasive in our lives that we tend to treat them as common sense, or even as facts, rather than as the beliefs they really are. These beliefs become a *cultural lens* through which we view events—a lens that may lead us to perceive other cultures' practices as somehow irrational and inferior to our own.

Teachers who work effectively with students from diverse backgrounds are keenly aware that their own cultural beliefs are just that—beliefs. And they make a concerted effort *not* to pass judgment on cultural practices and beliefs very different from their own, but rather to try to understand *why* people of other cultural groups think and act as they do (Banks et al., 2005; Rogoff, 2003).

* *Educate yourself about your students' cultural backgrounds.* One way to do this, of course, is to read as much as possible about various cultural groups. But in addition, effective teachers immerse themselves in students' daily lives and cultures—talking with students about their outside interests and activities, getting to know students' families, patronizing local businesses, and so on (Castagno & Brayboy, 2008; Ladson-Billings, 1995a; Moje & Hinchman, 2004). We can also benefit from observing other teachers who have been successful at working with culturally diverse students (Hilliard, 1995). Only when we immerse ourselves in a very different cultural environment can we truly begin to understand how we, too, are products of our own cultures and to appreciate the potential benefits of growing up in a very different one (Banks et al., 2005; Rogoff, 2003).

* *Be sensitive to the culture shock that recent immigrants may be experiencing.* In recent years, immigration has become a highly politicized topic in the United States and elsewhere. Whatever our own political views might be on the topic, we must realize that *all* students deserve our guidance and support in their efforts to acquire the knowledge and skills they will need to be successful in the adult world. Recent immigrant students may lack some of the skills and knowledge that non-immigrant students have acquired, and this can adversely affect their achievement (Martin, Liem, Mok, & Xu, 2012). Furthermore, media coverage about other parts of the world may make transitions more difficult for some immigrants than others. For example, when tensions are high between Western nations and countries in the Middle East, students who have immigrated from those countries may face particular challenges at school, such as being teased or ostracized by other students (Kumar, Warnke, & Karabenick, 2014).

For recent immigrants, guidance and support from teachers might include not only extra academic assistance, but also explicit instruction in the typical practices and customs—"how things are done"—of their new culture (Vang, 2010; Ward et al., 2001). Also, some students may require accommodations for their religious beliefs; for instance, we might discreetly give devout Muslim students a private place for their early afternoon prayer, and we might excuse them from vigorous physical exercise when they're fasting during Ramadan (Sirin & Ryce, 2010). In particular, immigrant students might need accommodations when taking certain tests; some recent research suggests that immigrant students especially might benefit from being allowed to take assessments using computer-based platforms, provided that the assessments are administered fairly and equitably to all students (Sonnleitner, Brunner, Keller, & Martin 2014).

Chapter 14 discusses strategies for assessing student learning.

* *Incorporate the perspectives and traditions of many cultures into the curriculum.* True multicultural education isn't limited to cooking ethnic foods, celebrating Cinco de Mayo, or studying famous African Americans during Black History Month. Rather, it integrates throughout the curriculum the perspectives and experiences of numerous cultural groups and gives all students reason for pride in their own cultural heritage. Students from diverse backgrounds are more likely to be motivated to do well in school—and to *actually* do well there—when they perceive the school curriculum and classroom activities to be relevant to their own cultures (Brayboy & Searle, 2007; Gay, 2010; Moje & Hinchman, 2004; Tyler et al., 2008). A primary school teacher who often has a majority of non-English-speaking children in her class at the beginning of each school year has described how she incorporates the students' diverse cultural backgrounds into her teaching: "We try to include all cultural celebrations throughout the year—Eid, Diwali, Chinese new year and so on. The lovely thing about teaching this age is children are still very naive to differences in nationality and religion and so are very accepting to all" (Eustice, 2012, paragraph 24).

It is important to recognize that exposure to novel cultures is beneficial to majority students as well. For example, kindergartners and first graders who share classrooms with children who are nonnative speakers of English (and who are learning to speak English) tend to have lower levels of behavioral problems and better social skills than children with fewer English language learners in their classrooms (Gottfried, 2014).

As teachers we can incorporate content from diverse cultures into many aspects of the school curriculum. Following are examples:

- In language arts, study the work of authors and poets from a variety of ethnic groups (e.g., study the lyrics of popular hip-hop songs).

- In math and science, draw on students' experiences with their community's building, hunting, farming, and cooking practices.

- In social studies, look at different religious beliefs and their effects on people's behaviors (e.g., see Figure 4.2).

- In history, look at wars and other major events from diverse perspectives (e.g., the Native American perspective on European settlers' westward migration, the Spanish perspective on the Spanish–American War, the Japanese perspective on World War II).

- In music, explore tonal and rhythmic differences in music from different world regions.

- In both history and current events, consider such issues as discrimination and oppression. (J. M. Hughes, Bigler, & Levy, 2007; J. Kim, 2011; Lipka, Yanez, Andrew-Ihrke, & Adam, 2009; McIntyre, 2010; NCSS Task Force on Ethnic Studies Curriculum Guidelines, 1992; K. Schultz, Buck, & Niesz, 2000)

In our exploration of diverse cultures, we should look for commonalities as well as differences. For example, in the elementary grades we might study how people in various countries celebrate children's birthdays. In the secondary grades it can be beneficial to explore issues that adolescents of all cultures face: gaining the respect of elders, forming trusting relationships with peers, and finding a meaningful place in society. One important goal of multicultural education should be to communicate that, underneath it all, people are more alike than different (Brophy, Alleman, & Knighton, 2009; Ulichny, 1996).

MyEdLab
Video Example 4.1.
Teachers work effectively with culturally diverse students by becoming aware of their cultural backgrounds and creating culturally inclusive classroom environments.

Look for commonalities as well as differences among people from different cultural backgrounds.

FIGURE 4.2 In this paper for her language arts and social studies classes, 13-year-old Melinda explains what she has learned about Japan's Shinto religion and how in some ways it relates to her own life.

Shinto gods are called Kami. It is believed that these spirits are found in the basic forces of fire, wind, and water. Most influence agriculture and this of course was how the earliest people survived. They relied on what they grew to live. So the gods had to help them grow their crops or they died. It seems natural for people to worship things that will help them survive, and worshiping forces that affect what you grow was the common practice in early history. These basic forces even affect the survival of modern people. We all still need agriculture to live and forces of nature really determine whether crops grow or not.

Shintoists never developed strong doctrines, such as the belief in life after death that many other religions have. However they have developed some moral standards such as devotion, sincerity, and purity. . . .

All Shintoists have a very good and simple set of rules or practice. They want to be honorable, have feelings for others, support the government, and keep their families safe and healthy. I think these are good principles for all people, whether they practice a religion or not. . . .

Students should be encouraged to contribute to the multicultural curriculum—for example, by bringing in photographs and favorite foods from home and by expressing their varying experiences and perspectives without fear of ridicule or censure (Gollnick & Chinn, 2009; Jiang, 2010). Ultimately, we should help students realize that diverse cultural groups have much to learn from one another. As an example, students might be surprised to discover that several practices underlying many democratic governments—such as sending delegates to represent particular groups, allowing only one person in a governing council to speak at a time, and keeping government and military bodies separate—were adopted from Native American practices in the 1700s (Rogoff, 2003; Weatherford, 1988).

Build on students' strengths, and adapt instructional methods to their preferred ways of learning and behaving. Classroom strategies that build on students' existing knowledge, skills, and accustomed ways of learning and behaving are collectively known as **culturally responsive teaching**. For example, if students regularly collaborate with others at home and in the community, we should make frequent use of cooperative group activities (Castagno & Brayboy, 2008; Hurley, Allen, & Boykin, 2009; Ladson-Billings, 1995a). If, in their informal interactions with peers, students are accustomed to talking simultaneously and elaborating on one another's ideas, we might ask them to answer questions in chorus rather than as individuals (K. H. Au, 1980). And if students' home environments are high-energy ones in which several activities often take place simultaneously—as is sometimes true in African American and Hispanic families—we might create a similarly high-energy, multi-activity classroom environment (Tyler et al., 2008).

Educators also need to remember that students' cultural backgrounds influence their behaviors and beliefs. When teachers lose sight of the strong influence of culture on students, they often underestimate students' intellectual potential, academic achievement, and language abilities (Hilliard, 1992; Tyler, Boykin, & Walton, 2006). For example, some African American students may harbor doubts about the economic value of education (Mickelson, 1990). An awareness of the fact that some students feel this way can help teachers to potentially understand why a student might become disengaged from academics.

Work hard to break down students' stereotypes of particular ethnic groups. Although we and our students should certainly be aware of real differences among various ethnic groups, it's counterproductive to hold a **stereotype**—a rigid, simplistic, and inevitably inaccurate caricature—of any particular group. Even the most open-minded of us are sometimes prone to holding ethnic stereotypes, as you might discover in the following exercise.

Stress that people from diverse cultures can all benefit from considering one another's perspectives.

Chapter 11 discusses how beliefs about the value of education in general, and of specific subject areas, affect students' motivation.

EXPERIENCING FIRSTHAND
PICTURE THIS #1

Form a picture in your mind of someone from each of the following three places. Make note of the *first* image that comes to mind in each case:

> The Netherlands (Holland)
> Mexico
> Hawaii

Now answer yes or no to each of these questions:

- Was the person from the Netherlands wearing wooden shoes?
- Was the person from Mexico wearing a sombrero?
- Was the person from Hawaii wearing a hula skirt or flower lei?

If you answered *yes* to any of the three questions, then one or more of your images reflected an ethnic stereotype. Most people in the Netherlands, Mexico, and Hawaii *don't* routinely wear such stereotypical attire.

In the preceding exercise, your stereotypes involved only superficial qualities. Yet people's stereotypes can also include notions about typical personality characteristics and behaviors. Some stereotypes—for instance, perceptions of a certain group as being "stupid," "lazy," or "aggressive"—are derogatory and certainly *not* conducive to productive cross-group interactions.

Researchers have identified several possible origins of counterproductive stereotypes. In some instances family members, friends, or popular media communicate stereotypes through prejudicial remarks, practices, avoiding eye contact, and caricatures (Branch, 1999; Castelli, De Dea, & Nesdale, 2008; Nesdale, Maass, Durkin, & Griffiths, 2005; Theobald & Herley, 2009). In other cases a history of conflict and animosity between two groups may lead children to conclude that people in the opposing group have undesirable qualities (Pitner, Astor, Benbenishty, Haj-Yahia, & Zeira, 2003). Occasionally stereotypes appear in curriculum materials and classroom instruction—as happens, for instance, when American children role-play the first Thanksgiving by dressing up in paper-bag "animal skins," painting their faces, and wearing feathers on their heads (Bigler & Liben, 2007; Brayboy & Searle, 2007). And sometimes students simply have little or no knowledge about a cultural group very different from their own. For example, when a Muslim girl wears a head scarf to school, a thoughtless classmate might ask, "Are you bald? Is there something wrong with your hair?" (McBrien, 2005a, p. 86; Sirin & Ryce, 2010).

At a minimum, unflattering stereotypes lead to misunderstandings among members of diverse cultural groups. When left uncorrected, they can also lead to overtly discriminatory and malicious behaviors—ethnic jokes, racial taunts, social exclusion, and so on (Killen, 2007; Pfeifer, Brown, & Juvonen, 2007). We also need to think about the stereotypes that we as teachers may hold, and consider how those stereotypes might affect out interactions with our students. For example, some teachers provide feedback differentially to minority students, giving less criticism and more praise to minority students than to majority students (Harber et al., 2012). Although this might be well intentioned, we need to be aware that we may be sending different messages to our students when we vary feedback. Students who are frequent victims of others' misunderstandings and prejudice are more likely than their peers to become chronically ill or depressed (Allison, 1998; G. H. Brody et al., 2006; Tatum, 1997). Negative stereotypes can also turn inward in a phenomenon known as **stereotype threat**: Students become overly anxious in domains in which their group stereotypically does poorly and, as a result, perform more poorly than they otherwise would (J. Aronson & Steele, 2005; Walton & Spencer, 2009).

As teachers, we must work hard to correct students' inaccurate and demeaning stereotypes of various cultural and ethnic groups, and we must vigorously address any acts of prejudice and discrimination we witness in the classroom and elsewhere. The Into the Classroom feature "Addressing Students' Stereotypes and Prejudices" offers several concrete strategies. By learning to appreciate multicultural differences within a single classroom, students take an important step toward appreciating the multicultural nature of the world at large.

🍎 *Bring cultural diversity to culturally homogeneous classrooms.* When students attend school only with peers who are culturally very similar to themselves, they may hold especially naive and potentially counterproductive stereotypes about other cultural and ethnic groups (McGlothlin & Killen, 2006; Pfeifer et al., 2007). In such situations we may have to take students beyond school boundaries, either physically or vicariously. For instance, we might engage students in community action projects that provide services to particular ethnic groups—perhaps in preschools, nursing homes, or city cultural centers (Sleeter & Grant, 1999). Alternatively, we might initiate a sister schools program in which students from two ethnically different communities regularly communicate, exchanging letters, photographs, stories, local news items, and the like (Koeppel & Mulrooney, 1992).

🍎 *Foster democratic ideals, and empower students to bring about meaningful change.* Any multicultural education program must include such democratic ideals as human dignity, equality, justice, and appreciation of diverse viewpoints (Gay, 2010; Gollnick & Chinn, 2009; NCSS Task Force on Ethnic Studies Curriculum Guidelines, 1992). We better prepare students to function effectively in a democratic society when we help them understand that virtually every nation includes numerous cultures and that such diversity provides a richness of ideas and perspectives that will inevitably yield a more creative, productive society overall. Such understanding is reflected in the writing sample in Figure 4.3, written by a student who was attending a rural, culturally homogenous high school in New Hampshire. The student's words were genuine; after earning his diploma, he spent 2 years in a very different cultural environment—a community in rural Brazil—before attending college.

Teaching respect for diverse perspectives doesn't necessarily mean that we treat all beliefs as equally acceptable. For instance, we should certainly not embrace a culture that blatantly

Chapter 11 looks more closely at stereotype threat.

Into The Classroom

Addressing Students' Stereotypes and Prejudices

🍎 **Use curriculum materials that represent all cultures and ethnic groups as competent, legitimate participants in mainstream society, rather than as exotic curiosities who live in a separate world.**

A history teacher peruses a history textbook to make sure it portrays members of all ethnic groups in a nonstereotypical manner. He supplements the text with readings that highlight the important roles that members of various ethnic groups have played in history.

🍎 **Assign literature depicting peers from diverse cultural backgrounds.**

As part of a research project in England, several elementary school teachers read to students a series of stories involving close friendships between English children and refugees from other countries. Following this experimental intervention, the students express more positive attitudes toward refugee children than do control-group students who have not heard the stories.

🍎 **Explore the nature and complexity of various dialects.**

A high school language arts class examines some unique features of a local African American dialect, including various forms of the verb *to be*. For example, African American members of the class explain that the word *is* is often dropped in simple descriptive sentences (e.g., "He a handsome man") and that the word *be* is sometimes used to indicate a constant or frequently occurring characteristic (e.g., "He be talking" describes someone who talks a lot).

🍎 **Conduct class discussions about prejudice and racism that exist in the school and local community.**

A middle school in a suburban community creates a number of mixed-race focus groups in which students regularly convene to share their views about interracial relations at the school. Although some students of European American ancestry initially feel uncomfortable talking about this topic with their minority-group peers, once the ice has been broken, greater cross-cultural understanding and communication result.

🍎 **Expose students to successful role models from various ethnic backgrounds.**

A teacher invites several successful professionals from minority groups to speak with her class about their careers. When some students seem especially interested in one or more of these careers, she arranges for the students to spend time with the professionals in their workplaces.

🍎 **Assign small-group cooperative projects in which students from diverse backgrounds must combine their unique talents to achieve a common goal.**

A fourth-grade teacher has small cooperative groups design and conduct schoolwide surveys soliciting other students' opinions on various topics (e.g., ideas for school fundraisers, preferences for cafeteria menu items, etc.). The teacher intentionally creates groups that are culturally heterogeneous, knowing that the group members will draw on diverse friendship networks in seeking volunteers to take the surveys. In addition, he makes sure that every member of a group has something unique to offer in survey design or data analysis—perhaps knowledge of word processing software, artistic talent, or math skills.

🍎 **Emphasize that some people affiliate with two or more cultural groups and that individual members of any single group are often very different from one another in behaviors, beliefs, and values.**

In a geography unit on major world religions, a middle school teacher regularly points out that members of any single religion often have very different customs. "For example," he says, "some Muslim women dress in much the same way that women in this country do; others also wear head scarves in addition to regular, modern clothes; and still others dress in a burqa that covers everything except their hands. Usually the women wear a scarf or burqa to show modesty about their bodies. In fact, some Jewish women, too, wear head scarves to show that they are modest, but many others don't."

Sources: Adger et al., 2007; Barbarin, Mercado, & Jigjidsuren, 2010; Boutte & McCormick, 1992; L. Cameron, Rutland, Brown, & Douch, 2006 (refugee stories example); Dovidio & Gaertner, 1999; Gutiérrez & Rogoff, 2003; Hulit & Howard, 2006, pp. 345–346 (dialect example); Mohan, 2009; Oskamp, 2000; Pfeifer et al., 2007; K. Schultz et al., 2000 (focus groups example); Tatum, 1997.

---

violates some people's basic human rights. Respect does mean, however, that we and our students should try to understand another cultural group's behaviors within the context of its overall beliefs and assumptions.

Ideally, a democracy also provides a context in which students can bring about meaningful change. Students should be encouraged to challenge the status quo and strive for social justice—perhaps regarding such issues as substandard housing, poor voter turnout in certain neighborhoods, or misuse of natural resources (Ladson-Billings, 1995a; Lipman, 1995). For example, in some high schools in the Navajo Nation of the American Southwest, students have taken on controversial commercial practices (e.g., excessive tree cutting, landscape-scarring mining practices) that threaten their community's long-term well-being; they've conducted library research, interviewed community leaders, prepared written reports, and presented their findings at public meetings (Nelson-Barber & Estrin, 1995). Service learning

FIGURE 4.3 In an essay for his American history class, 16-year-old Randy reveals his appreciation of cultural differences.

> To me, diversity is not only a fact of life, but it is life. To be different and unique is what allows people to live a fulfilling life. To learn and admire other people's differences is perhaps one of the keys to life and without that key, there will be too many doors that will be locked, keeping you out and not allowing you to succeed. To learn that a majority of one kind in one place may be a minority of another kind in another place can help to initiate an outlook on life that promotes perspective and reason of any situation.

projects such as these seem to instill a "can-do" spirit and optimism that all citizens can have a significant impact on the quality of their own and other people's lives (Eccles, 2007; Kahne & Sporte, 2008; Tate, 1995).

> MyEdLab **Self-Check 4.1**
>
> MyEdLab **Application Exercise 4.1.** In this interactive exercise you can practice identifying cultural and ethnic differences among students.
>
> MyEdLab **Application Exercise 4.2.** In this interactive exercise you can practice applying what you have learned about teaching strategies that underlie culturally responsive teaching.

Gender Differences

In their academic abilities, boys and girls are probably more similar than you think. But in other respects they may be more different than you realize.

RESEARCH FINDINGS REGARDING GENDER DIFFERENCES

Researchers have identified a number of gender differences in the physical, cognitive, personal, and social domains.

PHYSICAL ACTIVITY AND MOTOR SKILLS

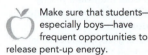 Make sure that students—especially boys—have frequent opportunities to release pent-up energy.

Generally, boys are temperamentally predisposed to be more active than girls. Thus, they have more trouble sitting still for long periods and are less likely to enjoy sedentary activities such as reading (W. O. Eaton & Enns, 1986; Newkirk, 2002). Before puberty, boys and girls seem to have similar *potential* for physical and psychomotor growth, although girls have a slight edge in fine motor skills (e.g., handwriting). But overall, boys develop their physical and motor skills more, perhaps through participation in organized sports (Eccles, 2005; J. R. Thomas & French, 1985). After puberty, boys have a biological advantage in height and muscular strength: They're taller and, because of increased levels of the male sex hormone testosterone, they're stronger (Halpern, 2006; Hyde, 2005; J. R. Thomas & French, 1985).

Such differences are hardly justification for favoring either gender when enhancing students' physical fitness, of course. Physical education curricula and sports programs should provide equal opportunities for boys and girls to maximize their motor skills and physical well-being.

COGNITIVE AND ACADEMIC ABILITIES

On average, boys and girls perform similarly on tests of general intelligence, in part because experts who construct the tests eliminate items that favor one group or the other (Halpern & LaMay, 2000). Researchers sometimes do find differences in more specific cognitive abilities, however. The most consistently observed gender difference is in **visual–spatial ability**, the ability to imagine and mentally manipulate two- and three-dimensional figures. As an example of what this ability involves, try the next exercise.

EXPERIENCING FIRSTHAND
MENTAL ROTATION

Are the three drawings shown here different rotations of the *same* object, or do they represent two or more *different* objects?

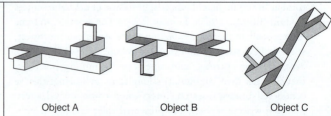

Object A   Object B   Object C

To correctly answer this question, you must "rotate" the objects in your head. If you mentally rotate Object B 180 degrees, you can see that it represents the same three-dimensional configuration as Object A. But if you rotate the right side of Object C down a bit and toward you, you can see that it's *not* the same as Object A; instead, it's a mirror image. Thus, Objects A and B are the same object; Object C is different. On average, males show greater proficiency in such visual–spatial thinking, even in infancy (Gallagher & Kaufman, 2005; Quinn & Liben, 2008). In contrast, females seem to have the advantage in certain verbal skills; for instance, girls have, on average, larger vocabularies and can more quickly think of the words they need to express their thoughts (Halpern, 2004, 2006; Halpern & LaMay, 2000; Lippa, 2002).

However, most gender differences in specific cognitive abilities tend to be *quite small,* with considerable overlap between the two groups (e.g., look once again at Figure 4.1). In addition, boys sometimes show greater *variability* in cognitive abilities than girls do, causing more boys than girls to demonstrate extremely high or low ability levels relative to their age-group (Halpern et al., 2007; Halpern & LaMay, 2000; Valla & Ceci, 2011). Instruction also may equalize some of these relatively small differences; for example, when female students receive instruction on how to select appropriate strategies to solve various spatial problems, the relations of visual–spatial gender differences to achievement are lessened (Stieff, Dixon, Ryu, Kumi, & Hegarty, 2014).

Even though ability levels may be similar, girls consistently earn higher grades in school (Halpern et al., 2007; Halpern & LaMay, 2000). If achievement is measured by achievement tests rather than grades, research findings are inconsistent. When differences are found, girls typically have an advantage in reading and writing, and after puberty boys tend to have the upper hand in complex mathematical problem solving (Halpern, 2006; Halpern & LaMay, 2000; Lindberg, Hyde, Petersen, & Linn, 2010; J. P. Robinson & Lubienski, 2011; Valla & Ceci, 2011). Not only are gender differences in visual–spatial, verbal, and mathematical performance quite small, but some researchers have found them to be getting *smaller* in recent years. In other words, boys and girls are becoming increasingly similar in their academic performance (Hyde, Lindberg, Linn, Ellis, & Williams, 2008; Leaper & Friedman, 2007; Spelke, 2005). Thus, in general, we should expect boys and girls to have similar academic aptitudes for different subject areas.

Nevertheless, recent research suggests that some gender differences in mathematics are attributable to the fact that female students are more likely to worry and experience anxiety than are males, and such feelings can interfere with those female students' ability to focus on and effectively think about complex mathematics problems (Ganley & Vasilyeva, 2014). In addition, results of a recent study indicate that when female students take a math test immediately before taking a verbal test, they tend to perform worse than do males on the math test; however, when the students take the verbal test first, the females perform as well or better than males on the math test (Smeding, Dumas, Loose, & Régner, 2013). This is most likely because the females experienced stereotype threat when the math test was presented first, and this affected their performance. Therefore, we should be aware that gender differences can result from many causes, including some seemingly insignificant instructional decisions.

EXPERIENCE WITH TECHNOLOGY

As societies worldwide are gaining increasing access to computers and wireless technologies, boys and girls alike are becoming increasingly proficient with technology—for example, they're apt to stay in frequent contact with peers by texting and sending photographs on cell phones and by posting messages on social networking websites such as Facebook and Instagram (Greenhow, Robelia, & Hughes, 2009; Valkenburg & Peter, 2009). But overall, boys seem to spend more of their leisure time with technology than girls do. Boys are more likely to play video games, a pastime that may interfere with their reading and writing development but enhances their visual–spatial ability and probably also their comfort and expertise with computers (Feng, Spence, & Pratt, 2007; Ivory, 2006; Lucas & Sherry, 2004; Weis & Cerankosky, 2010). When using educational technology in school, boys may be more confident initially because they may have had more experience using similar technology; however, girls adapt well and generally benefit equally from educational technology (Nietfeld, Shores, & Hoffmann, 2014).

MOTIVATION IN ACADEMIC ACTIVITIES

On average, girls are more concerned about doing well in school: They're more engaged in classroom activities, more diligent in completing school assignments, and more likely to graduate

MyEdLab
Video Example 4.2.
Most gender differences in specific cognitive abilities are small. Effective, unbiased instruction may equalize differences.

Expect boys and girls to have similar aptitudes for all academic subject areas.

We will discuss motivation in much greater detail in Chapters 10 and 11.

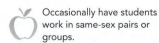

Make a special effort to motivate boys—for instance, by incorporating their personal interests into classroom activities.

Help girls understand that taking academic risks and making mistakes reflect their willingness to take on challenges and stretch their abilities in new directions.

Chapter 3 examines aggression in greater detail.

Communicate that showing emotion is a natural human trait that is appropriate for males as well as females.

Accommodate girls' affiliative nature by providing numerous opportunities for cooperative group work.

Occasionally have students work in same-sex pairs or groups.

from high school (H. M. Marks, 2000; Marsh, Martin, & Cheng, 2008; McCall, 1994; J. P. Robinson & Lubienski, 2011). Furthermore, girls are more interested in getting a college education than are boys, and in many countries more females than males earn college degrees (Halpern et al., 2007; National Science Foundation, 2007). However, this eagerness to achieve academically leads girls to prefer tasks at which they know they can succeed, and some find academic failure devastating. On average, boys are more willing to take on academic challenges and risks and more likely to take their failures in stride (Dweck, 2000; Yu, Elder, & Urdan, 1995).

SENSE OF SELF

Beginning in the upper elementary or middle school grades, boys appear to have a slightly more positive sense of self than do girls. This gender difference seems to be partly due to boys' tendency to *over*estimate their abilities and possibly also to girls' tendency to *under*estimate theirs (Hyde, 2007; Lundeberg & Mohan, 2009; Pajares, 2005). Boys' and girls' self-perceptions also tend to be consistent with stereotypes about what males and females are good at, especially in adolescence. Boys tend to rate themselves more highly in mathematics and sports, whereas girls tend to rate themselves more highly in reading and social studies. Such differences in self-perceptions persist even when boys' and girls' actual ability levels are *equal* (D. A. Cole, Martin, Peeke, Seroczynski, & Fier, 1999; Herbert & Stipek, 2005; Leaper & Friedman, 2007; Wigfield, Byrnes, & Eccles, 2006).

INTERPERSONAL BEHAVIORS AND RELATIONSHIPS

One of the most consistently observed gender differences involves aggression. In early childhood and throughout the elementary and secondary school years, boys are more physically aggressive than girls, with the difference being especially large for *unprovoked* aggression (Card, Stucky, Sawalani, & Little, 2008; Hyde, 2007; Pellegrini, 2011). However, girls can be equally aggressive in a nonphysical way—for instance, by spreading rumors or snubbing peers (Crick, Grotpeter, & Bigbee, 2002; French, Jansen, & Pidada, 2002; Pellegrini & Archer, 2005). Some of their victims can be emotionally devastated by such treatment (Rudolph, Caldwell, & Conley, 2005). Girls also may be more likely than boys to engage in cyberbullying by using the Internet (Connell, Schell-Busey, Pearce, & Negro, 2013).

Consistent differences are also seen in boys' and girls' interpersonal activities and relationships. Boys tend to congregate in large groups that engage in rough-and-tumble play, organized group games, and physical risk-taking activities (Maccoby, 2002; Pellegrini, Kato, Blatchford, & Baines, 2002; A. J. Rose & Smith, 2009). They enjoy competition and can be fairly assertive in their efforts to achieve their goals (Benenson et al., 2002; Eisenberg, Martin, & Fabes, 1996; Maccoby, 2002). They may often try to hide their true emotions in social situations, putting up a tough, "nothing-can-bother-me" front (Lippa, 2002; Pollack, 2006).

Whereas boys are apt to be competitive, girls are more likely to be affiliative and cooperative. Thus, they tend to form closer relationships with their teachers and to achieve at higher levels when classroom activities involve cooperation rather than competition (Inglehart, Brown, & Vida, 1994; Wentzel, Battle, Russell, & Looney, 2010). When working with instructional software, girls like to form relationships with their virtual "teachers," and those relationships, even though they are with a computer-generated character, may help to improve attitudes and motivation in subjects such as mathematics (Kim & Lim, 2013). Girls also seem to be more attuned to others' mental states and more sensitive to the subtle, nonverbal messages—the body language—that others communicate (Bosacki, 2000; Deaux, 1984). Girls spend much of their leisure time with one or two close friends, with whom they may share their innermost thoughts and feelings (Leaper & Friedman, 2007; A. J. Rose & Smith, 2009). Although girls can be assertive in making their wishes known, they're also concerned about resolving conflicts and maintaining group harmony, and so they may sometimes subordinate their own needs to those of others (Benenson et al., 2002; Leaper & Friedman, 2007; Rudolph et al., 2005).

CLASSROOM BEHAVIORS

In part because boys tend to be physically more active than girls, they're more likely to misbehave in class (Altermatt, Jovanovic, & Perry, 1998; Gay, 2006; Sadker & Sadker, 1994). Boys talk more and ask more questions, sometimes without waiting to be called on. They also tend to dominate small-group discussions and work sessions. Girls are more reticent classroom participants. They're less likely to publicly volunteer ideas and ask questions, perhaps for fear of looking stupid or perhaps because they worry that looking too smart will reduce their popularity (Jovanovic & King, 1998; Sadker & Sadker, 1994; Théberge, 1994; Wentzel, 2009). Girls are more likely to express their opinions in small-group rather than large-group discussions, and they're more likely to assume the role of leader (thereby developing valuable leadership skills) in same-sex groups (Fennema, 1987; MacLean, Sasse, Keating, Stewart, & Miller, 1995; Théberge, 1994).

CAREER ASPIRATIONS

Historically, boys have had more ambitious career aspirations than girls have. In recent years, however, many girls—especially those in Western countries—have also begun to set their sights on challenging professions. Often, boys and girls alike focus on careers that are stereotypically "appropriate" for their gender, in part because they have greater self-confidence about their ability to succeed in such careers (Bandura, Barbaranelli, Caprara, & Pastorelli, 2001; Leaper & Friedman, 2007; Weisgram, Bigler, & Liben, 2010). Students' general life goals come into the picture as well: Girls are more likely than boys to consider how their career choices might mesh with their desires to work with people (rather than objects) and to raise a family (Diekman, Brown, Johnston, & Clark, 2010; Eccles, 2009).

Some gender differences are especially prevalent for particular age-groups. Table 4.1 identifies differences you're apt to see at various grade levels and offers relevant classroom strategies for accommodating these differences.

ORIGINS OF GENDER DIFFERENCES

Obviously, heredity determines basic physical differences between males and females; some are present at birth, some emerge at puberty. And because of inherited differences in sex-related hormones—especially estrogen for girls and testosterone for boys—girls reach puberty earlier and boys eventually become taller and stronger. Hormones may account for certain nonphysical gender differences as well. The gender difference in physical aggression appears to be related to testosterone levels (Lippa, 2002; S. Moore & Rosenthal, 2006). Hormones may also play a role in the small differences observed in visual–spatial and verbal abilities, possibly by affecting neurological development in different areas of the brain (Valla & Ceci, 2011; Vuoksimaa et al., 2010). Hormones even seem to influence children's preferences for male-stereotypical versus female-stereotypical behaviors (Auyeung et al., 2009; Hines et al., 2002).

Yet environmental factors clearly play a role as well, often by interacting with and amplifying existing biology-based gender differences (Lippa, 2002; Nuttall, Casey, & Pezaris, 2005). Virtually every culture teaches children that some behaviors are more appropriate for males and others more appropriate for females, as the following exercise may show you.

EXPERIENCING FIRSTHAND
PICTURE THIS #2

Form a picture in your mind of each of the following individuals. Make note of the *first* image that comes to mind in each case:

Secretary	Scientist
Bank president	Fashion model
Elementary school teacher	Building contractor

Which individuals did you picture as male, and which did you picture as female?

If you're like most people, your secretary, teacher, and fashion model were females, and your bank president, scientist, and building contractor were males. Gender stereotypes persist throughout our society, and even preschool children are aware of them (Bornholt, Goodnow, & Cooney, 1994; Eisenberg et al., 1996; Nosek & Smyth, 2011).

Numerous aspects of society conspire to socialize growing children to conform to gender stereotypes. For example, many adults believe—and communicate the message—that boys are "naturally" better in some domains (e.g., math) and that girls are "naturally" better in others

DEVELOPMENTAL TRENDS

TABLE 4.1 • Gender-Related Characteristics at Different Grade Levels

GRADE LEVEL	AGE-TYPICAL CHARACTERISTICS	EXAMPLE	SUGGESTED STRATEGIES
K–2	• Physical abilities, general intelligence, and more specific cognitive abilities roughly equivalent for boys and girls • More self-control in girls than in boys, leading to girls' easier adjustment to a classroom environment • Rigid stereotypes about gender-appropriate behavior; eagerness to conform to these stereotypes • Play groups largely segregated by gender • Different themes in fantasy play (e.g., boys depict heroism, girls depict romance); play activities more active and forceful for boys than for girls	Most of the girls in a first-grade class can sit still during small-group reading instruction, but some of the boys quickly become fidgety and distracted. The boys are more likely to be attentive in their reading groups if they can physically act out a story they're reading.	• Expect and encourage equal achievement in all areas of the academic curriculum. • Give students whatever structure they may need to stay on task in order to acquire basic skills, but also give them numerous opportunities to release pent-up energy. • Provide materials for a wide range of play activities (e.g., household items, dress-up clothes, toy trucks, building blocks, balls). • Monitor students' play activities for potentially dangerous behaviors; provide guidance about which actions are and are not safe.
3–5	• Gender differences in self-evaluations of math ability, with boys rating themselves more highly than girls despite equal math achievement • Play groups largely segregated by gender • Organized large-group games more common for boys than for girls • More competition, aggression, and risk taking in boys than in girls • Onset of puberty earlier for girls (average age 10) • Tendency for some early-maturing girls to feel out of sync with peers, putting them at greater risk for depression	During recess, many of the boys in a fourth-grade class organize a game of baseball or soccer. A few girls join in, but most of the girls stand on the sidelines and talk with one or two friends.	• Assure students that boys and girls have equal potential in all areas of the academic curriculum. • Provide materials for group games (balls, bats, soccer goal nets, etc.). • Set and enforce reasonable limits on play behaviors so that students' physical safety is ensured. • Be especially sensitive and supportive as girls show signs of puberty (e.g., allow trips to the restroom as needed).
6–8	• Onset of puberty later for boys (average age 11½) • Greater physical ability for boys than for girls; participation in sports more widespread and prestigious for boys • Emergence of gender differences in overall self-esteem and assessments of physical attractiveness and athletic competence, with self-ratings being higher for boys and preoccupation with physical appearance being greater for girls • Increasing flexibility about which behaviors are gender-appropriate, especially for girls • Tendency for boys' social groups to be larger and less intimate than girls' • More emotional distress for girls than for boys when interpersonal relationships go badly; tendency for boys to try to hide feelings of sadness and distress	A student named Jason explains how he often hides his feelings at school: "If something happens to you, you have to say, 'Yeah, no big deal,' even when you're really hurting . . . I've punched so many lockers in my life, it's not even funny. When I get home, I'll cry about it."	• Respect students' modesty and need for privacy when they must change clothes or take a shower in physical education or after-school sports. • Encourage students to gain skills in domains stereotypically associated with the other gender (e.g., teach cooking and woodworking to boys and girls alike). • Encourage both boys and girls to pursue extracurricular sports activities; encourage attendance at both boys' and girls' sports events. • In appropriate contexts, teach good grooming habits and other skills for presenting oneself well to others. • Communicate to boys that occasionally showing emotion and vulnerability is both manly and healthy.
9–12	• Gradual improvement in girls' self-assessments of physical attractiveness • Greater interest in a college education among girls than among boys • Boys more likely to avoid academic work than girls. • Tendency for boys to aspire more to hands-on professions (e.g., working with tools and machines) and for girls to aspire more to social or artistic occupations (e.g., teaching, counseling, writing) • Prosocial behavior seen more frequently in girls than in boys, despite equal ability to act prosocially • Substance abuse and casual sexual intercourse more common in boys than in girls • Depression and eating disorders more common in girls than in boys	Most members of a high school service club are girls. The club plans two community service projects for the year: making monthly after-school trips to a local nursing home and conducting a schoolwide fundraiser to buy holiday gifts for low-income children.	• Encourage students to cross stereotypical boundaries in course selection (e.g., girls taking advanced math, boys taking creative writing). • Provide information about the benefits of a college education (e.g., invite recent high school graduates and adult college graduates from similar cultural groups to those of the student population to come and share their college experiences). • Expose students to diverse occupations and professions through guest lectures, trips to community businesses and agencies, and the like. • Work with colleagues and parents to vigorously address unhealthful and risky out-of-school behaviors. • Alert the school counselor when you suspect substance abuse, serious depression, an eating disorder, or some other potentially life-threatening condition.

Sources: E. M. Anderman, 2012; Benenson & Christakos, 2003; Binns, Steinberg, Amorosi, & Cuevas, 1997; Bussey & Bandura, 1992; Card, Stucky, Sawalani, & Little, 2008; D. A. Cole et al., 2001; Crouter, Whiteman, McHale, & Osgood, 2007; Davenport et al., 1998; Davila, 2008; Eisenberg et al., 1996; Evans-Winters & Ivie, 2009; Fabes, Martin, & Hanish, 2003; M. E. Ford, 1996; Grusec & Hastings, 2007; Halpern, 2004, 2006; Halpern et al., 2007; Hankin, Mermelstein, & Roesch, 2007; M. S. Hardy, 2002; J. R. Harris, 1995; Harter, 1999; Hayward, 2003; Herbert & Stipek, 2005; Hyde, 2005; Hyde & Durik, 2005; Leaper & Friedman, 2007; Liben & Bigler, 2002; Lippa, 2002; Maccoby, 2002; Matthews, Ponitz, & Morrison, 2009; T. M. McDevitt & Ormrod, 2013; S. Moore & Rosenthal, 2006; Passolunghi, Rueda Ferreira, & Tomasetto, 2014; Pollack, 2006, p. 72 (Jason example); Ponitz, Rimm-Kaufman, Brock, & Nathanson, 2009; M. Rhodes & Gelman, 2008; Rogoff, 2003; A. J. Rose & Smith, 2009; Rudolph et al., 2005; R. M. Ryan & Kuczkowski, 1994; Sadker & Sadker, 1994; Seiffge-Krenke, Aunola, & Nurmi, 2009; Skoog, & Stattin, 2014; J. R. Thomas & French, 1985; Wigfield, Byrnes, & Eccles, 2006; Wigfield, Eccles, & Pintrich, 1996; Zambo & Brozo, 2009 (reading group example).

(e.g., reading), even in cases where no gender differences in achievement exist (Bleeker & Jacobs, 2004; Eccles, 2009; Herbert & Stipek, 2005). The toys that children get also are often marketed specifically for boys and girls; results of a recent study indicated that toys marketed on the Disney store website vary greatly by color, with bold-colored toys (e.g., red, black, brown, or gray) marketed toward boys, and pastel-colored toys (e.g., pink and purple) marketed toward girls (Auster & Mansbach, 2012). Such gender-stereotypical toys and games can also have impact: The dolls and board games that girls often get foster verbal and social skills, whereas the building blocks and soccer balls that boys get are more apt to foster visual–spatial skills (Feng et al., 2007; Frost, Shin, & Jacobs, 1998; Liss, 1983; Lytton & Romney, 1991).

Boys' and girls' personality characteristics, too, are socialized to some degree. Especially in cultural groups that espouse traditional gender roles, boys are often reinforced—by adults and peers alike—for being assertive and aggressive, whereas girls are encouraged to be restrained and nurturing (Leaper & Friedman, 2007; Manning & Baruth, 2009; Rothbart, 2011). And television and video games often portray males as aggressive leaders and successful problem solvers, whereas females are depicted as demure, obedient followers (Furnham & Mak, 1999; Leaper & Friedman, 2007; M. K. Miller & Summers, 2007; T. L. Thompson & Zerbinos, 1995).

As young children become increasingly aware of the typical characteristics and behaviors of boys, girls, men, and women, they gradually pull their knowledge together into self-constructed understandings, or gender schemas, of how males and females are different. These gender schemas, in turn, become part of their sense of self and guide them in their choices and behaviors. By the time children reach school age, much of the pressure to act "appropriately" for their gender comes from within rather than from others (Bem, 1981; Eccles, 2009; Ruble, Martin, & Berenbaum, 2006).

Because gender schemas are self-constructed, their contents vary considerably from one individual to another (Liben & Bigler, 2002). For example, in adolescence some girls incorporate into their "female" schema unrealistic standards of beauty presented in popular media (films, fashion magazines, Internet sites, etc.). As girls compare themselves to these standards, they almost invariably come up short, and their self-assessments of physical attractiveness decline. In an effort to achieve the super-thin bodies they believe to be ideal, they may fall victim to eating disorders (Attie, Brooks-Gunn, & Petersen, 1990; Weichold, Silbereisen, & Schmitt-Rodermund, 2003). Likewise, some teenage boys go out of their way to meet self-constructed macho standards of male behavior by putting on a tough-guy act at school and bragging (perhaps accurately, but more often not) about their many sexual conquests (Pollack, 2006; K. M. Williams, 2001a).

Not all students have rigid or unrealistic stereotypes of what their gender should be like, of course. In fact, as students get older, many become increasingly flexible about what males and females can and should do. Those with more flexible gender schemas are more likely to pursue counterstereotypical interests and career paths (Liben & Bigler, 2002; C. L. Martin & Ruble, 2004).

MAKING APPROPRIATE ACCOMMODATIONS FOR GENDER DIFFERENCES

Despite many teachers' best intentions to treat male and female students equitably, subtle inequities continue. For example, teachers tend to give more attention to boys, partly because boys ask more questions and present more discipline problems. Teachers give boys more feedback—praise and criticism alike—than they give girls (Altermatt et al., 1998; Eisenberg et al., 1996; Gay, 2006; Halpern et al., 2007; S. M. Jones & Dindia, 2004). Teachers also tend to overestimate boys' abilities and underestimate girls' abilities in some subject areas, such as math (American Friends of Tel Aviv University, 2015).

The Into the Classroom feature "Promoting Gender Equity" offers several general suggestions for equitably fostering the learning and development of both sexes. At the same time, gender differences sometimes *do* warrant differential treatment of girls and boys. For example, girls are likely to improve their visual–spatial ability if we give them frequent opportunities to engage in activities requiring visual–spatial thinking (B. M. Casey et al., 2008; Gallagher & Kaufman, 2005). Girls also are more likely to benefit from computer software used during mathematics instruction when such programs include female characters and when those programs provide help options for users (Arroyo, Burleson, Tai, Muldner, & Woolf, 2013). Meanwhile, boys are more likely to improve their literacy skills if we allow them to pursue typical "boy" interests (e.g., sports, adventure) while reading and writing (Newkirk, 2002). In recent years, some educators have advocated for single-sex schools.

Self-imposed adherence to gender stereotypes is an example of self-socialization, a concept described in Chapter 3.

Acknowledge that some differential treatment of girls and boys is appropriate, especially if it helps to *reduce* gender gaps in particular abilities and predispositions.

Into The Classroom

Promoting Gender Equity

🍎 **Use your knowledge of typical gender differences to create greater equity for males and females, not to form expectations about how well males and females are likely to perform in various activities.**
An elementary physical education teacher realizes that most of the girls in her class probably haven't had as much experience as the boys in throwing a baseball or softball overhand, so she gives the girls extra instruction and practice in the overhand throw.

🍎 **When planning lessons and instructional strategies, consider typical interests and activity levels of both boys and girls.**
A sixth-grade math teacher teams up with his school's information technology teacher to create a month-long unit in which students learn how to use Game Maker, software that enables them to create simple video games using a variety of animated characters, graphics, and background music. The students then work in small groups to design games that will help them practice a particular mathematical concept or skill. At the end of the unit, each group demonstrates its game for the class, and the teachers post the games to their class websites so that students can play them at home.

🍎 **Use curriculum materials that represent both genders in a positive and competent light; include materials that portray both genders competently engaging in counterstereotypical behaviors.**
An English teacher assigns Harper Lee's *To Kill a Mockingbird*, in which an attorney named Atticus Finch is portrayed as a gentle, affectionate, and compassionate man, and his daughter Scout is portrayed as a courageous and adventuresome 8-year-old. The teacher also assigns Zora Neale Hurston's *Their Eyes Were Watching God*, in which an African American woman grows from a teenager who depends on others to meet her needs into a self-sufficient woman who can easily fend for herself.

🍎 **Monitor yourself to see whether you are unintentionally treating boys and girls in ways that limit the learning opportunities of one gender.**
A chemistry teacher decides to count the number of times he calls on boys and girls during class. He finds that he calls on boys more than three times as frequently as girls, partly because the boys raise their hands more often. Therefore he institutes a new procedure: He alternates between boys and girls when he calls on students, and he sometimes calls on students who aren't raising their hands.

Although there may be some social benefits to such settings, however, math and science achievement do not appear to be affected by attending a single-sex school (Pahlke, Hyde, & Mertz, 2013).

We must also help students recognize that gender stereotypes are just that—*stereotypes*—and don't necessarily limit what males and females can or should be. For example, we can:

🍎 Expose students to same-gender adults and peers who excel in domains commonly associated with the opposite gender.

🍎 Talk about the importance of all academic subject areas for students' future success.

🍎 Explain the historical roots of stereotypes. For instance, explain that differing expectations for males and females are a holdover from an era when many jobs outside the home required considerable strength (and thus were better suited for men) and jobs inside the home could easily be combined with breast-feeding (and thus were better suited for women).

🍎 Engage students in discussions about the adverse consequences of rigid gender roles—noting, for example, that adhering to such roles limits people's options and results in a lot of talent going to waste. (Bem, 1983, 1984; Evans-Winters & Ivie, 2009; Fennema, 1987; Huguet & Régner, 2007; A. Kelly & Smail, 1986; Pollack, 2006)

> MyEdLab **Self-Check 4.2**
>
> MyEdLab **Application Exercise 4.3.** In this interactive exercise you can practice identifying strategies for accommodating gender differences in the classroom.

Socioeconomic Differences

The concept of socioeconomic status (SES) encompasses a number of variables, including family income, parents' education levels, and parents' occupations. A family's socioeconomic status—whether high-SES, middle-SES, or low-SES—gives us a sense of family members' standing in the community: what type of neighborhood they live in, how much influence they have on political decision making, what educational opportunities are available to them, what resources they have available in their homes, and so on.

Students' school performance is correlated with their socioeconomic status: Higher-SES students tend to have higher academic achievement, and lower-SES students tend to be at greater risk for dropping out of school (J.-S. Lee & Bowen, 2006; Sirin, 2005; Tucker-Drob, 2013). As students from lower-SES families move through the grade levels, they tend to fall further and further behind their higher-SES peers (American Psychological Association, 2012; Farkas, 2008; Jimerson, Egeland, & Teo, 1999). Lower-SES students often live in neighborhoods with fewer economic and educational resources, both of which contribute to lower achievement for these students (Dupere, Leventhal, Crosnoe, & Dion, 2010). When researchers find achievement differences among students from different ethnic groups, the differences in the students' socioeconomic status—*not* their cultural differences—seem to be mostly to blame (Byrnes, 2003; N. E. Hill, Bush, & Roosa, 2003; Murdock, 2000).

Life certainly isn't perfect for students from high-SES homes (Luthar, 2006; Luthar & Latendresse, 2005). Some high-income parents have such high expectations for their children's achievement that the children suffer from significant anxiety and depression. In addition, some high-income parents have demanding jobs that keep them both physically and emotionally distant from their children, thereby limiting the guidance and support they provide. But by and large it's children who live in poverty, especially *chronic* poverty, who face the most significant obstacles to academic success and personal well-being.

EXPERIENCING FIRSTHAND
HOMEWORK ON THE INTERNET

Imagine that you are teaching fifth grade in an elementary school that has adopted a fully online mathematics program. Your school has adequate technology resources, and your students are able to work on computers in school every day. In addition, all of the homework assignments are completed online.

Cindy, a student in your class, approaches you and says "I don't have Internet at home." She then adds, "I don't even have a computer; my family says we can't afford one."

What should you do?

Unfortunately, this situation is not uncommon. As more schools are adopting curricula that are only provided online, access to the Internet is becoming essential. Nevertheless, students from low-SES neighborhoods are less likely to have this access. For some families, the only alternative is to take their children to local libraries to do their homework, and use computers that are available at those locations. Nevertheless, having to take a child to a library every night to do homework may be very stressful, particularly for parents who also work full time or do not have transportation. As teachers, we can provide students like Cindy with alternative resources. For example, we can print out the assignments for these students and send home paper copies.

CHALLENGES ASSOCIATED WITH POVERTY

Many, many children grow up in poverty, including more than *16 million* children (22%) in the United States (U.S. Census Bureau, 2010). Some of these children live in inner-city neighborhoods, but others live in rural areas or in modest apartments in wealthy suburbs. Some come from families that can meet life's basic necessities (e.g., food, warm clothing, adequate shelter) but have little money left over for luxuries. Many others live in extreme poverty; these students are the ones most at risk for academic failure and thus most in need of our attention and support.

Several factors tend to contribute to the generally lower school achievement of low-SES students. Students who face only one or two of these challenges often do quite well in school, but those who face many or all of them are at high risk for academic failure and other negative outcomes (Becker & Luthar, 2002; Gerard & Buehler, 2004; Grissmer, Williamson, Kirby, & Berends, 1998).

Poor nutrition and health.   Lower-income families have fewer financial resources to ensure that their children have adequate nutrition and health care. Poor nutrition in the early years of life (including the 9 months before birth) can lead to impairments in children's attention, memory, and learning ability (Aboud & Yousafzai, 2015; Noble, Tottenham, & Casey, 2005). Poor nutrition seems to influence school achievement both directly—for example, by hampering early brain development—and indirectly—for example, by leaving children listless and inattentive in class (Ashiabi & O'Neal, 2008; Sigman & Whaley, 1998). And inadequate health care means that some conditions that interfere with school attendance and performance, such as asthma and hearing problems, go unaddressed (Berliner, 2005).

Inadequate housing and frequent moves.   Many poor children live in tight quarters, perhaps sharing one or two rooms with several other family members (Hawkins, 1997; Hernandez, Denton, & Macartney, 2008). Furthermore, children who move frequently from one rental apartment to another must often change schools as well. In the process they lose existing social support networks—both with teachers and with peers—and may miss lessons on fundamental academic skills (Croninger & Valli, 2009; Gruman, Harachi, Abbott, Catalano, & Fleming, 2008; Hattie, 2009).

Exposure to toxic substances.   Especially when children live in poor, inner-city neighborhoods, their surroundings may expose them to excessive levels of environmental toxins that can seriously jeopardize their health and brain development (Hubbs-Tait, Nation, Krebs, & Bellinger, 2005; Koger, Schettler, & Weiss, 2005). For example, in old, badly maintained apartment buildings, children may be exposed to lead in the dust from deteriorating paint. In addition, the city water supply may contain pesticides or industrial waste, and the local air may be polluted by power plants and industrial incinerators.

Unhealthy social environments.   On average, low-SES neighborhoods and communities have higher frequencies of violence and vandalism, greater prevalence of alcoholism and drug abuse, and greater numbers of antisocial peers. Furthermore, there are fewer productive outlets for leisure time—libraries, recreation centers, sports leagues, and so on—and fewer positive adult role models. Such factors appear to be partly responsible for the lower academic achievement of students who live in poverty (Aikens & Barbarin, 2008; T. D. Cook, Herman, Phillips, & Settersten, 2002; Duncan & Magnuson, 2005; Leventhal & Brooks-Gunn, 2000; Milam, Furr-Holden, & Leaf, 2010; Nettles, Caughy, & O'Campo, 2008).

Emotional stress.   Students at all income levels experience stressful conditions at one time or another, but students from low-income families have more than their share. On average, low-SES homes are more chaotic and unpredictable than affluent ones. Children may wonder where their next meal is coming from or when the landlord might evict them for not paying rent. The preponderance of single-parent homes among low-SES families can come into play as well: A single parent may be too distracted by personal problems to offer much affection or consistent discipline. As a result of such factors, students from low-SES families show higher-than-average rates of depression and other emotional problems (Crosnoe & Cooper, 2010; G. W. Evans, Gonnella, Marcynyszyn, Gentile, & Salpekar, 2005; Foulds, Wells, & Mulder, 2014; Morales & Guerra, 2006; Parke et al., 2004). Sometimes, too, chronic stress adversely affects students' physical development, which in turn can hamper their cognitive development (G. W. Evans & Schamberg, 2009).

Not all children from low-income homes live in chronically stressful conditions, of course, and those whose families provide consistent support, guidance, and discipline generally enjoy good mental health (N. E. Hill et al., 2003; M. O. Wright & Masten, 2006). Nevertheless, we should continually be on the lookout for signs that certain students are experiencing unusual stress at home and then provide whatever support we can. In some instances effective support may involve nothing more than being a willing listener. In other cases we may want to consult with a school counselor, school psychologist, or social worker about possible support systems at school and resources in the local community.

Gaps in background knowledge.   Some students from low-SES families lack the basic knowledge and skills (e.g., knowledge of letters and numbers) on which successful school learning so often depends (Aikens & Barbarin, 2008; Brooks-Gunn, Linver, & Fauth, 2005; Siegler, 2008).

Help families apply for free and reduced-cost meal programs. Refer students with chronic health problems to the school nurse.

Provide emotional support and appropriate referrals when students seem to be undergoing exceptional stress at home.

Access to early educational opportunities that might foster such skills—books, computers, trips to zoos and museums, and so on—is always somewhat dependent on a family's financial resources. In addition, some parents have few basic academic skills that they might share with their children. However, as always, we must be careful not to overgeneralize. Some low-income parents have considerable education (perhaps a college degree) and may be well equipped to read to their children and provide other enriching educational experiences (Goldenberg, 2001; Raikes et al., 2006; Sidel, 1996).

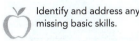
Identify and address any missing basic skills.

Lower-quality schools.   Unfortunately, the students who most need good schools are often least likely to have them. Schools in low-income neighborhoods and communities tend to receive less funding and, as a result, are often poorly equipped and maintained. Teacher turnover rates are high in these schools, and disciplinary tactics tend to be more harsh and less effective. Furthermore, some teachers at these schools have low expectations for students, offering a less-challenging curriculum, assigning less homework, and providing fewer opportunities to develop advanced thinking skills than do teachers in wealthier school districts (G. W. Evans, 2004; McLoyd, 1998; Pianta & Hamre, 2009; Raudenbush, 2009).

Of course, schools in low-income school districts don't have to be this way. In fact, we teachers can make a *huge* difference in the quality of children's educational experiences at even the poorest of schools. Consider a teacher whom researchers called Miss A (E. Pedersen, Faucher, & Eaton, 1978):

> Miss A taught at Ray School, an elementary school in a large, North American city. The school building—constructed like a fortress, with iron bars on its windows—was hardly appealing or welcoming. Its neighbors included old tenement buildings, a junkyard, and a brothel. Fewer than 10% of its students eventually completed high school.
>
> Nonetheless, Miss A worked wonders with the students in her first-grade classes. She showed obvious affection for them, insisted on appropriate behavior without ever losing her temper, and shared her lunch with those who hadn't brought one. She continually hammered home the importance of learning and education and had high expectations for achievement. She made sure her students learned to read, and she stayed after school with them whenever they needed extra help.
>
> Miss A's students got higher grades than students in other classes not only in their first-grade year but also for several years after that. On average, their IQ scores went *up* between third and sixth grade (one girl's score changed from 93 to 126), whereas the IQs of most students at Ray School went down. When researchers tracked down some of Miss A's students many years later, they found that these students were far more financially and professionally successful than the typical Ray graduate. And every single one of them remembered her name.

Be optimistic that you *can* make a difference in students' lives.

FOSTERING RESILIENCE

Thanks in part to teachers like Miss A, many students of low-income families succeed in school despite exceptional hardships. Some are **resilient students** who acquire characteristics and coping skills that help them rise above their adverse circumstances. As a group, resilient students have likable personalities, a positive sense of self, and ambitious goals, and they believe that success comes with hard work and a good education (S. Goldstein & Brooks, 2006; Schoon, 2006; Werner & Smith, 2001).

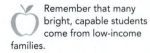
Remember that many bright, capable students come from low-income families.

Researchers have learned a great deal about factors that can foster resilience in students from challenging backgrounds. With their findings in mind, we offer the following suggestions.

Be a dependable source of academic and emotional support. Resilient students usually have one or more individuals in their lives whom they trust and can turn to in difficult times (Masten, 2001; McLoyd, 1998; Werner, 1995, 2006). For example, resilient students often mention teachers who have taken a personal interest in them and been instrumental in their school success (R. M. Clark, 1983; McMillan & Reed, 1994; D. A. O'Donnell, Schwab-Stone, & Muyeed, 2002). As teachers, we're most likely to promote resilience in low-SES students when we show that we like and respect them, are available and willing to listen to their concerns, hold high expectations for their performance, and provide the encouragement

MyEdLab
Video Example 4.3.

Students living in poverty face many challenges. Their basic needs for food, shelter, and clothing may not be met. They often move and change schools, experience emotional stress, and develop gaps in academic knowledge. Teachers can foster resilience by developing caring relationships.

and support they need to succeed both inside and outside the classroom (Kincheloe, 2009; Masten & Coatsworth, 1998; Milner, 2006; Schoon, 2006).

🍎 *Build on students' strengths.* Although some students from lower-SES backgrounds may lag behind in basic academic skills, they're apt to bring many strengths to the classroom. For example, these students are often quite clever at improvising with everyday objects. If they hold part-time jobs to help their families make ends meet, they may have a good understanding of the working world. If they are children of single, working parents, they may know far more than their classmates about cooking, cleaning house, and taking care of younger siblings. Their own scarce resources are likely to have instilled genuine empathy for and generosity toward other people in need. And many of these students are quite knowledgeable about certain aspects of popular culture—characters and plot lines in television shows, lyrics from current songs, and so on (Freedom Writers, 1999; Kraus, Piff, & Keltner, 2011; Lareau, 2003; Torrance, 1995).

As teachers, then, we must remember that students who have grown up in poverty may, in some respects, have more knowledge and skills than their economically advantaged peers. Such knowledge and skills can often provide a basis for teaching classroom subject matter (Schoon, 2006; Varelas & Pappas, 2006). Furthermore, students who are willing to talk about challenges they have faced can sensitize their classmates to serious inequities in today's society.

🍎 *Identify and provide missing resources and experiences important for successful learning.* Some students from very poor families lack basic essentials—such as nutritious meals, warm clothing, adequate health care, and school supplies—that will be important for their academic success. Many government programs and community agencies can help to provide such essentials. School districts offer free and reduced-cost meal programs for children from low-income families. Charitable organizations often distribute warm winter jackets gathered from annual clothing drives. Many communities have low-cost health clinics. And some office supply stores and large discount chains donate notebooks, pens, and other school supplies to children who need them.

Beyond connecting low-income students and families with community resources, we should identify any basic experiences that students may not have had. Field trips to zoos, farms, the mountains, or the ocean may be in order. And of course, we should identify and teach any basic skills that, for whatever reason, students haven't yet acquired. When we do so, we're likely to see significant improvements in students' classroom performance (S. A. Griffin, Case, & Capodilupo, 1995; G. Phillips, McNaughton, & MacDonald, 2004; Siegler, 2009). However, we must be careful not to focus *exclusively* on basic skills, especially when doing so means a fair amount of drill and practice. Students' academic progress will suffer over the long run if they don't also have frequent opportunities to engage in complex academic tasks—reading for understanding, mastering new technologies, solving real-world problems, and so on (Cazden, 2001; Reis, McCoach, Little, Muller, & Kaniskan, 2011).

🍏 Balance any needed instruction in basic skills with challenging and engaging real-world activities.

WORKING WITH HOMELESS STUDENTS

Children of homeless families typically face far greater challenges than other students from low-income families. Many have chronic physical problems, limited social support networks, significant mental health issues, and inappropriate behaviors. Some may be reluctant to come to school because they lack bathing facilities and suitable clothing, and some may even be runaways. Others may have moved so frequently from one school to another that they have large gaps in their academic skills (Coe, Salamon, & Molnar, 1991; McLoyd, 1998; P. M. Miller, 2011; Polakow, 2007).

As teachers, we too face extra challenges when teaching students who live in homeless shelters. Following are several suggestions for giving these students the support they may need to achieve academic and social success at school (Pawlas, 1994):

🍎 Pair new students with classmates who can provide guidance and assistance—for example, by explaining school procedures and making introductions to other students.

🍎 Provide a notebook, clipboard, or other portable "desk" on which students can do their homework at the shelter.

- 🍎 Find adult or teenage volunteers to serve as tutors at the shelter.
- 🍎 Meet with students' parents at the shelter rather than at school.
- 🍎 Share copies of homework assignments, school calendars, and newsletters with shelter officials.

When we use such strategies, however, we must keep in mind that students and their families are apt to feel embarrassed about their homeless status (Polakow, 2007). Accordingly, showing respect for their privacy and self-esteem must be a high priority. If you believe that a student may be homeless because she may have run away from home, contact professionals in your school (e.g., school social workers, school counselors, or school psychologists) who may be able to assist by finding appropriate resources for the student. Sometimes these individuals can be admitted into a temporary facility for homeless or runaway youth, which may provide short-term benefits (Slesnick, Dashora, Letcher, Erdem, & Serovich, 2009).

> MyEdLab **Self-Check 4.3**
>
> MyEdLab **Application Exercise 4.4.** In this exercise you can apply what you have learned about helping students with socioeconomic differences succeed in the classroom by fostering resilience with emotional and academic support.

Students at Risk

Students at risk are those with a high probability of failing to acquire the minimum academic skills necessary for success in the adult world. Many students at risk drop out before high school graduation, and many others graduate without mastery of basic skills in reading or mathematics (e.g., Boling & Evans, 2008; Laird, Kienzl, DeBell, & Chapman, 2007; U.S. Department of Education, 2015). Some students are at risk for dropping out of school earlier than are others. Results of a national study of students who were in the ninth grade during the 2009 academic year indicated that 2.7% of those students had dropped out of high school by the time they should have been in the 11th grade.

A common assumption is that the reasons for dropping out lie primarily in the students themselves (V. E. Lee & Burkam, 2003). But as we will see, school characteristics also play a significant role.

Some schools have been referred to as "dropout factories" (American Psychological Association, 2012). These schools have extraordinarily high dropout rates, and many are in areas of high poverty. Data suggest that in the United States, there are about 2,000 high schools in which the ninth-grade class decreases by at least 40% by the time those students should be high school seniors (Balfanz & Legters, 2004).

CHARACTERISTICS OF STUDENTS AT RISK

Students at risk come from all socioeconomic levels, but children of poor, single-parent families are especially likely to leave school before high school graduation. Boys are more likely than girls to drop out, and African Americans, Hispanics, and Native Americans are more likely than European American and Asian American students to drop out. Also, students in large cities and rural areas are more likely to drop out than students in the suburbs are; graduation rates in some big cities are less than 40% (C. Chapman, Laird, & KewalRamani, 2010; Hardré & Reeve, 2003; L. S. Miller, 1995; National Research Council, 2004).

Students at risk, especially those who eventually drop out, typically have some or all of the following characteristics:

- *A history of academic failure.* On average, students who drop out have poorer reading and study skills, achieve at lower levels, have less confidence in their academic ability, and are more likely to have repeated a grade than their classmates who graduate. Consistent patterns of low achievement are sometimes seen as early as third grade (Christle, Jolivette, & Nelson, 2007; Fan & Wolters, 2012; Hattie, 2009; Korhonen, Linnanmäki, & Aunio, 2014; Suh, Suh, & Houston, 2007).

- *Emotional and behavioral problems.* Potential dropouts tend to have lower self-esteem than their more successful classmates. They're also more likely to exhibit serious behavioral problems (e.g., fighting, substance abuse) both in and out of school. Often their close friends are low-achieving and, in some cases, antisocial peers (Battin-Pearson et al., 2000; Garnier, Stein, & Jacobs, 1997; Jozefowicz, Arbreton, Eccles, Barber, & Colarossi, 1994; Suh et al., 2007).

- *Lack of psychological attachment to school.* Students at risk for academic failure are less likely to identify with their school or to perceive themselves as being a vital part of the school community. For example, they engage in few extracurricular activities and are apt to express dissatisfaction with school in general (Christenson & Thurlow, 2004; Hymel, Comfort, Schonert-Reichl, & McDougall, 1996; Rumberger, 1995).

- *Increasing disengagement with school.* Dropping out isn't necessarily an all-or-nothing event. Many high school dropouts show lesser forms of dropping out many years before they officially leave school. Future dropouts are absent from school more frequently than their peers, even in the elementary grades. In addition, they're more likely to have been suspended from school and to show a long-term pattern of dropping out, returning to school, and dropping out again (Christenson & Thurlow, 2004; Suh et al., 2007).

The characteristics just described certainly aren't surefire indicators of which students will drop out, however. For example, some dropouts come from two-parent, middle-income homes, and some are actively involved in school activities almost until the time they drop out (Hymel et al., 1996; Janosz, Le Blanc, Boulerice, & Tremblay, 2000).

WHY STUDENTS DROP OUT

Chapter 15 looks more closely at the effects of high-stakes testing.

Students drop out for a variety of reasons. Some have little family and peer encouragement and support for school success. Others have extenuating life circumstances; perhaps they have medical problems, take a job to help support the family, become depressed, or get pregnant. Many simply become dissatisfied with school: They find the school environment unwelcoming or dangerous, perceive the curriculum to be boring and personally irrelevant, become victims of teasing or bullying, are absent often, or doubt that they can pass the high-stakes achievement tests on which graduation depends (Balfanz, Herzog, & Mac Iver, 2007; Brayboy & Searle, 2007; Cornell, Gregory, Huang, & Fan, 2013; Hardré & Reeve, 2003; Hursh, 2007; Quiroga, Janosz, Bisset, & Morin, 2013).

Sadly, teacher behaviors can enter into the picture as well. For example, a teacher might communicate low expectations for students' achievement either explicitly (e.g., by telling them that their chances of earning passing grades are slim) or implicitly (e.g., by brushing off their requests for assistance on assigned tasks). Students are more likely to drop out when they perceive their teachers to be uninterested in helping them succeed (Becker & Luthar, 2002; Farrell, 1990; Suh et al., 2007).

SUPPORTING STUDENTS AT RISK

MyEdLab
Video Example 4.4.

Students at risk often have a history of academic failure and feel little or no attachment to their school. Teachers and schools can make a difference by creating a culture of caring support and making systemic efforts to engage these students academically.

Because students who are at risk for academic failure are a diverse group of individuals with a diverse set of needs, there is no single strategy that can keep all of them in school until high school graduation (Christenson & Thurlow, 2004; Janosz et al., 2000). Nevertheless, effective school and classroom practices will go a long way in helping these students stay on the road to academic success and high school graduation. Following are several suggestions based on research findings.

- *Identify students at risk as early as possible.* We begin to see indicators of dropping out, such as low school achievement and high absenteeism, as early as elementary school. And other signs—such as disruptive behavior and lack of involvement in school activities—often appear years before students officially withdraw from school. Therefore it's quite possible to identify at-risk students early in their school careers and take steps to prevent or remediate academic difficulties before they become insurmountable. Schools can integrate methods for tracking these at-risk students into their data systems so that the students' progress over time can be easily tracked. For students at risk, prevention, early intervention, and long-term support are more effective than later, short-term efforts (Brooks-Gunn, 2003; Christenson & Thurlow, 2004; Institute of Education Sciences, 2008).

🍎 *Create a warm, supportive school and classroom atmosphere.* Teachers and schools that have high success rates with students at risk tend to be those that communicate a sense of caring, concern, and high regard for students (Christenson & Thurlow, 2004; Hamre & Pianta, 2005; Pianta, 1999). Particularly useful is the provision of an adult advocate for at-risk students; these advocates are specific individuals who are assigned to at-risk students. The relationships that students develop with these advocates can be effective in identifying resources to help the students with both short-term and longer-term needs (Institute of Education Sciences, 2008).

🍎 *Make long-term, systematic efforts to engage students in the academic curriculum.* Students are more likely to stay in school and more likely to learn and achieve at high levels if they think their classes are worth their time and effort (e.g., L. W. Anderson & Pellicer, 1998; Institute of Education Sciences, 2008; S. M. Miller, 2003; Ramey & Ramey, 1998; Suh et al., 2007). The Into the Classroom feature "Engaging Students at Risk in the Academic Curriculum" offers several concrete examples of what we might do.

🍎 *Encourage and facilitate identification with school.* Students are far more likely to stay in school if they have an emotional attachment to their school and believe that they're important members of the school community (Christenson & Thurlow, 2004; Fredricks, Blumenfeld, & Paris, 2004). Following are several strategies that researchers have found to be effective:

> Chapter 13 offers many strategies for creating warm, emotionally supportive schools and classrooms.

Into The Classroom

Engaging Students at Risk in the Academic Curriculum

🍎 **Pique students' interest with stimulating activities.**
In a unit on the physics of sound, a middle school science teacher shows students how basic principles of sound reveal themselves in popular music. On one occasion the teacher brings in a guitar and explains why holding down a string at different points along the neck of the guitar creates different frequencies and thus different notes.

🍎 **Make the curriculum relevant to students' lives and needs—for example, through service learning activities.**
A math teacher at an inner-city middle school consistently encourages her students to identify and work to solve problems in their community. One of her classes expresses concern about the many liquor stores located near the school and the questionable customers and drug dealers the stores attract. The students use yardsticks and maps to calculate the distance of each store from the school, gather information about zoning restrictions and other city government regulations, identify potential violations, meet with a local newspaper editor (who publishes an editorial describing the situation), and eventually meet with state legislators and the city council. As a result of the students' efforts, city police begin to monitor the liquor stores more closely, major violations are identified (leading to the closing of two stores), and the city council makes it illegal to consume alcohol within 600 feet of the school.

🍎 **Create a community of learners—a classroom in which students and teachers work collaboratively to increase everyone's understanding.**
In a high school science class's unit on weather, small groups of students specialize in different topics (e.g., humidity, wind, air pressure). Each group conducts research about its topic in the library and on the Internet and then prepares a lesson to teach students in other groups what it has learned.

🍎 **Use students' strengths to promote a positive sense of self.**
A low-income, inner-city elementary school forms a singing group (the Jazz Cats) for which students must try out. The group performs at a variety of community events, and the students enjoy considerable visibility for their talent. Group members exhibit increased self-esteem, improvement in other school subjects, and greater teamwork and leadership skills.

🍎 **Communicate high expectations for short-term and long-term academic success.**
A math teacher at a low-income, inner-city high school recruits students to participate in an intensive math program. The teacher and students work on evenings, Saturdays, and vacations, and all of them later pass the Advanced Placement calculus exam. (This real-life example is depicted in the 1988 film *Stand and Deliver*.)

🍎 **Provide extra support for academic success.**
A middle school homework program meets every day after school in Room 103, where students find their homework assignments on a shelf. Students follow a particular sequence of steps to do each assignment (assembling materials, having someone check their work, etc.) and use a checklist to make sure they don't skip any steps. Initially, a supervising teacher closely monitors what they do, but with time and practice the students are able to complete their homework with only minimal help and guidance.

Sources: J. P. Allen & Antonishak, 2008; E. M. Anderman & L.H. Anderman, 2014; L. W. Anderson & Pellicer, 1998; Belfiore & Hornyak, 1998 (homework program example); Christenson & Thurlow, 2004; Cosden, Morrison, Albanese, & Macias, 2001; Evans-Winters & Ivie, 2009; L. S. Fuchs, D. Fuchs, et al., 2008; Jenlink, 1994 (Jazz Cats example); Kincheloe, 2009; Ladson-Billings, 1994a; Mathews, 1988 (inner-city math program example); Suh et al., 2007; Tate, 1995 (liquor store example).

🍎 Encourage participation in athletic programs, extracurricular activities, and student government. In some instances, this may mean providing extra supports to allow participation, such as assistance with transportation or supplementing the cost of a uniform. This strategy is especially important when students are having academic difficulties, because it provides an alternative way of experiencing school success.

🍎 Involve students in school policy and management decisions.

🍎 Give students positions of responsibility in managing school activities.

🍎 Monitor students' attendance, and when students are persistently absent from school, discuss the absences with the student, and consult with others (e.g., school counselors) to intervene if necessary. (Eccles, 2007; Finn, 1989; Garibaldi, 1992; Newmann, 1981; M. G. Sanders, 1996)

In general, then, the most effective programs for students at risk are those that would be ideal for *any* student.

MyEdLab **Self-Check 4.4**

MyEdLab **Application Exercise 4.5.** In this interactive exercise you can practice identifying ways to work with students who are at risk and help them experience academic and social success.

---

4 What Have You Learned?

We now return to the chapter's learning outcomes and identify key points associated with each one. As we do so, we must remember three critical principles regarding the group differences described in this chapter: There is *considerable individual variability within any group, a great deal of overlap between any two groups, and additional variability across locations.*

■ **4.1: Describe frequently observed between-group differences and within-group variability for various cultural and ethnic groups; also describe the teacher attitudes and strategies that underlie culturally responsive teaching.** Cultural and ethnic-group differences may be seen in language and dialect, talkativeness and verbal assertiveness, eye contact, personal space, responses to questions, comfort with public performance, views about teasing, attitudes toward cooperation and competition, use of technology, family relationships and expectations, conceptions of time, and worldviews. For students from cultural and ethnic minority groups, there is often some degree of cultural mismatch between the home and school environments, and teachers' misinterpretations of students' behaviors can exacerbate this mismatch. All students benefit when we promote increased understanding of cultural and ethnic differences and foster social interaction among students from diverse groups.

■ **4.2: Describe the nature and origins of typical gender differences in school-age children and adolescents, and explain how you can best accommodate such differences in your classroom.** On average, males and females have similar academic abilities but differ somewhat in physical activity levels, experiences with technology, motivation, sense of self, interpersonal relationships, classroom behavior, and career aspirations. Biological differences (e.g., gender-related hormone levels and subtle differences in brain development) account for a few gender differences, but socialization (which can amplify small biology-based differences) is probably at the root of many others. As teachers, we may occasionally need to tailor instructional strategies to the unique characteristics of boys versus girls; in general, however, we should hold equally high expectations for both sexes and make sure that both have equal opportunities to develop in all areas of the school curriculum.

■ **4.3: Identify challenges that students from low-income families often face; also identify several strategies through which you can foster their resilience and help them be successful at school.** Numerous factors can contribute to the generally lower achievement of students from low-income families, including poor nutrition and housing, unhealthy physical and social environments, emotional stress, lower-quality schools, gaps in basic knowledge and skills, and homelessness. Despite such challenges, many children from low-income backgrounds have a positive sense of self and do well in school; such *resilient students* often have one or more individuals in their lives whom they trust and can turn to in difficult times. As teachers, we can help students in lower socioeconomic groups succeed in the classroom by building on their many strengths and providing the academic and emotional support they may sometimes need to overcome their adverse circumstances.

■ **4.4: Explain how you might recognize students who are at risk for academic failure and dropping out of school, and identify strategies for helping these students get on the path to academic and social success.** *Students at risk* are those with a high probability of failing to acquire the minimum academic skills necessary for success in the adult world; they may graduate from high school without having learned to read or write, or they may drop out before graduation. To help such students succeed at school, we should identify them as early as possible, make the curriculum relevant to their needs and interests, communicate high expectations for academic success, assign an advocate to work specifically with each student when possible, provide sufficient support to make such success possible, and encourage involvement in school activities.

Practice for Your Licensure Exam

The Active and the Passive

Ms. Stewart has noticed that only a few students actively participate in her middle school science classes. When she asks a question, especially one that requires students to draw inferences from information presented in class, the same hands always shoot up. She gives the matter some thought and realizes that all of the active participants are of European American descent and most of them are boys.

She sees the same pattern in students' involvement in lab activities. When she forms small groups for particular lab assignments, the same students (notably, the European American males) always take charge. The females and minority-group males take more passive roles, either providing assistance to the group leaders or else just sitting back and watching.

Ms. Stewart is a firm believer that students learn much more about science when they participate in class and when they engage in hands-on activities. Consequently, she is concerned about the lack of involvement of many of her students. She wonders whether they really even care about science.

1. **Constructed-response question:**

   Effective teachers place a high priority on *equity*; that is, they ensure that their classroom practices are not biased in ways that enhance some students' achievement more than others'. In this situation the European American boys appear to be benefiting more from instruction than their classmates are. Using what you know about group differences, identify at least three possible reasons that minority-group students are not actively participating in classroom lessons.

2. **Multiple-choice question:**

   Three of the following explanations are possible reasons that the boys in Ms. Stewart's class are participating more than the girls. Which alternative *contradicts* research findings on gender differences?

   a. On average, boys are more motivated to get good grades.

   b. On average, boys are more physically active in their classes.

   c. On average, boys tend to be more confident about their abilities.

   d. On average, boys are more likely to speak up without waiting to be called on.

3. **Constructed-response question:**

   Describe three different strategies you might use to increase the participation of both girls and minority-group students in Ms. Stewart's class.

MyEdLab **Licensure Exam 4.1**

PRAXIS Go to Appendix C, "Matching Book Content and Ebook Activities to the Praxis Principles of Learning and Teaching Tests," to discover sections of this chapter that may be especially applicable to the Praxis tests.

Fotosearch/Glow Images

5

Individual Differences and Special Educational Needs

Learning Outcomes

5.1 Describe various perspectives on the nature of intelligence, and identify several ways in which you can nurture intelligence in your own students.

5.2 Explain how students' cognitive styles and dispositions might influence their classroom performance.

5.3 Identify implications of the U.S. Individuals with Disabilities Education Act (IDEA) for your own work as a teacher.

5.4 Explain how you might adapt your instruction and classroom practices to the unique strengths and limitations of students with various disabilities.

5.5 Explain how you might nurture the development of students who show exceptional gifts and talents.

CASE STUDY: TIM

In elementary school, Tim earned reasonable grades despite poor reading comprehension skills. Although he often appeared to be in a daze during classroom activities, he was generally well behaved. In middle school his grades began to decline, and teachers complained of his spaciness and tendency to daydream. He had trouble staying on task in class and was so disorganized that he seldom completed homework. When Tim reached high school, he seemed unable to cope with the independence his teachers expected of students, and so he failed several 9th- and 10th-grade classes.

Now, as a 17-year-old 11th grader, Tim undergoes an in-depth psychological evaluation at a university diagnostic clinic. An intelligence test yields a score of 96, reflecting average ability, and measures of social and emotional adjustment are also within an average range. However, measures of attention consistently show this to be an area of weakness. Tim explains that he has trouble ignoring distractions and must find a very quiet place to do his schoolwork. Even then, he says, he often has to reread something several times to grasp its meaning. (Based on Hathaway, Dooling-Litfin, & Edwards, 2006, pp. 410–412)

- Tim's attention problems have obviously been interfering with his academic achievement. But if you look closely at the facts presented in the case, you might realize that Tim also has strengths on which teachers can build. What particular characteristics might be working in Tim's favor?
- As a teacher, how might you adapt your instructional strategies and classroom environment to accommodate Tim's unique needs?

The clinic evaluation team eventually concludes that Tim has attention-deficit hyperactivity disorder, or ADHD. (Like Tim, some students identified as having ADHD exhibit attention problems *without* hyperactivity.) The team suspects that a learning disability might be at the root of the problem but doesn't have sufficiently precise diagnostic techniques to determine this with certainty. On the plus side, Tim is certainly motivated to do well in school: He's well behaved in class, seeks out quiet places to study, and may read something several times in an effort to make sense of it. With appropriately modified instruction and settings—for example, teaching Tim basic organizational skills, breaking a single complex task into several shorter and simpler ones, and giving him a quiet place to read and study—Tim can more readily stay on task and complete assignments (Barkley, 2006; Meltzer, 2007).

Teachers have many diverse responsibilities, and meeting the needs of students like Tim may make prospective teachers feel somewhat anxious. As we will see, students show significant individual differences in cognitive abilities, personalities, physical skills, and so on. In this chapter we'll look at individual differences in intelligence, cognitive styles, and dispositions. We'll then consider *students with special needs*—students who, like Tim, are different enough from their peers that they require specially adapted curriculum materials, instructional practices, or both. As we go along, we'll find that the most effective instruction tends to be differentiated instruction—instruction that is tailored to align with each student's current knowledge, skills, and needs.

Intelligence

It is common for teachers, parents, and others to be involved in conversations about students' intelligence, and many of us use that term often. However, there are a variety of ways to talk about intelligence. As teachers, we need to be aware that this is a complex topic. As we will discuss, measures of intelligence can be very useful, but overinterpretation of these scores can sometimes be harmful to our students. Theorists define and conceptualize *intelligence* in a variety of ways, but most agree that it has several distinctive qualities:

- It is *adaptive:* It can be used flexibly to respond to a variety of situations and problems.
- It is related to *learning ability:* People who are intelligent in particular domains learn new information and skills in those domains more quickly and easily than people who are less intelligent in those domains.
- It involves the *use of prior knowledge* to analyze and understand new situations effectively.
- It involves the complex interaction and coordination of *many different mental processes.*
- It is *culture specific.* What is considered to be intelligent behavior in one culture isn't necessarily intelligent behavior in another culture. (Dai, 2010; Laboratory of Comparative Human Cognition, 1982; J. Li, 2004; Neisser et al., 1996; Saklofske, van de Vijver, Oakland, Mpofu, & Suzuki, 2015; Sternberg, 1997, 2004, 2007; Sternberg & Detterman, 1986)

With these qualities in mind, we offer an intentionally broad definition of intelligence: the ability to apply prior knowledge and experiences flexibly to accomplish challenging new tasks.

For most theorists intelligence is somewhat different from what a person has actually learned (e.g., as reflected in school achievement). At the same time, intelligent thinking and behavior *depend* on prior learning. Intelligence, then, isn't necessarily a permanent, unchanging characteristic; it can be modified through experience and learning.

THEORETICAL PERSPECTIVES OF INTELLIGENCE

Some psychologists have suggested that intelligence is a single, general ability that people have to varying degrees and apply in a wide range of activities. Others have disagreed, citing evidence that people can be more or less intelligent on different kinds of tasks, at different points in development, and in different contexts. The theories of intelligence we examine in this section reflect these diverse perspectives on the nature of intelligence.

SPEARMAN'S CONCEPT OF *g*

Imagine that you give a large group of students a wide variety of tests—some measuring verbal skills, others measuring visual–spatial thinking, still others measuring mathematical problem solving, and so on. Chances are that the test scores would all correlate with one another to some degree: Students who score high on one test would tend to score high on the other tests as well. The correlations would be strong among tests of very similar abilities; those among tests of distinctly different abilities would be weaker. For example, a student who scored very high on a vocabulary test would probably score high on other measures of verbal ability but might have only modest success in solving math problems (McGrew, Flanagan, Zeith, & Vanderwood, 1997; Neisser et al., 1996; Spearman, 1904).

Charles Spearman (1904, 1927) drew on such findings to propose that intelligence comprises both (1) a single, pervasive reasoning ability (a *general factor*) that is used across the board and (2) a number of more specific abilities, such as problem-solving ability and abstract reasoning (*specific factors*). The general factor and any relevant specific factors work together during the execution of particular tasks.

Many contemporary psychologists believe that sufficient evidence supports Spearman's concept of a general factor in intelligence—often known simply as Spearman's *g*. Underlying it, they suspect, may be a general ability to process information quickly and efficiently (Bornstein et al., 2006; Coyle, Pillow, Snyder, & Kochunov, 2011; Haier, 2003). A general ability to control and direct one's thinking may also be involved (Cornoldi, 2010; H. L. Swanson, 2008).

CATTELL'S FLUID AND CRYSTALLIZED INTELLIGENCES

Several decades after Spearman's groundbreaking work, Raymond Cattell (1963, 1987) found evidence for two distinctly different components of general intelligence (*g*). First, people differ in fluid intelligence, their ability to acquire knowledge quickly, use abstract reasoning abilities, and adapt to new situations effectively. Second, they differ in crystallized intelligence, the knowledge and skills they've accumulated from their experiences, schooling, and culture. Fluid intelligence

As we consider the roles of the central executive and metacognition in Chapter 6 and Chapter 7, respectively, we'll look more closely at how people can control and direct their own thought processes.

is more important for new, unfamiliar tasks, especially those that require rapid decision making and involve nonverbal content. Crystallized intelligence is more important for familiar tasks, especially those that depend heavily on language and prior knowledge. Cattell suggested that fluid intelligence is largely the result of inherited biological factors, whereas crystallized intelligence depends on both fluid intelligence and experience and thus is influenced by both heredity and environment.

EXPERIENCING FIRSTHAND
CRYSTALLIZED AND FLUID INTELLIGENCE

Consider the following two questions (Roberts & Lipnevich, 2012):

1. What is the next number in this sequence: 1 2 1 4 1 6 1 8?
2. What is the meaning of the word *peripatetic*?

One of these questions assesses fluid intelligence, whereas the other assesses crystallized intelligence. Can you tell which is which? Question 1 assesses fluid intelligence; a student has to reason abstractly to figure out the next number in the sequence; in contrast, question 2 represents crystallized intelligence, because knowledge of the meaning of the word *peripatetic* is something that a student would have learned—the answer could not be determined through any form of reasoning.[1] Both of these types of intelligence are important and valuable, but as you can see, they are also quite different.

CATTELL–HORN–CARROLL THEORY OF COGNITIVE ABILITIES

Some theorists have built on Cattell's distinction to suggest that intelligence may have three layers, or *strata* (Ackerman & Lohman, 2006; Carroll, 1993, 2003; D. P. Flanagan & Ortiz, 2001; Horn, 2008). In this *Cattell–Horn–Carroll theory of cognitive abilities,* the top stratum is general intelligence, or *g.* Underlying it in the middle stratum are 9 or 10 more specific abilities (including crystallized and fluid intelligence)—processing speed, general reasoning ability, general world knowledge, ability to process visual input, and so on—that encompass fluid and/or crystallized intelligence to varying degrees. And underlying *these* abilities in the bottom stratum are more than 70 very specific abilities, such as reading speed, mechanical knowledge, and number and richness of associations in memory. The Cattell–Horn–Carroll theory is the most researched and most widely accepted theory of intelligence among individuals who work with school-aged children and adolescents, and many of the IQ assessments currently in use are based on this theory (Kyllonen, 2015). The Cattell–Horn–Carroll theory is too complex to describe in detail here, but you should be aware that psychologists are increasingly finding it useful in predicting and understanding students' achievement in various content domains (e.g., J. J. Evans, Floyd, McGrew, & Leforgee, 2001; Phelps, McGrew, Knopik, & Ford, 2005; B. E. Proctor, Floyd, & Shaver, 2005; Proctor, 2012).

 Keep in mind that different students are likely to be intelligent in different ways.

GARDNER'S MULTIPLE INTELLIGENCES

Howard Gardner (1983, 1999, 2011; Gardner & Hatch, 1990) suggests that people have at least eight distinctly different abilities, or *multiple intelligences,* that are relatively independent of one another (see Table 5.1). In his view there may also be a ninth (existential) intelligence dedicated to philosophical and spiritual issues (e.g., Who are we? Why do we die?). However, because evidence for it is weaker than that for the other intelligences (Gardner, 1999, 2000a, 2003), we have omitted it from the table.

Gardner presents some evidence to support the existence of these distinctly different intelligences. For instance, he describes people who are quite skilled in one area, perhaps in composing music, yet have seemingly average

Attention to detail in 10-year-old Luther's drawing of a plant suggests some talent in what Gardner calls *naturalist* intelligence.

---

[1]The next numbers in the sequence would be 1 and 10; *peripatetic* means roaming or traveling (when used as an adjective) and a person who roams or travels (when used as a noun).

TABLE 5.1 • Gardner's Multiple Intelligences

TYPE OF INTELLIGENCE	EXAMPLES OF RELEVANT BEHAVIORS
Linguistic intelligence: Ability to use language effectively	• Making persuasive arguments • Writing poetry or contributing to a blog • Noticing subtle nuances in meanings of words
Logical–mathematical intelligence: Ability to reason logically, especially in mathematics and science	• Solving mathematical problems quickly • Generating mathematical proofs • Formulating and testing hypotheses about observed phenomena[a]
Spatial intelligence: Ability to notice details of what one sees and to imagine and manipulate visual objects in one's mind	• Creating mental images • Manipulating mental images • Drawing a visual likeness of an object • Seeing subtle differences among visually similar objects
Musical intelligence: Ability to create, comprehend, and appreciate music	• Playing a musical instrument • Composing a musical work • Identifying the underlying structure of music
Bodily–kinesthetic intelligence: Ability to use one's body skillfully	• Dancing • Playing basketball • Performing pantomime
Interpersonal intelligence: Ability to notice subtle aspects of other people's behaviors	• Reading other people's moods • Detecting other people's underlying intentions and desires • Using knowledge of others to influence their thoughts and behaviors
Intrapersonal intelligence: Awareness of one's own feelings, motives, and desires	• Identifying the motives guiding one's own behavior • Using self-knowledge to relate more effectively with others
Naturalist intelligence Ability to recognize patterns in nature and differences among various life-forms and natural objects	• Identifying members of particular plant or animal species • Classifying natural forms (e.g., rocks, types of mountains) • Applying one's knowledge of nature in such activities as farming, landscaping, or animal training

[a]This example may remind you of Piaget's theory of cognitive development. Many of the stage-specific characteristics that Piaget described reflect logical–mathematical intelligence.
Sources: Gardner, 1983, 1999.

abilities in other areas. He also points out that people who suffer brain damage sometimes lose abilities that are restricted primarily to one intelligence. One person might show deficits primarily in language, whereas another might have difficulty with tasks that require spatial reasoning.

Among psychologists, reviews of Gardner's theory are mixed (Roberts & Lipnevich, 2012). Some theorists don't believe that Gardner's evidence is sufficiently compelling to support the notion of eight or nine distinctly different abilities (N. Brody, 1992; Corno et al., 2002; Sternberg, 2003; Waterhouse, 2006). Others agree that people may have a variety of relatively independent abilities but argue for different distinctions than those Gardner makes (e.g., note the second-stratum abilities in the Cattell–Horn–Carroll theory just described). Still others reject the idea that abilities in certain domains, such as in music or bodily movement, are really "intelligences" per se (Bracken, McCallum, & Shaughnessy, 1999; Sattler, 2001).

Despite researchers' lukewarm reception of Gardner's theory, many educators have wholeheartedly embraced it because of its optimistic view of human potential. Gardner's perspective encourages us to use many different teaching methods so that we can capitalize on students' diverse talents to help them learn and understand classroom subject matter (L. Campbell, Campbell, & Dickinson, 1998; Gardner, 2000b; Kornhaber, Fierros, & Veenema, 2004).

Whether or not human beings have eight or more distinctly different intelligences, they certainly benefit when they're encouraged to think about a particular topic in two or more distinctly different ways—perhaps using both words and mental images (R. E. Mayer, 2011b; Moreno, 2006). We won't always want to teach to students' strengths, however. We must also give students tasks that encourage them to address and thereby strengthen their areas of weakness (Sternberg, 2002).

Present classroom subject matter using a variety of approaches to capitalize on students' diverse abilities, but also give them tasks that require them to work on areas of weakness.

STERNBERG'S THEORY OF SUCCESSFUL INTELLIGENCE

Robert Sternberg (e.g., 1998, 2004, 2012; Sternberg et al., 2000) has speculated that people may be more or less intelligent in three different domains. His Triarchic Theory of Intelligence (also sometimes referred to as the *Theory of Successful Intelligence*) focuses on how our skills and abilities in these domains help us to achieve our short-term and long-term goals. *Analytical intelligence* involves making sense of, analyzing, contrasting, and evaluating the kinds of information and problems often seen in academic settings and on intelligence tests. *Creative intelligence* involves imagination, invention, and synthesis of ideas within the context of new situations. *Practical intelligence* involves applying knowledge and skills effectively to manage and respond to everyday problems and social situations. Sternberg has argued that traditional views of intelligence have focused too narrowly on academic success, and have neglected the role of intelligence in our everyday lives.

In addition, Sternberg proposes that intelligent behavior involves an interplay of three factors, all of which vary from one occasion to the next (Sternberg, 1985, 1997, 2003):

- *The environmental context in which the behavior occurs.* Different behaviors may be more or less adaptive and effective in different cultures. For example, learning to read is an adaptive response in industrialized societies yet largely irrelevant to certain other cultures.

- *The relevance of prior experiences to a particular task.* Prior experiences can enhance intelligence in either of two ways. In some cases extensive practice with a particular kind of task enables students to perform that task with increasing speed and efficiency—that is, with greater *automaticity*. For example, as children get more practice multiplying double-digit numbers (e.g., 32×55), their speed and efficiency at solving such problems increases. In other instances, students are able to draw on what they've learned in previous situations to help them with *new* tasks. For example, students may apply algebraic principles learned in math classes to problems in physical science.

Chapter 6 looks more closely at automaticity.

- *The cognitive processes required by the task.* Numerous cognitive processes are involved in intelligent behavior: separating important information from irrelevant details, identifying possible problem-solving strategies, seeing relationships among seemingly different ideas, and so on. Different cognitive processes may be more or less important in different contexts, and an individual may behave more or less intelligently depending on the specific cognitive processes needed at the time.

There is some evidence that the three components of the theory of successful intelligence can be measured, and that assessments in these domains are related to important educational outcomes (Sternberg, 2010; Sternberg et al., 2014). In addition, recent research from the field of neuroscience suggests that similar processes are involved in creative and intellectual thinking (Silvia, 2015; Sternberg, 2003). However, empirical research supporting these three components is limited at this time (Roberts & Lipnevich, 2012). Nevertheless, the theory reminds us that students' ability to behave intelligently may vary considerably depending on the cultural context, previously learned knowledge and skills, and the cognitive processes that a task involves.

DEVELOPMENTAL VIEWS OF INTELLIGENCE

Theories of cognitive development portray children as becoming increasingly intelligent over time; for example, with age and experience children gain greater proficiency in abstract thinking (Jean Piaget's theory) and effective use of complex cultural tools (Lev Vygotsky's theory). Yet with the possible exception of Sternberg's triarchic theory—which points out the importance of prior experiences—the perspectives of intelligence described so far don't really consider how intelligence might take different forms at different points in development (Dai, 2010).

Chapter 2 describes Piaget's and Vygotsky's theories of development.

Some psychologists working in the area of giftedness suggest that not only is intelligence somewhat specific to particular domains but also that its basic nature changes with age and experience. From this perspective, the developmental course of exceptional abilities and talents is as follows:

1. Initially (typically in childhood), people show exceptional *potential* in a certain domain, perhaps in reading, math, or music.

2. With appropriate instruction, guidance, and practice opportunities, people show exceptional *achievement* in the domain.

3. If people continue to pursue the domain and practice domain-specific tasks over a lengthy time period (typically into adulthood), they may eventually gain considerable *expertise and eminence*, to the point that their accomplishments are widely recognized (Dai, 2010; Subotnik, Olszewski-Kubilius, & Worrell, 2011).

In addition, increases in more general cognitive abilities are related to experiences such as school attendance, work experiences, and other life events (Kyllonen, 2015). Here, then, we see a very dynamic view of intelligence: Although its roots may be in certain natural endowments, over the long run intelligence requires both environmental nurturance and personal perseverance (Dai, 2010; Subotnik et al., 2011)

DISTRIBUTED INTELLIGENCE

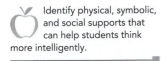

Identify physical, symbolic, and social supports that can help students think more intelligently.

MyEdLab
Video Example 5.1.

Children can think and behave more intelligently when they acquire the cognitive tools of their culture, such as strategies for organizing and graphing data.

Many psychologists are beginning to realize that not only does a supportive environmental context enhance people's intelligence over time, but in fact it can facilitate intelligent behavior in the here and now. People are far more likely to think and behave intelligently when they have assistance from their physical, cultural, and social environments—an idea that is sometimes called **distributed intelligence** (e.g., Hutchins, 1995; Pea, 1993; Perkins, 1995). People can "distribute" a challenging task—that is, they can pass some of the cognitive burden onto something or someone else—in at least three ways. First, they can use physical objects, especially technology (e.g., tablets, calculators, computers), to handle and manipulate large amounts of information. In particular, having a smartphone available virtually at any time and in any place affords students the opportunity to access information and various tools. Second, they can represent and think about the situations they encounter by using their culture's various symbolic systems—words, charts, diagrams, and so on—and other cognitive tools. And third, they can work with other people to explore ideas and solve problems—as we've often heard, two heads are (usually) better than one. In fact, when students work together on complex, challenging tasks and problems, they teach one another strategies and ways of thinking that can help each of them think even *more* intelligently on future occasions (Kuhn, 2001b; Palincsar & Herrenkohl, 1999; Slavin, 2011).

From a distributed-intelligence perspective, then, intelligence is a highly variable, context-specific ability that increases when appropriate environmental supports are available. It certainly isn't an immutable trait that learners "carry around" with them, nor is it something that can be easily measured and then summarized with one or more test scores. However, psychologists coming from other theoretical perspectives often *do* try to measure intelligence, as we'll see now.

MEASURING INTELLIGENCE

When a student consistently struggles with certain aspects of the school curriculum, as Tim does in the opening case study, psychologists sometimes find it helpful to get a measure of the student's general level of cognitive functioning. Such measures are commonly known as **intelligence tests**. To get a sense of what intelligence tests are like, try the following exercise.

EXPERIENCING FIRSTHAND
MOCK INTELLIGENCE TEST

Answer each of these questions:

1. What does the word *penitence* mean?
2. How are a goat and a beetle alike?
3. What should you do if you get separated from your family in a large department store?
4. What do people mean when they say, "A rolling stone gathers no moss"?

5. Complete the following analogy:

These test items are modeled after items on many contemporary intelligence tests. Often the tests include a mixture of verbal tasks (such as items 1 through 4) and less verbal, more visual tasks (such as item 5).

Scores on intelligence tests were originally calculated using a formula that involves division. Hence, they were called intelligence quotient scores, or **IQ scores**. Although we still use the term IQ, intelligence test scores are no longer based on the old formula. Instead, they're determined by comparing a student's performance on a given test with the performance of others in the same age-group. This is a very important point—an IQ score is reflective of a student's cognitive abilities at a particular age, compared to students of the same age. A score of 100 indicates average performance on the test: Students with this score have performed better than half of their age-mates but not as well as the other half. Scores well below 100 indicate below-average performance on the test; scores well above 100 indicate above-average performance.

Figure 5.1 shows the percentages of students getting scores at different points along the scale (e.g., 12.9% get scores between 100 and 105). Notice that the curve is high in the middle and low at both ends, indicating that scores close to 100 are far more common than scores considerably higher or lower than 100. For example, if we add up the percentages in different parts of Figure 5.1, we find that approximately two-thirds (68%) of students score within 15 points of 100 (i.e., between 85 and 115). In contrast, only 2% of students score as low as 70, and only 2% score as high as 130. Such a many-in-the-middle-and-few-at-the-extremes distribution of scores seems to characterize a wide variety of human characteristics. Hence, psychologists have created a method of scoring intelligence test performance that intentionally yields this distribution.

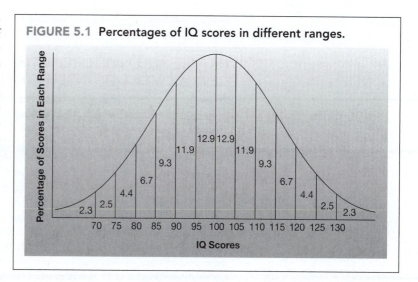

FIGURE 5.1 **Percentages of IQ scores in different ranges.**

In the opening case study, Tim's performance on an intelligence test yields an IQ score of 96, which we can now make some sense of. As you can see in Figure 5.1, a score of 96 is so close to 100 that we should consider it to be well within an average range.

Researchers are still studying intelligence and designing new assessments of intelligence. It has become particularly apparent in recent years that other noncognitive variables (e.g., motivation and persistence) are related to intelligence. In addition, new techniques are being developed to account for the fact that some individuals work quickly through assessments (and thus may complete more of the assessment, but may commit more errors because of going quickly), whereas other test takers are more slow and deliberate, and may achieve greater levels of accuracy, but not complete as many items (van der Linden, 2007).

If you have taken a course in descriptive statistics, you may realize that IQ scores are *standard scores* based on the *normal distribution*. Chapter 15 explains these concepts.

IQ SCORES AND SCHOOL ACHIEVEMENT

Studies repeatedly show that performance on intelligence tests is correlated with school achievement. On average, children with higher IQ scores earn higher course grades, do better on standardized achievement tests, and complete more years of education (N. Brody, 1997; Duckworth, Quinn, & Tsukayama, 2012; Sattler, 2001). Data suggest that these tests are predictive of success in higher education as well (Kuncel & Hezlett, 2007).

It's important to keep three points in mind about this IQ–achievement relationship. First, intelligence doesn't necessarily *cause* achievement; it is simply correlated with it. Even though students with high IQs typically perform well in school, we cannot conclusively say that their high achievement is actually the result of their intelligence. Intelligence probably does play an important role in school achievement, but so, too, do many other factors—motivation, quality of instruction, family and neighborhood resources, peer-group expectations, and so on. Second, the relationship between IQ scores and achievement is an imperfect one, with many exceptions to the rule. For a variety of reasons, some students with high IQ scores don't perform well in the classroom, and others achieve at higher levels than we would predict from their IQ scores alone. For example, recent research suggests that the relation between intelligence and achievement is affected by sleep—when students do not get enough sleep on any given night, intelligence and achievement aren't as closely correlated as they might otherwise be (Erath, Tu, Buckhalt, & El-Sheikh, 2015). Third and most important, we must remember that an IQ score simply reflects a

Don't use students' IQ scores to make long-term predictions about school achievement.

child's performance on a particular test at a particular time—it's *not* a permanent characteristic etched in stone—and that some change is to be expected over time.

NATURE AND NURTURE IN THE DEVELOPMENT OF INTELLIGENCE

Research tells us that heredity probably plays some role in intelligence. For instance, identical twins tend to have more similar IQ scores than nonidentical (fraternal) twins do, even when the twins are adopted at birth by different parents and grow up in different homes. This is *not* to say, however, that children inherit a single IQ gene that determines their intellectual ability. Rather, they probably inherit a variety of characteristics that in one way or another affect particular cognitive abilities and talents (O. S. P. Davis, Haworth, & Plomin, 2009; Horn, 2008; Kan, Wicherts, Dolan, & van der Maas, 2013; Kovas & Plomin, 2007).

Environmental factors influence intelligence as well, sometimes for the better and sometimes for the worse. Poor nutrition in the early years of development (including the 9 months before birth) leads to lower IQ scores, as does a mother's excessive use of alcohol during pregnancy (Neisser et al., 1996; Ricciuti, 1993; Sigman & Whaley, 1998). Moving a child from a neglectful, impoverished home environment to a more nurturing, stimulating one (e.g., through adoption) can result in IQ gains of 15 points or more (Beckett et al., 2006; Capron & Duyme, 1989; van IJzendoorn & Juffer, 2005). Effective, too, are long-term intervention programs designed to help children acquire basic cognitive and academic skills (e.g., F. A. Campbell & Burchinal, 2008; Kağitçibaşi, 2007). Even simply *going to school* has a positive effect on IQ scores (Ceci, 2003; Ramey, 1992), and attending an academically rigorous school may be particularly related to gains in intelligence, even during adolescence (Becker, Lüdtke, Trautwein, Köller, & Baumert, 2012). Furthermore, worldwide, there has been a slow but steady increase in people's performance on intelligence tests—a trend that is probably due to better nutrition, smaller family sizes, better schooling, increasing cognitive stimulation (through increased access to technology, reading materials, etc.), and other improvements in people's environments (Flynn, 2007; E. Hunt, 2008; Neisser, 1998).

The question of how *much* nature and nurture each play a role in influencing intelligence has been a source of considerable controversy over the years. But in fact, genetic and environmental factors interact in their influences on cognitive development and intelligence in ways that can probably never be disentangled. First of all, genes require reasonable environmental support to do their work. In an extremely impoverished environment—one with a lack of adequate nutrition and stimulation—heredity may have little to say about children's intellectual growth, but under better circumstances it can have a significant influence (Ceci, 2003; D. C. Rowe, Jacobson, & Van den Oord, 1999; Turkheimer, Haley, Waldron, D'Onofrio, & Gottesman, 2003). Second, heredity seems to affect how susceptible or impervious a child is to particular environmental conditions (Rutter, 1997). For instance, some students—such as those with certain inherited disabilities, like Tim in the opening case study—may need a quiet, well-structured learning environment in which to acquire good reading comprehension skills, but other students might pick up good reading skills regardless of the quality of their environment. Third, children tend to seek out environmental conditions that match their inherited abilities (O. S. P. Davis et al., 2009; W. Johnson, 2010; Scarr & McCartney, 1983). For example, children who inherit exceptional quantitative reasoning ability may enroll in advanced math courses and in other ways nurture their inherited talent. Children with average quantitative ability are less likely to take on such challenges and thus have fewer opportunities to develop their mathematical skills.

INTELLIGENCE AND THE BRAIN

See Chapter 2 for more information on the structure, development, and plasticity of the human brain.

Intelligence—at least that aspect of intelligence that can be measured by IQ tests—does seem to have some basis in the brain (Karama et al., 2011). A high level of intelligence also seems to involve ongoing, efficient interactions among numerous brain regions (Jung & Haier, 2007), Research conducted by neuroscientists suggests that numerous components of intelligence are related to the brain and its development, including basic cognitive skills in young children, memory, attention, reading, and mathematics ability (Byrnes, 2012). Although heredity appears to play some role in these differences, the extent to which they are the result of nature, nurture, or a nature–nurture interaction remains to be seen (Jung & Haier, 2007). And in any case, we must remember that the human brain has considerable ability to restructure itself—that is, it has *plasticity*—throughout childhood and adulthood.

CULTURAL AND ETHNIC DIVERSITY IN INTELLIGENCE

Historically, some ethnic groups in the United States have, *on average,* performed better than other ethnic groups on intelligence tests. Most experts agree that such group differences in IQ scores are probably due to differences in environment and, more specifically, to economic circumstances that affect the quality of prenatal and postnatal nutrition, availability of stimulating books and toys, access to educational opportunities, and so on (Brooks-Gunn, Klebanov, & Duncan, 1996; Byrnes, 2003; McLoyd, 1998). Furthermore, various groups have become increasingly *similar* in average IQ score in recent years—a trend that can be attributed only to more equitable environmental conditions (Dickens & Flynn, 2006; Neisser et al., 1996).

Yet it's important to note that different cultural groups have somewhat different views about what intelligence *is* and may therefore nurture somewhat different abilities in their children (Saklofske et al., 2015). Many people of European descent think of intelligence primarily as an ability that influences children's academic achievement and adults' professional success. In contrast, people in many African, Asian, Hispanic, and Native American cultures think of intelligence as involving social as well as academic skills—maintaining harmonious interpersonal relationships, working effectively together to accomplish challenging tasks, and so on (Greenfield et al., 2006; J. Li & Fischer, 2004; Sternberg, 2004, 2007). In Buddhist and Confucian societies in the Far East (e.g., China, Taiwan), intelligence also involves acquiring strong moral values and making meaningful contributions to society (J. Li, 2004; Sternberg, 2003).

Cultural groups differ, too, in the behaviors that they believe reflect intelligence. For example, many traditional measures of intelligence take speed into account on certain test items: Children score higher if they respond quickly as well as correctly. Yet people in some cultures tend to value thoroughness over speed and may be skeptical when tasks are completed very quickly (Sternberg, 2007). As another example, many people in mainstream Western culture interpret strong verbal skills as a sign of intelligence, but for many Japanese and many Inuit people of northern Quebec, talking a lot indicates immaturity or low intelligence (Crago, 1988; Minami & McCabe, 1996; Sternberg, 2003). One Inuit teacher had this concern about a boy whose language was quite advanced for his age-group:

> Do you think he might have a learning problem? Some of these children who don't have such high intelligence have trouble stopping themselves. They don't know when to stop talking. (Crago, 1988, p. 219)

As teachers, then, we must be careful not to assume that our own views of intelligence are shared by the students and families of cultures very different from our own.

BEING SMART ABOUT INTELLIGENCE AND IQ SCORES

Whatever its nature and origins may be, intelligence appears to be an important factor in students' ability to learn and achieve in the classroom. Accordingly, we must have a good grasp of how we can best nurture students' intellectual growth and how we can reasonably interpret their performance on intelligence tests and use that information wisely. Following are several recommendations.

- *Place higher priority on developing—rather than on determining—intelligence.* As we've seen, intelligence is hardly a fixed, unchangeable characteristic: Environmental factors, including schooling, can lead to increases in children's measured intelligence. And the notion of distributed intelligence suggests that virtually all students can act more intelligently when they have tools, symbolic systems, and social groups to assist them. As teachers, we should think more about *enhancing and supporting* students' intelligence than about measuring it (Dai, 2010; P. D. Nichols & Mittelholtz, 1997; Posner & Rothbart, 2007; B. Rhodes, 2008).

- *Think of intelligence tests as useful but imperfect measures.* Intelligence tests aren't magical instruments that mysteriously determine a learner's true intelligence—if, in fact, such a thing as

Assume that when children from diverse ethnic groups all have reasonably stimulating environments, they have equal potential to develop their intellectual abilities.

When meeting with students' parents, remember that those from diverse backgrounds may value different aspects of intelligence.

"true" intelligence exists. Instead, these tests are simply collections of questions and tasks that psychologists have developed in order to get a handle on how well students can think, reason, and learn at a particular point in time. Used in conjunction with other information, they can often give us a general idea of a student's current cognitive functioning. To interpret IQ scores appropriately, however, we must be aware of their limitations:

- Different kinds of tests can yield somewhat different scores.

Young children's distractibility during a testing session decreases the *reliability* of any test scores obtained (see Chapter 14 and Chapter 15).

- A student's performance on any test will inevitably be affected by many temporary factors—general health, time of day, distracting circumstances, and so on. Such factors are especially influential for young children, who are apt to have high energy levels, short attention spans, and little interest in sitting still for more than a few minutes.

- Test items typically focus on certain skills that are important in mainstream Western culture—especially in school settings—and on tasks that can be accomplished within a single, short testing session. They don't necessarily tap into skills that are more highly valued and nurtured in other cultures, nor do they tap into skills that involve lengthy time periods (e.g., planning ahead, making wise decisions) or highly specific areas.

- Some students may be unfamiliar with the content or types of tasks involved in particular test items and may perform poorly on those items as a result.

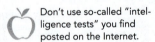 Be skeptical of any IQ scores obtained for recent immigrants and other students who were not fluent in English when tested. In general, never base expectations for students' achievement *solely* on IQ scores.

- English language learners—students who have only limited proficiency in English as a result of growing up in a non-English-speaking environment—are at an obvious disadvantage when an intelligence test is administered in English. Thus, their IQ scores will typically be poor indicators of what they will be able to do once their English improves. (Dirks, 1982; Heath, 1989; Neisser et al., 1996; Olvera, & Gómez-Cerrillo, 2014; Perkins, 1995; Stanovich, 2009; Sternberg, 2007; Sternberg, Grigorenko, & Kidd, 2005)

Obviously, then, we must be skeptical of IQ scores obtained for students who come from diverse cultural backgrounds, know little English, or were fairly young at the time of assessment.

Use the results of more focused measures when you want to assess specific abilities. Whenever we obtain and use IQ scores, we're buying into the idea that a general factor, or *g*, underlies students' school performance. But given the multifaceted nature of intelligence, no single test can possibly give us a complete picture of a student's abilities. If we want to estimate a student's potential for success in a particular domain—say, in mathematics—we're probably better off using measures of more specific abilities (Ackerman & Lohman, 2006; Horn, 2008; McGrew et al., 1997). However, we urge you to rely *only* on instruments available from well-respected test publishers. Tests you might find on the Internet—for instance, tests that claim to be measures of Gardner's multiple intelligences—have typically undergone little or no research scrutiny, making their results questionable at best. Keep in mind, too, that intelligence tests should be administered only by school psychologists and other professionals who have been specifically trained in their use.

Don't use so-called "intelligence tests" you find posted on the Internet.

Look for behaviors that reveal exceptional talents within the context of a student's culture. For example, among students who have grown up in predominantly African American communities, intelligence might be reflected in oral language, such as colorful speech, creative storytelling, or humor. For students from Native American cultures, intelligence might be reflected in interpersonal skills, highly skilled craftsmanship, or an exceptional ability to notice and remember subtle landmarks in one's physical environment (Dai, 2010; Sternberg, 2005; Torrance, 1989).

As teachers, then, we must be careful not to limit our conception of intelligence only to students' ability to succeed at traditional academic tasks and to perform well on traditional intelligence tests. One alternative is *dynamic assessment:* Rather than assess what students already know and can do, we might teach them something new and see how quickly and easily they master it (Feuerstein, Feuerstein, & Falik, 2010; Haywood & Lidz, 2007; Sternberg, 2007).

Chapter 14 provides more details about dynamic assessment.

Remember that many other factors also affect students' classroom achievement. Most measures of intelligence focus on specific things that a student *can* do, with little consideration of what a student is *likely* to do. For instance, intelligence tests don't evaluate the extent to which students are willing to view a situation from multiple perspectives, examine data with a critical eye, try hard even when faced with a difficult question, or actively take charge of their own learning. Yet such traits are often just as important as intellectual ability in determining success on academic and real-world tasks (Duckworth & Seligman, 2005; Kuhn, 2001a; Perkins, Tishman, Ritchhart, Donis, & Andrade, 2000). Even teachers' expectations for students can have small effects on students' intelligence test scores (Raudenbush, 1984). In the next section we'll examine forms that these *cognitive styles* and *dispositions* might take.

Chapter 11 discusses the relations between teacher expectations and student achievement.

MyEdLab **Self-Check 5.1**

MyEdLab **Application Exercise 5.1.** In this interactive exercise you can practice identifying ways in which teachers nurture intelligence in their diverse students.

Cognitive Styles and Dispositions

Students with the same general level of intelligence often approach classroom tasks and think about classroom topics differently. Some of these individual differences reflect cognitive styles, over which students don't necessarily have much conscious control. Others reflect dispositions, which students voluntarily and intentionally bring to bear on their efforts to master school subject matter. Don't agonize over the distinction between the two concepts, because their meanings overlap considerably. Both involve not only specific cognitive tendencies but also personality characteristics (Furnham, 2012; Messick, 1994b; Zhang & Sternberg, 2006). Dispositions also have a motivational component—an I-*want*-to-do-it-this-way quality (Kuhn, 2001a; Perkins & Ritchhart, 2004; Stanovich, 1999).

DO STUDENTS HAVE DISTINCT LEARNING STYLES?

Over the past few decades, psychologists and educators have examined a wide variety of cognitive styles, sometimes instead using the term *learning styles*. You probably have heard of educators discussing students as perhaps being "visual learners" or "auditory learners." The notion behind learning styles is that if teachers adjust instruction to meet the favored learning styles of individual students, then learning will be enhanced. Thus, if a "visual learner" is provided with extra visual materials when learning about a new topic, that student's learning will be improved.

Despite the popularity of this idea among educators, there is virtually no evidence that adapting instruction to students' learning styles has any effect on their actual learning (Curry, 1990; R. E. Mayer & Massa, 2003; Nieto & Bode, 2008; Rogowsky, Calhoun, & Tallal, 2015; Roher & Pashler, 2012; Snider, 1990). Many of the styles that have been identified and assessment instruments that have been developed don't hold up under the scrutiny of researchers (Cassidy, 2004; Krätzig & Arbuthnott, 2006; Messick, 1994b). Learning "styles" are basically just preferences; some students may indicate that they prefer to learn through listening, whereas others may indicate that they prefer to learn visually. Nevertheless, these preferences are just that—preferences. It is not the case that students with one preferred style cannot learn just as well when information is presented in other ways.

In fact, adapting instruction to students' preferred learning styles, or even telling students that they may have a learning style, may prove to be detrimental to learning. Consider the following example:

Harper is a sixth grader who does very well in school. On her mid-year report card, Harper's science teacher noted, "Harper does a great job in class; I just wish that she would participate more in our discussions." When Harper's parents asked her why she did not participate more in class, she responded that "the guidance counselor came in and gave us a test on our learning styles; she told me that I'm a visual learner. Since I am a visual learner, I don't really need to talk to learn; I just watch."

Why is this situation troubling? First, as we noted before, assessments of learning styles are generally not scientifically verified (and these "styles" are really just preferences). Second, and more disturbing, Harper has interpreted the information about being a visual learner as suggesting that she perhaps is weak in other areas, and thus does not need to learn with other modalities. If Harper is a quiet student, then we might recommend greater verbal interaction so that she can further develop her verbal skills; however, her naïve interpretation of the information about her visual learning style may actually cause her to talk even less!

DOES IT MAKE SENSE TO TEACH TO STUDENTS' "RIGHT BRAINS" OR "LEFT BRAINS"?

As a teacher you will probably hear about lessons, materials, and curricula that have been developed based on the latest findings from neuroscience; sometimes this is referred to as *brain-based learning* or *brain-based education*. Neuroscience is a growing area of research with exciting new discoveries emerging all the time; however, most researchers agree that it is too early to be applying this research to daily classroom instruction.

One area that has received much attention is the notion of adapting instruction to the "left brain" or the "right brain." Neuroscientists, in fact, have completely debunked the idea that we might teach to students' "left brains" or "right brains": Even the simplest of everyday thinking tasks requires the left and right hemispheres of the brain to work together (Bressler, 2002; Gonsalves & Cohen, 2010; Haxby et al., 2001; Kalbfleisch & Gillmarten, 2013; Organization for Economic Cooperation and Development, 2015).

ANALYTIC AND HOLISTIC THINKING

One dimension of cognitive style worthy of our attention, however, is a distinction between analytic and holistic thinking. In *analytic* thinking, learners tend to break new stimuli and tasks into their component parts and to see these parts somewhat independently of their context. In *holistic* thinking, learners tend to perceive situations as integrated, indivisible wholes that are closely tied to their context. Researchers have found cultural differences here: People from mainstream Western culture tend to be analytic thinkers, whereas people from East Asian cultures think more holistically (Park & Huang, 2010; Varnum, Grossmann, Kitayama, & Nisbett, 2010). In general, logical and scientific reasoning requires analytic thinking, but holistic thinking can help learners identify associations and relationships among seemingly very different phenomena. For example, holistically minded Chinese scientists identified the underlying cause of the ocean's tides—the moon's gravitational pull on any large body of water—many centuries before more narrowly focused, earth-centered European scientists did (Nisbett, 2009).

In contrast to the mixed research findings regarding cognitive styles and learning styles, research on dispositions has yielded more consistent and fruitful results. Some kinds of dispositions are clearly beneficial for classroom learning:

- *Stimulation seeking:* Eagerly interacting with one's physical and social environment in order to gain new experiences and information
- *Need for cognition:* Regularly seeking and engaging in challenging cognitive tasks
- *Critical thinking:* Consistently evaluating information or arguments in terms of their accuracy, credibility, and worth, rather than accepting them at face value
- *Open-mindedness:* Flexibly considering alternative perspectives and multiple sources of evidence, and suspending judgment for a time rather than leaping to immediate conclusions (Cacioppo, Petty, Feinstein, & Jarvis, 1996; DeBacker & Crowson, 2008, 2009; Furnham, 2012; Halpern, 2008; Kang et al., 2009; Raine, Reynolds, & Venables, 2002; Southerland & Sinatra, 2003; Stanovich, 1999; West, Toplak, & Stanovich, 2008)

Such dispositions are often positively correlated with students' learning and achievement, and many theorists have suggested that they play a causal role in what and how much students learn. In fact, dispositions sometimes overrule intelligence in their influence on long-term achievement (Dai & Sternberg, 2004; Kuhn & Franklin, 2006; Perkins & Ritchhart, 2004). For instance, children who eagerly seek out physical and social stimulation as preschoolers later become better readers and earn better grades in school (Raine et al., 2002). Students with a high need for

Don't plan instruction based on results you might get from easily available and aggressively marketed "learning style" inventories or "brain-based curricula."

MyEdLab
Video Example 5.2.

Some learners tend to use analytic thinking, but others use holistic thinking. Teachers can use strategies that facilitate the types of thinking required for specific learning tasks and help students learn to think both analytically and holistically.

Chapter 7 describes critical thinking more thoroughly.

cognition learn more from what they read and are more likely to base conclusions on sound evidence and logical reasoning (Cacioppo et al., 1996; Dai, 2002; P. K. Murphy & Mason, 2006). And students who critically evaluate new evidence and open-mindedly listen to diverse perspectives show more advanced reasoning capabilities and are more likely to revise their beliefs in the face of contradictory information (DeBacker & Crowson, 2009; G. Matthews, Zeidner, & Roberts, 2006; Southerland & Sinatra, 2003).

Researchers haven't yet systematically addressed the origins of various dispositions. Perhaps inherited temperamental differences (e.g., in stimulation seeking) are involved (Raine et al., 2002). Beliefs about the underlying nature of knowledge—for instance, the belief that knowledge is fixed and unchanging, on the one hand, or dynamic and continually evolving, on the other—may also play a role (P. M. King & Kitchener, 2002; Kuhn, 2001b; Mason, 2003). And almost certainly teachers' actions and the general classroom atmosphere they create—for example, whether students are encouraged to pursue intriguing topics, take risks, and think critically—make a difference (Flum & Kaplan, 2006; Gresalfi, 2009; Kuhn, 2001b, 2006). In the following classroom interaction, a teacher actually seems to *discourage* any disposition to think analytically and critically about classroom material:

Children differ in their desires for intellectual stimulation and challenging cognitive tasks.

Beliefs about the underlying nature of knowledge are known as *epistemic beliefs* (see Chapter 7).

> Write this on your paper . . . it's simply memorizing this pattern. We have meters, centimeters, and millimeters. Let's say . . . write millimeters, centimeters, and meters. We want to make sure that our metric measurement is the same. If I gave you this decimal, let's say .234 m (yes, write that). In order to come up with .234 m in centimeters, the only thing that is necessary is that you move the decimal. How do we move the decimal? You move it to the right two places. . . . Simple stuff. (Turner, Meyer, et al., 1998, p. 741)

Undoubtedly this teacher means well, but notice the noncritical attitude she communicates: "Write this . . . it's simply memorizing this pattern." The Into the Classroom feature "Promoting Productive Dispositions" offers strategies that are more likely to be effective.

MyEdLab **Self-Check 5.2**

MyEdLab **Application Exercise 5.2.** This interactive exercise allows you to practice identifying teaching strategies that promote productive dispositions.

Educating Students with Special Needs in General Education Classrooms

As teachers, we can typically accommodate many students' varying abilities and dispositions within the context of a single curriculum and everyday classroom lessons. But we're also likely to have **students with special needs**—students who are different enough from their peers that they require specially adapted instructional materials and practices to help them maximize their learning and achievement. Some of these students have cognitive, personal, social, or physical disabilities that adversely affect their performance in a typical classroom. Others, instead, are so advanced in a particular domain—that is, they are *gifted*—that they gain little from grade-level activities and assignments.

Into The Classroom

Promoting Productive Dispositions

🍎 **Communicate your own eagerness to learn about and master new topics.**

In a unit on poetry, a middle school English teacher says, "In our culture we're accustomed to poems that rhyme and have a steady beat. But many centuries ago the Japanese developed a very different form of poetry. This form, called *haiku*, is really cool. I'll give you some of my favorite examples, and then as a class we'll create some new haiku."

🍎 **Model open-mindedness about diverse viewpoints and a willingness to suspend judgment until all the facts are in.**

In a lesson about the properties of air—especially the fact that it takes up space—a first-grade teacher asks her students to predict whether the inside of a glass will get wet or stay dry when it is pushed upside down into a bowl of water. After the glass has been immersed, students come to different conclusions about the wetness or dryness of its inside. The teacher responds, "Uh-oh. Now we have two different opinions. We are going to have to figure out how to solve this problem." She devises a simple strategy—stuffing a crumpled paper towel into the glass and then re-immersing it in the water—to get more conclusive evidence.

🍎 **Conduct learning activities in which students collaborate to address intriguing, multifaceted issues.**

A few weeks before a national presidential election, a high school social studies teacher says to his class, "Many of the campaign ads we see on television now are harshly criticizing opposing candidates, and some of them may be misrepresenting the facts. In your cooperative groups today, you'll be looking at transcripts of three political ads, one each from a different candidate's campaign. Each group has at least two laptops or tablets with wi-fi. Your job is to be fact checkers—to search the Internet for credible websites that can either confirm or disconfirm what the candidates are saying about their own records or those of their opponents. Tomorrow we'll compare the findings of various groups."

🍎 **Ask students to evaluate the quality of scientific evidence, and scaffold their efforts sufficiently that they can reach appropriate conclusions.**

Working in pairs, fifth graders conduct "experiments" in a computer program that simulates the effects of various factors (amount of rainfall, rate of snowmelt, type of soil, etc.) on local flooding. To guide students' inquiry, the program asks them to form and then test specific hypotheses, and it occasionally asks them if a particular series of tests has controlled for other potentially influential factors.

Sources: Strategies based on discussions by de Jong, 2011; Gresalfi, 2009; Halpern, 1998; Kuhn, 2001b; Perkins & Ritchhart, 2004; vanSledright & Limón, 2006.

In the United States, most students with special educational needs are in general education classrooms for part or all of the school day—a practice known as **inclusion** (U.S. Department of Education, National Center for Education Statistics, 2010). In fact, federal legislation mandates that students with disabilities be educated in neighborhood schools and, ideally, in regular classrooms to the greatest extent possible.

PUBLIC LAW 94-142: INDIVIDUALS WITH DISABILITIES EDUCATION ACT (IDEA)

In 1975 the U.S. Congress passed Public Law 94-142, which is now known as the **Individuals with Disabilities Education Act (IDEA)**. This act has been amended and reauthorized several times since then, most recently in 2004 under the name *Individuals with Disabilities Education Improvement Act*. It currently grants educational rights from birth until age 21 for people with cognitive, emotional, or physical disabilities. It guarantees several rights for students with disabilities:

- *A free and appropriate education.* All students with disabilities are entitled to a free educational program designed specifically to meet their unique educational needs.

- *Fair and nondiscriminatory evaluation.* A multidisciplinary team conducts an in-depth evaluation of any student who may be eligible for special services. The team's makeup depends on the student's needs but typically consists of two or more teachers, any appropriate specialists, and the student's parent(s) or guardian(s). Using a variety of tests and other evaluation tools, school personnel conduct a complete assessment of potential disabling conditions. Evaluation procedures must take a student's background and any suspected physical or communication difficulties into account. For example, tests must be administered in a student's primary language.

- *Education in the least restrictive environment.* To the greatest extent possible, students with disabilities should be included in the same academic environment, extracurricular activities, and social interactions as their nondisabled peers. That is, they must have the **least restrictive environment**, the most typical and standard educational environment that, with sufficient supplementary aids and support services, can reasonably meet their needs. Exclusion from general education is warranted only when others' safety would be jeopardized or when, even with proper support and assistance, a student can't make appreciable progress in a general education setting.

- *Individualized education program (IEP).* When an individual aged 3 to 21 is identified as having a disability, the multidisciplinary team collaboratively develops an instructional program, called an individualized education program (IEP), tailored to the individual's strengths and weaknesses (see Figure 5.2). The IEP is a written statement that the team continues to review and, if appropriate, revise at least once a year—more frequently if conditions warrant. IEP meetings are most effective when they (a) are well planned and (b) have a designated meeting facilitator, a clear agenda, and ground rules for how to run the meeting, and when participants (c) have sufficient knowledge about these meetings and avoid using jargon (Diliberto & Brewer, 2014).

- *Due process.* IDEA mandates several practices that ensure that students' and parents' rights are preserved throughout the decision-making process. For instance, parents must be notified in writing before the school takes any action that might change their child's educational program. If the parents and school system disagree on the most appropriate placement for a child, mediation or a hearing can be used to resolve the differences.

IDEA has had a significant impact on the nature of special education. More and more, teachers are realizing that truly inclusive practices require differentiated instruction for *all* students, not just those with formally identified needs. And rather than provide specialized instruction in a separate classroom, many special education teachers now partner with regular classroom teachers to jointly teach all students—both those with disabilities and those without.

POTENTIAL BENEFITS AND DRAWBACKS OF INCLUSION

Despite the mandates of IDEA, inclusive practices for students with disabilities have been controversial. Some experts argue that students are most likely to develop normal peer relationships and social skills when they participate fully in their school's overall social life. But others worry that when students with special needs are in a regular classroom for the entire school day, they can't get the intensive specialized instruction they may need. Furthermore, nondisabled classmates may stigmatize, avoid, or bully students who appear to be odd or incompetent in some way (Blake, Lund, Zhou, Kwok, & Benz, 2012; Hamovitch, 2007).

Numerous research studies have suggested that attending general education classes for part or all of the school day can have several positive outcomes for students with disabilities:

- Academic achievement equivalent to (and sometimes higher than) that in a self-contained classroom

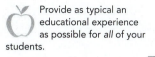

Provide as typical an educational experience as possible for *all* of your students.

MyEdLab
Video Example 5.3.

The Individuals with Disabilities Education Act (IDEA) grants educational rights to students with disabilities. When these students are included in the general education classroom, their individualized education program (IEP) is developed by a multidisciplinary team.

FIGURE 5.2 Components of an individualized education program (IEP).

In the United States, any IEP written for a student with a disability must include the following information:

- *Current performance:* Information about the student's current school achievement levels, including classroom tests and assignments, teachers' and specialists' observations, and results of individually administered assessments.

- *Annual goals:* objectives or benchmarks for the school year related to the student's academic, social, behavioral, and/or physical needs.

- *Special education and related services:* The special services, supplementary aids, and program modifications that will be provided in order to help the student meet the annual goals.

- *Participation with nondisabled children:* If applicable, explanation of the extent to which the student will *not* participate in regular classroom and extracurricular activities.

- *Measurement of progress:* Information regarding how the student's progress will be monitored and how parents will be informed of this progress.

- *Participation in state and district-wide tests:* Explanation of any modifications or exclusions with respect to regularly administered achievement tests and, if applicable, description of any alternative measures of achievement.

- *Dates and places:* Information regarding when and where services will begin and how long they will continue.

- *Transition services:* For any student aged 14 (or younger, if appropriate), any special services needed for reaching post-school goals and preparing to leave school.

Source: U.S. Department of Education, Office of Special Education and Rehabilitative Services, 2000.

- More appropriate classroom behavior, better social skills, and more frequent interaction with nondisabled peers
- Better sense of self *if* the school environment is one in which all students accept and respect individual differences among their peers (Halvorsen & Sailor, 1990; Hamovitch, 2007; Hattie, 2009; P. Hunt & Goetz, 1997; MacMaster, Donovan, & MacIntyre, 2002; Slavin, 1987; Soodak & McCarthy, 2006; Stainback & Stainback, 1992)

We're especially likely to see such outcomes when students understand the nature of their disabilities and when instruction and materials are tailored to students' specific needs, perhaps in their regular classrooms or perhaps in short resource-room sessions (e.g., H. L. Swanson, Hoskyn, & Lee, 1999). Appropriate assistive technology—electronic devices and other equipment that can enhance students' abilities and performance—is also extremely valuable in helping students successfully participate in the curriculum and social life of general education classrooms.

Nondisabled students often benefit from inclusive practices as well. For example, they may be able to take advantage of special supports designed for students with disabilities—perhaps detailed study guides or supplementary explanations (C. M. Cole et al., 2004). Furthermore, they acquire an increasing awareness of the heterogeneous nature of the human race and discover that individuals with special needs are in many respects very much like themselves (P. Hunt & Goetz, 1997; D. Staub, 1998). One of us authors often thinks about her son Jeff's friendship with Evan, a classmate with severe physical and cognitive disabilities, during their third-grade year. A teacher had asked Jeff to be a special friend to Evan, interacting with him at lunch and whenever possible. Although largely unable to speak, Evan always made it clear through gestures and expressions that he was delighted to spend time with his friend, giving Jeff—who was quite shy—a boost in social self-confidence. Several years later Jeff reflected on this friendship:

> It made me realize that Evan was a person too. It made me realize that I could have a friendship with a boy with disabilities. Doing things that made Evan happy made me happy as well. I knew that *Evan* knew that we were friends.

It's essential, of course, that nondisabled students treat classmates who have disabilities in respectful and supportive ways and, better still, forge friendships with these classmates. As teachers, we can do several things to nurture good relationships between students:

- Explicitly point out the strengths of a student with a disability.
- Ask students with and without disabilities to assist others in their areas of strength.
- Plan academic and recreational activities that require cooperation.
- Encourage students with disabilities to participate in extracurricular activities and community events. (Bassett et al., 1996; DuPaul, Ervin, Hook, & McGoey, 1998; Hamovitch, 2007; Madden & Slavin, 1983; Turnbull, Pereira, & Blue-Banning, 2000)

There are advantages and drawbacks to inclusion for classroom teachers as well. On the positive side, the inclusion of students with disabilities can lead to greater acceptance of individuals with disabilities among other students and increased opportunities for students to work in diverse groups and explain concepts to one another. Nevertheless, the inclusion of students with disabilities in regular classrooms does introduce some challenges for teachers. For example, teachers may need to differentiate instruction to a greater degree, prepare alternative materials for some students, and spend extra time with students with disabilities.

IDENTIFYING STUDENTS' SPECIAL NEEDS: RESPONSE TO INTERVENTION AND PEOPLE-FIRST LANGUAGE

Experts don't completely agree about how to define various categories of special needs—especially those not involving obvious physical conditions—or about how best to identify students who fit into each category. In the United States, IDEA provides specific identification criteria for various disabilities. Students with disabilities who don't meet IDEA's criteria are often eligible for special educational services under Section 504 of the Rehabilitation Act of 1973 (sometimes referred to simply as *Section 504*). This act stipulates that institutions that benefit from federal funding (including public schools) can't discriminate against individuals on the basis of a disability.

Procedures for assessing and accommodating students' disabilities are less prescriptive in Section 504 than they are in IDEA—a situation that can be either advantageous or disadvantageous, depending on the circumstances.

One approach to identification that is gaining increasing support (and that is endorsed in the 2004 reauthorization of IDEA) involves determining response to intervention (RTI). In this approach, a teacher keeps an eye out for any student who has exceptional difficulty with basic skills in a certain domain (e.g., in reading or math) despite normal whole-class instruction *and* intensive follow-up small-group instruction that have both been shown *by research* to be effective for most children. Such a student is referred for in-depth assessments of various characteristics and abilities. If the assessment rules out obvious disabling conditions (e.g., significant genetic abnormalities, sensory impairments), the student is assumed to have a cognitive impairment—often, but not always, falling within the category of learning disabilities—and is therefore eligible for special services (e.g., Fletcher & Vaughn, 2009; L. S. Fuchs & Fuchs, 2009; Mellard & Johnson, 2008).

Whenever we identify a student as having a particular disability, however, we run the risk of focusing other people's attention on weaknesses rather than on the student's many strengths and age-typical characteristics. To minimize such an effect, special educators urge us all to use people-first language when referring to students with disabilities—in other words, to mention the person *before* the disability. For instance, we might say *student with a learning disability* rather than *learning-disabled student* or *student who is blind* rather than *blind student*.

In upcoming sections of the chapter, we group students with special needs into five general categories. Table 5.2 lists the specific kinds of special needs that fall within each category. Disabilities covered by IDEA appear in red in the table.

 Use people-first language when talking about students with disabilities.

MyEdLab **Self-Check 5.3**

MyEdLab **Application Exercise 5.3.** This interactive exercise allows you to practice identifying instructional adaptations tailored to the specific strengths and weaknesses of a student with special needs.

Students with Specific Cognitive or Academic Difficulties

Some students with special educational needs show no outward signs of physical disability yet have cognitive difficulties that interfere with their ability to learn certain kinds of academic material or perform certain kinds of classroom tasks. Such students include those with learning disabilities, attention-deficit hyperactivity disorder, and speech and communication disorders.

LEARNING DISABILITIES

Although there are varying definitions of learning disabilities, students with learning disabilities have significant difficulties in one or more specific cognitive processes that can't be attributed to cultural or linguistic diversity, generally delayed cognitive development, emotional problems, sensory impairment, or environmental deprivation. Such difficulties often appear to result from specific and possibly inherited brain dysfunctions (American Psychiatric Association, 2013; N. Gregg, 2009; K. Pugh & McCardle, 2009). Figure 5.3 lists several forms that a learning disability might take.

COMMON CHARACTERISTICS

In general, students with learning disabilities are different from one another in many more ways than they are similar. They typically have many strengths but may also face challenges:

- Poor reading and writing skills
- Ineffective learning and memory strategies
- Trouble concentrating on and completing assigned tasks, especially in the face of distractions
- Poor sense of self and low motivation for academic tasks, especially in the absence of individualized assistance in areas of difficulty

MyEdLab
Video Example 5.4.

In the general education classroom, teachers adapt instructional strategies to meet the learning needs of students with various difficulties and disabilities.

STUDENTS IN INCLUSIVE SETTINGS

TABLE 5.2 • General and Specific Categories of Students with Special Needs (Specific Categories Listed in Red Are Covered by IDEA)

GENERAL CATEGORY	SPECIFIC CATEGORIES	DESCRIPTION
Students with specific cognitive or academic difficulties: These students exhibit an uneven pattern of academic performance; they may have unusual difficulty with certain kinds of tasks yet perform quite successfully on other tasks.	Learning disabilities	Difficulties in specific cognitive processes (e.g., in perception, language, or memory) that cannot be attributed to other disabilities, such as mental retardation, emotional or behavioral disorders, or sensory impairments
	Attention-deficit hyperactivity disorder (ADHD) (not specifically covered by IDEA, but students are often eligible for special services under the IDEA category Other Health Impairments)	Disorder marked by either or both of these characteristics: (1) difficulty focusing and maintaining attention and (2) frequent hyperactive and impulsive behavior
	Speech and communication disorders	Impairments in spoken language (e.g., mispronunciations of certain sounds, stuttering, or abnormal syntactical patterns) or in language comprehension that significantly interfere with classroom performance
Students with social or behavioral problems: These students exhibit social, emotional, or behavioral difficulties serious enough to interfere significantly with their academic performance.	Emotional and behavioral disorders	Emotional states and behaviors that are present over a substantial period of time and significantly disrupt academic learning and performance
	Autism spectrum disorders	Disorders marked by impaired social cognition, social skills, and social interaction, as well as repetition of certain idiosyncratic behaviors; milder forms (e.g., Asperger syndrome) associated with normal development in other domains; extreme forms associated with delayed cognitive and linguistic development and highly unusual behaviors
Students with general delays in cognitive and social functioning: These students exhibit low achievement in virtually all academic areas and have social skills typical of much younger children.	Intellectual disabilities (mental retardation)	Significantly below-average general intelligence and deficits in adaptive behavior (i.e., in practical and social intelligence); deficits are evident in childhood and typically appear at an early age.
Students with physical or sensory challenges: These students have disabilities caused by diagnosed physical or medical problems.	Physical and health impairments	Physical or medical conditions (usually long-term) that interfere with school performance as a result of limited energy and strength, reduced mental alertness, or little muscle control
	Visual impairments	Malfunctions of the eyes or optic nerves that prevent normal vision even with corrective lenses
	Hearing loss	Malfunctions of the ear or associated nerves that interfere with the perception of sounds within the frequency range of normal speech
Students with advanced cognitive development: These students have unusually high ability in one or more areas.	Giftedness (not covered by IDEA unless a disability is also present)	Unusually high ability or aptitude in one or more domains, usually within the academic curriculum, requiring special educational services to help students meet their full potential

- Poor motor skills
- Poor social skills (Estell et al., 2008; Gathercole, Lamont, & Alloway, 2006; N. Gregg, 2009; Job & Klassen, 2012; K. Pugh & McCardle, 2009; Swanson, in press; Waber, 2010)

By no means do such characteristics describe *all* students with learning disabilities. For instance, some are attentive in class, and some are socially skillful and popular with peers.

Sometimes learning disabilities reflect a mismatch between students' developing abilities, on the one hand, and grade-level expectations for performance, on the other (Waber, 2010). For instance, as students reach middle school, they're typically expected to work with little or no supervision, yet students with learning disabilities don't always have the time management skills they need to get things done (N. Gregg, 2009). In high school classes, learning may require

---

FIGURE 5.3 Examples of cognitive processing deficiencies in students with learning disabilities.

Perceptual difficulty. Students may have trouble understanding or remembering information they receive through a particular modality, such as vision or hearing.

Memory difficulty. Students may have less capacity for remembering information over either the short or long run (i.e., they may have problems with either *working memory* or *long-term memory*).

Metacognitive difficulty. Students may have difficulty using effective learning strategies, monitoring progress toward learning goals, and in other ways directing their own learning.

Oral language processing difficulty. Students may have trouble understanding spoken language or remembering what they have been told.

Reading difficulty. Students may have trouble recognizing printed words or comprehending what they read; extreme form is known as *dyslexia*.

Written language difficulty. Students may have problems in handwriting, spelling, or expressing themselves coherently on paper; an extreme form is known as *dysgraphia*.

Mathematical difficulty. Students may have trouble thinking about or remembering information involving numbers; an extreme form is known as *dyscalculia*.

Social perception difficulty. Students may have trouble interpreting others' social cues and signals and thus may respond inappropriately in social situations.

Music processing difficulty. Students may have little sensitivity to differences in pitch and be unable to recognize familiar tunes; an extreme form is known as *amusia*.

---

reading and studying sophisticated textbooks, yet the average high school student with a learning disability reads at a fourth- to fifth-grade level and has few, if any, effective study strategies (Cutting, Eason, Young, & Alberstadt, 2009; Meltzer & Krishnan, 2007).

The following exercise can give you a sense of how these students might feel under such circumstances.

EXPERIENCING FIRSTHAND
A READING ASSIGNMENT

Read the following passage carefully. You'll be tested on its contents later in the chapter.

> Personality research needs to refocus on global traits because such traits are an important part of everyday social discourse, because they embody a good deal of folk wisdom and common sense, because understanding and evaluating trait judgments can provide an important route toward the improvement of social judgment, and because global traits offer legitimate, if necessarily incomplete, explanations of behavior. A substantial body of evidence supporting the existence of global traits includes personality correlates of behavior, interjudge agreement in personality ratings, and the longitudinal stability of personality over time. Future research should clarify the origins of global traits, the dynamic mechanisms through which they influence behavior, and the behavioral cues through which they can most accurately be judged. (Funder, 1991, p. 31)

How well do you think you will perform on the upcoming test about this passage?

The passage you just read is a fairly typical one from *Psychological Science*, a professional journal written for people with advanced education (e.g., doctoral degrees) in psychology. Hence, it was written well above a typical college student's reading level. We won't *really* test you on the passage's contents, but we authors hope that the exercise gave you a feel for the frustration that high school students with learning disabilities might experience. For many students with learning disabilities, completing school assignments may constantly seem like fighting an uphill battle. Perhaps for this reason, a higher-than-average percentage of students with learning disabilities drop out of school before graduation (N. Gregg, 2009).

ADAPTING INSTRUCTION

Instructional strategies for students with learning disabilities must be tailored to students' specific strengths and weaknesses. If you become a regular classroom teacher, you will quite likely partner with a special educator when you have students with learning disabilities in your classes. You and the special educator will work collaboratively to adapt your instruction at times. Several strategies should benefit many of these students:

💿 *Minimize distractions.* Because many students with learning disabilities are easily distracted, we should minimize the presence of other stimuli that might compete for their attention—for example, by pulling down window shades if other classes are playing outside and by asking students to clear away materials they don't immediately need (Buchoff, 1990).

💿 *Present new information in an explicit and well-organized manner.* Most students with learning disabilities learn more successfully when instruction directly communicates what they need to learn, rather than requiring them to draw inferences and synthesize ideas on their own. Frequent and carefully structured practice of important skills is also critical (Fletcher, Lyon, Fuchs, & Barnes, 2007; J. A. Stein & Krishnan, 2007; U.S. Department of Education, 2014).

💿 *Present information in multiple sensory modalities.* Because some students with learning disabilities have trouble learning through a particular sensory modality, we need to think broadly about the modalities we use to communicate information. Thus we might incorporate videos, graphics, and other visual materials, and we might encourage students to audiotape lectures. And, when teaching children to recognize letters, we might have them not only look at the letters but also trace large, textured letter shapes with their fingers (Florence, Gentaz, Pascale, & Sprenger-Charolles, 2004; J. A. Stein & Krishnan, 2007; J. W. Wood & Rosbe, 1985).

💿 *Present stimulating, novel materials,* which may be particularly helpful in preventing students from getting bored and maintaining their attention while reading (Beike & Zentall, 2012). For example, stories that have a surprising turn of events may be particularly beneficial for the engagement of students with learning disabilities during reading.

FIGURE 5.4 Seven-year-old Daniel's attempt to write "I trust a policeman."

I trust a policeman.

Chapter 6 and Chapter 7 provide many strategies for helping students study and learn.

💿 *Analyze students' errors for clues about processing difficulties.* As an example of this strategy, look at 7-year-old Daniel's attempt to write "I trust a policeman" in Figure 5.4. Daniel captured several sounds correctly, including the "s" and final "t" sounds in *trust* and all of the consonant sounds in *policeman.* However, he misrepresented the first two consonant sounds in *trust,* replacing the *t* and *r* with an *N.* He also neglected to represent most of the vowel sounds, and two of the three vowels he did include (*I* for the article *a* and the *E* near the end of *policeman*) are incorrect. We might suspect that Daniel has difficulty hearing all the distinct sounds in spoken words and matching them with the letters he sees in written words. Such difficulties are quite common in students with significant reading disabilities (Goswami, 2007; N. Gregg, 2009; K. Pugh & McCardle, 2009).

💿 *Teach study skills and learning strategies.* Many students with learning disabilities benefit from being taught specific strategies for completing assignments and remembering subject matter (Joseph & Konrad, 2009; Meltzer, 2007; Wilder & Williams, 2001). For example, we might teach them strategies for taking notes and organizing homework, and we can teach them specific *mnemonics,* or memory tricks, to help them remember facts (see Figure 5.5).

💿 *Provide paper or electronic scaffolding that can support students as they study and work.* We might develop study guides, outlines, or graphics that help students identify and interrelate important concepts and ideas. We could provide a copy of a high-achieving classmate's lecture notes. And we can teach students how to use the grammar and spell checkers in word processing software (N. Gregg, 2009; Mastropieri & Scruggs, 1992; Meltzer, 2007).

ATTENTION-DEFICIT HYPERACTIVITY DISORDER (ADHD)

Virtually all students are apt to be inattentive, hyperactive, and impulsive at one time or another. But those with **attention-deficit hyperactivity disorder (ADHD)** typically have significant and chronic deficits in these areas, as reflected in the following identification criteria:

• *Inattention.* Students may have considerable difficulty focusing and maintaining attention on assigned tasks, especially when appealing alternatives are close at hand. They may have trouble listening to and following directions, and they may often make careless mistakes.

- *Hyperactivity.* Students may seem to have an excess amount of energy. They're apt to be fidgety and may move around the classroom at inappropriate times.
- *Impulsivity.* Students almost invariably have trouble inhibiting inappropriate behaviors. They may blurt out answers, begin assignments prematurely, or engage in risky or destructive behaviors without thinking about potential consequences. (American Psychiatric Association, 2000; Barkley, 2006; Gatzke-Kopp & Beauchaine, 2007; N. Gregg, 2009)

Students with ADHD don't necessarily show all three of these characteristics. For instance, some are inattentive without also being hyperactive, as is true for Tim in the opening case study. But all students with ADHD appear to have one characteristic in common: an *inability to inhibit inappropriate thoughts, inappropriate actions, or both* (Barkley, 2006, 2010; B. J. Casey, 2001; Nigg, 2010). Tim, for example, is easily distracted by his thoughts and daydreams when he should be focusing on a classroom lesson.

The prevalence of ADHD in the United States may surprise you. First, boys are about twice as likely as are girls to be diagnosed with ADHD. In the United States approximately 6.4 million students are diagnosed with ADHD at some point in time. In addition, these diagnoses have increased by 53% over the past decade (National Center for Learning Disabilities, 2014). The increase in diagnoses is due to a number of factors, including greater awareness of ADHD and thus more frequent diagnoses.

In many instances, ADHD appears to be the result of brain abnormalities that limit students' ability to focus their attention and control their behaviors (e.g., Kadziela-Olech, Cichocki, Chwiesko, Konstantynowicz, & Braszko, 2015). Sometimes these abnormalities are inherited, but sometimes, instead, they're the result of toxic substances in children's early environments—perhaps high lead content in the paint dust of old buildings (Accardo, 2008; Barkley, 2010; Faranoe et al., 2005; Gatzke-Kopp & Beauchaine, 2007; Nigg, 2010).

COMMON CHARACTERISTICS

In addition to inattentiveness, hyperactivity, and impulsivity, students identified as having ADHD may have characteristics such as these:

- Exceptional imagination and creativity; exceptionally detailed memories
- Certain specific cognitive processing difficulties (e.g., see Figure 5.6) and low school achievement
- Problems with planning and time management
- Classroom behavior problems (e.g., disruptiveness, noncompliance)
- Poor social skills and interpersonal difficulties
- Increased probability of substance abuse in adolescence (Barkley, 2006; Gatzke-Kopp & Beauchaine, 2007; S. Goldstein & Rider, 2006; N. Gregg, 2009; Hallowell, 1996; Skowronek, Leichtman, & Pillemer, 2008; Tarver, Daley, & Sayal, 2014)

Students' attention, hyperactivity, and impulsiveness problems may diminish somewhat in adolescence, but they don't entirely disappear, making it difficult for students to handle the increasing demands that come in high school; for many, ADHD continues into and sometimes throughout adulthood (Tarver, Daley, & Sayal, 2014). Accordingly, students with ADHD are at greater-than-average risk for dropping out of school (Barkley, 2006; S. Goldstein & Rider, 2006; N. Gregg, 2009; E. L. Hart, Lahey, Loeber, Applegate, & Frick, 1995). ADHD continues to be a life-long issue for some individuals (Tarver et al., 2014).

ADAPTING INSTRUCTION

Some students with ADHD take medication that helps them control their symptoms. But medication alone is rarely sufficient to enable classroom success; individually tailored educational interventions are also in order (Purdie, Hattie, & Carroll, 2002). The strategies previously listed for students with learning disabilities can often be helpful

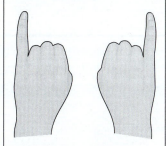

FIGURE 5.5 A mnemonic for remembering the letters *b* and *d*.

Young children with learning disabilities often confuse lowercase b and d. By clenching their fists as shown here and "reading" their hands in the normal left-to-right direction, they can more easily remember the difference: b comes first in both the alphabet and the fists.

FIGURE 5.6 Like many students with ADHD, 10-year-old Joshua has specific cognitive processing difficulties. Although he has the math skills of a typical fifth grader, he has delayed reading comprehension and writing skills, as reflected in the book report shown here. Josh can more easily express his thoughts orally.

I am just doce withbook. I really like ths book that I chose and it was a good chose. She dose not go back to San Fransico and find her peo pals. She stay io the Artic. , I would be sared too and cold. Mya X has survied there. about done.

for students with ADHD. Researchers and practitioners have offered several additional suggestions:

🍎 *Modify students' work environments and schedules.* Students with ADHD do better in a work environment that features minimal distractions, some degree of structure, and ongoing teacher monitoring. And ideally, students should have most academic subjects and challenging tasks in the morning rather than in the afternoon, as the symptoms of ADHD tend to get progressively worse as the day goes on (Barkley, 2006; N. Gregg, 2009).

🍎 *Explicitly facilitate attention and concentration.* Students may benefit from soundproof headphones or "white noise" machines that block out potentially distracting sounds, or, for a low-tech alternative, we might encourage them to move to a new location if their current one presents too many distractions (Buchoff, 1990; N. Gregg, 2009). Also, some computer programs give students practice in focusing and keeping their attention on specific stimuli (e.g., Klingberg, Keonig, & Bilbe, 2002; Rueda, Rothbart, McCandliss, Saccomanno, & Posner, 2005). Even using colored highlighting to point out particularly relevant information in reading materials or math problems may improve performance (Kercood, Zentall, Vinh, & Tom-Wright, 2012).

🍎 *Provide outlets for excess energy.* To help students control excess energy, we should intersperse quiet academic work with frequent opportunities for exercise (Pellegrini & Bohn, 2005; Pfiffner, Barkley, & DuPaul, 2006). We might also give students a settling-in time after recess or lunch—perhaps reading an excerpt from a high-interest book or article—before asking them to engage in an activity that involves quiet concentration (Pellegrini & Horvat, 1995).

🍎 *Help students organize and use their time effectively.* For example, we can show them how to prioritize activities, create to-do lists, and establish a daily routine that they post on their desks. We can break large tasks into smaller ones and set a short time limit for each subtask. And we can provide a folder in which students transport homework assignments to and from school (Buchoff, 1990; N. Gregg, 2009; Pfiffner et al., 2006).

SPEECH AND COMMUNICATION DISORDERS

Specific language impairments are described in Chapter 2.

Speech and communication disorders are impairments in spoken language or language comprehension that significantly interfere with students' academic performance. Examples include persistent articulation problems (e.g., see Figure 5.7), stuttering, abnormal syntactical patterns, and difficulty understanding other people's speech. By the time children reach the first grade, about 5% have noticeable speech disorders (National Institute of Deafness and Other Communication Disorders, 2010). Sometimes, but not always, these children have difficulty perceiving and mentally processing particular aspects of spoken language—a subcategory of speech and communication disorders known as *specific language impairments.* And often—but again, not always—the source of the disorder can be traced to heredity or brain abnormalities (Bishop, 2006; J. L. Locke, 1993; Spinath, Price, Dale, & Plomin, 2004).

COMMON CHARACTERISTICS

Although some students with speech and communication disorders have other disabilities as well, many of them are in most ways just typical students. Nevertheless, the following characteristics are fairly common:

• Reluctance to speak; embarrassment and self-consciousness when speaking
• Difficulties in reading and writing (Fey, Catts, & Larrivee, 1995; Heward, 2009; LaBlance, Steckol, & Smith, 1994; Rice, Hadley, & Alexander, 1993)

ADAPTING INSTRUCTION

Usually a trained specialist will work with students to help them improve or overcome their speech and communication difficulties. Although students may display deficits in only one noticeable part of speech, the specialist quite likely will intervene and work on a variety of aspects of speech (Owens, Farinella, & Metz, 2015). Nevertheless, general education teachers can assist in several ways:

FIGURE 5.7 Seven-year-old Isaac receives speech therapy at school to address his consistent mispronunciation of certain sounds (such as pronouncing "th" as "v"). In his writing, he sometimes spells words as he says them rather than as he hears them (for instance, he writes *ven* for *then*).

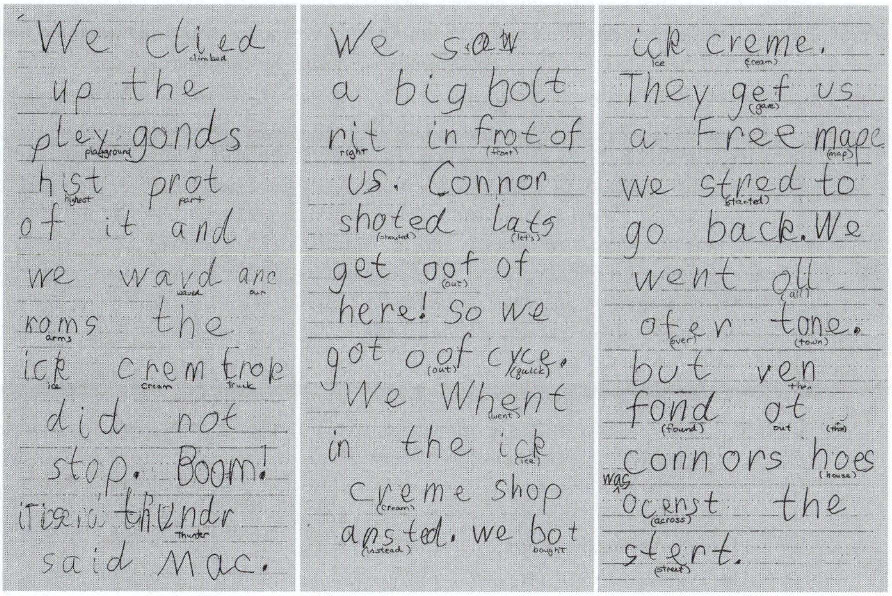

We clied (climbed) up the pley gonds (playground) hist (highest) prot (part) of it and we wavd (waved) anc (our) roms (arms) the ick crem (cream) trok (truck) did not stop. Boom! iTizig thundr (thunder) said Mac.

We saw a big bolt nit (right) in frot of (front) us. Connor shoted (shouted) lats (lets) get oof of (out) here! So we got o of (out) cyce (quick). We Whent (went) in the ick creme (cream) shop apsted (instead). we bot (bought)

ick creme (cream). They gef (gave) us a Free mape (map) we stred to (started) go back. We went oll (all) ofer (over) tone (town). but ven (then) fond (found) ot (out) connors hoes (house) was ocenst (across) the stert (street).

- *Encourage regular oral communication.* Students with speech and communication disorders need as much practice in classroom-based public speaking as their classmates do. Thus, we should encourage them to talk in class, provided that doing so doesn't create exceptional stress (Hallahan, Kauffman, & Pullen, 2009; Patton, Blackbourn, & Fad, 1996). We also should provide models of sentences and phrases that are easy for the child to understand, but also grammatically correct (Owens et al., 2015).

- *Listen patiently.* When students have trouble expressing themselves, we might be tempted to assist them, perhaps by finishing their sentences for them. But we help them more when we allow them to complete their own thoughts, and we must encourage their classmates to be equally patient (Heward, 2009; Patton et al., 1996). One of the authors of this book had a friend during adolescence who stuttered. In order to help the student, friends often would complete sentences for him when he was struggling to articulate a thought; however, when it was pointed out that it would be more helpful to listen patiently and allow the friend to complete his sentence for himself, conversations with the friend got much easier.

- *Ask for clarification when a message is unclear.* If we haven't entirely understood what students are saying, we should explain what we *did* understand and ask for clarification of the rest. Honest feedback helps students learn how well they're communicating (Patton et al., 1996).

- *Use augmentative and alternative communication (AAC) when students have little or no oral language.* Some forms of AAC involve computer technology; for example, a laptop or computer tablet might have a touchscreen that "speaks" when a student puts a finger on particular words or symbols. Others are nonelectronic; for example, we might give students a set of pictures or teach them some gestures they can use to represent their thoughts (Beukelman & Mirenda, 2005). For those of us who don't have easy access to speech experts, assessments and interventions can be provided via the Internet (Waite, Theodoros, Russell, & Cahill, 2010, 2012).

GENERAL RECOMMENDATIONS

In addition to the strategies described in the preceding pages, several general ones apply to many students with specific cognitive or academic difficulties:

🍎 *Get an early start on appropriate interventions.* When students lack basic concepts and skills on which their future learning will depend, intensive instruction to fill in the gaps—and the earlier, the better—can often make a significant difference in their achievement over the long run (L. S. Fuchs et al., 2005; Waber, 2010; Wanzek & Vaughn, 2007).

🍎 *Take skill levels into account when assigning reading materials.* Even after intensive reading instruction, many students with specific cognitive or academic difficulties continue to have poor reading skills. Thus, we may sometimes need to identify alternatives to standard grade-level textbooks for presenting academic content. For example, we might reduce the amount of required reading, substitute materials written on a simpler (yet not babyish) level, or present information through some medium other than printed text—perhaps audiotapes or text-to-speech computer software (N. Gregg, 2009; Mastropieri & Scruggs, 2007). Students may also need extra guidance and support when assignments require them to find and read information on the Internet (Sampson, Szabo, Falk-Ross, Foote, & Linder, 2007).

🍎 *Clearly describe expectations for academic performance.* Students will have an easier time accomplishing classroom tasks if they're told, in concrete and precise terms, exactly what's expected of them (Meltzer & Krishnan, 2007). For example, before students begin a science lab activity, we might first remind them to carefully follow the steps described on the lab sheet, then review safety precautions, and finally provide a written list of components that should be included in lab reports.

🍎 *Take steps to enhance self-confidence and motivation.* Students with a long history of failure at academic tasks need to see that they're making progress and that they do some things quite well. For instance, we can give them daily or weekly goals we know they can attain. We can also have them keep journals in which they describe the successes they've achieved each day. And, of course, we should give them opportunities to do tasks at which they excel (Buchoff, 1990; J. A. Stein & Krishnan, 2007).

MyEdLab **Application Exercise 5.4.** This interactive exercise gives you the opportunity to practice applying instructional adaptations and classroom practices that meet unique needs of students with specific cognitive or academic difficulties.

Students with Social or Behavioral Problems

For more information about matching instructional strategies to students' temperaments, see the section on *goodness of fit* in Chapter 3.

Many students have minor social, emotional, or behavioral difficulties at one time or another, particularly during times of unusual stress or major life changes. Often these problems are temporary ones that require only a little extra support from caring adults and peers. At other times problems are more enduring but *don't* reflect a disability. Perhaps a student's temperament is a poor fit with a teacher's instructional strategies—for instance, an especially fidgety child may perform poorly on lengthy seatwork assignments—or perhaps a teacher simply hasn't made clear the expectations and rules for classroom behavior (Keogh, 2003; Mehan, 1979). In such situations students' problems may decrease or disappear with a change in instructional practices or classroom management strategies.

However, some students show a pattern of engaging in behaviors that consistently interfere with their learning and performance *regardless* of the teacher and the classroom environment. In this section we'll look at two groups of students who fit into this category: those with emotional and behavioral disorders and those with autism spectrum disorders.

EMOTIONAL AND BEHAVIORAL DISORDERS

Students with emotional and behavioral disorders become identified as students with special needs—and therefore qualify for special educational services—when their problems have a substantial negative impact on classroom learning. Nevertheless, in the United States, some students do not receive adequate services; although these students represent between 3% and 6% of the population of students, less than 1% receive special education services under this categorization (Lane, Menzies, Kalberg, & Oakes, 2012). Symptoms of emotional and behavioral disorders typically fall into one of two broad categories. **Externalizing behaviors** have direct or indirect effects on other people; examples include aggression, defiance, stealing, and general lack of self-control. **Internalizing behaviors** primarily affect the student with the disorder; examples include severe anxiety or depression, exaggerated mood swings, withdrawal from social interaction, and eating disorders. Students with externalizing behaviors—who are more likely to be boys than girls—are more likely to be referred for evaluation and possible special services. However, students with internalizing behaviors—who are more likely to be girls than boys—can be just as much at risk for school failure (Angold, Worthman, & Costello, 2003; Gay, 2006; Hayward, 2003). These disorders need to be taken seriously, because, in addition to school failure, students with externalizing and internalizing behaviors are more at risk for serious mental health issues, including thinking about or attempting suicide (Peter & Roberts, 2010).

Some emotional and behavioral disorders result from environmental factors, such as stressful living conditions, child maltreatment, or family alcohol or drug abuse (P. T. Davies & Woitach, 2008; D. Glaser, 2000; Maughan & Cicchetti, 2002). But biological causes (e.g., inherited predispositions, chemical imbalances, brain injuries) may also be involved, either by themselves or through interaction with environmental conditions (Dodge, 2009; Raine, 2008; Yeo, Gangestad, & Thoma, 2007). Some students with a genetic predisposition for an emotional or behavioral disorder exhibit few, if any, signs until adolescence, as the following case illustrates:

> As a ninth grader, Kirk was a well-behaved, likeable student who earned As and Bs and showed particular promise in science and math. But in 10th grade, his grades began to decline, and he increasingly exhibited hostile and defiant behaviors. When Kirk failed three classes during the fall of his 12th-grade year, the school principal convened a meeting with him, his parents, and his faculty advisor to discuss how to help Kirk get back on track. At the meeting the principal described several occasions on which Kirk had acted disoriented, belligerent, and seemingly "high" on drugs. Despite his strong desire to attend college the following year, Kirk sat at the meeting smirking (seemingly gleeful about his predicament) and focusing his attention on sorting pieces of trail mix in a bowl on the conference room table. By the end of the meeting, the principal was so infuriated that she expelled him from school.
>
> Over the next few weeks, Kirk's mental condition and behavior continued to deteriorate, to the point that he was soon arrested, placed in a juvenile detention facility, and eventually hospitalized in the state mental institution.

Kirk was ultimately diagnosed with *bipolar disorder,* a condition that is usually inherited and is characterized by excessive mood swings (hence, the disorder is sometimes called manic depression) and in some cases (like Kirk's) by distorted thought processes. Bipolar disorder often doesn't appear until adolescence, even though its biological underpinnings have been present since birth (Griswold & Pessar, 2000).

When students have emotional or behavioral disorders, their inappropriate behaviors interfere not only with academic achievement but also with peer relationships, leading to social as well as academic failure. Some of these students may seek the companionship of the few peers who will accept them—peers who typically behave in similarly inappropriate ways and may introduce one another to drugs, alcohol, or criminal activity (J. Snyder et al., 2008; Webber & Plotts, 2008). Sadly, many youth who have emotional or behavioral disorders do not receive the services and supports that they need. Often boys with externalizing behaviors receive support, but others sometimes do not receive sufficient services (Hallahan, Kauffman, & Pullen, 2015).

COMMON CHARACTERISTICS

Students with emotional and behavioral disorders differ considerably in their abilities and personalities. However, in addition to the difficulty in maintaining healthy peer relationships just mentioned, you may observe one or more of the following characteristics:

- Frequent absences from school
- Deteriorating academic performance with increasing age

MyEdLab
Video Example 5.5.

Some students consistently disrupt the classroom environment with inappropriate behavior and have difficulty forming and maintaining peer relationships. Teachers can take steps to help these students learn appropriate behaviors and give them a sense that they have some control over their circumstances.

Report suspicions about child maltreatment *immediately* to school administrators or child protective services.

- Often, but not always, below-average intelligence
- Low self-esteem
- Aggressive or withdrawn behaviors
- Little or no empathy for others' distress
- Significant substance abuse (Grinberg & McLean-Heywood, 1999; Harter, 1999; Kauffman & Landrum, 2013; Leiter & Johnsen, 1997; McGlynn, 1998; Richards, Symons, Greene, & Szuszkiewicz, 1995; Turnbull, Turnbull, & Wehmeyer, 2010; Webber & Plotts, 2008)

Some students with emotional and behavioral disorders have other special needs as well, including learning disabilities, ADHD, or giftedness (Fessler, Rosenberg, & Rosenberg, 1991; Gatzke-Kopp & Beauchaine, 2007; Webber & Plotts, 2008).

ADAPTING INSTRUCTION

There is promising research indicating that some specific drug treatments are quite helpful to some children and adolescents with emotional and behavioral disorders (Konopasek & Forness, 2014); however, environmental supports are also important. Effective interventions must be tailored to each student's unique needs, but several strategies can benefit many of these students:

- *Show an interest in students' well-being and personal growth.* A good first step in helping students with emotional and behavioral disorders is simply showing that we care about them (Chang & Davis, 2009; Clarke et al., 1995; Heward, 2009). For example, we can greet them warmly when we see them, express concern when they seem upset or overly stressed, and lend a supportive ear when they want to share their opinions or frustrations. And we can take students' personal interests into account when planning instruction and assignments.

- *Give students a sense that they have some control over their circumstances.* Some students, especially those who are frequently defiant, often respond to efforts to control them by behaving even *less* appropriately. With such students it's important to avoid power struggles in which only one person wins and the other inevitably loses. Instead, we must create situations in which we ensure that students conform to classroom expectations yet feel that they have some control over what happens to them. For example, we can teach them techniques for observing and monitoring their own actions, with the goal of developing more productive classroom behavior. We can also give them choices, within reasonable limits, about what tasks to accomplish in particular situations (Chang & Davis, 2009; Kern, Dunlap, Childs, & Clark, 1994; Lane, Falk, & Wehby, 2006).

- *Make sure that students are learning basic skills.* Students with emotional and behavioral disorders often are inattentive and off-task, and thus less engaged with their academic work. Thus, these students may not develop some basic skills (e.g., basic reading or mathematical skills) that are important for all future learning. It is important to identify these disorders early, and to work collaboratively with special educators to meet these students' social and academic needs (Nelson, Benner, & Bohaty, 2014).

- *Be alert for signs that a student may be contemplating suicide.* In the United States, suicide is the third-leading cause of death for adolescents; occasionally even younger students take their own lives (Goldston et al., 2008; Westefeld et al., 2010). Warning signs include the following:

  - Sudden withdrawal from social relationships
  - Increasing disregard for personal appearance
  - Dramatic personality change (e.g., sudden elevation in mood)
  - Preoccupation with death and morbid themes
  - Overt or veiled threats (e.g., "I won't be around much longer")
  - Actions that indicate putting one's affairs in order (e.g., giving away prized possessions) (Granello & Granello, 2006; Wiles & Bondi, 2001)

  As teachers, we must take any of these warning signs seriously and seek help *immediately* from trained professionals, such as school psychologists or counselors.

It's also essential, of course, that we help students with emotional and behavioral disorders acquire more appropriate behaviors. We describe strategies for doing so after the discussion of autism spectrum disorders in the next section.

AUTISM SPECTRUM DISORDERS

The central, defining features of autism spectrum disorders are marked impairments in social cognition (e.g., perspective taking, interpreting other people's body language), social skills, language usage, and social interaction. Many students with these disorders prefer to be alone and form weak, if any, emotional attachments to other people. Some students develop limited abilities to use language, whereas others' language usage is more fully developed. Common, too, are repetitive behaviors (often very odd ones rarely seen in age-mates) and inflexible adherence to certain routines or rituals (American Psychiatric Association, 2000; Lord, 2010; Pelphrey & Carter, 2007; Tager-Flusberg, 2007). Autism spectrum disorders are prevalent; in the United States, an estimated 1 out of every 68 children has been identified as having autism spectrum disorder, with five times as many diagnoses in boys as in girls (Centers for Disease Control, 2014).

Aside from similarities in social impairments and repetitive behaviors, individuals with autism spectrum disorders differ considerably in the severity of their condition—hence the term *spectrum*. In Asperger syndrome, a fairly mild form, students usually have normal language skills and average or above-average intelligence. In severe cases, which are often referred to simply as *autism,* children have major delays in cognitive development and language and may exhibit certain bizarre behaviors—perhaps constantly rocking or waving fingers, continually repeating what someone else has said, or showing unusual fascination with a very narrow category of objects (American Psychiatric Association, 2000; Lord, 2010).

The vast majority of autism spectrum disorders are probably caused by abnormalities in the brain. Some researchers have observed abnormalities in *mirror neurons*—neurons that probably underlie people's perspective-taking abilities (Gallese, Gernsbacher, Heyes, Hickok, & Iacoboni, 2011). Other researchers have discovered abnormalities in interconnections among various parts of the brain—for example, in connections between parts that enable logical reasoning or inhibition of impulses, on the one hand, and parts that underlie emotions and emotional processing, on the other (Cherkassky, Kana, Keller, & Just, 2006; I. L. Cohen, 2007; Kana, Keller, Minshew, & Just, 2007). Recent studies suggest that multiple regions of the brain are involved in autism spectrum disorders (Byrnes, 2012). Although some have speculated that autism may be cause by childhood vaccines, there is *no* evidence that there is any association of vaccines with autism (Institute of Medicine, 2011; Maglione et al., 2014). Also, students with autism spectrum disorders may be either undersensitive or oversensitive to environmental stimulation (Ratey, 2001; R. C. Sullivan, 1994; D. Williams, 1996). Temple Grandin, a woman who has gained international prominence as a designer of livestock facilities, recalls what it was like to be a child with autism:

Mirror neurons are described in more detail in Chapter 3.

> From as far back as I can remember, I always hated to be hugged. I wanted to experience the good feeling of being hugged, but it was just too overwhelming. It was like a great, all-engulfing tidal wave of stimulation, and I reacted like a wild animal. . . . When I was little, loud noises were also a problem, often feeling like a dentist's drill hitting a nerve. They actually caused pain. I was scared to death of balloons popping, because the sound was like an explosion in my ear. (Grandin, 1995, pp. 63, 67)

COMMON CHARACTERISTICS

In addition to the traits already described, students with autism spectrum disorders may have characteristics such as these:

- Strong visual–spatial thinking skills and exceptional awareness of visual details
- Unusual ability to maintain attention and focus during distractions
- Good memory for a set of unrelated facts
- Difficulty planning and organizing a future course of action
- Strong need for a consistent, predictable environment (I. L. Cohen, 2007; M. Dawson, Soulières, Gernsbacher, & Mottron, 2007; Gernsbacher, Stevenson, Khandakar, & Goldsmith,

2008; Grandin & Johnson, 2005; Lord, 2010; Meltzer, 2007; Pelphrey & Carter, 2007; Tager-Flusberg, 2007)

Occasionally students with autism exhibit *savant syndrome,* possessing an extraordinary ability (e.g., exceptional mathematical, artistic, or musical talent) that is quite remarkable in contrast to other aspects of their mental functioning (I. L. Cohen, 2007; L. K. Miller, 2005; Treffert & Wallace, 2002).

ADAPTING INSTRUCTION

Children with Asperger syndrome are typically in general education classes. Students with autism spectrum disorders also can sometimes participate in general education classes for all or part of the day, although inclusion of these students can be complex, so the support of a special educator often may be necessary (Crosland & Dunlap, 2012). As with other exceptionalities, it is important to include parents in discussions about the most appropriate setting for their children. The mother of a first grader with autism, who advocated for her son to be in a classroom that also had non-special-education students, noted that "If he was in a program that was just with other autistic children, there would be no way for him to pick up the behaviors of typically developing children" (Crane, 2010).

Many of the classroom strategies described in earlier sections are applicable for such students. Two additional strategies are helpful as well:

- *Maximize consistency in the classroom layout and weekly schedule.* Many students with autism spectrum disorders feel more comfortable when their environments and schedules are predictable. At the beginning of the school year, then, we should arrange furniture and equipment in ways that will be serviceable throughout the school year, making adjustments later only if absolutely necessary. And to the greatest extent possible, we should schedule recurring activities at the same times each day or on particular days of the week. If the schedule must change for some reason, we should alert students well in advance (Dalrymple, 1995).

- *Use visual approaches to instruction.* Because students with autism spectrum disorders often have strong visual–spatial skills but may have impaired language skills, a heavy emphasis on visual materials may be in order (Ozonoff & Schetter, 2007; C. C. Peterson, 2002; Quill, 1995). We might use objects, pictures, and photographs to convey ideas about academic topics, or we might use some sort of visual cue to signal the start of a new activity.

GENERAL RECOMMENDATIONS

Although the causes of emotional and behavioral disorders and those of autism spectrum disorders are usually quite different, students with these disabilities can benefit from some of the same classroom interventions. Certainly we want to promote success on academic tasks, perhaps by using instructional strategies presented earlier for students with specific cognitive or academic difficulties. Following are additional suggestions:

- *Insist on appropriate classroom behavior.* Although certain students with disabilities may be more prone to counterproductive classroom behaviors than most of their peers, teachers clearly *can* help them behave in productive ways—for instance, by putting reasonable limits on their behavior and imposing consequences when they go beyond those limits (Evertson & Weinstein, 2006; Webber & Plotts, 2008). The Creating a Productive Classroom Environment feature "Encouraging Appropriate Behavior in Students with Social or Behavioral Problems" offers several useful strategies.

You can find strategies for fostering social cognition and perspective taking in Chapter 3.

- *Foster social cognition and effective interpersonal skills.* Students with social or behavioral problems often benefit from training in social cognition and perspective taking. Explicit instruction in and reinforcement of social skills can also be quite powerful. And of course, students need numerous opportunities to *practice* their new skills (e.g., Chan & O'Reilly, 2008; Myles & Simpson, 2001; Nikopoulos & Keenan, 2004; Schrandt, Townsend, & Poulson, 2009; Theimann & Goldstein, 2004).

- *Be persistent, and look for gradual improvement rather than overnight success.* Many students with social or behavioral problems will initially resist our efforts to help them. They may begin to recognize the value of our guidance and support only when they see the natural

Encouraging Appropriate Behavior in Students with Social or Behavioral Problems

Make expectations for behavior clear and specific.
A teacher reminds a student, "You can't borrow Mary's bottle of glue without getting her permission. Check with Mary first to make sure it's all right for you to use her things. If Mary says no, ask someone else."

Specify and follow through on consequences for appropriate and inappropriate behaviors.
A teacher tells a student, "Sam, you know that certain four-letter words, such as the two you just used, are unacceptable in this classroom. You also know the consequence for such behavior, so please go to the time-out corner for 10 minutes."

Give feedback about specific behaviors rather than general areas of performance.
A teacher tells a student, "You did a good job in study hall today. You focused your attention on your homework, and you didn't retaliate when Jerome accidentally brushed past you on his way to my desk."

Try to anticipate problems and nip them in the bud.
A student has occasional temper tantrums that disrupt the entire class. Although the tantrums seemingly occur at random, his teacher eventually realizes that his ears always turn red just before an outburst. With this knowledge, she can divert the student's attention to a punching bag whenever a tantrum is imminent, thereby letting him unleash his feelings with only minimal distraction to others.

Sources: Hallahan et al., 2009; Heward, 2009; Myles & Simpson, 2001; Ormrod & McGuire, 2007 (temper tantrum example); Webber & Plotts, 2008.

consequences of their changing behavior—for example, when they start to make new friends or get along better with their teachers. Their progress may be slow, but by focusing on small improvements, we and our students alike can be encouraged by the changes we *do* see, rather than being discouraged by problems that persist.

Students with General Delays in Cognitive and Social Functioning

When we use the term *student with general delays in cognitive and social functioning,* we're talking about any student who shows a consistent pattern of developmental delays, regardless of whether the student has been identified as having a disability. Educators sometimes use the term *slow learner* to describe a student who obtains intelligence test scores in the 70s and has noticeable difficulties in most or all parts of the curriculum. A student with especially pronounced difficulties may be identified as having an intellectual disability.

INTELLECTUAL DISABILITIES

You're undoubtedly familiar with the term *mental retardation.* In recent years, however, many special educators have instead advocated for the term intellectual disability in reference to students who show pronounced delays in most aspects of cognitive and social development. More specifically, students with intellectual disabilities exhibit *both* of the following characteristics (Luckasson et al., 2002):

- *Significantly below-average general intelligence.* These students have intelligence test scores that are quite low—usually no higher than 70, reflecting performance in the bottom 2% of their age-group. In addition, these students learn slowly and show consistently poor achievement in virtually all academic subject areas.

- *Deficits in adaptive behavior.* These students behave in ways that we would expect of much younger children. Their deficits in adaptive behavior include limitations in *practical intelligence*—that is, managing the ordinary activities of daily living—and *social intelligence*—that is, conducting themselves appropriately in social situations.

The preceding characteristics must be evident in childhood. Thus, a person who shows them beginning at age 18, perhaps as the result of a serious head injury, would *not* be classified as having an intellectual disability.

Intellectual disabilities are often caused by genetic conditions. For example, most children with Down syndrome have delayed cognitive and social development. Other cases are due to biological but noninherited causes, such as severe malnutrition or excessive alcohol consumption during the mother's pregnancy or oxygen deprivation during birth. In other situations, environmental factors, such as parental neglect or an extremely impoverished and unstimulating home environment may be at fault (Beirne-Smith, Patton, & Kim, 2006).

COMMON CHARACTERISTICS

Like students in any category of special needs, students with intellectual disabilities have differing personalities, strengths, and needs. Nevertheless, many of them are apt to exhibit characteristics such as the following:

- Sociability and a genuine desire to belong and fit in at school
- Less general knowledge about the world
- Poor reading and language skills
- Short attention span
- Poor memory; few or no effective learning and memory strategies
- Difficulty drawing inferences and understanding abstract ideas
- Difficulty generalizing something learned in one situation to a new situation
- Immature play behaviors and interpersonal skills
- Delayed motor skills; conditions that adversely affect performance in physical activities (e.g., heart defects, poor muscle tone) (Beirne-Smith et al., 2006; Bergeron & Floyd, 2006; Carlin et al., 2003; Heward, 2009; F. P. Hughes, 1998; Tager-Flusberg & Skwerer, 2007)

ADAPTING INSTRUCTION

With proper support, many students with mild intellectual disabilities can learn basic skills in reading, writing, and math, perhaps even mastering components of a typical fifth- or sixth-grade curriculum (Hallahan et al., 2009; Heward, 2009). Many special programs also are available for students with mild intellectual disabilities, sometimes involving partnerships with local universities (Nephin, 2014). Most of the strategies previously described in this chapter can be useful for these students. Here are several additional strategies to keep in mind:

- 🍎 *Pace instruction slowly and set short-term goals to ensure success.* When working with a student who has an intellectual disability, we should move through new topics and tasks slowly enough—and with enough support and repetition—that the student can eventually master them. Students with intellectual disabilities typically have a long history of failure at academic tasks. Thus, they need frequent success experiences to learn that, with hard work, they *can* succeed at many tasks. By setting short-term, easy-to-reach goals, students will be more likely to experience success, and be motivated to continue to engage in similar activities (Feuerstein et al., 2010; Fidler, Hepburn, Mankin, & Rogers, 2005; Heward, 2009; Sands & Wehmeyer, 2005).

- 🍎 *Provide considerable scaffolding to promote effective cognitive processes and desired behaviors.* We can develop simple study guides that tell students exactly what to focus on as they study. We can be explicit in our directions to perform various tasks—for instance, saying "John, go to the office, give Mrs. Smith the absentee sheet, and come back here." And we can provide handheld, teacher-programmed prompters—which go by such labels as *visual assistant* and *digital memory aid*—to help students remember the things they need to do (Beirne-Smith et al., 2006; Mastropieri & Scruggs, 1992; Patton et al., 1996, p. 105; Turnbull et al., 2010).

- 🍎 *Include vocational and general life skills in the curriculum.* For most students with intellectual disabilities, training in life and work skills is an important part of the high school curriculum. Such training is most likely to be effective when it takes place in realistic settings that closely resemble those in which students will find themselves once they leave school (Beirne-Smith et al., 2006; Turnbull et al., 2010). One successful program provides opportunities for adolescents to learn a variety of farming and farm-related skills. Participants are able to learn about planting, harvesting, and even the retail aspects of farming, including

MyEdLab
Video Example 5.6.

Students with intellectual disabilities experience difficulties in most or all parts of the curriculum and exhibit deficits in adaptive behavior. Many of these students are sociable and eager to fit in at school.

MyEdLab
Video Example 5.7.

Students with physical or sensory challenges vary in their strengths and limitations. In the general education classroom, teachers build on student strengths and adapt the environment to minimize limitations.

opportunities to sell produce at the farm's store (Bacon, 2014). The students report that they enjoy these opportunities, and the acquisition of these skills often leads to future employment.

MyEdLab **Application Exercise 5.5.**
In this interactive exercise you can practice identifying teaching strategies that help students with behavioral problems to function effectively and learn in the general education classroom.

Students with Physical or Sensory Challenges

Some students with special needs have obvious physical disabilities caused by medically detectable physiological conditions. These include physical and health impairments, visual impairments, and hearing loss. A small subset of them have severe and multiple disabilities that require significant adaptations and highly specialized services; such students are typically accompanied by child-specific teacher aides or other specialists when attending general education classrooms.

PHYSICAL AND HEALTH IMPAIRMENTS

Physical and health impairments are general physical or medical conditions (usually long term) that interfere with school performance to such a degree that special instruction, curricular materials, equipment, or facilities are necessary. Students in this category may have limited energy and strength, reduced mental alertness, or little muscle control. Examples of conditions that might qualify students for special services are traumatic brain injury, spinal cord injury, cerebral palsy, epilepsy, cancer, and acquired immune deficiency syndrome (AIDS).

COMMON CHARACTERISTICS

It's hard to generalize about students with physical and health impairments because their conditions are so very different from one another. Nevertheless, several common characteristics are noteworthy:

- Low stamina and a tendency to tire easily
- Varying degrees of intellectual functioning (many of these students have learning ability similar to that of nondisabled peers)
- Lower levels of academic achievement as a result of frequent school absences
- Fewer opportunities to experience and interact with the outside world in educationally important ways (e.g., less use of public transportation, fewer visits to museums and zoos)
- Possible low self-esteem, insecurity, social isolation from peers, or heavy dependence on adults, depending partly on how parents and others have responded to their impairments (Heward, 2009; Patton et al., 1996; J. W. Wood, 1998; Yeo & Sawyer, 2005)

ADAPTING INSTRUCTION

Although we won't necessarily need to modify the academic curriculum for students with physical and health impairments, we will definitely want to make certain accommodations:

- *Be sensitive to specific limitations, and accommodate them flexibly.* One student may require extra time with a writing assignment and perhaps should not be held to the same standards of neatness and legibility. Another may need to respond to test questions orally rather than on paper. Still another might tire easily and need to take frequent breaks.
- *Know what to do in emergencies.* A student with acute asthma may have trouble breathing; a student with diabetes may go into insulin shock; a student with epilepsy may have a grand mal seizure; a student who is HIV positive might get a cut and bleed. We should consult with school medical personnel ahead of time so that we are prepared to respond calmly and appropriately in such life- and health-threatening situations.

🍎 *If students and parents give permission, educate classmates about the nature of students' disabilities.* Many children treat peers with physical disabilities kindly and respectfully, but some others do not. Sometimes peers are simply ignorant about the nature of a disability, and giving them accurate information can help them become more accepting and supportive (e.g., R. White & Cunningham, 1991).

VISUAL IMPAIRMENTS

Students with visual impairments have malfunctions of their eyes or optic nerves that prevent normal vision even with corrective lenses. Some students are totally blind, others see only fuzzy patterns of light and dark, and still others have a restricted visual field (*tunnel vision*) that allows them to see just a very small area at a time. Visual impairments are caused by congenital abnormalities in or damage to either the eye or the visual pathway to the brain. Vision is essential to the development of many cognitive abilities, including reading from print, understanding spatial relationships, and comprehension of concepts (Smith, Polloway, Doughty, Patton, & Dowdy, 2016). When students have visual impairments, these abilities may be delayed, and that could affect learning in all academic subjects.

COMMON CHARACTERISTICS

Students with visual impairments are apt to have many or all of these characteristics:

- Normal functioning of other senses (hearing, touch, etc.)
- General learning ability similar to that of nondisabled students, although visual memory and concept development may be delayed or impaired
- More limited vocabulary, expressive and receptive language, and general world knowledge, in part because of fewer opportunities to experience the outside world in educationally important ways (e.g., less exposure to maps, films, and other visual material)
- Delayed motor development; reduced capability to imitate others' behaviors
- Inability to observe other people's body language and other nonverbal cues, leading to occasional misunderstanding of others' messages and immature social behaviors
- Uncertainty and anxiety (especially in chaotic environments, such as the lunchroom or playground) as a result of having no visual knowledge of ongoing events
- In the primary grades, less knowledge about the conventions of written language (direction of print, punctuation, etc.) (M. Harris, 1992; Heward, 2009; Hobson, 2004; Patton et al., 1996; Smith et al., 2016; Tompkins & McGee, 1986; Turnbull et al., 2010; Tuttle & Tuttle, 1996)

ADAPTING INSTRUCTION

Specialists typically give students training in Braille, orientation and mobility, and specially adapted computer technology. But general education teachers play important roles as well, as reflected in the following strategies:

🍎 *Orient students ahead of time to the physical layout of the classroom.* Students should have a chance to explore the classroom before other students arrive—ideally, before the first day of class. At that time we can help students locate important objects (e.g., wastebasket and pencil sharpener) and point out special sounds (e.g., the buzzing of a wall clock) to help students get their bearings (J. W. Wood, 1998). We also need to support students when furniture or objects in the classroom are moved to new locations during the school year. Computer-generated virtual environments can now be created and presented to individuals prior to their immersion in a new environment, and the use of such software can improve navigation skills (Connors, Chrastil, Sánchez, & Merabet, 2014).

🍎 *Use visual materials with sharp contrast.* Some students with partial sight can use visual materials with clearly distinguishable features, such as enlarged documents on computer screens and the large-print books available at most libraries. Students' eyes may tire quickly, however, so we should limit use of visual materials to short time periods (Heward, 2009; Patton et al., 1996).

🍎 *Depend heavily on other modalities*. Print-reading computer software and portable print-reading devices easily translate most printed text into spoken language. Many novels, school textbooks, and published curriculum materials are available in Braille, many other books are available in audio form (e.g., see www.learningally.org), and volunteers can sometimes be enlisted to convert still other written materials into Braille or audiotape. We can also conduct hands-on activities involving objects that students can feel and manipulate, and we can involve students in projects that involve oral presentations. For example, we might use plastic relief maps that portray mountains, valleys, and coastlines in three dimensions, perhaps embellishing them with pin pricks to indicate country borders and small dabs of nail polish to indicate major cities.

🍎 *Allow extra time for learning and performance*. Learning by hearing often takes more time than learning by seeing. When students *look* at something, they perceive a great deal of information at once and thus learn many commonplace relationships (e.g., between the sight of a cat and the sound it makes). When they must *listen* to it, however, they receive it sequentially—only one piece at a time—and often without obvious interconnections (Ferrell, 1996; Heward, 2009; M. B. Rowe, 1978).

🍎 *Teach learning strategies to your students*. Visually impaired students in particular can benefit from explicit instruction in various strategies (Smith et al., 2016). Whereas other students can acquire some of these strategies through observation, visually impaired students will need extra support in learning many strategies. In addition, some strategies (e.g., highlighting important text while reading) will not be possible for students with severe visual impairments; nevertheless, alternative strategies often are available. Collaborative partnerships with special educators are particularly beneficial in these situations.

HEARING LOSS

Students with **hearing loss** have a malfunction of the ears or associated nerves that interferes with the perception of sounds within the frequency range of normal human speech. Two to three of every 1,000 children born in the United States have detectable hearing loss at birth (National Institute on Deafness and Other Communication Disorders, 2014). Students who are completely *deaf* have insufficient sensation to understand any spoken language, even with the help of a hearing aid. Students who are *hard of hearing* understand some speech but experience exceptional difficulty in doing so.

COMMON CHARACTERISTICS

Most students with hearing loss have normal intellectual abilities (Braden, 1992; Schirmer, 1994). However, they may have characteristics such as these:

- Delayed language development because of reduced exposure to spoken language, especially if the impairment was present at birth or emerged early in life
- Proficiency in sign language, such as American Sign Language (ASL) or finger spelling
- Some ability to read lips (*speechreading*)
- Less oral language than that of hearing classmates; perhaps a monotonous, hollow quality to speech
- Less developed reading skills, especially if language development has been delayed
- Less general world knowledge because of reduced exposure to spoken language
- Some social isolation, more limited social skills, and reduced perspective-taking ability as a result of a reduced ability to communicate (Bassett et al, 1996; Chall, 1996; P. L. Harris, 2006; Heward, 2009; C. C. Peterson, 2002; M. B. Rowe, 1978; Schick, de Villiers, de Villiers, & Hoffmeister, 2007; Turnbull et al., 2010)

ADAPTING INSTRUCTION

Specialists typically provide training in such communication skills as American Sign Language, finger spelling, and speechreading. With these additions (and possibly some remedial instruction in reading and vocabulary), a normal school curriculum is appropriate for most students with hearing loss. However, several accommodations can facilitate students' success in general education classrooms:

🍎 *Minimize irrelevant noise.* Even when students can benefit from hearing aids, what they hear is often diminished or distorted; consequently, it's helpful to minimize potentially distracting sounds. For example, carpeting and bulletin boards can absorb some extraneous noise, and fans and pencil sharpeners should be located as far away as possible.

🍎 *Supplement auditory presentations with visual information and hands-on experiences.* We can write important points on the chalkboard, illustrate key ideas with pictures, provide reading materials that duplicate lectures, and ask an aide or student volunteer to take notes on in-class discussions. We can also provide speech-to-text software, which enables students to translate spoken words into written language with reasonable accuracy. And we can use concrete activities (e.g., role-playing historical events) to make abstract ideas more understandable.

🍎 *Communicate in ways that help students hear and speechread.* Students who are hard of hearing are most likely to understand us when we speak in a normal tone of voice (not overly loud) and pronounce words distinctly but otherwise normally. To help students speechread, we should speak only while facing them and never while sitting in a dark corner or standing in front of a window or bright light (Gearheart, Weishahn, & Gearheart, 1992; J. W. Wood, 1998).

🍎 *Teach American Sign Language and finger spelling to classmates.* To facilitate communication with students who have hearing loss, other class members should gain some competence in American Sign Language and finger spelling. One of us authors once taught at a school where *every* student—those with hearing loss and those without—received instruction in signing. One girl in the author's class was totally deaf yet quite popular with her peers, thanks to everyone's ability to communicate easily.

GENERAL RECOMMENDATIONS

In addition to the strategies just identified for specific physical disabilities, several more general strategies are useful with all students who have physical or sensory challenges:

🍎 *Ensure that all students have access to important educational resources and opportunities.* Such access may involve modifying instructional materials (e.g., obtaining large-print copies of textbooks), adjusting a classroom's physical arrangement (e.g., widening aisles and placing bulletin board displays at eye level to accommodate students in wheelchairs), or making special arrangements that enable students to participate in field trips or sports activities.

🍎 *Provide assistance only when students really need it.* Out of their eagerness to help students with physical and sensory challenges, many adults inadvertently perform tasks and solve problems that these students are perfectly capable of handling on their own. Yet one of our goals for these students should be to promote their independence, not their dependence on others (Wehmeyer et al., 2007).

🍎 *Use assistive technology to facilitate learning and performance.* We've already mentioned the value of print-reading software and speech-to-text software for students with sensory challenges. In addition, some computer printers can create Braille documents, enabling students with visual impairments to read their own class notes and compositions. Specially adapted joysticks and voice recognition systems can supplement or replace computer keyboards for students with limited muscle control. And machines known as augmentative communication devices provide synthesized speech for students incapable of producing normal speech.

MyEdLab **Self-Check 5.4**

MyEdLab **Application Exercise 5.6.**
In this interactive exercise you can practice identifying adaptations that improve learning for students with sensory challenges and strategies that build on their strengths.

Students with Advanced Cognitive Development

Many students are apt to have advanced abilities, either in specific subject areas or across the curriculum, that warrant attention and encouragement. Some students—those who are *gifted*—are so far above the norm that special educational services are often appropriate. We often will encounter gifted students in our classes; as we'll see, there are numerous considerations in adapting instruction to engage and challenge gifted students.

GIFTEDNESS

In general, **giftedness** is unusually high ability or aptitude in one or more areas (e.g., in math, science, creative writing, or music) to such a degree that special educational services are necessary to help the student meet his or her full potential. In most instances giftedness is probably the result of both a genetic predisposition and environmental nurturing (Dai, 2010; Simonton, 2001; Winner, 2000b). In some cases, however, special gifts and talents are largely the result of intensive practice and mentoring (Ericsson, 2003; Gladwell, 2006). The identification of a child as gifted is often a reflection of the values of one's society. Thus, a student who is gifted in sculpting might not be identified as such in a community in which sculpting (or art, more generally) is not valued (Subotnik, Olszewski-Kubilius, & Worrell, 2011).

Giftedness is not included in IDEA. In the United States, the Jacob K. Javits Gifted and Talented Student Education Act of 1987 (reauthorized in 1994 and 2001) encourages but doesn't necessarily mandate special educational services for students who are gifted. Many state governments also either encourage or mandate such services. School districts often use multiple criteria—sometimes including intelligence test scores, sometimes not—to identify students who show exceptional promise in general academic ability, specific academic fields, creativity, or the arts. A current debate is whether gifted education should be to develop eminence and talent, or to provide opportunities for students to develop newly emerging talents (Subotnik & Rickoff, 2010).

COMMON CHARACTERISTICS

Students who are gifted vary considerably in their unique strengths and talents, and those who show exceptional talent in one area may have only average ability in another (Winner, 2000b). Nevertheless, many students who are gifted have characteristics such as these:

MyEdLab
Video Example 5.8.

Students with advanced cognitive development vary considerably in their gifts and talents, but they generally have the ability to learn more quickly and independently than peers. They often have high standards for performance and high motivation to accomplish challenging tasks.

- Advanced vocabulary, language, and reading skills
- Extensive general knowledge about the world
- Ability to learn more quickly, easily, and independently than peers
- Advanced and efficient cognitive processes and learning strategies
- Considerable flexibility in ideas and approaches to tasks
- High standards for performance (sometimes to the point of unhealthy perfectionism)
- High motivation to accomplish challenging tasks; boredom during easy tasks
- Strong interest in the area in which strengths have been identified
- Positive self-concept, especially with regard to academic endeavors
- Average or above-average social development and emotional adjustment (although a few extremely gifted students may have difficulties because they are so *very* different from their peers) (Dai, 2010; Mendaglio, 2010; Parker, 1997; Shavinina & Ferrari, 2004; Steiner & Carr, 2003; Subotnik et al., 2011; Subotnik, Olszewski-Kubilus, & Worrell. 2012; Winner, 2000a, 2000b)

To some degree, the nature of giftedness depends somewhat on where students are in their developmental journeys (Dai, 2010; D. J. Matthews, 2009). In the preschool and early elementary years, giftedness might take the form of precociousness in certain general domains; for example, a first grader might be reading sixth-grade-level books or exhibit exceptional facility with numbers. By the upper elementary and secondary grades, some students are likely to show exceptional achievement in very specific areas—perhaps in creative writing, computer technology, or music.

Yet we must keep in mind that students who are gifted may also have one or more disabilities; for instance, they may have dyslexia or Asperger syndrome. In planning instruction for such students, we must address their disabilities as well as their unique gifts.

ADAPTING INSTRUCTION

Exceptional talents and achievement levels typically require ongoing environmental nurturance and support, in the forms of both differentiated instruction and access to appropriate resources and practice opportunities. Furthermore, many high-achieving students become bored or frustrated when school assignments don't challenge them, and others become so accustomed to the "easy A" that they have trouble coping with the mistakes they're likely to make when they venture into new areas (Dai, 2010; Mendaglio, 2010; Parker, 1997). With such points in mind, we offer the following recommendations:

- *Provide individualized tasks and assignments.* Different students are apt to need special services in very different areas—for example, in math, creative writing, or studio art. Some students who are gifted, especially those with only a limited background in English, may also need training in certain basic skills (C. R. Harris, 1991; Udall, 1989).

- *Form study groups of students with similar interests and abilities.* In some cases a study group might explore a topic in greater depth and with more sophisticated analysis than other students (an *enrichment* approach). In other instances a study group might simply move through the standard school curriculum at a more rapid pace (an *acceleration* approach). Enrichment and acceleration are both beneficial for gifted students, and they are not mutually exclusive—courses can potentially be both accelerated and enriching simultaneously (Rogers, 2002; Subotnik et al., 2011). Students benefit both academically and socially from increased contact with peers who have similar interests and talents (Hattie, 2009; J. A. Kulik & Kulik, 1997; McGinn, Viernstein, & Hogan, 1980).

- *Teach complex cognitive skills within the context of specific subject areas.* Programs designed to enhance students' creativity, critical thinking, or other complex skills separately from specific content domains tend to have only limited impact. Teaching complex thinking skills within the context of specific topics—for example, creativity in writing or reasoning and problem-solving skills in science—is more likely to be effective (Dai, 2010; M. C. Linn, Clement, Pulos, & Sullivan, 1989; Moon, Feldhusen, & Dillon, 1994; Stanley, 1980).

- *Provide opportunities for independent study and service learning projects.* Independent study and community service projects in areas of interest are often beneficial and motivating for high-ability students, provided that they have the work habits, study strategies, and research skills they need to use their time and resources effectively (Candler-Lotven, Tallent-Runnels, Olivárez, & Hildreth, 1994; Terry, 2008). However, even if students are working on projects of this nature, it is important that gifted students have clear goals, and are provided with continuous feedback as they progress toward these goals (Callahan, Moon, Oh, Azano, & Hailey, 2015).

- *Seek outside resources.* When students have high abilities in domains outside our own areas of expertise, it's often helpful to identify suitable mentors elsewhere in the school district or in the community at large—perhaps at a local university, government office, private business, or volunteer community group (Ambrose, Allen, & Huntley, 1994; Piirto, 1999; Seeley, 1989).

- *Keep in mind that students with exceptional cognitive abilities aren't necessarily advanced in other aspects of their development.* Most students with special gifts and talents have the same personal and emotional concerns as their average-ability age-mates (D. J. Matthews, 2009). For example, gifted sixth graders making the transition to middle school are likely to have the typical thoughts and feelings of a young adolescent: whether they'll fit in with a new peer group, whom to sit with at lunch, and so on. They may worry that their peers will see their exceptional ability levels as odd or in some other way unacceptable (Mendaglio, 2010). And they're likely to be surprised or anxious when they discover that they must exert considerable effort to master challenging new skills and that they sometimes make errors in the process (Mendaglio, 2010). For such reasons, high-ability students are likely to need as

From the perspective of Vygotsky's theory (Chapter 2), when gifted students are given the same assignments as their average-ability peers, they're unlikely to be working within their zone of proximal development and therefore are unlikely to make significant cognitive advancements.

Working with a mentor often takes the form of a cognitive apprenticeship (see Chapter 2).

much emotional support as their classmates, and they may occasionally need gentle reminders that only new challenges can truly help them grow and that new skills require practice, regardless of innate levels of ability.

MyEdLab **Self-Check 5.5**

MyEdLab **Application Exercise 5.7.** In this interactive exercise you can apply what you have learned about nurturing the development of students who show exceptional gifts and talents.

Considering Diversity When Identifying and Addressing Special Needs

Sadly, a disproportionately large number of minority-group students are identified as having disabilities, especially specific cognitive disabilities, general intellectual disabilities, and emotional and behavioral disorders (McLoyd, 1998; U.S. Department of Education, 2006; VanTassel-Baska, 2008). Most theorists attribute the differing identification rates to environmental conditions that often accompany low socioeconomic status: higher-than-normal exposure to environmental toxins, poor nutrition, inadequate medical care, limited access to enriching educational resources, and so on (e.g., Dyson, 2008; Jacoby & Glauberman, 1995; McLoyd, 1998). Also, English language learners are identified as having learning disabilities or intellectual disabilities more often than native English speakers—a finding that probably reflects students' difficulty in understanding and responding to items on language-based diagnostic tests (A. L. Sullivan, 2008).

The higher-than-average identification rates for minority-group students pose a dilemma for educators. On the one hand, we don't want to assign a label such as *intellectual disability* or *emotional disorder* to students whose classroom performance and behavior may be due largely to their challenging living conditions. On the other hand, we don't want to deprive these students of special educational services that might help them learn and achieve more successfully over the long run. In such situations we must conduct fair and nondiscriminatory evaluations of students' needs, and if students qualify under a special-needs category, we must create IEPs to meet those needs. We should consider these categories of special needs as *temporary* classifications that may no longer be applicable as students' classroom performance improves. *All* students, with and without disability classifications, have changing needs that evolve over time, and federal law requires that IEPs be revisited at least once a year.

In addition to being overrepresented in programs for students with disabilities, members of some minority groups are underrepresented in programs for gifted students (D. Y. Ford, 2012, 2014; Graham, 2009; VanTassel-Baska, 2008). Furthermore, when students from underrepresented groups are identified for participation in gifted education programs, teachers often need to carefully mentor and monitor students to encourage them to remain in these programs (Moore, Ford, & Milner, 2011). On average, students from cultural and ethnic minority groups are at a disadvantage when traditional tests of ability are used to identify giftedness—in some cases because they've had little experience with the kinds of tasks that appear on those tests (Rogoff, 2003). It's critical, then, that we be on the lookout for other signs of giftedness, including the following:

- Exceptional talent in a specific area (e.g., in music or video game design)
- Ability to learn quickly from experiences
- Exceptional communication skills (e.g., articulateness, richness of language)
- Originality and resourcefulness in thinking and problem solving
- Ability to generalize concepts and ideas to new, seemingly unrelated situations (Dai, 2010; Haywood & Lidz, 2007; Winner, 1996)

For the growth of our society over the long run, it's imperative that we nurture the many gifted students in *all* cultural and ethnic groups.

Especially when working with students identified as having cognitive, emotional, or behavioral difficulties, think of their disability labels as *temporary* classifications that may no longer be applicable as classroom performance improves.

Look beyond IQ scores in identifying students who may be gifted; for instance, look for specialized talents, richness of language, an ability to learn new things quickly, and exceptional resourcefulness in solving problems.

General Recommendations for Working with Students Who Have Special Needs

Although students with special educational needs vary widely in their abilities and disabilities, several recommendations apply across the board:

Chapter 14 and Chapter 15 offer numerous suggestions for accommodating disabilities in assessments.

MyEdLab
Video Example 5.9.

Students are complex and sometimes bring unique combinations of talents and special needs to the classroom. Teachers must look beyond IQ scores to identify students who may be gifted, and look beyond a student's disability to recognize exceptionality.

Such choice making can enhance both *self-regulation and autonomy*, discussed in Chapter 10 and Chapter 11, respectively.

- *Be flexible in approaches to instruction and assessment.* Even when students clearly fall within a particular category of special needs, we can't always predict which instructional methods will be most effective for each of them. If we don't succeed with a particular approach, we should try again, but we might also want to try *differently*. Furthermore, we must keep open minds about how we assess students' achievement; depending on the nature of their disabilities, we may need to give them extra time, let them audiotape responses, tailor assessment tasks to an individualized curriculum, and so on (Royer & Randall, 2012).

- *Seek new technologies that can facilitate students' learning and performance.* As we've seen, assistive technology takes a wide variety of forms—spell checkers, handheld prompters, speech-to-text software, and so on—and exciting new technologies emerge every year. Software also is becoming readily available so that students with disabilities can work with technology that is now fairly common in schools, such as iPads (Chai, Vail, & Ayres, 2015). Frequent searches of the Internet can alert us to recent innovations (e.g., search for "assistive technology devices" on Google or Yahoo!).

- *Unless there is reason to do otherwise, hold the same expectations for students with disabilities as for other students.* Sometimes a disability makes it difficult or impossible for students to accomplish certain tasks, and we have to modify our expectations and assessment practices accordingly. Aside from such situations, however, we should generally have the same expectations for students with special needs that we have for other students. Rather than think of reasons that a student *can't* do something, we should think about how we can help the student *do* it. When partnering with a special educator, both the classroom teacher and the special educator need to hold similar high expectations, while simultaneously partnering to provide appropriate supports for the student.

- *Identify and teach the prerequisite knowledge and skills students may not have acquired because of their disabilities.* As either a direct or indirect result of certain disabilities, some students lack the knowledge and skills essential for their school success. For instance, students with visual impairments haven't been able to observe many of the cause-and-effect relationships that form a foundation for learning science—such as the changes in the appearance of wood when it's burned (Ferrell, 1996; M. B. Rowe, 1978). Students also may need assistance using online texts and materials (Greer, Rowland, & Smith, 2014). And students whose medical conditions have limited their contact with peers may have had few opportunities to acquire effective interpersonal skills.

- *Consult and collaborate with specialists.* School districts usually employ a variety of specialists, including special educators, counselors, school psychologists, nurses, speech pathologists, and physical and occupational therapists. Some students leave the classroom for part of the day to work with these individuals. However, in today's inclusive schools many special services are provided within a regular classroom context by teachers and specialists working in close collaboration.

- *Communicate regularly with parents.* In accordance with IDEA, parents are part of the multidisciplinary team that determines the most appropriate program for a student with special needs. Parents can often tell us what works and what doesn't, and they can alert us to certain conditions or events at home that may trigger problem behaviors in class. Furthermore, we can bring about desired behavioral changes more effectively if the same expectations for behavior exist both at school and at home.

- *Include students in planning and decision making.* Programs for most students with special needs—especially those with disabilities—are so highly structured that students have little say regarding what and how they learn. But increasingly, educators are recognizing the importance of letting *all* students make some choices about their academic goals and curriculum (Algozzine, Browder, Karvonen, Test, & Wood, 2001; Prout, 2009; Wehmeyer et al., 2007).

👋 *Keep your eyes open for students who may qualify for special services.* The more we work with students in a particular age-group, the more we learn about their age-typical abilities and behaviors. Hence, we teachers are in an excellent position to identify children who in one way or another are *not* typical. Although specialists usually conduct the in-depth assessments necessary to identify particular special needs, the job of referring students for such assessments—and thereby gaining them access to the specialized services they may need—is ultimately up to teachers in general education classrooms.

👋 *Work with your other students toward acceptance and support of students with special needs.* As we've already noted elsewhere in the chapter, many students with disabilities have trouble being accepted by and developing friendships with peers in their classes (de Boer, Pijl, Post, & Minnaert, 2013). As teachers, having a student with any type of exceptionality in our classroom is a wonderful opportunity for our other students. When a child or adolescent learns about various disabilities firsthand, and learns to respect and value these differences, such respect may last a lifetime.

5 What Have You Learned?

Let's now review key points related to each of the chapter's learning outcomes.

■ **5.1: Describe various perspectives on the nature of intelligence, and identify several ways in which you can nurture intelligence in your own students.** Intelligence involves the ability to apply prior knowledge and experiences flexibly to accomplish challenging tasks; it's apt to manifest itself differently in different cultures. Some psychologists believe that intelligence is a single, biology-based entity that influences students' learning and performance across a wide variety of tasks and subject areas—a belief that's reflected in the use of IQ scores as general estimates of cognitive ability. Others disagree, proposing that intelligence consists of a number of somewhat independent abilities or, instead, that intelligent behavior varies considerably depending on a child's age and environmental support systems. As teachers, we must remember that human intelligence can and does change over time, especially with appropriate instruction and practice opportunities.

■ **5.2: Explain how students' cognitive styles and dispositions might influence their classroom performance.** *Cognitive styles* and *dispositions* are general inclinations to approach tasks in particular ways—for instance, to think analytically or holistically or to approach new ideas in an open-minded or close-minded manner. We can encourage productive styles and dispositions through the messages we give about classroom subject matter (e.g., "Does the evidence support what scientists are saying about this topic?") and by modeling curiosity and enthusiasm for learning.

■ **5.3: Identify implications of the U.S. Individuals with Disabilities Education Act (IDEA) for your own work as a teacher.** Students with special needs are those students who are different enough from their classmates that they require specially adapted instructional materials and practices to help them maximize their cognitive and social development. Increasingly, students with special needs are being educated in general education classrooms for part or all of the school day; in the United States, such *inclusion* is in part the result of a mandate of the Individuals with Disabilities Education Act (IDEA). Students with special needs are most likely to flourish in general education settings when instruction and materials are individualized to address any missing basic skills but also present challenges that spur developmental advancements.

■ **5.4: Explain how you might adapt your instruction and classroom practices to the unique strengths and limitations of students with various disabilities.** Students with specific cognitive or academic difficulties include those with learning disabilities, those with attention-deficit hyperactivity disorder (ADHD), and those with speech and communication disorders. Many instructional strategies must be tailored to students' specific difficulty areas, but some strategies are widely applicable; for instance, virtually all of these students benefit from early interventions, clear expectations for performance, and feedback that documents ongoing progress.

Students with social or behavioral problems include those with emotional and behavioral disorders (which might involve either externalizing or internalizing behaviors) and those with autism spectrum disorders. Many students with these disabilities benefit from training in interpersonal skills. They may also perform more successfully in a structured environment in which appropriate behaviors are clearly identified and consequences for desired and undesired behaviors are consistently administered.

Some students have general delays in cognitive and social functioning, and some of these students are formally diagnosed as having an intellectual disability. Effective instruction for these students usually involves a slow pace with considerable scaffolding and, eventually, explicit training in vocational and general life skills.

Students with physical and sensory challenges include those with physical and health impairments (conditions that result in reduced energy, alertness, or muscle control), visual impairments, or hearing loss. Although recommended instructional strategies vary considerably depending on students' specific disabilities, all of these students should have appropriate assistive technologies and access to the same educational resources and opportunities as their nondisabled peers.

■ **5.5: Explain how you might nurture the development of students who show exceptional gifts and talents.** Most students identified as gifted require individualized instruction that challenges them to stretch their existing abilities in new directions. We must be open-minded about how we identify such students, as giftedness may take different forms in different cultural and ethnic groups. Strategies for promoting the achievement of gifted students include forming small study groups on specific topics, teaching complex cognitive skills within the context of various academic subject areas, and providing opportunities for independent study and service learning either within or outside of school walls.

Practice for Your Licensure Exam

Quiet Amy

As a veteran kindergarten teacher, Mr. Mahoney knows that many kindergartners initially have difficulty adjusting to the school environment, especially if they haven't previously attended day care or preschool. But Amy is giving him cause for concern. Amy never speaks, either to him or to the other children, even when she is directly spoken to. On the infrequent occasions when she wants to communicate, she does so primarily by looking and pointing at something or someone in the room. Amy also has trouble following simple directions, almost as if she hasn't heard what she's been asked to do. And she seems distracted during daily storybook readings and science lessons. The only activities that give her pleasure are arts and crafts. She may spend hours at a time working with construction paper, crayons, scissors, and glue, and her creations are often the most inventive and detailed in the class.

Mr. Mahoney suspects that Amy may have a disability that qualifies her for special services. To get permission for an in-depth evaluation of her abilities and needs, he and the school psychologist visit Amy's mother, a single woman raising five other children as well. "Amy doesn't talk at home either," the mother

admits. "I work two jobs to make ends meet, and I haven't been able to spend as much time with her as I'd like. Her brothers and sisters take good care of her, though. They always seem to know what she wants, and they make sure she gets it."

1. **Multiple-choice question:**

   Mr. Mahoney suspects that Amy may qualify for special educational services. If she does, in which of the following categories of special needs is she *least* likely to fall?

   A. Hearing loss

   B. Autism spectrum disorders

   C. Speech and communication disorders

   D. Attention-deficit hyperactivity disorder

2. **Constructed-response question:**

   Amy's evaluation will undoubtedly take several weeks to complete. In the meantime, what strategies might Mr. Mahoney use to improve Amy's classroom behavior and performance? Describe at least three different things he might do. Be specific and concrete in your descriptions.

   | MyEdLab **Licensure Exam 5.1** |

PRAXIS Go to Appendix C, "Matching Book Content and Ebook Activities to the Praxis Principles of Learning and Teaching Tests," to discover sections of this chapter that may be especially applicable to the Praxis tests.

michaeljung/Fotolia

6

Learning, Cognition, and Memory

Learning Outcomes

6.1 Distinguish among four distinct approaches to the study of human learning, and summarize one of these approaches—cognitive psychology—in terms of five basic assumptions.

6.2 Describe and illustrate the key components that many psychologists believe may characterize the human memory system.

6.3 Apply your knowledge of long-term memory storage in identifying effective strategies for enhancing students' learning.

6.4 Explain how students' self-constructed beliefs can sometimes interfere with effective learning, and identify several ways of helping students productively revise such beliefs.

6.5 Describe several factors that influence students' ability to recall what they have previously learned; also describe several reasons why students may either forget or incorrectly remember what they have learned.

6.6 Give examples of the diversity in cognitive processes you are likely to see in students, in some cases as a result of students' cultural backgrounds or special educational needs.

CASE STUDY: BONES

In biology class Kanesha has been struggling to learn the names of the bones in the human body, from head (cranium) to toe (metatarsus). She has learned a few bones quickly and easily. For example, she realizes that, logically, the *nasal bone* should form part of the nose, and she remembers the *humerus* (upper arm bone) by thinking of it as being just above one's funny ("humorous") bone. But she's still confused about some of the other bones. For example, the *tibia* and *fibula* have similar-sounding names and are both located in the lower leg. And she keeps thinking that the *sternum* (at the front of the chest) is actually in the back of the body, just as the stern of a boat is at its rear. She also has trouble remembering bones whose names don't provide any clues about their location. The coccyx, ulna, sacrum, clavicle, and patella could be just about anywhere in the body, it seems.

To prepare for an upcoming quiz, Kanesha looks at a diagram of the human skeleton and whispers the name of each bone to herself several times. She also writes each name on a sheet of paper. "These terms will certainly sink in if I repeat them enough times," she tells herself. But Kanesha scores only 70% on the quiz. As she looks over her incorrect answers, she sees that she confused the tibia and the fibula, labeled the ulna as "clavicle," put the sternum in the wrong place, and completely forgot about the coccyx, sacrum, and patella.

- Why are some bones easier for Kanesha to remember than others? Which ones would be easiest for *you* to remember? What do your answers to these questions suggest about the nature of human learning?

Kanesha seems to have an easier time learning bone names she can relate to things she already knows. In particular, she relates *nasal bone* to *nose* and *humerus* to *funny bone.* She applies her existing knowledge in trying to learn *sternum* as well, but her strategy backfires because a boat's *stern* is at its back end, whereas the sternum is in front of the chest cavity. Kanesha also has trouble with bone names she can't connect to anything in her previous experiences. Over the course of a lifetime, human beings learn many, many new pieces of information and many, many new behaviors. But as a general rule, people have an easier time learning and remembering things they can readily and appropriately connect to their existing knowledge and skills.

For our discussion in this book, we'll define **learning** as a long-term change in mental representations or associations as a result of experience. Let's divide this definition into its three parts. First, learning is a *long-term change,* in that it isn't just a brief, transitory use of information—such as remembering a person's phone number only long enough to make a phone call—but it doesn't necessarily last forever. Second, learning involves *mental representations or associations;* at its core, it's a phenomenon that takes place in the brain. Third, learning is a change *due to experience,* rather than the result of physiological maturation, fatigue, use of alcohol or drugs, or onset of mental illness.

Psychologists have been studying the nature of learning for more than a century and in the process have taken a variety of theoretical perspectives. Table 6.1 summarizes four general ones, listed largely in the order in which they've gained influence in the field of psychology as a whole. We authors urge you *not* to think of these perspectives as being mutually exclusive. In fact, they tend to complement one another, and together they give us a richer picture of human learning—and also give us many more strategies for facilitating learning in instructional settings—than any single perspective could give us alone.

MyEdLab

Content Extension 6.1. In this supplementary reading, you can learn how psychologists' theories of human learning have evolved over time.

COMPARE/CONTRAST

TABLE 6.1 • General Theoretical Approaches to the Study of Learning	
THEORETICAL PERSPECTIVE	**GENERAL DESCRIPTION**
Behaviorism	Early behaviorists argued that because thought processes cannot be directly observed and measured, it is difficult to study thinking objectively and scientifically. Thus, most behaviorists downplay the role of cognitive processes in learning and instead focus on two things that researchers *can* observe and measure: people's behaviors (*responses*) and the environmental events (*stimuli*) that precede and follow those responses. Learning is viewed as a process of acquiring and modifying associations among stimuli and responses, largely through a learner's direct interactions with the environment. Behaviorism has been especially helpful in identifying effective strategies for encouraging productive classroom behaviors.
Social cognitive theory	Historically, social cognitive theorists have focused largely on the ways in which people learn from observing one another. Environmental stimuli affect behavior, but cognitive processes (e.g., *awareness* of stimulus–response relationships, *expectations* about future events) also play significant roles. Often people learn through *modeling*—that is, they watch and imitate what others do. Whether people learn and perform effectively is also a function of their *self-efficacy*, the extent to which they believe they can successfully accomplish a particular task or activity. As social cognitive theory has evolved over time, it has increasingly incorporated the concept of *self-regulation*, in which people take charge of and direct their own actions. Social cognitive theory has had a significant impact on our understanding of motivation as well as of human learning.
Cognitive psychology	Although they don't deny that the environment plays a critical role in learning, cognitive psychologists concern themselves with what goes on *inside* learners, focusing on the cognitive processes involved in learning, memory, and performance. From observations of how people execute various tasks and behave in various situations, these theorists make inferences about how people may perceive, interpret, and mentally manipulate the information they encounter. Many cognitive psychologists speculate about what internal mechanisms underlie human cognition (e.g., *working memory* and *long-term memory*) and about how people mentally process new information (e.g., through *elaboration* and *visual imagery*); this approach is called information processing theory. Other cognitive theorists (such as the developmental theorist Jean Piaget) focus on how individual learners create knowledge through their interactions with the environment; this approach is known as individual constructivism.
Contextual theories	Contextual theorists place considerable emphasis on the influence of learners' physical and social environments on cognition and learning. But rather than talk about specific stimuli (as behaviorists do), they focus on more general factors—physical, social, and cultural—that support "thoughtful" (i.e., cognition-based) learning. Some contextual theorists (such as the developmental psychologist Lev Vygotsky) suggest that young learners initially use sophisticated thinking strategies in social interactions and gradually *internalize* these strategies for their own, personal use; this approach is known as sociocultural theory. Other contextual theorists emphasize that by working together, two or more people can often gain better understandings than anyone could gain alone; this approach is sometimes called social constructivism. Still other theorists propose that various ways of thinking are inextricably tied to particular physical or social circumstances; this approach goes by a variety of labels, including situated learning and distributed cognition.

In this chapter we'll look primarily at what goes on *inside* the learner. In doing so, we'll draw from cognitive psychology, a large body of research that addresses numerous mental phenomena that underlie human behavior, including perception, memory, forgetting, and reasoning.

Basic Assumptions of Cognitive Psychology

At the core of cognitive psychology are several basic assumptions about how people learn.

- *Cognitive processes influence what is learned.* The specific things people mentally do as they try to interpret and remember what they see, hear, and study—that is, their cognitive processes—have a profound effect on what they specifically learn and remember. For example, in the opening case study, Kanesha thinks about the nasal bone and humerus in ways that should help her remember them. However, she thinks about the sternum in a way that *interferes* with her ability to remember it correctly, and she gives little or no thought to why certain other bones have particular names. The extent to which Kanesha thinks about the material she needs to learn—and also *how* she thinks about it—affects her performance on the quiz.

- *People's cognitive processes can sometimes be inferred from their behaviors.* Historically, some psychologists—especially behaviorists—have argued that we can't directly observe people's thinking and therefore can't study it objectively and scientifically. Cognitive psychologists disagree, suggesting that by observing people's responses to various objects and events, it's possible to draw reasonable *inferences*—to make educated guesses—about the cognitive processes that probably underlie the responses. As an example of how we might learn about people's cognitive processes by observing their behaviors, try the following exercise.

EXPERIENCING FIRSTHAND
REMEMBERING 12 WORDS

Read the 12 words below *one time only.* Then cover up the page, and write down the words in the order they come to mind.

shirt	table	hat
carrot	bed	squash
pants	potatoes	stool
chair	shoe	bean

Did you write down the words in the order in which you had read them? Probably not. If you're like most people, you recalled the words by category—perhaps clothing first, then vegetables, then furniture. From the order in which you wrote the words (i.e., from your *behavior*), we can draw an inference about an internal cognitive process that occurred as you learned the words: You mentally *organized* them into categories.

- *People are selective about what they mentally process and learn.* We human beings are constantly bombarded with information. Consider the many stimuli you're encountering at this very moment—for instance, the many letters on this page, the many others objects you can see while you're reading, the many sounds reaching your ears, and the various articles of clothing touching your skin. You've probably been ignoring most of these stimuli until just now, when you were specifically asked to think about them.

  It's useful to distinguish between *sensation*—one's ability to detect stimuli in the environment—and *perception*—one's interpretation of stimuli. For reasons you'll discover a bit later, it's virtually impossible to perceive (interpret) everything the body senses. Because learners can handle only so much information at a given time, they must choose a few things to focus on and ignore the rest.

  As an analogy, consider the hundreds of items a typical adult receives in the mail each year, not only in paper form from the post office but also in electronic form through email. Do you open, examine, and respond to every piece of mail? Probably not. Chances are that you process a few key items, inspect other items long enough to know that you don't need them, and discard still others without even opening them.

  In much the same way, students encounter a great deal of new information every day—information delivered by way of teacher instruction, textbooks, bulletin boards, classmates' behaviors, smartphones, and so on. They must inevitably make choices about which pieces of information are important for them. They select a few stimuli to examine and respond to in depth, give other stimuli only a cursory glance, and ignore other stimuli altogether.

- *Meanings and understandings are not derived directly from the environment; instead, they are constructed by the learner.* Like Kanesha, people often create their own unique understandings about a topic—understandings that may or may not be accurate. The process of **construction** lies at the core of many cognitive theories of learning: Learners take numerous, separate pieces of information and use them to create a general understanding, interpretation, or recollection of some aspect of their world (e.g., Brainerd & Reyna, 2005; Lin & He, 2012; Neisser, 1967). Learning theories that focus primarily on the nature of this constructive process are collectively known as **constructivism**. Some constructivist theories focus primarily on how learners idiosyncratically construct knowledge *on their own* (rather than in collaboration with other people); such theories fall into a subcategory known as **individual constructivism**.

To experience the process of construction firsthand, try the following exercise.

EXPERIENCING FIRSTHAND
THREE FACES

Look at the three black-and-white figures shown here. What do you see in each one? Most people perceive the figure on the left to be that of a woman, even though many of her features are missing. Enough features are visible—an eye, parts of the nose, mouth, chin, and hair—that you can construct a meaningful perception from them. Is enough information available in the other two figures for you to construct two more faces? Construction of a face from the figure on the right may take a while, but it can be done.

Source: Figures from "Age in the Development of Closure Ability in Children" by C. M. Mooney, 1957, *Canadian Journal of Psychology, 11*, p. 220. Copyright 1957 by Canadian Psychological Association. Reprinted with permission.

Objectively speaking, the three configurations of black splotches leave a lot to the imagination. The woman in the middle is missing half of her face, and the man on the right is missing the top of his head. Yet knowing what human faces typically look like may have been enough to enable you to mentally add the missing features and perceive complete pictures. Curiously, once you've constructed faces from the figures, they then seem obvious. If you were to close this book now and not pick it up again for a week or more, you would probably see the faces almost immediately, even if you had had considerable difficulty perceiving them originally.

As teachers, we must remember that students won't necessarily learn information exactly as we present it to them. In fact, they'll each interpret classroom subject matter in their own, idiosyncratic ways. And occasionally they may construct *mis*information, as Kanesha does when she counterproductively connects the *sternum* to the stern of a boat.

- *Maturational changes in the brain enable increasingly sophisticated cognitive processes with age.* With the advent of new technologies for studying the brain, psychologists have teamed with experts in neurology and medicine to learn more and more about how the brain functions and how it changes with age and experience. This body of research, known as either **neuropsychology** or **cognitive neuroscience**, has enabled cognitive psychologists to test various hypotheses about the precise nature of human learning and thinking. Furthermore, it has revealed that the human brain changes in many significant ways over the course of childhood and adolescence. Such changes are almost certainly one key reason why children become capable of increasingly effective cognitive processes, such as longer attention spans and enhanced ability to organize and integrate information (Atkins, Bunting, Bolger, & Dougherty, 2012; Kuhn, 2006; C. A. Nelson, Thomas, & de Haan, 2006). But rather than propose distinct stages of cognitive development (as Jean Piaget did), most cognitive psychologists believe that children's cognitive development can best be characterized as gradual *trends*. As we proceed through the chapter, we'll identify a number of developmental trends in children's cognitive processes.

Table 6.2 summarizes the assumptions just described and can help you apply them to your own teaching practice.

Chapter 2 describes several ways in which the human brain matures over the course of childhood and adolescence; it also describes Jean Piaget's theory of cognitive development.

PRINCIPLES/ASSUMPTIONS

TABLE 6.2 • Basic Assumptions of Cognitive Psychology and Their Educational Implications

ASSUMPTION	EDUCATIONAL IMPLICATION	EXAMPLE
Influence of cognitive processes	Encourage students to think about classroom subject matter in ways that will help them remember it.	When introducing the concept *mammal*, ask students to identify many examples of mammals.
Behavior as a reflection of cognitive processes	Ask students to explain their reasoning, and look closely at what they do and say to make educated guesses about how they are thinking about classroom topics.	When a student says that 16 + 19 = 25 and that 27 + 27 = 44, hypothesize that the student is forgetting to regroup—that is, when she adds 7 + 7, she forgets to carry the 1 in 14 to the tens column—and provide additional instruction about the regrouping process.
Selectivity about what is learned	Help students identify the most important things for them to learn. Also help them understand *why* these things are important.	Give students questions they should try to answer as they read their textbooks. Include questions that ask them to apply what they read to their own lives.
Construction of meanings and understandings	Provide experiences that will help students make sense of the topics they're studying, and regularly monitor students' understandings.	When studying Nathaniel Hawthorne's *The Scarlet Letter*, have students convene in small groups to discuss possible reasons that the Reverend Dimmesdale refuses to acknowledge that he is the father of Hester Prynne's baby.
Increasing capacity for sophisticated cognitive processes with age	Take into account strengths and limitations of students' cognitive processing capabilities at different age levels.	When teaching kindergartners basic counting skills, accommodate their short attention spans by keeping verbal explanations brief and conducting a variety of active, hands-on counting activities.

MyEdLab **Self-Check 6.1**

A Model of Human Memory

Cognitive psychologists have offered many explanations of how people mentally process and remember new information and events—explanations that fall into the general category of **information processing theory**. Some early explanations portrayed human thinking and learning as being similar to the ways computers operate. It has since become clear, however, that the computer analogy is too simple: People often think about and interpret information in ways that are hard to explain in the relatively simplistic, one-thing-always-leads-to-another ways that are typical for computers (e.g., Hacker, Dunlosky, & Graesser, 2009a; G. Marcus, 2008; Minsky, 2006).

Central to information processing theory is the concept of **memory**. In some instances we'll use this term to refer to learners' ability to mentally save previously learned knowledge or skills over a period of time. In other instances we'll use it when talking about a particular location where learners put what they learn—perhaps in *working memory* or *long-term memory*.

The process of putting what is being learned into memory is called **storage**. For example, each time you go to class, you undoubtedly *store* some of the ideas presented in a lecture or class discussion. You may store other information from class as well—perhaps the name of the person sitting next to you (George), the shape and size of the classroom (rectangular, about 15 by 30 meters), or the pattern of the instructor's shirt (a ghastly combination of orange and purple splotches). Yet learners rarely store information exactly as they receive it. Instead, they engage in **encoding**, modifying the information in some way. For instance, when listening to a story, you might imagine what certain characters look like—thus encoding some verbal input as visual images. And when you see your instructor's orange and purple shirt, you might think, "My instructor desperately needs a wardrobe makeover"—thus assigning a specific *meaning* and *interpretation* to what you've seen.

At some point after storing a piece of information, you may discover that you need to use it. The process of remembering previously stored information—that is, finding it in memory—is called **retrieval**. The following exercise illustrates this process.

EXPERIENCING FIRSTHAND

RETRIEVAL PRACTICE

See how quickly you can answer each of the following questions:

1. What is your name?
2. What is the capital of France?
3. In what year did Christopher Columbus first sail across the Atlantic Ocean to reach the New World?
4. When talking about appetizers at a party, we sometimes use a French term instead of the word *appetizer.* What is that French term, and how is it spelled?

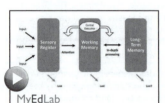

MyEdLab
Video Explanation 6.1.
This 16-minute video provides an animated explanation of the three-component model depicted in Figure 6.1.

As you probably noticed when you tried to answer these questions, retrieving some kinds of information from memory—your name, for instance—is quick and easy. Other things—perhaps the capital of France (Paris) and the year of Columbus's first voyage across the Atlantic (1492)—can be retrieved only after some thought and effort. Still other pieces of information, even though you may have stored them in memory at one time, may be almost impossible to retrieve. Perhaps the correct spelling of *hors d'oeuvre* falls into this category.

Despite their common use of such terms as *storage, encoding,* and *retrieval,* information processing theorists don't all agree about the precise nature of human memory. However, many suggest that memory has three key components: a sensory register, a working (short-term) memory, and a long-term memory. A three-component model of human memory, based loosely on one proposed by Atkinson and Shiffrin in 1968 with modifications to reflect more recent research findings, is presented in Figure 6.1. The model oversimplifies the nature of memory to some degree (more about this point later), but it provides a good way to organize much of what we know about how memory works.

Please note that in referring to three components of memory, we're *not* necessarily referring to three separate parts of the brain. The model of memory we describe here has been derived largely from studies of human behavior, rather than from studies of the brain.

THE NATURE OF THE SENSORY REGISTER

If you have ever played with a lighted sparkler at night, then you've seen the tail of light that follows a sparkler as you wave it about. If you have ever daydreamed in class, you may have noticed that when you tune back in to a lecture, you can still hear the three or four words that were spoken just *before* you started paying attention to your instructor again. The sparkler's tail and the words

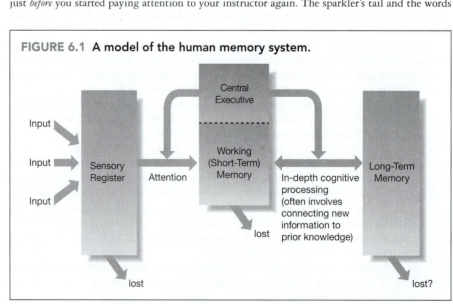

FIGURE 6.1 A model of the human memory system.

that linger aren't actually out there in the environment. Instead, they're recorded in your sensory register.

The **sensory register** is the component of memory that holds the information you receive— the *input*—in more or less its original, *un*encoded form. Thus, visual input is stored in a visual form, and auditory input is stored in an auditory form (e.g., Coltheart, Lea, & Thompson, 1974; Cowan, 1995). The sensory register has a *large capacity:* It can hold a great deal of information at any one time.

That's the good news. The bad news is that information stored in the sensory register doesn't last very long (e.g., Cowan, 1995; Dahan, 2010; Wingfield & Byrnes, 1981). Visual information (i.e., what you see) probably lasts for less than a second. For example, one of us authors (Jeanne) can never spell out her entire first name with a sparkler: The *J* always fades before she gets to the first *n,* no matter how quickly she writes in the night air. Auditory information (i.e., what you hear) probably lasts slightly longer, perhaps for 2 or 3 seconds. To keep information for any time at all, then, learners need to move it to *working memory.* Whatever information isn't moved is probably lost, or forgotten.

MOVING INFORMATION TO WORKING MEMORY: THE ROLE OF ATTENTION

Sensory information, such as the light cast by a sparkler, doesn't last very long no matter what we do. But we can preserve a memory of it by encoding it in some minimal way—for instance, by "seeing" (i.e., perceiving) the letters *Jea* in a sparkler's curlicue tail. In the model of memory presented in Figure 6.1, the first step in this process is **attention**: *Whatever someone mentally pays attention to moves into working memory.* If information in the sensory register doesn't get a person's attention, it presumably disappears from the memory system.

Paying attention involves directing not only the appropriate sensory receptors (in the eyes, ears, etc.) but also the *mind* toward whatever needs to be learned and remembered. Imagine yourself reading a textbook for one of your classes. Your eyes are moving down each page, but you're thinking about something altogether different—a recent argument with a friend, a high-paying job advertised on the Internet, or your growling stomach. What will you remember from the textbook? Absolutely nothing. Even though your eyes have been focused on the words in the book, you haven't been *mentally* attending to the words.

Young children's attention often moves quickly from one thing to another and is easily drawn to objects and events unrelated to the task at hand. For example, although decorating walls with colorful pictures and other images can make a kindergarten classroom more appealing for children, a *lot* of colorful décor is likely to distract many kindergartners from their lessons (Fisher, Godwin, & Seltman, 2014). As children grow older, they become better able to focus their attention on a particular task and keep it there, and they're less distracted by irrelevant thoughts and events. Yet even adult learners can't keep their minds on a single task *all* the time (E. Barron, Riby, Greer, & Smallwood, 2011; S. M. Carlson & Moses, 2001; Immordino-Yang, Christodoulou, & Singh, 2012).

Even when learners *are* paying attention, they can attend to only a very small amount of information at any one time. In other words, attention has a *limited capacity* (Cherry, 1953; Cowan, 2007). For example, if you're sitting in front of your television set with your textbook open in your lap, you can attend to a *Big Bang Theory* rerun playing on TV *or* to your book, but not to both simultaneously. And if, in class, you're preoccupied with your instructor's desperate need for a fashion makeover, you're unlikely to be paying attention to the lecture itself.

Exactly *how* limited is the limited capacity of human attention? People can often perform two or three well-learned, automatic tasks at once. For example, you can walk and chew gum simultaneously, and you can probably drive a car and drink a cup of coffee at the same time. But when a stimulus or event is detailed and complex (as both textbooks and *Big Bang Theory* reruns are) or when a task requires considerable thought (as understanding a lecture and driving a car on an icy mountain road would), then people can usually attend to only *one* thing at a time. Despite our best efforts, we human beings are *not* very good at multitasking (Foerde, Knowlton, & Poldrack, 2006; Lien, Ruthruff, & Johnston, 2006).

As teachers, we must remember that attention isn't just a behavior; it's also a mental process. The Into the Classroom feature "Getting and Keeping Students' Attention" presents several effective strategies for keeping students' minds on classroom topics.

Into The Classroom

Getting and Keeping Students' Attention

🍎 **Create stimulating lessons in which students *want* to pay attention.**

In a unit on nutrition, a high school biology teacher has students determine the nutritional value of various menu items at a popular local fast-food restaurant.

🍎 **Get students physically involved with the subject matter.**

A middle school history teacher plans a day late in the school year when all of his classes "go back in time" to the American Civil War. In preparation for the event, the students spend several weeks learning about the Battle of Gettysburg, researching typical dress and meals of the era, gathering appropriate clothing and equipment, and preparing snacks and lunches. On the day of the "battle," students assume various roles, such as Union or Confederate soldiers, government officials, journalists, doctors, nurses, merchants, and homemakers.

🍎 **Incorporate a variety of instructional methods into lessons.**

After explaining how to calculate the areas of squares and rectangles, a fourth-grade teacher has her students practice calculating areas in a series of increasingly challenging word problems. She then breaks the class into three- to four-member cooperative groups, gives each group a tape measure and calculator, and asks the students to calculate the area of their irregularly shaped classroom floor. To complete the task, the students must divide the room into several smaller rectangles, compute the area of each rectangle separately, and add the subareas together.

🍎 **Provide frequent breaks from sedentary activities, especially when working with students in the elementary grades.**

To provide practice with the alphabet, a kindergarten teacher occasionally has students make letters with their bodies. For example, one girl stands with her arms extended up and out to make a Y, and two boys bend over and join hands to form an M.

🍎 **In the middle school and high school grades, encourage students to take notes.**

In a middle school science class, different cooperative groups have been specializing in and researching various endangered species. As each group gives an oral report about its species to the rest of the class, the teacher asks students in the audience to jot down questions about things they would like to know about the animal. Upon the completion of their prepared report, members of the presenting group respond to their classmates' questions.

🍎 **Minimize distractions, especially when students must work quietly and independently.**

The windows of several classrooms look out onto an area where a new parking lot is being created. Teachers in those classrooms have noticed that many students are being distracted by the construction activity outside. The teachers ask the principal to request that the construction company work elsewhere on the day that an important statewide assessment is scheduled to be administered.

Sources: Some strategies based on Di Vesta & Gray, 1972; Kiewra, 1989; Ku, Chan, Wu, & Chen, 2008; Pellegrini & Bjorklund, 1997; M. I. Posner & Rothbart, 2007.

THE NATURE OF WORKING (SHORT-TERM) MEMORY

Working memory is the component of human memory where we hold attended-to information for a short time while we try to make sense of it. Working memory is also where much of our active cognitive processing occurs. For instance, it's where we think about the content of a lecture, analyze a textbook passage, or solve a problem. Basically, this is the component that does most of the mental work of the memory system—hence its name, *working* memory.

Rather than being a single entity, working memory probably has several components for holding and working with different kinds of information—for example, visual information, auditory information, and the underlying meanings of events—as well as a component that integrates multiple kinds of information. As shown in Figure 6.1, working memory may also include a **central executive** that focuses attention, oversees the flow of information throughout the memory system, selects and controls complex voluntary behaviors, and inhibits counterproductive thoughts and actions (Baddeley, 2001; Banich, 2009; Logie, 2011). Such processes—collectively known as **executive functions**—improve over the course of childhood and adolescence (largely as a result of brain maturation) and significantly enhance students' academic performance (Atkins et al., 2012; J. R. Best & Miller, 2010; Masten et al., 2012).

Information stored in working memory doesn't last very long—perhaps 5 to 20 seconds at most—unless the learner consciously does something with it (e.g., Baddeley, 2001; L. R. Peterson & Peterson, 1959; W. Zhang & Luck, 2009). Accordingly, this component is sometimes called *short-term memory.* For example, imagine that you need to call a neighbor, so you look up the neighbor's number in a telephone directory. Because you've paid attention to the number, it's presumably in your working memory. But then you discover that you can't find your cell phone. You have no paper and pencil handy. What do you do to remember the number until you have access to a phone?

When learners consciously and intentionally control their own thought processes, they are engaging in metacognition, discussed in depth in Chapter 7.

If you're like most people, you probably repeat it to yourself over and over again. This process, known as **maintenance rehearsal**, keeps information in working memory for as long as you're will- ing to continue talking to yourself. But once you stop, the number will disappear fairly quickly.

The amount of information children can hold in working memory increases a bit with age, probably as a result of both brain maturation and the acquisition of more effective cognitive pro- cesses (Barrouillet & Camos, 2012; Ben-Yehudah & Fiez, 2007; Kail, 2007). Yet even adults have only so much "room" to simultaneously hold and think about information. To see what we mean, put your working memory to work for a moment in the following exercise.

EXPERIENCING FIRSTHAND
DIVISION PROBLEM
Try computing the answer to this division problem in your head:

$$59\overline{)49{,}383}$$

Did you find yourself having trouble remembering some parts of the problem while you were dealing with other parts? Did you ever arrive at the correct answer of 837? Most people can't solve a division problem with this many digits unless they write it down. Working memory just doesn't have enough space both to hold all that information and to perform mathematical calcula- tions with it. Like attention, working memory has a *limited capacity*—perhaps just enough for a telephone number or very short grocery list (Cowan, 2010; Logie, 2011; G. A. Miller, 1956).

Virtually any learning activity imposes a **cognitive load**—a certain amount of information that learners must simultaneously think about, along with certain *ways* that they must think about it, in order to make sense of and remember what they're studying (R. E. Mayer, 2011b; Plass, Moreno, & Brünken, 2010; Sweller, 1988, 2008). As teachers, then, when we design and conduct lessons, we must consider just how much of a load students' working memories can rea- sonably handle at any given time. For example, we should minimize information that's irrelevant to the topic at hand. We should pace the presentation of important information slowly enough that students have time to effectively process what they're seeing and hearing. And we might re- peat the same idea several times (perhaps rewording it each time), stop to write important points on the board, and provide several examples and illustrations.

> Keep the limited capac- ity of working memory in mind when designing and conducting lessons.

We authors sometimes hear students talking about putting class material in "short-term memory" so that they can do well on an upcoming exam. Such a statement reflects the common misconception that this component of memory lasts for several hours, days, or weeks. Now you know otherwise. Working memory is obviously *not* the place to leave information that you need for an exam later in the week or even information you need for a class later in the day. For such infor- mation, storage in long-term memory—the final component of the memory system—is in order.

MOVING INFORMATION TO LONG-TERM MEMORY: CONNECTING NEW INFORMATION WITH PRIOR KNOWLEDGE

In the model of memory depicted in Figure 6.1, the arrow between working memory and long- term memory points in both directions. Effectively storing new information in long-term memory usually involves connecting it to relevant information that's *already* in long-term memory—a process that requires bringing the "old" information back into working memory. The following exercise can give you an idea of how this might happen.

EXPERIENCING FIRSTHAND
LETTERS AND A PICTURE

1. Study the two strings of letters below until you can remember each string perfectly:

   AIIRODFMLAWRS   FAMILIARWORDS

2. Study the picture shown here until you can reproduce it accurately from memory.

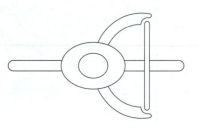

No doubt the second letter string was easier to learn because you could relate it to something you already knew: the words *familiar words*. How easily were you able to learn and remember the picture? Do you think you could draw it from memory a week from now? Do you think you could remember it more easily if it had the title "Bird's Eye View of a Cowboy Riding a Bicycle"? The answer to the last question is almost certainly yes, because the title would help you relate the picture to familiar shapes, such as those of a bicycle and a cowboy hat (e.g., see Bower, Karlin, & Dueck, 1975).

THE NATURE OF LONG-TERM MEMORY

Long-term memory is where learners store their general knowledge and beliefs about the world, the things they've learned from formal instruction (e.g., the capital of France, the correct spelling of *hors d'oeuvre*), and their recollections of events in their personal lives. It's also where learners store their knowledge about how to perform various actions, such as how to dribble a basketball, use a cell phone, and do long division.

Much of the information stored in long-term memory is interconnected. To see what we mean, try the next exercise.

EXPERIENCING FIRSTHAND
STARTING WITH A HORSE

What's the first word that comes to mind when you see the word *horse?* And what word does that second word remind you of? And what does the third word remind you of? Beginning with the word *horse,* follow your train of thought, letting each word remind you of a new word or short phrase, for a sequence of at least eight words or phrases. Write down the sequence of things that come to mind.

You probably found yourself easily following a train of thought from the word *horse,* perhaps something like the route that one of us authors followed:

horse → cowboy → lasso → rope → knot → Girl Scouts → cookies → chocolate

The last word in your sequence might be one with little or no obvious relationship to horses. Yet you can probably see a logical connection between each pair of items in the sequence. Related pieces of information tend to be associated with one another in long-term memory, perhaps in a network similar to the one depicted in Figure 6.2.

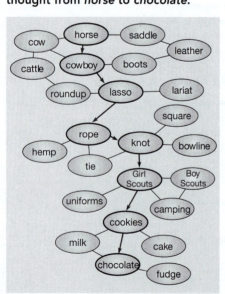

FIGURE 6.2 A possible train of thought from *horse* to *chocolate*.

Information stored in long-term memory lasts much, much longer than information stored in working memory—perhaps it lasts a day, a week, a month, a year, or a lifetime, depending on a variety of factors that we'll examine in upcoming sections of the chapter. In addition to its indefinitely long duration, long-term memory seems to be capable of holding as much information as a learner needs to store there. There's probably no such thing as "running out of room." In fact, for reasons you'll discover shortly, the more information already stored in long-term memory, the easier it is to learn new things.

LEARNING, MEMORY, AND THE BRAIN

Historically, theorists and researchers have believed that the physiological basis for most learning and memory lies in changes in the interconnections among neurons— in particular, in forming new synapses, strengthening existing ones, or eliminating counterproductive ones (e.g., M. I. Posner & Rothbart, 2007; Siegel, 2012; Trachtenberg et al., 2002). In addition, some learning may involve the formation of new neurons, especially in a small, seahorse-shaped structure in the middle of each side of the brain—a structure called the *hippocampus*—and possibly also in certain areas of the cortex. New learning experiences appear to enhance the survival rate and maturation of the young neurons; without such experiences, these neurons slowly die away (Leuner et al., 2004; C. A. Nelson et al., 2006; Spalding et al., 2013).

Within the last few years, some researchers have begun to speculate that certain star-shaped cells in the brain, known as astrocytes, are just as important as neurons—possibly even more important—in learning and memory. Figure 6.3 illustrates the general nature of an astrocyte and its connections with both neurons and the local blood supply. In human beings, astrocytes far outnumber neurons, have many connections with one another and with neurons, and appear to have considerable control over what neurons do and don't do and how much neurons communicate with one another. A normal brain produces many new astrocytes throughout its life span (X. Han et al., 2013; Koob, 2009; Oberheim et al., 2009).

As for *where* learning occurs, the answer is: many places. Key in the process is the *cortex,* the large, lumpy structure that covers the top and sides of the brain. The part of the cortex that's right behind the forehead—the *prefrontal cortex*—seems to be the primary headquarters for working memory and its central executive, although all of the cortex may be active to a greater or lesser extent in interpreting new input in light of previously acquired knowledge (Chein & Schneider, 2012; Gonsalves & Cohen, 2010; Huey, Krueger, & Grafman, 2006; Nee, Berman, Moore, & Jonides, 2008). The hippocampus is also actively involved in learning, in that it pulls together the information it simultaneously receives from various parts of the brain (Bauer, 2002; Squire & Alvarez, 1998).

As you might guess, a healthy brain is essential for effective learning. The Applying Brain Research feature "Enhancing Students' Brain Functioning" presents four general recommendations that are grounded in brain research.

CRITIQUING THE THREE-COMPONENT MODEL

As mentioned earlier, the three-component model just described oversimplifies—and probably overcompartmentalizes—the nature of human memory. For example, attention may be an *integral part* of working memory, rather than the separate entity depicted in Figure 6.1 (Cowan, 2007; Kiyonaga & Egner, 2014; Oberauer & Hein, 2012). Furthermore, studies conducted by neuropsychologists and other researchers have yielded mixed results about whether working memory and long-term memory are distinctly different entities (e.g., Baddeley, 2001; Nee et al., 2008; Öztekin, Davachi, & McElree, 2010; Talmi, Grady, Goshen-Gottstein, & Moscovitch, 2005).

Some psychologists have proposed that working memory and long-term memory simply reflect different **activation** states of a single memory (e.g., J. R. Anderson, 2005; Cowan, 1995; Ruchkin, Grafman, Cameron, & Berndt, 2003). According to this view, all information stored in memory is in either an active or inactive state. Active information, which may include both incoming information and information previously stored in memory, is what people are currently paying attention to and thinking about—information we've previously described as being in working memory. As attention shifts, other pieces of information in memory become activated, and the previously activated information gradually becomes inactive. The bulk of information stored in memory is in an inactive state, such that people aren't consciously aware of it; this is information we've previously described as being in long-term memory.

Despite its imperfections, the three-component model can help us remember aspects of human learning and memory that we teachers should take into account as we plan and teach lessons. For example, the model highlights the critical role of *attention* in learning, the *limited capacity* of attention and working memory, the *interconnectedness* of the knowledge learners acquire, and the importance of *relating* new information to things learned previously.

> MyEdLab **Self-Check 6.2**
>
> MyEdLab **Application Exercise 6.1.** In this exercise, you can apply your knowledge of memory's key components to various classroom scenarios.

Long-Term Memory Storage

Regardless of whether there are three truly distinct components of memory, we human beings remember a great many things for a considerable length of time—often for our entire life spans. In this sense, at least, a good deal of what we know and can do is in long-term memory.

Astrocytes are one variety of the brain's glial cells, described in Chapter 2.

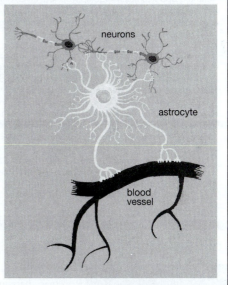

FIGURE 6.3 Two neurons, an astrocyte, and their interconnections.

neurons

astrocyte

blood vessel

Applying Brain Research

Enhancing Students' Brain Functioning

We urge you to be cautious when you read books, articles, and websites about "brain-based learning," because many of them are speculative at best. Following are four recommendations that have a solid foundation in neuropsychological research.

Provide regular intellectual stimulation. New challenges and learning opportunities—age-appropriate ones, of course—seem to enhance brain functioning, in part by nourishing existing neurons, synapses, and astrocytes and in part by stimulating the growth of new ones (Koob, 2009; C. A. Nelson et al., 2006).

Remember that the brain also needs time for rest and reflection. When it comes to stimulation, it's entirely possible to have too much of a good thing. Although we certainly don't want students to be bored during the school day, we should occasionally give them some mental downtime in which their minds can productively wander a bit—perhaps to ponder ideas they've recently learned or to reflect on their feelings regarding class assignments and upcoming assessments. For example, asking students to keep journals in which they write about their accomplishments and feelings can encourage regular self-reflection and enhance both mental health and academic achievement over the long run (Immordino-Yang et al., 2012).

Encourage physical exercise. Physical exercise appears to be good for brain health, especially if it includes aerobic activities that keep the cardiovascular system in good working order. A particular benefit is enhancement of the functioning of the central executive—that component of working memory that controls attention, oversees the general flow of information throughout the memory system, and inhibits counterproductive thoughts (Bryck & Fisher, 2012; Castelli, Hillman, Buck, & Erwin, 2007; Tomporowski, Davis, Miller, & Naglieri, 2008).

Encourage and enable students to get enough sleep. Unfortunately, typical school schedules, especially their early-morning starting times, are poor matches with the sleeping patterns of many high school students. As you well know, a good night's sleep improves mental alertness and can help people ward off germs that intend to do them harm. But in addition, sleep helps to firm up, or *consolidate*, new memories, rendering them more memorable over the long run (Dinges & Rogers, 2008; Kirby, Maggi, & D'Angiulli, 2011; J. D. Payne & Kensinger, 2010; Rasch & Born, 2008). Although we teachers may not have control of the timing of the school day, we can do other things that may enable them to sleep well. For example, we might give them at least 2 or 3 days to complete homework assignments, and we can teach them strategies for overcoming any inclinations to procrastinate on doing their schoolwork.

ENHANCEDetext
Video Example 6.1.

As you listen to 16-year-old Josh in this short video, think about how his teachers might help him juggle his homework obligations with his brain's need for sleep.

It appears that information stored in long-term memory can be encoded in a variety of forms (e.g., Barsalou, Simmons, Barbey, & Wilson, 2003; Brainerd & Reyna, 2005; Sadoski & Paivio, 2001). Some information may be encoded in a *verbal* form, perhaps as actual words. Things you remember word for word (e.g., your name, your address, certain song lyrics) are all verbally encoded. Other information may be encoded as *imagery*—as it appears perceptually. For example, if, in your mind, you can see the face of a relative, hear that person's voice, or conjure up a mental whiff of the person's favorite perfume or aftershave lotion, you're retrieving images. Finally, a great deal of information in long-term memory is probably encoded *semantically*—as a set of underlying meanings.

All of the preceding examples are instances of **declarative knowledge**—knowledge that relates to the nature of *how things are, were, or will be*. Declarative knowledge encompasses both general world knowledge (collectively known as *semantic memory*) and recollections of specific life experiences (collectively known as *episodic memory*). Not everything in long-term memory is declarative in nature, however. People also acquire **procedural knowledge**; that is, they learn *how to do things* (e.g., J. R. Anderson, 1983; Phye, 1997; Tulving, 1983). You probably know how to ride a bicycle, wrap a birthday present, and multiply a three-digit number by a two-digit number. To perform such actions successfully, you must adapt your behavior to changing conditions. For example, when you ride a bike, you must be able to turn left or right when an object blocks your path, and you must be able to come to a complete stop when you reach your destination. Accordingly, procedural knowledge often includes information about how to respond under different circumstances—it involves knowing *when to do certain things* (either physically or mentally). In such instances it's also known as **conditional knowledge**.

Most declarative knowledge is **explicit knowledge**: Once we recall it, we're quite conscious of what it is we know. But a good deal of procedural knowledge is **implicit knowledge**: We can't consciously recall or explain it, but it affects our thinking or behavior nonetheless (P. A. Alexander, Schallert, & Reynolds, 2009; J. R. Anderson, 2005; M. I. Posner & Rothbart, 2007). Another difference is that declarative knowledge can sometimes be learned very quickly, perhaps after a single presentation, whereas procedural knowledge is often acquired slowly and only with considerable practice.

HOW KNOWLEDGE CAN BE ORGANIZED

As we consider the nature of long-term memory storage, it's helpful to remember that, to a considerable degree, learners *construct* their knowledge and understandings. In the process of constructing knowledge, learners often create well-integrated entities that encompass particular ideas or groups of ideas. For example, beginning in infancy, human beings form **concepts** that enable them to categorize objects and events (G. Mandler, 2011; J. M. Mandler, 2007; Quinn, 2002). Some concepts, such as *butterfly, chair,* and *backstroke,* refer to a fairly narrow range of objects or events. Other concepts are fairly general ones that encompass many more-specific concepts. For example, the concept *insect* includes ants, bees, and butterflies (e.g., see Figure 6.4). The concept *swimming* includes the backstroke, dog paddle, and butterfly. As you can see, some words (such as *butterfly*) can be associated with two very different, more general concepts (such as *insects* and *swimming*) and so might lead someone to follow a train of thought such as this one:

horse → cowboy → lasso → rope → knot → Girl Scouts → camping
→ outdoors → nature → insect → butterfly → swimming

By combining numerous objects or events into single entities, concepts take some of the strain off of working memory's limited capacity (G. Mandler, 2011; Oakes & Rakison, 2003). For instance, the concept *molecule* takes very little "space" in working memory despite the many things we know about molecules, such as their composition and very tiny size. The Into the Classroom feature "Teaching Concepts" offers suggestions for fostering concept learning in a variety of academic disciplines.

Learners also pull some concepts together into general understandings of what things are typically like. Such understandings are sometimes called **schemas** (e.g., Rumelhart & Ortony, 1977; Schraw, 2006; Sweller, 2010). For example, let's return once again to the concept *horse.* You know what horses look like, of course, and you can recognize one when you see one. Hence, you have a concept for *horse.* But now think about the many things you know *about* horses. What do they eat? How do they spend their time? Where are you most likely to see them? You can probably retrieve many facts about horses, perhaps including their fondness for oats and carrots, their love of grazing and running, and their frequent appearance in pastures and at racetracks. The various things you know about horses are closely interrelated in your long-term memory in the form of a "horse" schema.

People have schemas not only about objects but also about events. When a schema involves a predictable sequence of events related to a particular activity, it's sometimes called a **script**. The next exercise provides an example.

EXPERIENCING FIRSTHAND
JOHN

Read the following passage *one time only.*

> John was feeling bad today so he decided to go see the family doctor. He checked in with the doctor's receptionist, and then looked through several medical magazines that were on the table by his chair. Finally the nurse came and asked him to take off his clothes. The doctor was very nice to him. He eventually prescribed some pills for John. Then John left the doctor's office and headed home. (Bower, Black, & Turner, 1979, p. 190)

You probably had no trouble making sense of the passage because you've been to a doctor's office yourself and have a schema for how those visits usually go. You can therefore fill in a number of details that the passage doesn't tell you. For example, you probably inferred that John actually *went* to the doctor's office, although the story omits this essential step. Likewise, you probably concluded that John took off his clothes in the examination room, *not* in the waiting room, even though the story doesn't tell you where John did his striptease. When critical information is missing, as is true in the story about John, schemas and scripts often enable learners to fill in the gaps in a reasonable way.

On a much larger scale, human beings—young children included—construct general understandings and belief systems, or **theories**, about particular aspects of the world (Gelman, 2003;

The idea that some concepts are nested within other, more general ones might remind you of the discussion of *class inclusion* in Chapter 2.

FIGURE 6.4 In his classification of a butterfly as an *insect,* 8-year-old Noah identifies one characteristic that all insects have—six legs—but correctly doesn't mention wings, which are optional.

Into The Classroom

Teaching Concepts

🍎 **Give a definition.**
A high school geometry teacher defines a *sphere* as "the set of points in three-dimensional space that are equidistant from a single point."

🍎 **Highlight the characteristics that all or most examples of a concept possess.**
A teacher illustrates the concept *insect* with a line drawing that emphasizes its three body parts, three pairs of legs, and two antennae in bold black lines. The drawing downplays other, irrelevant characteristics that might be visible, such as the insect's color and the presence of wings.

🍎 **Present a best example—a prototype that captures the key elements of the concept.**
To illustrate the concept *democracy*, a social studies teacher describes a hypothetical, ideal government.

🍎 **Present a wide range of examples in diverse contexts.**
A music teacher plays a *primary chord* in several keys, first on a piano and then on a guitar.

🍎 **Present nonexamples, especially near misses, to show what the concept is not.**
When a teacher describes what a *mammal* is, he explains why frogs and lizards don't fall into this category.

🍎 **Ask students to identify examples and nonexamples from among numerous possibilities.**
A language arts teacher gives students a list of sentences and asks them to identify the sentences that contain a *dangling participle*.

🍎 **Ask students to generate their own examples of the concept.**
A teacher asks students to think of examples of *adjectives* they frequently use in their own speech.

🍎 **Show students how various concepts are related to one another—their similarities and differences, their hierarchical relationships, and so on.**
A science teacher explains that the concepts *velocity* and *acceleration* have somewhat different meanings, even though they both involve speed.

Sources: R. M. Best, Dockrell, & Braisby, 2006; Brophy, Alleman, & Knighton, 2009; Carmichael & Hayes, 2001; R. G. Cook & Smith, 2006; R. M. Gagné, 1985; Ormrod, 2016; Rosch, 1977; B. H. Ross & Spalding, 1994; Tennyson & Cocchiarella, 1986.

Keil & Newman, 2008; Wellman & Gelman, 1998). Such theories include many concepts and the relationships among them (e.g., correlation, cause–and–effect). To see what some of your own theories are like, try the next exercise.

■■ **EXPERIENCING FIRSTHAND**
COFFEEPOTS AND RACCOONS

Consider each of the following situations:

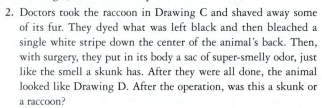

1. People took a coffeepot that looked like Drawing A. They removed the handle, sealed the top, took off the top knob, sealed the opening to the spout, and removed the spout. They also sliced off the base and attached a flat piece of metal. They attached a little stick, cut out a window, and filled the metal container with birdseed. When they were done, it looked like Drawing B. After these changes, was this a coffeepot or a bird feeder?

2. Doctors took the raccoon in Drawing C and shaved away some of its fur. They dyed what was left black and then bleached a single white stripe down the center of the animal's back. Then, with surgery, they put in its body a sac of super-smelly odor, just like the smell a skunk has. After they were all done, the animal looked like Drawing D. After the operation, was this a skunk or a raccoon?

(Both scenarios based on Keil, 1989, p. 184)

■■

Chances are, you concluded that the coffeepot was transformed into a bird feeder but that the raccoon was still a raccoon despite its cosmetic makeover and stinky surgery. Now how is it possible that the coffeepot could be made into something entirely different, whereas the raccoon could not? Even young children seem to make a basic distinction between human-made objects (e.g., coffeepots, bird feeders) and biological entities (e.g., raccoons, skunks) (Gelman & Kalish, 2006; Inagaki & Hatano, 2006; Keil, 1986, 1989). For instance, human-made objects are defined largely by the *functions* they serve (e.g., brewing coffee, feeding birds), whereas biological entities are defined primarily by their origins (e.g., the parents who brought them into being, their DNA). Thus, when a coffeepot begins to hold birdseed rather than coffee, it becomes a bird feeder because its function has changed. But when a raccoon is cosmetically and surgically altered to look and smell like a skunk, it still has raccoon parents and raccoon DNA and so can't possibly *be* a skunk.

By the time children reach school age, they've already constructed basic theories about their physical, biological, social, and psychological worlds (Flavell, 2000; Geary, 2005; Torney-Purta, 1994; Wellman & Gelman, 1998). They've also constructed preliminary theories about the nature of their own and other people's thinking. In general, self-constructed theories help children make sense of and remember personal experiences, classroom subject matter, and other new information (Gelman, 2003; Reiner, Slotta, Chi, & Resnick, 2000; Wellman & Gelman, 1998). Yet because children's theories often evolve with little or no guidance from more knowledgeable individuals, they sometimes include erroneous beliefs about the world that can wreak havoc with new learning (more about this point later in the chapter).

A child's theory of mind is an example of a self-constructed theory (see Chapter 3).

HOW DECLARATIVE KNOWLEDGE IS LEARNED

Especially when talking about the kinds of declarative knowledge acquired at school, learning theorists distinguish between two general forms of long-term memory storage processes—rote learning and meaningful learning—and among more specific storage processes that differ considerably in their effectiveness (see Table 6.3).

ROTE LEARNING

Learners engage in rote learning when they try to learn and remember something without attaching much meaning to it. For example, in the "Letters and a Picture" exercise presented earlier, you would be engaging in rote learning if you tried to remember the letter string FAMILIARWORDS simply as a list of isolated letters or if you tried to remember the cowboy/bicycle drawing as a collection of random, unrelated lines and curves.

One common form of rote learning is rehearsal, repeating something over and over within a short time frame (typically a few minutes or less), either by saying it aloud or by continuously thinking about it in an unaltered, verbatim fashion. Earlier we described how maintenance rehearsal—verbally repeating something over and over—helps us keep information in working memory indefinitely. Contrary to what many students think, however, rehearsal is *not* a very effective way of storing information in *long-term* memory. If a learner repeats something often enough, it might eventually "sink in," but the process is slow, laborious, and not much fun. Furthermore, for reasons we'll identify later, people who use rehearsal and other forms of rote learning often have trouble remembering what they've learned (J. R. Anderson, 2005; Craik & Watkins, 1973; McDermott & Naaz, 2014).

COMPARE/CONTRAST

TABLE 6.3 • Long-Term Memory Storage Processes

PROCESS	DEFINITION	EXAMPLE	EFFECTIVENESS
Rote learning: Learning primarily through repetition and practice, with little or no attempt to make sense of what is being learned			
Rehearsal	Repeating information verbatim, either mentally or aloud	Word-for-word repetition of a formula or definition	Relatively ineffective: Storage is slow, and later retrieval is difficult
Meaningful learning: Making connections between new information and prior knowledge			
Elaboration	Embellishing on new information based on what one already knows	Generating possible reasons that prominent people in history made the decisions they did	Effective if associations and additions made are accurate and productive
Organization	Making connections among various pieces of new information	Thinking about how one's lines in a play relate to the play's overall story line	Effective if organizational structure is legitimate and consists of more than just a list of discrete facts
Visual imagery	Forming a mental picture of something, either by actually seeing it or by envisioning how it might look	Imagining how various characters and events in a novel might have looked	Individual differences in effectiveness; especially beneficial when used in combination with elaboration or organization

Verbally rehearsing information is probably better than not actively processing it at all, and rehearsal may be one of the few strategies students can use when they have little prior knowledge to draw on to help them understand new material (E. Wood, Willoughby, Bolger, & Younger, 1993). For example, in the opening case study Kanesha resorts to rehearsal in her efforts to remember such seemingly nonsensical bone names as the coccyx, clavicle, and patella. Ideally, however, we should encourage students to engage in meaningful learning whenever possible.

MEANINGFUL LEARNING

Cognitive psychologists' concept of meaningful learning should remind you of Piaget's concept of *assimilation* (see Chapter 2).

In contrast to rote learning, meaningful learning involves recognizing a relationship between new information and something already stored in long-term memory. Whenever we use such words as *comprehension* and *understanding,* we're talking about meaningful learning. In the vast majority of cases, meaningful learning is more effective than rote learning for storing information in long-term memory (R. E. Mayer, 1996; Sweller, 2010; Wittrock, 1974). It's especially effective when learners relate new ideas not only to what they already know about the world but also to what they know or believe about *themselves*—for instance, to self-descriptions or personal life experiences (Heatherton, Macrae, & Kelley, 2004; Kesebir & Oishi, 2010; Rogers, Kuiper, & Kirker, 1977).

Meaningful learning takes a variety of forms. Three forms that researchers have studied in depth are elaboration, organization, and visual imagery. All three are *constructive* in nature: They involve combining several pieces of information into a meaningful whole.

Elaboration. In elaboration, learners use their prior knowledge to embellish on a new idea, thereby storing *more* information than was actually presented. For example, when one of us authors took a course in Mandarin Chinese in high school, she learned that the Chinese word *wǒmen* means "we." "Aha!" she thought to herself, "the sign on the restroom that *we* girls use says *wǒmen*" (albeit without the tone mark over the *o*). Similarly, a student who reads that a certain species of dinosaurs had powerful jaws and sharp, pointed teeth might correctly deduce that those dinosaurs were meat eaters. And when a student learns that the crew on Columbus's first trip across the Atlantic threatened to revolt, the student might speculate, "I bet the men were really frightened when they continued to travel west day after day without ever seeing signs of land."

As we'll see later in the chapter, learners sometimes elaborate on new information in inaccurate and counterproductive ways. On average, however, the more students elaborate on new material—that is, the more they use what they already know to help them understand and interpret new material—the more effectively they will store and remember it. Thus, students who regularly elaborate on what they learn in school usually show higher achievement than those who simply take information at face value (J. R. Anderson, 2005; McDaniel & Einstein, 1989; Paxton, 1999; Waters, 1982).

Encourage students to go beyond the specific information they have learned—for instance, to draw inferences, speculate about possible implications, or defend a position about a controversial topic. Occasionally have students work in pairs or small groups to formulate and ask one another elaborative questions.

One effective way to encourage elaboration in the classroom is to have students talk or write about a topic—for instance, to summarize what they've learned, relate new concepts to their personal experiences, or express and defend certain positions on controversial topics (e.g., Bangert-Drowns, Hurley, & Wilkinson, 2004; Shanahan, 2004). Another good strategy is to ask questions that require students to expand on something they've just learned—questions such as "How would you use . . . to . . . ?" and "What do you think would happen if . . . ?" (A. King, 1992, p. 309; McCrudden & Schraw, 2007). Still another approach is to have students work in pairs or small groups to formulate and answer their *own* elaborative questions. Different researchers call such group questioning either *elaborative interrogation* or *guided peer questioning* (Dunlosky, Rawson, Marsh, Nathan, & Willingham, 2013; A. King, 1994, 1999; Ozgungor & Guthrie, 2004). In the following dialogue, fifth graders Katie and Janelle are working together to study class material about tide pools. Katie's job is to ask Janelle questions that encourage elaboration:

> *Katie:* How are the upper tide zone and the lower tide zone different?
>
> *Janelle:* They have different animals in them. Animals in the upper tide zone and splash zone can handle being exposed—have to be able to use the rain and sand and wind and sun—and they don't need that much water and the lower tide animals do.

Katie: And they can be softer 'cause they don't have to get hit on the rocks.

Janelle: Also predators. In the spray zone it's because there's predators like us people and all different kinds of stuff that can kill the animals and they won't survive, but the lower tide zone has not as many predators.

Katie: But wait! Why do the animals in the splash zone have to survive? (A. King, 1999, p. 97)

Notice that the two girls are continually relating the animals' characteristics to survival in different tide zones, and eventually Katie asks why animals in the splash zone even *need* to survive. Such analyses are quite sophisticated for fifth graders. Just imagine what high school students might be able to do as they become increasingly capable of abstract and hypothetical thinking!

Organization. On average, we humans learn and remember a body of new information more easily when we pull it together in some reasonable way (e.g., McNamara & Magliano, 2009; Nesbit & Adesope, 2006; D. H. Robinson & Kiewra, 1995). Such organization involves making connections among various pieces of new information and forming an overall cohesive structure. For example, a learner might group information into categories, as you probably did in the "Remembering 12 Words" exercise near the beginning of the chapter.

An even better way of organizing information is to identify interrelationships among its various parts. For instance, when learning about *velocity, acceleration, force,* and *mass* in a physics class, a student might better understand these concepts by seeing how they're interconnected—perhaps by learning that velocity is the product of acceleration and time ($v = a \times t$) and that an object's force is determined by both its mass and its acceleration ($f = m \times a$). The trick is not simply to memorize the formulas (that would be rote learning) but rather to make sense of the relationships that the formulas represent.

It's often helpful to give students specific structures they can use to organize information. For example, the weblike note-taking form shown in Figure 6.5 can help elementary students organize what they learn about tarantulas. Another effective structure is a two-dimensional matrix or table that enables students to compare several items with respect to various characteristics—for instance, how various geographical regions differ in topography, climate, economic activities, and cultural practices (R. K. Atkinson et al., 1999; Kiewra, DuBois, Christian, & McShane, 1988; D. H. Robinson & Kiewra, 1995). A third approach is to teach students how to create concept maps—diagrams that depict the concepts of a unit and their interrelationships (Hattie, 2009; Nesbit & Adesope, 2006; Novak, 1998). Figure 6.6 shows concept maps that two different students might construct after a lesson about gorillas. The concepts themselves are circled, and their interrelationships are indicated by lines with words or short phrases. Several concept-mapping software programs (e.g., Kidspiration, MindMapper Jr.) are available for creating and modifying concept maps quickly and easily.

Not only can self-constructed organizational structures help students learn more effectively, but they can also help teachers *assess* students' learning. For example, the concept map on the left side of Figure 6.6 reveals only spotty, fragmented knowledge about gorillas. Furthermore, the student has two ideas that need correction. First, contrary to a common stereotype, gorillas don't regularly swing from trees, although young ones may occasionally climb a tree to escape danger. Second, gorillas aren't especially "fierce" creatures. For the most part, they live a peaceful existence within their family group; they get nasty (e.g., by beating their chests) only when an unfamiliar human being, non-family-member gorilla, or other potential encroacher threatens their territory.

Visual imagery. Earlier we mentioned imagery as one possible way in which information might be encoded in

Chapter 2 describes the development of abstract and hypothetical thinking in adolescence.

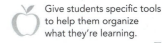
Explicitly show how various ideas are interrelated.

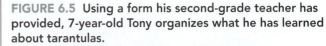
Give students specific tools to help them organize what they're learning.

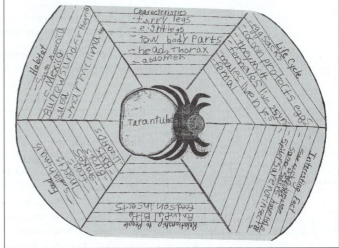

FIGURE 6.5 Using a form his second-grade teacher has provided, 7-year-old Tony organizes what he has learned about tarantulas.

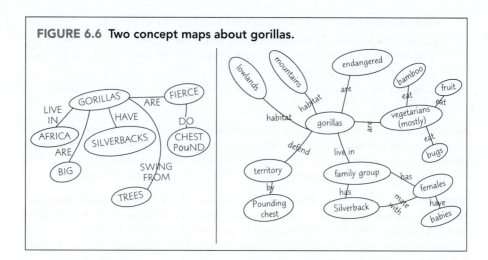

FIGURE 6.6 Two concept maps about gorillas.

long-term memory. Many research studies have shown that visual imagery—forming mental pictures of objects or ideas—can be a highly effective method of storing information (Sadoski & Paivio, 2001; D. L. Schwartz & Heiser, 2006; Urgolites & Wood, 2013). To show you how effective visual imagery can be, the next exercise will teach you a few words in Mandarin Chinese.

■▶ EXPERIENCING FIRSTHAND

FIVE CHINESE WORDS

Try learning these five Chinese words by forming the visual images we describe (don't worry about learning the tone marks over the words):

Chinese Word	English Meaning	Image
fáng	house	Picture a *house* with *fangs* growing on its roof and walls.
mén	door	Picture a restroom *door* with the word MEN painted on it.
kè	guest	Picture someone giving someone else (the *guest*) a *key* to the house.
fàn	food	Picture a plate of *food* being cooled by a *fan*.
shū	book	Picture a *shoe* with a *book* sticking out of it.

Now find something else to do for a couple of minutes. Stand up and stretch, get a glass of water, or use the restroom. But be sure to come back to your reading in just a minute or two.

Now that you're back, cover the list of Chinese words, English meanings, and visual images. Then try to remember what each word means:

kè   fàn   mén   fáng   shū

Did the Chinese words remind you of the visual images you stored? Did the images, in turn, help you remember the English meanings? You may have remembered all five words easily, or you may have remembered only one or two. People differ in their ability to use visual imagery: Some form images quickly and easily, whereas others form them only slowly and with difficulty (Behrmann, 2000; J. M. Clark & Paivio, 1991; Kosslyn, 1985).

In the classroom we can encourage the use of visual imagery in several ways. We can ask students to imagine how certain events in literature or history might have looked (Johnson-Glenberg, 2000; Sadoski & Paivio, 2001). We can provide visual materials (pictures, charts,

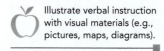 Illustrate verbal instruction with visual materials (e.g., pictures, maps, diagrams).

graphs, etc.) that illustrate important but possibly abstract ideas (R. K. Atkinson et al., 1999; R. Carlson, Chandler, & Sweller, 2003; Verdi, Kulhavy, Stock, Rittschof, & Johnson, 1996). We can also ask students to create their *own* illustrations or diagrams of the things they're studying, such as 9-year-old Trisha has done in Figure 6.7 (Edens & Potter, 2001; Schwamborn, Mayer, Thillmann, Leopold, & Leutner, 2010; van der Veen, 2012; Van Meter & Garner, 2005).

Visual imagery can be especially powerful when used in combination with other forms of encoding. For example, students more readily learn and remember information they receive in both a verbal form (e.g., a lecture or textbook passage) and a graphic form (e.g., a picture, map, or diagram) (R. E. Mayer, 2011b; Moreno, 2006; Winn, 1991). They're also likely to benefit from being explicitly asked to represent information both verbally and visually.

FIGURE 6.7 This drawing by 9-year-old Trisha effectively illustrates the water cycle.

DEVELOPMENTAL TRENDS IN STORAGE PROCESSES FOR DECLARATIVE INFORMATION

Meaningful learning—relating new information to prior knowledge—probably occurs in one form or another at virtually all age levels. More specific strategies—such as rehearsal, organization, and visual imagery—are fairly limited in the early elementary years but increase in both frequency and effectiveness over the course of childhood and adolescence. The frequency of elaboration—especially as a process that learners *intentionally* use—picks up a bit later, often not until adolescence, and is more common in high-achieving students. Table 6.4 provides more detailed information on the nature of long-term memory storage processes at different grade levels.

HOW PROCEDURAL KNOWLEDGE IS LEARNED

Some of the procedures people learn—for example, baking a cake, serving a volleyball, and driving a car with a stick shift—consist primarily of overt behaviors. Many others—for example, writing a persuasive essay, solving for x in an algebraic equation, and surfing the Internet—have a significant mental component as well. Many procedures involve a combination of physical behaviors and mental activities.

Procedural knowledge ranges from relatively simple actions (e.g., using scissors or correctly holding a pencil) to far more complex skills. Complex procedures usually aren't learned in one fell swoop. Instead, they're acquired slowly over a period of time, often only with a great deal of practice (Ericsson, 2003; Macnamara, Hambrick, & Oswald, 2014; Proctor & Dutta, 1995).

People appear to learn simple physical procedures primarily as actual behaviors—in other words, as specific actions that, with practice, are strengthened and gradually refined (Ennis & Chen, 2011; Féry & Morizot, 2000; Willingham, 1999). Yet many complex skills, especially those that have a mental component, may also be learned as declarative knowledge—in other words, as *information* about how to do something (J. R. Anderson, 1983; Baroody, Eiland, Purpura, & Reid, 2013; Beilock & Carr, 2004). Learners may initially use their declarative knowledge to guide them as they perform a new skill, but to the extent that they must do so, their performance is apt to be slow and laborious and to require a lot of concentration—that is, it can consume considerable working memory capacity. As learners continue to practice the skill, their declarative knowledge gradually evolves into procedural knowledge, perhaps eventually to the point that they can perform the activity quickly, efficiently, and effortlessly (we'll look at such *automaticity* more closely a bit later). People who show exceptional talent in a particular skill domain—say, in figure skating or playing the piano—typically practice a great deal, often a minimum of 3 to 4 hours a day over a period of 10 years or more (Ericsson, 1996; Horn, 2008).

Some of the storage processes we've already discussed play a role in acquiring procedural knowledge as well as declarative knowledge. For instance, verbally rehearsing a sequence of

MyEdLab
Video Example 6.2.

With age and experience, children become increasingly strategic in their efforts to remember new information. What strategies do 6-year-old Brent, 12-year-old Colin, and 16-year-old Hilary say they use to remember a list?

DEVELOPMENTAL TRENDS

TABLE 6.4 • Typical Long-Term Memory Storage Processes at Different Grade Levels

GRADE LEVEL	AGE-TYPICAL CHARACTERISTICS	EXAMPLE	SUGGESTED STRATEGIES
K–2	• Organization of physical objects as a way to remember them • Emergence of rehearsal to remember verbal material; used infrequently and relatively ineffectively • Emerging ability to use visual imagery to enhance memory, especially if an adult suggests this strategy • Few intentional strategic efforts to learn new things	At the end of the school day, a first-grade teacher reminds students that they need to bring three things to school tomorrow: an object that begins with the letter *W* (for a phonics lesson), a signed permission slip for a field trip to a local historic site, and a warm jacket to wear on the field trip. Six-year-old Cassie briefly mumbles "jacket" to herself a couple of times and naively assumes she'll remember all three items without any further mental effort.	• Get students actively involved in topics, perhaps through hands-on activities, engaging reading materials, or fantasy play. • Relate new topics to students' prior experiences. • Model rehearsal as a strategy for remembering things over the short run. • Provide pictures that illustrate verbal material. • Give students short notes they can take home to help them and their parents remember items that need to be brought to school.
3–5	• Spontaneous, intentional, and increasingly effective use of rehearsal to remember things for a short time period • Increasing use of organization as an intentional learning strategy for verbal information • Increasing effectiveness in the use of visual imagery as a learning strategy	As 10-year-old Jonathan studies for an upcoming quiz on clouds, he looks at the photos of four different kinds of clouds in his science book and says each one's name aloud. Then he repeats the four cloud types several times: "Cumulus, cumulonimbus, cirrus, stratus. Cumulus, cumulonimbus, cirrus, stratus. Cumulus, cumulonimbus, cirrus, stratus."	• Emphasize the importance of making sense of, rather than memorizing, information. • Encourage students to organize what they're studying; suggest possible organizational structures for topics. • Provide a variety of visual aids to facilitate visual imagery, and suggest that students create their own drawings or visual images of things they need to remember.
6–8	• Predominance of rehearsal as a learning strategy • Greater abstractness and flexibility in categories used to organize information • Emergence of elaboration as an intentional learning strategy	Two middle school students, Raj and Owen, are studying for a quiz on various kinds of rocks. "Let's group them somehow," Raj says. Owen suggests grouping them by color (gray, white, reddish, etc.). But after further discussion, the boys agree that sorting them into *sedimentary, igneous,* and *metamorphic* would be a more strategic approach.	• Suggest questions that students might ask themselves as they study; emphasize questions that promote elaboration (e.g., "Why would _____ do that?" "How is _____ different from _____?"). • In assignments and quizzes, assess true understanding rather than rote memorization.
9–12	• Continuing reliance on rehearsal as an intentional learning strategy, especially by low-achieving students • Increasing use of elaboration and organization to learn, especially by high-achieving students	In her high school world history class, Kate focuses her studying efforts on memorizing names, dates, and places. Meanwhile, Kate's classmate Janika likes to speculate about the personalities and motives of such historical characters as Alexander the Great, Napoleon Bonaparte, and Adolf Hitler.	• Ask thought-provoking questions that engage students' interest and help students see the relevance of topics to their own lives. • Have students work in mixed-ability cooperative groups, in which high-achieving students can model effective learning strategies for low-achieving students.

Sources: Bjorklund & Coyle, 1995; Bjorklund & Jacobs, 1985; Bjorklund, Schneider, Cassel, & Ashley, 1994; Cowan, Saults, & Morey, 2006; DeLoache & Todd, 1988; Gaskins & Pressley, 2007; Gathercole & Hitch, 1993; Kosslyn, Margolis, Barrett, Goldknopf, & Daly, 1990; Kunzinger, 1985; Lehmann & Hasselhorn, 2007; Lucariello, Kyratzis, & Nelson, 1992; Marley, Szabo, Levin, & Glenberg, 2008; L. S. Newman, 1990; P. A. Ornstein, Grammer, & Coffman, 2010; Plumert, 1994; Pressley, 1982; Pressley & Hilden, 2006; Schneider & Pressley, 1989.

steps in a motor skill enhances people's ability to perform the skill (Weiss & Klint, 1987). Illustrations or live demonstrations of a procedure, which presumably foster visual imagery, are also beneficial (Kitsantas, Zimmerman, & Cleary, 2000; SooHoo, Takemoto, & McCullagh, 2004; Zimmerman & Kitsantas, 1999). In fact, imagining *oneself* performing a new skill (e.g., executing a basketball shot or gymnastics move) can enhance acquisition of the skill, although this strategy obviously isn't as effective as actual practice (Feltz, Landers, & Becker, 1988; Kosslyn, 1985; SooHoo et al., 2004).

Perhaps the most effective way to teach new procedures is to model them for students, including both the overt behaviors and the internal thought processes involved (e.g., Rittle-Johnson, 2006; Schunk, 1998). The Into the Classroom feature "Helping Students Acquire New Procedures" illustrates several additional strategies for facilitating procedural learning.

Chapter 8 explains how some procedural knowledge is an integral part of a culture's *communities of practice.* Chapter 10 offers suggestions for effectively modeling new behaviors for students.

Into The Classroom

Helping Students Acquire New Procedures

🫛 **Help students understand the logic behind the procedures they are learning.**

As a teacher demonstrates the correct way to swing a tennis racket, she asks her students, "Why is it important to have your feet apart rather than together? Why is it important to hold your arm straight as you swing?"

🫛 **When skills are especially complex, break them into simpler tasks that students can practice one at a time.**

Knowing how overwhelming the task of driving a car can initially be, a driver education teacher begins behind-the-wheel instruction by having students practice steering and braking in an empty parking lot. Only later, after students have mastered these skills, does she have them drive in traffic on city streets.

🫛 **Provide mnemonics that can help students remember a sequence of steps.**

A math teacher shows students how to multiply in the expression

$$(3x + 4)(2x + 5)$$

by working out the steps on the board. As she goes along, she explains what she's doing: "The word *FOIL* can help you remember what you need to do. You begin by multiplying the two *first* terms inside the parentheses—that would be $3x \times 2x$, or $6x^2$. Then you multiply the two *outer* terms—$3x \times 5$—which gives you $15x$. After that, you multiply the two *inner* terms—$4 \times 2x$—which gives you $8x$. Finally, you multiply the two *last* terms—4×5, which equals 20. Add them all together, and you get $6x^2 + 23x + 20$."

🫛 **Give students many opportunities to practice new skills, and provide the feedback they need to help them improve.**

A science teacher asks his students to write lab reports after each week's lab activity. Because many of his students have had little or no prior experience in scientific writing, he writes numerous comments as he grades the reports. Some comments describe the strengths he sees, and others provide suggestions for making the reports more objective, precise, or clear.

Sources: P. A. Alexander & Judy, 1988; J. R. Anderson, Reder, & Simon, 1996; Baroody et al., 2013; Beilock & Carr, 2004; Ennis & Chen, 2011; Hattie & Timperley, 2007; Hecht, Close, & Santisi, 2003; Macnamara et al., 2014; Proctor & Dutta, 1995; Shute, 2008; van Merriënboer & Kester, 2008.

ROLES OF PRIOR KNOWLEDGE AND WORKING MEMORY IN LONG-TERM MEMORY STORAGE

Students are more likely to engage in meaningful learning when they have a relevant **knowledge base**—that is, when they have existing knowledge to which they can connect whatever new information and skills they're trying to master. When, in contrast, they have little relevant knowledge on which to build, they're apt to struggle in their efforts to make sense of new material, as Kanesha sometimes does while studying bone names for her biology quiz.

Occasionally students' prior knowledge interferes with something they need to learn; this is the case when Kanesha tries to remember where the sternum is located. In general, however, a relevant knowledge base helps students learn and remember new material more effectively than they would otherwise (e.g., P. A. Alexander, Kulikowich, & Schulze, 1994; Booth & Newton, 2012; Kintsch, 2009). For example, students will better understand scientific principles if they've already seen those principles in action either in their personal lives or in the classroom, and they'll better understand how large some dinosaurs were if they have previously seen life-sized dinosaur skeletons at a natural history museum.

🍎 Provide concrete experiences (lab experiments, museum visits, etc.) to which students can relate more abstract ideas.

Students' prior knowledge contributes to their learning in several ways:

- It helps them determine what is most important to learn and therefore helps them direct their *attention* appropriately.

- It enhances their ability to *elaborate* on information—for example, to fill in missing details, clarify ambiguities, and draw inferences.

- It provides a framework for *organizing* new information. (Bjorklund, Muir-Broaddus, & Schneider, 1990; Haskell, 2001; Rumelhart & Ortony, 1977; P. T. Wilson & Anderson, 1986)

Children's knowledge about the world grows by leaps and bounds every year; on average, then, older students have more knowledge to help them understand and elaborate on new ideas and events than younger ones do. When young children have more knowledge than their elders, however, they often have the upper hand (Chi, 1978; Flavell, Miller, & Miller, 2002; Kail, 1990; Rabinowitz & Glaser, 1985).

Children don't all acquire the *same* knowledge bases, of course, and their differing knowledge can lead them to construct different meanings from the same situation. The next exercise illustrates this point.

EXPERIENCING FIRSTHAND
ROCKY

Read the following passage *one time only:*

> Rocky slowly got up from the mat, planning his escape. He hesitated a moment and thought. Things were not going well. What bothered him most was being held, especially since the charge against him had been weak. He considered his present situation. The lock that held him was strong but he thought he could break it. He knew, however, that his timing would have to be perfect. Rocky was aware that it was because of his early roughness that he had been penalized so severely—much too severely from his point of view. (R. C. Anderson, Reynolds, Schallert, & Goetz, 1977, p. 372)

Now summarize what you've just read in two or three sentences.

What did you think the passage was about? A prison escape? A wrestling match? Or perhaps something else altogether? When a longer version of this passage was used in an experiment with college students, many physical education majors interpreted it as a wrestling match, but music education majors—most of whom had little or no knowledge of wrestling—were more likely to think it was about a prison break (R. C. Anderson et al., 1977).

Yet it isn't enough that students have the knowledge they need to make sense of new material. They must also be *aware* that some of their existing knowledge is relevant. They must retrieve that knowledge from long-term memory while thinking about the new material, so that *they have both the old and the new in working memory at the same time and thus can make the appropriate connections* (Bellezza, 1986; Glanzer & Nolan, 1986; Kalyuga, 2010).

As teachers, we should use students' existing knowledge as a starting point whenever we introduce a new topic. Furthermore, we should explicitly remind students of things they know that bear directly on a topic of classroom study—an instructional strategy known as **prior knowledge activation** (Machiels-Bongaerts, Schmidt, & Boshuizen, 1993; Resnick, 1989; Spires & Donley, 1998). For instance, we might begin a first-grade unit about plants by asking students to describe what their parents do to keep flowers or vegetable gardens growing. In a secondary English literature class, we might introduce Sir Walter Scott's *Ivanhoe* (in which Robin Hood is a major character) by asking students to tell the tale of Robin Hood as they know it. We should also remember that students from diverse cultural backgrounds may have somewhat different knowledge bases, and adjust our starting points accordingly (E. Fox, 2009; Nelson-Barber & Estrin, 1995; Pritchard, 1990).

Furthermore, we should encourage students to retrieve relevant knowledge *on their own* as they study. One approach is to model this strategy for students. For example, we might read aloud a portion of a textbook, stopping occasionally to tie an idea in the text to something previously studied in class or to something in our own personal experience. We can then encourage students to do likewise, giving suggestions and guiding their efforts as they proceed. Especially when working with students in the elementary grades, we might also want to provide specific questions that encourage students to reflect on their existing knowledge and beliefs as they read and study—for instance, asking themselves, "What do I already know about this topic?" and "Might I discover that something I think about this topic isn't correct?" (Baer & Garrett, 2010; Spires & Donley, 1998; H. Thompson & Carr, 1995).

Begin instruction with what students already know, and help them make connections between the "new" and the "old."

As students begin a reading assignment, encourage them to think about what they already know and believe about a topic.

ENCOURAGING A MEANINGFUL LEARNING SET AND CONCEPTUAL UNDERSTANDING

We can't always blame students when they take a relatively meaning*less* approach to their studies. Inadvertently, some teachers tend to encourage students to learn school subjects by rote. Think back to your own experiences in school. How many times were you allowed to define a word by repeating its dictionary definition, rather than being expected to explain it in your own words? In fact, how many times were you *required* to learn something word for word? And how many times did an exam assess your knowledge of facts or principles without ever assessing your ability to relate those facts and principles to everyday life or to things you learned in previous lessons or courses? When assignments and assessments require memory of isolated facts—and perhaps even require word-for-word recall—students are apt to engage in rote rather than meaningful learning, believing that a rote-learning approach will yield them better grades (Crooks, 1988; N. Frederiksen, 1984b; M. C. Linn & Eylon, 2011; L. Shepard, Hammerness, Darling-Hammond, & Rust, 2005).

As teachers, we should not only encourage meaningful learning through the strategies previously described—asking students to logically organize the things they're studying, think of new examples, speculate about implications, and the like—but we should also communicate that school topics are to be *understood* rather than memorized. In other words, we should encourage students to adopt a meaningful learning set. For example, we might frequently ask students to explain their reasoning, and our assignments and assessment tasks should require true understanding rather than rote memorization (Ausubel, Novak, & Hanesian, 1978; Middleton & Midgley, 2002; L. Shepard et al., 2005).

Ideally, students should gain a conceptual understanding of classroom topics; that is, they should form many logical connections among related concepts and principles. For example, rather than simply memorize basic mathematical computation procedures, students should learn how those procedures reflect underlying principles of mathematics. And rather than learn historical facts as lists of unrelated people, places, and dates, students should place those facts within the context of major social and religious trends, migration patterns, economic conditions, human personality characteristics, and other relevant phenomena. The more interrelationships students form within the subject matter they're learning—in other words, the better they *organize* it—the more easily they'll be able to remember and apply it later on (Baroody et al., 2013; M. C. Linn & Eylon, 2011; J. J. White & Rumsey, 1994).

Constructing an integrated understanding of any complex topic inevitably takes time. Accordingly, many experts advocate the principle *Less is more: Less* material studied thoroughly (rather than superficially) is learned *more* completely and with greater understanding (e.g., Brophy et al., 2009; M. C. Linn, 2008; Sizer, 2004). Following are several more specific strategies for promoting conceptual understanding of classroom subject matter:

- Organize units around a few core ideas or themes, always relating specific content back to this core.
- Explore each topic in depth—for example, by considering many examples, examining cause–and–effect relationships, and discovering how specific details relate to more general principles.
- Regularly connect new ideas to students' personal experiences and to things students have previously learned at school.
- Emphasize that conceptual understanding is far more important than knowledge of specific facts—not only through the statements you make but also through the questions you ask, the assignments you give, and the criteria you use to evaluate achievement.
- Ask students to teach what they've learned to others. Teaching others encourages them to focus on and pull together main ideas in ways that make sense. (Brophy, 2004; Brophy et al., 2009; Hatano & Inagaki, 1993; Middleton & Midgley, 2002; Perkins & Ritchhart, 2004; Roscoe & Chi, 2007; VanSledright & Brophy, 1992; J. J. White & Rumsey, 1994)

USING MNEMONICS IN THE ABSENCE OF RELEVANT PRIOR KNOWLEDGE

Some things are hard to make sense of—that is, hard to learn meaningfully. For instance, why do bones in the human body have such names as *fibula, humerus,* and *ulna?* Why is *Au* the chemical symbol for gold? Why is Augusta the capital of the state of Maine? From most students' perspectives, there's no rhyme or reason to such facts.

When students have trouble finding relationships between new material and their prior knowledge, or when a body of information seemingly has no organizational structure (as is true for many lists), special memory tricks known as mnemonics can help students remember classroom

FIGURE 6.8 Common mnemonic techniques.

Verbal Mediation

A **verbal mediator** is a word or phrase that creates a logical connection, or bridge, between two pieces of information. Verbal mediators can be used for paired pieces of information such as foreign language words and their English meanings, countries and their capitals, chemical elements and their symbols, and words and their spellings. Following are examples:

Information to Be Learned	Verbal Mediator
Handschuh is German for "glove."	A glove is a *shoe* for the *hand*.
Quito is the capital of Ecuador.	*Mosquitoes* are at the *equator*.
Au is the symbol for gold.	*Ay, you* stole my *gold* watch!
The word *principal* (a school administrator) ends with the letters *pal* (not *ple*).	The *principal* is my *pal*.
The *humerus* bone is the large arm bone above the elbow.	The *humorous* bone is just above the *funny* bone.
Amendment *2* to the U.S. Constitution is the right to *bear arms*.	A *bear* has *two arms*.

Keyword Method

Like verbal mediation, the **keyword method** aids memory by making a connection between two things. This technique is especially helpful when there is no logical verbal mediator to fill the gap—for example, when there is no obvious sentence or phrase to relate a foreign language word to its English meaning. The keyword method involves two steps, which we can illustrate using the Spanish word *amor* and its English meaning, "love":

1. Identify a concrete object to represent each piece of information. The object can be either a commonly used symbol (e.g., a heart to symbolize *love*) or a sound-alike word (e.g., a suit of armor to represent *amor*). Such objects are *keywords*.
2. Form a mental picture—that is, a visual image—of the two objects together. For example, to remember that *amor* means *love*, we might picture a knight in a suit of armor with a huge red heart painted on his chest.

You used the keyword method when you completed the "Five Chinese Words" exercise earlier in the chapter. Here are additional examples:

Information to Be Learned	Visual Image
Das Pferd is German for *horse*.	Picture a *horse* driving a *Ford*.
Augusta is the capital of Maine.	Picture a *gust of* wind blowing through a horse's *mane*.
Tchaikovsky composed the ballet *Swan Lake*.	Picture a *swan* swimming on a *lake*, wearing a *tie* and *coughing*.

Superimposed Meaningful Structure

A larger body of information, such as a list of items, can often be learned by superimposing a meaningful visual or verbal organizational structure on it—for instance, a familiar shape, word, sentence, rhythm, poem, or story. The following are examples of such **superimposed meaningful structures**:

Information to Be Learned	Superimposed Meaningful Structure
The shape of Italy	A boot
The five Great Lakes (Huron, Ontario, Michigan, Erie, Superior)	HOMES
Lines on the treble clef (E G B D F)	Elvis's Guitar Broke Down Friday, *or* Every Good Boy Does Fine.
The distinction between stalagmites and stalactites	When the "mites" go up, the "tites" come down.
The number of days in each month	Thirty days has September, . . .

Superimposed meaningful structures can be used to remember procedures as well as declarative information. Here are three examples:

Procedure to Be Learned	Superimposed Meaningful Structure
Shooting a free throw in basketball	BEEF: Balance the ball, Elbows in, Elevate the arms, Follow through.
Simplifying a complex algebraic expression	Please Excuse My Dear Aunt Sally: First, simplify terms within **p**arentheses, then terms with an **e**xponent, then terms to be **m**ultiplied or **d**ivided, and finally terms to be **a**dded or **s**ubtracted.
Turning a screw (clockwise to tighten, counterclockwise to loosen)	Righty, tighty, lefty, loosey.

material more effectively. Three commonly used mnemonics—verbal mediation, the keyword method, and superimposed meaningful structures—are described in Figure 6.8.

Research consistently supports the effectiveness of using mnemonics in learning (e.g., R. K. Atkinson et al., 1999; M. S. Jones, Levin, Levin, & Beitzel, 2000; Pressley, Levin, & Delaney, 1982; Soemer & Schwan, 2012). Their effectiveness lies in their conformity with a basic principle of long-term memory storage: Learners find some sort of meaning—even if that "meaning" is a bit contrived—in what might otherwise be nonsensical information. The artificial organization structure that some mnemonics provide is an additional plus. Imposing rhythm on a body of information—for instance, embedding the information in a song or hip-hop lyrics—is one way of giving it structure and can be especially beneficial when music is a significant part of students' cultures (B. A. Allen & Boykin, 1991; Barton, Tan, & Rivet, 2008; Tyler, Uqdah, et al., 2008).

> Suggest helpful mnemonics when new information is difficult to learn meaningfully, and teach students how to create their own mnemonics.

MyEdLab **Self-Check 6.3**

MyEdLab **Application Exercise 6.2.** In this exercise, you can apply what you have learned about long-term memory storage processes as you watch a high school geography lesson.

When Knowledge Construction Goes Awry: Addressing Learners' Misconceptions

When learners construct their own understandings, there's no guarantee that they'll construct accurate ones. Occasionally they may instead construct misconceptions—beliefs that are inconsistent with commonly accepted and well-validated explanations of phenomena or events. For example, in science, some of students' beliefs might be at odds with data collected over the course of decades or centuries of scientific research. And in history, students' understandings of certain events might be inconsistent with existing historical records and artifacts from the time period in question. Figure 6.9 presents misconceptions that researchers have often observed in students—not only in children and adolescents, but occasionally in college students as well.

In many instances students' misconceptions arise out of their own well-intended efforts to make sense of the things they see—for example, a sun and moon that seem to "travel" across the sky. But society and culture can foster misconceptions as well. Sometimes common expressions in language misrepresent the true nature of physical events. For instance, when we talk about the sun "rising" and "setting," children might easily conclude that the sun revolves around the earth, rather than vice versa. Sometimes people infer incorrect cause-and-effect relationships between two events simply because the events often occur at the same time—a problem of mistaking correlation for causation. In addition, fairy tales and cartoons may misrepresent what we know to be true in, say, physics or paleontology—as examples, you've probably watched cartoon bad guys run off cliffs and remain suspended in the air until they realize there's nothing holding them up, and perhaps you've seen cartoon cavemen riding on dinosaurs. And unfortunately, it's sometimes the case that students acquire erroneous ideas from textbooks, teachers, the Internet, or the general social and cultural group in which they live (A. C. Butler, Zaromb, Lyle, & Roediger, 2009; Cho, 2010; Glynn, Yeany, & Britton, 1991; Levstik, 2011; M. C. Linn & Eylon, 2011; Marcus, 2008; Wiser & Smith, 2008).

Regardless of how students' misconceptions originate, they can wreak havoc on new learning. As a result of elaborating on new information—a process that usually facilitates learning—students may interpret or distort the information to be consistent with what they already "know" and thus continue to believe what they've always believed. For example, one 11th-grade physics class was studying the idea that an object's mass and weight do *not,* by themselves, affect the speed at which the object falls. Students were asked to build egg containers that would keep eggs from breaking when dropped from a third-floor window. They were told that on the day of the egg drop, they would record the time it took for the eggs to reach the ground. Convinced that heavier objects fall faster, a student named Barry added several nails to his egg's container. Yet when he dropped it, classmates timed its fall at 1.49 seconds—a time very similar to that for other students' lighter containers. Rather than acknowledge that light and heavy objects fall at the same rate, Barry explained the result by rationalizing that "the people weren't timing real good" (Hynd, 1998a, p. 34).

> If you took the OOPS test in Chapter 1, you may have discovered some of your own misconceptions about human learning and development.

FIGURE 6.9 Common student beliefs and misconceptions.

In Biology

- Plants use their roots to take in "food" (e.g., water, nutrients) from the soil. (From the perspective of biology, plants produce their own food through photosynthesis.)
- Vision involves something moving outward from the eye toward the object being seen. (In reality, the opposite is true: Light rays bounce off the object to the eye.)

In Astronomy

- The sun revolves around the earth. It "rises" in the morning and "sets" in the evening, at which point it "goes" to the other side of the earth.
- The earth is shaped like a round, flat disk, with people living on its top, or a hollowed-out sphere, with people living on a horizontal surface in its middle.
- Space has an absolute "up" and "down"; people standing at the South Pole will fall off the earth.

In Climatology

- The four seasons are the result of the earth's distance from the sun; the earth is closer to the sun in the summer, farther away in the winter. (In fact, distance from the sun is largely irrelevant; seasons are the result of the angle at which the sun's rays hit different parts of the earth's surface.)

In Physics

- Objects exist for a purpose; for example, some rocks are pointy so that animals that live nearby can scratch themselves when they have an itch.
- Any moving object has a force acting on it. For example, a ball thrown in the air continues to be pushed upward by the force of the throw until it begins its descent. (In reality, force is needed only to change the direction or speed of an object; otherwise, *inertia* is at work.)
- If an astronaut were to open the hatch while traveling in outer place, he or she would be "sucked out" by the vacuum in space. (In reality, the astronaut would be blown out by the air inside the spacecraft.)

In Mathematics

- Multiplication always leads to a bigger number. (This principle holds true only when the multiplier is larger than 1.)
- Division always leads to a smaller number. (This principle holds true only when the divisor is larger than 1.)
- Parallelograms must be slanted; rectangles must have widths different from their lengths. (In reality, parallelograms can have right angles, in which case they're also rectangles; rectangles can have four equal sides, in which case they're also squares.)

In History

- Early human beings lived at the same time that dinosaurs did.
- Christopher Columbus was the first person to believe that the world is round rather than flat.

In Geography and Social Studies

- The lines separating countries or states are marked on the earth.
- Erosion is largely something that happened in the past; for example, the Grand Canyon is no longer eroding.
- People are poor only because they don't have enough money to "buy" a job; giving a poor person a small amount of money will make the person rich.

Sources: Brewer, 2008; Brophy et al., 2009; Chi, 2008; De Corte, Greer, & Verschaffel, 1996; Delval, 1994; diSessa, 1996; H. Gardner, Torff, & Hatch, 1996; Haskell, 2001; Hynd, 2003; Kelemen, 1999, 2004; V. R. Lee, 2010; Martínez, Bannan-Ritland, Kitsantas, & Baek, 2008; Masters et al., 2010; K. J. Roth & Anderson, 1988; Sneider & Pulos, 1983; Tirosh & Graeber, 1990; Vosniadou & Brewer, 1987; Vosniadou, Vamvakoussi, & Skopeliti, 2008; Winer & Cottrell, 1996.

When students have misunderstandings such as Barry's, we must work hard to promote conceptual change, a process of revising or overhauling an existing theory or belief system in such a way that new, discrepant information can be better understood and explained. Don't let the term *conceptual* mislead you here: For the most part, we're talking about changing tightly interconnected sets of ideas rather than changing single, isolated concepts.

OBSTACLES TO CONCEPTUAL CHANGE

Teachers often present new information with the expectation that it will easily replace students' erroneous beliefs about a topic. And in fact some misconceptions are easily corrected. Yet students of all ages can hold quite stubbornly to certain counterproductive beliefs about the world, even after considerable instruction that explicitly contradicts those beliefs. Theorists have offered several possible explanations about why students' misconceptions can be so resistant to change.

- *Students' existing beliefs affect their interpretations of new information.* Thanks to the processes of meaningful learning and elaboration—processes that usually facilitate learning—learners are more likely to interpret new information in ways that are consistent with what they already "know" about the world. For example, after one 4-year-old dinosaur enthusiast read a book about how increasingly cold temperatures may have contributed to the dinosaurs' extinction, he speculated that "they did not know how to put on their sweaters" (M. C. Linn & Eylon, 2011, p. 1). Presumably, he eventually rejected his "sweater" hypothesis, but in many cases people continue to believe some or all of what they've always believed despite convincing evidence to the contrary (Andiliou, Ramsay, Murphy, & Fast, 2012; Brewer, 2008; Kalyuga, 2010; Kendeou & van den Broek, 2005).

  Furthermore, people of all ages (even college students!) tend to actively *look* for information that confirms their existing beliefs and to ignore or discredit contradictory evidence—a phenomenon known as **confirmation bias** (Chinn & Buckland, 2012; Hynd, 1998b; P. K. Murphy & Mason, 2006). For example, when students in a high school science lab observe results that contradict what they expected to happen, they might complain, "Our equipment isn't working right," or "I can never do science right anyway" (Minstrell & Stimpson, 1996, p. 192).

- *Students' existing beliefs may be more consistent with their everyday experiences.* Well-established scientific theories are often fairly abstract and sometimes seem to contradict everyday reality (D. B. Clark, 2006; M. C. Linn, 2008; Wiser & Smith, 2008). For example, in physics, although the law of inertia tells us that force is needed to *start* an object in motion but not to *keep* it in motion, we know from experience that if we want to move a heavy object across the floor, we must continue to push it until we get it where we want it (Driver, Asoko, Leach, Mortimer, & Scott, 1994). And although virtually any piece of matter has some weight, a very small piece of Styrofoam may feel weightless in our hands (C. L. Smith, 2007).

- *Some beliefs are integrated into a cohesive whole, with many interconnections among ideas.* In such circumstances, changing misconceptions involves changing a tightly organized set of understandings—perhaps a personally constructed theory or perhaps an entire *worldview*—rather than a single belief (Lewandowsky, Ecker, Seifert, Schwarz, & Cook, 2012; J. L. McClelland, 2013; P. K. Murphy & Mason, 2006; Rosengren, Brem, Evans, & Sinatra, 2012). For example, the belief that the sun revolves around the earth may be part of a more general earth-centered view of things, perhaps one that includes the moon, stars, and other heavenly bodies revolving around the earth as well. In reality, of course, the moon revolves around the earth, the earth revolves around the sun, and other stars aren't directly involved with the earth in one way or another. Yet the earth-centered view is a much easier one to understand and accept—on the surface, at least—and everything seems to fit so nicely together.

  You can find more information about people's worldviews in Chapter 4 and Chapter 8.

- *Students may fail to notice an inconsistency between new information and their existing beliefs.* Sometimes this happens because students learn the new information in a rote manner, without relating it to things they already know and believe. In other instances it occurs because existing misconceptions take the form of *implicit knowledge*—knowledge that students aren't consciously aware of. In either circumstance, students don't realize that the material they're studying contradicts their current understandings, and thus they may continue to apply their misconceptions when interpreting new situations (Fernbach, Rogers, Fox, & Sloman, 2013; P. K. Murphy, 2007; Sinatra, Kienhues, & Hofer, 2014; Strike & Posner, 1992).

- *Students may have a personal or emotional investment in their existing beliefs.* For one reason or another, students may be especially committed to certain beliefs, perhaps insisting "This theory is what I believe in! Nobody can make me change it!" (Mason, 2003, p. 228). In some instances their beliefs may be an integral part of their religion or culture. In other cases students may interpret information that contradicts their existing understandings as a threat to their self-esteem. In either situation, students may cling to their current understandings even more tightly than they had before encountering more valid and productive explanations (Lewandowsky et al., 2012; Linnenbrink & Pintrich, 2003; Porat, 2004; Rosengren et al., 2012; Sherman & Cohen, 2002).

PROMOTING CONCEPTUAL CHANGE

For the reasons just identified, promoting conceptual change can be quite a challenge. Not only must we help students learn new things, but we must also help them *un*learn—or at least *inhibit*—their existing beliefs. Following are strategies that seem to have an impact, especially when used in combination.

- 🍎 *Identify existing misconceptions before instruction begins.* As teachers, we can more easily address students' misconceptions when we know what they *are* (P. K. Murphy & Alexander, 2008). Thus, we should probably begin any new topic by assessing students' current beliefs about the topic—perhaps simply by asking a few informal questions and probing further if students' initial explanations are vague. As an example, an 11-year-old once described rain as "water that falls out of a cloud when the clouds evaporate." The response had an element of truth—evaporation is an essential process in cloud formation—but wasn't quite on target: Rain actually results a bit later in the water cycle as a result of *condensation*. A series of follow-up questions eventually revealed a rather unique understanding: The water "comes down at little times like a salt shaker when you turn it upside down. It doesn't all come down at once 'cause there's little holes [in the cloud] and it just comes out" (Stepans, 1991, p. 94). This conception of a cloud as a salt shaker is hardly consistent with scientific views of rain and should definitely be addressed during instruction.

  Informal preassessments of students' current understandings will be especially important in your first few years of teaching. As you gain experience teaching a particular topic year after year, you may eventually find that you can anticipate what students' prior beliefs and misbeliefs about the topic are likely to be.

- 🍎 *Look for and then build on kernels of truth in students' current understandings.* Often students' current understandings have a partly-right-and-partly-wrong quality (diSessa, 1996, 2006; Vosniadou, 2008). For example, the 11-year-old with the salt-shaker explanation of rain correctly knew that evaporation is somehow involved in the water cycle, and such knowledge would be a good starting point for further instruction. Among other things, a teacher might (1) help the child understand how evaporation and condensation are essentially opposite processes that involve either changing from liquid form to vapor form (evaporation) or vice versa (condensation); and (2) explain how a cloud actually is *water itself* rather than a shakerlike water container.

- 🍎 *Convince students that their existing beliefs need revision.* We can more effectively promote conceptual change when we help students discover why their existing conceptions are inadequate. In Jean Piaget's terminology, we need to create *disequilibrium,* perhaps with strategies such as these:

  - 🍏 Present phenomena and ask questions that lead students to find weaknesses in their current understandings.
  - 🍏 Have students conduct experiments to test various hypotheses and predictions.
  - 🍏 Ask students to propose several possible explanations for puzzling phenomena and to discuss the pros and cons of each one.
  - 🍏 Show how one explanation of an event or phenomenon is more plausible (i.e., makes more sense) than others.
  - 🍏 Have students apply the new ideas to real-life situations and problems. (Beardsley, Bloom, & Wise, 2012; Chinn & Malhotra, 2002; Chinn & Samarapungavan, 2009; D. B. Clark, 2006; Lewandowsky et al., 2012; M. C. Linn & Eylon, 2011; P. K. Murphy & Mason, 2006; Pine & Messer, 2000; Sinatra & Pintrich, 2003; C. L. Smith, 2007; Vosniadou, 2008)

  Such strategies might encompass a wide variety of instructional methods, including demonstrations, hands-on activities, teacher explanations, small-group or whole-class discussions, and writing assignments. All of these strategies have one thing in common: a focus on meaningful learning rather than rote memorization.

🍎 *Motivate students to learn correct explanations.* Students will be most likely to engage in meaningful learning and undergo conceptual change when they're motivated to do so. At a minimum, they must be interested in the subject matter, see it as useful in helping them achieve their personal goals, set their sights on mastering it, and have sufficient self-confidence to believe they *can* master it. Furthermore, the classroom should be socially and emotionally *supportive* of conceptual change. For example, students must feel confident that (1) their teacher and classmates won't ridicule them for their initially erroneous or partly-right-but-partly-wrong ideas and (2) the ultimate goal of a lesson is understanding the subject matter rather than simply performing well on a quiz or assignment (Hatano & Inagaki, 2003; Pintrich, Marx, & Boyle, 1993; Sinatra & Mason, 2008).

Chapter 11 describes many strategies for motivating students to master classroom subject matter.

🍎 *Monitor what students say and write for signs of persistent misconceptions.* Some misconceptions and only-partly-correct understandings may persist despite our best efforts. Throughout a lesson, then, we should often check students' beliefs about the topic at hand, looking for subtle signs that their understanding isn't completely on target and giving corrective feedback when necessary. As an illustration, imagine a lesson about human vision that includes the following general principles:

- The retina of the human eye detects light rays that reach it; the eye sends information about these light rays to the brain for interpretation.
- A person sees an object when light rays (1) travel from the sun or other light source to the object, (2) bounce off of the object, and then (3) travel to the retina.
- Light rays bounce off of some (opaque) objects but go through other (transparent) objects.

A common misconception in both children and adults is that vision involves something going *out from the eye to the object,* rather than vice versa (K. J. Roth & Anderson, 1988; Winer & Cottrell, 1996; Winer, Cottrell, Gregg, Fournier, & Bica, 2002). Therefore, this misconception is something we would want to be on the lookout for throughout the lesson. For instance, we might show students the drawing in Figure 6.10 and ask them whether the girl can see the car. Several of them might respond, "No, she can't see through it" or "It's opaque." The phrase *see through* is one that people often use when talking about transparent objects, but it implies that something is traveling from—not *to*—the eye. We would thus want to ask follow-up questions to pin down their reasoning: "What do you mean, she can't see *through* it?" "What does *opaque* mean?" and "What are the light rays doing?"

Assessment of students' comprehension is important *after* a lesson as well. We're more likely to detect and correct misconceptions when we ask students to *explain* and *apply* what they've learned, rather than just asking them to spit back memorized facts, definitions, and formulas (D. B. Clark, 2006; Pine & Messer, 2000; K. J. Roth, 1990). Even so, we must remember that true and lasting conceptual change may take considerable time and instruction—perhaps several years' worth—especially if it involves overhauling a complex, interrelated set of student-constructed ideas (J. L. McClelland, 2013; Vosniadou, 2008).

FIGURE 6.10 Can the girl see the car? If not, why not?

🍎 Remember that true and lasting conceptual change about complex phenomena can take considerable time and instruction.

MyEdLab **Self-Check 6.4**

MyEdLab **Application Exercise 6.3.** In this exercise, you can apply what you have learned about conceptual change as you watch a first-grade science lesson.

Long-Term Memory Retrieval

As you've already discovered, some of the information stored in long-term memory is easily retrieved later on. Other pieces of information are harder to find, and still others may never be found at all. Retrieving information from long-term memory appears to involve following a pathway of associations; it's a process of mentally going down Memory Lane. One idea reminds us of another idea—that is, one idea *activates* another—the second idea reminds us of a third idea, and so on. The process is similar to what happened when you followed your train of thought from the word *horse* earlier in the chapter. If the pathway of associations eventually leads us to what we're trying to remember, we do indeed remember it. If the path takes us in another direction, we're out of luck.

Learners are more likely to remember something later on if, in the process of storing it, they connect it with something else in long-term memory. Ideally, the new and the old have a logical relationship. To illustrate this idea, let's return once again to all that mail you routinely get in your mail and email boxes. Imagine that, on average, you receive five important items—five things you really want to save—each day. That adds up to more than 1,800 items a year. Over the course of 15 years, you would have more than 27,000 important things stashed somewhere in your home, on your computer, or in a back-up storage mechanism.

Imagine that one day you hear that stock in a clothing company (Mod Bod Jeans) has tripled in value. You remember that your wealthy Aunt Agnes bought you some Mod Bod stock for your birthday several years ago, and you presumably decided that the paperwork documenting her purchase was important enough to save. But where in the world did you put it? How easily you find it—in fact, whether you find it at all—depends on how you've been storing your mail as you've accumulated it. If you've been storing it in a logical, organized fashion—for instance, maybe you've put all the bills you've paid by regular mail on a closet shelf, all banking and investment paperwork in alphabetical order in a file drawer, and all electronic documents from family and friends in labeled folders on your computer—you should quickly find Aunt Agnes's gift. But if you simply tossed each day's mail and email messages randomly about, you'll be searching for a long, long time, possibly without ever finding a trace of the Mod Bod stock.

Like a home with 15 years' worth of mail, long-term memory contains a great deal of information. And like your search for the Mod Bod purchase, the ease with which information is retrieved from long-term memory depends somewhat on whether the information has been stored in a logical place—that is, whether it's connected to related ideas. By making connections to existing knowledge—that is, by engaging in meaningful learning—we'll know where to look for information when we need it. Otherwise, we may never retrieve it again.

FACTORS AFFECTING RETRIEVAL

Even when people connect new information to their existing knowledge base, they can't always find it when they need it. We now look at several factors affecting retrieval from long-term memory.

MULTIPLE CONNECTIONS WITH EXISTING KNOWLEDGE AND A VARIETY OF CONTEXTS

Sometimes learners acquire and practice certain behaviors and ways of thinking in a very limited set of environments—say, in their science or civics classes. When this happens, the learners may associate those behaviors and ways of thinking *only* with those particular environments and thus fail to retrieve what they've learned when they're in other contexts (Day & Goldstone, 2012; Greeno, Collins, & Resnick, 1996; Gresalfi & Lester, 2009; Kirsh, 2009). This tendency for some responses and cognitive processes to be associated with and retrieved in some contexts but not others is often called situated learning or situated cognition. For example, if students associate principles of geometry only with math classes, they may not retrieve those principles at times when geometry would come in handy—say, when trying to determine whether a 10-inch pizza that costs $8.00 is a better value than an 8-inch pizza that costs $6.00.

In general, learners are more likely to retrieve information when they have *many* possible pathways to it—in other words, when they have associated the information with many other things they know and with many different contexts in which they might use it. Making multiple connections is like using cross-references in your mail storage system. You may have filed the Mod Bod paperwork in your banking/investments file drawer, but you may also have written its location on notes-to-self you've put in other places—perhaps with your birth certificate (after all, you received the stock on your birthday) and in a computer folder of family documents and photos (because a family member gave you the stock). By looking in one of these logical places, you'll discover where to find the Mod Bod documentation.

As teachers, we can help students more effectively remember classroom subject matter over the long run if we show how it relates to *many* other things they already know. For example, we can show them how new material relates to one or more of the following:

- Concepts and ideas within the same subject area (e.g., showing how multiplication is related to addition)
- Concepts and ideas in other subject areas (e.g., talking about how scientific discoveries have affected historical events)
- Students' general knowledge of the world (e.g., relating the concept of *inertia* to how passengers are affected when a car quickly turns a sharp corner)
- Students' personal experiences (e.g., finding similarities between the family feud in *Romeo and Juliet* and students' own interpersonal conflicts)
- Students' current activities and needs outside the classroom (e.g., showing how persuasive writing skills might be used to craft an essay for a college application)

> Help students connect important ideas to a variety of disciplines and real-world situations.

DISTINCTIVENESS

Learners are more likely to remember things that are unique in some way—for instance, things that are new, unusual, or a bit bizarre (R. R. Hunt & Worthen, 2006). For example, second graders are more likely to remember a visit to the local firehouse than, say, their teacher's explanation of what an *adverb* is. And when U.S. high school students recall what they've learned about events leading up to the American Revolution, they're more likely to remember the Boston Tea Party—a unique and colorful illustration of colonists' dissatisfaction with British taxation policies—than, say, the Quartering Act or the publication of Thomas Paine's *Common Sense*. Certainly, learners are more likely to *pay attention* to distinctive information, increasing the odds that they store it in long-term memory in the first place. But even when attention and initial learning have been the same, distinctive information is easier to retrieve than dull-and-ordinary information (Craik, 2006; Mather & Sutherland, 2011).

> Make important ideas distinctive in some way, perhaps by illustrating them with vivid examples or engaging hands-on experiences.

EMOTIONAL OVERTONES

As learners pay attention to and think about new information, their thoughts and memories sometimes become emotionally charged—a phenomenon called **hot cognition**. For example, learners might get excited when they read about advances in science that could lead to effective treatments for cancer, spinal cord injuries, or mental illness. Or they might feel sadness and empathy when they read about poor living conditions in certain parts of the world. And they will, we hope, get angry when they learn about atrocities committed against African American slaves in the pre–Civil War days of the United States or about large-scale genocides carried out in more recent times in Europe, Africa, and Asia.

When information is emotionally charged in such ways, learners are more likely to pay attention to it, continue to think about it for an extended period, and repeatedly elaborate on it (Bower, 1994; Heuer & Reisberg, 1992; M. I. Posner & Rothbart, 2007; Zeelenberg, Wagenmakers, & Rotteveel, 2006). And over the long run, learners can usually retrieve material with high emotional content more easily than they can recall relatively nonemotional information (LaBar & Phelps, 1998; Phelps & Sharot, 2008; Reisberg & Heuer, 1992).[1] It appears that students' emotional reactions to classroom topics become integral parts of their network of associations in long-term memory (Bower & Forgas, 2001; Siegel, 2012).

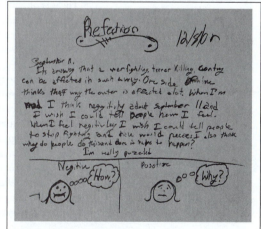

Information and events that evoke strong emotional reactions often remain vivid in memory for quite some time. In this reflection in a class journal, written more than a year after the 9/11 terrorist attacks on the World Trade Center and Pentagon, 12-year-old Amaryth still has strong feelings about the attacks.

---

[1] Some psychologists have suggested that people may occasionally have trouble retrieving highly anxiety-arousing memories. Such *repression*, if it truly occurs, is most likely to involve memories for traumatic personal events (M. C. Anderson et al., 2004; Erdelyi, 2010; Pezdek & Banks, 1996). It's unlikely to be a factor in the retrieval of classroom subject matter.

Convey your own enthusiasm for a topic.

Academic subject matter certainly doesn't need to be dry and emotionless. In addition to presenting subject matter that evokes students' emotions, we can promote hot cognition by revealing our own feelings about a topic. For instance, we might bring in newspaper articles and other outside materials about which we're excited, or we might share the particular questions and issues about which we ourselves are concerned (Brophy, 2004; R. P. Perry, 1985).

REGULAR PRACTICE

As noted earlier, rehearsal—mindlessly repeating information over and over within the course of a few seconds or minutes—is a relatively *in*effective way of getting information into long-term memory. But by "regular practice" here, we mean repetition over a *lengthy* time span: reviewing and using information and skills at periodic intervals over the course of a few weeks, months, or years. When practice is spread out in this manner—ideally in a variety of contexts—people of all ages learn something better and remember it longer (Karpicke, 2012; Lindsey, Shroyer, Pashler, & Mozer, 2014; Rohrer & Pashler, 2010).

When learners continue to practice things they've already mastered, they eventually achieve **automaticity**: They can retrieve what they've learned quickly and effortlessly and can use it almost without thinking (J. R. Anderson, 2005; Pashler, Rohrer, Cepeda, & Carpenter, 2007; Proctor & Dutta, 1995). As an example, think of driving a car, a complicated skill that you can probably perform easily. Your first attempts at driving many years ago may have required a great deal of mental effort. But perhaps now you can drive without having to pay much attention to what you're doing. Even if your car has a standard transmission that frequently requires stepping on a clutch and shifting gears, driving is, for you, an automatic activity.

Learning some knowledge and skills to a level of automaticity has a second advantage as well. Remember that working memory has a limited capacity: The active, consciously thinking part of the human memory system can handle only so much at a time. When much of its capacity must be used for recalling isolated facts or carrying out simple procedures, little room is left for addressing more complex situations or tasks. One key reason for learning some facts and procedures to the point of automaticity, then, is to free up working memory capacity for complex tasks and problems that require those simpler facts and procedures (De La Paz & McCutchen, 2011; L. S. Fuchs et al., 2013; Kalyuga, 2010; Limpo & Alves, 2013). For example, second graders who are reading a story can better focus their efforts on understanding it if they don't have to sound out words like *before* and *after*. High school chemistry students can more easily interpret the expression Na_2CO_3 (sodium carbonate) if they don't have to stop to think about what the symbols *Na, C,* and *O* represent.

Unfortunately, automaticity is achieved in only one way: practice, practice, and more practice. Practice doesn't necessarily make perfect, but it does make knowledge more durable and more easily retrievable. When learners use information and skills frequently, they essentially pave their retrieval pathways—in some cases creating superhighways. This is *not* to say that we should continually assign drill-and-practice exercises involving isolated facts and procedures (e.g., see Figure 6.11). Such activities promote rote (rather than meaningful) learning, are often boring, and are unlikely to convince students of the value of the subject matter (Mac Iver, Reuman, & Main, 1995). A more effective approach is to routinely incorporate basic knowledge and skills into a variety of meaningful and enjoyable activities, such as problem-solving tasks, brainteasers, group projects, and games.

Occasionally conduct activities in which students review and practice things they've learned in previous weeks, months, or years.

RELEVANT RETRIEVAL CUES

If you were educated in North America, then at one time or another you probably learned the names of the five Great Lakes. Yet at any given moment you might have trouble retrieving all five, even though they're all still stored somewhere in your long-term memory. Perhaps Lake Michigan doesn't come to mind when you retrieve the other four. The *HOMES* mnemonic presented in Figure 6.8 provides a **retrieval cue**—a hint about where to "look" in long-term memory. The mnemonic tells you that one lake begins with the letter *M,* prompting you to search among the *M* words you know until (we hope) you find *Michigan.* Learners are more likely to retrieve information when relevant retrieval cues are present to start their search of long-term memory in the right direction (e.g., Morris, Bransford, & Franks, 1977; Tulving & Thomson, 1973).

Providing retrieval cues is often useful in the classroom, especially when students have trouble recalling information that might help them remember or apply *other* information. For example, if a student asks what the symbol *Au* stands for, we might respond by saying "One day we talked about how *Au* comes from the Latin word *aurum*. Can you remember what *aurum* means?" Another example comes from Jess Jensen, a former teacher intern of one of us authors. A student in her eighth-grade history class had been writing about the Battle of New Orleans, which was a decisive victory for the United States in the War of 1812. The following exchange took place:

> **Student:** Why was the Battle of New Orleans important?
>
> **Jess:** Look at the map. Where is New Orleans?
>
> [The student finds New Orleans.]
>
> **Jess:** Why is it important?
>
> **Student:** Oh! It's near the mouth of the Mississippi. It was important for controlling transportation up and down the river.

In the early grades, teachers typically provide many retrieval cues for their students; for instance, they remind students about tasks they need to do at certain times ("I hear the fire alarm. Remember, we must all walk quietly during a fire drill"). But as students grow older, they must develop greater independence, relying more on themselves and less on their teachers for the things they need to remember. At all grade levels we can teach students ways of providing retrieval cues for *themselves*. For example, if we expect first graders to get a permission slip signed, we might ask them to write a reminder on a piece of masking tape that they put on their jacket or backpack. If we give junior high school students a major assignment due in several weeks, we might suggest that they tape a note with the due date to their bedside table or add one or more reminders to their cell phone calendar. One 10th grader developed several effective retrieval cues, each appropriate for certain situations:

> Homework is written down in my agenda book. If it is something to do when I get home, I will write it on my hand. If I have something to do in the next few days, I write it on a note card in my wallet, and whenever I go to get money, I will think to do it.

WAIT TIME

Wait time is the length of time a teacher allows to pass after the teacher or a student says something before the teacher says something else. In many classrooms, wait time is insufficient for most students to retrieve information that might be relevant to a teacher's or classmate's question or comment. For instance, when teachers ask one or more students a question, many wait for only a very short time—perhaps a second or less—and if they don't get a response, they ask someone else the same question, rephrase the question, or answer the question themselves. Many teachers are equally reluctant to let more than a second elapse after students answer questions or make comments in class; they're apt to jump in very quickly to respond to a student comment or ask another question (Jegede & Olajide, 1995; M. B. Rowe, 1974, 1987).

Students benefit tremendously simply from being given a little time to think. When teachers instead allow at least *3 seconds* of wait time, more students participate in class—this is especially true for females and minority-group members—and students begin to respond to one another's comments and questions. In addition, students are more likely to support their reasoning with evidence or logic and more likely to speculate when they don't know an answer. Furthermore, they're more motivated to learn classroom subject matter, thereby increasing actual learning and decreasing behavior problems. Such changes are due, in part, to the fact that with increased wait time, *teachers'* behaviors change as well. Teachers ask fewer simple questions (e.g., those requiring recall of facts) and more thought-provoking ones (e.g., those requiring elaboration). They also modify the direction of discussion to accommodate students' comments and questions, and they allow their classes to pursue a topic in greater depth than they had originally anticipated. Moreover, their expectations for many students, especially low-achieving ones,

Provide retrieval cues when appropriate. Also, teach students to develop their own retrieval cues for things they must remember to do.

FIGURE 6.11
Occasional rote practice of numerals and letters can be helpful in promoting automaticity, but too much conveys the message that learning basic skills is boring and tedious. Here 5-year-old Gunnar has practiced writing numerals 1 through 9. Notice that he got practice in writing 9 *backward!*

Give students time to think about and formulate responses to challenging questions.

begin to improve (Castagno & Brayboy, 2008; Giaconia, 1988; M. B. Rowe, 1974, 1987; Tharp, 1989; Tobin, 1987).

When our objective is simple recall—when students need to retrieve classroom material very quickly, to "know it cold"—then wait time should be short. Students may sometimes benefit from rapid-fire drill and practice to learn information and skills to automaticity. But when our instructional goals include more complex processing of ideas and issues, a longer wait time may give both our students and us the time everyone needs to think things through.

WHY LEARNERS SOMETIMES FORGET

Fortunately, people don't need to remember everything they've stored. For instance, you may have no reason to remember the Internet address of a website you looked at yesterday, the plot of last week's episode of a certain television show, or the due date of an assignment you turned in last semester. Much of the information learners encounter is, like junk mail, not worth keeping, and forgetting it enables learners to get rid of needless clutter. But sometimes learners have trouble recalling what they *do* need to remember. Here we look at several possible explanations for why students may sometimes forget important information.

FAILURE TO STORE OR CONSOLIDATE INFORMATION IN LONG-TERM MEMORY

As we've seen, a great deal of the information students encounter never reaches long-term memory. Perhaps students didn't pay attention in the first place, so the information never went beyond the sensory register. Or perhaps after attending to it, students didn't continue to process it, so it went no further than working memory.

Even when information does reach long-term memory, it needs some time to "firm up" in the brain—a process called **consolidation** (Rasch & Born, 2008; Wixted, 2005). A good night's sleep after learning something new seems to facilitate this process (see the earlier Applying Brain Research feature). And an event that interferes with consolidation—such as a serious brain injury—may cause someone to forget things that happened several seconds, minutes, hours, or even longer prior to the event (Bauer, DeBoer, & Lukowski, 2007; Wixted, 2005).

DECAY

Historically, many psychologists believed that once information is stored in long-term memory, it remains there permanently in some form (Loftus & Loftus, 1980). More recently, however, some psychologists have come to the conclusion that information can slowly weaken and eventually disappear—that is, it can **decay**—especially if it isn't used regularly (e.g., Altmann & Gray, 2002; Brainerd & Reyna, 2005; Schacter, 1999).

INSUFFICIENT SEARCH OF LONG-TERM MEMORY

A man at the supermarket looks familiar, but you can't remember who he is or where you met him. He smiles at you and says, "Nice to see you again." Gulp! You desperately search your long-term memory for his name, but you've clearly forgotten who he is. A few days later you have a bowl of chili for dinner. The chili reminds you of the Chili for Charity supper at which you worked a few months back. Of course! You and the man at the supermarket had stood side by side serving chili to hundreds of people that night. Oh yes, you now recall, his name is Melville Herman.

Like you, students often have retrieval difficulties: They simply can't find something that's actually in long-term memory (e.g., Schacter, 1999). Sometimes they may stumble on the information later, while looking for something else. But at other times they never do retrieve it, perhaps because they've learned it by rote or don't have sufficient retrieval cues to guide their memory search.

INTERFERENCE

Sometimes people can easily retrieve things they've learned but don't know what goes with what. To experience this phenomenon yourself, try the following exercise.

EXPERIENCING FIRSTHAND
SIX CHINESE WORDS

Following are six more Mandarin Chinese words and their English meanings (for simplicity's sake, we've omitted the tone marks over the words). Read the words two or three times, and try to store them in your long-term memory. But don't do anything special to learn the words—for instance, don't intentionally develop mnemonics to help you remember them.

Chinese	English
jung	middle
ting	listen
sung	deliver
peng	friend
ching	please
deng	wait

Now cover up the list of words and test yourself. What is the Chinese word for *friend?* For *please?* For *listen?* For *wait?*

Did you find yourself getting confused, perhaps forgetting which English meaning went with each Chinese word? If you did, you were the victim of interference. The various pieces of information you stored in memory were interfering with one another—essentially, they were getting mixed up in your head. Interference is especially likely to occur when items are similar to one another and when they're learned in a rote rather than meaningful or mnemonic-based fashion (Dempster, 1985; Healey, Campbell, Hasher, & Ossher, 2010; Lustig, Konkel, & Jacoby, 2004). Interference was probably at work when Kanesha struggled to remember *tibia* and *fibula*—two similar-sounding bones in the lower leg—in the opening case study.

RECONSTRUCTION ERROR

Have you and a friend ever remembered the same event quite differently, even though the two of you were equally active participants at the time? Were you and your friend both certain of the accuracy of your own memories and convinced that the other person remembered incorrectly? Constructive processes in retrieval might explain this difference of opinion. Retrieval isn't necessarily an all-or-nothing phenomenon. Sometimes learners retrieve part of the information they're seeking but can't recall the rest. They may logically but incorrectly fill in the gaps using their general knowledge and assumptions about the world. This form of forgetting—which might be better labeled as *misremembering*—is called reconstruction error (Levstik, 2011; Roediger & McDermott, 2000; Schacter, 1999).

Recalling an event we've previously experienced often affects our later memory for the event, especially if we verbally describe the event and perhaps embellish on it in some way (Karpicke, 2012; E. J. Marsh, 2007; Seligman, Railton, Baumeister, & Sripada, 2013). Neurologically speaking, by recalling the event, we're also revising and *reconsolidating* it in the brain—that is, we're firming it up anew—with a mixture of information we actually received and our elaborations of it (Finn & Roediger, 2011; Schacter, 2012; Schiller et al., 2010).

All of these explanations of forgetting underscore the importance of instructional strategies presented earlier: We must make sure students are paying attention, help them relate new material to things they already know, and give them frequent opportunities to review, practice, and apply the material.

> When important details are difficult to fill in logically or might easily be confused with one another, make sure students learn them well.

MyEdLab **Self-Check 6.5**

MyEdLab **Application Exercise 6.4.** In this exercise, you can apply what you have learned about long-term memory to various classroom scenarios.

Diversity in Cognitive Processes

Children and adolescents differ considerably in the various factors that influence their ability to learn and remember in the classroom, including their attention spans, working memory capabilities, long-term memory storage processes, and prior knowledge. For example, on average, girls have a slight edge over boys in keeping their attention focused on classroom activities and in performing certain kinds of memory tasks, such as remembering lists and specific life events (Das, Naglieri, & Kirby, 1994; Halpern, 2006; Halpern & LaMay, 2000). And students of both genders vary in their general ability to think about, encode, and respond to new events and ideas quickly and easily. Some of this variability is the result of differences in working memory capacity and executive functioning. Students with a smaller overall capacity and minimal ability to mentally control what they're thinking about often have trouble remembering instructions, tackling complex tasks, and keeping their minds on a task at hand—all of which adversely affect their academic achievement levels (Alloway, Gathercole, Kirkwood, & Elliott, 2009; DeMarie & López, 2014; Miyake & Friedman, 2012). Working memory and executive functioning difficulties are especially common in children who have grown up in chronically stressful living conditions, often as a result of living in extreme poverty (G. W. Evans & Schamberg, 2009; Masten et al., 2012; Noble, McCandliss, & Farah, 2007).

Another important source of diversity in cognitive processing is cultural background. Different cultures foster somewhat different ways of looking at physical and social events—different worldviews—that influence how students interpret classroom subject matter. For example, students whose cultures have taught them to strive to live in harmony with their natural environment may struggle with a science curriculum that urges them to *change* their environment in some way (Atran, Medin, & Ross, 2005; Medin, 2005). And whereas students of European ancestry are apt to view the Europeans' migration to North America in the 1600s and 1700s as a process of *settlement,* students with Native American backgrounds might instead view it as increasing *invasion* (Banks, 1991; VanSledright & Brophy, 1992).

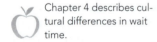 Expose students to multiple and possibly equally valid perspectives of historical and current events.

Children's varying cultural backgrounds may also have prepared them to handle different kinds of learning environments and tasks. For instance, African American and Hispanic students are more likely than European American students to be comfortable in environments in which several activities are going on at once and can more easily shift their attention from one activity to another (Correa-Chávez, Rogoff, & Mejía Arauz, 2005; Tyler, Uqdah, et al., 2008). Students from North American, East Asian, and Middle Eastern cultures are apt to have had experience rote-memorizing specific facts and written materials (perhaps in the form of multiplication tables, poems, or religious teachings), whereas students from certain cultures in Africa, Australia, and Central America may have been encouraged to remember oral histories or particular landmarks in the local terrain (L. Chang et al., 2011; Rogoff, 2001, 2003; Rogoff et al., 2007; Q. Wang & Ross, 2007).

Chapter 4 describes cultural differences in wait time.

The importance of wait time depends partly on students' cultural backgrounds as well. For example, some Native American students may wait several seconds before responding to a question as a way of showing respect for an adult (Castagno & Brayboy, 2008; Gilliland, 1988). And English language learners—students who have grown up in a non-English-speaking environment and are still developing their proficiency in English—are apt to require more mental translation time than their native-English-speaking peers (Igoa, 2007).

To maximize each student's learning and achievement in the classroom, we must take such individual and group differences into account. For example, we should be especially careful to engage the interest of—and also minimize distractions for—those students whose attention easily wanders. In addition, in our attempts to promote meaningful learning and other effective storage processes, we should relate classroom subject matter to the diverse background experiences that students have had. And we must allow sufficient wait time after questions and comments so that all students can actively think about and elaborate on topics of discussion.

FACILITATING COGNITIVE PROCESSING IN STUDENTS WITH SPECIAL NEEDS

Some diversity in learning and cognitive processes is the result of certain disabilities, on the one hand, or giftedness, on the other. For example, some students with disabilities have particular trouble attending to and effectively processing classroom subject matter. This is certainly true for

STUDENTS IN INCLUSIVE SETTINGS

TABLE 6.5 • Facilitating Cognitive Processing in Students with Special Educational Needs

CATEGORY	CHARACTERISTICS YOU MIGHT OBSERVE	SUGGESTED STRATEGIES
Students with specific cognitive or academic difficulties	• Deficiencies in one or more specific cognitive processes (e.g., perception, organization of related ideas into an integrated whole) • Distractibility, inability to sustain attention for some students • Difficulty screening out irrelevant stimuli • Less working memory capacity or less efficient use of working memory • Difficulty remembering multi-step instructions • Impulsivity in responding to classroom tasks • Exceptionally detailed memory for personally experienced events (for some students with ADHD)	• Analyze students' errors as a way of identifying possible processing difficulties. • Identify weaknesses in specific cognitive processes, and provide instruction that enables students to compensate for these weaknesses. • Minimize distracting stimuli, and make sure you have students' attention before beginning instruction. • Intersperse activities requiring sustained attention with opportunities for physical exercise. • Divide complex tasks into several simpler parts, and present instructions one step at a time. • Encourage greater reflection before responding—for instance, by reinforcing accuracy rather than speed. • Present information in an organized fashion and frequently make connections to students' prior knowledge. • Teach mnemonics for important but hard-to-remember facts. • When appropriate, provide concrete memory aids that remind students of what they've learned. • Capitalize on students' strengths (e.g., detailed knowledge about certain topics).
Students with social or behavioral problems	• Limited ability to focus attention because of off-task thoughts and behaviors (for some students with emotional and behavioral disorders) • Difficulty shifting attention quickly (for some students with an autism spectrum disorder) • Exceptional ability to attend to small details; may be reflected in unusually detailed memory and drawings (for some students with an autism spectrum disorder) • Impulsivity; less ability to inhibit inappropriate social behaviors (sometimes due to neurological deficits) • Possible difficulties in other cognitive processes (e.g., undiagnosed learning disabilities)	• Capture students' attention by relating instruction to their personal interests. • Nurture and capitalize on the visual-memory and artistic strengths that some students with an autism spectrum disorder may have. • Refer students to a school psychologist for evaluation and diagnosis of possible learning disabilities. • As appropriate, use strategies listed previously for students with specific cognitive or academic difficulties.
Students with general delays in cognitive and social functioning	• Slower cognitive processing • Difficulty with attention to task-relevant information • Reduced working memory capacity or less efficient use of working memory • Less intentional control of cognitive processes • Smaller knowledge base on which to build new learning • Greater difficulty retaining information for long time periods	• Keep instructional materials simple, emphasizing relevant stimuli and minimizing irrelevant stimuli. • Provide clear instructions that focus students' attention on desired behaviors (e.g., "Listen," "Write," "Stop"). • Pace instruction to allow students enough time to think about and process information adequately (e.g., provide ample wait time after questions). • Assume little prior knowledge about new topics (i.e., begin at the beginning).
Students with physical or sensory challenges	• Normal cognitive processing ability in most students • Less-developed knowledge base to which new information can be related, due to limited experiences in the outside world • Better-than-average ability to recall details of abstract shapes (for older students who are deaf but proficient with sign language)	• Assume equal ability for acquiring new information and skills unless you have good reason to do otherwise. • Provide assistive technologies that enable students to circumvent their sensory or physical challenges. • Provide basic life experiences that students may have missed because of their disabilities.
Students with advanced cognitive development	• Greater ability to attend to tasks for extended periods • More rapid cognitive processing • Greater intentional control of cognitive processes • Larger knowledge base, with specific contents dependent on students' cultural backgrounds • More interconnections among ideas in long-term memory; greater conceptual understanding of classroom material • More rapid retrieval of information from long-term memory	• Proceed through topics more quickly or in greater depth. • Create interdisciplinary lessons to foster integration of material in long-term memory.

Sources: Barkley, 2006; Beirne-Smith, Patton, & Kim, 2006; Bulgren, Schumaker, & Deshler, 1994; Cattani, Clibbens, & Perfect, 2007; Chapman, Gamino, & Mudar, 2012; B. Clark, 1997; Courchesne et al., 1994; DeMarie & López, 2014; Fletcher, Lyon, Fuchs, & Barnes, 2007; Gathercole, Lamont, & Alloway, 2006; Geary, Hoard, Byrd-Craven, Nugent, & Bailey, 2012; Grandin & Panek, 2014; N. Gregg, 2009; Heward, 2009; J. Johnson, Im-Bolter, & Pascual-Leone, 2003; G. R. Lyon & Krasnegor, 1996; Meltzer, 2007; Mercer & Pullen, 2005; Metcalfe, Harvey, & Laws, 2013; S. Moran & Gardner, 2006; Piirto, 1999; M. I. Posner & Rothbart, 2007; Rabinowitz & Glaser, 1985; Skowronek et al., 2008; H. L. Swanson, Cooney, & O'Shaughnessy, 1998; Turnbull, Turnbull, & Wehmeyer, 2010.

Chapter 5 identifies specific categories of special needs that fall within the five general categories listed in Table 6.5.

FIGURE 6.12 In a science activity in his third-grade class, 9-year-old Nicholas copied the scientific principle "No two pieces of matter can occupy the same space at the same time" onto a sheet of paper. He and a lab partner then filled a cup with water and dropped, one at a time, more than a dozen small metal cubes into the cup. Here Nick recorded his observations with both words and a drawing.

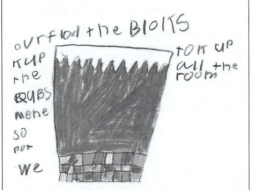

students with learning disabilities (who, by definition, have deficits in specific cognitive processes), and it's often true for students with attention-deficit hyperactivity disorder (ADHD) and general intellectual disabilities as well. In contrast, many children with autism spectrum disorders can be *very* attentive, sometimes to the point that they have trouble shifting to new tasks. And on average, gifted students have a longer attention span and can process new ideas more rapidly and elaboratively than many of their classmates. Table 6.5 identifies commonly observed cognitive processing differences in students who have special educational needs.

As teachers, we must keep in mind that students with disabilities almost invariably have strengths as well as weaknesses. For example, some students with ADHD have a keen memory for events they've personally experienced and may generate more detailed narratives than their nondisabled classmates (Skowronek, Leichtman, & Pillemer, 2008). And some students with autism spectrum disorders notice and remember many subtle nuances in the things they see and may produce highly detailed and skillful drawings that are unusual for their age-group (I. L. Cohen, 2007; S. Moran & Gardner, 2006).

The far-right column of Table 6.5 presents many useful strategies for working with students who have special educational needs. The first of these—analyzing students' errors for clues about possible processing difficulties—is illustrated in 9-year-old Nicholas's lab report in Figure 6.12. Nick's description of what he observed can be translated as "We poured so many cubes [that] the cup overflowed. The blocks took up all the room." We can only speculate about why Nick wrote up the left side of the glass, across the top, and then down the other side. One possible explanation is that, with his limited language skills, Nick hadn't yet mastered the conventional direction of written English. This hypothesis seems unlikely, however, as other samples of Nick's writing (not shown here) correctly begin at the top of the page and proceed downward. Another possibility is that Nick was thinking about the direction of the water flow (up and out) as he wrote and either intentionally or unintentionally followed the water's direction in his writing. His limited working memory capacity may have been a factor here: Perhaps he had insufficient mental "room" to think simultaneously about his observations plus the spellings of words and conventions of written English.

Virtually all students occasionally have trouble learning or remembering class material. Accordingly, many of the instructional strategies in Table 6.5 need not be limited to use with students with special needs. *All* students can benefit from guidance and support that enable them to process information more effectively.

MyEdLab Self-Check 6.6

6 What Have You Learned?

As a way of summing up our discussion of learning and cognitive processes in this chapter, we now return to the chapter's learning outcomes.

■ **6.1: Distinguish among four distinct approaches to the study of human learning, and summarize one of these approaches—cognitive psychology—in terms of five basic assumptions.** In general, *learning* is a long-term change in mental representations or associations as a result of experience. Over the past century, psychologists have offered a variety of

perspectives on human learning, many of which fall into one of four general categories: behaviorism, social cognitive theory, cognitive psychology, and contextual theories. As teachers, we can be most effective when we're theoretically eclectic—that is, when we draw from all of these perspectives to maximally facilitate students' learning and achievement.

Cognitive psychologists propose that the things learners do *mentally* with new subject matter determine how effectively they learn and remember it. Learners' cognitive processes can often be inferred from overt behaviors—for instance, from the ways in which learners recall information they've previously encountered. Learners must be selective about the information they process in any depth, and they use the information they've focused on to construct their own, somewhat idiosyncratic understandings of physical and social phenomena. To some degree, the sophistication and effectiveness of learners' cognitive processes depend on brain maturation over the course of childhood and adolescence.

■ **6.2: Describe and illustrate the key components that many psychologists believe may characterize the human memory system.** Many cognitive theorists propose that human memory has three components. A *sensory register* provides temporary storage for incoming information, holding new input for 2 or 3 seconds at most. By paying attention to information, learners move it to *working memory*, where they actively think about and make sense of it. Attention and working memory have a limited capacity; hence, students can pay attention to and think about only a small amount of information at any one time. Furthermore, information stored in working memory has a short duration (typically less than half a minute) and so must be processed further to promote storage in *long-term memory*. Long-term memory has an extremely large capacity and an indefinitely long duration. This particular model of memory has its flaws—for example, some brain research indicates that working memory and long-term memory aren't as distinctly different as the model suggests—but it can help us remember many aspects of learning and memory that we should take into account when planning and delivering instruction.

■ **6.3: Apply your knowledge of long-term memory storage in identifying effective strategies for enhancing students' learning.** Long-term memory contains both information *(declarative knowledge)* and skills *(procedural knowledge)*. A good deal of it is organized—often as concepts that are, in turn, integrated into more general schemas, scripts, and theories. To effectively acquire the kinds of declarative knowledge the school curriculum encompasses, learners should ideally engage in meaningful learning, perhaps by elaborating on or organizing new information or perhaps by engaging in visual imagery. In some cases, acquiring procedural knowledge involves learning and refining various physical behaviors; in other cases, it involves gradually converting declarative knowledge into either physical or mental actions. How effectively learners store new information and skills depends, in part, on how much they already know about the topic at hand. In the absence of relevant prior knowledge, mnemonics can enhance learners' memory for things that are important for them to remember.

■ **6.4: Explain how students' self-constructed beliefs can sometimes interfere with effective learning, and identify several ways of helping students productively revise such beliefs.** Although meaningful learning is usually beneficial, it can occasionally lead students to misinterpret classroom material, especially if they currently have erroneous or only partly correct beliefs about the topic or phenomenon they're studying. Some misconceptions may persist despite lessons

and activities that present information to the contrary, in part because students are cognitively and emotionally predisposed to confirm (rather than discredit) what they currently believe and in part because students' current beliefs may be integrated into cohesive theories that can't easily be unraveled and revised. As teachers, we're more likely to promote conceptual change when we determine what misconceptions students have before instruction begins, build on kernels of truth in students' existing understandings, convince students that revision is both warranted and within their grasp, and monitor what students say and write for especially persistent misunderstandings.

■ **6.5: Describe several factors that influence students' ability to recall what they have previously learned; also describe several reasons why students may either forget or incorrectly remember what they have learned.** Retrieving information from long-term memory appears to be a process of following pathways of associations. In general, classroom subject matter is more memorable if it has emotional overtones or in some other way is unique and distinctive. Furthermore, students are more likely to be successful in recalling what they've learned if they've connected it with many other things they know, if they've used it frequently (and perhaps learned it to automaticity), if their environment provides retrieval cues that send them down the right memory "path," and if they're given sufficient wait time to conduct a fruitful long-term memory search. Even under the best of circumstances, however, students sometimes forget or misremember what they've studied, perhaps as a result of insufficient consolidation, lack of use (resulting in gradual decay), restricted memory search, interference from competing memories, or reconstruction error.

■ **6.6: Give examples of the diversity in cognitive processes you are likely to see in students, in some cases as a result of students' cultural backgrounds or special educational needs.** Many components of the human memory system—including attention span, working memory capacity, executive functioning, long-term memory storage processes, and prior knowledge—can vary significantly from one student to another, and as a result students have varying abilities to learn and remember classroom subject matter. Students' cognitive processes differ, in part, as a function of their cultural worldviews, the kinds of learning tasks and environments to which they're accustomed, and their proficiency with the language in which instruction is being conducted. In addition, some diversity may be the result of certain disabilities. For example, students with attention-deficit hyperactivity disorder have trouble keeping their attention on any single task for lengthy periods, whereas some students with autism spectrum disorders may have trouble shifting their attention to new tasks. Yet at one time or another, all students are likely to have difficulty understanding and mastering particular topics. By identifying and facilitating cognitive processes that are most likely to lead to effective learning, teachers can better help *all* students achieve classroom success.

Practice for Your Licensure Exam

Vision Unit

Ms. Kontos is teaching a unit on human vision to her fifth-grade class. She shows her students a diagram of the various parts of the human eye, such as the lens, cornea, pupil, retina, and optic nerve. She then explains that people can see objects because light

A

from the sun or another light source bounces off those objects and into their eyes. To illustrate this idea, she shows them Picture A.

"Do you all understand how our eyes work?" she asks. Her students nod that they do.

The next day Ms. Kontos gives her students Picture B.

She asks students to draw one or more arrows on the picture to show how light enables the child to see the tree. More than half of the students draw arrows something like the one shown in Picture C.

B

C

Source: Case based on a study by J. F. Eaton, Anderson, and Smith, 1984.

1. **Constructed-response question:**

Obviously, most of Ms. Kontos's students have not learned what she thought she had taught them about human vision.

A. Explain why many students believe the opposite of what Ms. Kontos has taught them. Base your response on contemporary principles and theories of learning and cognition.

B. Describe two different ways in which you might improve on this lesson to help students gain a more accurate understanding of human vision. Base your strategies on contemporary principles and theories of learning and cognition.

2. **Multiple-choice question:**

Many elementary school children think of human vision in the way that Ms. Kontos's fifth graders do—that is, as a process that originates in the eye and goes outward toward objects that are seen. When students revise their thinking to be more consistent with commonly accepted scientific explanations, they are said to be:

a. acquiring a new script

b. revising their worldview

c. undergoing conceptual change

d. acquiring procedural knowledge

MyEdLab **Licensure Exam 6.1**

PRAXIS Go to Appendix C, "Matching Book Content and Ebook Activities to the Praxis Principles of Learning and Teaching Tests," to discover sections of this chapter that may be especially applicable to the Praxis tests.

7

Complex Cognitive Processes

Learning Outcomes

7.1 Explain how learners' metacognitive knowledge and skills influence their learning and academic achievement; also explain how you can promote metacognitive development in your own students.

7.2 Describe various forms that transfer might take and the conditions in which transfer is most likely to occur, and apply research findings about transfer to your classroom practices.

7.3 Describe four general factors that influence problem-solving performance; also describe teaching strategies you can use to help students successfully solve both well-defined and ill-defined problems.

7.4 Identify several instructional strategies that can encourage students to think creatively as they tackle new tasks and problems.

7.5 Describe several different forms that critical thinking might take, and explain how you can help students critically evaluate what they see, hear, and read both inside and outside the classroom.

7.6 Give examples of diversity you might see in creativity, critical thinking, and other complex thinking processes as a result of students' cultural backgrounds, disabilities, or advanced cognitive development.

CASE STUDY: TAKING OVER

When an eighth-grade math teacher goes on maternity leave midway through the school year, substitute teacher Ms. Gaunt takes over her classes. In accordance with Massachusetts state standards, the students are expected to master many mathematical concepts and procedures, including working with exponents and irrational numbers, graphing linear equations, and applying the Pythagorean theorem. But many of the students haven't yet mastered more basic concepts and operations, such as percentages, negative numbers, and long division. A few haven't even learned such number facts as $6 \times 3 = 18$ and $7 \times 8 = 56$.

Before long, Ms. Gaunt discovers that many students have beliefs and attitudes that also impede their learning progress. For example, some think that a teacher's job is to present material in such a way that they "get it" immediately and will remember it forever. Thus, they neither work hard to understand the material nor take notes during classroom explanations. And most students are concerned only with getting the right answer as quickly as possible. They depend on calculators to do their mathematical thinking for them and complain when Ms. Gaunt insists that they solve a problem with pencil and paper rather than a calculator. Students rarely check to see whether their solutions make logical sense. For instance, in a problem such as this one:

> Clifford can type 35 words a minute. He needs to type a final copy of his English composition, which is 4,200 words long. How long will it take Clifford to type his paper?

a student might submit an answer of 147,000 minutes—an answer that translates into more than 100 days of around-the-clock typing—and not give the outlandishness of the solution a second thought. (It would actually take Clifford 2 hours to type the paper.)

In mid-April, Ms. Gaunt begins moving through lessons more rapidly so that she can cover the mandated eighth-grade math curriculum before the upcoming statewide math competency exam. "Students can't do well on the exam if they haven't even been exposed to some of the required concepts and procedures," she reasons. "Mastery probably isn't possible at this point, but I should at least *present* what students need to know. Maybe this will help a few of them with some of the test items."

- Why are the students having trouble mastering the eighth-grade math curriculum? Can you identify at least three different factors that appear to be interfering with students' learning?

Source: Case used courtesy of a friend who wishes to be anonymous; "Ms. Gaunt" is a pseudonym.

One factor, of course, is students' lack of prerequisite knowledge and skills on which the eighth-grade curriculum depends. For instance, if students haven't learned basic number facts—let alone achieved automaticity for them—even simple word problems may exceed their working memory capacity. But students' beliefs about learning and problem solving are also coming into play. In their minds, learning should come quickly and easily if the teacher does her job. They seem not to realize that understanding classroom subject matter is an active, constructive process involving considerable effort on their part and that certain strategies (e.g., taking notes) can enhance their learning. And they view mathematical problem solving as a quick, mindless enterprise that involves plugging numbers into a calculator and writing down the result, rather than a step-by-step process that requires logical reasoning and frequent self-checking.

Study skills and problem solving are examples of complex cognitive processes, processes in which learners go far beyond the specific information they're studying, perhaps to apply it to a new situation, use it to solve a problem or create a product, or critically evaluate it. Mastering basic facts and skills is important, to be sure. But learners gain little if they can't also *do some-thing* with what they've learned. In this chapter we'll look at a variety of complex cognitive processes, including transfer, problem solving, creativity, and critical thinking. But we'll begin with a particular set of complex processes that in one way or another influences all of the others: metacognition.

Metacognition and Learning Strategies

Two key ingredients of metacognition are theory of mind and self-regulation, described in Chapter 3 and Chapter 10, respectively.

The term metacognition literally means "thinking about thinking." It encompasses knowledge and beliefs about the general nature of human cognitive processes, reflection on one's *own* cognitive processes, and intentional engagement in behaviors and thought processes that enhance learning and memory. For example, you've undoubtedly learned by now that you can acquire only so much information so fast—you can't possibly absorb the contents of an entire textbook in an hour. You've also discovered that you can learn information more quickly and recall it more easily if you put it into some sort of organizational framework. Perhaps, too, you've learned that you need to periodically check yourself to make sure you remember and understand what you've read.

The more learners know about thinking and learning—that is, the greater their *metacognitive awareness*—the better their learning and achievement is likely to be (Eason, Goldberg, Young, Geist, & Cutting, 2012; B. Hofer & Pintrich, 2002; Schneider, 2010). Furthermore, students who have a more advanced understanding of learning and thinking—for instance, students who realize that one's knowledge of a topic continues to evolve over time—are more likely to undergo conceptual change when it's warranted (Mason, 2010; Sinatra & Pintrich, 2003).

As children grow older, they become increasingly aware of their own thinking and learning processes and increasingly realistic about what they can learn and remember in a given time period (see Table 7.1). With this growing self-awareness come more sophisticated study strategies. Truly effective strategies emerge quite slowly, however, especially if young learners don't get guidance from teachers, parents, or other adults about how to study and learn (J. E. Barnett, 2001; Schommer, 1994a; Schneider, 2010; Veenman, 2011).

EFFECTIVE LEARNING STRATEGIES

An important component of metacognition is *controlling* one's own thinking and learning to some degree. Thanks, in part, to maturational changes in the brain, children and adolescents gradually become more capable of controlling and directing their cognitive processes in their efforts to learn something new (Chein & Schneider, 2012; Eigsti et al., 2006; Kuhn & Franklin, 2006). When learners *intentionally* use a certain approach to learning and remembering something, they're using a learning strategy.

Chapter 6 describes the development of basic long-term memory storage processes (e.g., see Table 6.4).

Information processing theorists have described several processes that may facilitate long-term memory storage, including rehearsal, elaboration, organization, and visual imagery. As children grow older, they increasingly discover the potential benefits of these processes and use them more frequently (P. A. Ornstein, Grammer, & Coffman, 2010; Pressley & Hilden, 2006). Children gradually acquire additional strategies as well. For example, consider the simple idea that you need to devote more study time to more difficult material; children don't use this seemingly obvious strategy until the fourth or fifth grade (Schneider, 2010). With age and experience, children also become more aware of which strategies are effective in different situations. Even so, many students of all ages—college students included!—seem relatively uninformed about effective learning strategies (Lovett & Flavell, 1990; Schneider, 2010; Schommer, 1994a; Short, Schatschneider, & Friebert, 1993).

TABLE 7.1 • Metacognition at Different Grade Levels

GRADE LEVEL	AGE-TYPICAL CHARACTERISTICS	EXAMPLE	SUGGESTED STRATEGIES
K–2	• Awareness of thought in oneself and others, albeit in a simplistic form; limited ability to reflect on the specific nature of one's own thought processes • Considerable overestimation of what has been learned and how much can be remembered • Belief that learning is a relatively passive activity • Belief that the absolute truth about any topic is "out there" somewhere, waiting to be discovered	An adult tells 6-year-old Brent that she will read him a list of 12 words; she then asks him to predict how many he'll be able to remember. Brent predicts "about 8 or 9 . . . maybe all of them," but in fact recalls only 6. Later, when the adult asks him what he did to try to remember the words, he says only "Think" and "Holded it, hold it in the brain." MyEdLab **Video Example 7.1.** You can observe Brett's explanation here.	• Talk often about thinking processes (e.g., "I *wonder* if . . ." "How might you *remember* to . . .?"). • Provide opportunities for students to experiment with their memories (e.g., playing "I'm going on a trip and I'm going to pack . . .," in which each student repeats items previously mentioned and then adds another item to the list). • Introduce simple learning strategies (e.g., rehearsal of spelling words, repeated practice of motor skills).
3–5	• Increasing ability to reflect on the nature of one's own thought processes • Some overestimation of memory capabilities • Emerging realization that learning is an active, constructive process and that people may misinterpret what they observe • Continuing belief in an absolute truth "out there"	After reading several explanations of how ancient humans migrated from Asia to North America, a cooperative learning group in a combined fifth- and sixth-grade classroom includes the following points in its summary of what it has learned: "The more that we learn, the more we get confused about which is fact and which is fiction . . . We have made [our] own theories using information we found and trying to make sense of it."	• Provide simple techniques (e.g., self-test questions) that enable students to monitor their learning progress. • Examine scientific phenomena through hands-on activities and experimentation; ask students to make predictions about what will happen and to debate competing explanations for what they observe.
6–8	• Few and relatively ineffective study strategies (e.g., poor note-taking skills, little or no self-monitoring of comprehension) • Belief that "knowledge" about a topic consists largely of a collection of discrete facts • Increasing realization that knowledge can be subjective and that conflicting perspectives may each have some validity (e.g., "people have a right to form their own opinions") • Increasing differentiation among the underlying natures of various content domains (e.g., thinking that math involves right vs. wrong answers whereas social studies allows for diverse opinions)	The students in Ms. Gaunt's eighth-grade math class rarely take notes to help them remember new concepts and procedures, and most are more concerned about getting correct answers than about making sense of mathematical operations (see the opening case study).	• Teach and model effective strategies within the context of various subject areas. • Scaffold students' studying efforts (e.g., provide a structure for note taking, give students questions to answer as they study). • Introduce multiple perspectives about topics (e.g., asking whether Christopher Columbus was a brave explorer in search of new knowledge or, instead, an entrepreneur in search of personal wealth). • Explicitly ask students to reflect on their beliefs about the nature of various academic disciplines (e.g., "Can a math problem sometimes have two *different* right answers?").

(continued)

TABLE 7.1   (Continued)

GRADE LEVEL	AGE-TYPICAL CHARACTERISTICS	EXAMPLE	SUGGESTED STRATEGIES
9–12	• Growing (but incomplete) knowledge of study strategies that are effective in different situations; persistent use of rote rehearsal by some students • Increasing mastery of covert learning strategies (e.g., intentional use of elaboration, comprehension monitoring) • Increasing recognition that knowledge involves understanding interrelationships among ideas • Increasing recognition that mastering a topic or skill takes time and practice (rather than happening quickly as a result of innate ability) • Emerging understanding that conflicting perspectives should be evaluated on the basis of evidence and logic (seen in a small minority of high school students)	When 16-year-old Hilary is asked to describe the things she does to help her remember school subject matter, she says, "When I'm trying to study for tests, I try to associate the things I'm trying to learn with familiar things . . . with the Spanish words, I'll try to think of the English word that it sounds like . . . sometimes if I can't find any rule, then I just have to memorize it, just try to remember it, just go over it a lot." MyEdLab **Video Example 7.2.** You can observe Hilary's explanation here.	• Continue to teach and model effective learning strategies; ask students to describe their strategies to one another. • Develop classroom assignments and assessments that emphasize understanding, integration, and application, rather than recall of discrete facts. • Present various subject areas as dynamic entities that continue to evolve with new discoveries and theories. • Have students weigh pros and cons of various explanations and documents using objective criteria (e.g., hard evidence, logical reasoning processes).

Sources: Agarwal, D'Antonio, Roediger, McDermott, & McDaniel, 2014; Andre & Windschitl, 2003; Astington & Pelletier, 1996; J. E. Barnett, 2001; Bendixen & Feucht, 2010; Buehl & Alexander, 2006; Chandler, Hallett, & Sokol, 2002; Elder, 2002; Flavell, Friedrichs, & Hoyt, 1970; Flavell, Miller, & Miller, 2002; Hatano & Inagaki, 2003; Hewitt, Brett, Scardamalia, Frecker, & Webb, 1995, p. 7 (migration example); P. M. King & Kitchener, 2002; Ku, Chan, Wu, & Chen, 2008; Kuhn, 2009; Kuhn, Garcia-Mila, Zohar, & Andersen, 1995; Kuhn & Park, 2005; Kuhn & Weinstock, 2002; Lovett & Flavell, 1990; McCrudden & Schraw, 2007; Meltzer, Pollica, & Barzillai, 2007; Muis, Bendixen, & Haerle, 2006; P. A. Ornstein, Grammer, & Coffman, 2010; Schneider, 2010; Schommer, 1994a, 1997; Short, Schatschneider, & Friebert, 1993; J. W. Thomas, 1993a; vanSledright & Limón, 2006; Wellman, 1985, 1990; J. P. Williams, Stafford, Lauer, Hall, & Pollini, 2009.

Some learning strategies are **overt strategies**; in other words, they're behaviors we can actually see. Others, such as elaborating and forming visual images, are **covert strategies**; they're internal mental processes we often *can't* see (Kardash & Amlund, 1991).

OVERT STRATEGIES

Successful learning and classroom achievement are partly the result of certain behaviors, such as keeping a calendar for assignments and due dates, devoting part of every evening to schoolwork, and asking questions in times of confusion. One especially effective overt strategy is *writing* about classroom subject matter (Bangert-Drowns, Hurley, & Wilkinson, 2004; P. D. Klein, 1999; Shanahan, 2004). Here we look at research on two writing-based learning strategies: taking notes and creating summaries.

Taking notes.   By the time students reach the upper elementary or middle school grades, note-taking skills begin to play a role in their classroom achievement. In general, students who take more notes learn and remember classroom subject matter better. However, the *quality* of the notes is equally important. Useful notes typically reflect the main ideas of a lesson or reading assignment (A. L. Brown, Campione, & Day, 1981; Kiewra, 1985, 1989; J. Lee & Shute, 2010). Ideally, too, students should be *making sense* of the information they're writing down—perhaps elaborating on it in some way—rather than just copying it in a rote, word-for-word manner (P. A. Mueller & Oppenheimer, 2014).

Despite the advantages of note taking, many young adolescents take few or no class notes unless specifically instructed to take them (recall the infrequent note taking in Ms. Gaunt's eighth-grade math class). And the notes they do take differ considerably in quality. For example, Figure 7.1 shows the notes that two students took about King Midas in a Greek mythology unit

FIGURE 7.1 Two students' class notes on King Midas, taken in a seventh-grade language arts unit on Greek mythology.

Story Note taking Form

Title: King Midas and the golden touch
Author: _____

I. Characters (write a few notes after each character's name to describe them, make a abbreviation after the character's name for further notes)

a. King Midas- King of Phrygia
b. Silenus- a demigod
c. Dionysus- god of whine
d. Daughter of King Midas
e. _____
f. _____
g. _____
h. _____
i. _____

II. Setting (write a few notes after the place to describe it, try to discover the time period)

a. _____
b. _____
c. _____

III. Events   Silenus was

a. Someone traring up km's rosebushs
b. Silenus tutored dionysus, dionysus wateher over Sil
c. silenus got a feast from Km, silenus stayed for awhile
d. Dionysus wants to pay Km for being nice to silenus
   Dionysus gives him a wish.
e. Km picks gold now everything he touches turns to gold
f. Km turns daughter to gold Km washes everything
   in the Pactolus loses gold tuch.

IV. Conflict (what is the problem, who is involved)

a. _____
b. _____

V. Solution (how did the problem work itself out, was there a lesson to learn)

a. _____
b. _____

Story Note taking Form

Title: King midas and the goldentouch
Author: _____

I. Characters (write a few notes after each character's name to describe them, make a abbreviation after the character's name for further notes)

a. King Midas
b. first guard
c. Second guard
d. Silenus
e. Dionysus
f. Daughter of the King
g. Ala
h. _____
i. _____

II. Setting (write a few notes after the place to describe it, try to discover the time period)

a. Castle
b. _____
c. _____

III. Events

a. sylinus destroys roses
b. King gets him
c. _____
d. _____
e. _____
f. _____

IV. Conflict (what is the problem, who is involved)

a. every thing he touches turns to gold
b. _____

V. Solution (how did the problem work itself out, was there a lesson to learn)

a. _____
b. _____

in their seventh-grade language arts class. The notes on the left provide a good overall synopsis of the King Midas story and might reasonably help the student remember the story fairly accurately. In contrast, the notes on the right are probably too brief and disjointed to be useful.

Especially when students are first learning how to take notes in class, we should scaffold their efforts by giving them an idea about which things are most important to include (Meltzer, Pollica, & Barzillai, 2007; Pressley, Yokoi, van Meter, Van Etten, & Freebern, 1997). One approach is to provide a specific structure to use, such as the one shown in Figure 7.1. Another strategy, especially if students are novice note takers, is to occasionally check their notebooks for accuracy and appropriate emphasis and then to give constructive feedback.

Scaffold students' early note-taking efforts.

Creating summaries. Many research studies have shown that writing a summary of material being studied can enhance students' learning and memory (A. King, 1992; R. E. Mayer, 2010b; Wade-Stein & Kintsch, 2004). Creating a good summary is a fairly complex process, however. At a minimum it includes distinguishing between important and unimportant information, synthesizing details into more general ideas, and identifying critical interrelationships. It's not surprising, then, that many middle school and high school students have trouble writing good summaries (Dunlosky, Rawson, Marsh, Nathan, & Willingham, 2013; Hidi & Anderson, 1986).

Ask students to summarize what they're learning, and scaffold their early efforts.

Probably the best way of helping students acquire this strategy is to ask them frequently to summarize what they hear and read. Initially we should scaffold the process for them—for example, by providing compare/contrast tables they can fill in as they read or having them develop summaries in collaboration with peers (Spörer & Brunstein, 2009; J. P. Williams, Stafford, Lauer, Hall, & Pollini, 2009). Computer software is also available to scaffold the summarizing process (e.g., Wade-Stein & Kintsch, 2004).

COVERT STRATEGIES

Students' overt strategies—allocating some time for studying in their daily schedules, taking notes, summarizing, and so on—are probably valuable only to the extent that effective cognitive processes, or *covert strategies*, underlie them (Kardash & Amlund, 1991). For example, high-achieving students tend to benefit more from note taking than low-achieving students, perhaps

MyEdLab

Video Example 7.3.

What strategies does this second-grade teacher use to help her students gain skill in summarizing short stories?

because the high-achieving students are more likely to elaborate on and organize what they're learning as they take notes (Kiewra, Benton, & Lewis, 1987; Ku, Chan, Wu, & Chen, 2008). In addition to engaging in meaningful learning processes (e.g., elaboration, organization), two covert strategies that may be especially critical for effective classroom learning and achievement are (1) accurately identifying important information and (2) regularly self-monitoring learning.

Identifying important information.   The human memory system isn't a video or audio recorder; it simply can't take in and retain *all* the information a typical classroom curriculum presents. Thus, students must be quite selective when they're studying. The things they choose to study—whether main ideas and essential supporting details or, instead, isolated facts and trivia—inevitably affect their learning and school achievement (Dee-Lucas & Larkin, 1991; J. A. Dole, Duffy, Roehler, & Pearson, 1991; R. E. Reynolds & Shirey, 1988).

Students often have trouble identifying the most important information in a lesson or reading assignment, especially when they don't know very much about the topic at hand. Many use relatively superficial strategies in choosing what to focus on—for instance, zeroing in on definitions and formulas, taking notes only on things their teacher writes on the board, or reading only the first sentence of each paragraph of a textbook—and miss critical ideas as a result.

 Let students know what things are most important to learn and remember.

As teachers, we can, of course, simply tell students exactly what they should study. But we can also highlight important ideas through more subtle means:

- Provide a list of learning objectives for a lesson.
- Write key concepts and relationships on the board.
- Ask questions that focus students' attention on central ideas.

Students—low-achieving ones especially—are more likely to learn the essential points of a lesson when such prompts are provided for them (Kiewra, 1989; McCrudden & Schraw, 2007; R. E. Reynolds & Shirey, 1988; Schraw, Wade, & Kardash, 1993). As students become better able to distinguish between important and unimportant information on their own, we can gradually phase out our guidance.

Regularly monitoring learning.   One very powerful learning strategy is comprehension monitoring, a process of periodically checking oneself for recall and understanding. How well do *you* monitor your comprehension? The following exercise can help you find out.

EXPERIENCING FIRSTHAND
LOOKING BACK

Stop for a minute and ask yourself this question:

What have I learned from this chapter so far?

Quickly jot down what you can recall.

Now go back and look at the pages preceding this one. Do the notes you've just written include all of the key points presented in those pages? Is there something you thought you understood but realize now that you don't? Is there something you never learned at all—perhaps something you were supposedly "reading" when your mind was thinking about something entirely different?

Successful learners continually monitor their comprehension both *while* they study something and at some point *after* they've studied it (Hacker, Dunlosky, & Graesser, 2009b). Furthermore, when they realize that they don't understand, they take steps to correct the situation, perhaps by rereading a section of a textbook or asking a question in class. In contrast, low achievers rarely check themselves or take appropriate action when they don't comprehend something. For example, they're unlikely to reread paragraphs they haven't understood the first time around (L. Baker & Brown, 1984; Haller, Child, & Walberg, 1988; Veenman, 2011).

Many children and adolescents engage in little or no comprehension monitoring (J. A. Dole et al., 1991; McKeown & Beck, 2009; Nokes & Dole, 2004). When they don't monitor their learning and comprehension, they don't know what they know and what they don't know; consequently, they may think they've mastered something when they really haven't. Although this illusion of knowing is especially common in young children, it's seen in learners at all levels, even college students. As paper-and-pencil exams become increasingly prevalent at upper grade levels, an illusion of knowing can lead students to overestimate how well they'll perform on these assessments (Hacker, Bol, Horgan, & Rakow, 2000; Stone, 2000; Zimmerman & Moylan, 2009). For example, we authors occasionally have students come to us expressing frustration with low test scores. "I knew the material so well!" they might say. But as we begin to talk with them about the exam material, it usually becomes clear that they have only vague understandings of some ideas and incorrect understandings of others.

Comprehension monitoring doesn't have to be a solitary activity, of course. If students work in small study groups, they can easily test one another on classroom material and may detect gaps or misconceptions in one another's understandings (Bol, Hacker, Walck, & Nunnery, 2012; Dunning, Heath, & Suls, 2004; Vaughn et al., 2011). Ideally, the questions they ask one another should encourage them to elaborate on rather than simply recall what they're studying. For example, we might teach them to ask questions beginning with such phrases as *Explain why, What do you think would happen if,* and *What is the difference between* (A. King, 1992, p. 309).

Yet to be truly effective learners, students must ultimately learn how to test *themselves* as well. One effective strategy is self-explanation, in which students frequently stop to explain to themselves what they're studying (Berthold & Renkl, 2009; Fonseca & Chi, 2011; McNamara & Magliano, 2009). Another, similar approach is self-questioning, in which students periodically stop to ask themselves questions—essentially internalizing the mutual question-asking process they may have previously used in small-group study sessions. Their self-questions should, of course, include not only simple, fact-based questions but also elaborative ones (Bugg & McDaniel, 2012; Dunning et al., 2004; Wong, 1985).

Teach students strategies for monitoring their own and others' learning progress.

This internalization of the question-asking process should remind you of Vygotsky's theory of cognitive development (see Chapter 2).

FACTORS AFFECTING STRATEGY USE

As we've seen, students become increasingly capable of using effective learning strategies as they grow older, in part because they can better control and direct their cognitive processes. With age, too, comes an ever-expanding knowledge base that supports students' efforts to engage in elaboration, identify important information, and effectively monitor their comprehension. Several other factors also influence students' choice and use of various strategies, as reflected in the following principles.

- *Learning strategies depend partly on the learning task at hand.* In some situations teachers may assign tasks for which truly effective learning strategies are either counterproductive or impossible. For instance, if we insist that facts and definitions be learned verbatim, students will understandably be reluctant to engage in elaboration and other meaningful learning processes (Turner, 1995; Van Meter, Yokoi, & Pressley, 1994). And if we expect students to master a great deal of material for a single exam, they may have to devote their limited study time to getting only a superficial impression of everything or to studying only the easy material they're confident they can master (Son & Schwartz, 2002; J. W. Thomas, 1993b). Sometimes working memory's limited capacity discourages metacognitive processing: If a learning task involves thinking about a lot of information all at once—that is, if it imposes a heavy cognitive load—students may have insufficient "room" in working memory to use strategies that might otherwise be effective (Kalyuga, 2010; H. S. Waters & Kunnmann, 2010).

- *Students are likely to acquire and use new, more effective strategies only if they realize that their current strategies are not working.* Students will come to such a conclusion only if they have been regularly monitoring their comprehension in previous learning tasks and have become aware of their learning difficulties. Comprehension monitoring, then, doesn't just affect students' understanding of classroom subject matter—it also plays a pivotal role in the development of *other* metacognitive strategies (Kuhn, Garcia-Mila, Zohar, & Andersen, 1995; Lodico, Ghatala, Levin, Pressley, & Bell, 1983; Loranger, 1994). In some cases, too, feedback that students haven't yet mastered a learning task will spur them to adopt more effective strategies, at least for the short run (Starr & Lovett, 2000).

- *Students' beliefs about the nature of knowledge and learning influence their strategy choices.* One of us authors once had a conversation with her son Jeff, then an 11th grader, about the Canadian

Studies program that a local university had just added to its curriculum. Jeff's comments revealed a very simplistic view of what history is:

Jeff: The Canadians don't have as much history as we [Americans] do.

Mom: Of course they do.

Jeff: No they don't. They haven't had as many wars.

Mom: History's more than wars.

Jeff: Yeah, but the rest of that stuff is really boring.

Once Jeff reached college, he discovered that history is a lot more than wars and other "really boring" stuff. In fact, he majored in history and now, as a middle school teacher, actually *teaches* history. But it's unfortunate that he had to wait until college to discover the true nature of history as an academic discipline.

Children and adolescents have misconceptions about other subject areas as well. For example, in the opening case study, Ms. Gaunt's students think that math consists simply of a bunch of procedures that yield single right answers but don't necessarily have to make sense. Furthermore, many students have misconceptions about the general nature of learning. For instance, Ms. Gaunt's students think they should be able to learn mathematical concepts and procedures quickly and easily—with little or no effort on their part—so long as their teacher does her job.

Students' beliefs about the nature of knowledge and learning are collectively known as **epistemic beliefs** (you may also see the term *epistemological* beliefs). Such beliefs often influence studying and learning (Bendixen & Feucht, 2010; B. Hofer & Pintrich, 1997; Muis, 2007). For example, when students believe that learning happens quickly in an all-or-none fashion—as Ms. Gaunt's students apparently do—they're apt to think they've mastered something before they really have. Furthermore, they tend to give up quickly in the face of failure and express discouragement or dislike regarding the topic they're studying. In contrast, when students believe that learning is a gradual process that often takes time and effort, they're likely to use a wide variety of learning strategies as they study and to persist until they've made sense of the material (D. L. Butler & Winne, 1995; Kardash & Howell, 2000; Muis, 2007; Schommer, 1990, 1994b).

As another example of variability in learners' epistemic beliefs, some students believe that when they read a textbook, they're passively soaking up many separate pieces of information from the page. In contrast, other students recognize that learning from reading requires them to construct their own meanings by actively interpreting, organizing, and applying new information. Learners who realize that reading is a constructive, integrative process are more likely to engage in meaningful learning as they read and to undergo conceptual change when they encounter ideas that contradict their existing understandings (Mason, Gava, & Boldrin, 2008; Muis, 2007; Schommer-Aikins, 2002; Sinatra & Pintrich, 2003).

Epistemic beliefs tend to evolve over the course of childhood and adolescence (Kuhn & Park, 2005; Muis, Bendixen, & Haerle, 2006; Schommer, Calvert, Gariglietti, & Bajaj, 1997). Children in the elementary grades typically believe in the certainty of knowledge: They think that for any topic there's an absolute truth "out there" somewhere. As they reach high school, some of them—and *only* some—begin to realize that knowledge is a subjective entity and that different perspectives on a topic can occasionally be equally valid. Additional changes can occur over the course of the high school grades. For example, 12th graders are more likely than 9th graders to believe that knowledge consists of complex interrelationships rather than discrete facts and that most learning happens gradually over time rather than in a quick, one-shot effort. And throughout adolescence, students' epistemic beliefs become increasingly specific to particular content domains (Buehl & Alexander, 2006; Muis et al., 2006). For example, students may believe that, in math, answers are always either right or wrong (again recall Ms. Gaunt's students) but that in social studies conflicting perspectives might all have some validity. Such developmental trends are reflected in some of the entries in Table 7.1.

As teachers, we must communicate to students what we ourselves know to be true about knowledge and learning:

- Knowledge involves not only knowing facts, concepts, and ideas but also understanding interrelationships among these things.
- Learning involves active construction of knowledge, rather than just a passive absorption of it.
- Knowledge doesn't always mean having clear-cut answers to difficult, complex issues, and in some cases it involves critically evaluating available evidence relative to a particular point of view.
- Mastering a body of information or a complex skill often requires hard work and persistence.
- Human beings' collective knowledge about any topic or phenomenon is a dynamic, ever-evolving entity; thus, acquiring such knowledge must, by necessity, be an ongoing effort over the course of one's lifetime.

Communicate that genuinely useful knowledge tends to be complex rather than simple and that learning can require considerable thought and effort.

We should communicate such messages not only in what we say but also in what we *do*, such as in the questions we ask, the activities we assign, and the ways in which we assess students' learning. For example, we can have students address complex issues and problems that have no clear-cut right or wrong answers. We can teach students strategies for gathering data and testing competing hypotheses. We can ask students to compare several explanations of a particular phenomenon and consider the validity and strength of evidence supporting each one. And we can show students, perhaps by presenting puzzling phenomena, that their current understandings—and in some cases even those of experts in the field—don't yet adequately explain all of human experience (Andre & Windschitl, 2003; Bendixen & Feucht, 2010; Kuhn, 2009; Muis et al., 2006; Reznitskaya & Gregory, 2013; vanSledright & Limón, 2006). When we do such things, we increase the likelihood that students will apply effective learning strategies, critically evaluate classroom subject matter, and undergo conceptual change when appropriate (Bendixen & Feucht, 2010; B. Hofer & Pintrich, 2002; Sinatra & Pintrich, 2003).

We must be careful how far we take such strategies, however. When students are firmly rooted in *learning-involves-facts-that-I-can-get-only-from-an-expert* beliefs, they may initially find little of value in—and so may gain little from—lessons that emphasize diverse perspectives and offer few solid answers. Nudging students toward more sophisticated beliefs about the nature of knowledge can take time, gentle prodding, and persistence, as well as a classroom atmosphere in which students feel comfortable questioning their own and others' beliefs (Andre & Windschitl, 2003; Rule & Bendixen, 2010).

- *Different motives and goals call for different strategies.* Motivational factors clearly influence the extent to which students use effective strategies to learn and study. Some students may be more interested in getting by with a passing grade than truly mastering classroom material. Others may think that meaningful learning and other effective strategies involve too much time and effort to be worthwhile. Still others may have so little faith in their learning ability that they expect to do poorly regardless of the strategies they use (P. A. Alexander, Graham, & Harris, 1998; Mason, 2010; Nolen, 1996; Palmer & Goetz, 1988).

The discussion of motivation in Chapter 11 identifies many things teachers can do to overcome such impediments to successful learning and achievement.

- *Ongoing instruction and guidance about effective strategies enhances learning and achievement.* With every transition to a higher educational level, teachers expect students to learn more material and to think about it in more sophisticated ways. Thus, the simple learning strategies children acquire in elementary school (e.g., rehearsal) become less and less effective with each passing year. All too often, however, teachers teach academic content areas—history, biology, math, and so on—without also teaching students how to *learn* in those content areas. When left to their own devices, most students develop effective strategies very slowly (if at all) and thus, over the years, encounter increasing difficulty in their attempts to master classroom subject matter. And when they *don't* master it, they may not know why they've failed or how to improve their chances of success the next time around

Into The Classroom

Promoting Effective Learning and Study Strategies

🍎 **When teaching academic content, simultaneously teach students how to effectively study and remember it.**

When a second-grade teacher presents the new spelling words for the week, he asks students to practice writing each word once by itself and once in a sentence. He also asks students to think about how some of the words are spelled similarly to words they already know (e.g., "The word *clown* ends in the letters *o-w-n*. What other words have you learned that end with those letters?"). And he teaches his students the mnemonic "*I* before *E* except after *C* . . ." to help them remember the spellings of such words as *believe* and *receive*.

🍎 **Suggest a wide variety of overt and covert strategies (e.g., taking notes, thinking of new examples, creating mnemonics, summarizing, taking self-check quizzes), each of which is apt to be useful in different situations and for different purposes.**

A high school social studies teacher acknowledges that some aspects of geography, such as the names of European capital cities, can be hard to remember. She suggests the keyword mnemonic and illustrates this process with the capital of Belgium, which is Brussels: "Think of a large *bell* with eyes and a mouth, and picture it eating some *Brussels* sprouts." But in addition, the teacher points out that many aspects of geography make sense and should be understood rather than memorized. For example, when presenting a map of Europe one day, she says, "Notice how most European capitals are on major rivers. Why do you suppose this is the case?"

🍎 **Scaffold students' attempts to use new strategies— for instance, by modeling the strategies, giving clues about when to use them, and providing feedback regarding productive and unproductive strategy use.**

A seventh-grade language arts teacher gives her students note-taking forms they can use to take notes in a unit on Greek mythology (see Figure 7.1).

🍎 **Explain the usefulness of various strategies in an age-appropriate way.**

A high school history teacher asks his class, "Who can tell me why the American colonists were so upset about the Quartering Act of 1765? We talked about that last week. Does anyone remember?" When no one responds, the teacher continues, "A lot of kids don't realize this, but we human beings can't always remember everything we're taught. It's time we started getting serious about taking notes in this class." The teacher gives some initial pointers on how and when to take notes and continues to scaffold the students' note taking over the course of the school year, sometimes simply by saying, "This is an important point, so you should be sure to include it in your notes."

🍎 **Ask students to self-reflect about their learning progress and the strategies they are using to master classroom subject matter.**

A high school math teacher regularly asks students to write in their "learning journals," in which they identify important ideas of a lesson, make connections between things they're learning and things they already know, self-reflect on the quality of their current understandings, and plan follow-up strategies that might enhance their mastery of the material.

🍎 **Occasionally ask students to study instructional material in pairs or small cooperative learning groups.**

In a unit on the human muscular system, seventh graders are given "starters" (e.g., "Describe _____ in your own words"; "Compare _____ with respect to _____") to help them formulate elaboration-promoting questions to ask a study partner. The students then break into pairs to study together. Many of them generate and are able to answer such elaborative questions as "Why are muscles important?" and "How are the skeletal muscles and the cardiac muscles the same?"

🍎 **Have students share their strategies with one another.**

At a school that serves a large number of minority-group students who are at risk for academic failure, faculty and students create a Minority Achievement Committee (MAC) program designed to make academic achievement a high priority. Participation in the program is selective (i.e., students must show a commitment to academic improvement) and prestigious. In regular meetings, high-achieving 11th and 12th graders describe, model, and encourage many effective strategies, and they help younger students who are struggling with their schoolwork.

Sources: P. A. Alexander et al., 1998; Azevedo & Witherspoon, 2009; J. E. Barnett, Di Vesta, & Rogozinski, 1981; Bulgren, Marquis, Lenz, Deshler, & Schumaker, 2011; Glogger, Schwonke, Holzäpfel, Nückles, & Renkl, 2012 (learning journals example); Hacker et al., 2009b; Hattie et al., 1996; Kahl & Woloshyn, 1994; A. King, Staffieri, & Adelgais, 1998 (muscular system example, pp. 139, 141); Kucan & Beck, 1997; Kuhn et al., 1995; McCrudden & Schraw, 2007; McGovern, Davis, & Ogbu, 2008 (Minority Achievement Club example); Meltzer et al., 2007; Nokes & Dole, 2004; S. G. Paris & Winograd, 1990; Pressley, Borkowski, & Schneider, 1987; Pressley et al., 1992; Pressley & Hilden, 2006; Rosenshine, Meister, & Chapman, 1996; Starr & Lovett, 2000; J. W. Thomas, 1993a; Vaughn et al., 2011; Veenman, 2011; Vygotsky, 1978; C. E. Weinstein, Goetz, & Alexander, 1988; C. E. Weinstein & Hume, 1998; Wentzel, 2009; E. Wood et al., 1999.

(Hacker et al., 2000; Hamman, Berthelot, Saia, & Crowley, 2000; Nokes & Dole, 2004; O'Sullivan & Joy, 1994).

Using effective learning strategies makes such a difference in students' classroom achievement that we mustn't leave the development of these strategies to chance. How can we help students *learn how to learn?* The Into the Classroom feature "Promoting Effective Learning and Study Strategies" presents several research-based strategies. The most important of the strategies presented there is the first one: *When teaching academic content, simultaneously teach students how to effectively study and remember it.* Students are more likely to use effective learning and study strategies when those strategies are taught not in separate study-skills classes but rather as integral parts of everyday instruction about specific academic topics (Hattie, Biggs, & Purdie, 1996; S. G. Paris & Paris, 2001; Pressley, Harris, & Marks, 1992; Veenman, 2011).

METACOGNITIVE STRATEGIES IN THE DIGITAL AGE

In many traditional modes of instruction—teacher lectures and explanations, textbook readings, and the like—teachers or other knowledgeable individuals are largely in control of what students study and in what order they study it. In the 21st-century digital age, however, many instructional materials take the form of hypermedia, in which students can go from one electronic "page" to another one of their own choosing simply by clicking on a word, icon, or "button" on the screen. Hypermedia can be found both in prepackaged instructional software programs and in expert-designed instructional Internet websites. And, of course, the Internet itself is a virtually boundless form of hypermedia.

Acquiring new information from the Internet and other forms of hypermedia requires not only the kinds of learning strategies previously described but a few additional ones as well. Among other things, effective learners must do most or all the following when they use computer-based materials to acquire new information:

- Identify potentially productive keywords to use in a search for particular information
- Make good choices about paths and hotlinks to follow
- Critically evaluate the information and potential *mis*information they find on various websites (more on this issue in the discussion of critical thinking near the end of the chapter)
- Monitor their progress toward achieving key goals for their learning efforts
- Make adjustments in their goals and search strategies as new information comes to light
- Compare, contrast, and synthesize information obtained from two or more sources (Afflerbach & Cho, 2010; P. A. Alexander & the Disciplined Reading and Learning Research Laboratory, 2012; Azevedo & Witherspoon, 2009; Leu, O'Byrne, Zawilinski, McVerry, & Everett-Cacopardo, 2009)

Many people of all ages don't have such skills, especially if they have little prior knowledge about a topic or naively assume that everything posted on the Internet must be "fact" (J. A. Greene, Hutchinson, Costa, & Crompton, 2012; P. A. Kirschner & van Merriënboer, 2013; Niederhauser, 2008). As you might guess, then, most elementary and secondary school students need considerable teacher guidance and scaffolding to learn effectively from hypermedia-based instructional resources.

Fortunately, some software programs are now emerging that explicitly scaffold students' learning strategies during computer-based instruction and online research (Azevedo, 2005; Koedinger, Aleven, Roll, & Baker, 2009; B. Y. White & Frederiksen, 2005). For example, a program might occasionally encourage students to set goals for their learning or ask them to identify causal relationships among concepts (Azevedo & Witherspoon, 2009; Graesser, McNamara, & VanLehn, 2005). And as students search the Internet for resources about a particular topic, computer-based scaffolding might occasionally remind them about their goal(s) in conducting the research or about the criteria they should use to evaluate the content of a particular website (Afflerbach & Cho, 2010; Quintana, Zhang, & Krajcik, 2005).

A good example of hypermedia with metacognitive scaffolding is *Betty's Brain,* a computer-based learning environment in which students read several resources about a topic, such as body temperature regulation or climate change, and then create a concept map representing the cause-and-effect relationships they discover in the resources. Students are told that a virtual "child" named Betty has to learn about the topic and that they can help her learn through the map they create as Betty's "teacher." Like a good teacher, they should also periodically assess her understanding with questions or a quiz. If Betty doesn't perform well, students can work to improve her understanding, and in the process they learn a great deal about the topic themselves. For example, Figure 7.2 shows an in-progress unit on climate change. The student/teacher has made some inappropriate causal links in her concept map, leading computer-based Betty to perform poorly on assessments. A virtual "mentor" (Mr. Davis) has stepped in to provide guidance about how to identify cause-and-effect relationships in a small section of text. Here the student has just correctly identified a relationship—*sea ice decreases absorbed light energy*—and Mr. Davis has suggested a good next step. (For more information about *Betty's Brain,* see Leelawong & Biswas, 2008; Segedy, Kinnebrew, & Biswas, 2013; also go to teachableagents.org.)

Chapter 8 describes specific ways in which teachers can scaffold students' use of the Internet and other hypermedia.

MyEdLab
Video Example 7.4.

In what specific ways does this third-grade teacher scaffold Luis's Internet search about leopards?

FIGURE 7.2 In this screenshot from *Betty's Brain,* a student has at this point created an inadequate concept map of cause-and-effect relationships impacting climate change. "Mr. Davis" has stepped in to provide scaffolding and feedback to guide the student.

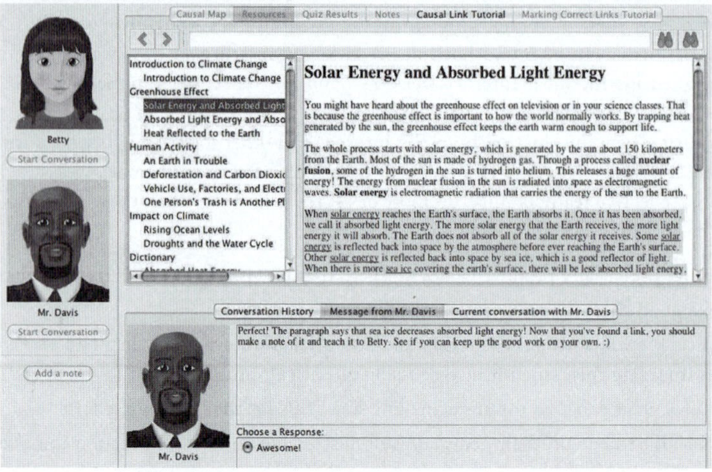

The *Betty's Brain* system has been developed by the Teachable Agents Group at Vanderbilt University with financial support from the Institute for Educational Sciences and the National Science Foundation.

DIVERSITY, DISABILITIES, AND EXCEPTIONAL ABILITIES IN METACOGNITION

Researchers have observed cultural differences in students' epistemic beliefs—in particular, their beliefs about what it means to *learn* something. From the perspective of mainstream Western culture, learning is largely a mental enterprise: People learn in order to understand the world and acquire new skills and abilities. But for many people in China, learning also has moral and social dimensions: It enables an individual to become increasingly virtuous and honorable and to contribute in significant ways to the betterment of society.

Researchers have uncovered other cultural differences in learners' epistemic beliefs as well. For instance, beginning in middle school, students in the United States are more likely to question the validity of an authority figure's claims than are students in the Far East. In contrast, students in Far Eastern countries (e.g., Japan and Korea) are apt to believe that knowledge is cut-and-dried and can be effectively gained from authority figures (Kuhn & Park, 2005; Qian & Pan, 2002). Yet Asian learners—and also Asian American learners—have an advantage in another respect: Compared to their European American counterparts (who sometimes expect quick results with little work), students of Asian heritage are more likely to believe that mastering complex academic topics is often a slow, effortful process requiring diligence, persistence, and a combination of rote and meaningful learning (Dahlin & Watkins, 2000; J. Li, 2005; Morelli & Rothbaum, 2007; Schommer-Aikins & Easter, 2008; Tweed & Lehman, 2002).

ACCOMMODATING STUDENTS WITH SPECIAL NEEDS

We're especially likely to see diversity in metacognition in students who have special educational needs. Table 7.2 presents characteristics you might see in these students. Notice that many students with cognitive disabilities—and some with emotional and behavioral disorders as well—may exhibit little knowledge and use of effective learning strategies. In contrast, students who are gifted typically have more sophisticated learning strategies than their peers do.

For many students with disabilities, we may have to teach metacognitive skills explicitly and with considerable scaffolding—that is, with close guidance and assistance in the use of specific learning strategies (e.g., Boyle, 2011; Meltzer, 2007). For example, we might provide

Remember that students' learning strategies and beliefs about learning may be partly the result of their cultural backgrounds.

Chapter 5 identifies specific categories of special needs that fall within the five general categories listed in Tables 7.2 and 7.3 in this chapter.

STUDENTS IN INCLUSIVE SETTINGS

TABLE 7.2 • Promoting Metacognitive Development in Students with Special Educational Needs

CATEGORY	CHARACTERISTICS YOU MIGHT OBSERVE	SUGGESTED STRATEGIES
Students with specific cognitive or academic difficulties	• Less metacognitive awareness or control of learning • Use of few and relatively inefficient learning strategies • Increased strategy use after explicit instruction in strategies	• Teach effective learning and reading strategies (e.g., taking notes, using mnemonics, identifying main ideas and general themes) within the context of lessons about particular topics. • Model effective strategies and scaffold students' efforts to use them (e.g., provide outlines to guide note taking, ask questions that encourage activation of prior knowledge).
Students with social or behavioral problems	• Limited metacognitive awareness of one's processing difficulties (for some students) • Few effective learning strategies (for some students)	• Provide guidance in using effective learning and study strategies (e.g., verbally model strategies, give outlines that guide note taking).
Students with general delays in cognitive and social functioning	• Lack of metacognitive awareness or control of learning • Lack of learning strategies, especially in the absence of strategies training	• Teach relatively simple learning strategies (e.g., rehearsal, specific mnemonics), and give students ample practice in using them.
Students with physical or sensory challenges	• No consistently observed deficits in metacognitive knowledge or strategies; specific deficits sometimes due to sensory impairments	• Address any deficits in metacognition with strategies you would use with nondisabled students, making appropriate accommodations for physical and sensory limitations.
Students with advanced cognitive development	• Use of relatively sophisticated learning strategies in comparison with peers	• Don't assume that students have adultlike learning strategies; assess their existing strategies and, as appropriate, encourage more effective strategies (e.g., elaboration, comprehension monitoring). • Provide opportunities for self-directed learning if students clearly have effective learning strategies they can use with little teacher guidance.

Sources: Beirne-Smith, Patton, & Kim, 2006; Boyle, 2011; Campione, Brown, & Bryant, 1985; B. Clark, 1997; Edmonds et al., 2009; E. S. Ellis & Friend, 1991; Graham & Harris, 1996; N. Gregg, 2009; Grodzinsky & Diamond, 1992; Heward, 2009; Mastropieri & Scruggs, 2007; McGlynn, 1998; Meltzer, 2007; Mercer & Pullen, 2005; Piirto, 1999; Pressley, 1995; Scruggs & Mastropieri, 1992; H. L. Swanson, 1993; Turnbull, Turnbull, & Wehmeyer, 2010; Waber, 2010; Wong, 1991.

partially filled-in outlines to guide students' note taking (e.g., see Figure 7.3). We might also tell students when particular strategies (e.g., elaboration, comprehension monitoring) are appropriate and model the use of such strategies with specific classroom subject matter. Finally, we must give students opportunities to practice their newly acquired strategies, along with feedback about how effectively they are using each one.

As teachers, we must remember that our students are likely to learn differently—and often less efficiently and successfully—than we do. Almost all of them can benefit from acquiring more sophisticated understandings of what knowledge and learning involve and from regularly practicing effective strategies for mastering school subject matter.

> Keep in mind that your students are apt to be less effective learners than you are.

> MyEdLab **Self-Check 7.1**
>
> MyEdLab **Application Exercise 7.1.** In the interview shown in this video, you can learn a few things about 12-year-old Colin's learning strategies, metacognitive awareness, and epistemic beliefs. Then, with such information in mind, you can speculate about possible ways of fostering Colin's metacognitive development.

Transfer

How students think about and study school subject matter has implications not only for how well they can understand and remember it but also for how effectively they can *use and apply* it later on. Here we're talking about **transfer**: the extent to which knowledge and skills acquired in

FIGURE 7.3 Example of a partially filled-in outline that can guide students' note taking

MUSCLES

A. Number of Muscles

   1. There are approximately _____ muscles in the human body.

B. How Muscles Work

   1. Muscles work in two ways:

      a. They _____, or shorten.

      b. They _____, or lengthen.

C. Kinds of Muscles

   1. _____ muscles are attached to the bones by _____ .

      a. These muscles are _____ (voluntary/involuntary).

      b. The purpose of these muscles is to _____

         _____ .

   2. _____ muscles line some of the body's _____ .

      a. These muscles are _____ (voluntary/involuntary).

      b. The purpose of these muscles is to _____

         _____ .

   3. The _____ muscle is the only one of its kind.

      a. This muscle is _____ (voluntary/involuntary).

      b. The purpose of this muscle is to _____

         _____ .

one situation affect a person's learning or performance in a subsequent situation. Following are examples:

- Elena speaks both English and Spanish fluently. When she begins a French course in high school, she immediately recognizes many similarities between French and Spanish. "Aha," she thinks, "what I know about Spanish will help me learn French."

- In her middle school history class, Stella discovers that she does better on quizzes when she takes more notes. She decides to take more notes in her science class as well, and once again the strategy pays off.

- Ted's fifth-grade class has been working with decimals for several weeks. His teacher asks, "Which number is larger, 4.4 or 4.14?" Ted recalls something he knows about whole numbers: Numbers with three digits are larger than numbers with only two digits. "The larger number is 4.14," he mistakenly concludes.

In most cases prior learning *helps* learning or performance in another situation. Such **positive transfer** takes place when Elena's Spanish helps her learn French and when Stella's practice with note taking in history class improves her performance in science class. In some instances, however, existing knowledge or skills *hinder* later learning. Such **negative transfer** is the case for Ted, who transfers a principle related to whole numbers to a situation in which it doesn't apply: comparing decimals.

Sometimes we see **specific transfer**, in which the original learning task and the transfer task overlap in content. For example, Elena should have an easy time learning to count in French because the numbers (*un, deux, trois, quatre, cinq* . . .) are very similar to the Spanish ones she already knows (*uno, dos, tres, cuatro, cinco* . . .). At other times we may see **general transfer**, in which learning in one situation affects learning and performance in a somewhat dissimilar situation. Consider, for example, Stella's strategy of taking more notes in science because of her success with note taking in history. History and science don't overlap much in content, but a strategy acquired in one class helps with learning in the other.

Historically, research studies have shown that when application of academic subject matter is involved, specific transfer occurs far more often than general transfer (S. M. Barnett & Ceci, 2002; W. D. Gray & Orasanu, 1987). In fact, the question of whether general transfer occurs at all has been the subject of considerable debate over the years. Many early educators believed that subject areas requiring considerable attention to precision and detail (e.g., math, Latin, and formal logic) might somehow strengthen students' minds and thereby enable students to tackle other, unrelated tasks more easily. This formal discipline perspective of transfer persisted throughout the first several decades of the 20th century. For instance, in the 1960s, when one of us authors was a high school student hoping to gain admission to a prestigious college, she was advised to take both French and Latin—the only two languages the school offered. "Why should I take Latin?" she asked. "I can use it only if I attend Catholic mass or run across phrases like 'caveat emptor' or 'e pluribus unum.'" The guidance counselor pursed her thin red lips and gave a look suggesting that she knew best. "Latin will discipline your mind," the counselor said. "It will help you learn better."

Most research has discredited this mind-as-muscle notion of transfer (Haskell, 2001; Perkins & Salomon, 1989; E. L. Thorndike, 1924). For example, practice in memorizing poems doesn't necessarily make one a faster poem memorizer (James, 1890). And studying computer programming, although often a worthwhile activity in its own right, doesn't necessarily help a person with dissimilar kinds of logical tasks (R. E. Mayer & Wittrock, 1996; Perkins & Salomon, 1989).

Rote memorization tasks such as this one have little or no benefit, because neither the information to be learned nor the "mental exercise" involved is likely to transfer to future situations. Furthermore, such tasks communicate the message that schoolwork is a waste of time.

We're more likely to see general transfer when we broaden our notion of transfer to include application of general academic skills and learning strategies that can be applied to a wide variety of topics and contexts (e.g., reading comprehension, persuasive writing, and note taking) (J. R. Anderson, Greeno, Reder, & Simon, 2000; S. M. Barnett & Ceci, 2002; Perkins, 1995; M. I. Posner & Rothbart, 2007). Furthermore, general beliefs, attitudes, and dispositions related to learning and thinking—for instance, recognition that learning often requires hard work, as well as open-mindedness to diverse viewpoints—can have a profound impact on later learning and achievement across multiple domains, and so clearly illustrate general transfer at work (Cornoldi, 2010; De Corte, 2003; K. J. Pugh & Bergin, 2006; D. L. Schwartz, Bransford, & Sears, 2005). And some students develop a general desire to apply what they learn in the classroom—that is, they have a *spirit of transfer*—that consistently resurfaces in later instructional contexts (Goldstone & Day, 2012; Haskell, 2001; Volet, 1999).

Chapter 5 describes open-mindedness and other general dispositions that positively influence students' learning and achievement.

FACTORS AFFECTING TRANSFER

Ideally, *positive* transfer to real-world contexts should be a major goal in classrooms at all grade levels. When learners can't use their basic math skills to compute correct change or balance a checkbook, when they can't use their knowledge of English grammar in a job application or business report, and when they can't apply their knowledge of science to an understanding of personal health or environmental problems, then we have to wonder whether the time spent learning these things might have been better spent doing something else.

Although both specific and general transfer do occur, students often *don't* apply the academic content they learn in particular classes to other classes or to out-of-school situations (Levstik, 2011; R. E. Mayer & Wittrock, 1996; Perkins & Salomon, 2012; Renkl, Mandl, & Gruber, 1996). Naturally, students are more likely to transfer what they learn at school when they approach each classroom topic with a deliberate intention to apply it. But several other factors also influence the probability of transfer, often because they influence learners' ability to *retrieve* what they've learned when they need to use it.

- *Meaningful learning promotes better transfer than rote learning.* Instructional time is clearly an important variable affecting transfer: The more time students spend studying a particular

Teach important topics in depth, with a focus on true understanding rather than rote memorization.

You have previously seen the less-is-more principle in Chapter 6.

topic, the more likely they are to apply what they've learned on future occasions. Ideally, students should gain a *conceptual understanding* of the topic—that is, they should have the many things they've learned appropriately organized and interrelated in long-term memory. Here we see an example of the general principle *Less is more:* Students are more likely to transfer their school learning to new situations, including those beyond the classroom, when they study a few things in depth and learn them meaningfully instead of studying many topics superficially (Brooks & Dansereau, 1987; Haskell, 2001; M. C. Linn, 2008; Schmidt & Bjork, 1992).

The *less-is-more* principle is clearly being violated in the opening case study. Ms. Gaunt decides that she must move fairly quickly if she is to cover the entire eighth-grade math curriculum, even if it means that few students will master any particular topic or procedure. Given the upcoming statewide math exam, she may have little alternative, but her students are unlikely to *use* what they're learning on future occasions.

- *Both positive and negative transfer are more common when a new situation appears to be similar to a previous one.* Perceived similarity increases the chances that a new situation will provide retrieval cues that point learners in the right direction as they search long-term memory for potentially relevant knowledge and skills (Bassok, 2003; Day & Goldstone, 2012; Haskell, 2001). For instance, when Elena first encounters number words in her French class (*un, deux, trois*), the words should quickly trigger recall of similar-sounding Spanish words (*uno, dos, tres*).

However, we should note that the similarity of two situations, although usually promoting positive transfer, can sometimes lead to negative transfer instead. To see what we mean, try the following exercise.

EXPERIENCING FIRSTHAND
A DIVISION PROBLEM

Quickly estimate an answer to this division problem:

$$60 \div 0.38$$

Is your answer larger or smaller than 60? If you applied your knowledge of division by whole numbers, you undoubtedly concluded that the answer is smaller than 60. In fact, the answer is approximately 158, a number much *larger* than 60. Does this exercise remind you of Ted's erroneous conclusion—that 4.14 is larger than 4.4—based on his knowledge of how whole numbers can be compared? Even at the college level, many students show negative transfer of whole-number principles to situations involving decimals and fractions (M. Carr, 2010; Karl & Varma, 2010; Ni & Zhou, 2005). Working with decimals appears, on the surface, to be similar to working with whole numbers. The only difference—a very important one, as it turns out—is a tiny decimal point.

To minimize the likelihood that our students *negatively* transfer some of what they've previously learned, we must be sure to point out differences between two superficially similar topics. For example, Ted's teacher might have identified some of the specific ways in which decimals are different from whole numbers. As another example, we authors find that students in our educational psychology classes often have trouble correctly understanding certain concepts (e.g., *maturation, socialization, short-term memory*) because the meanings of these words in psychology are quite different from their meanings in everyday conversation. So when we first introduce one of these concepts, we take great pains to contrast the different meanings. Even so, students' everyday meanings regularly can intrude into their thinking about course content, especially if they don't continually monitor their own thinking and understanding.

When concepts might be easily confused, explicitly point out their differences.

- *General principles and theories are more easily transferred than discrete facts and task-specific procedures.* Some knowledge of specific facts and procedures is indispensable; for instance, students should know what 2 + 3 equals, where to find Africa on a globe, and how to draw a right angle. Yet by themselves, specific facts and procedures have only limited usefulness in new situations. On average, general principles, rules, and theoretical explanations are more widely applicable than isolated bits of information and how-to-do-something-specific procedures (S. M. Barnett & Ceci, 2002; Bransford & Schwartz, 1999; Haskell, 2001; Kalyuga, Renkl, & Pass, 2010). The more we can emphasize general principles—for example, that adding two positive whole numbers always yields a larger number, that the cultures of various nations are influenced by their locations and climates, and that *cut, copy,* and *paste* functions are commonplace in computer applications—the more we facilitate students' ability to transfer what they learn. This is *not* to say, however, that we should always *begin* an instructional unit by teaching an abstract principle. Often it's better to begin with specific, concrete examples that engage students' interest and make immediate sense to them and only later introduce the general principle at work (Nathan, 2012; D. L. Schwartz, Chase, & Bransford, 2012).

Especially as they get older, some students acquire an ability to apply general principles to topics quite different from those they've previously studied. For example, in one research study, fifth graders and college students were asked to develop a plan for increasing the population of bald eagles, an endangered species in their state (Bransford & Schwartz, 1999). None of the students in either age-group had previously studied strategies for eagle preservation, and the plans that both groups developed were largely inadequate. Yet in the process of developing their plans, the college students addressed more sophisticated questions than the fifth graders did. In particular, the fifth graders focused on the eagles themselves (e.g., How big are they? What do they eat?), whereas the college students looked at the larger picture (e.g., What type of ecosystem supports eagles? What about predators of eagles and eagle babies?) (Bransford & Schwartz, 1999, p. 67). Thus, the college students were drawing on an important principle they had acquired in their many years of science study: Living creatures are more likely to survive and thrive when their habitat supports rather than threatens them.

- *Transfer is more common when information and skills are perceived as being relevant to diverse disciplines and real-world situations.* Unfortunately, many students tend to think of academic subject areas as *context bound*—that is, as being distinct disciplines that are completely separate from one another and from real-world concerns (P. A. Alexander & Judy, 1988; S. M. Barnett & Ceci, 2002; Perkins & Simmons, 1988; Renkl et al., 1996). For example, when baking cookies, an 11-year-old might ask a parent, "Do two one-quarters make two fourths? I know it does in math but what about in cooking?" (K. J. Pugh & Bergin, 2005, p. 16).

The context-bound nature of some school learning may prevent students from retrieving what they've learned in situations where it might be useful. A classic study with high school students (Saljo & Wyndhamn, 1992) provides an illustration. Students were asked to figure out how much postage they should put on an envelope that had a certain weight, and they were given a table of postage rates that would enable them to determine the correct amount. When students were given the task in a social studies class, most used the postage table to find the answer. But when students were given the task in a math class, most of them ignored the postage table and tried to calculate the postage, in some cases figuring it to several decimal places. Thus, the students in the social studies class were more likely to solve the problem correctly, perhaps because they were well accustomed to looking for information in tables and charts in their social studies courses. In contrast, many of the students in the math class drew on strategies they associated with math, using formulas and performing calculations, and thus overlooked the more efficient and accurate approach.

Fortunately, not all school learning remains "stuck" in school or in a particular classroom. People often apply some skills they've probably learned at school—such as reading, arithmetic, and map interpretation—to everyday, real-world tasks. But we can *increase* the transferability of school subject matter by regularly relating it to other disciplines and to the outside world (R. E. Clark & Blake, 1997; Perkins & Salomon, 2012; J. F. Wagner, 2010). For instance, we might show students how human digestion provides a justification for categorizing food into several basic food groups or how principles of economics have indirect impacts on global climate change.

- *Numerous and varied opportunities for practice increase the probability of transfer.* The more that students practice using what they've learned to address new tasks and problems—and the more *diverse* those tasks and problems are—the greater the probability that students will

Emphasize general principles more than discrete facts, but first present concrete examples that can provide a foundation for more abstract ideas.

The context-bound nature of some knowledge and skills learned in schools should remind you of the discussion of situated learning and cognition in Chapter 6.

Regularly relate topics in one academic discipline to other academic disciplines and to the nonacademic world.

apply school subject matter in future situations, including those outside the classroom (Gijbels, Dochy, Van den Bossche, & Segers, 2005; Gresalfi & Lester, 2009; J. F. Wagner, 2010). Especially helpful are **authentic activities**—activities similar or identical to those that students will eventually encounter in real-world contexts. For example, when students are learning basic arithmetic principles, they might be asked to apply those principles in determining best buys at a discount store, dividing items equitably among friends, and running a school book sale. Arithmetic will then be associated in long-term memory with all of these situations, and when the need arises to determine which of two purchases yields the most for the money, relevant mathematical procedures should be readily retrieved. Ideally, students should discover that much of what they learn at school truly has wide applicability—in other words, school topics become *context free* (A. Collins, Brown, & Newman, 1989; Cox, 1997; Perkins & Salomon, 1989).

- *Transfer increases when the cultural environment encourages and expects transfer.* All too often, it seems, students are encouraged to acquire school subject matter for mysterious purposes—for example, "You'll need to know this in college" or "It will come in handy later in life." Ideally, we should instead create a **culture of transfer**—a learning environment in which applying school subject matter to new situations, cross-disciplinary contexts, and real-world problems is both the expectation and the norm. For instance, we might regularly encourage students to ask themselves *How might I use this information?* as they listen, read, and study (R. A. Engle, Lam, Meyer, & Nix, 2012; Gresalfi & Lester, 2009; Haskell, 2001; Perkins & Salomon, 2012; Pea, 1987).

> MyEdLab **Self-Check 7.2**
>
> MyEdLab **Application Exercise 7.2.** In this exercise, you can apply what you have learned about transfer to various classroom scenarios.

Margin notes:

🍎 Give students many opportunities to apply classroom content to authentic, real-world tasks.

Chapter 8 discusses authentic activities in more detail.

🍎 Create a classroom culture in which transfer is both the expectation and the norm.

Problem Solving

Problem solving involves using—that is, *transferring*—existing knowledge and skills to address an unanswered question or troubling situation. The world presents many, many problems that differ widely in content and scope, as illustrated in the next exercise.

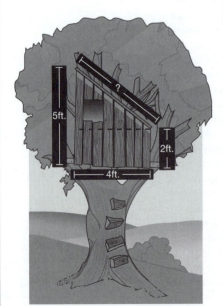

FIGURE 7.4 How long do the roof planks of this treehouse need to be?

■■ EXPERIENCING FIRSTHAND
FOUR PROBLEMS

How many of these problems can you solve?

1. You buy two apples for 25 cents each and one orange for 40 cents. How much change will you get back from a dollar bill?

2. You're building a treehouse with the shape and dimensions illustrated in Figure 7.4. You need to buy planks for a slanted roof. How long must the roof planks be to reach from one side of the treehouse to the other?

3. As a teacher, you want to illustrate the idea that metal battleships float even though metal is denser (and thus heavier) than water. You don't have a toy boat made of metal. What can you use instead to demonstrate that a metal object with a hollow interior can float on water?

4. Tropical rainforests provide homes for many species of animals and plants—including some plants useful in modern medicine—and they help to reduce the rapid increase in carbon dioxide in the earth's atmosphere. Yet each day tens of thousands of acres of tropical rainforest disappear, largely as a result of farmers' efforts to create new farmland by slashing and burning existing vegetation. What steps might be taken to curtail this alarming rate of deforestation?

Sometimes problems are straightforward and easy to solve. Problem 1 requires only simple addition and subtraction procedures, which readily yield a correct solution: 10 cents. Problem 2 (Figure 7.4) is more difficult, partly because you probably don't encounter such problems very often. But if you've studied geometry, you've almost certainly learned the Pythagorean theorem: In any right triangle, the square of the hypotenuse equals the sum of the squares of the other two sides. Looking at the top part of the treehouse (from the dashed line upward) as a triangle, we can find the length for the roof planks (x) this way:

$$(\text{Slanted side})^2 = (\text{Horizontal side})^2 + (\text{Vertical side})^2$$
$$x^2 = 4^2 + (5 - 2)^2$$
$$x^2 = 16 + 9$$
$$x^2 = 25$$
$$x = 5$$

Problems don't always have a single correct solution, of course. For instance, a variety of objects might be used to solve Problem 3; a metal pie plate and a bucket are two possibilities. And you might identify several possible ways of addressing Problem 4, but you probably wouldn't know which ones could successfully curtail rainforest destruction until you actually implemented them.

Problems differ considerably in the extent to which they're clearly specified and structured. At one end of this clarity-and-structure continuum is the **well-defined problem**, in which the goal is clearly stated, all information needed to solve the problem is present, and only one correct answer exists. Calculating correct change after a purchase (Problem 1) and determining the length of planks needed for a treehouse roof (Problem 2) are well-defined problems. At the other end of the continuum is the **ill-defined problem**, in which the desired goal is unclear, information needed to solve the problem is missing, or several possible solutions may exist. Finding a suitable substitute for a metal ship (Problem 3) is somewhat ill defined: Many objects might serve as a ship substitute, and some might work better than others. The rainforest destruction problem (Problem 4) is even less defined: The goal (curtailing deforestation) is ambiguous, we're missing a lot of information that would help us solve the problem (e.g., what alternatives might replace farmers' slash-and-burn practices?), and there's no single correct solution. On average, ill-defined problems are harder to solve than well-defined ones.

Most problems presented in school are well defined. As an example, let's return to the typing problem in the opening case study:

> Clifford can type 35 words a minute. He needs to type a final copy of his English composition, which is 4,200 words long. How long will it take Clifford to type his paper?

Notice that all the information needed to solve the problem is provided, and there's no irrelevant information to lead students astray. And if Clifford continues to type at the same pace, there's only one correct answer. Yet the real world presents ill-defined problems far more often than well-defined ones, and students need practice in dealing with them. Furthermore, when students regularly encounter ill-defined problems in the school curriculum, they may acquire more sophisticated epistemic beliefs—in particular, they may begin to realize that many topics and issues don't have easy, clear-cut right and wrong answers (Rule & Bendixen, 2010).

 Give students guidance and practice in dealing with ill-defined problems.

Taking the perspective of cognitive psychology (especially information processing theory), you might think of problem solving as involving five basic steps:

1. Encoding the problem
2. Retrieving one or more strategies that might be useful in solving the problem
3. Choosing the most appropriate strategy or set of strategies
4. Carrying out the chosen strategy or strategies
5. Evaluating the quality of the problem solution obtained (steps based loosely on Polya, 1957)

Cognitive factors we've previously identified as affecting transfer—such as thorough understanding of a topic and perceived relevance of new information to diverse contexts—certainly affect learners' ability to carry out these steps successfully. Researchers have identified additional factors related to four general categories: problem encoding, problem-solving strategies, working memory capacity, and metacognition.

PROBLEM ENCODING

At Step 1 in the problem-solving process, learners might mentally represent a problem—that is, they might *encode* it—in a variety of ways. As an example, try to solve the problem in the following exercise.

EXPERIENCING FIRSTHAND
PIGS AND CHICKENS

See if you can solve this problem before you read any further:

> Old MacDonald has a barnyard full of pigs and chickens. Altogether there are 21 heads and 60 legs in the barnyard (not counting MacDonald's own head and legs). How many pigs and how many chickens are running around the barnyard?

If you're having trouble figuring out the answer, think about the problem this way:

> Imagine the pigs standing upright on their two hind legs, with their two front legs raised over their heads. Therefore, both the pigs and the chickens are standing on two legs. Figure out how many legs are on the ground and how many must be in the air. From this information, can you determine the number of pigs and chickens in the barnyard?

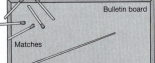

Some ways of encoding a problem enable more successful problem solving than others do.

Because there are 21 heads, there must be 21 animals. Thus, there must be 42 legs on the ground (21 × 2), which leaves 18 pigs' legs in the air (60 − 42). There must therefore be 9 pigs (18 ÷ 2) and 12 chickens (21 − 9).

There are several ways you might approach the pigs-and-chickens problem. But if you initially had trouble solving it—perhaps because your algebra skills are rusty—you may have struggled to encode it in a way that led you to an easy solution. Students often have difficulty solving mathematical word problems because they don't know how to translate the problems into procedures they've studied (K. Lee, Ng, & Ng, 2009; R. E. Mayer, 1992; Walkington, Sherman, & Petrosino, 2012).

At other times students may encode a problem in a seemingly logical way that nevertheless fails to yield a workable result. As an example, take a stab at the next problem.

EXPERIENCING FIRSTHAND
CANDLE PROBLEM

How might you stand a candle upright in front of a bulletin board attached to the wall? You don't want the candle to touch the bulletin board, because the flame might singe the board. Instead, you need to place the candle about a centimeter away from the board. How can you accomplish the task using some or all of the following materials: a small candle (birthday cake size), a metal knitting needle, matches, a box of thumbtacks, and a 12-inch ruler?

Source: Based on Duncker, 1945.

As it turns out, the ruler and knitting needle are useless in solving the problem. Piercing the candle with the knitting needle will probably break the candle, and you're unlikely to have much luck balancing the ruler on a few tacks. (One of us authors speaks from experience here, as some of her own students have unsuccessfully tried both strategies.) The easiest solution is to turn the thumbtack box upside down or sideways, attach it to the bulletin board with tacks, and then attach the candle to the top of the box with either a tack or melted wax. Many people don't consider this possibility because they encode the box only as a *container of tacks* and so overlook its potential use as a candle stand. When learners encode a problem in a way that limits possible solutions, they're the victims of a *mental set*. Mental sets, then, interfere with Step 2 in the problem-solving process: retrieving potentially useful strategies from long-term memory.

Mental sets sometimes emerge when learners practice solving a particular kind of problem (e.g., doing subtraction problems in math or applying the formula $E = mc^2$ in physics) without also practicing other kinds of problems at the same time. Such repetitive practice can lead students to encode problems in a particular way without really thinking about them—in other words, it can lead to automaticity in encoding. Although automaticity in the basic information and skills needed for problem solving is often an advantage because it frees up working memory capacity (more about this point shortly), automaticity in *encoding* problems can lead students to solve them incorrectly (Luchins, 1942; Rohrer & Pashler, 2010; D. L. Schwartz et al., 2012).

Several teaching strategies can help students effectively encode problems, without falling victim to counterproductive mental sets:

- Present problems in a concrete form; for example, provide real objects that students can manipulate, or present an illustration of a problem's components.
- Encourage students to make problems concrete *for themselves*; for example, encourage them to draw a picture or diagram.
- Highlight aspects of problems that students can competently solve, and when those elements appear again in a different problem, point out that the same information can be applied or the same approach to problem solution can be used.
- Give problems that look different on the surface yet require the same or similar problem-solving procedures.
- Mix the kinds of problems that students tackle in any single practice session.
- Have students work in cooperative groups to identify several ways of representing a single problem—perhaps as a formula, a table, and a graph. (Anzai, 1991; Brenner et al., 1997; Z. Chen, 1999; Dunlosky et al., 2013; L. S. Fuchs et al., 2003; R. E. Mayer, 1992; Mayfield & Chase, 2002; Prawat, 1989; Rohrer & Pashler, 2010; Sherman & Bisanz, 2009; Turner, Meyer, et al., 1998)

PROBLEM-SOLVING STRATEGIES: ALGORITHMS AND HEURISTICS

At the heart of successful problem solving are the *strategies* learners have available to them, as reflected in Steps 2, 3, and 4 of the problem-solving process described earlier. Some problems can be successfully solved with an **algorithm**—a specific sequence of steps that guarantees a correct solution. For example, by dividing 4,200 by 35, we can easily determine that Clifford will need 120 minutes (2 hours) to type his English composition. And by using the Pythagorean theorem and simple algebra, we can correctly calculate the length of a treehouse's slanted roof.

Yet the world presents many problems for which no algorithms exist. There are no rules we can follow to identify a substitute metal ship, no set of instructions to help us address worldwide rainforest destruction. In fact, few algorithms exist for solving problems outside the domains of mathematics and science. In the absence of an algorithm, learners must use one or more **heuristics**—general problem-solving strategies that may or may not yield a successful outcome. For example, one heuristic we might use in solving the deforestation problem is this: Identify a new behavior that adequately replaces the problem behavior (i.e., identify another way that rainforest farmers can successfully address their survival needs).

Both types of problem-solving strategies—algorithms and heuristics alike—are often specific to particular content domains. But here are several general problem-solving heuristics that can be helpful in a variety of contexts:

- *Identify subgoals.* Break a large, complex task into two or more specific subtasks that can be more easily addressed.
- *Round complex numbers up or down.* Estimate mathematical solutions by converting hard-to-work-with numbers to simpler ones.
- *Use paper and pencil.* Draw a diagram, list a problem's components, or jot down potential solutions or approaches.
- *Draw an analogy.* Identify a situation analogous to the problem situation, and derive potential solutions from the analogy.

- *Brainstorm.* Generate a wide variety of possible approaches or solutions—perhaps including some that might seem outlandish or absurd—without initially evaluating any of them. After a lengthy list has been created, evaluate each item for its potential relevance and usefulness.
- *"Incubate" the situation.* Let a problem remain unresolved for a few hours or days, allowing time for a broad search of long-term memory for potentially productive approaches. (Baird et al., 2012; J. E. Davidson & Sternberg, 1998, 2003; De Corte, Op't Eynde, Depaepe, & Verschaffel, 2010; Halpern, 1997; Minsky, 2006; Sweller, 2009; Zhong, Dijksterhuis, & Galinsky, 2008)

TEACHING PROBLEM-SOLVING STRATEGIES

Occasionally students develop problem-solving strategies on their own. For instance, many children invent simple addition and subtraction strategies long before they encounter arithmetic at school (Bermejo, 1996; Ginsburg, Cannon, Eisenband, & Pappas, 2006; Siegler & Jenkins, 1989). But without some formal instruction in effective strategies, even the most inventive students may occasionally resort to unproductive trial and error to solve problems. Following are research-based recommendations for teaching problem-solving strategies:

For Teaching Algorithms

- Describe and demonstrate specific procedures and the situations in which each can be used.
- Provide worked-out examples of algorithms being applied, and ask students to explain what is happening at each step.
- Help students understand why particular algorithms are relevant and effective in certain situations.
- When a student's application of an algorithm yields an incorrect answer, look closely at what the student has done, and locate the trouble spot (e.g., see Figure 7.5).

For Teaching Both Algorithms and Heuristics

- Teach problem-solving strategies within the context of specific subject areas—*not* as a topic separate from academic content.
- Have students tackle problems within the context of authentic activities. For example, in **problem-based learning**, students acquire new knowledge and skills while working on a complex problem similar to one that might exist in the outside world.
- Engage in joint problem-solving activities with students, modeling effective strategies and guiding students' initial efforts.
- Provide scaffolding for difficult problems; for example, break them into smaller and simpler problems, give hints about possible strategies, or provide partial solutions.
- Have students solve especially challenging problems in pairs or small groups, in which they share ideas about strategies, model various approaches for one another, and discuss the merits of each approach. (Barron, 2000; Belland, 2011; M. Carr, 2010; Hmelo-Silver, 2004; Hung, Jonassen, & Liu, 2008; Kapur & Bielaczyc, 2012; R. E. Mayer, 1985; Nathan, 2012; Renkl, 2011; Rittle-Johnson, 2006; D. L. Schwartz, Lindgren, & Lewis, 2009; Wentzel & Watkins, 2011)

WORKING MEMORY AND PROBLEM SOLVING

Remember, working memory has a limited capacity: At any one time it can hold only a few pieces of information and accommodate only so much cognitive processing. If a problem requires dealing with a lot of information at once or manipulating that information in a very complex way—when the *cognitive load* is high—working memory capacity may be insufficient for effective problem processing (K. Lee et al., 2009; Moreno & Park, 2010; H. L. Swanson, Jerman, & Zheng, 2008). Thus, working memory places an upper limit on Step 4 in the problem-solving process: successfully carrying out chosen strategies.

Learners can overcome the limits of working memory in at least two ways. One obvious strategy is to create an external record of needed information—for example, by writing it on a

---

FIGURE 7.5 Thirteen-year-old Malika incorrectly simplifies the expression 6(2x + y) + 2(x + 4y) as 14x + 10y. The correct answer is 14x + 14y. Where did Malika go wrong?

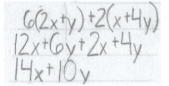

You may recall from an exercise in Chapter 6 just how difficult it can be to solve a long division problem in your head.

 Encourage students to write parts of a problem on paper.

piece of paper (as we sometimes do with long division problems). Another approach is to learn some skills to automaticity—in other words, to learn them so well that they can be retrieved quickly and easily (N. Frederiksen, 1984a; R. E. Mayer & Wittrock, 2006; Sweller, 1994).

Make sure students learn basic problem-solving skills to a level of automaticity.

METACOGNITION IN PROBLEM SOLVING

Successful problem solving often involves considerable metacognitive involvement. Especially when problems are fairly complex and challenging, effective problem solvers tend to engage in metacognitive process at all five steps of the problem-solving process—for example, by doing the following:

- Identifying one or more goals that must be accomplished to solve the problem
- Breaking the problem into two or more subproblems
- Planning a systematic, sequential approach to solving the problem and its subproblems
- Continually monitoring and evaluating their progress toward the problem-solving goal(s)
- Identifying obstacles that may be impeding their progress
- Changing to a new strategy if the current one isn't working
- Scrutinizing the final solution to make sure that it's logical and realistic (M. Carr, 2010; J. E. Davidson & Sternberg, 1998, 2003; Dominowski, 1998; Kirsh, 2009)

Such actions enable learners to use problem-solving strategies flexibly and to determine when particular strategies aren't appropriate. In contrast, *in*effective problem solvers tend to apply problem-solving procedures mindlessly, without any real understanding of what they're doing or why they're doing it. In the opening case study, Ms. Gaunt's students rarely critique their problem solutions for logical sense; thus, they may not recognize that typing a 4,200-word paper is unlikely to take 100 days.

To some extent, students' metacognitive problem-solving processes depend on their conceptual understanding of the subject matter (M. Carr & Biddlecomb, 1998; J. E. Davidson & Sternberg, 1998; Rittle-Johnson & Star, 2009). Yet students also benefit from instruction and guidance in metacognitive strategies. Following are several strategies we teachers can use:

- Ask students to explain what they're doing and why they're doing it as they work on a problem.
- Give students questions they can ask themselves as they work on a problem (e.g., "Am I getting closer to my goal?" "Why is this strategy the best one to use?").
- Help students to identify common errors in their problem solving and to check regularly for these errors.
- Ask students to reflect on their problem solutions to determine whether the solutions make sense within the context of the original problems. (M. Carr, 2010; Dominowski, 1998; Johanning, D'Agostino, Steele, & Shumow, 1999; A. King, 1999; Kramarski & Mevarech, 2003, p. 286; Roditi & Steinberg, 2007; Siegler, 2002)

Such approaches can be especially effective when students work on challenging problems with one or more classmates and must explain and defend their reasoning to their peers.

USING COMPUTER TECHNOLOGY TO TEACH PROBLEM-SOLVING SKILLS

The strategies we've considered thus far have been predominantly "low tech." But we can also capitalize on computer technology to foster problem-solving skills. Following are several possibilities:

- Use computer-based **intelligent tutoring systems**—software that provides individualized instruction and guidance related to a particular topic and set of skills—to teach mathematical and scientific reasoning and problem solving (e.g., see Figure 7.6).
- Show students how to use spreadsheets and graphing programs to manipulate and analyze large bodies of data.
- Use computer simulations that allow students to formulate hypotheses, design experiments to test the hypotheses, and interpret the virtual results.

FIGURE 7.6 In an intelligent tutoring system called *AnimalWatch*, middle school students apply math and science to solve problems about at-risk animal species and their environments. A screen from the system is shown here.

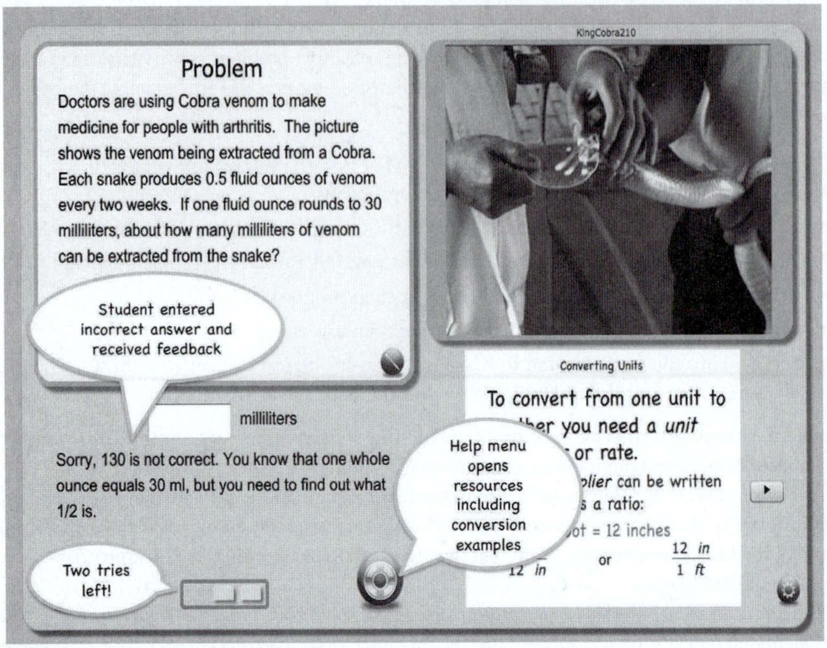

Screenshot courtesy of Carole Beal. Copyright © by Carole Beal. Reprinted with permission. Go to www.animalwatch.org for more information.

You can see another example of an intelligent tutoring system—My Science Tutor—in Figure 12.9 in Chapter 12.

🍎 Present complex real-world-like problems (i.e., authentic activities) that students must solve. (Beal, Arroyo, Cohen, & Woolf, 2010; Cognition and Technology Group at Vanderbilt, 1990, 1996; Kuhn & Dean, 2005; VanLehn, 2011; Vye et al., 1998; W. Ward et al., 2013)

Many software packages and Internet resources can help us with the last of these strategies: presenting complex real-world problems. Some of these are available commercially (e.g., you might check out online descriptions of *Civilization, SimCity,* and *Harvest Moon*). And for the budget-minded, many Internet websites provide free access to both traditional and authentic problem-solving activities appropriate for children and adolescents (e.g., see nsf.gov, smithsonianeducation.org). Such electronic resources—which often take the form of an interactive game or simulation—can both engage and sustain students' interest and help them apply what they're learning in school to adult-world contexts (B. Hoffman & Nadelson, 2010; Squire, 2011; Tobias, Fletcher, Dai, & Wind, 2011).

MyEdLab **Self-Check 7.3**

MyEdLab **Application Exercise 7.3.** In this exercise, you can observe and analyze the use of a complex, ill-defined problem in a high school history class.

Creativity

Creativity, like problem solving, is a form of transfer, because it involves applying previously learned knowledge or skills to a new situation. Psychologists have offered varying opinions about its nature, but in general creativity has two components:

- *New and original behavior:* Behavior not specifically learned from someone else
- *A productive result:* An outcome appropriate for, and in some way valuable to, one's culture (e.g., Beghetto & Kaufman, 2010; Runco & Chand, 1995; R. K. Sawyer, 2003)

To illustrate these two components, let's say that one of your instructors is conducting a lesson on creativity and wants a creative way of keeping students' attention. One possible approach would be to come to class stark naked. This approach certainly meets the first criterion for creativity (it's new and original) but not the second criterion (it isn't appropriate in our culture). An alternative strategy might be to give students several challenging problems that require creative thinking. This approach is more likely to meet both criteria: Not only is it a relatively original way of teaching, but it's also appropriate and productive for students to learn about creativity by exploring the process firsthand.

Many complex tasks involve both problem solving and creativity. But the two processes differ somewhat in the extent to which they involve convergent thinking versus divergent thinking, both of which are illustrated in Figure 7.7. To successfully tackle a problem, we typically pull together two or more pieces of information into an integrated whole that resolves the problem. This combining of information into a single idea or product is known as convergent thinking. In contrast, when we engage in creativity, we often begin with a single idea and take it in a variety of directions, at least one of which leads to something that's new, original, and culturally appropriate. This process of generating many different ideas from a single starting point is known as divergent thinking. To see the difference firsthand, try the next exercise.

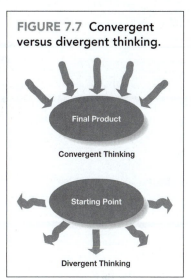

FIGURE 7.7 Convergent versus divergent thinking.

EXPERIENCING FIRSTHAND
CONVERGENT AND DIVERGENT THINKING

On a sheet of paper, write your responses to each of the following:

1. Why are houses more often built with bricks than with stones?
2. What are some possible uses of a brick? Try to think of as many different and unusual uses as you can.
3. Add improvements to the wagon drawing so that the object will be more fun to play with.

Source: Items 2 and 3 modeled after Torrance, 1970.

To answer the first question, you must use convergent thinking to pull together the things you know about bricks, stones, and building construction. But the other two items require divergent thinking about a single object: You must consider how a brick might be used in different contexts and how different parts of the wagon might be embellished—with some of your responses being novel and unique.

Contrary to a popular belief, creativity is *not* a single entity that people either have or don't have. Rather, it's probably a combination of many specific thinking processes, motives, and behaviors. Among other things, creative individuals tend to have the following characteristics:

- Considerable knowledge relevant to the task at hand
- Ability to interpret problems and situations in a flexible, open-minded manner and to combine existing information and ideas in new ways
- Passion for—and thus a willingness to invest a good deal of time and effort in—what they're doing
- Persistence in trying out various approaches, with acceptance of the many failures and dead-ends that they're likely to encounter before finally creating a satisfactory product (Amabile, 1996; Csikszentmihalyi, 1996; Leung, Maddux, Galinsky, & Chiu, 2008; Runco & Chand, 1995; Russ, 1993; Simonton, 2004, 2011; Weisberg, 1993)

Furthermore, creativity is often specific to particular situations and content areas (Dai, 2010; Glover, Ronning, & Reynolds, 1989; Runco, 2004). For example, students might show creativity in art, writing, or science but won't necessarily be creative in all of these areas.

FOSTERING CREATIVITY

Certain aspects of creative thinking may have their roots in hereditary factors, but environmental factors play an equally important role in the development of creativity (Esquivel, 1995; Ripple, 1989; Simonton, 2000). In fact, because creativity requires considerable expertise and fairly sophisticated thought processes, learners are apt to become increasingly creative as they grow older, gain diverse experiences and perspectives—ideally including *multicultural* experiences and perspectives—and have numerous opportunities to experiment with objects and ideas (Hatano & Oura, 2003; Leung et al., 2008; Simonton, 2004).

Research studies suggest several strategies for promoting creativity in classroom contexts:

* *Show students that creative thoughts and behaviors are valued.* One way to do this is to encourage and reward unusual ideas and responses. For example, we can assign activities that require students to generate a wide variety of ideas, and we can express excitement when students complete a project or assessment task in a unique and unusual manner. Engaging in creative activities ourselves also shows that we value creativity (Beghetto & Kaufman, 2010; Lubart & Mouchiroud, 2003; Runco, 2004; Sternberg, 2010).

* *Focus students' attention on internal rather than external rewards.* Students are more creative when they engage in activities they enjoy and when they have reason to take pride in their accomplishments (Hennessey, 2010; Lubart & Mouchiroud, 2003). To foster creativity, then, we should occasionally give students opportunities to explore their own interests—those they will gladly pursue without having to be prodded. We can also foster creativity by downplaying the importance of grades, focusing students' attention instead on the internal satisfaction their creative efforts bring (Hennessey, 2010; Perkins, 1990). For instance, we might say this to students in an art class:

> Please don't worry too much about grades. As long as you use the materials appropriately and give each assignment your best shot, you will do well in this class. The important thing is to find an art form that you enjoy and through which you can effectively express your perceptions and feelings.

Such a statement is intended to encourage intrinsic motivation, a concept discussed in depth in Chapter 11.

* *Promote mastery of a subject area.* Creativity in a particular subject area is more likely to occur when students have considerable mastery and conceptual understanding of a topic (Amabile & Hennessey, 1992; Haskell, 2001; Simonton, 2000). For example, if we want students to apply scientific principles in a creative manner—perhaps as they complete an experiment for the school science fair or develop a realistic solution to a local environmental problem—we should make sure that they know those principles *well.*

* *Ask thought-provoking questions.* Students are more likely to think creatively when we pose higher-level questions—questions that require them to use previously learned information in new ways. Questions that require divergent thinking can be especially helpful (Perkins, 1990; Sternberg, 2010). For example, in history lessons we might ask such questions such as these:
  * *In a lesson on the Pony Express as a method of U.S. mail delivery in the 1860s:* "In what different ways might people have carried mail across the country at that time?" (Feldhusen & Treffinger, 1980)
  * *In a lesson on Angkor Wat, an enormous stone temple complex built in the 12th century in what is now Cambodia:* "How might the Khmer people have built these temples using massive blocks (400 pounds each) with no cement?" (courtesy of Jeffrey Ormrod)

* *Teach and encourage cognitive and metacognitive strategies that support creative thinking.* Explicit instruction in some of the strategies that creativity requires can definitely have an impact (Hattie, 2009). Following are several examples of such strategies:

  * Brainstorming ideas, perhaps in collaboration with peers; deferring judgment until after a lengthy list has been generated

  * Focusing attention on gradual progress toward a goal, rather than expecting an immediate solution

  * Identifying and addressing specific obstacles that may be impeding progress (Baer & Garrett, 2010; Beghetto & Kaufman, 2010; Sternberg, 2010)

🍎 *Give students the freedom and security they need to take risks.* To be creative, students must be willing to take risks—something they're unlikely to do if they're afraid of failing (Amabile, 1996; Houtz, 1990; Sternberg, 2010). To encourage risk taking, we can allow students to engage in certain activities without evaluating their performance. For example, in response to the question presented earlier about how 12th-century Khmer people might have built large stone temples at Angkor Wat, a student at an English-speaking school in Thailand was quite creative in his response, as his teacher reported:

> Several students drew a long wooden ramp on which they would drag the giant blocks. I asked them what would probably happen as soon as they started dragging the block up this ramp (i.e., the block would break the ramp and come crashing down). So one student drew poles under his ramp to support it. I pointed out that this would work only at very low levels because the trees in the area were small and weak. His next idea was to use wood and bamboo to make the ramp stronger, but I suggested that the structure still wouldn't be strong enough to bear the load. He came back a few minutes later with another idea. He still had the ramp, but underneath it for support he had drawn in a few elephants. I urged him to reflect on his new idea: "Even if you can get the elephants to stand still and put a ramp on their backs, elephants are only about this tall. [I showed their height with my hand.] Angkor Wat is 213 feet tall. How are you going to support the ramp between about 6 feet and 213 feet?" His response was to stack the elephants on top of each other. (Example courtesy of Jeffrey Ormrod. Copyright © by Jeffrey Ormrod. Reprinted by permission.)

Granted, the student's ultimate solution wasn't realistic, but he was definitely thinking in an innovative, divergent manner—"outside the box"—and his teacher had created a classroom atmosphere in which he felt comfortable doing so.

We can further encourage risk taking by urging students to think of their mistakes and failures as an inevitable—but usually temporary—aspect of the creative process (Hennessey & Amabile, 1987; J. C. Kaufman & Beghetto, 2009). For example, when students are writing a short story, we might give them several opportunities to get our feedback and perhaps also the feedback of their peers before they turn in a final product.

🍎 *Provide the time and resources that creativity requires.* Students need time to experiment with new materials and ideas, think in divergent directions, and make mistakes. And in many instances they can be more creative if they have a variety of physical and social resources on which to draw—perhaps paper and pencil, computer software, the Internet, ample space in which to work, and the ideas and support of classmates. Occasional gentle guidance from a teacher can also boost creative thinking (Fairweather & Cramond, 2010; Sternberg, 2010).

Ideally, students should reflect on and carefully evaluate the results of their creative endeavors (Dai, 2010; Fairweather & Cramond, 2010). In other words, productive creative thinking also requires critical thinking—our next topic.

MyEdLab **Self-Check 7.4**

MyEdLab **Application Exercise 7.4.** In this exercise, you can observe and analyze a ninth-grade language arts assignment designed to foster both summarization skills and creativity.

Critical Thinking

Different theorists define critical thinking somewhat differently, but for our purposes here we'll define critical thinking as evaluating the accuracy, credibility, and worth of information and lines of reasoning. Critical thinking is reflective, logical, and evidence-based. It also has a purposeful quality to it—that is, the learner thinks critically in order to achieve a particular goal (Beyer, 1985; Bonney & Sternberg, 2011; Halpern, 2008; Moon, 2008).

Critical thinking can take a variety of forms, depending on the context. The following exercise presents four possibilities.

EXPERIENCING FIRSTHAND
COLDS, CARS, CHANCE, AND CHEER

Read and respond to each of the following situations:

1. It's autumn, and the days are becoming increasingly chilly. You see the following advertisement:

   Aren't you tired of sniffles and runny noses all winter? Tired of always feeling less than your best? Get through a whole winter without colds. Take Eradicold Pills as directed. (R. J. Harris, 1977, p. 605)

   Should you go out and buy a box of Eradicold Pills?

2. You have a beat-up old car and have invested several thousand dollars to get it in working order. You can sell the car in its present condition for $1,500, or you can invest a couple of thousand dollars more on repairs and then sell it for $3,000. What should you do? (modeled after Halpern, 1998)

3. You have been rolling a typical six-sided die (i.e., one member of a pair of dice). You know that the die isn't heavier on one side than another, and yet in the past 30 rolls you haven't rolled a number 4 even once. What are the odds that you'll get a 4 on the next roll?

4. This research finding was presented by Dr. Edmund Emmer at the annual conference of the American Educational Research Association in 1994:

   Teachers who feel happy when they teach are more likely to have well-behaved students (Emmer, 1994).

   If you're a teacher, do such results suggest that you should try to feel happy when you enter the classroom each morning?

In each of these situations, you had to evaluate information and make some sort of judgment. In Item 1, we authors hope you weren't tempted to buy Eradicold Pills, because the advertisement provided no proof that they reduce cold symptoms. It simply included the suggestion to "Take Eradicold Pills as directed" within the context of a discussion of undesirable symptoms—a common ploy in persuasive advertising.

As for Item 2, it makes more sense to sell the car now. If you sell the car for $3,000 after making $2,000 worth of repairs, you'll make $500 less than you would otherwise. Many people mistakenly believe that their past investments justify making additional ones, when in fact past investments are irrelevant to the present circumstances (Halpern, 1998).

In Item 3 the chance of rolling a 4 on an evenly balanced die is—as always—one in six. The outcomes of previous rolls are irrelevant, because each roll is independent of the others. But when a 4 hasn't shown up even once in 30 rolls, many people believe that a 4 is long overdue and so greatly overestimate its probability—a misconception known as the *gambler's fallacy*.

Now what about making sure that you're happy each time you enter the classroom (Item 4)? One common mistake people make in interpreting research results is to think that an association (*correlation*) between two things means that one of those things must *cause* the other. In fact, however, a correlation between two variables doesn't necessarily indicate a cause-and-effect relationship. Possibly teacher happiness does improve students' classroom behavior, but there are other potential explanations for the correlation as well. For instance, perhaps good student behavior makes teachers feel happy (rather than vice versa), or perhaps teachers who feel upbeat use more effective teaching techniques and can better keep students on task as the result of using those techniques (Emmer, 1994).

The four situations presented in the preceding exercise illustrate several forms that critical thinking can take (Halpern, 1997, 1998, 2008; Nussbaum, 2008):

- *Verbal reasoning:* Understanding and evaluating persuasive techniques found in oral and written language. You engaged in verbal reasoning when deciding whether to purchase Eradicold Pills.

Our analysis of Item 4 might remind you of the discussion of correlation versus causation in Chapter 1.

- *Argument analysis:* Discriminating between reasons that do and don't support a conclusion. You engaged in argument analysis when you considered possible pros and cons of investing an additional $2,000 in car repairs.
- *Probabilistic reasoning:* Determining the likelihood and uncertainties associated with various events. You engaged in probabilistic reasoning when you determined the probability of rolling a 4 on the die.
- *Hypothesis testing:* Judging the value of data and research results in terms of the methods used to obtain them and their potential relevance to certain conclusions. When hypothesis testing includes critical thinking, it involves considering questions such as these:
  - Was an appropriate instrument used to measure a particular outcome?
  - Have other possible explanations or conclusions been eliminated?
  - Can the results obtained in one situation be reasonably generalized to other situations?

You engaged in hypothesis testing when you evaluated Dr. Emmer's findings about teacher happiness.

Some theorists have argued that critical thinking involves a general set of cognitive skills that learners can apply broadly in many different contexts (e.g., Ennis, 1996). But in fact, the nature of critical thinking is somewhat specific to various content domains. In writing, critical thinking might involve reading the first draft of a persuasive essay to look for errors in logical reasoning or for situations in which opinions haven't been sufficiently justified. In science, it might involve revising existing theories or beliefs to account for new evidence—that is, it may involve conceptual change. In history, it might involve drawing inferences from historical documents, attempting to determine whether things *definitely* happened a particular way or only *maybe* happened that way.

As you might guess, critical thinking skills emerge gradually over the course of childhood and adolescence (Amsterlaw, 2006; Kuhn & Franklin, 2006; Pillow, 2002). Yet all too often, students at all grade levels—and even many well-educated adults—take the information they see in textbooks, in news reports, on the Internet, and elsewhere at face value. In other words, they engage in little or no critical thinking as they consider the accuracy, credibility, and worth of the information they encounter (Kuhn, 2009; Marcus, 2008; Metzger, Flanagin, & Zwarun, 2003; Sinatra, Kienhues, & Hofer, 2014).

To some degree, learners' tendencies to think or not think critically depend on certain personality characteristics: On average, critical thinkers are open-minded, enjoy intellectual challenges, and can emotionally handle the idea that they might occasionally be wrong about a topic (Halpern, 2008; Moon, 2008; Schraw, McCrudden, Lehman, & Hoffman, 2011). Learners' epistemic beliefs also come into play. Learners are more likely to look analytically and critically at new information if they believe that even experts' understanding of a topic continues to evolve as new evidence accumulates. They're *un*likely to engage in critical thinking if, instead, they believe that knowledge is an absolute, unchanging entity (P. M. King & Kitchener, 2002; Kuhn, 2001a; Muis & Franco, 2009; Schommer-Aikins, 2002).

FOSTERING CRITICAL THINKING

To become effective life-long learners, students must learn that not all sources of information can be trusted—that some messages presented through various media are either misleading or downright wrong. In our current era of ever-expanding information technology and social media, taking a critical stance toward new information is now more important than ever. For example, although entries in the popular website Wikipedia are generally accurate, they occasionally include inaccuracies added by nonexperts. Furthermore, virtually anyone can post personal beliefs and opinions somewhere on the Internet—often presenting these things as irrefutable "facts"— and it's quite easy to be taken in. Unfortunately, many people at all age levels naively assume that almost everything they read on the Internet is fact (Manning, Lawless, Goldman, & Braasch, 2011; Metzger, Flanagin, & Zwarun, 2003; Wiley et al., 2009).

Perhaps because critical thinking encompasses such a variety of cognitive skills, strategies for encouraging it are many and varied. Some of the factors that promote metacognition, transfer, and problem solving are applicable to teaching critical thinking as well. Embeddedness of thinking-skills instruction within the context of specific academic disciplines, collaborative group tasks, authentic activities—all of these things can help learners think more critically. Following are more specific theory- and research-based recommendations:

- Teach fewer topics, but in greater depth—the *less-is-more* principle once again.
- Encourage some intellectual skepticism—for instance, by urging students to question and challenge the ideas they read and hear—and communicate the epistemic belief that people's knowledge and understanding of any single topic will continue to change over time.
- Overtly model critical thinking—for instance, by thinking aloud while analyzing a persuasive argument or scientific report.
- Give students many opportunities to practice critical thinking—for instance, by identifying flaws in the arguments of a persuasive essay, evaluating the quality and usefulness of a scientific report, and using evidence and logic to support a particular viewpoint.
- Have students debate controversial issues from several perspectives, and occasionally ask them to defend a perspective quite different from their own.
- Help students understand that critical thinking involves considerable mental effort but that its benefits make the effort worthwhile.
- Embed critical thinking skills within the context of authentic, real-world problems and issues as a way of helping students retrieve those skills later on, both in the workplace and in other aspects of adult life. (Afflerbach & Cho, 2010; Bonney & Sternberg, 2011; Chinn, Anderson, & Waggoner, 2001; Derry, Levin, Osana, & Jones, 1998; Halpern, 1998; Heyman, 2008; Kardash & Scholes, 1996; Kuhn, 2015; Kuhn & Crowell, 2011; Monte-Sano, 2008; Moon, 2008; Muis & Duffy, 2013; Nussbaum, 2008; Nussbaum & Edwards, 2011; Sandoval, Sodian, Koerber, & Wong, 2014; Yang & Tsai, 2010)

We might also ask students to consider questions such as these when reading printed materials or gaining information from Internet websites:

- Who produced this document/website? Does the author have well-substantiated (as opposed to self-proclaimed) expertise about the topic? What biases or predispositions might the author have?
- What persuasive technique is the author using? Is it valid, or is it designed to mislead the reader?
- What assumptions underlie the assertions and arguments presented?
- What evidence and/or reasons support the conclusion? What evidence and/or reasons *don't* support it?
- Is the information consistent with what you've learned from other sources? If not, in what ways is it different? How might you reconcile the inconsistencies?
- What actions might you take to improve the design of this study? (Questions based on suggestions by De La Paz & Felton, 2010; Halpern, 1998; S. A. Stahl & Shanahan, 2004; Wiley et al., 2009)

An Internet search will probably lead you to several computer software programs allegedly designed to promote critical thinking skills. Some of these programs may be effective, whereas others may not be. When considering them for possible use in your classroom, keep in mind that like all complex cognitive processes, critical thinking skills are probably most effectively learned—and most likely to be transferred to new situations—when they're practiced within the context of specific academic topics (e.g., De La Paz & Felton, 2010; Kuhn & Franklin, 2006; Yang & Tsai, 2010).

The Into the Classroom feature "Fostering Critical Thinking" presents examples of what teachers might do in language arts, history, and science. In this age of widespread access to multiple sources of information—some legitimate, some of questionable value, and some completely bogus—critical thinking skills are now more *critical* than ever.

Teach and encourage critical thinking skills in diverse disciplines across the school curriculum.

MyEdLab **Self-Check 7.5**

MyEdLab **Application Exercise 7.5.** In this exercise, you can apply what you have learned about critical thinking to a classroom lesson.

Into The Classroom

Fostering Critical Thinking

Teach elements of critical thinking.

In a unit on persuasion and argumentation, a junior high school language arts teacher explains that a sound argument meets three criteria: (a) The evidence presented to justify the argument is accurate and consistent; (b) the evidence is relevant to and provides sufficient support for the conclusion; and (c) little or no information has been omitted that, if present, would lead to a contradictory conclusion. The teacher then has students practice applying these criteria to a variety of persuasive and argumentative essays.

Foster epistemic beliefs that encourage critical thinking.

Rather than teaching history as a collection of facts to be memorized, a high school history teacher portrays the discipline as an attempt by informed but inevitably biased scholars to interpret and make sense of historical events. On several occasions he asks his students to read two or three different historians' accounts of the same incident and to look for evidence of personal bias in each one.

Teach students skills for effectively presenting and evaluating arguments for various opinions on a controversial topic.

Students in a second-grade class read Shel Silverstein's *The Giving Tree*, a children's book in which a boy and an apple tree form a friendship. Throughout his childhood, the boy in the story regularly plays in the tree and eats her apples. As he grows older, his desires grow more sophisticated and he gradually takes parts of the tree—first all of her apples, then all of her branches, and finally her trunk, at which point only a small stump remains. After reading the book, the teacher scaffolds a discussion about whether the boy's actions were ethically appropriate. Initially, each student is asked to state an opinion on the matter. The students are then asked four questions:

- Why do you agree with that side?
- Can you be sure that you are right?
- Is it possible you could learn something new that would make you change your mind?
- What would someone from the other side say if he or she were trying to convince you that he or she was right?

Embed critical thinking skills within the context of authentic activities.

In a unit on statistical and scientific reasoning, an eighth-grade science class studies concepts related to probability, correlation, and experimental control. Then, as part of a simulated legislative hearing, the students work in small groups to develop arguments for or against a legislative bill concerning the marketing and use of vitamins and other dietary supplements. To find evidence to support their arguments, the students apply what they've learned about statistics and experimentation as they read journal articles and government reports regarding the possible benefits and drawbacks of nutritional supplements.

Teach students how to evaluate the accuracy of information posted on Internet websites.

On an educational website called "All About Explorers," elementary students practice distinguishing between credible and questionable information while searching for facts about well-known early explorers. For example, as students look for information about Christopher Columbus, they visit a bogus "website" that describes Columbus as having been born in 1951 but dying in 1906—a timeline that obviously makes no sense—and asserts that the king and queen of Spain called Columbus on his toll-free number.

Sources: Derry et al., 1998 (statistics example based on this study); Halpern, 1997 (criteria for a sound argument); Paxton, 1999 (bias in history example); C. M. Walker, Wartenberg, & Winner, 2013, p. 1340 (*Giving Tree* example). "All About Explorers," is a teacher-created website at www.allaboutexplorers.com.

Diversity in Creativity, Critical Thinking, and Other Complex Cognitive Processes

We might reasonably speculate that Western schools' focus on meaningful learning and conceptual understanding enhances students' ability to be creative: One recent study with college students found students from a European American background to be especially proficient in solving math problems requiring creative thinking (Schommer-Aikins & Easter, 2008). Perhaps more significant, however, has been the finding that experiences in *two or more cultures* enhance creative thinking and behaviors. Quite possibly, such a multicultural background exposes learners to a broader range of concepts, ideas, and perspectives from which to draw when trying to think about a topic or problem in nontraditional ways (Leung et al., 2008).

Critical thinking is another complex cognitive process that seems to depend somewhat on students' cultural backgrounds. Some cultures place high value on respecting one's elders or certain religious leaders, and in doing so, they may foster the belief that "truth" is a cut-and-dried entity that is best gained from authority figures (Losh, 2003; Qian & Pan, 2002; Tyler, Uqdah, et al., 2008). Furthermore, a cultural emphasis on maintaining group harmony may discourage children from hashing out differences in perspectives, which critical thinking often entails (Kağitçibaşi, 2007; Kuhn & Park, 2005). Perhaps as a result of such factors, critical thinking may be less common in some groups (e.g., in some traditional Asian and Native American communities and in some fundamentalist religious groups) than in others (Chinn & Buckland, 2012; Kuhn, Daniels, & Krishnan, 2003; Kuhn & Park, 2005; Tyler, Uqdah, et al., 2008).

In some situations, then, we must walk a fine line between teaching students to critically evaluate persuasive arguments and scientific evidence, on the one hand, and to show appropriate respect and strive for group harmony in their community and culture, on the other. One potentially effective approach is to suggest that students pose questions in a nonthreatening way, perhaps like this: "What if someone were to criticize your idea by saying _____? How might you respond?"

Teach students tactful and respectful ways of critiquing other people's arguments and viewpoints.

ACCOMMODATING STUDENTS WITH SPECIAL NEEDS

In addition to differences that might be a function of cultural background, researchers have observed differences in complex thinking skills for students with various disabilities and for students who have advanced cognitive abilities. Table 7.3 presents some of the characteristics you're likely to see in students with special educational needs, along with recommendations for working with these students.

MyEdLab **Self-Check 7.6**

STUDENTS IN INCLUSIVE SETTINGS

TABLE 7.3 • Promoting Advanced Thinking Skills in Students with Special Educational Needs

CATEGORY	CHARACTERISTICS YOU MIGHT OBSERVE	SUGGESTED STRATEGIES
Students with specific cognitive or academic difficulties	• Difficulty in transferring learned information to new situations • Difficulties in problem solving, perhaps because of limited working memory capacity, inability to identify important aspects of a problem, inability to retrieve appropriate problem-solving strategies, or limited metacognitive problem-solving skills	• Encourage and scaffold transfer of school topics. • Model effective problem-solving strategies, and scaffold students' efforts to use them (e.g., point out significant pieces of information in word problems, teach questions that students should ask themselves as they work their way through problems). • Present simple problems at first, then gradually move to more difficult problems as students gain proficiency and self-confidence. • Teach techniques for minimizing the load on working memory during problem solving (e.g., writing parts of a problem on paper, drawing a diagram of the problem).
Students with social or behavioral problems	• Deficiencies in social problem-solving skills	• Teach strategies for solving social problems (e.g., taking a multistep approach that includes defining the specific problem, identifying several possible solutions, and predicting the likely outcomes of each one).
Students with general delays in cognitive and social functioning	• Difficulty in transferring information and skills to new situations • Few effective problem-solving strategies • Little, if any, ability to think creatively or critically about classroom topics	• Teach new information and skills in the specific contexts and situations in which students should be able to use them. • Present simple problems and guide students through each step needed to solve them.
Students with physical or sensory challenges	• No consistent deficits in complex cognitive processes; deficits sometimes due to students' limited experiences with tasks that require such processes	• Address any deficits in complex processes using strategies you would use with nondisabled students, making appropriate accommodations for physical and sensory limitations.
Students with advanced cognitive development	• More frequent transfer of learning to new situations • Greater effectiveness in problem solving, more sophisticated problem-solving strategies, greater flexibility in strategy use, and less susceptibility to mental sets • Interest in addressing general problems of society • Divergent thinking (e.g., asking unusual questions, giving novel responses) • Greater facility with critical thinking	• Place greater emphasis on complex processes (e.g., transfer, problem solving) within the curriculum. • Teach advanced thinking skills within the context of specific classroom topics rather than in isolation from academic content. • Accept and encourage divergent thinking, including unanticipated yet appropriate responses. • Encourage critical analysis of ideas, opinions, and evidence.

Sources: Beirne-Smith et al., 2006; Brownell, Mellard, & Deshler, 1993; B. Clark, 1997; DuPaul & Eckert, 1994; E. S. Ellis & Friend, 1991; N. R. Ellis, 1979; S. Goldstein & Rider, 2006; K. R. Harris, 1982; Heward, 2009; Kercood, Zentall, Vinh, & Tom-Wright, 2012; M. C. Linn, Clement, Pulos, & Sullivan, 1989; Maker, 1993; Mastropieri & Scruggs, 2007; Meichenbaum, 1977; Mendaglio, 2010; Mercer & Pullen, 2005; Piirto, 1999; Pulos & Linn, 1981; Slife, Weiss, & Bell, 1985; Stanley, 1980; Torrance, 1989; Turnbull et al., 2010; Weissberg, 1985.

7 What Have You Learned?

If we focus classroom activities on learning isolated facts and if we also use assessment techniques that emphasize knowledge of those facts, students will naturally begin to believe that school learning is a process of absorbing information in a rote fashion and regurgitating it later on. But if we instead focus class time and activities on *doing things with* information—for instance, applying, analyzing, and critically evaluating it—then students should acquire the cognitive processes and skills that will serve them well in the world beyond the classroom. With these points in mind, let's return to the learning outcomes presented at the beginning of the chapter.

◼ **7.1: Explain how learners' metacognitive knowledge and skills influence their learning and academic achievement; also explain how you can promote metacognitive development in your own students.** *Metacognition* includes both the beliefs students have about their own cognitive processes and their attempts to strategically regulate those processes to maximize learning and memory. Some effective learning strategies, such as taking notes and writing summaries, are overt ones easily seen in students' behaviors. Others, such as identifying important ideas and self-monitoring comprehension, are covert ones that take place mostly or entirely inside students' heads. Students' use or nonuse of effective strategies depends, in part, on the particular learning task at hand and also, in part, on (a) students' ability to reflect on the effectiveness of previous strategies, (b) their beliefs about the nature of knowledge and learning (i.e., their *epistemic beliefs*), and (c) their ultimate goals for learning and classroom performance. As teachers, we should promote students' metacognitive development at the same time that we teach them academic subject matter—for example, by providing guidance and scaffolding in note taking, elaborative processing, and summarizing, and by having students use new strategies in small-group activities. Students are especially likely to need our guidance and scaffolding when they engage in learning activities that require considerable student decision making, such as activities involving hypermedia in instructional software or on the Internet.

◼ **7.2: Describe various forms that transfer might take and the conditions in which transfer is most likely to occur, and apply research findings about transfer to your classroom practices.** Transfer occurs when something learned in one situation either helps or hinders learning or performance in another situation; these two phenomena are known as *positive transfer* and *negative transfer,* respectively. Some instances of transfer involve applying specific facts to a similar situation; for example, a student might apply her knowledge of French vocabulary words in a Spanish class. Other instances involve general transfer of knowledge, skills, or attitudes to a very different situation; for example, a student might apply study strategies learned in a history class to a science class and, after gaining self-confidence in one class, might bring that self-confidence to other classes as well. Students are more likely to transfer what they learn when they engage in meaningful learning (rather than rote learning), when they see the relevance of classroom material to diverse disciplines and real-world situations (rather than seeing it as context-bound), and when they have many opportunities to use the material in new ways.

◼ **7.3: Describe four general factors that influence problem-solving performance; also describe teaching strategies you can use to help students successfully solve both well-defined and ill-defined problems.** Schools have traditionally focused attention on solving well-defined problems, yet the outside world presents many ill-defined problems that students must also learn how to tackle. To be successful problem solvers, students must (a) encode problems in ways that lead them in potentially useful directions in long-term memory, (b) master both step-by-step procedures for particular situations (algorithms) and more general problem-solving strategies (heuristics), (c) compensate for the limits of working memory (e.g., by learning basic skills to automaticity), and (d) consciously self-direct and self-monitor the overall problem-solving process. As teachers, we can help students become more effective problem solvers in a number of ways—for example, by scaffolding their attempts to solve new and complex problems (perhaps in technology-based simulations), mixing up the kinds of problems we ask them to solve in any single lesson or unit, and asking them to explain what they're doing as they work through a problem.

◼ **7.4: Identify several instructional strategies that can encourage students to think creatively as they tackle new tasks and problems.** Creativity involves new and original behavior that leads to an appropriate and productive result; it's probably a combination of many thinking processes and behaviors that each may or may not come into play in different situations and content areas. We're more likely to see creative thinking and behavior when we show students that we value creativity, focus their attention on internal rather than external rewards, help them master essential knowledge and skills, teach them metacognitive strategies that support creative thinking, ask thought-provoking questions, encourage risk taking, and provide the time and resources that creativity requires.

◼ **7.5: Describe several different forms that critical thinking might take, and explain how you can help students critically evaluate what they see, hear, and read both inside and outside the classroom.** Critical thinking involves evaluating the accuracy, credibility, and worth of information and lines of reasoning. It can take a variety of forms depending on the

(Continued)

situation, and it requires not only (a) a number of cognitive skills (e.g., argument analysis, probabilistic reasoning, hypothesis testing) but also (b) a general disposition to approach new ideas in a thoughtful, evaluative manner and (c) a belief that humankind doesn't have all the answers regarding many important topics. As teachers, we should encourage and model a certain amount of intellectual skepticism, give students many opportunities to engage in critical analysis of classroom subject matter, and ask questions that encourage students to carefully scrutinize and evaluate the ideas they encounter in written documents, classroom discussions, and Internet websites.

■ **7.6: Give examples of diversity you might see in creativity, critical thinking, and other complex thinking processes as a result of students' cultural backgrounds, disabilities,**

or advanced cognitive development. Students exhibit considerable diversity in the extent and nature of their complex cognitive thinking processes. For example, students from some cultural backgrounds may be unaccustomed to thinking in divergent, creative ways about complex problems. Students from other backgrounds may have been discouraged from critically evaluating what their elders tell them. Many students with special educational needs may have acquired few (if any) effective learning and problem-solving strategies and thus need considerable scaffolding in their early attempts at using such strategies. In contrast, students who show advanced cognitive development tend to be metacognitively sophisticated learners, and they may be quite adept at solving problems and thinking critically and creatively without much teacher assistance.

Practice for Your Licensure Exam

Interview with Charlie

Seventeen-year-old Charlie has been earning As in his high school classes; now, at the end of his 11th-grade year, he has a 4.0 grade point average. He has particular interests in science and technology; in fact, in addition to challenging coursework at school, Charlie has taken several computer courses at a local community college. His mother says, "He invests a lot of time in projects (writing papers, reports, etc.) but doesn't crack open a book to read or study often."

One afternoon Charlie has the following discussion with an adult:

Adult: Why do you think your grades have been so good?

Charlie: I do the homework, and I do well on the tests. I don't really study—I just make sure to focus on the homework and make sure it makes sense to me. . . . What I do depends on the circumstances. For math and chemistry, just doing homework and going over it with friends during lunch or something helps. That's about all I do for studying.

Adult: What do you mean, "make sure it makes sense"?

Charlie: If I look at the problem and I know the process of how to do it, like in math and chemistry.

Adult: Let's say that a teacher assigns a textbook chapter for you to read sometime in the next three days. What things would you do—in your head, that is—when you read the chapter?

Charlie: Depends on the book and the class. Probably just skim it. Is the teacher just telling us to read it, or are there questions with it? I think about those things.

We have a textbook in my computer programming class. I go through the chapter, look at examples and the [computer] code. I don't look at the other stuff.

Adult: I haven't heard you talk about trying to memorize anything.

Charlie: We do have to memorize. If I write it down once—a formula or something—and can use it in a few problems, I get it.

Adult: Do you ever use flashcards?

Charlie: Flashcards wouldn't work for what I do.

Adult: How do you know when you've really learned something—I mean, really learned it—and will remember it for a long time?

Charlie: When I do a couple of problems and they don't seem as hard . . . when I can get the right answer every time.

Adult: Your teachers probably expect you to do a lot of things outside of class, right? How do you make sure you get them all done?

Charlie: Making lists is really helpful, of everything that's due.

Adult: So what do you do with the lists?

Charlie: I either do things as soon as possible or else procrastinate, do it the night before. Sometimes I have a free block at the end of the day to do it. Or I go home and do my chemistry right away. Or I might wait until the last minute. It depends on whether I'm hanging out with friends.

1. **Multiple-choice question:**

   Charlie says, "I don't really study—I just make sure to focus on the homework and make sure it makes sense to me." Which one of the following terms most accurately describes the nature of this statement?

   a. Algorithm
   b. Metacognition
   c. Critical thinking
   d. Divergent thinking

2. **Multiple-choice question:**

   Which one of the following statements is the best example of *comprehension monitoring*?

   a. "Depends on the book and the class. Probably just skim it."
   b. "I go through the chapter, look at examples and the [computer] code. I don't look at the other stuff."
   c. "When I do a couple of problems and they don't seem as hard . . . when I can get the right answer every time."
   d. "I either do things as soon as possible or else procrastinate, do it the night before. Sometimes I have a free block at the end of the day to do it."

3. **Constructed-response question:**

   Would you characterize Charlie's learning strategies as involving *rote learning* or *meaningful learning?* Use excerpts from the interview to support your answer.

   MyEdLab **Licensure Exam 7.1**

PRAXIS Go to Appendix C, "Matching Book Content and Ebook Activities to the Praxis Principles of Learning and Teaching Tests," to discover sections of this chapter that may be especially applicable to the Praxis tests.

Ian Shaw/Alamy

8

Learning and Cognition in Context

Learning Outcomes

8.1 Describe five basic assumptions underlying contextual theories of learning, and apply these assumptions to classroom practice.

8.2 Contrast the benefits of expert–novice interactions with the benefits of peer interactions; explain how you might enhance students' learning through both kinds of interactions.

8.3 Explain how learners' cultural backgrounds can influence their interpretations of new information and experiences; also explain how learners can effectively begin to participate in one or more communities of practice.

8.4 Describe key elements of society that impact learning, and explain how authentic activities can enhance learners' performance in their out-of-school lives.

8.5 Describe the unique roles that digital technologies and the Internet can play in classroom instruction.

8.6 Apply your knowledge of learning, cognition, and effective instructional practices to various academic content domains.

CASE STUDY: IT'S ALL IN HOW YOU LOOK AT THINGS

In a research study by Susan Mosborg (2002), high-achieving 12th-grade history students learned about a 1996 court case involving a school district that had been regularly broadcasting prayers and Bible classes over the high school's loudspeaker system. The students read two newspaper articles about the case. One article, a front-page news story, presented the two opposing perspectives in the case: that of a mother who was suing the school district (arguing that the practice violated her daughter's right to religious freedom) and that of the school superintendent (who argued that the broadcasts legitimately manifested the school's right to free speech). The second article, an editorial, lamented the court's decision to rule in favor of the mother and suggested that the decision would force people to practice their religion behind closed doors, "in the closet."

When students reflected on the articles in light of what they'd previously learned about American history, they reached varying conclusions. For example, a student named Jacob thought the decision reflected society's general moral decline:

> The nation's Christian heritage to me says a lot about the decline of a lot of things in our country. Over the last century, in particular, morals and beliefs have changed quite a bit and fragmented lots of different groups. And I think a lot of that can be attributed to the fact that we've kind of forgotten and strayed away from Christian belief, from prayer. (Mosborg, 2002, p. 333)

Meanwhile, a student named Howard interpreted the court decision as reflecting progress toward greater religious choice:

> Despite the assertion that the government was never linked to the church, it really was a lot more back in colonial times . . . . If you didn't believe in Puritanism, if you did something that was against their morals, but not yours, you were put in jail for it . . . . And I think we've come a long way since then. (Mosborg, 2002, p. 333)

- Why might the two boys have interpreted the same information in such radically different ways? What principles of learning and cognition might you draw on to help you make sense of their diverging perspectives?

———————————————————

As cognitive psychologists have explained, human learning typically involves *meaningful* learning—connecting new information and experiences to existing knowledge and beliefs about the world. Often, in fact, people engage in *elaboration*, embellishing on and sometimes distorting new input so that it's a good fit with their current understandings. To the extent that different people retrieve different knowledge and beliefs in any given situation, they're likely to interpret that situation in very different ways. For example, Jacob may have retrieved information about undesirable behaviors in the 20th century—perhaps the rise of organized crime in the 1920s or the increasing popularity of illegal drugs beginning in the late 1960s. In contrast, Howard apparently retrieved his knowledge of the rigidity and intolerant religious practices of many Puritans in the Massachusetts Bay Colony of the 17th century.

But *why* did the boys retrieve different prior knowledge and elaborate on the information in distinctly different ways? In her study, Mosborg (2002) discovered one important factor that seemed to make a difference: the broader social context in which students had grown up. Some students in the study were, like Jacob, attending an interdenominational religious school that stressed adherence to certain principles of Christianity. Other students, like Howard, attended a more secular private school that focused only on traditional academic disciplines. Presumably the students' schools reflected their parents' priorities, beliefs, and values—all of which the parents wanted to pass along to their children.

Learning always take place within particular *contexts*—for instance, within a particular classroom environment, social group, culture, and society. Furthermore, in those societies where children attend school, instruction is typically divided into discrete content domains—such as reading, math, science, and history—that involve somewhat idiosyncratic kinds of knowledge and skills. Such social and content-specific contexts for learning are the subjects of this chapter.

Basic Assumptions of Contextual Theories

Cognitive psychology is described in Chapter 6.

Cognitive theories of learning—information processing theory, individual constructivism, and related perspectives—tell us a great deal about how human beings learn and develop. But in recent decades psychologists have become increasingly aware that people's learning and development are inextricably dependent on and bound to various physical, social, and cultural contexts. Many of these psychologists have been influenced by Russian psychologist Lev Vygotsky's early theory of cognitive development and American psychologist Urie Bronfenbrenner's subsequent bioecological systems theory; hence, as you will soon discover, the e-book version of this chapter includes links to resources that depict key ideas in Vygotsky's and Bronfenbrenner's theories.

Contextual theories of learning vary considerably in the particular contexts they emphasize. Even so, they tend to share most or all of the following assumptions.

- *The brain functions in close collaboration with—rather than in isolation from—the rest of the body.* Obviously the brain can't function without good nutrition and the health of the rest of the body, and it gets new information from the eyes, ears, and other sensory organs. But in addition, thinking and learning are often intimately intertwined with a learner's physical actions and reactions. For example, when we think about throwing a baseball, we activate parts of the brain that control arm and hand muscles involved in throwing even if we aren't actually moving those muscles (Spunt, Falk, & Lieberman, 2010). And when we're pondering complex situations—perhaps math problems or perhaps the shapes and locations of various objects in space—gesturing with our hands or arms can sometimes help us think and talk about the situations more effectively (Alibali, Spencer, Knox, & Kita, 2011; Goldin-Meadow & Beilock, 2010; Segal, Tversky, & Black, 2014).

- *Acquired knowledge and skills are often tied to specific physical, social, or cultural activities and environments.* People don't always use what they've learned in situations where it might be relevant—a phenomenon known as situated learning or situated cognition. In some cases, people have associated new information and skills only with particular kinds of tasks or problems; for example, they might be accustomed to using their knowledge of algebra in a math class but *not* accustomed to using it—and hence they don't retrieve it—in relevant real-world activities such as constructing a treehouse, sewing a new vest, or choosing a sensible mortgage plan. In other cases, people may simply find it *easier* to use newly learned ideas or skills in certain contexts because these contexts provide physical, social, or cultural support for applying the new knowledge—as you'll see in the discussions of the next two assumptions.

- *Learners often think and perform more effectively when they can offload some of the cognitive burden onto something or someone else.* As you should recall from information processing theory, active cognitive processing takes place in working memory, which—*by itself*—can handle only a small amount of information at any one time. For complex tasks, then, it's helpful to shift some of the cognitive load elsewhere—an idea that's sometimes referred to as distributed cognition or distributed intelligence (e.g., Pea, 1993; Salomon, 1993; E. R. Smith & Conrey, 2009).

One way to "distribute" the cognitive load is to use physical objects—for instance, by writing parts of a problem on paper or using a calculator to carry out multistep computations. A second way is to organize and interpret the many concrete facts of a situation—the "raw data," as it were—using concepts, principles, strategies, and other cognitive tools that one's cultural group has developed to address common problems. For example, we might use a *calendar* to keep track of upcoming appointments and other commitments, or we might draw a *line graph* to see if a particular region's average annual rainfall has substantially increased or decreased over the past few decades.

Still a third way to distribute the cognitive load is to share it with other individuals. When learners spread a challenging task or problem across many minds, they can draw on multiple knowledge bases and ideas. For example, we might convene a group of people to brainstorm possible solutions to a local, national, or international problem. Furthermore, in virtually any social group, different people gain expertise in different topics—some become medical doctors, others become engineers, and so on—thereby distributing the group's collective knowledge base.

- *Learners sometimes learn more effectively when they collaborate with others to co-construct meaning.* We've just mentioned how learners can reduce their own cognitive burden, in part, by sharing a task or problem with others. An additional advantage of multilearner collaboration is that, as a group, learners can often make better sense of a situation than they might do on their own. For example, think about times when you've worked cooperatively with classmates to make sense of confusing academic material. Perhaps by sharing various possible interpretations, your group jointly constructed a better understanding of the material than any one of you could have constructed on your own. Unlike individually constructed knowledge, which might differ considerably from one individual to another, socially constructed knowledge is shared by two or more people simultaneously. A perspective known as social constructivism focuses on such collective efforts to impose meaning on the world.

  Joint meaning-making doesn't necessarily have to occur in a single learning session, however. In some cases it proceeds gradually over the course of several days or weeks—or even over the course of many decades or centuries. For example, such academic disciplines as mathematics, science, history, economics, and psychology have evolved as the result of long-term collaborations among many individuals. Through these disciplines, people have developed concepts (e.g., *pi* [π], *molecule,* and *revolution*) and principles (e.g., *Pythagorean theorem, supply–and–demand,* and the *limited capacity of working memory*) to simplify, organize, and explain certain aspects of the world or its inhabitants. Literature, music, and the fine arts help us impose meaning on the world as well—for instance, by trying to portray the thoughts and feelings that characterize human experience. Here we see one very critical role that *culture* plays in knowledge construction: To the extent that different groups of people use different concepts and principles to explain their physical experiences and to the extent that they have unique bodies of literature, music, and art to capture their psychological experiences, they'll inevitably see the world in diverse ways.

- *With the help and guidance of more knowledgeable individuals, learners benefit from the accumulated wisdom of their cultural group.* Through its ongoing co-construction of meanings and development of new tools and strategies, any long-standing social group becomes increasingly effective and efficient in tackling challenging tasks and problems. As the group gains new members—often through the birth of new generations—it maintains its effectiveness and efficiency by indoctrinating the new members into its typical ways of interpreting and responding to various situations. Contextual perspectives that emphasize the role of society and culture in promoting learning and development (including Vygotsky's early theory of cognitive development) are collectively known as sociocultural theory.

  In virtually any culture, adults and other more experienced individuals continually help growing children make sense of and respond to new situations in ways the culture deems to be appropriate and productive. In other words, adults *mediate* new situations for children. Over time, children gradually internalize adults' ways of interpreting and addressing day-to-day events until they themselves become the experts who guide future generations.

Here we are revisiting concepts discussed in previous chapters, including *working memory* and *cognitive load* (Chapter 6), *distributed intelligence* (Chapter 5), and *cognitive tools* (Chapter 2).

Chapter 2 describes Lev Vygotsky's early sociocultural theory, including the processes of mediation and internalization.

MyEdLab
Content Extension 8.1.

For our readers who haven't yet learned about Bronfenbrenner's ecological systems theory, this supplementary reading describes and illustrates some of his key ideas.

You can also find a discussion of Bronfenbrenner's bioecological systems theory in Chapter 2.

A sociocultural perspective can help us understand Jacob's and Howard's differing interpretations of the school prayer issue in the opening case study. Although both boys had grown up in the United States—and, in fact, in the same part of the country—their parents and schools had probably passed along somewhat different ways of looking at religion and its role in human society. For Jacob, prayer and other Christian traditions provided essential foundations for people's overall well-being, whereas for Howard, legitimate religious beliefs and practices might take a wide variety of forms.

Table 8.1 summarizes the five assumptions, along with some of their implications for instruction. Taken together, the assumptions involve three general layers of context. In particular, people think and learn within the contexts of (1) their physical bodies, (2) their immediate physical and social environments, and (3) the broader cultures and societies in which they live (see Figure 8.1). Keep in mind, however, that the three layers of context *interact and influence one another,* as reflected in the two-way arrows in the figure. Furthermore, all of them *change over time*—for instance, the body's physical capabilities change, access to helpful resources and social collaborators changes, and new technological innovations are becoming increasingly available.

Our focus in the rest of the chapter will be on Layers 2 and 3—more specifically, on how thinking and learning are influenced by learners' immediate social environments and broader culture and society, as well as by the various tools and knowledge bases that culture and society have created to enhance human performance. As you may realize, our discussions of these layers have been heavily influenced by the various layers and systems that Urie Bronfenbrenner has described in his bioecological systems theory.

As we look at various environmental influences on what learners know, think, and can do, however, we mustn't throw our knowledge of learners' internal cognitive processes out the window. Instead, we must continually remember that contextual factors work *in conjunction with*

PRINCIPLES/ASSUMPTIONS

TABLE 8.1 • **Basic Assumptions of Contextual Theories and Their Educational Implications**

ASSUMPTION	EDUCATIONAL IMPLICATION	EXAMPLE
Brain–body interdependence	Encourage students to use their bodies to help them think about and remember classroom subject matter.	As students try to understand the difference between folded and fault-block mountains, suggest that they use their hands to simulate what the earth's shifting tectonic plates do to create these two different types of mountains.
Situated nature of learning and cognition	Have students apply new knowledge and skills to real-world, authentic tasks.	Ask students to design and conduct experiments in which they apply scientific procedures (e.g., isolation and control of variables) to questions relevant to their personal lives and interests; provide sufficient scaffolding to enable them to do so in scientifically valid ways.
Distributed nature of learning and cognition	Teach students how to use various physical and cognitive tools (e.g., technology, algebraic procedures) to help them more effectively gain new knowledge and solve new problems. Also, teach them skills that can effectively enable them to collaborate with others and draw on the wisdom of experts.	Teach students how to use a search engine such as Google or Bing to find information relevant to a particular topic. Also teach them how to distinguish between websites that present valid, well-documented information, on the one hand, and websites that present erroneous "facts" or highly biased opinions, on the other.
Collaborative co-construction of meaning	Convene small groups in which students discuss complex issues with no obvious right and wrong answers.	Assign students to four-member groups that discuss the pros and cons of increasing taxes in their community. Ask each group to (1) divide into pairs, with one pair identifying pros and the other pair identifying cons; (2) make a combined list of the pros and cons; and (3) develop a tax policy that takes both pros and cons into account.
Guidance from more advanced individuals	Teach new concepts and principles that can help students make better sense of new and potentially puzzling situations.	Use principles of chemistry to explain why water expands when it freezes—a phenomenon that has implications for food storage, road construction, and other important aspects of human society.

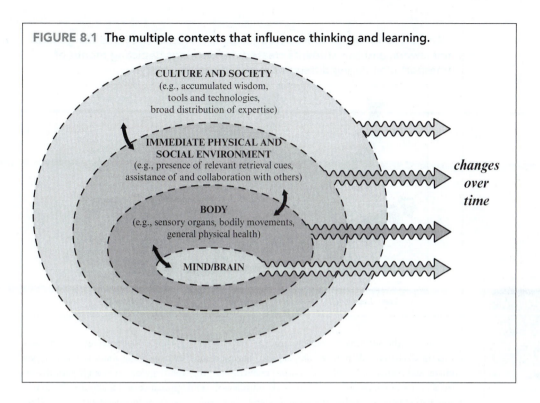

FIGURE 8.1 **The multiple contexts that influence thinking and learning.**

learners' internal cognitive processes—for instance, processes related to long-term memory storage and retrieval, metacognition, and problem solving (e.g., Kirsh, 2009; Sawyer & Greeno, 2009; Zusho & Clayton, 2011).

MyEdLab **Self-Check 8.1**

Social Interactions as Contexts

Certainly people sometimes learn new things on their own, perhaps by experimenting with the physical objects around them or perhaps simply by thinking and *re*thinking about things they've previously observed. Yet most human learning is in one way or another a very social enterprise, involving interaction with more advanced individuals, with equal-ability peers, or both.

INTERACTIONS WITH MORE ADVANCED INDIVIDUALS

Young learners are most likely to construct a productive understanding of the world when adults and other advanced individuals share with them the many concepts, principles, theories, and other cognitive tools that society has developed to explain the physical and psychological aspects of human experience (Driver, 1995; Sweller, Kirschner, & Clark, 2007; Vygotsky, 1934/1986). For example, children can learn a great deal about various biological species and fragile ecosystems—and are likely to acquire positive attitudes toward science—when firsthand observations in class or on field trips are accompanied by scientific explanations of the phenomena at hand (e.g., Patrick, Mantzicopoulos, & Samarapungavan, 2009; Zaragoza & Fraser, 2008). Any explanation that helps learners relate what they're observing to particular concepts, principles, or theories is a mediated learning experience.

Teach concepts, principles, and theories that help students make sense of their observations and experiences.

Adults and other advanced individuals help young learners in another important way as well: They introduce new cognitive and metacognitive strategies and guide learners in how to use these strategies, perhaps in a group instructional setting or perhaps in a one-on-one apprenticeship. For instance, in the elementary grades a teacher and students might co-construct a timeline that organizes information about different modes of transportation over the course of human history (Brophy, Alleman, & Knighton, 2009); Figure 8.2 is an example of such a co-constructed

FIGURE 8.2 In this co-constructed timeline, a teacher provided the general framework, and two students created the drawings depicting modes of transportation during different periods in human history.

Long, Long Ago   Long Ago   Modern Times

MyEdLab
Video Explanation 8.1.
This video describes and illustrates some of Lev Vygotsky's key ideas about how adults and other advanced individuals can enhance children's thinking and cognitive development.

Regularly engage students in small-group or whole-class discussions that encourage them to exchange views and build on one another's ideas.

Chapter 7 describes epistemic beliefs in greater depth.

timeline. In the secondary grades a teacher and students might collaboratively create two-dimensional charts to help them compare and contrast what they're learning about the topography, climate, and economic resources of various countries or geographic regions. Through joint discussions and use of strategies—typically with considerable adult guidance and scaffolding at first—learners gradually internalize the strategies and can begin using them independently (A. Collins, 2006; Dennen & Burner, 2008; Rogoff, 1990).

INTERACTIONS WITH PEERS

Learners benefit in somewhat different ways when, in an effort to make sense of new information and experiences, they share their ideas and perspectives with equal-ability peers:

- They must clarify and organize their thoughts well enough to explain and justify them to others.
- They tend to elaborate on what they've learned—for example, by drawing inferences, generating hypotheses, and formulating questions to be answered.
- They are exposed to the views of others, who may have more accurate understandings or culturally different—and yet equally valid—perspectives.
- They may discover flaws and inconsistencies in their own thinking.
- They can model effective ways of thinking about and studying academic subject matter for one another.
- With the support of their peers, they can gain practice in more sophisticated learning and reasoning skills, which they can eventually begin to use on their own.
- They can also gain practice in the argumentation skills that experts in various disciplines use to advance the frontiers of knowledge—for instance, presenting evidence in support of conclusions and examining the strengths and weaknesses of various explanations.
- They may acquire more advanced *epistemic beliefs*—more sophisticated views of the nature of knowledge and learning. For example, they may begin to realize that genuine understanding involves acquiring an integrated set of ideas about a topic and that such knowledge is likely to evolve gradually over time. (Andriessen, 2006; Bendixen & Rule, 2004; Chinn, 2006; Hatano & Inagaki, 2003; K. Hogan, Nastasi, & Pressley, 2000; D. W. Johnson & Johnson, 2009b; A. King, 1999; Kuhn, 2015; Kuhn & Crowell, 2011; P. K. Murphy, Wilkinson, & Soter, 2011; Nussbaum, 2008; Reznitskaya & Gregory, 2013; B. B. Schwarz, Neuman, & Biezuner, 2000; Sinatra & Pintrich, 2003; C. L. Smith, 2007; Vygotsky, 1978; Wentzel & Watkins, 2011)

Peer-group discussions about academic subject matter have social and motivational benefits as well as cognitive ones. Discussing a topic with classmates can help students acquire more effective interpersonal skills (Certo, 2011; Y. Li et al., 2007; N. M. Webb & Farivar, 1994). It can also have an energizing effect on students and instill a genuine desire to understand a topic better (Hacker & Bol, 2004; P. K. Murphy & Mason, 2006). Controversial topics can be especially motivating for them, provided that they can effectively resolve their differences without alienating one another (Chinn, 2006). Clearly, then, students have a great deal to gain from conversing with one another regularly about classroom subject matter.

CREATING A COMMUNITY OF LEARNERS

With the benefits of student dialogue in mind and with a goal of promoting social co-construction of meaning, some psychologists and educators have suggested that we create communities of learners, classes in which teachers and students collaborate to build a body of knowledge about a topic and help one another learn about it. A class that operates as a community of learners is likely to have certain characteristics:

- All students are active participants in classroom activities.
- The primary goal is to acquire a body of knowledge on a specific topic, with students contributing to and building on one another's efforts and, typically, creating one or more products representing that knowledge (e.g., a theory, oral presentation, or web page).
- Students draw on many resources—books, magazines, the Internet, and one another—in their efforts to learn about the topic.
- Discussion and collaboration among two or more students occur regularly and play key roles in learning.
- Diversity in students' interests and rates of progress is expected and respected.
- Students and teacher coordinate their efforts in helping one another learn; no one has exclusive responsibility for teaching others.
- Everyone is a potential resource for others; different individuals are likely to serve as resources on different occasions, depending on the topics and tasks at hand. In some cases, individual students focus on particular topics and become local experts on them. Occasionally people outside the classroom share their expertise as well.
- The teacher provides some guidance and direction for classroom activities, but students also contribute guidance and direction.
- Mechanisms are in place through which students can share what they've learned with others.
- Constructive questioning and critiquing of one another's work is commonplace.
- The process of learning is emphasized as much as—and sometimes more than—the finished product(s). (Bielaczyc & Collins, 2006; A. L. Brown & Campione, 1994; Campione, Shapiro, & Brown, 1995; A. Collins, 2006; R. A. Engle, 2006; Rogoff, Matusov, & White, 1996; Scardamalia & Bereiter, 2006; Wells, 2011)

Create a community atmosphere in which peer collaboration and mutual support are integral parts of classroom learning and achievement.

In one example of how a community of learners can be structured (A. L. Brown & Campione, 1994), students are divided into small groups to study different subtopics falling under a general theme; for instance, subtopics for the theme *changing populations* might be *extinct, endangered, artificial, assisted,* and *urbanized.* Each group conducts research and prepares teaching materials related to its subtopic. The class then reassembles into new groups that include at least one representative from each of the previous groups. Within these new groups, the students teach one another what they've learned. Such an approach, in which different students master different topics and then share their knowledge with classmates, is sometimes called the jigsaw technique.

Another approach is to use a computer network to promote a community of learners (Bereiter & Scardamalia, 2006; G. Stahl, Koschmann, & Suthers, 2006; J. Zhang, Scardamalia, Reeve, & Messina, 2009). In this electronic environment, students create a variety of documents—perhaps brief notes, lengthier reports, problem solutions, diagrams, or short stories—and post their work as computer files that their classmates can read, react to, and possibly modify or build on. Students also interact in an ongoing computer-based chat room in which they present questions or issues to which their classmates respond. For example, students might jointly wrestle with the puzzling fact that heat melts some solids but burns others, or they might critique various theories about how human beings first migrated to and then spread throughout North and South America (e.g., Hewitt, Brett, Scardamalia, Frecker, & Webb, 1995; Hewitt & Scardamalia, 1998).

Working in communities of learners can give students a sense of the strategies that scientists and other scholars use to advance the frontiers of knowledge: They conduct individual and collaborative research, share ideas, and build on and critique one another's findings and conclusions. And in fact, participating in such communities appears to promote fairly complex thinking and knowledge-building processes, often for extended time periods (A. L. Brown & Campione, 1994, 1996; R. A. Engle, 2006; R. A. Engle & Conant, 2002; Scardamalia & Bereiter, 2006). Participating in a community of learners is also highly motivating for students, who may insist on going to school even when they're sick and may express regret when the school year ends (Rogoff, 1994; Turkanis, 2001).

In addition to the cognitive and motivational benefits, working in a community of learners can foster effective peer relationships and social skills. It can also help create a *sense of community* in the classroom—a sense that teachers and students have shared goals, are mutually respectful and supportive of one another's efforts, and believe that everyone makes an important contribution to classroom learning.

A community of learners can be especially useful when we have a diverse student population (Kincheloe, 2009; Ladson-Billings, 1995b; Rothstein-Fisch & Trumbull, 2008). Such a community values the contributions of all students, using everyone's individual backgrounds, cultural perspectives, and unique abilities to enhance the overall learning and achievement of the class. It also provides a context in which students can form friendships across the lines of ethnicity, gender, socioeconomic status, and disability—friendships that are critical for students' social development and multicultural understandings.

However, we must also note potential weaknesses of communities of learners, as well as of peer-group discussions more generally. Some students may dominate interactions, and others (e.g., English language learners) may participate little or not at all (Walshaw & Anthony, 2008; T. White & Pea, 2011). Furthermore, particularly if what students learn is limited to the knowledge they personally acquire and share with one another, some of them may pass along their biases, misconceptions, and ineffective strategies to their classmates (A. L. Brown & Campione, 1994; Hynd, 1998b; E. R. Smith & Conrey, 2009). Obviously, then, when we conduct classroom discussions or structure our classrooms as communities of learners, we must carefully monitor student interactions to make sure that everyone is meaningfully participating and that students ultimately acquire *accurate* understandings of the topic they're studying.

You can learn more about creating a sense of community in Chapter 13.

MyEdLab **Self-Check 8.2**

MyEdLab **Application Exercise 8.1.** In this exercise, you can apply what you have learned about the benefits of social interactions as you watch a book-making activity in a first-grade classroom.

Cultures as Contexts

Almost any long-standing social group develops some sort of culture, which includes behaviors and beliefs that are passed from old members to new ones, from generation to generation. Culture is a phenomenon that is largely—although not exclusively—unique to the human species (M. Cole & Hatano, 2007). Through its culture a human social group ensures that each new generation acquires and presumably benefits from the wisdom that preceding generations have accumulated. By passing along this collective knowledge base, a cultural group increases the chances that it will survive and thrive over the long run.

Especially in large, complex societies, learners typically have exposure to and involvement in two or more cultural groups simultaneously. For example, most learners in North America are immersed in what is often called *mainstream Western culture,* which encourages literacy, knowledge of various academic disciplines, and, in its 21st-century form, proficiency in digital technologies. Despite its name, mainstream Western culture also pervades many other countries around the world. But many learners are likely to be active participants in other cultures as well, such as those associated with particular ethnic or religious groups.

Some aspects of cultural knowledge are concrete and easily observable. Such is the case when people use paper and pencil, equations, diagrams, or computers to help them analyze data or solve problems. But other aspects of cultural knowledge are so abstract and pervasive that they're taken for granted and easily overlooked as contextual factors affecting learning. For example, consider the concepts *north, south, east,* and *west.* You've probably used these concepts frequently to help you find your way around the countryside or on a map. Despite their seemingly obvious relationship to Mother Earth, these concepts are creations that some cultures—and only some cultures—provide. Culture's influence on learning and thinking is so strong that researchers have observed cultural differences—small, subtle ones, to be sure—in brain organization and functioning (Park & Huang, 2010).

As culturally experienced individuals explain various phenomena to newer members of a cultural group, they must inevitably focus more on certain aspects of the phenomena than on other aspects. In the process of doing so, young learners discover that certain things are especially important to think about and remember, and these things typically reflect the cultural group's perspectives and priorities. For example, when European American mothers recall past events with their children, they often speculate about the thoughts and feelings of the participants. In contrast, Asian mothers are more likely to talk about social norms and expectations, such as how someone might have behaved more appropriately. Such differences are consistent with the priorities and values of these two cultures (MacDonald, Uesiliana, & Hayne, 2000; Mullen & Yi, 1995; Q. Wang & Ross, 2007). As another example, recall once again Jacob's and Howard's differing interpretations of a court case regarding school prayer. People's religious beliefs are often an integral part of their specific cultural environments.

SCHEMAS, SCRIPTS, AND WORLDVIEWS AS ASPECTS OF CULTURE

As cognitive psychologists have suggested, developing learners draw on their experiences to construct schemas and scripts—general understandings of what things are typically like and how common activities typically unfold. Many schemas and scripts are unique to particular cultures. The exercise we present now illustrates this point.

You have previously learned about schemas and scripts in Chapter 6.

 EXPERIENCING FIRSTHAND
THE WAR OF THE GHOSTS

Read the following story *one time only:*

> One night two young men from Egulac went down to the river to hunt seals, and while they were there it became foggy and calm. Then they heard war-cries, and they thought, "Maybe this is a war-party." They escaped to the shore, and hid behind a log. Now canoes came up, and they heard the noise of paddles, and saw one canoe coming up to them. There were five men in the canoe, and they said:
>
> "What do you think? We wish to take you along. We are going up the river to make war on the people."
>
> One of the young men said: "I have no arrows."
>
> "Arrows are in the canoe," they said.
>
> "I will not go along. I might be killed. My relatives do not know where I have gone. But you," he said, turning to the other, "may go with them."
>
> So one of the young men went, but the other returned home.
>
> And the warriors went on up the river to a town on the other side of Kalama. The people came down to the water, and they began to fight, and many were killed. But presently the young man heard one of the warriors say, "Quick, let us go home: that Indian has been hit." Now he thought: "Oh, they are ghosts." He did not feel sick, but they said he had been shot.
>
> So the canoes went back to Egulac, and the young man went ashore to his house, and made a fire. And he told everybody and said, "Behold I accompanied the ghosts, and we went to fight. Many of our fellows were killed, and many of those who attacked us were killed. They said I was hit, and I did not feel sick."
>
> He told it all, and then he became quiet. When the sun rose he fell down. Something black came out of his mouth. His face became contorted. The people jumped up and cried.
>
> He was dead. (F. C. Bartlett, 1932, p. 65)

Now cover the story, and write down as much of it as you can remember.

Compare your own rendition of the story with the original. What differences do you notice? Your version is almost certainly the shorter of the two, and you probably left out many details. But did you also find yourself distorting certain parts of the story so that it made more sense to you?

As a Native American ghost story, "The War of the Ghosts" may be inconsistent with some of the schemas and scripts you've acquired, especially if you were raised in a nonNative American culture. In an early study of long-term memory (F. C. Bartlett, 1932), students at England's Cambridge University were asked to read the story twice and then to recall it at various times later on. Students' recollections of the story often included additions and distortions that made the story more consistent with English culture. For example, people in England rarely go "to the river to hunt seals" because seals are saltwater animals and most rivers have fresh water. Students might therefore say that the men went to the river to *fish*. Similarly, the ghostly element of the story didn't fit comfortably with the religious beliefs of most Cambridge students and so was often modified. When one student was asked to recall the story 6 months after he had read it, he provided the following account:

> Four men came down to the water. They were told to get into a boat and to take arms with them. They inquired, "What arms?" and were answered "Arms for battle." When they came to the battle-field they heard a great noise and shouting, and a voice said: "The black man is dead." And he was brought to the place where they were, and laid on the ground. And he foamed at the mouth. (F. C. Bartlett, 1932, pp. 71–72)

Notice how the student's version of the story leaves out many of its more puzzling aspects—puzzling, at least, from his own cultural perspective.

When students from diverse cultural backgrounds come to school with somewhat different schemas and scripts, they may interpret the same classroom materials or activities differently and in some cases may have trouble making sense of a particular lesson or reading assignment (e.g., Lipson, 1983; R. E. Reynolds, Taylor, Steffensen, Shirey, & Anderson, 1982; Steffensen, Joag-Dev, & Anderson, 1979). As teachers, then, we need to find out whether students have the appropriate schemas and scripts to understand whatever topic we're teaching. When students *don't* have such knowledge, we may sometimes need to back up and help them acquire it before we forge ahead with new material.

Learners' schemas and scripts tend to be specific to particular topics. In contrast, their worldviews—their general beliefs and assumptions about reality—can influence their meaning-making in a great many domains (Koltko-Rivera, 2004; Lewandowsky, Oberauer, & Gignac, 2013). Following are examples of assumptions that a worldview might encompass:

- Life and the universe came into being through random acts of nature *or* as part of a divine plan and purpose.
- Objects in nature (rocks, trees, etc.) have some degree of consciousness *or* are incapable of conscious thought.
- Human beings are at the mercy of the forces of nature *or* should strive to master the forces of nature *or* must learn to live in harmony with nature.
- People are most likely to enhance their well-being by relying on scientific principles and logical reasoning processes *or* by seeking guidance and support from sources beyond the realm of scientific and logical thought.
- People's successes and failures in life are the result of their own actions *or* divine intervention *or* fate *or* random occurrences.
- The human world is fair and just—good deeds ultimately bring rewards, and misdeeds are eventually punished—*or* is not necessarily fair and just. (M. Cole & Hatano, 2007; E. M. Evans, Rosengren, Lane, & Price, 2012; Furnham, 2003; Gifford, 2011; Keil & Newman, 2008; Koltko-Rivera, 2004; Medin, 2005)

To a considerable degree, such beliefs and assumptions are culturally transmitted, with different cultures communicating somewhat different beliefs and assumptions either explicitly through their words or implicitly through their actions (Berti, Toneatti, & Rosati, 2010; M. Cole & Hatano, 2007; Kitayama, 2002; Losh, 2003).

Determine whether students have appropriate schemas and scripts to understand the topic at hand.

Worldviews are often such an integral part of everyday thinking that people take them for granted and usually aren't consciously aware of them. In many cases, then, worldviews encompass *implicit knowledge* rather than explicit knowledge. Nevertheless, they influence learners' interpretations of current events and classroom subject matter. For example, if students believe that the world and its inhabitants are guided and protected by an omniscient and benevolent Greater Being, they're less likely to believe that global climate change is real or poses a significant threat to human society (Feinberg & Willer, 2011). And if students' culture consistently emphasizes the importance of accepting and living in harmony with nature as it is, they might struggle with a science curriculum that explores how human beings might manipulate and gain control over natural events (Atran, Medin, & Ross, 2005; Medin, 2005).

In some cases, academic subject matter may conflict with students' most core beliefs—and ultimately with the very essence of who they are as individuals. For example, students who strongly believe in the divine creation of humankind may readily dismiss any suggestion that the human race has evolved from more primitive species (E. M. Evans et al., 2012; Southerland & Sinatra, 2003). And students whose cultures view certain historical battles as involving good guys triumphing over bad guys—or vice versa—may disregard more balanced perspectives in which each side had legitimate needs and concerns (K. Jacoby, 2008; Levstik, 2011; Porat, 2004). Hence, students' worldviews can sometimes interfere with their ability to undergo legitimate conceptual change. Under such circumstances a more achievable goal may be to help students *understand* (rather than *accept*) academic scholars' explanations and lines of reasoning (Feinberg & Willer, 2011; Southerland & Sinatra, 2003).

As teachers, we must remember that we, too, have certain worldviews—often implicit, below-the-surface ones—that influence what and how we think about our physical and social worlds. For example, we may place greater value on the importance of objective scientific investigations as a source of new knowledge than some of our students do (Thanukos & Scotchmoor, 2012). And many of us are apt to think that the practices of certain cultural groups are in some way inferior to those of mainstream Western culture (Banks et al., 2005). Difficult as it might sometimes be to do so, we must continually reflect on our own cultural beliefs and acknowledge that they influence what and how we teach—sometimes for the better but sometimes to the detriment of our students' learning and development.

When students' world-views are central to their sense of identity, recognize that they may steadfastly hold on to their existing beliefs. In such cases, focus on helping them understand—rather than accept—experts' explanations and lines of reasoning.

COMMUNITIES OF PRACTICE AS ASPECTS OF CULTURE

Any cultural group passes along not only certain ways of interpreting the world but also certain ways of doing things. In other words, different cultures teach somewhat different kinds of *procedural knowledge.* Some procedural knowledge is task- or topic-specific and is conveyed directly and explicitly—for example, "Here's how to write a cursive *A,*" and "Let me show you how to do long division." But cultures typically also pass along a good deal of procedural knowledge within the context of **communities of practice**—groups of people who share common interests and goals and regularly interact and coordinate their efforts in pursuit of those interests and goals (Lave, 1991; Nolen, 2011; Sawyer & Greeno, 2009; Wenger, 1998). Communities of practice tend to adhere to certain standards for action and interaction—standards that are often unwritten understandings rather than explicitly stated rules. For example, in the adult world of mainstream Western culture, people in various professions—medicine, law, scientific research, and so on—tend to communicate regularly with one another and to support one another in particular ways. In most cases, new members of a community of practice learn the acceptable ways of doing things primarily by actively *participating* in the group. Often a learner begins by participating only at the fringe of the group, perhaps by doing menial chores or by assisting or apprenticing with a more experienced group member. In other words, a novice is gradually introduced to the ways of the group through **legitimate peripheral participation** (Lave & Wenger, 1991). Participation is *legitimate* in the sense that the novice contributes in genuine, authentic ways to the group's overall effort. It's *peripheral* in that it involves only small tasks at the outer edge, or periphery, of the action.

Communities of practice are hardly limited to adult professional groups. For instance, volunteer organizations (e.g., Habitat for Humanity, the American Red Cross) and organized youth groups (e.g., Boy Scouts and Girl Scouts) are essentially communities of practice as well. Schools, too, are communities of practice, in that they have certain prescribed ways of doing things in order to accomplish particular goals—for example, following schedules, completing assignments, and meeting deadlines.

We teachers must certainly help students learn the expectations of their educational community. But in addition, we can help students learn the ways of various adult professional communities, and of the adult world more generally, by having students actually participate in adult activities—perhaps by encouraging part-time internships with local businesses or collaborative efforts with public service organizations. Initially their participation might involve only easy tasks that are closely guided and supported, but as students gain more knowledge and skills they should also gain more responsibility and independence.

Encourage involvement in local businesses and public service organizations as a way of introducing students to the skills and commonly accepted practices of the adult world.

> MyEdLab **Self-Check 8.3**
>
> MyEdLab **Application Exercise 8.2.** In this exercise, you can practice reconciling students' personal cultural beliefs and practices with the academic and behavioral expectations of classrooms in mainstream Western culture.

Society and Technology as Contexts

A concept related to culture, but also somewhat distinct from it, is **society**: a very large, enduring social group that has fairly explicit social and economic structures, as well as collective institutions and activities. For instance, virtually any nation is a society, in that it has a government that regulates some of its activities, a set of laws identifying permissible and unacceptable behaviors, a monetary system that allows members to exchange goods and services, and well-established means of communication among its members.

A society influences its members' learning in a variety of ways, including through the resources it provides, the activities it supports, and the general messages it communicates (e.g., Bronfenbrenner, 2005; Gauvain & Munroe, 2009). For example, a society's infrastructure—such as its roads, power plants, and telephone and cable lines—enables the movement of people and goods over great distances and regular collaboration among its residents. Various media (newspapers, television, the Internet, etc.) convey information, ideas, opinions, and messages (often subtle ones) about desired behaviors and group stereotypes. And schools provide formal structures through which children and adults alike acquire knowledge and skills that will presumably enhance their personal and professional success.

One noteworthy aspect of any society is its **distributed knowledge**: Different people have expertise in different topics, and so society members must rely on one another in order to maximize both their individual success and the success of the overall group. To be truly effective participants in society, then, people must learn how to seek out the expertise they may occasionally need to (a) tackle challenging problems and (b) distinguish between true experts, on the one hand, and individuals who only *claim* to be experts, on the other (Bromme, Kienhues, & Porsch, 2010).

As teachers, virtually anything we do with students should in one way or another enhance their long-term success in adult society. But here we focus on two particular topics about which educational psychologists have had a great deal to say in recent years: authentic activities and technological innovations.

MyEdLab
Video Example 8.1.

What strategies does this elementary school teacher use to teach children about some of the roles that their society plays in their personal lives?

AUTHENTIC ACTIVITIES

In industrialized societies, children are largely separated from the adult workplace, and thus they have little exposure to the kinds of tasks they'll eventually need to perform when they themselves reach adulthood (Rogoff, 2003). Accordingly, many learning theorists recommend that teachers make frequent use of **authentic activities**—activities similar or identical to those that students will eventually encounter in the outside world (e.g., Barab & Dodge, 2008; Edelson & Reiser, 2006; Greeno, Collins, & Resnick, 1996). Such activities can have several benefits. For one thing, by working in naturalistic contexts, using the physical and social resources that such contexts offer (e.g., tools, other people), students should be able to accomplish more than they would accomplish in relatively artificial and simplistic classroom tasks. Second, complex authentic tasks are likely to promote meaningful learning rather than rote memorization of new information and procedures. Finally, because they resemble real-world tasks and problems, authentic activities should help students make mental connections between school subject matter and out-of-school situations, and these connections should help students retrieve and apply—that is, *transfer*—what they've learned to new settings and problems.

See Chapter 7 for a discussion of factors affecting transfer.

Many research studies have confirmed the effectiveness of authentic activities (e.g., Gijbels, Dochy, Van den Bossche, & Segers, 2005; Hung, Jonassen, & Liu, 2008). For example, students' writing skills may show greater improvement in both quality and quantity when, instead of completing traditional workbook writing exercises, they write stories, essays, and letters to real people (E. H. Hiebert & Fisher, 1992). Students gain a more complete understanding of how to use and interpret maps when, instead of answering workbook questions about maps, they construct their *own* maps (M. Gregg & Leinhardt, 1994a). And students are more likely to check their solutions to math problems—in particular, to make sure their solutions make logical sense—when they use math for real-life tasks (Cognition and Technology Group at Vanderbilt, 1993; De Corte, Greer, & Verschaffel, 1996).

 Incorporate classroom subject matter into real-world tasks.

Authentic activities can also be highly motivating for students (M. Barnett, 2005; Marks, 2000; Wirkala & Kuhn, 2011). As an example, consider one high school student's recollection of a ninth-grade moon-tracking activity:

> It was the first time I can remember in school doing something that wasn't in the textbook ... like we were real scientists or something. We had to keep data sheets, measure the time and angle of the moonrise every day for a month. It drove my mom nuts because sometimes we'd be eating dinner, and I'd look at my watch and race out the door! We had to measure the river near us to see how it was affected by the moon. . . I went down to the river more than I have in my whole life, I think. Then we had to do the calculations, that was another step, and we had to chart our findings. The test was to analyze your findings and tell what they meant about the relationship of the tides and the moon.... I felt that I did something real, and I could see the benefit of it. (Wasley, Hampel, & Clark, 1997, pp. 117–118)

By placing classroom activities in real-world contexts, we help students discover the reasons why they're learning academic subject matter. Accordingly, authentic activities may be especially valuable in working with students who are at risk for academic failure (L. W. Anderson & Pellicer, 1998; Christenson & Thurlow, 2004; Tate, 1995).

Authentic activities can be developed for virtually any area of the curriculum. For example, we might ask students to do the following:

- Write an editorial
- Participate in a debate
- Design an electrical circuit
- Converse in a foreign language
- Make a video
- Perform in a concert
- Plan a personal budget
- Create a classroom website

In some instances authentic activities take the form of **problem-based learning** or **project-based learning**, in which students acquire new knowledge and skills as they work on complex problems or projects similar to those they might find in the outside world (Hmelo-Silver, 2004, 2006; Krajcik & Blumenfeld, 2006; Wirkala & Kuhn, 2011). Occasionally authentic activities may also involve **service learning**—that is, they involve projects that directly or indirectly enhance the quality of life in the outside community (W.-M. Roth, 2011; Thapa, Cohen, Guffey, & Higgins-D'Alessandro, 2013). To be effective in enhancing students' learning—and to be sources of pleasure and success rather than sources of frustration and failure—most complex authentic activities require considerable teacher guidance and support (Hmelo-Silver, Duncan, & Chinn, 2007; Mergendoller, Markham, Ravitz, & Larmer, 2006).

Authentic activities are possibly most beneficial when they promote complex thinking skills—for instance, synthesizing information, forming and testing hypotheses, or solving problems—and when their final outcomes are multifaceted and somewhat unpredictable (Newmann & Wehlage, 1993; S. G. Paris & Turner, 1994). Nevertheless, they should be sufficiently simple that they don't impose an unmanageable cognitive load—in other words, they shouldn't be so complex that students find them overwhelming (Kester, Paas, & van Merriënboer, 2010; Plass, Kalyuga, & Leutner, 2010). The Into the Classroom feature "Conducting Authentic Activities" offers several strategies that researchers and experienced educators have found to be effective.

Into The Classroom

Conducting Authentic Activities

🍎 **Simplify the task sufficiently to be appropriate for students' age levels and cognitive abilities.**

At a school in Seattle, Washington, students in kindergarten and the first and second grades work cooperatively with researchers to monitor dog "poop" along a nature trail in an important watershed area. Once every 2 months, the students and several adult volunteers count and map the various dog deposits they find on the trail and within 7 feet to either side. Midway through the school year, the students place plastic-bag dispensers at various locations near the trail and continue their bimonthly monitoring in order to determine whether the dispensers and bags have any effect. Not only do the students gain an awareness of the harmful effects of pollution on natural resources, but they also gain confidence in their ability to have a positive impact on the health of their local environment.

🍎 **Choose a task that requires students to integrate and apply what they've learned in two or more subject areas.**

A third-grade class creates a "publishing company" that provides a variety of printed materials (announcements, programs, banners, etc.) for activities and performances throughout their school. Students engage in many typical business activities; for instance, they interview for various jobs in the company, make sales calls to solicit business from other classes, design customer order forms, edit and proofread their work, and conduct customer satisfaction surveys.

🍎 **Communicate that there is no single best or right approach or solution for a task.**

A teacher of a high school life skills class gives students a list of prices of many items (meats, fruits, vegetables, milk, etc.) available at the local grocery store. Using the list, the food pyramid, and a budget of $30, students must plan a healthful breakfast, lunch, and dinner for a family of four for one day.

🍎 **Encourage students to experiment with new ideas and strategies.**

A fifth-grade class has been studying a number of common plants and animals indigenous to their area. The students work in groups of two or three to create informational displays about several species for the city museum. Their teacher helps each group brainstorm ideas about how it might effectively portray a particular plant or animal for the general public.

🍎 **Communicate high expectations for students' performance but provide enough scaffolding to ensure students' success.**

All 92 eighth graders at a middle school are required to contribute in a meaningful way to the annual eighth-grade musical. Some students are members of the cast, whereas others are involved in scenery construction, costume design, or lighting. Faculty members supervise each aspect of the project and provide guidance and assistance as needed, but the students are largely responsible for the quality of the production. As students from different social groups work with one another, social barriers and ill feelings between popular and unpopular students begin to break down. By opening night the class has acquired a sense of cohesiveness and overall class spirit, and collectively the students take much pride in their successful production.

Sources: Edelson & Reiser, 2006; Hmelo-Silver et al., 2007; Kester et al., 2010; Kornhaber, Fierros, & Veenema, 2004 (publishing business example); Mergendoller et al., 2006; Newmann & Wehlage, 1993; S. G. Paris & Turner, 1994; Pickens, 2006 (dog poop example); Plass, Kaluyga, & Leutner, 2010; M. Thompson & Grace, 2001 (class play example).

MyEdLab **Self-Check 8.4**

TECHNOLOGICAL INNOVATIONS

Strictly speaking, *technology* includes any humanmade application of scientific knowledge for a practical purpose. But the focus here will be on *digital technologies*—those that enable us to electronically store, manipulate, and transmit information. (The word *digital* refers to the fact that the information is stored in the form of many, many 0s and 1s, collectively known as *bits*.) Computer hardware and software, cell phones, video cameras, video game systems, and the Internet are all examples of digital technologies.

As these technologies have become more widely available and affordable, they've also become more pervasive in modern-day societies. For example, although precise statistics on cell phone usage are virtually impossible to obtain, the majority of middle school and high school students in North America and western Europe appear to have their own cell phones, and many of them are proficient in using their phones not only to make calls but also to send text messages, take and send photographs, and post opinions and photos on social networking sites such as Facebook and Instagram. For most adolescents, the primary motive for using cell phones and other new technologies is to initiate and maintain social relationships, especially with peers (Ito et al., 2009; Valkenburg & Peter, 2009; Warschauer, 2011).

Recent technological innovations have increasingly enabled people around the world to access that *distributed knowledge* of which we spoke earlier. Gone are the days when quick access to important information required people to either (a) effectively store it in their own long-term memories or on personal bookshelves or (b) travel to a public library or other physical source of knowledge about a particular topic. Instead, people can gain needed information about almost any subject area—and sometimes they gain *mis*information—with a few simple keystrokes on an Internet search engine such as Google, Bing, or Yahoo! The overall learning environment of the early 21st century is indeed a very different one from that of the mid-20th century.

TECHNOLOGY IN LEARNING AND INSTRUCTION

When learning takes place in an electronic environment, it's sometimes called e-learning. But regardless of what we call it, the many technologies available in 21st-century societies can enhance learning in numerous ways:

- *Instruction can seamlessly integrate several media and multiple pedagogical strategies.* For example, instructional software programs often integrate written text with graphics, videos, simulations, exercises, and assessments. And *interactive smartboards*—large wall-mounted displays connected to a computer and projector—are increasingly replacing traditional chalkboards and whiteboards. Not only can these boards display the contents of a computer screen— perhaps a video, a set of instructions, or an Internet website—but in addition, class members can electronically write and draw on them, with the products being transmitted to and saved on the computer.

  Even many textbooks (including this one!) take a digital form these days. Digital textbooks might include not only traditional text and graphics but also videos, audio recordings, practice exercises, and links to dictionary and glossary entries. Students can electronically "search" for particular words or concepts, highlight sections of particular interest or importance, and add personal notes related to the content.

- *Instruction itself can be delivered from afar.* For example, students can participate in classroom activities when they must be absent from school for extended periods, perhaps because of a chronic illness or significant injury. Also, students can take courses that aren't available in their local school districts—perhaps Advanced Placement high school courses or college coursework appropriate for their ability levels. Collectively, such forms of instruction are known as distance learning.

- *Instruction can more easily be individualized to accommodate students' unique needs.* For example, Internet-based research projects allow students to pursue topics of personal interest in considerable depth. And software programs known as intelligent tutoring systems help students master knowledge and skills in various content domains—for instance, in reading, math, and science—by giving them ongoing, individually tailored guidance, hints, and feedback as they study new concepts and procedures. When well designed, these software programs can be as effective as one-on-one human tutors in helping students learn (Ma, Adesope, Nesbit, & Liu, 2014; Steenbergen-Hu & Cooper, 2013; VanLehn, 2011; W. Ward et al., 2013).

- *Learners can manipulate data in a variety of ways while also keeping their cognitive load within reasonable limits.* As teachers, we must remember that complex thinking tasks can impose a significant burden on working memory. In line with the notion of *distributed cognition,* digital technologies can carry some of the cognitive burden and free up some working memory capacity for problem solving and creativity. For example, students can use computer spreadsheets and graphing software to explore and examine the effects of different values of x in an algebraic equation. And they can use concept-mapping software such as Kidspiration or MindMapper Jr. for Kids—sometimes called *mind-mapping* programs—to try out various ways of organizing and interrelating new material. Ideally, technology can provide an electronic "playground" in which students can experiment with and expand on ideas (J. A. Langer, 2011; Spiro & DeSchryver, 2009).

- *Diverse bodies of knowledge are within easy reach, especially on the Internet, and can be searched on an as-needed basis.* Most schools in mainstream Western culture have computers with Internet connections located either in individual classrooms or in separate computer resource rooms. Some schools also provide laptops or computer tablets (e.g., iPads) that students can use as individuals or in small groups. Outside of school, many students can find computers at libraries and other public places. And as their cell phones increasingly become multifunction *smartphones,* they can access the Internet wirelessly (i.e., through *wifi*) at libraries, coffee shops, and other wireless "hotspots."

Consider the many ways in which technology might help students think more creatively and resourcefully about complex issues and problems.

You can find examples of intelligent tutoring systems in Chapter 7 and Chapter 12.

- *Teachers and learners can easily communicate and collaborate with one another.* Technology can certainly enhance communication and collaboration within a single classroom. For example, course management systems such as Blackboard and Moodle provide means through which teachers can post materials and assignments, students can upload their work for feedback or evaluation, and all class members can regularly interact through classroom discussion boards or chat rooms. Another good resource is Google Apps for Education, through which schools can create a separate email account for every student, post school and classroom calendars with scheduled activities and due dates, and upload documents to which teachers and students alike can contribute. In addition, teachers and their students can create class-specific *wikis,* websites on which individual class members can add to, edit, or rearrange material previously contributed by other members. Popular wiki-creation websites include wikispaces.com, web.com, and wix.com.

  Thanks to the Internet, individual students or entire classes can also communicate and collaborate with students or classes in other locations—even in other nations (e.g., see iearn. org). One good vehicle for doing so is Skype (skype.com), through which people at two different locations can both see and hear each other on any computer, tablet, or smartphone that has a built-in video camera and microphone.

  Finally, teachers are increasingly communicating and collaborating with *one another* via the Internet. For example, many teachers share lesson plans and other instructional strategies they've found to be effective (e.g., see www.tappedin.org or www.oercommons.org). Some teachers have even written electronic textbooks that other teachers can use and modify for their own purposes (e.g., see ck12.org).

- *Technology offers many means of providing authentic activities.* One strategy mentioned earlier—creating a class wiki—can be a highly authentic activity for students. Other possibilities include creating class newsletters, videos, or video games (e.g., see sploder.com, arisgames. org, or yoyogames.com/studio). Also, students can post their poems and short stories online for people elsewhere to read and critique. And through well-designed simulations, they can design and carry out virtual scientific "experiments" to test their theories about cause-and-effect relationships in the physical world.

- *Some technology-based instructional strategies effectively blur the lines between "work" and "play."* Well-designed technology-based instruction is highly interactive and can keep students motivated and engaged for lengthy periods. Some educators and software developers are now developing challenging video games that electronically immerse students in simulated environments in which they act as, say, tribal chiefs in 4000 BC, 20th-century urban planners, or farmers (e.g., look for online descriptions of *Civilization, SimCity,* and *Harvest Moon,* respectively). In the process of playing these games, students can learn a great deal about history, geography, and other academic content domains (Squire, 2011; Tobias & Fletcher, 2012; Wouters, van Nimwegen, van Oostendorp, & van der Spek, 2013). Also, students can acquire athletic skills and develop physical fitness through hardware and software in which they virtually engage in such activities as dancing, tennis, and baseball—an approach that's sometimes called *exergaming* (Shayne, Fogel, Miltenberger, & Koehler, 2012).

As we incorporate digital technologies and the Internet into instruction, however, we must give students the guidance they need to use these things effectively. Following are general suggestions:

- Don't assume that instruction is better only because it involves technology. Instead, make sure that the technological tools you use *enhance* students' thinking and learning in some way.

- Remember that some students may have had little or no experience with technology. As needed, teach them any basic skills they haven't yet mastered—perhaps how to send an email message; how to conduct a simple Internet search; or how to create, edit, and save a word processing document.

- Structure activities sufficiently that students aren't easily distracted by irrelevant information and activities (e.g., clicking on unproductive links or Internet websites, or going to personal Facebook pages).

Set up Internet websites that foster ongoing classroom communication both in and outside of school.

MyEdLab
Video Example 8.2.

In this technology-based interaction, high school students in Hawaii and New Hampshire learn from one another about the histories of their respective states. The discussion you see here occurs after the students have already communicated via an electronic discussion board. What benefits might students gain from this real-time interaction?

🍎 Teach and insist on appropriate social etiquette for cross-communication, and monitor students' entries for content; especially be on the lookout for bullying and other antisocial messages. (Arnesen, Elstad, Christophersen, & Vavik, 2014; Bellanca & Stirling, 2011; N. Carr, 2011; R. E. Clark, Yates, Early, & Moulton, 2009; Rivers, Chesney, & Coyne, 2011; Warschauer, 2011)

In addition, we must remember that use of the Internet requires literacy skills far beyond those necessary for more traditional reading and writing tasks, as we'll discover in an upcoming section on technological literacy.

> MyEdLab **Self-Check 8.5**

Academic Content Domains as Contexts

In the early millennia of human civilization, cultures and societies focused largely on teaching children knowledge and skills related to basic survival (hunting, growing crops, cooking, etc.), and experts in such areas as woodworking, metalwork, and medicine often taught their knowledge to new generations through one-on-one apprenticeships. But as cultural groups developed writing systems and constructed increasingly complex understandings of their physical, biological, and social worlds, they began to establish formal schools that could more efficiently pass their cultural creations along to future generations. One way in which schools made the ever-expanding knowledge base more manageable for instruction was to subdivide it into various academic disciplines, such as reading, writing, mathematics, science, history, and geography.

To some degree, different academic content domains require different thinking skills. For example, effective reading requires automatic retrieval of the meanings of thousands of words in one's language, whereas mathematical problem solving requires precisely thinking about quantities and flexibly manipulating symbols that represent them. Furthermore, various subject areas may depend more or less heavily on different parts of the brain (Dehaene, 2007; Katzir & Paré-Blagoev, 2006; Norton, Kovelman, & Pettito, 2007; Plumert & Spencer, 2007; Posner & Rothbart, 2007).

In a very real way, then, different content domains are additional *contexts* in which students learn, and strategies for effectively teaching the subject matter can vary significantly from one domain to another. In upcoming sections we'll consider four general content domains: literacy, mathematics, science, and social studies. By no means do these topics cover all of the academic curriculum; for example, physical education, music, and the visual and performing arts are also disciplines in their own rights and enhance children's development and general well-being in many ways (e.g., J. H. Davis, 2008).

In discussing the four domains separately, we authors don't mean to imply that each domain should be consistently taught in isolation from the others. On the contrary, instruction is often more effective when it simultaneously incorporates two or more domains—perhaps teaching reading in conjunction with science or teaching writing in conjunction with history (e.g., Martínez, Bannan-Ritland, Kitsantas, & Baek, 2008; Monte-Sano, 2008). Furthermore, several general principles of learning apply to *all* domains:

🍎 Regularly consider how you might integrate two or more content domains in instruction, perhaps in collaboration with other teachers.

- Learners use the information they receive from various sources to construct their own, unique understandings.
- Learners' interpretations of new information and events are influenced by what they already know and believe about the world.
- With age and development, learners acquire metacognitive strategies and epistemic beliefs that influence their thinking and performance within a domain.
- Learners often gain greater understanding and greater metacognitive sophistication in a domain when they work collaboratively with peers.

Table 8.2 illustrates how each of these principles can be seen in each of the domains we'll consider in this section of the chapter.

COMPARE/CONTRAST

TABLE 8.2 • Applying General Principles of Learning in Different Content Domains				
PRINCIPLE	**LITERACY**	**MATHEMATICS**	**SCIENCE**	**SOCIAL STUDIES**
Constructive processes in learning	Good readers go beyond the information explicitly presented on the page—for instance, by drawing inferences, making predictions, and identifying underlying themes. Effective writing involves more than simply transcribing one's knowledge and beliefs on paper; rather, it involves constructively recasting ideas in such a way that others can more readily understand them.	Beginning with a basic understanding of quantity, numbers, and counting, learners build an increasingly complex and integrated understanding of mathematical concepts and principles.	Learners can better understand and apply scientific ideas and findings when they construct general theories and models that integrate many concepts and principles related to particular topics.	Mastery of history, geography, and related domains involves reading maps and historical documents to construct integrated understandings of cause-and-effect relationships among people, events, and features of the physical environment.
Influence of prior knowledge and beliefs	Learners use what they already know about a topic to help them construct meaning from text, and they write more effectively about topics they know well.	Mathematics is an especially hierarchical discipline in which many advanced concepts and principles build on ideas learned in earlier years.	Learners often construct their own theories about natural phenomena long before they have formal instruction about these phenomena. Such theories sometimes interfere with their ability to learn more scientifically acceptable explanations.	Learners learn social studies more effectively when they can relate historical events and geographical phenomena to their own personal experiences.
Metacognitive strategies and epistemic beliefs	Good readers understand that reading involves active meaning making; they monitor their comprehension and engage in processes that are likely to enhance it (e.g., setting goals and asking questions that they try to answer as they read). Good writers set goals for their writing, consider what their audience is likely to know about a topic, and focus on enhancing organization and clarity as they revise what they've written.	Effective problem solvers monitor their progress toward problem solutions. They also have epistemic beliefs conducive to problem-solving success; for example, they recognize that mathematical procedures make logical sense and know that they may need to try several different approaches before they can obtain reasonable answers.	Learners' beliefs about the nature of science influence how they study and learn science; for example, those who believe that science consists of isolated facts are likely to focus on meaningless memorization. Furthermore, learners' ability to conduct valid experiments is influenced by the extent to which they ask themselves questions about their observations and interpretations (e.g., "Have I confirmed my prediction?").	A true understanding of history involves the recognition that a great deal of historical "knowledge" is interpretive rather than factual. A true understanding of geography involves the recognition that locations of various physical features and human creations are not random—rather, that human settlement and activity patterns are largely a function of local environmental conditions.
Collaboration with peers	Learners more effectively construct meaning from what they read when they discuss reading material with their classmates. They write more effectively when their peers read and critique their work and when they collaborate on writing projects.	Learners gain a better understanding of math when they tutor classmates or younger children. They gain greater metacognitive awareness of their problem-solving strategies—and they may also modify inappropriate ones—when they must explain and justify their reasoning to others.	Learners often revise misconceptions about scientific phenomena and acquire more sophisticated scientific reasoning processes when they jointly wrestle with puzzling findings and critique one another's conclusions.	Learners can more effectively practice advanced reasoning skills (e.g., evaluating and integrating information presented in multiple historical documents) when they work in partnership with peers.

LITERACY

The word *literacy* has two distinct meanings. In its narrower sense, it refers to one's reading and writing abilities. In its broader sense, it refers to one's general ability to understand and communicate meanings using the various concepts and symbols of a particular community of practice—perhaps that of physicists, musicians, or computer programmers. For now we'll be focusing on the narrower sense of the word: reading and writing. But we must remember that success in virtually any academic discipline requires mastery of its discipline-specific concepts and symbols.

Children's reading and writing skills obviously build on their knowledge of spoken language. But in addition, children must learn the relationships between how words sound and are produced in speech, on the one hand, and how they look and are written on paper, on the other. Children must also master nuances of the written symbol system that have no counterparts in spoken language, such as punctuation marks and appropriate uses of uppercase and lowercase letters.

Through storybook reading and other activities at home, many children—but not all of them—come to school knowing a few things about written language. For example, they may know that spoken language is represented in a consistent fashion in writing, that reading proceeds from left to right and from the top of the page to the bottom, and that each alphabet letter is associated with particular sounds in spoken language. They may be able to write part or all of their own names, and they may recognize logos of popular products and commercial establishments, such as Coke and McDonald's. Taken together, such knowledge and skills—collectively known as emergent literacy—lay a basic foundation for reading and writing (A.W. Gottfried, Schlackman, Gottfried, & Boutin-Martinez, 2015; Serpell, Baker, & Sonnenschein, 2005). And reading and writing, in turn, provide important foundations for learning most other academic disciplines, especially in the middle and secondary school grades (E. Fox & Alexander, 2011; Martínez et al., 2008; C. Shanahan, 2004; H. L. Swanson, 2006).

As a topic of formal instruction, reading is taught primarily in elementary school. Writing instruction continues in secondary school language arts classes. Yet effective reading and writing strategies tend to take somewhat different forms in different academic disciplines. For example, reading a textbook in a math class is quite different from reading a newspaper article in a social studies class (recall Jacob's and Howard's conflicting interpretations of a court decision in the opening case study), and writing a short story is quite different from writing a science lab report. As teachers, then, we should teach reading and writing within the context of a variety of content domains—not only in language arts classes but also in math, science, and social studies classes.

Teach literacy skills across the academic curriculum.

THE NATURE OF SKILLED READING

Reading is a multifaceted process that involves considerable knowledge and abilities:

- *Sound and letter recognition:* A large body of research indicates that phonological awareness—hearing distinct sounds, or *phonemes*, within a spoken word (e.g., detecting the sounds "guh," "ay," and "tuh" in the word *gate*)—is an essential element of successful reading, especially in the beginning stages of learning to read. And, of course, learners must be able to recognize alphabet letters in various fonts and in both uppercase and lowercase forms (Anthony & Francis, 2005; Boscardin, Muthén, Francis, & Baker, 2008; Hulme, Bowyer-Crane, Carroll, Duff, & Snowling, 2012).

- *Word decoding skills:* Readers inevitably encounter words they don't recognize. In such instances they must draw on letter–sound relationships, familiar prefixes and root words, common spelling patterns, and context clues to decipher the words (Goswami, 2007; Nagy, Berninger, & Abbott, 2006; Rayner, Foorman, Perfetti, Pesetsky, & Seidenberg, 2001).

- *Automatic word recognition:* When learners must use their limited working memory capacity to decode and interpret *many* individual words, they have little or no mental "room" left to use in gaining an overall understanding of what they're reading. Ultimately, word recognition must become automatic in two ways: Learners must be able to (a) identify most words in a split second, without having to decode them letter by letter; and (b) immediately retrieve the words' meanings (Curtis, 2004; Klauda & Guthrie, 2008; H. L. Swanson & O'Connor, 2009).

- *Meaning construction:* Effective reading is a constructive process: Good readers go far beyond the words themselves, identifying main ideas, drawing inferences, deriving applications, and so on. Sophisticated readers also find symbolism in works of fiction, evaluate the quality of evidence in persuasive essays, and identify assumptions or philosophical perspectives that underlie editorials. Meaning construction can be especially challenging when learners must integrate what they read from two or more distinct texts, as Jacob and Howard must do in the opening case study (Cromley & Azevedo, 2007; E. Fox & Alexander, 2011; Gaskins, Satlow, & Pressley, 2007; Kintsch, 2009).

MyEdLab
Video Example 8.3.
What metacognitive reading strategies are illustrated or described by the teachers in this video?

Teach and scaffold reading skills even in the secondary grades.

- *Metacognitive oversight:* Good readers metacognitively "supervise" their own reading. For example, they set goals regarding what they want to learn, focus attention on parts they deem to be important, and continually self-assess their understanding and memory of what they've read. And ultimately, good readers understand that reading involves actively *making* meaning, rather than mindlessly "absorbing" meaning from the page (Bråten, Britt, Strømsø, & Rouet, 2011; Gaskins et al., 2007; Pressley & Harris, 2006).

It shouldn't surprise you to learn that the amount of knowledge learners already have about a topic enhances their ability to comprehend what they read (Beck, McKeown, Sinatra, & Loxterman, 1991; Britton, Stimson, Stennett, & Gülgöz, 1998). For example, second graders who already know a lot about spiders remember more when they read a passage about spiders, and they can draw inferences more readily than their less knowledgeable classmates (Pearson, Hansen, & Gordon, 1979). Similarly, eighth graders who know more than their peers about a particular period in history can more readily draw inferences from new material about that period (Vidal-Abarca, Martínez, & Gilabert, 2000). Helpful, too, is knowledge about the structures that various types of literature typically follow; for example, the events described in works of fiction usually follow a chronological sequence, and persuasive essays usually begin with a main point and then present evidence to support it (Byrnes, 1996; Cain, Oakhill, & Bryant, 2004; Leon, 2008).

As learners grow older and gain more experience as readers, they become increasingly able to understand what they read, in part because they (a) gain automaticity in word recognition, (b) acquire more effective learning strategies and metacognitive processes, and (c) have a larger knowledge base on which to draw as they read. Table 8.3 lists typical characteristics of readers at different grade levels. Nevertheless, we must keep in mind that students at any single grade level differ widely in their reading skills; for example, some high school students have poor word decoding skills and little ability to make sense of what they read (Curtis, 2004; Felton, 1998; N. Gregg, 2009). As teachers, then, we should nurture students' reading development at *all* grades.

THE NATURE OF SKILLED WRITING

As you might guess, learners who are better readers also tend to be better writers. This correlation is partly due to the fact that general language ability—such as knowledge and effective use of vocabulary and various grammatical structures—provides a foundation for both reading and writing. Furthermore, practice in reading promotes vocabulary development and greater awareness of how words are spelled. And regular reading familiarizes learners with common ways in which fiction and nonfiction texts are structured (De La Paz & McCutchen, 2011; Rayner et al., 2001; T. Shanahan & Tierney, 1990). But effective writing involves additional processes as well:

- *Goal setting:* Good writers determine what they want to accomplish in their writing—perhaps to entertain, describe, report, or persuade—and have a good sense of the audience for whom they're writing (Graham, 2006; Scardamalia & Bereiter, 1986; Sitko, 1998).

- *Identification and organization of relevant knowledge:* Whether they're writing fiction or nonfiction, good writers identify what they already know about a topic and then, if necessary, supplement it with additional research. Typically they also spend a fair amount of time organizing their ideas before they write (Benton, 1997; Berninger, Fuller, & Whitaker, 1996; R. T. Kellogg, 1994).

- *Focus on communication rather than mechanics:* Good writers have typically learned the basic mechanics of writing (handwriting, spelling, punctuation, etc.) to automaticity, thereby leaving "room" in working memory to focus on effectively communicating their intended message (Benton, 1997; Limpo & Alves, 2013). In their initial drafts, skilled writers focus on conveying their ideas in ways that will help readers readily grasp their meaning; for example, they begin with what they think readers are likely to know and systematically lead readers toward better understandings. In other words, good writers engage in knowledge transforming. In contrast, less skilled writers engage in knowledge telling, writing thoughts in the order in which they retrieve them from long-term memory, with little concern for helping readers understand and learn (Bereiter & Scardamalia, 1987; Graham, Harris, & Olinghouse, 2007; McCutchen, 1996). The essays in Figure 8.3 illustrate the difference.

DEVELOPMENTAL TRENDS

TABLE 8.3 • **Typical Reading Skills at Different Grade Levels**			
GRADE LEVEL	**AGE-TYPICAL CHARACTERISTICS**	**EXAMPLE**	**SUGGESTED STRATEGIES**
K–2	• Before school entry, considerable differences in emergent literacy skills; for some students, lack of understanding that true reading involves constructing meaning from text • Increasing knowledge of letters and letter–sound correspondences; increasing ability to hear individual phonemes within words (phonological awareness) • Increasing focus on gaining meaning from text • Beginning of silent reading (around grade 2)	When asked if something she's just read makes sense to her, 6-year-old Marissa replies, "What I read never makes sense. The teacher just gives us books so we can practice reading words—they don't have to make sense."	• Emphasize that written language is intended to communicate ideas and that true reading involves making sense of print; for example, ask students questions about what they've read. • Jointly read a variety of storybooks, including some that tell stories with which students are familiar. • Teach letter–sound correspondences through storybooks, games, rhymes, and enjoyable writing activities. • Have students listen to or read animated multimedia storybooks on a desktop or tablet computer.
3–5	• Growing sight-word vocabulary, leading to greater reading fluency • Increasing ability to draw inferences from text • Increasing ability to learn from nonfiction, but with only limited metacognitive awareness and use of effective learning strategies • Tendency to take things in print at face value, without critically evaluating the content	As 10-year-old Gerrit reads about the Industrial Revolution in his history textbook, he focuses on specific facts. In doing so, he doesn't grasp the big picture—how people's entire way of life changed as a result of technological innovations at the time.	• Encourage students to read for meaning. • Assign well-written trade books (e.g., children's paperback novels) appropriate for students' reading levels. • Provide explicit instruction in how to read textbooks effectively. • Engage students in small-group or whole-class discussions of what they're reading. Focus on interpretation, drawing inferences, and speculation. • For students who continue to struggle with reading, explicitly teach word decoding skills within the context of meaningful reading activities.
6–8	• Automaticity in recognizing most common words • Increasing ability to identify main ideas in text • Emerging ability to go beyond the literal meanings of text • Increasing involvement of metacognitive processes that enhance understanding (e.g., comprehension monitoring)	When 12-year-old Dominic reads Harper Lee's *To Kill a Mockingbird*, he is appalled by the blatantly racist attitudes of some of the characters in the book.	• Assign age-appropriate reading materials in various content domains; provide scaffolding (e.g., questions to answer) to guide students' thinking and learning as they read. • Continue explicit instruction in effective reading strategies, with an emphasis on metacognitive processes (e.g., identifying important information, monitoring comprehension). • Begin to explore classic works of poetry and literature. • Seek the advice and assistance of specialists to help promote the reading skills of low-ability readers.
9–12	• Automaticity in recognizing many abstract and discipline-specific words • Ability to consider multiple viewpoints about a single topic • Some ability to critically evaluate the content of text, but often without all the knowledge and skills necessary to evaluate it appropriately • Considerable individual differences in sophistication of metacognitive reading strategies	For a high school science assignment, 16-year-old Lily searches the Internet for websites about global climate change. The websites she finds present conflicting results: Some stress that climate change is significant and the result of human activity, whereas others reject such claims. Lily knows that the websites can't *all* be right, but she doesn't have the expertise to distinguish between well-controlled research studies and poorly executed ones.	• Expect that many students can learn effectively from textbooks and other reading materials, but continue to scaffold reading assignments, especially for poor readers. • Ask students to read multiple printed and/or Internet sources on a single topic; guide them in their efforts to compare, contrast, and synthesize what they read. • Jointly discuss and interpret classic works of poetry and literature.

Sources: Afflerbach & Cho, 2010; Anthony & Francis, 2005; Chall, 1996; Gaskins et al., 2007 (Marissa example, pp. 196–197); Hulme et al., 2012; Jetton & Dole, 2004; Nagy, Berninger, Abbott, Vaughan, & Vermeulen, 2003; Nokes, Dole, & Hacker, 2007; R. E. Owens, 2008; Pressley & Harris, 2006; Serpell et al., 2005; Slavin, Lake, Chambers, Cheung, & Davis, 2009; Stuebing, Barth, Cirino, Francis, & Fletcher, 2008; van den Broek, Lynch, Naslund, Ievers-Landis, & Verduin, 2003; Verhallen, Bus, & de Jong, 2006.

FIGURE 8.3 Working in small groups, fourth graders wrote these two essays to help younger children learn about electric circuits. Notice how the first group's untitled piece simply presents a series of facts. In contrast, the second group's piece anticipates what young children might and might not already know about circuits, uses language appropriate for young children, and gives a concrete example.

Example of knowledge telling:

Electric circuits are wires that when it's closed electricity flows through and it's circular. A generator is a magnet that spins around in coils. It powers up a city or town. A conductor is what makes electricity. It powers up electrical things.

Example of knowledge transforming:

Electric Circuits They'll Shock You

You have energy inside of you that allows you to walk, run, jump, etc. There's also another source of energy, electrical energy. It lets you turn on your light, run your computer, listen to the radio, and many other things.

But before you experiment let us caution you that electricity can be very dangerous so don't experiment without adult supervision. Here are some safety precautions for when you experiment: Never touch the copper part of a wire. Do NOT leave liquid substances near electrical equipment. Do not open a battery without protection (it contains acid).

Now that you know the rules let me tell you about electricity. When you turn on your light that means you have made a circuit flow, when you turn off the light that means you broke the circuit. How does a light bulb light you ask? Well you have to have a complete circuit. Let all the equipment touch each other. The wires must touch the battery. The battery must touch the light. The light must touch the battery.

If you don't understand how the circuit breaks, here is an example. When you are using the refrigerator, you open it, and all the air comes out. When you are not using the refrigerator, you close it, and the air no longer comes out.

Now that you know about electricity it won't shock you the way it works.

Source: Excerpts from "Children as Thinkers Composing Scientific Explanations" by Marilyn J. Chambliss, paper presented at the annual meeting of the American Educational Research Association, April 1998. Copyright © 1998 by Marilyn J. Chambliss. Reprinted with permission of the author.

- *Revision:* Good writers almost invariably revise what they've written, often several times. Although they certainly look for problems related to spelling and grammar, they focus on enhancing organization and clarity while keeping in mind the overall goals of their writing (De La Paz & McCutchen, 2011; Fitzgerald, 1992; K. R. Harris, Santangelo, & Graham, 2010).

- *Metacognitive regulation of the overall writing effort:* Throughout the writing process, good writers are metacognitively active: They monitor their progress and the effectiveness of what they've written, addressing questions such as these:

  - Am I achieving my goal(s) for writing this piece?
  - Am I following a logical train of thought?
  - Am I giving examples to illustrate my ideas?
  - Am I supporting my opinions with valid arguments?

The answers to such questions influence their subsequent courses of action (Hacker, Keener, & Kircher, 2009; K. R. Harris et al., 2010).

The nature and quality of students' writing evolve in many ways throughout the elementary and secondary school years. In the early elementary grades, writing projects typically involve narratives: Students write about their personal experiences and create short, fictional stories. They have a hard time writing for an imagined audience and, as a result, engage almost exclusively in knowledge telling rather than knowledge transforming. And they're still working on basic skills in spelling, punctuation, and grammar—skills that can consume much or all of their working memory capacity (Graham et al., 2007; Hemphill & Snow, 1996; McCutchen, 1996).

In the upper elementary grades, writing mechanics are becoming automatic, enabling students to devote more effort to communicating their thoughts effectively. Furthermore, students begin to think about how their readers might respond to what they've written and so are more apt to proofread and revise their work. At this point, however, they do little planning before they begin to write, and their writing continues to involve more knowledge telling than knowledge transforming (Graham, 2006; R. E. Owens, 2008).

In the secondary grades, students are better able to analyze and synthesize their thoughts as they write, and thus they're more skillful in writing research papers and argumentative essays. At this point, too, although many students continue to engage in knowledge telling, knowledge transforming becomes more common. And students become more metacognitively involved in the writing process, especially when given instruction and guidance in effective metacognitive writing strategies (Graham & Perin, 2007; K. R. Harris et al., 2010; Spivey, 1997).

PROMOTING READING AND WRITING DEVELOPMENT

Explicit instruction in basic reading skills facilitates reading development, especially for poor readers (e.g., C. M. Connor et al., 2013; Ehri, Dreyer, Flugman, & Gross, 2007; Rayner et al., 2001). To become truly effective readers, students must master the most basic components of reading, such as word recognition, to a level of automaticity—something that comes primarily through practice, practice, practice (Ehri, Nunes, Stahl, & Willows, 2001; Stanovich, 2000). One approach, obviously, is to provide drill-and-practice activities—workbook exercises, flash cards, and the like—but many students find such activities dull and boring (E. H. Hiebert & Raphael, 1996; J. C. Turner, 1995). Better are basic-skills activities that genuinely engage and challenge students. For example, to promote phonological awareness in young children, we might conduct a game of "Twenty Questions" (e.g., "I'm thinking of something in the room that begins with the letter *B*") or ask children to bring something from home that begins with the letter *T*. And to foster greater automaticity in word recognition, we might simply engage students in a variety of authentic reading activities (Ehri, 1998; Share, 1995).

Under no circumstances should we postpone teaching reading comprehension until basic skills are automatic. To do so would be to communicate the message that reading is a meaningless, tedious task, rather than a source of enlightenment and pleasure (Serpell et al., 2005). In an approach known as *whole-language instruction,* some educators have suggested that virtually all basic literacy skills (e.g., knowledge of letter–sound relationships, root words, and common spelling patterns) be taught entirely within the context of reading children's books and other authentic written materials. Whole-language approaches are often quite effective in promoting emergent literacy, such as letter recognition and familiarity with the nature and purposes of books (Purcell-Gates, McIntyre, & Freppon, 1995; Sacks & Mergendoller, 1997; S. A. Stahl & Miller, 1989). On the downside, however, letter–sound relationships and phonological awareness are often short-changed in strictly whole-language instruction (Juel, 1998; Rayner et al., 2001; T. A. Roberts & Meiring, 2006). When working with novice readers, then, we probably need to strike a balance between whole-language and basic-skills activities (Claessens, Engel, & Curran, 2014; Cummins, 2007; Rayner et al., 2001).

Authenticity is important in writing assignments as well. Students write more frequently, and in a more organized and communicative (i.e., knowledge-transforming) manner, when they can write for a real audience—perhaps their classmates or perhaps peers on the Internet—and when they're interested in their topic (Benton, 1997; Garner, 1998; Graham, 2006). For example, Figure 8.4 shows excerpts from a story that 9-year-old Cooper wrote and illustrated in his third-grade class; his teacher had the story's text and artwork bound into a book that Cooper's classmates and family could read.

We must remember, too, that skilled reading and writing are both complex activities that involve considerable scaffolding. Following are examples of what we might do:

Maximize the authenticity of reading and writing tasks, but teach basic skills separately if students might not otherwise master them.

For Reading

- Especially for novice readers, provide multimedia books to which students can listen while reading along.
- Remind students of things they already know about a topic.
- Have students meet in pairs to retell or summarize short sections of what they've just read.
- Have students ask one another teacher-like questions about something they've all read (e.g., "Why do you think Alice did that?" "What do you think the author might talk about in the next section?").
- Provide outlines or graphics that students can use to organize what they're reading.

FIGURE 8.4 Excerpts from 9-year-old Cooper's book "The Boy Who Built an Igloo," created as a project in his third-grade class.

One bright winter morning, a boy went outside to build an igloo. He was so excited! He decided to build the igloo in his front yard. He started with the walls and built them his own height.

He said to himself, "This is going to be an awesome igloo."

🍎 Explicitly teach strategies for comparing, contrasting, and evaluating multiple texts that give competing messages. (Alfassi, 2004; De La Paz, 2005; D. Fuchs, Fuchs, Mathes, & Simmons, 1997; J. T. Guthrie et al., 2004; Hacker, Dunlosky, & Graesser, 2009b; Palincsar & Brown, 1984; Spörer & Brunstein, 2009; Verhallen, Bus, & de Jong, 2006)

For Writing

🍎 Ask students with limited writing skills (especially young children) to dictate rather than write their stories.

🍎 Ask students to set specific goals for their writing, and help them organize their thoughts before beginning to write.

🍎 Help students brainstorm ideas for communicating effectively.

🍎 Provide an explicit structure for students to follow as they write (e.g., for a persuasive essay, ask students to include a main argument, supporting arguments, and rebuttals to possible counterarguments).

🍎 Suggest that children initially focus on communicating clearly and postpone attention to writing mechanics (e.g., spelling, punctuation) until later drafts.

🍎 Provide specific questions that students should ask themselves as they critique their writing (e.g., "Do I follow a logical train of thought?").

🍎 Encourage use of word processing programs, voice recognition software, and other writing software that can support effective writing.

🍎 Have students work in small groups to either (a) critique one another's work or (b) co-write stories and essays. (Benton, 1997; L. K. Clarke, 1988; Ferretti, Lewis, & Andrews-Weckerly, 2009; Graham, McKeown, Kiuhara, & Harris, 2012; Graham & Perin, 2007; K. R. Harris et al., 2010; Larkin, 2008; McLane & McNamee, 1990; Quinlan, 2004; Sitko, 1998)

The "Essay Checklist" presented in Figure 2.8 of Chapter 2 is an example of a structure that can guide students' writing.

The Into the Classroom feature "Promoting Reading and Writing Development" presents concrete examples of effective strategies.

TECHNOLOGICAL LITERACY

Use of digital technologies and the Internet requires literacy knowledge and skills beyond those involved in traditional paper-based reading and writing tasks, including the following:

• *Use of common functions:* Some functions are essential in using a wide variety of computer applications. For example, learners must know how to "open," "cut," "paste," and "save," and how to search for desired information or locations in a document.

• *Use of device-specific operating systems:* Most learners who have cell phones know such basics as how to make a phone call, send a text message, or add a friend's contact information to an

Into The Classroom

Promoting Reading and Writing Development

🍎 **Help students develop phonological awareness.**

A kindergarten teacher suggests to his class, "Let's see how many words we can think of that rhyme with the word *gate*. I'll write the words on the board. Let's see if we can think of at least eight words that rhyme with *gate*."

🍎 **Help students develop automaticity in word recognition and spelling, but do so within the context of authentic reading and writing activities as much as possible.**

A second-grade teacher has several poor readers read Dr. Seuss's *The Cat in the Hat*, a book that repeatedly uses many of the same words (e.g., *cat*, *hat*, *thing*).

🍎 **Give students some choices in what they read and write about.**

A fourth-grade teacher gives students several options of paperback books they might read during their free time, being sure to include books that address students' diverse interests (e.g., animals, mysteries, science fiction).

🍎 **Have students discuss with peers the things they are reading and writing.**

A middle school teacher has students meet in small groups to read aloud the short stories they've written. As each student

reads his or her story, other group members ask questions for clarification and make suggestions about how to make the story better. Later, students revise their stories with their peers' comments in mind.

🍎 **Scaffold students' efforts as they work on increasingly challenging reading and writing tasks.**

A high school English teacher gives students a format to follow when writing a research paper: an introductory paragraph that describes the topic of the paper, at least three different sections within the paper that address different aspects of the topic (each one beginning with a new heading), and a "Conclusion" section that summarizes and integrates the main ideas of the paper.

🍎 **Address reading and writing skills in all areas of the curriculum.**

An eighth-grade social studies teacher gives students an article to read from *Time* magazine. Knowing that the reading level of the article may be challenging for many of her students, she gives them specific questions to answer as they read the article.

Sources: Botelho, Cohen, Leoni, Chow, & Sastri, 2010; Cromley & Azevedo, 2007; Graham et al., 2012; J. T. Guthrie et al., 2004; K. R. Harris et al., 2010; Jetton & Dole, 2004; Monte-Sano, 2008; Reis, McCoach, Little, Muller, & Kaniskan, 2011; Slavin et al., 2009; Stuebing et al., 2008; J. P. Williams, Stafford, Lauer, Hall, & Pollini, 2009.

address book. But to be technologically literate in the 21st century—especially as electronic books (e-books) become increasingly common—learners must also be able to find their way around the various applications of personal computers and tablets.

- *Use of specific computer applications:* For example, word processing software, spreadsheets, and presentation software (e.g., PowerPoint) are now commonplace in many elementary and secondary school classrooms. And various Internet-based communication applications—such as email, chat rooms, discussion boards, and wikis—all involve not only basic reading and writing skills but also application-specific knowledge.

- *Effective search for relevant and credible Internet websites:* Learners must know how to use Internet search engines and identify appropriate keywords to initiate a search. They must be able to determine whether particular Internet websites are relevant or irrelevant to particular tasks and questions. They must critically evaluate each website they find in order to make reasonable judgments about the validity of its content. And they must often pull together what they learn from various sources into an integrated, organized whole.

Perhaps through past experiences with cell phones, video games, or home computers, many students come to school with some of these skills. Yet others don't have the basics—for instance, they may not know how to turn a particular device on and off—and so we must certainly teach them what they don't know. Yet even students who seem to be technologically sophisticated may lack all the cognitive skills they need to *learn* effectively from technology. Learning from Internet websites can be especially problematic for them, for several reasons. First, they may have trouble sorting through the hundreds of sites that an Internet search yields in order to determine which ones are truly relevant to their questions and needs. Second, they may not have the knowledge and skills they need to discriminate between sites that present objective information, on the one hand, and those that convincingly offer biased social or political propaganda, on the other. Third, they may not know how to organize and synthesize the separate bits of information they've found on various sites. Finally, they may not have the self-motivating "stick-to-it-iveness" that lengthy and

🍎 Remember that some students may lack basic skills related to digital technologies.

Some of these skills involve *critical thinking* (see Chapter 7). The final one—stick-to-it-iveness—involves *self-regulation* (see Chapter 10).

occasionally frustrating Internet searches can involve (Afflerbach & Cho, 2010; K. Hartley & Bendixen, 2001; Leu, O'Byrne, Zawilinski, McVerry, & Everett-Cacopardo, 2009; Manning, Lawless, Goldman, & Braasch, 2011).

Clearly, then, students often need considerable scaffolding as they conduct online research about classroom topics, especially with regard to the *metacognitive* strategies they should use in the process. Following are a few suggestions:

> Scaffold students' early research on the Internet, and monitor their explorations to ensure that they don't venture into inappropriate websites and subject matter.

- 🍎 Use a database or search engine that restricts the websites to which students have access (e.g., EBSCO Information Services's "Searchasaurus" search engine).
- 🍎 Provide specific questions students should try to answer as they read.
- 🍎 Also provide questions students should consider in evaluating the credibility of a website's content (e.g., "Does a reputable organization sponsor the website?" "What evidence supports this point of view?").
- 🍎 Give students structured practice in comparing and contrasting websites that present diverse and possibly contradictory perspectives.
- 🍎 Ask students to write summaries of what they've learned from multiple websites, perhaps in collaboration with peers. (Afflerbach & Cho, 2010; P. A. Alexander & the Disciplined Reading and Learning Research Laboratory, 2012; Bromme et al., 2010; Gil, Bråten, Vidal-Abarca, & Strømsø, 2010; Manning et al., 2011; Wiley et al., 2009)

In doing these things, we enhance students' general information literacy—their knowledge and skills related to finding, using, evaluating, organizing, and presenting information acquired from diverse sources.

MATHEMATICS

Mathematics includes several subdomains (e.g., arithmetic, algebra, geometry, statistics) that use various methods for representing and solving quantitative problems. Central to all of them are the following knowledge and skills:

- *Understanding numbers and counting:* Obviously learners must know number words (*one, two, three . . .*), the written symbols that represent them (*1, 2, 3 . . .*), and their correct sequence. In addition, they must understand that, when counting objects, you must count each object once—and only once—until all objects have been included in the count. Learners eventually construct the mental equivalent of a *number line* on which positive whole numbers and then, later, negative whole numbers are spaced at equidistant intervals (see Figure 8.5). Learners must also become able to mentally approximate where fractions and decimals lie along this mental number line. Such understandings provide the basic foundation on which virtually all other mathematical concepts, principles, and procedures rest (Booth & Newton, 2012; Case & Okamoto, 1996; A. R. Edwards, Esmonde, & Wagner, 2011; Gallistel & Gelman, 1992; Göbel, Watson, Lervåg, & Hulme, 2014).

FIGURE 8.5 A genuine understanding of numbers and mathematics requires constructing a mental number line on which all numbers are spaced at equidistant intervals.

- *Understanding central concepts and principles:* For example, learners must master such concepts as *negative number*, *right angle*, and *variable* and such principles as "A negative times a negative equals a positive" and "The three angles of a triangle always equal 180°."

- *Mastering problem-solving procedures:* Many of these procedures are specific algorithms that, when correctly applied, always yield an accurate solution. For example, such is the case for doing long division, multiplying and dividing fractions, and solving for *x* in algebraic equations. But general problem-solving heuristics (e.g., identifying subgoals, drawing diagrams, rounding complex numbers up or down) often come into play as well. To be truly proficient mathematicians, learners can't simply apply such procedures in a rote, meaningless fashion; rather, they must *make sense* of the procedures so that they can use them in appropriate circumstances (Baroody, Eiland, Purpura, & Reid, 2013; Hecht & Vagi, 2010; Rittle-Johnson, Siegler, & Alibali, 2001).

See Chapter 7 for a more detailed discussion of algorithms and heuristics in problem solving.

- *Encoding problems appropriately:* An essential step in solving a problem is to encode it—to think of it as being a certain *kind* of problem and then represent it with relevant mathematical symbols. For example, a learner might identify one problem as requiring simple addition and another as requiring solving for an unknown variable in a quadratic equation. Ideally, learners apply their mathematical knowledge and skills in encoding and solving real-world problems as well as the more traditional word problems they typically encounter in school (De Corte et al., 1996; Geary, 2006).

- *Metacognitive oversight and regulation of problem solving:* Like virtually any other complex cognitive task, successful mathematical problem solving involves metacognitive processes. The learner must set one or more goals for a problem-solving task, monitor the effectiveness of various problem-solving strategies, and carefully scrutinize final solutions to determine whether they're logical ones (M. Carr, 2010; De Corte, Op't Eynde, Depaepe, & Verschaffel, 2010; L. S. Fuchs et al., 2003).

Even as young infants, we human beings seem to have a basic ability to think in terms of quantities and relative proportions, but our systematic ways of counting, measuring, and symbolically manipulating quantities are cultural creations that not all cultural groups share (Halford & Andrews, 2006; McCrink & Wynn, 2007; Saxe & Esmonde, 2005). When children are regularly exposed to numbers and counting, many of them come to school knowing how to count—at least to 10, and often well beyond (Ginsburg, Cannon, Eisenband, & Pappas, 2006). They may also have self-constructed simple procedures for adding and subtracting small quantities of objects. For example, if they want to add three objects to a group of five objects they might begin with *five* and then count the smaller group: "Five, six, seven, eight" (Bermejo, 1996; Siegler & Jenkins, 1989). By and large, however, more sophisticated mathematical knowledge and skills come from formal instruction, especially at school.

Despite ongoing math instruction throughout the elementary and secondary grades, many students seem to have particular difficulty with mathematics as a content domain. To some degree, their difficulty may lie in their limited ability to think about proportions (e.g., decimals, ratios) and abstract concepts removed from everyday reality (e.g., *pi, infinity*) (Byrnes, 1996; Siegler et al., 2012; Tournaire & Pulos, 1985). Encoding problems mathematically can pose an additional challenge, especially if students have learned concepts and procedures only in a rote, meaningless manner (M. Carr, 2010; Clement, 1982; Geary, 2006). For example, students of all ages tend to have trouble encoding relational problems—problems in which only comparative numbers are given—and hence are often unable to solve problems such as this one:

> Laura is 3 times as old as Maria was when Laura was as old as Maria is now. In 2 years Laura will be twice as old as Maria was 2 years ago. Find their present ages. (R. E. Mayer, 1982, p. 202)

Even college students have trouble encoding and solving this problem (R. E. Mayer, 1982). (Laura is 18 and Maria is 12.)

Unfortunately, too, many elementary and secondary school students don't metacognitively reflect on what they're doing as they work on mathematical problems (M. Carr, 2010; Roditi & Steinberg, 2007). To see how metacognitively reflective *you* are when you do math problems, try the next exercise.

EXPERIENCING FIRSTHAND
BUSING THE BAND

Take a minute to solve this problem. Feel free to use a calculator if you have one handy.

> The Riverdale High School marching band is traveling to Hillside High School to perform in the half-time show at Saturday's football game. The school buses owned by the Riverdale School District can transport 32 passengers each. There are 104 students in the Riverdale band. How many buses will the band director need in order to transport the band to Hillside on Saturday?

Is your answer 3.25? If so, think about that for a moment. How is it possible to have 3.25 *buses*? The band director must actually request four buses for Saturday's game. If you fell into our trap, you're not alone. Many students develop the habit of solving word problems based on the numbers alone and overlook the realities with which they're dealing (De Corte et al., 1996).

See Chapter 7 for a more general discussion of epistemic beliefs and their influence on learning.

Compounding the issue is that students are apt to have fairly naive epistemic beliefs about the nature of mathematics. The following misconceptions are common:

- Mathematics is a collection of meaningless procedures that must simply be memorized and recalled as needed.
- Math problems always have one and only one right answer.
- There's only one correct way to solve any particular math problem.
- Mathematical ability is largely a genetically endowed gift: Some people are naturally good at math, whereas others are not. (De Corte et al., 2010; Muis, 2004; Richland, Stigler, & Holyoak, 2012; Schoenfeld, 1988, 1992)

PROMOTING LEARNING IN MATHEMATICS

Unfortunately, many students focus largely on rote memorization of concepts and procedures when they study math (M. Carr, 2010; De Corte et al., 2010). Following are general strategies for promoting more meaningful learning and conceptual understanding:

In Chapter 2 of the e-text, you can see a video example of how a fourth-grade teacher uses manipulatives to help students understand the process of adding fractions that have different denominators.

- When formally introducing addition and subtraction, encourage students to use effective strategies they've already constructed on their own (e.g., counting on fingers), but also foster gradual automaticity for addition and subtraction facts.
- Have students apply fundamental concepts and procedures in working with concrete objects and computer simulations.
- Use a number line to help students understand how whole numbers and fractions relate to one another.
- Occasionally have students play games in which they must use their growing knowledge about numbers—for instance, board games that involve counting spaces along a path or using "money" to buy and sell things.
- Combine problems requiring different strategies (e.g., subtraction, multiplication) into a single practice set.
- Present problems that include irrelevant as well as relevant information.
- Present complex, real-world problems with multiple possible answers; have students work on them in small groups and explain their reasoning to one another.
- Encourage students to use calculators and computers to assist them in solving problems, especially after they've mastered the basic skills and procedures they're now offloading onto technology (e.g., adding a lengthy set of numbers).
- Present worked-out examples to illustrate multistep problem-solving procedures (e.g., solving for x in a quadratic equation).
- Teach and scaffold effective metacognitive processes (e.g., have students ask themselves such questions as "Am I closer to my goal?" and "Does this solution make sense?").
- Have students tutor classmates or younger children in math, thereby encouraging the tutors to elaborate on and better clarify *for themselves* what they've learned. (Carbonneau, Marley, & Selig, 2013; M. Carr, 2010; B. Clarke, Gersten, & Newman-Gonchar, 2010; De Corte et al., 2010; L. S. Fuchs, Fuchs, et al., 2008; Geary, 2006; Greeno et al., 1996; S. Griffin & Case, 1996; J. Hiebert et al., 1996; Inglis & Biemiller, 1997; Lampert, Rittenhouse, & Crumbaugh, 1996; R. E. Mayer, 1999; Ramani, Siegler, & Hitti, 2012; Renkl & Atkinson, 2010; Rittle-Johnson, 2006; Rittle-Johnson & Star, 2009; Roditi & Steinberg, 2007; Rohrer & Pashler, 2010; Sarama & Clements, 2009; Siegler, 1989)

SCIENCE

As a discipline, science has two major goals: to both describe and explain what people observe in nature. At its core is the basic assumption that the world is somewhat predictable—that the phenomena we human beings observe are various manifestations of general patterns and cause-and-effect relationships. Also central is the *scientific method*, which includes a number of more specific cognitive processes with a common element: a conscious intention to both acquire and evaluate new knowledge and explanations.

Key to scientific reasoning are the following:

- *Hypothesis formation and testing:* Scientists begin with tentative conjectures—hypotheses—about the nature of the world, its inhabitants, and the broader universe. Then, to the extent possible, they systematically test their hypotheses by separating and controlling variables that may possibly influence other variables. Good scientists look not only for evidence that confirms a particular hypothesis but also for evidence that might *disconfirm* it.

- *Careful, objective documentation of observations:* Scientists keep careful records of their observations. Ideally, they categorize and/or measure the things they observe in consistent, objective ways.

- *Construction of theories and models:* Scientific inquiry is a very constructive process. Often it involves constructing **theories**—organized bodies of concepts and principles intended to explain certain phenomena. It may also involve constructing **models**—physical or symbolic representations that show how certain entities might be interrelated parts of a larger system. For example, you've probably seen physical models of the sun and planets in our solar system, and you've undoubtedly seen graphic models of various phenomena in textbooks; Figure 8.1 in this chapter is an example.

- *Metacognitive reflection:* Good scientists think not only about the nature of things but also about the nature of *their thinking* about things. For example, they continually ask themselves whether they're being objective in their observations, whether their evidence adequately supports their hypotheses and conclusions, and where there might be holes or inconsistencies in their theories and models (Kuhn & Pearsall, 2000; M. C. Linn & Eylon, 2011; Metz, 2004; B. White, Frederiksen, & Collins, 2009).

- *Advanced epistemic beliefs about the nature of scientific knowledge:* Good scientists understand that theories and models are, at best, incomplete and potentially flawed constructions of reality and that, more generally, scientific understandings must continue to change and evolve as new evidence comes in (Kuhn, 2009; M. C. Linn, Songer, & Eylon, 1996; Wiser & Smith, 2008).

- *Conceptual change when warranted:* Good scientists continually revise their beliefs and understandings as credible new evidence and theories appear on the scene. In general, they keep open minds about the nature of phenomena and cause-and-effect relationships.

If you have previously read Chapter 2, you may have done the "Pendulum Problem" exercise, which requires separating and controlling variables.

In this pencil drawing, 9-year-old Corey portrays his science lab as one in which his teacher prescribes particular steps to follow. Ultimately, however, Corey must come to understand the true *nature* of science—that it comprises an integrated set of concepts, theories, strategies, and other cognitive tools for systematically investigating and explaining the physical, biological, and social worlds in which we live.

Children begin to construct theories about their physical and biological worlds long before they reach school age, but these early, self-constructed theories don't necessarily jibe with contemporary scientific thinking (Goldberg & Thompson-Schill, 2009; Vosniadou, 2008). For example, consider 7-year-old Rob's theory about mountain formation:

> ***Adult:*** How were the mountains made?
>
> ***Rob:*** Some dirt was taken from outside and it was put on the mountain and then mountains were made with it.
>
> ***Adult:*** Who did that?
>
> ***Rob:*** It takes a lot of men to make mountains, there must have been at least four. They gave them the dirt and then they [the mountains] made themselves all alone.
>
> ***Adult:*** But if they wanted to make another mountain?
>
> ***Rob:*** They pull one mountain down and then they could make a prettier one. (Piaget, 1929, p. 348)

Sometimes children's early theories are the results of their day-to-day observations; for example, Rob has probably observed construction workers making visible changes to his local environment. In other instances children's theories emerge from explicit teachings or more implicit worldviews of their cultures. In any case, children rarely come to school as "blank slates" when it comes to science. With formal instruction and informal learning experiences, their scientific knowledge gradually aligns itself with that of the adult scientific community, but misconceptions persist,

See Chapter 6 for more detailed information on children's early theories and common misconceptions.

especially when scientists' explanations are exceptionally abstract or seemingly conflict with children's personal experiences or cultural worldviews.

So, too, do children's scientific reasoning abilities change with age, experience, and formal instruction. For example, elementary school students can often distinguish between experiments that do and don't adequately control variables, yet they're apt to have trouble controlling variables in their *own* experiments—a task that requires them to keep track of several things simultaneously and thus may tax their limited working memory capacity (Barchfeld, Sodian, Thoermer, & Bullock, 2005; Bullock & Ziegler, 1999; Metz, 2004, 2011). Middle school and high school students are better able to separate and control variables than elementary school children, but even they occasionally have trouble doing so. Furthermore, in their hypothesis testing, they tend to focus on and test hypotheses they think are correct and to ignore evidence that contradicts their hypotheses or for some other reason strikes them as implausible. Such *try-to-prove-what-I-already-believe* thinking is known as confirmation bias (Barchfeld et al., 2005; Koslowski, 2012; Kuhn & Franklin, 2006).

As you might guess, students' metacognitive sophistication in scientific thinking also improves with age and instruction (Kuhn, 2009; Kuhn & Franklin, 2006; Sandoval, Sodian, Koerber, & Wong, 2014). For example, students become increasingly aware of the tentativeness of science—an idea clearly evident in this explanation by Giulana, an eighth grader:

> We can say it's true now, but tomorrow another scientist may say "I've found another document that proves something else" and then we'll have two different things and we'll no longer know which is true and which is false. When the atom was discovered, it was considered the smallest particle, but now the quark's been discovered. What we believed before, now we don't believe anymore because the quark is smaller. Perhaps in fifty years' time an even smaller particle will turn up and then we'll be told that what we believed in before was false. It's really something to do with progress. (Mason, 2003, p. 223)

At the same time, good scientific thinkers understand that good theories aren't fly-by-night speculations that have come out of thin air—that, instead, they're based on substantial bodies of evidence (Chinn & Buckland, 2012; Sandoval et al., 2014).

PROMOTING LEARNING IN SCIENCE

Certainly science instruction should introduce students to the many fundamental concepts, principles, and theories the discipline has developed to explain everyday experiences—for instance, why people get sick, why water expands when it freezes, and why (thanks to a solar eclipse) the sky might suddenly turn dark in the middle of the day. But in addition, we must attune students to the dynamic, ever-changing nature of science and foster the reasoning skills that will enable them both to draw appropriate conclusions from others' research findings and to conduct valid research studies themselves. Educated individuals understand that science isn't undisputed fact—that, instead, it simply reflects society's best efforts to make sense of the world—and that almost anyone can make significant contributions to humankind's collective knowledge base.

The Into the Classroom feature "Promoting Mathematical and Scientific Reasoning Skills" presents several general strategies useful in both math and science instruction. Following are additional strategies that researchers have found to be effective in teaching science.

- Ask students to explain their current beliefs and theories about a phenomenon; listen carefully both for elements of truth on which you can build and for unproductive misconceptions that require revision.
- Illustrate relationships among concepts and principles using live demonstrations, physical models, paper-and-pencil diagrams, or computer simulations.
- Present phenomena that are inconsistent with students' current understandings—for example, by showing how a wool blanket (something students associate with warmth) can actually help keep a cold drink cool.
- Have students design and carry out experiments to test various hypotheses about cause-and-effect relationships.
- When experiments with real-world objects and events are impractical or impossible, have students test their hypotheses in computer-simulated environments.

MyEdLab
Video Example 8.4.

Students can develop their emerging science and math skills when, with age-appropriate scaffolding, they conduct their own experiments about self-chosen topics and then report their findings to others. In what ways might the science fair project depicted in this video have helped the girls acquire greater expertise in scientific reasoning? In what ways have the girls also applied certain math skills?

Into The Classroom

Promoting Mathematical and Scientific Reasoning Skills

🍎 **Take students' general cognitive development into account when teaching concepts and principles.**
A fourth-grade teacher asks students to conduct experiments to find out what conditions influence the growth of sunflower seeds. He knows that his students probably have only a limited ability to separate and control variables, so he asks them to study the effects of just two things: the amount of water and the kind of soil. He has the students keep their growing plants on a shelf by the window, where temperature and amount of sunlight will be the same for all the plants.

🍎 **Use concrete manipulatives, analogies, and computer simulations to illustrate abstract ideas.**
A high school physics teacher has learned from experience that even though her students are, in theory, capable of abstract thought, they're still apt to have trouble understanding this principle: *When an object rests on a surface, the object exerts a force on the surface, and the surface also exerts a force on the object.* To illustrate the principle, she places a book on a large spring. The book compresses the spring somewhat, but not completely. "So you see, class," she says, "the book pushes down on the spring, and the spring pushes up on the book. An object compresses even a table or other hard surface on which it rests—not so much that you'd notice—and the surface pushes back in response."

🍎 **Ask students to apply math and science to real-world problems.**
With the help of a local scientist, a fifth-grade class conducts a study of its town's drinking water, taking small samples from various sources, examining the contents under a microscope, tabulating the results, and comparing its findings to recommended safety standards.

🍎 **Pose problems that are relevant to students' local cultures.**
In an inner-city neighborhood where colorful street art is highly valued, a high school math teacher gives small cooperative groups the following problem:

> Your sister loves street art. You would like to re-create one of her favorite pieces for her birthday. You decide to create a

poster board replica of this piece even though you're not an artist. Suddenly a deeper side of the image strikes you.

> This is going to be easy! You notice the tip of his nose at (0,0), the bottom lip (0,–2) . . . Where is his right eye, . . . the bottom of his chin, . . . the large patch of grass? What is the domain and range? Explain your reasoning. Try creating a replica on poster board.

🍎 **Ask students to identify several strategies or hypotheses regarding a particular task or problem and to explain and justify their ideas to one another.**
A middle school math teacher is beginning a unit on how to divide numbers by fractions. After students convene in small groups, she says, "You've already learned how to multiply one fraction by another. For example, you've learned that when you multiply $\frac{1}{3}$ by $\frac{1}{2}$, you get $\frac{1}{6}$. But now imagine that you want to *divide* $\frac{1}{3}$ by $\frac{1}{2}$. Do you think you'll get a number smaller than $\frac{1}{3}$ or larger than $\frac{1}{3}$? And what kind of number might you get? Discuss these questions within your groups. In a few minutes we'll all get back together to talk about the ideas you've come up with."

🍎 **Foster metacognitive strategies that students can use to regulate their experimentation and problem solving.**
When a high school science teacher has students conduct lab experiments, he always has them keep three questions in mind as they work: (a) As I test the effects of one variable, am I controlling for possible effects of other variables? (b) Am I seeing anything that supports my hypothesis? (c) Am I seeing anything that contradicts my hypothesis?

🍎 **Have students use mathematics and scientific methods in other content domains.**
A junior high school social studies teacher asks students to work in small groups to conduct experiments regarding the effects of smiling on other people's behavior. As the groups design their experiments, he reminds them about the importance of separating and controlling variables, and he insists that each group identify an objective means of measuring the specific behavior or behaviors that it intends to study. Later, he has the groups tabulate their results and report their findings to the rest of the class.

Sources: Boxerman, 2009; D. E. Brown & Clement, 1989 (book-on-spring example); M. Carr, 2010; Clement, 2008; De Corte et al., 2010; Graesser, McNamara, & VanLehn, 2005; Kuhn & Dean, 2005; Lampert et al., 1996; Lehrer & Schauble, 2006; M. C. Linn & Eylon, 2011; L. E. Matthews, Jones, & Parker, 2013, p. 136 (street art example); Metz, 2011; Morra, Gobbo, Marini, & Sheese, 2008; Sandoval et al., 2014; Sarama & Clements, 2009; Singer, Marx, Krajcik, & Chambers, 2000; C. L. Smith, 2007; Snir, Smith, & Raz, 2003.

🍎 Scaffold students' efforts to separate and control variables and to draw appropriate conclusions. For example, ask questions that focus their attention on critical aspects of what they're observing and nudge their thinking in appropriate directions.

🍎 Engage students in small-group or whole-class discussions in which they propose and try to justify various explanations for empirical findings.

🍎 Explicitly draw students' attention to results that contradict their predictions and expectations; ask students to explain and in other ways make sense of those results. (Boxerman, 2009; Chinn & Buckland, 2012; D. B. Clark, 2006; Clement, 2008; Eberbach & Crowley, 2009; Furtak, Seidel, Iverson, & Briggs, 2012; M. C. Linn & Eylon, 2011; Lorch et al., 2014; R. E. Mayer, 2008; Metz, 2011; Sandoval et al., 2014; Snir, Smith, & Raz, 2003; Zohar & Aharon-Kraversky, 2005)

Chapter 6 describes additional strategies for promoting conceptual change.

Such strategies not only help students gain new understandings about their physical and biological worlds but can also help them revise certain *mis*understandings. In other words, such strategies can promote conceptual change.

SOCIAL STUDIES

The term *social studies* encompasses content domains concerned with the nature of human societies and social relationships, both past and present. Our focus here will be on two domains that are especially prominent in elementary and secondary school curricula: history and geography.

THE NATURE OF HISTORICAL KNOWLEDGE AND THINKING

At its core, history is very much a socioculturally transmitted body of knowledge. Furthermore, as the opening case study illustrates, different cultural groups are likely to put their own spins on history, portraying past events in ways that are consistent with their beliefs and worldviews. For example, in the United States, European American students tend to view U.S. history as being guided by principles of freedom and democracy, whereas African American students are more likely to view it as being marked by racism and violations of basic human rights (T. Epstein, 2000; T. Epstein & Shiller, 2009). Such diverse interpretations are almost certainly the result of how various people and media in one's cultural group and larger society have described historical events (J. M. Hughes, Bigler, & Levy, 2007; Levstik, 2011; Porat, 2004; vanSledright & Limón, 2006).

A solid mastery of history, both as a body of knowledge and as an academic discipline, requires several abilities and processes:

- *Comprehending the nature of historical time:* Constructing legitimate understandings of history requires an abstract comprehension of the lengthy time span across which human events may have occurred—a time span far beyond any individual's personal experience.

- *Perspective taking:* Truly making sense of history requires recognizing that even highly influential and respected people (e.g., George Washington, Winston Churchill, Martin Luther King, Jr.) weren't perfect: They had their own foibles and fallibilities, and they made mistakes. Furthermore, historical figures lived in particular cultural and social contexts that profoundly influenced their thoughts and actions. Good historians try to put themselves in historical figures' shoes—to perceive events as those individuals might reasonably have perceived them (P. Lee & Ashby, 2001).

- *Drawing inferences from historical documents:* History textbooks often describe historical events in a matter-of-fact manner, communicating the message that "This is what happened." In reality, however, historians often don't know exactly how particular events unfolded. Instead, they construct reasonable interpretations of events after looking at a variety of historical documents that might offer conflicting accounts of what transpired (Leinhardt, Beck, & Stainton, 1994; Paxton, 1999; vanSledright & Limón, 2006).

- *Identifying possible cause-and-effect relationships among events:* Mastery of history includes not only knowledge and interpretations of events but also a sense of how some events—perhaps certain political decisions, religious movements, or economic downturns—may have directly or indirectly led to *other* events (van Drie, van Boxtel, & van der Linden, 2006).

- *Evaluating the credibility of various documents and interpretations:* Some historical documents are reasonably objective and accurate accounts of historical events and trends; government census records from past decades are an example. But many other documents—newspaper articles, personal diaries, and the like—reflect the opinions and biases of their authors. Competent historians take such biases into account when drawing their conclusions about events, but they also understand—metacognitively—that their own and others' interpretations aren't necessarily the best or only ones (Paxton, 1999; van Drie et al., 2006; vanSledright & Limón, 2006).

By and large, such abilities and processes require a fair amount of abstract thinking, and so learners acquire them only gradually over the course of development. For instance, in the early elementary grades, children tend to have little understanding of historical time and of the complexity of historical changes (Barton & Levstik, 1996; Ormrod, Jackson, Kirby, Davis, & Benson, 1999). They might refer to events that happened "a long, long time ago" or "in the old days" but have virtually no conception of the time span in question. And they tend to lump historical events into two general categories: those that happened very recently and those that happened many years ago. Not until about fifth grade do students show a reasonable ability to sequence historical events and to attach them to particular time periods (Barton & Levstik, 1996).

Other abstract notions continue to challenge students even in adolescence. Many high school students struggle with the ideas that history involves perspectives as well as facts and that historical figures may have been influenced by social and cultural factors very different from their own. And without explicit instruction and guidance, they have trouble effectively reconciling conflicting data that various historical accounts yield (Levstik, 2011; Nokes et al., 2007; S. A. Stahl & Shanahan, 2004).

THE NATURE OF GEOGRAPHICAL KNOWLEDGE AND THINKING

The discipline of geography is concerned not only with where various natural features and cultural groups are located but also with why and how they got there. For example, geographers study how rivers and mountain ranges end up where they do, why people are more likely to settle in some locations than in others, and how people in various locations make their livings and interact with one another.

The following abilities are key elements of knowledge and thinking in geography:

- *Understanding maps as symbolic representations:* An essential cognitive tool in geography is, of course, the *map*. Learners must understand that maps symbolically depict spatial relationships among various physical and/or humanmade features in a given geographic area. They must also understand that different maps are drawn to different scales, reflecting various ratios between graphic representations and reality.

- *Identifying interrelationships among people and their environments:* For example, skilled geographers recognize that people tend to migrate from places with limited or decreasing resources to places with more plentiful resources. And people are more likely to settle in areas that are easily accessible by water or land—perhaps those along navigable rivers or near major roadways.

- *Acknowledging cultural differences and their implications for human behavior patterns:* Geographers are acutely aware of how cultural beliefs and practices can have widespread influences on people's behavior. For example, a group's beliefs about forbidden foods can put limitations on the crops and livestock being raised. And the Chinese concept of *feng shui* directs some individuals to locate and orient buildings in ways that effectively align with certain spiritual forces.

Learners' facility in interpreting and using maps depends in part on the sociocultural context in which they've been raised. Maps are commonplace in some cultures, nonexistent in others. Even in a society that uses maps extensively, children have varying degrees of experience with geography and maps. For instance, children whose families travel quite a bit tend to have greater appreciation of distance, more familiarity with diverse landscapes, and a better understanding of how maps are used (Liben & Myers, 2007; Trawick-Smith, 2003).

When children in the early elementary grades look at large-scale maps—perhaps those depicting a state or country—they tend to take what they see somewhat literally. For example, they may think that lines separating states and countries are actually painted on the earth or that an airport denoted by a picture of an airplane has only one plane. Young children also have trouble maintaining a sense of scale and proportion when interpreting maps. For example, they might deny that a road could actually be a road because "it's not fat enough for two cars to go on" or insist that a mountain depicted on a three-dimensional relief map can't possibly be a mountain because "it's not high enough" (Liben & Myers, 2007, p. 202). As children get older, and especially as they reach adolescence, they become more proficient in dealing with the symbolic and proportional nature of maps (Forbes, Ormrod, Bernardi, Taylor, & Jackson, 1999; Liben & Myers, 2007; L. J. Myers & Liben, 2008).

Despite their growing proficiency with maps, children and adolescents alike tend to have somewhat narrow epistemic beliefs about geography as a discipline. Typically, they conceive of geography as being little more than the names and locations of various countries, capital cities, rivers, mountain ranges, and so on—perhaps, in part, because teachers often present geography

Into The Classroom

Enhancing Learning in History and Geography

🍎 **Help students organize and integrate the things they are learning.**

During a unit on ancient civilizations (e.g., Mesopotamia, Egypt, Greece, Rome), a middle school social studies teacher has students mark the location of each civilization on a map of the Eastern Hemisphere. She also has them develop a timeline that depicts the rise and fall of various civilizations.

🍎 **Ask students to draw inferences from maps and historical documents and to support their inferences with evidence.**

A high school geography teacher displays a map showing European countries and their capital cities. "Notice how almost all of the capital cities are located either by seaports or on major rivers," he points out. "Why do you suppose that is?"

🍎 **Identify cause-and-effect relationships.**

A high school history teacher asks students to consider the questions, "Why was Pearl Harbor such an important location to control?" and "What effects did the Japanese bombing of Pearl Harbor have on the course and final outcome of World War II?"

🍎 **Encourage empathy for people from diverse cultures and different time periods.**

A third-grade teacher encourages students to imagine themselves as Native Americans who are seeing Europeans for the first time. "You see some strange-looking men sail to shore on big boats—boats much larger than the canoes your own people use. As the men get out of their boats and approach your village, you see that they have very light skin; in fact, it's almost white. Furthermore, some of them have yellow hair and blue eyes. 'Strange colors for hair and eyes,' you think to yourself. How might you feel as these people approach you?"

🍎 **Scaffold productive metacognitive processes.**

An eighth-grade history teacher has students read several historical documents related to European Americans' westward expansion in North America during the 1800s. The teacher gives students some questions to consider as they read and compare the documents—for example, "What was each author's purpose?" "Do you find evidence of bias?" "Is an event described differently in different documents?"

🍎 **Have students tackle challenging tasks in pairs or small groups.**

Students in an advanced high school history class work in pairs to (1) read multiple documents related to a historical event and then (2) write an essay evaluating the trustworthiness of the documents and defending a particular narrative about the event itself.

Sources: Brophy et al., 2009; Davison, 2011; De La Paz, 2005, p. 145 (westward expansion example); Enyedy, 2005; M. Gregg & Leinhardt, 1994b; J. M. Hughes et al., 2007; Liben & Downs, 1989a; Monte-Sano, 2008; Nokes et al., 2007; S. A. Stahl & Shanahan, 2004; van Drie et al., 2006; Wolfe & Goldman, 2005; E. A. Yeager et al., 1997.

this way (Bochenhauer, 1990; Peck & Herriot, 2015; vanSledright & Limón, 2006). Even in the high school years, students rarely reflect on why various locations have the physical features they do or on how the economic and cultural practices of various social groups might be partly the result of their physical environments.

PROMOTING LEARNING IN SOCIAL STUDIES

The Into the Classroom feature "Enhancing Learning in History and Geography" presents several general strategies for teaching these two disciplines. Following are more specific instructional strategies to keep in mind:

For History

🍎 In the early elementary grades, focus instruction on students' own personal histories and on events that have occurred locally and in the recent past.

🍎 In the upper elementary grades, introduce students to primary historical sources, such as diaries, letters, and newspaper articles.

🍎 In the middle school and secondary grades, have students read multiple accounts of significant historical events and then draw conclusions both about what *definitely* happened and about what *might* have happened.

🍎 Have "journalists" (two or three students) role-play interviewing people (other students) who "participated" in various ways in a historical event.

🍎 Role-play family discussions and decision making during critical times (e.g., British soldiers demand to be housed in American colonists' homes, or a 14-year-old son wants to enlist and go off to war).

🍎 Have students write fictional diary or journal entries from the perspective of a particular time period or historical figure.

Figure 3.4 in Chapter 3 presents a student's fictional journal entries written from the perspective of a slave owner in the pre–Civil War United States.

Ask students to consider how things might have been different if certain events had *not* taken place. (Afflerbach, VanSledright, & Dromsky, 2003; Brophy & Alleman, 1996; Brophy et al., 2009; Byrnes, 1996; Leinhardt et al., 1994)

For Geography

Have students create maps of their school building or local neighborhood (e.g., see Figure 8.6).

Provide explicit instruction in common map symbols (e.g., compass rose, special dots designating capital cities, contour lines depicting elevation).

In the upper elementary or middle school grades, introduce the concept of *scale* in maps (e.g., 1 inch per mile, 1 centimeter per 10 kilometers).

Emphasize the complex, dynamic interrelationships among the earth's physical features and human activity (e.g., why towns and roads were constructed in particular locations).

Teach students how to use age-appropriate mapping websites and software (e.g., Google Earth). (Brophy et al., 2009; Egbert, 2009; Enyedy, 2005; M. Gregg & Leinhardt, 1994a; Liben & Downs, 1989a, 1989b; National Geographic Education Project, 1994)

For Social Studies in General

Focus on key principles—*big ideas*—that underlie social studies (e.g., basic human needs and motives, adaptation, interdependence, globalization).

Relate concepts and principles to students' everyday experiences.

Avoid characterizing individuals and groups as simplistic, one-dimensional figures, and vigorously combat stereotypes of any particular group in history or the modern-day world.

Assign works of fiction that realistically depict people living in particular times and places.

Engage students in authentic activities related to what they're learning (e.g., creating a museum display, analyzing political attack ads on television). (Brayboy & Searle, 2007; Brophy et al., 2009; A. Collins, Hawkins, & Carver, 1991; M. McDevitt & Chaffee, 1998; NCSS, 1994; Olsen, 1995)

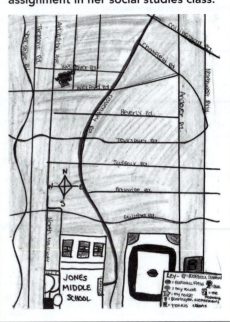

FIGURE 8.6 Twelve-year-old Mary Lynn constructed this local map for an assignment in her social studies class.

TAKING STUDENT DIVERSITY INTO ACCOUNT

As we teach reading and writing, we must remember that students will have had varying experiences with literacy at home. For example, the lives of some students may have been filled with storybooks and bedtime reading, whereas the lives of others may have involved more oral storytelling. Especially in the primary grades, then, we must not assume that children have mastered alphabet letters and other basics of written language. In addition, some children's families speak a language other than English at home, and other children's families speak a dialect of English quite different from the Standard English that's typically used in classrooms. Effective reading and writing instruction—and, in fact, literate activities in any content domain—takes such backgrounds into account (Janzen, 2008; Klingner & Vaughn, 2004; Serpell et al., 2005).

When teaching math and science, we must keep in mind that these two disciplines have, historically, been considered largely "male" domains. Even in this 21st century, the boys in our classes are, on average, more likely to believe they can be successful in these areas; this tends to be the case even though there are no substantial gender differences in *ability* in math and science (Herbert & Stipek, 2005; Leaper & Friedman, 2007; Wigfield, Byrnes, & Eccles, 2006). We must regularly convey the message that both content domains are important for girls as well as boys. We should also use instructional strategies that encourage males and females alike to become actively involved in talking about, applying, and mastering math and science; for instance, such strategies might involve hands-on activities and small-group discussions.

Traditionally, too, females have been given short shrift in history—as have most minority groups—in the sense that history textbooks tend to focus largely on the activities and

Address any missing emergent literacy skills within the context of engaging activities, such as alphabet games and high-interest storybook reading. Encourage students to write in their native dialect in appropriate contexts, such as in poems and short stories.

Chapter 4 describes the nature of dialects and Standard English; it also summarizes research regarding gender differences in various content domains.

Take extra steps to motivate and encourage females to achieve in math and science, and include the important roles of women and minority groups in history lessons.

Remember that students' differing cultural backgrounds and early experiences may influence their understanding of both history and geography.

accomplishments of European American males (Berkin, Crocco, & Winslow, 2009; Levstik, 2011). Accordingly, we may often need to supplement texts with materials that paint a more inclusive picture of our multicultural heritage. Furthermore, we must remember that students' meaning-making in social studies will, in part, be a function of the cultures in which they've been raised and the early family experiences they've had. For example, students with Japanese ancestry are likely to have a very different perspective on President Harry Truman's decision to bomb Hiroshima than students with European ancestry. And, of course, some students have had little or no experience with diverse cultural environments and far-away places. A friend of one of us authors once took students from a lower-income, inner-city Denver neighborhood on a field trip to the Rocky Mountains. Even though these children had seen the Rockies many times from downtown Denver, on seeing them up close for the first time some of them were amazed at how big they were. And a few of them were surprised to discover that the white stuff on the mountaintops was snow!

ACCOMMODATING STUDENTS WITH SPECIAL NEEDS

Many students with special needs have difficulties with reading and writing. The majority of poor readers—whether they've been identified as having a learning disability, attention-deficit hyperactivity disorder (ADHD), or some other disability—appear to have a significant deficit in phonological awareness: They have trouble hearing the individual sounds in words and connecting those sounds with letters. A few poor readers have other cognitive processing deficits; for example, they may have greater-than-average difficulty retrieving words and word meanings based on what they see on the page. In extreme forms, such reading difficulties are known as dyslexia, a disability that often has biological roots (Goswami, 2007; Shaywitz, Mody, & Shaywitz, 2006; Snowling, Gallagher, & Frith, 2003; Stanovich, 2000; Wimmer, Landerl, & Frith, 1999).

Chronic difficulties with literacy can have wide-ranging effects, not only for success in other academic disciplines but also for self-esteem. Tom, a second grader, describes his feelings when first trying to learn how to read in first grade:

> I falt like a losr. Like nobad likde me. I was afrad then kais wod tec me. Becacz I wased larning wale . . . I dan not whet to raed. I whoe whte to troe a book it my mom. (*I felt like a loser. Like nobody liked me. I was afraid that kids would tease me. Because I wasn't learning well ... I did not want to read. I would want to throw a book at my mom.*) (Knapp, 1995, p. 9)

Help students with disabilities find joy in literacy activities—ideally with authentic reading and writing activities.

To minimize the academic and psychological damage, we should address students' reading and writing deficits as early as possible, ideally with deliberate and intensive training in both basic skills (e.g., letter recognition, phonological awareness) and more complex processes (e.g., metacognitive skills in reading, composition skills in writing) (e.g., Elbro & Petersen, 2004; N. Gregg, 2009; Meltzer, 2007; Vadasy, Sanders, & Peyton, 2006). In addition, students with chronic literacy difficulties must find *joy* in reading and writing. For example, one especially popular series of paperback novels, Rick Riordan's "Percy Jackson and the Olympians," features a boy with dyslexia and ADHD whose disabilities actually work in his favor in his adventures with various godlike characters based on ancient Greek mythology.

Chapter 5 identifies specific categories of special needs that fall within the five general categories listed in Table 8.4.

Students' exceptional difficulties with academic subject matter aren't necessarily limited to reading and writing; for instance, some students with learning disabilities continuously struggle with basic concepts and procedures in mathematics (Geary, Hoard, Nugent, & Bailey, 2012; A. J. Wilson & Dehaene, 2007). When working with students who have special educational needs, then, we must typically make accommodations throughout the school curriculum, as the suggestions in Table 8.4 illustrate.

MyEdLab **Self-Check 8.6**

MyEdLab **Application Exercise 8.3.** In this exercise, you can integrate what you have learned about literacy and various content domains as you observe classroom activities in math, history, and science.

STUDENTS IN INCLUSIVE SETTINGS

TABLE 8.4 • Facilitating Learning in Various Content Domains for Students with Special Educational Needs

CATEGORY	CHARACTERISTICS YOU MIGHT OBSERVE	SUGGESTED STRATEGIES
Students with specific cognitive or academic difficulties	• Difficulties in word recognition and reading comprehension, often as a result of poor phonological awareness • Difficulties in handwriting and spelling; possible difficulties in composition skills as well • Less proficiency in learning from the Internet, due to poor literacy skills • Tendency to focus on mechanics (rather than meaning) when revising written work • Greater-than-average difficulty learning and remembering basic facts in math, science, and social studies	• Explicitly teach sound–print relationships. • Assign engaging reading materials that are appropriate for students' reading skills. • Provide extra scaffolding for paper-based and electronic reading assignments (e.g., shorten assignments, identify main ideas, have students look for answers to specific questions). • Provide extra scaffolding for writing activities (e.g., ask students to set goals for their writing, give students a specific structure to follow as they write, encourage use of word processing programs with grammar and spell checkers). • Use concrete manipulatives to teach math and science. • Use mnemonics to help students remember basic facts.
Students with social or behavioral problems	• Less motivation to achieve academic success in some or all content domains • For some students, achievement two or more years below grade level in one or more content domains	• Have students read and write about topics of personal interest. • Ask students to apply math, science, and social studies to situations relevant to their own lives. (Also use strategies listed for students with specific cognitive or academic difficulties.)
Students with general delays in cognitive and social functioning	• Delayed language development, with resulting delays in literacy skills • Smaller-than-average knowledge base to which new information can be related • Difficulty remembering basic facts • Lack of learning strategies such as rehearsal or organization • Reasoning abilities characteristic of younger children (e.g., inability to think abstractly in the secondary grades)	• Minimize reliance on reading materials as a way of presenting new information. • Provide experiences that help students learn the basic knowledge and skills that other students may have already learned on their own. • Have students conduct simple scientific experiments in which they need to consider only one or two variables at a time. (Also use strategies listed for students with specific cognitive or academic difficulties.)
Students with physical or sensory challenges	• Less advanced reading and writing skills, especially if students have hearing loss • Less awareness of the conventions of written language, especially if students have visual impairments • Fewer outside experiences and less general world knowledge upon which instruction in math, science, and social studies can build	• Locate Braille or audio texts for students with visual impairments; also encourage use of text-to-speech software. • When students have difficulty with motor coordination, allow them to dictate their stories and compositions. • Conduct demonstrations and experiments to illustrate basic scientific concepts and principles. • Use drama and role-playing to illustrate historical events. • If students have limited vision, enlarge images on a computer screen; if they are blind, use three-dimensional relief maps and embellish two-dimensional maps with dried glue or nail polish.
Students with advanced cognitive development	• Development of reading at an early age • Advanced reading comprehension skills • More sophisticated writing abilities • Greater ability to construct abstract and integrated understandings	• Provide challenging tasks (e.g., higher-level reading assignments, more advanced writing assignments). • Form study groups in which students can pursue advanced topics in particular domains.

Sources: Bassett et al., 1996; Beike & Zentall, 2012; Curtis, 2004; De La Paz & McCutchen, 2011; Ferretti, MacArthur, & Dowdy, 2000; Garner, 1998; Geary et al., 2012; N. Gregg, 2009; Hallenbeck, 1996; Hulme & Joshi, 1998; Mastropieri & Scruggs, 1992, 2000; Page-Voth & Graham, 1999; Piirto, 1999; Rayner et al., 2001; Salend & Hofstetter, 1996; Sampson, Szabo, Falk-Ross, Foote, & Linder, 2007; H. L. Swanson, Cooney, & O'Shaughnessy, 1998; Tompkins & McGee, 1986; Turnbull, Turnbull, & Wehmeyer, 2010; D. K. Wood, Frank, & Wacker, 1998.

8 What Have You Learned?

Let's now return to the chapter's learning outcomes as a way of reviewing and summarizing the chapter's discussions of various contexts for learning.

■ **8.1: Describe five basic assumptions underlying contextual theories of learning, and apply these assumptions to classroom practice.** Thinking and learning always take

(Continued)

place within certain contexts; in particular, they're inextricably intertwined with the learner's physical body, immediate physical and social environment, and broader culture and society. Taken as a whole, contextual theories rest on at least five assumptions. First, the brain functions in close conjunction with the rest of the body—for instance, with one's sensory systems, overt physical actions, and general bodily well-being. Second, acquired knowledge and skills are often linked to, or *situated* in, specific activities and environments. Third, learners frequently think and perform more effectively when they can offload, or *distribute,* some of their cognitive burden onto physical objects, symbolic systems, or other people. Fourth, learners are sometimes more effective when they collaborate with other people in thinking and learning tasks; such collaborative efforts can take place either at a single point in time or sequentially over a lengthy period. And fifth, learners benefit greatly from the collective wisdom of their culture and society.

■ **8.2: Contrast the benefits of expert–novice interactions with the benefits of peer interactions; explain how you might enhance students' learning through both kinds of interactions.** Learners gain many benefits from the guidance of teachers and other more advanced individuals. Such individuals can *mediate* new experiences for learners, helping them attach meaningful concepts, principles, and other productive interpretations to what they see and hear. These individuals also introduce learners to new cognitive and metacognitive strategies and scaffold learners' efforts to use them effectively.

Interactions with peers have a different set of advantages. For example, when equal-ability learners collaboratively discuss and apply new subject matter, they must clarify, organize, and elaborate on what they've learned sufficiently that they can explain it to others. Furthermore, when they encounter conflicting ideas coming from peers, they may reexamine their own perspectives and possibly revise their views to achieve more accurate and complete understandings. And active discussions of classroom subject matter provide a means through which learners can observe and acquire more advanced ways of thinking and more sophisticated views of the nature of knowledge.

One instructional strategy gaining research support is creating a *community of learners*—a classroom in which teachers and students collaborate to build a body of knowledge about a topic and help one another learn about it. In such a context, face-to-face and online interactions and feedback are common, as are collective efforts at meaning-making.

■ **8.3: Explain how learners' cultural backgrounds can influence their interpretations of new information and experiences; also explain how learners can effectively begin to participate in one or more communities of practice.** Any long-standing social group has a *culture,* which includes behaviors and beliefs that older, more experienced group members pass along to newer members. A learner's culture influences the ways in which the learner thinks about and interprets virtually any new situation. From day-to-day experiences and interactions within the culture, the learner acquires general schemas and scripts regarding what things are typically like and how common activities typically unfold. In addition, a culture passes along certain worldviews—all-encompassing sets of beliefs and assumptions about the very nature of reality and human existence. Occasionally students from certain cultural backgrounds may not have the schemas and scripts they need to effectively make sense of classroom material; at other times students may hold certain worldviews that are inconsistent with scientific theories or that distort their understandings of historical events.

Cultures typically include *communities of practice*—groups of people who share common interests and goals (e.g., making sick people well, conducting research about certain topics, or creating works of art) and regularly interact and coordinate their efforts in pursuit of those interests and goals. In general, people best gain competence in a community of learners by actively participating in it, usually at the fringe of an activity at first and then gradually becoming more centrally involved as competence increases.

■ **8.4: Describe key elements of society that impact learning, and explain how authentic activities can enhance learners' performance in their out-of-school lives.** A *society* is a very large, enduring social group that has fairly explicit social and economic structures, as well as collective institutions and activities. Any society influences learning in a number of ways—for instance, through the resources it provides, the activities it supports, and the general messages it communicates. Furthermore, different members of society have different areas of expertise, and so its members must rely on one another for their individual and collective success.

One critical way of preparing students for their eventual participation in adult society is engaging them in *authentic activities*—those that resemble tasks in the outside world. For example, authentic activities may involve solving complex, real-world problems, working on multifaceted projects, or engaging in community service. Such activities foster meaningful learning of classroom subject matter and increase the odds that students will eventually apply what they've learned to future tasks and problems outside of school.

■ **8.5: Describe the unique roles that digital technologies and the Internet can play in classroom instruction.** Recent technological advancements (especially those based on digital technologies) offer many benefits for instructional practice. They enable seamless integration of multiple media and pedagogical strategies into instruction, which can be simultaneously delivered to students in distant locations and individualized for different students' unique abilities and needs. Also, appropriately designed and scaffolded software can provide mechanisms through which students can manipulate complex data sets and bodies of information without being overwhelmed by the cognitive load. Furthermore, the Internet puts information about many topics within easy reach and allows teachers and students to communicate and collaborate easily and frequently. Finally, some technology-based instructional programs simulate real-world or fantasy environments that engage students in highly motivating learning and problem-solving tasks.

■ **8.6: Apply your knowledge of learning, cognition, and effective instructional practices to various academic content domains.** Different content domains involve somewhat different kinds of knowledge; for instance, reading and writing involve knowledge related to verbal language, whereas mathematics involves knowledge related to counting and measurement. The various domains also require different kinds of thinking and reasoning skills; for instance, scientific investigations require forming hypotheses and testing them through careful separation and control of variables, whereas historical research involves critically evaluating and comparing potentially biased accounts of events and then constructing defensible explanations of what may have transpired.

The chapter offers many strategies for teaching reading, writing, math, science, and social studies; underlying a good number of them are some common themes. First, we must scaffold students' efforts to construct reasonable meanings from various sources—for instance, from textbooks, Internet websites, historical documents, and maps. Second, we must help students acquire metacognitive processes and epistemic beliefs that will enhance their competencies in various content areas. For example, students must learn how to set goals and monitor their progress in reading, writing, and mathematical problem solving, and they must come to understand that science and social studies are evolving disciplines in which theories (and sometimes even basic "facts") may continue to change as new evidence comes in. And third, we can often help students acquire more sophisticated understandings, reasoning processes, and metacognitive skills by having them work collaboratively with peers to tackle complex issues and tasks.

Practice for Your Licensure Exam

The Birth of a Nation

Ms. Jackson has asked her second graders to write an answer to this question: *The land we live on has been here for a very long time, but the United States has been a country for only a little more than 200 years. How did the United States become a country?* Following are some of the children's responses:

> *Meg:* The United States began around two hundred years ago. The dinosors hav ben around for six taosine years ago. Christfer klumbis salde the May flowr.

> *Sue:* The pilgrums we're sailing to some place and a stome came and pushed them off track and they landed we're Amaraca is now and made friends with the indens and coled that spot AMARACA!

> *Matt:* It all staredid in eginggind they had a wore. Thein they mad a bet howevery wone the wore got a ney country. Called the united states of amarica and amaricins wone the wore. So they got a new country.

> *Lisa:* We wone the saver wore. It was a wore for fradam and labrt. One cind of labraty is tho stashow of labrt. We got the stashew of labraty from england. Crastaver calbes daskaved Amaraca.

1. **Constructed-response question:**

   Despite the many misspellings, the children have clearly learned some things about written language. Identify at least three aspects of written language that most or all of the students appear to have mastered.

2. **Multiple-choice question:**

   Which one of the following pairs of word spellings best reflects possible difficulty with *phonological awareness*, especially with regard to consonants?

   a. Meg spells *sailed* as "salde" and *flower* as "flowr."

   b. Sue spells *Pilgrims* as "pilgrums" and *called* as "coled."

   c. Matt spells *started* as "staredid" and *war* as "wore."

   d. Lisa spells *civil* as "saver" and *discovered* as "daskaved."

3. **Multiple-choice question:**

   Which one of the following statements best characterizes the content of these writing samples?

   a. The children have set clear goals for their writing efforts.

   b. The children appear to have a good sense of the audience for whom they're writing.

   c. The children are engaging in knowledge telling rather than knowledge transforming.

   d. The children have pulled together what they have learned about American history into coherent understandings.

MyEdLab **Licensure Exam 8.1**

PRAXIS Go to Appendix C, "Matching Book Content and Ebook Activities to the Praxis Principles of Learning and Teaching Tests," to discover sections of this chapter that may be especially applicable to the Praxis tests.

Monashee Frantz/Glow Images

9

Behaviorist Views of Learning

Learning Outcomes

9.1 Describe five basic assumptions underlying behaviorist views of learning, and apply these assumptions to classroom practices.

9.2 Explain how learners can acquire involuntary responses through classical conditioning and how you might help a student overcome classically conditioned emotional responses that interfere with classroom performance.

9.3 Describe the effects that various kinds of consequences can have on behavior.

9.4 Apply behaviorist principles to encourage productive student behaviors and discourage undesirable ones.

9.5 Accommodate students' personal and cultural backgrounds and special needs in your application of behaviorist principles.

CASE STUDY: THE ATTENTION GETTER

James is the sixth child in a family of nine children. He likes many things; for instance, he likes rock music, comic books, basketball, and strawberry ice cream. But more than anything else, James likes attention.

James is a skillful attention getter. He gets his teacher's attention by making outrageous remarks in class, throwing paper airplanes across the room, and refusing to turn in assignments. He gets his classmates' attention by teasing them, poking them, and writing obscenities on restroom walls. And by the middle of the school year, James's antics are regularly earning him trips to the school office, where he gets the assistant principal's attention at least once a week.

- Why might James be choosing inappropriate behaviors, rather than more productive ones, in order to get attention? What general principle of learning might explain his behavior?

As you consider James's situation, think back to your own experiences as a student in elementary and secondary school. Which students received the most attention: those who behaved well or those who behaved poorly? Chances are, your teachers and classmates paid the most attention to *mis*behaving students (Landrum & Kauffman, 2006; J. C. Taylor & Romanczyk, 1994). James has undoubtedly learned that if he wants to be noticed—if he wants to stand out in a crowd—he must behave in ways that are hard to ignore.

Throughout our lives we learn many, many new behaviors. In this chapter we'll examine a theoretical perspective known as behaviorism, which focuses on how people's immediate environments bring about changes in their behavior. We'll also use behaviorist ideas to understand how, as teachers, we can help students acquire behaviors that are more complex, productive, or prosocial than the ones they exhibit when they first enter our classrooms.

Basic Assumptions of Behaviorism

When psychologists first began systematically studying human learning and behavior in the late 1880s, much of their work involved asking people to "look" inside their heads and describe what they were mentally doing (e.g., Ebbinghaus, 1885/1913; Galton, 1880; James, 1890). But beginning in the early 1900s, some psychologists criticized this approach as being subjective and scientifically unsound. In their minds, the human mind was a *black box* that couldn't be opened for inspection. Instead, these psychologists began to focus on two things that could be observed and objectively measured: local conditions and events—that is, environmental stimuli (sometimes abbreviated as S)—and learners' behaviors, or responses (sometimes abbreviated as R). This focus gave rise to the behaviorist movement, which dominated much of psychology in the middle decades of the 20th century, especially in North America.

In later decades, psychologists became increasingly inventive in their efforts to study thinking processes with scientific rigor, and many left the behaviorist approach behind for more cognitively oriented approaches. Nevertheless, behaviorism is still very much alive and well, in large part because behaviorist concepts and principles can be quite useful in helping people of all ages acquire productive behaviors in classrooms and other settings. It's important, then, that we teachers include behaviorist principles and strategies among the cognitive tools we use in our approaches to instruction and classroom management.

Underlying the behaviorist perspective are several key assumptions.

- *People's behaviors are largely the result of their experiences with stimuli in their immediate environments.* Many early behaviorists suggested that, with the exception of a few simple reflexes, a person is born as a "blank slate" (or in Latin, *tabula rasa*), with no inherited tendency to behave one way or another. Over the years the environment "writes" on this slate, slowly molding, or conditioning, the person into someone who has unique characteristics and ways of behaving.

As we have learned from other theoretical perspectives—especially cognitive, neuropsychological, and contextual views—children's behaviors and achievements depend to some extent on genetically driven neurological changes and are also heavily influenced by the general culture(s) and society in which the children are growing up. Yet children's specific past and present environments can have significant impacts as well. We teachers can often use this basic principle to our advantage: By changing students' classroom environments, we may also be able to change their behaviors for the better.

- *Learning involves a behavior change.* Whereas most contemporary psychologists think of *learning* as a mental phenomenon, many behaviorists think of it as a behavior change—in particular, learning is a *change in behavior as a result of experience.* Such a view of learning can often be useful in the classroom. Consider this scenario:

  > Your students look at you attentively as you explain a difficult concept. When you finish, you ask, "Any questions?" You look around the room, and not a single hand is raised. "Good," you think, "everyone understands."

  But *do* your students understand? On the basis of what you've just observed, you really have no idea whether they do or don't. Only observable behavior changes—perhaps an improvement in achievement test scores, a greater frequency of independent reading, or a decline in off-task behaviors—can ultimately tell us that learning has occurred.

- *Learning involves forming associations among stimuli and responses.* By and large, behaviorist principles focus on relationships among observable events. For example, the opening case study illustrates one important behaviorist principle: People are likely to learn and exhibit behaviors that bring about certain kinds of consequences. In particular, James has formed an association between his own disruptive behaviors *(responses)* and attention from other people (which is an environmental *stimulus* for James).

  If we were to take a strict black-box perspective here, we wouldn't concern ourselves with what's going on inside James's head at all. But in recent decades, it has become increasingly evident, even to behaviorists, just how difficult it is to omit thinking from explanations of learning and behavior. Accordingly, some behaviorists incorporate cognitive processes and other internal phenomena into their theoretical explanations. As you read this chapter, you'll find that we authors occasionally allude to internal phenomena in our discussion of behaviorist principles. In doing so, we're revealing our own biases as cognitively oriented psychologists, and some pure behaviorists might object.

- *Learning is most likely to take place when stimuli and responses occur close together in time.* When two events occur at more or less the same time—perhaps two stimuli are presented together, or perhaps a certain response is immediately followed by a certain stimulus—there is contiguity between them. The following examples illustrate contiguity:

  - One of your instructors (Professor X) scowls at you as she hands back an exam she has just corrected. You discover that you've gotten a D– on the exam, and your entire body tenses up. The next time Professor X scowls at you, that same bodily tension returns.

  - Another instructor (Professor Y) calls on you every time you raise your hand. Although you're fairly quiet in your other classes, you find yourself raising your hand and speaking up more frequently in this one.

  In the first situation, Professor X's scowl and the D– on your exam are presented more or less simultaneously. Here we see contiguity between two stimuli. In the second situation, your hand-raising response is followed immediately by Professor Y's request for your input. In this case we see contiguity between a response and a subsequent stimulus (although calling on you is a response that Professor Y makes, it's a *stimulus* for *you*). In both situations a behavior has changed: You've begun to tighten your muscles every time one instructor scowls, and you've learned to raise your hand and speak up more often in another instructor's class.

In contrast, the more cognitively oriented definition of learning presented in Chapter 6 and in the book's glossary is this one: "a long-term change in mental representations or associations as a result of experience."

PRINCIPLES/ASSUMPTIONS

TABLE 9.1 • Basic Assumptions of Behaviorism and Their Educational Implications

ASSUMPTION	EDUCATIONAL IMPLICATION	EXAMPLE
Influence of the environment	Create a classroom environment that encourages and supports desirable student behaviors.	When a student consistently has trouble working independently, quietly praise her every time she completes an assignment without having to be prompted.
Learning as a behavior change	Conclude that learning has occurred only when students exhibit a change in classroom performance.	Regularly assess students' knowledge and skills in various content domains, and look for ongoing progress in what they know and can do.
Focus on observable events (stimuli and responses)	Identify specific stimuli—including your own actions as a teacher—that may be influencing students' behaviors, either for better or for worse.	If a student frequently engages in disruptive classroom behavior, consider whether you might be encouraging such behavior by giving him attention every time he misbehaves.
Contiguity of events	If you want students to associate two events (stimuli, responses, or stimulus and response), make sure those events occur close together in time.	Include enjoyable yet educational activities in each day's schedule as a way of helping students associate school subject matter with pleasurable feelings.
Similarity of learning principles across species	Remember that research with nonhuman species often has relevance for classroom practice.	Reinforce a hyperactive student for sitting quietly for successively longer time periods—a *shaping* process based on early research studies with rats and pigeons.

- *Many species, including human beings, learn in similar ways.* Many behaviorist principles have been derived from research with nonhuman animals. For instance, as you'll see in a moment, our knowledge about classical conditioning first emerged from Ivan Pavlov's early work with dogs. And another well-known behaviorist, B. F. Skinner, worked almost exclusively with rats and pigeons. Students in our own educational psychology classes sometimes resent having human learning compared to that of laboratory rats. But, in fact, behaviorist principles developed from the study of nonhuman animals are often quite helpful in explaining human behavior.

Table 9.1 summarizes the five assumptions just described and draws general implications for classroom practice.

MyEdLab Self-Check 9.1

Building on Existing Stimulus–Response Associations: Classical Conditioning

Consider this situation:

> Alan has always loved baseball. But while he was up at bat in a game last year, he was badly hurt by a wild pitch. Now, although he still plays baseball, he gets anxious whenever it's his turn at bat, to the point that his heart rate increases and he often backs away from the ball instead of swinging at it.

One possible explanation of Alan's behavior is classical conditioning, a theory that explains how we sometimes learn new responses as a result of two stimuli being presented at approximately the same time. Alan experienced two stimuli—an oncoming baseball and its painful impact—almost simultaneously. The ways in which Alan now responds to a pitched ball—his physiological reactions and his backing away—are ones he didn't exhibit before his painful experience with the baseball. Thus, learning has occurred.

Classical conditioning was first described by Ivan Pavlov (e.g., 1927), a Russian physiologist who was conducting research about salivation. Pavlov often used dogs in his research projects and presented meat to get them to salivate. He noticed that the dogs frequently began to salivate as soon as they heard the lab assistant coming down the hall, even though they couldn't yet smell the meat that the assistant was bringing. Curious about this phenomenon, Pavlov conducted an experiment to examine more systematically how a dog might learn to salivate in response to a new stimulus. His experiment went something like this:

> Pavlov first flashes a light and sees that the dog doesn't salivate. Using the letters S for stimulus and R for response, we can symbolize Pavlov's first observation like this:
>
> S (light) ➔ R (none)
>
> Pavlov flashes the light a second time and presents meat immediately afterward. He repeats this procedure several more times, and the dog always salivates. The dog is demonstrating something it already knows how to do—salivate to meat—and hasn't yet learned anything new. We can symbolize Pavlov's second observation like so:
>
> S (light) ⎤
>   ⎥ ➔ R (salivation)
> S (meat) ⎦
>
> After a sequence of such light-and-meat pairings, Pavlov flashes only the light, with no meat within range of sight or smell. The dog salivates once again—in other words, it has *learned* a new response to the light stimulus. We can symbolize Pavlov's third observation this way:
>
> S (light) ➔ R (salivation)

In more general terms, classical conditioning proceeds as follows:

1. It begins with a stimulus–response association that already exists—in other words, an *unconditioned* S–R association. Pavlov's dog salivates automatically whenever it smells meat, and Alan becomes upset and backs away whenever he encounters an object that causes him pain. When a stimulus already leads to a particular response in the situation at hand, we say that an **unconditioned stimulus (UCS)** elicits an **unconditioned response (UCR)**.[1] The unconditioned response is typically an automatic, involuntary one over which the learner has little or no control.

2. Conditioning occurs when a **neutral stimulus**—one that doesn't elicit any particular response—is presented immediately before the unconditioned stimulus. In the case of Pavlov's dog, a light is presented immediately before the meat. In the case of Alan, a baseball is pitched immediately before the painful impact. Conditioning is especially likely to occur when both stimuli are presented together on several occasions and when the neutral stimulus occurs *only* when the unconditioned stimulus is about to follow (R. R. Miller & Barnet, 1993; Rachlin, 1991; Rescorla, 1967). Sometimes one pairing is enough, especially if the unconditioned stimulus is a very painful or frightening one.

3. Before long, the new stimulus also elicits a response—usually one that's very similar to the unconditioned response. At this point the neutral stimulus has become a **conditioned stimulus (CS)**, and the response to it has become a **conditioned response (CR)**. For example, Pavlov's dog acquires a conditioned response of salivation to a new, conditioned stimulus—the light. Likewise, Alan acquires conditioned responses of increased heart rate and backing away—both of which reflect *anxiety*—to a pitched baseball. Like the unconditioned response, the conditioned response is an involuntary one: It occurs automatically every time the conditioned stimulus is presented.

---

[1] In discussions of classical conditioning, behaviorists often use the word *elicit* (meaning "draw forth or bring out"), as we do here. The word conveys the idea that learners have little or no control over their classically conditioned responses. Also, you should note that the UCS–UCR association as described here could involve either a biologically built-in reflex or a connection that has been acquired earlier in the learner's life. Some behaviorists make the distinction between the two circumstances, referring to the latter form of classical conditioning as *higher-order conditioning*.

CLASSICAL CONDITIONING OF INVOLUNTARY EMOTIONAL RESPONSES

Classical conditioning can help us understand how people learn a variety of involuntary responses, especially responses associated with physiological processes, emotions, and other relatively "thoughtless" aspects of human functioning (e.g., Mineka & Zinbarg, 2006; J. B. Watson & Rayner, 1920). Following are three examples of how unpleasant emotional responses might be learned through classical conditioning. Notice that in each case two stimuli are presented together: One stimulus already elicits a response, and the second stimulus begins to elicit a similar response as a result of the pairing.

- Bryson falls into a swimming pool and almost drowns. A year later, when his mother takes him to the local recreation center for a swimming lesson, he cries hysterically as she tries to drag him to the side of the pool.

  UCS: inability to breathe   ➔   UCR: fear of asphyxiation
  CS: swimming pool   ➔   CR: fear of the pool

- Bobby misses a month of school because of illness. When he returns to school, he doesn't know how to do the long division problems his teacher is now assigning. After a number of frustrating experiences with the assignments, he begins to feel anxious whenever he encounters a division task.

  UCS: failure/frustration   ➔   UCR: anxiety in response to failure
  CS: long division   ➔   CR: anxiety about long division

- Beth's teacher catches her writing a note to a friend during class. The teacher reads the note to the entire class, revealing some very personal, private information that embarrasses her. Beth now feels extremely uncomfortable whenever she goes into that teacher's classroom.

  UCS: humiliation   ➔   UCR: embarrassment in response to humiliation
  CS: teacher/classroom ➔   CR: emotional discomfort in response to teacher/classroom

As teachers, we should create a classroom environment in which stimuli—including our own behaviors—are likely to elicit such pleasant responses as enjoyment or excitement, *not* fear or anxiety. When students associate school with pleasurable circumstances, they soon learn that school is a place they want to be. But when they encounter unpleasant stimuli in school—perhaps public humiliation or constant frustration and failure—they may eventually learn to fear or dislike a particular activity, subject area, teacher, or school in general.

> Create a classroom atmosphere in which students feel physically and psychologically safe and secure.

COMMON PHENOMENA IN CLASSICAL CONDITIONING

Two common phenomena in classical conditioning are generalization and extinction. As you'll discover later in the chapter, variations of these phenomena occur in instrumental conditioning as well.

GENERALIZATION

When people acquire a conditioned response to a new stimulus, they may respond in the same way to similar stimuli—a phenomenon known as generalization. For example, a boy who learns to feel anxious about long division problems may generalize the anxiety response to other kinds of math problems. And a girl who experiences humiliation in one classroom may generalize her feelings of embarrassment to other classrooms as well. Thus, we see a second reason that students should associate pleasant feelings with school subject matter: Students' reactions to a particular topic, activity, or context may generalize—that is, they may *transfer*—to other topics, activities, or contexts.

EXTINCTION

Pavlov discovered that conditioned responses don't necessarily last forever. By pairing a light with meat, he conditioned a dog to salivate to the light alone. But later, when he repeatedly flashed the light without following it with meat, the dog salivated less and less. Eventually, the dog no longer

MyEdLab
Video Example 9.1.

In the activity depicted in this video, students are examining environmental conditions that can affect the well-being of earthworms. What aspects of the activity might elicit pleasurable feelings?

salivated to the light flash. When a conditioned stimulus occurs repeatedly *in the absence of* the unconditioned stimulus—for example, when math is never again associated with failure or when a teacher is never again associated with humiliation—the conditioned response may decrease and eventually disappear. In other words, **extinction** can occur.

Many conditioned responses do fade over time. Unfortunately, many others do not. A child's fear of water or anxiety about math can persist for years. One reason that fears and anxieties persist is that learners tend to avoid situations that elicit negative emotional reactions. But if they stay away from a stimulus that makes them fearful, they never have a chance to experience the stimulus in the absence of the unconditioned stimulus with which it was originally paired. As a result, they have no opportunity to learn to be *un*afraid—no opportunity for the response to undergo extinction.

ADDRESSING COUNTERPRODUCTIVE EMOTIONAL RESPONSES

As teachers, how can we weaken conditioned responses that interfere with students' learning and performance? One effective way to extinguish a negative emotional reaction to a particular conditioned stimulus is to introduce the stimulus *slowly and gradually* while a student is happy, relaxed, or in some other way feeling good (M. C. Jones, 1924; Ricciardi, Luiselli, & Camare, 2006; Wolpe & Plaud, 1997). For example, if Bryson is afraid of water, we might begin his swimming lessons someplace where he feels at ease—perhaps on dry land or in a wading pool—and move to a deeper pool only as he begins to feel more comfortable. And if Bobby gets overly anxious every time he encounters a math problem, we might revert to very easy problems—those he can readily solve— and gradually increase the difficulty of his assignments only as he demonstrates greater competence and self-confidence.

There's nothing like success to help students feel good about being at school. One way to promote student success is to structure the classroom environment so that appropriate behaviors lead to desirable consequences and inappropriate behaviors do not, as we'll see in the next section.

> When a particular subject matter or task arouses anxiety, present it slowly and gradually while the learner is happy and relaxed.

MyEdLab **Self-Check 9.2**

MyEdLab **Application Exercise 9.1.** In this exercise, you can apply what you are learning about classical conditioning to a classroom scenario.

Learning from Consequences: Instrumental Conditioning

Mark is a student in Ms. Ferguson's geography class. Let's look at what happens to him during the first week in October:

- *Monday:* Ms. Ferguson asks students where Colombia is. Mark knows that Colombia is at the northern tip of South America. He sits smiling, with his hands in his lap, hoping to be called on. Instead, Ms. Ferguson calls on another student.

- *Tuesday:* Ms. Ferguson asks the class where Colombia got its name. Mark reasonably guesses that it was named after Christopher Columbus, so he raises his hand a few inches. Ms. Ferguson calls on another student.

- *Wednesday:* Ms. Ferguson asks the class why Colombia's official language is Spanish rather than, say, English or French. Mark knows that Colombians speak Spanish because many of the country's early European settlers came from Spain. He raises his hand high in the air. Ms. Ferguson calls on another student.

- *Thursday:* Ms. Ferguson asks the class why Colombia grows coffee but Canada doesn't. Mark knows that coffee can grow only in certain climates. He raises his hand high and waves it wildly back and forth. Ms. Ferguson calls on him.

- *Friday:* Whenever Ms. Ferguson asks a question Mark can answer, he raises his hand high and waves it wildly about.

Several of Mark's behaviors bring no results. But waving his hand wildly brings Mark the outcome he wants—a chance to speak in class—and so it increases in frequency.

When learners' behaviors either increase or decrease as a result of the consequences those behaviors bring about, instrumental conditioning is at work. Consequences that *increase* the behaviors they follow are reinforcers, and the act of following a particular response with a reinforcer is known as reinforcement. Conversely, consequences that *decrease* the behaviors they follow constitute punishment. Both reinforcers and punishments are environmental *stimuli* that influence behavior.

In his research with animals, one highly influential early behaviorist, B. F. Skinner, found consistent evidence that reinforcers increased the behaviors they followed but little evidence for the influence of punishing consequences (e.g., B. F. Skinner, 1938, 1953, 1954). Skinner used the term operant conditioning to refer to reinforcement-based learning—a term that essentially captures the *increase-in-behavior* half of our instrumental conditioning definition—and many behaviorists continue to use that term today. However, many other behaviorists have found that punishment can, under certain conditions, be quite effective in reducing inappropriate behaviors. Accordingly, we'll use the more inclusive term *instrumental conditioning* in the rest of the chapter.

Notice that we've defined both *reinforcer* and *punishment* in terms of their effects on behavior, rather than in terms of their relative pleasantness and desirability. Sometimes people engage in certain behaviors in order to get consequences that most of us would think of as unpleasant—consequences that we certainly wouldn't think of as "rewards." As an example, let's return to the opening case study. When James throws objects, makes outrageous comments, and pokes classmates, we can assume that his teacher is probably frowning at or scolding him, which we don't usually think of as desirable outcomes. Yet those consequences are leading to an increase in James's misbehaviors; thus, they're apparently reinforcing for him. Other people's attention, regardless of the form it might take, can be highly reinforcing for some students and often serves to maintain counterproductive classroom behaviors (McGinnis, Houchins-Juárez, McDaniel, & Kennedy, 2010; M. M. Mueller, Nkosi, & Hine, 2011; N. M. Rodriguez, Thompson, & Baynham, 2010).

Punishment, too, seems to be in the eye of the beholder. For example, some seemingly very desirable forms of attention, such as teacher praise, can be a must-to-avoid—and hence are actually punishment—for adolescents who don't want their peers to think of them as a "goodie-two-shoes" or teacher's pet (Burnett, 2001; Pfiffner, Rosen, & O'Leary, 1985).

CONTRASTING CLASSICAL CONDITIONING AND INSTRUMENTAL CONDITIONING

Classical conditioning and instrumental conditioning both involve stimuli and responses. But instrumental conditioning is different from classical conditioning in two important ways:

- *The response is voluntary rather than involuntary.* In classical conditioning, the response is involuntary: When a particular (conditioned) stimulus is present, the response usually follows automatically, with little choice on the learner's part. In instrumental conditioning, however, the response is typically voluntary: The learner can control whether or not to make it. For example, in the opening case study, James can choose whether to make inappropriate comments, toss paper airplanes, or tease classmates; nothing in his classroom environment is forcing him to do these things.

  The voluntary nature of responses in instrumental conditioning is an important one for teachers to keep in mind. In order for such conditioning to occur, *learners must first make a response.* Many educational applications of behaviorist principles, then, involve getting students physically and actively engaged in working with academic subject matter.

- *Learning occurs as a result of a stimulus that comes after—rather than before—the response.* Classical conditioning results from the pairing of two stimuli, one (the UCS) that initially elicits a response and another (the CS) that begins to elicit the same or a similar response. Thus, these two stimuli automatically *evoke* certain responses. In instrumental conditioning, however, the learner makes the first move, and an environmental stimulus (either a reinforcer or punishment) follows. Typically there's a contingency between the response and the consequence: The consequence almost always follows the response and seldom occurs when the response hasn't been made. For example, a teacher who praises students only when they

Get students physically and actively engaged in working with classroom topics.

behave appropriately is making reinforcement contingent on desired behavior. In contrast, a teacher who laughs at the antics of a chronically misbehaving student is providing reinforcement even when an acceptable response hasn't occurred; as a result, the student's behavior is unlikely to improve.

Don't confuse *contingency* with the term *contiguity* introduced near the beginning of the chapter. Contingency involves an if-this-happens-then-that-happens relationship. In contrast, contiguity simply involves two things happening at about the same time. Effective instrumental conditioning usually involves contiguity as well as contingency; that is, the consequence occurs almost immediately after the response (J. A. Kulik & Kulik, 1988; Rachlin, 1991). The immediacy of reinforcement or punishment after a response is especially important when working with young children. It's less critical for older children and adolescents, who are better able to make a mental connection between what they do *now* with what happens to them *later* (more on this point shortly).

THE VARIOUS FORMS THAT REINFORCEMENT CAN TAKE

Reinforcers come in all shapes and sizes, and different ones are effective for different individuals. We explore a few possibilities in the following exercise.

EXPERIENCING FIRSTHAND
WHAT WOULD IT TAKE?

1. Imagine that one of your instructors asks you if you'd be willing to spend an hour after class tutoring two classmates who are having trouble understanding course material. You have no other commitments for that hour, but you'd really like to spend the time at a nearby coffee shop where several friends are having lunch. What would it take for you to spend the hour tutoring your classmates instead of joining your friends? Would you do it to gain your instructor's approval? Would you do it for a tasty sandwich? How about if your instructor gave you $5? Would you do it simply because it made you feel good to be helping someone else? Write down a consequence—perhaps one we've just listed or perhaps a different one altogether—that would persuade you to help your classmates instead of meeting your friends.

2. A few weeks later, your instructor asks you to spend the weekend (8 hours a day on both Saturday and Sunday) tutoring the same two struggling classmates. What would it take this time to convince you to do the job? Would the instructor's approval do the trick? A couple of good sandwiches? Five dollars? Five *thousand* dollars? Or would your internal sense of satisfaction be enough? Once again, write down what it would take for you to agree to help your classmates.

There are no right or wrong answers to this exercise. Different people would agree to tutor classmates for different reasons. But you were probably able to identify at least one consequence in each situation that would entice you to give up your free time to help others.

PRIMARY VERSUS SECONDARY REINFORCERS

Some reinforcers, such as a sandwich, are **primary reinforcers**, because they address a basic, built-in biological or psychological need. Food, water, sources of warmth, and oxygen are all primary reinforcers. To some extent, physical affection and cuddling seem to address built-in needs as well, and for an adolescent addicted to an illegal substance, the next "fix" is a primary reinforcer (Harlow & Zimmerman, 1959; Lejuez, Schaal, & O'Donnell, 1998; Vollmer & Hackenberg, 2001).

Other reinforcers, known as **secondary reinforcers**, don't satisfy any physiological or other "prewired" need; instead, learners *learn* to appreciate them. Praise, money, good grades, and trophies are examples. Such stimuli may become reinforcing over time through their association with other stimuli that already have a reinforcing effect. For example, if praise is occasionally associated with a special candy treat from Mother, and if money often comes with a hug from Father, the praise and money eventually become reinforcing in and of themselves. In this way, seemingly unpleasant stimuli can become reinforcers. For instance, if James regularly associates a teacher's scolding with something he wants—more attention—then a scolding may indeed become a reinforcer in its own right.

Secondary reinforcers are far more common in classrooms than primary reinforcers. In fact, making primary reinforcers (e.g., lunch, restroom breaks) contingent on certain levels of performance is generally *not* good teaching practice. When we use secondary reinforcers, however, we must remember that they're *learned* reinforcers, and not everyone has come to appreciate them. Although most students respond positively to such consequences as praise and good grades, a few students may not.

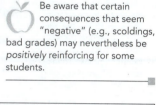

Keep in mind that not all students have learned to appreciate such secondary reinforcers as praise and good grades.

POSITIVE VERSUS NEGATIVE REINFORCEMENT

Up to this point, we've been talking about reinforcement as the *presentation* of a particular reinforcing stimulus. But in some cases we can also reinforce a behavior through the *removal* of a stimulus. Behaviorists use the terms *positive reinforcement* and *negative reinforcement,* respectively, for these two situations.

Positive reinforcement.   Whenever a particular stimulus is *presented* after a behavior and the behavior increases as a result, positive reinforcement has occurred. Don't be misled by the word *positive,* which in this case has nothing to do with the pleasantness or general desirability of the stimulus being presented. Positive reinforcement can occur even when the presented stimulus is one that others might think is *un*pleasant or *un*desirable. The word *positive* here simply means *adding* something to the situation. For example, some students may make a response to get a teacher's praise, but others (like James in the opening case study) may behave in a way that gets them a scolding. Most students will work for As, but a few may actually prefer Cs or even Fs. (As a school psychologist, one of us authors once worked with a high school student who used Fs as a way to get revenge on his overly controlling parents.) Depending on the individual, any one of these stimuli—praise, a scolding, an A, or an F—can be a positive reinforcer. Following are examples of the forms that positive reinforcement can take:

Be aware that certain consequences that seem "negative" (e.g., scoldings, bad grades) may nevertheless be *positively* reinforcing for some students.

Teachers' and peers' attention is often a *positive* reinforcer—that is, it *increases* the behavior it follows—even if the messages being communicated are intended to discourage the behavior.

- A *concrete reinforcer* is an actual object—something that can be touched (e.g., a snack, scratch-and-sniff sticker, or toy).

- A *social reinforcer* is a gesture or sign (e.g., a smile, attention, praise, or "thank you") that one person gives another, usually to communicate positive regard.

- An *activity reinforcer* is an opportunity to engage in a favorite pastime. Learners will often do one thing—even something they don't like to do—if it enables them to do something they enjoy. This phenomenon is sometimes called the Premack principle (Premack, 1959, 1963). For example, children with attention-deficit hyperactivity disorder (ADHD) are more likely to sit quietly during a lesson if they know that doing so will enable them to engage in a physically more lively activity afterward (Azrin, Vinas, & Ehle, 2007).

- A *token reinforcer* is a small, insignificant item (e.g., poker chip, specially marked piece of colored paper) that a learner can later use to "purchase" a desired object or privilege. It's often used in a *token economy,* a strategy to be described a bit later.

- Sometimes the simple message that an answer is correct or that a task has been done well— *positive feedback*—is reinforcement enough. In fact, sometimes even *negative* feedback can be reinforcing if the overall message is a positive one. The Creating a Productive Classroom Environment feature "Using Feedback to Improve Learning and Behavior" offers suggestions based on research by behaviorists, cognitive psychologists, and motivation theorists.

The reinforcers just listed are extrinsic reinforcers—those provided by the external environment (often by other people). Yet some positive reinforcers are intrinsic reinforcers—those that come from learners themselves or are inherent in tasks being performed. When students

MyEdLab
Video Example 9.2.

What kind of token reinforcer is being used in this special education classroom?

Creating a Productive Classroom Environment

Using Feedback to Improve Learning and Behavior

🍎 **Be explicit about what students are doing well—ideally, at the time they are doing it.**
When praising her students for appropriate classroom behavior, a second-grade teacher is quite specific about the actions for which she's commending them. For example, she says, "I like the way you're working quietly" and "You should see Ricky being so polite. Thank you, Ricky, for not disturbing the rest of the class."

MyEdLab
Video Example 9.3.

You can watch this second-grade teacher here.

🍎 **Give concrete guidance about how students can improve their performance.**
A high school physical education teacher tells a student, "Your time in the 100-meter dash wasn't as fast as it could have been. It's early in the season, though, and if you work on your endurance, I know you'll improve. Also, I think you might get a faster start if you stay low when you first come out of the starting blocks."

🍎 **Communicate optimism that students can improve.**
When a student in a middle school geography class gives her oral report on Mexico, she goes on at length about her family's recent trip to Puerto Vallarta, showing many photos, postcards, and souvenirs to illustrate her remarks. The other students soon become bored and communicate their displeasure through body language and occasional whispers across the aisles. At the end of class, the student is devastated that her report has been so poorly received. Her teacher takes her aside and gently says, "You included many interesting facts in your report, Julie, and all your pictures and artifacts really helped us understand Mexican culture. But you know how young teenagers are—they can have a pretty short attention span at times. I'll be assigning oral reports again next semester. Before you give yours, let's sit down and plan it so that your classmates will think, 'Wow, this is really interesting!'"

🍎 **Don't overwhelm students with too much feedback; tell them only what they can reasonably attend to and remember at the time.**
As a kindergarten teacher watches one of his students practice writing several alphabet letters, he helps the student hold her pencil in a way that gives her better control. He doesn't mention that she's writing her Bs and Ds backward; he'll save this information for a later time, after she has mastered her pencil grip.

🍎 **Minimize feedback when students already know exactly what they've done well or poorly.**
A high school math teacher has a student who has been getting poor grades in large part because of insufficient effort. When the student begins to buckle down and do his homework regularly, his quiz scores improve tremendously. As his teacher hands back his first quiz after his newfound diligence—a quiz on which he's earned a score of 96%—she says nothing but smiles and gives him a private thumbs-up.

🍎 **Teach students strategies for appropriately asking for teacher feedback.**
A fourth-grade teacher has two students with intellectual disabilities in her class. She knows that these students may need more frequent feedback than their classmates. She teaches them three steps to take when they need her assistance: (1) They should raise their hands or walk quietly to her desk; (2) they should wait patiently until she has time to speak with them; and (3) they should make their needs known (e.g., "How am I doing?" "What do I do next?").

Sources: Bangert-Drowns, Kulik, Kulik, & Morgan, 1991; Boyanton, 2010; D. L. Butler & Winne, 1995; Craft, Alberg, & Heward, 1998, p. 402 (fourth-grade example); Feltz, Chase, Moritz, & Sullivan, 1999; Hattie & Gan, 2011; Hattie & Timperley, 2007; K. A. Meyer, 1999; Narciss, 2008; Pintrich & Schunk, 2002; Schunk & Pajares, 2005; Shute, 2008; Stokes, Luiselli, Reed, & Fleming, 2010; Tunstall & Gipps, 1996.

engage in certain activities in the absence of any observable reinforcers—when they read an entire book without putting it down, do extra classwork without being asked, or practice with a neighborhood rock group into the wee hours of the morning—they're probably working for the intrinsic reinforcement that such activities yield. Intrinsic reinforcers are *not* observable events and thus don't fit comfortably within traditional behaviorist theory. Yet students clearly do engage in some behaviors solely for the intrinsic satisfaction their behaviors bring. For instance, in the earlier "What Would It Take?" exercise, if you agreed to help your classmates simply because doing so would make you feel good, you'd be working for an intrinsic reinforcer.

In classroom settings, positive feedback (an extrinsic reinforcer) and the feelings of pleasure and satisfaction that such feedback can bring (intrinsic reinforcers) are probably the most desirable forms of reinforcement. But we must remember that the classroom successes that yield such forms of reinforcement can occur only when instruction has been carefully tailored to individual skill levels and abilities and only when students have learned to value academic achievement. If students aren't motivated to achieve academic success for whatever reasons, then social reinforcers, activity reinforcers, and occasionally even concrete reinforcers can be used to increase desired behaviors.

Negative reinforcement.   Whereas positive reinforcement involves the presentation of a stimulus, negative reinforcement brings about the increase of a behavior through the *removal* of a stimulus—typically an unpleasant one, at least from the learner's perspective. The word *negative* here isn't a value judgment. It simply refers to the act of *taking away,* rather than adding, a stimulus.[2] When people make a response in order to get rid of something and the frequency of the response increases as a result, they're being negatively reinforced.

Imagine, for example, that you have a difficult assignment you must do for one of your classes. Because you don't like the assignment hanging over your head, you complete it and give it to your instructor well before its due date. After you turn it in, you feel much better: You've gotten rid of that annoying *worry* feeling. If you find yourself completing future assignments early as well, then you've been negatively reinforced for your complete-something-before-due-date behavior.

We can see another possible example of negative reinforcement in the opening case study. When James misbehaves, his teacher sometimes sends him to the assistant principal's office. By doing so, the teacher may be negatively reinforcing his troublesome behavior. In particular, James *gets out of class,* thereby removing a stimulus—some aspect of the classroom environment—that may be aversive for him. (If James likes spending time with the assistant principal, he's receiving positive reinforcement as well.) Whereas some students misbehave in class primarily to get attention (a positive reinforcer), others often misbehave to escape something they don't want to do, such as a difficult assignment, and their escape behavior is negatively reinforced (McComas, Thompson, & Johnson, 2003; M. M. Mueller et al., 2011; S. W. Payne & Dozier, 2013). Students may learn other escape behaviors as well, as one student with a learning disability revealed:

> When it comes time for reading I do everything under the sun I can to get out of it because it's my worst nightmare to read. I'll say I have to go to the bathroom or that I'm sick and I have to go to the nurse right now. My teacher doesn't know that I'll be walking around campus. She thinks I am going to the bathroom or whatever my lame excuse is. All I really want to do is get out of having to read. (Zambo & Brem, 2004, p. 5)

As teachers, we should use negative reinforcement rarely, if at all. Ideally, we want to create a classroom environment in which there are few stimuli that students want to escape. Nevertheless, we should recognize that negative reinforcement *does* have an effect on behavior. Some students may finish an assignment more to get it out of the way than for any intrinsic satisfaction the assignment brings. Others may engage in a variety of responses—perhaps misbehaving or identifying imaginary reasons for leaving the classroom—as a way of avoiding the assignment altogether. When certain responses enable students to eliminate or escape unpleasant stimuli, those responses will increase in frequency.

LOOKING AT REINFORCEMENT FROM A DEVELOPMENTAL PERSPECTIVE

Children's preferences for various kinds of reinforcers tend to change with age. For example, concrete reinforcers (e.g., stickers depicting popular cartoon characters, small trinkets) can be effective with young children, but teenagers are more likely to appreciate opportunities to interact with friends. Table 9.2 presents forms of reinforcement that may be especially effective at various grade levels.

An important developmental trend is evident in Table 9.2 as well: As children get older, they become better able to handle delay of gratification. That is, they can forego small, immediate reinforcers for the larger reinforcers that their long-term efforts may bring down the road (Atance, 2008; L. Green et al., 1994; Steinberg, Graham, et al., 2009). Whereas a preschooler or kindergartner is apt to choose a small reinforcer available *now* rather than a larger and more attractive reinforcer she can't get until tomorrow, an 8-year-old may be willing to wait a day or two for the more appealing item. Many adolescents can delay gratification for several weeks or even longer.

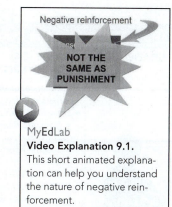

Negative reinforcement

NOT THE SAME AS PUNISHMENT

MyEdLab
Video Explanation 9.1.
This short animated explanation can help you understand the nature of negative reinforcement.

When students consistently behave in ways that enable them to avoid or escape certain activities, identify and address possible reasons that students find the activities aversive.

When working with young children, try to reinforce desired behaviors immediately, even if only by pointing out that a desired consequence will come later.

---

[2]You might draw an analogy between positive versus negative reinforcement and positive versus negative numbers. Positive numbers and positive reinforcement both add something to a situation. Negative numbers and negative reinforcement both *subtract* something from a situation.

DEVELOPMENTAL TRENDS

TABLE 9.2 • Effective Reinforcers at Different Grade Levels

GRADE LEVEL	AGE-TYPICAL CHARACTERISTICS	EXAMPLE	SUGGESTED STRATEGIES
K–2	• Preference for small, immediate reinforcers over larger, delayed ones • Examples of effective reinforcers: 　• Concrete reinforcers (e.g., stickers, crayons, small trinkets) 　• Teacher approval (e.g., smiles, praise) 　• Privileges (e.g., going to lunch first) 　• "Grown-up" responsibilities (e.g., taking notes to the main office)	When a kindergarten teacher asks children to choose between a small snack before morning recess or a larger one after recess, most of them clamor for the smaller, immediate snack.	• Give immediate praise for appropriate behavior. • Describe enjoyable consequences that may come later as a result of students' current behaviors. • Use stickers, handwritten smiley faces, and the like to reinforce students' efforts on their written work. • Have students line up for recess, lunch, or dismissal based on desired behaviors (e.g., "Table 2 is the quietest and can line up first"). • Rotate opportunities to perform classroom duties (e.g., feeding the goldfish, watering plants); make such duties contingent on appropriate behavior.
3–5	• Increasing ability to delay gratification (i.e., to put off small reinforcers in order to gain larger ones later on) • Examples of effective reinforcers: 　• Concrete reinforcers (e.g., snacks, pencils, small toys) 　• Teacher approval and positive feedback 　• "Good citizen" certificates 　• Free time (e.g., to draw or play games)	Nine-year-old Li-Mei glows with pride when her teacher praises her for helping a classmate with a challenging writing assignment.	• Use concrete reinforcers only occasionally, perhaps to add novelty to a classroom activity. • Award a certificate to a Citizen of the Week, explicitly identifying things the recipient has done especially well; be sure that every student gets at least one certificate during the school year. • Plan a trip to a local amusement park for students with good attendance records (especially useful for students at risk for academic failure).
6–8	• Increasing desire to have social time with peers • Examples of effective reinforcers: 　• Free time with friends 　• Acceptance and approval from peers 　• Teacher approval and emotional support (especially critical after the transition to middle school or junior high) 　• Specific positive feedback about academic performance (preferably given in private)	Students in a sixth-grade science class work diligently on an assigned lab activity, knowing that if they complete it before the end of the class session they can have a few minutes to talk with their friends.	• Make short periods of free time with peers contingent on accomplishing assigned tasks. • Spend one-on-one time with students, especially those who appear to be socially isolated. • Provide explicit feedback about what things students have done well (e.g., their use of colorful language in an essay or their prosocial behaviors with classmates).
9–12	• Increasing ability to postpone immediate pleasures in order to gain desired long-term outcomes • Concern about getting good grades (especially for students who are applying to selective colleges) • Examples of effective reinforcers: 　• Opportunities to interact with friends 　• Specific positive feedback about academic performance 　• Public recognition for group performance (e.g., newspaper articles about a club's public service work) 　• Positions of responsibility (e.g., being student representative to the Faculty Senate)	When 16-year-old Deon's friends ask him to go to the movies on a Thursday evening, he declines. "I have to study for tomorrow's history test," he tells them. "If I keep my grades up, I'll have a better chance of getting a good college scholarship."	• Acknowledge students' concerns about earning good grades, but focus their attention on the value of learning school subject matter for its own sake. • Be sure that good grades are contingent on students' own work; take precautions to ensure that cheating and plagiarism are *not* reinforced. • Publicize accomplishments of extracurricular groups and athletic teams in local news media. • Provide opportunities for independent decision making and responsibility, especially when students show an ability to make wise decisions.

Sources: E. M. Anderman & Mueller, 2010; L. H. Anderman, Patrick, Hruda, & Linnenbrink, 2002; Atance, 2008; Cizek, 2003; S. A. Fowler & Baer, 1981; L. Green, Fry, & Myerson, 1994; Hine & Fraser, 2002; Krumboltz & Krumboltz, 1972; Rimm & Masters, 1974; Rotenberg & Mayer, 1990; M. G. Sanders, 1996; Steinberg, Graham, et al., 2009; Urdan & Mestas, 2006; M.-T. Wang & Holcombe, 2010.

Some children and adolescents are better able to delay gratification than others. Those who are willing and able to postpone reinforcement are less likely to yield to temptation, more carefully plan their future actions, and achieve at higher levels at school (Bembenutty & Karabenick, 2004; Rothbart, 2011; Shoda, Mischel, & Peake, 1990). However, even 4- and 5-year-olds can learn to delay gratification for a few hours if their teachers tell them that rewards for desired behaviors (e.g., sharing toys with peers) will be coming later in the day and if they're engaging in enjoyable activities in the interim (S. A. Fowler & Baer, 1981; Newquist, Dozier, & Neidert, 2012). Teaching children effective waiting strategies—for instance, focusing attention on something else during the delay and using such self-talk as "If I wait a little longer, I'll get something better"—enhances their ability to postpone gratification as well (Binder, Dixon, & Ghezzi, 2000).

THE VARIOUS FORMS THAT PUNISHMENT CAN TAKE

Historically, the use of punishment in schools has been controversial, and in fact some forms of punishment do a great deal of harm. But under certain conditions, punishing consequences can be both effective and appropriate, especially when students seem to have little motivation to change their behavior for the better.

All punishing consequences fall into one of two categories. **Presentation punishment** involves presenting a new stimulus, presumably something that a learner finds unpleasant and doesn't want. Scoldings and teacher scowls—*if* they lead to a reduction in the behavior they follow—are instances of presentation punishment. **Removal punishment** involves removing an existing stimulus or state of affairs, presumably one that a learner finds desirable and doesn't want to lose. Loss of a privilege, a fine or penalty (involving the loss of money or previously earned points), and grounding (i.e., restriction from certain pleasurable outside activities) are all examples of removal punishment.[3]

Am I making this better, or worse?

MyEdLab
Video Explanation 9.2.
This short animated explanation can also help you learn to distinguish among positive reinforcement, negative reinforcement, and punishment.

Over the years, we authors have often seen or heard people use the term *negative reinforcement* when they're really talking about punishment. Remember, negative reinforcement is *reinforcement,* which increases a response, whereas punishment has the opposite effect. Table 9.3 can help you understand the distinction.

CONSEQUENCES THAT SERVE AS EFFECTIVE PUNISHMENTS

As a general rule, we should use only mild forms of punishment in the classroom. Researchers and educators have identified several mild consequences that can be effective in reducing classroom misbehaviors.

Verbal reprimands (scolding).　As is true for James in the opening case study, some students seem to thrive on teacher scolding because it brings them the attention they can't seem to get in other ways. But most students find verbal reprimands to be unpleasant and punishing (Landrum & Kauffman, 2006; Pfiffner & O'Leary, 1993; Van Houten, Nau, MacKenzie-Keating, Sameoto, & Colavecchia, 1982). In general, reprimands are most effective when they're immediate, brief, unemotional, and given in a quiet tone of voice. Whenever possible, we should reprimand students privately rather than publicly. When students are scolded in front of classmates, some may relish the peer attention, and others (e.g., many Native American and Hispanic students) may feel totally humiliated (Fuller, 2001).

Response cost.　The loss either of a previously earned reinforcer or of an opportunity to obtain reinforcement is known as **response cost**—a form of *removal punishment*. Response cost is especially effective when used in combination with reinforcement of appropriate behavior and when learners who make a few missteps within an overall pattern of desirable behavior lose only a *little bit* of what they've earned (Conyers et al., 2004; Landrum & Kauffman, 2006; E. L. Phillips, Phillips, Fixsen, & Wolf, 1971).

Logical consequences.　A **logical consequence** is something that follows naturally or logically from a student's misbehavior; in other words, it's punishment that fits the crime. For example, if a student destroys a classmate's possession, a reasonable consequence is for the student to

---

[3]You may sometimes see the terms *positive punishment* and *negative punishment* used instead of *presentation punishment* and *removal punishment,* respectively. But in the experiences of us authors, such terms can lead to the same value-judgment misinterpretation problem that exists for negative reinforcement: Many people mistakenly believe that positive punishment is somehow more desirable than negative punishment, which isn't necessarily the case.

COMPARE/CONTRAST

TABLE 9.3 • Distinguishing Among Positive Reinforcement, Negative Reinforcement, and Punishment

CONSEQUENCE	EFFECT	EXAMPLES
Positive reinforcement	Response *increases* when a new stimulus (presumably one the learner finds desirable) is *presented*.	• A student *is praised* for writing an assignment in cursive. She begins to write other assignments in cursive as well. • A student *gets lunch money* by bullying a girl into surrendering hers. He begins bullying his classmates more frequently.
Negative reinforcement	Response *increases* when a previously existing stimulus (presumably one the learner finds undesirable) is *removed*	• A student *no longer has to worry* about a research paper that he completed several days before the due date. He begins to do his assignments ahead of time whenever possible. • A student *escapes the principal's wrath* by lying about her role in recent school vandalism. After this incident she begins lying to school faculty whenever she finds herself in an uncomfortable situation.
Presentation punishment	Response *decreases* when a new stimulus (presumably one the learner finds undesirable) is *presented*.	• A student *is scolded* for taunting other students. She taunts others less frequently after that. • A student *is ridiculed by classmates* for asking what they perceive to be a stupid question during a lesson. He stops asking questions in class.
Removal punishment	Response *decreases* when a previously existing stimulus (presumably one the learner finds desirable) is removed.	• A student *is removed from the softball team for a week* for showing poor sportsmanship. She rarely exhibits poor sportsmanship in future games. • A student *loses points on a test* for answering a question in a creative but unusual way. He takes fewer risks on future tests.

replace it or pay for a new one. If two close friends talk so much that they aren't completing assignments, a reasonable consequence is for them to be separated. The use of logical consequences makes logical sense, and research vouches for its effectiveness (Dreikurs, 1998; Landrum & Kauffman, 2006; Nucci, 2001).

Positive-practice overcorrection. One desired result of administering punishment, of course, is that students learn more appropriate behavior in the process. **Positive-practice overcorrection** involves having a student repeat an action, this time doing it correctly, perhaps in an exaggerated form. For example, a student who runs dangerously down the school corridor might be asked to back up and then *walk* down the hall—perhaps at a normal pace, or perhaps very slowly. Similarly, a student in a drivers' education class who neglects to stop at a stop sign might be asked to drive around the block, return to the same intersection, and come to a complete stop—perhaps counting aloud to five—before proceeding. In general, positive-practice overcorrection is most likely to be effective when its duration is relatively short and when teachers portray it as a means for helping students acquire appropriate behavior rather than simply as punishment per se (Alberto & Troutman, 2013; R. G. Carey & Bucher, 1983; M. D. Powers & Crowel, 1985).

Time-out. A **time-out** is a specified period of time in which a student has no opportunity to receive the kinds of reinforcement to which other students have access. In a mild form, it might involve asking students to put their heads down on their desks or to sit away from other students, where they must quietly watch an enjoyable activity in which classmates are participating. For more significant infractions, it might involve placing a student for a short time in a separate place that's dull and boring—perhaps a remote corner of the classroom or playground.[4]

Time-outs have been used successfully to reduce a variety of noncompliant, disruptive, and aggressive behaviors. Keep in mind, however, that a time-out is apt to be effective only if ongoing

---

[4]Historically, many time-outs involved putting students in a separate, isolated room designed specifically for time-outs. This practice has largely fallen out of favor in public schools except in cases of significant behavior problems, such as physical aggression (Alberto & Troutman, 2013).

classroom activities are a source of pleasure and reinforcement for a student. If a time-out allows a student to escape difficult tasks or an overwhelming amount of noise and stimulation, it might actually be a form of negative reinforcement and thus *increase* undesirable behavior (J. M. Donaldson & Vollmer, 2011; McClowry, 1998; Pfiffner, Barkley, & DuPaul, 2006; Rortvedt & Miltenberger, 1994; A. G. White & Bailey, 1990).

In-school suspension. Like time-out, in-school suspension involves placing a student in a quiet, boring situation—in this case, in a separate room within the school building. It usually lasts one or more school days and involves close adult supervision. Students receiving in-school suspension spend the day working on their class assignments, enabling them to keep up with their schoolwork. But they have no opportunity for interaction with peers—an aspect of school that's reinforcing for most students.

Although in-school suspension programs haven't been systematically investigated through controlled research studies, educators report that these programs are often effective in reducing chronic behavior problems. They're typically most effective when suspension sessions include instruction in appropriate behaviors and missing academic skills and when the supervising teacher acts as a supportive resource rather than a punisher (Gootman, 1998; Huff, 1988; Pfiffner et al., 2006; J. S. Sullivan, 1989).

CONSEQUENCES THAT MAY UNDERMINE DESIRED BEHAVIOR CHANGES

Several forms of punishment are typically *not* recommended because they have adverse side effects, convey a counterproductive message, or actually serve as reinforcers for some students.

Physical punishment. Most experts advise against physical punishment for school-age children (e.g., W. Doyle, 1990; Hyman et al., 2006; Landrum & Kauffman, 2006). Furthermore, its use in the classroom is *illegal* in many places. Even mild physical punishment, such as a spank or slap with a ruler, can lead to such undesirable outcomes as resentment of the teacher, avoidance of school tasks, lying, aggression, vandalism, and truancy. When carried to extremes, physical punishment constitutes child abuse and can cause long-term physical damage, psychological problems, or both.

Psychological punishment. Any consequence that seriously threatens a student's self-esteem is psychological punishment and isn't recommended. Fear tactics, embarrassing remarks, and public humiliation can lead to some of the same side effects as physical punishment can—for instance, resentment, distraction from schoolwork, and truancy—and can inflict long-term psychological harm. By deflating students' sense of self, psychological punishment can also dampen their interest in classroom subject matter and expectations for future performance (Brendgen, Wanner, Vitaro, Bukowski, & Tremblay, 2007; J. Ellis, Fitzsimmons, & Small-McGinley, 2010; Hyman et al., 2006).

Extra classwork. Asking a student to complete makeup work for time missed in school is a reasonable and justifiable request. But assigning extra classwork or homework beyond that required for other students is inappropriate if it's assigned simply to punish a student for wrongdoing (H. Cooper, 1989; Corno, 1996). Such punishment has a very different side effect: It communicates the message that schoolwork is unpleasant.

Do *not* use physical punishment, public humiliation, or extra classwork to discourage undesirable behaviors.

Out-of-school suspension. Teachers and administrators are negatively reinforced when they suspend a problem student. After all, they get rid of something they don't want—a problem! But out-of-school suspension is usually *not* an effective means of changing a student's behavior. For one thing, being suspended from school may be exactly what the student wants, in which case inappropriate behaviors are being reinforced rather than punished. Also, because many students with chronic behavior problems tend to do poorly in their schoolwork, suspension involves a loss of valuable instructional time and interferes with any psychological attachment to school. Thus, it decreases students' chances for academic and social success even further and increases the probability that students will drop out before graduation (American Psychological Association Zero Tolerance Task Force, 2008; Christenson & Thurlow, 2004; Gregory, Skiba, & Noguera, 2010; Osher, Bear, Sprague, & Doyle, 2010).

Advocate for in-school alternatives to out-of-school suspension for wrongdoing.

CONSEQUENCES WITH MIXED REVIEWS

Two additional forms of punishment get mixed reviews regarding effectiveness. In some situations *missing recess* is a logical consequence for students who fail to complete their schoolwork during regular class time because of their off-task behavior. Yet research indicates that, especially at the elementary level, students can more effectively concentrate on school tasks if they have frequent breaks and opportunities to release pent-up energy (Maxmell, Jarrett, & Dickerson, 1998; Pellegrini & Bohn, 2005; Pellegrini, Huberty, & Jones, 1995). And although imposing *after-school detention* for serious misbehavior is common practice at many schools, some students simply can't stay after school hours, perhaps because they have transportation issues, must take care of younger siblings at home, or are justifiably afraid to walk through certain neighborhoods after dark (J. D. Nichols, Ludwin, & Iadicola, 1999). Unless we can address such concerns, imposing after-school detention isn't logistically feasible.

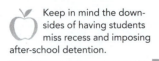 Keep in mind the downsides of having students miss recess and imposing after-school detention.

MyEdLab **Self-Check 9.3**

Strategies for Encouraging Productive Behaviors

As a prominent early behaviorist, B. F. Skinner was quite vocal in advocating for the application of behaviorist principles in classroom settings. He argued that punishment was a relatively *in*effective means of changing behavior—it might temporarily *suppress* a response but could never eliminate it—and thus urged teachers to focus their efforts on reinforcing desirable behaviors rather than punishing undesirable ones (e.g., B. F. Skinner, 1954, 1968; B. F. Skinner & Epstein, 1982). Following Skinner's lead, most contemporary behaviorists suggest that we emphasize the positive, looking for and reinforcing what's *right* with students' behavior.

As teachers, we must be sure that productive student behaviors—for instance, contributing to class discussions, working cooperatively with peers, and keeping work areas tidy—are reinforced in some way. At the same time, we should be careful *not* to reinforce counterproductive behaviors. If we repeatedly allow Carol to turn in assignments late because she says she forgot her homework and if we often let Caleb get his way by bullying his peers, then we're reinforcing—and hence increasing—Carol's irresponsibility and Caleb's aggressiveness.

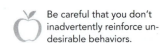 Be careful that you don't inadvertently reinforce undesirable behaviors.

USING REINFORCEMENT EFFECTIVELY

The following strategies are consistent with behaviorist principles and research findings.

 Specify desired behaviors at the outset. Before beginning a lesson or behavioral intervention, behaviorists identify the desired end results—the **terminal behaviors**—in specific, concrete, observable terms. Rather than talk about the need for students to "Learn world history," we might instead talk about them being able to "Describe the antecedents and outcomes of World War II." Rather than say that students should "Learn responsibility," we might instead talk about their need to "Follow instructions, bring the necessary books and supplies to class each day, and turn in assignments by the due dates." By specifying terminal behaviors up front, we give both ourselves and our students targets to shoot for, and we can better determine whether everyone is making progress toward them.

It's often important to specify quality as well as quantity. For instance, rather than reinforcing students simply for sitting quietly at their desks, we should also reinforce them for working productively during that time. And rather than reinforcing students for the number of books they read—which may encourage students to read many short, simple books—we should reinforce them for reading challenging materials appropriate for their ability levels.

In general, reinforcement solely for accomplishing a certain task, perhaps at a minimally acceptable level, focuses students' attention and effort more on completing the activity than on *learning* from it. Especially if we want students to engage in complex cognitive processes—for example, to think critically and creatively about a topic—then extrinsic reinforcement simply for task accomplishment can be counterproductive (E. M. Anderman & Anderman, 2010; Deci & Ryan, 1985; McCaslin & Good, 1996).

Specify the desired *quality* of complex terminal behaviors.

Educators are increasingly recognizing the importance of spelling out in advance the most important things that students should learn and achieve. You're apt to see a variety of terms for this idea—perhaps *instructional goals, objectives, outcomes, competencies, benchmarks,* and *standards.*

🍎 *Make sure that all students regularly receive reinforcement for desired behaviors.* In the opening case study, James engages in a variety of inappropriate behaviors as a means of gaining other people's attention. We might reasonably guess that James would prefer more pleasant interactions with adults and peers, yet for whatever reasons he seldom has such interactions—perhaps because his academic performance rarely gains his teacher's praise or perhaps because he lacks the social skills to make and maintain friendships. In working with James, then, his teacher should identify the academic and social skills he might be missing, help him acquire those skills, and then reinforce him for using them.

In our attempts to improve the behaviors of some students, however, we must be careful that we don't unintentionally slight other, equally deserving students. Furthermore, we must keep in mind that some students may be unable to exhibit particular behaviors through little or no fault of their own. Consider the case of an immigrant student who had to adjust very quickly from a 10:00–5:00 school day in Vietnam to a 7:45–3:45 school day in the United States:

> Every week on Friday after school, the teacher would give little presents to kids that were good during the week. And if you were tardy, you wouldn't get a present... . I would never get one because I would always come to school late, and that hurt at first. I had a terrible time. I didn't look forward to going to school. (Igoa, 1995, p. 95)

Ultimately school should be a place where *all* students can, in one way or another, earn reinforcement for appropriate behaviors and academic progress.

🍎 *Use extrinsic reinforcers only when desired behaviors will not otherwise occur.* It's neither possible nor necessary to provide extrinsic reinforcement for every good deed. Furthermore, many extrinsic reinforcements lose their effectiveness when used repeatedly (Michael, 2000; Murphy, McSweeney, Smith, & McComas, 2003). The best reinforcers are intrinsic ones, such as the pleasure one gets from reading, the pride one feels after completing a challenging task, and the internal satisfaction one feels while helping others. Students willingly engage in activities that are enjoyable or pique their curiosity, and they'll readily behave in ways that lead to feelings of mastery and accomplishment.

You should be aware, too, that *extrinsic reinforcement of an activity that students already find intrinsically reinforcing may undermine their enjoyment of the activity.* Some research has indicated that enjoyable activities can be increased through extrinsic reinforcement but will then *decrease* to a below-baseline frequency once the reinforcers are removed. Extrinsic reinforcers are most likely to have this adverse effect when students perceive them as being controlling or manipulative, rather than as promoting improvement and mastery (Deci & Moller, 2005; Lepper & Hodell, 1989; Reeve, 2006).

🍎 Communicate genuine appreciation for what students have done. Try not to come across as controlling or manipulative.

Yet many of the tasks students tackle in school—perhaps writing a persuasive essay, solving a complicated word problem, or learning how to play a clarinet—can be difficult and frustrating, especially at first. When students struggle with a task and encounter frequent failure, we should probably provide some extrinsic reinforcement (e.g., praise or free time) for small improvements. And when we find that we must break a complex task into small pieces that are easier to accomplish but less fulfilling in their own right—for instance, drill-and-practice activities that foster automaticity for basic math facts—we may need to reinforce a lot of small, seemingly trivial successes. However, once students have mastered tasks and skills to levels that bring them feelings of genuine accomplishment, extrinsic reinforcers may no longer be necessary (J. Cameron, 2001; Covington, 1992; Deci, Koestner, & Ryan, 2001; Hidi & Harackiewicz, 2000).

Extrinsic reinforcement for students who don't need it can undermine their sense of *autonomy* (see Chapter 11).

🍎 *Determine whether particular "reinforcers" are truly reinforcing for students.* Different students have different needs and desires—factors that underlie their *motivation*—that influence the effectiveness of various reinforcers (McGill, 1999; Michael, 2000; Rispoli et al., 2011). Accordingly, the use of reinforcement is far more productive when reinforcers are tailored

Chapter 11 describes students' typical needs and desires in depth.

to individual students. In some cases we can let students choose their *own* reinforcers and perhaps choose different reinforcers on different occasions. Children seem to prefer having some choice in the reinforcers for which they work (Geckeler, Libby, Graff, & Ahearn, 2000; Sran & Borrero, 2010; Tiger, Hanley, & Hernandez, 2006; Ulke-Kircuoglu & Kircaali-Iftar, 2010).

One useful strategy for a class with many chronic misbehavers is a token economy, in which students who exhibit desired behaviors receive tokens—perhaps specially printed "class dollars" or teacher-initialed checkmarks on a slip of paper—that they can collect and later use to "purchase" a variety of *backup reinforcers*—perhaps small treats, free time in a reading center, or a prime position in the lunch line. Often the tokens become effective reinforcers in and of themselves. Perhaps they become secondary reinforcers through repeated association with other reinforcing objects and events, or perhaps they're effective simply because they provide feedback that students are doing something well.

By and large, however, we should stay away from concrete reinforcers as much as possible. Such reinforcers can be expensive and distract students' attention away from their schoolwork. Fortunately, many less tangible reinforcers—such as positive feedback, special privileges, and favorite activities—and reinforcement at home for school behaviors can be quite effective with school-age children and adolescents (e.g., Feltz et al., 1999; Homme, deBaca, Devine, Steinhorst, & Rickert, 1963; Kelley & Carper, 1988). The Creating a Productive Classroom Environment feature "Identifying Effective Reinforcers for Different Students" offers some widely recommended strategies.

 Make response–consequence contingencies explicit. Reinforcement is typically more effective when students know exactly which behaviors will lead to which consequences. For example, kindergarten students are more likely to behave appropriately if they're told, "The quietest group will be first to get in line for recess." And high school students are more likely to complete their Spanish assignments if they know that regularly doing so will earn them a field trip to a local Cinco de Mayo festival.

One concrete way of communicating both behavioral expectations and response–reinforcement contingencies is a contingency contract. To develop such a contract, the teacher meets with a student to discuss a problem behavior (e.g., talking to friends during independent seatwork or speaking disrespectfully to classmates). The teacher and the student then identify and agree on desired behaviors that the student will demonstrate (e.g., completing seatwork assignments within a certain time frame or speaking with classmates in a friendly, respectful manner). The two also agree on one or more reinforcers (e.g., points earned toward a particular prize or privilege). Together the teacher and the student write and sign a contract that describes the desired behaviors and contingent reinforcers. Contingency contracts can be highly effective in improving a variety of academic and social behaviors (Kehle, Bray, Theodore, Jenson, & Clark, 2000; K. L. Lane, Menzies, Bruhn, & Crnobori, 2011; Wilkinson, 2003).

 Create conditions in which students can reinforce one another for academic achievements and productive classroom behaviors. In truly productive classrooms, not only teachers but also *peers* reinforce students for their efforts and achievements. Perhaps the most effective strategy here is to specifically *teach* students how to compliment one another for good work—for instance, by giving one another high-fives or fist-bumps (e.g., Beaulieu, Hanley, & Roberson, 2013).

In some cases, peer reinforcement might be one of the benefits of a group contingency, in which students are reinforced only when *everyone* in a particular group—perhaps even an entire class—achieves at a certain level or behaves appropriately. Following are two examples of whole-class contingencies:

- A class of 32 fourth graders was doing poorly on weekly spelling tests, with an average of only 12 students (38%) earning perfect test scores in any given week. Hoping for improvement, the teacher announced that any student with a perfect score would get free time later in the week, and the average number of perfect spelling tests rose to 25 (78%) a week. But then the teacher added a group contingency: Whenever the entire class achieved perfect spelling tests by Friday, the class could listen to the radio for 15 minutes. The group contingency produced an average of 30 perfect spelling tests (94%) a week (Lovitt, Guppy, & Blattner, 1969).

Use concrete reinforcers only if less tangible reinforcers are ineffective.

MyEdLab
Video Explanation 9.3.
This 5-minute video can help you identify instances of teacher and peer reinforcement in real classrooms.

Creating a Productive Classroom Environment

Identifying Effective Reinforcers for Different Students

🍎 **Give students choices among two or more alternatives.**

A high school teacher is working with a boy who has a significant intellectual disability and chronic behavior problems. On various occasions, she gives him different choices about which of two things he'd prefer to do. For example, she might give him a choice between (a) talking with her versus playing alone with favorite items, (b) working with her on an assigned task versus sitting by himself with nothing to do, or (c) working with her on an assigned task versus playing alone with favorite items. From the student's pattern of choices, the teacher concludes that her attention is an effective reinforcer for the student.

🍎 **Ask students (or perhaps their parents) about consequences they would find especially appealing.**

A first-grade teacher always includes his students in parent–teacher conferences. At one such conference, the teacher expresses his delight about the progress a student has made in the last few weeks but adds, "I've seen a lot of inconsistency in Janie's performance. Sometimes she works very hard, but at other times she doesn't put much effort into her schoolwork, and occasionally she doesn't complete assignments at all." Together, the teacher, Janie, and her parents agree that successfully completed assignments will earn her points toward the bicycle she has been asking her parents for.

🍎 **Make use of the Premack principle: Students will often engage in behaviors they don't especially enjoy so that they can do something else they *do* enjoy.**

After class one day, a ninth-grade teacher commends a student for his desire to make other people laugh. Then she points out the downside of his sense of humor: "Unfortunately, your jokes can distract your classmates from what they're supposed to be doing, and sometimes I have a hard time getting class discussions back on topic." She promises the student that if he can keep his attention and remarks focused on classroom subject matter throughout a class period, she'll give him the last 2 or 3 minutes of the period to tell the class a joke or two.

🍎 **Provide a small amount of free time contingent on desired behaviors.**

A fifth-grade teacher allows students to engage in favorite activities during the free time they earn each day. Some students work on a classroom computer, others work on art projects, and still others play board games in which they can practice basic math or literacy skills.

🍎 **Observe students' behaviors and written work, keeping a lookout for activities and consequences that students seem to appreciate.**

At home one night, 11-year-old Amie writes the entry below in the class journal that she and her teacher regularly use to communicate. The entry reveals that Amie clearly enjoys playing soccer; in other words, soccer is intrinsically reinforcing for her. It appears, too, that Amie appreciates attention from her coach, probably because (a) he might have her play more and (b) she would like feedback about what she's doing well and how she might improve her skills.

> Today I had a soccer game to see who would go to the state finals. Unfortunly we lost. I was very disapontated, not because we lost, but because my coach only put me in for 10 mins. I feel that the coach was ignoring me and was just focused on winning. I wish the coach would take notice of me on the side lines and not just focuse on winning.

Source: W. K. Berg et al., 2007 (student with intellectual disability example).

- Another fourth-grade teacher was dealing with an especially unruly class: In any given minute, chances were good that one or more students would be talking out of turn or getting out of their seats. In a desperate move, the teacher divided the class into two teams that competed in a "good behavior game." Every time that a student was observed talking out of turn or getting out of his or her seat, the student's team received a mark on the board. The team receiving fewer marks during a lesson won special privileges (e.g., having some free time or being first in the lunch line). If both teams had five marks or fewer, everyone won privileges. Misbehaviors dropped almost immediately to less than 20% of their initial frequency (Barrish, Saunders, & Wolf, 1969; also see Flower, McKenna, Bunuan, Muething, & Vega, 2014, for a review of many studies using such an approach).

Group contingencies are clearly effective in improving academic achievement and classroom behavior *if* everyone in the group is capable of making the desired responses (Heck, Collins, & Peterson, 2001; Kellam, Rebok, Ialongo, & Mayer, 1994; S. L. Robinson & Griesemer, 2006). Peer pressure, social reinforcers, and peer scaffolding also seem to play roles here. Many students encourage misbehaving classmates to behave appropriately and

🍎 When imposing a group contingency, make sure that everyone in the group is capable of making the desired response.

then reinforce those who do so. Furthermore, when students' own success is riding on the success of their peers, students who have mastered a topic begin to tutor students who are struggling (D. W. Johnson & Johnson, 1987; Pigott, Fantuzzo, & Clement, 1986; Slavin, 1983). Whenever we use group contingencies, however, we must closely monitor students' behaviors to make sure that any peer pressure is socially appropriate—for instance, that students aren't ridiculing or bullying their low-performing classmates.

◉ *Monitor students' progress.* Whenever we use reinforcement as a primary strategy for increasing desired behaviors—especially with students who have historically been performing poorly—we should ideally determine whether our efforts are bringing about the desired results. Behaviorists recommend that we assess the frequency of the desired terminal behavior both before and during our attempts to increase it. The frequency of a behavior *before* we intentionally begin reinforcement is its **baseline** level. Some behaviors occur frequently even when they're not being explicitly reinforced; others occur rarely or not at all.

By comparing the baseline frequency of a response with its frequency after we begin to reinforce it systematically, we can determine whether our strategy is actually having an effect. As an example, let's look once again at James in the opening case study. He rarely turns in classroom assignments; this is a behavior with a low baseline. An obvious reinforcer to use with James is attention—a consequence that, until now, has effectively reinforced such counterproductive behaviors as making inappropriate comments in class and throwing objects across the room. When we make our attention contingent on James's turning in assignments, rather than on his refusing to do so, we might see an almost immediate increase in the number of assignments we receive from James. But if we see no significant change, we might need to consider alternative reinforcers. We should also consider and address possible reasons—perhaps poor reading skills—why he might be trying to avoid his schoolwork.

◉ *Consider using mechanical or digital technologies as means of administering reinforcement and monitoring its effects.* Many small digital devices and cell phone applications enable teachers to reinforce productive behaviors in students with chronic behavior problems (you can find examples on the Internet by using a keyword phrase such as "mobile phone apps behavior management"). Simple mechanical clickers can help both teachers and students to monitor the frequency with which the students exhibit certain desired responses. And some Internet-based instructional programs provide "virtual" reinforcers as students make progress in acquiring basic academic skills (e.g., see readingeggs.com).

◉ *Administer reinforcement consistently until the desired behavior occurs at a desired rate.* As you might guess, desired responses increase more quickly when they're reinforced every time they occur—that is, when the responses lead to **continuous reinforcement**. Continuous reinforcement is most important when students are first learning new behaviors, perhaps when they begin a new school year or perhaps when they must tackle a challenging new task. In some instances we may need to begin by reinforcing *effort* (e.g., time on task) and switch to reinforcing *accuracy* only after students have gained some proficiency (Lannie & Martens, 2004).

◉ *Once a behavior is well established, gradually—but only gradually—wean students from extrinsic reinforcement.* Just as reinforced behaviors increase in frequency, *non*reinforced behaviors often *de*crease in frequency and may eventually disappear altogether. Like the decrease of a conditioned response in classical conditioning, the decrease and eventual disappearance of a nonreinforced response in instrumental conditioning is known as **extinction**.

Intrinsic reinforcement can, of course, maintain many productive behaviors over the long run, both at school and in the outside world. But as previously noted, students don't necessarily find *all* desired behaviors enjoyable in and of themselves. When certain behaviors have no intrinsic appeal, **intermittent reinforcement**—reinforcing a behavior on some occasions but not others—provides a viable alternative.

As an example, let's consider Molly and Maria, two students who rarely participate in class discussions. Their teacher, Mr. Oliver, decides to reinforce the girls for raising their hands. Each time Molly raises her hand, Mr. Oliver calls on her and praises her response. But when Maria raises her hand, Mr. Oliver isn't always looking in her direction; hence he

MyEdLab
Content Extension 9.1.
Different patterns of intermittent reinforcement have somewhat different effects on learning and extinction. You can learn more about their varying effects in this supplementary reading.

calls on her on some occasions but not others. Thus, Molly is getting continuous reinforcement and Maria is getting intermittent reinforcement. Other things being equal, Molly's hand raising should increase more rapidly than Maria's.

Now let's move ahead a few weeks. Thanks to Mr. Oliver's attentiveness to Molly and Maria, both girls are now regularly volunteering in class. Consequently, Mr. Oliver turns his attention to other quiet students and no longer reinforces Molly and Maria when they raise their hands. As you might expect, the girls begin to participate less often; in other words, we see signs of extinction. But which girl's class participation will extinguish more quickly?

If you predicted that Molly's volunteering will decrease more rapidly than Maria's, you're right. Responses that have previously been continuously reinforced tend to extinguish quickly once reinforcement stops. But because Maria has been receiving intermittent reinforcement, she's accustomed to being occasionally ignored and may not realize that reinforcement has stopped altogether. Behaviors that have been reinforced only intermittently decrease slowly, if at all, after reinforcement ceases. In other words, these behaviors can be more *resistant to extinction* (e.g., Ferster & Skinner, 1957; Freeland & Noell, 1999; Pipkin & Vollmer, 2009).

Once students have mastered a desired behavior and are using it regularly, then, we should continue to reinforce it intermittently, especially if it has no intrinsically reinforcing effect. Mr. Oliver doesn't need to call on Molly and Maria every time they raise their hands, but he should certainly call on them once in a while. In a similar manner, we might occasionally reinforce diligent study habits, completed homework assignments, prosocial behaviors, and so on—even for the best of students—as a way of encouraging these responses to continue.

When used purposefully and systematically, reinforcement can be a highly effective means of encouraging productive behaviors—*provided that* students have the physical, cognitive, and neurological capabilities necessary for performing the behaviors. For example, some children with physical disabilities may have insufficient physical stamina to attend to their classroom for lengthy time periods. And in the opening case study, perhaps James has poor reading skills that, because of shame or embarrassment, he wants to hide from his teacher and classmates. If so, he may sometimes misbehave to escape tasks that, to him, seem impossible. In some instances, then, we may need to supplement our use of reinforcement with individually tailored instruction, scaffolding, or modifications—typically by bringing strategies based on cognitive, contextual, or social cognitive theories of learning into the picture.

> After students have begun to exhibit a desired behavior regularly, continue to reinforce it intermittently to encourage persistence and prevent extinction.

> Determine whether physical, cognitive, or neurological factors may be interfering with students' ability to acquire certain behaviors or skills. When such factors are in play, use reinforcement only in combination with other strategies.

SHAPING NEW BEHAVIORS

What if a desired behavior has a baseline level of *zero?* How can we encourage a behavior that a student never exhibits at all, at least not in its ideal form? In such cases behaviorists suggest gradually shaping the behavior: reinforcing a series of responses—known as *successive approximations*—that increasingly resemble the terminal behavior. Shaping involves these steps:

1. Reinforce any response that in some way resembles the terminal behavior.
2. Reinforce a response that more closely approximates the terminal behavior (while no longer reinforcing the previously reinforced response).
3. Reinforce a response that resembles the terminal behavior even more closely.
4. Continue reinforcing closer and closer approximations to the terminal behavior.
5. Reinforce only the terminal behavior.

Each response in the sequence is continuously reinforced until it occurs regularly. Only at that point do we begin reinforcing a behavior that more closely approaches the desired end result. As an example, imagine that we have a second grader who can't seem to sit still long enough to get much of anything done. We'd ultimately like her to sit still for 20-minute periods, but we may first have to reinforce her for staying in her seat for just 2 minutes, gradually increasing the required sitting time as she makes progress.

> Shape a low-frequency behavior by reinforcing closer and closer approximations over time.

We can often use shaping to help students acquire complex physical and psychomotor skills. For example, in the early elementary grades teachers gradually shape students' handwriting skills—for instance, expecting increasingly small and well-shaped letters (see Figure 9.1). And in

FIGURE 9.1 **As Jeff moved through the elementary grades, his teachers gradually shaped his handwriting, in part by reducing the spacing between lines and, later, omitting some of the lines.**

Grade 1

I like to riyt.

Grade 2

One day Lonely was eating his brefisk

Grade 4

When we left Greeley I didnt want to go On the same day we stoped at a restrant. Then we went on In the ernen

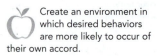

MyEdLab
Video Explanation 9.4.
This 4-minute video can enhance your understanding of both shaping and the transition from continuous to intermittent reinforcement.

secondary schools, physical education teachers and coaches may teach and expect increasingly proficient athletic skills (Harrison & Pyles, 2013; Stokes, Luiselli, & Reed, 2010).

In much the same way, we can use shaping—and teachers often do so—to teach students to work independently on assignments. We begin by giving first graders structured tasks that may take only 5 to 10 minutes to complete. As students move through the elementary school years, we expect them to work independently for longer periods and begin to give them short assignments to do at home. By the time students reach high school, they have extended study halls and complete lengthy assignments on their own after school hours. In the college years, student assignments require a great deal of independence and self-direction.

BRINGING ANTECEDENT STIMULI AND RESPONSES INTO THE PICTURE

In our discussion of instrumental conditioning so far, we've focused on the *consequences* of behaviors. But stimuli and responses that *precede* a desired behavior—antecedent stimuli and antecedent responses—can have effects as well. Here we'll look at several phenomena that involve antecedent stimuli, as well as one phenomenon (behavioral momentum) that involves antecedent responses.

CUEING

Students are more likely to behave appropriately when they get reminders—often called *cues* or *prompts*—that certain behaviors are expected (e.g., Northup et al., 1995; Shabani et al., 2002). Such cueing sometimes involves a nonverbal signal, such as flicking overhead lights off and on to remind students to use their "indoor voices." At other times it involves a verbal reminder about what students should be doing. Subtle hints are often effective for older students (e.g., "I see some art supplies that still need to be put away"), whereas more explicit hints may be necessary for younger children (e.g., "Table 3 needs to clean up its art supplies before it can go to lunch").

SETTING EVENTS

In cueing we use specific stimuli to prompt students to behave in particular ways. An alternative approach is to create an overall environment—a setting event—that's apt to evoke desired behaviors. For example, young children are more likely to interact with peers during free-play time if they have a relatively small area in which to play and if the toys available to them (e.g., balls, puppets) encourage cooperation and group activity (W. H. Brown, Fox, & Brady, 1987; Frost, Shin, & Jacobs, 1998; S. S. Martin, Brady, & Williams, 1991). Similarly, the nature of the games children are asked to play influences the behaviors they exhibit: Cooperative games promote cooperative behavior, whereas competitive games promote aggressive behavior (Bay-Hinitz, Peterson, & Quilitch, 1994).

Quickly and unobtrusively cue students about appropriate behaviors, perhaps through a flick of the light switch or brief verbal reminder.

Create an environment in which desired behaviors are more likely to occur of their own accord.

GENERALIZATION

Once children have learned that a response is likely to be reinforced in one set of circumstances (which serve as antecedent stimuli), they're apt to make the same response in similar situations. In other words, they show generalization. For example, after an especially fidgety student has learned to sit quietly and attentively for 20-minute periods in her second-grade classroom, she may generalize that behavior to her third-grade classroom the following year. And once a student has learned cursive writing at school, he's apt to use cursive in his out-of-school writing tasks. Generalization of newly acquired behaviors is most likely to occur when students have opportunities to practice them in diverse settings (Alberto & Troutman, 2013; Haring & Liberty, 1990; B. M. Johnson et al., 2006).

Provide opportunities for students to practice desired behaviors in a variety of settings.

This process of generalization should remind you of the generalization that occurs in classical conditioning: In both cases an individual learns a response to one stimulus and then responds in the same way to a similar stimulus. A key difference is one of learner control: Generalization involves an automatic, involuntary response in classical conditioning but a voluntary response in instrumental conditioning.

DISCRIMINATION

Sometimes responses are reinforced only when certain environmental conditions—that is, certain antecedent stimuli—are present. This ability to distinguish between conditions in which a particular behavior will and won't be reinforced is called discrimination. For example, teenage boys should certainly learn that slapping a peer on the fanny might be quite acceptable when celebrating an athletic victory with teammates but is *not* acceptable when greeting a female classmate in the hall. Some students may need explicit guidance about the circumstances in which particular behaviors are and are not likely to be reinforced.

It's occasionally helpful to use cueing to assist students in determining when certain behaviors are permissible. For example, in one study, children in three elementary classrooms were having trouble determining when they could and could not request a teacher's assistance. Their teachers began to wear green and red leis at different times and told them, "While I am wearing the green lei, I will be able to answer your questions. While I am wearing the red lei, I will not be able to answer your questions." This simple procedure minimized student requests at inopportune moments (Cammilleri, Tiger, & Hanley, 2008, p. 301; see Fisher, Rodriguez, & Owen, 2013, for a similar intervention).

Describe conditions under which certain behaviors are appropriate, and reinforce the behaviors only when they *are* appropriate.

BEHAVIORAL MOMENTUM

In many cases students are more likely to make desired responses if they're already making similar responses—a phenomenon known as behavioral momentum (Ardoin, Martens, & Wolfe, 1999; Belfiore, Lee, Vargas, & Skinner, 1997; Mace et al., 1988). For example, imagine that we have low-achieving adolescents who have a history of refusing to do math assignments. Such students are more likely to attempt difficult three-digit multiplication problems after they've first worked on a few simple one-digit problems (Belfiore et al., 1997). Similarly, we might ask students to tidy up a messy classroom after they've already cleaned their own desktops or to try a backward roll after they've successfully executed a forward roll. In general, we can promote behavioral momentum by assigning relatively easy or enjoyable tasks that lead naturally into more complex and potentially frustrating ones.

Take advantage of behavioral momentum, assigning easy tasks as a lead-in to similar but more challenging ones.

> MyEdLab **Application Exercise 9.2.** In this exercise, you can apply what you have learned about reinforcement to a variety of classroom scenarios.

Strategies for Discouraging Undesirable Behaviors

Our focus so far has been primarily on promoting desirable behaviors. But in addition, we must actively discourage *un*desirable behaviors—those that jeopardize students' classroom success or their classmates' well-being. Behaviorists have offered several possible approaches that we look at now.

CREATING CONDITIONS FOR EXTINCTION

 Identify and try to remove reinforcers that may be maintaining an undesirable behavior.

One way to reduce the frequency of an inappropriate response is simply to make sure it's never reinforced. For example, a class clown whose antics are ignored might stop distracting his class-mates, and a child who never gets what she wants by insulting others might begin to speak to them more respectfully.

There are several points to keep in mind about extinction, however. First, once reinforce-ment stops, a previously reinforced response may initially *increase* for a short time (Lerman & Iwata, 1995; McGill, 1999). For example, imagine you have a television set that works only when you bang on it once or twice. At some point something changes inside your TV that makes the banging ineffective; because you don't realize this at first, you bang it *many times and very hard* before you finally give up. In much the same way, students whose inappropriate behaviors have previously been reinforced may begin to behave even *less* appropriately once their original behav-iors are no longer working for them. Fortunately, such increases in misbehavior are usually tempo-rary, but they can certainly try our patience and perhaps tempt us into paying attention to—and thereby inadvertently reinforcing—the more extreme responses.

Second, if we ignore a student's misbehavior in an effort to extinguish it, we must be sure that we don't ignore the student altogether. Instead, we should give a misbehaving student attention for doing things *well* and also at random intervals throughout the school day (Austin & Soeda, 2008).

Third, we may sometimes have situations in which removing a reinforcer has no noticeable effect on a student's counterproductive behavior. Perhaps the behavior has previously been rein-forced only intermittently, thus making it fairly resistant to extinction (recall the earlier Molly-and-Maria example). Or perhaps the behavior is being reinforced in other ways—say, by class-mates' attention or the release of pent-up energy. In such cases, one or more of the strategies that follow are probably in order.

CUEING INAPPROPRIATE BEHAVIORS

 Use physical or verbal cues to discourage inappropri-ate behavior.

Just as we can use cueing to remind students about what they should be doing, we can also cue them about what they should *not* be doing. For example, we might use *body language*—perhaps making eye contact and raising an eyebrow—or *physical proximity*—moving closer to the student and standing there until the problem behavior stops. When subtlety doesn't work, a brief *verbal cue* may be in order—perhaps stating a student's name or (if necessary) pointing out an inappropri-ate behavior (e.g., "Lucy, put away your cell phone").

REINFORCING INCOMPATIBLE BEHAVIORS

Often we can reduce the frequency of an unproductive behavior simply by reinforcing an *alterna-tive* behavior. Ideally, the two behaviors are incompatible behaviors, in that they cannot both be performed at the same time. For example, try the following exercise.

EXPERIENCING FIRSTHAND
ASLEEP ON YOUR FEET

Have you ever tried to sleep while standing up? Horses can do it, but most of us humans really can't. In fact, there are many pairs of responses that are impossible to perform simultaneously. Take a minute to identify something you cannot possibly do when you perform each of these activities:

When you ...	You cannot simultaneously ...
Sit down	_____
Eat crackers	_____
Check messages on your cell phone	_____

Obviously there are many possible right answers. For instance, sitting is incompatible with stand-ing. Eating crackers is incompatible with singing—or at least with singing *well*. Checking your cell phone for new messages is incompatible with paying attention to a class lecture. In each case it's impossible to perform both activities at exactly the same time.

When our attempts at extinction or cueing are unsuccessful, reinforcement of one or more behaviors that are incompatible with a problem behavior is often quite effective (K. Lane, Falk, & Wehby, 2006; S. W. Payne & Dozier, 2013; Pipkin, Vollmer, & Sloman, 2010). This is the approach we're taking when we reinforce a hyperactive student for sitting quietly: Sitting is incompatible with getting-out-of-seat and roaming-around-the-room behaviors. It's also an approach we might use to deal with forgetfulness (we reinforce students when they remember to do what they're supposed to do), being off-task (we reinforce on-task behavior), and verbal abusiveness (we reinforce prosocial statements). And consider how we might deal with a chronic litterbug (Krumboltz & Krumboltz, 1972):

> Walt often leaves banana peels, sunflower seed shells, and other garbage in and outside the school building. When the school faculty establishes an Anti-Litter Committee, it puts Walt on the committee, and the committee eventually elects him as its chairman. Under Walt's leadership, the committee institutes an anti-litter campaign, complete with posters and lunchroom monitors, and Walt receives considerable recognition for the campaign's success. Subsequently, school personnel no longer find Walt's garbage littering the building and school grounds.

> Encourage and reinforce responses that are incompatible with undesirable behaviors.

USING PUNISHMENT WHEN NECESSARY

Some misbehaviors require an immediate remedy—for instance, they might interfere significantly with classroom learning or reflect total disregard for other people's rights and welfare. Consider this example:

> Bonnie doesn't handle frustration well. Whenever she encounters an obstacle she can't immediately overcome, she hits, punches, kicks, or breaks something. Once, during a class Valentine's Day party, she accidentally drops her cupcake. When she discovers that it's no longer edible, she throws her milk carton across the room, hitting another child on the head.

Bonnie's troublesome behaviors are hard to extinguish because they aren't being reinforced to begin with—at least not extrinsically. Also, there are no obvious incompatible responses that might be reinforced instead. And presumably Bonnie's teacher has often cued her about her inappropriate behaviors. When other strategies are inapplicable or ineffective, punishment is a potentially viable alternative.

> Use punishment when alternative approaches are inapplicable or have been ineffective.

A frequent criticism of punishment is that it's inhumane, or somehow cruel and barbaric. Indeed, certain forms of punishment, such as physical abuse and public humiliation, do constitute inhumane treatment. We must be *extremely careful* when we use punishment in the classroom. If administered judiciously, however, some forms of mild punishment can lead to rapid reductions in misbehavior without causing physical or psychological harm. And when we can decrease counterproductive classroom behaviors quickly and effectively—especially when those behaviors are harmful to self or others—punishment may, in fact, be one of the most humane approaches we can take (Lerman & Vorndran, 2002). Following are several guidelines for using punishment effectively and humanely.

- *Choose a consequence that is truly punishing without being overly severe.* Any unpleasant consequence must be strong enough to discourage students from engaging further in the punished behavior (Boyanton, 2010; Landrum & Kauffman, 2006; Lerman & Vorndran, 2002). But unnecessarily harsh punishments—those that far surpass the severity of the crime—are apt to lead to such undesirable side effects as resentment, hostility, aggression, and escape behavior. Furthermore, although severe punishment may quickly suppress a response, that response may reappear at its original level once the punisher has left the scene (Appel & Peterson, 1965; Azrin, 1960; Landrum & Kauffman, 2006). The ultimate purpose of administering punishment is to communicate that the limits of acceptable behavior have been exceeded, *not* to exact revenge and retaliation.

- *Inform students ahead of time that certain behaviors will be punished, and explain how those behaviors will be punished.* When students are informed of response–punishment contingencies ahead of time, they're less likely to engage in forbidden behaviors, and they're less likely to be surprised or resentful if punishment must be administered (Boyanton, 2010; Moles,

Understanding that one's own behaviors influence consequences is an example of an *attribution* (see Chapter 11).

1990). Ultimately, students must learn that their behaviors influence the consequences they experience—that they have some control over what happens to them.

• *Follow through with specified consequences.* A mistake some teachers make is to continually threaten punishment without ever following through. One warning is desirable, but repeated warnings are not. Consider the teacher who says, "If you bring that rubber snake to class one more time, I'll take it away!" but never does take away the snake. This teacher is giving the message that no response–punishment contingency really exists.

• *Administer punishment privately, especially when other students aren't aware of the transgression.* By administering punishment in private, we protect students from public embarrassment and humiliation. We also eliminate the possibility that the punishment will draw classmates' attention—a potential reinforcer for the very behavior we're trying to eliminate.

• *Emphasize that it's the behavior—not the student—that is unacceptable, and explain why it's unacceptable.* We must explain exactly why a certain behavior cannot be tolerated in the classroom—perhaps because it interferes with learning, threatens other students' safety or self-esteem, or damages school property. In other words, punishment should be accompanied by **induction.** Punishment is far more effective when accompanied by one or more reasons that the punished behavior is unacceptable (Hoffman, 1975, 2000; Parke, 1974; D. G. Perry & Perry, 1983).

Some mild forms of punishment, such as a brief time-out in a quiet corner away from peers, can reduce counterproductive behaviors, but we must monitor their effectiveness for different students.

Jamie Wilson/Fotolia

• *Administer punishment within the context of a warm, supportive interpersonal relationship.* Punishment is more effective when the person administering it has previously established a good working relationship with the student (Landrum & Kauffman, 2006; Nucci, 2001). The message should ultimately be this: "I care for you and want you to succeed, and your current behavior is interfering with your success."

• *Simultaneously teach and reinforce desirable alternative behaviors.* Punishment of misbehavior is almost always more effective when appropriate behaviors are being reinforced at the same time (Landrum & Kauffman, 2006; Lerman & Vorndran, 2002). Furthermore, by reinforcing desirable responses as well as punishing undesirable ones, we give students the positive, optimistic message that, yes, behavior can and will improve. Ultimately, the overall classroom atmosphere we create must be a positive one that highlights the *good* things students do.

• *Monitor the punishment's effectiveness.* Remember that punishment is defined by its effect on behavior. True punishment decreases the response it follows, typically quite rapidly (R. V. Hall et al., 1971; Landrum & Kauffman, 2006). If a given consequence doesn't decrease the response it's intended to punish, it may not be aversive to the individual being "punished." In fact, it may even be reinforcing.

> MyEdLab **Application Exercise 9.3.** In this exercise, you can apply what you have just learned about reducing unproductive behaviors to several classroom situations.

Addressing Especially Difficult Classroom Behaviors

Behaviorist principles can be extremely helpful in tackling difficult and chronic behavior problems. In this section we consider three related approaches for addressing especially challenging behaviors. Often they're planned and carried out by one or more teachers in consultation with a school psychologist or other specialist.

APPLIED BEHAVIOR ANALYSIS

Applied behavior analysis, or **ABA**, is a group of procedures that systematically apply behaviorist principles in changing behavior. (You might also see such terms as *behavior modification, behavior therapy,* and *contingency management.*) Applied behavior analysis is based on the assumptions that (a) behavior problems result from past and present environmental conditions and (b) modifying a learner's present environment will promote more productive behaviors.

Consistent with behaviorist traditions, teachers and therapists who use ABA focus on specific, concrete responses, which they call **target behaviors**. Sometimes interventions are aimed at increasing certain (presumably desirable) target behaviors; these are the *terminal behaviors* of which we've previously spoken. At other times interventions are designed to decrease certain (presumably undesirable) target behaviors.

When teachers and therapists use ABA to help a student acquire more appropriate classroom behavior, they typically use strategies such as these:

- Describe target behaviors in objectively measurable terms.
- Identify one or more effective reinforcers.
- Develop a specific intervention or treatment plan, which may involve reinforcement of desired behaviors, shaping, extinction, reinforcement of incompatible behaviors, punishment, or some combination of these.
- Give explicit instruction related to desired behaviors.
- Measure the frequency of target behaviors both before the intervention (i.e., at baseline level) and during the intervention in order to monitor the intervention's effectiveness; modify the program if necessary.
- Take steps to promote generalization of new behaviors (e.g., through practice in various realistic situations).
- Gradually phase out the treatment (e.g., through intermittent reinforcement) after desired behaviors are occurring regularly.

The systematic use of behaviorist strategies such as these can lead to significant improvements in academic performance and classroom behavior. For example, when we reinforce students for academic accomplishments, we're apt to see noticeable progress in such areas as reading, spelling, creative writing, and math. And when we reinforce appropriate classroom behaviors—perhaps paying attention to lessons, cooperating with classmates, or responding constructively to someone else's aggressive actions—misbehaviors decrease (S. N. Elliott & Busse, 1991; Evertson & Weinstein, 2006; Greer et al., 2013; Piersel, 1987).

One likely reason that ABA often works so well is that it gives students clear and consistent messages about which behaviors are acceptable and which are not. Another likely reason is that through the gradual process of *shaping,* students begin to practice new behaviors only when they're truly ready to acquire them; thus, their probability of achieving success and reinforcement is quite high.

FUNCTIONAL ANALYSIS

Traditional ABA focuses largely on changing response–reinforcement contingencies to bring about more appropriate behavior. Some behaviorists suggest that we also consider the purposes, or *functions,* that students' inappropriate behaviors may serve. Such an approach is known as **functional analysis** (you might also see the terms *functional assessment* and *functional behavioral assessment*). Functional analysis involves collecting data regarding the specific conditions (i.e., antecedent stimuli) in which students tend to misbehave and also the consequences (i.e., reinforcers, punishments, or both) that typically follow the misbehaviors. Thus, we would collect data related to the three parts of a stimulus–response–stimulus sequence, like this:

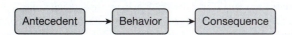

For example, we've speculated that in the opening case study, James misbehaves in order to get the attention he apparently can't get in more productive ways and possibly also to escape certain classroom tasks. Functional analyses have shown that students with chronic classroom behavior problems often misbehave when they're asked to do difficult or unpleasant tasks (this is the *antecedent*) and that their misbehavior either allows them to escape these tasks or gains them the attention of others (these are possible *consequences*) (McComas et al., 2003; M. M. Mueller et al., 2011; Van Camp et al., 2000).

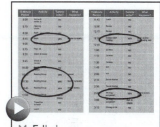

MyEdLab
Video Explanation 9.5.

This 19-minute video provides animated explanations of both ABA and functional analysis; it also provides concrete examples of how teachers might use these strategies in working with students who have chronic behavior problems.

When a student's problem behavior persists, try to identify functions that the behavior might serve for the student.

POSITIVE BEHAVIORAL INTERVENTIONS AND SUPPORTS

An approach known as **positive behavioral interventions and supports (PBIS)**[5] takes the process a step further: After identifying the purposes that inappropriate behaviors might serve, a teacher—or, more often, a team of teachers and other professionals—develops and carries out a plan to encourage appropriate behaviors. In particular, PBIS involves strategies such as these:

- Teach behaviors that can serve the same purpose as (and can therefore replace) inappropriate behaviors.
- Modify the school environment to minimize conditions that might trigger inappropriate behaviors.
- Establish a predictable daily routine as a way of minimizing anxiety and making the student feel more comfortable and secure.
- Give the student opportunities to make choices; in this way the student can often gain desired outcomes without having to resort to inappropriate behavior.
- Make adaptations in the curriculum, instruction, or both to maximize the likelihood of academic success (e.g., build on the student's interests, present material at a slower pace, or intersperse challenging tasks among easier and more enjoyable ones).
- Monitor the frequency of various behaviors to determine whether the intervention is working or, instead, requires modification. (Crone & Horner, 2003; Eber, 2002; Ruef, Higgins, Glaeser, & Patnode, 1998; Wheeler & Richey, 2014)

The following case study (summarized from DeVault, Krug, & Fake, 1996) provides an example of how functional analysis and PBIS support might be used in combination:

Nine-year-old Samantha had been identified as having a mild form of autism and moderate speech disabilities. She frequently ran out of her third-grade classroom, damaging school property and classmates' belongings in her flight. When an adult tried to intervene, she would fight back by biting, hitting, kicking, or pulling hair. On such occasions school personnel often asked her parents to take her home.

By systematically collecting data on Samantha's classroom performance, a team of teachers and specialists discovered that her misbehaviors typically occurred when she either was given or was expecting a difficult assignment. Departures from the regular schedule or the absence of favorite teachers further increased the frequency of misbehaviors.

The team hypothesized that Samantha's undesirable behaviors served two purposes: They (a) helped her escape unpleasant academic tasks and (b) enabled her to gain the attention of valued adults. The team suspected, too, that Samantha felt as if she had little or no control over classroom activities and that she yearned for more social interaction with her teachers and classmates.

Armed with this information, the team took several steps:

- Samantha was given a consistent and predictable daily schedule that included frequent breaks from potentially challenging academic tasks and numerous opportunities to interact with others.
- Samantha was given goal sheets from which she could choose the academic tasks she would work on, the length of time she would work on them, and the reinforcer she would receive for achieving each goal.
- Samantha was taught how to ask for help on challenging tasks.
- When Samantha felt she needed a break from academic work, she could ask to spend some time in the "relaxation room," a quiet and private space where she could sit in a beanbag chair and listen to soothing audiotapes.
- If Samantha tried to leave the classroom, an adult would place her immediately in the relaxation room, where she could calm down without a lot of adult attention.

---

[5]Historically, this approach has been known as *positive behavior support* (PBS), but special educators are increasingly using the term *positive behavioral interventions and supports* (PBIS), in part to avoid confusion with another "PBS"—the television network Public Broadcasting Service (K. R. Harris, personal communication, October 25, 2014).

- Samantha was given explicit instruction in how to interact appropriately with class-mates. Initially, she earned points for appropriate social behaviors and could trade them for special treats (e.g., a family trip to Dairy Queen or a video store). Eventually, her new social skills led to natural consequences—friendly interactions with peers—that made extrinsic reinforcers unnecessary.

Samantha's problem behaviors didn't disappear overnight, but they showed a dramatic decline over the next few months. By the time Samantha was 12 years old and in sixth grade, her grades consistently earned her a place on the honor roll, and she had a group of friends with whom she participated in extracurricular activities. Her teachers described her as being sociable, inquisitive, and creative. Her principal called her a "model student" (DeVault et al., 1996).

In recent years some schools have successfully instituted schoolwide positive behavioral interventions and supports programs that encourage productive behaviors in *all* students.[6] These programs typically include most or all of the following:

- Explicitly defining and teaching appropriate behaviors, including productive ways of getting desired outcomes (e.g., teacher attention)
- Designing a curriculum and implementing instructional practices tailored to students' current needs and ability levels
- Giving students opportunities to make choices
- Regularly reinforcing students for behaving appropriately, almost always with praise but often also with token reinforcers that can be traded for special prizes and privileges
- Providing considerable guidance and support (sometimes including individualized interventions) for students who need them
- Continually monitoring the program's effectiveness by examining office referrals, disciplinary actions, and other relevant data

Such steps often lead to dramatic changes in students' behavior and are especially helpful in schools that have historically had many discipline problems. Furthermore, teachers become more optimistic that they can truly make a difference in improving students' classroom behavior and academic achievement (Bradshaw, Mitchell, & Leaf, 2010; Ihlo & Nantais, 2010; T. J. Lewis, Newcomer, Trussell, & Richter, 2006; Osher et al., 2010; Warren et al., 2006).

Positive behavioral interventions and supports programs clearly have elements of behaviorist theory, including their focus on structuring an environment that reinforces desired behaviors and extinguishes undesirable ones. At the same time, they also incorporate contemporary theories of motivation, as reflected in their attempts to minimize anxiety, provide opportunities for choice making, and promote mastery of classroom tasks.

MyEdLab
Video Example 9.4.

Which components of schoolwide positive behavioral interventions and supports do you notice in the program described in this video?

The importance of doing such things will become clearer in the discussions of motivation and affect in Chapter 11.

> MyEdLab **Self-Check 9.4**
>
> MyEdLab **Application Exercise 9.4.** In this exercise, you can apply behaviorist strategies to address several chronic behavior problems.

Diversity in Student Behaviors and Reactions to Consequences

When we take a behaviorist perspective, we realize that every student brings a unique history of environments and experiences to the classroom, and such diversity is a key reason for the different behavior patterns we see. Some students may have associated particular stimuli with anxiety-arousing events (classical conditioning), and various students have undoubtedly been reinforced and punished—by parents, previous teachers, peers, and other community members—for different kinds of behaviors (instrumental conditioning). For example, some students may have been reinforced for completing tasks carefully and thoroughly, whereas others may have been reinforced

---

[6]You might see either "SWPBIS" or "SWPBS" used in reference to this approach.

for completing them quickly and with little regard for quality. Likewise, some students may have been reinforced for initiating interactions with age-mates, whereas others may have been punished (e.g., by peer rejection) for similar outgoing behaviors. In some instances, diversity in students' behaviors is the result of the different behaviors that various cultural groups encourage (i.e., reinforce) and discourage (i.e., punish) in children.

STUDENTS IN INCLUSIVE SETTINGS

TABLE 9.4 • Encouraging Appropriate Behaviors in Students with Special Educational Needs

CATEGORY	CHARACTERISTICS YOU MIGHT OBSERVE	SUGGESTED STRATEGIES
Students with specific cognitive or academic difficulties	• Inappropriate classroom behaviors (for some students) • Less ability to delay gratification (for students with ADHD) • Avoidance behaviors common when confronting challenging tasks • Difficulty discriminating among similar stimuli, especially when perceptual deficits exist	• Be explicit about and consistently reinforce desired classroom behaviors. • Emphasize differences among similar stimuli (e.g., the letters *b, d, p,* and *q*), and provide opportunities to practice making subtle discriminations. • Promote generalization of new responses (e.g., by pointing out similarities among different situations and by teaching skills in real-world contexts). • Have students work on assignments with classmates who are good role models and can encourage on-task behaviors.
Students with social or behavioral problems	• Inappropriate responses, especially in social situations; difficulty determining when and where particular responses are appropriate • A history of inappropriate behaviors being reinforced (e.g., intrinsically or by teacher attention) • Responsiveness to teacher praise if given in private (for students with emotional and behavioral disorders) • Little or no appreciation of others' praise and approval (for some students with autism) • Difficulty generalizing appropriate responses to new situations	• Explicitly and concretely describe desired behaviors. • Give precise feedback regarding students' behavior. • Reinforce desired behaviors using teacher attention, private praise, activity reinforcers, and group contingencies (for students with emotional and behavioral disorders). • Reinforce accomplishments immediately, using concrete reinforcers or activity reinforcers; combine them with praise so that praise eventually becomes reinforcing in and of itself (for students with severe forms of autism). • Shape desired behaviors over time; expect gradual improvement rather than immediate perfection. • Punish inappropriate behaviors (e.g., using time-out or response cost); implement positive behavioral interventions and supports for persistently challenging behaviors. • Promote generalization of new responses to appropriate situations (e.g., by teaching skills in real-world contexts and providing opportunities to role-play new responses).
Students with general delays in cognitive and social functioning	• Appreciation of and responsiveness to extrinsic reinforcers • Difficulty delaying gratification; behavior more likely to improve when reinforcement is immediate rather than delayed • Inappropriate responses in social situations • Difficulty discriminating between important and unimportant stimuli • Difficulty generalizing responses from one situation to another	• Explicitly teach and cue appropriate behaviors, but with the goal of having students eventually engage in such behaviors without external prompts. • Reinforce accomplishments immediately (e.g., using concrete reinforcers, activity reinforcers, praise). • Use continuous reinforcement during the acquisition of new responses. • Shape complex behaviors slowly over time; expect gradual improvement rather than immediate perfection. • Reprimand minor misbehaviors; use time-out or response cost for more serious and chronic misbehaviors. • Emphasize the stimuli to which you want students to attend. • Promote generalization of new responses (e.g., by teaching skills in real-world contexts and by reinforcing generalization).
Students with physical or sensory challenges	• Loss of some previously learned behaviors if students have had traumatic brain injury	• Shape desired behaviors slowly over time; expect gradual improvement rather than immediate perfection.
Students with advanced cognitive development	• Unusual and sometimes creative responses to classroom tasks	• Keep an open mind about acceptable responses to classroom assignments. • Encourage and reinforce creative responses.

Sources: Barbetta, 1990; Barbetta, Heward, Bradley, & Miller, 1994; Beirne-Smith, Patton, & Kim, 2006; Buchoff, 1990; J. O. Cooper, Heron, & Heward, 2007; Cuskelly, Zhang, & Hayes, 2003; E. S. Ellis & Friend, 1991; S. Goldstein & Rider, 2006; Grauvogel-MacAleese & Wallace, 2010; Hausman, Ingvarsson, & Kahng, 2014; Heward, 2009; Hobson, 2004; Hoerger & Mace, 2006; Landau & McAninch, 1993; Mercer & Pullen, 2005; M. M. Mueller et al., 2011; Neef et al., 2005; Patton, Blackbourn, & Fad, 1996; Pfiffner et al., 2006; Piirto, 1999; Pressley, 1995; Turnbull, Turnbull, & Wehmeyer, 2010.

Differences also exist in the consequences students find reinforcing, to some degree as a result of the cultures in which they've grown up. For instance, although many students from mainstream Western culture are apt to appreciate praise for their personal accomplishments, many students from Asian cultures are unaccustomed to public praise, preferring instead to have simple compliments given in private along with feedback that helps them improve on their weaknesses. And many Native American students may feel uncomfortable when praised for their work as individuals yet feel quite proud when they receive praise for group success—a preference that's consistent with the cooperative spirit of most Native American groups (Fuller, 2001; Hattie & Gan, 2011; Jiang, 2010; Kitayama, Duffy, & Uchida, 2007).

In some cultural groups, reprimands may be used to communicate concern and affection. For example, on one occasion a teacher in Haiti was reprimanding students for proceeding across a parking lot without her:

> *Teacher:* Did I tell you to go?
>
> *Children:* No.
>
> *Teacher:* Can you cross this parking lot by yourselves?
>
> *Children:* No.
>
> *Teacher:* That's right. There are cars here. They're dangerous. I don't want you to go alone. Why do I want you to wait for me, do you know?
>
> *Claudette:* Yes … because you like us. (Ballenger, 1992, p. 205)

> Keep in mind that students from some cultures are unaccustomed to public praise for their individual accomplishments.

ACCOMMODATING STUDENTS WITH SPECIAL NEEDS

The structured, systematic use of behaviorist principles—such as those manifested in positive behavioral interventions and supports—can be especially effective with students who have cognitive, social, or behavioral disabilities. Table 9.4 offers specific recommendations for working with students who have various special needs. Behaviorist strategies are often important components of students' individualized education programs (IEPs).

> Chapter 5 identifies specific categories of special needs that fall within the five general categories listed in Table 9.4.

MyEdLab **Self-Check 9.5**

---

9   What Have You Learned?

As a way of recapping our discussion of behaviorist principles, we now return to the chapter's learning outcomes.

■ **9.1: Describe five basic assumptions underlying behaviorist views of learning, and apply these assumptions to classroom practices.** Historically behaviorists have argued that internal mental processes cannot be studied objectively, and thus they have focused largely on stimuli in a learner's immediate environments (both past and present) and on a learner's responses to those stimuli. Many behaviorists view learning as a change in behavior (rather than as a mental change) and explain it in terms of specific stimulus–response associations. Key to forming such associations is close proximity in time (contiguity) between the stimuli and responses involved. Many behaviorist principles of learning apply equally to human beings and other animal species.

■ **9.2: Explain how learners can acquire involuntary responses through classical conditioning and how you might help a student overcome classically conditioned emotional responses that interfere with classroom performance.** Classical conditioning occurs when (a) one stimulus (the unconditioned stimulus) already elicits a particular response (the unconditioned response) and (b) that stimulus is presented in conjunction with another stimulus, usually on several occasions. Under these circumstances, the second (conditioned) stimulus begins to elicit a (conditioned) response as well. Classical conditioning is one possible explanation for why students may have unproductive emotional reactions in certain learning environments—say, in a math class or on the athletic field. As teachers, we should strive to create an instructional environment that conditions pleasure and relaxation responses to new tasks and activities, not an environment that elicits fear and anxiety.

■ **9.3: Describe the effects that various kinds of consequences can have on behavior.** By definition, a *reinforcing* stimulus increases the behavior it follows, whereas a *punishing* stimulus decreases the behavior. Taken together, these two effects are known as *instrumental conditioning,* although you may also see the term *operant conditioning* used in reference to the effects of a reinforcer.

Positive reinforcement is at work when a response increases after previously being followed by the presentation of a particular stimulus or event (e.g., a compliment or opportunity to engage in a favorite activity). Negative reinforcement is at work when a response increases after previously being followed by the *removal* of an *unpleasant* stimulus (e.g., a frustrating task or feeling of anxiety).

Negative reinforcement—which *increases* the behavior—shouldn't be confused with punishment, which can involve either the presentation of a stimulus (presumably one that a learner finds desirable) or the removal of a stimulus (presumably one that a learner wants to get rid of). Some forms of punishment (e.g., mild reprimands, time-outs) can be quite effective when used judiciously, whereas others (e.g., public humiliation, out-of-school suspension) are usually counterproductive.

■ **9.4: Apply behaviorist principles to encourage productive student behaviors and discourage undesirable ones.** We can increase the frequency of desired student behaviors either by reinforcing the behaviors whenever they occur or by gradually shaping them over time. Our use of reinforcement is more likely to be effective when we make response–consequence contingencies explicit and when we individualize reinforcers to match students' preferences. By itself, however, reinforcement can bring about behavior change only when students have the physical and cognitive *ability* to behave appropriately.

Students' behaviors are influenced not only by their consequences but also by antecedent events. For example, once students have learned a particular response to a particular stimulus, they may make the same response to similar stimuli. Seemingly similar situations occasionally call for very different behaviors, however, and so we must help students discriminate between occasions when certain responses are and are not appropriate. It's important, too, to create environments that readily evoke desired student behaviors and to introduce challenging tasks only after students have become comfortable performing similar but slightly easier ones.

Behaviorist principles offer several strategies for reducing nonproductive or counterproductive classroom behaviors.

As teachers, we might remove the consequences that reinforce an unwanted behavior (possibly resulting in extinction), cue students about inappropriate behavior, or reinforce responses that are incompatible with those we want to eliminate. In some cases, we may need to resort to punishment, especially if students' behaviors significantly interfere with classroom learning or jeopardize one or more students' welfare. We can maximize the effectiveness of punishment by adhering to certain guidelines in its use. For example, we should tell students ahead of time which behaviors are unacceptable and what the particular consequences will be, and we should administer punishment within the context of a warm, supportive relationship—one that communicates a genuine concern for students' well-being.

Applied behavior analysis, functional analysis, and positive behavioral interventions and supports (PBIS) are three overlapping approaches through which we can apply behaviorist principles in a systematic fashion. Such techniques are often effective in promoting academic achievement and appropriate classroom behavior, even in cases where other approaches haven't worked. In fact, PBIS can be effectively applied on a schoolwide basis to reduce discipline problems and enhance student achievement across the board.

■ **9.5: Accommodate students' personal and cultural backgrounds and special needs in your application of behaviorist principles.** Students in any single classroom have had different histories of reinforcement and different prior experiences with the stimuli they encounter at school; hence, they'll inevitably have varying reactions to the same tasks and situations. Students' cultural backgrounds may also have contributed to their diversity; for example, some students may appreciate praise only when it's given in private, and others may prefer reinforcement for group achievement rather than individual accomplishments.

Students with cognitive, social, or behavioral disabilities can especially benefit from the structured, consistent learning environments that behaviorists advocate. For example, a functional analysis can help us understand why a certain student is frequently aggressive or noncompliant and then enable us to plan an intervention that promotes more productive classroom behaviors. And consistent, explicit, and immediate use of reinforcement to shape increasingly complex behaviors can help students with cognitive disabilities acquire many new skills.

Practice for Your Licensure Exam

Hostile Helen

Mr. Washington has a close-knit group of friends in one of his high school vocational education classes. He is concerned about a particular student in this friendship group: a girl named Helen. Helen uses obscene language in class. She's also rude and disrespectful to Mr. Washington, and she taunts and insults classmates outside her own circle of friends. In addition, Helen is physically aggressive toward school property; for example, she sometimes defaces furniture, kicks equipment, and punches walls.

At first, Mr. Washington tries to ignore Helen's hostile and aggressive behaviors, but this strategy doesn't lead to any improvement in her behavior. He then tries praising Helen on those rare occasions when she does behave appropriately, but this strategy doesn't seem to work either.

1. Multiple-choice question:

Mr. Washington initially tries to ignore Helen's inappropriate behavior. This approach best reflects which one of the following concepts from behaviorism?

a. Extinction

b. Response cost

c. Functional analysis

d. Negative reinforcement

2. Multiple-choice question:

Later, Mr. Washington tries praising Helen for appropriate behaviors. This approach best reflects which one of the following behaviorist concepts?

a. Setting event

b. Discrimination

c. Reinforcement of incompatible behaviors

d. Positive behavioral interventions and supports

3. Constructed-response question:

Many research studies indicate that behaviorist principles *can* be effective in bringing about significant improvements in students' classroom behavior, yet neither of Mr. Washington's strategies has an effect on Helen's classroom behavior.

A. Suggest at least three different reasons why Mr. Washington's strategies might not be having much effect.

B. Describe how *you* might use behaviorist learning principles to bring about a behavior change in Helen. Be specific about what you would do.

MyEdLab **Licensure Exam 9.1**

PRAXIS Go to Appendix C, "Matching Book Content and Ebook Activities to the Praxis Principles of Learning and Teaching Tests," to discover sections of this chapter that may be especially applicable to the Praxis tests.

Jim Cummins/CORBIS/Glow Images

10 Social Cognitive Views of Learning

Learning Outcomes

10.1 Describe five basic assumptions of social cognitive theory and their classroom implications.

10.2 Use a social cognitive perspective to explain how mental processes can influence the effects of reinforcement and punishment.

10.3 Describe the potential effects of modeling on learners' behaviors, and explain how you can productively use modeling in instruction.

10.4 Describe the nature and origins of self-efficacy, and explain how you might enhance self-efficacy both in your students as developing learners and in yourself as a teacher.

10.5 Identify important components of self-regulated behavior and self-regulated learning, and apply your knowledge of self-regulation to help diverse learners effectively control their behavior, master academic subject matter, and address interpersonal problems.

10.6 Compare and contrast perspectives of learning associated with cognitive psychology, contextual theories, behaviorism, and social cognitive theory.

CASE STUDY: PARLEZ-VOUS FRANÇAIS?

Nathan is in French I only because his mother insisted that he take it. On the first day of class, Nathan notices that most of his classmates are girls and the few boys are students he doesn't know very well. He sits sullenly in the back, recalling that three male friends who took French last year got mostly Ds and Fs on quizzes and homework and that two of them dropped the class after one semester. "I do great in math and science," he tells himself, "but I'm just no good at learning languages. Besides, learning French is a *girl* thing."

Although Nathan comes to class every day, his mind often wanders as his teacher demonstrates correct pronunciations and explains simple syntactical structures. He makes feeble attempts at homework assignments but quickly puts them aside whenever he encounters something he doesn't immediately understand.

Sure enough, Nathan is right: He can't do French. He gets a D– on the first exam.

- What things has Nathan learned from observing the people around him? What things has he *not* learned, and why?
- In what general ways might observing other individuals influence learning?

Although Nathan hasn't learned much from his French teacher—partly because he hasn't been paying attention during lessons and partly because he hasn't put much effort into assignments—he's learned a few things from observing his *peers*. Knowing what happened to three male friends and seeing mostly girls in his class, he concludes that, as a boy, he's doomed to failure. We human beings learn a wide variety of behaviors by observing the people in our lives and in the media. We also learn which behaviors are likely to get us ahead—and which are not—by seeing their consequences for others. In part by watching what others do, we develop a sense of what our own capabilities are likely to be, and we begin to direct our behavior toward goals we think we can achieve.

In this chapter we explore social cognitive theory, a perspective that can help us understand what and how people learn by observing others and how, in the process, they begin to take control of their own behavior. Originally called *social learning theory,* social cognitive theory has its early roots in behaviorism and thus addresses the effects of reinforcement and punishment. Over the past few decades, however, it has increasingly incorporated cognitive processes into its explanations of learning and now includes a blend of ideas from behaviorism and cognitive psychology.

Social cognitive theory has developed in large part through the research efforts of Albert Bandura at Stanford University. You'll find references to Bandura and others who have built on his ideas (e.g., Dale Schunk, Barry Zimmerman) throughout the chapter.

Basic Assumptions of Social Cognitive Theory

Several basic assumptions underlie social cognitive theory:

- *People can learn by observing others.* From the perspective of behaviorism, learning is often a process of trial and error: Learners try many different responses, keep those that bring desired consequences, and leave unproductive ones behind. Social cognitive theorists argue that learners don't necessarily have to experiment in such a trial-and-error manner. Instead learners acquire many new responses simply by observing the behaviors of other individuals, or *models.* For example, a student might learn

Children learn many new behaviors simply by watching adults or peers perform them successfully.

Chapter 9 presents behaviorist perspectives of learning.

how to solve a long division problem, spell the word *synonym* correctly, or mouth off at a teacher simply by watching someone else do these things first.

- *Learning is an internal process that may or may not lead to a behavior change.* Rather than define learning as a change in behavior (as many behaviorists do), social cognitive theorists (like cognitive psychologists) view learning as a mental change that may or may not be reflected in the learner's present or future behavior. For example, you might try to dribble a basketball as soon as you watch someone else do it. You probably won't demonstrate that you've learned how to apologize tactfully until a later time when an apology is necessary. And you might *never* walk through campus nude, no matter how many times you see someone else do it.

- *Cognitive processes influence motivation as well as learning.* Like cognitive psychologists, social cognitive theorists recognize the importance of cognitive processes (e.g., attention, encoding) for learning and remembering new information. But they point out that cognition is also an important ingredient in *motivation.* For example, people set mental *goals* toward which they direct their behavior, and their goals are based to some degree on their *expectations* about what they might reasonably accomplish. People's beliefs about their own ability to execute certain behaviors or reach certain goals—their *self-efficacy*—influence how hard they try, how long they persist at challenging tasks, and ultimately how much they learn and achieve.

- *People and their environments mutually influence each other.* Some learning theorists, especially behaviorists, focus primarily on how environmental variables can influence learners. But the reverse is true as well: Learners influence their environments, often quite deliberately. To some degree learners influence their environments through their *behaviors.* For example, the responses they make (e.g., the classes they choose, the extracurricular activities they pursue, the company they keep) affect the learning opportunities they have and the consequences they experience. Mental processes, personality characteristics, and other things that learners "own" in some way—social cognitive theorists call these things *person* variables—come into play as well. For example, learners are apt to focus their attention on—and thus learn from—only certain aspects of their environment, and their idiosyncratic interpretations of why they've been reinforced or punished influence the specific effects that such consequences have.

FIGURE 10.1 In social cognitive theory, environmental, behavioral, and personal variables mutually influence one another.

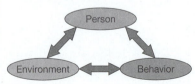

Ultimately, all three of these factors—environment, behavior, and person—influence one another in the manner shown in Figure 10.1. Social cognitive theorists use the term reciprocal causation when referring to this constant interplay among environment, behavior, and person variables (e.g., Bandura, 1989, 2008).

- *Behavior becomes increasingly self-regulated.* In the first few years of life, children's actions are controlled and guided to a considerable degree by others—by parents, older siblings, child-care providers, teachers, and so on. But as children grow older, most of them increasingly take charge of their lives, not only identifying particular goals toward which to strive but also directing and monitoring their behaviors and thought processes to accomplish their goals. In other words, most children increasingly engage in *self-regulation*.

Table 10.1 summarizes the assumptions just listed and offers examples of their implications for classroom practice.

MyEdLab **Self Check 10.1**

PRINCIPLES/ASSUMPTIONS

TABLE 10.1 • Basic Assumptions of Social Cognitive Theory and Their Educational Implications

ASSUMPTION	EDUCATIONAL IMPLICATION	EXAMPLE
Learning by observation	Help students acquire new behaviors more quickly by demonstrating those behaviors yourself.	Demonstrate appropriate ways to deal with and resolve interpersonal conflicts. Then ask students to role-play conflict resolution in small groups, and compliment those who use prosocial strategies.
Learning as an internal process that may or may not be reflected in behavior	Remember that new learning doesn't always reveal itself immediately but may instead be reflected in students' behaviors at a later time.	When one student engages in disruptive classroom behavior, take appropriate steps to discourage it. Otherwise, classmates who have witnessed the misbehavior may be similarly disruptive in the future.
Cognitive processes in motivation	Encourage students to set productive goals for themselves, especially goals that are challenging yet achievable.	When teaching American Sign Language to help students communicate with a classmate who is deaf, ask them to set goals for how many new words and phrases they can learn each week.
Reciprocal influences among environmental, behavioral, and personal variables	Encourage students to consider personal, behavioral, and contextual (environmental) variables so that they learn most effectively.	Describe the benefits of doing homework at the library instead of at a friend's house. If a student knows that she studies more effectively in quiet settings, she may benefit from this strategy.
Increasing self-regulation with age	Teach students strategies through which they can better control their own behavior and direct their own learning.	Give students concrete suggestions about how they can remind themselves to bring needed supplies to school each day.

The Social Cognitive View of Reinforcement and Punishment

Reinforcement and punishment are less critical in social cognitive theory than they are in behaviorism, but they do have several indirect effects on learning and behavior (e.g., Bandura, 1977, 1986; T. L. Rosenthal & Zimmerman, 1978). Cognitive factors come into play in these indirect effects, as reflected in the following ideas:

- *Consequences influence behavior only if learners are aware of the response–consequence contingency.* From a social cognitive perspective, reinforcement and punishment influence learners' behaviors only if the learners connect these consequences to specific things they've done (Bandura, 1986). As teachers, then, we should be very clear about what we're reinforcing and punishing, so that students know the real response–reinforcement contingencies operating in the classroom. For instance, if we give Sam an A on an essay but we don't tell him *why* he's earned that grade, he won't necessarily know how to get an A the next time. Thus we might accompany the A grade with feedback such as "You followed a logical train of thought and gave three good examples." And rather than simply tell Sandra "Good job!" after a basketball game, we might tell her that we were pleased with her high energy level and passing accuracy.

- *Learners form expectations about the likely consequences of future actions and then behave in ways they think will maximize desired results.* Learners often base such outcome expectations on

MyEdLab
Video Example 10.1.

Social cognitive theorists believe that mental processes influence the effects of reinforcement and punishment. If students receive specific feedback about behavior and performance (as exhibited in this video), then they understand and are influenced by the response–reinforcement contingencies in the classroom.

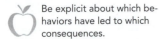

Be explicit about which behaviors have led to which consequences.

Be explicit about future response–reinforcement and response–punishment contingencies as well.

existing patterns of reinforcement, nonreinforcement, and punishment. For example, perhaps you've taken a course in which all exam questions came from the textbook, without a single question coming from class lectures. After the first exam, did you find yourself reading the textbook carefully but skipping class a lot? And perhaps you've taken a course in which exams were based almost entirely on lectures. In that situation, did you go to class regularly but hardly ever open your textbook? When a particular response is reinforced every time it's made, learners typically expect to be reinforced for behaving the same way in the future. In a similar manner, when a response frequently leads to punishment—as insulting an instructor or skipping class on a test day might—learners will probably expect that response to be punished on later occasions as well.

Sometimes, however, learners form expectations about future consequences on the basis of little or no hard data. For example, a high school student might erroneously believe that bragging about perfect test scores will gain him the admiration of his classmates (i.e., a reinforcer). Another student might believe that her classmates will ridicule and reject (i.e., punish) her for being smart, even though they wouldn't actually do so.

Expectations about future contingencies certainly affect learners' behaviors. They may or may not influence learning itself, as the following exercise can show you.

EXPERIENCING FIRSTHAND
DR. X

Think about a class you're taking now or have taken recently—not an online class but one that involves an instructor and students regularly convening in a single room. How many of the following questions can you answer about your instructor, whom we'll call "Dr. X"?

1. Is Dr. X right handed or left handed?
2. Is Dr. X a flashy dresser or more conservative one?
3. What kinds of shoes does Dr. X wear to class?
4. Does Dr. X wear a wedding ring?
5. Does Dr. X bring a briefcase to class each day?

If you've attended class regularly, you can probably answer at least two of these questions and possibly all five. But we're guessing that you've never mentioned what you've learned to anyone else, because you've had no reason to believe that demonstrating your knowledge about these matters would be reinforced. When learners *do* expect reinforcement for such knowledge, it suddenly surfaces. For example, when one of us authors teaches educational psychology, she takes a minute sometime during the semester to hide her feet behind the podium and ask her students what her shoes look like. They first look at her as if she has two heads, but after a few seconds of awkward silence, at least a half dozen of them (usually those who regularly sit in the first two rows) begin to describe her shoes, right down to the rippled soles, scuffed leather, and beige stitching.

Students learn many things in the classroom. They learn facts and figures, they learn ways of getting their teacher's attention, and they may even learn which classmate stores M&Ms in his desk or what kind of shoes their teacher wears to class. Of all the things they learn, they're most likely to demonstrate the things they think will bring reinforcement.

When learners choose to behave in a way that might bring future reinforcement, they're working for an **incentive**, which is never guaranteed. For instance, students never know that they're going to get an A on a test when they study for it or that they'll win a position on the student council simply because they run for office. An incentive is an expected or hoped-for consequence that may or may not actually occur.

• *Learners' expectations are influenced by what happens to other people as well as to themselves.* When one of us authors (Jeanne) was in the third grade, she entered a Halloween costume contest dressed as Happy Tooth, a character in several toothpaste commercials at the time. She didn't win the contest; a witch won first prize. So the following year she entered the same contest dressed as a witch, figuring she was a shoo-in for first place. She had experienced reinforcement *vicariously* rather than directly—that is, through watching what happened to someone else.

Learners who observe someone else being reinforced for a behavior are likely to exhibit that behavior more frequently themselves—a phenomenon known as vicarious reinforcement. For example, by watching the consequences their classmates' experience, students might learn that studying hard leads to good grades, that being elected to class office brings status and popularity, or that neatness counts. Conversely, when learners see someone else get punished for a behavior, they're *less* likely to behave that way themselves—a phenomenon known as vicarious punishment. For example, when a coach benches a football player for unsportsman-like conduct, other players are unlikely to behave similarly. Unfortunately, vicarious punishment can suppress desirable behaviors as well as undesirable ones. For instance, when a teacher belittles a student's question by calling it "silly," other students may be reluctant to ask questions of their own.[1] As teachers, we must be extremely careful that we don't vicariously reinforce undesirable behaviors or vicariously punish desirable ones. If we give too much attention to a misbehaving student, others who want our attention may misbehave as well. Or if we ridicule a student who volunteers an incorrect answer or erroneous belief, classmates will probably not be eager to voice their own ideas.

- *Expectations about future consequences affect how thoroughly and in what ways learners cognitively process new information.* To get a sense of how this might happen, try the next exercise.

■■ EXPERIENCING FIRSTHAND
■■ PLANNING AHEAD

Quickly skim the contents of the upcoming section on modeling to get a general idea of the topics it includes. Once you've done so, imagine yourself in each of these situations:

1. Your instructor announces, "The section on modeling won't be on your test, but please read it anyway." How thoroughly and carefully will you read that section?

2. The next day your instructor announces, "I misled you yesterday. Actually, half of next week's test will be on modeling." *Now* how thoroughly and carefully will you read that section?

If you don't expect to be reinforced for knowing about modeling, you may very well *not* read the chapter's discussion of it. (Perhaps you'll read it later, you tell yourself, but you have other things you need to do right now.) If, instead, you discover that getting an A in your educational psychology class depends on knowing the material about modeling really well, you're apt to read the material slowly and attentively, possibly trying to remember every detail.

When learners believe they'll be reinforced for learning something, they're more likely to pay attention to it and perhaps engage in elaboration, comprehension monitoring, and other effective cognitive processes. When they *don't* expect to be reinforced for learning something, they're far less likely to process it in any significant way. As an example of the latter situation, let's return to the opening case study. Nathan is convinced he can't learn French, thanks in part to his friends' low French grades (which served as vicarious punishment for him). As a result, Nathan pays little attention to what his teacher says in class, and he makes only halfhearted attempts to complete assignments. His low expectations almost guarantee poor performance—a self-fulfilling prophecy.

- *The nonoccurrence of an expected consequence—whether for oneself or for someone else—can have a reinforcing or punishing effect in and of itself.* What happens when learners' expectations aren't met—say, when an expected reinforcement never comes? When, as a fourth grader, Jeanne entered the Halloween costume contest as a witch, she lost once again—this time to a girl wearing a metal colander on her head and claiming to be *Sputnik,* the first satellite

You might read the section on modeling just because it is interesting to you; we will examine interest in Chapter 11.

---

[1]The effects of vicarious reinforcement and vicarious punishment are sometimes referred to as the *response facilitation effect* and *response inhibition effect*, respectively.

launched into space by what was then the Soviet Union. That was the last time she entered a Halloween contest. She had expected reinforcement and felt cheated because she didn't get it. Social cognitive theorists propose that the nonoccurrence of expected reinforcement is a form of punishment (e.g., Bandura, 1986). When people think that a certain response is going to be reinforced but the response *isn't* reinforced, they're less likely to exhibit the response in the future.

Just as the nonoccurrence of expected reinforcement is a form of punishment, the nonoccurrence of expected punishment is a form of reinforcement (Bandura, 1986). Perhaps you can think of a time when you broke a rule, expecting to be punished, but you got away with your crime. Or perhaps you can remember seeing a classmate cheating on a test without getting caught. When nothing bad happens after a forbidden behavior, people may actually feel as if the behavior has been reinforced.

Thus, when students work hard to achieve a desired result—perhaps a compliment, a high grade, or a special privilege—and the anticipated result doesn't materialize, they'll be unlikely to work as hard the next time around. And when students break school rules but aren't punished for doing so, they're likely to break the rules again—and so are other students who are aware that the behavior has gone unpunished.[2] It's important that we, as teachers, follow through with promised reinforcements for desirable student behaviors. It's equally important that we impose any reasonable consequences students have come to expect for inappropriate behaviors.

Follow through with the consequences students have been led to expect for certain behaviors.

See Chapter 9 for guidelines and cautions in the use of punishment.

MyEdLab **Self-Check 10.2**

MyEdLab **Application Exercise 10.1.** In this exercise you can apply your knowledge of the effects of reinforcement and punishment.

Modeling

As human beings, we have some ability to imitate others beginning early in infancy (S. S. Jones, 2007; Meltzoff, 2005; Nielsen & Tomaselli, 2010). In fact, the brain seems to be specially equipped for imitation. Certain neurons in the brain, appropriately called **mirror neurons**, become active either (1) when learners observe others engaging in a particular behavior or (2) when learners engage in that same behavior themselves. It appears, then, that our brains are prewired to make connections between observing and doing, thus enhancing our ability to learn new skills from our social and cultural surroundings (Arbib, 2005; Gallese, Gernsbacher, Heyes, Hickok, & Iacoboni, 2011; Hunter, Hurley, & Taber, 2013).

In general, a **model** can take one of three forms (Bandura, 1977, 1986). One form, of course, is a *live model*—an actual person demonstrating a particular behavior. But we can also learn from a *symbolic model*—a person or character portrayed in a book, film, television show, video game, or other medium. For example, many children model their behavior after football players, musicians, or such fictional characters as Harry Potter and Katniss Everdeen. In addition, youth today often are exposed to models more frequently than in the past; many of your students spend a lot of time using YouTube and other forms of social media, which are available anywhere and at any time via tablets, smartphones, and smart watches. Finally, we can learn from *verbal instructions*—descriptions of how to successfully execute certain behaviors—without another human being, either live or symbolic, being anywhere in sight.

Social cognitive theorists sometimes use the term **modeling** to describe what a model does (i.e., demonstrate a behavior) and at other times to describe what the observer does (i.e., imitate the behavior). To minimize confusion, we'll often use the verb *imitate* rather than *model* when referring to what the observer does.

---

[2]The tendency for learners to engage in forbidden behavior when they see others incur no adverse consequences for behaving that way is known as the *response disinhibition effect*. In this situation, the learners have presumably already mastered the behavior but the expectation of punishment has previously inhibited it. With the expectation no longer present, the behavior is *disinhibited* and may increase in frequency.

BEHAVIORS AND SKILLS THAT CAN BE LEARNED THROUGH MODELING

By observing what other people do, learners can, of course, acquire a wide variety of psychomotor skills, from relatively simple actions (e.g., brushing hair) to far more complex ones (e.g., performing dance routines or gymnastics skills) (Boyer, Miltenberger, Batsche, & Fogel, 2009; Vintere, Hemmes, Brown, & Poulson, 2004). But observations of other people also enable learners to acquire many behaviors with cognitive or emotional components. For example, learners are apt to do the following:

- Develop more sophisticated drawing skills when others demonstrate such skills, either in person or on videotape (Geiger, LeBlanc, Dillon, & Bates, 2010)

- Learn to fear particular stimuli or situations if others show fear in those circumstances (Mineka & Zinbarg, 2006)

- Better resist the enticements of a stranger when a peer has modeled resistance strategies (Poche, Yoder, & Miltenberger, 1988)

- Be less likely to tolerate racist statements if people around them refuse to tolerate such statements (Blanchard, Lilly, & Vaughn, 1991)

Students who are prominent members of the school community can be powerful models for many of their peers—perhaps for the better or perhaps for the worse, depending on the specific behaviors being modeled.

Considerable research has been conducted concerning the impact of models in three areas: academic skills, aggression, and productive interpersonal behaviors.

ACADEMIC SKILLS

Learners acquire many academic skills, at least in part, by observing what others do. For instance, they may learn how to solve long division problems or write a cohesive composition partly by observing how adults or peers do these things (Braaksma, Rijlaarsdam, & van den Bergh, 2002; K. R. Harris, Graham, Brindle, & Sandmel, 2009; Schunk & Hanson, 1985). Modeling of academic skills can be especially effective when the model demonstrates not only how to *do* a task but also how to *think about* the task—in other words, when the model engages in cognitive modeling (Schunk, 1998; Zimmerman, 2004, 2013). As an example, consider how a teacher might model the thinking processes involved in the long division problem in the margin:

> First I have to decide what number to divide 4 into. I take 276, start on the left and move toward the right until I have a number the same as or larger than 4. Is 2 larger than 4? No. Is 27 larger than 4? Yes. So my first division will be 4 into 27. Now I need to multiply 4 by a number that will give an answer the same as or slightly smaller than 27. How about 5? 5 × 4 = 20. No, too small. Let's try 6. 6 × 4 = 24. Maybe. Let's try 7. 7 × 4 = 28. No, too large. So 6 is correct.[3]

AGGRESSION

Numerous studies have indicated that children become more aggressive when they observe aggressive or violent models (Bandura, 1965; Ebesutani, Kim, & Young, 2014; Guerra, Huesmann, & Spindler, 2003). Children learn aggression not only from live models but also from the symbolic models they see in films, on television, and in video games—and possibly also from aggressive lyrics they hear in popular music (C. A. Anderson et al., 2003; Carnagey, Anderson, & Bartholow, 2007; Friedlander, Connolly, Pepler, & Craig, 2013). Furthermore, young learners' aggressive behaviors tend to take the same *forms* as the aggression they witness. Boys in particular are apt to copy other people's aggressive actions (Bandura, Ross, & Ross, 1963; Bushman & Anderson, 2001; Lowry, Sleet, Duncan, Powell, & Kolbe, 1995).

A classic study by Bandura, Ross, and Ross (1961) dramatically illustrates the power of modeling for both encouraging and *dis*couraging aggressive behavior. Preschoolers were taken,

MyEdLab
Video Example 10.2.

The teacher in this video teaches and models strategies for reading with expression. She also models speaking in a level one voice and other behaviors relevant to a productive learning environment.

---

[3]Extract from "Teaching Elementary Students to Self-Regulate Practice of Mathematical Skills with Modeling," by Dale H. Schunk, from *Self-Regulated Learning: From Teaching to Self-Reflective Practice*, edited by Dale H. Schunk and Barry J. Zimmerman, p. 146. Copyright © 1998 by Guilford Publications, Inc. Reprinted with permission.

one at a time, to a playroom containing a variety of toys and were seated at a table where they could draw pictures. While in the playroom, some of the children saw an aggressive model: An adult came in and behaved aggressively toward an inflatable punching doll—for example, kicking the doll in the air, hitting its head with a wooden mallet, and making statements such as "Pow!" and "Punch him in the nose." Other children instead observed a nonaggressive model: An adult came in and played constructively with building blocks. Still other children, who served as a control group in the study, saw no model at all in the playroom. The children were then led to another room where they were mildly frustrated: Just as they began to play with some attractive, entertaining toys, the toys were taken away. Finally, the children were taken to a third room that contained both nonaggressive and aggressive toys (including the punching doll and mallet). Children who had seen the aggressive model were the most aggressive of the three groups; in fact, they mimicked many of the behaviors they'd seen the aggressive model display. Children who had observed a nonaggressive model were even less aggressive than the no-model group. With regard to aggression, then, models can have an impact either way: Aggressive models lead to increased aggression in children, and nonaggressive models lead to decreased aggression.

PRODUCTIVE INTERPERSONAL BEHAVIORS

Learners acquire many interpersonal skills by observing and imitating others. For example, when they talk about literature in small groups, children may adopt one another's strategies for conducting discussions, perhaps learning how to solicit one another's opinions ("What do you think, Jalisha?"), express agreement or disagreement ("I agree with Kordell because . . ."), and justify a point of view ("I think it shouldn't be allowed, because . . .") (R. C. Anderson et al., 2001, pp. 14, 16, 25). And children with mild or moderate forms of an autism spectrum disorder are apt to play more effectively with age-mates after watching a videotape of a nondisabled peer using good social skills in play activities (Nikopoulos & Keenan, 2004).

Learners can also acquire prosocial behaviors in part through observation and modeling (R. Elliott & Vasta, 1970; Jordan, 2003). In one research study (Rushton, 1980), children observed an adult playing a game and reinforcing himself with tokens for good performance. Some children saw the adult donate half of his earned tokens to a poor boy named Bobby pictured on a poster in the room; other children observed the adult keep all his winnings for himself. After that, the children played the game and could reward themselves with tokens. The more tokens they earned, the better the prize they could purchase. They could make a donation to Bobby, but doing so meant lesser purchasing power for themselves. Children who had seen a generous model were more likely to give some tokens to Bobby than were children who had seen a selfish model—not only at that time but also in a follow-up session 2 months later.

Benevolent models in popular media can have a positive impact as well. Rather than encouraging aggression, some characters in books, television programs, and other popular media promote prosocial behaviors—those aimed at helping others rather than at enhancing personal well-being—and such models can prompt children and adolescents to behave similarly (D. R. Anderson, 2003; Gladding & Villalba, 2014; Jordan, 2003; Nucci, 2001; Rushton, 1980).

CHARACTERISTICS OF EFFECTIVE MODELS

Learners don't always imitate the people they see around them and in the media. Influential models typically have several characteristics (Bandura, 1986; T. L. Rosenthal & Bandura, 1978; Schunk, 1987). First, they're *competent* at the behavior or skill in question. Learners usually want to behave like people who do something well rather than poorly. For instance, children may try to imitate the basketball skills of a professional basketball player, and adolescents may make note of especially effective techniques they observe in art or literature. Even preschoolers have some ability to discriminate between competent and incompetent models (P. L. Harris & Want, 2005).

Second, influential models typically have *prestige and power*. Some effective models—a world leader, a renowned athlete, a popular rock star—are famous at a national or international level. The prestige and power of other models—a head cheerleader, the captain of the high school hockey team, the drum major in the marching band, a gang leader—may be more localized. As an example of such local influence, children are more likely to interact with students who have disabilities when they see popular classmates (rather than unpopular ones) initiating such interactions (Sasso & Rude, 1987).

In Chapter 12 we discuss *reciprocal teaching*, which is a good example of how students can acquire new skills through social interactions in the classroom.

Regularly expose students to prosocial models in literature, history, and other academic subject areas.

You can learn more about the development of prosocial behaviors in Chapter 3.

Third, and perhaps most important, influential models exhibit *behaviors relevant to learners' own circumstances.* Learners are most likely to adopt behaviors they believe will be useful for themselves and are within their own ability levels (Braaksma et al., 2002; Schunk & Hanson, 1985). And remember Nathan's belief that French is a "girl thing"? Learners must believe that a particular behavior is appropriate for their gender, with different individuals having varying views about which activities are "gender appropriate" (Grace, David, & Ryan, 2008; Leaper & Friedman, 2007).

As classroom teachers, we're likely to be perceived by most students as competent, prestigious, and powerful—that is, we're likely to be influential models. Thus, we "teach" not only by what we say but also by what we do. It's critical, then, that we model appropriate behaviors—for instance, showing enthusiasm about classroom topics and fairness in our dealings with all students—and *don't* model inappropriate ones. Our actions will often speak louder than our words (e.g., J. H. Bryan, 1975).

Yet our students won't always perceive our behaviors as being relevant to their own circumstances. For instance, students from cultures and socioeconomic groups very different from our own may think that certain topics have little value in their own lives and communities. Students of both genders may view certain content domains and careers as being only for males or "girl things." And students with disabilities may believe they're incapable of performing the skills that a nondisabled teacher demonstrates. Ideally, students need to see successful models who are similar to themselves in obvious ways—for instance, in race, cultural background, socioeconomic status, gender, and (if applicable) disability (C. L. Martin & Ruble, 2004; Pang, 1995; L. E. Powers, Sowers, & Stevens, 1995).

Expose students to successful male and female models from diverse cultural and socioeconomic backgrounds. Also expose them to models who have achieved success despite disabilities. Use technology (e.g., Skype) to virtually bring these individuals into your classroom to interact with your students.

ESSENTIAL CONDITIONS FOR SUCCESSFUL MODELING

Even with the presence of influential models, however, learners don't always acquire the behaviors and skills they see others demonstrate. Social cognitive theorists suggest that four conditions are necessary for successful learning from models: attention, retention, motor reproduction, and motivation (e.g., Bandura, 1986).

ATTENTION

To learn effectively, *the learner must pay attention to the model* and, in particular, to critical aspects of the modeled behavior. For instance, students must observe carefully as we show proper procedures in the science lab or demonstrate the elementary backstroke, and they must listen attentively as we pronounce *Comment allez-vous?* in a French class—something Nathan didn't do in the opening case study.

Chapter 6 presents many strategies for enhancing students' attention and retention, and Chapter 13 presents strategies for managing the classroom environment so that students are able to pay attention.

RETENTION

After paying attention, *the learner must remember what the model does.* As cognitive psychologists have discovered, students are more likely to recall information they've encoded in memory in more than one way—perhaps as both a visual image and a verbal representation (R. E. Mayer, 2011b; Moreno, 2006). As teachers, then, we may often want to describe what we're doing as we demonstrate behaviors. We may also want to give descriptive labels to complex behaviors that might otherwise be hard to remember (Vintere et al., 2004; Ziegler, 1987). For example, in teaching swimming, an easy way to help students remember the sequence of arm positions in the elementary backstroke is to teach them the labels *chicken, airplane,* and *soldier* (see Figure 10.2).

FIGURE 10.2 Often learners can more easily remember a complex, multifaceted behavior—such as the sequence of arm movements in the elementary backstroke—when the various components have verbal labels.

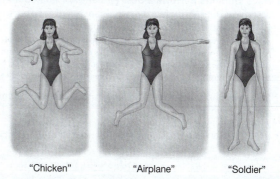

"Chicken"   "Airplane"   "Soldier"

MOTOR REPRODUCTION

In addition to attending and remembering, *the learner must be physically capable of reproducing the modeled behavior.* When a student lacks the ability to reproduce an observed behavior, motor reproduction obviously can't occur. For example, first graders who watch a teenager throw a softball don't have the muscular coordination to mimic the throw. And high school students who haven't yet learned to roll their *r*s will have trouble repeating the Spanish teacher's tongue twister: *Erre con erre cigarro, erre con erre barril. Rápido corren los carros del ferrocarril.*

It's often useful to have students imitate a desired behavior immediately after they see it modeled and to give them guidance and feedback that can help them improve their performance. This approach—sometimes known as *coaching*—is often more effective than modeling alone (S. N. Elliott & Busse, 1991; Kitsantas, Zimmerman, & Cleary, 2000; Schunk & Swartz, 1993). Thus a Spanish teacher could ask students to repeat the tongue twister right away, and acknowledge that it will feel and sound odd to make this sound, but that it will improve with practice. When considering this approach, however, we must keep in mind that students from some ethnic groups may prefer to practice new behaviors in private at first and show us what they've learned only after they've achieved reasonable mastery (Castagno & Brayboy, 2008; Suina & Smolkin, 1994).

 Into The Classroom

Promoting Learning Through Modeling

 Make sure you have students' attention when modeling a desired behavior.
A middle school science teacher wants to show his class how to prepare a slide of swamp water for inspection under a microscope. He meets with students in groups of three or four so that everyone can closely observe what he does.

 Describe what you are doing as you model a desired behavior.
As a fourth-grade teacher shows students how to use word processing software to edit their compositions, she explains every step she takes to insert new text, cut unwanted text, use the thesaurus and spell-check functions, and so on. She also distributes a handout that describes, step by step, how to perform each of these procedures, and she shows where to find important commands and functions on the computer screen.

 When teaching a complex behavior or sequence or behaviors, provide descriptive labels that students can repeat to themselves to help them remember what they need to do.
To help students remember the new dance steps she demonstrates, a dance teacher instructs them to say such things as "One, two, gallop, gallop" and "One leg, other leg, turn, and turn" while performing the steps.

 Have students perform a desired behavior immediately after you model it; give them guidance and feedback to help them improve their performance.
After an elementary art teacher shows students how to work effectively with watercolor paints, she walks around the classroom, giving pointers on how to blend colors for desired shades and how to keep differently colored areas from bleeding into one another.

 Show students how the skills you model can help them in their own lives.
After demonstrating how to use rounding to estimate sums, a middle school math teacher presents examples of how students might quickly estimate the total cost of several purchases at a local discount store.

 Invite respected professionals to the classroom to demonstrate skills in their areas of expertise.
A high school journalism teacher invites a local newspaper reporter to show students how he determines the sequence in which he presents information in a newspaper article.

 Show videos of skilled individuals performing complex psychomotor skills.
A gymnastics coach shows an aspiring young gymnast a video in which an expert performs a particular gymnastics skill. The coach also videotapes the child's execution of the skill. The coach and child then watch the two videos—sometimes pausing the videos at particular frames—to identify components of the skill in which the child could benefit from further practice.

 Have students read about or observe positive role models in such media as books and films.
In a unit on civic responsibility and community service, a high school social studies teacher has students read excerpts from Barack Obama's *Dreams from My Father*.

 Introduce students to models who have successfully crossed traditional gender boundaries in certain professions.
When exploring various professions over the course of the school year, a second-grade teacher invites several adults in the community—including a female police officer and a male nurse—to come to class and describe what they do in their jobs.

 Include competent children as well as adults in the role models you present.
Once a week, a kindergarten teacher invites one or two third graders to come and read storybooks to his class. The older children delight in their ability to show off their reading skills and work especially hard to make the stories lively and entertaining.

Sources: Boyer et al., 2009 (gymnastics example); R. L. Cohen, 1989; S. N. Elliott & Busse, 1991; Féry & Morizot, 2000; Gerst, 1971; Kitsantas et al., 2000; Mace, Belfiore, & Shea, 1989; Obama, 2004; T. L. Rosenthal, Alford, & Rasp, 1972; Schunk, 1989c; Schunk & Hanson, 1985; Schunk & Swartz, 1993; Shute, 2008; Vintere et al., 2004, p. 309 (dance example); Ziegler, 1987.

MOTIVATION

Finally, *the learner must be motivated to demonstrate the modeled behavior.* Some students may be eager to show what they've observed and remembered; for example, they may have seen the model reinforced for a certain behavior and thus have already been vicariously reinforced. But other students may not have any motivation to demonstrate something they've seen a model do, perhaps because they don't see the model's actions as being appropriate for themselves.

When all four factors—attention, retention, motor reproduction, and motivation—are present, modeling can be an extremely effective teaching technique. The Into the Classroom feature "Promoting Learning Through Modeling" offers several strategies that can maximize the effectiveness of modeling.

> MyEdLab **Self Check 10.3**
>
> MyEdLab **Application Exercise 10.2.** In this exercise you can observe cognitive modeling by the teacher and explain the effects on students.

Self-Efficacy

One important aspect of the fourth condition—motivation—is self-efficacy, and in this respect learners often differ considerably. In general, **self-efficacy** is a learner's self-constructed judgment about his or her ability to execute certain behaviors or reach certain goals. To get a sense of your own self-efficacy for various activities, try the following exercise.

EXPERIENCING FIRSTHAND
SELF-APPRAISAL

Take a moment to answer the following questions:

1. Do you believe you'll be able to understand and apply educational psychology by reading this book and thinking carefully about its content? Or do you believe you're going to have trouble with the material regardless of how much you study?

2. Do you think you could learn to execute a reasonable swan dive from a high diving board if you were shown how to do it and given time to practice? Or do you doubt that you could learn, no matter how much training and practice were involved?

3. Do you think you could walk barefoot over hot coals unscathed? Or do you think the soles of your feet would be burned to a crisp?

Learners are more likely to engage in certain behaviors when they believe they'll be able to execute the behaviors successfully—that is, when they have high self-efficacy for the behaviors (e.g., Bandura, 1997). For example, we hope you have high self-efficacy for learning educational psychology, believing that with careful thought about what you read, you'll be able to understand and apply its key principles. You may or may not believe that with instruction and practice, you could eventually execute a passable swan dive. You're probably quite skeptical that you could ever walk barefoot over hot coals, so we guess you have low self-efficacy regarding this endeavor. Obviously, then, self-efficacy plays a key role in learners' *outcome expectations* (i.e., predictions about the consequences that a particular behavior is likely to yield) for various courses of action.

Self-efficacy is a component of one's overall sense of self. It may seem similar to such concepts as *self-concept* and *self-esteem,* but it's different from these other two concepts in important ways (Bong & Skaalvik, 2003; Marsh, Xu, & Martin, 2012; Pietsch, Walker, & Chapman, 2003; Schunk & Pajares, 2005). When psychologists talk about self-concept and self-esteem (or self-worth), they're typically describing a fairly general self-view that pervades a broad range of activities (e.g., "Am I a good student?") and may encompass feelings as well as beliefs (e.g., "How proud am I of my classroom performance?"). In contrast, self-efficacy is more task or situation specific and involves judgments (rather than feelings) almost exclusively (e.g., "Can I learn how to solve quadratic equations?").

Table 10.2 provides a comparison of several self-related concepts discussed in this chapter.

See Chapter 3 for a discussion of other aspects of a learner's sense of self (e.g., self-concept, identity).

"SELF"-RELATED CONCEPTS

TABLE 10.2 • Comparison of "Self"-Related Concepts

TERM	DEFINITION	EXAMPLE
Self-efficacy	Belief that one is capable of executing certain behaviors or reaching certain goals. "Can I do this?"	When Lily's math teacher demonstrates converting decimals to fractions, Lily feels confident that she can accurately complete a set of practice examples.
Self-esteem or self-worth	Judgments and feelings about being a worthy and valued individual. "How do I feel about myself?"	Although George is disappointed not to be selected for a competitive scholarship, he still feels that he is a good person who is valued by his teachers.
Self-concept	A multidimensional view of the self across a broad range of characteristics, including strengths and weaknesses. "What am I like?"	"I'm a pretty analytic person," Antoinette muses, "math and physical sciences make a lot of sense to me, but I have to work harder at learning foreign languages."
Self-regulation	Process of setting goals for oneself and engaging in behaviors and cognitive processes that lead to goal attainment. "What am I trying to achieve? What do I need to do?"	Sofia wants to run her first half-marathon. She creates a training schedule, planning to gradually increase her distances over time, and records her progress.
Self-regulated learning	Self-regulation specifically related to learning opportunities.	Elijah has set himself the goal of earning an A grade on his science project. He reads the grading rubric carefully and divides the project into several small steps to make sure he completes everything on time. When he has questions about his project, he makes an appointment to meet with his science teacher.

HOW SELF-EFFICACY AFFECTS BEHAVIOR AND COGNITION

Learners' sense of self-efficacy affects their choice of activities, their goals, and their effort and persistence in classroom activities. Ultimately, then, it also affects their learning and achievement (Bandura, 1982, 2000; Lee, Lee, & Bong, 2014; Pajares, 2009; Schunk & Pajares, 2005; Zimmerman & Labuhn, 2012).

Choice of Activities   Imagine yourself on registration day, perusing the hundreds of courses in the semester schedule. You fill most of your schedule with required courses, but you have room for an elective. Only two courses are offered at the time slot you want to fill. Do you sign up for Advanced Psychoceramics, a challenging seminar taught by the world-renowned Dr. Josiah S. Carberry? Or do you sign up for an English literature course known across campus as being an "easy A"? Perhaps you find the term *psychoceramics* a bit intimidating, and you think you can't possibly pass such a course, especially if Dr. Carberry is as demanding as everyone claims. So you settle for the literature course, knowing it's one in which you can succeed.

Learners tend to choose tasks and activities at which they believe they can succeed and to avoid those at which they think they'll fail. Eventually they also place greater *value* on activities in which they think they'll do well (Bandura, 1986; Pajares, 2009).

Goals   Learners set higher goals for themselves when they have high self-efficacy in a particular domain. For example, adolescents' choices of careers and occupational levels often reflect subject areas in which they have high rather than low self-efficacy. On average, their choices tend to be consistent with traditional gender stereotypes: Boys are more likely to have high self-efficacy for (and so choose) careers in science and technology, whereas girls are more likely to have high self-efficacy for (and so choose) careers in education, health, and social services (Bandura, Barbaranelli, Caprara, & Pastorelli, 2001; Plante & O'Keefe, 2010).

Effort and Persistence   Learners with a high sense of self-efficacy are more likely to exert effort when attempting a new task, and they're more likely to persist—to "try, try again"—when they confront obstacles. In contrast, learners with low self-efficacy about a task will put in little effort and give up quickly in the face of difficulty. For example, in the opening case study, Nathan is convinced he can't learn French, and so he quickly abandons assignments when he encounters something he doesn't immediately understand.

Chapter 11 examines the development of value in greater detail.

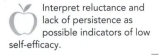 Interpret reluctance and lack of persistence as possible indicators of low self-efficacy.

Learning and Achievement   Learners with high self-efficacy tend to learn and achieve more than those with low self-efficacy, even when the two groups initially have similar ability levels (Bandura, 1986; Fast et al., 2010; Klassen, 2002; T. Williams & Williams, 2010). Learners with high self-efficacy may achieve at superior levels partly because they're more likely to engage in cognitive processes that promote learning—paying attention, elaborating, organizing, and so on (Berger & Karabenick, 2010; Bong & Skaalvik, 2003; Liem, Lau, & Nie, 2008; Schunk & Pajares, 2005).

MyEdLab
Video Example 10.3.
Learners' self-efficacy affects their effort and persistence in classroom activities. In this video, the teacher's scaffolding provides just the right amount of help for the student to feel that he can succeed with the task.

SOME OVERCONFIDENCE—BUT NOT TOO MUCH—CAN BE BENEFICIAL

Most 4- to 6-year-olds are quite confident about their ability to perform various tasks (R. Butler, 1990, 2005; Eccles et al., 1998). As they move through the elementary grades, however, they can better recall their past successes and failures, and they become increasingly aware of and concerned about how their performance compares with that of their peers. Presumably as a result of these changes, students gradually become less confident—although usually more realistic—about what they can and can't do (R. Butler, 2005; Dijkstra, Kuyper, van der Werf, Buunk, & van der Zee, 2008; Wigfield & Wagner, 2005).

Ideally learners should have a reasonably accurate sense of what they can and cannot accomplish, putting them in a good position to capitalize on their strengths and address their weaknesses (P. P. Chen, 2003; Försterling & Morgenstern, 2002; J. Wang & Lin, 2005). However, a tad of overconfidence can often be beneficial, because it may entice learners to take on challenging activities that will help them develop new skills and abilities (Assor & Connell, 1992; Bandura, 1997; Pajares, 2009). Within this context it's useful to distinguish between *self-efficacy for learning* ("I can learn this if I put my mind to it") and *self-efficacy for performance* ("I already know how to do this") (Lodewyk & Winne, 2005; Schunk & Pajares, 2004). Self-efficacy for learning—for what one can *eventually* do with effort—should be on the optimistic side, whereas self-efficacy for performance should be more in line with current ability levels.

Sometimes students—especially girls—*under*estimate their chances of success, perhaps because they've had a few bad experiences or are especially attuned to how their own performance falls short relative to that of peers (D. A. Cole, Martin, Peeke, Seroczynski, & Fier, 1999; Dijkstra et al., 2008; Schunk & Pajares, 2005). For example, a girl who gets a C in science from a teacher with exceptionally strict grading criteria may erroneously believe that she "just can't do" science. Or a new boy at school whose attempts at being friendly are rejected by two or three thoughtless classmates may erroneously believe that "no one" likes him and he cannot make friends. In such circumstances students set unnecessarily low goals for themselves and give up easily in the face of small obstacles.

But it's also possible to have too much of a good thing. When learners are *too* overconfident, they can set themselves up for failure by forming unrealistically high expectations or exerting insufficient effort to succeed. Moreover, students will hardly be inclined to address weaknesses they don't realize they have (Bandura, 1997; Sinatra & Mason, 2008; Sweeny, Carroll, & Shepperd, 2006; Zimmerman & Moylan, 2009).

FACTORS IN THE DEVELOPMENT OF SELF-EFFICACY

At least five distinct factors affect learners' self-efficacy: their previous successes and failures, their current emotional state, other people's messages, other people's successes and failures, and successes and failures that learners experience as members of a particular group (Bandura, 1986, 1997; Joët, Usher, & Bressoux, 2011; Usher & Pajares, 2009).

PREVIOUS SUCCESSES AND FAILURES

Without a doubt, the most important factor affecting learners' self-efficacy for an activity is the extent to which they've previously succeeded at that activity or similar ones (Bandura, 1986; Usher & Pajares, 2008; T. Williams & Williams, 2010). For example, Edward is more likely to believe he can learn to divide fractions if he has previously mastered fraction multiplication, and Elena will be more confident about learning to play rugby or field hockey if she's already acquired reasonable soccer skills. However, learners show developmental differences in *how far back* they look when they consider their prior successes and failures. Perhaps because of more limited cognitive abilities, children in the early elementary grades typically recall only their most recent

Adjust the initial difficulty of tasks to students' existing self-efficacy levels. Then gradually increase the challenge, providing structure to guide students' efforts.

FIGURE 10.3 Nine-year-old Sophie has been charting her monthly progress in remembering multiplication facts. Although she has had minor setbacks, her general progress is upward. (She was absent for February's assessment.)

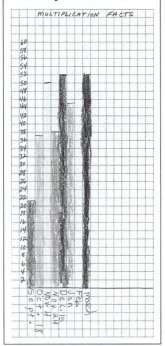

See Chapter 11 for a discussion of students' anxiety.

See Chapter 11 for a discussion of the benefits of helping students to achieve mastery.

Communicate your confidence in students' abilities even in your feedback about students' weaknesses.

experiences when predicting the likelihood of future success. In contrast, older children and adolescents are apt to consider a long-term pattern of prior successes and failures (Eccles et al., 1998).

As you can see, then, one important strategy for enhancing students' self-efficacy is to help them be successful at a variety of tasks in different content domains. Ideally we should tailor task difficulty to students' current self-efficacy levels: Students with little or no confidence in their ability to perform in a particular domain may initially respond more favorably if we give them tasks at which they'll almost certainly do well. But ultimately, students develop higher self-efficacy when they can successfully accomplish *challenging* tasks, perhaps initially with some degree of structure—that is, *scaffolding*—to increase the likelihood of successful performance (Falco, 2008; Lodewyk & Winne, 2005).

Nonetheless, mastery of important knowledge and skills, even fairly basic ones, often comes only slowly over time. Consequently, it's often important to define success in terms of *improvement* rather than mastery (R. Butler, 1998a; M.-T. Wang & Holcombe, 2010). In such instances we may need to provide concrete mechanisms that highlight day-to-day progress—for instance, giving students progress charts they can fill in themselves (e.g., see Figure 10.3), setting short-term goals that can reasonably be achieved, and providing frequent verbal or written feedback about the little things students are doing well.

Once students have developed a high sense of self-efficacy in a particular area, an occasional failure is unlikely to dampen their optimism much. In fact, when these students encounter small setbacks, they know they *can* succeed if they try, and they also develop a realistic attitude about failure—that at worst it's a temporary setback and at best it can give them useful information about how to improve their performance. In other words, students develop **resilient self-efficacy** (Bandura, 1989, 2008; Dweck, 2000).

CURRENT EMOTIONAL STATE

Learners' current emotional state—for instance, their general mood and the extent to which they feel anxious or stressed—can significantly affect their self-efficacy for the task at hand. For example, a student who feels excessively anxious or agitated during an important academic task may interpret that feeling as a sign of low ability for the task, even if the feeling has come from an unrelated source (Bandura, 1997; Schunk & Pajares, 2005; Usher & Pajares, 2009). The resulting low self-efficacy will, of course, undermine the student's performance, perhaps to the point that the task itself subsequently evokes anxiety and stress.

MESSAGES FROM OTHERS

When learners' successes aren't obvious, we can enhance their self-efficacy by explicitly pointing out ways in which they've previously done well or are now excelling. Occasionally we may also be able to boost their self-efficacy by giving them reasons to believe they can be successful in the future (Usher & Pajares, 2008). Statements such as "You can do this problem if you work at it" and "I bet Judy will play with you if you ask her" might give students a slight boost in self-confidence. We also can encourage our students to utilize feedback that is now often provided via technology in various online and computer-based learning environments (Miller, Doering, & Scharber, 2010). The effects of optimistic predictions will be modest and short lived, however, unless learners' efforts at a task ultimately *do* meet with success (Schunk, 1989a; Valentine, DuBois, & Cooper, 2004).

Even negative feedback can promote high self-efficacy *if* it gives guidance about how to improve and communicates confidence that improvement is likely—in other words, if it boosts *self-efficacy for learning* (Deci & Ryan, 1985; Narciss, 2008). For example, consider the following statement:

> In the first draft of your research paper, many of your paragraphs don't lead logically to the ones that follow. A few headings and transitional sentences would make a world of difference. Let's find a time to discuss how you might use these techniques to improve the flow of your paper.

The statement indirectly communicates the message "With a little effort and new strategies, I know you can do better."

In some cases we communicate our beliefs about learners' competence through our actions rather than our words. For example, if we offer after-school assistance to students who are struggling to master a particular mathematical procedure or musical technique, we're communicating that with a little persistence, improvement is possible. We must be careful not to go overboard, however. If we give struggling students more assistance than they really need, we may inadvertently communicate the message "I don't think you can do this on your own" (Schunk, 1989b). We also need to be careful not to single out individual students and unintentionally embarrass them by offering extra assistance. For example, if you want to encourage a specific student to come in after school for some extra help, make the suggestion privately, rather than in front of other students.

SUCCESSES AND FAILURES OF OTHER INDIVIDUALS

We often form opinions about our probability of success by observing the successes and failures of other people, especially those whose ability levels are seemingly similar to our own (Dijkstra et al., 2008; Usher & Pajares, 2008; Zeldin & Pajares, 2000). For example, you're more likely to enroll in Dr. Carberry's Advanced Psychoceramics class if most of your friends have done well in the course, but if, instead, numerous friends have dropped the course in frustration, you may suspect that your own chances of succeeding are pretty slim. Likewise, recall Nathan's pessimism about learning French in the opening case study—pessimism based largely on the experiences of three low-achieving friends.

Another way of enhancing learners' self-efficacy, then, is to point out that others like them have mastered the knowledge and skills at hand (Schunk, 1983, 1989c). For example, a class of chemistry students who seem overwhelmed by the many chemical symbols they must learn might be reassured with a statement such as this:

> I know it seems like a lot to learn in such a short time. My students last year thought so, too, but they found that they could learn the symbols within 3 weeks if they studied a few new symbols each day.

But even more than *telling* learners about others' successes, *seeing* is believing. Learners who actually observe similar-ability peers successfully reach a goal are especially likely to believe that they, too, can achieve the goal. Hence, students sometimes develop greater self-efficacy when they see a classmate model a behavior than when they see their teacher model it. In one study (Schunk & Hanson, 1985), elementary school students who were having trouble with subtraction were given 25 subtraction problems to complete. Students who had seen another student successfully complete the problems got an average of 19 correct, whereas those who saw a teacher complete the problems got only 13 correct, and those who saw no model at all correctly solved only 8! It may be even more beneficial for students to see one or more peers struggling with a task or problem at first—as they themselves might do—and then eventually mastering it (Kitsantas et al., 2000; Schunk, Hanson, & Cox, 1987; Schunk & Pajares, 2005). Presumably, observing such a coping model shows learners that success doesn't necessarily come easily—that they must work and practice to achieve success—and allows them to observe the strategies the model uses to gain proficiency.

What we *don't* want to do, however, is to *define* success in terms of how students' performance compares with that of their peers—perhaps identifying the "best" writer, science student, or basketball player. Whereas it is tempting to post charts indicating who has read the most books, who is the best behaved, or who ran the fastest in gym class, such comparisons set up competitive situations in which the majority of students must inevitably lose. Most students have higher self-efficacy and achieve at higher levels if they *don't* evaluate their own performance in terms of how they stack up against others (Graham & Golen, 1991; Shih & Alexander, 2000; Stipek, 1996).

SUCCESSES AND FAILURES AS PART OF A GROUP

Learners can often think more intelligently and acquire a more complex understanding of a topic when they collaborate with peers to master and apply classroom subject matter (e.g., D. W. Johnson & Johnson, 2009a; Pea, 1993; Slavin, 2011). Collaboration with peers has a possible additional benefit: Learners may have greater self-efficacy when they work in a group rather than alone. Such collective self-efficacy depends not only on students' perceptions of their own and others' capabilities but also on their perceptions of how effectively they can work together and coordinate their roles and responsibilities (Bandura, 1997, 2000; Jiang & Guo, 2002; Klassen & Usher, 2010).

Try not to give students more help than they actually need to succeed.

When you offer extra help to students, make the offer privately so that the students are not embarrassed.

Minimize students' awareness of classmates' performance levels.

See Chapter 8 and Chapter 12 for discussions of the benefits of cooperative learning activities.

Into The Classroom

Fostering Productive Self-Efficacy Levels

🍎 **Teach basic knowledge and skills to mastery.**
A biology teacher makes sure all students clearly understand the basic structure of DNA before moving to mitosis and meiosis, two topics that require a knowledge of DNA structure.

🍎 **Assure students that they can be successful at challenging tasks, and point out that others like them have been successful in the past.**
Early in the school year, students in beginning band express frustration in learning to play their instruments. Their teacher reminds them that, like themselves, students in last year's beginning band started out with little knowledge but eventually mastered their instruments. A few weeks later, the beginning band class attends a concert at which the school's advanced band (last year's beginning band class) play a medley from the *Harry Potter* movie series.

🍎 **Have students see peers with similar ability successfully accomplishing challenging tasks.**
To convince his students from low-income, minority-group families that they can do almost anything if they put their minds to it, a high school math teacher shows his class the film *Stand and Deliver*. The film depicts the true story of 18 Mexican American high school students from a low-income neighborhood in East Los Angeles who, through hard work and perseverance, earned college credit by passing the national Advanced Placement (AP) calculus exam.

🍎 **Help students track their progress on challenging tasks.**
As first graders are learning how to weave on small circular looms, one student approaches her teacher in tears, frustrated that her first few rows are full of mistakes. The teacher responds, "Look, Dorothy, this is the history, your own history, of learning to weave. You can look at this and say, 'Why, I can see how I began, here I didn't know how very well, I went over two instead of one; but I learned, and then—it is perfect all the way to the end!'" The student returns to her seat, very much comforted, and finishes her piece. She follows it with another, flawless one and proudly shows it to her teacher.

🍎 **After students have mastered basic skills, present some tasks at which they can succeed only with effort and perseverance.**
A physical education teacher tells his students, "Today we've determined how far each of you can go in the broad jump. We'll continue to practice good form a little bit each week. Some of your future efforts will be more successful than others, but let's see if every one of you can jump at least 2 inches farther when I test you again at the end of the month."

🍎 **Have students tackle especially challenging tasks in small, cooperative groups.**
A fifth-grade teacher has students work in groups of three or four to write research papers about early colonial life in North America. The teacher makes sure that the students in each group collectively have the skills in library research, writing, word processing, and art necessary to complete the task. She also makes sure that every student has some unique skills to contribute to the group effort.

🍎 **Have students set short-term (proximal) goals, so that they can experience success.**
A Spanish teacher realizes that his students are getting frustrated and feel like they are not learning how to speak or understand Spanish well. He asks them to set weekly short-term goals, rather than focusing on the longer-term goal of learning to speak Spanish. On Monday, he tells his students that "Our goal for the next 2 weeks is to learn how to count to 20 in Spanish; by the end of the week, you will be able to count forward, backward, by odd numbers, by even numbers, and even to do simple math problems in Spanish." At the end of the 2 weeks, the students are able to do this, and they feel great about what they have learned.

🍎 **If students are unrealistically overconfident—so much so that they don't exert the effort and strategies needed to master the material—help them learn how to accurately evaluate their current knowledge and skill levels.**
Many students at a technical school are quite confident that they're solving math problems correctly, even though their grades in the class have been poor. To help them more realistically assess their current understandings, a math teacher begins giving frequent short quizzes in which students have to predict their ability to correctly solve each problem before actually trying to solve it; they must also evaluate the accuracy of their problem solutions. Then, when they get back their graded quizzes, they get extra points for critiquing the accuracy of their problem-specific self-evaluations and for explaining and correcting their errors. Students in this class begin to achieve at higher levels.

Sources: Bandura, 1986, 1989, 1997, 2000; R. Butler, 1998a; Eccles et al., 1998; Friedel, Cortina, Turner, & Midgley, 2010; Hawkins, 1997, p. 332 (weaving example); Lodewyk & Winne, 2005; Mathews, 1988; Menéndez, 1988 (*Stand and Deliver* example); Schunk, 1983, 1984, 1989a, 1989c; Usher & Pajares, 2008; Zeldin & Pajares, 2000; Zimmerman & Moylan, 2009 (math example).

Whether we ask students to tackle challenging tasks as individuals or in small groups, we must keep in mind that the school day shouldn't necessarily pose one challenge after another. Such a state of affairs would be absolutely exhausting, and probably quite discouraging as well. Instead, we should strike a balance between easy tasks, which will boost students' self-confidence over the short run, and the challenging tasks so critical for an optimistic sense of self-efficacy for the long term (Spaulding, 1992; Stipek, 1996). The Into the Classroom feature "Fostering Productive Self-Efficacy Levels" presents several research-based strategies.

TEACHER SELF-EFFICACY

Not only should our students have high self-efficacy about their ability to succeed in the classroom, but so, too, should we teachers have high self-efficacy about our ability to *help* them succeed. Students are more likely to achieve at high levels when their teachers have confidence that they can help students master classroom topics (Skaalvik & Skaalvik, 2008; Tschannen-Moran, Woolfolk Hoy, & Hoy, 1998; Ware & Kitsantas, 2007). In fact, teacher efficacy is more strongly related to teachers' effective performance (as judged by independent observers) than are the teachers' personality characteristics (e.g., whether the teacher is outgoing or shy) (Klassen & Tze, 2014). Teachers' sense of efficacy, however, changes over time and situations. Not surprisingly, beginning teachers often feel increasingly confident in their abilities during their teaching practicum but then experience a decrease in their first year of teaching. Knowing that a sudden loss of confidence during the first year is quite common, and that your sense of efficacy will grow again with additional experience, can help you cope if this happens to you (L. Anderman & Klassen, 2016).

Some of this teacher confidence may take the form of collective teacher self-efficacy: When teachers at a school believe that, as a group, they can make a significant difference in the lives of children and adolescents, their students, too, have higher self-efficacy themselves and are more likely to achieve at high levels (Goddard, 2001; Goddard, Hoy, & Woolfolk Hoy, 2000; Tschannen-Moran et al., 1998).

When teachers have high self-efficacy about their effectiveness in the classroom—both individually and collectively—they influence students' achievement in several ways:

- They are more willing to experiment with new teaching strategies that can better help students learn.
- They set higher goals for students' performance.
- They put more effort into their teaching and are more persistent in helping students learn.
- They manage problem behaviors (e.g., bullying), more effectively, contributing to a more positive school culture. (Anderman & Klassen, 2016; Bandura, 1997; Skaalvik & Skaalvik, 2008; Sørlie & Torsheim, 2011; Tschannen-Moran et al., 1998; Veenstra, Lindenberg, Huitsing, Sainio, & Salmivalli, 2014)

Such effects should look familiar: Just as self-efficacy affects students' choice of activities, goals, effort, and persistence, so, too, does it affect *teachers'* choices, goals, effort, and persistence. And when teachers have high self-efficacy, particularly for instruction and behavior management, they are more satisfied with their jobs (Klassen & Chiu, 2010)!

As is true for students, however, it's possible for teachers to have too much of a good thing. Occasionally teachers have so much confidence in their existing knowledge and skills that they see little benefit in professional development activities that would enhance their effectiveness (Guskey, 1988; Middleton & Abrams, 2004; Tschannen-Moran et al., 1998). We teachers are *learners* as well, and we'll always have room for improvement in our classroom strategies.

Collaborate with colleagues to identify effective ways of fostering *all* students' academic and social success at school.

> MyEdLab **Self-Check 10.4**
>
> MyEdLab **Application Exercise 10.3.** In this exercise you can identify strategies that enhance self-efficacy in students as learners and in adults as teachers.

Self-Regulation

Although high self-efficacy can certainly enhance students' classroom performance, it's by no means the only thing that affects their performance. The notion that "just believing in yourself" is sufficient to bring success is a popular idea, but actually not strongly supported by research. As we will see, students must also master the knowledge and skills that make high performance levels possible. Some knowledge and skills are specific to particular topics and academic domains, but one set of skills—those related to self-regulation—can have a pervasive influence on students' achievement across the board. To get a sense of your own self-regulation skills, try the following exercise.

EXPERIENCING FIRSTHAND
SELF-REFLECTION ABOUT SELF-REGULATION

For each of the following situations, choose the alternative that most accurately describes your attitudes, thoughts, and behaviors as a college student. No one will see your answers except you, so be honest!

1. With regard to my final course grades, I'm trying very hard to
   a. Earn all As.
   b. Earn all As and Bs.
   c. Keep my overall grade point average at or above the minimally acceptable level at my college.

2. As I'm reading or studying a textbook,
   a. I often notice when my attention is wandering, and I immediately get my mind back on my work.
   b. I sometimes notice when my attention is wandering, but not always.
   c. I often get so lost in daydreams that I waste a lot of time.

3. Whenever I finish a study session,
   a. I write down how much time I've spent on my schoolwork.
   b. I make a mental note of how much time I've spent on my schoolwork.
   c. I don't really think much about the time I've spent on my schoolwork.

4. When I turn in an assignment,
   a. I usually have a good idea of the grade I'll get on it.
   b. I'm often surprised by the grade I get.
   c. I don't think much about the quality of what I've done.

5. When I do exceptionally well on an assignment,
   a. I feel good about my performance and might reward myself in some way.
   b. I feel good about my performance but don't do anything special for myself afterward.
   c. I don't feel much different than I did before I received my grade.

Regardless of how you answered Item 1, you could probably identify a particular goal toward which you're striving. Your response to Item 2 should give you an idea of how much you monitor and try to control your thoughts when you're studying. Your responses to Items 3 and 4 tell you something about how frequently and accurately you evaluate your performance. And your response to Item 5 indicates whether you're likely to reinforce yourself for desired behaviors. To the extent that we establish our own priorities and goals, take charge of our own thoughts and actions, and reflect on and evaluate our own behaviors, we are self-regulating individuals (e.g., Bandura, 2008).

Thanks, in part, to brain maturation over the course of childhood and adolescence, most learners become increasingly self-regulating as they grow older (more on this point in an Applying Brain Research feature later in the chapter). Table 10.3 presents typical advancements in the elementary and secondary school years. Some of the entries in the table, such as self-instructions and self-evaluation of actions, reflect self-regulation in *behavior*. Others, such as ability to control attention and self-motivation, reflect self-regulation in *learning*. We'll look here at both self-regulated behavior and self-regulated learning, as well as at self-regulated problem solving.

SELF-REGULATED BEHAVIOR

When we behave in particular ways and observe how our environment reacts—reinforcing some behaviors and punishing or otherwise discouraging others—we begin to distinguish between productive and unproductive responses, and most of us increasingly control and monitor our own actions (Bandura, 1986, 2008). In other words, we engage in self-regulated behavior. Self-regulated behavior has at least six important components, which are summarized in Figure 10.4. As you'll see, all six of them have cognitive elements as well as behavioral ones.

DEVELOPMENTAL TRENDS

TABLE 10.3 • Self-Regulation at Different Grade Levels

GRADE LEVEL	AGE-TYPICAL CHARACTERISTICS	EXAMPLE	SUGGESTED STRATEGIES
K–2	• Some internalization of adults' standards for behavior • Emerging ability to set self-chosen goals for learning and achievement • Some use of self-instructions (self-talk) to guide behavior • Some self-evaluation of effectiveness and appropriateness of actions; feelings of guilt about wrongdoings • Individual differences in self-control of impulses, emotions, and attention; peer relationships and classroom performance affected by amount of self-control in these areas	Most of the children in a kindergarten class can sit quietly and listen when their teacher reads a story-book. But a few of them squirm restlessly and occasionally poke or otherwise distract their classmates.	• Discuss rationales for classroom rules. • Show students how some behaviors can help them reach their goals and how other behaviors interfere with goal attainment. • Organize the classroom so that students can carry out some activities on their own (e.g., have reading centers where children can listen to storybooks on iPads). • When students show impulsiveness or poor control of emotions, provide guidelines and consistent consequences for behavior.
3–5	• Improving ability to self-assess performance and progress • Guilt and shame about unsatisfactory performance and moral transgressions • Emerging self-regulated learning strategies (e.g., conscious attempts to focus attention, ability to do short assignments independently at home) • Persistent difficulties with self-control for some students	Every Thursday evening, 8-year-old Logan studies for the weekly spelling test his teacher will give his class the following day. Sometimes he asks his father or older brother to test him on especially difficult words.	• Have students set specific, concrete goals for their learning. • Encourage students to assess their own performance; provide criteria they can use to evaluate their work. • Ask students to engage in simple, self-regulated learning tasks (e.g., small-group learning activities, short homework assignments); provide some structure to guide students' efforts. • Encourage students to use their peers as resources when they need help. • If students have continuing difficulty with self-control, teach self-instructions that can help them control their behavior.
6–8	• Increasing ability to plan future actions, due in part to increased capacity for abstract thought • Increasing mastery of some self-regulating learning strategies, especially those that involve overt behaviors (e.g., keeping a calendar of assignments and due dates) • Self-motivational strategies (e.g., minimizing distractions, devising ways to make a boring task more interesting and enjoyable, reminding oneself about the importance of doing well) • Decrease in help-seeking behaviors during times of confusion, especially if teachers appear to be aloof and nonsupportive	When Marie starts going to middle school, she asks her parents to by her a planner, because she wants to keep track of daily assignments and also plan for future tests and quizzes.	• Assign homework and other tasks that require age-appropriate independent learning. • Provide concrete strategies for keeping track of learning tasks and assignments (e.g., provide monthly calendars on which students can write due dates). • Provide concrete guidance about how to learn and study effectively (e.g., give students questions they should answer as they complete reading assignments at home). • Give students frequent opportunities to assess their own learning; have them compare your evaluations with theirs.
9–12	• More long-range goal setting • Continuing development of strategies for emotion regulation, especially in contexts that can evoke strong emotions (e.g., sports, theater productions) • Wide variability in ability to self-regulate learning, especially when out-of-school assignments conflict with attractive leisure activities; few self-regulating learning strategies among many low-achieving high school students • For a small number of older adolescents, persistent difficulties in self-control that can adversely affect classroom behavior and peer relationships	After moving from fairly small middle schools to a much larger, consolidated high school, some students diligently complete their homework each night. But others are easily enticed into more enjoyable activities with friends—hanging out at a local fast-food restaurant, instant-messaging on cell phones, and so on—and their grades decline significantly as a result.	• Relate classroom learning tasks to students' long-range personal and professional goals. • Encourage students to experiment with various emotion-control strategies through role-playing and drama. • Assign complex independent learning tasks, providing the necessary structure and guidance for students who are not yet self-regulating learners. • Have high-achieving students describe their strategies for resisting attractive alternatives and keeping themselves on task when doing homework.

Sources: Abrami, Venkatesh, Meyer, & Wade, 2013; Bronson, 2000; Brunstein & Glaser, 2011; Corno & Mandinach, 2004; Damon, 1988; Dunning, Heath, & Suls, 2004; Eccles, Wigfield, & Schiefele, 1998; Fries, Dietz, & Schmid, 2008; Hampson, 2008; M. Hofer, 2010; M. H. Jones, Estell, & Alexander, 2008; Kochanska, Gross, Lin, & Nichols, 2002; Larson & Brown, 2007; Marchand & Skinner, 2007; J. S. Matthews, Ponitz, & Morrison, 2009; Meichenbaum & Goodman, 1971; Meltzer et al., 2007; S. D. Miller, Heafner, Massey, & Strahan, 2003; S. G. Paris & Paris, 2001; Posner & Rothbart, 2007; Schneider, 2010; Valiente, Lemery-Calfant, Swanson, & Reiser, 2008; Wolters & Rosenthal, 2000.

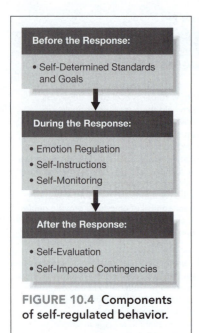

Before the Response:

- Self-Determined Standards and Goals

During the Response:

- Emotion Regulation
- Self-Instructions
- Self-Monitoring

After the Response:

- Self-Evaluation
- Self-Imposed Contingencies

FIGURE 10.4 Components of self-regulated behavior.

Self-chosen rather than other-chosen goals enhance one's sense of self-determination, an important prerequisite for intrinsic motivation (see Chapter 11).

Have students set some of their own goals in the classroom. Encourage them to set challenging yet realistic goals; caution them against always striving for perfection.

MyEdLab
Video Example 10.4.

As children grow older, most develop strategies for regulating their emotions. The strategies vary for 10-year-old Daniel, 13-year-old Crystal, and 15-year-old Greg.

SELF-DETERMINED STANDARDS AND GOALS

As self-regulating human beings, we tend to have general standards for our behavior—standards that serve as criteria for evaluating our performance in specific situations. We also establish certain goals that guide our actions and activity choices. Meeting our standards and reaching our goals give us considerable self-satisfaction, enhancing our self-efficacy and spurring us on to greater heights (Bandura, 1986, 1989).

Different individuals adopt different standards and goals for themselves, of course. Often their standards and goals are modeled after those of other people (Fitzsimmons & Finkel, 2010; E. A. Locke & Latham, 1990; R. B. Miller & Brickman, 2004). For example, at some high schools, many students want to go to the best college they possibly can, and their academic aspirations are contagious. But at a different high school, getting a job after graduation—or perhaps *instead* of graduation—might be the goal more commonly modeled by peers.

Students are typically more motivated to work toward goals they've chosen for themselves, rather than goals that others have imposed on them (e.g., Deci & Ryan, 1992; Fitzsimmons & Finkel, 2010; M. E. Ford, 1992). One way to help students develop self-regulation, then, is to provide situations in which they set their own goals. For example, we might ask them to decide how many addition facts they're going to learn by Friday, what topic they want to study for a research project, or which gymnastic skills they'd like to master.

Ideally we should encourage students to establish standards and goals that are challenging yet realistic. We might even want to provide incentives that encourage students to set and achieve challenging goals (i.e., **proximal goals**) (Stipek, 1996). Proximal goals are short-term goals that are achievable independently or with some support. Students who have high self-efficacy for a particular subject area (e.g., reading) will be more likely to set the goal of getting a good grade in that subject; that goal will encourage them to use self-regulatory strategies, which ultimately will led to higher achievement (Lee et al., 2014). At the same time, we must caution students that constant perfection is *not* a realistic goal—that occasional errors are inevitable in the pursuit of new and difficult tasks. Students who are satisfied only with flawless performance can't possibly live up to such an impossible standard and, as a result, may become excessively anxious or depressed (Bandura, 1986; Covington, 1992; Stoeber, Schneider, Hussain, & Matthews, 2014).

EMOTION REGULATION

A second important aspect of self-regulated behavior is **emotion regulation**, keeping in check or modifying any feelings that might lead to counterproductive responses—perhaps anger, resentment, or excessive excitement. Effective emotion regulation often involves a two-pronged approach (Buckley & Saarni, 2009; Pekrun, 2006; J. M. Richards, 2004). First, learners control the extent to which they *express their feelings*. In addition, self-regulating individuals often *reinterpret events* in order to put a positive spin on what might otherwise be anger- or sadness-inducing circumstances. For instance, a student who gets an unexpectedly low quiz score might treat it as a wake-up call to study more diligently in the future. And a student who doesn't make the varsity soccer team might think, "Maybe this is a blessing in disguise, because it gives me more time to help out at the Boys' Club after school."

On average, children and adolescents who can effectively control their emotions have more friends and better social skills (Aikins & Litwack, 2011; Eisenberg, Vaughan, & Hofer, 2009; Raver, 2014). In contrast, those who have trouble keeping their feelings in check are likely to be lonely and depressed; some exhibit behavior problems at school, and others become chronic victims of school bullies (Buckley & Saarni, 2009; Silk, Steinberg, & Morris, 2003).

SELF-INSTRUCTIONS

Sometimes learners simply need reminders of how to behave in particular situations. By teaching them how to use **self-instructions** to guide themselves through complex situations, we provide them with a means through which *they remind themselves* about appropriate actions. One effective approach involves five steps (Meichenbaum, 1977):

1. *Cognitive modeling:* The teacher models self-instruction by repeating instructions aloud while simultaneously performing the activity.

2. *Overt, external guidance:* The teacher repeats the instructions aloud while the learner performs the activity.

3. *Overt self-guidance:* The learner repeats the instructions aloud while performing the activity.

4. *Faded, overt self-guidance:* The learner whispers the instructions while performing the activity.

5. *Covert self-instruction:* The learner silently thinks about the instructions while performing the activity.

As you can see in these steps, the teacher initially serves as a model both for the behavior and for the self-instructions and then gradually transfers responsibility to the learner. Steps 3 through 5 in the process may remind you of Vygotsky's concepts of *self-talk* and *inner speech.*

Teaching self-instructions can be useful in helping students acquire and improve complex athletic skills (Hatzigeorgiadis, Zourbanos, Galanis, & Theodorakis, 2011). It can also be quite effective in working with students who consistently exhibit behavior problems, such as chronic impulsivity or dishonesty (Carter & Doyle, 2006; W. M. Casey & Burton, 1982; Meichenbaum, 1985). Furthermore, applications are now available for programming individualized self-instructions into a smartphone or other mobile devices (e.g., search the Internet for "self-talk apps") (Smith, Shepley, Alexander, Davis, & Ayres, 2015).

SELF-MONITORING

Another important aspect of self-regulation is to observe oneself in action—a process known as self-monitoring (or *self-observation*). To make progress toward important goals, learners must be aware of how well they're currently doing. And when they see themselves making progress, they're more likely to continue with their efforts (Schunk & Zimmerman, 1997).

Learners aren't always astute monitors of their own behavior, however. For instance, they may not be aware of how frequently they do something incorrectly or ineffectively or of how *in*frequently they do something well. Specific, concrete mechanisms can often enhance their self-monitoring. For example, if Raymond speaks out of turn too often, we can ask him to make a checkmark on a sheet of paper every time he catches himself talking at inappropriate times. And if Hillary has trouble staying on task during assigned activities, we can ask her to stop and reflect on her behavior every few minutes (perhaps with the aid of an egg timer or electronic beeper) to determine whether she was staying on task during each interval. Figure 10.5 illustrates the type of form we might give Hillary to record her observations.

Such self-focused observation and recording can bring about noticeable changes—sometimes quite dramatic ones—in learners' behavior. For example, self-monitoring can be used to increase students' participation in class and diligence in completing assignments. It's also effective in reducing aggression and such disruptive behaviors as talking out of turn and getting out of one's seat (Belfiore & Hornyak, 1998; Plavnick, Ferreri, & Maupin, 2010; Prater, Carter, Hitchcock, & Dowrick, 2011; Reid, Trout, & Schartz, 2005; Webber, Scheuermann, McCall, & Coleman, 1993).

Use of video technology can further enhance learners' self-monitoring capabilities (Bear, Torgerson, & Dubois-Gerchak, 2010; Hitchcock, Dowrick, & Prater, 2003; Prater et al., 2011). Consider, for example, the case of Charles, a highly intelligent fifth grader whose classroom behaviors—aggression, temper tantrums, regular refusals to complete schoolwork—had his parents and teachers totally exasperated. Nothing had worked with Charles—not traditional behaviorist techniques (e.g., systematic praise, time-outs, a token economy), counseling, or paper-and-pencil self-monitoring sheets. But when his special education teacher began videotaping and then showing him his behaviors in math class, he was appalled at what he saw: "Do I really look like that?" "Did

Vygotsky's theory is presented in Chapter 2.

 Teach students instructions they can use to guide themselves through difficult tasks.

Have students observe and record information about their own behavior.

FIGURE 10.5 Example of a self-monitoring sheet for staying on task.

Self-Observation Record for __*Hillary*__

Every ten minutes, put a mark to show how well you have been staying on task.

    +   means you were almost always on task
  1/2   means you were on task about half the time
  –   means you were hardly ever on task

9:00-9:10	9:10-9:20	9:20-9:30	9:30-9:40	9:40-9:50	9:50-10:00
+	+	–	+	½	–
10:00-10:10	10:10-10:20	10:20-10:30	10:30-10:40	10:40-10:50	10:50-11:00
½	–	*recess*	+	½	
11:00-11:10	11:10-11:20	11:20-11:30	11:30-11:40	11:40-11:50	11:50-12:00

I really say that?" "Turn it off!" Charles expressed a strong desire to be "normal," his classroom behaviors became noticeably more compliant and respectful, and he began to appreciate the praise, tokens, and other reinforcers he'd previously shunned (Bear et al., 2010, p. 83).

SELF-EVALUATION

Once students have set appropriate standards and objective methods of self-observation, ask them to evaluate their own performance.

To be truly self-regulating, learners must not only monitor but also *judge* their own behavior, as Charles obviously did when he watched the videotapes. In other words, they must engage in self-evaluation. Reasonably accurate self-evaluation depends on having appropriate standards for behavior, of course, and also on having relatively objective techniques for self-monitoring one's own actions. When learners have such prerequisites, we can use strategies such as the following:

- Have students write in daily or weekly journals in which they address the strengths and weaknesses of their performance.

- Arrange small-group peer conferences in which several students discuss their reactions to one another's work.

Chapter 15 offers recommendations for helping students create portfolios.

- Have students assemble portfolios of what they consider their best work, with a self-evaluation of each entry. (S. G. Paris & Ayres, 1994; S. G. Paris & Paris, 2001)

In addition, we can provide self-assessment instruments that show students what to look for as they evaluate their work, and we can occasionally have them compare their self-assessments with others' independent judgments of their performance (DuPaul & Hoff, 1998; Mitchem & Young, 2001; Reid et al., 2005; D. J. Smith, Young, West, Morgan, & Rhode, 1988). Figure 10.6 presents a form one teacher has used to help her students learn to evaluate their performance in a cooperative group activity.

FIGURE 10.6 After a cooperative group activity with three classmates, Ava and her teacher used the same criteria to rate Ava's performance and that of her group. With the two sets of ratings side by side, Ava could evaluate the accuracy of her self-assessments.

Project description ___Travel Guide___

Evaluate with a 1 for weak, a 2 for fair, a 3 for good, a 4 for very good, and a 5 for excellent.

Student	Teacher	
4	4	1. The task was a major amount of work in keeping with a whole month of effort.
5	4	2. We used class time quite well.
4	5	3. The workload was quite evenly divided. I did a fair proportion.
4	5	4. I showed commitment to the group and to a quality project.
5	4	5. My report went into depth; it didn't just give the obvious, commonly known information.
5	5	6. The project made a point: a reader (or viewer) could figure out how all of the details fit together to help form a conclusion.
5	5	7. The project was neat, attractive, well assembled. I was proud of the outcome.
4	5	8. We kept our work organized; we made copies; we didn't lose things or end up having to redo work that was lost.
5	4	9. The work had a lot of original thinking or other creative work.
4	4	10. The project demonstrated mastery of basic language skills—composition, planning, oral communication, writing.
45	45	Total

SELF-IMPOSED CONTINGENCIES

Self-imposed contingencies involve giving oneself reinforcement or punishment for one's behavior. For example, how do you feel when you accomplish a difficult task—perhaps earning an A in a challenging course or making a 3-point shot in a basketball game? And how do you feel when you fail in your endeavors—perhaps getting a D on an exam or thoughtlessly hurting a friend's feelings? When you accomplish something you've set out to do, especially if the task is complex and challenging, you probably feel quite proud of yourself and give yourself a mental pat on the back. In contrast, when you fail to accomplish a task, you're probably unhappy with your performance; you may also feel guilty, regretful, or ashamed (Harter, 1999; Krebs, 2008).

As children and adolescents become increasingly self-regulating, they, too, begin to reinforce themselves when they accomplish their goals—perhaps by feeling proud or telling themselves they did a good job. And they may punish themselves when they do something that doesn't meet their own performance standards—perhaps by feeling sorry, guilty, or ashamed. But self-imposed contingencies aren't necessarily confined to emotional reactions. Many self-regulating individuals reinforce themselves in far more concrete ways when they do something well (Bandura, 1977). One of the authors of this book (Jeanne) had a colleague who went shopping every time she completed a research article or report (she had one of the best wardrobes in town). Jeanne herself is more frugal: When she finishes writing each major section of a chapter, she either helps herself to a piece of chocolate or takes time to watch one of her favorite television game shows. As a result, Jeanne is chubbier than her colleague, but she has a wealth of knowledge of game-show trivia.

Thus, an additional way to help students become more self-regulating is to teach them self-reinforcement. When students begin to reinforce themselves for appropriate responses—perhaps giving themselves some free time, allowing themselves to engage in a favorite activity, or simply praising themselves—their study habits and classroom behavior can improve significantly (K. R. Harris, 1986; Hayes et al., 1985; Reid et al., 2005). In one research study, students who were performing poorly in arithmetic were taught to give themselves points when they did well on assignments; they could later use the points to "buy" a variety of items and privileges. Within a few weeks, these students were doing as well as their classmates on both in-class assignments and homework (H. C. Stevenson & Fantuzzo, 1986).

 Teach students to reinforce themselves for productive behavior.

The most diligent workers and highest achievers in the classroom, on the athletic field, and elsewhere are likely to be individuals who can effectively self-regulate their behavior (Duckworth & Seligman, 2005; Trautwein, Lüdtke, Kastens, & Köller, 2006; Zimmerman & Kitsantas, 2005). But we certainly don't have to leave the development of self-regulated behavior to chance. As we teach students strategies for taking charge of their own actions, we should keep several points in mind:

- Students must be physically and cognitively capable of achieving the goals they've set.
- Students must be motivated to change their behavior.
- Students' expectations for change must be realistic and practical; dramatic overnight improvements are rare.
- Students must have high self-efficacy for making the necessary changes.

Acquiring effective self-regulation skills is often a slow, gradual process, but with reasonable guidance and scaffolding, virtually all students can master them.

SELF-REGULATED LEARNING

To be truly self-regulating, learners must direct and monitor their learning as well as their behavior. In particular, self-regulated learning includes the following processes, many of which clearly involve metacognition:

See Chapter 7 for other aspects of metacognition.

- *Goal setting.* Self-regulating learners know what they want to accomplish when they read or study—perhaps to learn specific facts, gain a broad conceptual understanding of a topic, or simply acquire enough knowledge to do well on a classroom exam. Typically they tie their goals for a particular learning activity to longer-term goals and aspirations (Nolen, 1996; Winne & Hadwin, 1998; Wolters, 1998; Zimmerman & Moylan, 2009).
- *Planning.* Self-regulating learners determine ahead of time how best to use the time and resources they have available for learning tasks (Zimmerman & Moylan, 2009).

- *Self-motivation*. Self-regulating learners typically have high self-efficacy regarding their ability to accomplish a learning task successfully. They use a variety of strategies to keep themselves on task—perhaps embellishing the task to make it more fun, reminding themselves of the importance of doing well, or promising themselves a reward when they're finished (Pajares, 2009; Usher, 2009; Wolters, 2003).

- *Attention control*. Self-regulating learners try to focus their attention on the subject matter at hand and to clear their minds of potentially distracting thoughts and emotions (Harnishfeger, 1995; J. Kuhl, 1985; Winne, 1995).

- *Flexible use of learning strategies*. Self-regulating learners choose different learning strategies depending on the specific goals they hope to accomplish. For example, how they read a magazine article depends on whether they're reading it for entertainment or studying for an exam (Meltzer et al., 2007; van den Broek, Lorch, Linderholm, & Gustafson, 2001; Winne, 1995).

- *Self-monitoring*. Self-regulating learners continually monitor their progress toward their goals for studying—for instance, by frequently checking their understanding of and memory for what they're reading (i.e., monitoring comprehension). In addition, they change their learning strategies or modify their goals as necessary (D. L. Butler & Winne, 1995; Carver & Scheier, 1990; Zimmerman & Moylan, 2009).

- *Appropriate help-seeking*. Truly self-regulating learners don't necessarily try to do everything on their own. On the contrary, they recognize when they need other people's help and actively seek it out. They're especially likely to ask for the kinds of help that will enable them to work more independently in the future (R. Butler, 1998b; J. Lee & Shute, 2010; R. S. Newman, 2008; Zusho & Barnett, 2011).

- *Self-evaluation*. Self-regulating learners determine whether the things they've learned have helped them meet their goals. Ideally, they also use their self-evaluations to adjust their use of various learning strategies on future occasions (Schraw & Moshman, 1995; Winne & Hadwin, 1998; Zimmerman & Moylan, 2009).

As noted in Table 10.3, a few elements of self-regulated learning (e.g., conscious efforts to focus attention and completing short learning tasks independently) emerge in the upper elementary grades, and additional ones (e.g., planning, self-motivation) appear in the middle school and high school years. To some extent, self-regulated learning probably develops from opportunities to engage in age-appropriate independent learning activities and to observe other people modeling effective self-regulation strategies (S. G. Paris & Paris, 2001; Vye et al., 1998; Zimmerman, 2004). But if we take Vygotsky's perspective for a moment, we might suspect that self-regulated learning also has roots in socially regulated learning (Stright, Neitzel, Sears, & Hoke-Sinex, 2001; Vygotsky, 1934/1986; Zimmerman, 1998). At first, a teacher or parent might help children learn by setting goals for a learning activity, keeping the children's attention focused on the learning task, suggesting effective learning strategies, monitoring learning progress, and so on. Then, in co-regulated learning, the adult and children share responsibility for directing the various aspects of the learning process (McCaslin & Good, 1996; McCaslin & Hickey, 2001; Zimmerman, 2004). For example, a teacher and students might agree on the specific goals of a learning endeavor, or the teacher might prescribe criteria that students might use to self-evaluate their performance. The teacher might initially provide considerable scaffolding for the students' learning efforts and then gradually remove it as students become more proficient self-regulators. Alternatively, several learners of *equal ability* might collectively regulate a learning task, perhaps in a cooperative group activity (Hickey, 2011; Volet, Vaura, & Salonen, 2009). In such a situation, different learners can take on different responsibilities and monitor one another's progress.

When children and adolescents are self-regulating learners, they set more ambitious academic goals for themselves, learn more effectively, and achieve at higher levels in classrooms and computer-based learning environments (D. L. Butler & Winne, 1995; Corno et al., 2002; Greene & Azevedo, 2009; Mega, Ronconi, De Beni, 2014). Self-regulation becomes increasingly important in adolescence and adulthood, when many learning activities—reading, doing homework, seeking needed resources on the Internet, and so on—occur in isolation from other people and thus require considerable self-direction (Trautwein et al., 2006; Winne, 1995; Zimmerman & Kitsantas, 2005). Even at advanced grade levels, however, many students have few self-regulated learning skills, perhaps in part because traditional instructional practices do little to encourage them (S. G. Paris & Ayres, 1994; Winters, Greene, & Costich, 2008; Zimmerman & Risemberg, 1997).

PROMOTING SELF-REGULATED LEARNING

To promote self-regulated learning, we must, of course, teach students the kinds of cognitive processes that facilitate learning and memory—comprehension monitoring, elaborative self-questioning, and so on. In addition, researchers have suggested the following strategies:

- Encourage students to set some of their own goals for learning and then to monitor their progress toward those goals.

- Give students opportunities to work without teacher direction or assistance; include independent learning activities in which students study by themselves (e.g., seatwork assignments, homework), small-group activities in which students help one another learn (e.g., peer tutoring, cooperative learning), and technology-facilitated lessons that provide scaffolding.

- Occasionally assign activities in which students have considerable leeway regarding goals and use of time (e.g., research papers, creative projects).

- Teach time management strategies (e.g., setting aside specific times to study at home, prioritizing assignments based on difficulty and due dates).

- Provide the scaffolding students need to acquire self-regulation skills (e.g., give them checklists they can use to identify what they need to do each day and to determine when they've completed all assigned work).

- Model self-regulating cognitive processes by thinking aloud while using such processes, and then give students constructive feedback as they engage in similar processes.

- Encourage students to seek short-term, focused help to overcome temporary difficulties in understanding.

- Consistently ask students to evaluate their own performance, and have them compare their self-assessments to teacher assessments. (Belfiore & Hornyak, 1998; Bronson, 2000; Falco, 2008; Kitsantas, Dabbagh, Hiller, & Mandell, 2015; McCaslin & Good, 1996; McMillan, 2010; Meltzer et al., 2007; R. S. Newman, 2008; S. G. Paris & Paris, 2001; N. E. Perry, 1998; N. E. Perry, VandeKamp, Mercer, & Nordby, 2002; Schunk & Zimmerman, 1997; J. W. Thomas, 1993b; Winne & Hadwin, 1998; Wong, Hoskyn, Jai, Ellis, & Watson, 2008; Zimmerman & Risemberg, 1997)

SELF-REGULATED PROBLEM SOLVING

Effectively directing one's own efforts in tackling complex problems—that is, **self-regulated problem solving**—involves many of the same components as self-regulated learning: goal setting, self-motivation, attention control, self-monitoring, self-evaluation, and so on (Zimmerman & Campillo, 2003). And just as teacher scaffolding facilitates the development of self-regulated learning skills, so, too, does it facilitate the acquisition of self-regulated problem-solving strategies. For example, to encourage brainstorming and creativity in solving problems, we might suggest that students give themselves instructions such as these:

> I want to think of something no one else will think of, something unique. Be freewheeling, no hang-ups. I don't care what anyone thinks; just suspend judgment. I'm not sure what I'll come up with; it will be a surprise. The ideas can just flow through me. (Meichenbaum, 1977, p. 62)

We might also provide a general structure for students to follow as they approach complex problems—for example, by encouraging them to ask themselves such questions as "Why am I using this strategy?" and "Am I sure this answer makes sense?" (Berardi-Coletta, Buyer, Dominowski, & Rellinger, 1995; Desoete, Roeyers, & De Clercq, 2003).

Self-regulated problem solving is important not only for solving academic problems but for solving social problems as well. For instance, to help students deal more effectively with interpersonal conflicts, we might teach them to take these steps:

1. Define the problem.
2. Identify several possible solutions.

MyEdLab
Video Example 10.5.
Skills related to self-regulation have a pervasive influence on students' achievement. Strategies that encourage students to monitor their progress and stay on task enhance self-regulation.

Teach students the mental steps they can follow to solve complex problems more effectively.

3. Predict the likely consequences of each solution.

4. Choose the best solution.

5. Identify the steps required to carry out the solution.

6. Carry out the steps.

7. Evaluate the results. (S. N. Elliott & Busse, 1991; Meichenbaum, 1977; Weissberg, 1985; Yell, Robinson, & Drasgow, 2001)

Following such steps often helps students who have interpersonal problems—for instance, students who are either socially withdrawn or overly aggressive—to develop more effective social skills (K. R. Harris, 1982; Meichenbaum, 1977; Yell et al., 2001).

Another approach is to provide training in peer mediation, in which students *help one another* solve interpersonal problems. In this approach, students learn how to mediate conflicts among classmates by asking opposing sides to express their differing points of view and then work together to devise a reasonable resolution (Beaulieu, Hanley, & Roberson, 2013; M. Deutsch, 1993; D. W. Johnson & Johnson, 1996, 2006). In one study involving several second- through fifth-grade classrooms (D. W. Johnson, Johnson, Dudley, Ward, & Magnuson, 1995), students were trained to help peers resolve interpersonal conflicts by asking the opposing sides to do the following:

1. Define the conflict (the problem).

2. Explain their own perspectives and needs.

3. Explain the other person's perspectives and needs.

4. Identify at least three possible solutions to the conflict.

5. Reach an agreement that addresses the needs of both parties.

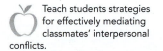

Teach students strategies for effectively mediating classmates' interpersonal conflicts.

Students took turns serving as mediator for their classmates, such that everyone had experience resolving the conflicts of others. As a result, the students more frequently resolved their *own* interpersonal conflicts in ways that addressed the needs of both parties, and they were less likely than students in an untrained control group to ask for adult intervention.

In peer mediation, then, we see another example of Vygotsky's notion that many effective cognitive processes have their roots in social interactions. In a peer mediation session, students model effective conflict resolution skills for one another, and they may eventually internalize the skills they use in solving others' problems to solve their *own* problems.

Peer mediation is most effective when students of diverse ethnic backgrounds, socioeconomic groups, and achievement levels all serve as mediators (Casella, 2001a; K. M. Williams, 2001b). It's appropriate primarily for small, short-term interpersonal problems, such as hurt feelings or conflicts over use of limited academic resources. Even the most proficient of peer mediators may be ill prepared to handle conflicts that involve deep-seated and emotionally charged attitudes and behaviors, such as homophobia and sexual harassment (Casella, 2001a). In such cases the guidance and intervention of teachers and other school personnel will probably be necessary.

DIVERSITY IN SELF-REGULATION

Some diversity in self-regulation—especially diversity related to effortful control—is the result of maturational changes in the brain (see the Applying Brain Research feature "Understanding and Accommodating Individual Differences in Self-Regulation"). Brain development progresses somewhat more quickly in females than in males—a trend that might partly explain girls' tendency to be more self-regulating than boys as early as kindergarten (Lenroot et al., 2007; Matthews, Ponitz, & Morrison, 2009).

But culture, too, seems to make a difference. Some cultural groups—for instance, many East Asian cultures—place particular importance on emotional restraint and self-discipline. Children growing up in these cultures are apt to be hard workers who can focus their attention and work independently on assigned tasks for long periods (X. Chen & Wang, 2010; P. M. Cole, Tamang, & Shrestha, 2006; Morelli & Rothbaum, 2007; Trommsdorff, 2009).

PROMOTING SELF-REGULATION IN STUDENTS AT RISK

Some students have few outside role models for effective study habits—few people in their out-of-school lives who can model the self-regulated learning skills they'll need to succeed in high school and postsecondary education (J. Chen & Morris, 2008). As a result, these students may have little

Applying Brain Research

Understanding and Accommodating Individual Differences in Self-Regulation

Learners' ability to regulate their behaviors and emotions depend largely on two areas in the front part of the brain—the *prefrontal cortex* and the *anterior cingulate cortex*—that continue to develop over the course of childhood, adolescence, and early adulthood (Velanova, Wheeler, & Luna, 2008). In normal brain development, these two areas gradually gain some control over a set of structures in the middle of the brain—including the *amygdala*—that are heavily involved in feeling and responding to emotions. To some degree, then, effective self-regulation requires maturational changes that come only slowly with development (M. D. Lewis & Stieben, 2004; Rothbart, 2011; Steinberg, 2009; Wisner Fries & Pollak, 2007).

Compounding the problem for adolescents is that the changing hormone levels accompanying puberty can increase their sensitivity and reactions to high-stress situations. For example, the increasing testosterone levels in teenage boys make some of them especially prone to impulsive aggressive responses (S. Moore & Rosenthal, 2006; E. Walker, Shapiro, Esterberg, & Trotman, 2010).

Yet in any single age-group, learners seem to differ considerably in their ability to regulate their behaviors, emotions, and cognitive processes. Some of this variability is the result of differences in an aspect of temperament known as effortful control, which appears to have its basis in the brain. In particular, some learners are better able than others to consciously restrain themselves from making impulsive responses when other, less dominant responses might be more productive (Bates & Pettit, 2007; Rothbart, 2011; Rothbart et al., 2007). Students who show high levels of effortful control can better plan ahead, focus their attention where they need to, and keep inappropriate emotional reactions in check. Such students also tend to be better behaved in class and to achieve at higher levels than their classmates with less self-control (Blair & Razza, 2007; Liew, McTigue, Barrois, & Hughes, 2008; Valiente, Lemery-Calfant, Swanson, & Reiser, 2008).

As you can see, then, some students may need more guidance and support than others in acquiring self-regulation skills. With this point in mind, we offer two suggestions:

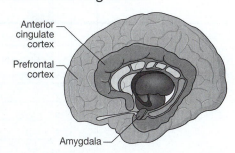

Anterior cingulate cortex
Prefrontal cortex
Amygdala

🔹 **Individualize the scaffolding students need to regulate their behaviors.** Some students are likely to need considerable structure to help them keep unproductive behaviors in check; for example, this will be true for many students who have been identified as having emotional and behavioral disorders. Clear rules for behavior, explicit response–consequence contingencies, and concrete mechanisms for self-monitoring and self-evaluation are often in order. Also useful are simple technological devices—such as small buzzers that a teacher or other adult can remotely activate—that either remind students of things they should be doing or give them feedback that they're doing something well (J. O. Cooper, Heron, & Heward, 2007).

🔹 **Teach strategies for keeping counterproductive emotions in check.** Especially when working with students who are prone to emotional volatility, we can provide concrete guidance about how they might control feelings that would lead them to behave in ways they'd later regret. For instance, we might suggest that they count to 10 and take a few deep breaths in order to calm down before responding to a provocation on the playground. And we can help them brainstorm possible "silver linings" in disappointing circumstances (K. L. Fletcher & Cassady, 2010; Silk et al., 2003).

knowledge about how to accomplish goals such as graduating from high school, attending college, and eventually becoming successful professionals (Belfiore & Hornyak, 1998; B. L. Wilson & Corbett, 2001). For example, in a study with low-income, inner-city middle school students (B. L. Wilson & Corbett, 2001), researchers found that many of the students aspired to professional careers (doctor, lawyer, teacher, etc.) yet misbehaved in class, inconsistently completed homework, and often skipped school. They had little idea about what it would take to do well in their studies, as this interview with one of the students reveals:

> *Adult:* Are you on track to meet your goals?
>
> *Student:* No. I need to study more.
>
> *Adult:* How do you know that?
>
> *Student:* I just know by some of my grades. [mostly Cs]
>
> *Adult:* Why do you think you will be more inclined to do it in high school?
>
> *Student:* I don't want to get let back. I want to go to college.
>
> *Adult:* What will you need to do to get better grades?
>
> *Student:* Just do more and more work. I can rest when the school year is over.[4]

---

[4]Dialogue from Listening to *Urban Kids: School Reform and the Teachers They Want*, by Bruce L. Wilson and Dick Corbett, p. 23. Copyright © 2001 by the State University of New York Press. State University of New York. Reprinted with permission. All rights reserved.

FIGURE 10.7 On this daily log sheet, 13-year-old Lea has kept track of her math assignments, their due dates, and her performance on them.

First Quarter

Math Grade Log		Name Lea Demers		Total
				(as needed)
Assignment		Due Date	Points/Points Possible	
1	Anagram Name	8-27	5/5	5/5
2	1-1 #2-42 even	8/26	5/5	10/10
3	Your Life in Math	8/27	5/5	15/15
4	1-2 #2-52 evens	8/30	5/5	20/20
5	1-3 #2-46 even	8/31	5/5	25/25
6	1-5 #1-36	9/1	5/5	30/30
7	Quiz 1-1 to 1-3	9/2	20/25	50/55
8	4-4's Problem	9/1	6/5	56/60
9	TI Programming A	9/3	5/5	61/65
10	Quiz 1-5 to 1-8	9/10	23/25	84/90
11	1-7 #1-48	9/7	5/5	89/95

Motivation and effort are important, to be sure, but so are planning, time management, regular self-monitoring and self-evaluation, and appropriate help-seeking—things about which this student seemed to have little knowledge (B. L. Wilson & Corbett, 2001).

Fortunately, explicit instruction in self-regulating strategies can help students at risk begin to acquire more effective study habits (Cosden, Morrison, Albanese, & Macias, 2001; Eilam, 2001; Graham & Harris, 1996; S. D. Miller et al., 2003). Sometimes instruction can take place in structured after-school homework programs, in which students have considerable scaffolding for such basic skills as keeping track of homework assignments and due dates, developing plans to complete all assignments in a timely manner, and locating helpful resources. But we can also provide scaffolding for self-regulated activities during regular school hours—for instance, distributing forms that students can use to keep track of what they've already done and still need to do. A daily log sheet, such as that presented in Figure 10.7, can help middle school students keep track of their math assignments and monitor their performance. The form has its limits, because it provides no place for students to record the types of problems they get wrong, the kinds of errors they make, or any other information that might help them improve. For students with few self-regulation strategies, however, using such a form can start them on the road to effective self-monitoring.

Sometimes we also will need to promote self-regulation in our students for helping them to achieve longer-term goals. For example, some students may conclude that they can't go to college because of financial constraints or because nobody else in the student's family has previously attended college. We can direct these students toward individuals (e.g., school counselors) who can inform them about scholarships and who can help them to develop short- and long-term plans that include self-regulatory strategies. In addition, there are programs available that can help *parents* to develop self-regulatory skills related to planning for the financial aspects of college and help students to prepare for college (a nice example of this can be found at http://www.iknowican.org /blueprinths.aspx).

SUPPORTING STUDENTS WITH SPECIAL NEEDS

Students with disabilities often grow up in tightly controlled and structured environments, and some of them have brain abnormalities that make self-regulation difficult. Thus many of these students may especially benefit from explicit instruction in self-regulation strategies and scaffolded opportunities to self-regulate some of their own activities (Coch, Dawson, & Fischer, 2007; Wehmeyer et al., 2007). For instance, we might encourage students with disabilities to set and strive for their own goals, especially goals that are concrete, specific, and accomplishable within a short time period. These students are also well served when we teach them self-monitoring, self-reinforcement, and self-regulated problem-solving skills (Butler, & Schnellert, 2015; Cunningham & Cunningham, 2006; Reid et al., 2005; J. R. Sullivan & Conoley, 2004).

Table 10.4 presents a social cognitive perspective of characteristics commonly seen in students with special needs, as well as strategies for promoting the academic and social success of these students.

Chapter 5 identifies specific categories of special needs that fall within the five general categories listed in Table 10.4.

STUDENTS IN INCLUSIVE SETTINGS

TABLE 10.4 • Applying Social Cognitive Theory with Students Who Have Special Educational Needs

CATEGORY	CHARACTERISTICS YOU MIGHT OBSERVE	SUGGESTED STRATEGIES
Students with specific cognitive or academic difficulties	• Difficulty predicting the consequences of specific behaviors • Low self-efficacy for academic tasks in areas where there has been a history of failure • Less self-regulation of learning and behavior • Difficulty setting appropriate goals	• Help students form more realistic expectations about the consequences of their behaviors. • Scaffold students' efforts on academic tasks to increase the probability of success. • Identify students' areas of strength, and give them opportunities to tutor peers in those areas. • Teach self-regulation strategies (e.g., goal setting and planning, self-monitoring, self-instructions, self-reinforcement).
Students with social or behavioral problems	• Unusual difficulty in learning from models and other aspects of the social environment (for many students with autism spectrum disorders) • Difficulties in planning a productive course of action and in predicting the likely consequences of specific behaviors • Friendships with peers who are poor models of effective social skills and prosocial behavior (for some students with emotional and behavioral disorders) • Less self-regulation of emotions and behaviors • Deficits in social problem solving	• Model appropriate classroom behaviors; combine modeling with explicit verbal instruction, and use visual aids to communicate desired behaviors. • Discuss possible consequences of various courses of action when social conflicts arise. • Provide opportunities for students to interact with peers who model effective social and prosocial behaviors. • Make video recordings of students as they exhibit appropriate and inappropriate behaviors; use videos of their appropriate behaviors as models for future actions. • Teach, demonstrate, and practice self-regulation strategies (e.g., self-monitoring, self-instructions, self-regulated problem solving). • Help students recognize and interpret other people's body language and other social cues.
Students with general delays in cognitive and social functioning	• Low self-efficacy for academic tasks • Tendency to watch others for guidance about how to behave • Low goals for achievement (possibly as a way of avoiding failure) • Little or no self-regulation of learning and behavior	• Scaffold students' efforts on academic tasks to increase the probability of success. • Model desired behaviors; identify peers who can also serve as good models. • Encourage students to set realistic yet somewhat challenging goals for achievement. • Promote self-regulation (e.g., by teaching self-monitoring, self-instructions, self-reinforcement).
Students with physical or sensory challenges	• Few opportunities to develop self-regulation skills because of health limitations and/or a tightly controlled environment	• Teach skills that promote self-sufficiency and independence. • Teach students to make positive self-statements (e.g., "I can do it!") to enhance their self-efficacy for acting independently.
Students with advanced cognitive development	• High self-efficacy for academic tasks • High goals for performance • More effective self-regulated learning • A history of easy successes and, hence, little experience dealing productively with failure (for some students)	• Provide the academic support that students need to reach high goals. • Provide opportunities for independent study. • Provide challenging tasks, including some at which students may initially fail; teach constructive strategies for dealing with failure (e.g., persistence, using errors to guide future practice efforts).

Sources: Asaro-Saddler & Bak, 2014; Bandura, 1989; Bear et al., 2010; Beirne-Smith, Patton, & Kim, 2006; Biemiller, Shany, Inglis, & Meichenbaum, 1998; Coch et al., 2007; Cunningham & Cunningham, 2006; Dapretto et al., 2006; E. S. Ellis & Friend, 1991; Fletcher, Lyons, Fuchs, & Barnes, 2007; Kehle, Clark, Jenson, & Wampold, 1986; Meltzer, 2007; Mercer & Pullen, 2005; J. R. Nelson, Smith, Young, & Dodd, 1991; Nikopoulos & Keenan, 2004; Piirto, 1999; Reid et al., 2005; Sands & Wehmeyer, 1996; Schumaker & Hazel, 1984; Schunk et al., 1987; Silk et al., 2003; J. R. Sullivan & Conoley, 2004; Turnbull, Turnbull, & Wehmeyer, 2010; Usher & Pajares, 2008; Webber & Plotts, 2008; Yell et al., 2001; Zimmerman, 2004.

COMPARE/CONTRAST

TABLE 10.5 •		Mutual Influences (Reciprocal Causation) Among Environment, Behavior, and Person		
		GENERAL EXAMPLES	**EXAMPLES IN LORI'S CASE: SCENE 1**	**EXAMPLES IN LORI'S CASE: SCENE 2**
Effect of Environment	**On behavior**	Reinforcement and punishment affect future behavior.	Teacher's ignoring Lori leads to future classroom failure.	New instructional methods lead to improved academic performance.
	On person	Feedback from others affects sense of self-efficacy.	Teacher's ignoring Lori perpetuates low self-efficacy.	New instructional methods capture Lori's interest and attention.
Effect of Behavior	**On environment**	Specific behaviors affect the amount of reinforcement and punishment received.	Poor classroom performance leads the teacher to meet privately with Lori and then eventually to ignore her.	Increasing self-regulation and better academic performance lead to more reinforcement from the teacher.
	On person	Success and failure affect expectations for future performance.	Poor classroom performance leads to low self-efficacy.	Increasing self-regulation and better academic performance lead to higher self-efficacy.
Effect of Person	**On environment**	Self-efficacy affects choices of activities and therefore also affects the specific environment encountered.	Attention to classmates rather than classroom activities affects the specific environmental stimuli and events perceived and experienced.	Attention to classroom activities leads to greater benefits derived from teacher's instruction.
	On behavior	Attention, retention, and motivation affect the degree to which a learner imitates behaviors modeled by others.	Attention to classmates rather than classroom activities leads to academic failure.	Greater self-efficacy and increased motivation lead to more persistent study habits.

REVISITING RECIPROCAL CAUSATION

We return now to a concept introduced at the beginning of the chapter: reciprocal causation. As we've explored social cognitive theory, we've identified how environmental factors (e.g., reinforcement, teacher scaffolding) can influence learners' behaviors. We've also identified personal factors (e.g., self-efficacy, self-determined standards and goals) that learners bring with them to new tasks, and those, too, affect learners' behaviors. From a social cognitive perspective, all three of these factors—environment, behavior, and person—mutually influence one another (e.g., Bandura, 2008). Several examples of these reciprocal influences are presented in the "General Examples" column in Table 10.5.

As a concrete illustration of how environment, behavior, and personal factors are continually intertwined, let's consider Scene 1 in the case of a student named Lori:

> Scene 1
>
> Lori often comes late to Mr. Broderick's seventh-grade social studies class, and she's usually ill prepared for the day's activities. In class she spends more time interacting with friends (e.g., whispering, passing notes) than engaging in assigned tasks. Lori's performance on most exams and assignments is unsatisfactory—when she turns in her work at all.
>
> In mid-October Mr. Broderick takes Lori aside to express his concern about her lack of classroom effort. He suggests that she could do better if she paid more attention in class. He also offers to work with her twice a week after school to help her understand class material. Lori is less optimistic, describing herself as "not smart enough to learn this stuff."
>
> For a week or so after meeting with Mr. Broderick, Lori seems to buckle down and exert more effort, but she never does stay after school for extra help. And before long she's back to her old habits. Mr. Broderick eventually concludes that Lori is a lost cause and decides to devote his time and effort to helping more motivated students.

Lori's low self-efficacy (a *person* factor) is probably one reason she spends so much class time engaged in task-irrelevant activities (*behaviors*). The fact that she devotes her attention (another *person* factor) to her classmates rather than to her teacher affects the particular stimuli she experiences (her *environment*). Lori's non-self-regulating behaviors and resulting poor performance on assignments and exams (*behaviors*) affect both her self-efficacy (*person*) and Mr. Broderick's treatment of her (*environment*). By eventually concluding that Lori is a lost cause, Mr. Broderick begins to ignore Lori (*environment*), contributing further to her failure (*behavior*) and even lower self-efficacy (*person*). The "Scene 1" column in Table 10.3 presents examples of such interactive effects. In general, Lori is showing signs of being at risk for long-term academic failure.

Now imagine that Mr. Broderick reads several research articles describing effective strategies for working with students like Lori. Midway through the school year, he makes the following changes in his classroom:

- He communicates clearly and consistently that he expects all his students to succeed.
- He incorporates students' personal experiences and interests into the study of social studies.
- He identifies specific, concrete tasks that students will accomplish each week.
- He provides explicit guidance for accomplishing each task.
- To teach simple self-regulation strategies, he asks students to set goals for each learning task, suggests that they reinforce themselves with 15 minutes of a favorite activity after finishing a homework assignment, and shows them how to track their progress on graph paper.
- After consulting with the school's reading specialist and school psychologist, he helps students develop more effective reading and learning strategies.
- He gives a short quiz every Friday so that students can self-assess what they've learned each week.
- When students perform well on weekly quizzes, he reminds them that they themselves are responsible for their performance; when they don't do well, he provides concrete suggestions for specific self-regulatory strategies that they can incorporate the next week.

Let's see what happens next, as we consider Scene 2:

Scene 2

By incorporating students' personal experiences and interests into daily lesson plans, Mr. Broderick captures Lori's interest and attention. She begins to realize that social studies has implications for her own life, and she becomes more involved in class activities. With the more structured assignments, better guidance about how to study class material, and frequent quizzes, Lori finds herself succeeding in a subject in which she previously experienced only failure. Mr. Broderick is equally pleased with her performance, and he frequently communicates his pleasure through his facial expressions, verbal feedback, and willingness to provide help whenever she needs it.

By the end of the school year, Lori is studying course material more effectively and completing her assignments regularly. She's actually looking forward to next year's social studies class, confident that she'll continue to do well.

Once again, we see the interplay among environment, behavior, and person. Mr. Broderick's new instructional methods (*environment*) engage Lori's attention (*person*), foster self-regulation, and enhance academic performance (*behaviors*). Lori's improved classroom performance, in turn, influences Mr. Broderick's treatment of her (*environment*) and her own self-efficacy (*person*). Her improved self-efficacy, her greater attention to classroom activities, and her increased motivation to succeed (all *person* variables) affect her ability to benefit from Mr. Broderick's instruction (*environment*) and her classroom success (*behavior*). The "Scene 2" column in Table 10.5 presents examples of such interactive effects.

MyEdLab **Self-Check 10.5**

MyEdLab **Application Exercise 10.4.** In this exercise, you can practice applying strategies that promote self-regulated learning in the classroom.

Comparing Theoretical Perspectives of Learning

For detailed discussions of the other three theoretical perspectives, see Chapter 6 and Chapter 7 (cognitive psychology), Chapter 8 (contextual theories), and Chapter 9 (behaviorism).

At this point in your study of human learning, you may have examined four general theoretical perspectives: cognitive psychology, contextual theories, behaviorism, and social cognitive theory. Table 10.6 identifies central ways in which these perspectives are similar and different. But we urge you to keep this point in mind: *Diverse perspectives of learning often complement rather than contradict one another, and together they give us a richer, more multifaceted picture of human learning than any single perspective can give us by itself.* All four perspectives are supported by research, and provide valuable guidance about how we can help students achieve in classroom settings.

MyEdLab **Self-Check 10.6**

COMPARE/CONTRAST

TABLE 10.6 • **Comparing the Four Perspectives of Learning**

ISSUE	COGNITIVE PSYCHOLOGY	CONTEXTUAL THEORIES	BEHAVIORISM	SOCIAL COGNITIVE THEORY
Learning is defined as...	An internal mental phenomenon that may or may not be reflected in behavior	A phenomenon that is often situated within a particular physical or social context	A behavior change	An internal mental phenomenon that may or may not be reflected in behavior
The focus of investigation is on...	Cognitive processes	Various layers of context (e.g., small groups, culture, society) that support learning and development	Stimuli and responses that can be readily observed	Both behavior and cognitive processes
Principles of learning describe how...	People mentally process new information and construct knowledge from their experiences	Physical, social, and cultural mechanisms influence learning and cognition	People's behaviors are affected by environmental stimuli	People's observations of those around them affect their behavior and cognitive processes
Consequences of behavior...	Are not a major focus of consideration	Are not a major focus of consideration	Must be experienced directly if they are to affect learning	Can be experienced either directly or vicariously
Learning and behavior are influenced...	Primarily by cognitive processes within the individual	Both by local environmental conditions and by broader cultural and social factors	Primarily by local environmental conditions	Partly by the environment and partly by cognitive processes (people become increasingly self-regulating—and therefore less controlled by the environment—over time)
Educational implications focus on how we can help students...	Process information in effective ways and construct accurate and complete knowledge about classroom topics	Acquire complex knowledge and skills within authentic, real-world contexts	Acquire more productive classroom behaviors	Learn by observing others, develop feelings of self-efficacy for academic tasks, and acquire effective self-regulation skills

10   What Have You Learned?

We now return to the chapter's learning outcomes to summarize key concepts, principles, and applications of social cognitive theory.

■ **10.1: Describe five basic assumptions of social cognitive theory and their classroom implications.** As a perspective that focuses on how people learn by observing others, social cognitive theory has built on ideas from both behaviorism and cognitive psychology. Social cognitive theorists view learning as an internal mental process (as cognitive psychologists do), but they also stress the important influences of response–consequence contingencies (as behaviorists do). Furthermore, the interplay of mental processes and environmental consequences has implications not only for learning but also for motivation. Ultimately environmental, behavioral, and personal factors all interact with one another in their effects on learning—a three-way interdependence known as *reciprocal causation*. With age, experience, and appropriate scaffolding, many learners can increasingly take charge of their own behaviors, academic learning, and interpersonal problems.

■ **10.2: Use a social cognitive perspective to explain how mental processes can influence the effects of reinforcement and punishment.** Social cognitive theorists' beliefs about how reinforcement influences learning and behavior are quite different from those of behaviorists. From a social cognitive perspective, reinforcement and punishment affect learning indirectly rather than directly, and consequences to one learner vicariously influence the behaviors of other learners as well. For example, students who observe a classmate being reinforced or punished for a particular behavior may conclude that engaging in that behavior will yield similar consequences for themselves. Furthermore, the nonoccurrence of expected reinforcement is punishing, and the nonoccurrence of expected punishment is reinforcing. As teachers, we should recognize that the consequences of students' behaviors are likely to influence the expectations students form, the ways in which they process information, and the choices they make.

■ **10.3: Describe the potential effects of modeling on learners' behaviors, and explain how you can productively use modeling in instruction.** Effective models can take one of three forms: living people, real or fictional characters portrayed in various media, or verbal instructions regarding how to successfully execute desired behaviors. Such models can encourage either productive behaviors and skills (e.g., math and writing competencies, interpersonal skills) or inappropriate ones (e.g., aggression). Four conditions are essential if students are to learn from models: attention to the model, retention (memory) of what the model does, capacity for motor reproduction of the modeled behavior, and motivation to exhibit the modeled behavior. Students often benefit more from models who are not only competent and prestigious but also similar to themselves in cultural background, socioeconomic status, gender, and (if applicable) disability.

■ **10.4: Describe the nature and origins of self-efficacy, and explain how you might enhance self-efficacy both in your students as developing learners and in yourself as a teacher.** Learners are more likely to engage and persist in certain activities when they believe they can perform or learn the activities successfully—that is, when they have high *self-efficacy*.

As teachers, we can enhance students' self-efficacy by giving them reasons to believe they can master school subject matter (e.g., by having them observe successful peer models) and by providing many opportunities to experience success working either as individuals or as part of a group. At the same time, we must remember that our *own* self-efficacy as teachers—our belief that with effort and effective instructional strategies we can definitely make a difference in students' lives—is an important factor in students' success.

■ **10.5: Identify important components of self-regulated behavior and self-regulated learning, and apply your knowledge of self-regulation to help diverse learners effectively control their behavior, master academic subject matter, and address interpersonal problems.** As children grow older, most of them become increasingly self-regulating. For example, they begin to set standards and goals for themselves, try to keep counterproductive emotions in check, and monitor and evaluate their own behaviors. With development, too, many children gradually acquire strategies for regulating their learning efforts. For example, they conscientiously plan how they might best use their time and resources, motivate themselves to stay on task as they work, apply and evaluate various study strategies, and seek help when they need it. They can be equally self-regulating in addressing interpersonal problems, identifying various possible solutions, and evaluating the end result of whatever solution they choose.

As teachers, we can foster the development of self-regulation skills in many ways—for instance, by asking students to set some of their own goals, providing explicit criteria with which they can evaluate their performance, and giving them age-appropriate independence in various situations and tasks. However, we must keep in mind that students in any single age-group vary considerably in their ability to control their behaviors and emotions, in part as a result of differences in brain maturation and temperament. Furthermore, some students may have had few outside role models for effective study habits. Some of our students, then, may need considerable guidance and support in their development of self-regulation skills.

■ **10.6: Compare and contrast perspectives of learning associated with cognitive psychology, contextual theories, behaviorism, and social cognitive theory.** Cognitive psychology, contextual perspectives, behaviorism, and social cognitive learning sometimes share and build on one another's ideas, but in other respects they offer competing views of how human beings learn. Key differences among the four perspectives include their definitions of learning; the nature of their research; their emphases on mental processes, influences of stimuli and consequences in one's immediate environment, or broader social and cultural contexts; and the specific implications they derive for instruction. As teachers, we must keep in mind that all four perspectives have useful applications for classroom practice.

Practice for Your Licensure Exam

Teacher's Lament

"Sometimes a teacher just can't win," complains Mr. Adams, a sixth-grade teacher. "At the beginning of the year, I told my students that homework assignments would count for 20% of their grades. Yet some students hardly ever turned in any homework, even though I continually reminded them about their assignments. After reconsidering the situation, I decided that I probably shouldn't use homework as a criterion for grading. After all, in this low-income neighborhood, many kids don't have a quiet place to study at home.

"So in November I told my class that I wouldn't be counting homework assignments when I calculated grades for the first report card. Naturally, some students—the ones who hadn't been doing their homework—seemed relieved. But the students who *had* been doing it were absolutely furious! And now hardly anyone turns in homework anymore."

1. Multiple-choice question:

Which one of the following statements best uses principles from social cognitive theory to explain why the students who had regularly been doing their homework were so upset?

a. Switching grading policies midstream, as Mr. Adams did, was a form of negative reinforcement.

b. The nonoccurrence of expected reinforcement for completing homework was a form of punishment.

c. By not giving credit for homework assignments, Mr. Adams significantly reduced students' self-efficacy regarding academic subject matter.

d. Reciprocal causation was at work: The students were essentially retaliating against their teacher for his unexpected change in grading policy.

2. Constructed-response question:

What might Mr. Adams do to encourage and help all students to complete homework assignments? Basing your discussion on principles of self-regulation, describe at least three different strategies in specific, concrete terms.

MyEdLab **Licensure Exam 10.1**

PRAXIS Go to Appendix C, "Matching Book Content and Ebook Activities to the Praxis Principles of Learning and Teaching Tests," to discover sections of this chapter that may be especially applicable to the Praxis tests.

Greatstock Photographic Library/Alamy

11

Motivation and Affect

Learning Outcomes

11.1 Draw on diverse theoretical perspectives to describe the multifaceted nature of motivation.

11.2 Explain how learners' needs, cognitive processes, and sociocultural environments can have significant impacts on their motivation and other types of needs, and apply your knowledge of these factors to classroom practice.

11.3 Describe how teachers' beliefs and behaviors affect student motivation.

11.4 Describe how various forms of affect are intertwined with motivation, learning, and cognition, and explain how you might promote productive affective states in students.

CASE STUDY: PASSING ALGEBRA

Fourteen-year-old Michael has been getting failing grades in his eighth-grade algebra class, prompting his family to ask graduate student Valerie Tucker to tutor him. In the first tutoring session, Michael tells Ms. Tucker that he probably won't pass the course because he has little aptitude for math and his teacher doesn't explain the subject matter very well. In his mind, he's powerless to change either his own ability or his teacher's instructional strategies, making continuing failure inevitable.

As Ms. Tucker works with Michael over the next several weeks, she encourages him to think more about what *he* can do to master algebra and less about what his teacher may or may not be doing to help him. She points out that he did well in math in earlier years and so certainly has the ability to learn algebra if he puts his mind to it. She also teaches him some strategies for understanding and applying algebraic principles. Michael takes a giant step forward when he finally realizes that his own efforts play a role in his classroom success:

> Maybe I can try a little harder. . . . The teacher is still bad, but maybe some of this other stuff can work.

When Michael sees gradual improvement on his algebra assignments and quizzes, he becomes increasingly aware that the specific strategies he uses are just as important as his effort:

> I learned that I need to understand information before I can hold it in my mind. . . . Now I do things in math step by step and listen to each step. I realize now that even if I don't like the teacher or don't think he is a good teacher, it is my responsibility to listen. I listen better now and ask questions more.

As Michael's performance in algebra continues to improve in later weeks, he gains greater confidence that he *can* master algebra after all, and he comes to realize that his classroom success is ultimately up to him:

> The teacher does most of his part, but it's no use to me unless I do my part. . . . Now I try and comprehend, ask questions and figure out how he got the answer. . . . I used to just listen and not even take notes. I always told myself I would remember but I always seemed to forget. Now I take notes and I study at home every day except Friday, even if I don't have homework. Now I study so that I know that I have it. I don't just hope I'll remember.[1]

- On what factors does Michael initially blame his failure? To what factors does he later attribute his success? How do his changing beliefs affect his learning strategies?
- What inferences about motivation might you draw from the case study? How might learners' cognitive processes influence their motivation? How might teachers' behaviors also have an impact?

---

1 This and preceding extracts from "Cycles of Learning: Demonstrating the Interplay Between Motivation, Self-Regulation, and Cognition," by Valerie G. Tucker and Lynley H. Anderman, paper presented at the annual meeting of the American Educational Research Association, April 1999, pp. 5–6. Copyright © 1999 by Valerie G. Tucker and Lynley H. Anderman. Reprinted with permission of the authors.

Michael initially believes he's failing algebra because of two things he can't control—his teacher's poor instruction and his own low ability—and so he exerts little effort in the class. But with Ms. Tucker's guidance, he discovers that increased effort and better strategies can make a big difference in his classroom performance. Suddenly Michael himself—not his teacher and not some genetically predetermined inability that lurks within him—is in control of the situation, and his confidence skyrockets.

In this chapter we'll discover that our students' beliefs, goals, and past experiences play key roles in their motivation—or apparent lack of it—to master classroom subject matter. We'll discover, too, that teachers' behaviors, beliefs, and attitudes can either enhance learners' motivation (perhaps by facilitating mastery, as Ms. Tucker does) or discourage it (perhaps by using ineffective instructional strategies, as Michael's teacher seemingly does). We'll also learn that many aspects of the classroom environment that teachers control can affect motivation. Finally, we'll also look at the nature of emotions—which psychologists often refer to as *affect*—and consider how they come into play in both learning and motivation.

The Nature of Motivation

In the first part of this chapter, we're going to look at some of the different ways researchers think about the nature of motivation. Motivation is a term that is often used very broadly. In general, motivation is something that energizes, directs, and sustains behavior; it gets people moving, points them in a particular direction, and keeps them going. More specifically, motivation has several effects:

- It directs behavior toward particular goals.
- It leads to increased effort and energy in pursuit of those goals.
- It increases initiation of and persistence in certain activities, even in the face of occasional obstacles and interruptions.
- It affects cognitive processes, such as what learners pay attention to and how much they think about and elaborate on academic content.
- It determines which consequences are reinforcing and punishing.

We often see students' motivation reflected in their *personal investment* and their cognitive, emotional, and behavioral *engagement* in certain activities. In general, then, motivation increases students' physical and cognitive time on task, an important factor affecting their learning and achievement in a particular domain (Fredricks, Blumenfeld, & Paris, 2004; Ladd & Dinella, 2009; J. Lee & Shute, 2010; Maehr & McInerney, 2004; E. Skinner, Furrer, Marchand, & Kindermann, 2008). Let's first consider the many questions that teachers might ask when trying to understand a student's lack of motivation:

▪▪ EXPERIENCING FIRSTHAND

Jodie is 14 years old, and her math teacher, Mr. Walters, feels that she is not motivated. Mr. Walters approaches you, as one of his teacher colleagues, and asks you to try to figure out why Jodie is not motivated. What questions would you ask Jodie to try to understand her lack of motivation? Keep your list of questions, because we will return to them later in the chapter. ▪▪

As you probably realized from thinking about Jodie's situation, teachers have many options to consider when thinking about how to best motivate their students. Researchers have approached the study of motivation from several angles, which are summarized in Table 11.1. Each of these theoretical perspectives provides pieces of the motivation "puzzle," offering useful ideas about how we can motivate students in classroom settings, and so we'll draw from all of them in the pages ahead.

Three general principles of motivation will underlie much of our discussion:

- *All children and adolescents are motivated in one way or another.* Occasionally we hear educators, policy makers, or the public at large talking about "unmotivated" students. In reality, all students have needs and desires they're motivated to satisfy. One student may be keenly interested

MyEdLab
Video Example 11.1.

Motivation is something that energizes, directs, and sustains behavior. Students in this video are learning about the nature of motivation by observing the thoughts, feelings, and actions of characters in stories.

in classroom topics and seek out challenging coursework, participate actively in class discussions, and earn high marks on projects. Another student may be more concerned with the social side of school, interacting frequently with classmates, attending many extracurricular activities, and perhaps running for an office in student government. Still another may be focused on athletics, excelling in physical education classes, playing or watching sports most afternoons and weekends, and faithfully following a physical fitness regimen. Yet another student—perhaps because of an undetected learning disability, shy temperament, or seemingly uncoordinated body—may be motivated to *avoid* academics, social situations, or athletic activities.

• *Motivation to do well in school is grounded in a variety of cognitive and sociocultural factors that evolve over time.* A common misconception is that students can turn their motivation "on" or "off" at will, much as one would flip a light switch. In fact, students' motivation to achieve—or *not* achieve—in a traditional academic curriculum is the result of many factors that don't easily change overnight. Some of these factors are cognitive in nature, such as students' short-term and long-term goals and their self-efficacy for learning academic topics. Others have social or cultural origins, such as the activities and values that students' families and local communities endorse. In the opening case study, Michael's self-efficacy for mastering math improves—but only *gradually*—as he discovers that by applying effort and good strategies, he can be successful in the class.

• *Conditions in the classroom and school play a major role in students' motivation to learn and achieve.* Motivation isn't necessarily something that learners bring *to* school; it can also arise from environmental conditions *at* school. When we talk about how the environment can enhance a learner's motivation to learn particular things or behave in particular ways, we're talking about situated motivation (S. G. Paris & Turner, 1994; Rueda & Moll, 1994; Turner & Patrick, 2008). As you'll see throughout the chapter, we teachers can do many things to motivate students to learn and achieve in ways that promote their long-term success and productivity. Even the seemingly "little" things we do—for instance, communicating genuine concern about students' academic and personal well-being and ensuring that their peers treat them respectfully—can have a significant long-term impact (Yeager & Walton, 2011).

As we show in Table 11.1, there are many different ways to think about motivation. As teachers, we need to understand that students' motivation is not simple and that there are many different influences that impact our students. In the following sections, we are going to introduce some key perspectives, and discuss ways teachers can shape positive motivational beliefs for their students.

INTRINSIC VERSUS EXTRINSIC MOTIVATION

A key distinction is between intrinsic and extrinsic motivation. A student who has intrinsic motivation engages in an activity because it is enjoyable and interesting; that is, the motivation is internal to the activity itself. In contrast, a student who has extrinsic motivation engages in an activity in order to receive a reward (like a good grade) or to avoid a punishment that comes from outside (external to) the activity itself.

Consider these two students in an advanced high school writing class:

• Sheryl is taking the class for only one reason: Earning an A or B in the class will help her earn a scholarship at State University, which she desperately wants to attend.

• Shannon has always liked to write. Doing well in the class will certainly help her get a scholarship at State University, but more important, she wants to become a better writer and knows that the skills she can gain will be useful in her future profession as a journalist. An additional bonus is that she's learning many new techniques for making her writing more vivid and engaging.

Sheryl has extrinsic motivation: She's motivated by factors external to herself and unrelated to the task at hand. Extrinsically motivated learners perform a task as a means to an end—perhaps the good grades, money, or recognition that particular activities and accomplishments bring—rather than as an end in itself. In contrast, Shannon shows intrinsic motivation: She's motivated by factors within herself and inherent in the task she's performing. Intrinsically motivated learners may engage in an activity because it gives them pleasure and a sense of fulfillment or seems to be the ethically and morally right thing to do. Some learners with high levels of intrinsic

COMPARE/CONTRAST

TABLE 11.1 • General Theoretical Approaches to the Study of Motivation	
THEORETICAL PERSPECTIVE	**GENERAL DESCRIPTION**
Trait theories	Relatively enduring characteristics and personality traits play a significant role in motivation. For example, learners have different *temperaments* that predispose them to either seek or avoid novel experiences and social situations. Furthermore, significant *individual differences* exist in learners' motives—for instance, in their desires to achieve at high levels, to interact frequently with other people, and to obtain other people's approval for their achievements and behaviors.
Behaviorist theories	Motivation is often the result of *drives:* internal states caused by a lack of something necessary for optimal functioning. Consequences of behavior (reinforcement, punishment) are effective to the extent that they either decrease or increase these drive states. In recent years some behaviorists have added a *purposeful* element to the behaviorist perspective: They suggest that learners intentionally behave in order to achieve certain end results.
Humanism	Learners have within themselves a tremendous *potential for psychological growth* and continually strive to fulfill this potential. When given a caring and supportive environment, learners strive to understand themselves, to enhance their abilities, and to behave in ways that benefit both themselves and others. Initially, humanism arose largely in reaction to behaviorists' environment-driven portrait of human motivation and was grounded largely in philosophy rather than in research findings. In recent years, however, a more research-based perspective known as positive psychology has begun to emerge.
Social cognitive theories	In the first few years of life, learners are motivated largely by the consequences that follow either their own behaviors or the behaviors of other people. With age and experience, they acquire *self-efficacy beliefs*—beliefs about their ability to achieve desired results in different domains. As many learners become increasingly self-regulating over time, they begin to set *goals* for themselves, and much of their motivation comes from within rather than from external consequences.
Cognitive theories	A variety of cognitive factors—sometimes in combination with emotional factors—affect learners' perceptions of themselves, of various topics, and of the world at large. Such perceptions, in turn, influence learners' inclinations to engage or not engage in particular tasks and activities. For example, learners tend to be more intrinsically motivated when they believe they have some control and choice in their activities—in other words, when they have a sense of *self-determination*. Also, learners identify what are, in their minds, the likely causes of their successes and failures, and these *attributions* influence their subsequent behaviors.
Contextual theories	Many aspects of motivation are the result of social and cultural factors, such as the behavioral norms that a peer group or overall culture endorses (which learners might gradually internalize) and the many formal and informal learning opportunities that learners' local community and broader society provide. Furthermore, motivation is often *situated* in particular contexts and content domains; for example, learners might be eager to learn technology skills when texting or playing video games with friends but have little interest in mastering math or science at school. Ultimately learners and the contexts in which they live and work dynamically influence each other, with learners choosing and changing their environments, and their environments, in turn, nurturing and in other ways influencing learners' specific interests and motives.

motivation become so focused on and absorbed in an activity that they lose track of time and completely ignore other tasks—a phenomenon known as flow (Csikszentmihalyi, 1990, 1996; Csikszentmihalyi, Abuhamdeh, & Nakamura, 2005; Shernoff & Csikszentmihalyi, 2009).

Learners are likely to experience beneficial effects when they're *intrinsically* motivated to engage in classroom activities. Intrinsically motivated learners willingly tackle assigned tasks and are eager to learn classroom material, are more likely to process information in effective ways (e.g., by engaging in meaningful learning), and are more likely to achieve at high levels. In contrast, extrinsically motivated learners may have to be enticed or prodded, may process information only superficially, and may be interested in performing only easy tasks and meeting minimal classroom requirements (M. Becker, McElvany, & Kortenbruck, 2010; Reeve, 2006; Schiefele, 1991; Taylor et al., 2014).

In the early elementary grades, students are eager and excited to learn new things at school. But sometime between grades 3 and 9, their intrinsic motivation to master school subject matter declines (A. E. Gottfried, Fleming, & Gottfried, 2001; Lepper, Corpus, & Iyengar, 2005; Otis, Grouzet, & Pelletier, 2005). This decline is probably the result of several factors. As students get older, they're increasingly reminded of the importance of good grades (extrinsic motivators) for promotion, graduation, and college admission, causing them to focus their efforts on earning high grade point averages. In addition, they become more cognitively capable of setting and striving for long-term goals, and they begin to evaluate school subjects in terms of their usefulness in meeting such goals (imagine a high school student who is studying chemistry, but mostly because she wants to become a doctor—her motivation to study chemistry here is clearly extrinsic). Furthermore, students may grow increasingly impatient with the overly structured, repetitive, and boring activities they often encounter at school (Battistich, Solomon, Kim, Watson, & Schaps, 1995; Larson, 2000; Shernoff, Csikszentmihalyi, Schneider, & Shernoff, 2003).

Many new teachers believe that intrinsic and extrinsic motivation represent opposite ends of a continuum; this is absolutely not the case! Often learners are simultaneously motivated by *both* intrinsic and extrinsic factors (J. Cameron & Pierce, 1994; Covington, 2000; Lepper et al., 2005). For example, although Shannon enjoys her writing course, she also knows that getting a good grade will help her get a scholarship at State U., and good grades and other external rewards for high achievement may confirm for her that she's mastering school subject matter (Hynd, 2003). Furthermore, in some situations, extrinsic motivation—perhaps in the form of extrinsic reinforcers for academic achievement or desired behavior—may be the only thing that can get students on the road to successful classroom learning and productive behavior. Yet ultimately motivation from *within* is what will sustain students over the long run.

Let's look at Figure 11.1. The columns represent low and high extrinsic motivation, and the rows represent low and high intrinsic motivation. Which of these four students do you think would be the most challenging to have in class? Most would probably agree that Steve would be rather difficult to teach. Steve is the type of student who has no intrinsic motivation and is not motivated by extrinsic incentives. Steve is basically a student who has given up. John doesn't like math, but he is still motivated by extrinsic rewards, whereas Ada does like math, but really doesn't care about any incentives. Janet is quite typical of high achieving students—she likes math, but also is motivated by grades. Many students who are focused on getting into college may have profiles similar to Janet's.

Extrinsic reinforcers appear to have no adverse effects when they're unexpected—for example, when students get special recognition for a community service project—or when the reinforcers aren't contingent on specific behaviors—for example, when they're used simply to make an activity more enjoyable. They can even be beneficial if used to encourage students not only to do something but also to do it *well*. When rewards convey information to students about why they have done well or have made considerable improvement (e.g., rewarding a student for using an appropriate strategy), they can enhance students' self-efficacy and focus students' attention on mastering the subject matter (E. M. Anderman & Dawson, 2011; J. Cameron, 2001; Deci & Moller, 2005; Reeve, 2006).

Sometimes students may initially find a new topic or skill boring or frustrating and thus may need external encouragement to continue (J. Cameron, 2001; Deci, Koestner, & Ryan, 2001; Hidi & Harackiewicz, 2000). On such occasions, one effective strategy is to praise students in a manner that communicates information but doesn't show an intent to control behavior (Deci, 1992; R. M. Ryan, Mims, & Koestner, 1983). Following are examples:

- "Your description of the main character in your short story is so detailed and vivid! It really makes her come alive."

See Chapter 9 if you need a refresher on the distinction between extrinsic and intrinsic reinforcers.

FIGURE 11.1 Intrinsic and extrinsic motivation are two distinct types of motivation, not opposite ends of a continuum.

		Extrinsic Motivation	
		Low	High
Intrinsic Motivation	Low	Steve does not like math, and incentives don't make him like it any more (he doesn't care if he gets a good grade).	John does not like math, but he is motivated in math class because he wants to get an "A" so he can get into a good college.
	High	Ada likes math and finds it very interesting, but she really doesn't care about the grades that she gets in math class.	Janet likes math and finds it interesting, but she also cares about her grades and wants to get an "A" so she can get into a good college.

• "Your poster clearly describes every step you took in your experiment. Your use of a bar graph makes your results easy to see and interpret."

Another strategy is to teach students to reinforce *themselves* for their accomplishments, a practice that clearly keeps control in students' hands.

Self-imposed reinforcement is an important aspect of self-regulated behavior (see Chapter 10).

Ideally we should rely on intrinsic reinforcers—such as students' own feelings of pride and satisfaction about their accomplishments—as often as possible. One problem with *extrinsic* reinforcers (e.g., praise, good grades) is that they can undermine intrinsic motivation, especially if students perceive them as controlling behavior and limiting choices (Deci & Moller, 2005; Lepper & Hodell, 1989; Reeve, 2006). Extrinsic reinforcers may also communicate the message that classroom tasks are unpleasant chores—why else would a reinforcer be necessary? (B. A. Hennessey, 1995; Stipek, 1993).

MyEdLab **Self-Check 11.1**

MyEdLab **Application Exercise 11.1.** In this exercise you can compare and contrast the types of motivation described by these students.

Early Views of Basic Human Needs

In considering general motivational processes, beyond academic motivation specifically, it is useful to remember that our students have certain basic needs they must address related to their physical survival; for example, they must regularly have food, water, and shelter.

An early model of human needs, proposed by Abraham Maslow, suggested that humans organize their needs in fairly consistent ways (e.g., Maslow, 1943, 1973, 1987). Maslow identified five basic human needs:

1. *Physiological:* Needs related to physical survival (food, water, shelter, etc.)
2. *Safety:* The need to feel safe and secure in one's environment
3. *Love and belonging:* The need to have affectionate relationships with others and to be accepted as part of a group
4. *Esteem:* The need to feel good about oneself (*self-esteem*) and also to believe that others also perceive oneself favorably (*esteem from others*)
5. *Self-actualization:* The need to reach one's full potential—to become all that one is capable of becoming

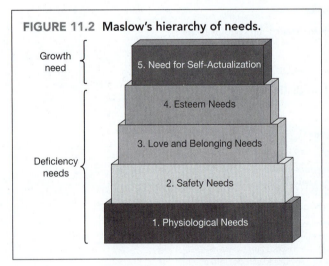

FIGURE 11.2 Maslow's hierarchy of needs.

Growth need {
5. Need for Self-Actualization

Deficiency needs {
4. Esteem Needs
3. Love and Belonging Needs
2. Safety Needs
1. Physiological Needs

Maslow proposed these needs are organized to form a hierarchy, as illustrated in Figure 11.2. Specifically, individuals try to satisfy their physiological needs first, then their need for safety, and still later their needs for love, belonging, and esteem. Only when such needs have been met do they strive for self-actualization, exploring areas of interest, learning simply for the sheer pleasure of it, and so on. Thus, students whose basic needs are insufficiently met are unlikely to be motivated by academic pursuit. For example, one of the authors once knew a boy living in a Philadelphia ghetto who was eager to go to school but often stayed home to avoid the violent gangs that hung out on the local street corner. This boy's need for safety took precedence over any need for self-actualization he might have had.

Unfortunately, Maslow's hierarchy of needs was based on very little hard evidence; thus, many theorists continue to regard his theory as being more conjecture than fact. Yet aspects of Maslow's theory clearly have some merit. It makes sense that learners will worry about their physical well-being and personal safety before trying to address more social needs (e.g., Kenrick, Griskevicius, Neuberg, & Schaller, 2010). And many people do seem to be eager to gain wisdom or creatively express themselves, consistent with Maslow's idea of self-actualization (Kesebir, Graham, & Oishi, 2010; C. Peterson & Park, 2010).

AROUSAL

Human beings appear to have a **need for arousal**—a need for some degree of stimulation (E. M. Anderman, Noar, Zimmerman, & Donohew, 2004; Berlyne, 1960; Heron, 1957; Labouvie-Vief & González, 2004). As an example, try the following exercise.

EXPERIENCING FIRSTHAND
TAKE FIVE

For the next 5 minutes, you're going to be a student who has nothing to do. *Remain exactly where you are,* put your book aside, and *do nothing.* Spend at least 5 minutes on this "task."

What kinds of reactions did you have during your 5-minute break? Did you fidget a bit, perhaps wiggling tired body parts or scratching newly detected itches? Did you interact in some way with something or someone else, perhaps tapping on a table or talking to another person in the room? Did you get out of your seat altogether—something we specifically asked you *not* to do? The exercise has, we hope, shown you that you tend to feel better when *something,* rather than nothing at all, is happening to you.

Not only do people seem to have a basic need for arousal, but they also strive for a certain *optimal level* of arousal at which they feel best (E. M. Anderman et al., 2004; Berlyne, 1960; Hsee, Yang, & Wang, 2010). Too little stimulation is unpleasant, but so is too much. You might enjoy watching a television game show or listening to music, but you'd probably rather not have three TV sets, five iPods, and a live rock band all blasting at you at once. Different people have different optimal levels: Some individuals are *sensation seekers* who thrive on physically thrilling and possibly dangerous experiences (Cleveland, Gibbons, Gerrard, Pomery, & Brody, 2005; V. F. Reyna & Farley, 2006); others prefer a quieter existence. You'll never catch someone who has a low need for sensation hang-gliding or bungee-jumping. Yet even someone who is not a high sensation seeker may still like a lot of *cognitive* stimulation in the form of regular exposure to new ideas, occasional debates about controversial issues, and so on (e.g., see Cacioppo, Petty, Feinstein, & Jarvis, 1996).

The need for arousal explains some of the motivation behind what our students do in the classroom. For instance, it explains why many students happily pull out a favorite book and read if they finish an in-class assignment before their classmates. But it also explains why students sometimes engage in off-task behaviors—for instance, passing notes and playing practical jokes—during lessons they find boring (Pekrun, Goetz, Daniels, Stupnisky, & Perry, 2010). Obviously, students are most likely to stay *on* task when classroom activities keep them sufficiently aroused so that they have little need to look elsewhere for stimulation.

Cognitive and Sociocultural Factors in Motivation

Let's return to the opening case study, in which Michael changes from a student who is failing algebra to one who pays close attention in class, regularly does his homework, and seeks help when he doesn't understand. Michael's initial beliefs about his math ability (i.e., his self-efficacy) and his explanations for his poor performance (low ability and poor instruction) contribute to a lackadaisical attitude: He simply *hopes* he'll remember—but usually forgets—his teacher's explanations. Later, when Michael's appraisal of the situation changes, he's a much more engaged and proactive learner.

Michael's dramatic turnaround illustrates both that *cognitive processes affect motivation* and that *motivation affects cognitive processes.* Yet the turnaround requires a significant change in Michael's social environment—in particular, a new tutor who helps him think in more productive ways both about mathematics as a content domain and about his ability to do well in that domain. As

Remember that students will be more eager to learn and master academic subject matter if they have met their more basic physiological and psychological needs.

MyEdLab
Video Example 11.2.
We all have a basic need for arousal. Teachers help students meet this need by planning classroom activitties that keep them continually active, either physically or cognitively.

Plan classroom activities that keep students continually active, either physically or cognitively.

we explore various elements of motivation in the upcoming sections, we'll see how cognition and motivation often interact in their effects on learning and behavior and how numerous sociocultural factors enter into the picture as well. A key element of all of these perspectives is that students' *beliefs and perceptions,* of themselves and their experiences, are critically important in shaping their future motivation and behavior. We'll also see that some of the cognitive and sociocultural perspectives on motivation focus on various needs of students; however, as you'll see, these newer conceptions of "needs" are more related to social contexts and cognitive processes than are some of the earlier conceptions of needs.

EXPECTANCIES AND VALUES

Many motivation-related beliefs and perceptions can be categorized as being related to either *expectancies* for success (Can I do this?) or *values* (Why should I do this?). As we discuss different theoretical perspectives, we will refer back to these key categories, even though they may focus on other important ideas. First, however, we discuss those theorists who have focused specifically on expectancies and values for explaining motivation for performing a particular task (e.g., Nagengast et al., 2011; Wigfield & Eccles, 2000; Wigfield & Karpathian, 1991).

This perspective suggests that, first, learners must have a high expectation, or **expectancy**, that they'll be successful. Certainly their prior history of success and failure at a particular task—and thus their self-efficacy—has a strong influence. But other factors also affect expectancies, including the perceived difficulty of a task, the availability of resources and support, the quality of instruction (recall Michael's complaint about his algebra teacher), and the amount of effort that will be necessary (Dweck & Elliott, 1983; Wigfield & Eccles, 1992; Zimmerman, Bandura, & Martinez-Pons, 1992). From such factors learners come to conclusions—perhaps accurate, perhaps not—about their chances of success.

Equally important and equally subjective is **task value**: Learners must believe there are benefits in performing a task. Theorists have suggested four possible reasons that value might be high or low: utility, importance, interest, and cost (Eccles, 2009; Wigfield & Eccles, 2000). Some activities have high value because they're seen as a means to a desired goal; that is, they have *utility.* For example, one of the authors' daughters found mathematics confusing and frustrating, but she struggled through 4 years of high school math because many colleges require that for admission. Other activities are valued because they're associated with desirable personal qualities; that is, they're viewed as *personally important* (note that this is different from the idea of being important for a grade or other goal). For example, a boy who wants to be smart and thinks that smart people do well in school will place a premium on academic success. Still other activities are valued simply because they bring pleasure and enjoyment; in other words, they're *interesting* (we will discuss interest in more detail later in the chapter).

However, we can also envision circumstances in which learners probably won't value an activity very much. Some activities may require a lot more effort than they're worth; this is the *cost* factor. For example, although you could eventually become an expert on some little-known topic (e.g., animal-eating plants of Borneo), gaining expertise might require far more time and energy than you're willing to expend. Other activities might seem costly as a result of their association with bad feelings. For example, if learners become frustrated often enough in their efforts to understand math, they may eventually try to avoid it whenever they can. Finally, some activities might seem valuable but conflict with other valued activities. For example, a high school student may view studying for a history exam as useful but also want to attend a friend's party; studying then comes at the cost of a preferred activity.

Students are likely to engage in a particular behavior only if they have some expectancy of success *and* find some value in the behavior. Although expectancies and values are both related to achievement, values affect the choices students make—for instance, which courses they select and whether they participate in extracurricular activities (Durik, Vida, & Eccles, 2006; Mac Iver, Stipek, & Daniels, 1991; Wigfield, Tonks, & Eccles, 2004).

In the early elementary years, students often pursue activities they find interesting and enjoyable, regardless of their expectancies for success (Wigfield, 1994). As they get older, however, their values and expectancies become somewhat interdependent. In particular, they increasingly attach value to activities for which they have high expectancy for success and that they think will help them meet long-term goals. At the same time, they begin to *devalue* the things they do

MyEdLab
Video Example 11.3.
Students' motivation is typically related to their expectancy for success and the task value. Mr. Stepien's plans and teaching strategies are likely to enhance both expectancy and value.

poorly (Jacobs, Lanza, Osgood, Eccles, & Wigfield, 2002; Wigfield, 1994). Sadly, the value students find in many school subjects declines markedly over the school years (Archambault, Eccles, & Vida, 2010; Jacobs et al., 2002; Wigfield et al., 2004). As one 16-year-old put it, "School's fun because you can hang out with your friends, but I know I won't use much of this stuff when I leave here" (Valente, 2001).

FOSTERING EXPECTANCIES AND VALUES IN THE CLASSROOM

As teachers, we must certainly give students reasons to expect success with classroom tasks—for instance, by providing the necessary resources, support, and strategies, as Ms. Tucker did in the opening case study. But we must also help students find value in school activities. Motivation theorists and experienced teachers have offered several suggestions for fostering genuine appreciation for academic subject matter:

> Enhance students' expectancies for success by providing the necessary resources, strategies, and support.

- Clearly identify the particular knowledge and skills that students will gain from lessons.
- Convey how certain concepts and principles can help students make better sense of the world around them.
- Ask students to write about how material that they are learning is relevant to their lives.
- Help students relate information and skills to their present concerns and long-term career goals.
- Embed the use of new skills within the context of real-world (i.e., authentic) and personally meaningful activities.
- Model how you yourself value academic activities—for example, by describing how you apply what you've learned in school.
- Above all, refrain from asking students to engage in activities with little long-term benefit—for instance, having them memorize trivial facts for no good reason or requiring them to read material that is clearly beyond their comprehension levels. (Ames, 1992; Brophy et al., 2009; G. L. Cohen, Garcia, Purdie-Vaughns, Apfel, & Brzustoski, 2009; Eccles, 2009; Hulleman, Godes, Hendricks, & Harackiewicz, 2010; Stefanou et al., 2004)

INTERESTS

One of the reasons students might value a topic or activity is because they find it interesting. When we say that learners have interest in a particular topic, we mean that they find it intriguing and engaging. Interest, then, is a form of intrinsic motivation. Interest is typically accompanied by cognitive arousal and such feelings as enjoyment and excitement (Ainley & Ainley, 2011; M. Hofer, 2010; Renninger, 2009).

Learners who are interested in a topic devote more time and attention to it and become more cognitively engaged in it—often both in and outside of school (Barron, 2006; Hidi & Renninger, 2006; M. A. McDaniel, Waddill, Finstad, & Bourg, 2000). They're also likely to learn it more meaningfully—for instance, by interconnecting ideas, drawing inferences, and identifying potential applications (Pintrich & Schrauben, 1992; Schraw & Lehman, 2001; Tobias, 1994). And unless they're emotionally attached to their current beliefs, learners who are interested in what they're studying are more likely to undergo conceptual change when it's warranted (Andre & Windschitl, 2003; Linnenbrink & Pintrich, 2003; Mason, Gava, & Boldrin, 2008). As you might guess, then, students who are interested in what they study show higher academic achievement and increased use of helpful self-regulatory strategies, and are more likely to remember the subject matter over the long run (Garner, Brown, Sanders, & Menke, 1992; Hidi & Harackiewicz, 2000; Lee, Lee, & Bong, 2014; Renninger, Hidi, & Krapp, 1992); in fact, the positive relations between interest and achievement begin during the preschool years (Fisher, Dobbs-Oates, Doctoroff, & Arnold, 2012).

Psychologists distinguish between two general types of interest. Situational interest is evoked by something in the immediate environment. Things that are new, different, or unexpected often generate interest, as do things with a high activity level or intense emotions. Children and adolescents also tend to be intrigued by topics related to people and culture (e.g., diseases, holidays), nature (e.g., dinosaurs, the sea), and popular media (e.g., television shows, games, contemporary music). Works of fiction and fantasy are more engaging when they include themes and characters with which readers can personally identify. Textbooks and other works of nonfiction are more interesting when they're easy to understand and when relationships among ideas are clear. And challenging tasks are often more interesting than easy ones—a fortunate state of affairs if, as Lev Vygotsky proposed, challenges promote cognitive growth (Ainley, 2006; J. M. Alexander, Johnson, Leibham, & Kelley, 2008; Hidi & Renninger, 2006; M. Hofer, 2010; Schraw & Lehman, 2001; Shernoff & Csikszentmihalyi, 2009; Zahorik, 1994).

Other interests lie within: Learners tend to have personal preferences about the topics they pursue and the activities in which they engage. Such personal interests are relatively stable over time and lead to consistent patterns in the choices learners make (J. M. Alexander et al., 2008; Nolen, 2007; Y.-M. Tsai, Kunter, Lüdtke, Trautwein, & Ryan, 2008; Wijnia, Loyens, Derous, & Schmidt, 2014). Even in the early elementary grades, many children have specific interests that persist over time—perhaps about reptiles, ballet, or computer technology. Often personal interest and knowledge perpetuate each other: Interest in a topic fuels a quest to learn more, and the increased knowledge and skills gained, in turn, promote greater interest (Barron, 2006; Blumenfeld et al., 2006; Nolen, 2007). Especially in adolescence, long-standing personal interests can be important components of a learner's sense of identity (Barron, 2006; M. Hofer, 2010).

Ultimately, personal interest is more beneficial than situational interest because it sustains engagement, effective cognitive processing, and improvement over the long run. Yet situational interest is important as well, because it captures learners' attention and often provides a seed from which a personal interest can grow (P. A. Alexander, Kulikowich, & Schulze, 1994; Durik & Harackiewicz, 2007; Hidi & Renninger, 2006; M. Mitchell, 1993).

PROMOTING INTEREST IN CLASSROOM SUBJECT MATTER

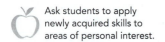

Ask students to apply newly acquired skills to areas of personal interest.

As teachers, we can temporarily pique students' interest, and perhaps also stimulate the beginnings of more enduring personal interests, through the activities we develop and the ways we present information. As teachers, we can certainly capitalize on students' personal interests by allowing some flexibility in the topics about which they read, learn, write, and study (e.g., see Figure 11.3). However, we need to be thoughtful in balancing opportunities for students to choose to further explore interesting topics with their prior experiences and knowledge about a topic (Patall, 2013). Following are several strategies that often evoke interest in classroom topics:

- Convey excitement, enthusiasm, and information about the usefulness of lessons.
- Occasionally incorporate novelty, variety, fantasy, or mystery into lessons and procedures.
- Encourage students to identify with historical figures or fictional characters and to imagine what these people might have been thinking or feeling.
- Provide opportunities for students to respond actively to the subject matter—perhaps by manipulating physical objects, collaborating with other students, creating new inventions, debating controversial issues, representing ideas in art or drama, or teaching something they've learned to peers. (Ainley, 2006; Brophy, Alleman, & Knighton, 2009; Certo, Cauley, & Chafin, 2003; Chinn, 2006; Hidi & Renninger, 2006; Hidi, Weiss, Berndorff, & Nolan, 1998; Kunter, Frenzel, Nagy, Baumert, & Pekrun, 2011; Pool, Dittrich, & Pool, 2011; Radel, Sarrazin, Legrain, & Wild, 2010; Wu, Anderson, Nguyen-Jahiel, & Miller, 2013; Zahorik, 1994)

Figure 11.4 presents examples of how we might promote intrinsic motivation in a variety of content domains.

SELF-DETERMINATION THEORY

Self-determination theory also addresses reasons why students might engage deeply with activities (rather than their expectations for success). These theorists suggest that people may also have additional needs; they focus on the need for competence, autonomy, and relatedness. As we mentioned at the

FIGURE 11.3 Students' personal interests can provide a motivating context in which to practice basic skills. Here 12-year-old Connor practiced research and graphing skills by surveying peers about a favorite topic: cars.

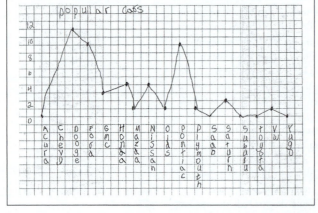

FIGURE 11.4 Examples of strategies for generating interest in various content domains.

- **Art:** Have students make a mosaic from items they've found on a scavenger hunt around the school building.

- **Biology:** Hold a class debate about the ethical implications of conducting medical research on animals.

- **Geography:** Present household objects not found locally, and ask students to guess where they might be from.

- **Health education:** In a lesson about alcoholic beverages, have students role-play being at a party and being tempted to have a beer or wine cooler.

- **History:** Have students read children's perspectives of historical events (e.g., Anne Frank's diary during World War II, Zlata Filipovic's diary during the Bosnian War).

- **Language arts:** examine lyrics in popular hip hop music, looking for grammatical patterns and literary themes.

- **Mathematics:** Have students apply their math skills in computer software programs that enable them to create fantasy sports teams or to solve authentic, real-world problems.

- **Music:** In a unit on musical instruments, let students experiment with a variety of simple instruments.

- **Physical education:** Incorporate steps from hip hop, swing, or country line dancing into an aerobics workout.

- **Physical science:** Challenge students to design and construct model airplanes (e.g., out of lightweight balsa wood strips) that will be able to fly a certain distance.

- **Reading:** Turn a short story into a play, with each student taking a part.

- **Spelling:** Occasionally depart from standard word lists, instead asking students to learn how to spell the names of favorite television shows or classmates' surnames.

- **Writing:** Ask students to create children's storybooks related to their own personal interests and experiences.

Sources: Some ideas derived from Alim, 2007; Barab, Gresalfi, & Ingram-Goble, 2010; Botelho, Cohen, Leoni, Chow, & Sastri, 2010; Brophy, 1986; A. Collins & Halverson, 2009; Lepper & Hodell, 1989; W.-M. Roth, 2011; Spaulding, 1992; Stipek, 1993; Wlodkowski, 1978.

beginning of this section, these needs have been framed in more social and cognitive terms than some of the earlier conceptions of needs (e.g., Maslow).

THE NEED FOR COMPETENCE

Human beings appear to have a **need for competence**—a need to believe they can deal effectively with their environment (Boggiano & Pittman, 1992; Elliot & Dweck, 2005; Reeve, Deci, & Ryan, 2004; R. White, 1959). To achieve this sense of competence, children spend a great deal of time exploring and trying to gain mastery over various aspects of their world.

One motivation theorist has proposed that a high priority for most people is *protecting* their general belief that, overall, they're good, capable individuals—something he calls **self-worth** (Covington, 1992). Occasionally some individuals seem more concerned about maintaining *consistent* self-perceptions, even if those self-perceptions are negative (J. Cassidy, Ziv, Mehta, & Feeney, 2003; Hay, Ashman, van Kraayenoord, & Stewart, 1999). By and large, however, viewing oneself favorably and demonstrating competence to others do appear to be high priorities (Rhodewalt & Vohs, 2005; Sedikides & Gregg, 2008; T. D. Wilson & Gilbert, 2008).

Other people's judgments and approval play a key role in children's development of a sense of competence and self-worth, especially in the early years (Harter, 1999; Rudolph, Caldwell, & Conley, 2005). Regularly achieving success in new and challenging activities—as Michael eventually does in the opening case study—is another important way of maintaining, perhaps even enhancing, a sense of competence and self-worth (Deci & Moller, 2005; N. E. Perry, Turner, & Meyer, 2006; Reeve et al., 2004).

But consistent success isn't always possible, especially when learners must undertake especially difficult tasks. In the face of such tasks, an alternative way to maintain self-worth is to *avoid failure,* because failure gives the impression of low ability (Covington & Müeller, 2001; Urdan & Midgley, 2001). Failure avoidance manifests itself in a variety of ways: Learners might refuse to engage in a task,

> *A Book That canged me*
>
> The Book that canged me was At The Plat With Ken Jriffey Jr. This Book canged me becouse it was my first book that had over onehondred pagis after that I read On The Cort With Mikeol Jorden. I asow liked it becouse it was by Matt Crister the frst spotswiter for Kids.

Mastering new challenges is one important means of gaining a sense of competence and self-worth. In writing about "A Book That C(h)anged Me," 8-year-old Anthony expresses pride in reading his first 100-page book. Notice Anthony's personal interest in sports: *At the Plat(e)* is about baseball, and *On the Co(u)rt* is about basketball.

minimize the task's importance, or set exceedingly low expectations for their own performance (Covington, 1992; Harter, 1990; Rhodewalt & Vohs, 2005).

When learners *can't* avoid tasks at which they expect to do poorly, they have several strategies at their disposal. They may make excuses that seemingly justify their poor performance (Covington, 1992; Urdan & Midgley, 2001). They may also do things that actually *undermine* their chances of success—a phenomenon known as self-handicapping. Self-handicapping takes a variety of forms, including the following:

🍎 *Reducing effort:* Putting forth an obviously insufficient amount of effort to succeed

🍎 *Setting unattainably high goals:* Working toward goals that even the most capable individuals couldn't achieve

🍎 *Taking on too much:* Assuming so many responsibilities that no one could possibly accomplish them all

🍎 *Procrastinating:* Putting off a task until success is virtually impossible

🍎 *Using alcohol or drugs:* Taking substances that will inevitably reduce performance (Covington, 1992; Hattie, 2008; Riggs, 1992; Urdan, Ryan, Anderman, & Gheen, 2002)

It might seem paradoxical that learners who want to be successful would actually try to undermine their own success. But if they believe they're unlikely to succeed no matter what they do—and especially if failure will reflect poorly on their intelligence and ability—such behaviors increase their chances of *justifying* the failure and thereby protecting their self-worth. Self-handicapping is seen as early as elementary school and becomes increasingly common in the high school and college years (Urdan, 2004; Urdan & Midgley, 2001; Wolters, 2003).

A comparison of self-worth and other "self" constructs is provided in Chapter 10.

Enhancing Students' Sense of Competence and Self-Worth
Strategies for enhancing students' general sense of self and more domain-specific self-efficacy should, of course, increase their sense of competence and self-worth. Following are three widely recommended strategies:

🍎 Help students achieve genuine success (rather than giving them hollow praise), especially on challenging tasks.

🍎 Give students concrete mechanisms through which they can track their progress over time, such as setting short-term goals and assessing whether those goals have been reached.

🍎 Minimize competitions and other situations in which students might judge themselves unfavorably in comparison with peers.

Chapter 3 and Chapter 10 describe these strategies in more detail.

Ideally, learners' sense of competence and self-worth should be based on a reasonably accurate appraisal of what they can and cannot accomplish. Learners who underestimate their abilities set unnecessarily low goals for themselves and give up easily after only minor setbacks. Those who overestimate their abilities—perhaps because they've been lavished with praise by parents or teachers or perhaps because school assignments have been consistently easy and unchallenging—may set themselves up for failure by forming unrealistically high expectations, exerting insufficient effort, or not addressing their weaknesses (Försterling & Morgenstern, 2002; Hattie & Gan, 2011; S. G. Paris & Cunningham, 1996; H. W. Stevenson, Chen, & Uttal, 1990).

As teachers, we're more likely to encourage students to tackle realistically challenging tasks—and thus enhance their sense of competence and intrinsic motivation—when we create an environment in which they feel comfortable taking risks and making mistakes (Clifford, 1990; Fredricks et al., 2004). We can also provide greater rewards for succeeding at challenging tasks than for achieving easy successes; for example, we might give students a choice between doing an easy task or a more difficult one but give them more points for accomplishing the difficult one (Clifford, 1990; Lan, Repman, Bradley, & Weller, 1994). Once students are intrinsically motivated, they seem to *prefer* challenges rather than easy tasks (Csikszentmihalyi et al., 2005; Reeve, 2006; Shernoff & Csikszentmihalyi, 2009). In general, challenges and intrinsic motivation mutually enhance one another, leading to a cycle of positive change.

Create an environment that encourages students to take academic risks—for instance, through the kinds of feedback you give and the criteria you use to assign grades. Make sure students know that they won't be punished or hurt their grade by taking such risks.

To date, most research on competence, self-worth, and self-handicapping has focused on academic tasks and accomplishments. We must keep in mind, however, that academic achievement isn't always the most important thing affecting students' sense of competence and self-worth. For many students such factors as physical appearance, peer approval, and social success are more influential (Eccles, Wigfield, & Schiefele, 1998; Rudolph et al., 2005). To the extent that we can, then, we should support students' successes in the nonacademic as well as the academic aspects of their lives.

Help students achieve a sense of competence in social as well as academic activities.

THE NEED FOR AUTONOMY

The need for autonomy reflects a desire for choice and self-direction regarding the things students do and the courses their lives take (d'Ailly, 2003; deCharms, 1972; Reeve et al., 2004; R. M. Ryan & Deci, 2000). When we think, "I'm doing this because I *want* to" or "because I'd *find it valuable*," we have a high sense of autonomy. In contrast, when we think, "I *have to*" or "I *should*," we're telling ourselves that someone or something else is making decisions for us. The following exercise provides an example.

EXPERIENCING FIRSTHAND
PAINTING BETWEEN THE LINES

Imagine that we give you a paintbrush, a set of watercolor paints, two sheets of paper (a fairly small one glued on top of a larger one), and some paper towels. We ask you to paint a picture of your house, apartment building, or dormitory and then give you the following instructions:

> You have to keep the paints clean. You can paint only on this small sheet of paper, so don't spill any paint on the big sheet. And you must wash out your brush and wipe it with a paper towel before you switch to a new color of paint, so that you don't get the colors all mixed up. In general, don't make a mess with the paints. (Koestner, Ryan, Bernieri, & Holt, 1984, p. 239)

How much fun do you think your task would be? After reading our rules, how eager are you to begin painting?

Our rules about painting are quite *controlling:* They make it clear that we're in charge of the situation and that you, as the artist, have little choice about how to go about your task. By diminishing your sense of autonomy, our rules would undermine any intrinsic motivation you might have to paint the picture, and you'd probably be less creative in your painting than you might be otherwise (Amabile & Hennessey, 1992; Koestner et al., 1984; Reeve, 2006).

Students with a sense of autonomy are more likely to be intrinsically motivated during classroom activities, to achieve at high levels, and to complete high school (Hardré & Reeve, 2003; Reeve, Bolt, & Cai, 1999; Shernoff, Knauth, & Makris, 2000; Vansteenkiste, Lens, & Deci, 2006). Even kindergartners seem to prefer classroom activities of their own choosing (E. J. Langer, 1997; Paley, 1984). For example, when students in Ms. Paley's kindergarten class are asked whether activities at the class painting table are "work" or "play," two of them respond as follows:

> *Clarice:* If you paint a real picture, it's work, but if you splatter or pour into an egg carton, then it's play.
>
> *Charlotte:* It's mostly work, because that's where the teacher tells you how to do stuff. (Paley, 1984, p. 31)

Enhancing Students' Sense of Autonomy As teachers, we can't always give students total freedom about what they will and won't do in the classroom. It's neither realistic nor helpful to suggest that all assigned tasks are just "play," because many tasks will—or at least *should*— require hard work and persistence in the face of obstacles. Nevertheless, we can do several things to enhance students' sense of autonomy at school:

Chapter 10 describes the nature and development of self-regulation skills.

 Provide opportunities for independent work and decision making. Opportunities to work and make decisions independently not only foster the development of self-regulation skills but also enhance learners' autonomy. For instance, we might have students study new topics through instructional software programs or tackle challenging tasks through small-group work, where they decide how to assign responsibilities. We also can give students considerable autonomy in the extracurricular activities we supervise (Larson, 2000; Stefanou, Perencevich, DiCintio, & Turner, 2004; Swan, Mitrani, Guerrero, Cheung, & Schoener, 1990).

Providing autonomy in activities doesn't mean removing all structure, however. Some scaffolding—tailored to students' developmental levels, of course—can further increase students' sense of autonomy. For example, we can establish general routines and procedures that students should follow as they work, thereby minimizing the need to give explicit instructions for every assignment. And we should describe our evaluation criteria in advance so that students know exactly what they'll need to do to be successful and monitor their progress toward those goals. (Ciani, Middleton, Summers, & Sheldon, 2010; Jang, Reeve, & Deci, 2010; Spaulding, 1992; M.-T. Wang & Holcombe, 2010)

One way to provide students with autonomy is to allow them to choose which questions to answer on tests. One of the authors used to give multiple-choice tests that did not offer students any choices. Thus instructions would read, "Answer the following 25 questions." However, an alternative was to give the students 30 questions, and instruct them to "Answer any 25 of the following 30 questions." Students could thus choose to skip any five questions (they did not get extra credit for answering the additional five items). Students greatly preferred to be able to choose which items to answer. Interestingly, students also seemed to take more ownership of incorrect answers; when students answered a question incorrectly, they knew that they had made the deliberate choice to answer the question, and often seemed to see the mistake as a learning opportunity. However, although this approach may enhance motivation, a downside is that it also reduces standardization of the test, which is important when a test is used for *summative* assessment purposes.

The necessity for standardization in summative assessments is discussed in Chapter 14 and Chapter 15.

🍎 *Present rules and instructions in an informational rather than controlling manner.* Virtually every classroom needs a few rules and procedures to ensure that students act appropriately and activities run smoothly. The challenge is to present these rules and procedures without communicating a message of *control*. Instead, we can present them as *information*—for instance, as conditions that can help students accomplish classroom objectives (Deci, 1992; Koestner et al., 1984; Reeve, 2009). Here are two examples:

- *Informational:* "We can make sure everyone has an equal chance to speak and be heard if we listen without interrupting and if we raise our hands when we want to contribute to the discussion."
- *Controlling:* "I'm giving you a particular format to follow when you do your math homework. If you use this format, it will be easier for me to find your answers and to figure out how I can help you improve."
- We should also acknowledge students' feelings about things they must do but would rather *not* do—thus communicating the message that their opinions matter (Deci & Ryan, 1985; Reeve, 2009).

🍎 *Give some choices about how to accomplish classroom goals.* Earlier in the chapter we noted that when students are limited in their choices, intrinsic motivation can suffer. However, as teachers, we can think creatively and realize that sometimes a variety of routes will lead to the same destination. For example, we might let students make choices, either individually or as a group—and within reasonable limits—about some or all of the following:

- Rules and procedures to make the class run more smoothly
- Specific topics for reading or writing projects
- Sequencing or due dates of assigned tasks
- Ways of achieving or demonstrating mastery of a particular skill (e.g., see Figure 11.5)
- Criteria by which some assignments will be evaluated (Ciani et al., 2010; Fairweather & Cramond, 2010; Meece, 1994; Patall, Cooper, & Wynn, 2010; Reed, Schallert, Beth, & Woodruff, 2004; A. C. Schmidt, Hanley, & Layer, 2009)

When students can make choices about such matters, they gain a sense of ownership about classroom activities, are more likely to be interested and engaged in what they're doing, and take genuine pride in their work (Deci & Ryan, 1992; Nolen, 2011; Patall et al., 2010; Schraw, Flowerday, & Lehman, 2001; Stefanou et al., 2004).

FIGURE 11.5 In this assignment, a sixth-grade language arts teacher enhances students' sense of autonomy by offering several options for demonstrating understanding of a science fiction book.

Choose One!

SCIENCE FICTION BOOK PROJECTS

_____ Write a "Dear Abby" letter from one of the main characters, in which he or she asks for advice on solving his or her main problem. Then answer the letter.

_____ Draw a time line of the main events of the book.

_____ Create a comic book or a comic strip page that features a major scene from the book in each box.

_____ Make a collage of objects and printed words from newspapers and magazines that give the viewer a feeling for the mood of the book.

_____ Your book probably takes place in an unusual or exotic setting, so illustrate and write a travel brochure describing that location.

_____ Imagine yourself as a scientist who has been asked to explain the unusual events in the book. Write up a report in scientific style.

_____ With other students who have read the same book, plan a bulletin board display. Write a plot summary; character and setting descriptions; discussions of special passages. Each group member must contribute one artistic piece—for example, new book cover, bookmark, poster, banner, some of the ideas listed above. Arrange the writing and artwork under a colorful heading announcing the book.

🍎 *Evaluate students' performance in a noncontrolling way.* As teachers, we must regularly evaluate students' accomplishments. But external evaluations can undermine students' intrinsic motivation, especially if they're communicated in a controlling manner (E. M. Anderman & Dawson, 2011; Deci & Moller, 2005). Ideally, we should present evaluations of students' work not as judgments to remind students of how they *should* perform but as information that can help them improve their knowledge and skills. And, of course, we can give students criteria by which they can evaluate *themselves*.

THE NEED FOR RELATEDNESS

The need for relatedness reflects the need to feel socially connected and to secure the love and respect of others (Connell & Wellborn, 1991; Fiske & Fiske, 2007; Reeve et al., 2004; R. M. Ryan & Deci, 2000). The need for relatedness seems to be especially strong in adolescence: Most teenagers spend a great deal of time interacting with peers, perhaps through face-to-face activities, instant messaging on smartphones, or social networking sites such as Instagram (Barron, 2006; Ito et al., 2009; A. M. Ryan & Patrick, 2001; Valkenburg & Peter, 2009).

At school the need for relatedness manifests itself in a variety of ways. Some students place a higher priority on interacting with friends than on getting schoolwork done (Dowson & McInerney, 2001; W. Doyle, 1986a; Wigfield, Eccles, Mac Iver, Reuman, & Midgley, 1991). They may also be concerned about projecting a favorable public image—that is, looking smart, popular, athletic, or cool. By looking good in the eyes of others, students not only satisfy their need for relatedness but also enhance their sense of self-worth (Harter, 1999; Juvonen, 2000). Yet another way in which they might address the need for relatedness is to work for the betterment of others—for example, by helping peers who are struggling with classroom assignments (Dowson & McInerney, 2001; Lawlor & Schonert-Reichl, 2008; Thorkildsen, Golant, & Cambray-Engstrom, 2008).

When the need for relatedness is satisfied, students feel a sense of belonging in their schools. School belonging is related to many important academic outcomes, including sustained academic engagement, less likelihood of feeling socially rejected, and better relationships with peers and

The Pythagorean theorem... blah blah blah the hypotenuse squared... blah blah blah

$a^2 + b^2 = c^2$

Texting on smartphones is one way that some students regularly address their need for relatedness.

Give students frequent opportunities to interact as they study classroom topics.

Continually communicate the message that you like and respect your students.

See the opening case study in Chapter 4 for a refresher on some cultural differences that you may observe related to Native American students.

teachers (L. Anderman & Freeman, 2004; Gillen-O'Neel & Fuligni, 2013). Feeling a sense of school belonging is particularly important for minority students; when minority students feel like they belong at their schools, they may be less likely to be absent, and may exert greater effort (Sanchez, Colon, & Esparza, 2005).

Enhancing Students' Sense of Relatedness and School Belonging Students are more likely to be academically motivated and successful—and more likely to stay in school rather than drop out—when they believe that their peers and teachers like and respect them, and care about their learning (Christenson & Thurlow, 2004; Furrer & Skinner, 2003; Patrick, Anderman, & Ryan, 2002; Roorda, Koomen, Spilt, & Oort, 2011). Ideally we should find ways to help students simultaneously learn academic subject matter *and* address their eagerness to interact with peers. Group-based activities—such as cooperative learning tasks, role-playing, and playful game-show contests among two or more teams of equal ability—provide the means through which students can satisfy their need for relatedness while also acquiring new knowledge and skills (Blumenfeld, Kempler, & Krajcik, 2006; D. W. Johnson & Johnson, 2009a; Wentzel & Wigfield, 1998).

Students' relationships with their teachers are just as important. Thus, we should show students that we enjoy being with them and are concerned about their academic achievement and personal well-being (M.-L. Chang & Davis, 2009; D. K. Meyer & Turner, 2006; Roorda et al., 2011). We can communicate our fondness and concern for them in numerous ways—for example, by expressing interest in their outside activities, providing extra help when they need it, and lending a sympathetic ear in stressful times. Such caring messages are especially important for students who are at risk for academic failure and dropping out of school (Anderman, Andrzejewski, & Allen, 2011; Christenson & Thurlow, 2004; Hamre & Pianta, 2005; Pianta, 1999).

It is particularly important to demonstrate academic (or "pedagogical") caring to our students (Wentzel, 1997). Students' motivation can be greatly enhanced when they believe their teacher truly cares about their individual learning. Academic caring can be conveyed to any student—even high-achieving students who often may be taken for granted. One of the authors of this book, who generally earned high grades in math, recalls an incident when a high school math teacher pulled him aside and said, "You only got a 90% on the unit test; what was going on with you, is anything wrong? I know you can do better than that." Although such statements may seem trivial, they demonstrate that we, as teachers, really notice what's going on with individual students.

DIVERSITY IN ADDRESSING NEEDS

The basic needs described earlier in the chapter (e.g., Maslow's hierarchy and the need for arousal) are probably universal among people throughout the world (e.g., Bao & Lam, 2008; Berlyne, 1960; Deci & Moller, 2005; Fiske & Fiske, 2007). However, researchers have identified distinct cultural differences in how people strive to address the three more socio-cognitive needs specifically included in self-determination theory.

ACHIEVING A SENSE OF COMPETENCE AND SELF-WORTH

In mainstream Western culture, achieving a sense of self-worth often involves *being good at* certain things and also *thinking* that one is good at these things. In such a context, learners are likely to engage in self-handicapping as a means of justifying poor performances. But not all cultures stress the importance of positive self-evaluations. For instance, many people in East Asian cultures place greater importance on how well other people view an individual as living up to society's standards for behavior. In such cultures the focus is more likely to be on correcting existing weaknesses—that is, on *self-improvement*—than on demonstrating current strengths (Heine, 2007; J. Li, 2005; Sedikides & Gregg, 2008).

ACHIEVING A SENSE OF AUTONOMY

The amounts and forms of autonomy seen as appropriate may differ considerably from group to group (d'Ailly, 2003; Fiske & Fiske, 2007; Rogoff, 2003). For example, adults in some Native American groups (e.g., those living in the Navajo Nation in the southwestern United States) give children more autonomy and control over decision making than do many adults in mainstream Western culture (Deyhle & LeCompte, 1999). In contrast, many Asian and African American parents give children *less* autonomy than other American adults, in some cases as a way of ensuring children's safety in potentially hostile environments (McLoyd, 1998; L. Qin, Pomerantz, & Wang, 2009; Tamis-Lemonda & McFadden, 2010).

Cultural differences have also been observed in one important aspect of autonomy: opportunities to make choices. In particular, although young people around the world find choice-making opportunities highly motivating, those from Asian cultures often prefer that people they trust (e.g., parents, teachers, respected peers) make the choices for them (Bao & Lam, 2008; Hufton, Elliott, & Illushin, 2002; Iyengar & Lepper, 1999). Perhaps Asian children see trusted others as people who can make *wise* choices, which will ultimately lead to greater learning and competence.

ACHIEVING A SENSE OF RELATEDNESS.

Researchers have found several cultural differences in how children and adolescents address their need for relatedness. In comparison with other groups, Asian children spend less time with peers and place greater importance on excelling in schoolwork and gaining others' approval (Dien, 1998; J. Li, 2005; Steinberg, 1996). Furthermore, whereas Asian students are apt to have friends who encourage academic achievement, some students from certain other ethnic groups (boys especially) may feel considerable peer pressure *not* to achieve at high levels, perhaps because high achievement reflects conformity to mainstream Western culture (Bergin & Cooks, 2008; B. B. Brown, 1993; Ogbu, 2008b).

An additional factor is family ties: Students from many cultural and ethnic groups have especially strong loyalties to family and may have been brought up to achieve for their respective communities, rather than just for themselves as individuals. Motivating statements such as "Think how proud your family will be!" and "If you get a college education, you can really help your community!" are likely to be especially effective for such students (C.-Y. Chiu & Hong, 2005; Fiske & Fiske, 2007; Kağitçibaşi, 2007; Timm & Borman, 1997).

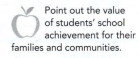

Point out the value of students' school achievement for their families and communities.

The need for relatedness can sometimes be at odds with the need for autonomy. In particular, achieving relatedness can involve doing what *others* want one to do, whereas achieving autonomy involves doing what one *personally* wants to do. Many people from Asian cultures resolve this apparent conflict by willingly agreeing to adjust personal behaviors and goals to meet social demands and maintain overall group harmony (Iyengar & Lepper, 1999; Kağitçibaşi, 2007; J. Li & Fischer, 2004; Savani, Markus, Naidu, Kumar, & Berlia, 2010).

INTERNALIZING VALUES AND MOTIVATIONAL BELIEFS OF ONE'S SOCIAL AND CULTURAL GROUPS

As children grow older, they tend to adopt many of the priorities and values of the people around them. Thus students tend to adapt many of the values and beliefs that they encounter in their experiences with their families, their schools, their peers, and their larger cultures. Such internalized motivation typically develops gradually over the course of childhood and adolescence, perhaps in the sequence depicted in Figure 11.6 (Deci & Moller, 2005; Deci & Ryan, 1995; R. M. Ryan & Deci, 2000). Initially children may engage in certain activities primarily because of the external consequences that result. For instance, they may do schoolwork to earn praise or to avoid being punished for poor grades. With time other people's approval becomes increasingly important for children's sense of self. Eventually children begin to internalize the pressure to perform certain activities and to see these activities as important in their own right. Such internalization of values is most likely to occur if adults who espouse those values (parents, teachers, etc.) do the following:

- Engage in and thereby model valued activities themselves.
- Provide a warm, responsive, and supportive environment (addressing children's need for relatedness).

FIGURE 11.6 Sequence in which internalized motivation may develop

1. External regulation: Learners are initially motivated to behave in certain ways, based primarily on the external consequences that will follow the behaviors; that is, the learners are extrinsically motivated.

2. Introjection: Learners begin to behave in ways that gain the approval of others, partly as a way of protecting and enhancing their sense of self. They feel guilty when they violate certain standards for behavior but do not fully understand the rationale behind these standards.

3. Identification: Learners now see some behaviors and activities as being personally important or valuable for them.

4. Integration: Learners integrate certain behaviors and activities into their overall system of motives and values. In essence, these behaviors become a central part of their identity and general sense of self.

Source: Based on Deci & Moller, 2005; Deci & Ryan, 1995.

Find a reasonable balance between giving students autonomy in their actions and imposing reasonable limits on their behavior.

- Offer some autonomy in decision making (addressing children's need for autonomy).
- Set reasonable limits for behavior and provide information about why certain behaviors are important. (Deci & Moller, 2005; Eccles, 2007; Gniewosz & Noack, 2012; Jacobs et al., 2005; R. M. Ryan, Connell, & Grolnick, 1992; R. M. Ryan & Deci, 2000)

Fostering the development of internalized motivation, then, involves striking a delicate balance between giving students opportunities to experience autonomy and providing guidance about desired behaviors.

In one respect, internalized motivation is similar to intrinsic motivation: Both forms of motivation arise from inside the learner rather than from outside factors in the immediate, here-and-now environment. But there's an important difference: Because intrinsic motivation seems to arise spontaneously within the learner, it can increase or decrease somewhat unpredictably. In contrast, because internalized motivation is a product of ongoing social and cultural factors and eventually becomes an integral part of learners' sense of self, it has considerable stability and is therefore fairly dependable over time (Otis et al., 2005; Reeve et al., 2004).

The more students have internalized the value of learning and academic success, the more cognitively engaged they become in school subject matter and the better their overall classroom achievement is likely to be. Internalized motivation is also an important aspect of self-regulated learning: It underlies a general work ethic in which learners spontaneously engage in activities that, although not always fun or immediately gratifying, are essential for reaching long-term goals (Assor, Vansteenkiste, & Kaplan, 2009; La Guardia, 2009; Ratelle, Guay, Vallerand, Larose, & Senécal, 2007; R. M. Ryan, et al., 1992; Walls & Little, 2005). In fact, when minority students in particular internalize the values associated with a particular career, they are more likely to intend to enter that career (Estrada, Woodcock, Hernandez, & Schultz, 2011).

Students also may internalize stereotypes that can undermine their motivation and achievement. For example, students may internalize stereotypical beliefs about gender differences (e.g., that boys are good at math and girls are good at language arts) in ways that negatively impact their expectancies for success and valuing of tasks. Thus, a female student may hear societal messages about boys being better at math than girls; however, the stereotype only will hurt her achievement if that message leads to changes in her motivational beliefs (Plante, de la Sablonnière, Aronson, & Théorêt, 2013).

ATTRIBUTIONS

Attributions are learners' self-constructed explanations of their successes and failures—their beliefs about *what causes what* in their personal lives. Learners are often eager to identify the probable causes of things that happen to them, especially when events are unexpected—for instance, when they get a low score on a class assignment after thinking they've done a good job (Stupnisky, Stewart, Daniels, & Perry, 2011; Tollefson, 2000; Weiner, 1986, 2000).

To gain insight into the kinds of attributions you yourself might form, try the following exercise.

EXPERIENCING FIRSTHAND
CARBERRY AND SEVILLE #1

1. Professor Josiah S. Carberry has just returned the first set of exams in your advanced psychoceramics class. You've gotten one of the few high test scores in the class: an A–. Why did you do so well when most of your classmates did poorly? Jot down several possible explanations for your high grade in Carberry's class.

2. An hour later you get the results of the first test in Professor Barbara F. Seville's sociocosmetology class, and you learn that you *failed* it! Why did you do so poorly? Jot down several possible reasons for your F on Seville's test.

3. You'll be taking second exams in both psychoceramics and sociocosmetology in about 3 weeks. How much will you study for each exam?

Here are some possible explanations for your A– in Carberry's class:

- You studied hard.
- You're a very intelligent human being.
- You have a natural talent for psychoceramics in particular.
- You were lucky that Carberry chose questions you could correctly answer.
- All those hours you spent brown-nosing Carberry in his office, asking questions about psychoceramics and requesting copies of the articles he's written (which you never actually read), really paid off.

In contrast, here are some possible reasons you failed the exam in Seville's class:

- You didn't study enough.
- You studied the wrong things.
- You've never had a knack for sociocosmetology.
- The student next to you was constantly distracting you with his wheezing and coughing.
- You were unlucky. If Seville had asked different questions, you'd have done better.
- It was a bad test: The questions were ambiguous and tested knowledge of trivial facts.

How much time you spend studying for the next exams will depend to some degree on how you've interpreted your previous test grades. Let's first consider your A–on Professor Carberry's exam. If you think you did well because you studied hard, you'll probably spend a lot of time studying for the second test as well. If you think you did well because you're smart or a natural whiz at psychoceramics, you may not study quite as much. If you believe your success was a matter of luck, you may hardly study at all, but you might wear your lucky sweater when you take the next exam. And if you think the A– reflects how much Carberry likes you, you may decide that time spent flattering him is more important than time spent studying.

Now let's consider your failing grade on Professor Seville's exam. Once again, your explanation of the grade will influence the ways in which you prepare for the second exam—if, in fact, you prepare at all. If you believe you didn't study enough or didn't study the right things, you may spend more time studying the next time. If you think your poor grade was due to a temporary situation—the student sitting next to you was distracting, or Seville asked the wrong questions—you may study in much the same way you did before, hoping you'll do better the second time around. If you believe your failure was due to your low aptitude for sociocosmetology or to the fact that Seville writes lousy tests, you may study even less than you did the first time. What good will it do to study when your poor test performance is beyond your control?

Learners form attributions for many events in their daily lives—not only about why they do well or poorly on tests and assignments but also about why they're popular or unpopular with peers, why they're skilled athletes or total klutzes, and so on. Their attributions vary in three primary ways (Weiner, 1986, 2000, 2004, 2005):

- *Locus: Internal versus external.*[2] Learners sometimes attribute the causes of events to *internal* things—to factors within themselves. Thinking that a good grade is due to your hard work and believing that a poor grade is due to your lack of ability are examples of internal attributions. At other times learners attribute events to *external* things—to factors outside themselves. Concluding that you received a scholarship because you were lucky and

MyEdLab
Video Example 11.4.

Teachers communicate controllable attributions to their students when they provide helpful feedback and teach strategies that help students improve and succeed in learning new skills.

---

[2] This dimension is sometimes referred to as *locus of control;* however, as you can see in the discussion here, *locus* and *control* are two distinct dimensions (Weiner, 1986, 2000).

interpreting a classmate's scowl as a sign of her bad mood (rather than a response to something you might have done to deserve it) are examples of external attributions.

- *Stability: Stable versus unstable.* Sometimes learners believe that events are due to *stable* factors—to things that probably won't change much in the near future. For example, if you believe that you do well in science because of your innate intelligence or that you have trouble making friends because you're unattractive, you're attributing events to stable, relatively long-term causes. But sometimes learners believe that events result from *unstable* factors—things that can change from one time to the next. Thinking that you won a tennis game because your opponent wasn't feeling well and believing you got a bad test grade because you were exhausted when you took the test are examples of attributions involving unstable factors.

- *Controllability: Controllable versus uncontrollable.* On some occasions learners attribute events to *controllable* factors—things they can influence and change. For example, if you think a classmate invited you to a party because you often smile at him and if you think you failed a test simply because you didn't study the right things, you're attributing these events to controllable factors. On other occasions learners attribute events to *uncontrollable* factors—to things over which they have no influence. If you think that you were chosen for the lead in the school play only because you look "right" for the part or that you played a lousy game of basketball because you were sick, you're attributing these events to uncontrollable factors.

In general, learners tend to attribute their successes to internal causes (e.g., high ability, hard work) and their failures to external causes (e.g., luck, other people's actions) (Mezulis, Abramson, Hyde, & Hankin, 2004; Rhodewalt & Vohs, 2005). By patting themselves on the back for things they do well and putting the blame elsewhere for poor performance, they can maintain their sense of self-worth. But when learners *consistently* fail at tasks—especially when they see their peers succeeding at the same tasks—they're apt to put the blame on a stable and uncontrollable internal factor: their own low ability (Covington, 1987; Y. Hong, Chiu, & Dweck, 1995; Schunk, 1990; Weiner, 1984).

HOW ATTRIBUTIONS INFLUENCE EMOTION, COGNITION, AND BEHAVIOR

Attributions influence a number of factors that either directly or indirectly affect learners' motivation. First, attributions influence learners' *emotional reactions to success and failure.* Learners are apt to feel proud about their successes and guilty and ashamed about their failures only if they attribute these outcomes to internal causes—for instance, to things they themselves have done. Unpleasant as guilt and shame might feel, such emotions often spur learners to address their shortcomings. If, instead, learners think someone else was to blame for an undesirable outcome, they're apt to be angry—an emotion that's unlikely to lead to productive follow-up behaviors (Hareli & Weiner, 2002; Pekrun, 2006).

Students are usually happy when they succeed at classroom tasks, but they also feel proud and satisfied if they attribute their successes to internal causes.

Second, attributions have an impact on *expectations for future success and failure.* When learners attribute their successes and failures to stable factors—perhaps to innate ability levels—they expect their future performance to be similar to their current performance. In contrast, when they attribute successes and failures to *un*stable factors—for instance, to effort or luck—their current success rate has little influence on future expectations. The most optimistic learners—those with the highest expectations for future success—are the ones who attribute their successes to stable, dependable (and usually internal) factors, such as innate ability and an enduring work ethic, and attribute their failures to unstable factors, such as lack of effort or inappropriate strategies (Dweck, 2000; S. J. Lopez, Rose, Robinson, Marques, & Pais-Ribeiro, 2009; McClure et al., 2011; Pomerantz & Saxon, 2001).

Third, attributions affect *effort and persistence.* Learners who believe their failures result from their own lack of effort (a controllable cause) are apt to try harder and persist in the face of difficulty. Learners who, instead, attribute failure to a lack of innate ability (an uncontrollable cause) give up easily and sometimes can't even perform tasks they've previously done successfully (Dweck, 2000; Feather, 1982; McClure et al., 2011; Weiner, 1984).

Finally, attributions influence *learning strategies and classroom performance.* Learners who expect to succeed in the classroom and believe that academic success is a result of their own actions are more likely to apply effective learning and self-regulation strategies, especially when they're *taught* these strategies. In contrast, learners who expect failure and believe that their academic performance is largely out of their hands often reject effective learning strategies in favor of rote-learning approaches (Mangels, 2004; D. J. Palmer & Goetz, 1988; Zimmerman, 1998). Given all of these effects, it shouldn't surprise you to learn that students with internal, controllable attributions for classroom success are more likely to achieve at high levels and graduate from high school (L. E. Davis, Ajzen, Saunders, & Williams, 2002; Dweck, Mangels, & Good, 2004; McClure et al., 2011; Pintrich, 2003).

Let's consider how some of the factors just discussed play out in the opening case study. Michael initially attributes his failure in algebra to both his own low ability and his teacher's poor instruction—attributions that probably evoke both shame and anger. Furthermore, because the perceived causes of his failure are both stable and out of his control, he expects future failure no matter what he does and therefore has little reason to exert much effort. As Michael acquires new study skills and gains a better understanding of algebra concepts and procedures, he achieves greater success and realizes that his success is the direct result of his own hard work. His new internal and controllable attributions lead him to use effective strategies and be a more self-regulating learner:

> Now I do things in math step by step and listen to each step. . . . I used to just listen and not even take notes. I always told myself I would remember but I always seemed to forget. Now I take notes and I study at home every day except Friday, even if I don't have homework. Now I study so that I know that I have it. I don't just hope I'll remember.[3]

DEVELOPMENTAL TRENDS IN ATTRIBUTIONS

Young children become increasingly able to distinguish among the various possible causes of their successes and failures: effort, ability, luck, task difficulty, and so on (Dweck & Elliott, 1983; Eccles et al., 1998; Nicholls, 1990). One distinction they come to understand is that between effort and ability. In the early elementary grades, children think of effort and ability as positively correlated: People who try harder are more competent. Thus they tend to attribute their successes to hard work and are usually optimistic about their chances for future success so long as they try hard. Sometime around age 9, they begin to understand that effort and ability often compensate for each other and that people with less ability may need to exert greater effort. Many begin to attribute their successes and failures to an inherited ability—for instance, intelligence—which they perceive to be fairly stable and beyond their control. If they're usually successful at school tasks, they have high self-efficacy for the tasks, but if they often fail, their self-efficacy is likely to plummet (Dweck, 1986; Eccles [Parsons] et al., 1983; Schunk, 1990). The following exercise demonstrates how students' beliefs about their abilities change as they move through elementary school:

See Chapter 2 if you need a refresher on the development of children's cognitive abilities.

EXPERIENCING FIRSTHAND
HOW DO I COMPARE?

Imagine presenting a picture of 30 circles on a piece of paper, where the circles are equally spaced starting at the top of the sheet and going to the bottom. Now imagine asking the following question to a student: *"These circles represent all of the students in your class. The top circle is the best reader, and the bottom circle is the worst reader in the class. Which circle represents you?"* How do you think a first

---

[3] Extract from "Cycles of Learning: Demonstrating the Interplay Between Motivation, Self-Regulation, and Cognition," by Valerie G. Tucker and Lynley H. Anderman, paper presented at the annual meeting of the American Educational Research Association, April 1999, pp. 5–6. Copyright © 1999 by Valerie G. Tucker and Lynley H. Anderman. Reprinted with permission of the authors.

grader would respond to this? A fifth grader? Most often, the first graders will put themselves at or near the top of the page, regardless of ability, whereas the fifth graders usually will think about the question and place themselves fairly accurately along the continuum (Nichols, 1978).

Attributions also are affected by various environmental cues. When a classroom task appears to be complex and exceptionally challenging—and especially if classmates are struggling with it as well—failure can easily be attributed to task difficulty rather than to internal causes. But if peers are performing a task with ease, learners are likely to attribute their own failures to low ability (Schunk, 1990; Weiner, 1984).

GOALS

Much of human behavior is directed toward particular goals. Some goals are short term and transitory (e.g., "I want to finish reading my dinosaur book"); others are long term and relatively enduring (e.g., "I want to be a paleontologist"). Children and adolescents typically have a wide variety of goals: Being happy and healthy, doing well in school, gaining popularity with peers, winning athletic competitions, and finding a long-term mate are just a few of the many possibilities (M. E. Ford & Smith, 2007; Schutz, 1994). Here we'll look at research related to several types of goals especially relevant to instructional settings.

ACHIEVEMENT GOALS

Early motivation theorists proposed that *achievement motivation* is a general trait that learners consistently exhibit in a wide variety of contexts. In contrast, most contemporary theorists believe that achievement motivation may be somewhat specific to particular tasks and occasions. It can also take different forms, depending on learners' specific goals. For example, let's consider what four different boys might be thinking during the first day of a basketball unit in Mr. Wesolowski's physical education class:

> *Jordan:* I'd like to show everyone what a great basketball player I am. If I stay near the basket, Travis and Tony will keep passing to me, and I can make a bunch of baskets.
>
> *Travis:* I hope I don't screw this up. If I shoot at the basket and miss, I'll look like a real loser. Maybe I should just stay outside the three-point line and keep passing to Tim and Tony.
>
> *Tony:* I really want to become a better basketball player. I'll ask Wesolowski to give me feedback about how I can improve my game. Maybe some of my friends will have suggestions as well.
>
> *Oliver:* I've always been a great basketball player and I always try to do my best when playing, but I'm out of shape and worried that I won't play up to my usual standards.

All four boys want to play basketball well—that is, they all have *achievement goals*. But they have different reasons for wanting to play well. Jordan is concerned mostly about impressing his teacher and classmates and so wants to maximize opportunities to demonstrate his skills. Travis, too, is concerned about the impression he'll make, but he just wants to make sure he doesn't look *bad*. In contrast, Tony isn't thinking about how his performance will appear to others. Instead, he's interested mainly in developing his basketball skills and doesn't expect immediate success. For Tony, making mistakes is an inevitable part of learning a new skill, not a source of embarrassment or humiliation. Oliver isn't think about others, but he is concerned that he won't perform as well as he thinks he should.

Jordan and Travis each have a **performance goal**, a desire to present themselves as competent in the eyes of others. More specifically, Jordan has a **performance-approach goal**: He wants to look good and receive favorable judgments from others. In contrast, Travis has a **performance-avoidance goal**: He wants to avoid looking bad and receiving unfavorable judgments. Both types of performance goals have an element of social comparison, with learners being concerned about how their accomplishments compare to those of their peers. Tony and Oliver's approaches to basketball illustrate **mastery goals**. Tony has a **mastery-approach goal**: He wants to become a better basketball player, and he is willing to work hard to do so. In contrast, Oliver has a

MyEdLab
Video Example 11.5.

A mastery approach helps students develop a healthy perspective about learning, effort, and failure.

mastery-avoidance goal: He is worried about not being able to play at his best. Neither Tony nor Oliver is concerned about how they appear to others—they both are more concerned about their own personal goals (Elliot & McGregor, 2001; Elliot, Murayama, & Pekrun, 2011; Régner, Escribe, & Dupeyrat, 2007; Senko, Hulleman, & Harackiewicz, 2011).

These four goals aren't necessarily mutually exclusive. Learners may simultaneously hold several of these goals (Luo, Paris, Hogan, & Luo, 2011; Murayama, Elliot, & Yamagata, 2011; Senko et al., 2011). Returning to our basketball example, we could imagine a fifth boy, Javier, who wants to improve his basketball skills *and* look good in front of his classmates *and* not come across as a klutz, *and* who worries that he won't live up to his self-standards.

Effects of Mastery and Performance Goals   In most instances, having mastery-approach goals is the optimal situation. As Table 11.2 illustrates, learners with mastery-approach goals tend to engage in the very activities that will help them learn: They pay attention in class, process information in ways that promote effective long-term memory storage, and learn from their mistakes.

COMPARE/CONTRAST

Table 11.2 • Typical Differences Between Learners with Mastery Versus Performance Goals	
LEARNERS WITH MASTERY GOALS (ESPECIALLY THOSE WITH MASTERY-APPROACH GOALS)	**LEARNERS WITH PERFORMANCE GOALS (ESPECIALLY THOSE WITH PERFORMANCE-AVOIDANCE GOALS)**
Are more likely to be actively engaged in classroom activities and intrinsically motivated to learn course material	Are more likely to be extrinsically motivated and more likely to cheat to obtain good grades
Believe that competence develops over time through practice and effort; persist in the face of difficulty	Believe that competence is a stable characteristic (people either have talent or they don't); think that competent people shouldn't have to try very hard; give up quickly when facing difficulty
Choose tasks that maximize opportunities for learning; seek out challenges	Choose tasks that maximize opportunities for showing competence; avoid tasks and actions that might reveal incompetence (e.g., asking for help)
Exhibit more self-regulated learning and behavior	Exhibit less self-regulation
Use learning strategies that promote true understanding and complex cognitive processes (e.g., elaboration, comprehension monitoring, transfer)	Use learning strategies that promote only rote learning (e.g., word-for-word memorization); may procrastinate on assignments
Are more likely to undergo conceptual change when confronted with convincing evidence that contradicts current beliefs	Are less likely to undergo conceptual change, in part because they are less likely to notice the discrepancy between new information and existing beliefs
React to easy tasks with feelings of boredom or disappointment	React to success on easy tasks with feelings of pride or relief
Seek feedback that accurately describes their ability and helps them improve	Seek feedback that flatters them
Have friends with whom they often collaborate to address academic or social problems	Collaborate with peers primarily when doing so can help them look competent or enhance their social status
Evaluate their own performance in terms of the progress they make	Evaluate their own performance in terms of how they compare with others
View errors as a normal and useful part of the learning process; use errors to improve performance	View errors as a sign of failure and incompetence; engage in self-handicapping to provide apparent justification for errors and failures
Are satisfied with their performance if they try hard and make progress	Are satisfied with their performance only if they succeed; are apt to feel ashamed and depressed when they fail
View a teacher as a resource and guide to help them learn	View a teacher as a judge and as a rewarder or punisher
Remain relatively calm during tests and other classroom assessments	Are often quite anxious about tests and other assessments
Are more likely to be enthusiastic about and become actively involved in school activities	Are more likely to distance themselves from the school environment
Are more likely to ask for help so that they can better understand what they are learning	Are more likely to ask for help so they can get finished with academic work as quickly as possible

Sources: Ablard & Lipschultz, 1998; E. M. Anderman & Maehr, 1994; L. H. Anderman & Anderman, 2009; Corpus, McClintic-Gilbert, & Hayenga, 2009; Dweck, 1986; ; Dweck, Mangels, & Good, 2004; Elliot et al., 2011; Gabriele, 2007; Graham & Weiner, 1996; Hardré, Crowson, DeBacker, & White, 2007; Kaplan & Midgley, 1999; Lau & Nie, 2008; Levy-Tossman, Kaplan, & Assor, 2007; Liem, Lau, & Nie, 2008; Linnenbrink & Pintrich, 2002, 2003; McGregor & Elliot, 2002; Middleton & Midgley, 1997; P. K. Murphy & Alexander, 2000; Nolen, 1996; Pekrun, Elliot, & Maier, 2006; Poortvliet & Darnon, 2010; Pugh & Bergin, 2006; Rawsthorne & Elliot, 1999; A.M. Ryan & Shim, 2012; Senko et al., 2011; Shim, Ryan, & Anderson, 2008; Sideridis, 2005; Sins et al., 2008; Skaalvik, 1997; Steuer & Dresel, 2011; Turner, Thorpe, & Meyer, 1998; Urdan, 2004; Urdan, Midgley, & Anderman, 1998; Wolters, 2004.

Furthermore, they have a healthy perspective about learning, effort, and failure: They realize that learning is a process of trying hard and continuing to persevere in the face of temporary setbacks. Consequently, these learners are the ones who are most likely to stay on task and who benefit the most from their classroom experiences. Mastery-approach goals are related to achievement, although some null results have been reported. Mastery-approach goals are particularly beneficial when they are experienced along with autonomy support (i.e., being able to make choices) (Benita, Roth, & Deci, 2014; Elliot et al., 2011; Keys, Conley, Duncan, & Domina, 2012; Kumar, Gheen, & Kaplan, 2002; Sins, van Joolingen, Savelsbergh, & van Hout-Wolters, 2008). Research on mastery-avoidance goals has been limited, but the limited research suggests that mastery-avoidance goals are related to maladaptive outcomes, such as increased anxiety and fear of failure (Sideridis, 2008).

In contrast, learners with performance goals—especially those with performance-*avoidance* goals—tend to steer clear of the challenges so important for learning, give up easily in the face of failure, and are apt to engage in self-handicapping when they expect to do poorly. Performance-*approach* goals are a mixed bag: They sometimes have positive effects, especially in combination with mastery-approach goals, spurring learners to achieve at high levels (Linnenbrink, 2005; Rawsthorne & Elliot, 1999; Wolters, 2004). Yet by themselves, performance-approach goals may be less beneficial than mastery-approach goals: Learners may exert only the minimum effort necessary, use relatively superficial learning strategies (e.g., rote memorization), and occasionally cheat on assessments. Performance-approach goals appear to be most detrimental when learners are younger (e.g., in the elementary grades) and have low self-efficacy for classroom tasks (E. M. Anderman, Griesinger, & Westerfield, 1998; Midgley, Kaplan, & Middleton, 2001; M.-T. Wang & Holcombe, 2010). Recent neurological studies suggest that areas of the brain associated with negative affect are active when performance-approach goals are prominent (Kim, Lee, Chung, & Bong, 2010). Performance goals are salient in students' minds when teachers spend much time emphasizing the importance of grades; this is particularly problematic when performance-avoidance goals are induced (Pulfrey, Buchs, & Butera, 2011).

Developmental Trends in Achievement Goals

In the preschool and early elementary years, children seem to focus largely on mastery-approach goals, but performance goals become increasingly prevalent at more advanced grade levels (Bong, 2009; Dweck & Elliott, 1983; Harter, 1992). By the time students reach high school, they may find pleasure in learning new things, but many are concerned primarily about getting good grades and prefer short, easy tasks to lengthier, more challenging ones. Performance goals are also common in team sports, where the focus often is more on winning and gaining public recognition than on developing new skills (G. C. Roberts, Treasure, & Kavussanu, 1997).

When children begin school at age 5 or 6, two things happen that gradually orient them more toward performance goals (Dweck & Elliott, 1983). For one thing, they now have many peers with whom to compare their own behaviors, and they may sometimes see themselves coming up short. In addition, children may have trouble evaluating their progress on complex academic skills and thus must rely on others (e.g., teachers) to make judgments about their competence. As children reach adolescence, two more factors kick in: They become increasingly concerned about what other people think of them, and they realize that performing at high levels—for instance, getting good grades—is critical for their future educational and professional opportunities (Anderman & Mueller, 2010; Covington & Müeller, 2001; Juvonen, 2000; Midgley, 1993).

Many teaching and coaching practices also contribute to the development of performance goals. Consider these common practices:

- Reinforcing students only for correct answers
- Posting only the "best" work on a bulletin board
- Grading tests on a curve
- Reminding students of the importance of good grades for college admissions
- Giving special recognition to sports teams that consistently defeat their rivals

All of these strategies are undoubtedly well intentioned, but they encourage students to focus their attention more on *demonstrating* competence than on *acquiring* it (E. M. Anderman & Mueller, 2010; Midgley, 2002). By the time students are approaching the end of high school, their achievement goals tend to remain relatively stable (Tuominen-Soini, Salmela-Aro, & Niemivirta, 2011).

Adolescents' increasing concern about other people's opinions of them may remind you of the *imaginary audience*, a concept presented in Chapter 3.

Fostering Productive Achievement Goals To some degree, performance goals (both performance-approach and avoidance) are probably inevitable in today's schools and in society at large. Learners may quite legitimately use their peers' performance as a criterion for evaluating their own ability levels, many colleges look at grade point averages and test scores when screening applicants, and many aspects of the adult world are inherently competitive in nature. Ultimately, however, mastery-approach goals are the ones most likely to lead to effective learning and performance over the long run.

Sometimes mastery-approach goals come from within, especially when students both value and have high self-efficacy for learning a topic (Liem, Lau, & Nie, 2008; P. K. Murphy & Alexander, 2000; Pajares, 2009). But the following classroom practices can also encourage mastery-approach goals:

- Show how mastery of certain topics is relevant to students' long-term personal and professional goals.
- Insist that students *understand,* rather than simply memorize, classroom material.
- Communicate the belief that effective learning requires exerting effort and making mistakes (and don't penalize students for taking risks and making mistakes!).
- Give students, and ask students to set, short-term, concrete goals—known as proximal goals—toward which to work; identify goals that are challenging yet accomplishable with reasonable effort (see Figure 11.7).
- Provide regular feedback that enables students to assess their progress toward goals.
- Offer specific suggestions about how students can improve.
- Give praise that focuses on content rather than on comparison with classmates.
- Encourage students to use their peers not as reference points for their own progress but rather as a source of ideas and assistance. (E. M. Anderman & Maehr, 1994; Brophy, 2004; Corpus, Tomlinson, & Stanton, 2004; E. A. Locke & Latham, 2006; Middleton & Midgley, 2002; R. B. Miller & Brickman, 2004; Page-Voth & Graham, 1999; N. E. Perry & Winne, 2004; Schunk & Pajares, 2005; Turner, Meyer, et al., 1998; Urdan et al., 2002; M.-T. Wang & Holcombe, 2010)

Focusing on mastery-approach goals, especially when these goals relate to students' own lives and needs, may especially benefit students from diverse ethnic backgrounds and students at risk for academic failure (E. S. Alexander, 2008; García, 1992; Wlodkowski & Ginsberg, 1995).

WORK-AVOIDANCE AND DOING-JUST-ENOUGH GOALS

As we've seen, learners sometimes want to avoid looking bad as they perform classroom tasks. But on other occasions they may want to avoid doing classroom tasks *at all,* or at least to invest as little effort as possible. In other words, learners may have a work-avoidance goal, often because they have low self-efficacy for the tasks at hand (Coddington & Guthrie, 2008; Dowson & McInerney, 2001; Urdan et al., 2002). Students use a variety of strategies to avoid classroom tasks—for instance, they might engage in disruptive behaviors, complain loudly about challenging assignments, or refuse to contribute to small-group activities (Dowson & McInerney, 2001; Gallini, 2000; Hemmings, 2004). Work-avoidance goals are related to poor cognitive engagement, low grades, and negative affect (King & McInerney, 2014).

A similar goal—but for a very different reason—is a doing-just-enough goal (McClure et al., 2011). In particular, students want to get reasonable school grades through the easiest possible routes, perhaps by rote-memorizing isolated facts, copying classmates' homework, or submitting research papers downloaded from the Internet. A doing-just-enough goal is in some respects a performance goal, but the focus isn't on demonstrating competence or hiding a lack of it. Instead, students simply have other priorities for their time—perhaps pursuing nonacademic interests or enhancing their relationships with peers (Hickey, 2011; M. Hofer, 2010; Wells, 2011). As you

FIGURE 11.7 With this handout, a middle school information technology teacher asks students to reflect on their current strengths and identify specific goals for improvement. This handout is for girls; boys get one with shorter hair.

Source: Created by and used with permission from Jeff Ormrod.

might guess, students with doing-just-enough goals have relatively low achievement levels (McClure et al., 2011; Tuominin-Soini et al., 2011).

When students actively avoid assigned tasks because of low self-efficacy, obviously the most effective strategy is to give them the guidance and support they need to improve their performance, as Ms. Tucker does in the opening case study. When, instead, they have doing-just-enough goals, we must help them find relevance in the subject matter and tie it to things that are important to them. For example, they might enhance their writing skills by writing about their own lives and exchanging their stories with peers on the Internet (Garner, 1998). Or they might apply scientific and mathematical concepts to document the ecological decline of their local environment and report their findings to the adult community (W.-M. Roth, 2011). Students with work-avoidance goals and doing-just-enough goals may ultimately be our biggest challenges, and we'll probably need to use a variety of motivational strategies—extrinsic reinforcement as well as strategies that promote interest and mastery-approach goals—to get them genuinely engaged in academic subject matter (Brophy, 2004).

> Use multiple strategies—including extrinsic reinforcement if necessary—to engage students who have work-avoidance and doing-just-enough goals.

SOCIAL GOALS

Earlier we noted that people have a need for relatedness—a need to feel socially connected with their fellow human beings. Consistent with this fundamental need, children and adolescents are apt to have a variety of social goals as they interact with other people. Such goals typically include some or all of the following:

- Forming and maintaining friendly or intimate social relationships
- Gaining other people's approval
- Establishing a balance between "fitting in" and "standing out" among one's peers
- Achieving status, popularity, and prestige among peers
- Becoming part of a cohesive, mutually supportive group; gaining a sense of belonging in the classroom
- Adhering to the rules and conventions of the group (e.g., being a good "class citizen")
- Meeting social obligations and keeping interpersonal commitments
- Assisting and supporting others and ensuring their welfare (Dowson & McInerney, 2001; M. E. Ford & Smith, 2007; Gray, 2014; Hinkley, McInerney, & Marsh, 2001; Kiefer & Ellerbrock, 2011; Patrick, Anderman, & Ryan, 2002; Schutz, 1994; Wentzel, Filisetti, & Looney, 2007)

The specific nature of students' social goals affects their classroom behavior and academic performance—sometimes for the better but sometimes for the worse. If students are seeking friendly relationships with classmates or are concerned about others' welfare, they may eagerly engage in such activities as cooperative learning and peer tutoring (Dowson & McInerney, 2001; Wentzel et al., 2007). But if they're more concerned about gaining the *approval* of their peers, they may go out of their way to behave in ways they think will please others, possibly compromising their own standards for behavior in the process and possibly also alienating peers because they're trying too hard to be liked (M. Bartlett, Rudolph, Flynn, Abaied, & Koerber, 2007; Boyatzis, 1973; Rudolph et al., 2005).

Meanwhile, of course, many students are also eager to form productive social relationships with their teachers. Ideally, we would hope that they see us teachers primarily as sources of support and guidance who can help them master academic subject matter and adjust comfortably to the school environment. But some may be more concerned with gaining our approval, in which case they're likely to shoot for performance goals and may self-handicap in activities at which they expect to do poorly (H. A. Davis, 2003; Hinkley et al., 2001; S. C. Rose & Thornburg, 1984).

LONG-TERM LIFE GOALS

Many children and adolescents give considerable thought to the kinds of lives they want to lead and set goals consistent with those hoped-for lives (J. Q. Lee, McInerney, Liem, & Ortiga, 2010; Mouratidis, Vansteenkiste, Lens, Michou, & Soenens, 2013; Oyserman, 2008). Key among these long-term goals, of course, are career goals. Young children set such goals with little thought and change them frequently; for instance, a 6-year-old may want to be a firefighter one week and a professional baseball player the next. But by late adolescence many young people have reached tentative and relatively stable decisions about the career paths they want to pursue (Lapan, Tucker, Kim, & Kosciulek, 2003; Marcia, 1980). Often their choices are based on a strong sense of competence in a particular domain and on personal and cultural values regarding important life pursuits (Plante & O'Keefe, 2010). Some adolescents also think about broader long-term goals, such as how one can have a positive impact on the world; when students consider both their career goals and such broader goals, they are likely to feel a greater sense of purpose and meaning in their lives (Yeager, Bundick, & Johnson, 2012).

Students' long-term goals can certainly direct them toward particular curricular and extracurricular activities at school—perhaps in science, music, or athletics. Three teaching strategies can capitalize on those goals:

Many children begin thinking about long-term goals as early as the preschool and early elementary years. Here 7-year-old Ashton explains why he wants to be a surgeon. His explanation reflects social goals as well as a career goal.

- Have students brainstorm the kinds of knowledge and abilities they're likely to need to accomplish their goals, and how they might obtain and master such knowledge.

- Also have students brainstorm possible obstacles they might encounter in pursuit of their goals, along with specific ways they might overcome those obstacles.

- Regularly tie school subject matter to students' personal goals; for example, conduct activities in which they can authentically apply classroom topics to tasks related to their chosen professions. (Gay, 2010; Nolen, 2011; Oyserman, 2008)

But in addition, we must keep in mind that many students don't have the self-regulation skills to keep themselves on track toward meeting their long-term goals, perhaps because they have few self-regulating role models in their outside lives (R. B. Miller & Brickman, 2004; Oyserman, 2008; B. L. Wilson & Corbett, 2001). Another key strategy, then, is to teach and scaffold such skills—scheduling sufficient time for studying, saying "no" to appealing but nonproductive leisure-time activities, self-imposing reinforcement for completing specific tasks, and so on. At the same time, students will probably have greater stick-to-itiveness if they also build enjoyable leisure activities into their schedules. Expecting them to totally deny themselves life's little pleasures isn't likely to be either productive or realistic (M. Hofer, 2010).

Urge students to build enjoyable leisure activities into their daily schedules, perhaps by making those activities contingent on completing specific academic tasks.

COORDINATING MULTIPLE GOALS

Most students have numerous goals and use a variety of strategies to juggle them (Conley, 2012; Covington, 2000; Darnon, Dompnier, Gilliéron, & Butera, 2010; Dodge, Asher, & Parkhurst, 1989; Urdan & Maehr, 1995). Sometimes students find activities that allow them to address two or more goals simultaneously; for example, they can address both achievement goals and social goals by forming a study group to prepare for a test. Sometimes students pursue one goal while temporarily putting others on the back burner; for example, they might complete a required reading assignment while bypassing more interesting but unassigned material. And occasionally students may modify their idea of what it means to achieve a particular goal; for instance, an ambitious high school student who initially hopes to earn all As in three advanced classes may eventually concede that earning Bs in two of them may be more realistic.

In other situations students may entirely abandon one goal in order to satisfy another, conflicting one (M. Hofer, 2010; McCaslin & Good, 1996; Phelan et al., 1994). For example, students who want to do well in school may choose *not* to perform at their best in order to maintain relationships with peers who don't value academic achievement (B. B. Brown, 1993; Ogbu, 2008b). And students with mastery-approach goals in particular content domains may find that the multiple demands of school coerce them into focusing on performance goals (e.g., getting good grades) rather than studying the subject matter as thoroughly as they'd like. Brian, a junior high school student, expresses his concern about leaving his mastery-approach goals behind as he strives for performance goals:

I sit here and I say, "Hey, I did this assignment in five minutes and I still got an A+ on it." I still have a feeling that I could do better, and it was kind of cheap that I didn't do my best and I still got this A. . . . I think probably it might lower my standards eventually, which I'm not looking forward to at all. . . . I'll always know, though, that I have it in me. It's just that I won't express it that much. (S. Thomas & Oldfather, 1997, p. 119)

Naturally, our students will be most successful when their multiple goals all lead them in the same direction (M. E. Ford, 1992; Wentzel, 1999). For example, students might work toward mastery-approach goals by learning and practicing new skills within the context of group projects (thus meeting their social goals) and with evaluation criteria that allow for taking risks and making mistakes (thus also meeting their performance goals). Students are *un*likely to strive for mastery-approach goals when assignments ask little of them (recall Brian's concern about the minimal requirements for an A), when we insist that they compete with one another for resources or high test scores (thereby interfering with their social goals), or when any single failure has a significant impact on their final grades (thereby thwarting their progress toward performance goals).

MINDSETS

As children and adolescents develop and have more experiences of successes and failures in school, they develop beliefs about their abilities and their own personal intelligence. Some of our students may believe that they truly can succeed at a difficult task, because they believe that their minds or brains have the ability to acquire new information and skills; but other students may feel that their intelligence is fixed to some extent, and that they just may not have the ability to learn certain topics well (or more generally, just to learn!). Let's explore what this might feel like with a brief exercise.

EXPERIENCING FIRSTHAND
EXPLORING MINDSETS

Think about an area in your life in which you have been very successful (e.g., playing tennis; learning mathematics; playing a musical instrument; baking gourmet pastries). Write down what you think about your potential to learn more about this area and to develop new, complex skills in this area. Now think about an area in your life in which you feel that you have no talent at all (e.g., perhaps as a writer, as a professional opera singer, as a track and field star, etc.). Write down what you think about your potential to learn more about this topic and to develop your skill sets in this area.

Now take a look at your responses. You probably wrote that you feel that you do have the potential to learn more in the area in which you have previously experienced successes, whereas you probably wrote that you are not confident about your potential to excel in the area in which you perceive that you lack talent. When we believe that our ability to learn something is possible and that our potential to improve our skills is high, we have what is known as a **"growth" mindset**. This means that we truly believe that we can learn, grow, and excel in this area, and that practice will lead to improvements and learning—that our brains are physically capable of mastering new topics and skills at virtually any age level—and that practice will lead to improvements in learning.

In addition, you might have written something about your lack of confidence in your ability to excel in the area in which you believe that you lack talent. When we believe that our ability to learn something is limited, we have what is known as a **"fixed" mindset**. This means that we believe that we simply do not have the capacity to excel in a particular academic area and that our intelligence can't improve, even with practice. If you again think about the human brain, it means we believe that our brains are just not capable of learning in certain areas, as Sarah reveals in her description of her problems in math:

My dad is very good at math, and my brother, I, and my mom aren't good at math at all, we inherited the "not good at math gene" from my mom and I am good in English but I am not good in math. (K. E. Ryan, Ryan, Arbuthnot, & Samuels, 2007, p. 5)

Students with a growth mindset are likely to adopt mastery-approach goals in the classroom, to work hard at their studies, and to earn increasingly high grades and standardized test

Consider how your classroom practices might help students address multiple goals simultaneously.

Be careful that you don't confuse the mindsets we describe here with the mental sets described in Chapter 7.

scores. In contrast, students with a fixed mindset often adopt performance goals, quickly lose interest in a topic that doesn't come easily to them, self-handicap in the face of failure, and earn lower grades over time (Blackwell, Trzesniewski, & Dweck, 2007; J. A. Chen & Pajares, 2010; Dweck & Leggett, 1988; Dweck & Molden, 2005; Good, Aronson, & Inzlicht, 2003).

Some of our students may have a *generalized* growth mindset, meaning that they believe that they can probably learn anything if they work hard. It is important to remember that although some of our students may have a general growth mindset, they still may not want to learn about topics that they are not interested in or do not value. In other cases, our students may hold a growth mindset in only certain domains (e.g., a student might have a growth mindset in mathematics but not in reading).

This also holds true for fixed mindsets. We need to be particularly cognizant of students who hold a generalized fixed mindset. If a student believes that no matter what, she simply is not a good learner (e.g., because she just does not have a "smart brain"), that belief may have a detrimental impact on motivation and achievement across all academic areas.

Fortunately there are some strategies that teachers can use to facilitate the development of a growth mindset in their students:

- Set short-term, easy-to-reach goals (proximal goals), so that students experience success even in areas that they find challenging. This will increase their self-efficacy, and encourage a growth mindset.

- Tell your students a bit about how the brain works. Help them to understand that when *anything* is learned, new connections are made, and that this happens for everyone; thus everyone has the potential to learn.

- Teach students that intelligence is in fact malleable—we can often dispel beliefs about the fixed nature of intelligence by simply making students aware of the benefits of a growth mindset.

- Avoid grouping students by ability whenever possible. When we use ability grouping, we are sending a message to our students about our beliefs about their capabilities. A student who is always in the low-level reading group is likely to develop a fixed mindset toward reading. One alternative is allowing students to choose groups based on interests, rather than assigning groups solely based on ability.

MASTERY ORIENTATION VERSUS LEARNED HELPLESSNESS

As children grow older, they gradually develop predictable patterns of attributions and expectations for their future performance. Consider these two students, keeping in mind that *their actual ability level is the same.*

- Jared is an enthusiastic, energetic learner. He works hard at school activities and takes obvious pleasure in doing well. He likes challenge, especially the brainteaser problems his teacher assigns as extra-credit work each day. He can't always solve the problems, but he takes failure in stride and is eager for more problems the following day.

- Jerry is an anxious, fidgety student who doesn't have much confidence in his ability to accomplish school tasks successfully. In fact, he often underestimates what he can do: Even when he has succeeded, he doubts that he can do it again. He prefers filling out drill-and-practice worksheets that help him practice skills he's already mastered, rather than attempting new tasks and problems. As for those daily brainteasers Jared likes so much, Jerry sometimes takes a stab at them but gives up quickly if the answer isn't obvious.

Over time, some learners, like Jared, develop an "I can do it" attitude known as a mastery orientation—a general sense of optimism that they can master new tasks and succeed in a variety of endeavors. A mastery orientation is similar to a mastery-approach goal, but a mastery orientation is a general positive orientation toward learning, whereas mastery-approach goals are goals related to mastering specific content areas (e.g., the goal of mastering verb conjugation in Spanish). Other learners, like Jerry, develop an "I *can't* do it" attitude known as learned helplessness—a general sense of futility about their chances for future success. You might think of this distinction, which really reflects a continuum rather than an either–or dichotomy, as a difference between

MyEdLab
Video Example 11.6.

Teachers can use strategies that facilitate the development of a growth mindset in students. Ms. McDaniels sees a difference in the mindset of her students as a result of such strategies.

Chapter 5 presents psychologists' varying perspectives on the origins of intelligence.

Portray intelligence and domain-specific abilities as characteristics that can change with effort and persistence.

optimists and *pessimists* (Boman, Furlong, Shochet, Lilles, & Jones, 2009; C. Peterson, 1990, 2006; Seligman, 1991).

Even when learners initially have equal ability levels, those with a mastery orientation behave in ways that lead to higher achievement over the long run. In particular, they set ambitious goals, seek challenging situations, have a growth mindset, and persist in the face of failure. Learners with learned helplessness behave very differently. Because they underestimate their ability, they set goals they can easily accomplish, avoid the challenges likely to maximize their learning and cognitive growth, have a fixed mindset, and respond to failure in counterproductive ways (e.g., giving up quickly) that almost guarantee future failure (Dweck, 2000; Graham, 1989; S. J. Lopez et al., 2009; C. Peterson, 2006; Seligman, 1991).

By age 5 or 6, some children begin to show a consistent tendency either to persist at a task and express confidence that they can master it, on the one hand, or to abandon a task quickly and say they don't have the ability to do it (Burhans & Dweck, 1995; Ziegert, Kistner, Castro, & Robertson, 2001). However, children younger than 8 rarely exhibit extreme forms of learned helplessness, perhaps because they still believe that success is due largely to their own efforts (Eccles et al., 1998; Lockhart, Chang, & Story, 2002; S. G. Paris & Cunningham, 1996). By early adolescence a general sense of helplessness becomes more common. Some middle schoolers believe they can't control the things that happen to them—for instance, they're apt to have a fixed mindset—and are at a loss for strategies about how to avert future failures (Dweck, 2000; S. G. Paris & Cunningham, 1996; C. Peterson, Maier, & Seligman, 1993). In the opening case study, Michael's initial pessimism about his chances of future success in his algebra class suggests some degree of learned helplessness, at least about mathematics.

Strategies we've previously identified for enhancing self-efficacy, growth mindsets, and a sense of competence (e.g., promoting mastery on challenging tasks) should promote a mastery orientation as well. In addition, students should know that they have a variety of resources—their teachers, their peers, instructional software, volunteer tutors, and so on—to which they can turn in times of difficulty. In general, students must have sufficient academic support to believe "I can do this if I really want to."

When working with students who have learned helplessness, be consistent and persistent in your efforts to help them succeed.

MyEdLab
Video Example 11.7.

In general, how learners feel depends on whether their needs are being met and their goals are being accomplished. Student differences are seen in the interviews of 10-year-old Daniel, 13-year-old Crystal, and 15-year-old Greg.

DIVERSITY IN COGNITIVE AND SOCIOCULTURAL FACTORS AFFECTING MOTIVATION

In the preceding sections we've already seen individual differences in personal interests, values, achievement goals, and general attributional style. Here our focus will be on diversity in students of various cultural and ethnic backgrounds, genders, and income levels, as well as in students with special educational needs. Table 11.3 summarizes developmental trends in attributions and other aspects of motivation.

CULTURAL AND ETHNIC DIFFERENCES

Most cultural and ethnic groups place high value on getting a good education (P. J. Cook & Ludwig, 2008; Fuligni & Hardway, 2004; Phalet, Andriessen, & Lens, 2004; Spera, 2005). But researchers have observed differences in more specific values related to school learning. For example, many Asian cultures (e.g., in China, Japan, and Russia) emphasize learning for learning's sake: With knowledge come personal growth, better understanding of the world, and greater potential to contribute to society. Important for these cultures, too, are hard work and persistence in academic studies, even when the content isn't intrinsically enjoyable (Hufton et al., 2002; J. Li, 2006; Morelli & Rothbaum, 2007). Students from European American backgrounds are less likely to be diligent when classroom topics have little intrinsic appeal, but they often find value in academic subject matter that piques their curiosity and in assignments that require creativity, independent thinking, or critical analysis (Hess & Azuma, 1991; Kuhn & Park, 2005; Nisbett, 2009).

Learners from diverse cultural backgrounds may also define academic success differently and, as a result, may set different achievement goals. For example, on average, Asian American students aim for higher grades than do students from other ethnic groups, in part to win their parents' approval and in part to bring honor to their families (Nisbett, 2009; Steinberg, 1996). Even so, Asian American students—and African American students as well—tend to focus more on mastery-approach goals (i.e., truly understanding what they're studying) than European American students do (Freeman, Gutman, & Midgley, 2002; Qian & Pan, 2002; Shim & Ryan,

DEVELOPMENTAL TRENDS

Table 11.3 • Motivation at Different Grade Levels

GRADE LEVEL	AGE-TYPICAL CHARACTERISTICS	EXAMPLE	SUGGESTED STRATEGIES
K–2	• Focus more on acquiring competence than on self-evaluating it • Rapidly changing interests for many students; more stable interests for others • Pursuit of interesting and enjoyable activities regardless of expectancy for success • Tendency to attribute success to hard work and practice, leading to optimism about what can be accomplished	Six-year-old Alex loves learning about lizards. He often draws lizards during his free time, and when he goes to the school library, he invariably looks for books about lizards and other reptiles. One day, with his teacher's permission, he brings his pet iguana to class and explains the things he must do to keep it healthy.	• Engage students' interest in classroom topics through hands-on, playlike activities. • Entice students into reading, writing, and other basic skills through high-interest books and subject matter (e.g., animals, superheroes, princes and princesses). • Show students how they're improving over time; point out how their effort and practice are contributing to their improvement.
3–5	• Increasing tendency to self-evaluate competence, in part by observing how one's own performance compares to that of peers • Emergence of fairly stable personal interests • Increasing focus on performance goals • Increasing belief in innate ability as a significant and uncontrollable factor affecting learning and achievement • Increasing awareness of the kinds of attributions that will elicit positive reactions from others (e.g., "I didn't feel well during the test"); decrease in verbalized attributions that peers might interpret as boastful and arrogant	During a gymnastics unit in physical education, 9-year-old Marta watches her classmates as they perform forward and backward rolls, handstands, and cartwheels. She willingly executes the rolls, but when she has trouble getting her legs up for a handstand, she quickly gives up, saying, "I can't do handstands and cartwheels—not like Jessie and Sharonda can."	• Allow students to pursue personal interests in independent reading and writing tasks. • Encourage students to judge their performance based on their own improvement, rather than on how it compares with that of peers. • Demonstrate your own fascination and enthusiasm about classroom topics; communicate reasons why many topics are worth learning about for their own sake. • Identify strengths in every student; provide sufficient support to enable students to gain proficiency in areas of weakness.
6–8	• Decline in general sense of competence (relative to peers) in many academic domains • Increasing tendency to self-handicap as a way of maintaining self-worth during difficult tasks • Increasing interest in activities that are stereotypically "gender appropriate" • Increasing tendency to value activities associated with long-term goals and high expectancies for success • For many students, decline in perceived value of many content domains (e.g., English, math, music, sports) • Increasing focus on social goals (e.g., interacting with peers, making a good impression)	Thirteen-year-old Regina has always liked math. But now that she's in an advanced eighth-grade math class, she's starting to worry that her peers might think she's a "math geek." She diligently does her math homework each night and earns high grades on assignments and quizzes, but she rarely raises her hand in class to ask or answer questions. And when her friends ask her about the class, she rolls her eyes and says that she's in the class only because "Dad made me take it."	• Promote interest in classroom topics by presenting puzzling phenomena and building on students' personal interests. • Focus students' attention on their improvement; minimize opportunities for them to compare their performance to that of classmates. • Relate classroom subject matter to students' long-term goals (e.g., through authentic activities). • Provide opportunities for social interaction as students study and learn (e.g., through role-playing activities, class debates, cooperative learning projects).
9–12	• Increasing integration of certain interests and values into one's overall sense of self • For most students, prevalence of performance goals (e.g., getting good grades) rather than mastery goals • Increase in cheating as a means of accomplishing performance goals • Increasing focus on postgraduation goals (e.g., college, careers); for some students, insufficient self-regulation strategies to achieve these goals	Sixteen-year-old Randall wants to become a pediatric oncologist—as he puts it, "a cancer doctor who can help kids with leukemia, like my sister had." He knows he needs good grades in order to get into a prestigious college and then medical school, yet he has trouble saying no when his friends ask him to go to a basketball game the night before an important biology test. And when he gets home after the game, he spends an hour on Facebook instead of studying.	• Provide opportunities to address interests and values through out-of-class projects and extracurricular activities (e.g., community service work). • Make it possible for students to attain good grades through reasonable effort and effective strategies; minimize competitive grading practices, such as grading on a curve. • Discourage cheating (e.g., by giving individualized assignments and monitoring behavior during in-class assessments), and impose appropriate consequences when cheating occurs. • Teach self-regulation strategies that can help students reach their long-term goals.

Sources: J. M. Alexander et al., 2008; Archambault et al., 2010; Blumenfeld et al., 2006; Bong, 2009; Brophy, 2008; Cizek, 2003; Corpus et al., 2009; Dijkstra, Kuyper, van der Werf, Buunk, & van der Zee, 2008; Dotterer, McHale, & Crouter, 2009; Eccles et al., 1998; Hidi, Renninger, & Krapp, 2004; Jacobs, Davis-Kean, Bleeker, Eccles, & Malanchuk, 2005; Jacobs et al., 2002; Juvonen, 2000; LaFontana & Cillessen, 2010; Lepper et al., 2005; Nolen, 2007; Patrick et al., 2002; Shute, 2008; Urdan, 2004; Wigfield, 1994; Wigfield, Byrnes, & Eccles, 2006; Wigfield et al., 1991; B. L. Wilson & Corbett, 2001; Wolters, 2003; Youniss & Yates, 1999.

2006). And students brought up in cultures that value group achievement over individual achievement (e.g., many Asian, Native American, Mexican American, and Pacific Islander cultures) tend to focus their mastery-approach goals not on how much they alone can improve but instead on how much they *and their peers* can improve—or in some instances on how much their individual actions can contribute to the betterment of the larger social group or society (C.-Y. Chiu & Hong, 2005; Kağitçibaşi, 2007; J. Li, 2005, 2006).

Learners' cultural and ethnic backgrounds influence their attributions as well. For instance, students from families with traditional Asian cultural beliefs are more likely than students from mainstream Western culture to attribute classroom success and failure to unstable factors—effort in the case of academic achievement, and temporary situational factors in the case of appropriate or inappropriate behaviors (J. Li & Fischer, 2004; Lillard, 1997; Weiner, 2004). Also, some studies have found a greater tendency for African American students to develop a sense of learned helplessness about their ability to achieve academic success. To some extent, racial prejudice may contribute to their learned helplessness: Students may begin to believe that because of the color of their skin, they have little chance of success no matter what they do (G. H. Brody et al., 2006; Graham, 1989; van Laar, 2000).

GENDER DIFFERENCES

In general, girls are more concerned than boys are about doing well in school: They work harder on assignments, earn higher grades, and more often graduate from high school (Elmore & Oyserman, 2012; H. M. Marks, 2000; Marsh, Martin, & Cheng, 2008; McCall, 1994; J. P. Robinson & Lubienski, 2011). But some students perceive certain domains (e.g., writing, music) to be "for girls" and other domains (e.g., math, science) to be "for boys," dampening their interest and self-efficacy in seemingly opposite-gender content areas and thereby limiting their career options (Eccles, 2005; Jacobs et al., 2002; Leaper & Friedman, 2007; Plante et al., 2013; Weisgram, Bigler, & Liben, 2010). Students' long-term life goals come into the picture as well: Girls are more likely than boys to consider how their career choices might mesh with their desires to work with people (rather than objects) and to raise a family (Diekman, Brown, Johnston, & Clark, 2010; Eccles, 2009).

Another commonly observed gender difference is the tendency for girls (especially high-achieving girls) to be more discouraged by failure experiences than boys are (Dweck, 1986, 2000). We can explain this difference, at least in part, by looking at gender differences in attributions. Some research results indicate that boys tend to attribute their successes to a fairly stable ability and their failures to a lack of effort, thus revealing an "I know I can do this" attitude. Girls show the reverse pattern: They attribute their successes to effort and their failures to lack of ability, believing "I don't know whether I can keep on doing it because I'm not very good at this type of thing." Such differences are most often observed in stereotypically male domains (e.g., math, sports) and can appear even when boys' and girls' previous levels of achievement in the domains have been equivalent (Leaper & Friedman, 2007; McClure et al., 2011; Stipek, 1984; Vermeer, Boekaerts, & Seegers, 2000).

As we work to encourage high levels of motivation in all of our students, we may want to focus our efforts in somewhat different directions for males and females. For boys, who have less concern about doing well in school, we may need to stress the importance of academic achievement for their long-term life goals and make a particular effort to pique their interest in classroom activities. For girls, we may have to go the extra mile to convince them that their classroom successes are the result not only of their efforts but also of their natural abilities—a stable and dependable internal attribution—and that they have "what it takes" to be successful in traditionally male domains.

SOCIOECONOMIC DIFFERENCES

Many students from low-income backgrounds want to do well in school (Payne, 2005; Shernoff, Schneider, & Csikszentmihalyi, 2001; B. L. Wilson & Corbett, 2001). However, teachers' attitudes, instructional practices, and relationships with students have a significant influence on whether these students choose to pursue academic success; this is especially true for students at high risk for academic failure (L. W. Anderson & Pellicer, 1998; Kumar et al., 2002; Maehr & Anderman, 1993; Murdock, 1999). Students from low-income families are apt to flourish in schools in which teachers have high expectations for achievement, engage students in high-interest activities and subject matter, emphasize mastery-approach goals over performance goals, and make students feel that they're valued members of the classroom community (Hom & Battistich, 1995; Juvonen, 2006; Osterman, 2000; Patrick, Ryan, & Kaplan, 2007).

> Help boys discover the relevance of their classroom learning and performance to their long-term goals. Encourage girls to consider a wide range of career options and foster their self-efficacy for success in traditionally male domains.

It's equally important that we increase the perceived value of school activities by making them relevant to students' personal lives and needs (P. A. Alexander et al., 1994; Knapp, Turnbull, & Shields, 1990; Wlodkowski & Ginsberg, 1995). All too often, students at schools in low-income neighborhoods encounter instruction that focuses on basic skills and rote learning and thus is unlikely to entice even the most motivated students (B. E. Becker & Luthar, 2002; Pianta & Hamre, 2009). The following interview with middle school students in an inner-city Philadelphia school illustrates the problem:

> *Adult:* How often do you write in English class?
>
> *Student:* Every day.
>
> *Adult:* What kinds of things are you writing?
>
> *Student:* We copy notes from the board and we do dictionary work. We also answer questions from our workbook.
>
> *Adult:* Do you ever write your own stories?
>
> *Student:* No.[4]

Such instruction is not only unengaging but also unlikely to prepare students for the demands of a challenging high school or college curriculum (Ogbu, 2003; Suskind, 1998).

It's essential that we help students acquire the skills and strategies they'll need to achieve their long-term goals for higher education and rewarding careers: complex thinking skills, self-regulation strategies, and so on. In addition, if students have had little direct contact with college life or high-income professions, we must promote a realistic understanding of what college achievement and professional success involve. When speaking with a group of middle school boys who hoped to go to college, one researcher encountered considerable naiveté about college life:

> I asked them what they thought college was like. The response was nearly unanimous—it was all about partying—drinking, smoking weed, and hanging out. Never did it come up that they would attend classes or do homework. College meant partying, and that was why they wanted to go. (K. M. Williams, 2001a, p. 106)

Such misconceptions are perhaps not surprising if we consider how college life is often portrayed in television and films. For adolescent viewers, college parties certainly yield more interesting plot lines than going to class and studying at the library.

ACCOMMODATING STUDENTS WITH SPECIAL NEEDS

Students with special educational needs are typically among those who show the greatest diversity in motivation. For example, students with learning disabilities or general intellectual disabilities may be easily discouraged by challenging tasks; some may even show signs of learned helplessness if their efforts consistently meet with failure (Jacobsen, Lowery, & DuCette, 1986; Mercer & Pullen, 2005; Seligman, 1975). In contrast, students who are gifted may become easily bored or annoyed if classroom activities *don't* challenge their abilities (Bleske-Rechek, Lubinski, & Benbow, 2004; Winner, 2000b). Table 11.4 presents these and other motivational characteristics in students with special needs.

Remember that meaningful, personally relevant classroom tasks are especially important for motivating students from lower-income backgrounds.

Communicate that academic success requires hard work not only in the secondary grades but in college as well.

Chapter 5 identifies specific categories of special needs that fall within the five general categories listed in Table 11.4.

MyEdLab **Self-Check 11.2**

MyEdLab **Application Exercise 11.2.** In this exercise you can explain in social and cognitive terms why Mr. Stepien's strategies meet students' needs and enhance their levels of engagement.

MyEdLab **Application Exercise 11.3.** In this exercise you can identify goal setting strategies and their effect on student motivation and achievement.

STUDENTS IN INCLUSIVE SETTINGS

TABLE 11.4 • Enhancing Motivation in Students with Special Educational Needs

CATEGORY	CHARACTERISTICS YOU MIGHT OBSERVE	SUGGESTED STRATEGIES
Students with specific cognitive or academic difficulties	• Less intrinsic motivation to succeed at academic tasks, due in part to a low sense of self-efficacy and competence • Reluctance to ask questions or seek assistance, especially in the secondary grades • Little or no persistence when confronting difficult tasks • Tendency to attribute poor achievement to low ability rather than to more controllable factors; learned helplessness regarding some classroom tasks	• Use extrinsic reinforcers to encourage effort and achievement; gradually phase out reinforcers as students show signs of intrinsic motivation. • Establish short-term goals for achievement that students perceive as being challenging yet accomplishable. • Offer assistance when you think students may really need it, but refrain from offering help when you know students are capable of succeeding on their own. • Teach effective learning strategies and encourage students to attribute their successes to such strategies.
Students with social or behavioral problems	• Desire to succeed in the classroom, despite behaviors that seemingly indicate a lack of motivation • Tendency to interpret praise as an attempt at control (for students who exhibit defiance or oppositional behavior) • Stronger desire for power over classmates than for establishing friendships (for some students with emotional and behavioral disorders) • Little or no apparent interest in social interaction (for some students with autism spectrum disorders) • Perception of classroom tasks as having little relevance to personal needs and goals • Tendency to attribute negative consequences to uncontrollable factors (things "just happen")	• Provide the guidance and support students need to succeed at classroom tasks. • When students are concerned about control issues, use subtle reinforcers (e.g., leave notes commending productive behaviors) rather than more obvious and seemingly controlling ones. • Offer some choices about activities and reinforcers in order to increase a sense of self-determination. • Help students discover the benefits of equitable and prosocial interactions with peers. • Relate the curriculum to students' specific needs and interests. • Teach behaviors that lead to desired consequences; stress cause-and-effect relationships between actions and outcomes.
Students with general delays in cognitive and social functioning	• On average, less intrinsic motivation than nondisabled age-mates; occasional curiosity about certain topics • Responsiveness to extrinsic motivators • Tendency to give up easily in the face of difficulty • Limited or no ability to conceptualize long-term goals • Tendency to attribute poor achievement to low ability or to external sources rather than to more controllable factors; in some situations, a sense of learned helplessness	• Use extrinsic reinforcers to encourage productive behaviors; gradually phase out reinforcers as students show signs of intrinsic motivation. • Reinforce persistence as well as success. • Set specific, short-term (proximal) goals for performance; ask students to set some of their own goals as well. • Help students see the relationship between their own actions and resulting consequences.
Students with physical or sensory challenges	• Low sense of self-determination about the course of their lives • Fewer opportunities to satisfy the need for relatedness, especially with peers	• Teach self-regulating behaviors and independence skills. • Identify classmates who can serve as "study buddies" to help students with assigned tasks or provide companionship at lunch and recess. • Collaborate with parents to promote interaction with classmates outside school.
Students with advanced cognitive development	• High self-efficacy and sense of competence • Eagerness for challenges; boredom when classroom tasks don't challenge their abilities • Persistence in the face of failure (although some may give up easily if they aren't accustomed to failure) • Possible self-handicapping if there is a strong desire to affiliate with low-achieving peers • Social isolation (for some students who are exceptionally gifted) • Variety of interests, sometimes pursued with a passion • Higher than average goal-directedness • Internal, optimistic attributions for classroom achievement • Tendency to adopt an entity view of intelligence; can lead to learned helplessness if failure is encountered after an early string of successes (especially for girls)	• Provide opportunities for students to pursue complex tasks and activities over an extended period. • Give assignments that students find stimulating and challenging. • Keep students' exceptional achievements confidential if their friends don't value high achievement. • Provide opportunities to pursue individual interests, perhaps with other students who have similar interests or perhaps in an apprenticeship with an outside mentor. • Encourage students to set high goals without expecting perfection.

Sources: Beirne-Smith, Patton, & Kim, 2006; Brophy, 2004; B. Clark, 1997; Covington, 1992; Dai, 2010; G. Dawson & Bernier, 2007; Dunlap et al., 1994; Dweck, 2000; Foster-Johnson, Ferro, & Dunlap, 1994; S. Goldstein & Rider, 2006; T. L. Good & Brophy, 1994; D. A. Greenspan, Solomon, & Gardner, 2004; Heward, 2009; Jacobsen et al., 1986; Knowlton, 1995; Mendaglio, 2010; Mercer & Pullen, 2005; Patrick, 1997; Patton, Blackbourn, & Fad, 1996; Piirto, 1999; S. Powell & Nelson, 1997; Prout, 2009; Robertson, 2000; G. F. Schultz & Switzky, 1990; Shavinina & Ferrari, 2004; Turnbull, Turnbull, & Wehmeyer, 2010; Ulke-Kurcuoglu & Kircaali-Iftar, 2010; Wehmeyer et al., 2007; Winner, 1997, 2000a, 2000b; Wong, 1991.

Effects of Teacher Attributions and Expectations on Students' Motivation

Students are not the only ones who make attributions. Teachers also make attributions about their students' behavior and achievement. These teacher beliefs are strongly related to teachers' subsequent interactions with their students (M.-L. Chang & Davis, 2009; Turner, Warzon, & Christensen, 2011). Imagine that a student, Linda, fails to finish an assignment on time. Her teacher, Mr. Smith, might conclude that Linda (1) didn't try very hard, (2) used her time poorly, or (3) wasn't capable of doing the task. The conclusion he draws will depend on his prior beliefs about Linda—for instance, whether he thinks she (1) is lazy and unmotivated, (2) is both motivated and capable of doing the work but hasn't yet acquired effective self-regulation skills, or (3) has little innate capacity for learning.

Teachers' attributions for students' current behaviors affect their expectations for students' future performance; those expectations, in turn, affect future attributions (Weiner, 2000). And their attributions and expectations both affect the teaching strategies they use with particular students. For example, if Mr. Smith thinks Linda is "unmotivated," he might use some sort of incentive—perhaps offering free time later in the day—to entice her into completing assignments on time. If, instead, he thinks Linda lacks self-regulation skills, he might strive to teach her such skills. But if he thinks Linda has insufficient intelligence to master classroom topics, he may do very little to support her learning. Thus the beliefs that we form about our students are related to our subsequent interactions with our students.

Teachers typically draw conclusions about their students early in the school year, forming opinions about each one's strengths, weaknesses, and potential for academic success. In many cases teachers size up their students fairly accurately: They know which ones need help with reading skills, which ones have short attention spans, and so on, and then adapt instruction and assistance accordingly (Goldenberg, 1992; T. L. Good & Brophy, 1994; T. L. Good & Nichols, 2001). Yet even the best teachers can make errors in their judgments. For example, teachers often underestimate the abilities of students who come from certain minority groups or from low-income families (Ready & Wright, 2011; Rubie-Davies, Hattie, & Hamilton, 2006; Sirin & Ryce, 2010; van den Bergh, Denessen, Hornstra, Voeten, & Holland, 2010).

Furthermore, many teachers have a *fixed mindset* about their students' abilities as learners: They believe that students' achievement typically depends on relatively enduring, uncontrollable ability levels (Dweck & Molden, 2005; Oakes & Guiton, 1995; C. Reyna, 2000). Thus they form fairly stable expectations for students' performance, which in turn lead them to treat students differently. When teachers have high expectations for students, they present more challenging tasks and topics, interact with students more frequently, and give more positive and specific feedback. In contrast, when teachers have low expectations for certain students, they present easy tasks, offer few opportunities for speaking in class, and provide only limited feedback (Babad, 1993; T. L. Good & Brophy, 1994; Graham, 1990; R. Rosenthal, 1994, 2002).

Teachers' attributions for students' performance often reveal themselves in the things they say to students (Dweck & Molden, 2005; Weiner, 2000). Consider the following interpretations of a student's success:

- "You did it! You're so smart!"
- "Your hard work has really paid off, hasn't it?"
- "It's clear that you really know how to study."
- "Terrific! This is certainly your lucky day!"

And now consider these interpretations of a student's failure:

- "Maybe this just isn't something you're good at. Perhaps we should try a different activity."
- "Why don't you practice a little more and then try again?"
- "Let's come up with some strategies that might work better for you."
- "Maybe you're just having a bad day."

All of these comments are presumably intended to make a student feel good. But notice the different attributions they imply—in some cases, stable and uncontrollable abilities (being naturally

Continually ask yourself whether you are giving inequitable treatment to students for whom you have low expectations. Also reflect on your beliefs about students' intelligence: Are you taking growth-mindset perspective that gives you optimism about future progress?

smart or incapable); in other cases, controllable and therefore changeable behaviors (hard work, lack of practice, effective or ineffective study strategies); and in still other cases, external, uncontrollable causes (a lucky break, a bad day).

Teachers communicate their attributions for students' successes and failures in more subtle ways as well—for example, through the emotions they convey (M.-L. Chang & Davis, 2009; C. Reyna & Weiner, 2001; Weiner, 2005). They're often sympathetic and forgiving when children fail for uncontrollable reasons (illness, lack of ability, etc.) but frequently get angry when children fail simply because they didn't try very hard. As an example, let's return once more to the opening case study, in which Michael is initially doing poorly in his eighth-grade algebra class. Imagine that you are Michael's teacher. Imagine, too, that you believe Michael has low ability: He just doesn't have a "gift" for math. When you see him consistently getting Ds and Fs on assignments and quizzes, you might reasonably conclude that his poor performance is beyond his control, leading you to communicate pity and sympathy in your interactions with him. But now imagine, instead, that you believe Michael has *high* math ability: He definitely has what it takes to do well in your class. When you see his poor marks on assignments and quizzes, you naturally assume he isn't trying very hard. In your eyes Michael has complete control over the amount of effort he exerts; thus, you might express anger or annoyance when he doesn't do well. With such an attribution, some teachers might even punish him for his poor performance (C. Reyna & Weiner, 2001).

HOW TEACHER ATTRIBUTIONS AND EXPECTATIONS AFFECT STUDENTS' ACHIEVEMENT

MyEdLab
Video Example 11.8.
A classroom climate of respect and risk-taking enhances students' motivation to learn.

Most students readily pick up on their teachers' subtle messages about their own and others' abilities (R. Butler, 1994; T. L. Good & Nichols, 2001; R. S. Weinstein, 2002). When teachers repeatedly convey low-ability messages, students may begin to see themselves as their teachers do, and to behave accordingly (Marachi, Friedel, & Midgley, 2001; Murdock, 1999; van den Bergh et al., 2010). In such cases, teachers' attributions and expectations can lead to a **self-fulfilling prophecy**: What teachers expect students to achieve becomes what students actually *do* achieve.

A classic study by Rosenthal and Jacobson (1968) provides an example. Near the end of the school year, researchers administered something they called the "Harvard Test of Inflected Acquisition" to elementary school students in a low-income neighborhood. Just before school resumed the following fall, the researchers gave teachers the names of students who, according to the test results, would probably show dramatic achievement gains during the school year. In fact, the researchers had chosen these academic "spurters" at random—essentially pulling their names out of a hat. Despite the researchers' bogus predictions, the chosen children made greater achievement gains during the school year than their nonchosen classmates, and teachers rated these children in more favorable terms (e.g., as being more intellectually curious). The results were especially dramatic for children in grades 1 and 2.

Certainly teacher expectations don't always lead to self-fulfilling prophecies. In some cases teachers follow up on their initially low assessments of students' abilities by offering the instruction and assistance that students need to improve, and students *do* improve. In other cases students may develop an "I'll show *you*" attitude that spurs them on to greater effort and achievement than a teacher anticipated. In still other cases assertive parents step in and offer evidence that their children are more capable than a teacher initially thought (Dweck & Molden, 2005; Goldenberg, 1992; T. L. Good & Nichols, 2001).

When one of the authors of this book was a beginning teacher, his new colleagues went through all of his class rosters with him and gave him much prior information about his students. He was told about their prior achievement, their behavior, their family backgrounds, and just about anything else that his colleagues could think of. Providing such information can be helpful to an educator, but it also can set up self-fulfilling prophecies. For example, if a new teacher is told that "Johnny cheats on tests," then the teacher may view Johnny as being dishonest from the start; if Johnny had decided to change his ways, he might have a difficult time escaping his prior reputation if all of the sordid details are passed down to new teachers. On the other hand, this is certainly relevant information to share with colleagues. Thus the decision about whether or not to provide such information to colleagues is complex; we need to weigh the implications of providing this information, and make careful decisions.

Research studies have revealed that teachers' expectations—whether for individual students or for an entire class of students—*do* have an effect on achievement (Hattie, 2009; R. Rosenthal, 2002). On average, girls, students from low-income families, and students from ethnic minority groups are more susceptible to teacher expectations than are boys from European American backgrounds. Teacher expectations also appear to have a greater influence in the early elementary school years (grades 1 and 2), the first year of secondary school and, more generally, the first few weeks of school—in other words, at times when students are entering new and unfamiliar school environments (de Boer, Bosker, & van der Werf, 2010; Hinnant, O'Brien, & Ghazarian, 2009; Jussim, Eccles, & Madon, 1996; Kuklinski & Weinstein, 2001).

As teachers, we're most likely to motivate students to achieve at high levels when we attribute their successes and failures to things over which either they or we have control and when, as a result, we have realistically optimistic expectations for their performance. The Into the Classroom feature "Forming Productive Attributions and Expectations for Student Performance" presents several research-based strategies. However, we must be careful when we attribute either success or failure to students' *effort*. There are at least two occasions when effort attributions can backfire. To see what we mean, try the next exercise.

> Be especially careful not to form unwarranted expectations for students at transition points in their academic careers.

EXPERIENCING FIRSTHAND
CARBERRY AND SEVILLE #2

1. Imagine that Professor Carberry wants you to learn to spell the word *psychoceramics* correctly. He gives you 10 minutes of intensive training in spelling the word and then praises you profusely for spelling it correctly. In which of the following ways would you be most likely to respond?

   a. You're delighted that he approves of your performance.
   b. You proudly show him that you've also learned how to spell *sociocosmetology*.
   c. You wonder, "Hey, is this all he thinks I can do?"

2. Now imagine that you drop by Professor Seville's office to find out why you did so poorly on her sociocosmetology exam. She smiles warmly and suggests that you simply try harder next time. But you tried as hard as you could the *first* time. Which one of the following conclusions would you be most likely to draw?

   a. You need to try even harder next time.
   b. You need to exert the same amount of effort the next time and keep your fingers crossed that you'll make some lucky guesses.
   c. Perhaps you just weren't meant to be a sociocosmetologist.

Chances are good that you answered *c* to both questions. Let's first consider the situation in which Carberry spent 10 minutes teaching you how to spell *psychoceramics*. When students succeed at a very easy task and are then praised for their effort, they may get the unintended message that their teacher doesn't have much confidence in their ability (Graham, 1991; Schunk & Pajares, 2004). Attributing students' successes to effort is apt to be beneficial only when students have, in fact, exerted a great deal of effort.

Now consider the second scenario, in which Seville encouraged you to try harder even though you'd previously studied very hard indeed. When students fail at a task on which they've expended a great deal of effort and are then told that they didn't try hard enough, they're likely to conclude that they simply don't have the ability to perform the task successfully (Curtis & Graham, 1991; Robertson, 2000; Stipek, 1996). In such circumstances it's usually better to attribute their failure to ineffective strategies. Students can and do acquire more effective learning and study strategies over time, especially when they're specifically trained to use these strategies. By teaching effective strategies, we not only promote students' academic success but we also foster the belief that they can *control* their success (Miranda, Villaescusa, & Vidal-Abarca, 1997; C. E. Weinstein, Hagen, & Meyer, 1991).

> Chapter 7 offers suggestions for teaching learning and study strategies.

Into The Classroom

Forming Productive Attributions and Expectations for Student Performance

🍎 **Remember that teachers can definitely make a difference.**
The teachers at a historically low-achieving middle school in a poor, inner-city neighborhood meet once a month to learn about teaching strategies that are especially effective with children from low-income families. They experiment with various strategies in their own classrooms and share especially effective strategies at their group meetings.

🍎 **Look for strengths in every student.**
A 9-year-old girl who lives in a homeless shelter seems to have learned little about punctuation and capitalization, and her spelling is more typical of a first grader than a fourth grader. Nonetheless, the stories she writes often have unusual plot twists and creative endings. Her teacher suspects that her frequent moves from one school to another have left big gaps in her knowledge of written language and so finds a parent volunteer who can work with her on her writing several times a week.

🍎 **Consider multiple possible explanations for students' low achievement and classroom misbehavior.**
Several seventh-grade teachers are sharing their experiences with a student who, at age 8, suffered a traumatic brain injury when he fell off a kitchen counter and landed on his head. His art and music teachers describe him as very disruptive in class and believe that he intentionally misbehaves in order to draw attention to himself. In contrast, his math and science teachers have found that he can easily stay on task—and can often achieve at average to above-average levels—so long as they provide reasonable structure for assignments and classroom behavior. They also realize that some children with brain injuries have trouble inhibiting inappropriate behaviors through no fault of their own.

🍎 **Communicate optimism about what students can accomplish.**
In September a high school teacher tells his class, "Next spring I will ask you to write a 15-page research paper. Fifteen pages may seem like a lot now, but in the next few months we'll work on the various skills you'll need to research and write your paper. By April, 15 pages won't seem like a big deal at all!"

🍎 **Objectively assess students' progress, and be open to evidence that contradicts your initial assessments of students' abilities.**
A kindergarten teacher initially has low expectations for the daughter of migrant workers, a girl named Lupita who has previously had little access to books, toys, and other educational resources. When a video camera captures Lupita's strong leadership ability and skill in assembling puzzles, the teacher realizes that she has considerable potential and works hard to help her acquire the math and literacy skills she'll need to be successful in first grade.

🍎 **Attribute students' successes to a combination of high ability and controllable factors such as effort and learning strategies.**
In a unit on basketball, a middle school physical education teacher tells students, "From what I've seen so far, you all have the capability to play a good game of basketball. And it appears that many of you have been regularly practicing after school."

🍎 **Attribute students' successes to effort only when they have actually exerted considerable effort.**
A teacher observes that his students have completed a particular assignment more quickly and easily than he expected. He briefly acknowledges their success and then moves on to a more challenging task.

🍎 **Attribute students' failures to factors that are controllable and easily remedied.**
A high school student seeks his teacher's advice about how he might improve his performance in her class. "I know you can do better than you have been, Frank," she replies. "I wonder if part of the problem might be that with your part-time job and all of your extracurricular activities, you just don't have enough time to study. Let's sit down before school tomorrow and look at what and how much you're doing to prepare for class."

🍎 **When students fail despite obvious effort, attribute their failures to a lack of effective strategies and help them acquire such strategies.**
A student in an advanced science class is having difficulty with the teacher's challenging weekly quizzes. The student works diligently on her science every night and attends the after-school help sessions her teacher offers, but to no avail. The teacher observes that the student is trying to learn the material by rote—an ineffective strategy for answering the higher-level questions typically presented on the quizzes—and teaches her strategies that promote more meaningful learning.

🍎 **Explicitly teach students to form productive attributions for their successes and failures.**
A boy with a learning disability has particular trouble with mathematics. As his special education teacher works with him on developing his math problem-solving skills, she urges him to make self-talk statements that attribute failures to temporary setbacks he can overcome with more effort and different strategies—for example, "I mustn't give up. I need to use a different approach and see if that one might work better."

Sources: Brophy, 2006; Carrasco, 1981 (Lupita example); Curtis, 1992; Dweck, 2000, 2009; J. W. Fowler & Peterson, 1981; Hattie, 2009; Hawley, 2005 (brain injury example); J. A. Langer, 2000; Pressley, Borkowski, & Schneider, 1987; Robertson, 2000; Roeser, Marachi, & Gehlbach, 2002; Skaalvik & Skaalvik, 2008; R. S. Weinstein, Madison, & Kuklinski, 1995.

A TARGETS Mnemonic for Remembering Motivational Strategies

Many strategies for enhancing students' motivation in the classroom can be summed up in seven words or phrases: task, autonomy, recognition, grouping, evaluation, time, and social support (L. H. Anderman & Anderman, 2009; J. L. Epstein, 1989; Maehr & Anderman, 1993). This multifaceted TARGETS approach to motivation is presented in Table 11.5. If you look closely at the entries in the table, you'll find that they reflect many of the concepts we've addressed in the preceding sections. And especially if you look at Column 2, you'll be convinced, as we are, that teachers clearly *can* make a difference—in fact, a very sizable one—not only in promoting students' learning but in enhancing their motivation as well.

MyEdLab **Self-Check 11.3**

MyEdLab **Application Exercise 11.4.** In this exercise you can associate teacher feedback with attributions students are likely to make about achievement.

MyEdLab **Application Exercise 11.5.** In this exercise you can practice identifying and explaining strategies used by Mr. Boone that have a significant impact on student motivation.

PRINCIPLES/ASSUMPTIONS

TABLE 11.5 • Seven "TARGETS" Principles of Motivation

PRINCIPLE	EDUCATIONAL IMPLICATIONS	EXAMPLE
Classroom **tasks** affect motivation.	• Present new topics through tasks that students find interesting and engaging. • Encourage meaningful rather than rote learning. • Relate activities to students' lives and goals. • Provide sufficient support to enable students to be successful.	• Ask students to conduct a scientific investigation about an issue that concerns them.
The amount of **autonomy** students have affects motivation, especially intrinsic motivation.	• Give students some choice about what and how they learn. • Teach self-regulation strategies. • Solicit students' opinions about classroom practices and policies. • Have students take leadership roles in some activities.	• Let students choose among several ways of accomplishing an instructional goal, being sure that each choice offers sufficient scaffolding to make success likely.
The amount and nature of the **recognition** students receive affect motivation.	• Acknowledge not only academic successes but also personal and social successes. • Commend students for improvement as well as for mastery. • Provide concrete reinforcers for achievement only when students are not intrinsically motivated to learn. • Show students how their own efforts and strategies are directly responsible for their successes.	• Commend students for a successful community service project.
The **grouping** procedures in the classroom affect motivation.	• Provide frequent opportunities for students to interact (e.g., cooperative learning activities, peer tutoring). • Plan small-group activities in which all students can make significant contributions. • Teach the social skills that students need to interact effectively with peers.	• Have students work in small groups to tackle a challenging issue or problem for which there are two or more legitimate solutions.
The forms of **evaluation** in the classroom affect motivation.	• Make evaluation criteria clear; specify them in advance. • Minimize or eliminate competition for grades (e.g., don't grade on a curve). • Give specific feedback about what students are doing well. • Give concrete suggestions about how students can improve. • Teach students how to evaluate their own work.	• Give students concrete criteria with which they can evaluate the quality of their own writing.
How teachers schedule **time** affects motivation.	• Give students enough time to achieve mastery of important topics and skills. • Let students' interests dictate some activities. • Include variety in the school day (e.g., intersperse high-energy activities among more sedentary ones). • Include opportunities for independent learning in the school day.	• After explaining a new concept, engage students in a hands-on activity that lets them see the concept in action.
The amount of **social support** students believe they have in the classroom affects motivation.	• Create an atmosphere of caring, respect, and support among all class members. • Convey affection and respect for every student, along with a genuine eagerness to help every student succeed. • Create situations in which all students feel comfortable participating actively in classroom activities (including students who are excessively shy, students who have limited academic skills, students who have physical disabilities, etc.).	• When working with students who seem chronically disengaged from lessons, identify their specific areas of strength and provide opportunities for them to showcase their expertise in the classroom.

Sources: L. H. Anderman & Anderman, 2009; L. H. Anderman, Andrzejewski, & Allen, 2011; L. H. Anderman, Patrick, Hruda, & Linnenbrink, 2002; J. L. Epstein, 1989; Maehr & Anderman, 1993; Patrick et al., 1997.

Applying Brain Research

Understanding Why and How Emotions Influence Learning

A key brain structure in affect is the *amygdala*, an almond-shaped part of the limbic system, which lies in the middle of the brain. We humans have two amygdalae, one each in our left and right hemispheres. The amygdala is especially active in unpleasant feelings (e.g., fear, stress, anger, and depression) and in automatic emotional reactions (e.g., impulsive aggression).

The amygdala has many interconnections with brain structures that underlie and support learning and cognition, including the hippocampus, anterior cingulate cortex, and prefrontal cortex. For one thing, the amygdala alerts us to stimuli in our environment that might in some way threaten our survival. In addition, it enables us to associate particular emotions with particular stimuli or memories. As a result, affective reactions are often closely intertwined with human thinking and learning (Adolphs & Damasio, 2001; Kuhbandner, Spitzer, & Pekrun, 2011; Phelps & Sharot, 2008; M. I. Posner & Rothbart, 2007).

A good deal of emotion-based learning takes the form of *implicit knowledge*—knowledge over which we have little or no conscious awareness and control. For example, such out-of-awareness knowledge might lead us to feel anxious in certain situations without knowing *why* we feel anxious, and it can sometimes lead us to make decisions that are neither rational nor productive (Damasio, 1994; Marcus, 2008; Minsky, 2006; Sapolsky, 2005).

With the close interconnections between emotion and cognition in mind, we offer two general recommendations:

🍎 **Remember that, for better or for worse, learning often involves acquiring emotions as well as knowledge and skills.** Students' feelings are integral parts of what they "know" about various topics and events (Bower & Forgas, 2001; Clore, Gasper, & Garvin, 2001; Minsky, 2006). Sometimes this knowledge is beneficial, but at other times it can work against students' best interests. For example, we would certainly like students to know that reading a good book can be a source of pleasure, but it's not helpful for them to "know" that mathematics is apt to evoke only frustration and anxiety.

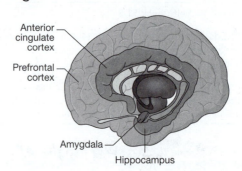

Create conditions that foster arousal and attention without generating undue stress. Early in the chapter we suggested that humans may have a basic need for arousal—a basic need for either physical or cognitive stimulation—but that we also like our arousal to be at a certain optimal level that feels good. Arousal has an emotional element as well, and at very high levels it can feel quite unpleasant. High, stressful arousal levels increase activity in the amygdala in ways that interfere with the functioning of more "rational" structures such as the hippocampus and prefrontal cortex. Furthermore, lengthy periods of high stress—as might be true for someone who lives in chronically dangerous conditions—can cause permanent damage to the prefrontal cortex (Nisbett, 2009; Sapolsky, 2005).

In the classroom, piquing students' interest and engagement in classroom topics and activities can effectively capitalize on the "good" side of arousal. In contrast, creating constant stress about doing well—and continually reminding students of the negative ramifications of *not* doing well—will adversely affect students' learning, development, and general well-being, quite possibly for the long term.

Affect and Its Effects

A close partner of motivation is **affect**: the emotions and general moods that a learner brings to bear on a task. Virtually any form of affect has both psychological elements (subjective feelings) and physiological elements (changes in heart rate, perspiration, muscular tension, etc.). Some forms of affect—such as happiness, excitement, and pride—feel both psychologically and physiologically pleasant. Other forms—such as fear, anger, and shame—feel both psychologically and physiologically aversive.

Affect has its basis in the brain, of course; the Applying Brain Research feature "Understanding How and Why Emotions Influence Learning" provides more details. Furthermore, each form of affect probably has a specific function (Izard, 2007; Minsky, 2006; Tamir, 2009). For example, when we face a dangerous situation, our fearful reaction includes an increased heart rate and muscular tension that spur us to take action, typically a response involving either *fight* or *flight.* In contrast, when we find ourselves enjoying the company of others, we're apt to smile, laugh, and in other ways nurture interpersonal relationships.

HOW AFFECT AND MOTIVATION ARE INTERRELATED

Without doubt, people's automatic emotional reactions to certain events—for instance, a quick, fearful retreat from someone who is wielding a gun or knife—are designed to keep them alive.

But affect also plays a significant role in the more planful, goal-directed aspects of human motivation. As a general rule, people act in ways they think will help them feel happy and comfortable rather than sad, confused, or angry, although they may occasionally work themselves into an angry frenzy as a way of helping them achieve certain outcomes (Mellers & McGraw, 2001; Tamir, 2009; J. L. Tsai, 2007).

Some emotions, known as self-conscious emotions, are closely tied to people's self-evaluations and thus affect their sense of self-worth (M. Lewis & Sullivan, 2005; Pekrun, 2006). When people evaluate their own actions and accomplishments as being consistent with their culture's standards for appropriate and desirable behavior, they're apt to feel pride. When, in contrast, they see themselves as failing to live up to those standards—for instance, when they thoughtlessly cause harm to someone else—they're apt to feel guilt and shame.

Affect and motivation are interrelated in other ways as well. For instance, intrinsic motivation is closely connected with pleasure and enjoyment. Learners tackle challenging tasks more willingly and effectively when they enjoy what they're doing, and their successful efforts often bring on feelings of excitement and pride (Linnenbrink & Pintrich, 2004; Pekrun, Goetz, Titz, & Perry, 2002; Shernoff & Csikszentmihalyi, 2009). Learners are especially likely to feel excited about their successes if they didn't expect to be successful, but they'll also experience more intense negative emotions about their failures—and often about the activity in question—if they didn't expect to fail (Bower & Forgas, 2001; Shepperd & McNulty, 2002). Their specific reactions will depend on how they *interpret* the outcomes of events—in particular, whether they hold themselves, other people, environmental circumstances, or something else responsible for what has happened (recall the earlier discussion of *attributions*).

Another emotion we mustn't overlook is boredom—a generally unpleasant feeling that results from a lack of stimulation and arousal (Pekrun et al., 2010). Boredom-inducing activities can take a variety of forms: They might be either too easy or too difficult for learners' current ability levels, or they might involve repetitive, monotonous tasks that seemingly have little relevance to learners' lives. Learners who are bored in their current environment will either seek to escape it or else create their own stimulation—perhaps in the form of passing notes across the aisle or checking their cell phones for recent text messages. In classroom settings, then, students who are bored with the topic at hand are unlikely to pay much attention to or benefit from instructional activities. In addition, when students are bored, achievement suffers, and this lowered achievement leads to additional boredom (Daschmann, Nett, Wimmer, Goetz, & Stupnisky, 2010; Nett, Goetz, & Hall, 2011; Pekrun et al., 2010, Pekrun, Hall, Goetz, & Perry, 2014). A student who is neither intrinsically nor extrinsically motivated may very well be bored (see Figure 11.1).

HOW AFFECT IS RELATED TO LEARNING AND COGNITION

As the Applying Brain Research feature reveals, brain structures that underlie affect and those that support cognition are closely interconnected. It's not surprising, then, that learners' affective reactions are often inextricably intertwined with their thinking and learning (Damasio, 1994; D. K. Meyer & Turner, 2002). For example, while learning how to perform a task, students simultaneously learn whether or not they like doing it (Zajonc, 1980). And students who feel frustrated and anxious when they struggle to master new material (as Michael initially does in the opening case study) may acquire a dislike for the topic (Carver & Scheier, 1990; Goetz, Frenzel, Hall, & Pekrun, 2008; Stodolsky, Salk, & Glaessner, 1991). Sixteen-year-old Megan expressed her feelings about mastery and non-mastery this way:

> When I haven't learned something I tend to say that I hate it, because I don't understand it. When I am excited and can have a discussion about something is when I know that I fully understand and have studied enough on that topic. (Quote courtesy of Brian Zottoli)

Learners can also associate specific topics and pieces of information with certain emotions—a phenomenon known as hot cognition. On average, learners are more likely to pay attention to, think actively about, and remember emotionally charged information (Bower, 1994; Heuer & Reisberg, 1992; Zeelenberg, Wagenmakers, & Rotteveel, 2006). Sometimes the nature of a topic itself evokes hot cognition, perhaps because it invokes feelings of sympathy for people in dire straits or a sense of outrage about blatant violations of some people's basic human rights.

Information that conflicts with what learners currently know or believe can also evoke hot cognition. In particular, such information can cause learners considerable mental discomfort, something that Piaget called *disequilibrium* but many contemporary theorists call cognitive dissonance. This dissonance typically leads learners to try to resolve the inconsistency in some way, perhaps undergoing conceptual change or perhaps ignoring or discrediting the new information (Buehl & Alexander, 2001; Harmon-Jones, 2001; Zohar & Aharon-Kraversky, 2005). A contemporary example is the heated debates over climate change. Whereas scientists generally agree that the Earth's climate is changing, there is much debate about this issue, resulting in the expression of a variety of emotions (Sinatra, Kardash, Taasoobshirazi, & Lombardi, 2012).

How effectively learners think about and make sense of new information also depends on their overall affective state—their general *mood*—while they're studying. They're most likely to engage in meaningful learning and think creatively about a topic if they're in an emotionally positive frame of mind. If, instead, they feel generally sad, frustrated, or bored, they're apt to process new information in superficial, inflexible ways—for instance, through mindless rehearsal (Ahmed, van der Werf, Kuyper, & Minnaert, 2013; Efklides, 2011; Fredrickson, 2009; Pekrun, 2006; R. E. Snow, Corno, & Jackson, 1996). As classroom teachers, we should remind our students that their moods affect their ability to study—thus we can tell our students that if they are in a very bad mood, they might want to put off studying until a later time (but not put it off indefinitely!).

One critical way to promote positive affect in the classroom, of course, is to address students' needs (e.g., for competence, relatedness, etc.). Researchers have suggested several additional ways in which we might increase positive affect:

- Occasionally incorporate gamelike features into classroom tasks and activities (e.g., crossword puzzles for practicing new spelling words, a television game-show format for a history class review).
- Adjust task difficulty to a level that students believe they can handle.
- Have students ask themselves questions that help them focus on the positive aspects of classroom activities and school in general (e.g., "What excites me about ___?" "What did I enjoy about ___?"). (Brophy, 2004; Pekrun, 2006; Townsend, 2008)

One form of affect—anxiety—can have either positive or negative effects on learning and cognition, depending on the circumstances. Because so many students experience anxiety at school, and because instructional practices and the classroom environment can contribute significantly to students' anxiety levels, we'll look at this particular form of affect more closely.

ANXIETY IN THE CLASSROOM

Imagine that, as a college student enrolled in Professor Carberry's advanced psychoceramics course, you must give a half-hour presentation about psychoceramic califractions today. You've read several books and numerous articles on your topic and undoubtedly know more about psychoceramic califractions than any of your classmates. Furthermore, you've meticulously prepared note cards to which you can refer during your presentation. As you sit in class waiting for your turn to speak, you should be feeling calm and confident. But instead you're a nervous wreck: Your heart is pounding wildly, your palms are sweaty, and your stomach is in a knot. When you are finally called to the front of the room, you have trouble remembering what you planned to say and can't read your note cards because your hands are shaking so much. It's not as if you *want* to be nervous about speaking in front of your class, and you can't think of a single reason that you *should* be nervous. You're an expert on your topic, you're not having a bad-hair day, and your peers aren't likely to snicker or throw rotten tomatoes if you make a mistake. So what's the big deal?

You're a victim of anxiety: You have a feeling of uneasiness and apprehension about an event because you're not sure what its outcome will be. Anxiety has both cognitive and affective aspects (R. Carter, Williams, & Silverman, 2008; E. Hong, O'Neil, & Feldon, 2005; Tryon, 1980). Its cognitive aspect involves *worry*—troubling thoughts and beliefs about whether a situation can be effectively dealt with. Its affective aspect involves *emotionality*, which includes both physiological changes (e.g., muscular tension, a rapid heartbeat, increased perspiration) and such behavioral responses as restlessness and pacing. Anxiety is similar to fear, in the sense that both involve high

Get students emotionally involved with classroom subject matter.

MyEdLab
Video Example 11.9.
A teacher's expectations for an individual student or an entire class have an effect on achievement. Ms. McDaniel holds high expectations and reduces anxiety by helping students attribute success and failure to things over which they have control.

levels of arousal. But the two emotions are different in one important respect: Although we're usually afraid of something in particular (e.g., a roaring lion or intense thunder storm), we usually don't know exactly why we're anxious (Lazarus, 1991).

Almost everyone is anxious at one time or another. Many students become anxious just before a test they know will be difficult, and most get nervous before speaking to a large group. Such temporary feelings of anxiety are instances of state anxiety. However, some students are anxious much of the time, even when the situation isn't especially dangerous or threatening. For example, some students get excessively nervous even before very easy exams, and others may be so anxious about mathematics that they can't concentrate on even the simplest math assignment. A learner who shows a pattern of responding with anxiety even in nonthreatening situations has trait anxiety, a chronic condition that often hampers performance.

HOW ANXIETY AFFECTS LEARNING AND PERFORMANCE

Imagine, for a moment, that you aren't anxious at all—not even the teeniest bit—about your grade in Carberry's psychoceramics class. Will you study for his tests? Will you turn in his assignments? If you have no anxiety whatsoever, you might not even buy the textbook or go to class, and you probably won't get a very good grade in the course.

A small amount of anxiety often improves performance: It's facilitating anxiety. A little anxiety spurs learners into action—for instance, making them go to class, complete assignments, and study for exams (see Figure 11.8). In contrast, a great deal of anxiety usually interferes with effective performance: It's debilitating anxiety. Excessive anxiety distracts learners and interferes with their attention to the task at hand.

At what point does anxiety stop facilitating and begin to debilitate performance? Very easy tasks—those that learners can do almost without thinking (e.g., running)—are typically facilitated by a high level of anxiety. But more difficult tasks—those that require considerable thought and mental effort—are best performed with only a small or moderate level of anxiety (Landers, 2007; Sapolsky, 2005; Yerkes & Dodson, 1908). A high level of anxiety in a complex situation can interfere with several aspects of cognition critical for successful learning and performance:

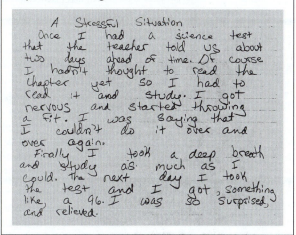

FIGURE 11.8 This writing sample by 14-year-old Loretta illustrates how anxiety can sometimes improve learning and achievement

A Stressful Situation
Once I had a science test that the teacher told us about two days ahead of time. Of course I hadn't thought to read the chapter yet so I had to read it and study. I got nervous and started throwing a fit. I was saying that I couldn't do it over and over again.
Finally I took a deep breath and study as much as I could. The next day I took the test and I got, something like, a 96. I was so surprised, and relieved.

- Paying attention to what needs to be learned and using working memory effectively
- Processing information effectively (e.g., elaborating on or organizing it)
- Retrieving and using previously learned information and skills (Eysenck, 1992; K. L. Fletcher & Cassady, 2010; Hagtvet & Johnsen, 1992; Sarason, 1980; Vukovic et al., 2013)

Anxiety is especially likely to interfere with such cognitive processes when a task places heavy demands on either working memory or long-term memory—for instance, when a task involves problem solving or creativity. In such situations learners may be so preoccupied with the possibility of doing poorly that they can't keep their minds on what they need to accomplish (Ashcraft, 2002; Beilock, 2008; K. L. Fletcher & Cassady, 2010; Turner, Thorpe, & Meyer, 1998; Zeidner & Matthews, 2005).

When asking students to perform difficult tasks, encourage them to do their best, but don't make them unnecessarily anxious about their performance.

SOURCES OF ANXIETY

Learners sometimes develop feelings of anxiety about particular situations through the process of classical conditioning. They're also more likely to experience anxiety, especially debilitating anxiety, when they face a threat, a situation in which they believe they have little or no chance of succeeding. In contrast, learners can experience *facilitating* anxiety when they face a challenge—when they believe they can probably succeed with reasonable effort. Given learners' varying ability levels, tasks that promote facilitating anxiety for some of them can promote debilitating anxiety for others (E. M. Anderman & Dawson, 2011; Combs, Richards, & Richards, 1976; Csikszentmihalyi & Nakamura, 1989; Deci & Ryan, 1992).

Classical conditioning is described in Chapter 9.

Children and adolescents are apt to have some degree of anxiety—possibly facilitating, possibly debilitating—in many of the following circumstances:

- *A situation in which physical safety is at risk*—for example, being regularly exposed to violence at school or in the neighborhood
- *A situation in which self-worth is threatened*—for example, hearing unflattering remarks about one's race or gender
- *Concern about physical appearance*—for example, feeling too fat or too thin, or reaching puberty either earlier or later than peers
- *A new situation*—for example, moving from one school to another midway through the school year
- *Judgment or evaluation by others*—for example, receiving a low grade from a teacher or being disliked or excluded by peers
- *Frustrating subject matter*—for example, having a history of difficulty with one or more content domains (as is true for many students with learning disabilities)
- *Technology*—for example, not knowing how to use the hardware or software required for assigned classroom tasks
- *Excessive classroom demands*—for example, being expected to learn a great deal of material in a very short time
- *Classroom tests*—for example, facing a high-stakes test that affects one's chances for promotion or graduation
- *Physical challenges*—for example, being required to do push-ups in front of one's classmates
- *Concern about the future*—for example, not knowing how to make a living after high school graduation (Benner & Graham, 2009; Cassady, 2004, 2010a; Chabrán, 2003; Covington, 1992; DuBois, Burk-Braxton, Swenson, Tevendale, & Hardesty, 2002; N. J. King & Ollendick, 1989; Martinez & Huberty, 2010; G. Matthews, Zeidner, & Roberts, 2006; Phelan, Yu, & Davidson, 1994; Stipek, 1993; Walton & Cohen, 2007; K. M. Williams, 2001a; Zeidner & Matthews, 2005)

Learners' particular concerns change somewhat as they grow older. Table 11.6 describes developmental trends in anxiety, as well as in affect more generally, across childhood and adolescence. For many children, one highly anxiety-arousing period is the transition from elementary school to secondary school—usually at the beginning of middle school or junior high but in some cases at the beginning of high school. We look at this issue next.

A MULTIPLE WHAMMY: MAKING THE TRANSITION TO A SECONDARY SCHOOL FORMAT

Elementary school classrooms are often warm, nurturing places in which teachers get to know 20 to 30 students very well. Students in elementary classrooms also get to know *one another* quite well: They often work together on academic tasks and may even see themselves as members of a classroom "family." But somewhere around fifth to seventh grade, many students move from elementary school to a middle school or junior high school. As they do so, they simultaneously encounter numerous changes in the nature of their schooling:

- The school is larger and has more students.
- Students have several teachers, and each teacher has many students. Thus teacher–student relationships are more superficial and less personal than in elementary school, and teachers have less awareness of how well individual students are understanding and mastering classroom subject matter.
- There is more whole-class instruction, with less individualized instruction that takes into account each student's academic needs.
- Classes are less socially cohesive. Students may not know their classmates very well and thus may be reluctant to ask peers for assistance.
- Students have fewer opportunities to make choices about the topics they pursue and the tasks they complete. At the same time, they have more independence and responsibility regarding their learning. For example, they may have relatively unstructured assignments to

DEVELOPMENTAL TRENDS

TABLE 11.6 • Affect at Different Grade Levels

GRADE LEVEL	AGE-TYPICAL CHARACTERISTICS	EXAMPLE	SUGGESTED STRATEGIES
K–2	• Possible culture shock and intense anxiety upon beginning school, especially if students have had little or no formal preschool experience • Possible separation anxiety when parents first leave the classroom (especially in the first few days of kindergarten) • Reduced anxiety when teachers and other adults are warm and supportive • Only limited control of overt emotional behaviors (e.g., may cry easily if distressed or act impulsively if frustrated)	Although Jeff has attended preschool since age 2, he's quite nervous about going to kindergarten. On his first day at the "big kids' school," he's reluctant to say good-bye to his mother. When Mom finally tells him she has to leave, he bursts into tears—a reaction that some of his classmates will taunt him about for several years.	• Ask parents about routines followed at home; when appropriate, incorporate these routines into classroom procedures. • If possible, provide an opportunity for students to meet you a few days or weeks before school begins. • Be warm, caring, and supportive with all students (but check school policies about hugs and other forms of physical affection). • Address inappropriate behaviors gently but firmly.
3–5	• Increasing control of overt emotional behaviors • Emergence of math anxiety for some students, especially if they receive little or no assistance with math tasks • Tendency for close friends (especially girls) to talk about and ruminate on negative emotional events; continues into adolescence • Possible stress as a result of others' racist and sexist behaviors (e.g., racial slurs, unkind remarks about emerging sexual characteristics); continues into adolescence	For 9-year-old Tina, basic arithmetic procedures with whole numbers are easy to understand. But she can make no sense of the new procedures she's learning for fractions—how to find common denominators, divide one fraction by another, and so on—and becomes increasingly frustrated when her attempts to solve fraction problems yield incorrect answers. Her aversion to math soon leads her to avoid the subject whenever possible, both in and outside of school.	• Ensure that students master basic concepts and procedures before proceeding to more complex material that depends on those concepts (especially important in teaching math, a subject area in which advanced knowledge and skills build on more basic ones). • Monitor students' behaviors for signs of serious anxiety or depression; talk with students privately if they seem overly anxious or upset, and consult with the school counselor if necessary. • Insist on respect for all class members' characteristics, feelings, and backgrounds; don't tolerate racist or sexist remarks or actions.
6–8	• General decline in positive, upbeat emotions; extreme mood swings, partly as a result of hormonal changes accompanying puberty • Increased anxiety and potential depression accompanying the transition to middle school or junior high school • Decrease in enjoyment of school (especially for boys) • Increasing anxiety about peer relationships and social acceptance	At the beginning of seventh grade, 12-year-old Jeannie moves from a small, close-knit elementary school to a large junior high school. At her new school she knows only a few students in each class, and her teachers present themselves as cold, no-nonsense disciplinarians. Jeannie struggles in her efforts to make new friends and feels awkward when she must occasionally sit by herself in the cafeteria. Before long, she regularly complains of stomachaches so that she can stay home from school.	• Expect mood swings, but monitor students' behavior for signs of long-term depression. • Make a personal connection with every student; express confidence that students can succeed with effort, and offer support that can facilitate success. • Design activities that capture students' interest in the subject matter; relate topics to students' personal lives and goals. • Provide opportunities for students to form supportive friendships with classmates (e.g., assign cooperative group projects).
9–12	• Continuing emotional volatility (especially in grades 9 and 10) • Increasing ability to reflect on and control extreme emotional reactions, due in part to ongoing brain maturation • Considerable anxiety about school if transition to a secondary school format has been delayed until high school • Susceptibility to serious depression in the face of significant stress • Increasing prevalence of debilitating anxiety regarding tests, especially high-stakes tests • Feelings of uncertainty about life after graduation	In a text message to a classmate, 15-year-old Jonathan reveals his crush on a popular cheerleader. The classmate thinks the message is amusing ("I can't believe that loser thinks he has a chance with the head cheerleader!") and forwards it to more than 50 members of the sophomore class. Jonathan is at a loss about how to cope with his humiliation and contemplates suicide as the only solution to the problem. (*Teachers should* **immediately** *report any suspicions of planned suicides to school personnel who can effectively intervene.*)	• Be especially supportive if students have just made the transition from an elementary school format (e.g., show personal interest in students' well-being, teach effective study skills). • Take seriously any signs that a student may be considering suicide (e.g., overt or veiled threats, such as "I won't be around much longer"; actions that indicate "putting one's affairs in order," such as giving away prized possessions). • Give frequent classroom assessments so that no single test score is a "fatal" one; help students prepare for high-stakes tests. • Present multiple options for postgraduation career paths.

Sources: Arnett, 1999; Ashcraft, 2002; Benes, 2007; Benner & Graham, 2009; Chabrán, 2003; DuBois et al., 2002; Eccles & Midgley, 1989; Elkind, 1981; Gentry, Gable, & Rizza, 2002; K. T. Hill & Sarason, 1966; Hine & Fraser, 2002; Kerns & Lieberman, 1993; Kuhl & Kraska, 1989; Lapsley, 1993; Larson & Brown, 2007; Larson, Moneta, Richards, & Wilson, 2002; D. K. Meyer & Turner, 2006; Midgley, Middleton, Gheen, & Kumar, 2002; Roderick & Camburn, 1999; A. J. Rose, 2002; Rudolph, Lambert, Clark, & Kurlakowsky, 2001; Seiffge-Krenke, Aunola, & Nurmi, 2009; R. E. Snow et al., 1996; Spear, 2000; R. M. Thomas, 2005; Tomback, Williams, & Wentzel, 2005; Wiles & Bondi, 2001.

be accomplished over a 2- or 3-week period, and they must take the initiative to seek help when they're struggling.

- Teachers place greater emphasis on demonstrating (rather than acquiring) competence, reflecting a shift from mastery-approach goals to performance goals. Thus mistakes are more costly for students.

- Standards for assigning grades are more rigorous, so students may earn lower grades than they did in elementary school. Grades are often assigned on a comparative and competitive basis, with only the highest-achieving students getting As and Bs.

- There is an increase in the use of between-class ability grouping. Thus students are more likely to label each other as "smart" or "not smart" in different subject areas.

- High-stakes tests—tests that affect promotion to the next grade level—become increasingly common. (E. M. Anderman & Mueller, 2010; H. A. Davis, 2003; Dijkstra et al., 2008; Eccles & Midgley, 1989; Hine & Fraser, 2002; Midgley, Middleton, Gheen, & Kumar, 2002; Wentzel & Wigfield, 1998; Wigfield et al., 2006; Yeung, Lau, & Nie, 2011)

Furthermore, previously formed friendships can be disrupted as students move to new (and perhaps differing) schools (Pellegrini & Long, 2004; Wentzel, 1999). And of course, students are also dealing with the physiological changes that accompany puberty and adolescence.

This multiple whammy of changes often leads to decreased confidence, a lower sense of self-worth, less intrinsic motivation, and considerable anxiety. Focus on peer relationships increases, and academic achievement drops. Some students become quite depressed or emotionally disengaged from the school environment, increasing the odds that they eventually will drop out of school (E. M. Anderman & Mueller, 2010; G. L. Cohen & Garcia, 2008; Danner, 2011; Eccles & Midgley, 1989; Gentry et al., 2002; Urdan & Maehr, 1995).

If students remain in a small elementary school environment in early adolescence, rather than moving to a larger middle or junior high school, their emotions and motivation are more likely to remain healthy and productive (E. M. Anderman, 1998, 2002; Midgley et al., 2002; Rudolph, Lambert, Clark, & Kurlakowsky, 2001). By the time they reach ninth grade, however, they almost inevitably make the transition to a secondary school format, where they experience many of the changes that their peers elsewhere experienced a few grades earlier (Benner & Graham, 2009; Hine & Fraser, 2002; Midgley et al., 2002; Tomback et al., 2005).

Students who make a smooth transition to secondary school are more likely to be successful there and, as a result, are more likely to graduate from high school. As teachers, the particular school environment we create for adolescents can make a world of difference for their personal, social, and academic well-being (E. M. Anderman & Mueller, 2010; M.-T. Wang & Holcombe, 2010). The Into the Classroom feature "Easing the Transition to Middle and Secondary School" suggests several strategies for teachers in the middle school and high school grades.

Alamy

Students entering the middle school grades face new challenges—more stringent evaluation criteria, less individualized instruction, greater competition in classes and sports, and so on— while also undergoing the unsettling physiological changes of puberty.

Chapter 3 offers specific recommendations for promoting productive interactions with peers.

KEEPING STUDENTS' ANXIETY AT A FACILITATIVE LEVEL

Even when students aren't making a significant transition from one educational setting to another, they may have many reasons to be anxious at school. We can address their concerns about social matters—for instance, their worries about peer relationships—by teaching social skills and planning activities that foster frequent and productive student interactions. And we can address their concerns about an uncertain future by teaching skills that will be marketable in the adult world and providing assistance with college applications.

But perhaps most important, we must take steps to ensure that students don't become overly anxious about classroom tasks and subject matter. Because anxiety is—like all emotions— largely beyond students' immediate control, simply telling them to calm down is unlikely to be effective. The key is to prevent rather than "cure" debilitating anxiety. Following are several strategies that should keep students' anxiety at a facilitative level:

- Communicate clear, concrete, and realistic expectations for performance.
- Match instruction to students' cognitive levels and capabilities (e.g., use concrete materials to teach math to students not yet capable of abstract thought).

Into The Classroom

Easing the Transition to Middle and Secondary School

- **Provide a means through which every student can feel part of a small, close-knit group.**
  During the first week of school, a ninth-grade math teacher forms three- to four-member *base groups* that provide support and assistance for one another throughout the school year. At the beginning or end of every class period, the teacher gives group members 5 minutes to help one another with questions and concerns about daily lessons and homework assignments.

- **Find time to meet one on one with every student.**
  Early in the school year, while students are working on a variety of cooperative learning activities, a middle school social studies teacher schedules individual appointments with each of his students. In these meetings he searches for interests that he and his students share and encourages the students to seek him out whenever they need help with academic or personal problems. Throughout the semester he continues to touch base with individual students (often during lunch or before or after school) to see how they're doing.

- **Teach students the skills they need to be successful independent learners.**
  After discovering that few of her students know how to take effective class notes, a high school science teacher distributes a daily notes "skeleton" that guides them through the note-taking process. The skeleton includes headings such as "Topic of the Lesson," "Definitions," "Important Ideas," and "Examples." As students' class notes improve over the course of the school year, the teacher gradually reduces the amount of structure she provides.

- **Assign grades based on mastery, not on comparisons with peers, and provide reasonable opportunities for improvement.**
  A junior high school language arts teacher requires students to submit two drafts of every essay and short story he assigns; he gives students the option of submitting additional drafts as well. He judges each composition on several criteria, including quality of ideas, organization and cohesiveness, word usage, grammar, and spelling. He explains and illustrates each of these criteria and gives ample feedback on every draft that students turn in.

- **Observe for students who do not fit in with others and are excluded.**
  A group of middle school teachers notice that there are a few students who do not seem to be making friends, and often sit by themselves in the cafeteria. The teachers decide to form "discussion tables" in the cafeteria, where students can join a group to discuss various topics while eating lunch (e.g., current events, sports, video games, etc.). The teachers approach the students who always eat by themselves and invite them to join one of the discussion tables.

- When students have a high level of trait anxiety, provide considerable structure to guide their activities.

- Provide supplementary sources of support for learning challenging topics and skills until mastery is attained (e.g., provide additional practice, individual or computerized tutoring, or a structure for taking notes).

- Teach strategies that can help students improve their overall learning and performance (e.g., effective study skills and self-regulation strategies).

- Assess students' performance independently of how well their classmates are doing, and encourage students to assess their own performance in a similar manner.

- Provide feedback about specific behaviors, rather than global evaluations of performance.

- Remind students that sometimes physiological reactions to academic work (e.g., feeling your heart beat faster or perspiration) may be signs of positive engagement ("your heart sometimes beats faster when you're really enjoying the work"), rather than signs of debilitating anxiety.

- Allow students to correct errors so that no single mistake is ever a "fatal" one. (E. M. Anderman & Dawson, 2011; Brophy, 1986; K. L. Fletcher & Cassady, 2010; Hattie & Timperley, 2007; Huberty, 2008; Jain & Dowson, 2009; Pekrun, 2006; Shute, 2008; Stipek, 1993; Strain, Azevedo, & D'Mello, 2013; Tryon, 1980; Zeidner, 1998)

Chapter 14 offers specific strategies for keeping students' anxiety at reasonable levels during tests and other classroom assessments.

DIVERSITY IN AFFECT

Some people seem to be consistently more emotionally upbeat than others—an individual difference variable that's probably rooted in biology to some degree (Costa & McCrae, 1992; C. Peterson, 2006). In addition, researchers have observed some consistent differences in affect in students of different cultural and ethnic backgrounds, genders, and socioeconomic levels.

CULTURAL AND ETHNIC DIFFERENCES

On average, cultural groups differ in the degree to which they show their feelings in their behaviors and facial expressions. For example, whereas Americans and Mexicans are often quite expressive, people from East Asian cultures tend to be more reserved and may be reluctant to confide in other people in times of sadness or distress (Camras, Chen, Bakeman, Norris, & Cain, 2006; P. M. Cole & Tan, 2007; H. S. Kim, Sherman, & Taylor, 2008). Cultures probably differ most in the extent to which they tolerate overt expressions of anger. Mainstream Western culture encourages children to act and speak up if someone infringes on their rights and needs, and expressing anger in a nonviolent way is considered quite acceptable. In many Southeast Asian cultures, however, any expression of anger is viewed as potentially undermining adults' authority or disrupting social harmony (Adam, Shirako, & Maddux, 2010; Mesquita & Leu, 2007; J. L. Tsai, 2007). Children brought up in some Buddhist communities are encouraged to not even *feel* anger (P. M. Cole, Bruschi, & Tamang, 2002; P. M. Cole, Tamang, & Shrestha, 2006). For example, if unfairly embarrassed or accused, a child who has grown up in the Tamang culture of Nepal might respond, "Tilda bomo khaba?" ("Why be angry?"), because the event has already occurred and being angry about it serves no purpose (P. M. Cole et al., 2002, p. 992).

Even seemingly "positive" emotions aren't always viewed favorably. Some cultures that place a high priority on social harmony discourage children from feeling pride about personal accomplishments, because such an emotion focuses attention on an individual rather than on the overall group (Eid & Diener, 2001). And for some cultural groups, joy and happiness can sometimes be too much of a good thing. For example, many Chinese and Japanese advocate striving for contentment and serenity—relatively calm emotions—rather than joy (Kagan, 2010; Mesquita & Leu, 2007; J. L. Tsai, 2007).

Finally, learners from various cultural backgrounds may have somewhat different sources of anxiety. For instance, some children and adolescents from Asian American families may feel so much family pressure to perform well in school that they experience debilitating test anxiety (Pang, 1995). Students who are clearly in the racial or ethnic minority at their school—for example, African American students at a predominantly European American school, or vice versa—may be especially anxious about whether their majority-group classmates will accept them without prejudice (G. L. Cohen & Garcia, 2008). And recent immigrants are often anxious about a variety of things in their new country: how to behave, how to interpret other people's behaviors, how to make friends, and, more generally, how to make sense of the strange new culture in which they now find themselves (P. M. Cole & Tan, 2007; Dien, 1998; Igoa, 1995).

Anxiety may be at the root of a phenomenon known as **stereotype threat**, which can lead students from stereotypically low-achieving groups to perform more poorly on classroom assessments than they otherwise would simply because they're aware that their group traditionally *does* do poorly (J. Aronson & Steele, 2005; K. E. Ryan & Ryan, 2005; J. L. Smith, 2004). When students are aware of the unflattering stereotype—and especially when they know that the task they're performing reflects their ability in an important domain—their heart rate and other physiological correlates of anxiety go up and their performance goes down (McKown & Weinstein, 2003; Osborne & Simmons, 2002; Walton & Spencer, 2009). We're more likely to see the negative effects of stereotype threat when students interpret their performance as an evaluation of their general competence and self-worth (P. G. Davies & Spencer, 2005; Huguet & Régner, 2007; McKown & Weinstein, 2003). Furthermore, stereotype threat is more likely to arise when students have a fixed mindset (Dweck et al., 2004; Good, et al., 2003; Osborne, Tillman, & Holland, 2010).

GENDER DIFFERENCES

In general, girls express their emotions more openly than boys do. However, girls sometimes hide angry feelings in order to preserve social harmony, whereas boys are often quite willing to show their anger (Eisenberg, Martin, & Fabes, 1996; Lippa, 2002; Sadker & Sadker, 1994). Girls are also more anxious about their classroom performance, which may partly explain their greater diligence in schoolwork (Marsh et al., 2008; Pomerantz, Altermatt, & Saxon, 2002). For instance, girls are more prone to test anxiety than boys are; some become victims of stereotype threat, earning lower scores than they should on tests in stereotypically "male" domains such as math (Ben-Zeev et al., 2005; E. Hong et al., 2005; Huguet & Régner, 2007). Visuospatial working memory

---

Keep in mind that some students may have been socialized to hide their emotions.

Be especially sensitive to sources of anxiety for particular cultural and racial groups and for recent immigrants.

Seek professional assistance with anger management training if a student frequently lashes out in anger.

may be particularly affected in girls when they experience anxiety (Ganley & Vasilyeva, 2014). But girls and boys alike can experience considerable stress at school, especially in adolescence—perhaps about academic struggles, broken friendships, or romantic relationships—and they don't always have productive strategies for coping with their disappointments (Frydenberg & Lewis, 2000; Seiffge-Krenke et al., 2009). Clearly, then, students of both genders may sometimes need extra social and emotional support.

Be especially supportive when a student experiences extreme stress at school or elsewhere.

SOCIOECONOMIC DIFFERENCES

Students from low-income families are, on average, more prone to anxiety and depression than their higher-income classmates (Ashiabi & O'Neal, 2008; G. W. Evans, Gonnella, Marcynyszyn, Gentile, & Salpekar, 2005; Morales & Guerra, 2006). Furthermore, students in low-income school districts are especially at risk for making a rough transition from elementary to secondary school (Ogbu, 2003; Roderick & Camburn, 1999). Accordingly, students from low socioeconomic backgrounds are apt to have a greater-than-average need for our emotional and social support, and they are the ones who are most likely to benefit from a consistently warm and nurturing classroom environment (B. E. Becker & Luthar, 2002; Masten, 2001; Milner, 2006).

Be especially attentive to the emotional needs of children from low-income families.

In bringing our discussion of motivation and affect to a close, we must emphasize once again an important point: We teachers can—and *should*—make a significant difference in the lives of children and adolescents. Through the academic and social skills we teach them, the general classroom atmosphere we create for them, and the individualized instructional and emotional support we give them, we can greatly enhance their ability to be both productive and happy.

Motivating Students in Any Environment

So how can we use all of this information? One of the issues that teachers often face is that some of the motivation theories seem to contradict each other. You might be wondering how you can promote intrinsic motivation and lower test anxiety while simultaneously working in a school that gives out many rewards or that mandates a great deal of testing.

These are normal concerns, and teachers who are most effective at motivating their students understand that they need to use a balanced approach. Few educators work in environments where they can guarantee a classroom environment that will allow them to solely emphasize adaptive components of motivation theories. Let's look at an example of this struggle.

EXPERIENCING FIRSTHAND
PROMOTING POSITIVE MOTIVATIONAL BELIEFS

Mr. Murphy is a middle school social studies teacher; he works in a school where there is much mandated testing. Many of the parents are focused on getting their children prepared for admission into competitive colleges. In addition, the school has an honor society, and membership in the honor society elevates the social status of students. Nevertheless, Mr. Murphy feels frustrated sometimes, because he wants to promote positive motivational beliefs in his students, but he often feels that the context of his school inhibits his efforts. What can Mr. Murphy do to promote positive motivational beliefs?

Mr. Murphy's problems are not unique. Most educators work in environments where school policies and local contexts make it difficult to develop positive motivational beliefs. As teachers we need to promote desirable motivational beliefs within such contexts; this may seem impossible, but it actually is not. If we promote productive motivational beliefs as much as possible, we can truly help struggling students. Figure 11.9 offers some suggestions for how to promote a positive motivational climate, even when other factors may seem to frustrate your efforts.

MyEdLab **Self-Check 11.4**

FIGURE 11.9 Strategies to promote positive motivational climates in any setting.

HOW TO PROMOTE...	STRATEGIES THAT CAN BE USED IN ANY ENVIRONMENT:
High Expectancies	Set short-term goals so that students experience success.
	Hold high expectations while also providing support so that students can meet your expectations.
Achievement Values	Present examples of how content that you are teaching is important in the real world.
	Give examples of careers in which the content is important.
	Allow students to explore topics of personal interest.
	When students get frustrated, give them concrete examples of why it is worth their time to persist with a task.
Adaptive Attributions	Carefully think about the feedback that you provide to students when they get a bad grade.
	Convey the message that all learners have to persist and try hard.
	When students make maladaptive attributions (e.g., "I failed because I'm stupid"), correct these beliefs by redirecting them toward more appropriate attributions (e.g., "You failed because you didn't study for the test effectively—let's develop a study plan so this doesn't happen again.")
Endorsement of Mastery-Approach Goals	When possible, eliminate time constraints and strict deadlines.
	Allow students who have not mastered content and who get a poor grade on an assignment to redo the assignment and have it re-graded.
	Encourage and reward students for taking on challenging assignments.
Low Anxiety	Don't talk too much about tests.
	When students are working on difficult tasks, encourage them to take breaks.
	Offer positive feedback while students are working on challenging tasks to show them that they are making progress.
	If a student is extremely stressed by a particular exam or assignment, consider an alternate approach to assessment (e.g., instead of a timed test in class, allow the student to take the test after school and to have additional time).
Belongingness	Use cooperative learning techniques and other group activities in which all group members play important roles.
	If you see any signs of bullying or social exclusion, deal with those promptly (see Chapter 13).
	If a student appears to not interact with others, tactfully find ways to involve that student in group activities.
	Encourage students who are natural leaders to work with you to create a positive classroom environment.
	Use a wide variety of assessments in determining students' grades (i.e., don't just focus on a few high-stakes exams).

11   What Have You Learned?

We now return to the chapter's learning outcomes and identify some key points related to each one. Recall the exercise at the beginning of the chapter where you came up with a set of questions that you might ask Jodie to try to figure out why she was not motivated in math. How many questions did you write? Now that we have discussed the multifaceted aspects of academic motivation, you may see that your original list was not comprehensive

enough. Here are some questions that might be asked, based on the topics that we examined:

- Is math interesting?
- Do you like math?
- Is math useful?
- Is it worth your time to do math homework?

- When you get a bad grade on a math assignment, why does that happen?
- Do you get anxious when you take math tests?
- Do you think you'll be successful in your math class this year?
- Do you feel like you fit in with the other kids in your math class?

■ **11.1: Draw on diverse theoretical perspectives to describe the multifaceted nature of motivation.** Motivation energizes, directs, and sustains behavior; for instance, it focuses learners' attention on certain goals, influences what and how learners cognitively process information, and determines the specific consequences that are likely to be reinforcing. *Extrinsic motivation* is based on factors external to learners and unrelated to the task at hand, whereas *intrinsic motivation* arises from conditions within learners themselves or from factors inherent in the task. For the most part, intrinsic motivation leads to more effective learning, both in the short term and over the long haul (Taylor et al., 2014).

■ **11.2: Explain how learners' needs, cognitive processes, and sociocultural environments can have significant impacts on their motivation and other types of needs, and apply your knowledge of these factors to classroom practice.** Humans have basic needs for physical survival (e.g., food and water), but also have several other types of needs related to their psychological well-being. One is the need for *arousal*—a need for a certain level of physical and cognitive stimulation. People also have a need for *competence* and *self-worth*—a need to believe that they can deal effectively with their surroundings and are, overall, good, capable individuals. Third, people have a need for *autonomy*—a need to believe that they have some autonomy and control regarding the course of their lives. And finally, people seem to have a need for *relatedness*—a need to feel loved, respected, and socially connected to others. As teachers, we're most likely to foster students' intrinsic motivation to master academic subject matter when we also address their needs— for example, by conducting stimulating and peer-interactive activities, giving them age-appropriate autonomy in their work, and scaffolding their efforts in challenging tasks.

Many forms of motivation have both cognitive and sociocultural elements. For example, learners' *interests* in certain topics—whether temporarily induced situational interests or longer-term personal ones—can emerge from learners' own intellectual curiosity, from unusual or puzzling events, or from a general environment in which inquiry and creativity are encouraged. Learners should also find *value* in certain activities and have an *expectancy* that they can be successful in those activities. Learners' values are especially impacted by their sociocultural environment: When conditions are right—when the environment is warm and responsive, with an age-appropriate balance between autonomy and guidance—learners gradually internalize some of the values of people around them.

Learners' self-constructed explanations of why various things happen to them—their *attributions*—influence their learning and performance as well. As students move through the grade levels, many of them increasingly attribute their successes and failures to a relatively fixed, uncontrollable ability; those students who, in contrast, believe they can improve their performance with hard work and more effective strategies achieve at higher levels over the long run.

Learners typically have a number of *goals,* including achievement goals (perhaps to master particular topics and skills or perhaps to demonstrate competence in a particular area), work-avoidance goals, social goals, and long-term life goals. Sometimes learners can accomplish multiple goals simultaneously, but in other cases they can't; for instance, learners can address both their achievement goals and their social goals by forming a study group for a challenging high school course, but it's quite difficult to master a topic while also avoiding hard work. As teachers, we should encourage mastery-approach goals as much as possible—for example, by insisting on genuine understanding of classroom material and by communicating that learning involves exerting effort and making mistakes—but we must also help students achieve other goals important for their well-being, such as certain performance goals, social goals, and long-term life goals.

Learners also approach academic tasks with different mindsets. When students have a growth mindset, they believe that they have the ability to learn new information (even complex information) if they work hard and practice. In contrast, when students have a fixed mindset, they believe that their abilities are limited, and that there are certain topics that they simply can't learn. As teachers, we can encourage students to adopt a growth mindset by allowing them to experience success and by reminding them about their potential as learners.

■ **11.3: Describe how teachers' beliefs and behaviors affect student motivation.** As teachers, we form beliefs about why our students achieve at different levels and display different abilities (i.e., attributions). These attributions affect our interactions with students, and ultimately may affect students' future motivation and achievement. We communicate our beliefs to our students both directly (e.g., via comments that we make to them) and indirectly (e.g., through our emotions or nonverbal communications). If we repeatedly convey to students that we believe that their abilities are limited, we may create self-fulfilling prophecies, wherein our expectations for our students actually affect their academic performance. We teachers can foster more optimistic and productive attributions, in part, by conveying the message—not only through our words but also through our actions—that students can, indeed, have considerable control over their destinies.

■ **11.4: Describe how various forms of affect are intertwined with motivation, learning, and cognition, and explain how you might promote productive affective states in students.** The emotions and general moods that learners bring to bear on a task—collectively known as *affect*—are closely intertwined with motivation; for example, how learners feel depends on whether their needs are being met. Affect is closely connected with learning and cognition as well; for example, learners typically learn and remember more when they're emotionally as well as cognitively involved in classroom topics.

One particular form of affect—anxiety—has particular implications for classroom learning. A small amount of anxiety often facilitates learning and performance, but a great deal of anxiety typically impedes them, especially when difficult tasks are involved. In most circumstances, we should strive to keep students' anxiety at a low to moderate level—for example, by clearly communicating expectations for achievement and by ensuring that students have a good chance of being successful with reasonable effort.

Practice for Your Licensure Exam

When "Perfect" Isn't Good Enough

Mrs. Gaskill's second graders are just beginning to learn how to write the letters of the alphabet in cursive. Every day Mrs. Gaskill introduces a new cursive letter and shows her students how to write it correctly. She also shows them some common errors in writing the letter—for instance, claiming that she's going to make the "perfect f" but then making it much too short and crossing the lines in the wrong place—and the children delight in finding her mistakes. After the class explores the shape of a letter, Mrs. Gaskill asks her students to practice the letter, first by writing it in the air using large arm movements and then by writing it numerous times on lined paper.

Meanwhile, Mrs. Gaskill has decided to compare the effects of two kinds of praise on the children's performance. She has placed a small colored sticker on each child's desk to indicate membership in one of two groups. When children in Group 1 write a letter with good form, she gives them a happy-face token, says "Great!" or "Perfect!" and either smiles at them or gives them a pat on the back. When children in Group 2 write a letter with good form at least once, she gives them a happy-face token and says something like "You sure are working hard," "You can write beautifully in cursive," or "You are a natural at this." When children in either group fail to meet her standards for cursive writing, she gives them whatever corrective feedback they need.

Thus, the only way in which Mrs. Gaskill treats the two groups differently is in what she says to them when they do well, either giving them fairly cryptic feedback (for Group 1) or telling them that they are trying hard or have high ability (for Group 2). Despite such a minor difference, Mrs. Gaskill finds that the children in Group 2 say they enjoy cursive writing more, and they use it more frequently in their spelling tests and other writing tasks. Curiously, too, the children in Group 1 often seem disappointed when they receive their seemingly positive feedback. For instance, on one occasion a girl who writes beautifully but has the misfortune of being in Group 1 asks, "Am *I* a natural at this?" Although the girl consistently gets a grade of "+" for her cursive writing, she never writes in cursive voluntarily throughout the 3-week period in which Mrs. Gaskill conducts her experiment. (Study described by Gaskill, 2001)

1. **Multiple-choice question:**

   Which one of the following observations best supports the conclusion that the children in Group 2 have greater *intrinsic* motivation than the children in Group 1?

   a. The children in Group 2 get more detailed feedback.

   b. The children in Group 2 seem happier when Mrs. Gaskill reinforces them.

   c. The children in Group 1 seem disappointed about the feedback they get.

   d. The children in Group 2 use cursive writing more frequently in other assignments.

2. **Constructed-response question:**

   Explain why the praise given to Group 2 might be more motivating than the praise given to Group 1. Base your explanation on contemporary principles and theories of motivation.

3. **Constructed-response question:**

   Might the feedback given to Group 1 ("e.g., Great!" "Perfect") be more effective if Mrs. Gaskill used it for all, rather than just some, of her students? Explain your reasoning.

   > MyEdLab **Licensure Exam 11.1**

PRAXIS Go to Appendix C, "Matching Book Content and Ebook Activities to the Praxis Principles of Learning and Teaching Tests," to discover sections of this chapter that may be especially applicable to the Praxis tests.

12

Instructional Strategies

CASE STUDY: WESTWARD EXPANSION

Martin Quinn's sixth-grade class is studying the great westward expansion in North America during the middle 1800s. Today's lesson is about a typical journey west in a covered wagon. Mr. Quinn begins by projecting a 19th-century U.S. map on a screen at the front of room. "Many people traveled by steamship up the Missouri River to the town of Independence," he says, and he uses a pointer to trace the route on the map. "Then they continued west in a covered wagon until they reached their final destination—maybe Colorado, Oregon, or California." He now shows several old photographs of people traveling in covered wagons and says, "A typical covered wagon was about 4 feet wide and maybe 10 or 12 feet long." He has two students use masking tape to mark a 4-by-10-foot rectangle on the classroom carpet. "How much room would a wagon with these dimensions give you for your family and supplies?" The students agree that people would have to be quite choosy about what they brought with them on the trip west.

"All right," Mr. Quinn continues, "let's think about the kinds of things you would need to pack in your wagon. Let's start with the kinds of food you'd want to bring and how much of each one you should pack." He divides the students into groups of three or four members each and has them brainstorm what might seem to be a reasonable grocery list. After a few minutes, he writes each group's suggestions on the board.

At this point, Mr. Quinn clicks on an Internet link and projects an electronic copy of John Lyle Campbell's pamphlet, *Idaho: Six Months in the New Gold Regions: The Emigrant's Guide*, published in 1864. "This pamphlet provided advice for a party of four men who might be traveling west to seek their fortunes in the quartz mining boom in Idaho." The pamphlet lists many things that the students haven't thought of and suggests much larger amounts than the students have estimated. For example, it recommends 12 sacks of flour, 400 pounds of bacon, 100 pounds of coffee, 15 gallons of vinegar, 50 pounds of lard, and "one good cow for milking purposes."

"What do you think about the list?" Mr. Quinn asks. "Does it make sense?" The students have varying opinions: "Fifty pounds of lard—eeuuww, gross! Isn't that stuff really bad for your arteries or something?" "We way underestimated our flour." "I don't understand why they needed to bring so much coffee." "The cow's a good idea, though."

Mr. Quinn's next question is, "*Why* did people need all these things? Let's talk about that for a bit."

- What specific instructional strategies does Mr. Quinn use to engage and motivate his students? What strategies does he use to help them learn and remember the content of the lesson?

To engage and motivate his students, Mr. Quinn arouses situational interest through a physical activity (students mark a "wagon" on the carpet), creates cognitive dissonance (the list in the pamphlet doesn't entirely match the ones the students have generated), and makes the lesson a very social, interactive one. And he promotes learning and understanding, in part, by encouraging visual imagery and elaboration—for example, by making the subject matter concrete and vivid (through the old photographs and masking-tape wagon)

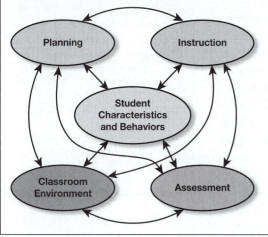

FIGURE 12.1 Planning, instruction, the classroom environment, classroom assessment practices, and students' characteristics and behaviors are all closely intertwined.

Chapter 13 presents strategies for creating a productive classroom environment. Chapter 14 and Chapter 15 present assessment strategies.

Choose instructional strategies and assessment methods that reflect the desired end results of instruction.

and by asking students to speculate about why such things as lard and coffee might have been important to have.

Effective instruction requires knowledge and use of evidence-based practices—those methods and strategies that research has consistently shown to be effective in helping students learn and achieve. It also requires considerable *planning:* We must decide in advance both what needs to be accomplished and how best to accomplish it, and we must continue to revise our plans—mentally, at least—as a lesson or instructional unit proceeds. Not only are planning and instruction closely connected but they're also intertwined with two other critical aspects of classroom practice: creating a productive environment for learning and assessing students' performance. Furthermore, planning, instruction, the classroom environment, and assessment practices both influence and are influenced by students' characteristics and behaviors (see Figure 12.1). As we make our day-to-day decisions in the classroom, we must *always* take into account what we know about each of our students.

General Principles that Can Guide Instruction

Historically many theorists and practitioners have looked for—and in some cases believe that they have found—the single best way to teach children and adolescents. In reality, *there is no single best approach to instruction.* Instead, effective teachers adhere to several general principles as they plan and carry out instruction.

- *Effective teachers begin their instructional planning by determining what they ultimately want students to know and be able to do.* An increasingly popular approach is a backward design, in which teachers proceed through this sequence (Tomlinson & McTighe, 2006; Wiggins & McTighe, 2011):

1. Identify the desired end results in terms of knowledge and skills that students should attain—ideally including meaningful learning, conceptual understanding, and complex cognitive processes.

2. Determine acceptable evidence—in the form of performance on various classroom assessment tasks—to verify that students have achieved those results.

3. Plan learning experiences and instructional activities that enable students to master the knowledge and skills identfied in Steps 1 and 2.

  With such an approach, we essentially *begin at the end* and then choose assessment tasks and instructional strategies that are specifically related to that end (see Figure 12.2). For example, if the objective for a unit on addition is *rapid retrieval* of number facts, we might create a timed quiz to assess students' ability to recall the facts quickly and easily, and we might employ gamelike computer software to enhance students' automaticity for the facts. But if our objective is *application* of number facts, we may instead want to focus our assessment methods and instructional strategies on word problems or, better still, on activities involving real objects and hands-on measurements.

- *Effective teachers use a variety of instructional strategies, often within a single lesson.* The lesson in the opening case study includes graphic displays, a physical activity, a small-group cooperative learning task, an old pamphlet, and intriguing questions. This combination of instructional strategies engages students' interest and

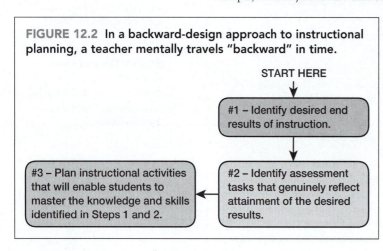

FIGURE 12.2 In a backward-design approach to instructional planning, a teacher mentally travels "backward" in time.

START HERE

#1 – Identify desired end results of instruction.

#2 – Identify assessment tasks that genuinely reflect attainment of the desired results.

#3 – Plan instructional activities that will enable students to master the knowledge and skills identified in Steps 1 and 2.

attention and helps students understand what 19th-century westward migration involved. Much of the lesson reflects teacher-directed instruction, in which a teacher calls most of the shots, choosing which topics will be addressed and carefully structuring students' activities. However, one of Mr. Quinn's strategies—having students develop grocery lists in small cooperative groups—reflects learner-directed instruction, in which students have considerable control regarding what they do and learn. Some educators use the terms *teacher-centered* versus *learner-centered* in reference to this distinction, but as Figure 12.1 illustrates, virtually all instructional strategies should focus (center) on students' characteristics and behaviors—for instance, by taking into account what students currently know and don't know, what their needs and motives are, and how instruction can best support their engagement in effective cognitive processes.[1]

Regardless of the specific terms we use, we must remember that the distinction being made here really reflects a *continuum* rather than an either-or situation, because instructional strategies can vary considerably in the degree to which teachers and students control the course of events. The relative amounts of teacher and student control can change even within a single lesson. For example, although Mr. Quinn poses specific questions for students to answer—a teacher-directed strategy—the questions are sufficiently open-ended that students' responses influence the nature of subsequent discussions.

- *Effective teachers help students make sense of, remember, and apply classroom subject matter.* Instruction can be effective only to the extent that it actively engages students in thinking about the subject matter; fosters meaningful learning and appropriate conceptual change; and encourages problem solving, critical thinking, and other complex cognitive processes. Good instruction also keeps students' cognitive load at a manageable level: At any particular moment, information and cognitive processing demands mustn't exceed students' limited working memory capacity (R. E. Mayer, 2011a; Sweller, 2010).

To see this principle in action, try the following exercise.

EXPERIENCING FIRSTHAND
FINDING PEDAGOGY IN ONE OF YOUR TEXTBOOKS

1. Look at two or three chapters in this book or another textbook that you've recently read. Identify places where the author has done specific things to help you learn and remember the material more effectively. What specific strategies did the author use to facilitate your cognitive processing?

2. In those same chapters, can you find places where you had trouble making sense of the ideas presented? If so, what might the author have done differently in those instances?

If you've chosen one or more chapters that we authors have written, we're hoping that the Experiencing Firsthand exercises have helped you relate new topics to your own knowledge and experiences. We're hoping, too, that the case studies, video examples, and interactive media activities have made abstract ideas more concrete and easy to understand. Perhaps some of the tables and graphics have helped you organize concepts and principles. But if you've found certain parts of a chapter confusing or hard to understand, we encourage you to let us know.

- *Effective teachers focus on knowledge and skills that are most likely to enhance students' long-term success both in and outside of school.* For example, rather than asking students to memorize trivial facts, effective teachers emphasize general themes, principles, and skills—sometimes known as *big ideas*—that are applicable to many topics and contexts (e.g., Brophy, Alleman, & Knighton, 2009; Wiggins & McTighe, 2011). Rather than simply chastising students for failing to complete homework assignments, effective teachers foster metacognitive strategies and self-regulation skills essential for self-guided, independent learning. And rather

---

[1]The American Psychological Association (APA) has identified 14 *Learner-Centered Psychological Principles* that encompass many fundamental principles of human learning, motivation, and development. You can find these principles by going to the APA's website (apa.org) and typing "learner-centered principles" in the search box.

than filling the entire school day with traditional drill-and-practice exercises, effective teachers often assign authentic activities—activities that in some way resemble those that students are likely to encounter in the outside world.

- *Effective teachers provide some structure and scaffolding for activities and assignments.* Even when lessons are largely learner directed, students typically need structure and guidance, especially with new and challenging tasks (e.g., Wise & O'Neill, 2009). The concept of *scaffolding* is useful here: We can provide a great deal of structure for tasks early in the school year, gradually removing it as students become better able to structure tasks for themselves. For example, when students first engage in cooperative learning activities, we might break down each group task into several subtasks, giving clear directions about how each subtask should be carried out and assigning every group member a particular role to serve in the group. As the school year progresses and students become more adept at working cooperatively with one another, we can gradually become less directive about how small-group tasks are accomplished.

- *Effective teachers capitalize on technological innovations to enhance students' learning and performance.* Interactive whiteboards, basic computer tools (e.g., word processing programs, electronic spreadsheets), topic-specific instructional software, educational websites—all of these innovations can potentially help students better understand and apply classroom subject matter. Yet, as is true for more traditional, "low-tech" instructional methods, such innovations can be effective only to the extent that they facilitate productive cognitive processes and provide sufficient scaffolding to foster students' success at new tasks and skills. Furthermore, they tend to have a greater impact when they're used in conjunction with—rather than as replacements for—more traditional methods involving face-to-face teacher–student interaction (Azevedo & Witherspoon, 2009; P. A. Kirschner & van Merriënboer, 2013; Tamin, Bernard, Borokhovski, Abrami, & Schmid, 2011).

- *Effective teachers take student diversity into account when planning and carrying out instruction.* Our choice of instructional strategies must, of course, be appropriate for students' current ability levels and existing knowledge related to the topics and skills at hand. We must take temperamental and motivational characteristics into consideration as well. For example, some children and adolescents have trouble sitting still and concentrating during lengthy lectures, and many students of all ages find hands-on activities more motivating and engaging than abstract textbook readings. And students with special educational needs often require accommodations tailored to their unique abilities and disabilities. Ideally, instruction is individually tailored for *all* students—a practice called differentiated instruction.

- *Effective teachers regularly assess and provide feedback about students' progress.* Assessment isn't something we do only at the end of instruction. It's also something we must do *throughout* instruction—a process known as formative assessment. Regularly determining students' ongoing understandings and skill levels—what they understand and misunderstand, what they can and cannot do—enables us to modify our instructional strategies in ways that maximize students' learning. It also enables us to provide the constructive feedback students may need to capitalize on their strengths, work on their weak spots, and, in general, be optimistic that they can ultimately achieve at high levels (Hattie & Gan, 2011; Narciss, 2008).

MyEdLab **Self-Check 12.1**

Planning for Instruction

Good teachers engage in considerable advance planning: They identify the information and skills they want students to acquire, determine an appropriate sequence in which to teach that knowledge, and develop classroom lessons and activities that will maximize learning and keep students motivated and on task. Ideally teachers also coordinate their plans with colleagues—for example, identifying common goals toward which everyone will strive or developing interdisciplinary units that involve two or more classes and subject areas. And they regularly share their plans and goals with their students. Especially when used in combination, such strategies can make a *big* difference in students' long-term learning and development (e.g., Hattie, 2009; Konstantopoulos & Chung, 2011; Pianta, Barnett, Burchinal, & Thornburg, 2009).

IDENTIFYING THE GOALS OF INSTRUCTION

An essential step in planning instruction is to identify the specific things students should accomplish during a lesson or unit, as well as the things they should accomplish over the course of a semester or school year. Educators use a variety of terms for such end results, including *goals, objectives, outcomes, competencies, benchmarks,* and *standards.* For example, each chapter in this book begins with *learning outcomes* that have guided our writing and can help readers anticipate and organize the chapter's various topics. In our discussion here, however, we'll typically use the term instructional goals when referring to desired general, long-term outcomes of instruction. We'll use the term instructional objectives when referring to more specific outcomes of a particular lesson or unit.

Consistent with the concept of *backward design,* identifying instructional goals and objectives should be the very first step in the instructional planning process. Our instructional strategies *must* be dictated by our short- and long-term goals for students' learning. Students, too, benefit from knowing our goals and objectives. When they know what we hope they'll accomplish, they can make more informed decisions about how to focus their efforts and allocate their study time, and they can more effectively monitor their comprehension as they read and study (Gronlund & Brookhart, 2009; McAshan, 1979). For example, if we tell students that we expect them to apply math concepts and procedures to practical, real-world situations, they'll probably think about and study math quite differently than if we tell them—or in some way imply—that they should rote-memorize definitions and formulas (a learning strategy that we authors certainly don't recommend!).

ALIGNING INSTRUCTIONAL GOALS WITH NATIONAL, INTERNATIONAL, AND STATE STANDARDS, INCLUDING (IF APPLICABLE) THE COMMON CORE STATE STANDARDS

People have varying opinions about the kinds of things students should learn in elementary and secondary school classrooms. For example, you may have heard people advocating for increasing students' knowledge of basic facts—a perspective sometimes called *back to the basics* or *cultural literacy* (e.g., Hirsch, 1996). Certainly some factual knowledge is essential for students' long-term academic and professional success. But equally essential are the complex cognitive processes (e.g., problem solving, critical thinking) and general *habits of mind* (e.g., scientific reasoning, drawing inferences from historical documents) that are central to various academic disciplines (Brophy et al., 2009; M. C. Linn, 2008; Monte-Sano, 2008; R. K. Sawyer, 2006).

One important source of guidance comes from content-area standards identified by national and international discipline-specific professional groups (e.g., National Council for Geographic Education, National Association for Music Education). Such standards are typically in the form of general statements regarding the knowledge and skills that students should acquire at various grade levels, as well as the characteristics that their accomplishments should reflect.

Also, in the United States, state departments of education—as well as some local school districts—have established comprehensive lists of standards in reading, writing, math, science, and social studies, and sometimes in such domains as art, music, foreign languages, and physical education, and teachers are expected to help students make significant progress toward these standards. Most U.S. states have jointly adopted a set of Common Core State Standards in mathematics and English language arts, and some are now signing on to the Next Generation Science Standards; you can find these standards on the Internet at corestandards.org and nextgenscience. org, respectively. Table 12.1 presents examples of reading skills identified in the Common Core State Standards for English Language Arts, along with instructional strategies potentially useful in helping students acquire those skills.

In recent years, many teachers, parents, and policy makers have voiced major concerns—in some cases, downright paranoia—about the use of the Common Core standards in their states and local school districts. By and large, the concerns that they've raised reflect a great deal of misinformation about the intent and implementation of these standards. In an effort to counter such misconceptions, we must stress a few basic facts about Common Core:

- Development of the standards was the joint initiative of many state governors and state commissioners of education in an effort to ensure that high school graduates in their states would be prepared for college and meaningful careers. The U.S. federal government was *not* involved in developing the standards, nor has it mandated their use in public schools.

DEVELOPMENTAL TRENDS

	EXAMPLES OF COMMON CORE STANDARDS FOR ENGLISH LANGUAGE ARTS	EXAMPLES OF INSTRUCTIONAL STRATEGIES THAT ADDRESS THESE STANDARDS
Grade 2	Ask and answer such questions as *who, what, where, when, why,* and *how* to demonstrate understanding of key details in a text. (RL.2.1)[a]	During "settling down" time immediately after lunch each day, read a chapter of a high-interest children's novel, stopping frequently to ask questions that require students to go beyond the text itself (e.g., ask students to speculate about what a character might be feeling).
	Recount stories, including fables and folktales from diverse cultures, and determine their central message, lesson, or moral. (RL.2.2)	Have several students create props for and act out a story they have recently read, with other class members serving as the audience. Follow up with a class discussion of important lessons that one or more story characters might have learned from events or challenges that they faced.
Grade 4	Refer to details and examples in a text when explaining what the text says explicitly and when drawing inferences from the text. (RL.4.1)	As a reading group discusses Carl Hiaasen's *Hoot,* ask students to speculate about how the plot might progress and to identify clues in the text that support their predictions.
	Explain events, procedures, ideas, or concepts in a historical, scientific, or technical text, including what happened and why, based on specific information in the text. (RI.4.3)	When students are reading a chapter in their history textbook, ask *why* questions that encourage cause-and-effect connections (e.g., "Why did Columbus's crew want to sail back to Europe after several weeks on the open sea?").
Grade 7	Analyze the structure an author uses to organize a text, including how the major sections contribute to the whole and to the development of the ideas. (RI.7.5)	Before students read a chapter in their science textbook, have them use its headings and subheadings to (1) create a general outline of the chapter and (2) generate questions they hope to answer as they read the chapter. Then, for homework, ask them to read and take notes on the chapter, using the outline and self-questions as guides for note taking.
	Trace and evaluate the argument and specific claims in a text, assessing whether the reasoning is sound and the evidence is relevant and sufficient to support the claims. (RI.7.8)	Give students an advertisement for a self-improvement product (e.g., a diet pill or exercise equipment); have them work in small cooperative learning groups to (1) identify the advertiser's motives and (2) evaluate the quality of evidence for the product's effectiveness.
Grades 11–12	Analyze and evaluate the effectiveness of the structure an author uses in his or her position or argument, including whether the structure makes points clear, convincing, and engaging. (RI.11–12.5)	Describe common techniques in persuasive writing, and have students identify the various persuasive techniques used in newspaper editorials.
	Determine an author's point of view or purpose in a text in which the rhetoric is particularly effective, analyzing how style and content contribute to the power, persuasiveness or beauty of the text. (RI.11–12.6)	Ask students to identify the unstated assumptions underlying two news magazines' depictions of the same event (e.g., an assumption that one group is good or right and another is bad or wrong).

[a] The letters "RL" indicate standards related to reading literature; the letters "RI" indicate standards related to reading informational text. The number or numbers before the period indicate the grade level; the number after the period indicates the particular standard for that grade level. For example, the first entry shown here, identified as "RL.2.1," is the first standard for grade 2 for reading literature.

Source: Entries in the column "Examples of Common Core Standards for English Language Arts" are from *Common Core State Standards.* © Copyright 2010. National Governors Association for Best Practices and Council of Chief State School Officers. Reprinted with permission. All rights reserved.

- The standards do *not* prescribe particular instructional methods; in fact, the developers have emphatically stated that local schools and teachers should make their own decisions about how best to help students strive to achieve the standards.

- The standards do *not* prescribe particular assessment tools for measuring students' achievement of the standards—for example, they do *not* require that students' achievement be assessed by one or more multiple-choice achievement tests. (Any tests that currently exist for this purpose have been developed by private companies and have *not* been endorsed by the developers of Common Core.)

The website corestandards.org addresses these and many other myths about Common Core; we authors strongly urge you to take a look at this website.

With the importance of considering content-area standards in mind, let's break the first step of a backward design into two substeps, as shown in Figure 12.3. In particular, we explicitly identify one or more standards we want our students to meet (Step 1a) and then pin down more specific outcomes we want an instructional unit to address (Step 1b). Only after we've done *both* of these things do we identify appropriate assessment tasks (Step 2) and plan our instructional strategies (Step 3).

We should also keep in mind that existing content-area standards focus almost exclusively on what students should achieve in reading, writing, and various academic content domains. They largely overlook goals that lie *outside* particular content areas—for instance, goals related to technological literacy, effective study strategies, self-regulation techniques, and good social skills. The International Society for Technology in Education

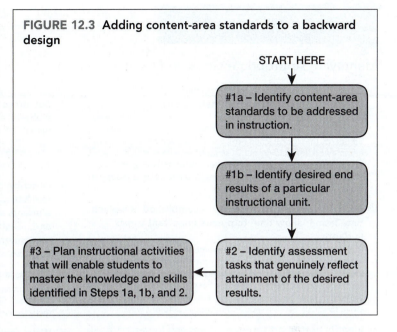

FIGURE 12.3 Adding content-area standards to a backward design

(ISTE) has developed standards that can help us enhance students' knowledge and skills related to digital technologies (go to iste.org/standards). But with an eye toward enhancing students' long-term academic social success both at school and in the outside world, we must also develop some of our *own* goals for students' achievements during their time in our classrooms.

WRITING USEFUL GOALS AND OBJECTIVES

Our goals and objectives are useful only to the extent that they provide concrete guidance as we plan instructional activities and assessment procedures. The Into the Classroom feature "Identifying Appropriate Goals and Objectives" offers suggestions for writing useful ones.

An especially important suggestion in the Into the Classroom feature is to *include goals and objectives with varying levels of complexity and sophistication.* One tool that can help us keep a broad view of what students should learn and be able to do is a 2001 revision of Bloom's taxonomy, a list of six general cognitive processes that vary in complexity:

1. *Remember:* Recognizing or recalling information learned at an earlier time and stored in long-term memory
2. *Understand:* Constructing meaning from instructional materials and messages (e.g., drawing inferences, identifying new examples, summarizing)
3. *Apply:* Using knowledge in a familiar or new situation
4. *Analyze:* Breaking information into its constituent parts and perhaps also identifying interrelationships among the parts
5. *Evaluate:* Making judgments about information using certain criteria or standards
6. *Create:* Putting together knowledge, procedures, or both to form a coherent, structured, and possibly original whole (L. W. Anderson & Krathwohl, 2001)[2]

Another helpful taxonomy can be found in *Understanding by Design* (e.g., Wiggins & McTighe, 2005, 2011), a popular resource for guiding teachers through the backward-design process. This taxonomy identifies six forms ("facets") that students' understanding of a topic might take:

1. *Explanation:* Integrating various bits of information into meaningful wholes (e.g., knowing the *hows* and *whys* of various facts and principles), drawing appropriate inferences, and possibly helping others understand the subject matter

MyEdLab
Content Extension 12.1.
In this supplmentary reading, you can find Bloom's original taxonomy, an expanded description of the 2001 revision, and two other classic taxonomies.

---

[2]Bloom's original taxonomy uses nouns rather than verbs: *knowledge, comprehension, application, analysis, synthesis, evaluation.* In the revision shown here, *create* replaces and subsumes *synthesis*, and *evaluate* moves from sixth to fifth place.

Into The Classroom

Identifying Appropriate Goals and Objectives

Consult state, national, and international standards, but don't rely on them exclusively.

In identifying instructional goals for the year, a middle school science teacher takes into account the Next Generation Science Standards (nextgenscience.org), which her state has adopted as a framework for guiding public schools' science curricula. In addition, she identifies specific objectives related to two issues directly affecting many students in her inner-city school district: poor nutrition and air pollution.

Be realistic about what can be accomplished in a given time frame; allow time to pursue important topics in depth.

Rather than expect students to remember a lot of discrete facts in social studies, a second-grade teacher identifies several "big ideas" students should master during the school year—for instance, the ideas that (a) all people have certain needs and desires that affect their behaviors and (b) different cultural groups may strive to satisfy those needs and desires in different ways.

Identify both short-term objectives and long-term goals.

A fourth-grade teacher wants students to learn how to spell at least 10 new words each week. He also wants them to write coherent and grammatically correct short stories by the end of the school year.

In addition to goals related to specific topics and content areas, identify goals related to students' general long-term academic success.

A middle school teacher knows that early adolescence is an important time for developing the learning and study strategies that students will need in high school and college. Throughout the school year, he continually introduces new strategies for learning and remembering classroom subject matter—for example, effective ways to organize class notes, mnemonic techniques for remembering important facts, and self-questions to answer while reading a textbook chapter—and regularly assesses students' progress in using these strategies.

Include goals and objectives with varying levels of complexity and sophistication.

A high school physics teacher wants students not only to understand various kinds of simple machines (e.g., levers, wedges) but also to recognize examples in their own lives (e.g., crowbars, spatulas) and to use these machines to solve real-world problems.

Consider physical, social, motivational, and affective outcomes as well as cognitive outcomes.

A physical education teacher wants her students to know the basic rules of basketball and to dribble and pass the ball appropriately. She also wants them to acquire a love of basketball, effective ways of working cooperatively with teammates, and a general desire to stay physically fit.

Describe goals and objectives not in terms of what the teacher will do during a lesson but in terms of what _students_ should be able to do at the _end_ of instruction—and, ideally, also in ways that point to appropriate assessment tasks.

A Spanish teacher knows that students often confuse the verbs _estar_ and _ser_ because both are translated into English as "to be." She identifies this objective for her students: "Students will correctly conjugate _estar_ and _ser_ in the present tense and use each one in appropriate contexts." She assesses students' ability to use the two verbs correctly through both paper–pencil quizzes and in-class conversations.

When writing short-term objectives, identify specific behaviors that will reflect accomplishment of the objectives.

In a unit on the food pyramid, a health teacher identifies this objective for students: "Students will create menus for a breakfast, lunch, and dinner that, in combination, include all elements of the pyramid in appropriate proportions."

When writing long-term goals that involve complex topics or skills, list a few abstract outcomes and give examples of specific behaviors that reflect each one.

Faculty members at a middle school identify this instructional goal for all students at their school: "Students will demonstrate effective listening skills, for example, by taking thorough and accurate notes, responding correctly to teacher questions, and seeking clarification when they don't understand."

Provide opportunities for students to identify goals and objectives of their own.

A high school art teacher asks students to choose a particular medium they'd each like to focus on during the semester (e.g., pastels, oils, clay) and to identify at least three skills they want to improve while working with the chosen medium. He helps students develop concrete goals toward which they'll work and specific criteria they can use to evaluate their progress.

Sources: Brophy, 2008; Brophy et al., 2009; N. S. Cole, 1990; Gronlund & Brookhart, 2009; M. D. Miller, Linn, & Gronlund, 2009; Pellegrino, Chudowsky, & Glaser, 2001; Popham, 2014; Wiggins & McTighe, 2011.

2. _Interpretation:_ Making sense of and identifying the underlying meanings of events, data, documents, and works of art and literature

3. _Application and adjustment:_ Using acquired knowledge in new situations and diverse contexts

4. _Perspective:_ Considering various points of view regarding an issue; trying to minimize bias in one's own analysis of the issue

5. _Empathy:_ Looking at a situation or issue from a particular individual's or group's vantage point, perhaps based on the individual's or group's feelings or general worldviews

6. *Self-knowledge:* Identifying gaps in one's own understandings, as well as personal prejudices that might distort one's views and interpretations

Neither of the preceding taxonomies provides exhaustive lists of what students should be able to do while learning classroom subject matter; for example, they don't include psychomotor skills. Nor do the particular sequences of items necessarily reflect a progression from simpler to more complex processes (L. W. Anderson & Krathwohl, 2001; Iran-Nejad & Stewart, 2010; Marzano & Kendall, 2007). Even so, the taxonomies can certainly remind us that there's much more to school learning and academic achievement than remembering discrete facts. More detailed, comprehensive taxonomies—which are too complex to present here—can provide additional guidance (e.g., see Marzano & Kendall, 2007).

The six items in the *Understanding by Design* taxonomy might remind you of concepts described elsewhere in the book: conceptual understanding (Item 1; see Chapter 6), critical thinking (Items 2 and 4; see Chapter 7), transfer (Item 3; see Chapter 7), perspective taking (Item 5; see Chapter 3), and metacognition (Item 6; see Chapter 7).

CONDUCTING A TASK ANALYSIS

In addition to identifying goals and objectives for instruction, we need to determine how best to break down complex topics and skills into manageable chunks. As examples, consider these four teachers:

- Ms. Begay, a third-grade teacher, plans to teach her students how to solve arithmetic word problems. She also wants to help them learn more effectively from reading materials.
- Mr. Marino, a middle school physical education teacher, wants his students to develop enough proficiency in basketball to feel comfortable playing either on organized basketball teams or in pick-up games in their neighborhoods.
- Mr. Wu, a junior high school music teacher, hopes to teach his new trumpet students how to play "Jingle Bell Rock" in time for the New Year's Day parade.
- Ms. Flores, a high school social studies teacher, is going to introduce her students to the intricacies of the federal judicial system.

All four teachers want to teach complex topics or skills. Accordingly, each of them should conduct a **task analysis**, identifying the essential behavioral or cognitive aspects of mastering a particular topic or skill. The task analyses can then guide the teachers in their selections of appropriate methods and sequences in which to teach the subject matter.

Figure 12.4 illustrates three general approaches to task analysis (Jonassen, Hannum, & Tessmer, 1989; also see R. E. Clark, Feldon, van Merriënboer, Yates, & Early, 2008):

- **Behavioral analysis.** One way of analyzing a complex task is to identify the specific behaviors required to perform it (much as a behaviorist might do). For example, Mr. Marino can identify the specific physical movements involved in dribbling, passing, and shooting a basketball. Similarly, Mr. Wu can identify the behaviors students must master in order to play a trumpet, such as how to correctly hold the instrument and how to blow into the mouthpiece.
- **Subject matter analysis.** Another approach is to break down the subject matter into the specific topics, concepts, and principles that it includes. For example, Ms. Flores can identify various aspects of the judicial system (concepts such as *innocent until proven guilty* and *reasonable doubt,* the roles that judges and juries play, etc.) and their interrelationships. And Mr. Wu can identify the basic elements of written music that his trumpet students must be able to interpret, such as the treble and bass clefs and whole, half, and quarter notes. Subject matter analysis is especially important when the subject matter being taught includes many interrelated concepts and ideas that students should learn meaningfully and with conceptual understanding.
- **Information processing analysis.** A third approach is to specify the cognitive processes involved in a task. As an illustration, Ms. Begay can identify the mental processes involved in successfully solving a word problem—for instance, correct encoding of the problem (e.g., determining whether it requires addition, subtraction,

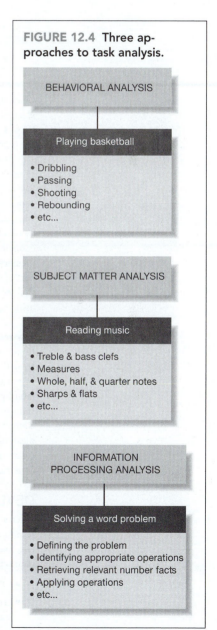

FIGURE 12.4 Three approaches to task analysis.

BEHAVIORAL ANALYSIS

Playing basketball

- Dribbling
- Passing
- Shooting
- Rebounding
- etc...

SUBJECT MATTER ANALYSIS

Reading music

- Treble & bass clefs
- Measures
- Whole, half, & quarter notes
- Sharps & flats
- etc...

INFORMATION PROCESSING ANALYSIS

Solving a word problem

- Defining the problem
- Identifying appropriate operations
- Retrieving relevant number facts
- Applying operations
- etc...

etc.) and rapid retrieval of basic number facts. Similarly, she can identify specific metacognitive strategies useful in reading comprehension, such as finding main ideas, elaborating, and self-questioning.

To get a taste of what a task analysis might involve, try the next exercise.

EXPERIENCING FIRSTHAND
PEANUT BUTTER SANDWICH

Conduct a task analysis for the process of making a peanut butter sandwich, as follows:

1. Decide whether your approach should be a behavioral analysis, a subject matter analysis, or an information processing analysis.

2. Using the approach you've selected, break the sandwich-making task into a number of small, teachable steps.

3. (Optional) If you're hungry and have the necessary materials close at hand, make an actual sandwich following the steps you've identified. Did your initial analysis omit any important steps?

Chances are good that you chose a behavioral analysis, because making a peanut butter sandwich is largely a behavioral rather than mental task. For example, you must know how to unscrew the lid of a peanut butter jar, get an appropriate amount of peanut butter on your knife, and spread the peanut butter gently enough that you don't tear the bread.

Conducting task analyses for complex skills and topics serves at least three important functions in instructional planning (Jonassen et al., 1989; R. E. Mayer, 2011a; Stokes, Luiselli, & Reed, 2010; van Merriënboer & Kester, 2008). First, when we identify a task's specific components—whether behaviors, concepts and ideas, or cognitive processes—we gain a better sense of what things students need to learn and the order in which to most effectively learn them. Second, a task analysis helps us choose appropriate instructional strategies. For example, if one necessary component of solving arithmetic word problems is rapid retrieval of math facts from long-term memory, repeated practice of the facts may be critical for developing automaticity. If another aspect of solving such problems is identifying the relevant operation(s) to apply (addition, subtraction, etc.), we must promote a true understanding of math concepts and principles, perhaps by using concrete manipulatives or authentic activities.

A third important function of a task analysis is determining what kind of *cognitive load* a new task might impose on students—in particular, whether or not certain aspects of a task might initially put a strain on students' limited working memory capacity. Sometimes the analysis will reveal that certain components of a task should be taught separately, one at a time. For instance, Mr. Wu may initially ask his beginning trumpet students to practice blowing into the mouthpiece correctly without worrying about the specific notes they produce. But on other occasions it might be both possible and desirable to teach the desired knowledge and behaviors entirely within the context of the overall task, in part because doing so makes the subject matter meaningful for students. For instance, Ms. Begay should almost certainly teach her students effective metacognitive processes in reading primarily within the context of authentic reading activities.

DEVELOPING A LESSON PLAN

After identifying specific goals for instruction—in part by taking into account any mandated or recommended content-area standards—and perhaps also conducting one or more task analyses, effective teachers develop one or more **lesson plans** to guide them during instruction. A lesson plan typically includes the following:

- The goal(s) or objective(s) of the lesson and, if applicable, relevant content-area standard(s)
- Instructional materials (e.g., textbooks, handouts, software programs) and equipment required

- Specific instructional strategies and the sequence in which they'll be used
- Assessment method(s) planned

Any lesson plan should also take into account the particular students who will be learning—their developmental levels, prior knowledge, cultural backgrounds, and (if applicable) disabilities and other special educational needs.

As a beginning teacher, you'll initially need to develop fairly detailed lesson plans that describe how you're going to help your students learn the subject matter in question (Calderhead, 1996; Corno, 2008; Sternberg & Horvath, 1995). For instance, when we authors first began teaching, we spent many hours each week writing down the information, examples, questions, and student activities we wanted to use in class during the following week. But as you gain experience teaching certain topics, you'll learn which strategies work effectively and which do not, and you may use some of the effective ones frequently enough that you can retrieve them quickly and easily from long-term memory. Consequently, as time goes on, you'll find that planning lessons becomes far less time consuming, and much of it becomes *mental* planning rather than planning on paper or a computer screen.

In planning lessons, teachers have many resources at their disposal, including experienced teachers' lesson plans in books and on the Internet. For example, the following websites offer lesson plans and related materials concerning a wide range of topics:

- Smithsonian Institution (smithsonianeducation.org)
- Educator's Reference Desk (eduref.org)
- Discovery Education (discoveryeducation.com)

In taking advantage of such resources, however, we must always keep in mind that *lessons should be closely tied to instructional goals and objectives.*

Generally speaking, a lesson plan is a guide rather than a recipe: It can and should be adjusted as events unfold. For example, during the course of a lesson, we may find that we need to back up and teach material we'd mistakenly assumed students had already mastered. And if students express considerable curiosity or have intriguing insights about a particular topic, we might want to capitalize on this unique opportunity—this teachable moment—and spend more time exploring the topic than originally planned.

As we proceed through the school year, our long-range plans may also change to some degree. For instance, we may find that our initial task analyses of certain topics are overly simplistic, or we may discover that our initial expectations for students' achievement are either unrealistically high or unnecessarily low. Both short-term and long-term lesson planning, then, must continue to be a work in progress.

> In your first few months of teaching, create fairly detailed lesson plans to guide you, but be flexible when circumstances call for adjustments.

CREATING A CLASS WEBSITE TO SHARE GOALS AND FACILITATE COMMUNICATION THROUGHOUT THE SCHOOL YEAR

Historically, a traditional practice at the high school and college levels has been to give students a printed syllabus that lists course topics, instructional goals, homework assignments, due dates, and scheduled assessments. But increasingly teachers at all levels are sharing such information—and much more—on class-specific Internet websites within their school's overall website. A variety of Internet resources are available to create such sites (e.g., see moodle.org). In the K–12 grades, students' parents typically have access to class websites as well.

As an example, Figure 12.5 shows the opening screen that teacher Jeff Ormrod created for one of his sixth-grade humanities classes. Notice that the course resources included two documents (a course outline and assessment criteria) that students could download. Scrolling further down in the website, students could learn about general goals for the class, get detailed information about various units and assignments, and find many more downloadable

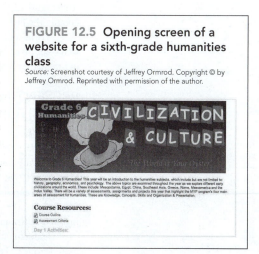

FIGURE 12.5 Opening screen of a website for a sixth-grade humanities class
Source: Screenshot courtesy of Jeffrey Ormrod. Copyright © by Jeffrey Ormrod. Reprinted with permission of the author.

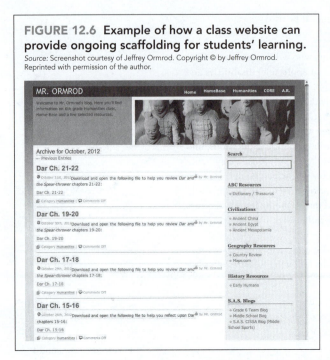

FIGURE 12.6 Example of how a class website can provide ongoing scaffolding for students' learning.
Source: Screenshot courtesy of Jeffrey Ormrod. Copyright © by Jeffrey Ormrod. Reprinted with permission of the author.

documents. Students could also interact in a class-specific electronic chat room, and they could upload their completed assignments to the website.

As Jeff has gained experience as a teacher, he has increasingly used his class websites as means through which to scaffold students' learning, as illustrated in Figure 12.6. As part of a unit on early humans, his class had been reading Marjorie Cowley's *Dar and the Spear-Thrower,* and Jeff had regularly posted study guides that encouraged students to elaborate on what they were reading—for example, by posing such questions as "Why does Dar decide to leave his clan to find the stranger?" and "Explain how the 'wind was his enemy.'" The sidebar on the right provided links to various online resources (e.g., Merriam-Webster's online dictionary) and schoolwide blogs.

Class websites provide one easy way for us to communicate regularly with students and their parents. They can't be the *only* way, however. Not all students and parents have easy access to computers and the Internet at home. And some individuals—parents especially—may simply not have the technological literacy they need to access and navigate through an Internet website. Accordingly, we should also provide hard copies of assignments we want students to do as homework and of information we want parents to know.

MyEdLab Self-Check 12.2

MyEdLab Application Exercise 12.1. In this exercise, you can see how one teacher aligned her instructional objectives for a lesson with some of the Common Core State Standards. You can also critique her effectiveness in communicating her objectives to her students.

MyEdLab Application Exercise 12.2. In this exercise, you can practice using a backward design in lesson planning.

Teacher-Directed Instructional Strategies

Teacher-directed instruction can include a variety of strategies. Much of it involves **expository instruction**, in which information is presented (i.e., *exposed*) in essentially the same form in which students are expected to learn it. Some elements of Mr. Quinn's lesson in the opening case study—notably the facts he presents and the things he presents on the screen—are expository in nature.

Yet as we'll see in upcoming sections, teachers can direct students' learning in other ways as well—for instance, by asking questions that get students thinking in particular ways or by assigning tasks that require students to practice and apply new skills.

PRESENTING NEW MATERIAL THROUGH TRADITIONAL EXPOSITORY METHODS: LECTURES AND TEXTBOOKS

Some theorists have criticized lectures and textbooks for putting students in a physically passive role (e.g., B. F. Skinner, 1968). But cognitive psychologists argue that students are often *mentally* active during such seemingly passive activities as listening and reading (Ausubel, Novak, & Hanesian, 1978; R. E. Mayer, 2011a; Weinert & Helmke, 1995). The degree to which students learn from expository instruction depends on the particular cognitive processes they engage in—for instance, the extent to which they pay attention, focus on meaningful rather than rote learning, and self-monitor their comprehension.

Unfortunately, lectures and textbooks don't always present information in ways that promote learning. For example, you can probably think of high school or college instructors whose lectures were dry, disorganized, confusing, or in some other way unmotivating and noninformative. And analyses of school textbooks in such diverse disciplines as history, geography, and science have found the focus of many texts to be on teaching specific facts, with little attention to helping students learn the facts in a meaningful way (I. L. Beck & McKeown, 1994, 2001; Brophy et al., 2009; M. C. Linn & Eylon, 2011).

The Into the Classroom feature "Effectively Using Expository Instruction" suggests several research-based strategies for promoting productive cognitive processes through explanations, lectures, and other expository approaches. Expository instruction has a distinct advantage: It enables us to present information quickly and efficiently. By itself, however, it doesn't allow us to assess students' progress in learning the subject matter. Whenever possible, then, we should use it in combination with other instructional strategies—perhaps asking questions and having students apply what they're studying in in-class and homework assignments.

Into The Classroom

Effectively Using Expository Instruction

Use an advance organizer—a verbal or graphic introduction that lays out the general organizational framework of upcoming material—to help students make meaningful connections among the things they learn.

A high school biology teacher introduces a unit on vertebrates by saying, "Vertebrates all have backbones. We'll be talking about five phyla of vertebrates—mammals, birds, reptiles, amphibians, and fish—that differ from one another in several ways, including whether their members are warm-blooded or cold-blooded; whether they have hair, scales, or feathers; and whether they lay eggs or bear live young."

Make ongoing connections between new information and things students already know, perhaps by drawing analogies between abstract ideas and students' everyday experiences.

A middle school geography teacher draws an analogy between how a glacier grows and how pancake batter behaves as it's poured into a frying pan: "As more and more substance is added to the middle, the edges spread farther and farther out."

Informally assess students' existing understandings of the topic to determine whether they have misconceptions that require conceptual change.

When beginning a unit on the solar system, a fourth-grade teacher asks her students, "What do we mean when we say that the sun *sets*? Does the sun really go *down* at the end of the day?" Several students respond that the sun does indeed go down and then travels to the other side of the world. The teacher isn't surprised—their misconception is a common one—but she works hard to show students that the earth's rotation gives the appearance of the sun moving around it, when actually the opposite is true: The earth revolves around the sun.

Present new ideas in a logical, organized manner that enables students to make appropriate interconnections among them.

While describing the contributions of various vitamins and minerals to people's health and well-being, a ninth-grade health teacher writes each nutrient and its benefits in a two-column table on the board.

Give numerous signals about the things that are most important for students to learn and remember.

When beginning a unit about the U.S. government system, a high school government teacher writes the phrase "Checks and Balances" on the board and underlines it with big, bold strokes. "This is a key principle that guided delegates to the Constitutional Convention as they wrote the Constitution. We're going to look at how each of the three branches of government—executive, legislative, and judicial—places limits on the power of the other two branches. Be sure to include at least four examples of checks and balances in your class notes for today." Later in the lesson, the teacher assigns a textbook chapter for homework and distributes a list of questions that students should be able to answer after they've finished reading the chapter.

Use visual aids to help students encode material visually as well as verbally.

In a lesson on western expansion in North America in the 1800s, a sixth-grade teacher shows photographs of typical covered wagons and wagon trains to help students get a sense of how arduous the westward migration might have been for many pioneer families.

Pace your presentation slowly enough to give students adequate time to think about and meaningfully process the information.

To demonstrate how to make a pinch pot from a ball of clay, an elementary school art teacher proceeds through the steps slowly and deliberately, explaining what he's doing every step of the way: "First I roll the clay into a nice round ball—as round as I can make it, with no cracks or rough edges. . . . Okay, see how I've done that? Now I hold the ball in both hands and gently push my thumbs into the middle, slowly pushing them farther and farther in, but being sure that I don't push them out the other side of the ball. . . . And then I gradually push the sides of the ball outward, continually turning the ball so that I make the sides of my pot an even thickness all the way around."

At the end of a lecture or reading assignment, summarize key points as a way of helping students organize the material and identify its main ideas.

A high school English teacher sums up a lesson on the poems of Emily Dickinson by describing the characteristics that make Dickinson's poetry so unique and powerful.

Sources: Bulgren, Deshler, Schumaker, & Lenz, 2000; Carney & Levin, 2002; Clement, 2008; Corkill, 1992; Dansereau, 1995; Edmonds et al., 2009; E. L. Ferguson & Hegarty, 1995; J. Hartley & Trueman, 1982; Ku, Chan, Wu, & Chen, 2008; J. R. Levin & Mayer, 1993; M. C. Linn & Eylon, 2011; Lorch, Lorch, & Inman, 1993; R. E. Mayer, 2010a; R. E. Mayer & Gallini, 1990; M. A. McDaniel & Einstein, 1989; Moreno, 2006; Newby, Ertmer, & Stepich, 1994; Pittman & Beth-Halachmy, 1997; R. E. Reynolds & Shirey, 1988; Sadoski & Paivio, 1994; Scevak, Moore, & Kirby, 1993; M. Y. Small, Lovett, & Scher, 1993; Verdi & Kulhavy, 2002; Wade, 1992; P. T. Wilson & Anderson, 1986; Winn, 1991; Wittwer & Renkl, 2008; Zook, 1991.

ASKING QUESTIONS AND GIVING FEEDBACK

Some teacher questions are lower-level questions that ask students to retrieve information in their existing knowledge base. Such questions have several benefits:

Ask lower-level questions to check for basic understanding and recall.

- They give us a good idea of students' current understandings and misconceptions about a topic.
- They help keep students' attention on the lesson in progress, especially when they require all students to respond to each question in some way.
- They help us assess whether students are learning class material successfully or, instead, are confused about particular points. (Even very experienced teachers sometimes overestimate what students are actually learning during expository instruction.)
- They give students the opportunity to monitor their *own* comprehension—to determine whether they understand the information being presented or, instead, should ask for help or clarification.
- When students are asked questions about material they have studied at an earlier time, they must review that material, which should promote greater recall later on. (Airasian, 1994; Brophy, 2006; F. W. Connolly & Eisenberg, 1990; P. W. Fox & LeCount, 1991; Lambert, Cartledge, Heward, & Lo, 2006; Wixson, 1984)

Following is an example of how one eighth-grade teacher promoted review of a lesson on ancient Egypt by asking questions:

MyEdLab
Video Example 12.1.

What purposes might questions be serving in the two lessons shown in this video—one in first-grade science and the other in middle school history?

> *Teacher:* The Egyptians believed the body had to be preserved. What did they do to preserve the body in the earliest times?
>
> *Student:* They dried them and stuffed them.
>
> *Teacher:* I am talking about from the earliest times. What did they do? Carey.
>
> *Carey:* They buried them in the hot sands.
>
> *Teacher:* Right. They buried them in the hot sands. The sand was very dry, and the body was naturally preserved for many years. It would deteriorate more slowly, at least compared with here. What did they do later on after this time?
>
> *Student:* They started taking out the vital organs.
>
> *Teacher:* Right. What did they call the vital organs then?
>
> *Norm:* Everything but the heart and brain.
>
> *Teacher:* Right, the organs in the visceral cavity. The intestines, liver, and so on, which were the easiest parts to get at.
>
> *Teacher:* Question?
>
> *Student:* How far away from the Nile River was the burial of most kings? (Aulls, 1998, p. 62)

At the end of the dialogue, a *student* asks a question, one that requests additional information. The student is apparently trying to elaborate on the material, perhaps speculating that only land a fair distance from the Nile would be dry enough to preserve bodies for a lengthy period. We can encourage such elaboration, as well as more complex cognitive processes, by asking higher-level questions—those that in some way require students to expand on the information they've learned (Brophy, 2006; Minstrell & Stimpson, 1996; Redfield & Rousseau, 1981). For instance, a higher-level question might ask students to think of their own examples of a concept, use a newly learned principle to solve a problem, or speculate about possible explanations for a cause-and-effect relationship. In the opening case study, Mr. Quinn poses such a question when he asks, "*Why did people need all these things?*" As another example, when a science class is studying the nature of air pressure at different altitudes, a teacher might ask questions about the following scenario in Rocky Mountain National Park, which has altitudes ranging from 1½ to more than 2 miles above sea level:

Ask higher-level questions to encourage elaboration and complex cognitive processes such as problem solving and critical thinking.

> A group of Girl Scouts went hiking in Rocky Mountain National Park. They noticed that it was harder to breathe when hiking in the mountains than when hiking in [hometown]. During the

hike, one girl opened a tube of suntan lotion that she bought in [hometown]. When she opened it, a small squirt of air and lotion shot out.

- Why did the girls have a hard time breathing?
- Why did the air and lotion squirt out of the tube? (Pugh, Schmidt, & Russell, 2010, p. 9)

Often we can simultaneously pose questions to *all* of our students. For example, we might ask a multiple-choice question and have students "vote" on various answers by raising their hands, holding up premade response cards, or using handheld electronic clickers that send signals to the class computer (Glass & Sinha, 2013; Lambert et al., 2006; Munro & Stephenson, 2009). However, we must give students adequate time to think about our questions and retrieve information relevant to possible answers. We must remember, too, that students from some cultural and ethnic backgrounds may intentionally allow several seconds to elapse before responding as a way of being courteous and showing respect for the speaker (Castagno & Brayboy, 2008; M. B. Rowe, 1987; Tharp, 1989).

> Have all students either manually or electronically "vote" on various answers to questions.

> The importance of such *wait time* is discussed in more detail in Chapter 4 and Chapter 6.

Unless we specifically want to have students deliberate about particular issues over a lengthy period, we should, of course, give them feedback about their responses to our questions. Furthermore, we must help students save face when an initial response is incorrect, perhaps by gently nudging them toward a better one. For example, in an elementary school lesson on the food pyramid, a student incorrectly answered that orange juice was a member of the "milk" group, and his teacher nudged him in the right direction with these hints:

> A Creating a Productive Classroom Environment feature in Chapter 9 offers additional strategies for giving feedback.

> Everything in the milk group comes from a cow. What does orange juice come from? . . . Orange juice comes from oranges. If it comes from oranges, which group is oranges? . . . Is it fruit or bread? (Brophy et al., 2009, p. 225)

PROVIDING PRACTICE THROUGH IN-CLASS ASSIGNMENTS

When we choose or create assignments for students, our number-one criterion must be to help students accomplish important instructional goals. Some goals may be at the *remember* or *understand* level in Bloom's taxonomy—for example, correctly conjugating the French verb *être* ("to be") or showing knowledge of current events around the globe. Other goals will be higher-level ones—for example, writing a well-organized persuasive essay or applying scientific principles to everyday phenomena and problems.

> Prioritize assignments based on their relevance to important instructional goals.

Especially when higher-level goals are involved, we should assign tasks that help students learn classroom material in a meaningful, integrated manner. Often we'll want to assign authentic activities, perhaps within the context of small cooperative groups in which students can share ideas, ask one another questions, and offer explanations of their thinking. Because authentic activities are typically less structured and more complex than traditional classroom tasks, they're apt to require a good deal of teacher scaffolding (Hmelo-Silver, 2006; Mergendoller, Markham, Ravitz, & Larmer, 2006; van Merriënboer, Kirschner, & Kester, 2003).

It usually isn't a good idea to fill the entire curriculum with authentic tasks, however. For one thing, students can often master basic skills more effectively when they practice them in relative isolation from more complex activities (J. R. Anderson, Reder, & Simon, 1996). For example, when learning to play the violin, students need to master their fingering before they join an orchestra, and when learning to play softball, students need to practice hitting, throwing, and catching the ball before they can have an enjoyable game. In addition, some authentic tasks are too expensive and time consuming to warrant regular use in the classroom (Bereiter & Scardamalia, 2006; M. M. Griffin & Griffin, 1994). It's probably most important that assignments encourage effective cognitive processing (e.g., organization, elaboration) and that students understand the relevance of what they're learning for larger tasks they'll face down the road (J. R. Anderson et al., 1996; Bransford et al., 2006).

Regardless of whether assignments are authentic or more traditional ones, we're most likely to facilitate students' learning and achievement when we:

- Clearly define each task and its purpose.
- Stimulate interest and cognitive engagement in the task.

Tasks that challenge students to "stretch" their existing abilities can optimally promote their cognitive development; see Vygotsky's concept of *zone of proximal development* in Chapter 2.

🍎 Begin at an appropriate difficulty level, ideally by assigning tasks that challenge students to "stretch" their existing knowledge and skills; accommodate diversity in students' abilities and needs. (Vygotsky's concept of *zone of proximal development* is helpful here.)

🍎 Increase difficulty and complexity—or gradually decrease scaffolding—as students gain proficiency.

🍎 Frequently monitor students' progress and give feedback that promotes further growth.

🍎 Assess students' work in ways that reward high quality but also allow for experimentation and risk taking.

🍎 Encourage students to reflect on and evaluate their own work. (Brophy et al., 2009; W. Doyle, 1983; Dymond, Renzaglia, & Chun, 2007; Edelson & Reiser, 2006)

When assigning tasks for students to complete at school, we might occasionally ask them to use one or more *computer tools,* as illustrated in the following examples:

- Word processing programs can enhance the quality of students' essays and short stories (e.g., see Figure 12.7).
- Database programs can help students organize information about trees or planets.
- Spreadsheets can enable students to predict changes in weather patterns or declines in endangered species populations.
- Concept-mapping and brainstorming software can help students generate and organize ideas as they study for a test or write a research paper.
- Music editors let students create musical compositions and experiment with different notes, keys, instrumental sounds, and time signatures.
- With geographic mapping software (known as *geographic information systems software,* or *GIS*), students can map data on pollutants or environmental wetlands. (Egbert, 2009; Guinee, 2003; Merrill et al., 1996; Sitko, 1998)

Have students use computer tools to complete tasks in various content domains.

We must keep in mind, however, that such tools are most likely to be effective when students have already acquired some automaticity in keyboarding and other basic computer skills.

GIVING HOMEWORK

Students can accomplish only so much during class time, and homework provides a means through which we can extend the school day. On some occasions we may want to use homework to give students extra practice with familiar information and procedures (perhaps as a way of promoting review and automaticity) or to introduce them to new but simple material (H. Cooper, 1989). In other situations we might give homework assignments that ask students to apply classroom material to their outside lives. For example, in a unit on lifestyle patterns, we might ask second graders to compare their own homes with homes of earlier time periods (e.g., caves, log cabins) and to identify modern conveniences that make their lives easier and more comfortable (Alleman & Brophy, 1998). On still other occasions we might encourage students to bring items or ideas from home (e.g., small biological specimens from the neighborhood, information about family ancestry) and use them as the basis for in-class activities (Alleman et al., 2010; Corno, 1996). When we ask students to make connections between classroom material and the outside world through homework assignments, we're potentially promoting transfer.

Doing homework appears to have a greater effect on achievement in the middle school and high school grades than in the elementary grades (H. Cooper, Robinson, & Patall, 2006). Although homework in elementary school may not enhance achievement very much, it can help students develop some of the study strategies and self-regulation skills they'll need in later years (H. Cooper & Valentine, 2001; Zimmerman, 1998). Without doubt, the *quality* of homework assignments—for instance, whether they encourage rote memorization or meaningful learning and whether students find them boring or engaging—makes an appreciable difference both in what and how much students learn and

FIGURE 12.7 Darren, a fifth grader who struggles with reading and writing, wrote this very cohesive paragraph with the help of a word processing program. A spell checker enabled him to spell most, but not all, of the words correctly. (He meant to use *very* and *sight*, not *vary* and *site*.)

When I was young it was almost impossible to read. One of my teachers told me I could learn to read if I worked hard. Learning to read was like climbing Mount Rushmore. It took a very long time but I finally got it. My Mom said she was vary proud. Reading was hard for me. It took five years for me to learn to read. Every day I would go to the learning center to learn my 400 site words. It was hard for me to learn these words but I did it. Reading is one of the most important things I have learned so far in my life.

in what kinds of learning and self-regulating strategies they develop (Dettmers, Trautwein, Lüdtke, Kunter, & Baumert, 2010; Trautwein, Lüdtke, Kastens, & Köller, 2006).

When assigning homework, we must remember that students are apt to differ considerably in the time and resources they have at home (e.g., reference books, Internet access), in the amount and quality of assistance they can get from parents and other family members, and in the extent to which they have the motivation and self-regulation strategies to keep themselves on task (Dumont et al., 2012; Eilam, 2001; Fries, Dietz, & Schmid, 2008; Xu, 2008). With these issues in mind, we authors offer the following guidelines:

- Use assignments primarily for instructional and diagnostic purposes; minimize the degree to which homework is used to assess learning and determine final class grades.

- Make homework sufficiently intriguing and challenging that students *want* to complete it; for example, give it an authentic, real-world quality, but don't make it so difficult that it leaves students confused and frustrated.

- Provide the information and structure students need to complete assignments with little or no assistance from others.

- Give a mixture of required and voluntary assignments. (Voluntary ones should help to give students a sense of autonomy and control, enhancing their intrinsic motivation.)

- Discuss homework assignments in class the following day or as soon after that as possible.

- When students have poor self-regulation skills or limited resources at home, establish supervised after-school homework programs. (Alleman et al., 2010; Belfiore & Hornyak, 1998; H. Cooper, 1989; Cosden, Morrison, Albanese, & Macias, 2001; Dettmers et al., 2011; Garbe & Guy, 2006; Patall, Cooper, & Wynn, 2010; Trautwein et al., 2006; Trautwein, Niggli, Schnyder, & Lüdtke, 2009)

We should remember, too, that homework is appropriate only to help students achieve important educational goals—*never* to punish students for misbehavior.

CONDUCTING DIRECT INSTRUCTION

Direct instruction incorporates all of the preceding strategies—expository instruction, asking questions, providing feedback, and giving in-class assignments and homework—to keep students continually and actively engaged in learning and applying classroom subject matter. To some extent, direct instruction is based on behaviorist ideas: It requires learners to make frequent responses and provides immediate reinforcement of correct responses through teacher feedback. But it also capitalizes on principles from cognitive psychology, including the importance of attention and long-term memory storage processes in learning, the limited capacity of working memory, and the value of learning basic skills to automaticity. Sociocultural theory comes into play as well, in that a teacher provides considerable scaffolding (especially at first) and might incorporate small-group activities into students' practice sessions.

Various experts describe and implement direct instruction somewhat differently. But in general, this approach involves small and carefully sequenced steps, fast pacing, and a great deal of teacher–student interaction. Each lesson typically involves most or all of the following components (Rosenshine, 2009; Rosenshine & Stevens, 1986):

1. *Review of previously learned material.* The teacher reviews relevant content from previous lessons, checks homework assignments involving that content, and reteaches any information or skills that students haven't yet mastered.

2. *Statement of the current lesson's objectives.* The teacher describes one or more concepts or skills that students should master in the lesson.

Assign homework to enhance automaticity of basic knowledge and skills, encourage review, introduce students to new but relatively simple material, or help students make connections between classroom subject matter and the outside world.

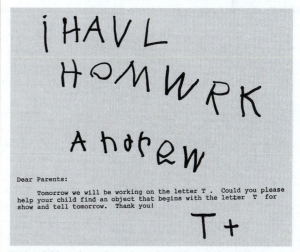

MyEdLab
Video Example 12.2.

What specific concerns does 16-year-old Josh have about homework? What might teachers do to address some of his concerns?

Giving extra homework as punishment for misbehavior communicates the message that schoolwork is unpleasant (see Chapter 9).

¡HAVL HOMWRK A hotQw

Dear Parents:
    Tomorrow we will be working on the letter T . Could you please help your child find an object that begins with the letter T for show and tell tomorrow. Thank you!

T +

Young children don't always have the self-regulation skills they need to complete homework on their own. Six-year-old Andrew and his teacher jointly constructed the homework reminder shown here.

3. *Presentation of new material in small, logically sequenced steps.* The teacher presents a small amount of information or a specific skill, perhaps through a verbal explanation, modeling, and one or more examples. The teacher may also provide an advance organizer, ask questions, or in other ways scaffold students' efforts to process and remember the material.

4. *Guided student practice and assessment after each step.* Students have numerous opportunities to practice what they're learning, perhaps by answering questions, solving problems, or performing modeled procedures. The teacher gives hints during students' early responses, provides immediate feedback about their performance, makes suggestions about how to improve, and provides additional instruction as needed. After students have completed guided practice, the teacher checks to be sure they've mastered the information or skill in question, perhaps by having them summarize what they've learned or answer a series of follow-up questions.

5. *Independent practice.* Once students have demonstrated some degree of competence, they engage in further practice either independently or in small cooperative groups. By doing so, they work toward achieving automaticity for the material in question.

6. *Frequent follow-up reviews.* Over the course of the school year, the teacher provides opportunities for students to review previously learned material, perhaps through homework assignments, writing tasks, or quizzes.

The teacher moves back and forth among these steps as necessary to ensure that all students are truly comprehending the subject matter.

Direct instruction is most suitable for teaching information and skills that are well defined and best taught in a step-by-step sequence (Rosenshine & Stevens, 1986; Spiro & DeSchryver, 2009). Because of the high degree of teacher–student interaction, it's often implemented more easily with small groups or in one-on-one tutoring sessions. Especially in such circumstances, it can lead to substantial gains in achievement (Rittle-Johnson, 2006; Watkins, 1997; Weinert & Helmke, 1995). Using direct instruction *exclusively* may be too much of a good thing, however, particularly if we don't vary instructional methods to maintain students' interest and engagement—for instance, if we just present one drill-and-practice worksheet after another (Mac Iver, Reuman, & Main, 1995; Wasley, Hampel, & Clark, 1997).

PROMOTING MASTERY

Imagine that a class of 27 students, listed in Figure 12.8, is beginning a unit on fractions. The class progresses through several lessons as follows:

Lesson 1: The class studies the basic idea that a fraction represents a part of a whole: The denominator indicates the number of pieces into which the whole has been divided, and the numerator indicates how many of those pieces are present. By the end of the lesson, 23 children understand what a fraction is. But Sarah, LaShaun, Jason K., and Jason M. are either partly or totally confused.

Lesson 2: The class studies the process of reducing fractions to lowest terms (e.g., $\frac{12}{20}$ can be reduced to $\frac{3}{5}$). By the end of the lesson, 20 children understand this process. But Alison, Reggie, and Jason S. haven't mastered the idea that they need to divide both the numerator and denominator by the same number. Sarah, LaShaun, and the other two Jasons still don't understand what fractions *are* and therefore have trouble with this lesson as well.

Lesson 3: The class studies the process of adding two fractions that have equal denominators (e.g., $\frac{1}{20} + \frac{11}{20} = \frac{12}{20}$). By the end of the lesson, 19 children can add fractions with the same denominator. However, Matt, Charlie, Maria F., and Maria W. keep adding the denominators together as well as the numerators (e.g., figuring that $\frac{1}{20} + \frac{11}{20} = \frac{12}{40}$). And Sarah, LaShaun, Jason K., and Jason M. continue to be puzzled about the general nature of fractions.

Lesson 4: The class combines the processes of adding fractions and reducing fractions to lowest terms. They must first add two fractions together and then, if necessary, reduce the sum to its lowest terms (e.g., after adding $\frac{1}{20} + \frac{11}{20}$, they must reduce the sum of $\frac{12}{20}$ to $\frac{3}{5}$). Here we lose Muhammed, Aretha, and

Explicitly teach basic skills, giving lots of scaffolded practice and frequent feedback. As students gain competence, provide less-structured practice activities.

FIGURE 12.8 How the sequential and hierarchical nature of knowledge about fractions can affect students' learning.

Students	Lesson 1: Concept of Fraction	Lesson 2: Reducing to Lowest Terms (Builds on Lesson 1)	Lesson 3: Adding Fractions with Same Denominators (Builds on Lesson 1)	Lesson 4: Adding Fractions & Reducing to Lowest Terms (Builds on Lessons 2 & 3)
Sarah	nonmastery	nonmastery	nonmastery	nonmastery
LaShaun	nonmastery	nonmastery	nonmastery	nonmastery
Jason K.	nonmastery	nonmastery	nonmastery	nonmastery
Jason M.	nonmastery	nonmastery	nonmastery	nonmastery
Alison	mastery	nonmastery	nonmastery	nonmastery
Reggie	mastery	nonmastery	nonmastery	nonmastery
Jason S.	mastery	nonmastery	nonmastery	nonmastery
Matt	mastery	mastery	nonmastery	nonmastery
Charlie	mastery	mastery	nonmastery	nonmastery
Maria F.	mastery	mastery	nonmastery	nonmastery
Maria W.	mastery	mastery	nonmastery	nonmastery
Muhammed	mastery	mastery	mastery	nonmastery
Aretha	mastery	mastery	mastery	nonmastery
Karen	mastery	mastery	mastery	nonmastery
Kevin	mastery	mastery	mastery	mastery
Nori	mastery	mastery	mastery	mastery
Marcy	mastery	mastery	mastery	mastery
Janelle	mastery	mastery	mastery	mastery
Joyce	mastery	mastery	mastery	mastery
Ming Tang	mastery	mastery	mastery	mastery
Georgette	mastery	mastery	mastery	mastery
LaVeda	mastery	mastery	mastery	mastery
Mark	mastery	mastery	mastery	mastery
Seth	mastery	mastery	mastery	mastery
Joanne	mastery	mastery	mastery	mastery
Rita	mastery	mastery	mastery	mastery
Shauna	mastery	mastery	mastery	mastery

→ = mastery of subject matter
-→ = nonmastery of subject matter

Karen because they keep forgetting to reduce the sum to its lowest terms. And of course, we've already lost Sarah, LaShaun, Alison, Reggie, Matt, Charlie, the two Marias, and the three Jasons on prerequisite skills. *We now have only 13 of our original 27 students understanding what they're doing—less than half the class!* (See the rightmost column of Figure 12.8.)

Mastery learning—a variation of direct instruction in which students must demonstrate competence in one topic before proceeding to the next—minimizes the likelihood of leaving some students behind as we proceed to increasingly challenging material (e.g., Bloom, 1981; L. S. Fuchs et al., 2005; Guskey, 1985, 2010; Zimmerman & Didenedetto, 2008). This approach is based on three assumptions:

- Almost every student can learn a particular topic to mastery.
- Some students need more time to master a topic than others.
- Some students need more assistance than others.

As you can see, mastery learning represents a very optimistic approach to instruction: It assumes that most children *can* learn school subject matter if given sufficient time and instruction to do so.[3]

In general, mastery learning includes the following components:

1. *Small, discrete units*. The subject matter is broken up into numerous lessons, with each lesson covering a small amount of material and aimed at accomplishing only a very small number of instructional objectives.

2. *A logical sequence*. Units are sequenced so that basic, foundational concepts and procedures are studied before more complex ones.

3. *Demonstration of mastery at the end of each unit*. Students move to a new unit only after they show mastery of the preceding one (e.g., by taking a quiz). Mastery is defined in specific, concrete terms (e.g., answering at least 90% of quiz items correctly).

4. *Additional activities for students needing extra help or practice to attain mastery*. Support and resources are tailored to individual needs and might include alternative approaches to instruction, different materials, specially tailored assignments, study groups, or individual tutoring.

To promote mastery of a topic, break the subject matter into small, logically sequenced units, assess students' mastery of each one, and provide additional instruction and practice as needed.

Students engaged in mastery learning often proceed through units at their own speed; hence different students may be studying different units at any given time. But it's also possible for an entire class to proceed through a sequence at the same rate: Students who master a unit more quickly than their classmates can pursue various enrichment activities, or they can serve as tutors for those still working on the unit (Block, 1980; Guskey, 1985).

The various elements of mastery learning are consistent with several theoretical perspectives. Behaviorists tell us that complex behaviors are often acquired more easily through *shaping*, whereby a simple response is reinforced until it occurs frequently (i.e., until it's mastered), then a slightly more difficult response is reinforced, and so on. Cognitive psychologists point out that information and skills that need to be retrieved rapidly or used in complex problem-solving situations must be practiced sufficiently to ensure automaticity. And as social cognitive theorists have noted, the ability to perform a particular task successfully and easily is likely to enhance students' sense of self-efficacy for performing similar tasks.

Mastery learning has several advantages over nonmastery approaches to instruction. In particular, students tend to have a better attitude toward the subject matter, learn more, and perform at higher levels on classroom assessments. The benefits are especially striking for low-ability students (Guskey, 2010; Hattie, 2009; C. C. Kulik, Kulik, & Bangert-Drowns, 1990; Shuell, 1996).

Mastery learning is most appropriate when the subject matter is hierarchical in nature—that is, when certain concepts and skills provide the foundation for future learning and genuine conceptual understanding. When instructional goals deal with such basics as word recognition, rules of grammar, arithmetic, or key scientific concepts, instruction designed to promote mastery learning may be in order. However, the very notion of mastery may be irrelevant to some

---

[3]Don't confuse mastery *learning* with mastery *goals*. Here we're talking about an instructional strategy. In contrast, mastery goals are an aspect of motivation: They reflect students' focus on gaining competence in the subject matter rather than on, say, simply getting a good grade.

long-term instructional goals. For example, skills related to critical thinking, scientific reasoning, and creative writing may continue to improve throughout childhood and adolescence without ever being completely mastered.

USING INSTRUCTIONAL WEBSITES

Internet search engines such as Google, Bing, and Yahoo! enable students and teachers to find instructional websites on virtually any topic. Many of these websites take the form of **hypermedia**, in that they enable students to look at a collection of topic-specific multimedia materials in a self-chosen sequence.

A good general informational resource for students is Wikipedia (wikipedia.org), an ever-expanding online encyclopedia to which virtually anyone can contribute about a limitless number of topics. Also, many government offices, public institutions, and private associations have websites that provide information, mini-lessons, and links to other relevant websites. Following are just a few of the innumerable possibilities:

U.S. Geological Survey (usgs.gov)

U.S. Census Bureau (census.gov)

National Aeronautic and Space Administration (nasa.gov)

National Museum of Natural History (mnh.si.edu)

The Knowledge Loom (knowledgeloom.org)

Khan Academy (khanacademy.org)

Web-based Scientific Inquiry Environment (WISE) (wise.berkeley.edu)

One especially noteworthy website on the preceding list is Khan Academy, which offers a large and growing collection of instructional videos on a wide variety of topics in math, science, economics, history, art, music, and computing.

Keep in mind, however, that students don't always have the self-regulation skills and technological literacy they need to learn effectively as they explore the many resources the Internet offers (Azevedo & Witherspoon, 2009; Warschauer, 2011; Winters, Greene, & Costich, 2008). Furthermore, the Internet doesn't have a good quality-control mechanism to ensure that information is accurate, especially when posted by individuals rather than by government agencies or professional organizations. (For example, entries in Wikipedia, although generally accurate, occasionally include inaccuracies added by nonexperts, and some individuals may intentionally "rewrite" history or science to advance a particular personal or political agenda.) An additional concern is that some students may venture into unproductive domains, perhaps finding research papers they can pass off as their own (this is plagiarism), stumbling on sites that preach racist attitudes or offer pornographic images, or sharing personal information with people who might jeopardize their well-being (Nixon, 2005; Schofield, 2006).

Clearly, then, students often need considerable scaffolding as they study a particular topic online, and their journeys into cyberspace should be closely monitored. Even in the secondary grades, students are apt to need considerable guidance about how to distinguish between helpful and unhelpful websites, sift through mountains of information in search of tidbits most relevant to their own purposes, critically evaluate the quality of the information they're finding, and synthesize what they discover into a cohesive, meaningful whole (Afflerbach & Cho, 2010; Egbert, 2009; P. A. Kirschner & van Merriënboer, 2013; Leu, O'Byrne, Zawilinski, McVerry, & Everett-Cacopardo, 2009).

One effective way to focus students' Internet searches is to post links to suitable websites on a class website. Alternatively, we might use or create a **webquest** activity, in which students can use a number of predetermined websites as they tackle an interesting and challenging task requiring higher-level thinking skills; WebQuest.org provides links to many examples. In using such strategies, we should give students explicit instructional objectives they need to accomplish as they conduct their Internet searches—for instance, by giving them specific questions to which they need to find answers (Niederhauser, 2008).

Also, many school computer systems now include a *remote desktop* feature that can help us both scaffold and monitor students' use of the Internet. With this feature, we can share our own computer screen with students and demonstrate how they should proceed with any online activity.

Scaffold students' early research on the Internet, and monitor their explorations to ensure that they don't venture into inappropriate websites and subject matter.

See Chapter 7 for recommendations about how to foster effective metacognitive skills and critical thinking skills relevant to Internet-based learning. See Chapter 8 for recommendations related to enhancing students' technological literacy skills.

The feature also allows us to view every student's computer screen from afar. If a particular student goes astray, we can lock the student's screen and send an appropriate message.

USING TECHNOLOGY TO INDIVIDUALIZE INSTRUCTION

The Internet provides limitless ways in which we can individualize instruction to match students' ability levels, interests, and needs. For instance, students can pursue personal interests through in-depth Internet searches, and many high schools now give credit for online courses offered by universities or other accredited agencies. Also, many instructional software programs—sometimes known as computer-based instruction (CBI)—are specifically designed to take individual differences into account. In their early forms in the 1970s, CBI programs were based largely on behaviorist principles of active responding, shaping, and reinforcement: Students progressed through a series of lockstep computer frames that presented small amounts of new information, asked for responses to questions, and then provided feedback. More contemporary programs typically reflect cognitivist principles as well as those of behaviorism: They capture and hold students' attention with engaging tasks and graphics, encourage meaningful learning, and present diverse examples and practice exercises that promote such complex cognitive processes as problem solving, critical thinking, and scientific reasoning. Students tend to remain physically and cognitively engaged with such programs, in large part because they must continually respond to questions and problems.

Some instructional software programs provide drill and practice of basic knowledge and skills (e.g., math facts, typing, fundamentals of music), helping students develop automaticity in these areas. Others, known as intelligent tutoring systems, skillfully guide students through complex subject matter and can anticipate and address a wide variety of misconceptions and learning difficulties (e.g., Beal, Arroyo, Cohen, & Woolf, 2010; W. Ward et al., 2013). Still others teach and scaffold complex study strategies, metacognitive skills, and self-regulation (Azevedo & Witherspoon, 2009; Graesser, McNamara, & VanLehn, 2005; Koedinger, Aleven, Roll, & Baker, 2009; Quintana, Zhang, & Krajcik, 2005; Wade-Stein & Kintsch, 2004).

A good example of an intelligent tutoring system is *My Science Tutor*, or *MyST,* in which students in the upper elementary grades have one-on-one conversations with "Marni," a computer-animated woman who both talks to them and—through the software's voice recognition and language-processing components—also listens to and understands what they say in response to her questions (W. Ward et al., 2013). Marni typically begins a conversation with a student by activating the student's prior knowledge about the topic, saying something such as "What have you been studying in science recently?" Then, after the topic of the lesson has been identified, Marni presents a series of illustrations, animations, and interactive simulations and asks more specific questions—for instance, she might ask, "So, what's going on here?" or "What could you do to . . . ?" (W. Ward et al., 2013, pp. 1118–1119). She tailors subsequent instruction to the student's current understandings and addresses any misconceptions she "thinks" they might have. Figure 12.9 presents examples of what a student might see on the computer screen in lessons on electric circuits and electromagnetism, respectively.

Well-designed programs can be quite effective in helping students learn academic subject matter (e.g., Slavin & Lake, 2008; Steenbergen-Hu & Cooper, 2013; Tamin et al., 2011). They can also be highly motivating, piquing situational interest and giving students the independence and frequent successes that can enhance their feelings of autonomy and competence (Blumenfeld, Kempler, & Krajcik, 2006; Snir, Smith, & Raz, 2003; Swan, Mitrani, Guerrero, Cheung, & Schoener, 1990). But one caveat is in order here: Too *much* independence in choice-making in a program can lead students to flounder aimlessly and not make much progress in their learning. Good CBI programs provide considerable guidance about what students should do at various steps along the way (Kanar & Bell, 2013; Karich, Burns, & Maki, 2014).

Computer-based instructional programs offer several advantages that we sometimes don't have with other forms of instruction. For one thing, CBI can seamlessly include animations, video clips, and spoken messages—components that aren't possible with traditional textbooks and other printed materials. Second, a computer can record and maintain ongoing data for every student, including such information as how far each of them has progressed in a program, how quickly they respond to questions, and how often they're right and wrong. With such data we can monitor each student's progress and identify students who appear to be struggling with the

Figure 7.6 in Chapter 7 presents another example of an intelligent tutoring system—AnimalWatch—that teaches both math and science skills in an authentic context.

FIGURE 12.9 In the intelligent tutoring system *My Science Tutor (MyST)*, elementary school students converse one on one with a virtual tutor, "Marni," who asks questions, "listens" to their answers, and tailors follow-up instruction accordingly. The screenshot on the left shows Marni asking a question about an animated electric circuit. The one on the right shows Marni "watching" and "listening" as a student experiments with an electromagnet, either increasing or decreasing the number of times the wire winds around the metal core to see its possible effects on the magnet's strength.

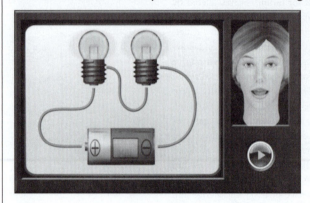
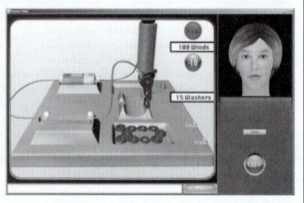

material. Finally, a computer can be used to provide instruction when flesh-and-blood teachers aren't available—for instance, in **distance learning**, in which learners receive much or all of their technology-based instruction at a location far away from that of their instructor.

To the extent that instructional websites and software programs give students control over the information they get and the order in which they get it, they're really midway along the teacher-directed–learner-directed continuum. We now turn to strategies that are even more learner-directed in nature.

MyEdLab **Self-Check 12.3**

MyEdLab **Application Exercise 12.3.** In this exercise, you can apply what you have learned about direct instruction to a third-grade reading lesson.

MyEdLab **Application Exercise 12.4.** In this exercise, you can observe and evaluate a middle school geometry lesson that uses an instructional website to teach the concept of *tessellation*.

Learner-Directed Instructional Strategies

By definition, learner-directed instruction places control of learning activities largely in students' hands. Yet for all but the most self-regulating of students, learner-directed instruction requires *some* teacher control and guidance, as we'll see in the upcoming sections.

STIMULATING AND GUIDING CLASS DISCUSSIONS

When students exchange ideas in whole-class or small-group discussions, they must elaborate on and organize their thoughts, may discover gaps and inconsistencies in their understandings, and may encounter explanations that are more accurate and useful than their own (e.g., D. W. Johnson & Johnson, 2009b; Reznitskaya & Gregory, 2013; Sinatra & Mason, 2008). Class discussions can be fruitful in virtually any academic discipline. For example, in language arts, students might discuss various interpretations of classic works of literature, addressing questions with no easy or definitive right answers (Applebee, Langer, Nystrand, & Gamoran, 2003; McGee, 1992; Wu, Anderson, Nguyen-Jahiel, & Miller, 2013). In social studies, discussing controversial topics (e.g., civil disobedience, capital punishment) can help students understand that diverse viewpoints on an issue may all have some legitimacy (D. W. Johnson & Johnson, 2009b; Kuhn & Crowell, 2011; Kuhn, Shaw, & Felton, 1997). And in science classes, discussions of various and conflicting explanations of observed phenomena can enhance students' scientific reasoning skills, promote conceptual change, and help students understand that science is a dynamic and continually evolving set of concepts and principles rather than just a collection of discrete facts (P. Bell & Linn, 2002; K. Hogan, Nastasi, & Pressley, 2000; M. C. Linn, 2008).

Although students typically do most of the talking in class discussions, teachers play critical roles, as illustrated in the following guidelines.

> Learners' beliefs about the nature of science are examples of *epistemic beliefs* (see Chapter 7).

* *Focus on topics that lend themselves to multiple perspectives, explanations, or approaches.* Such topics appear to have several benefits: Students are more likely to express their opinions, seek out new information that resolves seemingly contradictory data, reevaluate their positions on issues, and develop a meaningful and well-integrated understanding of the subject matter (Applebee et al., 2003; Jadallah et al., 2011; Sinatra & Mason, 2008; C. L. Smith, 2007).

* *Make sure students have enough prior knowledge about a topic to discuss it intelligently.* This knowledge might come either from previous class sessions or from students' personal experience. Often it comes from studying a particular topic in depth (Bruning, Schraw, & Ronning, 1995; Onosko, 1996).

* *Create a classroom atmosphere conducive to open debate and the constructive evaluation of ideas.* Students are more likely to share their ideas and opinions if their teacher is supportive of multiple viewpoints and if disagreeing with classmates is socially acceptable and psychologically "safe" (A.-M. Clark et al., 2003; Hadjioannou, 2007; Walshaw & Anthony, 2008). The following strategies can promote such an atmosphere:

  * Communicate that understanding a topic at the end of a discussion is more important than having a correct answer at the beginning of it.

  * Communicate that asking questions reflects curiosity, that differing perspectives on a controversial topic are both inevitable and healthy, and that changing one's opinion on a topic is a sign of thoughtful reflection.

  * Encourage students to explain and justify their reasoning and to try to understand one another's explanations.

  * Suggest that students build on one another's ideas whenever possible.

  * Encourage students to be open in their agreement or disagreement with classmates—that is, to agree to disagree—but to be critical of *ideas* rather than of people.

  * When students' perspectives reflect misconceptions or errors in reasoning, gently guide them toward more productive understandings.

  * Depersonalize challenges to a student's line of reasoning by framing questions in a third-person voice—for example, "What if someone were to respond to your claim by saying . . . ?"

  * Occasionally ask students to defend a position that's the opposite of what they actually believe.

  * Require students to develop compromise solutions that take into account opposing perspectives. (Cobb & Yackel, 1996; Hadjioannou, 2007; Hatano & Inagaki, 1993, 2003; Herrenkohl & Guerra, 1998; K. Hogan et al., 2000; D. W. Johnson & Johnson, 2009b; Kuhn, 2015; Lampert, Rittenhouse, & Crumbaugh, 1996; Nussbaum, 2008; Staples, 2007; Walshaw & Anthony, 2008; Webb et al., 2008)

When students become comfortable with disagreeing in a congenial way, they often find the interactions highly motivating (Certo, 2011; A.-M. Clark et al., 2003; Hadjioannou, 2007). One fourth grader, whose class regularly had small-group discussions about literature, put it this way:

> I like it when we get to argue, because I have a big mouth sometimes, and I like to talk out in class, and I get really tired of holding my hand up in the air. Besides, we only get to talk to each other when we go outside at recess, and this gives us a chance to argue in a nice way. (A.-M. Clark et al., 2003, p. 194)

🍎 *Create a class discussion board or chat room that enables students to converse about a topic or issue both in and out of school.* Such electronic mechanisms can be integral parts of a class website and—if students have Internet access at home—can easily extend the school day. Students should understand, however, that the rules for in-class discussions apply to electronic discussions as well. For example, students must accept that varying perspectives are both welcome and to be expected, and although they can certainly critique their classmates' ideas, they must do so respectfully and without ridicule (Bellanca & Stirling, 2011).

🍎 *Use small-group discussions as a way of encouraging all students to participate.* Students gain more from a class discussion when they actively participate in it (Lotan, 2006; P. K. Murphy, Wilkinson, Soter, Hennessey, & Alexander, 2009; A. M. O'Donnell, 1999). And they're more likely to speak openly when their audience is a handful of classmates rather than the class as a whole—a difference especially noticeable for girls and for students with disabilities (A.-M. Clark et al., 2003; Théberge, 1994). On some occasions, then, we may want to have students first discuss an issue in small groups—thereby allowing them to test and possibly gain support for their ideas in a relatively private context—before bringing them together for a whole-class discussion (Onosko, 1996).

🍎 *Provide a structure to guide the discussion.* Discussions are more productive when they have some sort of structure. For example, we might do the following:

🍎 Set a particular goal toward which students should work.

🍎 Assign different roles to different class members (e.g., some might serve as "recorders" of the group's discussion, others might evaluate the quality of evidence presented, and still others might evaluate the validity of conclusions).

🍎 Before conducting an experiment for the entire class to watch, ask students to make and defend predictions about what will happen; later, ask them to explain what actually happened and why. (I. L. Beck & McKeown, 2001; Calfee, Dunlap, & Wat, 1994; Hatano & Inagaki, 1991; Herrenkohl & Guerra, 1998; Nolen, 2011; Palincsar & Herrenkohl, 1999; C. L. Smith, 2007; B. Y. White & Frederiksen, 1998)

At the same time, we must recognize that the most effective group discussions are often those in which students have some control over the direction of discourse—perhaps asking their own questions, initiating new issues related to the topic, or taking a creative but risky approach or viewpoint (Aulls, 1998; M. M. Chiu, 2008; K. Hogan et al., 2000). Learner-directed discussions are also more likely to encourage effective group interaction skills (R. C. Anderson et al., 2001). For example, when elementary school students meet in small, self-directed groups to discuss children's literature, they can develop and model such skills as expressing agreement ("I agree with Kordell because . . ."), disagreeing tactfully ("Yeah, but they could see the fox sneak in"), justifying an opinion ("I think it shouldn't be allowed, because if he got to be king, who knows what he would do to the kingdom"), and seeking everyone's participation ("Ssshhh! Be quiet! Let Zeke talk!") (R. C. Anderson et al., 2001, pp. 16, 25; Certo, 2011; A.-M. Clark et al., 2003).

Ultimately, the amount of structure we impose must depend on how much scaffolding students need to have a productive discussion. For instance, we may want to be more directive with a small discussion group that seems to be unfocused and floundering than with one in which students are effectively articulating, critiquing, and building on one another's ideas (K. Hogan et al., 2000).

🍎 *Provide closure at the end of the discussion.* Even when the topic of discussion has no single right answer, a class discussion should have some form of closure that helps students tie various ideas together. For example, when we authors conduct discussions about controversial topics in our own classes, we often spend a few minutes at the end of class summarizing important ideas that students have identified. Another, more learner-directed approach is to have students themselves summarize the key issues, perhaps uploading their thoughts to a class website.

CONDUCTING RECIPROCAL TEACHING SESSIONS

Student discussions not only encourage students to think about and process classroom subject matter more thoroughly but can also promote more effective metacognitive strategies during reading and listening activities (A. L. Brown & Reeve, 1987; P. K. Murphy, Wilkinson, & Soter,

2011; Nussbaum, 2008). One form of discussion, **reciprocal teaching**, is especially effective in this regard. It focuses on promoting four metacognitive strategies:

- *Summarizing:* Identifying the gist and main ideas of a reading passage.
- *Questioning:* Asking oneself questions to make sure one understands a reading passage—that is, engaging in comprehension monitoring.
- *Clarifying:* Taking active steps to make sense of confusing or ambiguous parts of a passage, perhaps by rereading or making logical inferences.
- *Predicting:* Anticipating what is likely to come next based on cues in the text (e.g., headings) and ideas that have already been presented. (A. L. Brown & Palincsar, 1987; Palincsar & Brown, 1984, 1989; Palincsar & Herrenkohl, 1999)

In a typical reciprocal teaching session, a teacher and several students meet in a group to read a piece of text, occasionally stopping to discuss what they're reading. Initially the teacher leads the discussion, asking questions about the text to promote summarizing, questioning, clarifying, and predicting. But gradually the role of "teacher" is turned over to different students, who then take charge of the discussion and ask one another the kinds of questions their teacher has modeled. Eventually students can read and discuss a text almost independently of their teacher: They work together to construct meaning and check one another for comprehension and possible misunderstandings, and they become increasingly flexible in how they apply their newly acquired strategies (A. L. Brown & Palincsar, 1987; Palincsar & Herrenkohl, 1999).

In most instances of reciprocal teaching, students take turns reading sections of the text being discussed. Sometimes, however, the teacher reads the text, especially when working with novice readers. As an illustration, let's look at a reciprocal teaching session in which six first graders and their teacher are discussing a text about snowshoe rabbits. The teacher has just read a description of a mother rabbit giving birth to and caring for several babies. In the discussion that follows, a student named Kam takes the role of "teacher." As you read the dialogue, look for examples of summarizing, questioning, clarifying, and predicting—there's at least one instance of each.

> *Kam:* When was the babies born?
>
> *Teacher:* That's a good question to ask. Call on someone to answer that question.
>
> *Kam:* Robby? Milly?
>
> *Milly:* Summer.
>
> *Teacher:* What would happen if the babies were born in the winter? Let's think.
>
> [Several children make a number of responses, including "The baby would be very cold," "They would need food," "They don't have no fur when they are just born."]
>
> *Kam:* I have another question. How does she get the babies safe?
>
> *Kris:* She hides them.
>
> *Kam:* That's right, but something else. . . .
>
> *Teacher:* There is something very unusual about how she hides them that surprised me. I didn't know this.
>
> *Travis:* They are all in a different place.
>
> *Teacher:* Why do you think she does this?
>
> *Milly:* Probably because I heard another story, and when they're babies they usually eat each other or fight with each other.
>
> *Teacher:* That could be! And what about when that lynx comes?
>
> [Several children comment that that would be the end of all the babies.]
>
> *Travis:* If I was the mother, I would hide mine, I would keep them all together.
>
> *Kris:* If the babies are hidden and the mom wants to go and look at them, how can she remember where they are?
>
> *Teacher:* Good question. Because she does have to find them again. Why? What does she bring them?
>
> *Milly:* She needs to bring food. She probably leaves a twig or something.

When reading a story or textbook with students, ask questions that promote summarizing, questioning, clarifying, and predicting. Gradually turn the role of question-asking over to students.

Teacher: Do you think she puts out a twig like we mark a trail?

[Several children disagree and suggest that she uses her sense of smell. One child, recalling that the snowshoe rabbit is not all white in the winter, suggests that the mother might be able to tell her babies apart by their coloring.]

Teacher: So we agree that the mother rabbit uses her senses to find her babies after she hides them. Kam, can you summarize for us now?

Kam: The babies are born in the summer. . . .

Teacher: The mother . . .

Kam: The mother hides the babies in different places.

Teacher: And she visits them . . .

Kam: To bring them food.

Travis: She keeps them safe.

Teacher: Any predictions?

Milly: What she teaches her babies . . . like how to hop.

Kris: They know how to hop already.

Teacher: Well, let's read and see. (Used courtesy of A. Palincsar)[4]

Reciprocal teaching provides a mechanism through which both the teacher and the students can model effective reading and learning strategies; hence this approach has an element of social cognitive theory. But when we consider that we're encouraging effective cognitive processes by first having students practice them aloud in group sessions, we realize that sociocultural theory is also at work here: Students should eventually *internalize* processes they first use in their discussions with others. Furthermore, the structured nature of a reciprocal teaching session scaffolds students' efforts to make sense of what they read and hear. For example, in the preceding dialogue the teacher models elaborative questions and connections to prior knowledge (e.g., "What would happen if the babies were born in the winter?") and provides general guidance and occasional hints about how students should cognitively process the text ("Kam, can you summarize for us now?"). Also notice in the dialogue how students support one another in their efforts to make sense of what they are learning (e.g., Kam says, "That's right, but something else").

Reciprocal teaching promotes more effective reading and listening comprehension skills in students at all grade levels, and in English language learners as well as native English speakers (Alfassi, 2004; Johnson-Glenberg, 2000; Palincsar & Brown, 1989; Rosenshine & Meister, 1994; Slater, 2004). For example, in an early study of reciprocal teaching (Palincsar & Brown, 1984), six seventh graders with a history of poor reading comprehension participated in 20 reciprocal teaching sessions, each lasting about 30 minutes. Despite this relatively short intervention, students showed remarkable improvement in their reading comprehension skills. Furthermore, they generalized their new reading strategies to other classes, sometimes surpassing the achievement of their classmates.

We shouldn't think of reciprocal teaching as something that only reading teachers use. It's also been successfully used in science classes (where teachers have adapted it for whole-class discussions of passages in science textbooks) and math classes (where teachers have adapted it to help students make sense of complex word problems) (A. L. Brown & Palincsar, 1987; van Garderen, 2004). Furthermore, reciprocal teaching sessions can be conducted online as well as in the classroom (Reinking & Leu, 2008). Effectively using reciprocal teaching may take some practice, however. It may also require a concerted effort to make sure that students do, in fact, generate and model higher-level questions as well as lower-level ones (e.g., Hacker & Tenent, 2002).

CONDUCTING DISCOVERY AND INQUIRY ACTIVITIES

In **discovery learning**, students derive information for *themselves*—perhaps by randomly exploring and manipulating objects or perhaps by performing systematic experiments. Hands-on discovery experiences can often convey ideas that language alone can't fully communicate. For example, in the excerpt from a lab report shown in Figure 12.10, 10-year-old Berlinda describes what she has

---

[4]Excerpt by Annmarie Palincsar. Copyright © by Annemarie Palincsar. Reprinted with permission of the author.

learned about anatomy from a small-group dissection of several pig organs. Notice how her focus is largely on how the various organs *felt* when she touched them.

In his early theory of cognitive development, Jean Piaget suggested that effective discovery learning should be largely a child-initiated and child-directed effort. However, researchers have been finding that in classroom settings, students typically benefit more from carefully planned and structured activities that help them construct appropriate interpretations (Alfieri, Brooks, Aldrich, & Tenenbaum, 2011; M. C. Brown, McNeil, & Glenberg, 2009; Hardy, Jonen, Möller, & Stern, 2006; R. E. Mayer, 2004).

A variation of discovery learning, inquiry learning, typically has the goal of helping students acquire more effective *reasoning processes* either instead of or in addition to acquiring new information. For example, to help students learn to separate and control variables in scientific investigations, we might have them design and conduct experiments related to, say, factors affecting how fast a pendulum swings or how far a ball travels after rolling down an inclined plane. And we might foster critical thinking skills in history by having students read historical documents with the mind-set that they are reading *interpretations* rather than facts and therefore must look for evidence that either supports or disconfirms those interpretations. Such activities can often promote more advanced reasoning skills, especially when combined with appropriate instruction and scaffolding (Furtak, Seidel, Iverson, & Briggs, 2012; Levstik, 2011; Lorch et al., 2010; Monte-Sano, 2008).

Discovery and inquiry activities need not be limited to materials we have available in the classroom. When we have access to the Internet, our options for discovery and inquiry activities are virtually unlimited. For example, one of us authors and her middle school geography students once used the U.S. Geological Survey website (usgs.gov) to track the path of a hurricane as it made its way through the Caribbean and up the Atlantic Coast. Similarly, data available from the U.S. Census Bureau (census.gov) can enable students to explore issues related to population growth and poverty. And data from the Centers for Disease Control and Prevention (cdc.gov) can enable students to delve into issues related to cancer, air pollution, and other health-threatening conditions.

At the same time, we must note a few potential problems with discovery learning and inquiry learning activities. First, students don't always have sufficient reasoning and metacognitive skills to effectively direct their explorations and monitor their findings (de Jong, 2011; Plass, Kalyuga, & Leutner, 2010; B. White, Frederiksen, & Collins, 2009). Second, students may be overwhelmed by the many facets and subfacets of what they're observing—an issue of *cognitive load*—to the point that they can't adequately think about and sort through all the data available to them (Moreno & Park, 2010). Third, students may construct incorrect understandings from their discovery and inquiry activities; for instance, they may misinterpret or distort the evidence they gather in an experiment so that it seemingly "supports" their existing misconceptions (de Jong & van Joolingen, 1998; Karpov, 2003). Finally, such activities often take considerably more time than expository instruction, and teachers may feel torn between providing hands-on experiences, on the one hand, and covering all topics in a school-mandated curriculum, on the other (Klahr, 2009; M. C. Linn, 2008).

In our own experiences, we authors have found that students sometimes remember what they learn in hands-on activities so much more effectively than what they learn through expository instruction alone that the extra time we occasionally devote to these activities is time well spent—an instance of the *less-is-more* principle. The Into the Classroom feature "Effectively Using Discovery and Inquiry Learning Activities" offers several suggestions for maximizing the advantages and minimizing the potential shortcomings of these approaches.

USING TECHNOLOGY-BASED SIMULATIONS AND GAMES

Effective discovery and inquiry learning sessions don't necessarily have to involve actual physical objects or real-world data; they can instead involve experimentation in computer-based simulations. For example, children can learn a great deal about fractions with virtual "manipulatives" on a computer screen, and adolescents can systematically test various hypotheses that affect earthquakes or avalanches in a computer-simulated world. A particular advantage of simulations is that they can be designed in ways that keep students' cognitive load within reasonable bounds and

FIGURE 12.10 Ten-year Berlinda's report about her group's dissection of several pig organs.

> Our table was given an esophogus with felt wet and smooth. The main blood vessel which felt hard, almost as though someone had stuck a toothpick inside of it. The tracea which felt felt wet and slitely textured. The heart which, well you couldn't tell. Two lungs which felt a little bit like silly pudy.

MyEdLab
Video Example 12.3.

Effective hands-on discovery activities sometimes require considerable teacher scaffolding. What kinds of scaffolding does the teacher provide in this third-grade water-wheel-making activity?

Mistakenly finding evidence that supports existing misconceptions is a phenomenon known as *confirmation bias* (see Chapter 6 and Chapter 8).

See Chapter 6 if you need a refresher about the *less-is-more* principle.

Into The Classroom

Effectively Using Discovery and Inquiry Learning Activities

Identify a concept or principle about which students can learn something significant through interaction with their physical or social environment.

In a unit on erosion, a sixth-grade teacher sets a 4-foot-long tray at a slight incline at the front of the classroom. The tray contains quite a bit of sand at its higher end. In a series of experiments, students pour water into the tray's higher end and look at how varying water pressures and quantities differentially affect sand movement.

Make sure students have the necessary prior knowledge to make sense of what they observe.

A high school physics class studies basic principles of velocity, acceleration, and force. In a follow-up lab activity, students place metal balls of various weights and sizes at the top of an inclined plane and observe each ball's progress as it rolls down the slope. A computer attached to the plane enables the students to measure the rate of acceleration for each ball, thereby also enabling them to determine whether either weight or size influences acceleration. From the data, the students can draw conclusions about the effects of gravity.

Explicitly teach relevant reasoning processes, such as separation and control of variables in science or critical analysis of historical documents in history.

A high school history teacher gives students copies of 12 political cartoons that appeared in U.S. newspapers at various times during the Vietnam War. He first reminds students about previous lessons regarding the personal biases that underlie many human-created historical documents. He then explains the symbolic nature of political cartoons and common symbols used in them. Finally, he asks students to work in small cooperative groups to identify pro-war or anti-war messages in the cartoons, as well as possible trends in the cartoonists' opinions over time.

Show puzzling results to create disequilibrium and arouse curiosity.

A science teacher shows her class two glasses of water. In one glass an egg floats at the water's surface; in the other glass an egg rests on the bottom. The students hypothesize that one egg has more air inside and is lighter as a result. But then the teacher switches the eggs into opposite glasses. The egg that the students believe to be heavier now floats, and the supposedly lighter egg sinks to the bottom. The students are quite surprised and demand to know what's going on. (Ordinarily, water is less dense than an egg, so an egg placed in it will quickly sink. But in this situation, one glass contains saltwater—a mixture denser than an egg and thus capable of keeping it afloat.)

Simplify, structure, and guide the experience sufficiently that students proceed logically toward discoveries you want them to make.

To demonstrate the effects of prejudice, a middle school social studies teacher creates a situation in which some students experience the prejudice of classmates because of an arbitrarily chosen physical characteristic: an inability to roll their tongues. After 15 minutes—long enough for students to feel the sting of prejudice but not so long as to damage peer relationships—the teacher stops the activity and asks students to share their reactions to the experience.

Have students record their findings.

Students in a biology class collect data from a local stream and use handheld wireless computer-networking devices to send their findings to a central class computer. Once back in the classroom, the students consolidate and graph the data and look for general patterns and trends.

Help students relate their findings to concepts and principles in the academic discipline they are studying.

After students in a social studies class have collected data on average incomes and voting patterns in different counties within their state, their teacher asks, "How can we interpret these data given what we've learned about the relative wealth of members of the two major political parties?"

Actively address and correct any erroneous conclusions that students draw from their observations.

In a whole-class discovery activity regarding the nature of air, a first-grade teacher fills a glass with water and holds an index card across its top. When she turns the glass upside down and then gently removes her hand, the card continues to hold the water in the glass. The students are quite surprised, and some students suggest that the water is acting like "glue" that holds the card in place. The teacher gently nudges the students toward a better explanation: *Air* is holding the card *up*. She then has students work in small groups to explore this phenomenon on their own.

MyEdLab
Video Example 12.4.

This video shows the teacher and her students engaging in this discovery activity.

Sources: Boxerman, 2009 (erosion example); Bruner, 1966; de Jong & van Joolingen, 1998; N. Frederiksen, 1984a; Furtak et al., 2012; Hardy et al., 2006; P. A. Kirschner, Sweller, & Clark, 2006; Klahr, 2009; Leach & Scott, 2008; M. C. Linn & Eylon, 2011; Minstrell & Stimpson, 1996; Monte-Sano, 2008; Moreno, 2006; E. L. Palmer, 1965 (egg example); Pea & Maldonado, 2006 (stream example); Schwartz & Martin, 2004; B. Y. White & Frederiksen, 1998, 2005.

---

appropriately scaffold students' efforts (Baroody, Eiland, Purpura, & Reid, 2013; de Jong, 2011; Kuhn & Pease, 2010; Sarama & Clements, 2009).

Some technology-based simulations promote complex cognitive processes within seemingly authentic contexts, occasionally in the form of video games that students play alone or with peers. Following are examples:

Use well-designed computer simulations when hands-on activities are impractical or impossible.

- *Civilization.* Learners begin "living" several thousand years ago and, over many centuries, build an increasingly complex society. In an effort to survive and thrive, they must make decisions about food, natural resources, government, emerging technologies, and interactions with other social and cultural groups (civilization.com).

- *Science Court.* In a courtlike setting, learners confront common misconceptions about science, examine evidence, and make predictions (tomsnyder.com).

- *StockTrak.* Learners "invest" in various stocks in the stock market and track profits and losses in their virtual "portfolios" over time (stocktrak.com).

Such simulations are often both motivating and challenging—thereby keeping students on task for extended periods—and can significantly enhance students' reasoning and problem-solving skills (Barab, Gresalfi, & Ingram-Goble, 2010; de Jong, 2011; Kuhn & Pease, 2008; Tobias & Fletcher, 2011).

Sometimes Internet-based simulations involve many students—they may even involve many schools—working together on common problems. For example, in a simulation called GlobalEd (globaled.uconn.edu), middle school social studies classes become representatives for particular countries (e.g., one class might be France, and another might be Nigeria), with different members of a class tackling different global issues (e.g., international conflicts, human rights, environmental issues). Students study their countries and issues and then electronically communicate with representatives from other "countries" (i.e., students in other schools) to share perspectives and negotiate treaties. Not only does the simulation enhance students' understanding of global issues, but it also enhances their perspective-taking ability and interest in social studies as a discipline (Gehlbach et al., 2008).

In another, globally distributed simulation, Atlantis Remixed (ARX; atlantisremixed.org), students take on various roles (e.g., scientist, historian, mathematician) to tackle complex worldwide problems related to certain environmental or social issues, and they make decisions and take actions that have significant virtual "effects" on long-term outcomes (Barab, Gresalfi, & Arici, 2009; Barab et al., 2010). As an example, Figure 12.11 shows a screenshot in ARX's series called World Games; in this particular simulation, students examine water quality in an effort to determine why fish populations are declining in a three-dimensional fictional world.

FIGURE 12.11 This screenshot from Atlantis Remixed illustrates a technology-based simulation activity in which students examine water quality in an effort to determine why fish populations are declining in a three-dimensional virtual world. For more information about the many simulations in Atlantis Remixed, go to atlantisremixed.org.

CONDUCTING COOPERATIVE LEARNING ACTIVITIES

In your many years as a student, you've undoubtedly had a variety of incentives to do well in your classes. In the next exercise you'll consider three possibilities.

EXPERIENCING FIRSTHAND
PURPLE SATIN

Imagine yourself as a student in each of the three classrooms described here. How would you behave in each situation?

1. Mr. Alexander tells your class, "Let's find out which students can learn the most in this week's unit on the human digestive system. The three students getting the highest scores on Friday's quiz will get free tickets to the Purple Satin concert on Saturday." Purple Satin is a popular musical group you'd really like to see and hear in person, but the concert has been sold out for months.

2. Ms. Bernstein introduces her lesson this way: "I'm hoping that all of you will master the basics of human digestion this week. If you get a score of at least 90% on Friday's quiz, I'll give you a free ticket to the Purple Satin concert."

3. Mr. Camacho begins the same lesson like this: "Beginning today, you'll be working in groups of three to study the human digestive system. On Friday I'll give you a quiz to see how much you've learned. If all three members of your group score at least 90% on the quiz, your group will get free tickets to the Purple Satin concert."

In which class(es) are you likely to work hard to get free tickets to Purple Satin? How might you work *differently* in the three situations?

The first class (Mr. Alexander's) is obviously a very competitive one: Only the three best students are getting tickets to the concert. Will you try to earn one of those tickets? It all depends on what you think your chances are of being a top scorer on Friday's quiz. If you've been doing well on quizzes all year, you'll undoubtedly study harder than ever during this week's unit. If, instead, you've been doing poorly in class despite your best efforts, you probably won't work for something you're unlikely to get. But in either case, will you help your fellow students learn about the digestive system? Not if you want to go to the concert yourself!

In Ms. Bernstein's class there's no competition for concert tickets. As long as you get a score of 90% or higher on the quiz, you'll get a ticket. But will you help your classmates understand what the pancreas does or learn the difference between the large and small intestines? Maybe—*if* you have the time and are feeling altruistic.

Now consider Mr. Camacho's class. Whether or not you get a concert ticket depends on how well you *and two other students* score on Friday's quiz. Are you going to help those two students learn about salivation and digestive enzymes? And can you expect them, in turn, to help you understand where the liver fits into the whole system? Absolutely!

In cooperative learning,[5] students work in small groups to achieve a common goal. Unlike an individualistic classroom such as Ms. Bernstein's (where one student's success is unrelated to peers' achievement) or a competitive classroom such as Mr. Alexander's (where one student's success depends partly on the *failure* of others), students in a cooperative learning environment such as Mr. Camacho's work together to achieve joint successes. On some occasions cooperative groups are formed on a short-term basis to accomplish specific tasks—perhaps to study new material, solve a problem, or complete an assigned project. In other instances groups are formed to work toward long-term classroom goals. For example, base groups are cooperative groups that work together for an entire semester or school year, clarifying assignments for one another, helping one another with class notes, and giving one another a general sense of support and belonging in the classroom (D. W. Johnson & Johnson, 1991).

Consider creating cooperative *base groups* in which students can get support from two or three classmates throughout the school year.

---

[5]Some theorists distinguish between *cooperative* learning and *collaborative* learning, with different theorists drawing the dividing line somewhat differently. In this chapter, we're using cooperative learning broadly to include collaborative approaches to learning.

When students engage in cooperative learning, they reap the many benefits of student dialogue, including greater comprehension and integration of the subject matter, exposure to new strategies, and increased perspective taking. Furthermore, when students help one another learn, they provide scaffolding for one another's efforts and thus tend to have higher self-efficacy for accomplishing challenging tasks. And, of course, cooperative learning activities can provide valuable experience with the collaboration and negotiation skills that success in the adult world often requires (Good, McCaslin, & Reys, 1992; D. W. Johnson & Johnson, 2009a; A. M. O'Donnell & O'Kelly, 1994; Webb & Palincsar, 1996; J. R. White & McVeigh, 2010).

When designed and structured appropriately, cooperative learning activities can promote high achievement in students of all ability levels, including many who have historically been at risk for academic failure. They're especially suitable for complex, challenging tasks and problems in which group members can share the cognitive load and model effective learning and problem-solving strategies for one another. They can have other desirable outcomes as well, such as increased self-efficacy for academic success and more productive relationships with classmates from diverse ethnic and socioeconomic backgrounds (e.g., Ginsburg-Block, Rohrbeck, & Fantuzzo, 2006; F. Kirschner, Paas, & Kirschner, 2009; Lou, Abrami, & d'Apollonia, 2001; Pfeifer, Brown, & Juvonen, 2007; Qin, Johnson, & Johnson; R. J. Stevens & Slavin, 1995; Vaughn et al., 2011).

We should note some potential downsides of cooperative learning, however. Some students may be more interested in achieving social and performance goals (e.g., creating a good impression, getting the right answer quickly) than they are in mastering the material; consequently, they might be unwilling to ask for help or assist their classmates (Levy, Kaplan, & Patrick, 2000; Moje & Shepardson, 1998; Wentzel, 2009). In addition, students who do most of the work and most of the talking are likely to learn more than other group members (Gayford, 1992; Lotan, 2006; Webb, 1989). Furthermore, students may occasionally agree to use an incorrect strategy or method that a particular group member has suggested, or they may share misconceptions about a topic they're studying (Good et al., 1992; Stacey, 1992). And in some cases students simply don't have the skills to help one another learn (Ladd et al., 2014; Webb & Mastergeorge, 2003). Clearly, then, we must keep a close eye on group discussions, providing structure and guidance as necessary to promote maximal learning and achievement.

Following are several strategies that can enhance the effectiveness of cooperative learning groups.

🍎 *Form groups based on knowledge about which students are likely to work effectively with one another.* Cooperative groups are typically comprised of two to six members; groups of three to four students are especially effective (Hatano & Inagaki, 1991; Lou et al., 1996). In most cases we teachers should form the groups, identifying student combinations that will be productive (D. W. Johnson & Johnson, 1991; Lotan, 2006). Some advocates of cooperative learning suggest that groups be heterogeneous, with each group including high achievers and low achievers, boys and girls, and children of various ethnic backgrounds. Others disagree, arguing that too much heterogeneity makes students' differing ability levels obvious and discourages low-ability students from actively participating (Lotan, 2006; Moje & Shepardson, 1998; A. M. O'Donnell & O'Kelly, 1994; Webb, Nemer, & Zuniga, 2002).

Research regarding the effects of heterogeneous cooperative groups has yielded mixed results. Some studies indicate that heterogeneous groups benefit both high-achieving students (who can sharpen their knowledge by explaining it to peers) and low-achieving students (who benefit from hearing such explanations) (Lou et al., 1996; R. J. Stevens & Slavin, 1995; Webb, Nemer, Chizhik, & Sugrue, 1998; Webb & Palincsar, 1996). However, other studies indicate that high-achieving students *don't* always gain from working with low-achieving classmates and can occasionally even lose ground (D. M. Hogan & Tudge, 1999; Lou et al., 1996; Webb et al., 2002). Ideally, cooperative group activities require a sufficiently wide range of talents and skills that every group member has something unique and useful to contribute to the group's overall success (E. G. Cohen, 1994; Esmonde, 2009; Lotan, 2006).

🍎 *Give group members one or more common goals toward which to work.* Effective cooperative learning activities have clear, concrete goals regarding what each group should accomplish

Identify cooperative activities that require multiple talents and skills, and create groups in which all members can help one another and contribute meaningfully to the group's overall success.

FIGURE 12.12 To be effective, cooperative learning groups should work toward common goals. Here eighth-grade history teacher Mark Nichols identifies several things students need to accomplish as they prepare their group presentations about colonial America.

Group Responsibilities:

Groups will be established with 3-4 students.

Each group will be responsible for reading and thoroughly understanding their assigned sub-chapter.

Each group will prepare an outline of the chapter, which will be typed in final draft format. Copies will be made for each student in class.

Each group will create an artistic example of their material and a board game to be played at the end of the presentations.

The day before your group presentation you are to instruct the class to read your sub-chapter and prepare a homework assignment for the class.

A presentation of the material will be made to the class, which will include going over the homework assignment, the outline, and explanation of your creative display of the sub-chapter information. Class members are required to question the presenting group on their material.

An open-notes test will be given at the end of this unit in order to ensure understanding of the material.

MyEdLab
Video Example 12.5.

Watch this fifth-grade teacher conduct a class review of guidelines for cooperative group work. What particular benefits might his approach have?

(Crook, 1995; Slavin, Hurley, & Chamberlain, 2003). For example, one of us authors has a daughter, Tina, whose high school Spanish teacher once assigned a cooperative activity in which groups wrote and videotaped an episode of a television soap opera spoken entirely in Spanish. The students knew that these *telenovelas* would eventually be shown at an "Academy Awards" banquet for the students and parents, and "Oscars" would be presented for best picture, best screenplay, and so on. (Tina won for best actress—no surprise to Mom, given Tina's frequent displays of emotional drama at home.) Another example, used in an eighth-grade social studies class, is presented in Figure 12.12.

🍎 *Provide clear guidelines about how to behave.* Cooperative learning is more successful when students act respectfully and prosocially toward one another. Following are possible guidelines to give them:

- Listen to other group members politely and attentively.
- Ask questions when you don't understand something.
- Encourage other group members in their efforts, and offer assistance as needed.
- Address differences of opinion in respectful and constructive ways (e.g., I'm curious why you chose to begin with this . . .").
- Change your mind when others present persuasive arguments and evidence.
- Whenever possible, identify compromises that pull together differing perspectives. (Berger, 2003, p. 94; Deutsch, 1993; Gillies & Ashman, 1998; Lotan, 2006; Lou et al., 1996; A. M. O'Donnell & O'Kelly, 1994; Webb & Farivar, 1999)

🍎 *Structure tasks so that group members must depend on one another for success.* Students must believe that it's to their advantage to cooperate and help other group members learn. In some situations each student might have a unique and essential function within the group, perhaps serving as group leader, critic, bookkeeper, peacekeeper, or summarizer (Esmonde, 2009; D. W. Johnson & Johnson, 1991; Lotan, 2006). In other situations the **jigsaw technique** is useful: New information is divided equally among all group members, and each student must teach his or her portion to the others. A jigsaw approach can be quite effective *provided that* students give one another adequate instruction in the material they've studied (E. Aronson & Patnoe, 1997; Slavin, 2011).

When students are novices at cooperative learning, it's often helpful to give them a set of steps—a script to follow, if you will—that guides their interactions (Gillies, 2003; Ginsburg-Block et al., 2006; A. M. O'Donnell, 2006). In one simple approach, known as scripted cooperation, students work together in pairs to read and study expository text. One member of the pair might act as *recaller,* summarizing the contents of a textbook passage, while the other student acts as *listener,* correcting any errors and recalling additional important information. The two students switch roles for the subsequent passage. Such an approach can help students improve learning strategies such as elaboration, summarizing, and comprehension monitoring (Dansereau, 1988; A. M. O'Donnell, 1999).

- *Serve primarily as a resource and monitor.* Whenever we conduct a cooperative learning activity, we should provide any assistance and scaffolding necessary to keep groups on track toward meeting their goal (S. M. Williams, 2010). We must also monitor group interactions to ensure that they are productive and socially appropriate (D. W. Johnson & Johnson, 1991). For instance, if students seem to be buying into a classmate's misconception about a topic, a gentle intervention can steer a discussion in a more fruitful direction (e.g., "Lydia thinks such-and-such; do the rest of you agree with that?"). And if a student make hurtful remarks to a classmate, a reminder about the rules for behavior—and in some cases a request for an apology—may be in order. Too much intervention can be counterproductive, however: Students tend to talk less with one another when their teacher joins the group (E. G. Cohen, 1994).

- *Make students individually accountable for their achievement, but also reinforce them for group success.* Students are more likely to learn assigned subject matter during cooperative learning activities when they know they'll have to demonstrate individual mastery or accomplishment of the group's goal—for example, by answering questions in class, taking a quiz, or making a unique and easily identifiable contribution to an overall group product. Such an approach minimizes the likelihood that some students will do most or all of the work while others contribute little or nothing (Finn, Pannozzo, & Achilles, 2003; Ginsburg-Block et al., 2006; D. W. Johnson & Johnson, 2009a).

  But in addition, we might reinforce group members for the success of the group as a whole—a *group contingency* in action (Lou et al., 1996; Slavin, 2011). Such group rewards often promote higher achievement overall, perhaps because students have a vested interest in one another's performance and thus make a concerted effort to help fellow group members understand the subject matter (R. J. Stevens & Slavin, 1995). One commonly used approach is to give students a quiz over material they've studied in cooperative learning groups and award one or two bonus points if all group members perform at or above a certain level.

  See Chapter 9 for a discussion of group contingencies.

- *At the end of an activity, have groups evaluate their effectiveness.* After cooperative groups have accomplished their goals, we should have them look analytically and critically (perhaps with our assistance) at the ways in which they've functioned effectively and the ways in which they need to improve (E. G. Cohen, 1994; Deutsch, 1993; D. W. Johnson & Johnson, 2009a).

STRUCTURING PEER TUTORING SESSIONS

In peer tutoring, students who have mastered a topic teach those who haven't. Peer tutoring sometimes occurs spontaneously in cooperative learning activities, but we can also use it as an instructional strategy in its own right. On some occasions we might have students within a single class tutor one another. At other times we might have older students teach younger ones—perhaps fourth or fifth graders teaching students in kindergarten or first grade. Additionally, we might create a schoolwide tutoring program. One of us authors had such a program at her own high school; it was a highly successful one coordinated by the school's chapter of the National Honor Society.

Peer tutoring sessions can provide a context in which struggling students can more easily ask questions and get immediate feedback about their performance. But the tutors often benefit as well, in part because they can practice using and elaborating on their newly acquired knowledge and skills. Furthermore, in the process of directing and guiding other students' learning and problem solving, tutors may *internalize* these processes (as sociocultural theorists would predict) and thus become better able to direct and guide their *own* learning and problem solving. In other words, peer tutoring can foster greater self-regulation in the tutors. Accordingly, both the tutors and the students they tutor are likely to show significant academic gains (Biemiller, Shany, Inglis, & Meichenbaum, 1998; A. M. O'Donnell, 2006; Graesser, D'Mello, & Cade, 2011; D. R. Robinson, Schofield, & Steers-Wentzell, 2005; Roscoe & Chi, 2007; J. R. Sullivan & Conoley, 2004).

Peer tutoring has nonacademic benefits as well. Cooperation and other social skills improve, behavior problems diminish, and friendships form among students of different ethnic groups and between students with and without disabilities (Cushing & Kennedy, 1997; DuPaul, Ervin, Hook, & McGoey, 1998; Greenwood, Carta, & Hall, 1988; D. R. Robinson et al., 2005).

Following are several research-based recommendations for enhancing the effectiveness of peer tutoring.

🍎 *Make sure that tutors have mastered the material they are teaching and that they use sound instructional techniques.* In most cases, good tutors have a solid understanding of the subject matter they're teaching and can provide explanations that focus on meaningful (rather than rote) learning. Good tutors also use teaching strategies that are likely to promote learning; for instance, they ask questions, give hints, scaffold responses when necessary, and provide constructive feedback (L. S. Fuchs et al., 1996; Lepper, Aspinwall, Mumme, & Chabay, 1990; Roscoe & Chi, 2007).

Especially in the elementary grades, explicit training in tutoring skills can be helpful. For example, student tutors might be shown how to establish a good relationship with the students they're tutoring, how to break a task into simple steps, and how and when to give feedback (Fueyo & Bushell, 1998; Graesser et al., 2011; Inglis & Biemiller, 1997; D. R. Robinson et al., 2005).

🍎 *Provide a structure for students' interactions.* Providing a structure for tutoring sessions can often help students facilitate their classmates' learning (Fantuzzo, King, & Heller, 1992; L. S. Fuchs et al., 1996; Mathes, Torgesen, & Allor, 2001; Spörer & Brunstein, 2009). As an example, in one study (D. Fuchs, Fuchs, Mathes, & Simmons, 1997), 20 second- through sixth-grade classes participated in a program called Peer-Assisted Learning Strategies (PALS), designed to foster more effective reading comprehension skills. In each class, students were ranked with regard to their reading performance, and the ranked list was divided in half. The first-ranked student in the top half of the list was paired with the first-ranked student in the bottom half of the list, the second student in the top half was paired with the second student in the bottom half, and so on down the list. Through this procedure, students who were paired together had moderate but not extreme differences in reading level. Each pair read material at the level of the weaker reader and engaged in the following activities:

- *Partner reading with retell.* The stronger reader read aloud for 5 minutes, then the weaker reader read the same passage of text. Reading something that a higher-ability peer had previously just read presumably enabled the weaker reader to read the material easily. After the double reading, the weaker reader described the material the pair just read.

- *Paragraph summary.* The students both read a passage one paragraph at a time. Then, with help from the stronger reader, the weaker reader tried to identify the subject and main idea of the paragraph.

- *Prediction relay.* Both students read a page of text, and then, with help from the stronger reader, the weaker reader summarized the text and also made a prediction about what the next page would say. The students then read the following page, and the weaker reader would confirm or disconfirm the prediction, summarize the new page, and make a new prediction.

This procedure enabled students in the PALS program to make significantly more progress in reading than students who had traditional reading instruction, even though the amount of class time devoted to reading was similar for both groups. The researchers speculated that the superior performance of the PALS students was probably the result of students' more frequent opportunities to respond to what they were reading, more frequent feedback about their performance, and, in general, greater support for using effective reading strategies.

At the middle and secondary school levels, we can incorporate a tutoring component into paired study sessions by teaching students the kinds of questions they might ask one another as they jointly study science, social studies, and other academic disciplines. In one approach (A. King, 1997, 1999), students are given question "starters" to help them formulate higher-level questions (e.g., "What is the difference between ___ and ___?" "What do you think would happen to ___ if ___ happened?") (A. King, 1997, p. 230). In the following dialogue, two seventh graders use question starters as they work together to learn more about muscles, a topic that neither of them has previously known much about:

Jon: How does the muscular system work, Kyle?

Kyle: Well . . . it retracts and contracts when you move.

Jon: Can you tell me more? . . . Um, why are muscles important, Kyle?

Kyle: They are important because if we didn't have them we couldn't move around.

Jon: But . . . how do muscles work? Explain it more.

Kyle: Um, muscles have tendons. Some muscles are called skeletal muscles. They are in the muscles that—like—in your arms—that have tendons that hold your muscles to your bones—to make them move and go back and forth. So you can walk and stuff.

Jon: Good. All right! How are the skeletal muscles and the cardiac muscles the same? . . .

Kyle: Well, they're both a muscle. And they're both pretty strong. And they hold things. I don't really think they have much in common.

Jon: Okay. Why don't you think they have much in common?

Kyle: Because the smooth muscle is—I mean the skeletal muscle is voluntary and the cardiac muscle is involuntary. Okay, I'll ask now. What do you think would happen if we didn't have smooth muscles?

Jon: We would have to be chewing harder. And so it would take a long time to digest food. We would have to think about digesting because the smooth muscles—like the intestines and stomach—are *in*voluntary. . . .

Kyle: Yeah, well—um—but, do you think it would *hurt* you if you didn't have smooth muscles?

Jon: Well, yeah—because you wouldn't have muscles to push the food along—in the stomach and intestines—you'd get plugged up! Maybe you'd hafta drink liquid— just liquid stuff. Yuk. (A. King, Staffieri, & Adelgais, 1998, p. 141)

Notice how the boys ask each other questions that encourage elaboration and metacognitive self-reflection (e.g., "Why don't you think they have much in common?" "Do you think it would hurt you if you didn't have smooth muscles?"). Through such structured interactions, students at the same grade and ability levels can provide valuable scaffolding for one another's learning efforts (A. King et al., 1998).

🍎 *Be careful that your use of higher-achieving students to tutor lower-achieving students is not excessive or exploitative.* As we've seen, tutors often gain just as much from tutoring sessions as the students they're tutoring. Nevertheless, we mustn't assume that high-achieving students will always learn from a tutoring session. Instead, we should regularly monitor the effects of a peer-tutoring program to make sure that all students are reaping its benefits.

🍎 *Give all students opportunities to tutor other individuals.* This is often easier said than done, as a few students may show consistently lower achievement than most of their peers. One effective approach is to ask low-achieving students to tutor classmates with disabilities (Cushing & Kennedy, 1997; DuPaul et al., 1998; D. Fuchs et al., 1997). Another possibility is to teach low-achieving students specific tasks or procedures they can share with their higher-achieving, but in this case uninformed, classmates (E. G. Cohen, Lockheed, & Lohman, 1976; Webb & Palincsar, 1996). Still another is to have students teach basic skills to younger children (Inglis & Biemiller, 1997). In fact, students with significant social or behavioral problems (e.g., autism spectrum disorders, emotional and behavioral disorders) can make significant gains in both academic and social skills when they have opportunities to tutor children several years younger than they are (J. R. Sullivan & Conoley, 2004).

CONDUCTING TECHNOLOGY-BASED COLLABORATIVE LEARNING ACTIVITIES

Effective cooperative and collaborative activities don't necessarily have to be face to face. Through such mechanisms as email, chat software, class websites and blogs, electronic bulletin boards, and Skype, computer technology enables students to communicate with their peers (either locally or around the world), exchange perspectives, brainstorm and build on one another's ideas, and occasionally pull experts into the conversation. Students must understand, however, that the rules for in-class discussions apply to electronic discussions as well. For instance, students must accept that varying perspectives are both welcome and to be expected, and although they can certainly critique others' ideas, they must do so respectfully and without ridicule (Bellanca & Stirling, 2011; Kreijns, Kirschner, & Vermeulen, 2013).

Software created at the University of Toronto provides an example of how technology can enhance student interaction and collaborative learning. The software, called Knowledge Forum (knowledgeforum.com), provides a multimedia database that enables students to jointly construct a body of shared knowledge about a particular topic, perhaps aerodynamics, the American Civil War, or optics. In this electronic environment, students post their work in the form of reports, problem solutions, diagrams, flowcharts, short stories, and the like. Their classmates respond regularly, perhaps by giving feedback, building on ideas, offering alternative perspectives, or synthesizing what the group has been learning; sometimes a subject-matter expert gets involved in the conversation as well. The electronic nature of interactions gives students the time they may need to reflect on one another's ideas and may be especially welcoming for students who are shy or for other reasons feel uncomfortable communicating with peers more publicly. In essence, the software provides the foundation for a computer-based *community of learners* in which most students feel comfortable and psychologically "safe" (Hewitt & Scardamalia, 1996, 1998; Lamon, Chan, Scardamalia, Burtis, & Brett, 1993; Scardamalia & Bereiter, 2006).

Another option for technology-based collaborative learning is the GLOBE Program (globe.gov), through which student groups around the world collaborate on inquiry-based projects related to environmental and earth sciences. Students in participating schools and classrooms collect and analyze data about various environmental topics (e.g., climate change, watershed dynamics), write reports, and share their findings with students and professional scientists elsewhere.

As the Internet becomes increasingly accessible to learners worldwide, then, not only do we have limitless sources of information on which to draw, but we also have limitless mechanisms for communicating and collaborating with other people in faraway settings about issues of common interest. Multinational student–student collaborations are an excellent way to get young learners thinking and acting as *global* citizens as well as citizens of a particular community and country.

Chapter 8 describes communities of learners in more detail.

MyEdLab **Self-Check 12.4**

MyEdLab **Application Exercise 12.5.** In this exercise, you can explore various strategies for conducting a cooperative learning activity.

Taking Instructional Goals and Student Diversity into Account

Let's return to the first of the general principles presented at the beginning of the chapter: *Effective teachers begin their instructional planning by determining what they ultimately want students to know and be able to do.* Table 12.2 presents several general instructional goals we might have, along with potentially useful instructional strategies for accomplishing each one. Notice that many of the strategies we've examined in this chapter appear two or more times in the table, reflecting the multiple purposes for which they might flexibly be used.

To some degree, the instructional strategies we choose must also take into account students' ages and developmental levels. For example, strategies that involve a lot of active responding and frequent feedback (e.g., direct instruction, mastery learning) may be especially appropriate for younger students (Brophy et al., 2009; Rosenshine & Stevens, 1986). Lectures (which are often

COMPARE/CONTRAST

TABLE 12.2 • Choosing an Instructional Strategy	
WHEN YOUR GOAL IS TO HELP STUDENTS . . .	**CONSIDER USING . . .**
Master and review basic skills	• Direct instruction • Lower-level teacher questions • In-class assignments • Homework assignments in which students practice skills they have previously learned in class • Mastery learning • Instructional websites • Computer-based instruction (some programs) • Cooperative learning • Peer tutoring
Gain firsthand, concrete experience with a particular topic	• Authentic activities • Discovery or inquiry learning • Computer simulations
Gain a general, relatively abstract body of knowledge about a topic	• Lectures • Textbooks and other assigned readings • Instructional websites • Intelligent tutoring systems
Connect school subject matter to real-world contexts and problems	• Authentic activities • Appropriately designed and scaffolded homework assignments • Inquiry learning • Computer simulations • Technology-based collaborative learning
Acquire advanced understandings about a topic and/or develop complex cognitive processes (e.g., problem solving, critical thinking, scientific reasoning)	• Higher-level teacher questions • Authentic activities • Computer-based instruction (some programs) • Class discussions • Inquiry learning • Intelligent tutoring systems • Cooperative learning • Technology-based collaborative learning
Acquire increased metacognitive awareness and more effective reading comprehension and self-regulation strategies	• Age-appropriate homework assignments that foster independent study habits and scaffold metacognitive processes (e.g., self-questioning, self-monitoring) • Computer-based instruction (some programs) • Reciprocal teaching • Cooperative learning • Peer tutoring (which can enhance tutors' self-regulation skills)
Acquire technological literacy skills	• Regular use of a class website • Instructional websites • Computer-based instruction • Computer simulations • Technology-based collaborative learning
Acquire effective strategies for interacting and working with others	• Class discussions • Reciprocal teaching • Small-group inquiry learning • Multiplayer computer simulations and games • Cooperative learning • Peer tutoring • Technology-based collaborative learning

somewhat abstract) and complex homework assignments tend to be more effective with older students (Ausubel et al., 1978; H. Cooper et al., 2006).

The knowledge and skills that students bring to a topic must be considerations as well. Structured, teacher-directed approaches are probably most appropriate when students know little or nothing about the topic. But when students have mastered basic knowledge and skills—and especially when they're self-regulating learners—they should begin to direct some of their own

When choosing instructional strategies, take into account students' developmental levels, background knowledge, and self-regulation skills.

learning, perhaps in intelligent tutoring systems, small-group discussions, or technology-based collaborative activities.

In general, however, *all* students should have experience with a wide variety of instructional methods. For example, although some students may need a considerable amount of direct instruction to learn and practice basic skills, authentic activities—perhaps within the context of small cooperative groups—can give them a greater appreciation for the relevance and meaningfulness of classroom subject matter. Furthermore, too much time in structured, teacher-directed activities can minimize opportunities to choose what and how to study and learn and, as a result, can prevent students from developing the sense of autonomy so important for intrinsic motivation (Battistich, Solomon, Kim, Watson, & Schaps, 1995; Reeve, 2009).

CONSIDERING GROUP DIFFERENCES

Students' cultural and ethnic backgrounds may occasionally have implications for our choice of instructional strategies. For instance, students from cultures that place a high premium on interpersonal cooperation (e.g., as is true in many Hispanic and Native American communities) are apt to achieve at higher levels in classrooms with many interactive and collaborative activities (Castagno & Brayboy, 2008; García, 1994, 1995; Webb & Palincsar, 1996). In contrast, recent immigrants from some Asian countries may be more accustomed to teacher-directed instruction than to learner-directed classroom activities, and students who have only limited proficiency in English may be reluctant to speak up in class discussions (Igoa, 1995; Walshaw & Anthony, 2008). When working with English language learners, technology can often come to our assistance, perhaps in the form of bilingual software for teaching basic skills, English-language tutorials, and word processing programs with spell checkers and grammar checkers (Egbert, 2009; Merrill et al., 1996).

We must take gender differences into account as well. For example, video games that engage students in simulated real-world problems can often captivate boys who aren't otherwise motivated to master academic skills (Carr-Chellman, 2012). Meanwhile, although many boys thrive on competition, girls tend to do better when instructional activities are interactive and cooperative. However, girls can be intimidated by whole-class discussions; they're more likely to participate when discussions and activities take place in small groups (Théberge, 1994). Because boys sometimes take charge of small-group activities, we may occasionally want to form all-female groups. By doing so, we're likely to increase girls' participation in group activities and to encourage them to take leadership roles (Fennema, 1987; MacLean, Sasse, Keating, Stewart, & Miller, 1995; Slavin et al., 2003).

Our choice of instructional strategies can be especially critical when we work in schools in low-income, inner-city neighborhoods. Students in such schools often get a lot of drill-and-practice work in basic skills—work that's hardly conducive to fostering excitement about academic subject matter (R. Ferguson, 1998; Pianta & Hamre, 2009; Portes, 1996). Mastering basic information and skills is essential, to be sure, but we can frequently incorporate them into authentic activities and computer-based simulations and games in which students apply what they're learning to personal interests and real-world contexts (Eccles, 2007; Lee-Pearce, Plowman, & Touchstone, 1998; Squire, 2011). For example, in a curriculum called Kids Voting USA, students in kindergarten through grade 12 engage in age-appropriate lessons about voting, political parties, and political issues, and they relate what they learn to local election campaigns (M. McDevitt & Chaffee, 1998; Meirick & Wackman, 2004; also see kidsvotingusa.org). Depending on the grade level, students might conduct their own mock elections, analyze candidates' attacks on opponents, or give speeches about particular propositions on a ballot. Students who participate in the program are more likely to attend regularly to media reports about an election, initiate discussions about the election with friends and family members, and be knowledgeable about candidates and election results. In fact, their knowledge and excitement about politics is contagious, because even their *parents* begin to pay more attention to the news, talk more frequently about politics, and acquire more knowledge about candidates and political issues.

Interactive and collaborative strategies are particularly valuable when our instructional goals include promoting social development as well as academic achievement. As we've seen, such interactive approaches as cooperative learning and peer tutoring encourage friendly relationships across ethnic groups. Furthermore, collaborative activities—especially when they require multiple skills and abilities—can foster an appreciation for the various talents that students with diverse backgrounds can contribute (E. G. Cohen, 1994; E. G. Cohen & Lotan, 1995).

Identify teaching strategies that are compatible with students' cultural backgrounds.

Use cooperative approaches to enhance the achievement of females and of students whose cultural groups especially value cooperation.

ACCOMMODATING STUDENTS WITH SPECIAL NEEDS

We must often modify our instructional goals and strategies for students who have exceptional cognitive abilities or disabilities—an example of the *differentiated instruction* mentioned early in the chapter. For example, to ensure that all students are working on tasks appropriate for their current skill levels (i.e., tasks within each student's zone of proximal development), we may need to identify more basic instructional goals for some students (e.g., those with intellectual disabilities) and more challenging goals for others (e.g., those who are gifted). In addition, different instructional strategies may be more or less useful for students with different kinds of special needs. For instance, strictly expository instruction (e.g., a lecture or textbook chapter) can provide a quick and efficient means of presenting new ideas to students who process information quickly and abstractly but might be incomprehensible and overwhelming to students with low cognitive ability. Similarly, inquiry learning and discussion-based approaches are often effective in enhancing the academic achievement of students with high ability but may be detrimental to the achievement of lower-ability students who haven't yet mastered basic concepts and skills (Corno & Snow, 1986; Lorch et al., 2010). In contrast, mastery learning and direct instruction have been shown to be effective with students who have learning difficulties, but these approaches might prevent rapid learners from progressing at a rate commensurate with their potential (Arlin, 1984; Rosenshine & Stevens, 1986; J. A. Stein & Krishnan, 2007). Table 12.3 identifies some characteristics of students with special needs that might influence instructional decision making.

Include your instructional strategies in the individualized education programs (IEPs) you develop for students with special needs.

Chapter 5 identifies specific categories of special needs that fall within the five general categories listed in Table 12.3.

STUDENTS IN INCLUSIVE SETTINGS

TABLE 12.3 • Identifying Appropriate Instructional Goals and Strategies for Students with Special Educational Needs		
CATEGORY	**CHARACTERISTICS YOU MIGHT OBSERVE**	**SUGGESTED STRATEGIES**
Students with specific cognitive or academic difficulties	• Uneven patterns of achievement • Difficulty with complex cognitive tasks in some content domains • Difficulty processing or remembering information presented in particular modalities • Poor listening skills, reading skills, or both • Greater-than-average difficulty in completing homework assignments	• Tailor goals to individual students' strengths and weaknesses. • Identify the specific cognitive skills involved in a complex task; consider teaching each skill separately. • Use direct instruction, mastery learning, computer-based instruction, cooperative learning, and peer tutoring to help students master basic knowledge and skills. • Provide information through multiple modalities (e.g., videotapes, audiotapes, graphic materials); also provide advance organizers and study guides. • Have students use computer tools (e.g., grammar and spell checkers) to compensate for areas of weakness. • Assign homework that provides additional practice in basic skills; provide extra scaffolding (e.g., solicit parents' help, explicitly teach effective study habits). • Use reciprocal teaching to promote listening and reading comprehension strategies.
Students with social or behavioral problems	• Frequent off-task behaviors • Inability to work independently for extended periods • Poor social skills	• Use small-group direct instruction and peer tutoring as ways of providing one-on-one attention. • Keep unsupervised seatwork assignments to a minimum. • Use cooperative learning to foster social skills and friendships. • Give explicit guidelines about how to behave during interactive learning activities; closely monitor students' behavior in small groups. • As appropriate, use strategies previously listed for students with specific cognitive or academic difficulties.
Students with general delays in cognitive and social functioning	• Difficulty with complex tasks • Difficulty thinking abstractly • Need for a great deal of repetition and practice of basic information and skills • Limited ability to transfer information and skills to new situations	• Identify realistic goals related to both academic and social development. • Break complex behaviors into simpler responses that students can easily learn. • Present information in a concrete form (e.g., through hands-on experiences). • Provide extended practice in basic skills. • Embed skills within simple authentic tasks to promote transfer to the real world. • Use peer tutoring to promote friendships with nondisabled classmates; also identify skills these students can teach to classmates or younger students.

(Continued)

TABLE 12.3 • Continued		
CATEGORY	**CHARACTERISTICS YOU MIGHT OBSERVE**	**SUGGESTED STRATEGIES**
Students with physical or sensory challenges	• Average intelligence in most instances • Tendency to tire easily (for some) • Limited motor skills (for some) • Difficulty with speech (for some)	• Aim for instructional goals similar to those for nondisabled students unless there is a compelling reason to do otherwise. • Allow frequent breaks from strenuous or intensive activities. • Use instructional software (with any needed mechanical adaptations) to individualize instruction. • When students have trouble speaking, provide assistive technology that enables them to participate actively in group activities.
Students with advanced cognitive development	• Rapid learning • Greater frequency of responses at higher levels of Bloom's taxonomy (e.g., analysis, evaluation) • Greater ability to think abstractly; earlier appearance of abstract thinking • Greater conceptual understanding of classroom material • Ability to learn independently	• Identify goals and objectives that challenge students and encourage them to develop to their full potential. • Use expository instruction (e.g., lectures, advanced reading materials, instructional websites) as a way of transmitting abstract information about particular topics quickly and efficiently. • Provide opportunities to pursue topics in greater depth (e.g., through assigned readings, the Internet, or homogeneous cooperative learning groups). • Teach strategies that enable students to learn on their own (e.g., teach library skills, effective use of Internet websites, scientific methods of inquiry). • Ask predominantly higher-level questions. • Introduce students to safe Internet outlets where they can communicate with others who have similar interests and abilities. • Use advanced students as peer tutors only if both tutors and learners will benefit.

Sources: Strategies based on suggestions from T. Bryan, Burstein, & Bryan, 2001; Carnine, 1989; Connor, 2006; DuNann & Weber, 1976; Egbert, 2009; Fiedler, Lange, & Winebrenner, 1993; Fletcher, Lyon, Fuchs, & Barnes, 2007; Greenwood et al., 1988; Heward, 2009; C. C. Kulik et al., 1990; Mercer & Pullen, 2005; Merrill et al., 1996; Morgan & Jenson, 1988; Piirto, 1999; A. Robinson, 1991; Ruef, Higgins, Glaeser, & Patnode, 1998; Schiffman, Tobin, & Buchanan, 1984; Spicker, 1992; R. J. Stevens & Slavin, 1995; J. R. Sullivan & Conoley, 2004; Tarver, 1992; Turnbull, Turnbull, & Wehmeyer, 2010; J. W. Wood & Rosbe, 1985.

MyEdLab **Self-Check 12.5**

MyEdLab **Application Exercise 12.6.** In this exercise, you can apply what you have learned about planning and instruction to analyze an actual lesson plan.

12   What Have You Learned?

As a way of summarizing key ideas in the chapter, we now return to the chapter's learning outcomes.

◼ **12.1: Identify eight general principles that can guide your planning and instructional strategies.** As teachers, we must choose our strategies on the basis of our instructional goals and objectives, the specific topics we're teaching, and the unique characteristics of our students. More specifically, we should:

• Begin our planning with what we ultimately want students to achieve and then choose instructional strategies accordingly.

• Flexibly combine multiple strategies into each lesson or unit.

• Encourage and support cognitive processes through which students can effectively understand and apply classroom subject matter.

• Focus on knowledge and skills most important for students' long-term success.

• Provide structure and scaffolding appropriate for students' ability levels.

• Capitalize on technological innovations that can enhance students' performance.

• Take individual and group differences into account in instructional decision making.

• Regularly assess students' progress in order to both modify lesson plans and provide constructive feedback.

◼ **12.2: Describe important elements of instructional planning, and explain how and why planning and instruction must be closely intertwined.** Effective teachers engage in considerable advance planning, and they continually evaluate and modify their plans as the school year progresses. They identify the general instructional goals and more specific instructional objectives they would like students to accomplish, and they plan their lessons and instructional strategies accordingly. They conduct task analyses to break complex tasks into smaller and simpler components, and they develop lesson plans that spell out the instructional activities and assessments they'll use each day. And with the increasing availability of computer technology and the Internet in today's world, many teachers now create class-specific websites that enable them to communicate effectively with students and parents.

■ **12.3: Explain how you can effectively promote students' learning through teacher-directed instructional strategies.** In teacher-directed instruction, a teacher is largely in control of the content and course of a lesson. Teacher-directed strategies take multiple forms, but typically they involve some degree of *expository* instruction; that is, they present (expose) information in more or less the same form that students are expected to learn it. Lectures, textbooks, and other predominantly expository approaches are most effective when we apply basic principles of cognitive psychology—for example, when we show students how new material relates to their prior knowledge and help them encode ideas in multiple ways. Many teacher-directed strategies also include ongoing teacher–student interaction. For example, we can encourage students to elaborate on what they've learned through the questions we ask and the feedback we give, and we can provide practice and encourage complex cognitive processes (e.g., transfer, problem solving, critical thinking) through in-class assignments and homework. We can also combine several teacher-directed strategies into direct instruction and/or mastery learning sessions. Instructional websites and computer-based instruction—which often fall midway along the teacher-directed–learner-directed continuum—provide additional options for teaching a variety of academic topics and skills.

■ **12.4: Explain how you can also promote students' learning through more learner-directed strategies.** Learner-directed instruction is instruction in which students have considerable control regarding the specific issues they address and the ways they address them. Like teacher-directed instruction, it can take a variety of forms. For example, class discussions and technology-based collaborative learning provide arenas in which students can encounter multiple perspectives on complex or controversial topics and build on one another's ideas. Reciprocal teaching encourages more sophisticated metacognition and study skills by modeling and providing practice in effective reading strategies. Structured discovery learning and inquiry learning activities provide opportunities for students to self-construct new knowledge or develop advanced reasoning skills through in-depth observations and/or data analyses. Well-designed computer simulations and games can immerse students in virtual environments in which they apply classroom subject matter to real-world-like problems. Cooperative learning activities encourage students to work collaboratively on challenging tasks and to mutually support one another's efforts to learn and achieve. And peer-tutoring sessions can help both the tutor and the student being tutored gain better understandings of classroom subject matter.

■ **12.5: Choose appropriate instructional strategies for varying instructional goals and different kinds of students.** Different instructional goals and objectives often require somewhat different instructional strategies. For instance, whereas expository methods may be quite useful in teaching basic knowledge and skills, learner-directed approaches tend to be better for promoting complex cognitive processes such as problem solving and critical thinking. Students' unique characteristics, abilities, and circumstances are important considerations as well. For example, cooperative learning activities may be especially effective with students whose cultural backgrounds encourage cooperation rather than competition, and authentic activities and computer simulations can be quite motivating for students from low-income backgrounds.

Practice for Your Licensure Exam

Cooperative Learning Project

One Monday morning Ms. Mihara begins the unit "Customs in Other Lands" in her fourth-grade class. She asks students to choose two or three students with whom they would like to work to study a particular country. After the students have assembled into six small groups, she assigns each group a country: Australia, Colombia, Ireland, Greece, Japan, or South Africa. She tells the students, "Today we'll go to the school library, where your group can find information on the customs of your country, print out relevant materials you find on the Internet, and check out books and magazines you think might be useful. Every day over the next 2 weeks you'll have time to work with

your group. A week from Friday, each group will give an oral report to the class."

During the next few class sessions, Ms. Mihara runs into many more problems than she anticipated. She realizes that the high achievers have gotten together to form one of the groups, and many socially oriented, "popular" students have flocked to two others. The remaining two groups are comprised of whichever students were left over. Some groups get to work immediately on their task, others spend their group time joking and sharing gossip, and still others are neither academically nor socially productive.

As the unit progresses, Ms. Mihara hears more and more complaints from students about their task: "Janet and I are doing all the work; Karen and Mary Kay aren't helping at all," "Eugene thinks he can boss the rest of us around because we're studying Ireland and he's Irish," "We're spending all this time but just can't seem to get anywhere!" And the group reports at the end of the unit differ markedly in quality: Some are carefully planned and informative, whereas others are disorganized and have little substance.

1. **Constructed-response question:**

   Describe two things you might do to improve Ms. Mihara's cooperative learning activity. Base your improvements on research findings related to cooperative learning or on contemporary principles and theories of learning, development, or motivation.

2. **Multiple-choice question:**

   Ms. Mihara never identifies an instructional objective for her unit "Customs in Other Lands." Which one of the following statements reflects recommended guidelines about how instructional goals and objectives should be formulated?

   a. "The teacher should expose students to many differences in behaviors and beliefs that exist in diverse cultures (e.g., eating habits, ceremonial practices, religious beliefs, moral values)."

   b. "The teacher should use a variety of instructional practices, including (but not limited to) lectures, direct instruction, textbook readings, and cooperative learning activities."

   c. "Students should study a variety of cultural behaviors and beliefs, including those of countries in diverse parts of the world."

   d. "Students should demonstrate knowledge of diverse cultural practices—for example, by describing three distinct ways in which another culture is different from their own."

MyEdLab **Licensure Exam 12.1**

PRAXIS Go to Appendix C, "Matching Book Content and Ebook Activities to the Praxis Principles of Learning and Teaching Tests," to discover sections of this chapter that may be especially applicable to the Praxis tests.

Monkey Business/Fotolia

13

Creating a Productive Learning Environment

CASE STUDY: A CONTAGIOUS SITUATION

After receiving a teaching certificate in May, Ms. Cornell has accepted a position as a fifth-grade teacher. She has spent the summer identifying instructional goals for the year and planning lessons that should help students achieve those goals. Today, on the first day of school, she has jumped headlong into the curriculum she planned. But three problems quickly present themselves—in the forms of Eli, Jake, and Vanessa.

These three students seem determined to disrupt the class at every possible opportunity. They move around the room without permission, intentionally annoying others as they walk to the pencil sharpener or wastebasket. They talk out of turn, often in disrespectful ways, to their teacher and peers. They rarely complete assignments, preferring instead to engage in horseplay or practical jokes. They seem especially prone to misbehavior during downtimes in the daily schedule—for example, at the beginning and end of the day, before and after recess and lunch, and whenever Ms. Cornell is preoccupied with other students.

Ms. Cornell continues to follow her daily lesson plans, ignoring her problem students and hoping they'll eventually shape up. Yet the disruptive behavior continues, with the three of them delighting in one another's antics. Furthermore, the misbehavior begins to spread to other students. By the middle of October, Ms. Cornell's classroom is out of control, and the few students who are still interested in learning something are having a hard time doing so.

- In what ways has Ms. Cornell planned in advance for her classroom? In what ways has she *not* planned?

As a first-year teacher, Ms. Cornell is well prepared in some respects but not at all prepared in others. She has carefully identified her instructional goals and planned relevant lessons. But she has neglected to think about how she might keep students on task or how she might adjust her lessons based on how students are progressing. And she hasn't considered how she might nip behavior problems in the bud, before they begin to interfere with instruction and learning. In the absence of such planning, no curriculum can be effective—not even one grounded firmly in contemporary theories of learning, development, and motivation.

Learning always takes place within particular contexts—for instance, within particular physical settings, social groups, and cultures. In academic learning, one important context is, of course, the classroom. Skillful teachers not only choose instructional strategies that foster effective learning but also create a classroom environment that keeps students busily engaged in productive activities. They certainly deal with the inappropriate behaviors that occur, but their emphasis is on *preventing* such behaviors. As we explore classroom management strategies in this chapter, our focus, too, will be on prevention. We'll frequently return to the opening case study and consider how Ms. Cornell might have gotten the school year off to a better start.

Creating a Setting Conducive to Learning

In general, classroom management involves creating and maintaining a classroom environment conducive to students' learning and achievement. Students definitely learn more in some classrooms than in others. Consider these four classes as examples:

- Mr. Aragon's class is calm and orderly. Students work independently at their seats, and all of them appear to be concentrating on individually tailored tasks.

Occasionally students approach Mr. Aragon to seek clarification of an assignment or to get feedback about a task they've completed, and he quietly confers with them.

- Mr. Boitano's class is chaotic and noisy. A few students are doing their schoolwork, but most are engaged in nonacademic activities. One girl is painting her nails, a boy nearby is playing games on a smartphone, three students are exchanging gossip, and several others are attacking one another with paper clips and rubber bands.

- Mr. Cavalini's class is as noisy as Mr. Boitano's. But rather than exchanging gossip or waging battle, students are debating—often loudly and passionately—the causes of climate change. After 20 minutes of heated discussion, Mr. Cavalini stops the conversation, lists students' various arguments on the board, and then explains why there's no simple "correct" resolution of the issue.

- Mr. Durocher believes that students learn most effectively when rules for their behavior are clearly spelled out, so he has 53 rules that cover almost every conceivable occasion: "Always use a ballpoint pen with blue or black ink," "Don't submit assignments on torn-out pages from spiral notebooks," "Don't ask questions unrelated to the lesson," and so on. He punishes each infraction severely enough that students follow the rules to the letter. As a result, his students are a quiet and obedient bunch, but their achievement levels remain discouragingly low.

Two of these classrooms are quiet and orderly; the other two are active and noisy. But as you can see, the activity and noise levels are poor indicators of how much students are learning. Students are learning in Mr. Aragon's quiet class and in Mr. Cavalini's noisier one. Neither the students in Mr. Boitano's loud, chaotic battlefield nor those in Mr. Durocher's peaceful dictatorship seem to be learning much. A well-managed classroom is one in which students are consistently engaged in productive learning activities and in which students' behaviors rarely interfere with the achievement of instructional goals (Brophy, 2006; W. Doyle, 1990; Emmer & Evertson, 1981). It *isn't* one in which students' every moves are closely controlled.

Creating and maintaining an environment in which students are continually engaged in productive activities can be a challenging task. We must tend to the unique needs of many different students, must sometimes coordinate several activities at once, and must often make quick decisions about how to respond to unanticipated events. Furthermore, we must vary our classroom management techniques considerably depending on the particular instructional strategies in progress; for instance, direct instruction, hands-on activities, and cooperative learning all require somewhat different management techniques. It isn't surprising, then, that many beginning teachers mention classroom management as their number-one concern (Evertson & Weinstein, 2006; V. Jones, 1996; Veenman, 1984), and that some teachers who experience difficulties managing behavior consider leaving the profession (Marsh, 2015).

A good general model of effective classroom management is *authoritative parenting*. Authoritative parents tend to do the following:

- Provide a generally loving and supportive environment
- Hold high expectations and standards for children's behavior
- Explain why some behaviors are acceptable and others are not
- Consistently enforce reasonable rules for behavior
- Include children in decision making
- Provide age-appropriate opportunities for independence

As we explore classroom management strategies in this chapter, we'll often see one or more of these characteristics at work.

We've organized our discussion of preventive classroom management strategies around eight general strategies:

- Create a physical arrangement that helps to focus students' attention on classroom lessons and academic subject matter.
- Establish and maintain good working relationships with students.
- Create a psychological climate in which students feel emotionally safe and are intrinsically motivated to learn.

Chapter 3 discusses the benefits of authoritative parenting from a developmental perspective.

🍎 Set reasonable limits for behavior.

🍎 Plan activities that keep students on task and productive.

🍎 Regularly monitor what students are doing.

🍎 Modify instructional strategies when necessary.

🍎 Take developmental differences and student diversity into account in making classroom management decisions.

In the upcoming sections we'll identify specific ways to implement each of these strategies.

ARRANGING THE CLASSROOM

Good management begins well before the first day of class. As we arrange desks and chairs, decide where to put instructional materials and equipment, and think about where each student will sit, we should consider the effects that various arrangements are likely to have on students' behavior. For example, we might decide to allow students to choose their own seats, but then we need to be prepared for the fact that students will surely sit near their friends! The following strategies are especially helpful.

🍎 *Arrange furniture in ways that encourage student interaction when it's appropriate and discourage it when it's counterproductive.* In the past, student desks and chairs often were bolted to the floor in tidy rows—an arrangement that was compatible only with a traditional lecture format. Fortunately the great majority of classrooms now have movable furniture, giving us considerable flexibility in how we might arrange and occasionally rearrange things. Several clusters of desks and chairs facing one another are useful for small-group work, whereas traditional rows are often more effective in keeping students on task during individual assignments (K. Carter & Doyle, 2006). However, we should be sensitive to cultural differences here: Students who are accustomed to cooperating regularly with peers (e.g., students from many Native American communities) might find an everyone-faces-the-teacher arrangement strange and unnerving (Lipka, 1994). You may want to plan for flexibility so students can move to different positions for different types of activities.

Jeffery Ormrod

Ideally the classroom's furniture and physical layout should enable a variety of instructional strategies, including not only whole-group lectures and computer-based presentations but also small-group work, independent assignments, and hands-on physical activities. A classroom should also be well organized and visually appealing, but without presenting unnecessary distractions.

🍎 *Minimize possible distractions.* Certainly we want to make our classrooms visually appealing and enticing—for example, by putting colorful messages and posters on walls and bulletin boards—but we shouldn't bombard students with so much visual stimulation that they have trouble concentrating on their schoolwork. We should also arrange our classrooms in ways that minimize the likelihood of off-task behaviors—for instance, by establishing traffic patterns that allow students to move around the room without disturbing one another and by seating overly chatty friends on opposite sides of the room. If the doors to our classrooms have exposed windows to the hallway, we might consider covering the windows so that students are not distracted by those passing by. We should keep intriguing materials out of sight and reach until we need them, and we should always preview all materials to make sure that the content is appropriate (Emmer & Evertson, 2009; Hanley, Tiger, Ingvarsson, & Cammilleri, 2009; Sabers, Cushing, & Berliner, 1991).

🍎 *Arrange the classroom so that it's easy to interact with students.* Our arrangement of desks, tables, and chairs should make it easy for us to converse with virtually any student as necessary. It's often beneficial to place chronically misbehaving or uninvolved students close at hand: Students seated near us are more likely to pay attention, interact with us, and become actively involved in classroom activities. In addition to rearranging students' seats, we also can move our desks, bookshelves, computer stations, and other furnishings throughout the year when needed (G. A. Davis & Thomas, 1989; Strother, 1991; Woolfolk & Brooks, 1985).

 Place chronically misbehaving or uninvolved students close at hand.

🍎 *Identify locations that allow easy monitoring of students' behavior.* As we proceed through various lessons and activities—even when working with an individual or small groups—we should regularly be able to see *all* students (Emmer & Evertson, 2009; Gettinger & Kohler,

2006). By occasionally surveying the classroom for possible signs of confusion, frustration, or boredom, we can more easily detect minor student difficulties and misbehaviors before they develop into serious problems.

🍎 *Make appropriate changes for classwide use of technology.* If students are individually using laptops or computer tablets, we should arrange furniture *and* position ourselves in ways that enable us to monitor the contents of each student's computer screen. Also, we should ensure that we can continue to watch students' behavior when we are using classroom technology ourselves.

ESTABLISHING AND MAINTAINING PRODUCTIVE TEACHER–STUDENT RELATIONSHIPS

Research consistently indicates that the quality of teacher–student relationships is one of the most important factors—perhaps *the* most important factor—affecting students' emotional well-being, motivation, and learning. When students have positive, supportive relationships with teachers, they have more intrinsic motivation to learn, engage in more self-regulated learning, behave more appropriately, and achieve at higher levels (E. M. Anderman, Lane, Zimmerman, Cupp, & Phebus, 2009; J. N. Hughes, 2011; J. N. Hughes, Luo, Kwok, & Loyd, 2008; Pakarinen et al., 2014; Roorda, Koomen, Spilt, & Oort, 2011; Vitaro, Boivin, Brendgen, Girard, & Dionne, 2012).

Although some students may misbehave as a way of gaining our attention (this might be true for Eli, Jake, and Vanessa in the opening case study), in our own experiences as parents, teachers, and school psychologists, we've never met a child or adolescent who, deep down, didn't want to have positive, productive relationships with school faculty members. In addition, *we* also benefit from having good relationships with our students; indeed, when teachers establish productive relationships with students, we experience more positive emotions and are more engaged ourselves (Klassen, Perry, & Frenzel, 2012).

The following strategies must be central in our efforts to have productive working relationships with students.

🍎 *Regularly communicate caring and respect for students as individuals.* To some degree we can communicate affection and respect through the many little things we do each day (Allday, Bush, Ticknor, & Walker, 2011; Allday & Pakurar, 2007; L.H. Anderman, Andrzejewski, & Allen, 2011; Certo, Cauley, & Chafin, 2003). For example, we can give students a smile and warm greeting at the beginning of the day. We can compliment them when they get a flattering haircut, excel in an extracurricular activity, or receive recognition in the local newspaper. We can be good listeners when they come to school angry or upset. And we should certainly learn every student's name within the first few days of school. One high school student described caring teachers this way:

> You might see them in the hallway and they ask how you're doing, how was your last report card, is there anything you need. Or, maybe one day you're looking a little upset. They'll pull you to the side and ask you what's wrong, is there anything I can do. (Certo, Cauley, & Chafin, 2002, p. 15)

Such caring gestures can be especially important for students who have few, if any, supportive relationships at home (Juvonen, 2006; E. O'Connor, Dearing, & Collins, 2011; Reese, Jensen, & Ramirez, 2014).

🍎 *Remember that caring and respect involve much more than just showing affection.* Some beginning teachers erroneously think that good teaching involves little more than showing that they really like their students—in other words, being "warm and fuzzy" (L. H. Anderman, Patrick, Hruda, & Linnenbrink, 2002, p. 274; Goldstein & Lake, 2000; Patrick & Pintrich, 2001). In fact, to show students that we *truly* care about and respect them, we must take steps such as these:

🍎 Be well prepared for class, and always demonstrate a love of teaching.

🍎 Communicate high yet realistic expectations for performance, and provide the support students need to meet those expectations.

🍎 Include students in decision making and evaluation of their work.

🍎 Acknowledge that students can occasionally have an "off" day. (Certo et al., 2003; M.-L. Chang & Davis, 2009; H. A. Davis, 2003; Patrick, Kaplan, & Ryan, 2011; Wentzel, Battle, Russell, & Looney, 2010)

Another important strategy is to establish means through which students can communicate privately with us. One option, especially for older students, is email, perhaps through a class website or other online mechanism that prevents students from wandering into potentially inappropriate Internet sites. A low-tech alternative is a "What's Up?" form on which students might occasionally write and submit information about especially noteworthy or challenging events in their personal lives (A. K. Smith, 2009). A third possibility is the use of two-way *dialogue journals,* in which individual students and their teacher both write one or more times each week. Figure 13.1 shows several entries in 6-year-old Matt's journal; each entry is followed by a response (indented) from his first-grade teacher. Notice that Matt feels comfortable enough with his teacher to engage in playful one-upmanship ("I can go fastr then you"). Although his writing skills are far from perfect—for instance, he writes *especially downhill skiing* as "spshal don hilscein"—they're certainly adequate to communicate his thoughts. Notice, too, that his teacher doesn't correct his misspellings. Her primary purposes are to encourage him to write and to open the lines of communication; giving negative feedback about spelling here might interfere with both of these goals.

🍎 *Work hard to improve relationships that have gotten off to a bad start.* Occasionally students may come to us with an apparent chip on the shoulder, distrusting us from the start because of previous hurtful relationships with parents, teachers, or other adults (H. A. Davis, 2003; Hyman et al., 2006; Pianta, 1999). At other times we may get relationships off to a bad beginning through our own actions—perhaps because we've incorrectly attributed low achievement to lack of effort rather than lack of skill or perhaps because we've accused a temperamentally high-energy child of being intentionally disobedient (M.-L. Chang & Davis, 2009; B. K. Keogh, 2003; Silverberg, 2003). Occasionally, too, students might misinterpret something we say or do. For example, the first day that 8-year-old Darcy attended third grade at a new school, she accidentally got egg in her hair. Her teacher, Mrs. Whaley,

> 🍎 Establish mechanisms through which you can communicate regularly and privately with every student.

FIGURE 13.1 Two-way *dialogue journals* provide one effective means of maintaining one-on-one communication with all students. In these excerpts from 6-year-old Matt's journal, Matt and his first-grade teacher discover common outside interests.

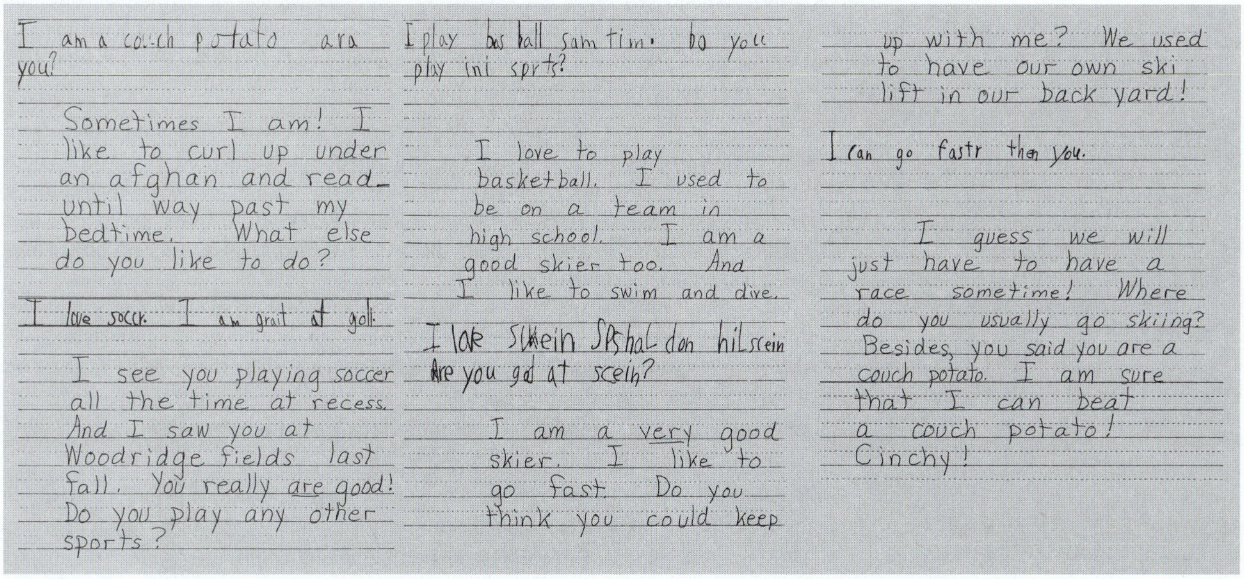

FIGURE 13.2 As her journal entries show, 8-year-old Darcy initially interpreted her teacher's casual remark to the school nurse in a way very different from the teacher's intended meaning. Fortunately, the teacher corrected the misunderstanding a few days later.

October 22
I went to a new school today. My teacher's name is Mrs. Whaley. I accidentally cracked an egg on my head. Mrs. Whaley told the nurse that I was a showoff and a nuisance. I got really sad and wanted to run away from school, but I didn't leave.

. . .

October 27
We presented our book reports today. I was the last one to present my book report. Whenever I did my book report, they laughed at me, but the teacher said they were laughing with me. I asked the teacher why she had called me a nuisance the first day. And she said, "Darcy, I didn't call you a nuisance. I was saying to Mrs. Larson that it was a nuisance to try to wash egg out of your hair." I was so happy. I decided to like Mrs. Whaley again.

took her to the nurse's office to have the egg washed out. As revealed in the journal entries in Figure 13.2, Darcy initially misinterpreted Mrs. Whaley's comment about the situation. Not until 5 days later did she gain a more accurate understanding of what Mrs. Whaley had said.

Unfortunately, students who have the poorest relationships with their teachers are often those most in need of good ones (Juvonen, 2006; Stipek & Miles, 2008; Wentzel, Donlan, Morrison, Russell, & Baker, 2009). Thus, regardless of the causes of nonproductive relationships, we must work hard to turn them into productive ones. The first step, of course, is to *identify* nonproductive relationships, recognizing signs such as these:

- We have hostile feelings (e.g., dislike, anger) toward a student.
- We rarely interact with a student.
- Our messages to a student usually involve criticism or faultfinding.
- We have a sense of learned helplessness about our ability to work effectively with a student. (Houts, Caspi, Pianta, Arseneault, & Moffitt, 2010; Pianta, 1999; Sutherland & Morgan, 2003)

Once we've identified troublesome relationships, several strategies can help us repair them:

- 🍎 Meet one on one with a student to talk openly about the problem and possible ways to fix it (more on this point later in the chapter).
- 🍎 Think actively—perhaps in a brainstorming session with one or more colleagues—about alternative hypotheses that might explain a student's behavior and about potential solutions
- 🍎 Spend time with a student in a relaxed, noninstructional context—perhaps a mutually enjoyable recreational activity or just chatting before or after school—that can allow more positive feelings to emerge. (M.-L. Chang & Davis, 2009; Pianta, 1999, 2006; Silverberg, 2003; Sutton & Wheatley, 2003)

CREATING AN EFFECTIVE PSYCHOLOGICAL CLIMATE

Caring and supportive teacher–student relationships are important contributors to the overall **classroom climate**—the general psychological environment that permeates classroom interactions. Ultimately we want a classroom in which students feel safe and secure, make learning a high priority, and are willing to take the risks and make the mistakes so critical for maximal cognitive growth (Hamre & Pianta, 2005; Hattie & Gan, 2011). Such an environment minimizes discipline problems and seems to be especially important for students at risk for academic failure and dropping out of school (Gregory et al., 2010; V. E. Lee & Burkam, 2003; Pianta, 1999). Following are several critical strategies.

- 🍎 *Establish a goal-oriented, businesslike, yet nonthreatening atmosphere.* We and our students must all recognize that we're in school to get certain things accomplished (G. A. Davis & Thomas, 1989). Effective classroom activities and tasks are typically interesting and engaging—occasionally even exhilarating—rather than tedious and boring. However, entertainment and excitement shouldn't be goals in and of themselves. Rather, they're means to a more important goal: mastering academic content.

Chapter 11 discusses the potential adverse effects of anxiety.

Despite our emphasis on business, the classroom atmosphere should never be uncomfortable or threatening, because students who are excessively anxious are unlikely to give us their best (Cassady, 2010a; Sapolsky, 2005). Strategies such as these enable us to be businesslike without being threatening:

- 🍎 Hold students accountable for achieving instructional objectives but without placing them under continual surveillance.
- 🍎 Point out students' errors and misconceptions within the context of messages that highlight their strengths (e.g., inquisitiveness, critical thinking skills) and ongoing progress.
- 🍎 Admonish students for misbehavior without holding grudges against them. (K. L. Fletcher & Cassady, 2010; Narciss, 2008; C. R. Rogers, 1983; Spaulding, 1992)

🍎 *Communicate and demonstrate that school tasks and academic subject matter have value.* As teachers, we give students messages about the value of school subject matter by both what we say and what we do (Brophy, 2008; W. Doyle, 1983). For example, if we ask students to spend hours each day engaged in what seems like meaningless busy work and if we assess learning primarily through tests that encourage rote memorization, we're indirectly telling students that classroom tasks are merely things that need to be "gotten over with" (E. H. Hiebert & Raphael, 1996; Stodolsky, Salk, & Glaessner, 1991). Furthermore, if we continually focus students' attention on performance goals—how their achievement compares to that of others— we may increase their anxiety about academic achievement and indirectly increase the frequency of disruptive behavior (Kumar, Gheen, & Kaplan, 2002; Marachi, Friedel, & Midgley, 2001; Patrick et al., 2011). If, instead, we continually communicate that learning classroom subject matter can help students make better sense of the world, if we assess learning in ways that require meaningful learning, and if we focus on how well each student is improving over time, we show students that mastering the subject matter can potentially enhance the quality of students' lives (Pugh, Linnenbrink-Garcia, Koskey, Stewart, & Manzey, 2010).

🍎 *Give students some control over classroom activities.* To make sure students accomplish important instructional goals, we must direct the course of classroom activities to some degree. Nevertheless, we can give students control over some aspects of classroom life—for example, through strategies such as these:

🍎 Create a regular routine for completing assignments, enabling students to do them with only minimal guidance.

🍎 Allow students to set their own deadlines for some assignments, enabling them to establish a manageable schedule.

🍎 Occasionally let students choose how to accomplish certain instructional goals and objectives, enabling them to set some of their own priorities. (Patall, Cooper, & Wynn, 2010; Spaulding, 1992)

Through such strategies, we promote the sense of autonomy so important for intrinsic motivation, along with the development of self-regulation skills so essential for students' long-term academic success.

🍎 *Promote a general sense of community and belongingness.* An increasingly popular instructional strategy is to create a *community of learners,* a classroom in which one or more teachers and their students collaborate to build a body of knowledge and help one another learn. Ultimately we also want to create a general **sense of community** in the classroom—a sense that we and our students have shared goals, are mutually respectful and supportive of one another's efforts, and believe that everyone makes an important contribution to classroom learning (Ciani, Middleton, Summers, & Sheldon, 2010; Hom & Battistich, 1995; Osterman, 2000). Creating a sense of community engenders feelings of **belongingness**: Students see themselves as important and valued members of the classroom (E. M. Anderman, 2002; L. Anderman & Freeman, 2004; J. Ellis, Fitzsimmons, & Small-McGinley, 2010).

When students share a sense of community, they're more likely to exhibit prosocial behavior, stay on task, be enthusiastic about classroom activities, and achieve at high levels. Furthermore, a sense of classroom community is associated with lower rates of emotional distress, disruptive classroom behavior, truancy, and dropping out (Hom & Battistich, 1995; Juvonen, 2006; Osterman, 2000; Patrick et al., 2007). And consistent experiences with caring and equitable classroom communities help students internalize attitudes essential for a successful democratic society, including a commitment to fairness and justice for everyone (C. A. Flanagan, Cumsille, Gill, & Gallay, 2007).

Perhaps the most important characteristic of a sense of classroom community is that students always treat one another with kindness and respect. Even when students must take issue with something that one of their classmates has said or done, they can do so tactfully and respectfully (e.g., see Figure 13.3). When classmates *aren't* kind and respectful—for example, when they ridicule or bully certain other class members—their victims are apt to withdraw either physically or mentally from classroom activities (Swearer, Espelage, Vaillancourt, & Hymel, 2010).

As teachers, we must make it clear that remarks or behaviors that deride or denigrate other class members are *totally unacceptable* both inside and outside the classroom. The

Chapter 11 discusses the importance of giving students a sense of autonomy.

MyEdLab
Video Example 13.1.

Students need to see the classroom as a community for learning and feel a sense of belonging. The teacher's neutral response to behavioral issues contributes to a positive climate and culture.

You can learn more about communities of learners in Chapter 8.

Create a sense of shared goals, interpersonal respect, and mutual support.

MyEdLab
Video Example 13.2.

A climate of mutual respect and support is conducive to learning. This teacher's choices about placement of students, helping behaviors, and differentiation create an atmosphere of shared goals and interpersonal respect.

Refuse to tolerate statements or behaviors that show lack of concern or respect for other class members.

See Chapter 3 for a discussion of socialization as an important factor in children's development.

MyEdLab
Video Example 13.3.

Establishing a few rules at the beginning of the year helps students learn behavioral expectations. Teachers create a productive environment for learning when they monitor and enforce the class rules consistently in an uncontrolling manner.

FIGURE 13.3 **Especially in the elementary grades, many students benefit from visual reminders about how to interact with classmates, as illustrated in these two posters displayed in a second-grade classroom.**

Words to Use

I don't like it when _____.

Can you not do _____?

Can you please stop _____?

I need a break and then I'll come back to talk about it.

Working with a Partner

Be polite.

Help each other.

Share.

Listen to your partner.

Be a good sport.

Take turns.

Talks about problems.

Speak respectfully.

Posters courtesy of Christina Fox.

Creating a Productive Classroom Environment feature "Creating and Enhancing a Sense of Classroom Community" offers several strategies that can enhance students' sense that they're important and valued members of the classroom.

SETTING LIMITS

In the opening case study, Ms. Cornell failed to provide guidelines for how students should behave—something she should have done the first week of school. Students must know that certain behaviors simply won't be tolerated, especially those that cause physical or psychological harm, damage school property, or interfere with others' learning and performance. And over the long run, setting reasonable limits on classroom behavior helps students become productive members of adult society. In other words, imposing limits on students' behavior is one important way in which schools help *socialize* children to work effectively in their cultural group.

As we set limits, however, we must remember that students are more likely to be intrinsically motivated to master classroom subject matter if we preserve their sense of autonomy. With this caution in mind, we offer the following recommendations.

🍎 *Establish a few rules and procedures at the beginning of the year.* Effective classroom managers establish and communicate certain rules and procedures right from the start. For example, they identify acceptable and unacceptable behaviors and describe the consequences of noncompliance. They develop consistent procedures and routines for such things as completing seatwork, asking for help, and turning in assignments. They have procedures in place for nonroutine events such as school assemblies, field trips, and fire drills. And in today's high-tech world, teachers need to have a clear policy about the use of personal cell phones and other handheld devices during class time. Taking time to clarify rules and procedures seems to be especially important in the early elementary grades, when students may not be familiar with how things are typically done at school (K. Carter & Doyle, 2006; W. Doyle, 1990; Gettinger & Kohler, 2006; K. L. Lane, Menzies, Bruhn, & Crnobori, 2011).

Ideally students should understand that rules and procedures aren't based on our personal whims but are, instead, designed to help the class run smoothly and efficiently. One way of promoting such understanding is to include students in decision making about the rules and procedures by which the class will operate. For example, we might solicit students' suggestions for making sure that unnecessary distractions are kept to a minimum and that everyone has a chance to speak during discussions. By incorporating students' ideas and listening to their concerns about the limits we set, we help them understand the reasons for—and also enhance their sense of ownership of—those limits (Evertson & Emmer, 2009; Fuller, 2001; M. Watson, 2008).

Creating a Productive Classroom Environment

Creating and Enhancing a Sense of Classroom Community

⬤ **Consistently communicate the message that all students deserve the respect of their classmates and are important members of the classroom community.**

A middle school language arts class has three students with reading disabilities that are obvious in much of the students' oral and written work in class. The teacher doesn't publicly identify the students with disabilities, because doing so would violate their right to confidentiality about their conditions. However, she frequently communicates the message that students at any grade level vary widely in their literacy skills—usually through no fault of their own—and continually stresses that it's the class's responsibility to help *everyone* improve their literacy skills.

⬤ **Create mechanisms through which students can all help to make the class run smoothly and efficiently.**

A kindergarten teacher creates several "helper" roles (e.g., distributing art supplies, feeding the class goldfish); he develops a tracking system to make sure he assigns roles to different students on a rotating basis.

⬤ **Emphasize such prosocial values as sharing and cooperation, and provide opportunities for students to help one another.**

As students work on in-class assignments each day, a seventh-grade math teacher often asks, "Who has a problem that someone else might be able to help you solve?"

⬤ **Make frequent use of interactive and collaborative teaching strategies.**

In assigning students to cooperative learning groups, a high school social studies teacher usually puts a student with poor social skills (e.g., a student with Asperger syndrome) in a group with two or three more socially proficient students. Before the groups begin their work, the teacher reminds students of the class's rules for cooperative group work, such as "Listen to others politely and attentively" and "Address differences of opinion in respectful and constructive ways."

⬤ **Solicit students' ideas and opinions, and incorporate them into class discussions and activities.**

A first-grade teacher regularly has students vote on the storybook she should read during "settling-down" time after lunch each day. She first reads the book that gets the most votes, but she assures students who voted differently that she'll read their choices later in the week, saying, "It's important that everyone has a say in what we read."

⬤ **Use competition only to create an occasional sense of playfulness in the class and only when all students have an equal chance of winning.**

A high school Spanish teacher assigns a long-term cooperative group project in which students write and videotape Spanish soap operas (*telenovelas*). A few weeks later the teacher holds an "Academy Awards Banquet"—a potluck dinner for the students and their families. At the banquet the teacher shows all the videos and awards a variety of "Oscars." She gives every group an Oscar for some aspect of their performance.

⬤ **Encourage students to be on the lookout for classmates on the periphery of ongoing activities—perhaps students with disabilities—and to ask these students to join in.**

Teachers at an elementary school all adhere to and enforce the same *no-exclusion* policy on the playground: Any student who wants to be involved in a play activity *can* be involved.

⬤ **Work on social skills with students whose interpersonal behaviors may victimize or alienate others.**

A third grader often behaves aggressively toward classmates who have something she wants. For example, when waiting for her turn at the class computer, she may yell "*I* need to use it now!" or, instead, shove its current user out of the chair. In a private conference, her teacher points out the importance of patience and turn taking and suggests several ways she might politely make her needs known (e.g., "When might you be finished with the computer? Can I use it after you're done?") The teacher also has the student practice the strategies in various role-playing scenarios.

Sources: C. Ames, 1984; M.-L. Chang & Davis, 2009; Evertson & Emmer, 2009; Hamovitch, 2007; D. Kim, Solomon, & Roberts, 1995; Lickona, 1991; Osterman, 2000; A. M. Ryan & Patrick, 2001; Sapon-Shevin, Dobbelaere, Corrigan, Goodman, & Mastin, 1998 (playground example); Stipek, 1996; Turnbull, Pereira, & Blue-Banning, 2000; M.-T. Wang & Holcombe, 2010; Wentzel et al., 2010.

Keep in mind that rules and procedures are easier to remember—and therefore easier to follow—if they're relatively simple and few in number (W. Doyle, 1986a; Emmer & Gerwels, 2006; K. L. Lane et al., 2011). Effective classroom managers tend to stress only the most important rules and procedures at the beginning of the school year and introduce additional rules and procedures as needed later. Figure 13.4 is an example of an easy-to-remember acronym that a high school teacher developed. You should also keep in mind that although some order and predictability is essential for student productivity, *too much* order can make a classroom a routine, boring place—one without any element of fun and spontaneity. We don't necessarily need rules and procedures for everything!

⬤ *Present rules and procedures in an informational rather than controlling manner.* We're more likely to maintain students' sense of autonomy if we present rules and procedures as items of information rather than as forms of control (Deci, 1992; Koestner, Ryan, Bernieri, & Holt, 1984; Reeve, 2009). This will require some planning and forethought for teachers, but it is well worth the effort;

"Remember, there is no SOOT allowed in our class!"
S = speaking out of turn or during quiet time
O = out of seat
O = other work
T = tardy

FIGURE 13.4 After a year of dealing with many behavioral problems, a new high school teacher developed this acronym to help students remember his class rules.

FIGURE 13.5 We are more likely to motivate students to follow classroom rules and procedures if we communicate those rules and procedures as information *without* conveying a desire to impose a lot of control.

We might say this (as information) . . .	Rather than this (as control)
"You'll finish your independent assignments sooner if you get right to work."	"Please be quiet and do your own work."
"As we practice for our fire drill, it's important to line up quickly and quietly so that we can hear the instructions we're given and will know what to do."	"When the fire alarm sounds, line up quickly and quietly, and then wait for further instructions."
"This assignment can help you develop the writing skills you'll need after you graduate. It's unfair to other authors to copy their work word for word, so we'll practice putting ideas into our own words and giving credit to authors whose ideas we borrow. Passing off another's writing as your own can lead to suspension in college or a lawsuit in the business world."	"Cheating and plagiarism are not acceptable in this classroom."
"Everyone needs to be in their seats when the bell rings at the start of class. There is a lot going on at the start of class, and when you are in your seats, you can get started on your work right away, and I can take attendance quickly. Then we'll get much more accomplished during class, and you'll be less likely to have homework."	"When the bell rings, you need to be seated and quiet."

we naturally think about rules and procedures in terms of controlling students, but we need to carefully balance behavior management with issues of engagement and motivation. Figure 13.5 provides several examples of rules and procedures presented in an informational manner. Each of these statements includes the reasons for imposing certain guidelines—a strategy that's likely to increase students' compliance. The following scenario provides a simple illustration of how giving a reason can make a noticeable difference:

> Gerard has little tolerance for frustration. Whenever he asks Ms. Donnelly for assistance, he wants it *now*. If she can't immediately help him, he screams, "You're no good!" or "You don't care!" and shoves other students' desks as he angrily walks back to his seat.

Refer to Chapter 11 for a reminder about the benefits of informational versus controlling messages.

> At one point during the school year, the class has a unit on interpersonal skills. One lesson addresses *timing*—the most appropriate and effective time to ask for someone's assistance. A week later, Gerard approaches Ms. Donnelly for help with a math problem. She is working with another student but briefly turns to Gerard and says, "Timing." She expects the usual screaming, but instead he responds, "Hey, Ms. D., I get it! I can ask you at another time!" He returns to his seat with a smile. (Based on Sullivan-DeCarlo, DeFalco, & Roberts, 1998, p. 81)

🍎 *Periodically review the usefulness of existing rules and procedures.* As the school year progresses, we may discover that some rules and procedures need revision. For example, we may find that rules about when students can move around the room are overly restrictive or that procedures for turning in homework don't accommodate students who must leave class early for doctors' appointments or certain extracurricular events.

When it's necessary to change classroom rules and procedures, include students in the decision making.

Regularly scheduled class meetings provide one mechanism through which we and our students can periodically review classroom rules and procedures (D. E. Campbell, 1996; Glasser, 1969; Striepling-Goldstein, 2004). Consider this scenario as an example:

> Every Friday afternoon Ms. Ayotte's students move their chairs into a circle for their weekly class meeting. First on the agenda is a review of the past week's successes, including both academic achievements and socially productive events. Next, the group identifies problems that have emerged during the week and brainstorms possible

ways to avert such problems in the future. Finally, the students consider whether existing class rules and procedures are serving their purpose, and, if not, the group either modifies existing rules and procedures or establishes new ones. During the first few meetings, Ms. Ayotte leads the discussions, but once students have become familiar and comfortable with the process, she relinquishes control of the meetings to one or another of her students on a rotating basis.

By providing frequent opportunities for students to review classroom policies, we find another way of giving them a sense of ownership about the policies. Furthermore, more advanced moral reasoning may gradually emerge, perhaps as a result of occasional moral dilemmas with which students must wrestle (Milner, 2006; Nucci, 2006, 2009; Power, Higgins, & Kohlberg, 1989).

You can learn more about the nature and benefits of moral dilemmas in Chapter 3.

🍎 *Acknowledge students' feelings about requirements.* There will undoubtedly be times when we must ask students to do things they would prefer not to do. Rather than pretend that students are eager to do what we've asked of them, we're better advised to acknowledge their displeasure and lack of motivation. For example, we might tell students that we know how difficult it can be to sit quietly during a lengthy school assembly or to spend an entire evening on a particular assignment. At the same time we can explain that the behaviors we're requesting of them can help them achieve their own long-term goals. By acknowledging students' feelings about tasks they'd rather not do but also pointing out the benefits, we increase the likelihood that students will willingly comply (Jang, Reeve, & Deci, 2010; Reeve, 2009).

🍎 *Enforce rules consistently and equitably.* Classroom rules are likely to be effective only if they're consistently enforced. For example, in the opening case study Ms. Cornell imposes no consequences when her three troublesome students misbehave. Not only do their antics continue, but other students follow suit, realizing that "anything goes" in Ms. Cornell's classroom. As social cognitive theorists have pointed out, imposing no adverse consequence for inappropriate behavior—especially when that consequence has been spelled out in advance—can actually be a form of *reinforcement* for the misbehavior (Bandura, 1986).

Chapter 10 describes social cognitive theory's perspectives on reinforcement and punishment.

Consistency in enforcing classroom rules should apply not only across occasions but also across *students.* As teachers, we may often like some students more than others (e.g., we're apt to prefer high achievers), but we must keep our preferences to ourselves. Students can be quite resentful of teachers who grant special favors to and overlook the rule infractions of a few favorite students (Babad, 1995; Babad, Avni-Babad, & Rosenthal, 2003; J. Baker, 1999). And students who are unfairly accused or punished are, of course, even more resentful, as one high school student explains:

Because like if you had a past record or whatever like in middle school if you got in trouble like at all, they would think that you're a slight trouble maker and if you got in trouble again, they would always . . . if you were anywhere that something bad happened or something against the rules or whatever, they pick you first because they think that you have a past. So they wouldn't like pick the kids that had never done anything. (Certo et al., 2002, p. 25)

Thus, consistency and equitable treatment for all students—or the lack thereof—have a significant effect on teacher–student relationships and overall classroom climate (Babad et al., 2003; Peter & Dalbert, 2010; Wentzel et al., 2010).

PLANNING ACTIVITIES THAT KEEP STUDENTS ON TASK

As effective teachers plan their lessons, they think not only about how to facilitate students' learning and productive cognitive processes but also how to keep students consistently on task. Optimal learning occurs when we provide both ample time for students to engage in academic tasks and an organized, responsive, and supportive environment (Connor et al., 2014). Certainly a key strategy is to motivate students to *want* to master classroom subject matter, but experienced educators have offered several other suggestions as well:

Chapter 11 presents strategies for motivating students to learn and achieve.

🍎 *Make sure students are always productively engaged in worthwhile activities.* Virtually all human beings have a basic *need for arousal*—a need for some degree of physical or cognitive stimulation. At school, children and adolescents should find their stimulation in ongoing tasks and activities. If, instead, they have a lot of free time on their hands, they'll generate stimulation of their own, sometimes in the form of misbehaviors.

Chapter 11 describes the need for arousal in more depth.

Effective classroom managers make sure that there's little unscheduled time in which nothing's going on. Following are several strategies for keeping students productively engaged:

- Have something specific for students to do each day, even on the first day of class.
- Have materials organized and equipment set up before class.
- Plan activities that ensure *all* students' involvement and participation.
- Maintain a brisk pace throughout each lesson, but without moving so quickly that students can't keep up.
- Present advance organizers at the beginning of each day or class period. Specifically, list the day's activities, and, when possible, the time allocated for each (although sometimes you will want to allow for flexibility if an activity may take longer than planned). Briefly review the accomplishments at the end of the day or the class period.
- Ensure that students' comments are relevant and helpful but not excessively long winded. For example, take chronic time-monopolizers aside for private discussions about giving classmates a chance to speak.
- Spend only short periods of class time assisting individual students unless other students are capable of working independently in the meantime.
- Ensure that students who finish an assigned task quickly have something else to do (e.g., reading a book or writing in a class journal). (W. Doyle, 1986a; Emmer & Evertson, 2009; Emmer & Gerwels, 2006; Gettinger, 1988; K. L. Lane et al., 2011; Munn, Johnstone, & Chalmers, 1990)

See Chapter 2 for a review of Vygotsky's notion of the zone of proximal development, which has implications for providing somewhat challenging tasks when students are working collaboratively with others.

- *Choose tasks at an appropriate difficulty level for students' knowledge and skills.* Students are more likely to work diligently at their classwork when they have activities and assignments appropriate for their current knowledge and skills—this may include challenging tasks, but the challenges need to be reasonable and teachers need to provide appropriate scaffolding so that students can experience success (Mac Iver, Reuman, & Main, 1995; J. W. Moore & Edwards, 2003; S. L. Robinson & Griesemer, 2006). They're apt to misbehave when they're asked to do things that they perceive—either accurately or not—to be exceptionally difficult. Hence, classroom misbehaviors are more often observed with students who have a history of struggling in their schoolwork (W. Doyle, 1986a; Miles & Stipek, 2006). In the opening case study, Eli, Jake, and Vanessa may very well have such a history of failure.

  Avoiding overly difficult tasks *doesn't* mean that we should plan activities so easy that students aren't challenged and learn nothing new. One strategy is to *begin* the school year with relatively easy tasks that students can readily complete. Such tasks enable students to practice normal classroom routines and procedures and gain a sense that they can succeed in and enjoy classroom activities. Once we've established a supportive classroom climate and made students comfortable with our procedures, we can gradually introduce more difficult and challenging assignments (W. Doyle, 1990; Emmer & Evertson, 2009).

Begin the school year with easy and familiar tasks, introducing more difficult ones after a supportive classroom climate has been firmly established.

- *Provide some structure for activities and assignments.* As an example of how important structure can be, try the following exercise.

EXPERIENCING FIRSTHAND
POP QUIZ

Complete these two tasks either on paper or on your computer:

- **Task A:** Using single words or short phrases, list six characteristics of an effective teacher.
- **Task B:** Explain the general effects of school attendance on children's lives.

Don't read further until you've either (1) completed each task or (2) spent at least 5 minutes on it. Once you've tackled the two tasks, answer each of the following questions:

1. For which task did you have a better understanding of what you were being asked to do?
2. During which task did your mind more frequently wander to irrelevant topics?
3. During which task did you engage in more off-task behaviors—perhaps looking around the room, doodling, or getting out of your seat?

We're guessing that you found the first task relatively straightforward, whereas the second wasn't at all clear-cut. Did the ambiguity of Task B lead to more irrelevant thoughts and off-task behaviors? Off-task behavior occurs more frequently when activities are so loosely structured that students don't have a clear sense of what they're supposed to do.

Effective teachers tend to give assignments with some degree of structure—not only sufficient scaffolding to support learning but also clear guidance about how to proceed, especially during the first few weeks of the school year (W. Doyle, 1990; Evertson & Emmer, 1982; Gettinger & Kohler, 2006). However, we need to strike a happy medium here: We don't want to structure tasks to the point that they require only basic skills and never allow students to make decisions. In addition to keeping students on task, we also want them to have a sense of autonomy, practice self-regulation skills, and develop and use complex cognitive processes—for example, to think analytically, critically, and creatively (W. Doyle, 1986a; J. D. Nichols, 2004; Weinert & Helmke, 1995).

🍎 *Plan for transition times in the school day.* In the opening case study, Eli, Jake, and Vanessa often misbehave at the beginning and end of the school day, as well as before and after recess and lunch. Misbehaviors occur most frequently during transition times—as students end one activity and begin a second or as they move from one classroom to another. Effective classroom managers take steps to ensure that transitions proceed quickly and without a loss of momentum (W. Doyle, 1984; Gettinger & Kohler, 2006). For example, they establish procedures for moving from one activity to the next, and they ensure that there's little slack time in which students have nothing to do. Recall the "advance organizer" that we suggested having available for students daily; such organizers can be used to facilitate transitions when these are used daily and consistently. Especially in the secondary grades, when students change classes every hour or so, effective classroom managers typically have a task for students to complete as soon as they enter the classroom. Consider these examples:

- An elementary school teacher has students follow the same procedure each day as lunchtime approaches: (1) Place completed assignments in the teacher's "In" basket, (2) put away supplies, (3) get out any home-packed lunches, and (4) line up quietly by the door.

- A middle school math teacher has students copy the night's homework assignment as soon as they come into class.

- As students first enter the classroom, a middle school social studies teacher always hands them a short "Do It Now" assignment. For example, on one occasion he hands out a map of U.S. states and state capitals and instructs students to identify place names that might have Native American names and those that probably have European roots—a task that leads to a class discussion on the origins of place names.

- Before each class period begins, a ninth-grade creative writing teacher writes a topic or question on the board (e.g., "My biggest pet peeve"). Students know that when they come to class, they should immediately begin to write on the topic or question of the day.

- A high school physical education teacher has students begin each class session with 5 minutes of stretching exercises.

Although very different in nature, all of these strategies share the common goal of keeping students focused on productive behaviors. When such strategies are used consistently, behavior problems are less likely to emerge.

Some students may have considerable trouble moving from one activity to another, especially if they're deeply engaged in what they're doing. Accordingly, it's often helpful to give students advance warning that a transition is coming, describe for them what the subsequent activity will be, and remind them of the usual procedures for switching from one task to another (K. Carter & Doyle, 2006; Emmer & Gerwels, 2006).

MONITORING WHAT STUDENTS ARE DOING

Effective teachers communicate something called **withitness**: They know—and their students *know* that they know—what students are doing at all times. These teachers regularly scan the classroom and make frequent eye contact with individual students. They know what misbehaviors are occurring *when* those misbehaviors occur, and they know who the perpetrators are. When we demonstrate withitness, especially at the beginning of the school year, students are more likely to stay on task and display appropriate classroom behavior. Not surprisingly, they're also more likely to achieve at high levels (Gettinger & Kohler, 2006; T. Hogan, Rabinowitz, & Craven, 2003; Kounin, 1970). It may seem difficult to develop a sense of "withitness" in busy classrooms; this takes time and practice. Videotaping yourself during student teaching experiences and later experiences and then analyzing those videotapes is an effective way to develop this important skill (Snoeyink, 2010).

MODIFYING INSTRUCTIONAL STRATEGIES

As should now be clear, principles of effective classroom management go hand in hand with principles of learning and motivation. When students are learning and achieving successfully and when they clearly want to pursue the class's instructional goals, they're apt to be busily engaged in productive activities for most of the school day. In contrast, when students have trouble understanding classroom subject matter or little interest in learning it, they're likely to exhibit the nonproductive or counterproductive classroom behaviors that result from frustration or boredom (W. Doyle, 1990; Pekrun, Goetz, Daniels, Stupnisky, & Perry, 2010).

When students misbehave, beginning teachers often think about what the students are doing wrong. In contrast, experienced teachers are more apt to think about what *they themselves* could do differently to keep students on task, and they modify their plans accordingly (Emmer & Stough, 2001; Sabers et al., 1991; H. L. Swanson, O'Connor, & Cooney, 1990). Thus, when behavior problems arise, we should think as the experts do, considering questions such as these:

- How can I change my instructional strategies to stimulate students' interest?
- Are instructional materials so difficult or unstructured that students are getting frustrated? Alternatively, are they so easy or lock-step that students are bored?
- What are students really concerned about? For example, are they more concerned about interacting with peers than in gaining new knowledge and skills? How can I address students' motives and goals while simultaneously helping them achieve classroom objectives?
- Are students' problem behaviors being reinforced socially? In other words, is a student misbehaving because she garners attention from others?

Answering such questions enables us to focus our efforts on our ultimate goal: helping students *learn.*

Occasionally students are justifiably preoccupied by current events on the local or national scene—perhaps a tragic car accident involving classmates or a contentious political event—to the point that they can't focus on classroom subject matter. In such circumstances we may want to abandon our lesson plans altogether, at least for a short time.

TAKING DEVELOPMENTAL DIFFERENCES INTO ACCOUNT

To some degree our students' age levels must influence our classroom management decisions. Behavior management is important for students of all ages, even those in preschool (Bulotsky-Shearer, Dominguez, & Bell, 2012). Many children in the early elementary grades haven't had enough experience with formal education to know all the unspoken rules that govern classroom interactions: Students should remain silent when a teacher or other adult is talking, only the student who is called on should answer a question, and so on (Mehan, 1979; R. K. Payne, 2005). In addition, children just beginning kindergarten or first grade may find their new school environment to be unsettling and anxiety arousing, as do many adolescents making the transition to middle school or high school. And children's social skills—which affect their ability to interact effectively with others—continue to develop with age. Table 13.1 presents these and other developmental considerations, along with recommendations for accommodating them in classroom practices.

TAKING INDIVIDUAL AND GROUP DIFFERENCES INTO ACCOUNT

Earlier we mentioned the importance of consistency and equity in enforcing classroom rules. But when it comes to preventing off-task behaviors and supporting more productive ones, optimal strategies may differ considerably from one student to another. For example, during independent

Continually monitor what students are doing, and let students know that *you* know what's going on in your classroom.

Consider whether instructional strategies or classroom assignments might be partly to blame for off-task behaviors.

Take developmental differences into account in planning your classroom management strategies.

Chapter 11 describes the many reasons that students so often find the transition to middle school or high school unsettling.

DEVELOPMENTAL TRENDS

TABLE 13.1 • Effective Classroom Management at Different Grade Levels			
GRADE LEVEL	**AGE-TYPICAL CHARACTERISTICS**	**EXAMPLE**	**SUGGESTED STRATEGIES**
K–2	• Anxiety about being in school, especially in the first few weeks and especially for students without preschool experience • Lack of familiarity with unspoken rules about appropriate classroom behavior • Short attention span and high level of distractibility • Little self-regulation • Desire for teacher affection and approval • Considerable individual differences in social skills	Immediately after lunch on the first day of school, a first-grade teacher gathers students at the front of the room for a storybook reading. Before she begins to read, she explains the importance of sitting quietly so that everyone can hear the story, and when students occasionally behave in ways that might distract others, she gently reminds them of appropriate classroom behaviors.	• Invite students and their parents to visit the classroom before the school year begins. • Especially during the first few weeks of school, place high priority on forming a warm, supportive relationship with every student. • Be explicit about acceptable classroom behavior; correct inappropriate behaviors gently but consistently. • Keep assigned tasks relatively short and focused. • Create a gathering place (e.g., a carpet) where students can sit close at hand for whole-class discussions. • Give students frequent opportunities to release pent-up energy. • Create areas where students can work independently on tasks of their choosing (e.g., a reading center where students can listen to storybooks on tape **or a computer**).
3–5	• Continuing desire for teacher approval, but with increasing concern about peer approval as well • Greater attentiveness to teachers who are emotionally expressive (e.g., teachers who often smile and show obvious concern in times of distress) • Increasing self-regulation skills • Gradually improving ability to reflect on one's own and others' thoughts and motives (i.e., increasing social cognition) • Increasing disengagement from school if students are consistently encountering academic or social failure	Nine-year-old Bailey is often disruptive and socially inappropriate in class—so much so that her classmates avoid her as much as possible. On several occasions her teacher takes her aside and respectfully requests more productive behavior. For example, on one occasion the teacher says, "Bailey, I'm very happy to have you in my class. But it would really help me—and I think it would help you, too—if you could raise your hand before you answer a question. That way, other kids also have a chance to answer questions."	• Use two-way journals to communicate regularly with students about academic and personal issues. • In both words and actions, frequently show students that you're concerned about their academic progress and emotional well-being. • Provide increasing opportunities for independent work, but with enough structure to guide students' efforts. • In times of disagreement or conflict among classmates, ask students to reflect on one another's thoughts and feelings. • Make an extra effort to establish close, supportive relationships with students who appear to be academically and socially disengaged.
6–8	• Considerable anxiety about the transition to middle school, often due to more distant and less supportive relationships with teachers • Decrease in intrinsic motivation to learn academic subject matter • Increasing tendency to challenge traditional school norms for behavior—for instance, norms regarding clothing and hairstyle (for some students) • Increase in cheating behaviors; cheating less common if students think teachers respect them and are committed to helping them learn • Heightened concern about ability to fit in and be accepted by peers • Increase in bullying behaviors	The son of a neglectful mother, 14-year-old D.J. has frequently moved from one relative's home to another. He's now spending a second year in seventh grade, where he's extremely disruptive and disrespectful. When he calls a classmate a "fag," his teacher takes him aside and says, "I won't tolerate that offensive word. But I know you're going through a lot at home, and I really want you to be successful here at school. How can I help?" D.J. admits he has gay friends who wouldn't like the word he just used, and his teacher's obvious concern for his well-being leads to better behavior in class. Furthermore, D.J. starts asking the teacher for help on assignments.	• Find occasions to interact with students outside of class (e.g., attend sports events, chaperone school dances). • Plan lessons that are engaging and relevant to students' lives and needs. • Prohibit modes of dress that may threaten students' safety and well-being (e.g., gang insignia, racist T-shirts, sexually revealing attire), but otherwise give students some freedom of expression in what they wear. • Provide sufficient academic support that students have no reason to cheat; nevertheless, be on the lookout for possible cheating. • Don't tolerate bullying and other forms of aggression; address their underlying causes. • Reach out to students who seem socially unconnected (e.g., invite them to join you for lunch in your classroom).

(Continued)

TABLE 13.1 • *(Continued)*			
GRADE LEVEL	**AGE-TYPICAL CHARACTERISTICS**	**EXAMPLE**	**SUGGESTED STRATEGIES**
 **9–12**	• Anxiety about the transition to high school, especially if the seventh and eighth grades were part of elementary school • Social and romantic relationships often a source of distraction • Considerable self-regulation ability in some but not all students • High incidence of cheating, in part because many peers communicate that it's acceptable • Disdain for classmates who work too hard for teacher approval (i.e., "brown-nosers") • Tendency for some adolescents to think that misbehavior will gain peers' admiration • Increase in violent behaviors, especially at schools in low-income neighborhoods	When a high school teacher sees 16-year-old Jerrod standing alone at a school dance, he approaches the boy to express empathy. "I remember my first school dance," the teacher tells him. "Boy, did I feel awkward! I was too shy to ask a girl to dance, and I was so afraid of making a fool of myself. What do you think we might do to make these events less intimidating?" Jerrod smiles and admits that he feels the same way his teacher once did, and they brainstorm ideas for helping students feel more comfortable at future dances.	• Remember that even in the high school grades, students achieve at higher levels when they have close, supportive relationships with teachers. • Regularly plan activities that involve social interaction; if possible, move desks and chairs to allow students to interact more easily. • When students have few self-regulation skills, provide guidance and support to help them stay on task. • Describe what cheating is and why it's unacceptable. • Communicate approval privately rather than publicly. • Proactively address violence (see the section "Addressing Aggression and Violence at School" later in the chapter).

Sources: Some characteristics and recommendations based on Blanton & Burkley, 2008; Blugental, Lyon, Lin, McGrath, & Bimbela, 1999; K. Carter & Doyle, 2006; Castagno & Brayboy, 2008; Cizek, 2003; Emmer & Gerwels, 2006; Espinoza & Juvonen, 2011; Fingerhut & Christoffel, 2002; Hamre & Pianta, 2005; J. N. Hughes, Luo, Kwok, & Loyd, 2008; Ladd, Herald-Brown, & Reiser, 2008; Mehan, 1979; Murdock, Hale, & Weber, 2001; E. O'Connor & McCartney, 2007; Pellegrini, 2002; many other ideas derived from discussions in earlier chapters.

seatwork assignments, some students may work quite well with classmates close by, whereas others may be easily distracted unless they can work in a quiet spot, perhaps near their teacher's desk. And during small-group work, some groups may function effectively on their own, whereas others may need considerable guidance and supervision.

See Chapter 3 for more information about individual differences in temperament.

One important individual difference factor affecting classroom behavior is *temperament:* the extent to which a student is naturally inclined to be energetic, irritable, impulsive, and so on. To be truly effective classroom managers, we must realize that students' vastly different classroom behaviors may be due, in part, to biological and psychological predispositions that aren't entirely within their control. Such a realization should influence our beliefs about why students are acting as they are—that is, it should influence our *attributions*—and these beliefs will, in turn, affect our willingness to adapt classroom strategies to foster productive classroom behavior (W. Johnson, McGue, & Iacono, 2005; B. K. Keogh, 2003; A. Miller, 2006; Rothbart, 2011).

CULTURAL AND ETHNIC DIFFERENCES

Students who've grown up in diverse cultural and ethnic groups aren't always familiar with the unspoken standards for behavior in Western schools (Igoa, 1995; Tyler et al., 2008). Furthermore, some students may be unfamiliar with questions and hints that only indirectly tell them how they should behave—for instance, "Sally, would you like to sit down?" Such students are apt to be better behaved (and also less confused) if we're more explicit in our requests—for instance, "Sally, please sit down and focus on your schoolwork" (Adger, Wolfram, & Christian, 2007; Woolfolk Hoy, & Weinstein, 2006, p. 186). In addition, some students may not be native speakers of English, and thus linguistic challenges may arise; such students simply may not understand rules and procedures because of limited experience with English.

MyEdLab
Video Example 13.4.

Some students from diverse backgrounds may need explicit guidance about how they should behave at school.

But perhaps most important for students from diverse backgrounds is a warm, supportive classroom atmosphere (Castagno & Brayboy, 2008; García, 1995; Meehan, Hughes, & Cavell, 2003). For example, African American students in one eighth-grade social studies class explained why they liked their teacher so much:

Remember that some students from diverse backgrounds may need explicit guidance about how they should behave at school.

"She lets us express our opinions!"

"She looks us in the eye when she talks to us!"

"She smiles at us!"

"She speaks to us when she sees us in the hall or in the cafeteria!" (Ladson-Billings, 1994a, p. 68)

Simple gestures such as these go a long way toward establishing the kinds of teacher–student relationships that lead to a productive learning environment. It's also essential that we create a sense of community in the classroom—a sense that we and our students share common goals and are mutually supportive of everyone's reaching those goals. This sense of community is consistent with the cooperative spirit evident in many Hispanic, Native American, and African American groups. It can also be reassuring to students who perceive themselves to be different in an obvious way and thus might have exceptional concerns about not fitting in with their peer group (G. L. Cohen & Garcia, 2008; Ladson-Billings, 1994a; Tyler et al., 2008).

GENDER DIFFERENCES

On average, girls form more affectionate and productive relationships with teachers than boys do (Hughes, Wu, Kwok, Villarreal, & Johnson, 2012; Tutwiler, 2007; Wentzel et al., 2010). A variety of reasons may underlie some boys' nonproductive relationships with teachers. Boys are more prone to physical aggression than girls, and they're more likely than girls to be oppositional and defiant when asked to engage in tasks they'd rather not do. And in general, boys are temperamentally more active and have less self-control, to the point that they may have trouble sitting still for lengthy periods (W. O. Eaton & Enns, 1986; Rothbart, 2011). As teachers we can deter aggressive behaviors, particularly in boys, if we are attuned to students' aggressive tendencies and to the social relationships among students in our classes (Ahn & Rodkin, 2014). Referring back to the concept of "withitness" mentioned earlier, we need to be aware of all of the academic events occurring in our classrooms, but also of the social interactions that occur. Notice what happened to one fourth grader (now a successful college professor) when his teacher took his temperament into consideration:

A warm, supportive classroom climate may be especially important for students from diverse ethnic backgrounds.

> One day when I was especially restless . . . I could see Miss Rickenbrood circling to the back of the room. . . . After a few minutes she leaned over and whispered in my ear, "Tom, would you like to go outside and run?"
>
> I was stunned. To go outside and run? On my own? When it wasn't recess? What could have possessed this woman to ignore all school rules and allow me to run? I said yes and quietly went to put on my coat. As I recall, I didn't actually run in the playground (people would be watching from inside the building), but stood outside in the doorway, in the cold, marveling at my freedom. I returned to class after about ten minutes, settled for the rest of the day. (Newkirk, 2002, pp. 25–26)

Make a special effort to establish good relationships with emotionally distant or chronically misbehaving students.

SOCIOECONOMIC DIFFERENCES

Having teachers' affection, respect, and support is even more important for students who face exceptional hardships at home—poverty, violent neighborhoods, homelessness, and so on. Some of these students may be prone to anger and disrespectful classroom behavior, undoubtedly as a result of their difficult circumstances outside of school (R. K. Payne, 2005). Yet when students from economically impoverished backgrounds have one or more caring, trustworthy adults in their lives—and when they regularly come to a classroom that's warm, predictable, and dependable—they often have a strong sense of self-worth and autonomy. Hence they're better equipped to succeed both at school and in the outside world. In other words, they're more likely to be *resilient*—to rise above their adverse circumstances (Abelev, 2009; B. E. Becker & Luthar, 2002; Masten, 2001; Polakow, 2007).

When students face exceptional challenges at home, make an extra effort to create an affectionate, supportive, predictable, and safe environment at school.

You can learn more about resilience in the discussion of *students at risk* in Chapter 4.

ACCOMMODATING STUDENTS WITH SPECIAL NEEDS

Most students with special needs can more easily adapt to a general education setting when the classroom is orderly and well structured. Even more so than their nondisabled peers, students with disabilities benefit from classrooms in which procedures for performing certain tasks are specified, expectations for student behavior are clear, and misbehaviors are treated consistently (Heward, 2009; Pfiffner, Barkley, & DuPaul, 2006; Scruggs & Mastropieri, 1994). Although some students with disabilities may need considerable guidance and support in order to behave appropriately,

Chapter 5 identifies specific categories of special needs that fall within the five general categories listed in Table 13.2.

unless there are extenuating circumstances, these students must incur the same consequences as everyone else when their behaviors are out of line. Table 13.2 offers many suggestions for accommodating students with special needs.

MyEdLab **Self-Check 13.1**

MyEdLab **Application Exercise 13.1.** In this exercise, you can describe strategies for setting limits and creating a productive climate for learning.

STUDENTS IN INCLUSIVE SETTINGS

TABLE 13.2 • Maintaining a Productive Classroom Environment for Students with Special Educational Needs

CATEGORY	CHARACTERISTICS YOU MIGHT OBSERVE	SUGGESTED STRATEGIES
Students with specific cognitive or academic difficulties	• Difficulty staying on task • Misbehaviors such as hyperactivity, impulsiveness, disruptiveness, and inattentiveness (in some students) • Poor time management skills and/or a disorganized approach to accomplishing tasks (in some students)	• Closely monitor students during independent assignments. • Make sure students understand their assignments; if appropriate, give extra time to complete them. • Make expectations for behavior clear, and enforce classroom rules consistently. • Reinforce (e.g., praise) desired behaviors immediately; be specific about the behaviors you are reinforcing. • For hyperactive students, plan short activities that help them settle down after periods of physical activity (e.g., after recess, lunch, or physical education). • For impulsive students, teach self-regulation skills (e.g., verbal self-reminders about appropriate behavior). • Teach strategies for organizing time and work (e.g., tape a schedule of daily activities to students' desks, provide folders that students can use to carry assignments to and from home).
Students with social or behavioral problems	• Frequent overt misbehaviors, such as acting out, aggression, noncompliance, destructiveness, or stealing (in some students) • Difficulty inhibiting impulses • Misbehaviors triggered by changes in the environment or daily routine or by sensory overstimulation (for some students with autism spectrum disorders) • Difficulty interacting effectively with peers • Difficulty staying on task • Tendency to engage in power struggles with teachers (for some students)	• Specify in precise terms what behaviors are acceptable and unacceptable in the classroom; establish and enforce rules for behavior. • Maintain a predictable schedule; warn students ahead of time about changes in the routine. • Use self-regulation techniques and behaviorist approaches to promote productive classroom behaviors. • Explicitly teach social skills. • Closely monitor students during independent assignments. • Give students a sense of self-determination about some aspects of classroom life; minimize use of coercive techniques. • Make an extra effort to show students that you care about them as individuals.
Students with general delays in cognitive and social functioning	• Occasional disruptive classroom behavior (for some students) • Dependence on others for guidance about how to behave • More appropriate classroom behavior when expectations are clear	• Establish clear, concrete rules for classroom behavior. • As necessary, remind students about appropriate behavior; keep directions simple. • Use structured behaviorist approaches to promote desired behaviors. • Give explicit feedback about what students are and are not doing appropriately.
Students with physical or sensory challenges	• Social isolation from classmates (for some students) • Difficulty accomplishing tasks as quickly as other students • Difficulty understanding directions and other spoken messages about desired behaviors (for students with hearing loss)	• Establish a strong sense of community within the classroom. • When appropriate, give extra time to complete assignments. • Keep unnecessary noise to a minimum if one or more students have hearing loss.
Students with advanced cognitive development	• Off-task behavior in some students, often due to boredom during easy assignments and activities	• Assign tasks appropriate to students' cognitive abilities.

Sources: Barkley, 2006; Beirne-Smith, Patton, & Kim, 2006; Buchoff, 1990; M.-L. Chang & Davis, 2009; B. Clark, 1997; Dai, 2010; Dempster & Corkill, 1999; S. C. Diamond, 1991; D. A. Granger, Whalen, Henker, & Cantwell, 1996; N. Gregg, 2009; Heward, 2009; Koegel, Koegel, & Dunlap, 1996; Mendaglio, 2010; Mercer & Pullen, 2005; Morgan & Jenson, 1988; Patton, Blackbourn, & Fad, 1996; Pellegrini & Horvat, 1995; Turnbull, Turnbull, & Wehmeyer, 2010; Winner, 1997.

Expanding the Sense of Community Beyond the Classroom

Students' learning and development depend not only on what happens inside the classroom but also on what happens in other parts of the school, in the neighborhood and community, and at home. To be most effective, we should coordinate our efforts with other influential individuals in students' lives—with other school faculty members, with professionals at community agencies, and especially with students' parents or other primary caregivers. Ideally we should think of such joint efforts as *partnerships* in which everyone is working together to promote students' long-term development and learning.

WORKING WITH OTHER FACULTY MEMBERS

It's important that all school faculty members communicate consistent messages and expectations using strategies such as these:

- Identify common goals regarding what students should learn and achieve.
- Work together to identify and overcome obstacles to students' achievement.
- Establish a common set of standards for students' behavior, along with systematic, schoolwide procedures for encouraging productive and respectful behaviors.
- Make a group commitment to promote equality and multicultural sensitivity throughout the school community. (Battistich, Solomon, Watson, & Schaps, 1997; K. L. Lane, Kalberg, & Menzies, 2009; J. Lee & Shute, 2010; Levine & Lezotte, 1995; T. J. Lewis, Newcomer, Trussell, & Richter, 2006)

One increasingly popular approach is schoolwide positive behavioral interventions and supports, in which school faculty members jointly and explicitly define, teach, and reinforce appropriate behaviors and provide varying levels of support tailored to students' needs (e.g., Ihlo & Nantais, 2010; Osher, Bear, Sprague, & Doyle, 2010; J. S. Warren et al., 2006).

Ideally, too, in addition to creating a sense of community within our individual classrooms, we should create an overall sense of school community—a shared belief that all teachers and students within a school are working together to help everyone learn and succeed (Battistich, Solomon, Kim, Watson, & Schaps, 1995, Battistich et al., 1997; M. Watson & Battistich, 2006). When a school has a genuine sense of community, students regularly get two very important messages: (1) All faculty members are working together to help students become informed and productive citizens; and (2) students can and should *help one another.* A sense of school community involves close student–student relationships not only within individual classrooms but also across classrooms and grade levels. Cross-class peer tutoring, participation in extracurricular activities, student involvement in school decision making, frequent use of school mascots and other traditional school symbols—all of these help to create a sense that students are members of a mutually supportive school "family" (Juvonen, 2006; Nucci, 2009; D. R. Robinson, Schofield, & Steers-Wentzell, 2005).

When teachers and students share an overall sense of school community, students have more positive attitudes toward school, are more motivated to achieve at high levels, exhibit more prosocial behavior, and interact more often with peers from diverse backgrounds. Furthermore, teachers have higher expectations for students' achievement and a greater sense of self-efficacy about their teaching effectiveness (Battistich et al., 1995, 1997; J. A. Langer, 2000). In fact, when teachers work together, they have higher *collective self-efficacy*—a belief that by working as a team, they can definitely have an impact on students' learning and achievement—and this collective self-confidence is correlated with students' academic performance (Goddard, Hoy, & Woolfolk Hoy, 2000; J. Lee & Shute, 2010; Sørlie, & Torsheim, 2011). Such a team spirit has an additional advantage for beginning teachers: It provides the support structure (scaffolding) they may need, especially when working with students who are at risk for school failure. New teachers report greater confidence in their ability to help students learn and achieve when they collaborate regularly with their colleagues (Chester & Beaudin, 1996).

Chapter 9 describes schoolwide positive behavioral interventions and supports in more detail.

Collaborate with colleagues to create an overall sense of school community.

Collective self-efficacy is a key concept in social cognitive theory (see Chapter 10).

WORKING WITH THE COMMUNITY AT LARGE

Students almost always have regular contact with other institutions besides school—possibly youth groups, community organizations, social services, churches, hospitals, mental health clinics, and local judicial systems. And some students live in cultural environments very different from our own. As teachers, we enhance our effectiveness if we understand the environments in which our students live and if we think of ourselves as integral members of a larger community that promotes children's and adolescents' long-term development. For example, we must educate ourselves about students' cultural backgrounds, perhaps by taking course work and getting involved in local community events (Castagno & Brayboy, 2008; McIntyre, 2010). We must also keep in contact with other people and institutions that play major roles in students' lives, coordinating our efforts whenever possible (J. L. Epstein, 1996; Kincheloe, 2009).

Work cooperatively with other agencies that play key roles in students' lives.

WORKING WITH PARENTS

Above all, we must work cooperatively with students' parents and other primary caregivers. Productive parent–teacher relationships may be especially important when working with students from diverse cultural backgrounds, and they're *essential* when working with students who have physical, cognitive, or behavioral disabilities (Hidalgo, Siu, Bright, Swap, & Epstein, 1995; Iruka, Winn, Kingsley, & Orthodoxou, 2011; Reschly & Christenson, 2009; Waasdorp, Bradshaw, & Duong, 2011).

We must keep in mind that families come in a variety of forms and that students' primary caregivers aren't always their parents. For example, in some ethnic minority communities, grandmothers take primary responsibility for raising children (Dantas & Manyak, 2010; Stack & Burton, 1993). To keep our discussion simple, we use the term *parents* in upcoming paragraphs, but we are, in fact, referring to all primary caregivers.

In the United States, the Individuals with Disabilities Education Act (IDEA) ensures parents' involvement in educational decision making for students with disabilities (see Chapter 5).

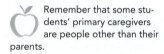

Remember that some students' primary caregivers are people other than their parents.

COMMUNICATING WITH PARENTS

We should open lines of communication with parents as soon as classes begin—perhaps even before that—and stay in regular contact with them throughout the school year. We should inform them of their children's accomplishments and keep them apprised of any behaviors that are consistently interfering with learning and achievement. Regular communication also provides a means through which parents can give *us* information, which might yield new ideas about how we might most effectively work with their children. In addition, regular communication enables us to coordinate our classroom strategies with those that parents use at home. Communications with parents should not only occur when students misbehave; in fact, communication can be particularly beneficial when we have *good* relationships with our students (McCormick, Cappella, O'Connor, & McClowry, 2013). Following are several common mechanisms for enhancing school–family communication.

MyEdLab
Video Example 13.5.

Regular communication with parents and other primary caregivers provides a means for giving and receiving information about the student's progress and needs.

Parent–Teacher Conferences   In most school districts, formal parent–teacher conferences are scheduled one or more times a year. We may often want to include students in conferences—essentially making them parent–teacher–student conferences—and in some instances we might even ask students to *lead* the conferences. By holding student-led conferences, we increase the likelihood that parents will come to the conferences, we encourage students to reflect on their own academic progress, and we give students practice in communication and leadership skills. Furthermore, teachers, students, and parents alike are apt to leave such meetings with a shared understanding of the progress that has been made and of subsequent steps that need to be taken. Even if students do lead the conferences, however, it is important for teachers to still play an active role, because parents want to get feedback from you! Figure 13.6 offers suggestions for conducting effective conferences.

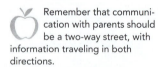

Remember that communication with parents should be a two-way street, with information traveling in both directions.

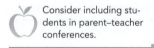

Consider including students in parent–teacher conferences.

Written Communication   Written communication can take a variety of forms. It can be a general welcome letter sent to students and parents before the school year begins. It can be a weekly checklist that documents a student's progress. It can be a quick, informal note or email acknowledging a significant accomplishment. Or it can be a newsletter that describes class activities, expectations for homework, and so on. All of these mechanisms have two things in common: They let parents know what's happening at school and convey a genuine desire to stay in touch with families.

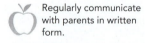

Regularly communicate with parents in written form.

A parent letter written by second-grade teacher Ann Reilly provides an illustration (see Figure 13.7). The letter was written on September 14, 2001, 3 days after terrorist attacks on the

---

FIGURE 13.6 Suggestions for conducting effective parent–teacher conferences.

Suggestions for Any Parent–Teacher Conference

- Schedule the conference at a time that accommodates parents' jobs and other obligations.

- Accommodate cultural differences. For example, invite extended family members who play key roles in caregiving, and include a trusted individual who can translate for non-native-English speakers.

- Prepare ahead of time. For example, review what you know about the student (e.g., academic progress, classroom behavior), organize your thoughts, create an agenda for the meeting, and have examples of the student's work on hand.

- Create a warm, nonjudgmental atmosphere. For example, express appreciation that the parents have come and encourage them to offer their thoughts and perspectives. Remember that your objective is to work cooperatively and constructively with parents to create the best educational program possible for their child. Also remember that some parents may have had bad personal experiences when they were students, so they may come into the conference expecting to have a difficult meeting.

- Describe your general goals and expectations for students.

- Avoid educational jargon with which parents may be unfamiliar; describe the student's performance in ways a noneducator can understand. If you report standardized test scores to parents, make sure that you can explain the scores to them and not just report numbers that may seem meaningless.

- Actively seek information. For example, ask parents to describe their child's strong points and favorite activities.

- Jointly explore possible ways in which you and parents might support one another's efforts to promote the student's development.

- End on a positive note—perhaps with a review of the student's many strengths and the progress he or she has made.

- Follow through with anything you have said you will do.

Additional Suggestions for a Student-Led Conference:

- Meet with the student ahead of time to agree on appropriate work samples to share.

- Model and role-play effective conferences in class, and give students time to practice with their classmates.

- Schedule a backup audience (e.g., a former teacher or trusted friend) who can sit in if the student's parents don't attend.

- Offer additional time in which you can meet without the student if the parents so desire.

- Talk with the student afterward about what went well and how the two of you might improve the next conference.

World Trade Center and Pentagon and during a week when students were taking a districtwide standardized test. The letter communicates a great deal of information: what topics the class is studying, how parents will get results of the standardized test, and why the class isn't talking much about the terrorist attacks. It communicates attitudes as well; for instance, Ms. Reilly is eager to keep the lines of communication with parents open, is approachable (she signs the letter "Ann"), and cares about how well her students are doing (e.g., "I don't like telling them that they are on their own" during classroom assessments). She also suggests several simple ways in which parents might contribute to the class: helping with spelling assessments, donating tissues, and providing instructions for making baby wipes. Because she teaches in a school district in which most parents have Internet access either at home or at work, she has given parents her email address. Suggesting the use of email would be less appropriate in communities where many families can't afford computers or parents have limited knowledge of English.

Class Websites   Many teachers now create class websites on which they post instructional goals, assignments, and so on; in fact, some schools now require the use of such websites. Typically teachers' websites are available to parents as well as students, but, as is true for email messages, they're most appropriate for parents who regularly use computers and the Internet.

See Chapter 12 for more information about constructing class websites.

Telephone Conversations   In the elementary grades, telephone calls are a useful way of introducing oneself at the start of the school year and following up on conferences that parents have missed (C. Davis & Yang, 2005; Striepling-Goldstein, 2004). And at all grade levels, telephone calls are often appropriate when something unusual has happened—for instance, when a student has either made a noteworthy step forward or, instead, has recently shown an unexpected decline in performance. Often, parents receive phone calls from teachers when something bad has happened—when a student gets a low grade or behaves badly; try to also call parents when something good happens—when students show improvement or do something nice for others, or just to "check in" and say that all is going well. When parents are aware of their children's successes and develop positive perceptions of their children's competence, the children's academic

Make a quick telephone call to inform parents of exciting new accomplishments or potential areas of concern.

FIGURE 13.7 An example of a teacher's letter to parents.

9/14/01

Dear Parents,

I have been lucky so far and have not had to go back for jury duty. I have two more weeks to go [in terms of possibly being summoned for duty] and hope I will continue to be in the classroom.

We have been trying to keep the routine pretty regular, despite one or two testing sessions per day. The children have been pretty focused, although it is difficult when they are unfamiliar with the format and look to us for help. I don't like telling them that they are on their own! We are done, thank goodness. I believe you will receive results in the mail.

Homework and spelling will resume next week. I could also use my regular volunteers to help get through the spelling assessments. The times you have been coming are still fine. Call or e-mail me if you need the available times for helping.

We finished our unit on germs and sanitation, although we did not get into any discussions about Anthrax. It seems that you are keeping the children protected at home from details of the scary news, as we are at school. We kept our discussions to common illnesses that they are aware of and how they can avoid them with proper sanitation.

A few classrooms are doing activities to raise money for many of the children involved in the tragedy. Sarah [the teacher intern] and I decided not to work with our children on a fundraiser because we don't want to get into anxiety-producing discussions. It is hard to help young children understand that they are safe where they are and that it is unlikely that they will be involved in such things.

Next week, we will be starting a Nutrition Unit and beginning to read some Halloween stories. We will continue working to become automatic with math facts, along with our regular routine of phonics lessons, DOL [daily oral language], reading, writing, spelling, etc.

We are running out of Kleenex and could use some donations. We would also like some boxes of baby wipes to use in cleaning hands and desks when there is not time for the entire class to wash. Someone mentioned to me that there is a homemade recipe for baby wipes out there somewhere. Is there a parent who knows and would be willing to share?

Have a great weekend.

Ann

Source: Text of "Dear Parents" letter dated September 14, 2001, by Ann L. Reilly. Copyright © 2001 by Anne L. Reilly. Reprinted with permission.

achievement benefits (Gut, Reimann, & Grob, 2013). Likewise, parents should feel free to call *us*. Because many parents are at work during the school day, it's often helpful to accept and encourage calls at home during the early evening hours.

Parent Discussion Groups   In some instances we may want to assemble a group of parents to discuss issues of mutual interest—perhaps specific topics that might be included in the class curriculum or effective strategies that parents can use to promote their children's academic, personal, and social development (J. L. Epstein, 1996; Fosnot, 1996; Rudman, 1993). Also, some teachers have successfully used parent *coffee nights* or *coffee mornings,* during which they explain a new instructional strategy, or *author teas,* during which students read poetry and short stories they have written.

Hold parent discussion groups for topics of general interest.

GETTING PARENTS INVOLVED IN SCHOOL ACTIVITIES

Ultimately the best means of communicating and collaborating with parents is to get them actively involved in school life and in children's learning, and perhaps get other family members involved as well. Students whose parents are involved in school activities have better attendance records, higher achievement, and more positive attitudes toward school. Although the reasons for these correlations aren't entirely clear, they appear to be due partly to the fact that parents who actively participate in school activities can more effectively coordinate their efforts at home with teachers' efforts in the classroom (N. E. Hill & Taylor, 2004; Hindman & Morrison, 2011; Lam, Chow-Yeung, Wong, Lau, & Tse, 2013; Monti, Pomerantz, & Roisman, 2014; Spera, 2005).

Parental involvement in school activities can take a variety of forms. For instance, we might:

- Invite parents to an open house or musical performance in the evening.
- Request parents' help with a weekend fundraiser.
- Seek volunteers to help with field trips, special projects, or individual tutoring during the school day.

- Use parents and other community members as resources to provide a multicultural perspective of the local community. (C. Davis & Yang, 2005; McCarty & Watahomigie, 1998; McIntyre, 2010; Minami & Ovando, 1995)

Many parents are apt to become involved in such activities only when they have a specific invitation to do so and when they know that school personnel genuinely want them to be involved (C. L. Green, Walker, Hoover-Dempsey, & Sandler, 2007; Serpell, Baker, & Sonnenschein, 2005). Some parents—especially those from certain minority groups or low-income families—may not take a general, open-ended invitation seriously. A personal invitation can often make all the difference, as one mother explained:

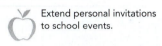

Extend personal invitations to school events.

> The thing of it is, had someone not walked up to me and asked me specifically, I would not hold out my hand and say, "I'll do it." . . . You get parents here all the time, black parents that are willing, but maybe a little on the shy side and wouldn't say I really want to serve on this subject. You may send me the form, I may never fill the form out. Or I'll think about it and not send it back. But you know if that principal, that teacher, my son's math teacher called and asked if I would . . . (A. A. Carr, 1997, p. 2)

Parents can also be invaluable in helping children with homework. Even parents who have few academic skills themselves can provide worthwhile support—for instance, by communicating the importance of doing well, providing a quiet place to study, and making television viewing contingent on homework completion. The more parents do such things, the higher their children's achievement is likely to be. Furthermore, many parents are open to teacher suggestions about how they might best be of assistance. Thus, you might help parents to understand that their involvement with homework will be particularly beneficial when they are perceived as supportive; conflict and interference with homework actually can be detrimental to achievement (Dumont et al., 2012; Dumont, Trautwein, Nagy, & Nagengast, 2014; S. Hong & Ho, 2005; J. Lee & Shute, 2010; J.-S. Lee & Bowen, 2006; Patall, Cooper, & Robinson, 2008; J. M. T. Walker & Hoover-Dempsey, 2006).

Offer suggestions about things parents might do to help their children with homework.

ENCOURAGING RELUCTANT PARENTS

Despite our best efforts, a few parents may remain uninvolved in their children's education; for example, they may never attend scheduled parent–teacher conferences. But before we jump too quickly to the conclusion that these parents are also *uninterested* in their children's education, we must recognize several possible reasons that parents might be reluctant to make contact with us. Some may have an exhausting work schedule or lack adequate child care. Others may know little English, have difficulty finding their way through the school system, or believe it's inappropriate to bother teachers with their concerns. Still others may have had such bad experiences when they themselves were students that they feel uncomfortable in a school building. And a few parents may be victims of mental illness or substance abuse, limiting their ability to support their children financially, academically, or otherwise (Bornstein & Cote, 2010; Carbrera, Shannon, West, & Brooks-Gunn, 2006; Cazden, 2001; Dantas & Manyak, 2010; J.-S. Lee & Bowen, 2006; Ogbu, 2003).

Identify alternative sources of academic support when a student's family is unable to provide it.

Experienced educators have offered numerous suggestions for getting reluctant parents more involved in their children's schooling:

- Make an extra effort to gain parents' trust and confidence—for instance, by demonstrating that their contributions are both helpful and appreciated.
- Encourage parents to be assertive when they have questions or concerns.
- Invite other important family members (e.g., grandparents, aunts, uncles) to participate in school activities, especially if a student's cultural group places high value on extended families.
- Offer suggestions about learning activities parents can easily do with their children at home.
- Find out what parents do exceptionally well (e.g., carpentry, cooking), and ask them to share their talents with students.
- Provide opportunities for parents to volunteer for jobs that don't require them to leave home (e.g., to be someone whom students can call when they're unsure of homework assignments).

- Identify specific individuals (e.g., bilingual parents) who can translate for those who speak little or no English.
- Make home visits *if* such visits are welcomed.
- Offer resources for parents at the school building—for instance, contacts with social and health services, or classes in English, literacy, home repairs, and crafts. (Castagno & Brayboy, 2008; Dantas & Manyak, 2010; C. Davis & Yang, 2005; J. L. Epstein, 1996; Finders & Lewis, 1994; Hidalgo et al., 1995; G. R. López, 2001; Salend & Taylor, 1993; M. G. Sanders, 1996; J. M. T. Walker & Hoover-Dempsey, 2006)

Another potentially effective strategy is to reinforce *parents* as well as students when the students do well at school. One administrator at a school serving many immigrant students put it this way:

> One of the things we do . . . is that we identify those students that had perfect attendance, those students that passed all areas of the [statewide achievement tests] and were successful. We don't honor the student, we honor the parents. We give parents a certificate. Because, we tell them, "Through your efforts, and through your hard work, your child was able to accomplish this." (G. R. López, 2001, p. 273)

A few parents may resist all of our efforts to get them involved. Especially in such circumstances, we must never penalize students for their parents' actions or inactions. And we must realize that as teachers, *we* are apt to be among the most important academic and emotional resources in these students' lives.

CONSIDERING CULTURAL DIFFERENCES WHEN WORKING WITH PARENTS

As we work with students' parents, we must be aware that people from different cultural and ethnic groups sometimes have radically different ideas about how—and also how *much*—to control their children's behavior. For example, many parents from Asian cultures expect children to obey adult authority figures without question; such parents often think that Western teachers are much too lenient with students (Dien, 1998; Hidalgo et al., 1995; Kağitçibaşi, 2007; Tamis-Lemonda & McFadden, 2010). In contrast, parents in some Native American cultures believe that children have a right to make their own decisions; from their perspective, good parenting involves providing gentle suggestions and guidance rather than insisting that children behave in certain ways (Deyhle & LeCompte, 1999). Some cultural and religious groups use ostracism in an effort to keep children in line: The child is ignored—for instance, given the "silent treatment"—for an extended period (K. D. Williams, 2001). We need to be wary of stereotyped comments suggesting that parents from some cultural groups do not want to be involved with schools; most parents do want to be involved in some way (e.g., J. T. M. Walker, Ice, Hoover-Dempsey, & Sandler, 2011).

We must realize that the vast majority of parents want what's best for their children and recognize the value of a good education. It's essential, then, that we not leave parents out of the loop when we're concerned about how their children are performing in school. And as we talk with them, we must listen to their attitudes and opinions with an open mind and try to find common ground on which to develop strategies for helping their children thrive in the classroom.

> **Give recognition to parents whose children do well or show improvement at school.**

> **Don't penalize students for things that their parents do or don't do.**

> **Communicate your confidence in each student's ability to succeed, as well as your commitment to working cooperatively with parents.**

MyEdLab **Self-Check 13.2**

MyEdLab **Application Exercise 13.2.** This exercise involves explaining how teachers can coordinate their efforts to maximize students' academic and personal development.

Dealing with Misbehaviors

Despite our best efforts to create a classroom environment that promotes learning, one or more of our students will occasionally behave in undesirable ways. For purposes of our discussion, we'll define a misbehavior as any action that can potentially disrupt learning and planned classroom activities, puts one or more students' physical safety or psychological well-being in jeopardy, or violates basic moral and ethical standards. Some misbehaviors are relatively minor and have little long-term impact on students' achievement. Such behaviors as talking out of turn, writing brief notes to classmates during a lecture, and submitting homework assignments after their due date—especially if these behaviors occur infrequently—generally fall in this category. Other misbehaviors are far more serious, in that they definitely interfere with the learning or well-being of one or more students. For example, when students scream at their teachers, hit classmates, or habitually refuse to participate in learning activities, then classroom learning—certainly that of the guilty party, and sometimes that of other students as well—can be adversely affected, as can the overall classroom climate.

Typically only a few students are responsible for the great majority of misbehaviors in any single class (W. Doyle, 2006). These students are apt to be among our greatest challenges, and it can be all too tempting to write them off as lost causes. Yet we must work vigorously to turn them in more productive directions: Without active interventions by teachers and other caring adults, students who are consistently disruptive or in other ways off task in the early grades may continue to show behavior problems later on (Dishion, Piehler, & Myers, 2008; Emmer & Gerwels, 2006; Vitaro, Brendgen, Larose, & Tremblay, 2005). In addition, new teachers in particular enjoy their work more and feel better about their jobs when they feel efficacious about managing student behavior (Dicke et al., 2014). As teachers, we need to plan ahead about how we'll address students' misbehaviors. We also need to take personal responsibility for behavior management in our classrooms—sometimes student learning outcomes suffer more because of teachers not knowing effective management techniques than because of the actual behaviors of the students (Hochweber, Hosenfeld, & Klieme, 2014). Although we must be consistent in the consequences we impose for blatant rule infractions (recall our earlier discussion of consistency and equity), a variety of strategies can be useful in reducing counterproductive behaviors over the long run. We need to be consistent in our delivery of various interventions to students; for example, low-income African American boys tend to be disciplined disproportionately more than are other students (Petras, Masyn, Buckley, Ialongo, & Kellam, 2011).

Here we'll examine six general strategies and their appropriate applications: ignoring a behavior, cueing a student, talking with a student in private, teaching self-regulation skills, conferring with parents, and planning and conducting a systematic intervention.

IGNORING CERTAIN BEHAVIORS

On some occasions our best course of action is *no* action, at least nothing of a disciplinary nature. For example, consider these situations:

- Dimitra rarely breaks classroom rules. But on one occasion, after you've just instructed students to work quietly and independently at their seats, you see her briefly whisper to the girl beside her. Other students don't seem to notice that she is temporarily disobeying your instructions.

- Henry is careless in chemistry lab and accidentally knocks over a small container of liquid—a harmless one, fortunately. He quickly apologizes and cleans up the mess.

Will these behaviors interfere with Dimitra's or Henry's academic achievement? Are they "contagious" behaviors that will spread to other students, as the horseplay did in Ms. Cornell's class? The answer to both questions is "Probably not."

Whenever we stop an instructional activity to deal with a misbehavior, even for a few seconds, we may disrupt the momentum of the activity and draw students' attention to a misbehaving classmate. Furthermore, by drawing other students' attention to a particular misbehavior, we may unintentionally be reinforcing it.

Ignoring misbehavior is often reasonable in circumstances such as these:

- When the behavior is a rare occurrence and probably won't be repeated

- When the behavior is unlikely to spread to other students

- When the behavior is the result of unusual and temporary conditions (e.g., the last day of school before a holiday, unsettling events in a student's personal life)

- When the behavior is typical for the age-group (e.g., kindergartners becoming restless after sitting for an extended time, sixth-grade boys and girls resisting holding one another's hands during dance instruction)

- When the behavior's natural consequence is unpleasant enough to deter a student from repeating it
- When the behavior isn't interfering with classroom learning (G. A. Davis & Thomas, 1989; W. Doyle, 1986a, 2006; Dreikurs, 1998; Munn et al., 1990; Silberman & Wheelan, 1980; Wynne, 1990)

Dimitra's behavior—briefly whispering to a classmate during independent seatwork—is unlikely to spread to her classmates (they don't see her do it) and probably isn't an instance of cheating (it occurs before she begins working on the assignment). Henry's behavior—knocking over a container of liquid in chemistry lab—has in and of itself resulted in an unpleasant consequence: He must clean up the mess. In both situations, then, ignoring the misbehavior is probably best.

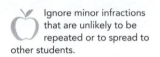

Ignore minor infractions that are unlikely to be repeated or to spread to other students.

CUEING STUDENTS

In some situations off-task behaviors, although not serious in nature, *do* interfere with learning and must be discouraged. Consider these situations as examples:

- As you're explaining a difficult concept, Marjorie is busily writing. At first you think she's taking notes, but then you see her pass the paper across the aisle to Kang. A few minutes later you see Kang pass the same sheet back to Marjorie. It appears that the two students are exchanging personal notes when they should be attending to the lesson.
- You've separated your class into small groups for a cooperative learning activity. One group is frequently off task and probably won't complete the assignment if the students don't get down to business soon.

Gently cue students about desired behaviors.

Effective classroom managers handle such minor behavior problems as unobtrusively as possible: They don't stop the lesson, distract other students, or call unnecessary attention to the inappropriate behavior. In many cases they use **cueing**: They give a brief signal—perhaps a stern look or a simple verbal directive—to communicate that the misbehavior has been noticed and should cease. Ideally such cues focus students' attention on what *should* be done rather than on what *isn't* being done (Evertson & Emmer, 2009; K. L. Lane et al., 2011). For instance, instead of chastising students for being overly noisy during a cooperative group activity, a teacher might say, "As you exchange ideas, remember to use your *indoor voices* so that you don't distract other groups."

MyEdLab
Video Example 13.6.

When teachers spend too much class time dealing with a single misbehaving students, other students get off task. This teacher's approach helps the groups stay on task and allows the disruptive students to use self-regulating behavior by removing herself from the group.

DISCUSSING PROBLEMS PRIVATELY WITH STUDENTS

Sometimes brief cues are insufficient to change a student's misbehavior. Consider these situations:

- Alonzo is almost always a few minutes late to your third-period algebra class. When he finally arrives, he takes several more minutes to pull his textbook and other class materials out of his backpack. You've often reminded him about the importance of coming to class on time, yet his tardiness continues.
- Tara rarely completes assignments; in fact, she often doesn't even *begin* them. On many previous occasions you've gently tried to get her on task, but usually without success. Today, when you look Tara in the eye and ask her point blank to get to work, she defiantly responds, "I'm not going to do it. You can't make me!"

In such situations, talking privately with the student is the next logical step. The discussion should be *private* for several reasons. First, as noted earlier, calling peers' attention to a problem behavior may actually reinforce the behavior rather than discourage it. Or, instead, the attention of classmates may cause a student to feel excessively embarrassed or humiliated—feelings that can make the student overanxious about coming to school in the future. Finally, when we spend too much class time dealing with a single misbehaving student, other students are apt to get off task as well (W. Doyle, 2006; Emmer & Gerwels, 2006; Scott & Bushell, 1974).

Speak privately with students about chronic behavior problems.

Private conversations give us an opportunity to explain why certain behaviors are unacceptable and must stop. They also give students a chance to explain why they behave as they do. For example, Alonzo might explain his chronic tardiness by revealing that he has diabetes and must check his blood sugar level between his second- and third-period classes. He can perform the procedure himself but would prefer to do it in the privacy of the school nurse's office. Meanwhile, Tara might describe her long-standing frustration with subject matter and assignments she perceives as being impossible to make sense of. A boy with a reading disability once voiced such frustration in an interview with a researcher:

> They [teachers] used to hand us all our homework on Mondays. One day my teacher handed me a stack about an inch thick and as I was walking out of class there was a big trash can right there and I'd, in front of everybody including the teacher, just drop it in the trash can and walk out. I did this because I couldn't read what she gave me. It was kind of a point that I wanted to get the teacher to realize. That while I'm doing it, inside it kind of like hurt because I really wanted to do it but I couldn't and just so it didn't look like I was goin' soft or anything like that I'd walk over to the trash and throw it in. (Zambo & Brem, 2004, p. 6)

Students' explanations often provide clues about how best to deal with their behavior over the long run. For example, given his diabetes, Alonzo's continued tardiness to class might be inevitable. Perhaps we could reassign him to a seat by the door, enabling him to join class unobtrusively when he arrives, and we might ask the student next to him to quietly fill him in on the lesson in progress. Tara's frustration with her schoolwork suggests that she needs additional scaffolding to help her succeed. It also hints at a possible undiagnosed learning disability that might warrant a referral to the school psychologist or other diagnostician.

Students won't always provide explanations that lead to such logical solutions, however. For example, it may be that Alonzo is late to class simply because he wants to spend more time in the hall with friends. Or perhaps Tara doesn't want to do her assignments because, as she says, "I'm sick and tired of other people always telling me what to do." In such circumstances it's essential that we not get into a power struggle with the student—a situation in which one person wins by dominating the other in some way. Several strategies can minimize the likelihood of a power struggle:

- Speak in a calm, matter-of-fact manner, describing the problem as you see it. ("You haven't turned in a single assignment in the past 3 weeks. You and I would both like for you to do well in my class, but that can't happen unless we *both* work to make it happen.")
- Present the problem as one involving unproductive behavior, *not* a personality flaw. ("You've come to class late almost every day this month.")
- Listen empathetically to what the student has to say, being openly accepting of his or her feelings and opinions. ("I get the impression that you don't enjoy my class very much; I'd really like to hear your concerns.")
- Summarize what you think the student has told you, and seek clarification if necessary. ("It sounds as if you'd rather not let your classmates know how much trouble you're having with your schoolwork. Is that the problem, or is it something else?")
- Give I-messages; that is, describe the effects of the problem behavior, including your personal reactions to it, in a calm, relatively nonaccusatory manner. ("When you come to class late each day, I worry that you're getting further and further behind, and I'm concerned that you don't seem to value your time in my classroom.")
- Give the student a choice from among two or more acceptable options. ("Would you rather try to work quietly at your group's table, or would it be easier if you sat somewhere by yourself to complete your work?")
- Especially when working with an adolescent, try to identify a solution that allows the student to maintain credibility in the eyes of peers. ("I suspect you might be worrying that your friends will think less of you if you comply with my request. What might we do to address this problem?") (Colvin, Ainge, & Nelson, 1997; Emmer & Evertson, 2009; Henley, 2010; Keller & Tapasak, 2004; K. Lane, Falk, & Wehby, 2006)

Ultimately we must communicate (1) our interest in the student's long-term school achievement, (2) our concern that the misbehavior is interfering with that achievement, and (3) our commitment to working cooperatively with the student to alleviate the problem.

TEACHING SELF-REGULATION SKILLS

Sometimes students simply need guidance in how they might better control their own behaviors. Consider these examples:

- Bradley's performance on assigned tasks is usually rather poor. You know he's capable of better work because he occasionally submits assignments of very high quality. The root of Bradley's problem seems to be that he's off task most of the time—perhaps sketching pictures of sports cars, mindlessly fiddling with objects he's found on the floor, or daydreaming. Bradley would really like to improve his academic performance but doesn't seem to know how to do it.

- Georgia often talks without permission—for instance, blurting out answers to questions, interrupting classmates who are speaking, and initiating off-task conversations at inopportune times. On several occasions you've spoken with Georgia about the problem, and she always vows to exercise more self-control in the future. Her behavior improves for a day or so, but after that her mouth is off and running once again.

Bradley's off-task behavior interferes with his own learning, and Georgia's excessive chattiness interferes with the learning of her peers. Cueing and private discussions haven't led to any improvement. But both Bradley and Georgia have something going for them: They *want* to change their behavior.

The discussion of social cognitive theory in Chapter 10 offers additional strategies for fostering self-regulation skills.

When students express concern about their problem behaviors, teaching self-regulation skills can be helpful. One valuable skill is *self-monitoring,* especially when students need a reality check about the severity of a problem. For example, Bradley may think he's on task far more often than he really is; thus we might give him a timer set to beep every 5 minutes and ask him to write down whether he's been on task each time he hears a beep. Similarly, Georgia may not realize how frequently she prevents her classmates from speaking; thus we might ask her to make a check mark on a tally sheet every time she talks without permission.

If self-monitoring alone doesn't do the trick, *self-instructions* might help Georgia gain some self-restraint in class discussions:

1. *Button* my lips (by holding them tightly together).
2. *Raise* my hand.
3. *Wait* until I'm called on.

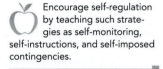

Encourage self-regulation by teaching such strategies as self-monitoring, self-instructions, and self-imposed contingencies.

In addition, both students might use *self-imposed contingencies* to give themselves a motivational boost. For example, Bradley might award himself a point for each 15-minute period he's been on task. Georgia might give herself 5 points at the beginning of each school day and then subtract a point each time she speaks out of turn. By accumulating a certain number of points, the two students could earn opportunities to engage in favorite activities.

Self-regulation strategies have several advantages. They help us avoid power struggles with students about who's in charge. They increase students' sense of autonomy and thus also increase their intrinsic motivation to learn and achieve in the classroom. When students notice that their own behaviors have improved, the self-regulation strategies are positively reinforced, thus increasing the likelihood that the students will continue to use those strategies in the future. And when we teach students to monitor and modify their own behavior, rather than depend on us to do it for them, we become free to do other things—for example, to teach!

CONFERRING WITH PARENTS

We may sometimes need to consult with students' parents or other primary caregivers about a serious or chronic behavior problem. Consider these situations:

- You give your students short homework assignments almost every night. Carolyn has turned in only about one-third of them. You're pretty sure she's capable of doing the work, and you know from previous parent–teacher conferences that her parents give her the time and support she needs to get assignments done. You've spoken with Carolyn several times about the problem, but she shrugs you off as if she doesn't really care whether she does well in your class.

- Students have often found things missing from their desks or personal storage bins shortly after Roger has been in the vicinity. A few students have told you that they've seen Roger take things that belong to others, and many of the missing objects have later turned up in Roger's possession. When you confront him about your suspicion that he's been stealing from classmates, he adamantly denies it. He says he has no idea how Cami's gloves or Ryan's baseball trading cards ended up in his desk.

Conferring with parents is especially important when students' behavior problems show a pattern over time and have serious implications for students' long-term academic or social success. In some cases a simple telephone call may be sufficient. For example, Carolyn's parents may be unaware that she hasn't been doing her homework (she's been telling them she doesn't have any) and may be able to take the steps necessary to ensure that it gets done. In other cases a conference may be necessary. For example, you may want to discuss Roger's suspected thefts with both Roger and his parent(s) together—something you can do more effectively when you all sit face to face in the same room.

Confer with parents about chronic problems that have serious implications for students' long-term success.

Some ways of talking with parents are far more effective than others. Put yourself in a parent's shoes in the following exercise.

EXPERIENCING FIRSTHAND
PUTTING YOURSELF IN A PARENT'S SHOES

Imagine you're the parent of a seventh grader named Tommy. As you and Tommy are eating dinner one evening, you get a telephone call.

You: Hello?

Ms. J.: This is Ms. Johnson, Tommy's teacher. May I talk with you for a few minutes?

You: Of course. What can I do for you?

Ms. J.: Well, I'm afraid I've been having some trouble with your son, and I thought you should know about it.

You: Really? What's the problem?

Ms. J.: Tommy hardly ever gets to class on time. When he does arrive, he spends most of his time talking with friends rather than paying attention to what I'm saying. It seems as if I have to speak to him three or four times every day about his behavior.

You: How long has all this been going on?

Ms. J.: For several weeks now. And the problem's getting worse rather than better. I'd really appreciate it if you'd talk with Tommy about the situation.

You: Thank you for letting me know about this, Ms. Johnson.

Ms. J.: You're most welcome. Good night.

You: Good night, Ms. Johnson.

Take a few minutes to jot down some of the things that, as a parent, you might be thinking after this conversation.

You may have had a variety of thoughts, possibly including these:

- Why isn't Tommy taking his schoolwork more seriously?
- Isn't Tommy doing anything *right?*
- Has Ms. Johnson tried anything besides reprimanding Tommy for his behavior? Or is she laying all of this on *my* shoulders?
- Tommy's a good kid. I should know, because I raised him. For some reason Ms. Johnson doesn't like him and so is finding fault with anything he does.

Only the first of these four reactions is likely to lead to a productive response on your part.

Notice how Ms. Johnson focused strictly on the negative aspects of Tommy's classroom performance. As a result, you (as Tommy's parent) may possibly have felt anger toward your son or guilt about your ineffective parenting skills. Alternatively, if you remained confident about your son's scholastic abilities and your own ability as a parent, you may have begun to wonder about Ms. Johnson's ability to teach and motivate seventh graders. Sadly, too many teachers reach out to parents only to talk about students' weaknesses—never their strengths—as the following interview with Jamal illustrates:

> *Adult:* Has your grandpa [Jamal's primary caregiver] come to school?
>
> *Jamal:* Yup, when the teachers call him.
>
> *Adult:* What did they call him for?
>
> *Jamal:* The only time they call him is when I am being bad, the teacher will call him, he will come up here and have a meeting with the teacher.
>
> *Adult:* If you are being good do the teachers call?
>
> *Jamal:* No. (Kumar et al., 2002, p. 164)

Ideally a teacher–parent discussion about problem behaviors is initiated within the context of an ongoing relationship characterized by mutual trust and respect and a shared concern for the student's learning and well-being. For example, a phone call to parents is most likely to yield productive results if we already have a good working relationship with them and are sure that they won't overreact with harsh, excessive punishment. Furthermore, when communicating with parents, our overall messages about their child should be positive and optimistic. For instance, we might describe negative aspects of a student's classroom performance within the context of the many things the student does *well*. (Rather than start out by complaining about Tommy's behavior, Ms. Johnson might have begun by saying that Tommy is a bright, capable young man with many friends and a good sense of humor.) And we must be clear about our commitment to working *together* with parents to help a student succeed in the classroom. The Into the Classroom feature "Talking with Parents About a Student's Misbehaviors" presents several strategies for effectively approaching parents about a challenging behavior problem.

CONDUCTING PLANNED, SYSTEMATIC INTERVENTIONS

Sometimes problem behaviors are so disruptive and persistent that they require a systematic effort to change them. Consider these situations:

- Tucker finds many reasons to roam about the room—he "has to" sharpen a pencil, "has to" get his homework out of his backpack, "has to" get a drink of water, and so on. As a result, Tucker gets very little work done and often distracts his classmates with his perpetual motion.
- Amelia's verbal abusiveness is getting out of hand. She frequently offends you and your other students with sexually explicit language. You've tried praising her on occasions when she's pleasant to others, and she seems to appreciate your doing so, yet her abusive remarks continue.

MyEdLab
Video Example 13.7.

When simple interventions are not successful, teachers often use more systematic interventions. One technique involves a social contract or written agreement between the teacher and the student.

Plan a systematic intervention when other, simpler interventions haven't been successful.

Imagine that both Tucker and Amelia are in your class. You've already spoken with each of them about their unacceptable behavior, yet you've seen no improvement. You've suggested self-regulation techniques, but neither student is interested in changing for the better. You've tried putting them in time-out for their actions, but Amelia seems to enjoy the time away from her schoolwork, and Tucker sometimes has a valid reason for getting out of his seat. Although both students' parents are aware of and concerned about their children's classroom behaviors, their efforts at home haven't had an impact. And after all, these are largely *school* problems rather than home problems. So what do you do now?

When simpler, short-term intervention strategies haven't been productive, individually tailored behaviorist approaches can be quite useful, perhaps in the form of *applied behavior analysis* or *positive behavioral interventions and supports*. Such approaches can be especially effective when combined with other strategies, such as fostering perspective taking, teaching effective social skills, and scaffolding self-regulation. Combining behaviorist principles with other, more cognitively oriented techniques is sometimes called **cognitive behavioral therapy** (e.g., Forman & Barakat, 2011; Platts & Williamson, 2000).

Into The Classroom

Talking with Parents about a Student's Misbehaviors

Consult with parents if a collaborative effort might bring about a behavior change.

At a parent–teacher–student conference, a high school math teacher expresses concern that a student often falls asleep in class. Because the student has a computer and a cable outlet in her room as well as a smartphone, her father speculates that perhaps she's surfing the Internet when she should be in bed. He looks at his daughter inquisitively, and her guilty facial expression confirms his suspicion. With the teacher's prompting, the father and the student identify an appropriate policy for home computer and phone use—one that includes moving the computer to another room, where its use can be more closely monitored.

Begin with a description of the child's many strengths.

In a phone conversation with a student's mother, a teacher describes several areas in which the student has made considerable progress and then asks for advice about strategies for helping the student stay on task and be more conscientious about completing his work.

Describe the problem in terms of inappropriate behaviors, not in terms of undesirable personality characteristics.

When describing a student's poor record of turning in homework assignments, her teacher says, "Carolyn has turned in only one-third of the homework I've assigned this year. Her attendance record is excellent, so I know she's been healthy, and she's certainly capable of doing the work." At no point does the teacher suggest that Carolyn is lazy, unmotivated, or stubborn.

Don't place blame; instead, acknowledge that raising children is rarely easy.

When talking with the mother of a middle school student, a teacher mentions that the student seems to be more interested in talking to friends than in getting her schoolwork done. The mother describes a similar problem at home: "Marnie's always been a much more social girl than I ever was. It's like pulling teeth just getting her off the phone to do her homework, and then we end up having a shouting match that gets us nowhere!" The teacher sympathetically responds, "Students seem to become especially concerned about social matters once they reach adolescence. How about if you, Marnie, and I meet some day after school to talk about the problem? Perhaps by working together the three of us can find a way to solve it."

Ask for information, and express your desire to work together to address the problem.

When a teacher discovers that a student has regularly been taking items from classmates' personal storage bins, she sets up an appointment to meet with the student and his grandmother (the student's primary caregiver). "I like Roger a lot," she says. "He has a great sense of humor, and his smile often lights up my day. I can't understand why he might want to 'borrow' items from other children without asking them first. His actions have cost him several friendships. Do either of you have any ideas about how we might tackle the problem? I'd like to do whatever I can to help Roger repair his reputation with his peers."

Agree on a strategy.

While reviewing a student's academic progress at a parent–teacher conference, an elementary teacher says, "Mark has a tendency to fiddle with things at his desk—for example, twisting paper clips, playing with rubber bands, or making paper airplanes—when he should be getting his work done. As a result, he often doesn't complete his assignments." The student's father replies, "I've noticed the same thing when he works on his homework, but I bring a lot of paperwork home from the office every night and don't have time to constantly hound him to stay on task." The teacher and father talk more about the problem and agree that reinforcement for completed assignments might be helpful. Mark will earn points for high scores that will help him "buy" the new bicycle he's been asking for.

Sources: Christenson & Sheridan, 2001; C. Davis & Yang, 2005; Emmer & Evertson, 2009; Evertson & Emmer, 2009; A. Miller, 2006; Woolfolk Hoy, Davis, & Pape, 2006.

How might we use behaviorist techniques to improve Tucker's classroom behavior? One approach would be to identify one or more effective reinforcers—given Tucker's constant fidgeting, opportunities for physical activity might be reinforcing—and then gradually shape more sedentary behavior. We might also give Tucker a reasonable allotment of "tickets" he can use to "purchase" permission to get out of his seat during class activities. An alternative strategy might be to conduct a *functional analysis* to determine the particular purpose that out-of-seat behaviors serve for Tucker. Perhaps they allow him to avoid difficult tasks or to release the physical energy his body seems to overproduce. If we discover that Tucker acts out only when he expects challenging assignments, we should provide the instruction and support he needs to accomplish those assignments successfully—for example, by teaching him effective learning strategies. If, instead, we find that Tucker's hyperactivity emerges in a wide variety of situations, we might suspect a physiological cause and give him numerous opportunities to release pent-up energy during the school day. Finally, Tucker might benefit from instruction and scaffolding regarding general organizational skills—in particular, assembling necessary supplies (notebooks, sharpened pencils, completed homework, etc.) before lessons begin.

Cognitive behavioral therapy could be helpful for Amelia as well. In this case we might suspect that Amelia lacks the social skills she needs to interact effectively with others; we might

See Chapter 9 for more information about behaviorist approaches to intervention, including applied behavior analysis, functional analysis, and positive behavioral interventions and supports.

therefore begin by teaching her such skills through modeling, role-playing, and so on. Once Amelia has gained some competence in interpersonal skills, we can begin to reinforce her for using them (perhaps with praise, as she has responded well to praise in the past). Meanwhile, the teacher should also punish any relapses into old, abusive behavior patterns (time-outs haven't previously worked with Amelia, but perhaps having her write apology notes to offended parties—a logical consequence—would help to drive home the message that some of her language is inappropriate).

Table 13.3 summarizes the six general strategies we've examined for addressing student misbehaviors, along with the circumstances in which each strategy is likely to be useful.

TAKING STUDENTS' CULTURAL BACKGROUNDS INTO ACCOUNT

> The section on cultural and ethnic differences in Chapter 4 can help you with this exercise.

As we determine which behaviors are truly unacceptable in our classrooms, we must remember that some behaviors that our own culture deems inappropriate may be quite appropriate in another culture. In the next exercise, we look at some examples.

EXPERIENCING FIRSTHAND
IDENTIFYING MISBEHAVIORS

As you read each scenario below, consider these questions:

- Would you classify the behavior as a *mis*behavior?
- What cultural group(s) might find the behavior appropriate?
- How might you deal with the behavior?

Scenarios:

1. A student is frequently late for school, sometimes arriving more than an hour after the school bell has rung.
2. Two students are sharing answers as they take a quiz.
3. Several students are exchanging insults that become increasingly derogatory.

Tardiness (Example 1) interferes with learning because the student loses valuable instructional time; thus, it might reasonably be construed as a misbehavior. However, a student who is chronically tardy may live in a community that doesn't observe strict schedules and timelines—a pattern common in some Hispanic and Native American communities. Furthermore, arrival time may not be entirely within the student's control; for instance, perhaps the student has household responsibilities or transportation issues that make punctuality difficult. A private conversation with the student, perhaps followed up by a conference with family members, might be the most effective way to determine the root of the problem and identify potential solutions.

> Inappropriately sharing answers also lowers the validity of a quiz score (see Chapter 14 and Chapter 15).

Sharing answers during a quiz (Example 2) is a misbehavior *if* students have been specifically instructed to do their own work. Because a quiz can help us determine what students have and haven't learned, inaccurate quiz scores affect our instructional planning and thus indirectly affect students' future learning. Although the behavior represents cheating to many people, it may reflect the cooperative spirit and emphasis on group achievement evident in the cultures of many Native American and Mexican American students. An adverse consequence is in order *if* we have previously explained what cheating is in a way that students understand and *if* we have clearly described the situations in which collaboration is and isn't appropriate—in other words, if the students know full well that their behavior violates classroom policy. But if we *haven't* laid such groundwork, we must take the incident as a lesson for ourselves about what we must do to prevent such behavior from occurring again.

> Remember that some behaviors that are unacceptable in your culture may be quite acceptable in a student's culture. When these behaviors interfere with classroom achievement, be patient and understanding as you help the student acquire behaviors consistent with school expectations.

Exchanging insults (Example 3) might be psychologically harmful for the students involved and might adversely affect the overall classroom climate. Alternatively, however, it might simply be an instance of *playing the dozens,* a playful verbal interaction involving creative one-upmanship common in some African American communities. How we handle the situation depends on the spirit in which the students seem to view the exchange. Their body language—whether they're smiling or scowling, whether they seem relaxed or tense—will tell us a great deal. If the insults truly signal escalating hostilities, immediate intervention is in order—perhaps separating the

PRINCIPLES/ASSUMPTIONS

TABLE 13.3 • Strategies for Addressing Inappropriate Classroom Behaviors		
STRATEGY	**SITUATIONS IN WHICH IT'S APPROPRIATE**	**EXAMPLES**
Ignoring the behavior	● The misbehavior is unlikely to be repeated. ● The misbehavior is unlikely to spread to other students. ● Unusual circumstances have temporarily elicited the misbehavior. ● The misbehavior doesn't seriously interfere with learning.	● One student discreetly passes a note to another student just before the end of class. ● A student accidentally drops her books, startling other students and temporarily distracting them from their work. ● An entire class is hyperactive on the last afternoon before spring break.
Cueing the student	● The misbehavior is a minor infraction but definitely interferes with students' learning. ● Behavior is likely to improve with a subtle reminder.	● A student forgets to close his notebook at the beginning of a test. ● Members of a cooperative learning group are talking so loudly that they distract other groups. ● Several students are exchanging jokes during an independent seatwork assignment.
Discussing the problem privately with the student	● Cueing has been ineffective in changing the behavior. ● If made clear, the reasons for the misbehavior might suggest possible strategies for addressing it.	● A student is frequently late to class. ● A student refuses to do certain kinds of assignments. ● A student shows a sudden drop in motivation for no apparent reason.
Promoting self-regulation	● The student has a strong desire to improve his or her behavior.	● A student doesn't realize how frequently she interrupts her classmates. ● A student seeks help in learning to control his anger. ● A student acknowledges that his inability to stay on task is adversely affecting the good grades he wants to get.
Conferring with parents	● A chronic behavior problem is likely to interfere with long-term academic and/or social success. ● The source of the problem may possibly lie outside school walls. ● Parents are likely to work collaboratively with school faculty members to bring about a behavior change.	● A student does well in class but rarely turns in required homework assignments. ● A student falls asleep in class almost every day. ● A student is caught stealing classmates' lunches.
Conducting a planned, systematic intervention	● The misbehavior has continued over a period of time and significantly interferes with student learning. ● Other, less intensive approaches (e.g., cueing, private conferences) have been ineffective. ● The student seems unwilling or unable to use self-regulation techniques.	● A student has unusual difficulty sitting still for age-appropriate time periods. ● A student's obscene remarks continue even though her teacher has spoken with her about the behavior on several occasions. ● A member of the soccer team displays bursts of anger and aggression that are potentially dangerous to other players.

students, imposing an appropriate consequence, and following up with a private conference. If, instead, the insults reflect creative verbal play, we may simply need to establish reasonable boundaries (e.g., "indoor" voices should be used, racial or ethnic slurs are unacceptable).

MyEdLab **Self-Check 13.3**

MyEdLab **Application Exercise 13.3.** In this exercise you can practice using your knowledge about dealing with misbehavior.

Addressing Aggression and Violence at School

In recent years the news media have focused considerable attention on violent school crime, and especially on school shootings, leading many people to believe that aggression in our schools is on the rise and that school buildings are generally unsafe. In reality, violent aggression involving serious injury or death is relatively rare on school grounds and, has, if anything, been *declining* rather than increasing, at least in the United States. Most aggression at school involves minor physical injury, psychological harm (e.g., sexual or racial harassment), or destruction of property (e.g., vandalization of student lockers) (Borum, Cornell, Modzeleski, & Jimerson, 2010; Centers for Disease Control, 2015; M. J. Mayer & Furlong, 2010; Robers, Zhang, Truman, & Snyder, 2012; U.S. Department of Education, 2014).

If we consider *only* violent aggression that causes serious injury or death, then school is probably the safest place that young people can be (DeVoe, Peter, Noonan, Snyder, & Baum, 2005; Garbarino, Bradshaw, & Vorrasi, 2002). Although more incidents may occur in larger schools, actual rates of such incidents are not strongly related to school size (Klein & Cornell, 2010). Furthermore, most schools now control access to their buildings; recent national data indicates that 88% of public schools control access, and 64% use security cameras (Robers et al., 2014). According to the National Center for Education Statistics (NCES), of the 1,336 homicides that occurred among school-aged youth in the 2010–2011 academic year, only 11 occurred at school (NCES, 2014). But if we consider *all* forms of aggression (mild as well as severe), then aggression among children and adolescents occurs more frequently at school than at any other location—especially in areas where adult supervision is minimal (e.g., hallways, restrooms, parking lots) (Astor, Meyer, & Behre, 1999; Casella, 2001b; Finkelhor & Ormrod, 2000). In addition, sometimes teachers are victimized at school, although these instances are not always physical (often they involve intimidation, bullying, or threats) (Espelage et al., 2013). The relative prevalence of aggression at school is almost certainly due to two factors. First, children and adolescents spend a great deal of time at school, more so than in any other place except home. Second, the sheer number of students attending even the smallest of schools makes some interpersonal conflict almost inevitable.

The roots of school aggression and violence are many and diverse. A variety of cognitive factors (e.g., lack of perspective taking, misinterpretation of social cues, poor social problem-solving skills) predispose some students to aggressive behavior (Coie & Dodge, 1998; Dodge et al., 2003; Troop-Gordon & Asher, 2005). Furthermore, some school- or neighborhood-specific cultures endorse the belief that defending one's reputation in the face of personal insults or indignities is a matter of "honor" that calls for aggressive action (R. P. Brown, Osterman, & Barnes, 2009; K. M. Williams, 2001a). Developmental factors come into play as well; for instance, many young children and a few adolescents have poor impulse control, and in early adolescence an unsettling transition to middle school can lead some students to bully weaker age-mates as a way of gaining social status with peers (Espelage, Holt, & Henkel, 2003; National Center for Education Statistics, 2007; Pellegrini, 2002). Some students are not tolerant of homosexual or bisexual tendencies, and may act in an aggressive or threatening manner to others as a result of homophobia (Poteat, O'Dwyer, & Mereish, 2012). Finally, aggression is a common reaction to frustration, and some students are repeatedly frustrated in their efforts to be academically and socially successful at school (G. Bender, 2001; Casella, 2001b; Miles & Stipek, 2006).

See Chapter 3 for more information about cognitive factors underlying aggression, as well as for recommendations on addressing the causes and emotional consequences of peer bullying.

A THREE-LEVEL APPROACH

Don't tolerate *any* form of aggression at school. For example, be on the look-out for bullying and other forms of psychological intimidation.

Regardless of the roots of the behavior, we mustn't tolerate *any* form of aggression or violence on school grounds. Students can learn and achieve at optimal levels only if they know they're both physically and psychologically safe at school. And if they *don't* feel safe, they're at increased risk for dropping out before high school graduation (Filax, 2007; Peguero & Bracy, 2014). To be truly effective in combating aggression and violence, we must address these challenges on three levels, depicted graphically in Figure 13.8 (Dwyer & Osher, 2000; Hyman et al., 2006; Ihlo & Nantais, 2010; H. M. Walker et al., 1996).[1]

---

[1] For a more in-depth discussion of the three levels, we urge you to read *Safeguarding Our Children: An Action Guide* by K. Dwyer and D. Osher (2000). You can download a copy from a variety of Internet websites, including http://www2.ed.gov/admins/lead/safety/actguide/index.html.

LEVEL I: CREATING A NONVIOLENT SCHOOL ENVIRONMENT

One-shot "antiviolence" campaigns have little lasting effect on school aggression and violence (Burstyn & Stevens, 2001). Instead, creating a peaceful, nonviolent school environment must be a long-term effort that includes numerous strategies:

- Make a schoolwide commitment to supporting *all* students' academic and social success.
- Provide a challenging and engaging curriculum; addresses cases of academic disengagement promptly.
- Form caring, trusting faculty–student relationships.
- Insist on genuine and equal respect—among students and faculty alike—for people of diverse backgrounds, races, and ethnic groups.
- Emphasize prosocial behaviors (e.g., sharing, helping, cooperating).
- Establish classroom-specific and schoolwide policies and practices that foster appropriate behavior (e.g., give clear guidelines for behavior, consistently apply consequences for infractions, provide instruction in effective social interaction and problem-solving skills). Make sure that classroom and school policies are aligned.
- Teach specific skills that students can use to intervene when they witness bullying.
- Provide mechanisms through which students can communicate their concerns about aggression and victimization openly and without fear of reprisal.
- Involve students in school decision making.
- Adopt ongoing violence prevention programs that are supported by solid research.
- Establish close working relationships with community agencies and families.
- Openly discuss safety issues. (Burstyn & Stevens, 2001; Dwyer & Osher, 2000; Learning First Alliance, 2001; Meehan et al., 2003; G. M. Morrison, Furlong, D'Incau, & Morrison, 2004; Pellegrini, 2002; S. W. Ross & Horner, 2009; Syvertsen, Flanagan, & Stout, 2009; J. S. Warren et al., 2006)

Most of these strategies should look familiar, as they've been mentioned frequently throughout this and other chapters of the book. The final strategy on the list—openly discussing safety issues—encompasses a variety of more specific strategies, such as these:

- Explain what bullying is (i.e., that it involves harassing and intimidating peers who can't easily defend themselves) and why it's unacceptable.
- Solicit students' input about potentially unsafe areas that require more faculty supervision (e.g., an infrequently used restroom or back stairwell).
- Convey willingness to hear students' complaints about troublesome classmates. (Such complaints can provide important clues about which students most need assistance and intervention.)
- Most important, take active steps to *address* students' safety concerns.

LEVEL II: INTERVENING EARLY FOR STUDENTS AT RISK

Usually, when educators use the term *students at risk,* they're referring to students who are at risk for academic failure. But students can be at risk for *social* failure as well. For instance, they may have few or no friends, be overtly bullied or rejected by many of their peers, or in other ways find themselves excluded from the social life of the school. Social failure can also include those students who are the perpetrators of violence and bullying, who can benefit from intervention.

FIGURE 13.8 A three-level approach to preventing aggression and violence in schools.

Provide Intensive Intervention for Students in Trouble

Intervene Early for Students at Risk

Create a Schoolwide Environment That Minimizes the Potential for Aggression and Violence

Source: Based on a figure in *Safeguarding Our Children: An Action Guide* (p. 3), by K. Dwyer and D. Osher, 2000, Washington, DC: U.S. Departments of Education and Justice, American Institutes for Research.

MyEdLab
Video Example 13.8.

Cultural differences and intolerance are often the source of aggressive behavior. Classroom and school policies for dealing with such behaviors, including bullying, should be aligned and enforced.

Provide individually tailored guidance and support for students who experience consistent social failure at school.

Perhaps 10% to 15% of students need some sort of minor intervention to help them interact effectively with peers, establish good working relationships with teachers, and become bona fide members of the school community (Ihlo & Nantais, 2010; K. L. Lane et al., 2011). Such intervention can't be a one-size-fits-all approach but must instead be tailored to students' particular strengths and needs. For some students, it might require instruction in effective social skills. For other students, it might mean getting them actively involved in school clubs or extracurricular activities. For still others, it may require a well-planned, systematic effort to encourage and reinforce productive behaviors, perhaps through applied behavior analysis or positive behavioral interventions and supports. Regardless of type, interventions are most effective when they occur *early* in the game—before students go too far down the path of antisocial behavior—and when they're developed by a multidisciplinary team of teachers and other professionals who bring various areas of expertise to the planning table (Crone, Horner, & Hawken, 2004; Dwyer & Osher, 2000; Osher et al., 2010).

LEVEL III: PROVIDING INTENSIVE INTERVENTION FOR STUDENTS IN TROUBLE

For a variety of reasons, minor interventions aren't always sufficient for a small percentage of students who are predisposed to be aggressive and violent. For example, some students have serious mental illnesses that interfere with their ability to think rationally, cope appropriately with everyday frustrations, and control impulses. Typically schools must work closely and collaboratively with other community groups—perhaps mental health clinics, police and probation officers, and social services—to help students at high risk for aggression and violence (Dwyer & Osher, 2000; Greenberg et al., 2003; Hyman et al., 2006).

As teachers, our frequent interactions with students put us in an ideal position to identify those children and adolescents most in need of intensive intervention and get them back on track for academic and social success. As you gain teaching experience, you'll begin to get a good sense of which characteristics are and aren't normal for a particular age-group. You should especially be on the lookout for the early warning signs of violence presented in Figure 13.9.

Keep the common warning signs of violence in mind. Use them as possible indicators that a student needs significant assistance to gain emotional well-being and social success.

Although we must be ever vigilant for signals that a student may be planning to cause harm to others, it's essential that we keep several points in mind. First, as mentioned earlier, extreme violence is *very rare* in schools; unreasonable paranoia about potential school violence will prevent us from working effectively with students. Second, the great majority of students who exhibit one or a few of the warning signs listed in Figure 13.9 *won't* become violent (U.S. Secret Service National Threat Assessment Center, 2000). And most important, we must *never* use the warning signs as a reason to unfairly accuse, isolate, or punish a student (Dwyer, Osher, & Warger, 1998). These signs provide a means of getting students help if they need it, not of excluding them from the education that all children and adolescents deserve.

ADDRESSING GANG-RELATED PROBLEMS

A frequent source of aggression at some schools is gang-related hostilities. Although gangs are more prevalent in low-income, inner-city schools, they're sometimes found in suburban and rural schools as well (Howell & Lynch, 2000; Kodluboy, 2004). It is important to remember that membership in a gang does not necessarily mean that such students will behave violently at school or solely interact with other gang members (Estrada, Gilreath, Astor, & Benbenishty, 2014; Gebo & Sullivan, 2014).

The three-level approach to combating school aggression and violence just described can go a long way toward suppressing violent gang activities, but we'll often need to take additional measures as well. Recommended strategies include these:

- Develop, communicate, and enforce clear-cut policies regarding potential threats to other students' safety.
- Identify the specific nature and scope of gang activity in the student population.

FIGURE 13.9 Early warning signs of possible violent behavior.

Experts have identified numerous warning signs that a student may possibly be contemplating violent actions against others. Any one of them alone is unlikely to signal a violent attack, but several of them *in combination* should lead us to consult with school administrators and specially trained professionals.

- *Social withdrawal:* Over time, a student interacts less and less frequently with teachers and with all or most peers.

- *Excessive feelings of isolation, rejection, or persecution:* A student directly or indirectly expresses the belief that he or she is friendless, disliked, or unfairly picked on; such feelings are sometimes the result of long-term physical or psychological bullying by peers.

- *Rapid decline in academic performance:* A student shows a dramatic change in academic performance and seems unconcerned about doing well. Cognitive and physical factors (e.g., learning disabilities, ineffective study strategies, brain injury) have been ruled out as causes of the decline.

- *Poor coping skills:* A student has little ability to deal effectively with frustration, takes the smallest affront personally, and has trouble bouncing back after minor disappointments.

- *Lack of anger control:* A student frequently responds with uncontrolled anger to even the slightest injustice and may misdirect anger at innocent bystanders.

- *Apparent sense of superiority, self-enteredness, and lack of empathy:* A student depicts himself or herself as smarter or in some other way better than peers, is preoccupied with his or her own needs, and has little regard for the needs of others. Underlying such characteristics may be low-esteem and depression.

- *Lengthy grudges:* A student is unforgiving of others' transgressions, even after considerable time has elapsed.

- *Violent themes in drawings and written work:* Violence predominates in a student's artwork, stories, or journal entries, and perhaps certain individuals (e.g., a parent or particular classmate) are regularly targeted in these fantasies. (Keep in mind that *occasional* violence in writing and art isn't unusual, especially for boys.)

- *Intolerance of individual and group differences:* A student shows intense disdain and prejudice toward people of a certain race, ethnicity, gender, sexual orientation, religion, or disability.

- *History of violence, aggression, and other discipline problems:* A student has a long record of seriously inappropriate behavior extending over several years.

- *Association with violent peers:* A student associates regularly with a gang or other antisocial peer group.

- *Inappropriate role models:* A student speaks with admiration about Satan, Adolf Hitler, Osama bin Laden, the Boston bombers, or some other malevolent figure.

- *Excessive alcohol or drug use:* A student who abuses alcohol or drugs may have reduced self-control. In some cases substance abuse signals significant mental illness.

- *Inappropriate access to firearms:* A student has easy access to guns and ammunition and may regularly practice using them.

- *Threats of violence:* A student has openly expressed an intent to harm someone else, perhaps in explicit terms or perhaps through ambiguous references to "something spectacular" happening at school on a particular day. ***This warning sign requires immediate action.***

Sources: Dwyer et al., 1998; O'Toole, 2000; U.S. Secret Service National Threat Assessment Center, 2000; M. W. Watson, Andreas, Fischer, & Smith, 2005.

- Consult with school and community support services to mediate between-gang and within-gang disputes.
- Forbid clothing, jewelry, and behaviors that signify membership in a particular gang (e.g., bandanas, shoelaces in gang colors, certain hand signs).[2]

As should be apparent from our discussion in this chapter, helping growing children and adolescents develop into successful, productive adults can occasionally be quite a challenge. But in our own experiences, discovering that you actually *can* make a difference in students' lives—including the lives of some who are at risk for academic or social failure—is one of the most rewarding aspects of being a teacher.

MyEdLab **Self-Check 13.4**

MyEdLab **Application Exercise 13.4.** In this exercise you can review strategies for reducing aggressive behavior.

---

[2]A potential problem with this strategy is that it may violate students' civil liberties. For guidance on how to walk the line between ensuring students' safety and giving them reasonable freedom of expression, see Kodluboy (2004) and Rozalski and Yell (2004).

13   What Have You Learned?

We now return to the chapter's learning outcomes to review some of the chapter's key ideas.

13.1: Describe numerous strategies for creating a classroom environment conducive to academic achievement and students' personal well-being. Effective teachers create a setting in which students are regularly engaged in planned tasks and activities and in which few student behaviors interfere with those tasks and activities. The physical arrangement of the classroom makes a difference, but more important is a psychological environment—*classroom climate*—in which students feel safe and secure, make learning a high priority, and are willing to take risks and make mistakes. Central to such a climate are (1) teacher–student relationships that communicate genuine caring and concern for every student and (2) an overall sense of community in the classroom and school—a sense that teachers and students have shared goals, are mutually respectful and supportive of one another's efforts, and believe that everyone makes an important contribution to learning. Creating a warm, supportive atmosphere and a sense of classroom community may be especially important for students in minority cultural groups, students from lower socioeconomic backgrounds, and students with disabilities. At the same time, we teachers must take charge to some extent, establishing rules and planning age-appropriate activities to ensure that students are continually working toward instructional goals and objectives.

13.2: Explain how you can coordinate your efforts with colleagues, community agencies, and parents to maximize students' academic and personal development. As teachers, we'll be most effective when we work cooperatively with other faculty members, other institutions, and parents to promote students' learning, development, and achievement. It's especially important to keep in regular contact with parents, sharing information in both directions about the progress students are making and coordinating efforts at school with those on the home front. We can keep the lines of communication open through a variety of mechanisms—for instance, through parent–teacher conferences, newsletters, class websites, and family activities at school. We may need to make an extra effort to establish productive working relationships with those parents who, on the surface, seem reluctant to become involved in their children's education.

13.3: Identify six general approaches to dealing with student misbehaviors and the circumstances and cultural contexts in which each approach might be appropriate. Despite our best efforts, students sometimes engage in behaviors that disrupt classroom learning, put one or more students' physical safety or psychological well-being in jeopardy, or violate basic moral and ethical standards. Some minor misbehaviors are best ignored, including those that probably won't be repeated, those that are unlikely to be imitated by other students, and those that occur only temporarily and within the context of unusual circumstances. Other minor infractions can be dealt with simply and quickly by cueing students or talking privately with them about our concerns. More serious and chronic behavior problems may require instruction in self-regulation skills, consultation with parents, or intensive, multifaceted interventions. Regardless of the approach we use in dealing with students' misbehaviors, we must take into account the fact that some of those behaviors may be the product of a particular cultural upbringing or the result of a specific disability.

13.4: Describe a three-level approach that can effectively reduce aggression and violence in the overall school community, as well as additional strategies you might use to address gang-related hostilities. Although violent crime in schools is on the decline, milder forms of aggression (e.g., minor physical injuries, psychological harm, destruction of property) continue to be common in and around schools. Some experts recommend a three-level approach to combating aggression and violence in schools. First, we must collaboratively create a schoolwide environment that makes aggression and violence unlikely—for instance, by establishing trusting teacher–student relationships, fostering a sense of caring and respect among students from diverse backgrounds, and providing mechanisms through which students can communicate their concerns without fear of reprisal. Second, we must intervene early for students who appear to be at risk for academic or social failure, providing them with the cognitive and social skills they need to be successful at school. And third, we must seek intensive intervention for a small number of students who are prone to violence, have a disabling mental illness, or in some other way are seriously troubled. If well-organized gangs have a significant presence in our schools, we may need to take additional measures as well.

Practice for Your Licensure Exam

The Good Buddy

Mr. Schulak has wanted to be a teacher for as long as he can remember. In his many volunteer activities over the years—coaching a girls' basketball team, assisting with a Boy Scout troop, teaching Sunday school—he has discovered how much he enjoys working with children. Children obviously enjoy working with him as well: Many occasionally call or stop by his home to shoot baskets, talk over old times, or just say hello. Some of them even call him by his first name.

Now that Mr. Schulak has completed his college degree and obtained his teaching certificate, he has accepted a teaching position at his hometown's middle school. He's delighted to find that he already knows many of his students, and he spends the first few days of class renewing his friendships with them. But by the end of the week, he realizes that his classes have accomplished little of an academic nature.

The next Monday Mr. Schulak vows to get down to business. He begins each of his five class sessions by describing his instructional goals for the weeks to come and then introduces the first lesson. Unfortunately, many of his students are resistant to settling down and getting to work. They want to move from one seat to another, talk with friends, use their phones, toss wadded-up paper "basketballs" across the room, and do anything *except* the academic tasks Mr. Schulak has in mind. In his second week as a new teacher, Mr. Schulak has already lost control of his classes.

1. **Constructed-response question:**

   Mr. Schulak is having considerable difficulty bringing his classes to order.

A. Identify two critical things that Mr. Schulak has *not* done to get the school year off to a good start.

B. Describe two strategies that Mr. Schulak might now use to remedy the situation.

2. **Multiple-choice question:**

   Mr. Schulak is undoubtedly aware that good teachers show that they care about and respect their students. Which one of the following statements describes the kind of teacher–student relationship that is most likely to foster students' learning and achievement?

   a. The teacher communicates optimism about students' potential for success and offers the support necessary for that success.

   b. The teacher spends a lot of time engaging in recreational activities with students after school and on weekends.

   c. The teacher focuses almost exclusively on what students do well and ignores or downplays what students do poorly.

   d. The teacher listens patiently to students' concerns but reminds them that he or she alone will ultimately decide what transpires in the classroom.

> MyEdLab **Licensure Exam 13.1**

PRAXIS Go to Appendix C, "Matching Book Content and Ebook Activities to the Praxis Principles of Learning and Teaching Tests," to discover sections of this chapter that may be especially applicable to the Praxis tests.

Blend Images/Alamy

14

Classroom Assessment Strategies

CASE STUDY: THE MATH TEST

Ms. Ford is teaching a middle school math class to students with low achievement levels. She has just returned a set of graded test papers, and the following discussion with her students ensues:

Ms. Ford: When I corrected these papers, I was really, really shocked at some of the scores. And I think you will be too. I thought there were some that were so-so, and there were some that were devastating, in my opinion.

Student: [Noise increasing.] Can we take them over?

Ms. Ford: I am going to give them back to you. This is what I would like you to do: Every single math problem that you got wrong, for homework tonight and tomorrow, it is your responsibility to correct these problems and turn them in. In fact, I will say this, I want this sheet back to me by Wednesday at least. All our math problems that we got wrong I want returned to me with the correct answer.

Student: Did anybody get 100?

Ms. Ford: No.

Student: Nobody got 100? [Groans]

Ms. Ford: OK, boys and girls, shhh. I would say, on this test in particular, boys and girls, if you received a grade below 75 you definitely have to work on it. I do expect this quiz to be returned with Mom or Dad's signature on it. I want Mom and Dad to be aware of how we're doing.

Student: No!

Student: Do we have to show our parents? Is it a requirement to pass the class?

Ms. Ford: If you do not return it with a signature, I will call home. (J. C. Turner, Meyer, et al., 1998, pp. 740–741)

- What information have the test results actually given Ms. Ford? What inferences does Ms. Ford make based on this information?
- What underlying messages does Ms. Ford communicate about the poor test scores? How might these messages affect students' motivation and the classroom climate?

The only thing Ms. Ford knows for sure is that her students have performed poorly on the test. From this fact she infers that they haven't mastered the knowledge and skills the test was designed to assess—an inference that's appropriate *only* if the test is a good measure of what the students have actually learned. When she tells them they must "work on it" and correct wrong answers as a homework assignment, she's putting the blame for their poor scores entirely on their shoulders. Furthermore, with her insistence that students get parents' signatures on the graded tests, she's focusing their attention on performance goals rather than mastery goals—demonstrating competence rather than actually *acquiring* it— and potentially raising students' anxiety to debilitating levels.

Classroom assessment practices are intertwined with virtually every other aspect of classroom functioning. They affect (a) our future planning and instruction (e.g., what we teach and how we teach it), (b) students' motivation and affect (e.g., what specific achievement goals they adopt and whether they feel confident or anxious), and (c) the

Chapter 11 describes the advantages of emphasizing mastery goals over performance goals.

How Ms. Ford tries to communicate students' test scores to parents is yet another issue, as you'll discover in Chapter 15.

Figure 12.1 in Chapter 12 graphically depicts the interrelationships of classroom assessment practices with planning, instruction, classroom management, and student characteristics.

overall classroom climate (e.g., whether it feels psychologically safe or threatening). Only when we consider the very integral roles that assessment plays in the classroom can we truly harness its benefits to help students accomplish important instructional goals. It's essential, then, that we give considerable thought to how we assess students' learning and achievement, both informally through daily observations of their behavior and more formally through preplanned assessment instruments and procedures.

The Many Forms and Purposes of Assessment

We begin our discussion of assessment with a definition:

> **Assessment** is a process of observing a sample of a student's behavior and drawing inferences about the student's knowledge and abilities.

Three words in this definition are especially important to note. First, assessment involves an observation of *behavior*. As behaviorists have pointed out, it's impossible to look inside students' heads and see what knowledge lurks there; we can see only how students perform in particular situations. Second, an assessment typically involves just a *sample* of behavior; we certainly can't observe and keep track of every single thing that every single student does during the school day. Finally, assessment involves drawing *inferences* from observed behaviors to make judgments about students' overall achievements and abilities—a tricky business at best. It's critical, then, that we select behaviors that can provide reasonably accurate estimates of what students know and can do.

Think of classroom assessments primarily as tools that can help you improve classroom instruction and students' learning. Let assessment results *guide*, rather than dictate, your decision making.

Notice that the definition doesn't include anything about decision making. By themselves, educational assessments are merely *tools* that can help people make decisions about students and sometimes about teachers, instructional programs, and schools as well. When people use these tools for the wrong purposes, or when they interpret assessment results in ways the results were never meant to be interpreted, it's the *people*—not the assessment instruments—that are to blame.

Classroom assessments vary in six key ways, which are summarized in Figure 14.1. Let's look more closely at each distinction.

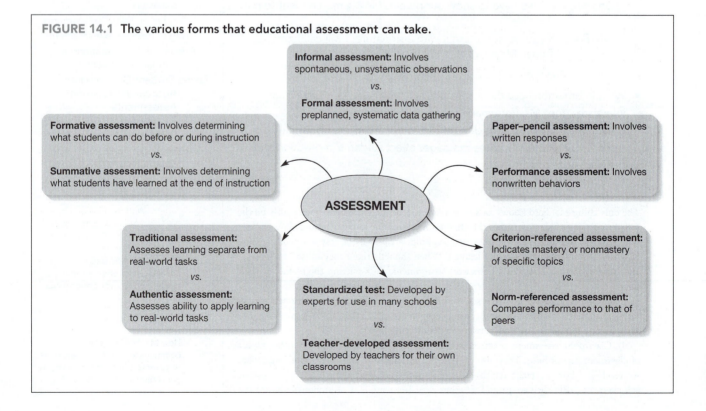

FIGURE 14.1 The various forms that educational assessment can take.

Informal assessment: Involves spontaneous, unsystematic observations
vs.
Formal assessment: Involves preplanned, systematic data gathering

Formative assessment: Involves determining what students can do before or during instruction
vs.
Summative assessment: Involves determining what students have learned at the end of instruction

Paper–pencil assessment: Involves written responses
vs.
Performance assessment: Involves nonwritten behaviors

Traditional assessment: Assesses learning separate from real-world tasks
vs.
Authentic assessment: Assesses ability to apply learning to real-world tasks

ASSESSMENT

Standardized test: Developed by experts for use in many schools
vs.
Teacher-developed assessment: Developed by teachers for their own classrooms

Criterion-referenced assessment: Indicates mastery or nonmastery of specific topics
vs.
Norm-referenced assessment: Compares performance to that of peers

Formative versus summative assessment.   A formative assessment involves determining what students know and can do *before or during instruction*. Ongoing formative assessments can help us determine what students already know and believe about a topic and whether they need further practice on particular skills, and we can develop or revise our lesson plans accordingly. In contrast, summative assessment involves conducting an assessment *after instruction* to make final determinations about what students have achieved. Summative assessments are used to determine whether students have mastered the content of a lesson or unit, what final grades we should assign, which students are eligible for more advanced classes, and the like.

Informal versus formal assessment.   An informal assessment involves a spontaneous, unplanned observation of something a student says or does. For example, when Mitchell asks "How come people in Australia don't fall into space?" he reveals a misconception about gravity. And when Jaffa continually squints when she looks at the board, we might wonder if she needs an eye exam. In contrast, a formal assessment is planned in advance and used for a specific purpose— perhaps to determine what students have learned from a geography unit or whether they can apply the Pythagorean theorem to real-world geometry problems. Formal assessment is *formal* in several respects: A particular time is set aside for it, students can prepare for it ahead of time, and it's intended to yield information about particular instructional goals or content-area standards.

The similar names for *formative* assessment and *formal* assessment are sometimes a source of confusion for our readers, but as you've just seen, the two terms refer to different things. Certainly formative assessments can also be formal ones, in that they're planned in advance to assess students' progress and can guide future instruction. But not all formative assessments are formal ones, and many formal assessments are used for summative rather than formative purposes.

Paper–pencil versus performance assessment.   As teachers, we may sometimes choose paper–pencil assessment, in which we present questions or problems that students must address on paper—or, perhaps, an electronic equivalent, such as in a word processing document. But we may also find it helpful to use performance assessment, in which students physically demonstrate their abilities—for example, by giving an oral presentation in a language arts class, singing in a concert, or taking prescribed safety precautions in a chemistry lab.

Traditional versus authentic assessment.   Historically, most educational assessments have focused on measuring knowledge and skills in relative isolation from real-world tasks. Spelling quizzes, math word problems, and physical fitness tests are examples of such traditional assessment. Yet ultimately students must be able to transfer their knowledge and skills to complex situations outside the classroom. The notion of authentic assessment—measuring students' knowledge and skills in a real-life (i.e., *authentic*) context—has gained considerable popularity in recent years. Keep in mind, however, that the distinction between traditional and authentic assessment really represents a *continuum* rather than an either–or situation: Assessment tasks can resemble real-world situations to varying degrees.

Some authentic assessment tasks involve paper and pencil or, alternatively, a word processing program. For example, we might ask students to write a letter to a friend or develop a school newspaper. But in many cases authentic assessment is based on nonwritten performance and closely integrated with instruction. For instance, we might ask students to bake a cake, converse in a foreign language, or successfully maneuver a car into a parallel parking space. Often teachers ask students to create *portfolios* that present a collection of authentic artifacts they've created—perhaps short stories, newspaper editorials, audiotapes of oral or musical performances, or videotapes of dramatic performances.[1]

Standardized tests versus teacher-developed assessments.   Sometimes classroom assessments involve tests developed by test construction experts and published for use in many different schools and classrooms. Such tests, commonly called standardized tests, can be helpful

MyEdLab
Video Explanation 14.1.
This 5-minute video contrasts summative versus formative assessment and gives concrete examples to illustrate each one.

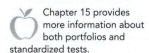

Chapter 15 provides more information about both portfolios and standardized tests.

---

[1]Educators aren't in complete agreement in their use of the terms *performance assessment* and *authentic assessment;* many treat them as synonyms. However, we authors find it useful to consider separately whether an assessment involves physical performance (rather than paper and pencil) and whether it involves a complex, real-world (authentic) task. Thus we are *not* using the two terms interchangeably.

in assessing students' general achievement and ability levels. But when we want to assess students' learning and achievement related to specific instructional objectives—for example, whether students have mastered long division or can apply what they've just learned in a social studies lesson—we'll usually want to construct our own teacher-developed assessments.

Criterion-referenced versus norm-referenced assessments. Some assessments, known as criterion-referenced assessments, are designed to tell us exactly what students have and haven't accomplished relative to predetermined standards or criteria. A simple example is a test covering a fourth-grade class's 20 spelling words for the week: A score of 20 indicates a perfect paper, a score of 15 indicates 15 correct spellings, and so on. With such a test, we would know precisely which words each student does and doesn't know how to spell.

In contrast, norm-referenced assessments reveal how well each student's performance compares with the performance of peers—perhaps classmates or perhaps age-mates across the nation. For example, ninth graders might take a nationwide mathematics test yielding percentile ranks that indicate how well each student has performed in comparison with other ninth graders around the country. Such scores don't tell us specifically what students have and haven't learned in math; instead, they tell us how well each student stacks up against others at the same age or grade level.

Strictly speaking, any assessment has the potential to tell us *both* what students have learned and how they compare with peers. In reality, however, experienced educators tend to construct the two types of assessments somewhat differently. Ideally, questions and tasks on a criterion-referenced assessment are closely tied to the curriculum and to the particular knowledge and skills we hope students have acquired. If all students have mastered the subject matter to the same degree, it's entirely possible for them all to get the same score. If we want to know how students *differ* from one another—and we'll soon identify some circumstances in which we would want to know that—we must have an instrument that will yield considerable variability in scores. In such an instrument, we're apt to have questions and tasks that vary widely in difficulty level, including some that only a few students can respond to correctly.

With the various kinds of assessments in mind, we now consider how we might use educational assessments for five interrelated purposes.

GUIDING INSTRUCTIONAL DECISION MAKING

Obviously formative assessments can guide our instructional decision making: They can help us determine a suitable point at which to begin instruction and give us ongoing information about the appropriateness of our instructional goals and the effectiveness of our instructional strategies. For example, if we find that almost all students are completing assignments quickly and easily, we might set our short-term goals and objectives a bit higher. Or if we discover that many students are struggling with important material we've presented only through verbal explanations, we might consider trying a different instructional approach—perhaps a more concrete, hands-on one.

Yet summative assessments, too, must guide our decision making to some degree. For example, any mandated standardized tests of students' general achievement levels in particular content domains must—for better or for worse—influence the topics and skills on which we focus in our teaching. Our own teacher-developed assessments should influence our instructional decision making as well, as we'll see in a discussion of *backward design* later in the chapter.

In Chapter 15, you'll learn more about such mandated assessments of achievement, especially with regard to their use in high-stakes testing and accountability.

DETERMINING WHAT STUDENTS HAVE LEARNED FROM INSTRUCTION

In most cases we'll need to use planned formal assessments—rather than more casual, informal ones—to determine whether students have achieved instructional goals or met certain content-area standards. Formal assessments of achievement are important in any mastery-learning approach to instruction, and they're essential for assigning final grades. School counselors and administrators, too, may use assessments of students' achievement levels to make placement decisions, such as which students are most likely to do well in advanced classes and which ones might need additional coursework in basic skills.

EVALUATING THE QUALITY OF INSTRUCTION

Final measures of student achievement are also useful in evaluating how effective instruction has been. When most students perform poorly after an instructional unit—as Ms. Ford's students did in the opening case study—we must consider not only what students might have done differently but also what we, as teachers, might have done differently. For example, perhaps we moved too quickly through material or provided insufficient opportunities for students to practice critical skills. In any event, consistently low assessment results should tell us that some modification of instruction is in order.

Use the results of classroom assessments not only to assess what students have learned but also to reflect on the effectiveness of your instructional strategies.

DIAGNOSING LEARNING AND PERFORMANCE PROBLEMS

Why is Levi having trouble learning to read? Why does Gretel misbehave every time we assign a challenging task? We ask such questions when we suspect that certain students might learn differently from their classmates and may possibly require special educational services. A variety of standardized tests have been designed specifically to identify the unique academic and personal needs that some students have. Most of these tests require explicit training in their use and thus are often administered and interpreted by specialists (school psychologists, counselors, speech and language pathologists, etc.). As a general rule, the tests tend to be norm-referenced rather than criterion-referenced in order to identify students who are well above or well below their age-group with respect to certain abilities or characteristics.

Yet teacher-developed assessments can provide considerable diagnostic information as well, especially when they reveal consistent error patterns and areas of difficulty (e.g., see Figure 14.2). In other words, teacher-developed assessments can—and ideally *should*—give us information we can use to help students improve.

Increasingly teachers are using short, formative assessments to determine whether certain students might have exceptional instructional needs. In this approach, known as **response to intervention (RTI)**, a teacher regularly assesses students' progress, keeping a lookout for students who have unusual difficulty acquiring certain basic skills (e.g., in reading or math) despite teachers' evidence-based practices in both whole-class instruction and follow-up small-group work. Note the importance of *evidence-based practices* here: The teacher must have used instructional strategies that research has shown to be effective for most students. The RTI approach has gained particular popularity as a means of identifying students who have learning disabilities, but it's potentially useful for other students as well (T. A. Glover & Vaughn, 2010; J. J. Hoover, 2009; Mellard & Johnson, 2008).

See Chapter 5 for more information about *response to intervention* as a diagnostic tool.

FIGURE 14.2 In these and other work samples, 7-year-old Casey shows consistent difficulty in making connections between the sounds he hears and the sounds he represents in his writing—a difficulty that in his case reflects a learning disability known as *dyslexia*.

PROMOTING LEARNING

Whenever we conduct formative assessments to help us develop or modify lesson plans, we're obviously using assessment to facilitate students' learning. But summative assessment can influence learning as well, and in several ways.

Classroom assessments should be closely aligned with important instructional goals—*not* measures of trivial, isolated facts.

Construct assessment instruments that reflect how you want students to think about and cognitively process information as they study.

Chapter 7 discusses epistemic beliefs in more detail.

- *Assessments can motivate students to study and learn.* On average, students study class material more, review it more regularly, and learn it better when they know they'll be tested on it or in some other way held accountable for it, rather than when they're simply told to learn it (Dempster, 1991; Haertel, 2013; Rohrer & Pashler, 2010). Yet *how* students are assessed is as important as *whether* they're assessed. Assessments are especially effective as motivators when they're criterion-referenced, are closely aligned with instructional goals and objectives, and challenge students to do their best (Mac Iver, Reuman, & Main, 1995; Maehr & Anderman, 1993; L. H. Meyer, Weir, McClure, & Walkey, 2008). Students' self-efficacy and attributions affect their perceptions of the challenge, of course: Students must believe that success on an assigned task is possible if they exert reasonable effort and use appropriate strategies.

  Although regular classroom assessments can be highly motivating, they are, in and of themselves, usually *extrinsic* motivators. Thus they may direct students' attention to performance goals and undermine any intrinsic motivation to learn, especially if students perceive them to be primarily an evaluation of their performance rather than a mechanism for helping them master useful topics and skills (Danner, 2008; Grolnick & Ryan, 1987; S. G. Paris & Turner, 1994; Shernoff, 2013).

  With the potentially motivating effects of classroom assessments in mind, let's return to the opening case study. With her focus on students' test scores and parents' approval or disapproval, Ms. Ford is fostering performance goals and extrinsic motivation. Furthermore, notice how controlling, even threatening, some of her statements are: "It is your responsibility to correct these problems and turn them in. . . . All our math problems that we got wrong I want returned to me with the correct answer. . . . If you do not return it with a [parent's] signature, I will call home." Such comments are likely to undermine students' sense of autonomy and will hardly endear students to mathematics as a content domain.

- *Assessments can influence students' cognitive processes as they study.* Different kinds of assessment tasks can lead students to study and learn quite differently (Carpenter, 2012; Corliss & Linn, 2011; N. Frederiksen, 1984b). For instance, students will typically spend more time studying the things they think will be addressed on an assessment than the things they think the assessment won't cover. Furthermore, their expectations about the kinds of tasks they'll need to perform and the questions they'll need to answer will influence whether they try to memorize isolated facts, on the one hand, or construct a meaningful, integrated body of information, on the other.

  As an example, look at the sixth-grade test about rocks shown in Figure 14.3. Part A (identifying rocks shown at the front of the room) might be assessing either basic knowledge or application (transfer) to new situations, depending on whether the students have seen those particular rock specimens before. The rest of the test clearly focuses on memorized facts and is likely to encourage students to engage in rote learning as they study for future tests. For instance, consider the last item: "Every rock has a _____." Students can answer this item correctly *only* if they've learned the material verbatim: The missing word here is "story."

  Classroom assessments can also influence students' views about the nature of various academic disciplines; that is, they can influence students' epistemic beliefs. For example, if we give quizzes that assess knowledge of specific facts, students are apt to conclude that a discipline is just that: a collection of undisputed facts. If, instead, we ask students to take a position on a controversial issue and justify their position with evidence and logic, they get a very different message: that the discipline involves an integrated set of understandings that must be supported with reasoning and are subject to change over time.

- *Assessments can provide valuable feedback about learning progress.* Simply knowing one's final score on a test or assignment isn't terribly helpful. To facilitate students' learning and

FIGURE 14.3 Much of this sixth-grade geology test focuses on knowledge of specific facts and may encourage students to memorize, rather than understand, information about rocks.

A. Write whether each of the rocks shown at the front of the room is a sedimentary, igneous, or metamorphic rock.
   1. _____
   2. _____
   3. _____

B. The following are various stages of the rock cycle. Number them from 1 to 9 to indicate the order in which they occur.
   ____ Heat and pressure
   ____ Crystallization and cooling
   ____ Igneous rock forms
   ____ Magma
   ____ Weathering and erosion into sediments
   ____ Melting
   ____ Sedimentary rock forms
   ____ Pressure and cementing
   ____ Metamorphic rock forms

C. Write the letter for the correct definition of each rock group.
   1. ____ Igneous
   2. ____ Sedimentary
   3. ____ Metamorphic

   a. Formed when particles of eroded rock are deposited together and become cemented.
   b. Produced by extreme pressures or high temperatures below the earth's surface.
   c. Formed by the cooling of molten rock material from within the earth.

D. Fill in the blank in each sentence.
   1. The process of breaking down rock by the action of water, ice, plants, animals, and chemical changes is called _____ .
   2. All rocks are made of _____ .
   3. The hardness of rocks can be determined by a _____ .
   4. Continued weathering of rock will eventually produce _____ .
   5. Every rock has a _____ .

[The test continues with several additional fill-in-the-blank and short-answer items.]

achievement—and also to enhance students' self-efficacy for mastering school subject matter—assessment feedback must include specific information about where students have succeeded, where they've had difficulty, and how they might improve (Andrade & Cizek, 2010; Hattie & Gan, 2011).

- *Assessments can serve as learning experiences in and of themselves.* In general, the very process of completing an assessment on classroom material helps students review the material and learn it better. Assessment tasks are especially valuable if they ask students to elaborate on or apply the material in a new way (Dunlosky, Rawson, Marsh, Nathan, & Willingham, 2013; Foos & Fisher, 1988; Rohrer & Pashler, 2010).

 Think about how assessment tasks might encourage new learning.

In general, then, sound assessment practices are closely tied to instruction: They reflect instructional goals and content-area standards, guide instructional strategies, and provide a means of tracking students' progress through the curriculum. In a very real sense, assessment *is* instruction: It gives students clear messages about what things are most important for them to accomplish and how best to accomplish them.

MyEdLab **Self-Check 14.1**

MyEdLab **Application Exercise 14.1.** In this exercise, you can examine a student artifact and form hypotheses about both the student's knowledge of numbers and his developing psychomotor skills.

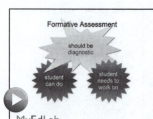

MyEdLab
Video Explanation 14.2.
This 15-minute video provides a good overview of effective formative assessments, along with illustrative examples of both rubrics and checklists.

Enhancing Learning Through Ongoing Assessments and Regular Feedback

As we've just seen in the preceding section, certain practices associated with summative assessment can have a significant positive impact on students' learning. But without doubt, it is our *formative assessments*—those that occur before or during instruction rather than after it—that have the greatest potential to enhance students' learning and achievement (Andrade & Cizek, 2010; Black & Wiliam, 1998; Wiliam, 2011).

Perhaps the most critical strategies for enhancing students' learning and achievement through our classroom assessments—formative and summative assessments alike—are these:

- Make assessment criteria explicit and concrete for students.
- Give students regular feedback about how they are progressing.
- Suggest concrete and realistic steps that students can take to improve.

Often we can accomplish these things, at least in part, by creating and distributing general scoring guides that identify key components of desired performance. In some instances we can use a simple **checklist** of characteristics that should be evident in students' work. For example, Figure 14.4 shows a checklist that one fourth-grade teacher has used for scoring students' performance on math word problems. Notice that the checklist includes both objectively scorable criteria (e.g., the correct answer) and more qualitative, subjectively scorable criteria (e.g., neatness of work, explanation of the problem solution).

When the focus of instruction is a complex, multifaceted topic or skill, we might instead use a **rubric**—a two-dimensional matrix that identifies criteria for assessing different components of students' performance, along with concrete descriptions of various levels of performance relative to each component. As an example, Figure 14.5 shows a possible rubric for evaluating various qualities in students' nonfiction writing. The criteria aren't completely objective—for instance, what do the words *occasionally, a few,* and *many* mean?—but they can help a teacher pin down the kinds of supplementary instruction and activities that some students may need. Rubrics are probably most useful when they have the following characteristics:

- They focus on only a few key attributes of skilled performance and describe these attributes in clear, concrete terms.

- They also focus on attributes that students can realistically acquire with appropriate instruction and practice.

FIGURE 14.4 In this checklist for scoring solutions to mathematics word problems in a fourth-grade class, both teacher and student evaluate various aspects of the student's performance.

Elements	Possible Points	Points Earned Self	Points Earned Teacher
1. You highlighted the question(s) to solve.	2	___	___
2. You picked an appropriate strategy.	2	___	___
3. Work is neat and organized.	2	___	___
4. Calculations are accurate.	2	___	___
5. Question(s) answered.	2	___	___
6. You have explained in words how you solved the problem.	5	___	___
Total	___	___	___

FIGURE 14.5 Possible rubric for evaluating students' nonfiction writing

Characteristic	Proficient	In Progress	Beginning to Develop
Correct spelling	Writer correctly spells all words.	Writer correctly spells most words.	Writer incorrectly spells many words.
Correct punctuation & capitalization	Writer uses punctuation marks and uppercase letters where, and only where, appropriate.	Writer occasionally (a) omits punctuation marks, (b) inappropriately uses punctuation marks, or (c) inappropriately uses uppercase/lowercase letters.	Writer makes many punctuation and/or capitalization errors.
Complete sentences	Writer uses complete sentences throughout, except when using an incomplete sentence for a clear stylistic purpose. Writing includes no run-on sentences.	Writer uses a few incomplete sentences that have no obvious stylistic purpose, or writer occasionally includes a run-on sentence.	Writer includes many incomplete sentences and/or run-on sentences; writer uses periods rarely or indiscriminately.
Clear focus	Writer clearly states main idea; sentences are all related to this idea and present a coherent message.	Writer only implies main idea; most sentences are related to this idea; a few sentences are unnecessary digressions.	Writer rambles, without a clear main idea; or writer frequently and unpredictably goes off topic.
Logical train of thought	Writer carefully leads the reader through his/her own line of thinking about the topic.	Writer shows some logical progression of ideas but occasionally omits a key point essential to the flow of ideas.	Writer presents ideas in no logical sequence.
Convincing statements/ arguments	Writer effectively persuades the reader with evidence or sound reasoning.	Writer includes some evidence or reasoning to support ideas/opinions, but a reader could easily offer counterarguments.	Writer offers ideas/ opinions with little or no justification.

Adapted from "Enhancing Learning Through Formative Assessments and Effective Feedback" (interactive learning module) by J. E. Ormrod, 2015, in *Essentials of Educational Psychology* (4th ed.). Copyright 2015, Pearson. Adapted by permission.

- They are applicable to many tasks within the content domain. (Arter & Chappuis, 2006; Popham, 2006, 2014)

Checklists and rubrics have at least three benefits. First, they give students clear targets toward which to shoot. Second, when well constructed, they enable us teachers to evaluate students' performance consistently and with reasonable objectivity (more about this point in an upcoming discussion of *reliability*). And third, they provide a means through which we can give students detailed feedback about the strengths and limitations of their performance—feedback that ideally can help them improve.

Using a checklist or rubric certainly isn't the only way of enhancing students' learning through classroom assessment practices. Other key strategies are these:

- Describe the instructional goals and objectives being assessed in clear, understandable language.
- Assess students' progress frequently rather than infrequently.

🍎 When giving an assessment, communicate a desire to enhance understanding and promote mastery, rather than to pass judgment.

🍎 Help students recognize important (yet possibly subtle) differences between genuine mastery and more superficial knowledge.

🍎 Engage students in constructive discussions of one another's work, with a focus on ideas for improvement.

🍎 Give students opportunities to revise their work based on feedback they've received. (Andrade & Cizek, 2010; Black & Wiliam, 1998; Chappuis, 2009; Hattie & Gan, 2011; McDaniel, Agarwal, Huelser, McDermott, & Roediger, 2011; Rohrer & Pashler, 2010; Szpunar, Jing, & Schacter, 2014)

Such strategies can be especially important when working with students who are at risk for academic failure (G. B. Hughes, 2010; Wiliam, 2011).

Still another formative assessment strategy is dynamic assessment, in which a teacher assesses students' ability to learn something *new,* typically in a one-on-one situation that includes instruction, assistance, or some other form of scaffolding. Such an approach reflects Vygotsky's *zone of proximal development* and can give us an idea of what students might be able to accomplish with appropriate structure and guidance. Dynamic assessment can provide a wealth of qualitative information about children's abilities, cognitive strategies, and approaches to learning. For example, it might give us insights into the following:

- Students' readiness for instruction in particular topics and skills
- Students' motivational and affective patterns (e.g., self-efficacy, achievement goals, attributions, anxiety)
- Students' work habits (e.g., impulsiveness, persistence, reactions to frustration and failure)
- Potential obstacles to students' learning (e.g., distractibility, poor reading comprehension skills, lack of effective self-monitoring and self-evaluation skills) (Feuerstein, Feuerstein, & Falik, 2010; L. S. Fuchs, Compton, et al., 2008; Hamers & Ruijssenaars, 1997; Haywood & Lidz, 2007; Seethaler, Fuchs, Fuchs, & Compton, 2012; Tzuriel, 2000)

See Chapter 2 for a memory refresher about Vygotsky's zone of proximal development.

INCLUDING STUDENTS IN THE ASSESSMENT PROCESS

As noted earlier, classroom assessments are typically extrinsic motivators that provide only externally imposed reasons for learning school subject matter. Yet students learn more effectively when they're *intrinsically* motivated, and they're more likely to be intrinsically motivated if they have some sense of autonomy about classroom activities. Furthermore, if students are to become self-regulating learners, they must acquire skills in self-monitoring and self-evaluation. For such reasons, we should think of assessment as something we do *with* students rather than *to* them (Andrade, 2010; Panadero & Jonsson, 2013; Reeve, Deci, & Ryan, 2004; L. Shepard, Hammerness, Darling-Hammond, & Rust, 2005).

Students become more skillful in self-assessment as they grow older (van Kraayenoord & Paris, 1997), but even students in the elementary grades have some ability to evaluate their own performance. Following are several strategies for including students in the assessment process and helping them develop important self-monitoring and self-evaluation skills:

🍎 Solicit students' ideas about assessment criteria and rubric design.

🍎 Provide examples of good and not-so-good products, and ask students to compare them on the basis of several criteria.

🍎 Communicate the importance of being introspective and candid regarding one's own strengths and shortcomings, so that teacher assistance can be most effective.

🍎 Have students compare self-ratings of their performance with teacher ratings (e.g., notice the "Self" and "Teacher" columns in Figure 14.4).

🍎 Ask students to write practice questions similar to those they might see on an upcoming paper–pencil test.

🍎 Have students keep ongoing records of their performance and chart their progress over time.

MyEdLab
Video Example 14.1.
What specific strategies does this first-grade teacher use to help students self-assess the quality of their own writing?

- Have students reflect on their work in daily or weekly journal entries, where they can keep track of knowledge and skills they have and haven't mastered, as well as learning strategies that have and haven't been effective.
- Have students compile a portfolio of their work, including self-reflective explanations of what the items in the portfolio reveal about their learning and achievement.
- Ask students to lead parent–teacher conferences. (Andrade, 2010; A. L. Brown & Campione, 1996; Chappuis, 2009; McMillan, 2010; S. G. Paris & Ayres, 1994; L. Shepard, 2000; Stiggins & Chappuis, 2012)

It's important, too, that we encourage productive attributions; for instance, students should genuinely believe that they can overcome their existing shortcomings with reasonable effort and good strategies (Andrade, 2010). And we should ask students to develop a follow-up action plan—to explicitly address the question *What do I need to do now?*—based on their assessment results. Such an action plan might include identifying answers to more specific questions such as these:

- What specific things do I need to do to improve?
- What resources and assistance do I need to help me improve?
- How will I know when I have reached my goal? (based on Chappuis, 2009)

USING DIGITAL TECHNOLOGIES IN FORMATIVE ASSESSMENT

Thanks to recent advances in both hardware and software, technology can now make our ongoing assessments of students' progress and achievement increasingly easy and effective. For instance, several Internet-based resources provide short formative assessments through which we can regularly monitor students' progress in literacy, math, or science. Following are four examples:

- Accelerated Reader (renaissance.com)
- AIMSweb (aimsweb.com)
- Diagnoser (diagnoser.com)
- DIBELS (Dynamic Indicators of Basic Early Literacy Skills; dibels.uoregon.edu)

Some of these resources provide means through which we can immediately enter students' responses onto a handheld digital device, such as a tablet computer or personal digital assistant (PDA); others present short assessments that students themselves complete on a laptop or desktop computer. The programs keep track of students' performance over time and, at our request, can quickly generate reports and graphs regarding both individual students and an entire class. Thus they're especially useful in *response-to-intervention* approaches to assessment (described earlier) and *curriculum-based measurement* (to be described a bit later in the section on content validity).

Many computer software programs can help *students* assess their work. For instance, some Internet-based programs are specifically designed to help students evaluate qualities of their written work; examples are Latent Semantic Analysis (LSA) (lsa.colorado.edu) and T. A. Toolbar (ta-toolbar.com). Such programs provide quick analyses of students' electronically written essays, short stories, and other compositions—whether students have used plausible word combinations, appropriate grammatical structures, and the like. Most word processing programs also provide this service to some degree through grammar checkers. Certainly we shouldn't let these programs replace human beings in evaluating students' written work; ultimately only *people* can reasonably evaluate the accuracy, organization, and logic of what students have written. However, when students use the programs for formative assessment purposes, they can gain substantive feedback that helps them improve the quality of their writing (Russell, 2010).

Other digital technologies can enhance students' self-assessment abilities as well. For example, class websites provide a good mechanism through which students can voluntarily upload early drafts of their work in order to get their peers' constructive feedback and suggestions. And in some cases we might use a videocamera or a laptop computer with a built-in video recorder. For instance, we might videotape a student's execution of a complex behavior and have the student apply certain criteria in self-evaluating the performance (Stokes, Luiselli, Reed, & Fleming, 2010).

Consider how you might use technology to help students assess themselves and give their classmates constructive feedback.

And at one middle school, students designed and built small models of wooden bridges, then videotaped their bridges as they placed a brick on top; analyzing the videos frame by frame, they could detect possible flaws in their bridge design (Warschauer, 2011).

MyEdLab **Self-Check 14.2**

MyEdLab **Application Exercise 14.2.** In this exercise, you can observe and analyze the strategies a third-grade teacher uses to give a child concrete and constructive feedback about her writing.

Important Qualities of Good Assessments

As a student, have you ever been assessed in a way you thought was unfair? If so, *why* was it unfair?

1. Did the teacher evaluate students' responses inconsistently?
2. Were some students assessed under more favorable conditions than others?
3. Was the assessment a poor measure of what you had learned?
4. Was the assessment so time consuming that after a while you no longer cared how well you performed?

In light of your experiences, what characteristics seem to be essential for good classroom assessment instruments and practices?

The four numbered questions just posed reflect, respectively, four *RSVP* characteristics of good classroom assessments: reliability, standardization, validity, and practicality. Such characteristics are important considerations for any assessment activity, but they're especially important when we're using summative assessments to make potentially life-changing decisions—for instance, decisions about final class grades, placements in advanced classes, and appropriate services for students with disabilities.

RELIABILITY

The reliability of an assessment instrument or procedure is the extent to which it yields consistent information about the knowledge, skills, or characteristics being assessed. To get a sense of what reliability involves, try the following exercise.

EXPERIENCING FIRSTHAND
FOWL PLAY

Consider this sequence of events in the life of biology teacher Ms. Fowler:

- *Monday.* After completing a lesson on the bone structures of both birds and dinosaurs, Ms. Fowler asks students to write an essay explaining why many scientists believe that birds are descended from dinosaurs. After school she tosses the pile of essays on the back seat of her cluttered Chevrolet.
- *Tuesday.* Ms. Fowler looks high and low for the essays both at home and in her classroom, but she can't find them anywhere.
- *Wednesday.* Because Ms. Fowler wants to use the students' essays to determine what they've learned, she asks the class to write the same essay a second time.
- *Thursday.* Ms. Fowler finally discovers Monday's essays on the back seat of her car.
- *Friday.* Ms. Fowler grades both sets of essays. She's surprised to find little consistency between them: Students who wrote the best essays on Monday didn't necessarily do well on Wednesday, and some of Monday's poorest performers did quite well on Wednesday.

Which results should Ms. Fowler use, Monday's or Wednesday's? Why?

When we assess students' learning and achievement, we must be confident that our assessment results will be essentially the same regardless of whether we give the assessment on Monday or Wednesday, whether the weather is sunny or rainy, or whether we evaluate students' responses while we're in a good mood or a foul frame of mind. Ms. Fowler's assessment instrument has poor reliability, because the results it yields are completely different from one day to another. So which day's results should she use? You've just been asked a trick question: There's no way of knowing which set is more accurate.

Any single assessment instrument will rarely yield *exactly* the same results for the same student on two different occasions, even if the knowledge or ability being assessed remains the same. Many temporary conditions unrelated to the knowledge or ability being measured are apt to affect students' performance and almost inevitably lead to some fluctuation in assessment results. For instance, the inconsistencies in Ms. Fowler's two sets of student essays might have been due to temporary factors such as these:

- *Day-to-day changes in students*—for example, changes in health, motivation, mood, and energy level

  A 24-hour flu was making the rounds among Ms. Fowler's students.

- *Variations in the physical environment*—for example, variations in room temperature, noise level, and outside distractions

  On Monday students who sat by the window in Ms. Fowler's class enjoyed peace and quiet, but on Wednesday they wrote their essays while noisy construction machinery was tearing up the pavement outside.

- *Variations in administration of the assessment*—for example, variations in instructions, timing, and the teacher's responses to students' questions

  On Monday a few students wrote the essay after school because they had attended a dress rehearsal for the school play during class time. Ms. Fowler explained the task more clearly to them than she had during class, and she gave them as much time as they needed to finish. On Wednesday a different group of students had to write the essay after school because of an across-town band concert during class time. Ms. Fowler explained the task very hurriedly and collected the essays before students had finished.

- *Characteristics of the assessment instrument*—for example, the length, clarity, and difficulty of tasks (e.g., ambiguous and very difficult tasks increase students' tendency to guess randomly)

  The essay topic—"Explain why many scientists believe that birds are descended from dinosaurs"—was an ambiguous one that students interpreted differently from one day to the next.

- *Subjectivity in scoring*—for example, judgments made on the basis of vague, imprecise criteria

  Ms. Fowler graded both sets of essays while watching *Chainsaw Murders at Central High* on television Friday night. She gave higher scores during kissing scenes, lower scores during stalking scenes.

All of the factors just listed lead to a certain amount of *error* in students' test scores and other assessment results. Rarely are assessment results dead-on measures of what students have learned and can do. Psychologists distinguish among different kinds of reliability, which take different error factors into account. *Test–retest reliability* is the extent to which an assessment instrument yields similar results over a short time interval. *Scorer reliability* is the extent to which two or more independent evaluators of students' performance agree in their judgments. *Internal consistency reliability* is the extent to which different parts of a single instrument all measure the same characteristic.

Whenever we draw conclusions about students' learning and achievement, we must be confident that the information on which we're basing our conclusions isn't overly distorted by temporary, irrelevant factors. Several strategies can increase the likelihood that an assessment yields reliable results:

Appendix B explains how we can determine each of these reliabilities. It also explains how we can estimate the amount of error that a particular assessment result might have.

- Include a variety of tasks, and look for consistency in students' performance on different tasks.
- Define each task clearly enough that students know exactly what they're being asked to do.
- Use a checklist or rubric that identifies specific, concrete criteria with which to evaluate students' performance.

🍏 Try not to let expectations for students' performance influence judgments of *actual* performance.

🍏 Avoid assessing students' achievement when they're unlikely to give their best performance—for example, when they're sick.

🍏 Administer the assessment in similar ways and under similar conditions for all students.

The last recommendation suggests that assessment procedures also be *standardized*, especially when—for whatever reason—students need to be compared to one another. We turn to this RSVP characteristic now.

STANDARDIZATION

The term standardization refers to the extent to which an assessment involves similar content and format and is administered and scored in the same way for everyone. Especially in norm-referenced summative assessments, students should all get the same instructions, perform identical or similar tasks, have the same time limits, and work under the same constraints. Furthermore, all students' responses should be scored using the same criteria. For example, unless there are extenuating circumstances, we shouldn't use tougher standards for one student than for another.

At the beginning of the chapter, we noted that many tests constructed and published by testing experts are called *standardized* tests. This label indicates that such tests have explicit procedures for administration and scoring that are consistently applied wherever the tests are used. Yet standardization is important in teacher-developed assessments as well: It reduces the amount of error in assessment results, especially error due to variation in test administration or subjectivity in scoring. The more an assessment is standardized for all students, then, the higher its reliability.

Equity is an additional consideration here: Under most circumstances, it's only fair to ask all students to be evaluated under similar conditions. We find an obvious exception to this guideline in the assessment of students with special educational needs; we'll consider appropriate accommodations for these students near the end of the chapter.

VALIDITY

Earlier you learned about *reliability*. The following exercise can help you determine how well you understand what reliability involves.

■■ EXPERIENCING FIRSTHAND
■ FTOI

One of us authors has recently developed a test called the FTOI: the Fathead Test of Intelligence. It consists of only a tape measure and a *table of norms* that shows how children and adults of various ages typically perform on the test. Administration of the FTOI is quick and easy. You simply measure a person's head circumference just above the eyebrows (firmly but not too tightly) and compare your measure against the average head circumference for the person's age-group. People with large heads (comparatively speaking) get high IQ scores. People with smaller heads get low scores.

Does the FTOI have high reliability? Answer the question before you read further.

■■

No matter how often you measure a person's head circumference, you're going to get a similar score: Fatheads will continue to be fatheads, and pinheads will always be pinheads. So the answer to our question is *yes:* The FTOI has high reliability because it yields consistent results. If you answered *no,* you were probably thinking that the FTOI isn't a very good measure of intelligence. But that's a problem with the instrument's *validity,* not with its reliability.

The validity of an assessment instrument is the extent to which it measures what it's intended to measure and allows us to draw appropriate inferences about the characteristic or ability in question. Does the FTOI measure intelligence? Are scores on a standardized, multiple-choice achievement test a good indication of whether students have mastered basic skills in reading and writing? Does students' performance at a school concert reflect what they've achieved in their instrumental music class? When our assessments don't do these things well—when they're poor measures of students' knowledge and abilities—we have a validity problem.

As noted earlier, many irrelevant factors are apt to influence how well students perform in assessment situations. Some of these—such as students' health, classroom distractions, and inconsistencies in scoring—are temporary conditions that lead to fluctuation in assessment results from one time to the next and thereby lower reliability. But other irrelevant factors—perhaps reading ability or chronic test anxiety—are more stable, and thus their effects on assessment results will be relatively constant. For example, if Joe has poor reading skills, he may get consistently low scores on multiple-choice achievement tests regardless of how much he has actually learned in science, math, or social studies. When assessment results continue to be affected by the same irrelevant variables, the *validity* of the results is in doubt.

Psychologists distinguish among different kinds of validity, which are important in different situations. Three kinds of particular interest to educators and other practitioners are content validity, predictive validity, and construct validity.

CONTENT VALIDITY

Classroom teachers should typically be most concerned with content validity—the extent to which assessment questions and tasks are a representative sample of the overall body of knowledge and skills being assessed. Assessments with high content validity are, like effective instruction, closely aligned with instructional goals and any relevant content-area standards. Different goals and standards often require different assessment strategies. In some situations—for example, when the desired outcome is the simple recall of facts—we might ask students to respond to a series of multiple-choice or short-answer questions on a paper–pencil or computer-administered quiz. In other situations—for example, when the goal is to critique a work of literature or to use principles of physics to explain everyday phenomena—essay tasks that require students to follow a logical line of reasoning might be appropriate. And for some skills—for example, reading aloud, cooking a hard-boiled egg, executing a front dismount from the parallel bars—only performance assessment can give us reasonable content validity. In the end, we'll probably find that we can best assess students' achievement with a combination of paper–pencil and performance assessments.

> Align classroom assessment instruments and procedures both with relevant content-area standards and with your own specific goals, objectives, and curriculum.

In most states in the United States, teachers must consider the Common Core State Standards as they identify appropriate assessments of students' progress in reading, writing, and mathematics. As an illustration, Table 14.1 presents examples of key reading skills identified in the Common Core State Standards for English Language Arts, along with relevant instructional lessons and tasks (Column 3) and assessment strategies (Column 4). Some of the entries in Column 4 can potentially serve as *formal summative assessment* tasks. But notice that the entries to their immediate left (in Column 3) also require students to do, say, or write something—thus providing opportunities for *informal assessment* or *formative assessment* of students' current knowledge and ongoing progress.

The first three columns in Table 14.1 previously appeared in Table 12.1.

One helpful framework for planning assessments with good content validity is a backward design, as illustrated in Figure 14.6. More specifically, we begin with what we ultimately want students to achieve in our classes: We consider any applicable content-area standards (Step 1a) and identify more specific instructional goals (Step 1b). We then identify one or more suitable methods to assess students' achievement of the desired end results (Step 2). Finally, we plan instructional strategies that will enable students to master the important knowledge and skills we've identified (Step 3)

You have previously learned about a backward design in Chapter 12. The diagram in Figure 14.6 should look familiar, as it's identical to the one presented in Figure 12.3.

Another strategy for enhancing content validity in *formative* assessments is curriculum-based measurement (CBM), which is especially useful both in basic skills instruction and in a response-to-intervention approach to identifying persistent learning problems. In this approach teachers regularly administer assessments that each focus on a single, specific skill in the curriculum (e.g., word recognition in reading, addition of 2-digit numbers) as a means of tracking individual students' progress. Each assessment is typically quite short (perhaps only 1 to 4 minutes in length) and yet can help teachers identify students who may need additional instruction in a certain skill in order to move forward. In recent years some of the computer software programs mentioned earlier, such as AIMSweb and DIBELS, have made CBM increasingly easy and powerful.

High content validity is, of course, also important whenever we're using an assessment instrument for *summative* assessment purposes—that is, to determine what knowledge and skills students have ultimately acquired from instruction. When a summative assessment addresses

TABLE 14.1 • Examples of How You Might Align Classroom Assessments with Common Core State Standards and Instruction at Different Grade Levels

GRADE LEVEL	EXAMPLES OF COMMON CORE STANDARDS FOR ENGLISH LANGUAGE ARTS	EXAMPLES OF INSTRUCTIONAL STRATEGIES THAT ADDRESS THESE STANDARDS *AND* PROVIDE A MEANS OF INFORMALLY ASSESSING STUDENTS' PROGRESS	EXAMPLES OF ASSESSMENTS THAT ALIGN WITH THE STANDARDS AND WITH CLASSROOM INSTRUCTION
Grade 2	Ask and answer such questions as *who, what, where, when, why,* and *how* to demonstrate understanding of key details in a text. (RL.2.1)[a]	During "settling down" time immediately after lunch each day, read a chapter of a high-interest children's novel, stopping frequently to ask questions that require students to go beyond the text itself (e.g., ask students to speculate about what a character might be feeling).	Meet with students in small groups and ask each group member to describe a story in his or her own words. Follow up with questions such as "What happened next?" and "Why did [a character] do that?" to determine the extent to which each student has understood important elements of the story.
	Recount stories, including fables and folktales from diverse cultures, and determine their central message, lesson, or moral. (RL.2.2)	Have several students create props for and act out a story they have recently read, with other class members serving as the audience. Follow up with a class discussion of important lessons that one or more story characters might have learned from events or challenges that they faced.	Give a reading group several age-appropriate Middle Eastern or Chinese folktales to read, and then ask the students, "What advice do you think this story is giving us?" Be sure that every group member answers the question, and communicate that there isn't necessarily a single right answer.
Grade 4	Refer to details and examples in a text when explaining what the text says explicitly and when drawing inferences from the text. (RL.4.1)	As a reading group discusses Carl Hiaasen's *Hoot,* ask students to speculate about how the plot might progress and to identify clues in the text that support their predictions.	After students have read the first few chapters of Natalie Babbitt's *Tuck Everlasting* (in which the Tuck family has drunk from a well that gives everlasting life), ask them to write an essay speculating on problems the Tucks' immortality might create for them. Later, after they learn that Mae Tuck has killed someone, ask them to speculate about the implications of her arrest and to back up their predictions with clues in the text.
	Explain events, procedures, ideas, or concepts in a historical, scientific, or technical text, including what happened and why, based on specific information in the text. (RI.4.3)	When students are reading a chapter in their history textbook, ask *why* questions that encourage cause-and-effect connections (e.g., "Why did Columbus's crew want to sail back to Europe after several weeks on the open sea?").	Ask students to create concept maps that show interrelationships (including cause and effect) among various events during a particular period in history.
Grade 7	Analyze the structure an author uses to organize a text, including how the major sections contribute to the whole and to the development of the ideas. (RI.7.5)	Before students read a chapter in their science textbook, have them use its headings and subheadings to (1) create a general outline of the chapter and (2) generate questions they hope to answer as they read the chapter. Then, for homework, ask them to read and take notes on the chapter, using the outline and self-questions as guides for note taking.	Ask students to write a two-page summary of a chapter in their science book, using chapter headings and subheadings to organize their discussion.
	Trace and evaluate the argument and specific claims in a text, assessing whether the reasoning is sound and the evidence is relevant and sufficient to support the claims. (RI.7.8)	Give students an advertisement for a self-improvement product (e.g., a diet pill or exercise equipment); have them work in small cooperative learning groups to (1) identify the advertiser's motives and (2) evaluate the quality of evidence for the product's effectiveness.	Have students examine an Internet website that promotes an allegedly health-promoting product. Ask them to identify, either orally or in writing, possible flaws in the evidence and logic the website uses to convince people to purchase the product.

(continued)

GRADE LEVEL	EXAMPLES OF COMMON CORE STANDARDS FOR ENGLISH LANGUAGE ARTS	EXAMPLES OF INSTRUCTIONAL STRATEGIES THAT ADDRESS THESE STANDARDS *AND* PROVIDE A MEANS OF INFORMALLY ASSESSING STUDENTS' PROGRESS	EXAMPLES OF ASSESSMENTS THAT ALIGN WITH THE STANDARDS AND WITH CLASSROOM INSTRUCTION
Grades 11–12	Analyze and evaluate the effectiveness of the structure an author uses in his or her position or argument, including whether the structure makes points clear, convincing, and engaging. (RI.11–12.5)	Describe common techniques in persuasive writing, and have students identify the various persuasive techniques used in newspaper editorials.	Ask students to (1) identify three specific persuasive techniques used in the U.S. Declaration of Independence and (2) explain their particular purposes and probable effectiveness in the American colonies in 1776.
	Determine an author's point of view or purpose in a text in which the rhetoric is particularly effective, analyzing how style and content contribute to the power, persuasiveness or beauty of the text. (RI.11–12.6)	Ask students to identify the unstated assumptions underlying two news magazines' depictions of the same event (e.g., an assumption that one group is good or right and another is bad or wrong).	Give students a magazine article describing a recent event in the national or international news. Ask them to underline five sentences that reveal the author's cultural and/or political biases and to describe those biases in a two-page essay.

ᵃThe letters "RL" indicate standards related to reading literature; the letters "RI" indicate standards related to reading informational text. The number or numbers before the period indicate the grade level; the number after the period indicates the particular standard for that grade level. For example, the first entry shown here, identified as "RL.2.1," is the first standard for grade 2 for reading literature.

Source: Entries in the column "Examples of Common Core Standards for English Language Arts" are from *Common Core State Standards.* Copyright © 2010 by National Governors Association Center for Best Practices and Council of Chief State School Officers. Reprinted with permission. All rights reserved.

multiple topics, concepts, and skills, we can't necessarily include each and every one of them in the assessment. But taken as a whole, the things we ask students to do in the assessment should comprise a *representative* sample of the content domain we're assessing. The most widely recommended strategy is to construct a blueprint that identifies the specific things we want to assess and the proportion of questions or tasks that should address each one. This blueprint often takes the form of a **table of specifications**: a two-way grid that indicates both what topics should be covered and what students should be able to *do* with each topic. Each cell of the grid indicates the relative importance of each topic–behavior combination, perhaps as a particular number or percentage of tasks to be included in the overall assessment. Figure 14.7 shows two examples. The table on the left, constructed for a 30-item paper–pencil quiz on addition, assigns different weights (i.e., different numbers of test items) to different topic–behavior combinations, with some combinations intentionally not being assessed at all. The table on the right, constructed for a high school physics unit on classical mechanics, instead uses percentages to identify the relative weights assigned to different topic–behavior combinations; the three behaviors it includes are based loosely on the first three processes in Bloom's taxonomy (*remember, understand, apply*). Both tables in Figure 14.7 intentionally place greater emphasis on some topic–behavior combinations than on others, but in other situations equal weightings across the board might be quite appropriate.

Content validity is important not only for teacher-developed assessments but also for any published achievement tests being used to assess students' abilities and academic progress. A table of specifications can help us in this situation as well, but this time we *start with the test* and then determine the degree to which it matches our curriculum. More specifically, we create a two-dimensional table that includes both the topics and the behaviors we want to assess. We look closely at the items in the test and count the number of items that fall into each cell in our table. (Sometimes the test publisher provides such a table.) We can then decide whether the test matches

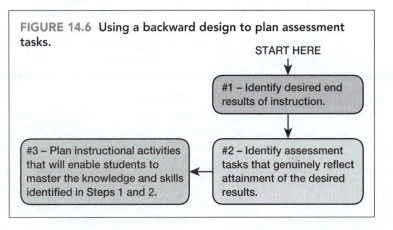

FIGURE 14.6 Using a backward design to plan assessment tasks.

START HERE

#1 – Identify desired end results of instruction.

#2 – Identify assessment tasks that genuinely reflect attainment of the desired results.

#3 – Plan instructional activities that will enable students to master the knowledge and skills identified in Steps 1 and 2.

To enhance the content validity of a summative assessment, develop a table of specifications that can guide your selection of topics and tasks.

Bloom's taxonomy is described in Chapter 12.

FIGURE 14.7 Two examples of a table of specifications.

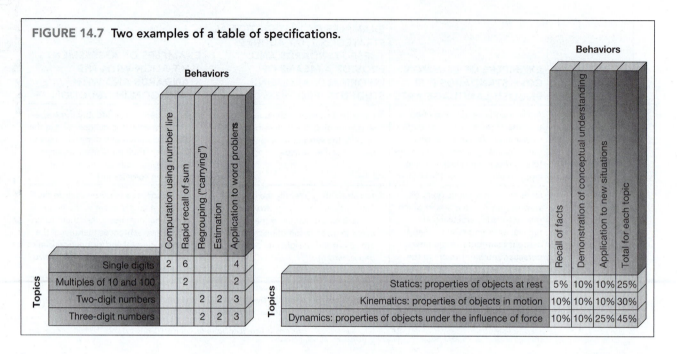

Topics \ Behaviors	Computation using number line	Rapid recall of sum	Regrouping ("carrying")	Estimation	Application to word problems
Single digits	2	6			4
Multiples of 10 and 100	2				2
Two-digit numbers			2	2	3
Three-digit numbers			2	2	3

Topics \ Behaviors	Recall of facts	Demonstration of conceptual understanding	Application to new situations	Total for each topic
Statics: properties of objects at rest	5%	10%	10%	25%
Kinematics: properties of objects in motion	10%	10%	10%	30%
Dynamics: properties of objects under the influence of force	10%	10%	25%	45%

our curriculum closely enough that it has content validity for our particular situation—that is, whether it reflects what we actually do in our classrooms.

Four words in the last sentence of the preceding paragraph—*for our particular situation*—are especially important to note. We can't *ever* say that a certain achievement test has high or low content validity in general. A test might have good content validity for the curriculum of some schools and classrooms but little or no content validity in other circumstances.

PREDICTIVE VALIDITY

Shantel is thinking about a career in mathematics. But even though she's doing well in her eighth-grade math class, she worries that she'll eventually have trouble with advanced courses in trigonometry and calculus. To get an idea of her chances for future math success, Shantel takes the Mathematics Aptitude Test (MAT) that her school counselor makes available to her. Shantel does quite well on the MAT, bolstering her confidence that she can succeed in a mathematics career. But does the MAT actually measure a student's potential for success as a mathematician? This is a question of **predictive validity**—the extent to which an assessment instrument accurately predicts future performance in some arena.

Publishers of standardized, norm-referenced ability tests often determine, mathematically, the accuracy with which test scores predict later success in certain domains. Keep in mind, however, that, as is true for content validity, a test has no *single* predictive validity. Its validity in a given situation depends on the specific behavior being predicted, the age-group being assessed (e.g., many tests have greater predictive validity for older students than for younger ones), and the amount of time between the test and the predicted performance.

See Appendix B for details about how predictive validity is calculated.

CONSTRUCT VALIDITY

In psychology, a *construct* is a hypothesized internal trait that can't be directly observed but must instead be inferred from consistencies we see in people's behavior. *Motivation, self-efficacy,* and *intelligence* are all constructs; we can't actually *see* any of these things but must instead draw conclusions about them from what students do and don't do. For example, we might use our observations of students' on-task and off-task behaviors to make inferences about their self-efficacy for various classroom topics and skills. Similarly, we might use students' performance on abstract reasoning tasks as evidence of their general intelligence.

By **construct validity**, then, we mean the extent to which an assessment instrument actually measures an abstract, unobservable characteristic. Construct validity is of most concern when we're trying to draw general conclusions about students' traits and abilities—perhaps when we're trying to identify certain disabling conditions that may require specialized instruction and support systems. The problem with the Fathead Test of Intelligence (FTOI) described earlier is one of poor construct validity: Despite its high reliability, the scores it yields have little—probably nothing—to do with intelligence.

How do we determine whether a test or other assessment instrument measures something we can't actually *see?* Assessment experts have developed a variety of strategies for doing so. For example, they might determine how well assessment results correlate with other measures of the same trait (e.g., do scores on one intelligence test correlate with scores on other IQ tests?). They might also find out whether older students perform better than younger students on instruments measuring traits that presumably increase with age (e.g., do 12-year-olds correctly answer more items on an intelligence test than 6-year-olds?). Or they might compare the performance of two groups known to be different with respect to the trait in question (e.g., do nondisabled 12-year-olds perform better on an intelligence test than 12-year-olds who have been identified as having an intellectual disability?). When data from a variety of sources are consistent with what we would expect if the instrument is a good measure of the characteristic in question, we conclude that it probably does have construct validity.

One principle applies to all three forms of validity: *Virtually any assessment tool is more valid for some purposes than for others.* A math achievement test may be a valid measure of how well students can solve arithmetic word problems but a terrible measure of how well they can apply arithmetic to real-life situations. And a paper–pencil quiz on the rules of tennis may accurately assess students' knowledge of how many games are in a set, what *deuce* means, and so on, but it probably won't tell us much about how well students can actually play the game.

PRACTICALITY

The final RSVP characteristic is **practicality**—the extent to which assessment instruments and procedures are easy to use. Practicality encompasses issues such as these:

- How much time will it take to develop the questions and/or tasks to be administered?
- Can the assessment be administered to many students at once, or is one-on-one administration required?
- Are expensive materials involved?
- How much time will the assessment take away from instructional activities?
- How quickly and easily can students' performance be evaluated?

There's often a trade-off between practicality and characteristics such as validity and reliability. For example, a true–false test on tennis would be easier to construct and administer, but a performance assessment in which students actually demonstrate their tennis skills—even though it would take more time and energy—would undoubtedly be a more valid measure of how well students have mastered the game.

The four RSVP characteristics of good assessments are summarized in Table 14.2. Of these, *validity is the most important:* We must use assessment techniques that validly assess students' achievement of instructional goals and objectives. Yet we should keep in mind that *reliability is a necessary condition for validity*, especially when summative assessments are involved. Reliability doesn't guarantee validity, however, as the earlier FTOI exercise illustrated. Standardization is most relevant to summative assessments, particularly norm-referenced ones in which each student's performance is evaluated in comparison with peers. Furthermore, standardization can enhance the reliability of assessment results and hence can indirectly enhance their validity. Practicality should be a consideration only when validity isn't lost in the process.

MyEdLab **Self-Check 14.3**

MyEdLab **Application Exercise 14.3.** In this exercise, you can practice using the four RSVP characteristics in evaluating a variety of classroom assessment strategies.

COMPARE/CONTRAST

TABLE 14.2 • RSVP Characteristics of Good Assessment			
CHARACTERISTIC	**DEFINITION**	**RELEVANT QUESTIONS TO CONSIDER**	**COMMENTS**
Reliability	The extent to which an assessment instrument or procedure yields consistent results for each student	• How much are students' scores affected by temporary conditions unrelated to the characteristic being assessed (*test–retest reliability*)? • Do different people score students' performance similarly (*scorer reliability*, also known as *interrater reliability*)? • Do different parts of a single assessment instrument lead to similar conclusions about a student's achievement (*internal consistency reliability*)?	Reliability is a necessary condition for validity and is especially important in summative assessments. It's less critical in short formative assessments that are used simply to guide instruction over the short term (e.g., those used in curriculum-based measurement).
Standardization	The extent to which an assessment instrument or procedure is similar for all students	• Are all students assessed on identical or similar content? • Are all students asked to perform the same types of tasks? • Is everyone given the same instructions? • Do all students have the same time limits? • Is everyone's performance evaluated using the same criteria?	Standardization is essential for legitimate and equitable comparisons among students (e.g., in norm-referenced tests). It's less important when assessments are used to guide and individualize instruction. Also, appropriate accommodations must be made for students with disabilities.
Validity	The extent to which an instrument or procedure actually assesses what it is intended to assess and enables appropriate inferences to be made	• Does the assessment tap into a representative sample of the content domain being assessed (*content validity*)? • Do students' scores predict their later success in a domain (*predictive validity*)? • Does an assessment accurately measure a particular psychological or educational characteristic (*construct validity*)?	Validity must be the most central concern in all classroom assessments. Assessment results are meaningless unless they're closely aligned with instructional goals and the academic curriculum.
Practicality	The extent to which an assessment instrument or procedure is easy and inexpensive to use	• How much class time does the assessment take? • How quickly and easily can students' responses be scored? • Is special training required to administer or score the assessment? • Does the assessment require specialized materials that must be purchased?	Especially when using summative assessments to make potentially life-altering decisions, practicality should be a consideration only to the extent that validity isn't seriously jeopardized. Brief formative assessments (e.g., in CBM) should be highly practical so that they don't consume much instructional time.

Assessing Students' Progress and Achievement Both Informally and Formally

Effective teachers regularly draw inferences both from their ongoing, spontaneous observations of students' behaviors and from students' performance on preplanned paper–pencil and performance tasks. We examine each of these strategies now.

INFORMALLY OBSERVING STUDENTS' BEHAVIORS

From our daily observations of students' classroom behaviors, we can discover a great deal about what students have and haven't learned, enabling us to make reasonable decisions about how future instruction should proceed. For example, we can:

- Ask questions during a lesson (see the Into the Classroom feature "Asking Questions to Assess Learning and Achievement Informally").
- Listen to what and how much students contribute to whole-class and small-group discussions; make note of the kinds of questions they ask.
- Have students write daily or weekly entries in personal journals.
- Observe how well students perform physical tasks.

Asking Questions to Assess Learning and Achievement Informally

🍎 **Direct questions to the entire class, not just to a few students who seem eager to respond.**

The girls in a high school science class rarely volunteer when their teacher asks questions. Although the teacher often calls on students who raise their hands, he occasionally calls on those who don't, and he makes sure that he calls on *every* student at least once a week.

🍎 **When a question has only a few possible answers, have students vote on the particular answers they think are correct.**

When beginning a lesson on dividing one fraction by another, a middle school math teacher writes this problem on the board:

$$(^3/_4 \div {}^1/_2) = ?$$

She asks, "Before we talk about how we solve this problem, how many of you think the answer will be less than 1? How many think it will be greater than 1? How many think it will be exactly 1?" She tallies the number of hands that go up after each question and then says, "Hmmm, most of you think the answer will be less than 1. Let's look at how we solve a problem like this. Then each of you will know whether you were right or wrong."

🍎 **Ask follow-up questions to probe students' reasoning.**

In a geography lesson on Canada, a fourth-grade teacher points to the St. Lawrence River on a map and asks, "Which way does the water flow, toward the ocean or away from it?" One student shouts out, "Away from it." "Why do you think so?" the teacher asks. The student's explanation reveals a common misconception: that rivers can flow only from north to south, never vice versa.

🍎 Identify the kinds of activities in which students engage voluntarily.

🍎 Watch for body language that may reflect students' feelings about particular classroom tasks.

🍎 Observe students' interactions with peers in class, at lunch, and on the playground.

🍎 Look at the relative frequency of on-task and off-task behaviors; look for patterns in *when* students are off task.

Informal assessment has several advantages. First and foremost, it gives us continuing feedback about the effectiveness of the day's instructional tasks and activities. Second, it's easily adjusted at a moment's notice; for example, when students reveal misconceptions about a topic, we can ask follow-up questions that probe their beliefs and reasoning processes. Third, informal assessment provides information that may either support or call into question the data we obtain from more formal assessments such as paper–pencil tests and quizzes; for instance, it might provide more optimistic assessments of English language learners. Finally, ongoing observations of students' behaviors provide clues about social, emotional, and motivational factors affecting students' classroom performance and may often be the only practical means through which we can assess such goals as "Shows courtesy" and "Enjoys reading."

RSVP CHARACTERISTICS OF INFORMAL ASSESSMENTS

When we get information about students' characteristics and achievements through informal means, we must be aware of the strengths and limitations of this approach with respect to reliability, standardization, validity, and practicality.

Reliability.   Most informal assessments are quite short, and such snippets of students' behavior aren't always reliable indicators of their overall accomplishments and dispositions. Perhaps we happen to ask Manuel the *only* question to which he doesn't know the answer. Perhaps we happen to notice Naomi being off task during the *only* time she's off task. Perhaps we misinterpret something Jacquie says after school. When we use informal assessment to draw conclusions about what students know and can do, we should base our conclusions on many observations over a long period. And given the fact that our long-term memories can never be totally accurate, dependable records of our observations, we should keep ongoing, written records of what we see and hear (M. D. Miller, Linn, & Gronlund, 2009; Stiggins & Chappuis, 2012).

Standardization.   Informal assessments can rarely, if ever, be standardized; for example, we're apt to ask different questions of different students, and we'll probably observe each student's behavior in different contexts. Hence such assessments definitely *don't* give us the same

🍏 Don't take any single observation of a student's behavior too seriously; instead, look for patterns over time.

🍏 Keep written records of what students say and do, especially if final assessments will depend heavily on in-class observations.

information for each student. In most cases, then, we can't make legitimate comparisons among students merely on the basis of a few casual observations.

Validity. Even when students' behavior is consistent over time, it won't always give us accurate data about what students know and can do. For example, Tom may intentionally answer questions incorrectly so that he doesn't come across as a know-it-all, and Margot may be reluctant to say anything because of a chronic stuttering problem. In general, when we use in-class questions to assess students' learning, we must keep in mind that some students—especially females and students from certain ethnic minority groups—will be less likely to respond than others. Meanwhile, other students may speak with such confidence that they lead us to believe they know more than they actually do (Castagno & Brayboy, 2008; Rogoff, 2003; Stiggins & Chappuis, 2012; Wentzel, 2009).

Teachers tend to evaluate well-behaved students as achieving at higher levels than badly behaved students, even when the students' actual academic achievement levels are the same.

Our personal biases and expectations can also come into play in our informal assessments (Carbonneau & Selig, 2011; Ritts, Patterson, & Tubbs, 1992; J. P. Robinson & Lubienski, 2011). As cognitive psychologists have revealed, we human beings typically impose meanings on what we see and hear based on things we already know or believe to be true. For instance, we're apt to expect academic or social competence from students we like or admire and thus perceive their actions in an overly positive light—a phenomenon known as the halo effect. In much the same way, we might expect inappropriate behavior from students with a history of misbehavior, and our observations might be biased accordingly—a phenomenon aptly called the horns effect.

In addition, despite our efforts to be impartial judges, any expectations we have for students based on their ethnic backgrounds or socioeconomic status can unfairly bias our judgments of their performance (Ready & Wright, 2011; van den Bergh, Denessen, Hornstra, Voeten, & Holland, 2010). In one experimental study (Darley & Gross, 1983), college students were told that they were participating in a study on teacher assessment methods and then shown a videotape of a fourth grader named Hannah. Two versions of the videotape gave differing impressions about Hannah's socioeconomic status: Her clothing, the kind of playground on which she played, and information about her parents' occupations indirectly conveyed to some students that she was from a high socioeconomic background and to others that she was from a low socioeconomic background. All students watched Hannah taking an oral achievement test (on which she performed at grade level) and were asked to rate her on several characteristics. Students who had been led to believe that Hannah came from a wealthy family rated her ability well above grade level, whereas students believing that she came from a poor family evaluated her as being below grade level. The two groups of students also rated Hannah's work habits, motivation, social skills, and general maturity differently.

Chapter 11 describes additional effects of teacher expectations.

Practicality. The greatest strength of informal assessment is its practicality. It involves little or none of our time either before or after the fact, except when we keep written records of our observations. It's also quite flexible: We can adjust our assessment procedures on the spot as circumstances change.

Treat the conclusions you draw from informal assessment as hypotheses that need confirmation through more formal means.

Despite the practicality of informal assessment, we've just noted serious problems regarding its reliability, standardization, and validity. Hence we should treat any conclusions we draw only as *hypotheses* that we must either confirm or disconfirm through other means. In the end, we must rely more heavily on preplanned, formal assessment techniques to determine whether our students have achieved instructional goals and met content-area standards.

USING PAPER–PENCIL ASSESSMENTS

When we need to conduct a formal assessment, paper–pencil assessment is typically easier and faster—and thus has greater practicality—than performance assessment. Questions that require brief responses—such as multiple-choice and short-answer questions—are often suitable for assessing students' knowledge of single, isolated facts. Paper–pencil tasks that require extended responses—such as essay questions and geometry proofs—more easily lend themselves to assessment of complex cognitive processes, such as logical reasoning, critical thinking, and problem solving. However, item type alone doesn't tell us whether we're assessing simple or complex thinking skills. For example, it's quite possible (and also quite common) for an essay question to ask students only to retrieve and explain things they've previously been taught, and some teachers are quite creative in writing multiple-choice questions that require students to apply classroom subject matter to new situations.

One important distinction to consider regarding various paper–pencil item formats is whether they involve recognition or recall. A recognition task (e.g., a multiple-choice, true–false, or matching question) asks students to identify a correct answer within the context of incorrect statements or irrelevant information. In contrast, a recall task (e.g., a short-answer question, word problem, or essay task) requires students to generate the correct answer themselves. When a recall task requires a lengthy response—and especially when it also involves elaborating on, analyzing, synthesizing, or applying information in new ways—it's sometimes called a constructed-response task.

Recognition items have two major advantages. First, we can often include a relatively large number of questions and tasks in a single assessment, enabling us to get a representative sample of a broad content domain and hence potentially increasing content validity. In addition, we can score students' responses quickly and consistently, thus addressing our need for practicality and reliability. However, recognition tasks tend to overestimate achievement: Students can sometimes guess correctly when they don't know the material very well.

When our instructional goal involves retrieving knowledge and skills *without* the benefit of seeing the correct answer within the context of distracting information, and especially when we want to examine students' reasoning processes—for instance, their ability to justify a particular point of view on a controversial topic—recall tasks generally have greater validity than recognition tasks. Also, students tend to study classroom material more thoroughly when they're preparing for recall rather than recognition test questions, and they remember the material better (D'Ydewalle, Swerts, & De Corte, 1983; Roediger & Karpicke, 2006; Rohrer & Pashler, 2010; G. Warren, 1979). But because students may require considerable time to respond to each recall item, we'll be able to present fewer items in a single assessment session (adversely affecting reliability) and will tap a more limited sample of the content domain (potentially affecting content validity). In addition, we'll typically take longer to score such items (a practicality issue) and will make more errors in scoring them (another reliability issue).

Use recognition tasks to assess students' ability to identify facts, especially when the content domain is large. Use recall tasks when it's important to assess students' ability to retrieve information on their own and use it in new ways.

CONSTRUCTING A PAPER–PENCIL ASSESSMENT

Most recognition assessment items take one of three basic forms:

- An *alternative-response item* is one for which there are only two or three possible answers (e.g., *true* versus *false, fact* versus *opinion*) for all items in a series.

- A *multiple-choice item* consists of a question or incomplete statement (the *stem*) followed by one correct answer and several incorrect alternatives (*distractors*).

- A *matching item* presents two columns of information; students must match each item in the first column with an appropriate item in the second.

Of these three formats, most assessment experts recommend multiple-choice items. Multiple-choice items have two advantages relative to other recognition items. First, the number of items students can answer correctly simply by guessing is relatively low, especially in comparison with alternative-response items. (For example, when multiple-choice items have five possible answers, students can get only about 20% of them correct through guessing alone.) Second, other things being equal, the multiple-choice format lends itself most readily to measuring complex thinking skills.

Recall items range widely in format and are essentially limited only by our imaginations. Some are quite simple and straightforward—for instance, "How much is two plus two?" and "What's the capital of France?" Others may call for considerable thought. For example, we might give students a problem that requires them to manipulate or synthesize data and develop a solution. Alternatively, we might give students new material (e.g., a table, graph, map, or section of text) and ask them to analyze and draw conclusions from it. Figure 14.8 presents an example.

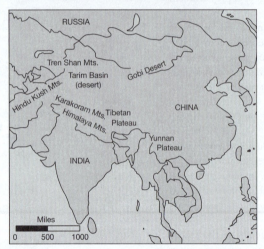

FIGURE 14.8 Example of an assessment item that requires students to analyze and draw conclusions from new material.

Using the map shown here, explain why early people living in Russia, China, and India developed distinctly different languages and cultures.

With RSVP characteristics of good assessments in mind, we offer the following general recommendations for constructing paper–pencil assessments.

🍎 *Combine multiple formats in a single assessment.* Often we'll want to assess students' ability to synthesize, evaluate, or in other ways elaborate on the things they've learned, and we can usually do this more easily with constructed-response tasks. Yet assessments consisting of only one or two lengthy constructed-response items don't always provide a representative sample of the topics and skills being assessed, and any errors in scoring a single item can seriously impact students' overall scores. A workable compromise is to combine both quick-response recognition and recall items— which allow broad sampling—and lengthier, constructed-response recall items—which better enable us to examine students' reasoning skills—in a single paper–pencil assessment. Also, we must keep in mind that paper–pencil assessments don't need to be entirely verbal in nature; they can also include visual materials, as the example in Figure 14.8 does.

🍎 *When assessing basic knowledge, rephrase ideas presented in class or reading materials.* If we want to encourage meaningful rather than rote learning as students prepare for a formal assessment, we must—let's repeat that, we *must*—create items for which word-for-word memorization is counterproductive. Consider, for example, a middle school language arts teacher who uses short multiple-choice quizzes to assess students' understanding of each week's new vocabulary words. Quiz items should never include the exact definitions students have been given. Maybe students have been given this definition for *manacle*: "Device used to restrain a person's hands or wrists." A question might look like this:

> Which one of the following words or phrases is closest in meaning to the word *manacle?*
>
> a. Insane
> b. Handcuffs
> c. Out of control
> d. Saltwater creature that clings to hard surfaces
> (*The correct answer is* b.)

🍎 *To assess complex cognitive processes, ask students to apply what they've learned to new situations.* When we present situations or problems that students have previously studied, students may respond correctly simply because they've memorized the answers. We can genuinely assess problem solving, critical thinking, and other complex cognitive processes only when we ask students to use their knowledge and skills in new contexts—that is, when they must *transfer* what they've learned. For example, we might ask students to:

- Critique the conclusions a researcher draws from a research study
- Identify a writer's underlying assumptions in arguing for a particular perspective
- Assess the credibility of information presented on an Internet website (Nitko & Brookhart, 2011)

Although constructed-response tasks are typically better suited for assessing transfer, with thought and creativity we can even create recognition items that assess transfer. The following multiple-choice question for a science unit on simple machines is an example:

> An inventor has just designed a new device for cutting paper. Which one of the following simple machines is this device most likely to include?
>
> a. A lever
> b. A movable pulley
> c. An inclined plane
> d. A wedge
> (*The correct answer is* d.)

🍎 *Define tasks clearly and unambiguously.* Regardless of whether students know how to correctly respond to assessment tasks, they should at least understand what we're asking them to do. The next exercise can show you what we mean.

EXPERIENCING FIRSTHAND
ASSESSING YOUR KNOWLEDGE OF ASSESSMENT

Your educational psychology instructor gives you a test that includes these questions:

1. List four qualities of a good classroom assessment.
2. Summarize the purposes of classroom assessment.

Take a few minutes to think about how you might answer each question. Jot down your thoughts about what you would include in your responses.

Was your answer to Question 1 as simple as "reliability, standardization, validity, and practicality"? Did you think you needed to explain each of the RSVP characteristics? Did you identify legitimate qualities of "goodness" other than the four RSVP characteristics? And what about Question 2? What purposes did you focus on, and how long do you think your actual summary might be? Words such as *list, qualities,* and *summarize* are hard to interpret and can be misleading.

🍎 *Provide guidance and structure for students' responses.* To some degree, we should do this by clearly defining the assessment task. For example, to assess students' knowledge of 18th-century American history, rather than ask them only to "List three causes of the American Revolution," we might instead ask them to do this:

> Identify three policies or events during the 1760s and/or 1770s that contributed to the outbreak of the American Revolution. For each one, explain in three to five sentences how it increased tension between England and the American colonies.

Alternatively, to assess students' ability to separate and control variables, we might give them a question such as this one:

> A physics student wants to study the rate at which a ball rolls down an inclined plane. The student wonders whether either the slope of the plane or the weight of the ball affects this rate. Describe an experiment the student could conduct. Be sure to include (a) the materials the student should use in the experiment, (b) at least two hypotheses the student might make, and (c) the steps the students should take to test the hypotheses. (Based on a general structure suggested by R. L. Johnson, Penny, & Gordon, 2009)

Such clarity and structure are especially important when a *lot* of information might potentially be relevant to a constructed-response task. Otherwise, students' responses can go in so many different directions that scoring them consistently and reliably is virtually impossible.

🍎 *Minimize the likelihood that students can guess correctly when they don't know the answer.* Assessment tasks have content validity only to the extent that they can help us accurately determine whether students have mastered the knowledge and skills being assessed. Poorly written items sometimes provide logical clues that enable even uninformed students to answer correctly. The following exercise provides examples.

EXPERIENCING FIRSTHAND
CALIFRACTIONS

Imagine that you're enrolled in Professor Carberry's psychoceramics course. Early in the semester, before you've had a chance to read the assigned chapter, Professor Carberry gives a surprise quiz on califractions. Below are the first three quiz items; there's only one correct answer for each one:

1. Because they are furstier than other califractions, califors are most often used to
   a. reassignment of matherugs
   b. disbobble a fwing
   c. mangelation
   d. in the burfews

2. Calendation is a process of
    a. combining two califors
    b. adding two califors together
    c. joining two califors
    d. taking two califors apart

3. The furstiest califraction is the
    a. califor
    b. calderost
    c. calinga
    d. calidater

You could possibly answer all three questions without knowing anything about califractions. Because Item 1 says "califors are most often used to . . .," the answer must begin with a verb and so must be Alternative *b* (Alternatives *a* and *c* begin with nouns—"reassign*ment*" and "mangela*tion*"—and *d* begins with a preposition). Item 2 includes three similar-meaning alternatives (*a, b, c*); because the item can have only one right answer, the correct choice must be *d*. And the answer to Item 3 must be *a* because Item 1 has already told you that califors are furstier than other califractions.

In constructing multiple-choice items and other recognition tasks, we should take care that all alternatives are equally logical choices in two respects: (a) They're grammatically parallel to one another and consistent with the stem and (b) only one of them is legitimately correct. Hence many experts recommend that we *not* use "all of the above" as an option in a multiple-choice question: If this is the correct answer (and it often is in teacher-written tests), the other alternatives must be correct as well, and students who have been told to choose the "correct" answer might reasonably be confused. A better strategy is to use one or more common misconceptions as distractors, as the following item about the causes of the seasons does:

> What is the *main* reason that it's colder in winter than in summer?
> a. Because the earth is in the part of its orbit farthest away from the sun
> b. Because the snow on the ground reflects rather than absorbs the sun's heat
> c. Because the sun's rays hit our part of the earth at more of an angle
> d. Because wind is more likely to come from one of the poles than from the Equator
> (*The correct answer is* c. *Alternative* a *is a common misconception.*)

Another strategy for minimizing correct guesses—one that's especially useful in constructed-response tasks—is to include information that's irrelevant to the answer. For example, at some point in your schooling you almost certainly learned how to calculate the area of a parallelogram. If you did, can you quickly calculate the area of the parallelogram shown here?

If you can recall the formula (Area = Base × Height), you should easily arrive at the answer (8 × 4, or 32 square cm). But if you've forgotten the procedure, you might be led astray by some of the information the figure provides. An additional advantage of including extraneous information is that it often enhances the real-life nature of an assessment task. The outside world typically presents a lot of information that has little or nothing to do with the task at hand, and students must ultimately be able to determine what information they actually need.

🍎 *Consider giving students access to reference materials.* In some cases we may want students to have only one resource—long-term memory—as they complete an assessment activity. But in other cases it may be appropriate to let them use reference materials as they work—perhaps a dictionary, map, magazine article, or class notes. An assessment task in which reference materials are allowed is especially appropriate when our objective is for students to find, analyze, or apply information rather than memorize it.

🍎 *Place shorter and easier items before more challenging ones.* Some students approach paper–pencil assessments strategically, answering quick and easy items first, regardless of the order in

---

Construct items that can help you determine whether certain misconceptions persist.

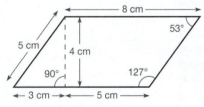

Reduce the likelihood of a correct guess—and also enhance the real-world nature of a task—by including irrelevant information.

which the items are sequenced. But other students tend to address items in the order they appear, sometimes spending so much time on one item (e.g., a lengthy essay) that they leave little time to tackle other, shorter ones. By beginning an assessment with short, relatively easy items, we can both (a) keep students' anxiety at a facilitative, productive level and (b) ensure that they demonstrate some of what they've learned before they get bogged down in especially challenging tasks.

- *Identify scoring criteria in advance.* We should identify correct responses—or at least the components of a good response—at the same time we develop our assessment tasks. To the extent that students' responses will require some professional judgment on our part, we might develop one or more checklists or rubrics to guide our scoring. We should also develop policies about what to do when students give partially correct answers, respond correctly but include additional *in*correct information, or write responses with numerous grammatical and spelling errors (more about the last of these issues shortly).

- *Consider using an electronic alternative to paper and pencil.* Some online resources and software programs enable us to create, administer, and score what have traditionally been paper–pencil assessment instruments. An example is Quia (quia.com/web), where we can create tests and quizzes using a variety of traditional paper–pencil item formats (e.g., multiple choice, true–false, short answer) and, if we like, include graphics or audio messages in one or more items. Students take an assessment on the computer and get immediate feedback once they've completed it; the website also records students' scores in a class database for us. In using resources such as Quia, we must of course, remember that they're limited largely to assessment tasks with clear-cut right and wrong responses, and they may not be suitable for students who have limited technological literacy or for some other reason find computers intimidating.

ADMINISTERING A PAPER–PENCIL ASSESSMENT

The validity of our classroom assessment instruments depends not only on how we construct them but also on how we administer them. Following are three general strategies that should increase the validity of our results when we administer a paper–pencil assessment.

- *Provide a quiet and comfortable environment.* Students are more likely to perform at their best when they have adequate lighting, reasonable work space, and minimal distractions. Such comfort factors may be especially important for students who are easily distracted, unaccustomed to formal assessments, or uninterested in exerting much effort—for instance, students who are at risk for academic failure and dropping out of school (Popham, 2006; Shriner & Spicuzza, 1995).

- *Encourage students to ask questions when tasks aren't clear.* Despite our best intentions, we may sometimes present assessment tasks that are ambiguous or misleading. Thus we should encourage students to seek clarification whenever they're uncertain about what we're asking them to do. Without such encouragement, some students—including many from ethnic minority groups—may be reluctant to ask questions during formal assessments (L. R. Cheng, 1987; C. A. Grant & Gomez, 2001; J. Li & Fischer, 2004).

- *Take reasonable steps to discourage cheating.* For a variety of reasons, the prevalence of cheating increases as students get older. Some students may be more interested in doing well on an assessment than in actually learning the subject matter; for them, performance goals predominate over mastery goals. Others may believe that teachers' or parents' expectations for their performance are unattainably high and that success is possible only if they *do* cheat. In addition, students may perceive certain assessments—especially paper–pencil tests—to be poorly constructed, arbitrarily graded, or in some other way a poor reflection of what they've learned. Often, too, peers may communicate through words or actions that cheating is quite acceptable (L. H. Anderman, Freeman, & Mueller, 2007; Cizek, 2003; Danner, 2008; E. D. Evans & Craig, 1990; Lenski, Husemann, Trautwein, & Lüdtke, 2010; Murdock, Miller, & Kohlhardt, 2004).

When students cheat, their assessment scores don't accurately reflect what they know and can do—hence, the scores have little or no validity. Furthermore, cheating can be habit forming if students discover that it enables them to get good grades with minimal effort

(Cizek, 2003). The best approach is prevention—making sure students don't cheat in the first place—through strategies such as these:

In the Weeks or Days Before the Assessment

- Focus students' attention on mastery goals rather than performance goals.
- Make success without cheating a realistic possibility.
- Use assessment instruments with obvious validity for important instructional goals.
- Create two or more instruments that are equivalent in form and content but have different answers (e.g., arrange the same set of multiple-choice questions in two different orders).
- Explain exactly what cheating is and why it's unacceptable; for instance, explain that cheating includes plagiarism, such as copying material word for word from the Internet without giving appropriate credit.
- Describe the consequence that will be imposed for cheating.

During the Assessment

- Insist that cell phones and other electronic devices be turned off and checked in at the classroom door.
- Have teacher-assigned seats during any assessments that require individual work rather than small-group work.
- Remain attentive to what students are doing throughout the assessment session, but without hovering over particular students.

Unfortunately, digital technologies now enable students to cheat in ways that weren't possible several decades ago. During quizzes, some ill-prepared students may try to communicate electronically to share answers (note the preceding recommendation about checking cell phones at the door). And when assignments require independent research in an unsupervised setting, a few students might try to pass off documents obtained on the Internet as being their own work. As teachers ourselves, we authors have found two strategies to be helpful in minimizing Internet-based plagiarism. First, we've designed assessment tasks that are so specific—and so tied to particular instructional goals—that documents found on the Internet don't meet the task requirements. Second, we've been vigilant for clues that point to questionable authorship—for example, sophisticated knowledge, vocabulary, and sentence structures that we don't typically see in our students' work.

If, despite reasonable precautions, cheating occurs, we must administer whatever consequence we've previously described. This consequence should be severe enough to discourage a student from cheating again yet not so severe that the student's motivation and chances for academic success are affected over the long run. Having the student honestly redo the task is one appropriate consequence; we might also ask the student to write a paper about the moral implications and negative repercussions of academic dishonesty (K. O'Connor, 2011). In general, we must remember that students' final grades should ultimately reflect *what they have learned*. For this reason, many assessment experts recommend that the consequence for cheating *not* be a failing final grade if a student has, in other assessments, demonstrated mastery of the subject matter (K. O'Connor, 2011; Stiggins & Chappuis, 2012).

Identify an appropriate consequence for cheating, one severe enough to discourage cheating yet not so severe that it undermines students' motivation and long-term success. Alert students to this consequence and administer it consistently when cheating occurs.

SCORING STUDENTS' RESPONSES TO A PAPER–PENCIL ASSESSMENT

As we evaluate students' performance on an assessment task, we must continue to be concerned about the four RSVP characteristics. Also, we must keep in mind that our most important goal isn't to evaluate students but rather to *help students learn*. Each of the following strategies is valuable in achieving one or both of these ends.

- *Strive for objectivity.* Some assessment tasks have clear right and wrong answers, but others (e.g., essays and lab reports) can require teacher judgments regarding quality. Whenever scoring involves considerable decision making, a scoring checklist or rubric can help us be reasonably objective in our evaluations. To be maximally useful, a rubric includes concrete descriptions of various levels of proficiency—rather than a simple rating scale of, say,

"Poor" to "Excellent"—and perhaps also includes examples of student work that illustrate each level.

- *To the extent possible, score grammar and spelling separately from the content of students' responses unless specifically assessing writing skills.* This recommendation is especially important when assessing students with limited writing skills, such as English language learners and students with disabilities (Hamp-Lyons, 1992; Scarcella, 1990; Valdés, Bunch, Snow, & Lee, 2005).

- *Before beginning to score, skim a few students' responses, looking for unanticipated responses and revising the criteria if necessary.* As a general rule, we should use the criteria we've previously told students we'll use. Occasionally, however, we may need to adjust one or more criteria—or perhaps add or subtract one or two criteria—to accommodate unexpected responses and enhance our ability to score all responses consistently, fairly, and reliably. Any adjustments should be made *before* we begin scoring, rather than midway through scoring a stack of papers.

- *Score item by item rather than paper by paper.* When scoring involves subjective decision making, we can score students' responses more reliably if we score them item by item—scoring all responses to the first question, then all responses to the second question, and so on.

- *Try not to let prior expectations for students' performance influence judgments of their actual performance.* The halo and horns effects described earlier can come into play in formal assessments as well as informal ones. The more variable and complex students' responses are on a paper–pencil assessment, the greater the difficulty we'll have in scoring responses objectively and reliably. Strategies such as shuffling papers after grading one question and using small self-stick notes to cover up students' names can help us prevent our expectations from inappropriately influencing our judgments.

- *Accompany any overall scores with specific feedback.* We must always keep in mind that all of our assessments—including our summative ones—can and should enhance students' *future* achievement. Accordingly, we should provide detailed comments that tell students what they've done well, where their weaknesses lie, and how they can improve. When students get only a single score or grade on an assessment, without an accompanying explanation of *why* their performance was evaluated as it was, they're likely to attribute the evaluation to something beyond their control—perhaps to their own innate ability or *in*ability, or perhaps to highly subjective and arbitrary teacher judgments—and to work toward performance goals rather than mastery goals (E. M. Anderman & Dawson, 2011; Stupnisky, Stewart, Daniels, & Perry, 2011).

RSVP CHARACTERISTICS OF PAPER–PENCIL ASSESSMENTS

How do paper–pencil assessments measure up in terms of the four RSVP characteristics? Let's consider each characteristic in turn.

Reliability.   When paper–pencil assessment tasks have definite right and wrong answers, we can usually evaluate students' responses with a high degree of consistency. In contrast, when we must make subjective judgments about the relative rightness or wrongness of students' responses, reliability inevitably goes down a bit.

Standardization.   As a general rule, paper–pencil instruments are easily standardized. We can give all students similar tasks and instructions, provide similar time limits and environmental conditions, and score everyone's responses in essentially the same way. Yet we must balance the need for standardization against other considerations. For example, we may need to tailor assessment tasks to the particular abilities and disabilities of students with special needs. And when assessing students' writing skills, we might sometimes let students choose a writing topic, perhaps as a way of increasing their sense of autonomy. We shouldn't go overboard in allowing student choices on summative assessments, however. For example, if we're giving two or three constructed-response questions, we will typically want to have all students answer *all* questions, rather than having them choose and respond to only one. If we give students choices in the questions they answer, they can avoid topics they haven't studied very well, and we might unintentionally score responses to one question more stringently than we score responses to another.

Standardize paper–pencil assessments as much as possible, but make appropriate accommodations for students with disabilities.

Validity.   When we ask questions that require only short, simple responses, we can sample students' knowledge about many topics within a short time period. In this sense, then, such questions can give us greater content validity. Yet such items won't always reflect our instructional goals. To assess students' ability to apply what they've learned to new situations and complex real-world problems, we may need to be satisfied with a few tasks requiring lengthy responses, even if those tasks provide a somewhat limited sample of the content domain.

Practicality.   Paper–pencil assessment is typically more practical than performance assessment; for example, we can assess all students at the same time, and in many cases we can score students' responses in a short time. Thus paper–pencil assessment should be our method of choice *if* it can yield a valid measure of what students know and can do. But when paper–pencil tasks aren't a good reflection of what students have learned, we may need to sacrifice practicality to gain the greater validity that a performance assessment provides.

USING PERFORMANCE ASSESSMENTS

A wide variety of performance tasks can be used to assess students' mastery of classroom subject matter. Here are just a few of the many possibilities:

- Playing a musical instrument
- Conversing in a foreign language
- Engaging in a debate about social issues
- Fixing a malfunctioning machine
- Role-playing a job interview
- Presenting research findings to a group of teachers, peers, and community members

Performance assessment lends itself especially well to the assessment of complex achievements, such as those that involve simultaneous use of multiple skills. It can also be quite helpful in assessing such complex cognitive processes as problem solving, creativity, and critical thinking. Furthermore, performance tasks are often more meaningful, thought provoking, and authentic—and thus often more motivating—than paper–pencil tasks (Darling-Hammond, Ancess, & Falk, 1995; DiMartino & Castaneda, 2007; R. L. Johnson et al., 2009; Khattri & Sweet, 1996; S. G. Paris & Paris, 2001).

CHOOSING APPROPRIATE PERFORMANCE TASKS

As is true for any assessment of students' achievement, our selection of appropriate performance assessment tasks must be closely aligned with our instructional goals and objectives. We must also consider whether a particular task will enable us to make reasonable generalizations about what our students know and can do in the content domain in question. Following are three distinctions that can help us zero in on the most appropriate tasks for our purposes.

Products versus processes.   Some performance assessments focus on tangible *products* that students create—perhaps a pen-and-ink drawing, scientific invention, or poster display. Others instead focus on the specific *processes and behaviors* that students exhibit—perhaps giving an oral presentation, demonstrating a forward roll, or playing an instrumental solo. Sometimes we might be interested in students' *thinking* processes. For example, if we want to determine whether students have acquired certain logical thinking abilities (e.g., conservation, separation, and control of variables), we might present tasks similar to those Jean Piaget used and, through a series of probing questions, ask students to explain their reasoning. And we can often learn a great deal about how students conceptualize and reason about scientific phenomena when we ask them to manipulate physical objects (e.g., chemicals in a chemistry lab, electrical circuit boards in a physics class), make predictions about what will happen under varying circumstances, and explain their results (Baxter, Elder, & Glaser, 1996; diSessa, 2007; Magnusson, Boyle, & Templin, 1994; Quellmalz & Hoskyn, 1997).

Individual versus group performance.   Many performance tasks require *individual* students to complete them with little or no assistance. Other tasks are sufficiently complex that they're best accomplished by a *group* of students. For instance, in high school social studies, we

Choose paper–pencil assessment over performance assessment *if* a paper–pencil instrument can yield a valid measure of students' achievement.

MyEdLab
Video Example 14.2.
This video shows a seventh-grade German teacher using computer technology for both instruction and performance assessment. Is the teacher conducting formative assessment or summative assessment?

Piaget's assessment strategy, known as the *clinical method*, is described more fully in Chapter 2.

FIGURE 14.9 Example of a group-based performance assessment task in a high school social studies class.

1. Use a map of your city or town to choose a 6- to 8-block neighborhood near your school.

2. Use both field studies and Google Earth to identify your neighborhood's types of housing, businesses, and public spaces and services (e.g., parks, schools, health care facilities). Also identify common modes of transportation, such as walking, bicycling, driving privately owned vehicles, and use of public transportation systems (e.g., buses, subways).

3. Conduct interviews with at least five residents and/or business owners in the neighborhood, asking them what things they think are "good" and "bad" about the neighborhood.

4. Using the information you have gathered in Steps 2 and 3, identify problems this neighborhood appears to have. For example, are buildings or roads in disrepair or in some other way unsafe? Do people have trouble getting from this neighborhood to other parts of your city or town? Are crime rates high?

5. As a cooperative group, write a report that both (a) describes your findings and (b) makes at least three recommendations for improving your neighborhood.

---

might assess students' mastery of certain concepts and skills by using a field-based cooperative group project like the one shown in Figure 14.9. Tasks such as these require students to collect data systematically, use the data to draw conclusions and make predictions, and, in general, think as local government officials and urban planners might think (Newmann, 1997).

One challenge in using group tasks for assessment purposes is determining how to evaluate each student's contribution. Often teachers consider individual students' behaviors and achievements—for instance, what and how much a student contributes to the group effort and how much the student has learned by the end of the project—in addition to or instead of the entire group's accomplishments (Lester, Lambdin, & Preston, 1997; Stiggins & Chappuis, 2012).

Restricted versus extended performance. Some performance tasks are quite short; that is, they involve *restricted performance.* For instance, we might ask each student in a beginning instrumental music class to play the C-major scale in brief, one-on-one sessions with us. Or we might ask students in a chemistry class to demonstrate mastery of basic safety procedures before beginning their lab experiments.

We assess *extended performance* when we want to determine what students are capable of doing over several days or weeks. Extended performance tasks might provide opportunities for students to collect data, engage in collaborative problem solving, and edit and revise their work. Many extended performance tasks embody authentic assessment: They closely resemble the situations and problems that students might eventually encounter in the outside world. Because extended performance tasks take a great deal of time, we should use them primarily for assessing achievement related to our most important and central instructional goals (Alleman & Brophy, 1997; Lester et al., 1997; Wiggins & McTighe, 2007).

PLANNING AND ADMINISTERING A PERFORMANCE ASSESSMENT

Many of the guidelines presented earlier for paper–pencil assessments are equally relevant to performance assessment. The following ones are especially important to keep in mind:

- Define tasks clearly and unambiguously.
- Identify scoring criteria in advance.
- Encourage students to ask questions when tasks aren't clear.

Three additional guidelines pertain primarily to performance assessments:

- *Consider incorporating the assessment into normal instructional activities.* We can sometimes make more efficient use of class time if we combine instruction and assessment into a single

FIGURE 14.10 In this "Birthday Graph" exercise, first-grade teacher Susan O'Byrne gained information about students' writing and graphing skills.

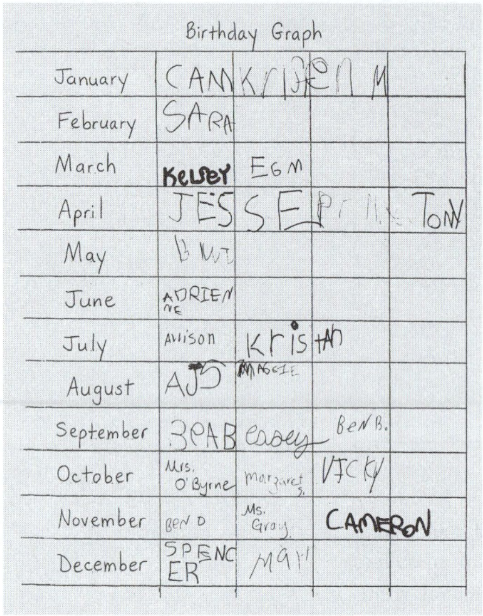

activity (Baxter et al., 1996; Boschee & Baron, 1993). For example, in a unit on bar graphs, a first-grade teacher gave each of her students a two-dimensional grid with the months of the year written in the leftmost column. She instructed students to write their own name in a box beside their birthday month and then to circulate around the room to get each classmate's signature in a box in the appropriate row. Ideally, this procedure would yield a horizontal bar graph depicting the number of children born in each month. The completed graph shown in Figure 14.10 reveals that some but not all students understood the nature of simple bar graphs. Many students (e.g., Cam, Allison, Spencer) wrote their names inside a single box on the grid. However, a few students (e.g., Kristen, Jesse, Kristah) used two boxes to write their names, perhaps because they either (a) hadn't mastered the idea that one person equals one box or (b) couldn't write small enough to fit their name inside a box and didn't know how to solve this problem. Also, one student (Meg, with a March birthday) hadn't yet learned that she must always write her name and other words in a left-to-right direction.

When we incorporate performance assessments into instructional activities, we must keep in mind that we won't be able to completely standardize conditions for all students, and we won't necessarily see students' best work. Furthermore, although it's quite appropriate to give students assistance or feedback during instruction, it may be *in*appropriate to do so during a summative assessment of what they've achieved. In some situations, then, we may want to conduct an assessment separately from instructional activities, announce it in advance, and give students guidance beforehand about how they can maximize their performance.

When using a performance assessment for summative assessment, keep the assessment separate from instruction.

◉ *Provide some structure to guide students' efforts, but not so much structure that it reduces the authenticity of the task.* Especially if we're conducting a summative assessment, we should probably structure performance assessments to some degree. For example, we can provide detailed directions about what students should accomplish, what materials and equipment they can use, and how much time they have to get the job done (Gronlund & Waugh, 2009; E. H. Hiebert, Valencia, & Afflerbach, 1994). Such structure helps to standardize the assessment and thus enables us to evaluate students' performance more reliably. A *lot* of structure can decrease the validity of a performance task, however. Imposing a great deal of structure is particularly problematic when we intend performance tasks to be authentic ones that resemble real-world situations—which often *don't* have much structure.

◉ *Plan classroom management strategies for the assessment activity.* As we conduct a performance assessment, we should put into practice two important principles of classroom management: Effective teachers are continually aware of what their students are doing (the notion of *withitness*), and they make sure that students are always productively engaged. When we can assess students' performance only individually or in small groups, we must make sure that other students are actively involved in a learning activity (L. M. Carey, 1994). For example, in an English class, when one student is giving an oral presentation, we might have the other students jot down notes about the topic being presented—facts they find interesting, ideas they disagree with, or questions they wonder about. Or in a unit on soccer, when a few students are demonstrating their ability to dribble and pass the ball as they run down the field, we might have other students work in pairs to practice their footwork.

Chapter 13 presents these and other guidelines for effective classroom management.

SCORING STUDENTS' RESPONSES IN A PERFORMANCE ASSESSMENT

Occasionally responses to performance assessment tasks are objectively scorable; for instance, we can easily time students' performance in a 100-meter dash and count students' errors on a typing test. But more often we'll find ourselves making subjective decisions as we assess students' performance. There are no clear-cut right or wrong responses when students give oral reports, create clay sculptures, or engage in heated debates on controversial issues. Consequently, if we aren't careful, our judgments may be unduly influenced by our expectations for each student.

Especially for summative performance assessments, we should create some sort of structured recording form that can guide us during the assessment process and later serve as a written record of what we've observed. The next four recommendations can help us design recording forms that should ensure reasonable validity and reliability in a performance assessment.

🍎 *When using several criteria to evaluate students' performance, describe each criterion in concrete terms, and develop a checklist or rubric to guide scoring.* Some performance tasks lend themselves well to checklists, whereas others are more effectively evaluated with rubrics. Figure 14.11 shows three simple examples. The two on the left, one for using varnish and the other for general work habits, are obviously checklists. The one on the right includes two simple rubric-like **rating scales** for evaluating the quality of students' performance in a science lab—that is, it assigns numbers to various points on two continua of quality. Both of these approaches can enhance the reliability of scoring and have instructional benefits as well: They identify specific areas of difficulty and thereby give students feedback about how performance can be improved.

🍎 *Decide whether analytic or holistic scoring better serves your purpose(s) in conducting the assessment.* When we need detailed information about students' performance, we may want to use **analytic scoring**, in which we evaluate various aspects of the performance separately, perhaps with a checklist or several rating scales. In contrast, when we need to summarize students' performance in a single score, we should probably use **holistic scoring**, in which we consider all relevant criteria but make a single judgment; for instance, we might have a single rating scale of "1" to "5" or "Poor" to "Proficient," along with concrete descriptions of what a student's performance along each point of the continuum looks like. Analytic scoring tends to be more useful in conducting formative assessments and promoting students' learning, whereas holistic scoring is often used in final, summative assessments.

FIGURE 14.11 Examples of task-specific scoring guides.

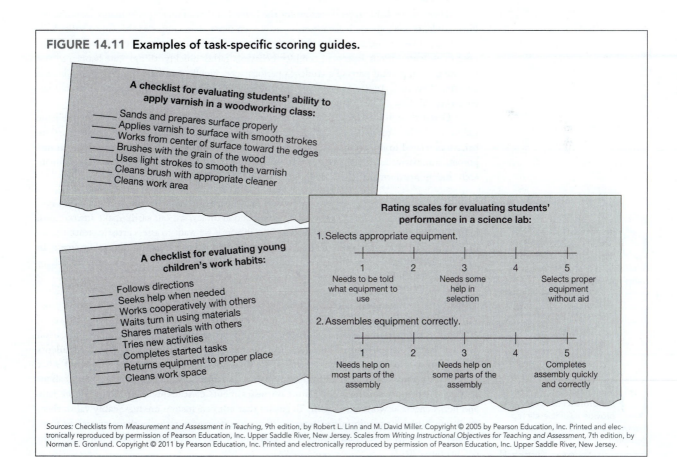

Sources: Checklists from *Measurement and Assessment in Teaching*, 9th edition, by Robert L. Linn and M. David Miller. Copyright © 2005 by Pearson Education, Inc. Printed and electronically reproduced by permission of Pearson Education, Inc. Upper Saddle River, New Jersey. Scales from *Writing Instructional Objectives for Teaching and Assessment*, 7th edition, by Norman E. Gronlund. Copyright © 2011 by Pearson Education, Inc. Printed and electronically reproduced by permission of Pearson Education, Inc. Upper Saddle River, New Jersey.

🍎 *Limit scoring criteria to the most important aspects of the desired response.* Scoring criteria should focus on aspects of the performance that are critical indicators of proficiency and most relevant to instructional goals and objectives (M. D. Miller et al., 2009; Wiggins, 1992). The criteria should also be relatively few in number (perhaps five or six) so that we can keep track of them as we observe each student's performance (Gronlund & Waugh, 2009; Popham, 2014). Remember the limited capacity of working memory: Human beings—including teachers!—can think about only so many things at a single time.

🍎 *Make note of any significant aspects of a student's performance that the scoring guide doesn't address.* Whenever we break down performance on a complex task into discrete behaviors, we can lose valuable information along the way (Delandshere & Petrosky, 1998). As we use scoring guides to assess student's achievement levels, then, we may occasionally want to jot down other noteworthy characteristics of students' performance. This aspect of our scoring process will be neither standardized nor reliable, of course, but it can sometimes be useful in identifying students' unique strengths and needs and can therefore assist us in future instructional planning.

RSVP CHARACTERISTICS OF PERFORMANCE ASSESSMENTS

Compared with traditional paper–pencil assessment, many performance assessment techniques are relative newcomers on the educational scene, and educators continue to wrestle with concerns related to reliability, standardization, validity, and practicality.

Reliability. Researchers have reported varying degrees of reliability in performance assessments. Assessment results are often inconsistent over time, and different teachers may rate the same performance differently (Crehan, 2001; P. J. Hay, 2008; Haywood & Lidz, 2007; R. L. Johnson et al., 2009).

There are probably several reasons for the low reliability of many performance assessments. First, students don't always behave consistently; even in a task as simple as shooting a basketball, a student is likely to make a basket on some occasions but not on others. Second, we sometimes need to evaluate various aspects of complex behaviors rather quickly; things may happen so fast that we miss important parts of a student's performance. Finally, one form of reliability—*internal consistency* (see Table 14.2)—is largely irrelevant when we're assessing complex, multifaceted behaviors (L. M. Carey, 1994; Parkes, 2001; Wiley & Haertel, 1996).

Given these limitations, a single performance assessment may very well *not* be a reliable indicator of what students have achieved. Accordingly, we should ask students to demonstrate behaviors related to important instructional goals on more than one occasion. And when an important summative assessment is involved, we should ideally have more than one rater evaluate each student's performance (R. L. Johnson et al., 2009; M. D. Miller et al., 2009).

Standardization. Some performance assessments are easily standardized, but others are not. If we want to assess students' keyboarding speed and accuracy, we can easily make instructions, tasks, and time limits the same for everyone. In contrast, if we want to assess artistic creativity, we may want to let students choose the materials they use and the particular products they create. In such nonstandardized situations, it's especially important to use multiple assessments and look for consistency in students' performance across several occasions.

🍎 Remember that a single performance assessment may not be a standardized or reliable indicator of what students have achieved.

Validity. As previously noted, performance assessment tasks can sometimes provide more valid indicators of what students have accomplished relative to instructional goals. However, students' responses to a *single* performance assessment task often are *not* a good indication of their overall achievement. Content validity is the issue here: If we have time for students to perform only one or two complex tasks, we may not get a representative sample of what they've learned and can do. In addition, any biases that affect our judgment (e.g., beliefs about particular students' abilities) can distort our assessments of students' performance—the halo and horns effects at work once again. To ensure that our conclusions are reasonably valid, then, we'll typically want to administer several different performance tasks, perhaps on two or more different occasions (S. Klassen, 2006; R. L. Linn, 1994; Messick, 1994a; Parkes, 2001; Stiggins & Chappuis, 2012).

🍎 Remember that a single performance task may not provide a sufficiently representative sample of the content domain.

Practicality.   Unfortunately, performance assessments are often less practical than more traditional paper–pencil assessments. Administering an assessment can be quite time consuming, especially when we must observe students one at a time or when they must perform relatively complex (perhaps authentic) tasks. In addition, we may need considerable equipment to conduct the assessment—perhaps enough for every student to have a personal set. Clearly, then, we must carefully consider whether the benefits of a performance assessment outweigh its impracticality. Ultimately the best strategy overall may be to use *both* paper–pencil and performance assessments when drawing conclusions about students' achievement.

> Think about how you might use a combination of paper–pencil and performance tasks to assess what students know and can do.

Table 14.3 presents a summary of our RSVP analyses of informal assessment, formal paper–pencil assessment, and formal performance assessment.

ADDITIONAL CONSIDERATIONS IN FORMAL ASSESSMENT

In our discussion of formal assessment so far, our focus has been on the design, administration, and scoring of particular paper–pencil and performance tasks. We now step back and look at more general issues related to formal assessment.

TEACHING TESTWISENESS

If you did well on the califractions quiz earlier in the chapter, you have some degree of **testwiseness**: You use test-taking strategies that enhance your test performance. Testwiseness includes strategies such as these:

- *Pinning down the task(s) to be performed*—for example, carefully reading the directions and every question
- *Using time efficiently*—for example, allocating enough time for each task and saving difficult items for last

COMPARE/CONTRAST

TABLE 14.3 • Evaluating RSVP Characteristics of Different Kinds of Summative Assessment				
KIND OF ASSESSMENT	**RELIABILITY**	**STANDARDIZATION**	**VALIDITY**	**PRACTICALITY**
Informal assessment	A single, brief assessment is not a reliable indicator of achievement. We must look for consistency in a student's performance across time and in different contexts.	Informal observations are rarely, if ever, standardized. Thus, we should not compare one student to another on the basis of informal assessment alone.	Students' public behaviors in the classroom aren't always valid indicators of their achievement (e.g., some students may try to hide high achievement from their peers; others may come from cultures that encourage listening more than talking).	Informal assessment is definitely practical: It's flexible and can occur spontaneously during instruction.
Formal paper–pencil assessment	Objectively scorable items are highly reliable. We can enhance the reliability of subjectively scorable items by specifying scoring criteria in concrete terms.	In most instances, paper–pencil instruments are easily standardized for all students. Giving students choices (e.g., regarding topics to write about or questions to answer) may increase motivation but reduces standardization.	Numerous questions requiring short, simple responses can provide a more representative sample of the content domain. But tasks requiring lengthy responses may sometimes more closely match instructional goals.	Paper–pencil assessment is usually practical: All students can be assessed at once, and no special materials are required.
Formal performance assessment	Performance assessment tasks are often difficult to score reliably. We can enhance reliability by specifying scoring criteria in concrete terms (e.g., with a checklist or rubric).	Some performance assessment tasks are easily standardized, whereas others are not.	Performance tasks may sometimes be more consistent with instructional goals than are paper–pencil tasks. However, a single performance task may not provide a representative sample of the content domain; several tasks may be necessary to ensure adequate content validity.	Performance assessment is typically less practical than other approaches: It may involve special materials, and it can take a fair amount of class time, especially if students must be assessed one by one.

- *Deductive reasoning*—for example, eliminating two alternatives that say the same thing and using information from one question to answer another
- *Avoiding sloppy errors*—for example, checking answers a second time and erasing stray pencil marks on a digitally scanned answer sheet
- *Guessing*—for example, eliminating obviously wrong alternatives and then guessing one of the others, or guessing randomly if time runs out and there's no penalty for guessing (Hong, Sas, & Sas, 2006; Millman, Bishop, & Ebel, 1965; Petersen, Sudweeks, & Baird, 1990; L. Shepard et al., 2005)

Give students practice in responding to unfamiliar test-item formats (e.g., multiple choice). Teach test-taking strategies, but not at the expense of shortchanging instruction in the knowledge and skills being assessed.

Certain aspects of testwiseness, such as guessing strategically and erasing stray pencil marks, are applicable primarily to paper–pencil recognition items (e.g., multiple-choice questions). But others, such as clarifying assigned tasks and carefully managing time, can make a difference in virtually any kind of formal classroom assessment.

As teachers, we must remember that many students—especially younger ones and those whose prior schooling has been in a different culture—may need explicit instruction in common item formats and useful test-taking strategies. At the same time, we should keep in mind that testwiseness typically has only a small impact on students' assessment scores. Furthermore, test-taking skills and student achievement are positively correlated: Students with many test-taking strategies tend to be higher achievers than students with few strategies. In other words, very few students get low test scores *only* because they're poor test takers. In most cases, then, we can best serve students by teaching them the knowledge and skills a given assessment is designed to measure, rather than spending an inordinate amount of time teaching them how to take tests (J. R. Frederiksen & Collins, 1989; Geiger, 1997; Scruggs & Lifson, 1985; L. Shepard et al., 2005).

Speed Tests!
Speed Tests make everyone a nervous reck before I pasted Speed Test I I would barle eat and had troble sleeping. Nows this very day I find out I pasted, Speed Test II and mayhe I pasted Speed Test III! Oh God please, oh please let me passe Speed Test II Effen if I never passi Speed Test 15 teen I want you to know I tried my hardest.

In this reflection on "Speed Tests"—those in which many questions must be answered in a very short time—8-year-old Connie describes how overwhelming test anxiety can be.

KEEPING TEST ANXIETY IN CHECK

A small amount of anxiety about tests and other important assessments can enhance performance. But some students become extremely anxious in assessment situations—they have test anxiety—to the point that their scores significantly underestimate what they've learned. Such students appear to be concerned primarily about the *evaluative* aspect of assessments, worrying that someone will find them to be "stupid" or in other ways inadequate. Test anxiety interferes not only with retrieval and performance at the time of an assessment but also with encoding and storage when learners are preparing for the assessment. Thus, highly test-anxious students don't just *test* poorly; they also *learn* poorly (Cassady, 2010b; Zeidner & Matthews, 2005).

Excessive, debilitating test anxiety is especially common in students from ethnic minority groups and in students with disabilities (R. Carter, Williams, & Silverman, 2008; Putwain, 2007; Whitaker Sena, Lowe, & Lee, 2007). On average, students with the highest test anxiety are those who've performed poorly in school in the past. One important strategy for helping students overcome excessive test anxiety, then, is to help them acquire the skills they need to master course material in the first place, including good study strategies and self-regulation skills. In addition, we must present classroom assessments in ways that motivate students to do their best without succumbing to debilitating anxiety levels. One middle school student, Jamaal, explained how his math teacher helped to keep his anxiety about assessments in check:

Minimize debilitating test anxiety by helping students master academic subject matter.

> Ms. Wheeler doesn't call it a test. She says, "It's a quiz, it's a worksheet, it's whatever you want it to be. Just make sure you do your best. It's a puzzle, it's a game. Just do your best." And [on] most tests she doesn't even put the word "Test" on it, or she doesn't tell us it's a test. It takes the pressure off so you can think about what you're doing more. (Usher, 2009, p. 303)

Table 14.4 presents some *dos* and *don'ts* for keeping students' test anxiety at productive levels.

ENCOURAGING RISK TAKING

Only when students feel free to take risks and make mistakes will they tackle the challenging tasks that can maximize their learning and cognitive development. We encourage risk

COMPARE/CONTRAST

TABLE 14.4 • Keeping Students' Anxiety at a Facilitative Level During Classroom Assessments	
WHAT TO DO	**WHAT *NOT* TO DO**
Point out the value of the assessment as a feedback mechanism to improve learning.	Don't stress the fact that students' competence is being evaluated.
Administer a practice assessment or pretest that gives students an idea of what the final assessment instrument will be like.	Don't keep the nature of the assessment a secret until the day it is administered.
Encourage students to do their best but not necessarily to expect perfection; for instance, say, "We're here to learn, and you can't do that without making mistakes."	Don't remind students that failing might have dire consequences.
Provide or allow the use of memory aids (e.g., a list of formulas or a single note card containing key facts) when instructional goals don't require students to commit information to memory.	Don't insist that students commit even trivial facts to memory.
Eliminate time limits unless speed is an important part of the skill being measured.	Don't give more questions or tasks than students can possibly respond to in the time allotted.
Continually survey the room, and be available to answer students' questions.	Don't hover over students, watching them closely as they complete the assessment.
Use unannounced assessments (i.e., pop quizzes) only for formative assessments (e.g., to determine an appropriate starting points for instruction).	Don't give occasional pop quizzes to motivate students to study regularly and to punish those who study very little, if at all.
Use the results of several assessments to make decisions (e.g., to assign grades).	Don't evaluate students on the basis of a single assessment.

Sources: Agarwal, D'Antonio, Roediger, McDermott, & McDaniel, 2014; Brophy, 1986, 2004 ("We're here to learn..." suggestion on p. 274); Cassady, 2010b; Cizek, 2003; Gaudry & Bradshaw, 1971; K. T. Hill, 1984; K. T. Hill & Wigfield, 1984; Sieber, Kameya, & Paulson, 1970; Spaulding, 1992; Stipek, 1993.

taking—and lower students' anxiety levels as well—when our assessment strategies give students some leeway to be wrong without penalty (Clifford, 1990; McMillan, 2010). Certainly no single assessment should ever be "sudden death" for a student who earns a low score. Following are three recommended strategies for encouraging risk taking during classroom assessments.

Assess students' achievement frequently rather than infrequently. Regular assessments are, of course, a key means by which we and our students can track students' progress and address areas of weakness needing attention. But frequent assessments—rather than infrequent ones—have several additional benefits. First, students are less likely to experience debilitating anxiety if they complete a number of assessments that each contribute only a small amount to their final grades. Second, frequent assessments motivate students—especially those with lower achievement levels—to study regularly. Third, when students no longer feel pressure to perform well on every quiz and assignment, they're less likely to cheat in order to get good grades. Finally and most importantly, students who are assessed frequently achieve at higher levels than students who are assessed infrequently (Crooks, 1988; E. D. Evans & Craig, 1990; J. A. Glover, 1989; McDaniel et al., 2011; Roediger & Karpicke, 2006; Rohrer & Pashler, 2010; Sax, 2010).

Provide opportunities to correct errors. Especially when an assessment includes most or all of the content domain in question, students can often increase their understanding of classroom subject matter when they're asked to correct errors they've previously made on an assessment task. For example, in an approach known as *mastery reform,* some math teachers have students correct their errors as follows:

1. *Identification of the error.* Students describe in a short paragraph exactly what they don't yet know how to do.

2. *Statement of the process.* Using words rather than mathematical symbols, students explain the steps involved in the procedure they're trying to master.

3. *Practice.* Students demonstrate their mastery of the procedure with three new problems similar to the problem(s) they previously solved incorrectly.

4. *Statement of mastery*. Students state in a sentence or two that they've now mastered the procedure.

By completing these steps, students can replace a grade on a previous assessment with the new, higher one. A high school math teacher once told one of us authors that this approach also had a more general, long-term benefit for his students: Many of them eventually incorporated the four steps into their regular, internalized learning strategies.

● *When appropriate, allow students to retake assessments.* Some students will invariably need more time than others to master a topic and may therefore need to be assessed on the same material more than once. In addition, students are less likely to have debilitating test anxiety if they know they can have another try if they need one. Retakes are obviously quite appropriate for most formative assessments, but they have certain disadvantages for summative assessments. When students know they can retake a summative assessment if they get a low score the first time, they may prepare less well than they would otherwise. Furthermore, if they're allowed to retake the *same* assessment a second time, they may work on the specific things the assessment covers without studying equally important but nonassessed material. (Remember, most assessment tasks can be only a small sample of the content in question.)

If we truly want students to master course material but also to take risks in their learning and classroom performance, we may want to make retakes a regular practice. To encourage students to take the first assessment seriously and to discourage them from focusing only on the content of specific test items as they study for the retake, we might construct two assessment instruments for the same content domain, using one as the initial assessment and the other for retakes (this is what one of us authors has routinely done in her undergraduate classes). If this strategy is too time consuming to be practical, we might allow students to redo the same assessment a second time and average the two scores earned.

EVALUATING AN ASSESSMENT AFTER THE FACT: ITEM ANALYSIS

Not only must we assess students' learning and achievement but we must also *assess our assessments*. In the process of scoring students' performance on an assessment, we may discover that some items or tasks simply don't provide the information we had hoped they would. For example, it may become obvious that one item isn't measuring the knowledge or skill we had in mind (a validity problem) and that another is hard to score consistently (a reliability problem that indirectly affects validity as well).

We can't always predict which items are going to be good ones and which are not. For this reason, assessment experts frequently recommend conducting an item analysis after an assessment has been administered and scored. Such an analysis typically involves an examination of both the difficulty level and the discriminative power of each item.

Item difficulty. The item difficulty (p) of an assessment item is simply the proportion of students who have responded correctly relative to the total number of students who took the assessment:

$$p = \frac{\text{Number of students getting the item correct}}{\text{Number of students taking the assessment}}$$

This formula yields a number between 0.0 and 1.0. A high *p* value indicates that the item was relatively easy for students; for example, a *p* of .85 means that 85% of the students answered it correctly. A low *p* value indicates that the item was difficult; for example, a *p* of .10 means that only 10% gave a correct response.

In criterion-referenced assessments, *p* values help us determine the degree to which students are accomplishing instructional goals and objectives. If most students have responded to an item correctly and we can rule out guessing and other factors that may have contributed to the high success rate, we can conclude that students have mastered the knowledge or skill the item represents. A low *p* value tells us either that students haven't learned what we're assessing or that the item doesn't accurately reflect what students *have* learned.

For norm-referenced assessments, *p* values are useful in a very different way: They help us determine which items have a difficulty level that is best for comparing the performance of individual students. In this situation, ideal *p* values are somewhere between .30 and .70, indicating that the items are difficult enough that some but not all students get them wrong. When, instead,

Conduct an item analysis as one source of evidence for the validity and reliability of an assessment instrument.

almost all students answer an item in the same way—either correctly (a very high p) or incorrectly (a very low p)—we get little or no information about how students differ from one another.

Item discrimination.   Imagine that you're scoring a 30-item multiple-choice test you've just given your class. You notice that the best students—those who've done well on most of the test—have answered Question 13 incorrectly. You also notice that several students who got very low test scores got Question 13 correct. This doesn't make sense: You'd expect the students who do well on any one item to be the same ones who perform well on the test overall. When the "wrong" students are getting an item correct—that is, when the item inaccurately identifies informed versus uninformed students—we have a problem with item discrimination (*D*).

To determine item discrimination, we use the approach just described. That is, we identify two groups of students, those who've gotten the highest overall scores and those who've gotten the lowest overall scores, putting about 20% to 30% of the total number of students in each group. We then compare the proportions of students in the two groups getting each item correct using this formula:

$$D = \frac{\text{Number of high-scoring students getting item correct}}{\text{Total number of high-scoring students}} - \frac{\text{Number of low-scoring students getting item correct}}{\text{Total number of low-scoring students}}$$

The D formula yields a number ranging from -1.0 to $+1.0$. Positive D values tell us that more high-scoring students than low-scoring students have done well on an item; in other words, the item discriminates between knowledgeable and unknowledgeable students, which is exactly what we want. In contrast, negative D values reflect circumstances similar to the situation with our hypothetical Question 13: Low-scoring students answered the item correctly, but high-scoring students didn't. A negative D is often a sign that something's wrong with the item; perhaps it misleads knowledgeable students to choose what was intended to be an incorrect response, or perhaps we've marked an incorrect answer on our scoring guide.

Let's return to an assumption we made in the Question 13 situation: The students who do well on any single item should be the same ones who perform well overall. Here we're talking about *internal consistency reliability*, the extent to which different parts of an assessment instrument all measure more or less the same thing. However, when the items or tasks on an assessment instrument are all designed to measure very *different* things—as is often true for performance assessments—D values are less helpful in evaluating an item's effectiveness.

Many teachers save good assessment items for use on future occasions, perhaps putting them in appropriately labeled documents or folders on their computers. As teachers accumulate items over the years, they eventually have a large enough collection that they don't have to use any one item very often.

> Follow up on negative *D* values; for example, disregard performance on items that high-achieving students have consistently responded to incorrectly and then recalculate students' overall scores.

> Save good test questions and assessment tasks for use in future years; take precautions to prevent students from getting unauthorized access to them.

MyEdLab **Self-Check 14.4**

MyEdLab **Application Exercise 14.4.** In this exercise, you can apply what you've learned in this chapter to evaluate various classroom assessment practices.

MyEdLab **Application Exercise 14.5.** In this exercise, you can identify possible developmental and motivational benefits of using checklists during performance activities.

Taking Student Diversity into Account in Classroom Assessments

As we've seen, standardization of assessment instruments and procedures is important for fairness, reliability, and (indirectly) validity in our assessment results. Yet standardization has a downside: It limits our ability to accommodate students' diverse backgrounds and needs, capitalize on their individual strengths, and help them compensate for areas of weakness.

Standardization in classroom assessment practices is essential if, for some reason, we need to compare a student's performance to that of others. But in many other situations—for example, when we're trying to ascertain an appropriate starting point for instruction or specific weaknesses that each student needs to address—standardization is less critical. In some instances, in fact, we may find that the best way of assessing one student's learning is a relatively *ineffective* way of assessing another's.

ACCOMMODATING GROUP DIFFERENCES

Let's remind ourselves of a few commonly observed differences, also remembering that these are only *average* differences:

You can find more information about these differences in Chapter 2 and Chapter 4.

- Boys tend to talk more in class than girls do.
- Girls tend to work harder on classroom assignments than boys do.
- Many students who have grown up in mainstream Western culture place high value on individual achievement, but those from some other cultures may be more accustomed to working as a group than to working alone.
- Many students brought up in mainstream Western culture are accustomed to showing others what they know and can do, but students from some cultural backgrounds may be more accustomed to practicing skills in private until they've achieved mastery.
- English language learners need considerable time—perhaps 5 to 7 years—to master the levels of English vocabulary and syntax necessary to fully understand and learn from English-based instruction.
- Some students from low-income families lack adequate nutrition and health care to perform their best at school.
- Students at risk for academic failure may perceive academic subject matter to have little relevance to their own lives.

Use assessment tasks that are sufficiently diverse in nature to give all students numerous opportunities to show what they have learned.

Chapter 15 provides more information about assessment bias.

All of these factors may, of course, affect students' ability to learn and achieve in the classroom. But they may also affect how students perform on our informal and formal assessments *independently* of their learning and achievement. This is just one of the many reasons that we should consider multiple assessments—as well as several different kinds of assessments—to assign grades and make other important decisions. In addition, we should scrutinize our assessment tasks to be sure that they don't unfairly put some students at a disadvantage because of diversity in their life experiences—a disadvantage known as *cultural bias* or, more generally, *assessment bias*. Ultimately our assessment practices must be fair and equitable for students of all groups and backgrounds.

ACCOMMODATING STUDENTS WITH SPECIAL NEEDS

Chapter 5 provides details about IDEA; it also identifies specific categories of special needs that fall within the five general categories listed in Table 14.5.

In the United States, the Individuals with Disabilities Education Act (IDEA) mandates that schools make appropriate accommodations for students with physical, mental, social, or emotional disabilities. This mandate applies not only to instruction but to assessment practices as well. Consequently, we may sometimes have to disregard our concern about standardization so that we can gain more *valid* assessments of what students with certain disabilities know and can do. For example, we may have to develop student-specific summative assessments for students whose individualized education programs (IEPs) identify instructional goals different from those of their peers. Suggestions for additional accommodations for students with special needs are presented in Table 14.5.

MyEdLab **Self-Check 14.5**

STUDENTS IN INCLUSIVE SETTINGS

TABLE 14.5 • Using Classroom Assessments with Students Who Have Special Educational Needs

CATEGORY	CHARACTERISTICS YOU MIGHT OBSERVE	SUGGESTED STRATEGIES
Students with specific cognitive or academic difficulties	• Poor listening, reading, and/or writing skills • Inconsistent performance due to off-task behaviors (for some students with learning disabilities or attention-deficit hyperactivity disorder) • Difficulty processing specific kinds of information • Higher-than-average test anxiety	• Make paper–pencil instruments easy to read and respond to; for instance, let students use word processing software to self-check written essays, space test items far apart, and have students respond to multiple-choice items directly on their test papers rather than on separate answer sheets. • If appropriate for the disability, provide extra time for students to complete assessment tasks and/or minimize reliance on literacy skills (e.g., read aloud paper–pencil test items and have students respond orally). • When students have a limited attention span, break lengthy assignments into several shorter tasks. • Provide extra scaffolding to guide students' efforts; give explicit directions about what students are expected to do. • Be sure students are motivated to do their best but not overly anxious. • Score responses separately for content and quality of writing. • Look at students' errors for clues about specific cognitive processing difficulties. • Use informal assessments to confirm or disconfirm the results of formal assessments.
Students with social or behavioral problems	• Inconsistent performance on classroom assessments due to off-task behaviors or lack of motivation (for some students)	• Make modifications in assessment procedures as necessary (see the strategies just presented for students with specific cognitive or academic difficulties). • Use informal assessments (e.g., observations of behavior) to confirm or disconfirm the results of formal assessments.
Students with general delays in cognitive and social functioning	• Slow learning and cognitive processing • Limited, if any, reading skills • Poor listening skills	• Be very explicit and concrete about what you're asking students to do. • Tailor any written assessment items to students' reading levels. • Use performance assessments that require little reading or writing. • Allow considerable time for students to complete assigned tasks.
Students with physical or sensory challenges	• Mobility problems (for some students with physical challenges) • Tendency to tire easily (for some students with physical challenges) • Less developed language abilities (for some students with hearing loss)	• Use written rather than oral assessments (for students with hearing loss). • Minimize reliance on visual materials (for students with visual impairments). • Use appropriate technology to facilitate students' performance. • Provide extra time for students to complete assessments. • Limit assessments to short time periods, and give frequent breaks. • Use simple language if students have language difficulties.
Students with advanced cognitive development	• Greater ability to perform exceptionally complex tasks • Unusual, sometimes creative responses to assessment tasks • Tendency to hide giftedness to avoid possible ridicule by peers (in some students)	• Use performance assessments to assess complex activities. • Establish scoring criteria that allow for unusual and creative responses. • Provide opportunities for students to demonstrate their achievements privately, especially if they're concerned that peers might disapprove of their exceptional ability level.

Sources: Barkley, 2006; Beirne-Smith, Patton, & Kim, 2006; D. Y. Ford & Harris, 1992; N. Gregg, 2009; R. L. Johnson et al., 2009; B. J. Lovett, 2010; Mercer & Pullen, 2005; D. P. Morgan & Jenson, 1988; Piirto, 1999; Sireci, Scarpati, & Li, 2005; Stein & Krishnan, 2007; Turnbull, Turnbull, & Wehmeyer, 2010; Whitaker Sena et al., 2007.

14   What Have You Learned?

Ongoing assessment of students' progress is—and *must* be—a critical part of our role as teachers. We now return to the chapter's learning outcomes as a way of revisiting key ideas about classroom assessment.

■ **14.1: Describe the various forms that classroom assessment can take and the various purposes it can serve for teachers**

and students. In general, *assessment* is a process of observing a sample of students' behavior and drawing inferences about their knowledge and abilities. It can take any number of forms: It might be formative or summative, informal or formal, paper–pencil or performance based, traditional or authentic, criterion-referenced or norm-referenced. Occasionally it takes the form of a standardized test, but far more often it consists of a teacher-developed instrument or procedure.

Classroom assessments serve a variety of interrelated purposes—perhaps to guide instructional decision making, determine students' achievement levels at the end of instruction, evaluate the quality of instruction, diagnose learning and performance problems, or promote students' short- and long-term learning and development. Regardless of our primary purposes in assessing students' knowledge and skills, we must remember that the nature of our assessment instruments will give students messages about what their learning priorities should be and how they should think about and study classroom subject matter. Not only is assessment closely interconnected with instruction, but in a very real sense it *is* instruction.

■ **14.2: Explain how you might enhance students' learning through frequent formative assessments and feedback.** Formative assessments are those that occur before or during instruction in order to (a) guide instructional decision making and (b) facilitate students' progress toward instructional goals. To be useful, formative assessments must closely reflect the subject matter to be mastered (i.e., they should have content validity) and yield information about what students currently can and can't do. One key strategy is to construct a rubric that identifies the characteristics and components of desired performance; such a rubric provides clear targets toward which to shoot. To most effectively promote students' learning and achievement over the long run, we should regularly include students in the assessment process—for example, by soliciting their ideas about evaluation criteria and by having them constructively critique their own and others' work. We should also consider how various digital technologies might facilitate our own and students' efforts to assess students' progress through the curriculum.

■ **14.3: Define and apply four important RSVP characteristics of good assessments: reliability, standardization, validity, and practicality.** As we identify our classroom assessment tasks and procedures, we should keep four characteristics in mind, especially when conducting summative assessments. First, a good assessment is *reliable*, yielding consistent results regardless of the circumstances in which we administer and score it. Second, it is *standardized*, in the sense that it has similar content and is administered and scored in a similar manner for everyone (excepting students who have certain extenuating circumstances). Third, it is *valid*, in that it's an accurate reflection of the knowledge or skills we're trying to assess. And fourth, it is *practical*, staying within reasonable costs and time constraints. No matter how well planned and executed, however, any single assessment almost invariably has limitations with respect to one or more of these characteristics. According, we must think of our classroom assessments as useful tools—but *imperfect* ones at best—that can guide us in our classroom decision making.

■ **14.4: Explain how you might conduct informal assessments, paper–pencil assessments, and performance assessments to assess students' learning and performance with reasonable reliability and validity.** We can sometimes assess achievement informally, perhaps by simply observing what students do and say in ongoing school activities. Informal assessment is flexible and requires little or no advance planning, but unfortunately it doesn't give us a representative sample of what students have learned, and our judgments will inevitably be biased by our existing beliefs about various students.

Whenever we must draw firm conclusions about what students have and haven't achieved—for example, when we assign final grades—we should base our conclusions largely on formal assessments that are reasonably valid and reliable. Especially important in this context is *content validity*: Our assessment tasks should provide a representative sample of what students have accomplished relative to instructional goals and objectives.

Paper–pencil assessment tasks take various forms; for instance, they might be multiple-choice questions, word problems, essays, or lab reports. Different formats are suitable for assessing different instructional goals, and each format has advantages and disadvantages. Performance assessment tasks are often more appropriate for assessing complex achievements that require the integration of many skills, and accomplishment of some instructional goals can be assessed *only* through direct observation of what students can physically do. Paper–pencil tasks and performance tasks alike yield more valid and reliable results when students have a clear understanding of what they're supposed to do and when their responses are evaluated as objectively as possible.

Several additional strategies can, in one way or another, impact the quality of classroom assessments. First, we must be sure that students have some test-taking know-how, or test-wiseness; for instance, they should have some sense of how to manage their time in any formal assessment task. Second, we should keep students' anxiety at productive, facilitative levels—for example, by emphasizing that learning is an ongoing process and inevitably involves making mistakes along the way. Third, our assessment practices must allow leeway for students to take the risks so essential for the pursuit of challenging topics and activities. Finally, after we've developed and used a particular assessment, an item analysis can help us determine whether the assessment results are reasonably representative of what students have learned.

■ **14.5: Describe individual and group differences that have implications for classroom assessment practices.** Although standardization of assessment instruments and procedures is important for fairness and reliability, it has a downside: It limits our ability to accommodate students' diverse characteristics, backgrounds, and abilities. Standardization is essential when we need to compare students' performances to one another in a norm-referenced manner. It's less important when we're trying to ascertain appropriate starting points for instruction or specific student weaknesses that need to be addressed, and it can sometimes be counterproductive when we're working with students who have disabilities.

Of the four RSVP characteristics, validity is the most critical one, and we can typically get a better handle on what students know and can do when we flexibly and open-mindedly assess their knowledge and skills in multiple ways.

Practice for Your Licensure Exam

Two Science Quizzes

Knowing that frequent paper–pencil quizzes will encourage students to study and review class material regularly, Mr. Bloskas tells his middle school science students that they'll have a quiz every Friday. As a first-year teacher, he has had little experience developing test questions; thus, he decides to use the questions in the test-item manual that accompanies the class textbook. The night before the first quiz, Mr. Bloskas selects 30 multiple-choice and true–false items from the manual, making sure that they cover the specific topics he has addressed in class.

Mr. Bloskas's students complain that the questions are "picky." As he looks carefully at his quiz, he realizes that they are right: The quiz measures nothing more than memorization of trivial details. So when he prepares the second quiz, he casts the test-item manual aside and writes two essay questions that ask students to apply principles they've studied to new, real-life situations.

The following Friday, students complain even more loudly about the second quiz: "This is too hard!" "We never studied this stuff!" "I liked the first quiz better!" Later, as Mr. Bloskas scores the essays, he's appalled to discover how poorly his students have performed.

1. **Constructed-response question:**

    When identifying classroom assessment tasks, teachers must be sure that the tasks have validity, especially *content validity*.

A. Compare Mr. Bloskas's two quizzes with respect to their content validity.

B. Describe a reasonable approach Mr. Bloskas might use to create quizzes that have good content validity for his classes.

2. **Multiple-choice question:**

    The following alternatives present four possible explanations for the students' negative reactions to the second quiz. Drawing on contemporary theories of learning and motivation, choose the most likely explanation.

    a. Multiple-choice and true–false items are more likely than essay questions to enhance students' sense of autonomy.

    b. Learners are most likely to behave and study in ways that they expect will lead to reinforcement.

    c. Multiple-choice and true–false items are apt to foster mastery goals, whereas essay questions are more likely to foster performance goals.

    d. Multiple-choice and true–false items almost always assess information in working memory, whereas essay questions usually assess information in long-term memory.

    MyEdLab **Licensure Exam 14.1**

PRAXIS Go to Appendix C, "Matching Book Content and Ebook Activities to the Praxis Principles of Learning and Teaching Tests," to discover sections of this chapter that may be especially applicable to the Praxis tests.

Blend Images/Alamy

15 Summarizing Students' Achievements and Abilities

CASE STUDY: B IN HISTORY

Ellie is the top student in Ms. Davidson's sixth-grade class. She is bright, motivated, and conscientious about completing her classwork, and she has consistently earned straight As on report cards in previous years.

At the end of the school day one Friday, Ms. Davidson tells her class, "As you all know, our first-quarter grading period ended last week. Today I have your report cards for you to take home to your parents. I'm especially proud of one student who always puts forth her best effort, and her grades are almost perfect." She smiles at Ellie with obvious affection and hands her a report card. "Here you are. Just one B, Ellie, in history. I'm sure you'll be able to bring it up to an A next quarter."

Despite the praise, Ellie is devastated. The B has blindsided her; she had no idea it was coming. Embarrassed beyond words, she successfully fights back tears but looks down at her desk while Ms. Davidson distributes the other report cards. When the final school bell rings, Ellie quickly gathers her backpack and heads out the door, forgoing the usual after-school good-byes to her friends.

- Ellie's parents are unlikely to be concerned about her single B; they're more worried about Ellie's younger brother, a second grader who still can't read and probably has an undiagnosed learning disability. Why, then, might Ellie be so upset? Can you think of at least two possible explanations?
- Was it appropriate for Ms. Davidson to announce Ellie's grades to the class? Why or why not?

Although Ellie undoubtedly knows that she has made occasional errors on history assessments, she apparently hasn't been aware of how those errors might add up to a B rather than an A. And with her past straight-A record, she has set an extremely high standard for herself. Only perfection is good enough—an unrealistic standard held by perhaps 25% of high-achieving sixth graders (Parker, 1997). In addition, Ms. Davidson has announced Ellie's imperfection to the entire class. As a young adolescent, Ellie isn't sure which is worse: that her peers know she has earned the highest grades in the class or that they know she's *not* perfect in history. Not only does Ms. Davidson's announcement make Ellie extremely uncomfortable, but it also violates Ellie's right to confidentiality. In fact, as we'll discover later in the chapter, making a student's grades public, as Ms. Davidson does, is illegal, at least in the United States.

As teachers, we must eventually determine what students have accomplished during an academic term or school year. As we do so, we must keep the four RSVP characteristics of good assessment in mind. In particular, any overall indicator of achievement should be *reliable*, reflecting a consistent pattern of achievement rather than a rare, chance occurrence. It should also be *standardized*: Except for extenuating circumstances (e.g., for some students with disabilities), the same assessment criteria should apply to everyone. In addition, any summary of achievement should be *valid*; that is, it should accurately reflect what students have learned and achieved. Finally, it must be *practical* in terms of the time and effort it requires.

Our first order of business in this chapter will be to consider how we might summarize students' performance on a single assessment instrument. After that, we'll consider ways to summarize students' achievement on a broader scale.

Summarizing the Results of a Single Assessment

On some occasions we might find it appropriate to describe in detailed written form how a student has performed on a particular assessment. But such an approach for every student and every assessment would be extremely time consuming—a significant practicality issue. More often, then, we'll need to have some easy way of summarizing students' performance on individual assessments, perhaps using numbers or letter grades. To simplify our discussion, we'll focus largely on numbers, which we'll call *scores*. The scores on individual assessments, whether teacher-developed instruments or standardized tests, typically take one of three forms: raw scores, criterion-referenced scores, and norm-referenced scores.

RAW SCORES

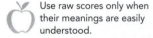
Use raw scores only when their meanings are easily understood.

A raw score is a score based solely on the number or percentage of points earned or items answered correctly. For example, a student who correctly answers 15 items on a 20-item multiple-choice test might get a score of 75%. A student who gets 3 points, 5 points, and 8 points on two essay questions and one performance task, respectively, might get an overall score of 16. Raw scores are easy to calculate, and they appear to be easy to understand. But in fact, we sometimes have trouble knowing what raw scores really mean. Are scores of 75% and 16 good scores or bad ones? Without knowing what kinds of tasks an assessment includes, we have no easy way of interpreting a raw score.

CRITERION-REFERENCED SCORES

As you might guess, criterion-referenced scores and norm-referenced scores are used, respectively, with criterion-referenced and norm-referenced assessments. More specifically, a criterion-referenced score indicates what students have achieved relative to specific instructional objectives or content-area standards. Some criterion-referenced scores are either–or scores indicating that a student has mastered or not mastered a skill, met or not met an objective, or passed or failed a unit. Figure 15.1 illustrates this approach in a beginning swimming class. If we wanted to assign numbers to a student's performance, we could give a "1" for every skill the student has mastered and a "0" for any nonmastered skill.

Other criterion-referenced scores indicate various levels of competence or achievement, in which case we might use a rating scale or rubric. As an example, Figure 15.2 presents excerpts from a rubric designed to assess six qualities of good nonfiction writing: correct spelling, correct punctuation and capitalization, complete sentences, clear focus, logical train of thought, and convincing statements/arguments. To keep things simple, the figure shows only two rows of the rubric—those for (a) punctuation and capitalization and (b) clear focus. If we wanted to assign numerical scores to a student's writing sample, we might use "3" to indicate a *proficient* rating, "2" to indicate *in progress,* and "1" to indicate *beginning to develop.* Such an approach is quite common as a strategy for assigning numerical scores to complex, multifaceted student products; however, its use is problematic, as we'll see in a moment.

Sometimes—and we need to stress the word *sometimes*—we can add up students' scores on individual criteria to obtain single, overall criterion-referenced scores. For example, we could do this with the swimming checklist shown in Figure 15.1. Students who get an overall score of 8—reflecting proficiency in all eight skills—are ready to move on to a more advanced class. But what if we want to add up a student's scores on all the criteria in a rubric for nonfiction writing? In this situation, we have two problems, both related to the *validity* of the overall scores we obtain. First, recall how we've just assigned scores of "3," "2," and "1" to the three levels of performance identified in the rubric. We can't really say that *proficient* is worth three times as much as *beginning to develop* and that *in progress* is midway in quality between the two other levels; the

---

FIGURE 15.1 Example of a criterion-referenced checklist for a beginning swimming class.

Beginner Swimmer Class
Springside Parks and Recreation Department

Students must demonstrate proficiency in each of the following:

- ☐ Jump into chest-deep water
- ☐ Hold breath under water for 8 seconds
- ☐ Float in prone position for 10 seconds
- ☐ Glide in prone position with flutter kick
- ☐ Float on back for 10 seconds
- ☐ Glide on back with flutter kick
- ☐ Demonstrate crawl stroke and rhythmic breathing while standing in chest-deep water
- ☐ Show knowledge of basic water safety rules

FIGURE 15.2 Two of the six evaluation criteria in a rubric for evaluating students' nonfiction writing.

Characteristic	Proficient	In Progress	Beginning to Develop
Correct punctuation & capitalization	Writer uses punctuation marks and uppercase letters where, and only where, appropriate.	Writer occasionally (a) omits punctuation marks, (b) inappropriately uses punctuation marks, or (c) inappropriately uses uppercase/lowercase letters.	Writer makes many punctuation and/or capitalization errors.
Clear focus	Writer clearly states main idea; sentences are all related to this idea and present a coherent message.	Writer only implies main idea; most sentences are related to this idea; a few sentences are unnecessary digressions.	Writer rambles, without a clear main idea; or writer frequently and unpredictably goes off topic.

Adapted from "Enhancing Learning Through Formative Assessments and Effective Feedback" (interactive learning module), by J. E. Ormrod, 2015, in *Essentials of Educational Psychology* (4th ed.). Copyright 2015, Pearson. Adapted by permission.

numbers we've used are strictly arbitrary ones.[1] Second, adding up all the scores to get a single score is based on the assumption that all criteria in the rubric are equally important—for instance, that using correct punctuation and capitalization is just as important as having a clear focus—when this assumption isn't necessarily correct. We authors have no immediate remedy for these two problems; we simply point out that it doesn't always make sense to use rubrics to obtain single criterion-referenced scores (also see Humphry & Heldsinger, 2014; Reddy & Andrade, 2010).

See Figure 14.5 in Chapter 14 for the complete writing rubric excerpted in Figure 15.2.

NORM-REFERENCED SCORES

A norm-referenced score is derived by comparing a student's performance on an assessment with the performance of others—perhaps that of classmates or perhaps that of students in a nationwide norm group. The scores for the comparison group comprise the norms for the assessment. A norm-referenced score might not tell us very much about what a student specifically knows and can do; instead, it tells us whether a student's performance is typical or unusual for his or her age or grade level.

Many published standardized tests yield norm-referenced scores. In some cases the scores are derived by comparing a student's performance with that of students at a variety of grade or age levels; such comparisons give us grade- or age-equivalent scores. In other cases the scores are based on comparisons only with students of the *same* age or grade; these comparisons give us either percentile scores or standard scores.

GRADE-EQUIVALENT AND AGE-EQUIVALENT SCORES

Imagine that Shawn takes a standardized test, the Reading Achievement Test (RAT). He gets 46 of the 60 test items correct; thus 46 is his raw score. We turn to the norms reported in the test manual and find the average raw scores for students at different grade and age levels, shown in Figure 15.3. Shawn's raw score of 46 is the same as the average score of 11th graders in the norm group, so he has a grade-equivalent score of 11. His score is also halfway between the average score of 16-year-old and 17-year-old students, so he has an age-equivalent score of about 16½. Shawn is 13 years old and in the eighth grade and so has obviously done well on the RAT.

---

[1] For readers who have a background in basic statistics, the problem here is one of trying to use numbers (which comprise a *ratio scale*) to quantify what might be an *ordinal scale*.

FIGURE 15.3 Hypothetical norm-group data for the Reading Achievement Test (RAT).

Norms for Grade Levels		Norms for Age Levels	
Grade	Average Raw Score	Age	Average Raw Score
5	19	10	18
6	25	11	24
7	30	12	28
8	34	13	33
9	39	14	37
10	43	15	41
11	46	16	44
12	50	17	48

In general, grade- and age-equivalent scores are determined by matching a student's raw score to that of a particular grade or age level in the norm group. A student who performs as well as the average second grader on a reading test will get a grade-equivalent score of 2, regardless of the student's actual grade level. A student who earns the same raw score as the average 10-year-old on a physical fitness test will get an age-equivalent score of 10, regardless of whether the student is 5, 10, or 15 years old.

Grade- and age-equivalent scores seem quite simple and straightforward. But they have a serious drawback: They give us no idea of the typical *range* of performance for students at a particular grade or age level. For example, a raw score of 34 on the RAT gives us a grade-equivalent score of 8, but obviously not all eighth graders will get raw scores of exactly 34. It's possible (and in fact quite likely) that many eighth graders will get raw scores several points above or below 34—yielding grade-equivalent scores of 9 or 7, perhaps even 10 or higher, or 6 or lower. Yet grade-equivalent scores are often used inappropriately as a standard for performance: Parents, school personnel, government officials, and the public at large may believe that *all* students should perform at grade level on an achievement test. Given that students' abilities vary considerably in most classrooms—and that, mathematically, students can't all score at average or above-average levels—this goal is virtually impossible to meet.

PERCENTILE SCORES

A percentile score—sometimes instead called a *percentile rank* or, more simply, a percentile—is the percentage of people at the *same* age or grade level getting a raw score less than or equal to the student's raw score. To illustrate, let's once again consider Shawn's performance on the RAT. Because Shawn is in the eighth grade, we would turn to the eighth-grade norms in the RAT test manual. If we discover that a raw score of 46 is at the 98th percentile for eighth graders, we know that Shawn has done as well as or better than 98% of eighth graders in the norm group. Similarly, a student getting a percentile score of 25 has performed better than 25% of the norm group, and a student getting a score at the 60th percentile has done better than 60%. It's important to note that a percentile score refers to a percentage of *people,* not to the percentage of correct items—a misconception that teacher education students sometimes have.

Percentile scores are relatively easy to understand and therefore used frequently in reporting test results. But they have a major weakness: They distort actual differences among students. For example, consider the RAT percentile scores of these four boys:

Student	Percentile Score
Ernest	45
Frank	55
Giorgio	89
Wayne	99

In *actual achievement*—at least as measured by the RAT—Ernest and Frank are probably very similar to one another even though their percentile scores are 10 points apart. However, a 10-point difference at the upper end of the scale probably reflects a substantial difference in achievement: Giorgio's percentile score of 89 tells us that he knows quite a bit (relative to his peers), but Wayne's percentile score of 99 tells us that he knows an exceptional amount.

In general, percentiles tend to *over*estimate differences in the middle range of the characteristic being measured: Scores a few points apart reflect similar achievement or ability. Meanwhile, percentiles *under*estimate differences at the upper and lower extremes: Scores only a few points apart often reflect significant differences in achievement or ability. We can avoid these problems by using standard scores.

STANDARD SCORES

The school nurse measures the heights of the 25 students in Ms. Oppenheimer's third-grade class; these heights are listed on the left side of Figure 15.4. The nurse then creates a graph of the

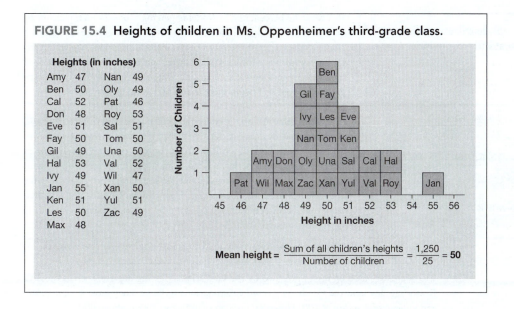

FIGURE 15.4 Heights of children in Ms. Oppenheimer's third-grade class.

Heights (in inches)			
Amy	47	Nan	49
Ben	50	Oly	49
Cal	52	Pat	46
Don	48	Roy	53
Eve	51	Sal	51
Fay	50	Tom	50
Gil	49	Una	50
Hal	53	Val	52
Ivy	49	Wil	47
Jan	55	Xan	50
Ken	51	Yul	51
Les	50	Zac	49
Max	48		

$$\text{Mean height} = \frac{\text{Sum of all children's heights}}{\text{Number of children}} = \frac{1,250}{25} = 50$$

children's heights, shown on the right side of Figure 15.4. Notice that the graph is high in the middle and low at both ends. This shape tells us that most of Ms. Oppenheimer's students are fairly average in height, with only a handful of students being very short (e.g., Pat, Amy, Wil) and just a few others being very tall (e.g., Hal, Roy, Jan).

Many educational and psychological characteristics—including many academic abilities—seem to show roughly the same pattern we see for height: Most people are close to average, with fewer and fewer people being counted as we move farther from the average. This theoretical pattern of educational and psychological characteristics, known as the normal distribution (or normal curve), is shown in the margin. Standard scores are based on the normal distribution: Many students have scores in the middle range, and only a few have very high or very low scores.

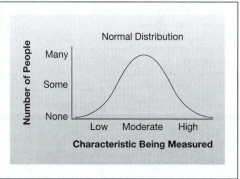

Before we examine standard scores more closely, we need to understand two numbers used to derive these scores: the mean and the standard deviation. The mean (M) is the *average* of a set of scores: We add all the scores together—counting any given score as many times as the number of people who have earned it—and divide by the total number of scores (or people) in the set. For example, if we add the heights of all 25 students in Ms. Oppenheimer's class and divide the sum by 25, we get a mean height of 50 inches (see the calculation at the bottom of Figure 15.4).

The standard deviation (SD) indicates the *variability* of a set of scores. A small number tells us that, generally speaking, the scores are close together, and a large number tells us that they're spread far apart. For example, third graders tend to be more similar in height than eighth graders; some eighth graders are less than 5 feet tall, whereas others may be almost 6 feet tall. The standard deviation for the heights of third graders is therefore smaller than the standard deviation for the heights of eighth graders. The formula for calculating a standard deviation is too complex to discuss in a book such as this one, but you can easily find it on the Internet. In any case, we don't need to know the formula in order to understand the role that a standard deviation plays in standard scores. (In case you're curious, the standard deviation for the heights of Ms. Oppenheimer's students is approximately 2.06.)

The mean and standard deviation can be used to divide the normal distribution into several parts, as shown in Figure 15.5. The vertical line in the middle of the curve shows the mean; for a normal distribution, it's both the midpoint and the highest point of the curve. The thinner lines to either side reflect the standard deviation: We count out 1 standard deviation higher and lower than the mean and mark those two spots with vertical lines, and then we count another standard deviation to either side and draw two more lines. When we divide a true normal distribution in

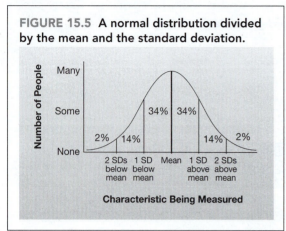

FIGURE 15.5 A normal distribution divided by the mean and the standard deviation.

this way, the percentages of students getting scores in each part are always the same. Approximately two-thirds (68%) get scores within 1 standard deviation of the mean (34% in each direction). As we go farther away from the mean, we find fewer and fewer students, with 28% being between 1 and 2 standard deviations away (14% on each side) and only about 4% being more than 2 standard deviations away (2% at each end).

Now that we better understand the normal distribution and two statistics that describe it, let's return to standard scores. A **standard score** reflects a person's position in the normal distribution: It tells us how far the person's performance is from the mean in terms of standard deviation units. Unfortunately, not all standard scores use the same scale: Scores used for various tests have different means and standard deviations. Five commonly used standard scores, depicted graphically in Figure 15.6, are the following:

- **IQ scores** are frequently used to report students' performance on intelligence tests. They have a *mean of 100* and, for most tests, a *standard deviation of 15*.

- **ETS scores** are used on tests published by the Educational Testing Service, such as the SAT Reasoning Test and the Graduate Record Examinations (GREs). They have a *mean of 500* and a *standard deviation of 100*. However, no scores fall below 200 or above 800.

- **Stanines** (short for *standard nines*) are often used in reporting standardized achievement test results. They have a *mean of 5* and a *standard deviation of 2*. Because they're always reported as whole numbers, each score reflects a *range* of test performance, indicated by the shaded and nonshaded portions of the upper-right-hand curve in Figure 15.6.

Figure 5.1 in Chapter 5 shows the distribution of IQ scores broken up by lines that each reflect one-third of a standard deviation (5 points). The lines for 85 and 115 are 1 standard deviation from the mean of 100. The lines for 70 and 130 are 2 SDs from the mean.

- **NCE scores** (short for *normal-curve-equivalent scores*) are increasingly being used in reporting standardized achievement test results. They have a *mean of 50* and a *standard deviation of 21.06*. However, it isn't possible to get a score of zero or below, nor is it possible to get a score of 100 or above.

- **z-scores** are the standard scores that statisticians most often use. They have a *mean of 0* and a *standard deviation of 1*.

FIGURE 15.6 Distributions of five types of standard scores.

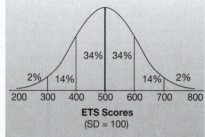

IQ Scores
(SD = 15)

ETS Scores
(SD = 100)

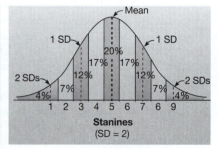

Stanines
(SD = 2)

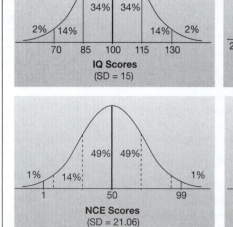

NCE Scores
(SD = 21.06)

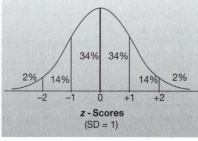

z - Scores
(SD = 1)

FIGURE 15.7 Computer printout revealing 12-year-old Ingrid's scores on standardized achievement tests in several content domains.

	STANINE	PERCENTILE	1	5	10	20	30	40	50	60	70	80	90	95	99
			WELL BELOW AVERAGE				BELOW AVERAGE	AVERAGE		ABOVE AVERAGE			WELL ABOVE AVERAGE		
READING COMPREHENSION	8	92											XXXXXXXXXXXXXX		
SPELLING	4	39					XXXXXXXXXXX								
MATH COMPUTATION	4	37					XXXXXXXXXX								
MATH CONCEPTS	5	57							XXXXXXXXXXX						
SCIENCE	8	90										XXXXXXXXXXXXXX			
SOCIAL STUDIES	7	84										XXXXXXXX			

NATIONAL PERCENTILE BANDS

The odd standard deviation for NCE scores (21.06) requires an explanation. It turns out that with this particular standard deviation, an NCE score of 1 is equivalent to a percentile score of 1 and, likewise, an NCE score of 99 is equivalent to a percentile score of 99. And, of course, an NCE score of 50 (being the mean and midpoint of the curve) is also a percentile score of 50. Thus NCE scores have the same overall range as percentile scores.

Typically the publishers of standardized achievement tests report students' test results using two or more types of scores. For example, Figure 15.7 presents a computer printout that lists both stanine scores and percentile scores for 12-year-old Ingrid in several content domains. The printout is admittedly a very dated one—as we'll see later, contemporary computer-generated reports tend to be much more complex—but its simplicity can better help you see how such scores might be represented. Ingrid's scores reveal average to below-average achievement in spelling and math computation, average to above-average achievement in math concepts, and well-above-average achievement in reading comprehension, science, and social studies. The "national percentile bands" (shown as rows of Xs within some of the green lines)—more commonly called **confidence intervals** or *confidence bands*—reflect the amount of error (due to imperfect reliability) that's likely to be affecting Ingrid's percentile scores.

You can learn more about confidence intervals in Appendix B.

Notice how the numbers at the bottom of the computer printout (1, 5, 10, 20, etc.) are unevenly spaced. Remember a point made earlier about percentile scores: They overestimate differences near the mean and underestimate differences at the extremes. The uneven spacing in the printout is the test publisher's way of showing this fact: It squishes the middle percentile scores closer together and spreads high and low percentile scores farther apart. In this way, the publisher tries to give students and parents an idea about where students' test scores fall in a normal distribution.

Table 15.1 provides a summary of raw scores, criterion-referenced scores, and norm-referenced scores.

USING CRITERION-REFERENCED VERSUS NORM-REFERENCED SCORES IN THE CLASSROOM

In most instances criterion-referenced scores communicate what we and our students most need to know: whether instructional goals and content-area standards are being achieved. Criterion-referenced scores can also focus students' attention on mastery goals and, by showing improvement over time, can enhance their self-efficacy for learning classroom subject matter. When criterion-referenced scores are hard to determine—perhaps because an assessment simultaneously addresses many instructional goals and objectives (something we authors don't generally recommend)—raw scores are usually the second-best choice for teacher-developed assessments. But we must remember an important point about raw scores: They don't often tell us very much about what students have and haven't specifically learned.

Use criterion-referenced scores to indicate mastery of specific instructional goals and objectives.

COMPARE/CONTRAST

TABLE 15.1 • Scores Used to Summarize the Results of a Single Assessment			
TYPE OF SCORE	**METHOD OF DETERMINING SCORE**	**USES**	**POTENTIAL DRAWBACKS**
Raw score	Counting the number (or calculating a percentage) of correct responses or points earned	Often used in teacher-developed assessment instruments	Scores may be difficult to interpret without knowledge of how performance relates either to a specific criterion or to a norm group.
Criterion-referenced score	Comparing performance to one or more criteria or standards for success	Useful when determining whether specific instructional goals or standards have been achieved	Concrete criteria for assessing mastery of complex skills are sometimes difficult to identify. Also, combining separate scores for different criteria into a single overall score may seriously jeopardize validity.
Grade- or age-equivalent score (norm-referenced)	Equating a student's performance to the average performance of students at a particular grade or age level	Useful when explaining norm-referenced test performance to people who are unfamiliar with standard scores	Scores are frequently misinterpreted (especially by parents), may be inappropriately used as a standard that all students must meet, and are often inapplicable when achievement is being assessed in adolescence or adulthood.
Percentile rank (norm-referenced)	Determining the percentage of students at the same age or grade level who have obtained the same score or lower scores	Useful when explaining norm-referenced test performance to people who are unfamiliar with standard scores	Scores overestimate differences near the mean and underestimate differences at the extremes.
Standard score (norm-referenced)	Determining how far the performance is from the mean (for the grade or age level) in terms of standard deviation units	More accurate in characterizing students' ability differences than grade-equivalent scores, age-equivalent scores, or percentile ranks	Scores are not easily understood by people who don't have some basic knowledge of statistics.

Norm-referenced scores—in everyday lingo, *grading on the curve*—may occasionally be appropriate if we truly need to know how students have performed relative to one another. For example, we might find these scores helpful when designating first chairs in an instrumental music class (best violinist, best trombone player, etc.) or when choosing the best entries for a regional science fair. We may also need to resort to a norm-referenced approach when assessing complex skills (e.g., writing poetry, demonstrating advanced athletic skills, or critically analyzing scientific research studies) that we can't really describe as "mastered" or "not mastered."

> Use norm-referenced scores only when you truly need to compare various students' performances.

We probably *shouldn't* use norm-referenced scores for teacher-developed assessments on a regular basis, however. Such scores create a competitive situation, because students do well only if their performance surpasses that of their classmates. Thus norm-referenced scores focus students' attention primarily on performance goals rather than on mastery goals and may possibly encourage students to cheat on assessment tasks. Furthermore, the competitive atmosphere that norm-referenced scores create is likely to undermine students' general *sense of community* as a class (E. M. Anderman, Griesinger, & Westerfield, 1998; Brophy, 2004; M.-T. Wang & Holcombe, 2010).

> Chapter 13 describes the many benefits of having a sense of community in the classroom.

MyEdLab **Self-Check 15.1**

MyEdLab **Application Exercise 15.1.** In this exercise, you can practice distinguishing between criterion-referenced and norm-referenced assessments.

Determining Final Class Grades

Especially in the upper elementary and secondary school years, most schools use letter or number grades to summarize students' overall achievement levels in various content domains. Such grades have several limitations. First, different teachers are apt to use varying criteria to assign grades; for instance, some are more lenient than others, and some stress rote memorization whereas others stress complex cognitive skills. Second, different students may be working to accomplish different instructional goals, especially in classes that include children of diverse backgrounds and needs. Third, typical grading practices promote performance goals rather than mastery goals and may encourage students to go for the "easy A" instead of taking risks. Finally, students under pressure to achieve high grades may resort to cheating (e.g., plagiarizing someone else's work) in order to attain those grades (Cizek, 2003; K. O'Connor, 2011; Pulfrey, Buchs, & Butera, 2011; L. Shepard, Hammerness, Darling-Hammond, & Rust, 2005; S. Thomas & Oldfather, 1997).

Despite their drawbacks, final class grades continue to be the most common method of summarizing students' classroom achievement. The following recommendations can enhance their validity and usefulness.

🍎 *Take the job of grading seriously.* Consider these scenarios:

- A high school math teacher makes numerous errors in calculating students' final grades. As a result, some of his students get lower grades than they've earned.
- A middle school Spanish teacher asks her teenage son to calculate her students' final grades. Some columns in her gradebook are only for scores on retests, so students who didn't need to retake tests have blanks in these columns. The son treats all blank spaces as zeros and thus gives grades of D or F to some of the highest achievers.

A math teacher who makes mathematical errors? A Spanish teacher who has her son determine final grades? Preposterous? No, both scenarios are true stories. Students' final class grades are often the *only* data that appear in their school records, so we must take the time and make the effort to ensure that they're accurate.

Many computer software programs and Internet websites provide electronic gradebooks that can help us with record keeping and grading; most online resources that support class websites (e.g., moodle.org) also include gradebooks. In addition to helping us keep track of a sizable body of assessment information, electronic gradebooks make it easy to keep students continually informed about their performance and progress. We can't use these gradebooks mindlessly, however. For example, if we make errors when entering information or don't take into account the idiosyncrasies of our record-keeping system, we might as well have the Spanish teacher's son calculate our grades for us!

🍎 *Base grades on achievement.* Tempting as it might be to reward well-behaved, cooperative students with good grades and to punish chronic misbehavers with Ds or Fs, grades should ultimately reflect how much students have *learned*. Awarding good grades simply for good behavior may mislead students and their parents to believe that students are making better progress than they really are. And awarding low grades as punishment for disruptive behavior leads students to conclude, perhaps with good reason, that their teacher's grading system is arbitrary and meaningless (Brookhart, 2004; Cizek, 2003; K. O'Connor, 2011; L. Shepard et al., 2005).

🍎 *Base grades on hard data.* Our informal judgments of students' current achievement levels will be imperfect assessments at best, and they can easily be influenced by other things we know about students—for example, how often they misbehave in class and what their past achievement levels have been (Carbonneau & Selig, 2011; J. P. Robinson & Lubienski, 2011; Südkamp, Kaiser, & Möller, 2012). For this reason and also for the sake of our students—who learn more and achieve at higher levels when we tell them what we expect in concrete terms—we should base grades on objective information derived from formal assessments, *not* on subjective impressions of what students appear to know.

🍎 *Use many assessments to determine grades, but don't count everything.* Using multiple assessments to determine final grades can help us compensate for the imperfect reliability and validity of any single assessment task. At the same time, we probably don't want to consider *everything* students do, in part because we want them to feel comfortable taking risks and making mistakes. Thus we may not want to include students' early efforts at new tasks, which are likely to involve considerable trial and error. Many assessments are more appropriately used for formative assessment purposes—to help students learn—than for summative assessment (Frisbie & Waltman, 1992; Nitko & Brookhart, 2011; L. Shepard et al., 2005).

Although overall class grades should be based on multiple sources of data, not everything needs to be graded. Furthermore, students must feel confident that they have some leeway to take risks and make errors.

Your class grades will be based on a gazillion assignments and a bazillion quizzes, and I'll be deducting points for any stupid things you might do in class . . .

🍎 *Assign criterion-referenced grades unless there is a compelling reason to do otherwise.* Many experts recommend that final grades reflect mastery of classroom subject matter and instructional goals—in other words, that final grades be criterion-referenced. Criterion-referenced grades are especially appropriate during the elementary years: Much of the elementary school curriculum consists of basic skills that are either mastered or not mastered, and there's little need to use grades as a basis for comparing students to one another.

The issue becomes more complicated at the secondary level: Students' grades are sometimes used to choose college applicants, award scholarships, and make other comparative decisions. Historically, then, some secondary school teachers have used norm-referenced grades—for instance, giving As to the top 10% of each class, Bs to the next 20%, Cs to the middle 40%, and so on. We authors personally recommend that high school grades be criterion-referenced to the extent that such is possible. The most critical decisions for which grades are used—decisions about promotion and graduation—should be based on students' mastery or nonmastery of the school curriculum, not on their standing relative to others. Furthermore, because different classes of students often differ in ability level, a strictly norm-referenced approach might assign a C grade to a student's performance in one class (e.g., Honors Math), whereas the same performance might warrant an A in another class (e.g., General Math). (Under such circumstances a student striving for a high grade point average would be foolish to enroll in the honors section.) Finally, only a very few students (i.e., the highest achievers) find a norm-referenced grading system motivating; most students quickly resign themselves to achieving at an average level at best (Ames, 1984; Graham & Golen, 1991; Shih & Alexander, 2000; Stipek, 1996).[2]

When setting up a criterion-referenced grading system, we should determine as concretely as possible what we want each grade to communicate. For example, if we're assigning traditional letter grades, we might use criteria such as the following:

Grade	*Criteria*
A	The student has a firm command of both basic and advanced knowledge and skills in the content domain. He or she is well prepared for future learning tasks.
B	The student has mastered all basic knowledge and skills. Mastery at a more advanced level is evident in some but not all areas. In most respects he or she is ready for future learning tasks.
C	The student has mastered basic knowledge and skills but has difficulty with more advanced aspects of the subject matter. He or she lacks a few prerequisites critical for future learning tasks.
D	The student has mastered some but not all of the basics in the content domain. He or she lacks many prerequisites for future learning tasks.
F	The student shows little or no mastery of instructional objectives and cannot demonstrate the most elementary knowledge and skills. He or she lacks most of the prerequisites essential for success in future learning tasks. (Based on criteria described by Frisbie & Waltman, 1992)

---

[2] Over the past several decades, teachers have gradually moved from norm-referenced grading (i.e., grading on the curve) to criterion-referenced grading. This focus on mastery of instructional goals and objectives, rather than on comparing students with one another, accounts in part for the increasing grade point averages (i.e., "grade inflation") about which some public figures complain. In fact, the gradual movement toward assigning students' grades based on absolute achievement levels rather than peer-group comparisons has probably yielded *increases* in the validity of students' final grades (Pattison, Grodsky, & Muller, 2013).

Only when final grades reflect criteria such as these can they legitimately be used for instructional decision making.

🍎 *Identify a reasonable grading system and stick to it.* Consider this situation:

> At the beginning of the school year, Ms. Giroux announces that final class grades will be based entirely on students' quiz scores. But after a few weeks she realizes that if she relies *only* on quiz scores, most students will get a D or F for the semester. To help students boost their grades, she asks them to turn in all previous homework assignments, which can contribute up to 20 percentage points toward final grades. The students protest loudly and angrily: Thinking there was no reason to keep completed assignments, many students have already discarded them.

If most students are getting Ds and Fs, something's definitely wrong. Perhaps Ms. Giroux's instructional methods aren't as effective as other approaches might be. Perhaps she's moving so quickly through the curriculum that students never have time to master a topic. Perhaps her quizzes reflect unrealistic expectations about what students should be able to do.

As teachers, we can't always anticipate how best to teach a new topic or how well students will perform on particular assessments. Nevertheless, if we want to give students a sense that they have some control over their grades—that is, if we want them to have internal, controllable attributions for their classroom performance—we must tell them early in the school year or semester what our grading criteria will be. In addition, by providing concrete information about how we'll be assigning grades, we avoid unpleasant surprises when students actually receive their grades (recall Ellie's sense of devastation in the opening case study). If we find that our initial criteria are overly stringent, we may need to lighten up in some way, perhaps by adjusting cutoffs or allowing retakes of critical assessments. But we must never change our criteria in midstream in a way that unfairly penalizes some students or imposes additional, unanticipated requirements.

🍎 *Accompany grades with qualitative information about students' performance.* Whether final grades take the form of letters or numbers, they are, at best, only general indicators of some *quantity* of what students have learned. Thus it's often helpful to accompany grades with *qualitative* information—for instance, information about students' particular academic strengths, work habits, attitudes, social skills, and unique contributions to the classroom community (e.g., see Figure 15.8). Students and parents alike often find such qualitative feedback just as informative as final class grades—sometimes even more informative. The feedback should be fairly explicit, however; comments such as "A pleasure to have in class" communicate little (Brookhart, 2004, p. 183).

> See Chapter 11 for a discussion of how students' attributions influence their motivation and learning.

CONSIDERING—OR NOT CONSIDERING—OTHER FACTORS IN GRADING

Some educators suggest that students be graded at least partly on the basis of how much they improve, how hard they try, how much extra work they do, or whether they've turned assignments in late (if at all). Most assessment experts disagree with this idea, as we'll see now.

Considering improvement. Many motivation theorists stress the importance of focusing students' attention more on their own improvement than on how their performance compares with that of peers. But assessment experts have made two good arguments against basing final grades solely on students' improvement over the course of a semester or school year. First, students who already show accomplishment of some of the year's instructional goals will have less room for improvement than their classmates. Second, when we use improvement as a criterion, students trying to "beat the system" may quickly realize that they can achieve high grades simply by performing as poorly as possible when the school year begins (Airasian, 1994; M. D. Miller, Linn, & Gronlund, 2009; Sax, 2010).

FIGURE 15.8 Examples of qualitative feedback one second-grade teacher gave her students at the end of the school year.

- To Amanda: You are a good friend to everyone in the class. You look out for people's feelings and work hard to make others feel good.

- To Andrea: You have a beautiful singing voice and are a very animated performer. You show self-confidence in all that you do.

- To Angus: You are always willing to lend a hand to teachers and peers alike. You have practical advice and reasonable solutions to many questions and situations that arise.

- To Charlotte: You are a very thoughtful worker. You always give 100% on everything you do. Your positive attitude and great work ethic are a wonderful addition to the class.

- To Colin: I love your sense of humor. You make me laugh with your great riddles and jokes. The humor in your stories is very creative and keeps your audience wanting to know more about the story.

How do we balance what motivation theorists recommend, on the one hand, with what assessment experts recommend, on the other? Following are several possible strategies:

- Assign greater weight to assessments conducted at the end of the semester or school year, after *all* students have had a reasonable opportunity to achieve instructional goals.
- Give students a chance to correct their errors and, in doing so, to demonstrate mastery.
- Administer retakes of assessments, perhaps using items or tasks different from those presented the first time.
- Reinforce improvement in other ways—for instance, with free time or special privileges. (Lester, Lambdin, & Preston, 1997; K. O'Connor, 2011; L. Shepard et al., 2005)

Considering effort. Most assessment experts urge us *not* to base final grades on the amount of effort students appear to exert in their studies. For one thing, students who begin the year already performing at a high level are penalized because they may not have to work as hard as their less knowledgeable classmates. Furthermore, student effort is something we can evaluate only subjectively and imprecisely at best (Brookhart, 2004; K. O'Connor, 2011; L. Shepard et al., 2005).

An alternative is to have students work for individualized instructional goals appropriate for their existing ability levels. Such an approach is workable *if,* when we report students' final grades, we also report the instructional goals on which the grades are based. In fact, this approach is widely used for students with special educational needs, whose goals are described in their individualized education programs (IEPs).

Obviously we enhance students' motivation when we explicitly acknowledge their effort. Some school systems have multidimensional grading systems that allow teachers to assign separate grades to the various aspects of students' classroom performance. Such mechanisms as brief written notes to parents, parent–teacher conferences, and letters of recommendation to colleges provide additional means by which we can describe the multifaceted nature of students' classroom performance.

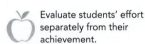

Evaluate students' effort separately from their achievement.

Giving extra credit.   As college professors we've occasionally had students appear at our office doors asking—sometimes begging—for an opportunity to improve their grades at the last minute by completing extra-credit projects. Our response is invariably *no,* and for a very good reason: Our course grades are based on the extent to which students achieve instructional goals for the course, as determined by their performance on assessments that are the same or equivalent (and therefore standardized and fair) for all students. Extra-credit projects assigned to only one or two students (typically those achieving at a low level) are insufficient to demonstrate mastery of the subject matter and aren't standardized for the entire class.

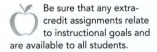

Be sure that any extra-credit assignments relate to instructional goals and are available to all students.

Extra-credit work is occasionally appropriate *provided that* (a) the work relates to instructional goals and (b) all students have the same opportunity to complete it (Padilla-Walker, 2006; L. Shepard et al., 2005). It *isn't* appropriate when its only purpose is to help a failing student earn a passing grade.

Addressing lateness and missing work.   Certainly we want students to learn to be punctual in submitting assignments, in part because it will be hard for them to complete all of their work at the last minute—and they're apt to learn less when they finally do it—and in part because a habit of meeting deadlines will be important for their success in the adult workplace. Nevertheless, students may occasionally have justifiable reasons for a late submission—perhaps because of a lengthy illness, an unexpected crisis at home, or unanticipated confusion about what an assignment requires.

A few students may consistently *not* turn in assignments, especially ones they've been asked to do outside of class. Some of these students may believe these assignments are pointless and irrelevant to their lives and needs. Others may be reluctant to admit that they don't have the basic knowledge and skills they need to complete the assignments. Still others may have poor self-regulation skills; for example, they may be easily enticed into nonacademic activities once they leave the school building.

With such issues in mind, experts recommend that we *not* take off points for late submissions or grade missing assignments as *zeroes* that enter into our final grade calculations. Remember, final grades should reflect *actual achievement* related to instructional goals and objectives. Strategies such as the following can be more productive:

- Explain why punctuality is important for students' long-term success.
- Solicit students' input about reasonable deadlines for assignments.
- Give students the extra guidance and support they might need to complete assignments in a timely manner.
- If the school grading system allows it, record a student's grade as "Incomplete" and describe the work the student must do in order to get a passing grade.
- Base *all* students' final grades on only a subset of summative assessment results; this final strategy works only if the subset can validly and reliably reflect all instructional goals. (Brookhart, 2004; Nitko & Brookhart, 2011; K. O'Connor, 2011)

INCLUDING STUDENTS IN THE GRADING PROCESS

Let's return to the opening case study, in which Ellie is blindsided by her B in history. Although Ellie has been informed of her scores on various assessments during the grading period, she apparently hasn't been aware of how those scores would be combined into an overall grade. Ms. Davidson has presumably been tracking Ellie's progress over time, but Ellie herself hasn't been doing so.

In previous chapters we've repeatedly seen the benefits of self-assessment for self-regulation and motivation. In the end, however, we teachers must be the ones to determine students' final grades, as most students are likely to give themselves grades based on what they would *prefer* rather than what they've objectively *earned* (e.g., see Figure. 15.9). Yet final grades shouldn't seemingly come out of the blue. Students must know, in advance and in concrete terms, our criteria for assigning grades, and we must frequently update students about their progress toward earning good ones, perhaps by using one of the electronic gradebooks described earlier. Under these conditions students *do* have a say in their grades—by working hard to master classroom subject matter.

FIGURE 15.9 In her rationale for getting an A for the term, 15-year-old Lexee focuses on effort, punctuality, and class participation rather than on achievement.

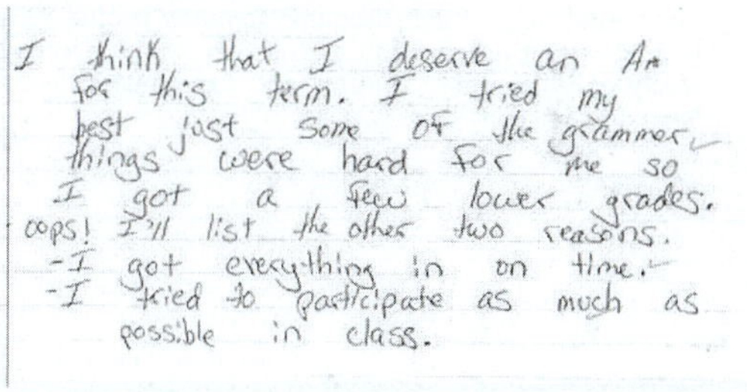

I think that I deserve an A+ for this term. I tried my best just some of the grammar things were hard for me so I got a few lower grades. oops! I'll list the other two reasons.
- I got everything in on time.
- I tried to participate as much as possible in class.

Using Portfolios

Whenever we boil down students' achievement into single letter or number grades, we lose valuable information about students' specific strengths and weaknesses, inclinations and disinclinations, and so on. In contrast, **portfolios**—collections of work systematically collected over a lengthy time period—can capture the complex, multifaceted nature of students' accomplishments and interests. Portfolios might include writing samples, student-constructed objects (e.g., sculptures, inventions), photographs, audiotapes, video recordings, technology-based creations (e.g., PowerPoint presentations, student-authored video games), or any combination of these.

Traditionally most portfolios have been actual physical entities that include various examples of students' work. But such a collection can sometimes be cumbersome and hard to transport from one place to another. An alternative is an **electronic portfolio** (sometimes simply called an *e-folio*) in which portfolio contents—perhaps including writing samples, audiovisual materials, or photographs of creations—are stored and presented via portable electronic storage devices (e.g., CDs, DVDs, flash drives) or an Internet-based storage service (e.g., a "cloud").

The items included in a portfolio are often called *artifacts*. Students typically decide for themselves which artifacts to include, perhaps with the guidance of a teacher or other mentor. This decision-making process can give students a sense of ownership of their portfolios, enhance their sense of autonomy, and bolster their intrinsic motivation to gain new knowledge and skills.

In addition to specific artifacts, most school portfolios include student reflections that (a) identify the purpose(s) and goals of the portfolio, (b) describe each artifact and the reason(s) it was included, and (c) summarize what the collection of artifacts reveals about the student's achievement. For example, in Figure 15.10, 14-year-old Kurt describes and evaluates the writing samples he has included in a portfolio for his eighth-grade language arts class; he has

> **FIGURE 15.10** In this self-reflection 14-year-old Kurt explains why he has chosen certain pieces to include in his eighth-grade language arts portfolio.
>
> SELF-ASSESSMENT
>
> The three pieces of writing in my portfolio that best represent who I am are: 1) "Author Ben Hoff," which is a story in the language of Ben Hoff; 2) "Quotes from *The Tao of Pooh*"; and 3) "Discrimination."
>
> What "Author Ben Hoff" shows about me as a learner or a writer is that I am able to analyze and absorb the types and styles of an author and then transfer what I learn onto paper in a good final understandable piece of writing. This piece has good description, a good plot line, gets the point across, has a basic setting, and is understandable. I did not change too much of this piece from one draft to the next except punctuation, grammar and spelling. I did, however, add a quote from *The Tao of Pooh*.
>
> "Quotes from *The Tao of Pooh*" shows that I am able to pull out good and significant quotes from a book, understand them, and put them into my own words. Then I can make them understandable to other people. This piece gets the point across well and is easy to understand. I really only corrected spelling and punctuation from one draft to the next.
>
> "Discrimination" shows me that I am learning more about discrimination and how it might feel (even though I have never experienced really bad discrimination). I found I can get my ideas across through realistic writing. This piece has good description and was well written for the assignment. Besides correcting some punctuation and spelling, I changed some wording to make the story a little more clear.
>
> For all three pieces, the mechanics of my writing tend to be fairly poor on my first draft, but that is because I am writing as thoughts come into my mind rather than focusing on details of grammar. Then my final drafts get better as I get comments and can turn my attention to details of writing.
>
> The four most important things that I'm able to do as a writer are to: 1) get thoughts pulled into a story; 2) have that story understandable and the reader get something from it; 3) have the reader remember it was a good piece of writing; and 4) like the piece myself.

included two or more drafts of each piece of writing to show how he has improved each one over time. Self-reflections encourage students to look at and judge their own work in ways that teachers typically do, thereby promoting the self-monitoring and self-evaluation skills so essential for self-regulated learning (Arter & Spandel, 1992; R. S. Johnson, Mims-Cox, & Doyle-Nichols, 2006; Vucko & Hadwin, 2004).

TYPES AND PURPOSES OF PORTFOLIOS

Portfolios take a variety of forms. Following are four types commonly used in school settings:

- *Working portfolio*—Shows competencies up to the present time; is dynamic in content, with new artifacts that show greater proficiency gradually replacing older, less skillful ones.
- *Developmental portfolio*—Includes several artifacts related to a particular set of skills; shows how a student has improved over time.
- *Course portfolio*—Includes assignments and reflections for a single course; typically also includes a summarizing reflection in which the student identifies his or her general accomplishments in the course.
- *Best-work portfolio*—Includes artifacts intended to showcase the student's particular achievements and unique talents. (R. S. Johnson et al., 2006; Spandel, 1997)

These categories aren't necessarily mutually exclusive. For example, a course portfolio might have a developmental component, showing how a student has improved in, say, persuasive writing or graphic design over the school year. And a best-work portfolio may be a work-in-progress for quite some time, thereby having the dynamic nature of a working portfolio.

Some portfolios are most appropriate for formative assessment, whereas others are appropriate for summative assessment. Developmental portfolios can show whether students are making reasonable progress toward long-term instructional goals; as such, they're often best used for formative assessment. Best-work portfolios are better suited for summative assessment; for example, they might be used to communicate students' final accomplishments to parents, school administrators, college admissions officers, or potential employers.

MyEdLab
Video Example 15.1.

What specific guidance does this high school art teacher give his students as they create their best-work portfolios?

BENEFITS AND LIMITATIONS OF PORTFOLIOS

Portfolios have several benefits, some of which we've already identified:

- They capture the multifaceted nature of students' achievements, with a particular emphasis on complex skills.

- They can show growth over time—something that a single assessment at a single time can't do.

- They can demonstrate students' performance in real-world, authentic activities (e.g., science experiments, service learning projects).

- They provide practice in self-monitoring and self-evaluation, thereby enhancing students' self-regulation skills.

- They give students a sense of accomplishment and self-efficacy about areas that have been mastered, while possibly also alerting students to areas needing improvement.

- They provide a mechanism through which teachers can easily intertwine assessment with instruction: Students often include products that their teachers have assigned primarily for instructional purposes.

- Because the focus of portfolios is on complex skills, teachers are more likely to *teach* those skills. (Banta, 2003; Darling-Hammond, Ancess, & Falk, 1995; DiMartino & Castaneda, 2007; R. S. Johnson et al., 2006; Paulson, Paulson, & Meyer, 1991; Spandel, 1997)

RSVP characteristics are often a source of concern with portfolios, however, especially if they're used to evaluate—rather than simply communicate—students' learning and achievement (Arter & Spandel, 1992; Banta, 2003; Haertel & Linn, 1996; R. S. Johnson et al., 2006). When portfolios must be scored in a holistic manner, the scoring is often unreliable, with different teachers rating them differently. In addition, there's an obvious standardization problem, because their contents can vary considerably from one student to another. Validity may or may not be an issue: Some portfolios may include enough work samples to adequately represent what students have accomplished relative to instructional goals, but others may be unrepresentative. And because portfolios are apt to take a great deal of teacher time, they're less practical than other methods of summarizing achievement. All of this isn't to say that we should shy away from using portfolios, but rather that we should be sure the potential benefits outweigh the downsides. And we must interpret them cautiously if we use them as summative reflections of what students have accomplished.

HELPING STUDENTS CONSTRUCT PORTFOLIOS

Creating a portfolio is typically a lengthy process that stretches out over several weeks or months; some best-work portfolios evolve over several years. So as not to overwhelm students by such a complex undertaking, it's often helpful to break the portfolio-construction process into a series of steps, scaffolding students' efforts at each step:

1. *Planning:* Decide on the purpose(s) the portfolio will serve (e.g., which instructional goals and/or content-area standards it will address and whether it will be used primarily for formative or summative assessment); identify a preliminary plan of attack for creating the portfolio.

2. *Collection:* Save artifacts that demonstrate progress toward or achievement of particular goals and standards.

3. *Selection:* Review the saved artifacts, and choose those that best reflect achievement of the specified goals and standards.

4. *Reflection:* Write explanations and self-evaluations of each artifact; describe how the artifacts show current competencies and growth over time; relate achievements to previously identified goals and standards.

5. *Projection:* Identify new goals toward which to strive.

6. *Presentation:* Share the portfolio with an appropriate audience (e.g., classmates, parents, college admissions officers). (Six steps based on R. S. Johnson et al., 2006)

The Into the Classroom feature "Summarizing Students' Achievements with Portfolios" offers and illustrates several suggestions for scaffolding students' efforts in creating portfolios.

MyEdLab
Video Example 15.2.
What benefits might this portfolio conference have for 8-year-old Keenan and her teacher?

Keep in mind the limitations of portfolios with respect to the RSVP characteristics.

Break the construction of portfolios into a sequence of several manageable steps.

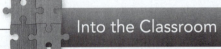

Into the Classroom

Summarizing Students' Achievements with Portfolios

🍎 **Identify in advance the specific purpose(s) for which a portfolio will be used.**

A third-grade teacher and her students agree to create portfolios that will show parents and other family members how much their writing skills improve over the school year. Throughout the year students save their fiction and nonfiction work, and eventually they choose pieces that best demonstrate mastery of some writing skills and progress on other skills. The children proudly present their portfolios at parent–teacher–student conferences at the end of the year.

🍎 **Align portfolio contents with important instructional goals and/or content-area standards.**

At a high school in Ohio, 12th graders complete graduation portfolios with three components, each of which reflects one or more of the school's instructional goals for all graduates:

- A *life-long-learning skills* section shows mastery of a student's key skills in writing, math, science, and at least one other content domain.
- A *democratic citizenship* section provides specific examples of how a student has been actively engaged in issues related to the local community or larger society (e.g., by contributing to a public service activity).
- A *career-readiness* section contains a résumé, letters of recommendation from teachers or other adults, and other documents that show preparedness for post-secondary education or the workplace.

🍎 **Ask students to select the contents of their portfolios; provide the scaffolding they need to make wise choices.**

A fifth-grade teacher meets one on one with each of his students to help them choose artifacts that best reflect their achievements for the year. To give the students an idea of the kinds of things they might include, he shows them several portfolios that students have created in previous years. He shares only those portfolios that previous students and parents have given him permission to use in this way.

🍎 **Identify specific criteria that should guide students' selections; possibly include students in the criteria identification process.**

A middle school geography teacher leads his class in a discussion of criteria that students might use to identify artifacts for a course portfolio. After reviewing the instructional goals for the course, the class agrees that the portfolio should include at least one artifact demonstrating each of the following:

- Map interpretation skills
- Map construction skills
- Understanding of interrelationships between physical environments and socioeconomic practices
- Knowledge of cultural differences within the nation
- Recognition that all cultures have many positive qualities

🍎 **Have students include reflections on the products they include.**

At the beginning of the school year, a ninth-grade journalism teacher tells students that they will be creating portfolios that show progress in journalistic writing during the semester. She asks them to save all of their drafts—"Even simple notes and sketchy outlines," she says. Later in the semester, as students begin to compile their portfolios, she asks them to look at their various drafts of each piece and to describe how the progression from one draft to the next shows their gradual mastery of journalistic skills. She occasionally assigns these reflections as homework so that students spread the portfolio construction task over a 4-week period and therefore don't leave everything until the last minute.

🍎 **Give students a general organizational scheme to follow.**

When a high school requires students to complete portfolios as one of their graduation requirements, students get considerable guidance from their homeroom teachers. These teachers also provide a handout describing the elements each portfolio should include: title page, table of contents, introduction to the portfolio's contents and criteria guiding artifact selection, distinct sections for each content domain included, and final reflection summarizing achievements.

🍎 **Determine whether a physical format or electronic format is more suitable for the circumstances.**

At a high school that places particular emphasis on visual and performing arts, students create electronic portfolios that showcase their talents in art, drama, dance, and/or instrumental music. They digitally photograph, videotape, or audiotape their projects and performances, and they create word processing documents that describe and evaluate each one. They then divide their electronic documents into several logical categories, each of which they put in a separate electronic folder on a flash drive, CD, or DVD.

🍎 **When using portfolios for summative assessments, develop a rubric to guide evaluation.**

At a high school in New York City, a key instructional goal is for students to acquire certain dispositions and thinking processes—which the school collectively calls *habits of mind*—in their academic work. One of these habits of mind is the use of credible, convincing evidence to support statements and positions. The school develops a four-point rating scale to evaluate students' work on this criterion. A score of 4 is given to work that reflects "Generalizations and ideas supported by specific relevant and accurate information, which is developed in appropriate depth." At the other end of the scale, a score of 1 is given to work that reflects "Mostly general statements; little specific evidence relating to the topic."

Sources: Darling-Hammond et al., 1995, p. 39 (New York City high school example); DiMartino & Castaneda, 2007 (Ohio high school example); R. L. Johnson, Penny, & Gordon, 2009; R. S. Johnson et al., 2006; Paulson et al., 1991; Popham, 2014; Spandel, 1997; Stiggins & Chappuis, 2012.

MyEdLab **Self-Check 15.2**

MyEdLab **Application Exercise 15.2** In this video case analysis, you can apply what you have learned about instructional strategies and human motivation to analyze the use of portfolios in a bilingual sixth-grade class.

Standardized Tests

A **standardized test** is one developed by test construction experts and published for use in many different schools and classrooms. Standardized tests are *standardized* in several ways: All students receive the same instructions, have the same time limits, respond to the same (or very similar) questions or tasks, and have their responses evaluated relative to the same criteria. These tests typically come with manuals that include the instructions to give students, the time limits to impose, and explicit scoring criteria to use. If the tests are norm-referenced—and many of them are—their manuals usually provide norms for various age or grade levels. Also, the manuals often provide information about test reliability for various populations and age-groups, as well as information from which we can draw inferences about test validity for our own situation and purposes.

TYPES OF STANDARDIZED TESTS

School districts use four kinds of standardized tests fairly frequently: tests of achievement, general scholastic aptitude and intelligence, specific aptitudes and abilities, and school readiness.[3]

ACHIEVEMENT TESTS

Standardized achievement tests are designed to assess how much students have learned from what they've specifically been taught. The test items are intended to reflect the curriculum common to most schools; for example, a history test will focus on national or world history rather than the history of a particular state or province. Many of these tests yield norm-referenced scores, although some tests now also yield criterion-referenced scores tied to particular national or state standards. The overall test scores reflect achievement in a broad sense: They tell us how much a student has learned in general about, say, mathematics or language mechanics—and perhaps whether the student has mastered certain basic skill areas—but won't necessarily give us information related to specific instructional objectives (e.g., multiplication of fractions or correct usage of uppercase versus lowercase letters).

Standardized achievement tests are useful in two primary ways. First, they tell us how well our own students' achievement compares with that of students elsewhere—information that may indirectly tell us something about the effectiveness of our instruction. Second, they help us track students' general progress over time and alert us to potential trouble spots. For example, imagine that Lucas gets average test scores year after year but then suddenly performs well below average in the ninth grade, even though the test and norm group are the same as in previous years. At this point we would want to ascertain whether the low performance is a temporary fluke—perhaps Lucas was sick on the test day—or, instead, due to more enduring factors that require attention.

Most standardized achievement tests are highly reliable; that is, they lead to fairly consistent results for individual students, especially for students in the upper elementary and secondary grades. However, our main concern whenever we assess achievement is *content validity*, which we need to determine for *our own situation*. We can determine the content validity of a standardized achievement test by comparing a table of specifications—one provided in the test manual or one we construct ourselves by analyzing the test items—to our own curriculum. A test has high content validity only if the topics—*and also* the thinking skills—emphasized in test items match our curriculum, instructional goals, and content-area standards.

GENERAL SCHOLASTIC APTITUDE AND INTELLIGENCE TESTS

Whereas achievement tests are designed to assess how much students have specifically learned from what they've presumably been taught, **scholastic aptitude tests** are designed to assess a general *capacity* to learn. Traditionally many of these tests have been called *intelligence tests*. However, some experts shy away from the latter term, in part because psychologists don't agree about what intelligence *is* and in part because many people mistakenly believe that IQ scores reflect inherited ability almost exclusively. Other commonly used terms are *general aptitude test, school ability test,* and *cognitive ability test*.

MyEdLab
Video Example 15.3
Standardized achievement test results can help teachers monitor students' progress, *provided that* they are closely aligned with important instructional goals and standards. What benefits and potential limitations of standards and standardized test scores do school administrators identify in this video?

Determine the content validity of a standardized achievement test for your own curriculum, instructional goals, and content-area standards.

---

[3] You can find examples of popular standardized tests at the websites for CTB and McGraw-Hill (ctb.com), Pearson (pearsonassessments.com), and Riverside Publishing (riverpub.com).

Regardless of what we call them, tests that fall into this category are used mainly for prediction—that is, to estimate how well students are likely to learn and perform in future academic situations. Typically these tests are designed to assess how much students have learned and deduced from their general, everyday experiences. For example, they may assess understanding of vocabulary words that most students are likely to have encountered at one time or another. They may include analogy items intended to assess how well students can recognize similarities among well-known relationships. They may ask students to analyze pictures or manipulate concrete objects. And most of them include measures of general knowledge and tasks that require deductive reasoning and problem solving.

You can learn more about intelligence tests and IQ scores in Chapter 5.

Like standardized achievement tests, scholastic aptitude tests tend to be quite reliable, especially for older students. Of greater concern, however, is their *predictive validity*—the accuracy with which they can help us estimate students' future achievement levels. Their predictive validity for future academic success varies considerably depending on the situation and population at hand, but in general you should think of these tests as providing only rough estimates of how students are likely to perform in school in the next 2 or 3 years; they're even *less* accurate in predicting students' academic and professional success over the long run. Keep in mind, too, that many factors not measured by these tests—for instance, motivation, self-regulation skills, and the quality of instruction—also influence students' learning and classroom performance (Dai, 2010; Duckworth & Seligman, 2005; Kuhn, 2001; Perkins, Tishman, Ritchhart, Donis, & Andrade, 2000).

SPECIFIC APTITUDE AND ABILITY TESTS

General scholastic aptitude tests are useful when we want to predict overall academic performance. But when we're interested in how well students are apt to perform in a particular content domain (e.g., math, music, or auto mechanics), **specific aptitude tests** are more useful. Some aptitude tests are designed to predict future performance in just one content domain. Others, called *multiple aptitude batteries,* yield subscores for a variety of domains simultaneously.

Specific aptitude tests are sometimes used to identify students who are most likely to benefit from certain domain-specific instructional programs (e.g., advanced math or science classes). They may also be used for counseling students about future educational plans and career choices. But two caveats are important to keep in mind when using these tests for such purposes. First, their predictive validity in academic contexts tends to be lower than that for general scholastic aptitude tests—that is, they yield only very rough estimates of students' future academic performance in the domain(s) in question. Second, they're based on the assumption that the ability being measured is a fairly stable one—an assumption that may or may not be accurate. Rather than trying to identify students with high aptitudes for particular subject areas, then, some educators argue that we should focus more on *developing* abilities in *all* students (Boykin, 1994; P. D. Nichols & Mittelholtz, 1997; Sternberg, 2002). Accordingly, specific aptitude tests now appear less frequently in wide-scale school testing programs than they once did.

SCHOOL READINESS TESTS

A **school readiness test** is designed to determine whether children have acquired knowledge and skills essential for success in kindergarten or first grade—for instance, knowledge of colors, shapes, letters, and numbers. When used in combination with other information, school readiness tests can be helpful if we're looking for significant developmental delays that require immediate attention (Bracken & Walker, 1997; Lidz, 1991). On their own, however, they have limited predictive validity: The scores they yield typically correlate only moderately with children's academic performance even a year or so later (Duncan et al., 2007; La Paro & Pianta, 2000; C. E. Sanders, 1997; Stipek, 2002).

Use the results of school readiness tests only for instructional planning—*not* for making decisions about which children are ready to begin school.

School readiness tests can often give us an idea of where to begin instruction with particular children. But as a general rule, we should *not* use them to identify children who should postpone formal schooling. By age 5 almost all children are probably ready for some form of structured educational program. Rather than focus on determining which children might have trouble in a particular educational curriculum and environment, we better serve children when we determine how to adapt the curriculum and environment to fit each child's developmental progress and particular needs (Farran, 2001; Lidz, 1991; Stipek, 2002).

Table 15.2 summarizes the four categories of standardized tests just described.

COMPARE/CONTRAST

TABLE 15.2 • Commonly Used Standardized Tests		
KIND OF TEST	**PURPOSE**	**RECOMMENDATIONS**
Achievement tests	To assess how much students have learned from what they have presumably been specifically taught	• Use these tests primarily for assessing broad areas of achievement rather than specific knowledge and skills.
Scholastic aptitude and intelligence tests	To assess students' general capability to learn; to predict their general academic success over the short run	• Use test scores as rough predictors of performance in the near future, *not* as predictors of learning potential over the long run. • Use tests designed for one-on-one administration if (a) a student's verbal skills are limited, (b) exceptional giftedness or a significant disability is suspected, or (c) a student has insufficient self-regulation skills to stay on task during paper–pencil or computer-administered tests.
Specific aptitude and ability tests	To predict how easily students are likely to learn in a specific content domain	• Use test scores as rough predictors of performance in the near future, *not* as predictors of learning potential over the long run. • Because predictive validities for many of these tests are low, use test scores only in combination with other information about students.
School readiness tests	To determine whether young children have the prerequisite skills to be successful in a typical kindergarten or first-grade curriculum	• Use test results only in combination with other information about children. • Use test results for instructional planning, *not* for deciding whether students are ready to begin formal schooling.

INDIVIDUAL VERSUS GROUP ADMINISTRATION OF STANDARDIZED TESTS

Some standardized tests are administered one on one. Such tests enable the examiner to observe a student's attention span, motivation, and other factors that may affect academic performance. For this reason, individually administered tests are typically used when identifying cognitive disabilities and other special educational needs.

When circumstances call for giving *all* students a standardized test, testing them as a group is usually the only practical approach. Fortunately, computer technology comes to our assistance in two distinct ways. For one thing, computers are routinely used to score a group test and generate reports about each student's performance. In addition, some tests come in computer-based rather than paper–pencil form. Computer-based standardized testing can provide several options that are either impractical or impossible with paper–pencil tests:

- It allows **adaptive testing**, which adjusts the difficulty level of items as students proceed through a test and can thereby zero in on students' specific strengths and weaknesses fairly quickly.
- It can include animations, simulations, videos, and audiotaped messages—all of which can expand the kinds of knowledge and skills that test items assess.
- It enables assessment of how students approach specific problems and how quickly they accomplish specific tasks.
- It allows the possibility of assessing students' abilities under varying levels of support (e.g., by providing one or more hints as needed to guide students' reasoning).
- It can provide on-the-spot scoring and analyses of students' performance.

Computer-based standardized tests tend to have reliability and validity levels similar to those of traditional paper–pencil tests. Their use should, of course, be limited to students who are familiar and comfortable with computers and have adequate keyboarding skills.

GUIDELINES FOR CHOOSING AND USING STANDARDIZED TESTS

As teachers, we may sometimes have input into the selection of standardized tests for our districts, and we'll often be involved in administering them. Following are guidelines for choosing and using a standardized test appropriately:

🍎 *Choose a test with high validity for your particular purpose and high reliability for students similar to your own.* We've examined four categories of standardized tests as if they're four distinctly different entities, but in fact the differences among them aren't always clear-cut. To some extent, all of these tests assess what a student has already learned, and all of them can be used to predict future performance. Our best bet is to choose the test that has the greatest validity for our particular purpose, regardless of what the test might be called. We also want a test that has been shown to be highly reliable with a population similar to ours.

🍎 *Make sure that the test's norm group is relevant to your own population.* Scrutinize the test manual's description of the norm group used for the test, with questions like these in mind:

- Does the norm group include students of both genders and students of the same ages, educational levels, and cultural backgrounds as those of your own students?
- Is it a representative sample of the population at large or in some other way appropriate for any comparisons you plan to make?
- Have the normative data been collected recently enough that they reflect how students typically perform in the current year?

When we determine norm-referenced test scores by comparing students with an *in*appropriate norm group, the scores are meaningless. For example, one of us authors recalls a situation in which teacher education students at a major state university were required to take basic skills tests in language and math. Because the tests had been normed on a high school population, the university students' performance was compared to that of high school seniors—a practice that made no sense whatsoever.

🍎 *Take students' ages and developmental levels into account.* A variety of irrelevant factors—such as motivation, self-regulation skills, and general energy level—affect students' performance on tests and other assessments. When these factors are relatively stable characteristics, they affect test validity. When they're temporary and variable from day to day (perhaps even hour to hour), they affect test reliability and thus also indirectly affect validity. Such sources of error in students' test scores and other assessment results are especially common in young children, who may have limited language skills, short attention spans, little motivation to do their best, and low tolerance for frustration. Furthermore, young children's erratic behaviors may make it difficult to maintain standardized testing conditions (Bracken & Walker, 1997; Messick, 1983; Wodtke, Harper, & Schommer, 1989).

In adolescence other variables can affect the validity of standardized test scores. For example, especially in high school, some students become quite cynical about the validity and usefulness of standardized paper–pencil tests. Thus they may read test items superficially, if at all, and a few may complete answer sheets simply by following a certain pattern (e.g., alternating between A and B) or filling in bubbles to make pictures or designs (S. G. Paris, Lawton, Turner, & Roth, 1991). Table 15.3 describes these and other developmental differences affecting students' performance on standardized tests.

🍎 *Make sure that students are adequately prepared to take the test.* In most instances we'll want to prepare students ahead of time for a standardized test. Several more specific strategies are widely recommended:

🍎 Explain the general nature of the test and the tasks it involves (e.g., if applicable, mention that students aren't expected to know all of the answers and that many students won't have enough time to respond to every item).

🍎 Encourage students to do their best, but without describing the test as a life-or-death matter.

🍎 Give students practice with the test's format and item types (e.g., demonstrate how to fill in electronically scored answer sheets).

🍎 Give suggestions about effective test-taking strategies; in other words, foster *testwiseness*. But don't overdo it; remember that your time is best spent helping students master the content domain being assessed.

🍎 Encourage students to get a full night's sleep and eat a good breakfast before taking the test.

🍎 *When administering the test, follow the directions closely, and report any unusual circumstances.* Once a test session begins, we should follow the test administration procedures to the letter,

See Chapter 14 for more information on testwiseness.

DEVELOPMENTAL TRENDS

TABLE 15.3 • Characteristics Affecting Standardized Test Performance at Different Grade Levels			
GRADE LEVEL	**AGE-TYPICAL CHARACTERISTICS**	**EXAMPLE**	**SUGGESTED STRATEGIES**
K–2	• Short attention span; significant individual differences in ability to stay focused on test items • Little intrinsic motivation to perform well on tests • Inconsistency in test performance from one occasion to another	One Saturday morning each spring, an elementary school conducts a "Kindergarten Roundup" at which it collects information about children who will be enrolling in kindergarten in the fall. Escorted by a parent, each child goes to various booths in the gym, where teachers conduct various short assessments of basic knowledge and emerging literacy skills. Some children willingly comply with the teachers' instructions, but others are bouncy and have trouble staying on task.	● Don't use school readiness tests to determine which children are "ready" for elementary school; instead, plan early school experiences that can prepare students for future academic learning. ● Leave assessment for diagnostic purposes (e.g., to identify students with special needs) in the hands of trained professionals who have experience in assessing young children. ● Don't make long-term predictions about achievement on the basis of standardized test scores. ● Use multiple measures when making important decisions about students' educational programs.
3–5	• Unquestioning acceptance of standardized tests as valid measures of ability or achievement • Increasing ability to stay focused on a paper–pencil assessment instrument • Increasing facility with computer-scored answer sheets • Considerable variability in knowledge and use of effective test-taking strategies	Students in a fourth-grade class work quietly and diligently on a statewide achievement test. Most of them address the questions in the order they appear in the test booklet, and some students spend so much time on especially difficult items that they must leave many questions still unanswered when the allotted time is up.	● Stress the value of standardized tests for tracking students' progress and identifying areas in which students may need extra instruction and support. ● Give students plenty of practice using computer-scored answer sheets. ● Explicitly teach basic test-taking strategies (e.g., skipping difficult test items and returning to them later if time allows).
6–8	• Increase in debilitating test anxiety (for some students) • Continuing variability in testwiseness • Emerging skepticism about the value of standardized tests (for some students)	When a junior high school homeroom teacher announces an upcoming national achievement test, a few low-achieving students argue that it will be a "complete waste of time" and insist that they won't take it seriously.	● Explain that standardized tests provide only a rough idea of what students know and can do; reassure students that test results won't be the only things affecting instructional decision making. ● Encourage students to do their best on a test; assure them that test results will be used not to judge them but rather to help them learn more effectively. ● Provide some practice in test-taking skills, but remember that students' performance depends more on their knowledge and abilities in content domains than on their general test-taking ability.
9–12	• Increasing cynicism about the validity and usefulness of standardized tests (especially common in low-achieving students) • Decreasing motivation to perform well on standardized tests; in some instances may reflect self-handicapping as a way of justifying poor performance	After a high school teacher has passed out test booklets, read the instructions, and started her stopwatch, one student puts down his pencil, slouches back in his chair, and looks absent-mindedly out the window. A few minutes later, he grabs his pencil and fills in bubbles on his answer sheet to spell his name: "JESSE."	● Acknowledge that standardized tests aren't perfect, but explain that they *can* help teachers and administrators assess school effectiveness and plan future instruction. ● Be alert for signs that a student may intentionally subvert an assessment or has already done so; speak privately with the student about his or her concerns and offer your support to enhance test performance.

Sources: Bracken & Walker, 1997; S. M. Carver, 2006; Dempster & Corkill, 1999; R. L. Johnson et al., 2009; Lidz, 1991; Messick, 1983; S. G. Paris et al., 1991; Petersen, Sudweeks, & Baird, 1990; Sarason, 1980; Scruggs & Lifson, 1985; Stipek, 2002.

distributing test booklets as directed, asking students to complete any practice items provided, keeping time faithfully, and responding to questions in the prescribed manner. If we don't replicate the conditions under which the norm group has taken a test, any norm-referenced scores derived from the test will be meaningless. When unanticipated events significantly alter the test environment (e.g., when electrical power unexpectedly goes out), they jeopardize the validity of the test results and must be reported. We should also make note of any students who are behaving in ways unlikely to lead to maximum performance—appearing exceptionally nervous, staring out the window for long periods, marking answers haphazardly, and so on (M. D. Miller et al., 2009).

INTERPRETING STANDARDIZED TEST SCORES

Thanks to increasingly sophisticated software programs, computer-generated reports of students' performance on standardized tests can be quite detailed and complex. Figure 15.11 presents a hypothetical example for a second grader we'll call "Sarah," who has recently taken both the Stanford Achievement Test Series and the Otis-Lennon School Ability Test. As you can see in the purple-and-white-striped section of the form, the Stanford yields scores related to students' overall achievement in a variety of content domains and subdomains; such a multidomain test is often called a *test battery*. The Otis-Lennon (at the bottom of the purple-and-white section) is designed to assess students' general cognitive abilities with respect to both *verbal* tasks (those that depend heavily on language skills) and *nonverbal* tasks (those that involve numbers, pictures, or graphical configurations).

At first glance, the report can be quite daunting, but let's make sense of some of the data presented in the top section. The "Number Correct" columns are Sarah's raw scores on the overall tests and various subtests within them. The PR-S scores are really two separate scores: The first two digits indicate a percentile score and the digit after the hyphen is a stanine score. The Stanford yields percentiles and stanines based on a national norm group of second graders; the Otis-Lennon yields two sets of percentiles and stanines, one set derived from the second-grade norms (the "Natl Grade PR-S") and the other derived from students in the norm group who are the same age as Sarah (the "Age PR-S"). We've previously explained the nature of NCE scores, and the SAI scores on the Otis-Lennon are based on the IQ-score scale we also described earlier ("SAI" refers to "School Ability Index"). We haven't specifically talked about scaled scores or what an AAC range might be, and we authors don't want to overwhelm our readers with too much information—in common texting lingo, "TMI"—so we're putting explanations of these columns in a footnote for readers who might be curious.[4]

Notice the "National Grade Percentile Bands" in the upper right part of the figure. These are *confidence intervals* intended to reflect the amount of error (and imperfect reliability) affecting Sarah's percentile scores. As is true in the simpler printout in Figure 15.7, the graph squishes middle-range percentile scores close together and spreads the high and low percentiles farther apart as a way of reflecting the scores' underlying normal distribution.

Despite the many numbers that standardized tests can yield, we must remember that students' scores on these tests are, at best, only *imprecise estimates* of what students generally know and can do, and they may have little or no validity for some students. We must be *extremely cautious*— and occasionally downright skeptical—in our interpretation of students' standardized test results, and we mustn't place too much stock in the *exact* scores that the tests yield. Following are three additional guidelines to keep in mind when interpreting and using standardized test scores.

🕯 *Have a clear and justifiable rationale for establishing any cutoffs for acceptable performance.* If we want to use test results to make *either–or* decisions—for instance, to determine whether a student should move to a more advanced math class or be exempt from a basic writing skills course—we must have a clear rationale for the cutoff scores we use. The process can be relatively easy for criterion-referenced scores, provided that they truly reflect mastery and nonmastery of the subject matter. It's far more difficult for norm-referenced scores: At what point does a student's performance become acceptable? At the 20th percentile? At a stanine of 6? Without more information about the knowledge and skills the scores represent, there's no easy way for determining a cutoff for acceptable scores.

> Remember that despite the apparent precision of standardized test scores, these scores are, at best, only imprecise estimates of students' abilities, and for some students the scores may be way off target.

---

[4]The "Scaled Scores" are statistical adjustments that reflect the difficulty level of a particular form of each test; they allow comparisons among students who have taken different forms of the tests, with some forms almost inevitably being slightly more difficult than others. "AAC Range" refers to "Ability-Achievement Comparison"; entries in this column indicate how Sarah's various achievement test scores compare with the Otis-Lennon's estimates of her general cognitive ability. For example, Sarah is "High" in her Math achievement scores, indicating that she has done better than have most students with Otis-Lennon scores similar to hers.

FIGURE 15.11 **Hypothetical report for a second grader's performance on the Stanford Achievement Test Series and the Otis-Lennon Ability Test.**

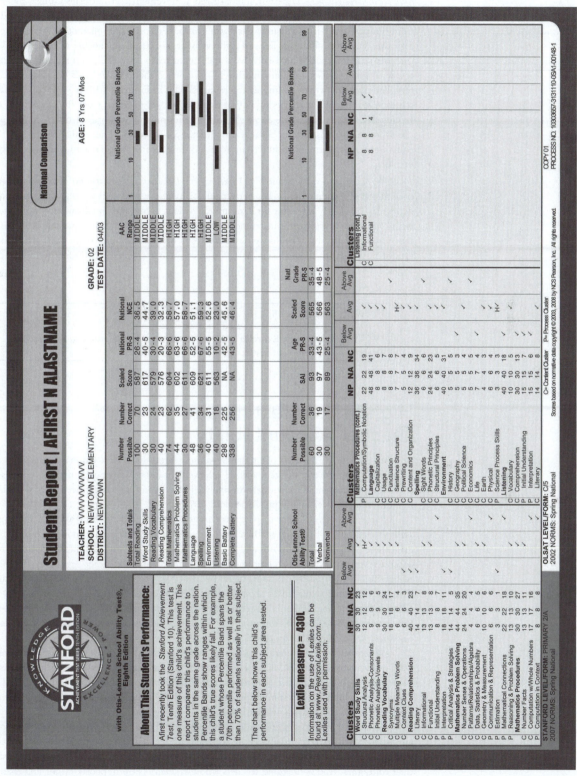

Appendix B offers additional insights on when and how we can compare a student's varying test scores.

🍎 *Compare two standardized test scores only when the scores have been derived from the same or equivalent norm group(s).* Different standardized achievement test batteries almost always have different norm groups; for example, scores on the Stanford Achievement Test Series are derived from comparisons with one particular norm group, whereas scores on another widely used battery, the Woodcock-Johnson Tests of Achievement, are based on another norm group. We can compare students' performance on two achievement tests—say, their performance on a reading test with their performance on a math test—*only* when the tests are parts of the same test battery. For example, when looking at the report shown in Figure 15.11, we can compare Sarah's scores in reading and math because all of these scores were derived from the same norm group. In contrast, we *can't* compare Sarah's reading scores on the Stanford with her math scores on the Woodcock-Johnson tests because any differences we might find could be the result of inequivalent norm groups rather than actual differences in Sarah's achievement in the two domains.

🍎 *Never use a single test score to make important decisions.* No test—no matter how carefully constructed and widely used—has perfect reliability and validity. Every test is fallible, and students may do poorly on a test for a variety of reasons. Thus, we should never—note the word *never*—use a single assessment instrument or a single test score to make important decisions about individual students. Nor should we use single test scores to make important decisions about large groups of students or about the teachers who teach them, for reasons we'll identify in the next few pages.

MyEdLab **Self-Check 15.3**

MyEdLab **Application Exercise 15.3.** In this interactive exercise, you can practice interpreting achievement test scores.

High-Stakes Testing and Teacher Accountability

In recent decades, a great deal of emphasis—almost certainly *too much* emphasis—has been placed on students' performance on standardized achievement tests. Many policy makers, business leaders, and other influential individuals routinely cite low scores on standardized tests as evidence of low achievement levels in our public schools.

Some students do seem to progress through several grade levels without acquiring basic skills in reading, writing, and math; a few graduate from high school without such skills. To address these problems, many states and school districts now use students' performance on tests or other assessments as a basis for promoting students to the next grade level or awarding high school diplomas. Typically educators begin by identifying certain instructional goals or standards that students' final achievement should reflect. They then assess students' performance levels at the end of instruction, and only those students whose performance meets the predetermined goals and standards move forward. You might see such labels as *minimum competency testing* and *outcomes-based education* used for this approach.

Whenever we use a single assessment instrument to make major decisions about students, we're using a high-stakes test. Because high-stakes tests are typically used to make judgments about *mastery* of school subject matter, they require criterion-referenced rather than norm-referenced scores. For example, a high-stakes test might yield a score such as "In progress," "Proficient," or "Advanced" with respect to a student's knowledge and skills in a particular subject area.

Sometimes students' scores on high-stakes tests are used to make important decisions not only about students but also about the students' *teachers*. For example, teachers whose students score at exceptionally high levels at the end of the school year might get higher pay raises that their colleagues. And nontenured teachers whose students perform poorly might find themselves without a teaching job the following year. Whenever teachers are evaluated on the basis of how their students perform on achievement tests, we're talking about teacher accountability.

THE U.S. NO CHILD LEFT BEHIND ACT

In the United States the No Child Left Behind Act of 2001—sometimes known simply as NCLB—mandates both high-stakes testing and accountability in all public elementary and secondary schools. It also mandates that states establish

> challenging academic content standards in academic subjects that —
> I. specify what children are expected to know and be able to do;
> II. contain coherent and rigorous content; and
> III. encourage the teaching of advanced skills (P.L. 107-110, Sec. 1111)

School districts must annually assess students in grades 3 through 8 and at least once during grades 10 through 12 to determine whether students are making *adequate yearly progress* in meeting state-determined standards in reading, math, and science. The nature of this progress is defined by the state (and thus differs from state to state), but assessment results must clearly show that all students—including those from diverse racial and socioeconomic groups—are making significant gains in knowledge and skills. (Students with diagnosed cognitive disabilities may be given alternative assessments, but these students must show improvement commensurate with their ability levels.) Schools that demonstrate progress receive rewards, such as teacher bonuses and increased funding. Schools that don't demonstrate progress are subject to sanctions and corrective actions (e.g., bad publicity, administrative restructuring, dismissal of staff members), and their students have the option of attending a better public school at the school district's expense. The U.S. Department of Education's website (ed.gov/nclb) provides more details.

The No Child Left Behind Act has been highly controversial and in many respects hasn't brought about the changes it was intended to generate (Forte, 2010; Mintrop & Sunderman, 2009; Polikoff, McEachin, Wrabel, & Duque, 2014). As this book goes to press in 2015, most U.S. states have gotten waivers from certain parts of the legislation. Waivers don't get states off the hook; rather, states must develop and implement their own comprehensive plans for improving instruction and significantly increasing students' achievement levels, especially for historically low-performing minority groups.

Systematic efforts to monitor schools' instructional effectiveness and students' academic progress are certainly well intentioned. Ideally they can help schools determine whether instructional methods need revision and whether teachers need retooling. They can also help teachers identify students who aren't acquiring the basic skills necessary for successful participation in the adult world. And the focus on improving *all* students' achievement levels is long overdue. However, the current emphasis on boosting students' test scores is fraught with difficulties in implementation, and solutions to these difficulties are only slowly emerging.

PROBLEMS WITH HIGH-STAKES TESTING

Experts have identified several problems with the use of high-stakes tests to make decisions about students, teachers, and schools.

🍎 *The tests don't always reflect important instructional goals.* High-stakes achievement tests don't always have good content validity for the contexts in which they're used. Even if well constructed, they may reflect only a small portion of a school's curriculum and instructional goals. For instance, the emphasis in NCLB and in some state- and district-level assessments is primarily on achievement in certain content domains (e.g., NCLB focuses on reading, math, and science), with little regard for achievement in other areas. Furthermore, the preponderance of multiple-choice and other objectively scorable items on many standardized tests limits the extent to which these tests assess complex cognitive skills and performance on authentic, real-world tasks (Hursh, 2007; M. G. Jones, Jones, & Hargrove, 2003; Leu, O'Byrne, Zawilinski, McVerry, & Everett-Cacopardo, 2009; Mintrop & Sunderman, 2009; R. M. Thomas, 2005).

🍎 *Teachers spend a great deal of time teaching to the tests.* When teachers are held accountable for their students' performance on a particular test, many of them understandably devote many class hours to the topics and skills the test assesses, and students may focus their studying accordingly. The result is often that students perform at higher levels on a high-stakes test *without* improving their achievement and abilities more generally. If a test truly measures the things that are most

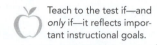

Teach to the test if—and *only* if—it reflects important instructional goals.

You can learn more about this math teacher's dilemma in the opening case study in Chapter 7.

important for students to learn—including problem solving, critical thinking, and other complex thinking skills—then focusing on those things is quite appropriate. But if the test primarily assesses only rote knowledge and simple skills, it can undermine the achievement gains we *really* want to see (W. Au, 2007; A. S. Finn et al., 2014; Jennings & Bearak, 2014; Quellmalz et al., 2013).

Sometimes, too, high-stakes tests are based on lengthy lists of prescribed competencies or standards—far too many for most students to master in a single school year. Thus teachers may try to cover many topics quickly, without giving students sufficient time and instruction to master any of them. As one eighth-grade math teacher put it when her class was facing a statewide math competency exam, "Mastery probably isn't possible at this point, but I should at least *present* what students need to know. Maybe this will help a few of them with some of the test items." Such superficial coverage is common when maximizing students' scores on high-stakes tests must be at the top of teachers' priority lists (W. Au, 2007; La Guardia, 2009; Plank & Condliffe, 2013; Valli & Buese, 2007).

🍎 *Teachers and schools may focus much of their attention on helping some students while shortchanging others.* The focus of NCLB and many state- and district-level assessment policies is on maximizing the number of students who meet certain minimal criteria for acceptable performance. Within such a context, the key to doing well as a school is to push as many low-achieving students as possible over the minimal cutoff for success. In the process, students who fall way below the cutoff and students who are already well above it may be given short shrift; for instance, schools may devote little instructional time or resources to students who are most in need of them (Balfanz, Legters, West, & Weber, 2007; A. D. Ho, 2008; Porter & Polikoff, 2007).

🍎 *School personnel have disincentives to follow standardized testing procedures and to assess the achievement of chronically low performers.* In a high-stakes situation, teachers and administrators sometimes conclude that *dis*honesty is the best policy. Imagine that, as a teacher or school administrator, you want to maximize your school's average test scores. Might you give students more than the allotted time to finish the test? Might you provide hints about correct answers or possibly even *give* students the correct answers? Might you find reasons to exempt certain students from taking the test—perhaps finding a place for them in a special education program or retaining them at a grade level where they won't be assessed? Such practices can occur when teachers and administrators are under pressure to raise a school's average test scores (Hursh, 2007; Mintrop & Sunderman, 2009; R. M. Ryan & Brown, 2005; R. M. Thomas, 2005).

A few years after NCLB was instituted, one of us authors spoke with a high school principal in a small rural school district in northern New England. Although this principal certainly saw benefits to regularly assessing students' progress in basic skills, he revealed that one group of minority students at his school had *not* shown the NCLB-mandated yearly progress during the preceding school year. "We have only five students in that particular group," he explained. "As a result of difficult family circumstances, one of the five—a 16-year-old—lives on his own and comes to school only about 40% of the time. His performance on the annual assessment pulled the average scores for his group way down. If we truly wanted our test results to look good for the group, we should just have let him drop out—something he was inclined to do anyway. Instead, we did everything we could to keep him in school." The school's decision was certainly in the student's best interest, but it was a costly one in terms of the achievement results it reported for the school year.

🍎 *Different criteria lead to different conclusions about which students and schools are performing at high levels.* When we base teacher retention, salary increases, school funding, and other incentives on students' test performance, what specific criterion do we use? A predetermined, absolute level of achievement? Improvement over time? Superior performance relative to other school districts? There's no easy answer to this question. Yet depending on which criterion we use, we'll reach different conclusions as to which students, teachers, and schools are and are not performing well. Compounding the problem is the fact that students in lower-income communities achieve at lower levels, on average, than those in higher-income communities even when both groups have excellent teachers and instructional programs (E. M. Anderman, Gimbert, O'Connell, & Riegel, 2015; Ballou, Sanders, & Wright, 2004; Mintrop & Sunderman, 2009).

🍎 *Too much emphasis is placed on punishing seemingly low-performing teachers and schools; not enough is placed on helping them improve.* Many advocates of school reform think that a quick, easy "fix" to students' low achievement levels is simply to reward teachers and schools whose students do well and to punish those whose students do poorly. This strategy is unlikely to be effective, especially if some of the factors affecting students' academic performance (health, family support, peer group norms, etc.) are beyond teachers' and administrators' control. In fact, there's *no* convincing evidence that simply holding school faculty accountable for students' performance on high-stakes assessments—without also providing sufficient support to make change possible—has a significant positive influence on teachers' instructional strategies or on students' learning and achievement. Furthermore, the threat of harsh consequences for insufficient improvements in test scores can adversely affect teachers' morale and lead some teachers, including some very good ones, to leave teaching altogether (A. B. Brown & Clift, 2010; Finnigan & Gross, 2007; Forte, 2010; Stringfield & Yakimowski-Srebnick, 2005).

🍎 *Students' motivation affects their performance on the tests, and consistently low test performance can, in turn, affect their motivation.* For a variety of reasons—perhaps because of low self-efficacy or external, uncontrollable attributions for academic achievement—some students have little motivation to do well on high-stakes tests, and others become so anxious that they *can't* do as well as they should (Chabrán, 2003; Siskin, 2003). Furthermore, when students get consistently low test scores—and especially when their scores pose obstacles to promotion and graduation—they may see little point in staying in school. Thus the use of high-stakes tests for high school graduation doesn't necessarily increase students' achievement levels. Instead, it can increase school dropout rates, especially for students from certain ethnic minority groups and students from low-income neighborhoods (Holme, Richards, Jimerson, & Cohen, 2010; M. G. Jones et al., 2003; Kumar, Gheen, & Kaplan, 2002; Plunk, Tate, Bierut, & Grucza, 2014; R. M. Ryan & Brown, 2005).

PRODUCTIVE STEPS FORWARD IN HIGH-STAKES TESTING

Public concern about students' achievement levels in elementary and secondary schools isn't going away any time soon, nor should it. Many students *are* achieving at low levels, especially those in low-income school districts, those in certain minority groups, and those with special educational needs. Hence we authors offer several potential solutions that, in combination, may help to alleviate the problems with high-stakes testing just identified.

🍎 *Assess those things most important for students to know and do.* If we're going to make important decisions about students, teachers, and schools based on assessment results, we must be sure we're assessing aspects of achievement most critical for students' long-term success both in school and in the adult world. For instance, students should not only acquire basic skills in literacy, math, and science but also gain a solid understanding of how their government works, what social factors affect the welfare and behaviors of their fellow human beings, and how they can productively use their leisure time and contribute to the general betterment of society (R. M. Thomas, 2005). We shouldn't pretend that assessing such things is easy, but it's essential if we're going to rely on assessment results to determine whether schools are truly meeting students' long-term needs.

🍎 *Educate the public about what standardized tests can and cannot do for us.* What we authors have recently seen and heard in the media leads us to think that many public figures and policy makers overestimate how much standardized achievement tests can tell us: They assume that such instruments are highly accurate, comprehensive measures of what students know and can do. True, these tests are usually developed by experts in test construction, but no test is completely reliable, and its validity will vary considerably depending on the context in which it's being used. It behooves all of us—whether we're teachers, school administrators, parents, or simply members of the general public—to learn about the limitations of standardized tests and educate our fellow citizens acordingly.

🍎 *Consider alternatives to traditional machine-scorable paper–pencil tests.* When a test will be administered to many students at once, it's likely to consist largely of machine-scorable recognition-item formats such as multiple-choice questions. Well-constructed multiple-choice tests certainly have the capacity to assess complex cognitive skills, but they inevitably limit how

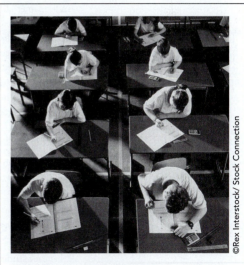

As teachers, we must help educate the public about the limitations of standardized tests, especially those that are used in making important decisions about students and instructional programs.

effectively we can assess certain skill areas, such as in writing and computer technology. Thus some experts argue that we should use authentic assessments either instead of or in addition to more traditional paper–pencil tests (e.g., E. L. Baker, 2007; DiMartino, 2007; L. Shepard et al., 2005). We should be aware, however, that states and school districts that have used authentic, performance-based assessments on a large scale have encountered problems with reliability and validity. As a society, then, we must tread cautiously as we move in this direction.

🍎 *Advocate for the use of multiple measures in any high-stakes decisions about students.* No matter what kind of assessment techniques we use, no single technique is likely to give us a comprehensive picture of what students have learned and achieved. Even if a single assessment could give us such a picture, perfect reliability is an elusive goal: Students' test results are inevitably subject to temporary swings in motivation, attention, mood, health, and other factors. To base life-altering decisions about students on a single test score is unconscionable.

🍎 *If tests are being used to measure teacher effectiveness, advocate for a focus on academic improvement rather than on age-group averages.* Assessing the degree to which each student makes progress during the school year may not be the best approach to assigning final grades (recall our earlier concerns about basing grades on improvement) but it is probably a reasonable approach to evaluating the effectiveness of teachers and schools. You may sometimes see the term **value-added assessment** used in reference to progress-based evaluation of teachers and schools.

Unfortunately, assessing students' improvement over a single school year isn't as easy as it might seem, especially when we're using standardized achievement tests. We can't just find the difference between beginning-of-year and end-of-year test scores and say, "Hey, Mr. Black's students showed bigger gains than Ms. Brown's students did, so Mr. Black must be the better teacher." For one thing, if we calculate the mathematical difference between two test scores with imperfect reliability and validity, the result will be a number with even *less* reliability and validity. Also, students can differ considerably in the *rates* at which they improve, with students from low-income families improving more slowly (on average) than their more economically advantaged peers. Furthermore, the particular school at which a teacher is working can have a major influence; for example, Mr. Black might be teaching at a newly built facility with many resources and a highly motivated student body, whereas Ms. Brown might be teaching in a dilapidated old school building with inadequate supplies and little or no sense of school community among students and faculty. Statisticians have developed a variety of mathematical methods for taking such factors into account in calculating improvement scores, but none of them has yet emerged as a tried-and-true approach to measuring teacher effectiveness (e.g., see American Statistical Association, 2014; E. M. Anderman et al., 2015; Ballou et al., 2004; McCaffrey, Lockwood, Koretz, & Hamilton, 2003).

So where does all of this leave us with respect to teacher accountability? At this point, we authors strongly urge educators with decision-making powers to move away from relying mainly on large-scale achievement tests as the primary indicators of student progress and teacher effectiveness. Ideally, educators should instead identify concrete, realistic instructional goals for students in a single school year—perhaps tailoring those goals to local students' strengths and needs and breaking them down into more specific and manageable short-term goals—and create reasonable criterion-referenced tasks to assess goal accomplishment (E. M. Anderman et al., 2015).

MyEdLab **Self-Check 15.4**

MyEdLab **Application Exercise 15.4.** In this exercise, you can analyze how one sixth-grade teacher strategically prepares students for a high-stakes test.

Taking Student Diversity into Account

Whenever students take standardized tests, their performance can be affected by factors that aren't necessarily related to the characteristics the tests are intended to assess. If two students have *learned equally* yet *perform differently* on an assessment, the information obtained has **assessment bias** and questionable validity. We have a biased assessment whenever either the specific contents of items or the general behaviors and skills required to do well give some students an unfair advantage over others.

CULTURAL BIAS IN TEST CONTENT

One especially noteworthy form of assessment bias is cultural bias. An assessment instrument has cultural bias if any of its items either offend or unfairly penalize some students on the basis of their ethnicity, gender, socioeconomic status, religion, or other group membership (e.g., Buck, Kostin, & Morgan, 2002; Popham, 2014). To get a sense of this phenomenon, try the following exercise.

▪▪ EXPERIENCING FIRSTHAND
HOW PRODUCTIVE WILL YOU BE?

Imagine that you're taking a test designed to estimate your general ability to make productive contributions to the society in which you live. Here are the first three questions on the test:

1. When you enter a hogan, in which direction should you move around the fire?

2. Why is turquoise often attached to a baby's cradleboard?

3. If you need black wool for weaving a rug, which one of the following alternatives would give you the blackest color?

   a. Dye the wool with a mixture of sumac, ochre, and piñon gum.

   b. Dye the wool with a mixture of indigo, lichen, and mesquite.

   c. Use the undyed wool of specially bred black sheep.

Try to answer these questions before you read further.

_____ ▪▪

Did you have trouble answering some or all of the questions? All three were written from the perspective of a particular culture—that of the Navajos. Unless you've had considerable exposure to this culture, you would probably perform poorly. The three answers are (1) clockwise, (2) to ward off evil, and (3) Alternative *a*—"Dye the wool with a mixture of sumac, ochre, and piñon gum" (Gilpin, 1968; Nez, 2011).

Is the test culturally biased? That depends. If the test is designed to assess your ability to succeed in a Navajo community, the questions might be quite appropriate. But if it's designed to assess your ability to accomplish tasks for which knowledge of Navajo culture is irrelevant, the questions have cultural bias.

Two points about cultural bias are important to note. First, the term includes biases related to *gender* and *socioeconomic status* as well as to culture and ethnicity. For example, consider the following hypothetical assessment items, one for a math test and the other for a test of writing skills:

1. As a member of his high school baseball team this year, Mark has hit the ball 17 times in the 36 times he's been at bat. Of those hits, only 12 got him safely to base; the other 5 were either fly balls or sacrifice bunts that resulted in outs. And in three of Mark's at-bats, poor pitches enabled Mark to walk to first base. Based on this information, calculate Mark's batting average for the year so far.

2. Would you rather swim in an ocean, a lake, or a swimming pool? Write a two-page essay defending your choice.

Question 1 assumes a fair amount of knowledge about baseball—knowledge that some students (especially boys) are more likely to have than other students. Question 2 would obviously be difficult for students who haven't gone swimming in all three situations and would be even more difficult for those who have never swum at all; students from low-income, inner-city families might easily fall into one of these two categories.

A second important point is that an assessment instrument is culturally biased if it *offends* a particular group. For example, imagine a test item that implies that girls are more intelligent than boys, and imagine another item that portrays people of a certain country in an unflattering light. Such questions have cultural bias because some students are likely to be offended by the items and thus may be distracted from doing their best. These students might also take the stereotypes to heart, which would adversely affect their sense of self.

An assessment instrument isn't necessarily biased simply because one group gets higher scores on it than another group. It's biased only if the groups' scores are different when the characteristic we're trying to measure *isn't* different for the groups or if the instrument has higher predictive validity for one group than for another. Yes, we may sometimes see group differences in students' scores on particular assessment instruments, but these differences often reflect inequities in students' backgrounds that will affect their future educational performance. For example, if, on average, high school boys are more likely than girls to earn extremely high scores on standardized math tests, the difference may be partly due to the fact that—again, on average—parents more actively encourage boys than girls to learn math (Bleeker & Jacobs, 2004; Halpern et al., 2007; Valla & Ceci, 2011). Similarly, if students from low-income families have had few opportunities to venture beyond their immediate neighborhoods (fewer trips to science museums, less educational travel to other states or countries, etc.), their more limited exposure to diverse environments is likely to impact both their test performance *and* their classroom achievement.

Most publishers of large-scale standardized tests employ individuals who represent numerous minority groups and who actively screen test items for possible sources of cultural bias. Furthermore, most scholastic aptitude tests show similar predictive validity for various ethnic and cultural groups, provided that the members of those groups are native English speakers (R. T. Brown, Reynolds, & Whitaker, 1999; Sattler, 2001; Zwick & Sklar, 2005). Nevertheless, any standardized test should be carefully scrutinized for any items that might be offensive to either gender or to any cultural group, as well as for items that might be more difficult for one group than another for reasons unrelated to the characteristic being measured. And, of course, we should continually be on the lookout for any unintentional cultural bias in the classroom assessment instruments that we construct ourselves.

> Scrutinize assessment instruments carefully for tasks that some students might find offensive or might have difficulty answering solely because of their ethnic background, gender, or socioeconomic status.

CULTURAL AND ETHNIC DIFFERENCES

Even when test content isn't culturally biased, traditional group-administered standardized tests—the paper–pencil variety that involve time limits and electronically scored answer sheets—put students from some cultural and ethnic backgrounds at a disadvantage. For example, timed tests that require answering many questions very quickly can be troublesome for Native American students whose communities have socialized them to carefully think and reflect before responding to questions (Tyler, Uqdah, et al., 2008). And children from some cultural backgrounds may have little prior experience with questions to which the adult already knows the answer (Adger, Wolfram, & Christian, 2007; Heath, 1989; Rogoff, 2003). In addition, debilitating test anxiety is more common among students from cultural and ethnic minority groups (R. Carter, Williams, & Silverman, 2008; G. E. García & Pearson, 1994; Putwain, 2007). One possible contributor to this anxiety is a phenomenon known as **stereotype threat**, in which students from stereotypically low-achieving groups perform more poorly on classroom assessments than they otherwise would simply because they're aware that their group traditionally *does* do poorly (J. Aronson & Steele, 2005; Osborne, Tillman, & Holland, 2010; J. L. Smith, 2004; Walton & Spencer, 2009).

For such reasons, less traditional assessment methods—perhaps dynamic assessment or portfolios—can often provide a more optimistic picture of minority-group students' achievements and abilities (Feuerstein, Feuerstein, & Falik, 2010; Haywood & Lidz, 2007; R. S. Johnson et al., 2006). When circumstances *require* traditional paper–pencil tests, students should have plenty of advance practice in taking them. And to ease students' anxiety, we should encourage them to think of the tests as only rough measures of abilities that will almost certainly improve with future schooling and effort (e.g., C. Good, Aronson, & Inzlicht, 2003).

See Chapter 11 for a more detailed explanation of stereotype threat.

See Chapter 14 for a description of dynamic assessment.

> When students' backgrounds put them at a disadvantage in traditional standardized tests, assess their achievements and abilities in other ways. If a standardized paper–pencil test is mandated, give students practice in taking that kind of test, and encourage them to think of the ability being measured as something that will improve with time and practice.

LANGUAGE DIFFERENCES AND ENGLISH LANGUAGE LEARNERS

The earlier section on cultural bias mentioned that most scholastic aptitude tests show similar predictive validity for various groups *provided that the members of those groups are native English speakers.* Without question, students' experience and facility with English affects their performance on English-based assessments of achievement and ability (Kieffer, Lesaux, Rivera, & Francis, 2009; Solórzano, 2008). Poor reading and writing skills are likely to interfere with success on paper–pencil tests, and poor speaking skills can adversely affect students' ability to perform well on oral exams. For example, students whose native language is Spanish perform better on math tests that are given in Spanish rather than English (J. P. Robinson, 2010). For immigrant students in particular, "any test in English is a test *of* English" (E. E. Garcia, 2005).

A particular concern is the use of high-stakes tests with English language learners. When children have learned a language other than English at home, it typically takes them considerable time—perhaps 5 to 7 years—to gain sufficient proficiency in English to perform at their best in English-speaking classrooms (Cummins, 2008; Dixon et al., 2012; Padilla, 2006). Yet many school districts require these students to take high-stakes tests in English when they have only a superficial understanding of the language. Clearly such a practice leads to significant underestimations of English language learners' academic achievement—in other words, the test scores may have poor content validity for these students (Carhill, Suárez-Orozco, & Páez, 2008; Forte, 2010; Solórzano, 2008).

Following are examples of practices we should advocate for English language learners, especially in high-stakes situations:

- Translate a test into a student's native language.
- Let students use a dictionary or other appropriate reference tool.
- Administer a test one on one, perhaps eliminating time limits, presenting questions orally, and allowing students to respond in their native language.
- Use alternative assessment methods (e.g., dynamic assessment, portfolios) to document achievement.
- Exclude students' test scores when computing averages that reflect the overall achievement of a school or a particular subgroup within the school. (Haywood & Lidz, 2007; R. S. Johnson et al., 2006; Kieffer et al., 2009; Solórzano, 2008; W. E. Wright, 2006)

> When students have limited proficiency in English, minimize the use of written or spoken English to assess knowledge and skills that are not primarily linguistic in nature.

ACCOMMODATING STUDENTS WITH SPECIAL NEEDS

We must keep students' unique needs and disabilities in mind whenever we want to assess their abilities and summarize their achievements. For example, if instructional goals for a student with a learning disability are different from those for nondisabled classmates, our grading criteria should be altered accordingly, perhaps to be in line with the student's IEP. However, letter grades alone communicate very little information about what students have specifically learned and achieved; if we change the criteria for a particular student, the grades may communicate even *less* information. Portfolios—perhaps including teacher checklists, photographs, audiotapes, and videotapes, as well as students' written work—can be quite helpful for conveying the progress and achievements of students with a variety of disabilities and special needs (Mastropieri & Scruggs, 2007; Venn, 2000).

We may also have to modify standardized testing procedures to accommodate students with special educational needs. In the United States the Individuals with Disabilities Education Act (IDEA) mandates appropriate accommodations for students' disabilities. Such accommodations might involve one or more of the following:

- For a student with limited proficiency in English, administer assessments in his or her native language.
- Modify the presentation format of the assessment (e.g., using Braille or American Sign Language to present test items and other assessment tasks).
- Modify the response format (e.g., dictating answers, allowing use of a word processor).
- Modify the timing (e.g., giving extra time or frequent breaks).
- Modify the assessment setting (e.g., having a student take a standardized paper–pencil test alone in a quiet room).
- Administer only part of an assessment.
- Use instruments different from those given to nondisabled classmates, to be more compatible with students' ability levels and needs. (American Educational Research Association, American Psychological Association, & National Council on Measurement in Education, 1999)

We can often use students' IEPs for guidance about appropriate accommodations for each student. Table 15.4 offers additional suggestions for using standardized tests with students who have special needs.

> Chapter 5 identifies specific categories of special needs that fall within the five general categories listed in Table 15.4.

STUDENTS IN INCLUSIVE SETTINGS

TABLE 15.4 • Using Standardized Tests with Students Who Have Special Educational Needs

CATEGORY	CHARACTERISTICS YOU MIGHT OBSERVE	SUGGESTED STRATEGIES
Students with specific cognitive or academic difficulties	• Poor listening, reading, and/or writing skills (for some students) • Tendency for test scores to underestimate overall achievement levels (if students have poor reading skills) • Inconsistent performance due to off-task behaviors (e.g., hyperactivity, inattentiveness), affecting reliability and validity of scores (for some students with learning disabilities or attention-deficit hyperactivity disorder) • Higher-than-average test anxiety	• Modify test administration procedures to accommodate disabilities identified in students' IEPs (e.g., when administering a district-wide essay test, allow students with writing disabilities to use a word processor and spell checker). • Have students take tests in a room with minimal distractions. • Make sure students understand what they're being asked to do. • Be sure students are motivated to do their best but not overly anxious about their performance. • Use classroom assessments (both formal and informal) to confirm or disconfirm results of standardized test results. • Record and report all modifications of standardized procedures.
Students with social or behavioral problems	• Inconsistent performance due to off-task behaviors or lack of motivation, affecting reliability and validity of scores (for some students)	• Modify test administration procedures to accommodate disabilities identified in students' IEPs (e.g., when students are easily distracted, administer tests individually in a quiet room). • Convince students that doing their best can in some way enhance their long-term well-being. • Use classroom assessments (both formal and informal) to confirm or disconfirm results of standardized test results. • Record and report all modifications of standardized procedures.
Students with general delays in cognitive and social functioning	• Slow learning and cognitive processing • Limited or nonexistent reading skills • Poor listening skills	• Choose assessments appropriate for students' cognitive abilities and reading and writing skills. • Minimize the use of assessments that are administered to an entire class at once; rely more on those that are administered one on one. • Make sure students understand what they're being asked to do.
Students with physical or sensory challenges	• Mobility problems (for some students with physical challenges) • Tendency to tire easily (for some students with physical challenges) • Less developed language skills, affecting reading and writing ability (for some students with hearing loss)	• Obtain modified test materials for students with visual impairments (e.g., large-print or Braille test booklets). • Modify test administration procedures to accommodate students' unique needs (e.g., have a sign language interpreter give directions to students with hearing loss, or have students with limited muscle control dictate their answers). • If reading and writing skills are impaired, read test items to students. • Break lengthy assessments into segments that can be administered on separate occasions. • Schedule tests at times when students feel rested and alert. • Record and report all modifications of standardized procedures. • Don't compare a student's performance to that of the norm group if significant modifications have been made.
Students with advanced cognitive development	• Greater interest and engagement in challenging tests • Tendency in some students to hide giftedness to avoid possible ridicule by peers • In some instances, ability levels beyond the scope of typical tests for the grade level	• Keep assessment results confidential. • When students consistently earn perfect or near-perfect scores (e.g., percentile ranks of 99), request individualized testing that can more accurately assess their very high ability levels. • Use dynamic assessments as an alternative to traditional ability tests to identify giftedness in students from diverse cultural or linguistic backgrounds.

Sources: Barkley, 2006; Beirne-Smith, Patton, & Kim, 2006; D. Y. Ford & Harris, 1992; A. W. Gottfried, Fleming, & Gottfried, 1994; N. Gregg, 2009; Haywood & Lidz, 2007; Mastropieri & Scruggs, 2007; Mercer & Pullen, 2005; M. S. Meyer, 2000; B. N. Phillips, Pitcher, Worsham, & Miller, 1980; Piirto, 1999; Pitoniak & Royer, 2001; J. A. Stein & Krishnan, 2007; Turnbull, Turnbull, & Wehmeyer, 2010; Venn, 2000; Whitaker Sena, Lowe, & Lee, 2007.

Whenever we modify assessment instruments or procedures for students with special needs, we must recognize that there's a trade-off between two of our RSVP characteristics. On the one hand, we're violating the idea that an assessment should be standardized with respect to content, administration, and scoring criteria. On the other hand, if we fail to accommodate the disabilities that some students have, we'll get results that have little validity. There's no magic formula for determining the right balance between standardization and validity for students with special needs. As teachers, we must use our best professional judgment—and perhaps also seek the advice of specialists—in each situation.

We must keep in mind, too, that modifying assessment instruments or procedures for a standardized test may render the test's norms irrelevant; hence any norm-referenced scores we derive may be uninterpretable. When our purpose is to *identify* students' learning and performance difficulties, standardized testing procedures and norm-referenced scores are often quite appropriate. But when we're concerned about how to modify instructional methods and materials to *address* those difficulties, criterion-referenced scores and a close inspection of students' responses to particular tasks and items may be more helpful.

> Keep in mind that published peer-group norms for a standardized test may no longer be applicable when the test is modified in a significant way.

MyEdLab **Self-Check 15.5**

Confidentiality and Communication About Assessment Results

Students' test scores, class grades, and other assessment results should be confidential, as the following exercise can illustrate.

EXPERIENCING FIRSTHAND
HOW WOULD YOU FEEL?

How would you feel if one of your instructors did the following?

- Returned test papers in the order of students' test scores, so that those with highest scores were handed out first, and you received yours *last*.

- Told your other instructors how poorly you had done on the test, so that they could be on the lookout for other stupid things you might do.

- Looked through your school records and discovered that you scored 87 on an IQ test you took last year and that a schoolwide personality test you unknowingly also took has revealed some unusual sexual fantasies.

You'd probably be outraged if your instructor did *any* of these things.

But exactly *how* confidential should students' assessment results be? When should people know the results of students' assessments, and who should know them? In the United States we get legal guidance on these questions from the Family Educational Rights and Privacy Act (FERPA), passed by the U.S. Congress in 1974. This legislation limits normal school testing practices primarily to the assessment of achievement and scholastic aptitude—two things that are clearly within the school's domain. Furthermore, it restricts access to students' assessment results to the few individuals who really need to know them: the students who earn them, their parents, and school personnel directly involved with students' education and well-being. Assessment results can be shared with other individuals (e.g., a family doctor or a psychologist in private practice) *only* if the student (if at least 18 years old) or a parent gives written permission. Following are implications of this legislative mandate for classroom practices:

- We *cannot* ask students to reveal their political affiliation, sexual attitudes, illegal behaviors, potentially embarrassing psychological problems, or family income. (An exception: Questions about income to determine eligibility for financial assistance are allowed.)

- We *cannot* post test scores in ways that allow students to learn one another's scores. (For example, we can't post scores in alphabetical order or according to birthdays or social security numbers.)

Keep students' assessment results confidential; for example, don't post assessment results in ways that allow students to discover how their classmates have performed.

- We *cannot* distribute papers in any way that allows students to observe one another's scores. (For example, we can't let students search through a stack of scored papers to find their own.)

Many educators initially interpreted FERPA as forbidding teachers to have students grade one another's test papers. In 2002, however, the U.S. Supreme Court ruled that this practice doesn't violate FERPA because the test scores obtained aren't yet a part of students' permanent school records.[5] Nevertheless, although students can certainly give one another feedback on tasks used for formative assessment purposes, we authors strongly urge you *not* to have students swap and grade quizzes or other assessments that yield obvious high and low scores.

Keeping students' assessment results confidential makes educational as well as legal sense. Low scores can be a source of shame and embarrassment—and are even more so if classmates know about them—and thus can increase students' anxiety levels about future assessments. Students with high scores can also suffer from having the results made public: At many schools it isn't cool to be smart, and high achievers may perform at lower levels to avoid risking peer rejection. Also, publicizing students' assessment results focuses students' attention on performance goals—how they appear to others—rather than on mastering the subject matter.

In the opening case study, Ms. Davidson announces Ellie's grades to the entire class. The teacher's remarks violate FERPA, which applies to final grades as well as to individual assessments. Furthermore, making Ellie's grades public isn't in Ellie's best interest. Rather than motivate her to work harder (she's already highly motivated), it distresses her to the point that she no longer feels comfortable in Ms. Davidson's classroom.

An additional provision of FERPA is that parents and students (if at least 18 years old) have the right to review test scores and other school records. And school personnel must present and interpret this information in a way that parents and students can understand.

COMMUNICATING ASSESSMENT RESULTS TO STUDENTS AND PARENTS

Consider what happens when students in Ms. Ford's middle school math class learn that many of them have done poorly on a recent quiz:

You can see more of this class discussion in the opening case study in Chapter 14.

> **Ms. Ford:** If you received a grade below 75 you definitely have to work on it. I do expect this quiz to be returned with Mom or Dad's signature on it. I want Mom and Dad to be aware of how we're doing.
>
> **Student:** No!
>
> **Student:** Do we have to show our parents? Is it a requirement to pass the class?
>
> **Ms. Ford:** If you do not return it with a signature, I will call home. (J. C. Turner, Meyer, et al., 1998, p. 741)

Ms. Ford wants parents to know that their children aren't doing well in her class, but her approach has three drawbacks. First, many students may find it easier to forge an adultlike signature than to deliver bad news to a parent. Second, parents who do see their children's test papers won't have much information to help them interpret the results. (Are the low scores due to little effort? Poor study strategies? Poor instruction?) And third, Ms. Ford focuses entirely on the problem—low achievement—without offering suggestions for *solving* it.

As teachers, we must think of ourselves as working in cooperation with students and parents for something that everyone wants: students' academic success. Our primary goal in communicating classroom assessment results is to share information that will help achieve that end—something Ms. Ford neglects to do. Furthermore, because many students have done poorly on the test, Ms. Ford should consider whether something *she* has done—or not done—might account for the low scores. For instance, perhaps she allocated insufficient class time to certain concepts and skills, used ineffective strategies in teaching them, or constructed an exceptionally difficult test.

---

[5]*Owasso Independent School District v. Falvo,* 534 U.S. 426.

When we need to report standardized test results, we face a different challenge: How do we explain the results to students and parents who know very little about such tests and the kinds of scores they yield? Following are several guidelines that assessment experts offered many years ago (Durost, 1961; Ricks, 1959) but are still relevant today.

🍎 *Make sure you understand the results yourself.* When conveying information about standardized test results, we need to know something about a test's reliability and validity for the situation in which we've used it. We also need to know the general nature of the test scores—for example, whether they're criterion-referenced or norm-referenced and, if norm-referenced, how to interpret them.

🍎 *Remember that in many cases it is sufficient to describe the test and students' performance in broad, general terms.* To illustrate, we might describe an achievement test as a general measure of how much a student has learned in science compared to what other students around the country have learned, or we might describe a scholastic aptitude test as something that provides a rough idea of how well a student is likely to do in a particular instructional program. It's sometimes possible to describe a student's performance without referring to specific test scores at all. For example, we might say, "Your daughter scores like students who do well in college math courses" or "Your son had more-than-average difficulty on the spelling subtest; this is an area in which he may need extra help in the next few years." However, if parents want to know their child's specific test scores, in the United States FERPA requires that we reveal them and help parents understand what they mean.

🍎 *When reporting specific test scores, emphasize scores that are least likely to be misinterpreted.* Many parents mistakenly believe that a child's grade-equivalent score reflects the grade level the child should actually be in; consequently they may argue for advanced placement of high-achieving children or feel distressed that low-achieving children are in over their heads. And many parents interpret scores labeled as "IQs" as reflecting a permanent, unchangeable ability rather than a rough estimate of a child's present cognitive functioning (recall that the printout in Figure 15.11 uses the label "SAI" for Otis-Lennon scores based on the IQ scale). By reporting other kinds of scores—perhaps percentile scores, stanines, or NCEs—we're less likely to have parents jumping to such erroneous conclusions. Many parents are familiar with percentile scores, and many others can easily grasp the notion of a percentile if it's explained to them. But because percentile scores misrepresent actual differences among students (i.e., by overestimating actual ability differences in the middle range and underestimating differences at the extremes), we may also want to provide stanine scores or NCEs. Although most parents are unfamiliar with standard scores in general, we can help them understand them using a concrete graphic, such as the one presented in Figure 15.12.

Also, when test results include confidence intervals, such as those depicted in the computer printouts previously shown in Figures 15.7 and 15.11, it's helpful to explain their general nature. By reporting confidence intervals along with specific test scores, we communicate an important point about classroom assessment: Any test score has some error associated with it.

Whenever we assess students' achievement and abilities, we must remember that our primary purpose is to *help students learn and achieve more effectively.* When students perform well on classroom assessments and standardized tests, we have cause for celebration, because we know that our instructional strategies are working as they should. But when students perform poorly, our primary concern—and that of students, parents, school administrators, and policy makers as well—should be how to improve the situation.

MyEdLab
Video Example 15.4.

In this video, two fifth-grade teachers prepare their classes for upcoming parent–teacher–student conferences in which students will present their portfolios to their parents. As you watch the video, identify several benefits that such student-led conferences might have.

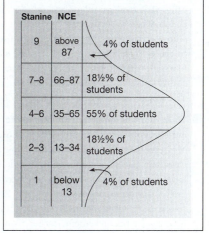

FIGURE 15.12 A graphic for helping parents understand stanines and NCE scores.

Stanine	NCE	
9	above 87	4% of students
7–8	66–87	18½% of students
4–6	35–65	55% of students
2–3	13–34	18½% of students
1	below 13	4% of students

MyEdLab **Self-Check 15.6**

MyEdLab **Application Exercise 15.5.** In this exercise, you will analyze one teacher's strategies for communicating the results of student assessments.

15   What Have You Learned?

Not only are the RSVP characteristics important for individual assessments, but they're also important—in fact, they're even *more* important—for summaries of students' general achievement and ability levels. Indicators of overall achievement should be reliable (reflecting a consistent pattern over time), standardized for all students (except in extenuating circumstances, such as when students have certain disabilities), valid (reflecting the actual achievement or abilities purportedly being measured), and practical (taking only a reasonable amount of time and effort). What's ultimately *most* important is that assessment results are sufficiently accurate and dependable that they can effectively guide decision making in classrooms and schools.

With these points in mind, we now return to the chapter's learning outcomes and review some of the chapter's key ideas.

15.1: Describe the nature, advantages, and disadvantages of three types of test scores: raw scores, criterion-referenced scores, and norm-referenced scores. Assessment scores take a number of forms, with different scores having distinctly different meanings. *Raw scores,* based on the number or percentage of items answered correctly or the number of points accumulated, have only limited utility unless they can be compared to a criterion for performance or to the performance of a norm group. *Criterion-referenced scores* tell us specifically what students know and can do. *Norm-referenced scores*— age and grade equivalents, percentile scores, and standard scores—enable us to compare our own students' performance to the performance of others. Because age and grade equivalents are often misinterpreted and percentiles distort actual ability differences among students, standard scores are preferable whenever we need to compare students to their peers.

15.2: Identify important guidelines to follow in summarizing students' achievement with final grades and portfolios. Most teachers eventually need to boil down the results of classroom assessments into general indicators of what students have learned. The most common procedure is to assign final grades that summarize what students have achieved over the course of the term or school year. Typically final grades should reflect actual achievement (rather than effort or some other subjective quality) and be based on hard data.

One significant weakness of final grades is that they communicate very little about what a student specifically has learned and can do. An alternative to grades—a *portfolio*—provides a means for representing the multifaceted, complex nature of students' accomplishments. When used to summarize students' achievement, portfolio contents should be closely tied to important instructional goals and standards, and students should have teacher guidance in choosing artifacts to include and organizing the final products.

15.3: Describe four different kinds of standardized tests, and explain how you might appropriately use and interpret these various tests. A wide variety of standardized tests are available for use in classrooms, including tests of achievement, general scholastic aptitude, specific aptitudes and abilities, and school readiness. As teachers, we must make sure that any standardized test we use meets the RSVP characteristics for our own situation and, if norm-referenced, has appropriate norms to which our students can be compared. Furthermore, we must take developmental factors into account when interpreting the results of standardized tests; for instance, young children's limited language skills and short attention spans make it more difficult to get valid assessments of their abilities, and some adolescents may be so cynical about the value of standardized tests that they put little thought or effort into their responses.

15.4: Explain how high-stakes testing and teacher accountability practices can affect instruction and classroom learning, and suggest several strategies for enhancing the benefits of these practices. Increasingly, standardized achievement tests are being used to make important decisions about students and to hold schools and individual teachers accountable for students' achievement levels. For example, in the United States the No Child Left Behind Act of 2001 mandates ongoing assessments of students' achievement in reading, math, and science; sanctions and corrective actions can be imposed on schools and faculty members not showing regular progress in these content domains. Many experts believe that such *high-stakes testing* and *accountability* create as many problems as they solve, but these practices are here to stay, at least for the short run. Thus, educators must become vocal advocates for reasonable, valid approaches to assessing students' overall progress and achievement and to evaluating teacher effectiveness, with an emphasis on enhancing instruction and learning rather than on punishing seemingly low-performing students, teachers, and schools.

15.5: Explain how you might accommodate group differences and special educational needs in your efforts to summarize students' achievement. Students' test scores and other assessment results can be affected by their ethnic- and cultural-group memberships, gender, and socioeconomic background in ways that impact the scores' reliability and validity. Furthermore, limited proficiency with the English language can interfere with some students' performance, as can cultural bias in the questions or tasks presented. Whenever we suspect that such factors may be affecting students' performance, we should interpret assessment results cautiously and look for other information that might either confirm or disconfirm those results. Furthermore, we should make reasonable accommodations for students' disabilities when administering tests to assess their achievement and abilities; such accommodations will increase the likelihood that the assessments yield useful information.

■ **15.6: Distinguish between circumstances in which you should and should not reveal students' assessment results, and explain how you can effectively communicate these results to students and parents.** For both legal and pedagogical reasons,

we must keep students' assessment results confidential, communicating assessment scores and other information only to the students themselves, to their parents, and to school personnel directly involved in the students' education and well-being. We must also describe assessment results in ways that students and parents can understand—for instance, by using graphics that illustrate the nature of various norm-referenced scores—and we must remember that the ultimate purpose of any assessment is to *help students learn and achieve more effectively*.

Practice For Your Licensure Exam

Can Johnny Read?

Ms. Beaudry is serving on a committee to study reading curricula in her school district. As part of her work with the committee, she plans to administer a standardized reading achievement test to determine whether her sixth graders have mastered the reading skills she's been trying to teach them this year. She's been given the opportunity to select the test from three instruments approved for purchase in her district. She scrutinizes the test manuals carefully and eliminates one test when she sees that it has poor test-retest reliability. She looks closely at tables of specifications for the other two tests and eventually selects the Comprehensive Reading Test (CRT) as the most reliable and valid measure for her own class.

Ms. Beaudry gives the test to her class, following the prescribed administration procedures closely. Because the test consists entirely of multiple-choice items, she can score the results quickly and easily that night. She computes each student's raw score and then turns to the norms in the test manual to obtain stanine scores. Her students' stanines range from 3 to 8. "Hmmm, what now?" she asks herself. "After all of this, I still don't know if my students have learned what I've been trying to teach them."

1. **Constructed-response question:**

   Ms. Beaudry chooses the wrong test for her purpose. What specifically does she do wrong?

2. **Multiple-choice question:**

   Ms. Beaudry uses tables of specifications to determine the validity of two of the tests for her own situation. Which one of the following statements best describes a typical table of specifications?

   a. It describes the ideal curriculum for a particular content domain and grade level.

   b. It provides specific, item-by-item scoring criteria that enable objective, reliable scoring.

   c. It indicates the topics covered by an assessment and the things that students should be able to do related to each topic.

   d. It presents the average performance of students at various grade and age levels, thereby enabling conversion of a raw score to one or more norm-referenced scores.

   MyEdLab **Licensure Exam 15.1**

PRAXIS Go to Appendix C, "Matching Book Content and Ebook Activities to the Praxis Principles of Learning and Teaching Tests," to discover sections of this chapter that may be especially applicable to the Praxis tests.

Appendix A

Describing Associations with Correlation Coefficients

- Do students with high self-esteem perform better in school than students with low self-esteem?
- As students move through the grade levels, do they become more intrinsically motivated to learn classroom subject matter or, instead, less intrinsically motivated to learn it?
- When students are given two different tests of general cognitive ability in the same week, how similar are their scores on the two tests likely to be?
- Are intellectually gifted students more emotionally well adjusted than their classmates of average intelligence?

Each of these questions asks about an association between two variables—whether it be an association between self-esteem and school achievement, between grade level and intrinsic motivation, between two tests of general cognitive ability, or between giftedness and emotional adjustment. The nature of such associations is sometimes summarized by a statistic known as a **correlation coefficient**.

A correlation coefficient is a number between –1 and +1; most correlation coefficients are decimals (either positive or negative) somewhere between these two extremes. A correlation coefficient for two variables tells us about both the direction and the strength of the association between the variables.

Direction. The direction of the association is indicated by the *sign* of the coefficient—in other words, by whether the number is positive or negative. A positive number indicates a *positive correlation:* As one variable increases, the other variable also increases. For example, there's a positive correlation between self-esteem and school achievement: Students with higher self-esteem achieve at higher levels (e.g., Marsh, Gerlach, Trautwein, Lüdtke, & Brettschneider, 2007). In contrast, a negative number indicates a *negative correlation:* As one variable increases, the other variable decreases instead. For example, there's a negative correlation between grade level and intrinsic motivation: On average, students in the upper grades (e.g., in junior high) have less intrinsic motivation to master classroom subject matter than younger students do (e.g., A. E. Gottfried, Fleming, & Gottfried, 2001). Figure A.1 graphically depicts the two correlations just described.

Strength. The strength of the association is indicated by the *size* of the coefficient. A number close to either +1 or –1 (e.g., +.89 or –.76) indicates a *strong* correlation: The two variables are closely related, so knowing the level of one variable allows us to predict the level of the other variable with considerable accuracy. For example, we often find a strong correlation between two tests of general cognitive ability given within a short time period: Students tend to get similar scores on both tests, especially if the tests cover similar kinds of content (e.g., McGrew, Flanagan, Zeith, & Vanderwood, 1997). In contrast, a number close to 0 (e.g., +.15 or –.22) indicates a *weak* correlation: Knowing the level of one variable allows us to predict the level of the other variable, but without much accuracy. For example, there's a weak association between intellectual giftedness and emotional adjustment: In general, students with higher measured intelligence levels (IQ scores) show better emotional well-being than students with lower scores (e.g., Janos & Robinson, 1985), but many students are exceptions to this general rule. Correlations in the middle range (e.g., those in the .40s and .50s, either positive or negative) indicate a *moderate* correlation.

As teachers, we will often encounter correlation coefficients in research articles in our professional books and journals. For instance, we might read that students' visual–spatial thinking

Figure A.1 Each face in these two graphs represents one student in a group of 50 students. The location of the face tells the extent to which a student is high or low on the two characteristics indicated. There is a *positive correlation* between self-esteem and school achievement: Students with higher self-esteem tend to achieve at higher levels. There is a *negative correlation* between grade level and intrinsic motivation: Students in higher grades tend to have less intrinsic motivation to learn school subject matter than students in lower grades do.

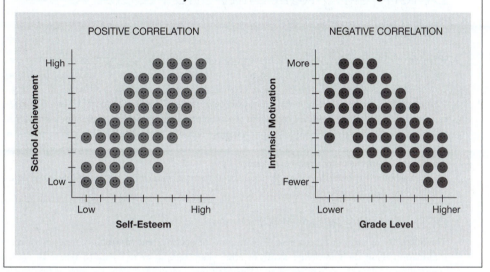

ability is positively correlated with their success in a math class or that there's a negative correlation between class size and students' achievement test scores. Whenever we see such evidence of correlation, we must remember one very important point: *Correlation does not necessarily indicate causation.* For example, we can't say that visual–spatial thinking ability specifically *leads to* greater mathematical ability, nor can we say that a large class size specifically *interferes with* classroom achievement. Each of these italicized phrases implies a causal relationship that doesn't necessarily exist. Only carefully designed *experimental studies* enable us to draw conclusions about the extent to which one thing causes or influences another.

Chapter 1 discusses the nature of experimental studies.

Many computer programs (including Microsoft Excel) are programmed to compute correlation coefficients. You can also find websites that enable you to calculate correlations and other simple statistics (e.g., see easycalculation.com). Computing a correlation coefficient by hand is complicated but certainly possible. If you're interested in learning more, you can easily find the formula through an Internet search or in most introductory statistics textbooks.

Appendix B

Determining Reliability and Predictive Validity

If you've read Appendix A, you've already learned something about **correlation coefficients**—statistics that indicate the strength and direction of an association between two variables. A correlation coefficient is always a number between −1 and +1. A coefficient close to either +1 or −1 (e.g., +.89 or −.76) indicates a strong correlation, whereas a number close to 0 (e.g., +.15 or −.22) indicates a weak correlation. A *positive* coefficient (i.e., one preceded by either a plus sign or no sign at all) indicates a positive relationship: As one variable increases, the other variable also increases. A negative coefficient (i.e., one preceded by a minus sign) indicates a negative relationship: As one variable increases, the other variable *decreases*.

Psychologists sometimes use correlation coefficients to determine the reliability and predictive validity of an assessment instrument.

DETERMINING RELIABILITY

The **reliability** of a test or other assessment instrument is the extent to which it yields consistent information about the knowledge, skills, or other characteristic we're trying to assess. To mathematically calculate the reliability of an assessment instrument, we begin by getting two scores on the same instrument for the same group of students. We can get these two sets of scores in at least three different ways, with each approach giving us a somewhat different angle on the instrument's reliability. If we use the same instrument to assess students on two different occasions, we get information about **test–retest reliability**: the extent to which the instrument yields similar results over a short time interval. If we ask two or more people to judge students' performance—for instance, to grade the same set of essays or rate the same gymnastic performance—we get information about **scorer reliability**: the extent to which different people agree in their judgments of students' performance. If we compute two or more subscores for different items on the same instrument and look at how similar those subscores are, we get information about **internal consistency reliability**: the extent to which different parts of the instrument all assess the same characteristic.

> The "Fowl Play" exercise in Chapter 14 provides an example of poor test–retest reliability.

Once we have two sets of scores for a single group of students, we can determine how similar the two sets are by computing a correlation coefficient; in this case, it's more frequently called a *reliability coefficient*. A reliability coefficient typically ranges from 0 to +1.[1] A number close to +1 indicates high reliability: The two sets of test scores are very similar. Although a perfect reliability coefficient of 1.00 is rare, many objectively scorable standardized achievement and ability tests have reliabilities of .90 or above, reflecting a high degree of consistency in the scores they yield. As reliability coefficients decrease, they indicate more error in the assessment results—error due to temporary, and in most cases irrelevant, factors. Publishers of standardized achievement and ability tests typically calculate and report reliability coefficients for the various scores and subscores the tests yield.

Estimating Error in Assessment Results. A reliability coefficient tells us, in general, the degree to which temporary errors contribute to fluctuations in students' assessment results. But how much error is apt to be present in a *single* score? In other words, how close is a particular student's score to what it really should be? A number known as the **standard error of measurement (SEM)**

---

[1] A negative coefficient is possible but would be obtained only when an *inverse* relationship between the two sets of scores exists—that is, when students who get the highest scores one time get the lowest scores the other time, and vice versa. Such an outcome is highly unlikely when calculating reliability.

allows us to estimate how close or far off the score might be. The standard error of measurement is calculated from the reliability coefficient; you can find details by searching for "calculating standard error of measurement" on the Internet. If you conduct such a search, however, be careful *not* to click on sites that address standard error of the *mean,* which is a statistic used for an entirely different purpose.

Let's look at a concrete example. Imagine that Susan takes an academic achievement test known as the Basic Skills Test (BST). Imagine, too, that with her current level of reading ability, Susan should ideally get a score of 40 on the BST Reading subtest. Susan's ideal score of 40 is her **true score**: This is what she would theoretically get if we could measure her reading achievement *with complete accuracy.* But Susan misinterprets a few test items, answering them incorrectly when in fact she knows the correct answers, so she actually gets a score of only 37. Because we can't see inside Susan's head, we have no way of determining what her true score is; we know only that she has earned a 37 on the test. To estimate the amount of error in her score, we consult the BST test manual and learn that the standard error of measurement for the Reading subtest is, let's say, 5 points. We can then guess that Susan's true score probably lies somewhere within a range that's 1 SEM to either side of her test score: 37 ± 5, or between 32 and 42.[2]

Because almost any assessment score includes a certain amount of error, assessment results are sometimes reported not as specific scores, but as a range, or **confidence interval.** (The term *confidence band* is sometimes used instead, especially in computer-generated test reports for students and parents; alternatively, you may see the term *national percentile band* if percentile scores are being reported.) A confidence interval typically extends 1 SEM to either side of the actual test score. By reporting confidence intervals along with specific test scores, we communicate an important point about students' test results: Any test score has some error associated with it. Figure B.1 shows how we might report Susan's scores on the Reading and other subtests of the BST. Notice that the confidence intervals for the different subtests are different lengths, because each subtest has a different standard error of measurement.

When we use a single SEM to determine the confidence interval, there's a 68% chance that the student's true score falls within that interval. If we instead use *two* SEMs to determine the interval (for Susan's reading score, such an interval would be 27 to 47), we can be 95% confident that the true score lies within it.[3]

If two or more test scores come from the same test battery—and thus involve the same norm group—we can use the 68% confidence intervals for the scores to make meaningful comparisons. Overlapping confidence intervals for any two subtests indicate that the student has performed equally well in the two areas. But if the intervals show no overlap, we can reasonably conclude that the student has done appreciably better in one area than the other. Using this approach with Susan's BST scores, we can conclude that Susan has performed best on the math and science subtests, less well on the social studies subtest, and least well on the reading and spelling subtests. We would *not* say that she has done better in science than in math or that she has done better in reading than in spelling, because the confidence intervals overlap for those two pairs of scores.

DETERMINING PREDICTIVE VALIDITY

The **predictive validity** of an assessment instrument (you may also see the term *criterion validity*) is the extent to which the instrument accurately predicts future performance in some domain. Publishers of standardized, norm-referenced ability tests often determine the accuracy with which test scores predict later success in certain content areas. To do so, they first give a test to a group of people; a few months or years later, they measure the same group's success or competence in the behavior being predicted (i.e., the criterion variable). They then calculate the correlation

---

[2]Technically speaking, the simple add-and-subtract approach I describe here applies only to standard scores; it's a bit more complicated for other norm-referenced scores, such as percentiles and grade- and age-equivalents. But for most of my readers, details might be TMI—too much information—in an introductory discussion of assessment such as this one.

[3]If you have some knowledge of descriptive statistics, it may help you to know that, when standard scores are being reported, the SEM is the standard deviation for the hypothetical distribution of all possible scores that a student with a particular *true* score might get.

Figure B.1 **A graphic representation of Susan's scores on the Basic Skills Test (BST).**

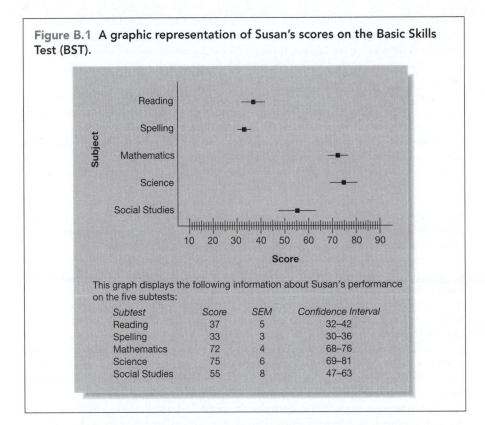

This graph displays the following information about Susan's performance on the five subtests:

Subtest	Score	SEM	Confidence Interval
Reading	37	5	32–42
Spelling	33	3	30–36
Mathematics	72	4	68–76
Science	75	6	69–81
Social Studies	55	8	47–63

coefficient between the test scores and the criterion behavior. As is true for a reliability coefficient, this *validity coefficient* is typically a number between 0 and +1, with higher numbers indicating greater predictive validity. Tests with relatively high predictive validity for a particular behavior (e.g., validity coefficients in the .60s and .70s are usually considered high) predict that behavior fairly well. Those with lower predictive validity (e.g., coefficients in the .30s and .40s) yield less accurate predictions.

Any test's predictive validity can vary considerably depending on the specific criterion variable being predicted; for example, many scholastic aptitude tests more accurately predict academic performance in the near future (e.g., within the next 2 or 3 years) than in the distant future. Predictive validity also depends somewhat on the age-group in question; for instance, validity coefficients tend to be higher for students in the upper elementary and secondary grades than they are for young children. Typical validity coefficients for general scholastic aptitude tests (including intelligence tests) range between .40 and .70. Those for specific aptitude tests often fall below .50.

Appendix C

Matching Book and MyEdLab® Content to the PRAXIS® *Principles of Learning and Teaching* Tests

In the United States, state teacher licensing requirements in many states include passing Praxis tests published by Educational Testing Service (ETS). Among the Praxis tests are four Principles of Learning and Teaching (PLT) tests, one each for teachers seeking licensure for early childhood and for grades K–6, 5–9, and 7–12. This text, *Educational Psychology: Developing Learners* addresses most of the topics covered in the PLT tests. The left column of Table C.1 presents the topics covered on the tests, as identified in *The Praxis Series: Official Guide* (Educational Testing Service, 2008, pp. 348–364). The middle column of the table indicates chapters and sections in *Educational Psychology: Developing Learners* that are relevant to these topics. The right column suggests relevant exercises and readings in.

*The Praxis Series*RTM Assessments* involve reading and analyzing case studies. For this reason, the case studies and "Practice for Your Licensure Exam" exercises presented in *Educational Psychology: Developing Learners* may be especially helpful as you prepare for these tests. The opening case study in each chapter is addressed in several places throughout the chapter. The "Practice for Your Licensure Exam" exercise presents a second case study and poses questions that encourage you to apply the chapter content. You will find additional case study material in some of the resources in.

You may also want to obtain your own copy of *The Praxis Series: Official Guide*. It provides practice case studies and offers suggestions for analyzing them and responding to test questions. You can purchase a copy through various online vendors, including the following:

- Educational Testing Service
  www.ets.org/store.html
- McGraw-Hill
  www.mhprofessional.com
- Amazon
  www.amazon.com
- Barnes and Noble
  www.barnesandnoble.com

At some of these websites, you may need to type "Praxis Official Guide" in the "Search" box.

TABLE C.1 • Matching Book and MyEdLab® Content to the PRAXIS® Principles of Learning and Teaching Tests

TOPICS IN THE PRAXIS PRINCIPLES OF LEARNING AND TEACHING (PLT) TESTS	LOCATION OF TOPICS IN ORMROD'S *EDUCATIONAL PSYCHOLOGY* (9TH ED.)	LOCATION OF TOPICS AND PRACTICE OPPORTUNITIES IN MyEdLab
I. Students as Learners		
A. Student Development and the Learning Process		
▶ Theoretical foundations about how learning occurs: how students construct knowledge, acquire skills, and develop habits of mind	**Chapter 2:** "The Multiple Layers of Environmental Influence: Bioecological Systems and the Importance of Culture" (pp. 23–25); "Piaget's Theory of Cognitive Development" (pp. 27–39); "Vygotsky's Theory of Cognitive Development" (pp. 39–48) **Chapters 6– 10:** Entire chapters (pp. 170–356)	**Supplementary Reading** "Content Extension 8.1" in Book-Specific Resources for Chapter 8
▶ Examples of important theorists: • Albert Bandura	**Chapter 10:** Entire chapter (pp. 322–356); especially see "Basic Assumptions of Social Cognitive Theory" (pp. 323–325)	
• Jerome Bruner	See Bruner citations in the Name Index.	
• John Dewey		
• Jean Piaget	**Chapter 2:** "Piaget's Theory of Cognitive Development" (pp. 27–39); "Contrasting Piaget's and Vygotsky's Theories" (p. 47); **Practice for Your Licensure Exam: "A Floating Stone"** (p. 55)	**Assignments and Activities: Understanding Research** exercise "Class Inclusion" in topic "Cognitive and Linguistic Development" **Building Teaching Skills and Dispositions** practice "Applying Piaget's Theory" in topic "Cognitive and Linguistic Development"
• Lev Vygotsky	**Chapter 2:** "Vygotsky's Theory of Cognitive Development" (pp. 39–47); **Practice for Your Licensure Exam: "A Floating Stone"** (p. 55)	**Building Teaching Skills and Dispositions** exercise "Using Cognitive Tools" in topic "Cognitive and Linguistic Development"
• Howard Gardner	**Chapter 5:** "Gardner's Multiple Intelligences" (pp. 131–132)	
• Abraham Maslow	**Chapter 11:** "Early Views of Basic Human Needs" (pp. 364–365)	
• B. F. Skinner	**Chapter 9: Case Study: "The Attention Getter"** (p. 289); "Learning from Consequences: Instrumental Conditioning" (pp. 294–304); "Strategies for Encouraging Productive Behaviors" (pp. 304–311)	**Supplementary Reading** "Content Extension 9.1" in Book-Specific Resources for Chapter 9 **Supplementary Reading** "Content Extension 12.1" in Book-Specific Resources for Chapter 12
▶ Important terms that relate to learning theory: • Constructivism	**Chapter 2:** "Piaget's Basic Assumptions" (pp. 29–30); "Social Construction of Meaning" (pp. 43–45); "Scaffolding" (pp. 45–46) **Chapter 6: Case Study: "Bones"** (p. 171); "Basic Assumptions of Cognitive Psychology" (pp. 172–175); "How Declarative Knowledge Is Learned" (pp. 185–189); "When Knowledge Construction Goes Awry: Addressing Learners' Misconceptions" (pp. 195–199); **Practice for Your Licensure Exam: "Vision Unit"** (p. 210) **Chapter 8:** "Basic Assumptions of Contextual Theories" (pp. 250–253)	**Building Teaching Skills and Dispositions** exercise "Knowledge Construction and Conceptual Change" in topic "Knowledge Construction" **Assignments and Activities: Understanding Research** exercise "Knowledge Construction in History" in topic "Knowledge Construction" **Supplementary Reading** "Content Extension 6.1" in Book-Specific Resources for Chapter 6
• Metacognition	**Chapter 7: Case Study: "Taking Over"** (p. 213); "Metacognition and Learning Strategies" (pp. 214–225); "Metacognition in Problem Solving" (p. 235); **Practice for Your Licensure Exam: "Interview with Charlie"** (pp. 246–247) **Chapter 8:** "Academic Content Domains as Contexts" (pp. 265–285); **Chapter 12:** "Conducting Reciprocal Teaching Sessions" (pp. 436–438)	**Building Teaching Skills and Dispositions** exercise "Encouraging Self-Regulation" in topic "Social Cognitive Perspectives" **Assignments and Activities: Understanding Research** exercise "Self-Discipline and Academic Achievement" in topic "Student Diversity"

TABLE C.1 • (Continued)

TOPICS IN THE PRAXIS PRINCIPLES OF LEARNING AND TEACHING (PLT) TESTS	LOCATION OF TOPICS IN ORMROD'S *EDUCATIONAL PSYCHOLOGY* (9TH ED.)	LOCATION OF TOPICS AND PRACTICE OPPORTUNITIES IN MyEdLab
I. Students as Learners		
A. Student Development and the Learning Process		
		Assignments and Activities: Understanding Research exercise "Teaching Reading Comprehension Strategies" in topic "Memory and Cognitive Processes" **Assignments and Activities: Understanding Research** exercise "High School Students' Study Strategies" in topic "Memory and Cognitive Processes"
• Readiness	**Chapter 2:** "Role of the Brain in Learning and Development" (pp. 25–27) **Chapter 15:** "School Readiness Tests" (pp. 558–559)	**Assignments and Activities: Understanding Research** exercise "Usefulness of School Readiness Tests" in topic "Assessment"
• Schemata	**Chapter 2:** "Piaget's Basic Assumptions" (pp. 29–30) **Chapter 6:** "How Knowledge Can Be Organized" (pp. 183–185)	
• Transfer	**Chapter 7:** "Transfer" (pp. 225–230)	
• Scaffolding	**Chapter 2:** "Scaffolding" (pp. 45–46) **Chapter 8:** Into the Classroom: "Promoting Reading and Writing Development" (p. 273); "Technological Literacy" (pp. 272–274) **Chapter 13:** "Planning Activities That Keep Students on Task" (pp. 467–469)	
• Bloom's taxonomy	**Chapter 12:** "Identifying the Goals of Instruction" (pp. 417–421)	**Supplementary Reading** "Content Extension 12.1" in Book-Specific Resources for Chapter 12
• Zone of proximal development	**Chapter 2:** "Vygotsky's Basic Assumptions" (pp. 39–42); "Considering Diversity from the Perspective of Vygotsky's Theory" (p. 43)	**Building Teaching Skills and Dispositions** exercise "Using Cognitive Tools" in topic "Cognitive and Linguistic Development"
• Intrinsic and extrinsic motivation	**Chapter 9:** "Positive Versus Negative Reinforcement" (pp. 297–299); "Using Reinforcement Effectively" (pp. 304–309) **Chapter 11:** Case Study: "Passing Algebra" (p. 359); "Intrinsic Versus Extrinsic Motivation" (pp. 361–364); "Internalizing Values and Motivational Beliefs of One's Social and Cultural Groups" (pp. 375–376); "Achievement Goals" (pp. 380–383); "Accommodating Students with Special Needs" (pp. 391–392); **Practice for Your Licensure Exam: "When 'Perfect' Isn't Good Enough"** (p. 410)	**Building Teaching Skills and Dispositions** exercise "Promoting Interest" in topic "Motivation and Affect" **Assignments and Activities: Understanding Research** exercise "Self-Discipline & Academic Achievement" in topic "Student Diversity"
▶ Human development in the physical, social, emotional, moral, and cognitive domains:	**Chapter 2– 3:** Entire chapters (pp. 20–94) **Chapters 4, 6– 15:** Developmental Trends tables (pp. 116, 190, 215–216, 269, 300, 341, 389, 403, 418, 471–472, 561) **Chapter 4:** "Origins of Gender Differences" (pp. 115–117) **Chapter 5:** "Developmental Views of Intelligence" (pp. 133–134); "Nature and Nurture in the Development of Intelligence" (pp. 136–137) **Chapter 6:** "Developmental Trends in Storage Processes for Declarative Information" (p. 189) **Chapter 8: Practice for Your Licensure Exam: "The Birth of a Nation"** (p. 287) **Chapter 9:** "Classical Conditioning of Involuntary Emotional Responses" (p. 293)	**Assignments and Activities: Understanding Research** exercise "Class Inclusion" in topic "Cognitive and Linguistic Development" **Supplementary Reading** "Content Extension 2.1" in Book-Specific Resources for Chapter 2

(continued)

TOPICS IN THE PRAXIS PRINCIPLES OF LEARNING AND TEACHING (PLT) TESTS	**LOCATION OF TOPICS IN ORMROD'S** *EDUCATIONAL PSYCHOLOGY* **(9TH ED.)**	**LOCATION OF TOPICS AND PRACTICE OPPORTUNITIES IN** MyEdLab
I. Students as Learners		
A. Student Development and the Learning Process		
	Chapter 10: "Factors in the Development of Self-Efficacy" (pp. 335–338); "Applying Brain Research: Understanding and Accommodating Individual Differences in Self-Regulation" (p. 349) Chapter 11: "Developmental Trends in Achievement Goals" (p. 382); Table 11.3 ("Developmental Trends: Motivation at Different Grade Levels" p. 389); "Applying Brain Research: Understanding Why and How Emotions Influence Learning" (p. 398) Chapter 13: "Taking Developmental Differences into Account" (p. 470) Chapter 15: "Guidelines for Choosing and Using Standardized Tests" (pp. 559–562)	
• The theoretical contributions of important theorists such as Erik Erikson, Lawrence Kohlberg, Carol Gilligan, Jean Piaget, Abraham Maslow, Albert Bandura, and Lev Vygotsky	Chapter 2: "The Multiple Layers of Environmental Influence: Bioecological Systems and the Importance of Culture" (pp. 23–25); "Piaget's Theory of Cognitive Development" (pp. 27–39); "Vygotsky's Theory of Cognitive Development" (pp. 39–48) Chapter 3: Figure 3.1 ("Erikson's eight stages of psychosocial development," p. 65); "Developmental Trends in Morality and Prosocial Behavior" (pp. 83–87); "Diversity in Moral and Prosocial Development" (pp. 88–89) Chapter 10: Entire chapter (pp. 322–356) Chapter 11: "Early Views of Basic Human Needs" (pp. 364–365)	**Building Teaching Skills and Dispositions** exercise "Using Cognitive Tools" in topic "Cognitive and Linguistic Development" **Assignments and Activities: Understanding Research** exercise "Self-Efficacy and Achievement" in topic "Social Cognitive Perspectives"
• The major progressions in each developmental domain and the ranges of individual variation within each domain	Chapter 2: "Piaget's Proposed Stages of Cognitive Development" (pp. 30–35); "Contemporary Extensions and Applications of Piaget's Theory" (pp. 36–39); "Language Development" (pp. 48–54) Chapter 3: "Developmental Changes in Sense of Self" (pp. 64–67); "Development of Peer Relationships and Interpersonal Understandings" (pp. 69–82); "Developmental Trends in Morality and Prosocial Behavior" (pp. 83–87) Chapters 2 – 4, 6 – 15: Developmental Trends tables (pp. 49–50, 68, 116, 190, 215–216, 269, 300, 341, 389, 403, 418, 471–472, 561)	**Building Teaching Skills and Dispositions** exercise "Encouraging Self-Regulation" in topic "Social Cognitive Perspectives" **Assignments and Activities: Understanding Research** exercise "Class Inclusion" in topic "Cognitive and Linguistic Development" **Supplementary Reading** "Content Extension 2.1" in Book-Specific Resources for Chapter 2
• The impact of students' physical, social, emotional, moral, and cognitive development on their learning and how to address these factors when making instructional decisions	Chapters 2– 3: See apple icons throughout Chapter 2: Case Study: **"Apple Tarts"** (p. 21); **Practice for Your Licensure Exam: "A Floating Stone"** (p. 55) Chapter 3: Case Study: **"Hidden Treasure"** (p. 57); **Practice for Your Licensure Exam:** *The Scarlet Letter*" (pp. 93–94) Chapter 5: "Emotional and Behavioral Disorders" (pp. 152–155); "Intellectual Disabilities" (pp. 157–159) Chapter 9: "Classical Conditioning of Involuntary Emotional Responses" (p. 293)	**Building Teaching Skills and Dispositions** exercise "Using Cognitive Tools" in topic "Cognitive and Linguistic Development" **Assignments and Activities: Understanding Research** exercise "Supporting Children at Risk" in topic "Student Diversity" **Assignments and Activities: Understanding Research** exercise "Need for Approval and Emotional Well-Being" in topic "Motivation and Affect" **Assignments and Activities: Understanding Research** exercise "Usefulness of School Readiness Tests" in topic "Assessment" **Supplementary Reading** "Content Extension 5.1" in Book-Specific Resources for Chapter 5

TABLE C.1 • (Continued)

TOPICS IN THE PRAXIS PRINCIPLES OF LEARNING AND TEACHING (PLT) TESTS	LOCATION OF TOPICS IN ORMROD'S *EDUCATIONAL PSYCHOLOGY* (9TH ED.)	LOCATION OF TOPICS AND PRACTICE OPPORTUNITIES IN MyEdLab
I. Students as Learners		
A. Student Development and the Learning Process		
• How development in one domain, such as physical, may affect performance in another domain, such as social	**Chapter 2:** "Role of the Brain in Learning and Development" (pp. 25–27) **Chapter 3:** "Temperament" (p. 58); "Developmental Changes in Sense of Self" (pp. 64–67); "Applying Brain Research: Understanding and Addressing Adolescent Risk Taking" (p. 67); "Social Cognition" (pp. 74–77); "Factors Influencing Moral and Prosocial Development" (pp. 87–88) **Chapter 4:** "Characteristics of Students at Risk" (pp. 123–124) **Chapter 6:** "Applying Brain Research: Enhancing Students' Brain Functioning" (p. 182) **Chapter 10:** "Applying Brain Research: Understanding and Accommodating Individual Differences in Self-Regulation" (p. 349) **Chapter 11:** "Applying Brain Research: Understanding Why and How Emotions Influence Learning" (p. 398)	**Building Teaching Skills and Dispositions** exercise "Perspective Taking & Social Skills" in topic "Personal, Social, & Moral Development" **Supplementary Reading** "Content Extension 2.1" in Book-Specific Resources for Chapter 2
B. Students as Diverse Learners		
▶ Differences in the ways students learn and perform:	**Chapter 2:** Diversity sections (pp. 36, 43, 50–51); "Second-Language Learning and English Language Learners" (pp. 51–54) **Chapter 3:** "Personality Development" (pp. 58–62); "Diversity" sections (pp. 67–69, 79, 88–89) **Chapters 4 – 5:** Entire chapters (pp. 96–168) **Chapter 6:** "Diversity in Cognitive Processes" (pp. 206–208) **Chapter 7:** "Diversity in Creativity, Critical Thinking, and Other Complex Cognitive Processes" (pp. 243–244) **Chapter 8:** "Schemas, Scripts, and Worldviews as Aspects of Culture" (pp. 257–259) **Chapter 9:** "Diversity in Student Behaviors and Reactions to Consequences" (pp. 317–319) **Chapter 10:** "Diversity in Self-Regulation" (pp. 348–351) **Chapter 11:** "Diversity in Cognitive and Sociocultural Factors Affecting Motivation" (pp. 374–376; 388–392); "Diversity in Affect" (pp. 405–407) **Chapter 12:** "Taking Instructional Goals and Student Diversity into Account" (pp. 448–452) **Chapter 13:** "Taking Individual and Group Differences into Account" (pp. 470–474); "Taking Students' Cultural Backgrounds into Account" (pp. 488–489) **Chapter 14:** "Taking Student Diversity into Account in Classroom Assessments" (pp. 535–537) **Chapter 15:** "Taking Student Diversity into Account" (pp. 568–573)	
▶ Differences in the ways students learn and perform:		
• Learning styles	**Chapter 5:** "Cognitive Styles and Dispositions" (pp. 139–141) **Chapter 6:** "Diversity in Cognitive Processes" (pp. 206–208)	**Assignments and Activities: Understanding Research** exercise "Self-Discipline & Academic Achievement" in topic "Student Diversity"
• Multiple intelligences	**Chapter 5:** "Gardner's Multiple Intelligences" (pp. 131–132)	

(continued)

TABLE C.1 • (Continued)		
TOPICS IN THE PRAXIS PRINCIPLES OF LEARNING AND TEACHING (PLT) TESTS	**LOCATION OF TOPICS IN ORMROD'S** *EDUCATIONAL PSYCHOLOGY* **(9TH ED.)**	**LOCATION OF TOPICS AND PRACTICE OPPORTUNITIES IN** MyEdLab
I. Students as Learners		
B. Students as Diverse Learners		
• Performance modes • Concrete operational thinkers • Visual and aural learners	**Chapter 2:** Table 2.1 ("Piaget's Proposed Stages of Cognitive Development" (p. 31); "Concrete Operations Stage" (pp. 32–33) **Chapter 5:** "Learning Disabilities" (pp. 145–148) **Chapter 6:** "Visual Imagery" (pp. 187–189) **Chapter 7: Practice for Your Licensure Exam: "Interview with Charlie"** (pp. 246–247)	**Assignments and Activities: Understanding Research** exercise "Teaching Reading Comprehension Strategies" in topic "Memory and Cognitive Processes"
• Gender differences	**Chapter 3:** "Gender Differences" sections (pp. 69, 79, 88) **Chapter 4:** "Gender Differences" (pp. 112–118); **Practice for Your Licensure Exam: "The Active and the Passive"** (p. 127) **Chapter 10: Case Study: "Parlez-Vous Français?"** (p. 323) **Chapter 11:** "Gender Differences" sections (pp. 390; 406–407) **Chapter 12:** "Considering Group Differences" (p. 450) **Chapter 13:** "Gender Differences" (p. 473) **Chapter 15:** "Cultural Bias in Test Content" (pp. 569–570)	
• Cultural expectations and styles	**Chapter 2:** "Considering Diversity from the Perspective of Vygotsky's Theory" (p. 43) **Chapter 3: Case Study: "Hidden Treasure"** (p. 57); "Family Dynamics" (pp. 58–60); "Cultural Expectations and Socialization" (p. 60); "Cultural and Ethnic Differences" sections (pp. 69, 79, 89) **Chapter 4: Case Study: "Why Jack Wasn't in School"** (p. 97); "Cultural and Ethnic Differences" (pp. 99–112); **Practice for Your Licensure Exam: "The Active and the Passive"** (p. 127) **Chapter 5:** "Cultural and Ethnic Diversity in Intelligence" (p. 137) **Chapter 6:** "Diversity in Cognitive Processes" (pp. 206–208) **Chapter 7:** "Diversity in Creativity, Critical Thinking, and Other Complex Cognitive Processes" (pp. 243–244) **Chapter 8: Case Study: "It's All in How You Look at Things"** (p. 249); "Cultures as Contexts" (pp. 256–260) **Chapter 9:** "Diversity in Student Behaviors and Reactions to Consequences" (pp. 317–319) **Chapter 10:** "Diversity in Self-Regulation" (pp. 348–352) **Chapter 11:** "Diversity in Cognitive and Sociocultural Factors Affecting Motivation" (pp. 374–376); "Diversity in Cognitive and Sociocultural Factors Affecting Motivation" (pp. 388–392); "Diversity in Affect" (pp. 405–407) **Chapter 12:** "Considering Group Differences" (p. 450) **Chapter 13:** "Taking Students' Cultural Backgrounds into Account" (pp. 488–489) **Chapter 14:** "Teaching Testwiseness" (pp. 531–532); "Accommodating Group Differences" (p. 536) **Chapter 15:** "Cultural Bias in Test Content" (pp. 569–570); "Cultural and Ethnic Differences" (p. 570)	**Building Teaching Skills and Dispositions** exercise "Accommodating Cultural Differences" in topic "Student Diversity" **Assignments and Activities: Understanding Research** exercise "Navigating Adolescence" in topic "Personal, Social, & Moral Development"
► Areas of exceptionality in student learning:	**Chapter 5:** Entire chapter (pp. 128–168); see especially **Case Study: "Tim"** (p. 129) and **Practice for Your Licensure Exam: "Quiet Amy"** (p. 168) **Chapters 6– 15:** Students in Inclusive Settings tables (pp. 207, 244, 285, 318, 351, 392, 451–452, 474, 537, 572) **Chapters 6– 15:** "Special Needs" sections (pp. 206–208, 244, 284–285, 319, 350–351, 391–392, 451–452, 473–474, 536–537, 571–573)	**Assignments and Activities: Understanding Research** exercise "Conducting a Functional Analysis" in topic "Behaviorist Perspectives" **Assignments and Activities: Understanding Research** exercise "Identifying Reinforcers Through Functional Analysis" in topic "Classroom Management"

TABLE C.1 • (Continued)		
TOPICS IN THE PRAXIS PRINCIPLES OF LEARNING AND TEACHING (PLT) TESTS	**LOCATION OF TOPICS IN ORMROD'S** *EDUCATIONAL PSYCHOLOGY* **(9TH ED.)**	**LOCATION OF TOPICS AND PRACTICE OPPORTUNITIES IN** MyEdLab
I. Students as Learners		
B. Students as Diverse Learners		
• Visual and perceptual differences	**Chapter 5:** Figure 5.3 ("Examples of cognitive processing deficiencies in students with learning disabilities," p. 147); "Autism Spectrum Disorders" (pp. 155–156)	
• Special physical or sensory challenges	**Chapter 5:** "Students with Physical or Sensory Challenges" (pp. 159–162)	
• Learning disabilities	**Chapter 5:** "Learning Disabilities" (pp. 145–148)	
• Attention deficit disorder (ADD); Attention deficit-hyperactivity disorder (ADHD)	**Chapter 5: Case Study: "Tim"** (p. 129); "Attention-Deficit Hyperactivity Disorder (ADHD)" (pp. 148–150)	
• Functional mental retardation	**Chapter 5:** "Intellectual Disabilities" (pp. 157–159)	**Supplementary Reading** "Content Extension 5.1" in Book-Specific Resources for Chapter 5
• Behavioral disorders	**Chapter 5:** "Emotional and Behavioral Disorders" (pp. 152–155)	**Simulation** exercise "Developing Behavior Change Plans" in topic "Classroom Management" **Assignments and Activities: Understanding Research** exercise "Identifying Reinforcers Through Functional Analysis" in topic "Classroom Management"
• Developmental delays	**Chapter 5:** "Students with General Delays in Cognitive and Social Functioning" (pp. 157–159)	
▶ Legislation and institutional responsibilities relating to exceptional students:		
• Americans with Disabilities Act (ADA)		
• Individuals with Disabilities Education Act (IDEA)	**Chapter 5:** "Public Law 94-142: Individuals with Disabilities Education Act (IDEA)" (pp. 142–143)	
• Inclusion, mainstreaming, and "least restrictive environment"	**Chapter 5:** "Educating Students with Special Needs in General Education Classrooms" (pp. 141–145) **Chapters 6– 15:** Students in Inclusive Settings tables (pp. 207, 244, 285, 318, 351, 392, 451–452, 474, 537, 572)	
• IEP (individual education plan), including what, by law, must be included in each IEP	**Chapter 5:** Figure 5.2 ("Components of an individualized education program (IEP)," p. 143) **Chapter 12:** "Accommodating Students with Special Needs" (pp. 451–452) **Chapter 14:** "Accommodating Students with Special Needs" (pp. 536–537) **Chapter 15:** "Considering Effort" (p. 552); "Accommodating Students with Special Needs" (pp. 571–573)	
• Section 504 of the Rehabilitation Act	**Chapter 5:** "Identifying Students' Special Needs: Response to Intervention and People-First Language" (pp. 144–145)	
• Due process	**Chapter 5:** "Public Law 94-142: Individuals with Disabilities Education Act (IDEA)" (pp. 142–143)	
• Family involvement	**Chapter 5:** "Public Law 94-142: Individuals with Disabilities Education Act (IDEA)" (pp. 142–143); "General Recommendations for Working with Students Who Have Special Needs" (pp. 166–167) **Chapter 13:** "Working with Parents" (pp. 476–480)	

(continued)

TOPICS IN THE PRAXIS PRINCIPLES OF LEARNING AND TEACHING (PLT) TESTS	LOCATION OF TOPICS IN ORMROD'S *EDUCATIONAL PSYCHOLOGY* (9TH ED.)	LOCATION OF TOPICS AND PRACTICE OPPORTUNITIES IN MyEdLab
I. Students as Learners		
B. Students as Diverse Learners		
▶ Approaches for accommodating various learning styles, intelligences, or exceptionalities, including:	**Chapter 5:** Entire chapter (pp. 128–168) **Chapter 6:** "Diversity in Cognitive Processes" (pp. 206–208) **Chapters 6– 15:** Students in Inclusive Settings tables (pp. 207, 244, 285, 318, 351, 392, 451–452, 474, 537, 572)	
• Differentiated instruction	**Chapter 12:** "General Principles that Can Guide Instruction" (pp. 414–416); "Accommodating Students with Special Needs" (pp. 451–452)	
• Alternative assessments	**Chapter 14:** "The Many Forms and Purposes of Assessment" (pp. 498–503); "Enhancing Learning Through Ongoing Assessments and Regular Feedback" (pp. 504–508); "Using Performance Assessments" (pp. 526–531) **Chapter 15:** "Using Portfolios" (pp. 553–556)	
• Testing modifications	**Chapter 14:** Table 14.5 "Students in Inclusive Settings" (p. 537) **Chapter 15:** "Accommodating Students with Special Needs" (pp. 571–573); Table 15.4 ("Students in Inclusive Settings: Using Standardized Tests with Students Who Have Special Educational Needs" p. 572)	
▶ The process of second-language acquisition and strategies to support the learning of students for whom English is not a first language	**Chapter 2:** "Second-Language Learning and English Language Learners" (pp. 51–54) **Chapter 12:** "Considering Group Differences" (p. 450) **Chapter 14:** "Informally Observing Students' Behaviors" (pp. 516–518); "Accommodating Group Differences" (p. 536) **Chapter 15:** "Language Differences and English Language Learners" (pp. 570–571)	
▶ How students' learning is influenced by individual experiences, talents, and prior learning, as well as language, culture, family, and community values, including:	**Chapter 2:** "The Multiple Layers of Environmental Influence: Bioecological Systems and the Importance of Culture" (pp. 23–25) **Chapter 5:** "Cognitive Styles and Dispositions" (pp. 139–141) **Chapter 6:** "Roles of Prior Knowledge and Working Memory in Long-Term Memory Storage" (pp. 191–192); "Diversity in Cognitive Processes" (pp. 206–208)	**Assignments and Activities: Understanding Research** exercise "Knowledge Construction in History" in topic "Knowledge Construction" **Supplementary Reading** "Content Extension 8.1" in Book-Specific Resources for Chapter 8
• Multicultural backgrounds	**Chapter 3: Case Study: "Hidden Treasure"** (p. 57); "Cultural Expectations and Socialization" (p. 60); Creating a Productive Classroom Environment box "Encouraging Positive Interactions Among Diverse Individuals and Groups" (p. 81) **Chapter 4: Case Study: "Why Jack Wasn't in School"** (p. 97); "Cultural and Ethnic Differences" (pp. 99–112) **Chapter 5:** "Cultural and Ethnic Diversity in Intelligence" (p. 137) **Chapter 8: Case Study: "It's All in How You Look at Things"** (p. 249); "Cultures as Contexts" (pp. 256–260) **Chapter 12:** "Considering Group Differences" (p. 450)	**Building Teaching Skills and Dispositions** exercise "Accommodating Cultural Differences" in topic "Student Diversity" **Assignments and Activities: Understanding Research** exercise "Navigating Adolescence" in topic "Personal, Social, & Moral Development"
• Age-appropriate knowledge and behavior	**Chapter 2:** "Piaget's Proposed Stages of Cognitive Development" (pp. 30–35); "Language Development" (pp. 48–54) **Chapter 3:** "Developmental Changes in Sense of Self" (pp. 64–67); "Perspective Taking" (pp. 75–76); "Developmental Trends in Morality and Prosocial Behavior" (pp. 83–87) **Chapters 4 – 15:** Developmental Trends tables (pp. 116, 190, 215–216, 269, 300, 341, 389, 403, 418, 471–472, 561)	

TABLE C.1 • (Continued)

TABLE C.1 • (Continued)

TOPICS IN THE PRAXIS PRINCIPLES OF LEARNING AND TEACHING (PLT) TESTS	LOCATION OF TOPICS IN ORMROD'S *EDUCATIONAL PSYCHOLOGY* (9TH ED.)	LOCATION OF TOPICS AND PRACTICE OPPORTUNITIES IN MyEdLab
I. Students as Learners		
B. Students as Diverse Learners		
• The student culture at the school	**Chapter 3:** "Roles of Peers in Children's Development" (pp. 69–71); "Common Social Groups in Childhood and Adolescence" (pp. 71–73); "Technology and Peer Relationships" (pp. 78–79) **Chapter 4:** "Navigating Different Cultures at Home and at School" (pp. 100–101) **Chapter 13:** "Addressing Aggression and Violence at School" (pp. 489–493)	**Simulation** exercise "Dealing with Situations Where Students Are Being Bullied/Harassed" in topic "Classroom Management" **Assignments and Activities: Understanding Research** exercise "Navigating Adolescence" in topic "Personal, Social, & Moral Development" **Assignments and Activities: Understanding Research** exercise "Cheating in High School Students" in topic "Assessment"
• Family backgrounds	**Chapter 3:** "Family Dynamics" (pp. 58–60) **Chapter 4:** "Socioeconomic Differences" (pp. 118–123)	**Assignments and Activities: Understanding Research** exercise "Supporting Children at Risk" in topic "Student Diversity"
• Linguistic patterns and differences	**Chapter 2:** "Language Development" (pp. 48–54)" **Chapter 5:** "Speech and Communication Disorders" (pp. 150–151) **Chapter 8: Practice for Your Licensure Exam: "The Birth of a Nation"** (p. 287)	
• Cognitive patterns and differences	**Chapter 5:** "Cognitive Styles and Dispositions" (pp. 139–141) **Chapter 6:** "Diversity in Cognitive Processes" (pp. 206–208) **Chapter 7: Practice for Your Licensure Exam: "Interview with Charlie"** (pp. 246–247)	**Assignments and Activities: Understanding Research** exercise "Self-Discipline & Academic Achievement" in topic "Student Diversity" **Assignments and Activities: Understanding Research** exercise "High School Students' Study Strategies" in topic "Memory and Cognitive Processes"
• Social and emotional issues	**Chapter 3:** "Personality Development" (pp. 58–62); "Development of a Sense of Self" (pp. 62–69); "Social Cognition" (pp. 74–77); "Aggression" (pp. 77–78); "Factors Influencing Moral and Prosocial Development" (pp. 87–88) **Chapter 5:** "Emotional and Behavioral Disorders" (pp. 152–155); "Autism Spectrum Disorders" (pp. 155–156) **Chapter 9:** "Classical Conditioning of Involuntary Emotional Responses" (p. 293) **Chapter 10:** "Emotion Regulation" (p. 342) **Chapter 11:** "Affect and Its Effects" (pp. 398–407) **Chapter 14:** "Keeping Test Anxiety in Check" (p. 532)	**Assignments and Activities: Understanding Research** exercise "Navigating Adolescence" in topic "Personal, Social, & Moral Development" **Assignments and Activities: Understanding Research** exercise "Need for Approval and Emotional Well-Being" in topic "Motivation and Affect"
C. Student Motivation and the Learning Environment		
▶ Theoretical foundations about human motivation and behavior:	**Chapter 11** Entire chapter (pp. 358–410)	
• Abraham Maslow	**Chapter 11:** "Early Views of Basic Human Needs" (pp. 364–365)	
• Albert Bandura	**Chapter 10:** Entire chapter (pp. 322–356)	
• B. F. Skinner	**Chapter 9: Case Study: "The Attention Getter"** (p. 289); "Learning from Consequences: Instrumental Conditioning" (pp. 294–304); "Shaping New Behaviors" (pp. 309–310)	**Supplementary Reading** "Content Extension 9.1" in Book-Specific Resources for Chapter 9 **Supplementary Reading** "Content Extension 12.1" in Book-Specific Resources for Chapter 12

(continued)

TABLE C.1 • (Continued)		
TOPICS IN THE PRAXIS PRINCIPLES OF LEARNING AND TEACHING (PLT) TESTS	**LOCATION OF TOPICS IN ORMROD'S** *EDUCATIONAL PSYCHOLOGY* **(9TH ED.)**	**LOCATION OF TOPICS AND PRACTICE OPPORTUNITIES IN** MyEdLab
I. Students as Learners		
C. Student Motivation and the Learning Environment		
► Important terms that relate to motivation and behavior:		
• Hierarchy of needs	**Chapter 11:** "Early Views of Basic Human Needs" (pp. 364–365)	
• Correlational and causal relationships	**Chapter 11: Case Study: "Passing Algebra"** (p. 359); "Attributions" (pp. 376–380)	
• Intrinsic motivation	**Chapter 9:** "Using Reinforcement Effectively" (pp. 304–309) **Chapter 11:** "Intrinsic Versus Extrinsic Motivation" (pp. 361–364); "Early Views of Basic Human Needs" (pp. 364–365); "Expectancies and Values" (pp. 366–367); "Interests" (pp. 367–368); "Achievement Goals" (pp. 380–383);	**Building Teaching Skills and Dispositions** exercises "Addressing Students' Basic Needs" and "Promoting Interest" in topic "Motivation and Affect" **Assignments and Activities: Understanding Research** exercise "Self-Discipline & Academic Achievement" in topic "Student Diversity"
• Extrinsic motivation	**Chapter 9:** "Learning from Consequences: Instrumental Conditioning" (pp. 294–304); "Using Reinforcement Effectively" (pp. 304–309) **Chapter 11:** "Intrinsic Versus Extrinsic Motivation" (pp. 361–364); "Achievement Goals" (pp. 380–383) **Chapter 14:** "Promoting Learning" (pp. 502–503)	
• Learned helplessness	**Chapter 11:** "Mastery Orientation Versus Learned Helplessness" (pp. 387–388)	
• Self-efficacy	**Chapter 3:** "Development of a Sense of Self" (pp. 62–69) **Chapter 10: Case Study: "Parlez-Vous Français?"** (p. 323); "Self-Efficacy" (pp. 333–339)	**Assignments and Activities: Understanding Research** exercise "Self-Efficacy and Achievement" in topic "Social Cognitive Perspectives"
• Operant conditioning	**Chapter 9:** "Learning from Consequences: Instrumental Conditioning" (pp. 294–304)	
• Reinforcement	**Chapter 9: Case Study: "The Attention Getter"** (p. 289); "The Various Forms That Reinforcement Can Take" (pp. 296–301); "Using Reinforcement Effectively" (pp. 304–309); "Reinforcing Incompatible Behaviors" (pp. 312–313) **Chapter 10:** "The Social Cognitive View of Reinforcement and Punishment" (pp. 325–328); **Practice for Your Licensure Exam: "Teacher's Lament"** (p. 356) **Chapter 13:** "Conducting Planned, Systematic Interventions" (pp. 486–488)	**Assignments and Activities: Understanding Research** exercise "Conducting a Functional Analysis" in topic "Behaviorist Perspectives"
• Positive reinforcement	**Chapter 9:** "Positive Reinforcement" (pp. 297–298)	**Assignments and Activities: Understanding Research** exercise "Identifying Reinforcers Through Functional Analysis" in topic "Classroom Management"
• Negative reinforcement	**Chapter 9:** "Negative Reinforcement" (p. 299)	**Assignments and Activities: Understanding Research** exercise "Identifying Reinforcers Through Functional Analysis" in topic "Classroom Management"
• Shaping successive approximations	**Chapter 9:** "Shaping New Behaviors" (pp. 309–310)	**Supplementary Reading** "Content Extension 12.1" in Book-Specific Resources for Chapter 12
• Prevention	**Chapter 9:** "Functional Analysis" (p. 315); Positive Behavioral Interventions and Supports" (pp. 316–317) **Chapter 13:** "Creating a Setting Conducive to Learning" (pp. 457–474); "Addressing Aggression and Violence at School" (pp. 489–493)	

TABLE C.1 • (Continued)

TOPICS IN THE PRAXIS PRINCIPLES OF LEARNING AND TEACHING (PLT) TESTS	LOCATION OF TOPICS IN ORMROD'S *EDUCATIONAL PSYCHOLOGY* (9TH ED.)	LOCATION OF TOPICS AND PRACTICE OPPORTUNITIES IN MyEdLab
I. Students as Learners		
C. Student Motivation and the Learning Environment		
• Extinction	**Chapter 9:** "Creating Conditions for Extinction" (p. 312); **Practice for Your Licensure Exam: "Hostile Helen"** (p. 321) **Chapter 13:** "Ignoring Certain Behaviors" (pp. 481–482)	
• Punishment	**Chapter 9:** "The Various Forms That Punishment Can Take" (pp. 301–304); "Using Punishment When Necessary" (pp. 313–314) **Chapter 10:** "The Social Cognitive View of Reinforcement and Punishment" (pp. 325–328); **Practice for Your Licensure Exam: "Teacher's Lament"** (p. 356)	
• Continuous reinforcement	**Chapter 9:** "Using Reinforcement Effectively" (pp. 304–309)	
• Intermittent reinforcement	**Chapter 9:** "Using Reinforcement Effectively" (pp. 304–309)	**Supplementary Reading** "Content Extension 9.1" in Book-Specific Resources for Chapter 9
▶ How knowledge of human motivation and behavior should influence strategies for organizing and supporting individual and group work in the classroom	**Chapter 11:** Entire chapter (pp. 358–410)	**Building Teaching Skills and Dispositions** exercise "Applying Behaviorist Principles" in topic "Behaviorist Perspectives" **Building Teaching Skills and Dispositions** exercise "Addressing Students' Basic Needs" in topic "Motivation and Affect" **Assignments and Activities: Understanding Research** exercise "Combining Achievement Goals" in topic "Motivation and Affect"
▶ Factors and situations that are likely to promote or diminish students' motivation to learn; how to help students become self-motivated	**Chapter 10:** "Self-Regulated Learning" (pp. 345–347); "Diversity in Self-Regulation" (pp. 348–351) **Chapter 11:** Entire chapter (pp. 358–410) **Chapter 13:** "Teaching Self-Regulation Skills" (p. 484)	**Building Teaching Skills and Dispositions** exercise "Promoting Interest" in topic "Motivation and Affect" **Simulation** exercise "Helping All Students Believe They Can Achieve" in topic "Classroom Management" **Assignments and Activities: Understanding Research** exercise "Navigating Adolescence" in topic "Personal, Social, & Moral Development" **Assignments and Activities: Understanding Research** exercises "Need for Approval and Emotional Well-Being" and "Combining Achievement Goals" in topic "Motivation and Affect" **Assignments and Activities: Understanding Research** exercise "Cheating in High School Students" in topic "Assessment"
▶ Principles of effective classroom management and strategies to promote positive relationships, co-operation, and purposeful learning, including:	**Chapters 3, 5, 9, 13:** "Creating a Productive Classroom Environment" boxes (pp. 61, 81, 157, 298, 307, 465) **Chapter 3:** "Social Cognition" (pp. 74–77); "Aggression" (pp. 77–78); "Promoting Healthy Peer Relationships" (pp. 80–82) "Encouraging Moral and Prosocial Development at School" (pp. 89–92)	**Building Teaching Skills and Dispositions** exercise "Applying Behaviorist Principles" in topic "Behaviorist Perspectives " **Building Teaching Skills and Dispositions** exercise "Maintaining On-Task Behavior" in topic "Classroom Management"

(continued)

TABLE C.1 • (Continued)

TOPICS IN THE PRAXIS PRINCIPLES OF LEARNING AND TEACHING (PLT) TESTS	LOCATION OF TOPICS IN ORMROD'S *EDUCATIONAL PSYCHOLOGY* (9TH ED.)	LOCATION OF TOPICS AND PRACTICE OPPORTUNITIES IN MyEdLab
I. Students as Learners		
C. Student Motivation and the Learning Environment		
	Chapter 8: "Creating a Community of Learners" (pp. 255–256) Chapter 11: "The Need for Relatedness" (pp. 373–374) Chapter 13: "Establishing and Maintaining Productive Teacher–Student Relationships" (pp. 460–462); "Creating an Effective Psychological Climate" (pp. 462–464); "Addressing Aggression and Violence at School" (pp. 489–493)	**Simulation** exercise "Developing Positive Teacher-Student Relationships with All Students" in topic "Classroom Management" **Simulation** exercise "Helping All Students Believe They Can Achieve" in topic "Classroom Management" **Assignments and Activities: Understanding Research** exercise "Supporting Children at Risk" in topic "Student Diversity"
• Establishing daily procedures and routines	Chapter 13: "Setting Limits" (pp. 464–467); **Practice for Your Licensure Exam: "The Good Buddy"** (p. 495)	
• Establishing classroom rules	Chapter 10: "The Social Cognitive View of Reinforcement and Punishment" (pp. 325–328) Chapter 13: "Setting Limits" (pp. 464–467)	**Simulation** exercise "Creating Classroom Behavioral Expectations" in topic "Classroom Management"
• Using natural and logical consequences	Chapter 9: "Logical Consequences" (pp. 301–302)	
• Providing positive guidance	Chapter 3: "Promoting Healthy Peer Relationships" (pp. 80–82) Chapter 9: "Shaping New Behaviors" (pp. 309–310); "Cueing Inappropriate Behaviors" (p. 312); "Reinforcing Incompatible Behaviors" (pp. 312–313); "Functional Analysis" (p. 315); Positive Behavioral Interventions and Supports" (pp. 316–317) Chapter 13: "A Three-Level Approach" (pp. 490–492)	**Simulation** exercise "Developing Behavior Change Plans" in topic "Classroom Management"
• Modeling conflict resolution, problem solving, and anger management	Chapter 10: "Self-Regulated Problem Solving" (pp. 347–348) Chapter 13: "Addressing Aggression and Violence at School" (pp. 489–493)	
• Giving timely feedback	Chapter 9: Creating a Productive Classroom Environment box "Using Feedback to Improve Learning and Behavior" (p. 298); "Cueing Inappropriate Behaviors" (p. 312) Chapter 11: "Fostering Productive Achievement Goals" (p. 383); **Practice for Your Licensure Exam: "When 'Perfect' Isn't Good Enough"** (p. 410) Chapter 12: Asking Questions and Giving Feedback (pp. 426–427) Chapter 13: "Cueing Students" (p. 482); "Discussing Problems Privately with Students" (pp. 482–483) Chapter 14: "Enhancing Learning Through Ongoing Assessments and Regular Feedback" (pp. 504–508)	
• Maintaining accurate records	Chapter 14: "RSVP Characteristics of Informal Assessments" (pp. 517–518) Chapter 15: "Determining Final Class Grades" (pp. 548–553)	
• Communicating with parents and caregivers	Chapter 13: "Working with Parents" (pp. 476–480); "Conferring with Parents" (pp. 484–486)	
• Using objective behavior descriptions	Chapter 9: "Using Reinforcement Effectively" (pp. 304–309); "Addressing Especially Difficult Classroom Behaviors" (pp. 314–317)	
• Responding to student misbehavior	Chapter 9: "Strategies for Discouraging Undesirable Behaviors" (pp. 311–314); "Addressing Especially Difficult Classroom Behaviors" (pp. 314–317)	**Simulation** exercise "Dealing with Situations Where Students Are Being Bullied/Harassed" in topic "Classroom Management"

TABLE C.1 • (Continued)

TOPICS IN THE PRAXIS PRINCIPLES OF LEARNING AND TEACHING (PLT) TESTS	LOCATION OF TOPICS IN ORMROD'S *EDUCATIONAL PSYCHOLOGY* (9TH ED.)	LOCATION OF TOPICS AND PRACTICE OPPORTUNITIES IN MyEdLab
I. Students as Learners		
C. Student Motivation and the Learning Environment		
	Chapter 13: "Dealing with Misbehaviors" (pp. 480–489); "Addressing Aggression and Violence at School" (pp. 489–493)	**Simulation** exercise "Responding to Student Disruptions" in topic "Classroom Management"
• Arranging of classroom space	**Chapter 13:** "Arranging the Classroom" (pp. 459–460)	
• Pacing and structuring the lesson	**Chapter 5:** "Intellectual Disabilities" (pp. 157–159) **Chapter 6:** "Wait Time" (pp. 203–204) **Chapter 12:** "Conducting a Task Analysis" (pp. 421–422); Into the Classroom box "Effectively Using Expository Instruction" (p. 425) **Chapter 13:** "Planning Activities That Keep Students on Task" (pp. 467–469)	
II. Instruction and Assessment		
A. Instructional Strategies		
▶ The major cognitive processes associated with student learning, including:	**Chapters 6– 7:** Entire chapters (pp. 170–210, 212–247) **Chapter 8:** "Academic Content Domains as Contexts" (pp. 265–285)	
• Critical thinking	**Chapter 5:** "Cognitive Styles and Dispositions" (pp. 139–141) **Chapter 7:** "Critical Thinking" (pp. 239–243) **Chapter 8:** "Technological Literacy" (pp. 272–274)	**Assignments and Activities: Understanding Research** exercise "Self-Efficacy and Achievement" in topic "Social Cognitive Perspectives"
• Creative thinking	**Chapter 7:** "Creativity" (pp. 236–239)	
• Higher-order thinking	**Chapter 7:** Entire chapter (pp. 212–247) **Chapter 8:** "Academic Content Domains as Contexts" (pp. 265–285) **Chapter 12:** "Identifying the Goals of Instruction" (pp. 417–421)	
• Inductive and deductive thinking	**Chapter 2:** "Piaget's Proposed Stages of Cognitive Development" (pp. 30–35) **Chapter 7:** "Critical Thinking" (pp. 239–243)	
• Problem-structuring and problem-solving	**Chapter 7:** Case Study: "Taking Over" (p. 213); "Problem Solving" (pp. 230–236) **Chapter 8:** "Mathematics" (pp. 274–276)	**Building Teaching Skills and Dispositions** exercise "Teaching Problem Solving Skills" in topic "Memory and Cognitive Processes"
• Invention	**Chapter 7:** "Creativity" (pp. 236–239)	
• Memorization and recall	**Chapter 6:** "Long-Term Memory Storage" (pp. 181–195); "Long-Term Memory Retrieval" (pp. 199–205) **Chapter 7: Practice for Your Licensure Exam: "Interview with Charlie"** (pp. 246–247)	**Building Teaching Skills and Dispositions** exercise "Facilitating Long-Term Memory Storage Processes" in topic "Memory and Cognitive Processes"
• Social reasoning	**Chapter 3:** "Social Cognition" (pp. 74–77); "Aggression" (pp. 77–78); "Developmental Trends in Morality and Prosocial Behavior" (pp. 83–87); "Gender Differences" (pp. 88–89); **Practice for Your Licensure Exam: "The Scarlet Letter"** (pp. 93–94)	**Building Teaching Skills and Dispositions** exercise "Fostering Perspective Taking and Social Skills" in topic "Personal, Social, & Moral Development"
• Representation of ideas	**Chapter 6:** "The Nature of Long-Term Memory" (p. 180); "How Knowledge Can Be Organized" (pp. 183–185); "How Declarative Knowledge Is Learned" (pp. 185–189)	**Building Teaching Skills and Dispositions** exercise "Knowledge Construction & Conceptual Change" in topic "Knowledge Construction" **Assignments and Activities: Understanding Research** exercise "Knowledge Construction in History" in topic "Knowledge Construction"

(continued)

TABLE C.1 • (Continued)

TOPICS IN THE PRAXIS PRINCIPLES OF LEARNING AND TEACHING (PLT) TESTS	LOCATION OF TOPICS IN ORMROD'S *EDUCATIONAL PSYCHOLOGY* (9TH ED.)	LOCATION OF TOPICS AND PRACTICE OPPORTUNITIES IN MyEdLab
II. Instruction and Assessment		
A. Instructional Strategies		
▶ Major categories of instructional strategies, including:	**Chapter 12:** "Teacher-Directed Instructional Strategies" (pp. 424–434); "Learner-Directed Instructional Strategies" (pp. 434–448); "Taking Instructional Goals and Student Diversity into Account" (pp. 448–452)	
• Cooperative learning	**Chapter 12:** "Conducting Cooperative Learning Activities" (pp. 442–445); **Practice for Your Licensure Exam: "Cooperative Learning Project"** (pp. 453–454)	
• Direct instruction	**Chapter 12:** "Conducting Direct Instruction" (pp. 429–430); "Promoting Mastery" (pp. 430–432)	
• Discovery learning	**Chapter 12:** "Conducting Discovery and Inquiry Activities" (pp. 438–440)	
• Whole-group discussion	**Chapter 8:** "Interactions with Peers" (pp. 254–255) **Chapter 12:** "Stimulating and Guiding Class Discussions" (pp. 434–436)	
• Independent study	**Chapter 5:** "Giftedness" (pp. 163–165; (see especially subsection "Adapting Instruction," p. 164) **Chapter 8:** "Technology in Learning and Instruction" (pp. 263–265) **Chapter 12:** "Giving Homework" (pp. 428–429); "Using Instructional Websites" (pp. 432–433); "Using Technology to Individualize Instruction" (pp. 433–434)	
• Interdisciplinary instruction	**Chapter 6:** "Multiple Connections with Existing Knowledge and a Variety of Contexts" (pp. 200–201) **Chapter 7:** "Factors Affecting Transfer" (pp. 227–230)	
• Concept mapping	**Chapter 6:** "Organization" (p. 187)	
• Inquiry method	**Chapter 8:** "Promoting Learning in Science" (pp. 278–280) **Chapter 12:** "Conducting Discovery and Inquiry Activities" (pp. 438–440); "Using Technology-Based Simulations and Games" (pp. 439–441)	
• Questioning	**Chapter 4:** "Responding to Questions" (pp. 103–104) **Chapter 7:** "Fostering Creativity" (pp. 238–239) **Chapter 12:** "Asking Questions and Giving Feedback" (pp. 426–427)	
• Play	**Chapter 2:** "Vygotsky's Basic Assumptions" (pp. 39–42) **Chapter 12:** "Using Technology-Based Simulations and Games" (pp. 439–441)	
• Learning centers		
• Small group work	**Chapter 2: Case Study: "Apple Tarts"** (p. 21) **Chapter 12:** "Conducting Cooperative Learning Activities" (pp. 442–445); "Structuring Peer Tutoring Sessions" (pp. 445–447)	**Assignments and Activities: Understanding Research** exercise "Teaching Reading Comprehension Strategies" in topic "Memory and Cognitive Processes"
• Revisiting	**Chapter 6:** "Regular Practice" (p. 202)	
• Reflection	**Chapter 10:** "Self-Evaluation" (p. 344) **Chapter 14:** "Including Students in the Assessment Process" (pp. 506–507)	
• Project approach	**Chapter 8:** "Authentic Activities" (pp. 260–262) **Chapter 12:** "Providing Practice Through In-Class Assignments" (pp. 427–428); "Conducting Cooperative Learning Activities" (pp. 442–445); **Practice for Your Licensure Exam: "Cooperative Learning Project"** (pp. 453–454)	

TABLE C.1 • (Continued)		
TOPICS IN THE PRAXIS PRINCIPLES OF LEARNING AND TEACHING (PLT) TESTS	**LOCATION OF TOPICS IN ORMROD'S** *EDUCATIONAL PSYCHOLOGY* **(9TH ED.)**	**LOCATION OF TOPICS AND PRACTICE OPPORTUNITIES IN** MyEdLab
II. Instruction and Assessment		
A. Instructional Strategies		
▸ Principles, techniques, and methods associated with various instructional strategies, including:	**Chapter 12:** Entire chapter (pp. 412–454)	**Building Teaching Skills and Dispositions** exercise "Identifying Effective Instructional Strategies" in topic "Planning and Instruction"
• Direct instruction:	**Chapter 12:** "Conducting Direct Instruction" (pp. 429–430)	**Building Teaching Skills and Dispositions** exercise "Facilitating Long-Term Memory Storage Processes" in topic "Memory and Cognitive Processes"
• Madeline Hunter's "Effective Teaching Model"		
• David Ausubel's "Advance Organizers"	**Chapter 12:** Into the Classroom box "Effectively Using Expository Instruction" (p. 425)	
• Mastery learning	**Chapter 12:** "Promoting Mastery" (pp. 430–432)	
• Demonstrations	**Chapter 8:** "Promoting Learning in Science" (pp. 278–280) **Chapter 10:** Into the Classroom box "Promoting Learning Through Modeling" (p. 332)	
• Mnemonics	**Chapter 6:** "Using Mnemonics in the Absence of Relevant Prior Knowledge" (pp. 193–195)	
• Note taking	**Chapter 7:** "Overt Strategies" (pp. 216–217)	
• Outlining	**Chapter 7:** "Accommodating Students with Special Needs" (pp. 224–225)	
• Use of visual aids	**Chapter 5:** "Visual Impairments" (pp. 160–161); "Hearing Loss" (pp. 161–162) **Chapter 6:** "Visual Imagery" (pp. 187–189) **Chapter 12:** Into the Classroom box "Effectively Using Expository Instruction" (p. 425)	
• Student-centered models:	**Chapter 12:** Learner-Directed Instructional Strategies (pp. 434–448)	
• Inquiry model	**Chapter 12:** "Conducting Discovery and Inquiry Activities" (pp. 438–440)	
• Discovery learning	**Chapter 12:** "Conducting Discovery and Inquiry Activities" (pp. 438–440)	
• Cooperative learning (pair-share, jigsaw, STAD, teams, games, tournaments)	**Chapter 12:** "Conducting Cooperative Learning Activities" (pp. 442–445)	
• Collaborative learning	**Chapter 8:** "Creating a Community of Learners" (pp. 255–256) **Chapter 12:** "Structuring Peer Tutoring Sessions" (pp. 445–447); "Conducting Technology-Based Collaborative Learning Activities" (p. 448)	**Assignments and Activities: Understanding Research** exercise "Effect of Ability Level" in topic "Planning and Instruction"
• Concept models (concept development, concept attainment, concept mapping)	**Chapter 6:** "How Knowledge Can Be Organized" (pp. 183–185); "Organization" (p. 187)	**Building Teaching Skills and Dispositions** exercise "Knowledge Construction & Conceptual Change" in topic "Knowledge Construction"
• Discussion models	**Chapter 2:** Case Study: "Apple Tarts" (p. 21) **Chapter 8:** "Creating a Community of Learners" (pp. 255–256) **Chapter 12:** "Stimulating and Guiding Class Discussions" (pp. 434–436)	**Assignments and Activities: Understanding Research** exercise "Teaching Reading Comprehension Strategies" in topic "Memory and Cognitive Processes"

(continued)

TABLE C.1 • (Continued)

TOPICS IN THE PRAXIS PRINCIPLES OF LEARNING AND TEACHING (PLT) TESTS	LOCATION OF TOPICS IN ORMROD'S *EDUCATIONAL PSYCHOLOGY* (9TH ED.)	LOCATION OF TOPICS AND PRACTICE OPPORTUNITIES IN MyEdLab
II. Instruction and Assessment		
A. Instructional Strategies		
• Laboratories	**Chapter 8:** "Promoting Learning in Science" (pp. 278–280) **Chapter 12:** "Conducting Discovery and Inquiry Activities" (pp. 438–440)	
• Project-based learning	**Chapter 8:** "Authentic Activities" (pp. 260–262) **Chapter 12:** "Conducting Cooperative Learning Activities" (pp. 442–445); **Practice for Your Licensure Exam: "Cooperative Learning Project"** (pp. 453–454)	
Simulations	**Chapter 12:** "Using Technology-Based Simulations and Games" (pp. 439–441)	
▶ Methods for enhancing student learning through the use of a variety of resources and materials:		
• Computers, Internet resources, Web pages, e-mail	**Chapter 5:** "Students with Physical or Sensory Challenges" (pp. 159–162; see especially subsection "General Recommendations" p. 162) **Chapter 7:** "Using Computer Technology to Teach Problem-Solving Skills" (pp. 235–236) **Chapter 8:** "Technological Innovations" (pp. 262–265) **Chapter 12:** "Creating a Class Website to Share Goals and Facilitate Communication Throughout the School Year" (pp. 423–424); "Providing Practice through In-Class Assignments" (pp. 427–428); "Using Instructional Websites" (pp. 432–433); "Using Technology to Individualize Instruction" (pp. 433–434); "Using Technology-Based Simulations and Games" (pp. 439–441); "Conducting Technology-Based Collaborative Learning Activities" (p. 448) **Chapter 14:** "Using Digital Technologies in Formative Assessment" (pp. 507–508)	
• Audiovisual technologies such as videotapes and compact discs	**Chapter 8:** "Technology in Learning and Instruction" (pp. 263–265) **Chapter 10:** "Self-Monitoring" (pp. 343–344)	
• Local experts	**Chapter 5:** "Giftedness" (pp. 163–165; see especially subsection "Adapting Instruction", pp. 164–165) **Chapter 8:** "Interactions with More Advanced Individuals" (pp. 253–254)	
• Primary documents and artifacts	**Chapter 8:** "Promoting Learning in Social Studies" (pp. 282–283)	
• Field trips	**Chapter 4:** "Fostering Resilience" (pp. 121–122) **Chapter 5:** "Students with Physical or Sensory Challenges" (pp. 159–162; see especially subsection "General Recommendations", p. 162)	
• Libraries	**Chapter 8:** "Technological Literacy" (pp. 272–274)	
• Service learning	**Chapter 3:** "Encouraging Moral and Prosocial Development at School" (pp. 89–92) **Chapter 8:** "Authentic Activities" (pp. 260–262)	
B. Planning instruction		
▶ Techniques for planning instruction to meet curriculum goals, including the incorporation of learning theory, subject matter, curriculum development, and student development:	**Chapter 12:** "General Principles That Can Guide Instruction"; (pp. 414–416); "Planning for Instruction" (pp. 416–424) **Chapter 13: Case Study: "A Contagious Situation"** (p. 457)	

TABLE C.1 • (Continued)		
TOPICS IN THE PRAXIS PRINCIPLES OF LEARNING AND TEACHING (PLT) TESTS	**LOCATION OF TOPICS IN ORMROD'S** *EDUCATIONAL PSYCHOLOGY* **(9TH ED.)**	**LOCATION OF TOPICS AND PRACTICE OPPORTUNITIES IN** MyEdLab
II. Instruction and Assessment		
B. Planning instruction		
• National and state learning standards	**Chapter 7:** Case Study: "Taking Over" (p. 213) **Chapter 12:** "Aligning Instructional Goals with National, International, and State Standards, Including (If Applicable) the Common Core State Standards" (pp. 417–419) **Chapter 14:** Table 14.1 ("Examples of How You Might Align Classroom Assessments with Common Core State Standards and Instruction at Different Grade Levels" pp. 512–513) **Chapter 15:** "High-Stakes Testing and Teacher Accountability" (pp. 564–568)	
• State and local curriculum frameworks	**Chapter 12:** "Aligning Instructional Goals with National, International, and State Standards, Including (If Applicable) the Common Core State Standards" (pp. 417–419) **Chapter 15:** "High-Stakes Testing and Teacher Accountability" (pp. 564–568)	
• State and local curriculum guides		
• Scope and sequence in specific disciplines	**Chapter 8:** "Academic Content Domains as Contexts" (pp. 265–285) **Chapter 12:** "Conducting a Task Analysis" (pp. 421–422)	
• Units and lessons— rationale for selecting content topics	**Chapter 12:** "Developing a Lesson Plan" (pp. 422–423)	**MyEdLab Application Exercises 12.1 and 12.2** in topic "Planning for Instruction"
• Behavioral objectives: affective, cognitive, psychomotor	**Chapter 12:** Into the Classroom box "Identifying Appropriate Goals and Objectives" (p. 420)	**Supplementary Reading** "Content Extension 12.1" in Book-Specific Resources for Chapter 12
• Learner objectives and outcomes	**Chapter 11:** "Achievement Goals" (pp. 380–383) **Chapter 12:** Into the Classroom box "Identifying Appropriate Goals and Objectives" (p. 420)	
• Emergent curriculum		
• Antibias curriculum	**Chapter 4:** "Creating a Culturally Inclusive Classroom Environment" (pp. 106–112)	
• Themes/projects	**Chapter 6:** "Encouraging a Meaningful Learning Set and Conceptual Understanding" (pp. 192–193) **Chapter 12:** "General Principles That Can Guide Instruction" (pp. 414–416)	
• Curriculum webbing		
▶ Techniques for creating effective bridges between curriculum goals and students' experiences:	**Chapter 12:** "General Principles That Can Guide Instruction" (pp. 414–416); "Planning for Instruction" (pp. 416–424)	
• Modeling	**Chapter 10:** "Modeling" (pp. 328–333)	
• Guided practice	**Chapter 2:** "Scaffolding" (pp. 45–46); "Guided Participation in Challenging New Activities" (p. 46); "Apprenticeships" (pp. 46–47) **Chapter 8:** "Communities of Practice as Aspects of Culture" (pp. 259–260)	
• Independent practice, including homework	**Chapter 10:** "Self-Regulated Learning" (pp. 345–347) **Chapter 12:** "Giving Homework" (pp. 428–429)	
• Transitions	**Chapter 13:** "Planning Activities That Keep Students on Task" (pp. 467–469)	**Simulation** exercise "Effectively Handling Transitions" in topic "Classroom Management"

(continued)

TABLE C.1 • (Continued)

TOPICS IN THE PRAXIS PRINCIPLES OF LEARNING AND TEACHING (PLT) TESTS	LOCATION OF TOPICS IN ORMROD'S *EDUCATIONAL PSYCHOLOGY* (9TH ED.)	LOCATION OF TOPICS AND PRACTICE OPPORTUNITIES IN MyEdLab
II. Instruction and Assessment		
B. Planning instruction		
• Activating students' prior knowledge	**Chapter 6:** "Roles of Prior Knowledge and Working Memory in Long-Term Memory Storage" (pp. 191–192) **Chapter 12:** Into the Classroom box "Effectively Using Expository Instruction" (p. 425)	**Assignments and Activities: Understanding Research** exercise "Knowledge Construction in History" in topic "Knowledge Construction"
• Anticipating preconceptions	**Chapter 6:** "When Knowledge Construction Goes Awry: Addressing Learners' Misconceptions" (pp. 195–199); **Practice for Your Licensure Exam: "Vision Unit"** (p. 210) **Chapter 12:** "Asking Questions and Giving Feedback" (pp. 426–427)	**Building Teaching Skills and Dispositions** exercise "Knowledge Construction & Conceptual Change" in topic "Knowledge Construction" **Assignments and Activities: Understanding Research** exercise "Knowledge Construction in History" in topic "Knowledge Construction"
• Encouraging exploration and problem-solving	**Chapter 2:** "Piaget's Basic Assumptions" (pp. 29–30); "Contrasting Piaget's and Vygotsky's Theories" (p. 47) **Chapter 7:** "Problem Solving" (pp. 230–236) **Chapter 12:** "Conducting Discovery and Inquiry Activities" (pp. 438–440)	**Building Teaching Skills and Dispositions** exercise "Teaching Problem Solving Skills" in topic "Memory and Cognitive Processes"
• Building new skills on those previously acquired	**Chapter 6:** "How Procedural Knowledge Is Learned" (pp. 189–191) **Chapter 9:** "Shaping New Behaviors" (pp. 309–310) **Chapter 12:** "Promoting Mastery" (pp. 430–432)	
• Predicting	**Chapter 8:** "Promoting Learning in Science" (pp. 278–280)	
C. Assessment Strategies		
▶ Measurement theory and assessment-related issues:	**Chapters 14– 15:** Entire chapters (pp. 496–539, 540–577)	
• Types of assessments	**Chapter 14:** "The Many Forms and Purposes of Assessment" (pp. 498–503)	**Building Teaching Skills and Dispositions** exercise "Assessing Students' Written Work" in topic "Assessment"
• Standardized tests, norm-referenced or criterion-referenced	**Chapter 14:** "The Many Forms and Purposes of Assessment" (pp. 498–503) **Chapter 15:** "Standardized Tests" (pp. 557–564); "High-Stakes Testing and Teacher Accountability" (pp. 564–568)	**Assignments and Activities: Understanding Research** exercise "Usefulness of School Readiness Tests" in topic "Assessment"
• Achievement tests	**Chapter 14:** "Assessing Learning and Performance Both Informally and Formally" (pp. 516–535) **Chapter 15:** "Achievement Tests" (p. 557); **Practice for Your Licensure Exam: "Can Johnny Read?"** (p. 577)	
• Aptitude tests	**Chapter 5:** "Measuring Intelligence" (pp. 134–136); "Being Smart about Intelligence and IQ Scores" (pp. 137–139) **Chapter 15:** "General Scholastic Aptitude and Intelligence Tests" (pp. 557–558); "Specific Aptitude and Ability Tests" (p. 558)	
• Structured observations	**Chapter 14:** "Using Performance Assessments" (pp. 526–531)	
• Anecdotal notes	**Chapter 14:** "Informally Observing Students' Behaviors" (pp. 516–518)	
• Assessments of prior knowledge	**Chapter 12:** Asking Questions and Giving Feedback" (pp. 426–427); Into the Classroom box "Effectively Using Expository Instruction" (p. 425)	
• Student response during a lesson	**Chapter 14:** "Informally Observing Students' Behaviors" (pp. 516–518)	

TABLE C.1 • (Continued)

TOPICS IN THE PRAXIS PRINCIPLES OF LEARNING AND TEACHING (PLT) TESTS	LOCATION OF TOPICS IN ORMROD'S *EDUCATIONAL PSYCHOLOGY* (9TH ED.)	LOCATION OF TOPICS AND PRACTICE OPPORTUNITIES IN MyEdLab
II. Instruction and Assessment		
C. Assessment Strategies		
• Portfolios	**Chapter 15:** "Using Portfolios" (pp. 553–556)	**Building Teaching Skills and Dispositions** exercise "Encouraging Self-Regulation" in topic "Social Cognitive Perspectives"
• Essays written to prompts	**Chapter 14:** "Using Paper–Pencil Assessments" (pp. 518–526)	
• Journals	**Chapter 13:** "Establishing and Maintaining Productive Teacher–Student Relationships" (pp. 460–462) **Chapter 14:** "Including Students in the Assessment Process" (pp. 506–507)	
• Self-evaluations	**Chapter 10:** "Self-Evaluation" (p. 344) **Chapter 14:** "Including Students in the Assessment Process" (pp. 506–507) **Chapter 15:** "Including Students in the Grading Process" (p. 553); "Using Portfolios" (pp. 553–556)	**Building Teaching Skills and Dispositions** exercise "Encouraging Self-Regulation" in topic "Social Cognitive Perspectives"
• Performance assessments	**Chapter 14:** "Using Performance Assessments" (pp. 526–531)	
• Characteristics of assessments:	**Chapter 14: Practice for Your Licensure Exam:** "Two Science Quizzes" (p. 539) **Chapter 15: Practice for Your Licensure Exam:** "Can Johnny Read?" (p. 577)	**Building Teaching Skills and Dispositions** exercise "Assessing Students' Written Work" in topic "Assessment"
• Validity	**Chapter 14:** "Validity" (pp. 510–515); "RSVP Characteristics of Informal Assessments" (pp. 517–518); "RSVP Characteristics of Paper–Pencil Assessments" (pp. 525–526); "RSVP Characteristics of Performance Assessments" (pp. 530–531) **Chapter 15:** "Using Portfolios" (pp. 553–556); "Guidelines for Choosing and Using Standardized Tests" (pp. 559–562)	**Assignments and Activities: Understanding Research** exercise "Usefulness of School Readiness Tests" in topic "Assessment"
• Reliability	**Chapter 14:** "Reliability" (pp. 508–510); "RSVP Characteristics of Informal Assessments" (pp. 517–518); "RSVP Characteristics of Paper–Pencil Assessments" (pp. 525–526); "RSVP Characteristics of Performance Assessments" (pp. 530–531) **Chapter 15:** "Using Portfolios" (pp. 553–556)	
• Norm-referenced	**Chapter 14:** "Criterion-Referenced Versus Norm-Referenced Assessments" (p. 500) **Chapter 15:** "Norm-Referenced Scores" (pp. 543–547); "Using Criterion-Referenced Versus Norm-Referenced Scores in the Classroom" (pp. 547–548); "Interpreting Standardized Test Scores" (pp. 562–564)	
• Criterion-referenced	**Chapter 14:** "Criterion-Referenced Versus Norm-Referenced Assessments" (p. 500) **Chapter 15:** "Criterion-Referenced Scores" (pp. 542–543); "Using Criterion-Referenced Versus Norm-Referenced Scores in the Classroom" (pp. 547–548); "Interpreting Standardized Test Scores" (pp. 562–564)	
• Mean, median, mode	**Chapter 15:** "Standard Scores" (pp. 544–547)	
• Sampling strategy	**Chapter 14:** "Content Validity" (pp. 511–514)	
• Scoring assessments:	**Chapter 14:** "Enhancing Learning Through Ongoing Assessments and Regular Feedback" (pp. 504–508); "Reliability" (pp. 508–510); "Scoring Students' Responses to a Paper–Pencil Assessment" (pp. 524–525); "Scoring Students' Responses in a Performance Assessment" (pp. 528–530)	

(continued)

TABLE C.1 • (Continued)

TOPICS IN THE PRAXIS PRINCIPLES OF LEARNING AND TEACHING (PLT) TESTS	LOCATION OF TOPICS IN ORMROD'S *EDUCATIONAL PSYCHOLOGY* (9TH ED.)	LOCATION OF TOPICS AND PRACTICE OPPORTUNITIES IN MyEdLab
II. Instruction and Assessment		
C. Assessment Strategies		
• Analytical scoring	**Chapter 14:** "Scoring Students' Responses in a Performance Assessment" (pp. 528–530)	
• Holistic scoring	**Chapter 14:** "Scoring Students' Responses in a Performance Assessment" (pp. 528–530)	
• Rubrics	**Chapter 14:** "Enhancing Learning Through Ongoing Assessments and Regular Feedback" (pp. 504–508); "Scoring Students' Responses to a Paper–Pencil Assessment" (pp. 524–525); "Scoring Students' Responses in a Performance Assessment" (pp. 528–530)	
• Reporting assessment results	**Chapter 15:** "Summarizing the Results of a Single Assessment" (pp. 542–548); "Communicating Assessment Results to Students and Parents" (pp. 574–575) **Appendix B:** "Estimating Error in Assessment Results" (pp. B-1–B-2)	
• Percentile rank	**Chapter 15:** "Percentile Scores" (p. 544)	
• Stanines	**Chapter 15:** "Standard Scores" (pp. 544–547)	
• Mastery levels	**Chapter 15:** "Criterion-Referenced Scores" (pp. 542–543)	
• Raw score	**Chapter 15:** "Raw Scores" (p. 542)	
• Scaled score	**Chapter 15:** "Interpreting Standardized Test Scores" (see footnote, p. 562)	
• Grade equivalent score	**Chapter 15:** "Grade-Equivalent and Age-Equivalent Scores" (pp. 543–544)	
• Standard deviation	**Chapter 15:** "Standard Scores" (pp. 544–547)	
• Standard error of measurement	**Appendix B:** "Estimating Error in Assessment Results" (pp. B-1–B-2)	
• Use of assessments	**Chapter 14:** "The Many Forms and Purposes of Assessment" (pp. 498–503)	
• Formative evaluation	**Chapter 1: Case Study: "The 'No D' Policy"** (p. 3) **Chapter 14:** "Enhancing Learning Through Ongoing Assessments and Regular Feedback" (pp. 504–508)	**Building Teaching Skills and Dispositions** exercise "Assessing Students' Written Work" in topic "Assessment"
• Summative evaluation	**Chapter 14:** "Assessing Students' Learning and Performance Both Informally and Formally" (pp. 516–535) **Chapter 15:** "Determining Final Class Grades" (pp. 548–553); "Achievement Tests" (p. 557); "High-Stakes Testing and Teacher Accountability" (pp. 564–568)	
• Diagnostic evaluation	**Chapter 8: Practice for Your Licensure Exam: "The Birth of a Nation"** (p. 287) **Chapter 14:** "Diagnosing Learning and Performance Problems" (p. 501); "Enhancing Learning Through Ongoing Assessments and Regular Feedback" (pp. 504–508)	
• Understanding measurement theory and assessment-related issues	**Chapter 14:** "Important Qualities of Good Assessments" (pp. 508–516); "Additional Considerations in Formal Assessment" (pp. 531–535) **Chapter 15:** "Considering—Or Not Considering—Other Factors in Grading" (pp. 551–553); "High-Stakes Testing and Teacher Accountability" (pp. 564–568); "Cultural Bias in Test Content" (pp. 569–570)	**Assignments and Activities: Understanding Research** exercise "Cheating in High School Students" in topic "Assessment"
• Interpreting and communicating results of assessments	**Chapter 15:** "Confidentiality and Communication About Assessment Results" (pp. 573–575)	

TABLE C.1 • (Continued)

TOPICS IN THE PRAXIS PRINCIPLES OF LEARNING AND TEACHING (PLT) TESTS	LOCATION OF TOPICS IN ORMROD'S *EDUCATIONAL PSYCHOLOGY* (9TH ED.)	LOCATION OF TOPICS AND PRACTICE OPPORTUNITIES IN MyEdLab
III. Communication Techniques		
▶ Basic, effective verbal and nonverbal communication techniques	**Chapter 1: Case Study: "The 'No D' Policy"** (p. 3) **Chapter 11:** "Enhancing Students' Sense of Autonomy" (pp. 371–373); "Effects of Teacher Attributions and Expectations on Students' Motivation" (pp. 393–396); **Practice for Your Licensure Exam: "When 'Perfect' Isn't Good Enough"** (p. 410) **Chapter 12:** "Creating a Class Website to Share Goals and Facilitate Communication Throughout the School Year" (pp. 423–424) **Chapter 13:** "Establishing and Maintaining Productive Teacher–Student Relationships" (pp. 460–462); "Creating an Effective Psychological Climate" (pp. 462–464); "Setting Limits" (pp. 464–467); "Working with Parents" (pp. 476–480); "Discussing Problems Privately with Students" (pp. 482–483) **Chapter 14: Case Study: "The Math Test"** (p. 497) **Chapter 15:** "Communicating Assessment Results to Students and Parents" (pp. 574–575)	**Simulation** exercise "Developing Positive Teacher Student-Relationships with All Students" in topic "Classroom Management"
▶ Effect of cultural and gender differences on communications in the classroom	**Chapter 4:** "Examples of Cultural and Ethnic Diversity" (pp. 101–106); "Research Findings Regarding Gender Differences" (pp. 112–115; see especially subsections "Interpersonal Behaviors and Relationships" p. 114 and "Classroom Behaviors" pp. 114–115)	
▶ Types of questions that can stimulate discussion in different ways for particular purposes:	**Chapter 12:** "Asking Questions and Giving Feedback" (pp. 426–427)	
• Probing for learner understanding	**Chapter 6:** "Elaboration" (pp. 186–187); "Promoting Conceptual Change" (pp. 198–199)	
• Helping students articulate their ideas and thinking processes	**Chapter 6:** "Wait Time" (pp. 203–204); "Promoting Conceptual Change" (pp. 198–199)	
• Promoting risk-taking and problem-solving	**Chapter 7:** "Problem Solving" (pp. 230–236); "Fostering Creativity" (pp. 238–239) **Chapter 13:** "Creating an Effective Psychological Climate" (pp. 462–464)	
• Facilitating factual recall	**Chapter 6:** "Factors Affecting Retrieval" (pp. 200–204)	**Assignments and Activities: Understanding Research** exercise "Knowledge Construction in History" in topic "Knowledge Construction"
• Encouraging convergent and divergent thinking	**Chapter 7:** "Creativity" (pp. 236–239)	
• Stimulating curiosity	**Chapter 2:** "Piaget's Basic Assumptions" (pp. 29–30); **Practice for Your Licensure Exam: "A Floating Stone"** (p. 55) **Chapter 11:** "Promoting Interest in Classroom Subject Matter" (p. 368) **Chapter 12:** "Conducting Discovery and Inquiry Activities" (pp. 438–440); "Using Technology-Based Simulations and Games" (pp. 439–441)	
• Helping students to question	**Chapter 7:** "Regularly Monitoring Learning" (pp. 218–219); "Critical Thinking" (pp. 239–243)	

(continued)

TABLE C.1 • (Continued)		
TOPICS IN THE PRAXIS PRINCIPLES OF LEARNING AND TEACHING (PLT) TESTS	**LOCATION OF TOPICS IN ORMROD'S** *EDUCATIONAL PSYCHOLOGY* (9TH ED.)	**LOCATION OF TOPICS AND PRACTICE OPPORTUNITIES IN** MyEdLab
III. Communication Techniques		
• Promoting a caring community	**Chapter 8:** "Creating a Community of Learners" (pp. 255–256) **Chapter 11:** "The Need for Relatedness" (pp. 373–374) **Chapter 13:** "Creating an Effective Psychological Climate" (pp. 462–464); "Working with Other Faculty Members" (p. 475)	
IV. Profession and Community		
A. The Reflective Practitioner		
▶ Types of resources available for professional development and learning:		
• Professional literature	**Chapter 1:** "Developing as a Teacher" (pp. 14–16)	**Supplementary Reading** "Content Extension 1.1" in Book-Specific Resources for Chapter 1
• Colleagues	**Chapter 13:** "Working with Other Faculty Members" (p. 475)	
• Professional associations	**Chapter 1:** "Developing as a Teacher" (pp. 14–16)	
• Professional development activities	**Chapter 1:** "Developing as a Teacher" (pp. 14–16)	
▶ Ability to read, understand, and apply articles and books about current research, views, ideas, and debates regarding best teaching practices	**Chapter 1: Case Study: "The 'No D' Policy"** (p. 3); "Teaching as Evidence-Based Practice" (pp. 4–6); "Understanding and Interpreting Research Findings" (pp. 6–12); "From Research to Practice: The Importance of Principles and Theories" (pp. 11–12); **Practice for Your Licensure Exam: "New Software"** (p. 18) **Appendix A:** "Describing Associations with Correlation Coefficients" (pp. A-1–A-2)	All **Assignments and Activities:** **Understanding Research** exercises in various topic areas **MyEdLab Application Exercise** 1.1 in topic "Understanding and Interpreting Research Findings" in Chapter 1.
▶ Why personal reflection on teaching practices is critical, and approaches that can be used to reflect and evaluate:	**Chapter 1: Case Study: "The 'No D' Policy"** (p. 3); "Conducting Action Research" (pp. 13–14); "Developing as a Teacher" (pp. 14–16) **Chapter 3: Case Study: "Hidden Treasure"** (p. 57) **Chapter 4:** "Creating a Culturally Inclusive Classroom Environment" (pp. 106–112) **Chapter 11:** "Effects of Teacher Attributions and Expectations on Students' Motivation" (pp. 393–396)	
• Code of ethics		
• Advocacy for learners	**Chapter 4:** "Supporting Students at Risk" (pp. 124–126)	
B. The Larger Community		
▶ The role of the school as a resource to the larger community:	**Chapter 13:** "Working with the Community at Large" (p. 476); "Getting Parents Involved in School Activities" (pp. 478–479)	
• Teacher as a resource	**Chapter 13:** "Communicating with Parents" (pp. 476–478)	

TABLE C.1 • (Continued)

TOPICS IN THE PRAXIS PRINCIPLES OF LEARNING AND TEACHING (PLT) TESTS	LOCATION OF TOPICS IN ORMROD'S *EDUCATIONAL PSYCHOLOGY* (9TH ED.)	LOCATION OF TOPICS AND PRACTICE OPPORTUNITIES IN MyEdLab
IV. Profession and Community		
B. The Larger Community		
▶ Factors in the students' environment outside of school (family circumstances, community environments, health and economic conditions) that may influence students' life and learning	**Chapter 2:** "The Multiple Layers of Environmental Influence: Bioecological Systems and the Importance of Culture" (pp. 23–25) **Chapter 3:** "Family Dynamics" (pp. 58–60) **Chapter 4: Case Study: "Why Jack Wasn't in School"** (p. 97); "Navigating Different Cultures at Home and at School" (pp. 100–101); "Family Relationships and Expectations" (p. 105); "Socioeconomic Differences" (pp. 118–123); "Students at Risk" (pp. 123–126) **Chapter 5:** "Nature and Nurture in the Development of Intelligence" (pp. 136–137) **Chapter 8:** "Basic Assumptions of Contextual Theories" (pp. 250–253); "Cultures as Contexts" (pp. 256–260)	**Supplementary Reading** "Content Extension 8.1" in Book-Specific Resources for Chapter 8
▶ Basic strategies for developing and utilizing active partnerships among teachers, parents/guardians, and leaders in the community to support the educational process:	**Chapter 5:** "General Recommendations for Working with Students Who Have Special Needs" (pp. 166–167) **Chapter 13:** "Expanding the Sense of Community Beyond the Classroom" (pp. 475–480); "Addressing Aggression and Violence at School" (pp. 489–493)	
• Shared ownership		
• Shared decision making	**Chapter 5:** "Public Law 94-142: Individuals with Disabilities Education Act (IDEA)" (pp. 142–143)	
• Respectful/reciprocal communication	**Chapter 13:** "Working with Parents" (pp. 476–480)	
▶ Major laws related to students' rights and teacher responsibilities:		
• Equal education		
• Appropriate education for students with special needs	**Chapter 5:** "Public Law 94-142: Individuals with Disabilities Education Act (IDEA)" (pp. 142–143)	**Supplementary Reading** "Content Extension 5.1" in Book-Specific Resources for Chapter 5
• Confidentiality and privacy	**Chapter 15: Case Study: "B in History"** (p. 541); "Confidentiality and Communication About Assessment Results" (pp. 573–575)	
• Appropriate treatment of students		
• Reporting in situations related to possible child abuse	**Chapter 3:** "Child Maltreatment" (p. 60)	

Glossary

accommodation. Process of responding to or thinking about a new object or event by either modifying an existing scheme or forming a new one.

acculturation. Gradual process of adopting the values and customs of a new culture.

action research. Research conducted by teachers and other school personnel to address issues and problems in their own schools or classrooms.

activation. Degree to which something in memory is being actively attended to and mentally processed.

actual developmental level. Upper limit of tasks that a learner can successfully perform independently.

adaptive behavior. Behavior related to daily living skills or appropriate conduct in social situations; used as a criterion for identifying students with intellectual disabilities.

adaptive testing. Computer-based assessment in which students' performance on early items determines which items are presented subsequently.

advance organizer. Introduction to a lesson that provides an overall organizational scheme for the lesson.

affect. Feelings, emotions, and moods that a learner brings to bear on a task.

African American English. Dialect of some African American communities that includes some pronunciations, idioms, and grammatical constructions different from those of Standard English.

age-equivalent score. Test score that matches a particular student's performance with the average performance of students of a certain age.

aggression. Action intentionally taken to hurt another either physically or psychologically.

algorithm. Prescribed sequence of steps that guarantees a correct problem solution.

analytic scoring. Scoring a student's performance on an assessment by evaluating various aspects of it separately.

antecedent response. Response that influences the probability that a certain *other* response will follow.

antecedent stimulus. Stimulus that influences the probability that a particular response will follow.

anxiety. Feeling of uneasiness and apprehension concerning a situation with an uncertain outcome.

applied behavior analysis (ABA). Systematic application of behaviorist principles in educational and therapeutic settings.

apprenticeship. Mentorship in which a novice works with an expert for a lengthy time period to learn how to accomplish increasingly complex tasks within a particular domain.

appropriation. Process of internalizing but also adapting the cognitive tools of one's culture for one's own use.

Asperger syndrome. Mild form of an autism spectrum disorder in which students have normal intelligence and language skills but show significant deficits in social cognition and social skills.

assessment. Process of observing a sample of a student's behavior and drawing inferences about the student's knowledge and abilities.

assessment bias. Factor in an assessment instrument or procedure that consistently and differentially influences students' performance for reasons unrelated to the characteristic being measured; reduces the validity of assessment results.

assimilation. Process of responding to or thinking about an object or event in a way that is consistent with an existing scheme.

assistive technology. Any electronic or nonelectronic device that can enhance certain abilities or performance areas for students with disabilities.

astrocyte. Star-shaped brain cell hypothesized to be involved in learning and memory; has chemically mediated connections with many other astrocytes and with neurons.

attachment. Strong, affectionate bond formed between a child and a caregiver.

attention. Focusing of mental processing on particular stimuli.

attention-deficit hyperactivity disorder (ADHD). Disorder marked by inattention, hyperactivity, impulsive behavior, or some combination of these characteristics.

attribution. Self-constructed causal explanation for a personally experienced or observed event, such as one's own or another person's success or failure.

authentic activity. Classroom activity similar to an activity that students are apt to encounter in the outside world.

authentic assessment. Assessment of students' knowledge and skills in a context similar to one that might be found in the outside world.

authoritarian parenting. Parenting style characterized by rigid rules and expectations for behavior that children are asked to obey without question.

authoritative parenting. Parenting style characterized by emotional warmth, high standards for behavior, explanation and consistent enforcement of rules, and inclusion of children in decision making.

autism spectrum disorders. Disorders marked by impaired social cognition, social skills, and social interaction, presumably due to a brain abnormality; extreme forms often associated with significant cognitive and linguistic delays and highly unusual behaviors.

automaticity. Ability to respond quickly and efficiently while mentally processing or physically performing a task.

backward design. Approach to instructional planning in which a teacher first determines the desired end result (i.e., what knowledge and skills students should acquire), then identifies appropriate assessments, and finally determines appropriate instructional strategies.

base group. Cooperative learning group in which students work together for an entire semester or school year to provide mutual support for one another's learning.

baseline. Frequency of a response before it is intentionally and systematically reinforced.

basic interpersonal communication skills (BICS). Proficiency in English sufficient for day-to-day conversation with English speakers but *not* sufficient for academic success in an English-only curriculum.

behavioral momentum. Increased tendency for a learner to make a particular response immediately after making similar responses.

behaviorism. Theoretical perspective in which learning and behavior are described and explained in terms of stimulus–response relationships.

belonging. Feeling that one is an important and valued member of a group.

belongingness. General sense that one is an important and valued member of the classroom or school.

bilingual education. Second-language instruction in which students are instructed in academic subject areas in their native language while simultaneously being taught to speak and write in the second language.

bioecological systems theory. Theory proposing that a child's everyday environments and the child's broader social and cultural contexts interact in their influences on the child's development.

Bloom's taxonomy. Taxonomy of six cognitive processes, varying in complexity, that lessons might be designed to foster.

boredom. Unpleasant affective state that results from lack of stimulation and arousal.

bully. Person who frequently threatens, harasses, or causes injury to particular peers.

central executive. Component of human memory that oversees the flow of information throughout the memory system.

challenge. Situation in which a learner believes that success is possible with sufficient effort.

checklist. List of characteristics that good performance on an assessment task should have.

child maltreatment. Consistent neglect or abuse of a child that jeopardizes the child's physical and psychological well-being.

classical conditioning. Form of learning in which a new, involuntary response is acquired as a result of two stimuli being presented close together in time.

class inclusion Recognition that an object simultaneously belongs to a particular category and to one of its subcategories.

classroom climate. Overall psychological atmosphere of the classroom.

classroom management. Establishment and maintenance of a classroom environment that's conducive to learning and achievement.

clinical method. Procedure in which an adult presents a task or problem and asks a child a series of questions about it, tailoring later questions to the child's previous responses.

clique. Moderately stable friendship group of perhaps 3 to 10 members.

co-regulated learning. Process through which an adult and child share responsibility for directing various aspects of the child's learning; alternatively, collaborative process in which one or more learners jointly support and monitor one another's learning progress.

cognitive academic language proficiency (CALP). Mastery of English vocabulary and syntax sufficient for English language learners to achieve academic success in an English-only curriculum.

cognitive apprenticeship. Mentorship in which an expert and novice work together on challenging tasks, with the expert providing guidance regarding how to *think* about the tasks.

cognitive behavioral therapy. Planned, systematic combination of behaviorist techniques and cognition-based strategies (e.g.,

modeling, self-regulation techniques) as a means of bringing about desired behaviors.

cognitive development. Development of increasingly sophisticated thinking, reasoning, and language with age.

cognitive dissonance. Feeling of mental discomfort caused by new information that conflicts with current knowledge or beliefs.

cognitive load. Cognitive burden that a particular learning activity places on working memory at any one time; includes both the amount of information learners must simultaneously think about and the specific cognitive processes learners must engage in to understand what they're studying.

cognitive modeling. Demonstrating how to think about as well as how to do a task.

cognitive neuroscience. Study of how various brain structures and functions are related to human learning and behavior; also known as *neuropsychology*.

cognitive process. Particular way of thinking about and mentally responding to a certain event or piece of information.

cognitive psychology. General theoretical perspective that focuses on the mental processes underlying learning and behavior; encompasses information processing theory, individual constructivism, and related perspectives.

cognitive style. Characteristic way in which a learner tends to think about a task and process new information; typically comes into play automatically rather than by choice.

cognitive tool. Concept, symbol, strategy, procedure, or other culturally constructed mechanism that helps people think about and respond to situations more effectively.

collective self-efficacy. People's beliefs about their ability to be successful when they work together on a task.

Common Core State Standards. Set of standards that most U.S. states have adopted to guide instruction and assessment in English-language arts and mathematics (see corestandards.org).

community of learners. Class in which teachers and students actively and collaboratively work to create a body of knowledge and help one another learn.

community of practice. Group of people who share common interests and goals and regularly interact and coordinate their efforts in pursuit of those interests and goals.

complex cognitive process. Cognitive process that involves going well beyond the information specifically learned; for example, it might involve analyzing, applying, or evaluating the information.

comprehension monitoring. Process of checking oneself to verify understanding and memory of newly acquired information.

computer-based instruction (CBI). Academic instruction provided by means of specially designed computer software and/or Internet websites.

concept. Mental grouping of objects or events that have something in common.

concept map. Diagram of concepts and their interrelationships; used to enhance learning and memory of a topic.

conceptual change. Significant revision of one's existing beliefs about a topic, enabling new, discrepant information to be better understood and explained.

conceptual understanding. Meaningfully learned and well-integrated knowledge about a topic, including many logical connections among specific concepts and ideas.

concrete operations stage. Piaget's third stage of cognitive development, in which adultlike logic appears but is largely limited to concrete objects and events.

conditional knowledge. Knowledge concerning appropriate ways to respond (physically or mentally) under various circumstances.

conditioned response (CR). Response that begins to be elicited by a particular (conditioned) stimulus through classical conditioning.

conditioned stimulus (CS). Stimulus that, through classical conditioning, begins to elicit a particular response as a result of being experienced in conjunction with another (unconditioned) stimulus.

conditioning. Term commonly used by behaviorists for *learning;* typically involves specific environmental events leading to the acquisition of specific responses.

confidence interval. Range around an assessment score reflecting the amount of error that might have influenced the student's performance on this particular occasion (reflecting imperfect reliability of the assessment instrument).

confirmation bias. Tendency to seek information that confirms rather than discredits current beliefs.

conservation. Recognition that if nothing is added or taken away, the amount stays the same, regardless of alterations in shape or arrangement.

consolidation. Neurological process in which newly acquired knowledge is firmed up in the brain; often takes several hours, sometimes even longer.

construct validity. Extent to which an assessment accurately measures an unobservable educational or psychological characteristic.

constructed-response task. Recall assessment task that requires a lengthy response; often also requires elaboration, analysis, synthesis, and/or application of learned information.

construction. Mental process in which a learner takes many separate pieces of information and uses them to build an overall understanding or interpretation.

constructivism. Theoretical perspective proposing that learners actively construct (rather than passively absorb) knowledge and beliefs from their experiences.

content-area standards. General statements regarding the knowledge and skills that students should gain and the characteristics that their accomplishments should reflect in a particular academic discipline.

content validity. Extent to which an assessment includes a representative sample of tasks within the content domain being assessed.

contextual theory. Theoretical perspective that focuses on how people's general physical, social, and/or cultural surroundings support their learning, development, and behavior.

contiguity. Occurrence of two or more events (e.g., two stimuli, or a stimulus and a response) at approximately the same time.

contingency. Situation in which one event happens only after another event has already occurred; one event is *contingent* on the other's occurrence.

contingency contract. Formal agreement between a teacher and a student that identifies behaviors the student will exhibit and the reinforcers that will follow.

continuous reinforcement. Reinforcement of a response every time it occurs.

control group. Group of people in a research study who are given either no intervention or a *placebo* treatment that is unlikely to have an effect on the dependent variable.

controversial student. Student whom some peers strongly like and other peers strongly dislike.

conventional morality. Uncritical acceptance of society's conventions regarding right and wrong behaviors.

conventional transgression. Action that violates a culture's general expectations regarding socially appropriate behavior.

convergent thinking. Process of pulling together several pieces of information to draw a conclusion or solve a problem.

cooperative learning. Approach to instruction in which students work with a small group of peers to achieve a common goal and help one another learn.

coping model. Model who initially struggles with a task but successfully overcomes obstacles.

correlation. Extent to which two variables are associated, such that when one variable increases, the other either increases or decreases somewhat predictably.

correlation coefficient. Statistic that indicates the strength and direction of an association between two variables.

correlational study. Research study that explores possible associations among two or more variables.

cortex. Upper part of the brain; primary site of complex, conscious thinking processes.

covert strategy. Learning strategy that is strictly mental (rather than behavioral) in nature and thus cannot be directly observed by others.

creativity. New and original behavior that yields a productive and culturally appropriate result.

criterion-referenced assessment. Assessment instrument designed to determine what students know and can do relative to predetermined standards or criteria.

criterion-referenced score. Assessment score that specifically indicates what a student knows or can do.

critical thinking. Process of evaluating the accuracy, credibility, and worth of information and lines of reasoning.

crowd. Large, loose-knit social group that shares certain common interests and behaviors.

crystallized intelligence. Knowledge and skills accumulated from prior experience, schooling, and culture.

cueing. Use of a verbal or nonverbal signal to indicate that a certain behavior is desired or that a certain behavior should stop.

cultural bias. Extent to which assessment tasks either offend or unfairly penalize some students because of their ethnicity, gender, or socioeconomic status.

cultural mismatch. Situation in which a student's home culture and the school culture hold conflicting expectations for behavior.

culturally responsive teaching. Use of instructional strategies that build on students' existing knowledge and skills and that accommodate their accustomed ways of behaving and learning.

culture. Behaviors and belief systems that members of a long-standing social group share and pass along to successive generations.

culture of transfer. Learning environment in which applying school subject matter to new situations, cross-disciplinary contexts, and real-world problems is both the expectation and the norm.

culture shock. Sense of confusion when a student encounters a new environment with behavioral expectations very different from those previously learned.

curriculum-based measurement (CBM). Use of frequent assessments to track students' progress in acquiring basic skills;

assessments are typically quite short (e.g., one to four minutes) and each focus on a specific skill.

cyberbullying. Engaging in psychological aggression via wireless technologies or the Internet.

debilitating anxiety. Anxiety of sufficient intensity that it interferes with performance.

decay. Gradual weakening of information stored in long-term memory, especially if the information is used infrequently or not at all.

declarative knowledge. Knowledge concerning the nature of how things are, were, or will be.

delay of gratification. Ability to forego small, immediate reinforcers in order to obtain larger ones later on.

descriptive study. Research study that enables researchers to draw conclusions about the current state of affairs regarding an issue but not about correlation or cause-and-effect relationships.

developmental milestone. Appearance of a new, more advanced behavior that indicates significant progress in a child's development.

dialect. Form of a language that has certain unique pronunciations, idioms, and grammatical structures and is characteristic of a particular region or ethnic group.

differentiated instruction. Practice of individualizing instructional methods—and possibly also individualizing specific content and instructional goals—to align with each student's existing knowledge, skills, and needs.

direct instruction. Approach to instruction that uses a variety of techniques (e.g., explanations, questions, guided and independent practice) in a fairly structured manner to promote learning of fundamental knowledge and skills.

discovery learning. Approach to instruction in which students construct their own knowledge about a topic through firsthand interaction with an aspect of their environment.

discrimination. Phenomenon in which a student learns that a response is reinforced in the presence of one stimulus but not in the presence of another, similar stimulus.

disequilibrium. State of being unable to address new events with existing schemes; typically accompanied by some mental discomfort.

disposition. General inclination to approach and think about learning and problem-solving tasks in a particular way; typically has a motivational component in addition to cognitive components.

distance learning. Technology-based instruction in which students are at a location physically separate from that of their instructor.

distributed cognition and intelligence. Enhancement of thinking through the use of physical objects and technology, concepts and symbols of one's culture, and/or social collaboration and support.

distributed knowledge. Distribution of expertise across various members of a social group, such that group members must rely on one another to maximize their personal and collective success.

divergent thinking. Process of mentally moving in a variety of directions from a single idea.

doing-just-enough goal. Desire to get reasonable school grades through the easiest possible routes—routes that may or may not involve actually learning classroom material.

dynamic assessment. Systematic examination of how easily and in what ways a student can acquire new knowledge or skills, usually within the context of instruction or scaffolding.

dyslexia. Inability to master basic reading skills in a developmentally typical time frame despite normal reading instruction; often has biological roots.

e-learning. Instruction and learning that occur largely or entirely within the context of digital technologies.

educational psychology. Academic discipline that (a) systematically studies the nature of learning, child development, motivation, and related topics and (b) applies its research findings to the identification and development of effective classroom practices.

effortful control. One's general ability to inhibit immediate impulses in order to think and act productively; believed to be a distinct aspect of temperament that has a biological basis in the brain.

elaboration. Cognitive process in which learners embellish on new information based on what they already know or believe.

electronic portfolio (e-folio). Portfolio compiled and available for inspection on a CD, DVD, flash drive, Internet-based storage service, or other electronic storage mechanism.

emergent literacy. Knowledge and skills that lay a foundation for reading and writing; typically develops from early experiences with written language.

emotion regulation. Process of keeping in check or intentionally altering feelings that might lead to counterproductive behavior.

emotional and behavioral disorders. Emotional states and behavior patterns that consistently and significantly disrupt academic learning and performance.

empathy. Experience of sharing the same feelings as someone in unfortunate circumstances.

encoding. Mentally changing the format of new information in order to think about it or remember it more easily.

English language learner (ELL). School-age child who is not fully fluent in English because of limited exposure to English prior to enrollment in an English-speaking school.

epistemic belief. Belief about the nature of knowledge or knowledge acquisition.

equilibration. Movement from equilibrium to disequilibrium and back to equilibrium, a process that promotes development of more complex thought and understandings.

equilibrium. State of being able to address new events with existing schemes.

ethnic group. People who have common historical roots, values, beliefs, and behaviors and who share a sense of interdependence.

ethnic identity. Awareness of one's membership in a particular ethnic or cultural group, and willingness to adopt behaviors characteristic of the group.

ETS score. Standard score with a mean of 500 and a standard deviation of 100.

evidence-based practice. Instructional method or other classroom strategy that research has consistently shown to bring about significant gains in students' development and/or academic achievement.

executive functions. General mental processes that human beings use to control what they pay attention to, think about, and learn; are presumed to occur within working memory.

expectancy. Belief about the likelihood of success in an activity, given present ability levels and external circumstances that may either help or hinder performance.

experimental study (experiment). Research study that involves both (a) the manipulation of one variable to determine its possible effect on another variable and (b) control of additional variables that might potentially have an impact on the outcome; allows conclusions about cause-and-effect relationships.

explicit knowledge. Knowledge that a person is consciously aware of and can verbally describe.

expository instruction. Approach to instruction in which information is presented in essentially the same form in which students are expected to learn it.

externalizing behavior. Symptom of an emotional or behavioral disorder that has a direct effect on other people (e.g., aggression, lack of self-control).

extinction. Gradual disappearance of an acquired response. In classical conditioning, it results from repeated presentation of a conditioned stimulus in the absence of the unconditioned stimulus; in instrumental conditioning, it results from repeated lack of reinforcement.

extrinsic motivation. Motivation resulting from factors external to the individual and unrelated to the task being performed.

extrinsic reinforcer. Reinforcer that comes from the outside environment, rather than from within the learner.

facilitating anxiety. Level of anxiety (usually relatively low) that enhances performance.

Family Educational Rights and Privacy Act (FERPA). U.S. legislation passed in 1974 that gives students and parents access to school records and limits other people's access to those records.

fixed mindset. Belief that one simply does not have the ability to learn in some areas.

flow. Intense form of intrinsic motivation, involving complete absorption in and concentration on a challenging activity.

fluid intelligence. Ability to acquire knowledge quickly and adapt effectively to new situations.

formal assessment. Preplanned, systematic attempt to ascertain what students know and can do.

formal discipline. View of transfer reflecting the idea that the study of rigorous subject matter enhances one's ability to learn other, unrelated things.

formal operational egocentrism. Inability of adolescents in Piaget's formal operations stage to separate their own abstract logic from the perspectives of others and from practical considerations.

formal operations stage. Piaget's fourth and final stage of cognitive development, in which logical reasoning processes can be applied to abstract ideas as well as to concrete objects.

formative assessment. Assessment conducted before or during instruction to facilitate instructional planning and enhance students' learning.

functional analysis. Examination of inappropriate behavior and its antecedents and consequences to determine one or more purposes (functions) that the behavior might serve for the learner.

g. Theoretical general factor in intelligence that influences one's ability to learn and perform in a wide variety of contexts.

gang. Cohesive social group characterized by initiation rites, distinctive colors and symbols, territorial orientation, and feuds with rival groups.

gender schema. Self-constructed, organized body of beliefs about characteristics and behaviors of males or females.

general transfer. Instance of transfer in which the original learning task and the transfer task are different in content.

generalization. Phenomenon in which a person learns a response to a particular stimulus and then makes the same response to a similar stimulus. In classical conditioning, it involves making a conditioned response to a stimulus similar to a conditioned stimulus; in instrumental conditioning, it involves making a voluntary response to a stimulus that is similar to one previously associated with a response–reinforcement contingency.

giftedness. Unusually high ability or aptitude in one or more areas, to such a degree that students require special educational services to help them meet their full potential.

glial cell. Cell in the brain that supports neurons or general brain functioning.

goodness of fit. Situation in which classroom conditions and expectations are compatible with students' temperaments and personality characteristics.

grade-equivalent score. Test score that matches a particular student's performance with the average performance of students at a certain grade level.

group contingency. Situation in which everyone in a group must make a particular response before reinforcement occurs.

group differences. Consistently observed differences (on average) among diverse groups of students (e.g., students of different genders or ethnic backgrounds).

growth mindset. Belief that one has the ability to learn, even about complex topics, if one practices much and works hard.

guided participation. Process in which a child gains new skills by working on a complex, meaningful task in close collaboration with an adult or more experienced peer.

guilt. Feeling of discomfort about having caused someone else pain or distress.

halo effect. Phenomenon in which people are more likely to perceive positive behaviors in someone they like or admire.

hearing loss. Malfunction of the ears or associated nerves that interferes with perception of sounds within the frequency range of normal human speech.

heuristic. General strategy that facilitates problem solving but doesn't always yield a viable solution.

high-stakes testing. Practice of using students' performance on a single assessment to make major decisions about students, school personnel, or overall school quality.

higher-level question. Question that requires students to use previously learned information in a new way—that is, to engage in one or more complex cognitive processes.

holistic scoring. Summarizing a student's performance on an assessment with a single score.

horns effect. Phenomenon in which people are more likely to perceive negative behaviors in someone for whom they have little affection or respect.

hostile attributional bias. Tendency to interpret others' behaviors as reflecting hostile or aggressive intentions.

hot cognition. Learning or cognitive processing that is emotionally charged.

hypermedia. Collection of computer-based and electronically linked multimedia materials (e.g., text, pictures, sound, animations) that students can examine in a sequence of their own choosing.

I-message. Statement that communicates the adverse effects of a student's misbehavior, including one's own reactions to it, in a calm, relatively nonaccusatory manner; its intent is to convey information, not to lay blame.

identity. Self-constructed definition of who one is and what things are important to accomplish in life.

ill-defined problem. Problem in which the desired goal is unclear, some information needed to solve the problem is missing, and/or several possible solutions to the problem may exist.

illusion of knowing. Thinking one knows something that one actually does *not* know.

imaginary audience. Belief that one is the center of attention in any social situation.

immersion. Second-language instruction in which students hear and speak that language almost exclusively in the classroom.

implicit knowledge. Knowledge that a person cannot consciously recall or explain but that nevertheless affects the person's thinking or behavior.

in-school suspension. Consequence for misbehavior in which a student is placed in a quiet, boring room within the school building, typically to do schoolwork under close adult supervision.

incentive. Hoped-for, but not guaranteed, future consequence of behavior.

inclusion. Practice of educating all students, including those with severe and multiple disabilities, in neighborhood schools and general education classrooms.

incompatible behaviors. Two or more behaviors that cannot be performed simultaneously.

individual constructivism. Theoretical perspective that focuses on how learners each construct their own idiosyncratic meanings from their experiences.

individual differences. Diversity in abilities and characteristics (intelligence, personality, etc.) among students at a particular age and within a particular gender or cultural group.

individualized education program (IEP). Written description of an appropriate instructional program for a student with special needs.

Individuals with Disabilities Education Act (IDEA). U.S. federal legislation granting educational rights from birth until age 21 for people with cognitive, emotional, or physical disabilities.

induction. Explanation of why a certain behavior is unacceptable, often with a focus on the pain or distress that someone has caused another.

informal assessment. Assessment that results from a teacher's spontaneous, day-to-day observations of how a student performs in class.

information literacy. Knowledge and skills that help a learner find, use, evaluate, organize, and present information about a particular topic.

information processing theory. Theoretical perspective that focuses on the specific ways in which learners mentally think about, or process, new information and events.

inner speech. Process of talking to and guiding oneself mentally rather than aloud.

inquiry learning. Approach to instruction in which students apply complex reasoning skills in their examination and interpretation of new phenomena and data sources.

instructional goal. Desired long-term outcome of instruction.

instructional objective. Desired outcome of a lesson or unit.

instrumental conditioning. Learning process in which a response either increases or decreases as a result of being followed by either reinforcement or punishment, respectively.

intellectual disability. Disability characterized by significantly below-average general intelligence and deficits in adaptive behavior, both of which first appear in infancy or childhood; also known as *mental retardation*.

intelligence. Ability to apply prior knowledge and experiences flexibly to accomplish challenging new tasks.

intelligence test. General measure of current level of cognitive functioning; often used to predict academic achievement in the short run.

intelligent tutoring system. Computer software program that provides individually tailored instruction and practice, supplemented with ongoing guidance and feedback, related to a particular topic and set of skills.

interest. Perception that an activity is intriguing and enticing; typically accompanied by both cognitive engagement and positive affect.

interference. Phenomenon whereby something stored in long-term memory inhibits one's ability to remember something else correctly.

intermittent reinforcement. Reinforcement of a response only occasionally, with some occurrences of the response *not* being reinforced.

internal consistency reliability. Extent to which different parts of an assessment instrument all assess the same characteristic.

internalization. Process through which a learner gradually incorporates socially based activities into his or her internal cognitive processes.

internalized motivation. Adoption of other people's priorities and values as one's own.

internalizing behavior. Symptom of an emotional or behavioral disorder that adversely affects the student with the disorder but has little or no direct effect on other people (e.g., depression, social withdrawal).

intrinsic motivation. Motivation resulting from internal personal characteristics or inherent in the task being performed.

intrinsic reinforcer. Reinforcer that is provided by the learner or inherent in the task being performed.

IQ score. Score on an intelligence test, determined by comparing a person's performance on the test with that of others in the same age-group; for most tests, it's a standard score with a mean of 100 and a standard deviation of 15.

IRE cycle. Adult–child interaction marked by adult initiation (usually involving a question), child response, and adult evaluation.

item analysis. Follow-up analysis of patterns in students' responses to various items in an assessment.

item difficulty (p). Index reflecting the proportion of students getting a particular assessment item correct.

item discrimination (D). Index reflecting the relative proportion of high-scoring versus low-scoring students getting a particular assessment item correct.

jigsaw technique. Instructional technique in which materials are divided among members of a cooperative group, with different students being responsible for learning different content and teaching it to other group members.

keyword method. Mnemonic technique in which a learner mentally connects two ideas by forming a visual image of one or more concrete objects (*keywords*) that either sound similar to or symbolically represent those ideas.

knowledge base. One's existing knowledge about specific topics and the world in general.

knowledge telling. Writing ideas in whatever order they come to mind, with little regard for communicating the ideas effectively.

knowledge transforming. Writing about ideas in a manner that intentionally helps a reader comprehend them.

learned helplessness. General, fairly pervasive belief that one is incapable of accomplishing tasks and has little or no control of the environment.

learner-directed instruction. Approach to instruction in which students have considerable control regarding the issues they address and the ways they address them.

learning. Long-term change in mental representations or associations as a result of experience.

learning disabilities. Deficiencies in one or more specific cognitive processes but not in overall cognitive functioning.

learning strategy. One or more cognitive processes used intentionally for a particular learning task.

least restrictive environment. Most typical and standard educational environment that can reasonably meet the needs of a student with a disability.

legitimate peripheral participation. Participation at the fringe of a community of practice as a way of gaining knowledge and skills related to the group's typical ways of doing things.

lesson plan. Predetermined guide for a lesson that identifies instructional goals or objectives, necessary materials, instructional strategies, and one or more appropriate assessments.

level of potential development. Upper limit of tasks that a learner can successfully perform with the assistance of a more competent individual.

logical consequence. Unpleasant consequence that follows naturally or logically from a student's misbehavior.

long-term memory. Component of memory that holds knowledge and skills for a relatively long time.

lower-level question. Question that requires students to retrieve and recite what they have learned in essentially the same form that they learned it.

maintenance rehearsal. Rapid repetition of a small amount of information to keep it fresh in working memory.

mastery-approach goal. Desire to acquire new knowledge and master new skills.

mastery-avoidance goal. Desire to avoid misunderstanding what one is learning.

mastery goal. Desire to understand and become proficient at what one is learning.

mastery learning. Approach to instruction in which students learn one topic thoroughly before moving to a subsequent one.

mastery orientation. General, fairly pervasive belief that one is capable of accomplishing challenging tasks.

maturation. Gradual, genetically driven acquisition of more advanced physical and neurological capabilities over the course of childhood and adolescence.

mean (M). Mathematical average of a set of scores.

meaningful learning. Cognitive process in which learners relate new information to things they already know.

meaningful learning set. Attitude that one can make sense of the information one is studying.

mediated learning experience. Discussion between an adult and a child in which the adult helps the child make sense of an event they are mutually experiencing.

memory. Ability to mentally save something that has been previously learned; also, the mental "location" where such information is saved.

mental set. Inclination to encode a problem in a way that excludes potential solutions.

metacognition. Knowledge and beliefs about the nature of human cognitive processes (including one's own), as well as conscious attempts to engage in behaviors and thought processes that increase learning and memory.

metalinguistic awareness. Ability to think consciously about the nature and functions of language.

mindset. Personal beliefs about one's ability to learn new information or skills.

mirror neuron. Neuron in the brain that fires either when a person is performing a particular behavior or when the person sees someone else perform the behavior.

misbehavior. Action that disrupts learning and planned classroom activities, puts students' physical safety or psychological well-being in jeopardy, or violates basic moral standards.

misconception. Belief that is inconsistent with commonly accepted and well-validated explanations of phenomena or events.

mixed-methods study. Research study that includes elements of both quantitative and qualitative research.

mnemonic. Memory aid or trick designed to help students learn and remember one or more specific pieces of information.

model. In science, physical or symbolic representation of a phenomenon that depicts its key components and important interrelationships. In social cognitive theory, real or fictional individual who demonstrates a behavior that learners might emulate; alternatively, a set of instructions for successfully executing the behavior.

modeling. Demonstrating a behavior for another person *or* observing and imitating another person's behavior.

moral dilemma. Situation in which two or more people's rights or needs may be at odds and the morally correct action is not clear-cut.

moral transgression. Action that causes harm or infringes on the needs or rights of others.

morality. One's general standards regarding right and wrong behaviors.

motivation. Inner state that energizes, directs, and sustains behavior.

multicultural education. Instruction that integrates the perspectives and experiences of numerous cultural groups throughout the curriculum.

myelination. Growth of a fatty sheath (myelin) around the axons of neurons, enabling faster transmission of electrical impulses.

NCE score (normal-curve-equivalent score). Standard score with a mean of 50 and a standard deviation of 21.06; an NCE score of 1 equals a percentile rank of 1, and an NCE score of 99 equals a percentile rank of 99.

need for arousal. Ongoing need for either physical or cognitive stimulation.

need for autonomy. Basic need to believe that one has some control regarding the course of one's life.

need for competence. Basic need to believe that one can deal effectively with one's overall environment.

need for relatedness. Basic need to feel socially connected to others and to secure others' love and respect.

negative reinforcement. Consequence that brings about the increase of a behavior through the removal (rather than the presentation) of a stimulus.

negative transfer. Phenomenon in which something learned at one time interferes with learning or performance at a later time.

neglected student. Student about whom most peers have no strong feelings, either positive or negative.

neo-Piagetian theory. Theoretical perspective that combines elements of Piaget's theory with more contemporary research and theories and suggests that development in specific content domains is often stagelike in nature.

neuron. Cell in the brain or another part of the nervous system that transmits information to other cells.

neuropsychology. Study of how various brain structures and functions are related to human learning and behavior; also known as *cognitive neuroscience*.

neurotransmitter. Chemical substance through which one neuron sends a message to another neuron.

neutral stimulus. Stimulus that does not presently elicit any particular response.

Next Generation Science Standards. Set of standards that some U.S. states have adopted to guide instruction and assessment in science (see nextgenscience.org).

No Child Left Behind Act (NCLB). U.S. legislation passed in 2001 that mandates regular assessments of basic skills to determine whether students are making adequate yearly progress relative to state-determined standards in reading, math, and science.

norm group. Group of individuals to which a student's performance on an assessment is compared; is ideally comprised of many people who, together, represent the diversity of the nation's population.

norm-referenced assessment. Assessment instrument that indicates how students perform relative to a peer group.

norm-referenced score. Assessment score that indicates how a student's performance compares with the performance of others.

normal distribution (normal curve). Theoretical pattern of educational and psychological characteristics in which most individuals score in the middle range and only a few score at either extreme.

norms. In assessment, data regarding the typical performance of various groups of students on a standardized test or other norm-referenced measure of a particular characteristic or ability.

operant conditioning. Learning process in which a response increases as a result of being followed by reinforcement; is one form of *instrumental conditioning*.

organization. Cognitive process in which learners make connections among various pieces of information they need to learn (e.g., by forming categories, identifying hierarchies, determining cause-and-effect relationships).

outcome expectation. Prediction regarding the consequence that a particular behavior is likely to yield.

overt strategy. Learning strategy that is at least partially evident in a learner's behavior (e.g., taking notes during a lecture).

paper–pencil assessment. Assessment in which students provide written responses to written items.

pedagogical content knowledge. Knowledge about effective methods of teaching a specific topic or content area.

peer contagion. Phenomenon in which certain behaviors, attitudes, and/or values spread from one child or adolescent to another, perhaps through modeling, peer reinforcement, social sanctions, or self-socialization.

peer mediation. Approach to conflict resolution in which a student (serving as a *mediator*) asks peers in conflict to express their differing viewpoints and then work together to devise a reasonable resolution.

peer tutoring. Approach to instruction in which one student provides instruction to help another student master a classroom topic.

people-first language. Language usage in which a student's disability is identified *after* the student is named.

percentile score (percentile). Test score indicating the percentage of peers in the norm group getting a raw score less than or equal to a particular student's raw score.

performance assessment. Assessment in which students demonstrate their knowledge and skills in a nonwritten fashion.

performance goal. Desire to demonstrate one's ability relative to others.

performance-approach goal. Desire to look good and receive favorable judgments from others.

performance-avoidance goal. Desire not to look bad or receive unfavorable judgments from others.

personal development. Development, with age, of distinctive behavioral patterns and increasingly complex self-understandings.

personal fable. Belief that one is completely unlike anyone else and so cannot be understood by others.

personal interest. Long-term, relatively stable interest in a particular topic or activity.

personal space. Personally or culturally preferred distance between people during social interaction.

personality. Characteristic ways in which a particular individual behaves, thinks, and feels in a wide range of circumstances.

perspective taking. Ability to look at a situation from someone else's viewpoint.

phonological awareness. Ability to hear the distinct sounds of which spoken words are comprised.

physical aggression. Action that can potentially cause bodily injury.

physical and health impairment. General physical or medical condition that interferes so significantly with school performance that special accommodations are required.

plasticity. Ability to reorganize in order to adapt to changing circumstances; term often used in describing the human brain.

popular student. Student whom many peers like and perceive to be kind and trustworthy.

portfolio. Collection of a student's work compiled systematically over a lengthy time period.

positive behavioral interventions and supports (PBIS). Variation of traditional applied behavior analysis that involves identifying the purposes of undesirable behaviors and encouraging alternative behaviors that more appropriately accomplish those purposes.

positive psychology. A perspective in psychology that focuses on happiness and positive outcomes, instead of on illness and dysfunctional thoughts and behaviors.

positive reinforcement. Consequence that brings about the increase of a behavior through the presentation (rather than the removal) of a stimulus.

positive transfer. Phenomenon in which something learned at one time facilitates learning or performance at a later time.

positive-practice overcorrection. Consequence of a poorly performed response in which a learner must repeat the response correctly and appropriately, perhaps in an exaggerated manner.

postconventional morality. Thinking in accordance with self-constructed, abstract principles regarding right and wrong behaviors.

practicality. Extent to which an assessment instrument or procedure is inexpensive and easy to use and takes only a small amount of time to administer and score.

preconventional morality. Lack of internalized standards about right and wrong behaviors; decision making based primarily on what seems best for oneself.

predictive validity. Extent to which the results of an assessment predict future performance in a particular domain; sometimes called *criterion validity.*

Premack principle. Phenomenon in which learners do less-preferred activities in order to engage in more-preferred activities.

preoperational egocentrism. Inability of children in Piaget's preoperational stage to look at a situation from another person's perspective; reflects a cognitive limitation, *not* a personality flaw.

preoperational stage. Piaget's second stage of cognitive development, in which children can think about objects and events beyond their immediate view but do not yet reason in logical, adultlike ways.

presentation punishment. Punishment involving presentation of a new stimulus, presumably one a learner finds unpleasant.

primary reinforcer. Consequence that satisfies a biologically or psychologically built-in need.

principle. Statement that identifies a fairly consistent finding regarding cause-and-effect related to a particular phenomenon.

prior knowledge activation. Process of reminding learners of what they already know relative to a new topic.

proactive aggression. Deliberate aggression against another as a means of obtaining a desired goal.

problem solving. Using existing knowledge and skills to address an unanswered question or troubling situation.

problem-based learning. Classroom activity in which students acquire new knowledge and skills while working on a complex problem similar to one that might exist in the outside world.

procedural knowledge. Knowledge concerning how to do something (e.g., a skill).

professional learning community. Schoolwide collaborative effort in which teachers and administrators share a common vision for students' learning and achievement and work together to bring about desired student outcomes.

project-based learning. Classroom activity in which students acquire new knowledge and skills while working on a complex, multifaceted project that yields a concrete end product.

prosocial behavior. Behavior directed toward promoting the well-being of people other than oneself.

proximal goal. Concrete goal that can be accomplished within a short time period; may be a stepping stone toward a long-term goal.

psychological aggression. Action intended to cause mental anguish or reduce self-esteem.

psychological punishment. Consequence that seriously threatens self-esteem and general psychological well-being.

punishment. Consequence (stimulus) that decreases the frequency of the response it follows.

qualitative research. Research yielding information that cannot easily be reduced to numbers; typically involves an in-depth examination of a complex phenomenon.

quantitative research. Research yielding information that is inherently numerical in nature or can easily be reduced to numbers.

quasi-experimental study. Research study that involves the manipulation of one variable to determine its possible effect on another variable, but without total control of additional variables that might have an impact on the outcome.

rating scale. Scoring guide in which different numbers are assigned to different degrees of quality in a student's performance on an assessment.

raw score. Assessment score based solely on the number or point value of correctly answered items.

reactive aggression. Aggressive response to frustration or provocation.

recall task. Assessment task in which one must retrieve information from long-term memory with only minimal retrieval cues.

reciprocal causation. Mutual cause-and-effect relationships among environment, behavior, and personal variables as these three factors influence learning and development.

reciprocal teaching. Approach to fostering reading and listening comprehension skills in which students take turns asking teacher-like questions of classmates.

recognition task. Assessment task in which one must identify correct information among incorrect statements or irrelevant information.

reconstruction error. Construction of a logical but incorrect "memory" by combining information retrieved from one's long-term memory with one's general knowledge and beliefs about the world.

recursive thinking. Thinking about what other people may be thinking about oneself, possibly through multiple iterations.

reflective teaching. Regular, ongoing examination and critique of one's assumptions and instructional strategies, and revision of them as necessary to enhance students' learning and development.

rehearsal. Cognitive process in which information is repeated over and over within a short time frame (typically a few minutes or less) as a possible way of learning and remembering it.

reinforcer. Consequence (stimulus) of a response that increases the frequency of the response it follows; the act of following a response with a reinforcer is known as **reinforcement.**

rejected student. Student whom many peers identify as being an undesirable social companion.

relational aggression. Action that can adversely affect interpersonal relationships; a form of psychological aggression.

reliability. Extent to which an assessment yields consistent information about the knowledge, skills, or characteristics being assessed.

removal punishment. Punishment involving withdrawal of an existing stimulus, presumably one a learner doesn't want to lose.

resilient self-efficacy. Belief that one can perform a task successfully even after experiencing setbacks.

resilient student. Student who succeeds in school and in life despite exceptional hardships at home.

response (R). Specific behavior that an individual exhibits.

response cost. Loss either of a previously earned reinforcer or of an opportunity to obtain reinforcement.

response to intervention (RTI). Approach to diagnosing significant learning difficulties in which students are identified for in-depth assessment after failing to master certain basic skills despite evidence-based whole-class and small-group instructional practices.

retrieval. Process of finding information previously stored in memory.

retrieval cue. Stimulus that provides guidance about where to "look" for a piece of information in long-term memory.

rote learning. Learning information in a relatively uninterpreted form, without making sense of it or attaching much meaning to it.

rubric. Two-dimensional table that includes two or more characteristics on one dimension and concrete criteria for rating them on the other dimension; useful in evaluating a multifaceted performance or product

scaffolding. Support mechanism that helps a learner successfully perform a challenging task (i.e., a task within the learner's zone of proximal development).

schema. Tightly organized set of facts about a specific topic.

scheme. Organized group of similar actions or thoughts that are used repeatedly in response to the environment.

scholastic aptitude test. Test designed to assess a general capacity to learn and used to predict future academic achievement.

school readiness test. Test designed to assess cognitive skills important for success in a typical kindergarten or first-grade curriculum.

schoolwide positive behavioral interventions and supports. Systematic use of behaviorist principles to encourage and reinforce productive behaviors in all students; typically involves multiple layers of support in order to accommodate the varying needs and behavior patterns of different students.

scorer reliability. Extent to which different people agree in their judgments of students' performance on an assessment; sometimes called *interrater reliability*.

script. Schema that involves a predictable sequence of events related to a common activity.

scripted cooperation. Technique in which cooperative learning groups follow a specified set of steps, or script, that guides members' verbal interactions.

secondary reinforcer. Consequence that becomes reinforcing over time through its association with another reinforcer.

self-conscious emotion. Affective state based on self-evaluations regarding the extent to which one's actions meet society's standards for appropriate and desirable behavior; examples are pride, guilt, and shame.

self-efficacy. Belief that one is capable of executing certain behaviors or reaching certain goals.

self-evaluation. Process of judging one's own performance or behavior.

self-explanation. Process of occasionally stopping to verbalize to oneself (and hence to better understand) material being read or studied.

self-fulfilling prophecy. Situation in which expectations for an outcome either directly or indirectly lead to the expected result.

self-handicapping. Behavior that undermines one's own success as a way of protecting self-worth during potentially difficult tasks.

self-imposed contingency. Self-reinforcement or self-punishment that follows a behavior.

self-instructions. Instructions that one gives oneself while performing a complex behavior.

self-monitoring. Process of observing and recording one's own behavior.

self-questioning. Process of asking oneself questions as a way of checking one's understanding of a topic.

self-regulated behavior. Self-chosen and self-directed behavior that leads to the fulfillment of personally constructed standards and goals.

self-regulated learning. Regulation of one's own cognitive processes and studying behaviors in order to learn successfully.

self-regulated problem solving. Use of self-directed strategies to address complex problems.

self-regulation. Process of setting goals for oneself and engaging in behaviors and cognitive processes that lead to goal attainment.

self-socialization. Tendency to integrate personal observations and others' input into self-constructed standards for behavior and to choose actions consistent with those standards.

self-talk. Process of talking to oneself as a way of guiding oneself through a task.

self-worth. General belief about the extent to which one is a good, capable individual.

sense of community. Shared belief that teacher and students have common goals, are mutually respectful and supportive, and all make important contributions to classroom learning.

sense of school community. Shared belief that all faculty and students within a school are working together to help everyone learn and succeed.

sense of self. Perceptions, beliefs, judgments, and feelings about oneself as a person; includes *self-concept* and *self-esteem.*

sensitive period. Age range during which environmental conditions have an especially strong influence on an aspect of a child's development (you may sometimes see the term *critical period*).

sensorimotor stage. Piaget's first stage of cognitive development, in which schemes are based largely on behaviors and perceptions.

sensory register. Component of memory that holds incoming information in an unanalyzed form for a very brief period of time (2 or 3 seconds at most, depending on the modality).

service learning. Activity that promotes learning and development through contributing to the general betterment of other people and the outside community.

setting event. Complex environmental condition that is likely to evoke certain voluntary behaviors.

severe and multiple disabilities. Combination of two or more disabilities that, taken together, require significant classroom adaptations and highly specialized educational services.

shame. Feeling of embarrassment or humiliation after failing to meet certain standards for moral behavior.

shaping. Process of reinforcing successively closer and closer approximations to a desired terminal behavior.

situated learning and cognition. Knowledge, behaviors, and thinking skills acquired and used primarily within certain contexts, with limited or no retrieval and use in other contexts; sometimes involves dependence on physical or social support mechanisms available only in certain contexts.

situated motivation. Phenomenon in which aspects of the immediate environment enhance motivation to learn particular things or behave in particular ways.

situational interest. Interest evoked temporarily by something in the environment.

social cognition. Process of thinking about how other people are likely to think, act, and react.

social cognitive theory. Theoretical perspective that focuses on how people learn by observing others and how they eventually assume control over their own behavior.

social constructivism. Theoretical perspective that focuses on people's collective efforts to impose meaning on the world.

social development. Development, with age, of increasingly sophisticated understandings of other people and of society as a whole, as well as increasingly effective interpersonal skills and more internalized standards for behavior.

social information processing. Mental processes involved in making sense of and responding to social events.

socialization. Process of molding a child's behavior and beliefs to be appropriate for his or her cultural group.

society. Very large, enduring social group that has fairly explicit social and economic structures and collective institutions and activities.

sociocognitive conflict. Situation in which one encounters and has to wrestle with ideas and viewpoints inconsistent with one's own.

sociocultural theory. Theoretical perspective emphasizing the importance of society and culture in promoting learning and development.

socioeconomic status (SES). One's general social and economic standing in society; encompasses family income, occupation, and educational level.

specific aptitude test. Test designed to predict future ability to succeed in a particular content domain.

specific language impairment. Disability characterized by abnormalities in the production or comprehension of spoken language, to the point that special educational services are required.

specific transfer. Instance of transfer in which the original learning task and the transfer task overlap in content.

speech and communication disorders. Impairments in spoken language or language comprehension that significantly interfere with classroom performance.

standard deviation (SD). Statistic indicating the amount of variability characterizing a set of scores.

Standard English. Form of English generally considered acceptable at school, as reflected in textbooks and grammar instruction.

standard error of measurement (SEM). Statistic estimating the amount of error in a test score or other assessment result.

standard score. Test score indicating how far a student's performance is from the mean in terms of standard deviation units.

standardization. Extent to which an assessment involves similar content and format and is administered and scored similarly for everyone.

standardized test. Test developed by test construction experts and published for use in many different schools and classrooms.

stanine. Standard score with a mean of 5 and a standard deviation of 2; always reported as a whole number between 1 and 9.

state anxiety. Temporary feeling of anxiety elicited by a threatening situation.

stereotype. Rigid, simplistic, and erroneous view of a particular group of people.

stereotype threat. Awareness of a negative stereotype about one's own group and accompanying uneasiness that low performance will confirm the stereotype; leads (often unintentionally) to lower-quality performance.

stimulus (S). Specific object or event that influences an individual's learning or behavior.

storage. Process of putting new information into memory.

students at risk. Students with a high probability of failing to acquire the minimal academic skills necessary for success in the adult world.

students with special needs. Students different enough from their peers that they require specially adapted instructional materials and practices to maximize their learning and achievement.

subculture. Group that resists the ways of the dominant culture and adopts its own norms for behavior.

subtractive bilingualism. Phenomenon in which complete immersion in a new-language environment leads to deficits in a child's native language.

summative assessment. Assessment conducted after instruction to assess students' final achievement.

superimposed meaningful structure. Familiar shape, word, sentence, poem, or story imposed on information in order to facilitate recall.

sympathy. Feeling of sorrow for another person's distress, accompanied by concern for the person's well-being.

synapse. Junction between two neurons that allows transmission of messages from one to the other.

synaptic pruning. Universal process in brain development in which many previously formed but rarely used synapses gradually wither away.

synaptogenesis. Universal process in brain development in which many new synapses form spontaneously.

table of specifications. Two-way grid indicating the topics to be covered in an assessment and the things students should be able to do with those topics.

target behavior. Specific, concrete response that a teacher or therapist wants to either increase or decrease by means of a systematic intervention.

task analysis. Process of identifying the specific behaviors, knowledge, or cognitive processes necessary to master a particular topic or skill.

task value. Belief regarding the extent to which an activity has direct or indirect benefits.

teachable moment. Situation or event (often unplanned) in which students might be especially predisposed to acquire particular knowledge or skills.

teacher accountability. Practice of using students' achievement test scores as measures of a teacher's effectiveness in the classroom.

teacher-developed assessment instrument. Assessment tool developed by an individual teacher for use in a specific classroom.

teacher-directed instruction. Approach to instruction in which the teacher is largely in control of the content and course of the lesson.

temperament. Genetic predisposition to respond in particular ways to one's physical and social environments.

terminal behavior. Form and frequency of a desired response that a teacher or therapist hopes to foster through reinforcement.

test anxiety. Excessive anxiety about a particular test or about assessment in general.

testwiseness. Test-taking know-how that enhances test performance.

test–retest reliability. Extent to which a particular assessment instrument yields similar results over a short time interval.

theory. Integrated set of concepts and principles developed to explain a particular phenomenon; may be constructed jointly by researchers over time or individually by a single learner.

theory of mind. Self-constructed understanding of one's own and other people's mental and psychological states (thoughts, feelings, etc.).

threat. Situation in which a learner believes there is little or no chance of success.

time on task. Amount of time that students are both physically and cognitively engaged in a learning activity.

time-out. Consequence for misbehavior in which a learner cannot interact with others and has no opportunity to receive the kinds of reinforcement to which classmates have access.

token economy. Technique in which desired behaviors are reinforced by small, insignificant items (tokens) that learners can use to "purchase" a variety of other, more desirable reinforcers.

traditional assessment. Assessment that focuses on measuring basic knowledge and skills in relative isolation from activities typical of the outside world.

trait anxiety. General pattern of responding with anxiety even in nonthreatening situations.

transfer. Phenomenon in which something a person has learned at one time affects how the person learns or performs in a later situation.

treatment group. Group of people in a research study who are given a particular experimental intervention (e.g., a particular method of instruction).

true score. Hypothetical score a student would obtain if an assessment measured a characteristic or ability with complete accuracy.

unconditioned response (UCR). Response that is already elicited by a particular (unconditioned) stimulus in the situation at hand.

unconditioned stimulus (UCS). Stimulus that already elicits a particular response in the situation at hand.

universals. Similar patterns in how children change and progress over time, regardless of their specific environment.

validity. Extent to which an assessment actually measures what it is intended to measure and allows appropriate inferences about the characteristic or ability in question.

value-added assessment. Approach to evaluating teacher and school effectiveness based on students' academic progress rather than on absolute achievement levels.

verbal mediator. Word or phrase that forms a logical connection, or mental "bridge," between two pieces of information.

vicarious punishment. Phenomenon in which a response decreases in frequency when another person is observed being punished for that response.

vicarious reinforcement. Phenomenon in which a response increases in frequency when another person is observed being reinforced for that response.

visual imagery. Process of forming a mental picture of an object or idea.

visual impairment. Malfunction of the eyes or optic nerves that prevents normal vision even with corrective lenses.

visual–spatial ability. Ability to imagine and mentally manipulate two- and three-dimensional figures.

wait time. Length of time a teacher pauses, after either asking a question or hearing a student's comment, before saying something.

webquest. Structured activity in which students use a number of teacher- or expert-chosen websites to tackle an engaging, challenging task that requires complex cognitive processes (e.g., problem solving, critical thinking).

well-defined problem. Problem in which the goal is clearly stated, all the information needed to solve the problem is present, and only one correct answer exists.

withitness. Classroom management strategy in which a teacher gives the impression of knowing what all students are doing at all times.

work-avoidance goal. Desire either to avoid classroom tasks or to complete them with minimal effort, often because of low self-efficacy for the tasks.

working memory. Component of memory that holds and actively thinks about and processes a limited amount of information for a short time.

worldview. General, culturally based set of assumptions about reality that influence understandings of a wide variety of phenomena.

zone of proximal development (ZPD). Range of tasks that a learner can perform with the help and guidance of others but cannot yet perform independently.

z-score. Standard score with a mean of 0 and a standard deviation of 1.

References

CHAPTER 1

Anderson, J. R. (2005). *Cognitive psychology and its implications* (6th ed.). New York, NY: Worth.

Barab, S. A., Gresalfi, M., & Ingram-Goble, A. (2010). Transformational play: Using games to position person, content, and context. *Educational Researcher, 39,* 525–536.

Baumert, J., Kunter, M., Blum, W., Brunner, M., Voss, T., Jordan, A., . . . Tsai, Y.-M. (2010). Teachers' mathematical knowledge, cognitive activation in the classroom, and student progress. *American Educational Research Journal, 47,* 133–180.

Berliner, D. C. (2001). Learning about and learning from expert teachers. *International Journal of Educational Research, 35,* 463–483.

Borko, H., & Putnam, R. T. (1996). Learning to teach. In D. C. Berliner & R. C. Calfee (Eds.), *Handbook of educational psychology* (pp. 673–708). New York, NY: Macmillan.

Bransford, J., Darling-Hammond, L., & LePage, P. (2005). Introduction. In L. Darling-Hammond & J. Bransford (Eds.), *Preparing teachers for a changing world: What teachers should learn and be able to do* (pp. 1–39). San Francisco, CA: Jossey-Bass/Wiley.

Bransford, J., Derry, S., Berliner, D., & Hammerness, K. (with Beckett, K. L.). (2005). Theories of learning and their roles in teaching. In L. Darling-Hammond & J. Bransford (Eds.), *Preparing teachers for a changing world: What teachers should learn and be able to do* (pp. 40–87). San Francisco, CA: Jossey-Bass/Wiley.

Brayboy, B. M. J., & Searle, K. A. (2007). Thanksgiving and serial killers: Representations of American Indians in schools. In S. Books (Ed.), *Invisible children in the society and its schools* (3rd ed., pp. 173–192). Mahwah, NJ: Erlbaum.

Bressler, S. L. (2002). Understanding cognition through large-scale cortical networks. *Current Directions in Psychological Science, 11,* 58–61.

Brouwer, N., & Korthagen, F. (2005). Can teacher education make a difference? *American Educational Research Journal, 42,* 153–224.

Carpenter, S. K. (2012). Testing enhances the transfer of learning. *Current Directions in Psychological Science, 21,* 279–283.

Cassady, J. C. (2010b). Test anxiety: Contemporary theories and implications for learning. In J. C. Cassady (Ed.), *Anxiety in schools: The causes, consequences, and solutions for academic anxieties* (pp. 7–26). New York, NY: Peter Lang.

Castagno, A. E., & Brayboy, B. M. J. (2008). Culturally responsive schooling for Indigenous youth: A review of the literature. *Review of Educational Research, 78,* 941–993.

Clotfelter, C. T., Ladd, H. F., & Vigdor, J. (2007). Who teaches whom? Race and the distribution of novice teachers. *Economics of Education Review, 24,* 377–392.

Cochran, K. F., & Jones, L. L. (1998). The subject matter knowledge of preservice science teachers. In B. J. Fraser & K. G. Tobin (Eds.), *International handbook of science education* (Pt. II, pp. 707–718). Dordrecht, Netherlands: Kluwer.

Desimone, L. M. (2009). Improving impact studies of teachers' professional development: Toward better conceptualizations and measures. *Educational Researcher, 38,* 181–199.

DuFour, R., DuFour, R., & Eaker, R. (2008). *Revisiting professional learning communities at work: New insights for improving schools.* Bloomington, IN: Solution Tree.

Feldon, D. F. (2007). Cognitive load and classroom teaching: The double-edged sword of automaticity. *Educational Psychologist, 42,* 123–137.

Fives, H., & Gill, M. G. (Eds.). (2015). *International handbook of research on teachers' beliefs.* New York, NY: Routledge.

Frederiksen, N. (1984b). The real test bias: Influences of testing on teaching and learning. *American Psychologist, 39,* 193–202.

Gage, N. L. (1991). The obviousness of social and educational research results. *Educational Researcher, 20*(1), 10–16.

Gee, J. P. (2010). Looking where the light is bad: Video games and the future of assessment. *Edge, 6,* 3–19.

Gentile, D. A. (2011). The multiple dimensions of video game effects. *Child Development Perspectives, 5*(2), 75–81.

Goldstein, L. S., & Lake, V. E. (2000). "Love, love, and more love for children": Exploring preservice teachers' understanding of caring. *Teaching and Teacher Education, 16,* 861–872.

Graesser, A. C., & Bower, G. H. (Eds.). (1990). *Inferences and text comprehension. The psychology of learning and motivation: Advances in research and theory* (Vol. 25). Orlando, FL: Academic Press.

Graham, P., & Ferriter, W. M. (2009). *Building a professional learning community at work: A guide to the first year.* Bloomington, IN: Solution Tree.

Gregoire, M. (2003). Is it a challenge or a threat? A dual-process model of teachers' cognition and appraisal processes during conceptual change. *Educational Psychology Review, 15,* 147–179.

Hammerness, K., Darling-Hammond, L., & Bransford, J. (with Berliner, D., Cochran-Smith, M., McDonald, M., & Zeichner, K.). (2005). How teachers learn and develop. In L. Darling-Hammond & J. Bransford (Eds.), *Preparing teachers for a changing world: What teachers should learn and be able to do* (pp. 358–389). San Francisco, CA: Jossey-Bass/Wiley.

Hattie, J. A. C. (2009). *Visible learning: A synthesis of over 800 meta-analyses relating to achievement.* London: Routledge.

Heck, A., Collins, J., & Peterson, L. (2001). Decreasing children's risk taking on the playground. *Journal of Applied Behavior Analysis, 34,* 349–352.

Hemmings, A. B. (2004). *Coming of age in U.S. high schools: Economic, kinship, religious, and political crosscurrents.* Mahwah, NJ: Erlbaum.

Henry, G. T., Bastian, K. C., & Fortner, C. K. (2011). Stayers and leavers: Early-career teacher effectiveness and attrition. *Educational Researcher, 40,* 271–280.

Hill, H. C., Blunk, M. L., Charalambous, C. Y., Lewis, J. M., Phelps, G. C., Sleep, L., & Ball, D. L. (2008). Mathematical knowledge for teaching and the mathematical quality of instruction: An exploratory study. *Cognition and Instruction, 26,* 430–511.

Hogan, T., Rabinowitz, M., & Craven, J. A., III. (2003). Representation in teaching: Inferences from research of expert and novice teachers. *Educational Psychologist, 38,* 235–247.

Holzberger, D., Philipp, A., & Kunter, M. (2013). How teachers' self-efficacy is related to instructional quality: A longitudinal analysis. *Journal of Educational Psychology, 105,* 774–786.

Johnson, B. (2001). Toward a new classification of nonexperimental quantitative research. *Educational Researcher, 30*(2), 3–13.

Kagan, J., & Snidman, N. (2007). Temperament and biology. In D. Coch, K. W. Fischer, & G. Dawson (Eds.), *Human behavior, learning, and the developing brain: Typical development* (pp. 219–246). New York, NY: Guilford.

Keogh, B. K. (2003). *Temperament in the classroom.* Baltimore, MD: Brookes.

Kirschner, P. A., & van Merriënboer, J. J. G. (2013). Do learners really know best? Urban legends in education. *Educational Psychologist, 48,* 169–183.

Konstantopoulos, S., & Chung, V. (2011). The persistence of teacher effects in elementary grades. *American Educational Research Journal, 48,* 361–386.

Kozhevnikov, M., Evans, C., & Kosslyn, S. M. (2014). Cognitive style as environmentally sensitive individual differences in cognition: A modern synthesis and applications in education, business, and management. *Psychological Science in the Public Interest, 15,* 3–33.

Krätzig, G. P., & Arbuthnott, K. D. (2006). Perceptual learning style and learning proficiency: A test of the hypothesis. *Journal of Educational Psychology, 98,* 238–246.

Krauss, S., Brunner, M., Kunter, M., Baumert, J., Blum, W., Neubrand, M., & Jordan, A. (2008). Pedagogical content knowledge and content knowledge of secondary mathematics teachers. *Journal of Educational Psychology, 100,* 716–725.

Ladson-Billings, G. (1995b). Toward a theory of culturally relevant pedagogy. *American Educational Research Journal, 32,* 465–491.

Langer, J. A. (2000). Excellence in English in middle and high school: How teachers' professional lives support student achievement. *American Educational Research Journal, 37,* 397–439.

Larrivee, B. (2006). The convergence of reflective practice and effective classroom management. In C. M. Evertson & C. S. Weinstein (Eds.), *Handbook of classroom management: Research, practice, and contemporary issues* (pp. 983–1001). Mahwah, NJ: Erlbaum.

Lundeberg, M. A., & Fox, P. W. (1991). Do laboratory findings on test expectancy generalize to classroom outcomes? *Review of Educational Research, 61,* 94–106.

Mayer, R. E., & Massa, L. J. (2003). Three facets of visual and verbal learners: Cognitive ability, cognitive style, and learning preference. *Journal of Educational Psychology, 95,* 833–846.

McDonald, B. O., Robles-Piña, R., & Polnick, B. (2011, April). *A comparison of urban middle school mathematics teachers with high student gain scores and low student gain scores.* Paper presented at the annual meeting of the American Educational Research Association, New Orleans, LA.

McIntyre, E. (2010). Issues in funds of knowledge teaching and research: Key concepts from a study of Appalachian families and schooling. In M. L. Dantas & P. C. Manyak (Eds.), *Home–school connections in a multicultural society: Learning from and with culturally and linguistically diverse families* (pp. 201–217). New York, NY: Routledge.

Mills, G. E. (2011). *Action research: A guide for the teacher researcher* (4th ed.). Upper Saddle River, NJ: Pearson.

Moje, E. B., & Hinchman, K. (2004). Culturally responsive practices for youth literacy learning. In T. L. Jetton & J. A. Dole (Eds.), *Adolescent literacy research and practice* (pp. 321–350). New York, NY: Guilford.

Morelli, G. A., & Rothbaum, F. (2007). Situating the child in context: Attachment relationships and self-regulation in different cultures. In S. Kitayama & D. Cohen (Eds.), *Handbook of cultural psychology* (pp. 500–527). New York, NY: Guilford Press.

Ogbu, J. U. (2003). *Black American students in an affluent suburb: A study of academic disengagement.* Mahwah, NJ: Erlbaum.

Perry, N. E., Turner, J. C., & Meyer, D. K. (2006). Classrooms as contexts for motivating learning. In P. A. Alexander & P. H. Winne (Eds.), *Handbook of educational psychology* (2nd ed., pp. 327–348). Mahwah, NJ: Erlbaum.

Posner, M. I., & Rothbart, M. K. (2007). *Educating the human brain.* Washington, DC: American Psychological Association.

Raudenbush, S. W. (2009). The *Brown* legacy and the O'Connor challenge: Transforming schools in the images of children's potential. *Educational Researcher, 38,* 169–180.

Richardson, V. (2003). Preservice teachers' beliefs. In J. Raths & A. C. McAninch (Eds.), *Teacher beliefs and classroom performance: The impact of teacher education* (pp. 1–22). Greenwich, CT: Information Age.

Roderick, M., & Camburn, E. (1999). Risk and recovery from course failure in the early years of high school. *American Educational Research Journal, 36,* 303–343.

Rothbart, M. K. (2011). *Becoming who we are: Temperament and personality in development.* New York, NY: Guilford.

Sadler, P. M., Sonnert, G., Coyle, H. P., Cook-Smith, N., & Miller, J. L. (2013). The influence of teachers' knowledge on student learning in middle school physical science classrooms. *American Educational Research Journal, 50,* 1020–1049.

Shipman, S., & Shipman, V. C. (1985). Cognitive styles: Some conceptual, methodological, and applied issues. In E. W. Gordon (Ed.), *Review of research in education* (Vol. 12, pp. 229–291). Washington, DC: American Educational Research Association.

Shulman, L. S. (1986). Those who understand: Knowledge growth in teaching. *Educational Researcher, 15*(2), 4–14.

Skaalvik, E. M., & Skaalvik, S. (2008). Teacher self-efficacy: Conceptual analysis and relations with teacher burnout and perceived school context. In H. W. Marsh, R. G. Craven, & D. M. McInerney (Eds.), *Self-processes, learning, and enabling human potential* (pp. 223–247). Charlotte, NC: Information Age.

Smith, A. K. (2009). *The art of possibility: Creating more successful learners.* Malibu, CA: Center for Collaborative Action Research, Pepperdine University. Retrieved from http://cadres.pepperdine.edu/ccar/projects.school.html

Squire, K. (2011). *Video games and learning: Teaching and participatory culture in the digital age.* New York, NY: Teachers College Press.

Stone, N. J. (2000). Exploring the relationship between calibration and self-regulated learning. *Educational Psychology Review, 12,* 437–475.

Thiede, K. W., Griffin, T. D., Wiley, J., & Redford, J. S. (2009). Metacognitive monitoring during and after reading. In D. J. Hacker, J. Dunlosky, & A. C. Graesser (Eds.), *Handbook of metacognition in education* (pp. 85–106). New York, NY: Routledge.

Tobias, S., & Fletcher, J. D. (Eds.). (2011). *Computer games and instruction.* Charlotte, NC: Information Age.

Tyler, K. M., Uqdah, A. L., Dillihunt, M. L., Beatty-Hazelbaker, R., Connor, T., Gadson, N., . . . Stevens, R. (2008). Cultural discontinuity: Toward a quantitative investigation of a major hypothesis in education. *Educational Researcher, 37,* 280–297.

Woolfolk Hoy, A., Davis, H., & Pape, S. J. (2006). Teacher knowledge and beliefs. In P. A. Alexander & P. H. Winne (Eds.), *Handbook of educational psychology* (2nd ed., pp. 715–737). Mahwah, NJ: Erlbaum.

CHAPTER 2

Adesope, O. O., Lavin, T., Thompson, T., & Ungerleider, C. (2010). A systematic review and meta-analysis of the cognitive correlates of bilingualism. *Review of Educational Research, 80,* 207–245.

Adger, C. T., Wolfram, W., & Christian, D. (2007). *Dialects in schools and communities* (2nd ed.). New York, NY: Routledge.

Aitchison, J. (1996). *The seeds of speech: Language origin and evolution.* Cambridge, England: Cambridge University Press.

Andriessen, J. (2006). Arguing to learn. In R. K. Sawyer (Ed.), *The Cambridge handbook of the learning sciences* (pp. 443–459). Cambridge, England: Cambridge University Press.

Ash, D. (2002). Negotiations of thematic conversations about biology. In G. Leinhardt, K. Crowley, & K. Knutson (Eds.), *Learning conversations in museums* (pp. 357–400). Mahwah, NJ: Erlbaum.

Bebko, J. M., Burke, L., Craven, J., & Sarlo, N. (1992). The importance of motor activity in sensorimotor development: A perspective from children with physical handicaps. *Human Development, 35*(4), 226–240.

Beck, S. R., Robinson, E. J., Carroll, D. J., & Apperly, I. A. (2006). Children's thinking about counterfactuals and future hypotheticals as possibilities. *Child Development, 77,* 413–426.

Benton, S. L. (1997). Psychological foundations of elementary writing instruction. In G. D. Phye (Ed.), *Handbook of academic learning: Construction of knowledge* (pp. 235–264). San Diego, CA: Academic Press.

Berk, L. E. (1994). Why children talk to themselves. *Scientific American, 271,* 78–83.

Bialystok, E. (1994). Representation and ways of knowing: Three issues in second language acquisition. In N. C. Ellis (Ed.), *Implicit and explicit learning of languages* (pp. 549–569). London: Academic Press.

Bialystok, E. (2001). *Bilingualism in development: Language, literacy, and cognition.* Cambridge, England: Cambridge University Press.

Bialystok, E., Craik, F. I. M., Green, D. W., & Gollan, T. H. (2009). Bilingual minds. *Psychological Science in the Public Interest, 10,* 89–129.

Bishop, D. V. M. (2006). What causes specific language impairment in children? *Current Directions in Psychological Science, 15,* 217–221.

Bishop, D. V. M., McDonald, D., Bird, S., & Hayiou-Thomas, M. E. (2009). Children who read words accurately despite language impairment: Who are they and how do they do it? *Child Development, 80,* 593–605.

Bivens, J. A., & Berk, L. E. (1990). A longitudinal study of the development of elementary school children's private speech. *Merrill-Palmer Quarterly, 36,* 443–463.

Blair, K. F., & Schwartz, D. L. (2012). A value of concrete learning materials in adolescence. In V. F. Reyna, S. B. Chapman, M. R. Dougherty, & J. Confrey (Eds.), *The adolescent brain: Learning, reasoning, and decision making* (pp. 95–122). Washington: American Psychological Association.

Bortfeld, H., & Whitehurst, G. J. (2001). Sensitive periods in first language acquisition. In D. B. Bailey, Jr., J. T. Bruer, F. J. Symons, & J. W. Lichtman (Eds.), *Critical thinking about critical periods* (pp. 173–192). Baltimore, MD: Brookes.

Brainerd, C. J. (2003). Jean Piaget, learning research, and American education. In B. J. Zimmerman & D. H. Schunk (Eds.), *Educational psychology: A century of contributions* (pp. 251–287). Mahwah, NJ: Erlbaum.

Bressler, S. L. (2002). Understanding cognition through large-scale cortical networks. *Current Directions in Psychological Science, 11,* 58–61.

Bronfenbrenner, U. (2005). *Making human beings human: Bioecological perspectives on human development.* Thousand Oaks, CA: Sage.

Bronfenbrenner, U., & Ceci, S. J. (1994). Nature–nurture reconceptualized in developmental perspective: A bioecological model. *Psychological Review, 101,* 568–586.

Bronfenbrenner, U., & Morris, P. A. (1998). The ecology of developmental processes. In W. Damon (Series Ed.) & R. M. Lerner (Vol. Ed.), *Handbook of child psychology: Vol. 1. Theoretical models of human development* (5th ed., pp. 993–1028). New York, NY: Wiley.

Brown, J. S., Collins, A., & Duguid, P. (1989). Situated cognition and the culture of learning. *Educational Researcher, 18*(1), 32–42.

Brown, M. C., McNeil, N. M., & Glenberg, A. M. (2009). Using concreteness in education: Real problems, potential solutions. *Child Development Perspectives, 3,* 160–164.

Bruer, J. T. (1999). *The myth of the first three years: A new understanding of early brain development and lifelong learning.* New York, NY: Free Press.

Bruer, J. T., & Greenough, W. T. (2001). The subtle science of how experience affects the brain. In D. B. Bailey, Jr., J. T. Bruer, F. J. Symons, & J. W. Lichtman (Eds.), *Critical thinking about critical periods* (pp. 209–232). Baltimore, MD: Brookes.

Bryck, R. L., & Fisher, P. A. (2012). Training the brain: Practical applications of neural plasticity from the intersection of cognitive neuroscience, developmental psychology, and prevention science. *American Psychologist, 67,* 87–100.

Byrnes, J. P. (1996). *Cognitive development and learning in instructional contexts.* Boston, MA: Allyn & Bacon.

Byrnes, J. P. (2001). *Minds, brains, and learning: Understanding the psychological and educational relevance of neuroscientific research.* New York, NY: Guilford.

Byrnes, J. P. (2007). Some ways in which neuroscientific research can be relevant to education. In D. Coch, K. W. Fischer, & G. Dawson (Eds.), *Human behavior, learning, and the developing brain: Typical development* (pp. 30–49). New York, NY: Guilford.

Byrnes, J. P., & Fox, N. A. (1998). The educational relevance of research in cognitive neuroscience. *Educational Psychology Review, 10,* 297–342.

Cairns, H. S. (1996). *The acquisition of language* (2nd ed.). Austin, TX: Pro-Ed.

Capelli, C. A., Nakagawa, N., & Madden, C. M. (1990). How children understand sarcasm: The role of context and intonation. *Child Development, 61,* 1824–1841.

Carey, S. (1978). The child as word learner. In M. Halle, J. Bresnan, & G. A. Miller (Eds.), *Linguistic theory and psychological reality* (pp. 264–293). Cambridge, MA: MIT Press.

Carey, S. (1985). *Conceptual change in childhood.* Cambridge, MA: MIT Press.

Carhill, A., Suárez-Orozco, C., & Páez, M. (2008). Explaining English language proficiency among adolescent immigrant students. *American Educational Research Journal, 45,* 1045–1079.

Case, R. (1985). *Intellectual development: Birth to adulthood.* Orlando, FL: Academic Press.

Case, R., & Mueller, M. P. (2001). Differentiation, integration, and covariance mapping as fundamental processes in cognitive and neurological growth. In J. L. McClelland & R. S. Siegler (Eds.), *Mechanisms of cognitive development: Behavioral and neural perspectives* (pp. 185–219). Mahwah, NJ: Erlbaum.

Case, R., & Okamoto, Y., in collaboration with Griffin, S., McKeough, A., Bleiker, C., Henderson, B., & Stephenson, K. M. (1996). The role of central conceptual structures in the development of children's thought. *Monographs of the Society for Research in Child Development, 61*(1, Serial No. 246).

Chapman, M. (1988). *Constructive evolution: Origins and development of Piaget's thought.* Cambridge, England: Cambridge University Press.

Chein, J. M., & Schneider, W. (2012). The brain's learning and control architecture. *Current Directions in Psychological Science, 21,* 78–84.

Chen, X., Anderson, R. C., Li, W., Hao, M., Wu, X., & Shu, H. (2004). Phonological awareness of bilingual and monolingual Chinese children. *Journal of Educational Psychology, 96,* 142–151.

Chinn, C. A., Anderson, R. C., & Waggoner, M. A. (2001). Patterns of discourse in two kinds of literature discussion. *Reading Research Quarterly, 36,* 378–411.

Chomsky, N. (1972). *Language and mind* (enlarged ed.). San Diego, CA: Harcourt Brace Jovanovich.

Chomsky, N. (2006). *Language and mind* (3rd ed.). Cambridge, England: Cambridge University Press.

Cole, M. (1990). Cognitive development and formal schooling: The evidence from cross-cultural research. In L. C. Moll (Ed.), *Vygotsky and education* (pp. 89–110). New York, NY: Cambridge University Press.

Cole, M. (2006). Culture and cognitive development in phylogenetic, historical and ontogenetic perspective. In W. Damon, R. M. Lerner (Series Eds.), D. Kuhn, & R. Siegler (Vol. Eds.), *Handbook of child psychology: Vol. 2. Cognition, perception, and language* (6th ed., pp. 636–683). New York, NY: Wiley.

Cole, S. W. (2009). Social regulation of human gene expression. *Current Directions in Psychological Science, 18,* 133–137.

Collier, V. P. (1992). The Canadian bilingual immersion debate: A synthesis of research findings. *Studies in Second Language Acquisition, 14,* 87–97.

Collins, A. (2006). Cognitive apprenticeship. In R. K. Sawyer (Ed.), *The Cambridge handbook of the learning sciences* (pp. 47–60). Cambridge, England: Cambridge University Press.

Collins, A., Brown, J. S., & Newman, S. E. (1989). Cognitive apprenticeship: Teaching the crafts of reading, writing, and mathematics. In L. B. Resnick (Ed.), *Knowing, learning, and instruction: Essays in honor of Robert Glaser* (pp. 453–494). Mahwah, NJ: Erlbaum.

Comeau, L., Cormier, P., Grandmaison, É., & Lacroix, D. (1999). A longitudinal study of phonological processing skills in children learning to read in a second language. *Journal of Educational Psychology, 91,* 29–43.

Coplan, R. J., & Arbeau, K. A. (2009). Peer interactions and play in early childhood. In K. H. Rubin, W. M. Bukowski, & B. Laursen (Eds.), *Handbook of peer interactions, relationships, and groups* (pp. 143–161). New York, NY: Guilford.

Corriveau, K., Pasquini, E., & Goswami, U. (2007). Basic auditory processing skills and specific language impairment: A new look at an old hypothesis. *Journal of Speech, Language, and Hearing Research, 50,* 647–666.

Cromer, R. F. (1987). Language growth with experience without feedback. *Journal of Psycholinguistic Research, 16,* 223–231.

Cummins, J. (2000). *Language, power, and pedagogy: Bilingual children in the crossfire.* Clevedon, England: Multilingual Matters.

Cummins, J. (2008). BICS and CALP: Empirical and theoretical status of the distinction. In B. Street & N. H. Hornberger (Eds.), *Encyclopedia of language and education* (2nd ed., Vol. 2, pp. 71–83). New York, NY: Springer.

Curtiss, S. (1977). *Genie: A psycholinguistic study of a modern-day "wild child."* New York, NY: Academic Press.

Davidson, C. N. (2011). *Now you see it: How the brain science of attention will transform the way we live, work, and learn.* New York, NY: Viking.

DeCasper, A. J., & Fifer, W. P. (1980). Of human bonding: Newborns prefer their mothers' voices. *Science, 208,* 1174–1176.

Dennen, V. P., & Burner, K. J. (2008). The cognitive apprenticeship model in educational practice. In J. M. Spector, M. D. Merrill, J. van Merriënboer, & M. P. Driscoll (Eds.), *Handbook of research on educational communications and technology* (3rd ed., pp. 425–439). New York, NY: Erlbaum.

Diamond, A., Barnett, W. S., Thomas, J., & Munro, S. (2007). Preschool program improves cognitive control. *Science, 318,* 1387–1338.

Diaz, R. M. (1983). Thought and two languages: The impact of bilingualism on cognitive development. In E. W. Gordon (Ed.), *Review of research in education* (Vol. 10. pp. 23–54). Washington, DC: American Educational Research Association.

diSessa, A. A. (2006). A history of conceptual change research. In R. K. Sawyer (Ed.), *The Cambridge handbook of the learning sciences* (pp. 265–281). Cambridge, England: Cambridge University Press.

diSessa, A. A. (2007). An interactional analysis of clinical interviewing. *Cognition and Instruction, 25,* 523–565.

Dixon, L. Q., Zhao, J., Shin, J.-Y., Wu, S., Su, J.-H., Burgess-Brigham, R., . . . Snow, C. (2012). What we know about second language acquisition: A synthesis from four perspectives. *Review of Educational Research, 82,* 5–60.

Doyle, A. (1982). Friends, acquaintances, and strangers: The influence of familiarity and ethnolinguistic backgrounds on social interaction. In K. Rubin & H. Ross (Eds.), *Peer relationships and social skills in childhood* (pp. 229–252). New York, NY: Springer-Verlag.

Duff, P. A. (2001). Language, literacy, content, and (pop) culture: Challenges for ESL students in mainstream courses. *Canadian Modern Language Review, 58*(1), 103–132.

Egbert, J. (2009). *Supporting learning with technology: Essentials of classroom practice.* Upper Saddle River, NJ: Pearson/Merrill Prentice Hall.

Elliott, D. J. (1995). *Music matters: A new philosophy of music education.* New York, NY: Oxford University Press.

Empson, S. B. (1999). Equal sharing and shared meaning: The development of fraction concepts in a first-grade classroom. *Cognition and Instruction, 17,* 283–342.

Espinosa, L. (2007). English-language learners as they enter school. In R. Pianta, M. Cox, & K. Snow (Eds.), *School readiness and the transition to kindergarten in the era of accountability* (pp. 175–196). Baltimore, MD: Brookes.

Espinosa, L. M. (2008, January). *Challenging common myths about young English language learners.* (FCD Policy Brief No. 8). New York, NY: Foundation for Child Development.

Ferretti, R. P., MacArthur, C. A., & Dowdy, N. S. (2000). The effects of an elaborated goal on the persuasive writing of students with learning disabilities and their normally achieving peers. *Journal of Educational Psychology, 92,* 694–702.

Feuerstein, R., Feuerstein, R. S., & Falik, L. H. (2010). *Beyond smarter: Mediated learning and the brain's capacity for change.* New York, NY: Teachers College Press.

Fischer, K. W., & Bidell, T. R. (2006). Dynamic development of action, thought, and emotion. In R. M. Lerner (Ed.), *Handbook of child psychology. Vol. 1: Theoretical models of human development* (6th ed., pp. 319–399). New York, NY: Wiley.

Fischer, K. W., & Daley, S. G. (2007). Connecting cognitive science and neuroscience to education: Potentials and pitfalls in inferring executive processes. In L. Meltzer (Ed.), *Executive function in education: From theory to practice* (pp. 55–72). New York, NY: Guilford.

Fischer, K. W., & Immordino-Yang, M. H. (2002). Cognitive development and education: From dynamic general structure to specific learning and teaching. In E. Lagemann (Ed.), *Traditions of scholarship in education* (pp. 1–55). Chicago, IL: Spencer Foundation.

Flavell, J. H. (1994). Cognitive development: Past, present, and future. In R. D. Parke, P. A. Ornstein, J. J. Rieser, & C. Zahn-Waxler (Eds.), *A century of developmental psychology* (pp. 569–587). Washington, DC: American Psychological Association.

Flieller, A. (1999). Comparison of the development of formal thought in adolescent cohorts aged 10 to 15 years (1967–1996 and 1972–1993). *Developmental Psychology, 35,* 1048–1058.

Fujimura, N. (2001). Facilitating children's proportional reasoning: A model of reasoning processes and effects of intervention on strategy change. *Journal of Educational Psychology, 93,* 589–603.

Gallimore, R., & Tharp, R. (1990). Teaching mind in society: Teaching, schooling, and literate discourse. In L. C. Moll (Ed.), *Vygotsky and education: Instructional implications and applications of sociohistorical psychology* (pp. 175–205). Cambridge, England: Cambridge University Press.

García, E. (1995). Educating Mexican American students: Past treatment and recent developments in theory, research, policy, and practice. In J. A. Banks & C. A. M. Banks (Eds.), *Handbook of research on multicultural education* (pp. 372–387). New York, NY: Macmillan.

Garcia, E., & Jensen, B. (2009). Early educational opportunities for children of Hispanic origins. *Social Policy Report, 23*(2), 3–19.

Gauvain, M. (2001). *The social context of cognitive development.* New York, NY: Guilford.

Geary, D. C. (1998). What is the function of mind and brain? *Educational Psychology Review, 10,* 377–387.

Geary, D. C. (2008). An evolutionarily informed education science. *Educational Psychologist, 43,* 179–195.

Genesee, F. (1985). Second language learning through immersion: A review of U.S. programs. *Review of Educational Research, 55,* 541–561.

Gentner, D., & Namy, L. L. (2006). Analogical processes in language learning. *Current Directions in Psychological Science, 15,* 297–301.

Gershkoff-Stowe, L., & Thelen, E. (2004). U-shaped changes in behavior: A dynamic systems perspective. *Journal of Cognition and Development, 1*(5), 11–36.

Giedd, J. N., Stockman, M., Weddle, C., Liverpool, M., Wallace, G. L., Lee, N. R., . . . Lenroot, R. K. (2012). Anatomic magnetic resonance imaging of the developing child and adolescent brain. In V. F. Reyna, S. B. Chapman, M. R. Dougherty, & J. Confrey (Eds.), *The adolescent brain: Learning, reasoning, and decision making* (pp. 15–35). Washington, DC: American Psychological Association.

Girotto, V., & Light, P. (1993). The pragmatic bases of children's reasoning. In P. Light & G. Butterworth (Eds.), *Context and cognition: Ways of learning and knowing* (pp. 134–156). Mahwah, NJ: Erlbaum.

Gonsalves, B. D., & Cohen, N. J. (2010). Brain imaging, cognitive processes, and brain networks. *Perspectives on Psychological Science, 5,* 744–752.

Goodman, C. S., & Tessier-Lavigne, M. (1997). Molecular mechanisms of axon guidance and target recognition. In W. M. Cowan, T. M. Jessell, & S. L. Zipursky (Eds.), *Molecular and cellular approaches to neural development* (pp. 108–137). New York, NY: Oxford University Press.

Gopnik, M. (Ed.). (1997). *The inheritance and innateness of grammars.* New York, NY: Oxford University Press.

Goswami, U., & Pauen, S. (2005). The effects of a "family" analogy on class inclusion reasoning by young children. *Swiss Journal of Psychology, 64*(2), 115–124.

Grant, C. A., & Gomez, M. L. (2001). *Campus and classroom: Making schooling multicultural* (2nd ed.). Upper Saddle River, NJ: Merrill/Prentice Hall.

Haenan, J. (1996). Piotr Gal'perin's criticism and extension of Lev Vygotsky's work. *Journal of Russian and East European Psychology, 34*(2), 54–60.

Halford, G. S., & Andrews, G. (2006). Reasoning and problem solving. In W. Damon, R. M. Lerner (Series Eds.), D. Kuhn, & R. Siegler (Vol. Eds.), *Handbook of child psychology: Vol. 2. Cognition, perception, and language* (6th ed., pp. 557–608). New York, NY: Wiley.

Hardy, I., Jonen, A., Möller, K., & Stern, E. (2006). Effects of instructional support within constructivist learning environments for elementary school students' understanding of "floating and sinking." *Journal of Educational Psychology, 98,* 307–326.

Harris, K. R., Graham, S., & Mason, L. H. (2006). Improving the writing, knowledge, and motivation of struggling young writers: Effects of self-regulated strategy development with and without peer support. *American Educational Research Journal, 43,* 295–340.

Harris, K. R., Santangelo, T., & Graham, S. (2010). Metacognition and strategies instruction in writing. In H. S. Waters & W. Schneider (Eds.), *Metacognition, strategy use, and instruction* (pp. 226–256). New York, NY: Guilford.

Haxby, J. V., Gobbini, M. I., Furey, M. L., Ishai, A., Schouten, J. L., & Pietrini, P. (2001). Distributed and overlapping representations of faces and objects in ventral temporal cortex. *Science, 293,* 2425–2430.

Hennessey, M. G., & Beeth, M. E. (1993). *Students' reflective thoughts about science content: A relationship to conceptual change learning.* Paper presented at the meeting of the American Educational Research Association, Atlanta, GA.

Herrell, A., & Jordan, M. (2004). *Fifty strategies for teaching English language learners* (2nd ed.). Upper Saddle River, NJ: Merrill/Prentice Hall.

Hiebert, J., Carpenter, T. P., Fennema, E., Fuson, K. C., Wearne, D., Murray, H., . . . Human, P. (1997). *Making sense: Teaching and learning mathematics with understanding.* Portsmouth, NH: Heinemann.

Hoff, E. (2003). The specificity of environmental influence: Socioeconomic status affects early vocabulary development via maternal speech. *Child Development, 74,* 1368–1378.

Hoff-Ginsberg, E. (1997). *Language development.* Pacific Grove, CA: Brooks/Cole.

Hutt, S. J., Tyler, S., Hutt, C., & Christopherson, H. (1989). *Play, exploration, and learning: A natural history of the pre-school.* London: Routledge.

Huttenlocher, P. R., & Dabholkar, A. S. (1997). Regional differences in synaptogenesis in human cerebral cortex. *Journal of Comparative Neurology, 387,* 167–178.

Hyde, K. L., Lerch, J., Norton, A., Forgeard, M., Winner, E., Evans, A. C., & Schlaug, G. (2009). Musical training shapes structural brain development. *Journal of Neuroscience, 29,* 3019–3025.

Igoa, C. (1995). *The inner world of the immigrant child.* Mahwah, NJ: Erlbaum.

Igoa, C. (2007). Immigrant children: Art as a second language. In S. Books (Ed.), *Invisible children in the society and its schools* (3rd ed., pp. 117–140). Mahwah, NJ: Erlbaum.

Inhelder, B., & Piaget, J. (1958). *The growth of logical thinking from childhood to adolescence* (A. Parsons & S. Milgram, Trans.). New York, NY: Basic Books.

Janzen, J. (2008). Teaching English language learners in the content areas. *Review of Educational Research, 78,* 1010–1038.

Jitendra, A. K., Star, J. R., Rodrigues, M., Lindell, M., & Someki, F. (2011). Improving students' proportional thinking using schema-based instruction. *Learning and Instruction, 21,* 731–745.

Johnson, D. W., & Johnson, R. T. (2009b). Energizing learning: The instructional power of conflict. *Educational Researcher, 38,* 37–51.

Johnson, W. (2010). Understanding the genetics of intelligence: Can height help? Can corn oil? *Current Perspectives in Psychological Science, 19,* 177–182.

Jusczyk, P. W. (1995). Language acquisition: Speech sounds and phonological development.

In J. L. Miller & P. D. Eimas (Eds.), *Handbook of perception and cognition: Vol. 11. Speech, language, and communication* (pp. 261–301). Orlando, FL: Academic Press.

Kaminski, J. A., & Sloutsky, V. M. (2012). Representation and transfer of abstract mathematical concepts in adolescence and young adulthood. In V. F. Reyna, S. B. Chapman, M. R. Dougherty, & J. Confrey (Eds.), *The adolescent brain: Learning, reasoning, and decision making* (pp. 67–93). Washington, DC: American Psychological Association.

Karmiloff-Smith, A. (1979). Language development after five. In P. Fletcher & M. Garman (Eds.), *Language acquisition: Studies in first language development* (pp. 307–323). Cambridge, England: Cambridge University Press.

Karmiloff-Smith, A. (1993). Innate constraints and developmental change. In P. Bloom (Ed.), *Language acquisition: Core readings* (pp. 563–590). Cambridge, MA: MIT Press.

Kieffer, M. J. (2008). Catching up or falling behind? Initial English proficiency, concentrated poverty, and the reading growth of language minority learners in the United States. *Journal of Educational Psychology, 100,* 851–868.

Kitayama, S., & Cohen, D. (Eds.). (2007). *Handbook of cultural psychology.* New York, NY: Guilford.

Klaczynski, P. A. (2001). Analytic and heuristic processing influences on adolescent reasoning and decision-making. *Child Development, 72,* 844–861.

Klahr, D. (2001). Time matters in cognitive development. In J. L. McClelland & R. S. Siegler (Eds.), *Mechanisms of cognitive development: Behavioral and neural perspectives* (pp. 291–301). Mahwah, NJ: Erlbaum.

Kolb, B., Gibb, R., & Robinson, T. E. (2003). Brain plasticity and behavior. *Current Directions in Psychological Science, 12,* 1–5.

Koob, A. (2009). *The root of thought.* Upper Saddle River, NJ: Pearson.

Krashen, S. D. (1996). *Under attack: The case against bilingual education.* Culver City, CA: Language Education Associates.

Kuhl, P. K. (2004). Early language acquisition: Cracking the speech code. *Nature Reviews Neuroscience, 5,* 831–843.

Kuhl, P. K., Conboy, B. T., Padden, D., Nelson, T., & Pruitt, J. (2005). Early speech perception and later language development: Implications for the "critical period." *Language Learning and Development, 1,* 237–264.

Kuhn, D. (2006). Do cognitive changes accompany developments in the adolescent brain? *Perspectives on Psychological Science, 1,* 59–67.

Kuhn, D., & Franklin, S. (2006). The second decade: What develops (and how)? In W. Damon, R. M. Lerner (Series Eds.), D. Kuhn, & R. Siegler (Vol. Eds.), *Handbook of child psychology: Vol. 2. Cognition, perception, and language* (6th ed., pp. 953–993). New York, NY: Wiley.

Kuhn, D., & Pease, M. (2008). What needs to develop in the development of inquiry skills? *Cognition and Instruction, 26,* 512–599.

Lai, C. S. L., Fisher, S. E., Hurst, J. A., Vargha-Khadem, F., & Monaco, A. P. (2001). A forkhead-domain gene is mutated in a severe speech and language disorder. *Nature, 413*(6855), 519–523.

Lampert, M., Rittenhouse, P., & Crumbaugh, C. (1996). Agreeing to disagree: Developing sociable mathematical discourse. In D. R. Olson & N. Torrance (Eds.), *The handbook of education and human development: New models of learning, teaching, and schooling* (pp. 731–764). Cambridge, MA: Blackwell.

Lautrey, J. (1993). Structure and variability: A plea for a pluralistic approach to cognitive development. In R. Case & W. Edelstein (Eds.), *The new structuralism in cognitive development: Theory and research on individual pathways* (pp. 101–114). Basel, Switzerland: Karger.

Lave, J., & Wenger, E. (1991). *Situated learning: Legitimate peripheral participation.* Cambridge, England: Cambridge University Press.

Lee, C. D. (2005). Intervention research based on current views of cognition and learning. In J. E. King (Ed.), *Black education: A transformative research and action agenda for the new century* (pp. 45–71). Washington, DC: American Educational Research Association.

Lee, C. D. (2010). Soaring above the clouds, delving the ocean's depths: Understanding the ecologies of human learning and the challenge for education science. *Educational Researcher, 39,* 643–655.

Lee, S. (1985). Children's acquisition of conditional logic structure: Teachable? *Contemporary Educational Psychology, 10,* 14–27.

Liben, L. S., & Myers, L. J. (2007). Developmental changes in children's understanding of maps: What, when, and how? In J. M. Plumert & J. P. Spencer (Eds.), *The emerging spatial mind* (pp. 193–218). New York, NY: Oxford University Press.

Lichtman, J. W. (2001). Developmental neurobiology overview: Synapses, circuits, and plasticity. In D. B. Bailey, Jr., J. T. Bruer, F. J. Symons, & J. W. Lichtman (Eds.), *Critical thinking about critical periods* (pp. 27–42). Baltimore, MD: Brookes.

Linn, M. C. (2008). Teaching for conceptual change: Distinguish or extinguish ideas. In S. Vosniadou (Ed.), *International handbook on conceptual change* (pp. 694–722). New York, NY: Routledge.

Linn, M. C., Clement, C., Pulos, S., & Sullivan, P. (1989). Scientific reasoning during adolescence: The influence of instruction in science knowledge and reasoning strategies. *Journal of Research in Science Teaching, 26,* 171–187.

Locke, J. L. (1993). *The child's path to spoken language.* Cambridge, MA: Harvard University Press.

Lorch, R. F., Jr., Lorch, E. P., Calderhead, W. J., Dunlap, E. E., Hodell, E. C., & Freer, B.

D. (2010). Learning the control of variables strategy in higher and lower achieving classrooms: Contributions of explicit instruction and experimentation. *Journal of Educational Psychology, 102,* 90–101.

Lorch, R. F., Lorch, E. P., Freer, B. D., Dunlap, E. E., Hodell, E. C., & Calderhead, W. J. (2014). Using valid and invalid experimental designs to teach the control of variables strategy in higher and lower achieving classrooms. *Journal of Educational Psychology, 106,* 18–35.

Lovell, K. (1979). Intellectual growth and the school curriculum. In F. B. Murray (Ed.), *The impact of Piagetian theory: On education, philosophy, psychiatry, and psychology* (pp. 191–208). Baltimore, MD: University Park Press.

Maratsos, M. (1998). Some problems in grammatical acquisition. In W. Damon (Series Ed.), D. Kuhn, & R. S. Siegler (Vol. Eds.), *Handbook of child psychology: Vol. 2. Cognition, perception, and language* (5th ed., pp. 421–466). New York, NY: Wiley.

Mareschal, D., Johnson, M. H., Sirois, S., Spratling, M. W., Thomas, M. S. C., & Westermann, G. (2007). *Neuroconstructivism: Vol. 1. How the brain constructs cognition.* Oxford, England: Oxford University Press.

Marsh, H. W., Hau, K.-T., & Kong, C.-K. (2002). Multilevel causal ordering of academic self-concept and achievement: Influence of language of instruction (English compared with Chinese) for Hong Kong students. *American Educational Research Journal, 39,* 727–763.

Mayer, R. E. (2004). Should there be a three-strikes rule against pure discovery learning? *American Psychologist, 59,* 14–19.

Maynard, A. E., & Greenfield, P. M. (2003). Implicit cognitive development in cultural tools and children: Lessons from Maya Mexico. *Cognitive Development, 18,* 489–510.

McBrien, J. L. (2005b). Educational needs and barriers for refugee students in the United States: A review of the literature. *Review of Educational Research, 75,* 329–364.

McCarty, T. L., & Watahomigie, L. J. (1998). Language and literacy in American Indian and Alaska Native communities. In B. Pérez (Ed.), *Sociocultural contexts of language and literacy* (pp. 69–98). Mahwah, NJ: Erlbaum.

McClelland, J. L. (2001). Failures to learn and their remediation: A Hebbian account. In J. L. McClelland & R. S. Siegler (Eds.), *Mechanisms of cognitive development: Behavioral and neural perspectives* (pp. 97–121). Mahwah, NJ: Erlbaum.

McClelland, J. L., Fiez, J. A., & McCandliss, B. D. (2002). Teaching the /r/–/l/ discrimination to Japanese adults: Behavioral and neural aspects. *Physiology and Behavior, 77,* 657–662.

McDevitt, T. M., & Ford, M. E. (1987). Processes in young children's communicative functioning and development. In M. E. Ford & D. H. Ford (Eds.), *Humans as self-constructing living systems: Putting the framework to work* (pp. 145–175). Mahwah, NJ: Erlbaum.

McDevitt, T. M., Spivey, N., Sheehan, E. P., Lennon, R., & Story, R. (1990). Children's beliefs about listening: Is it enough to be still and quiet? *Child Development, 61,* 713–721.

McGivern, R. F., Andersen, J., Byrd, D., Mutter, K. L., & Reilly, J. (2002). Cognitive efficiency on a match to sample task decreases at the onset of puberty in children. *Brain and Cognition, 50*(1), 73–89.

McNeil, N. M., & Uttal, D. H. (2009). Rethinking the use of concrete materials in learning: Perspectives from development and education. *Child Development Perspectives, 3,* 137–139.

Mechelli, A., Crinion, J. T., Noppeney, U., O'Doherty, J., Ashburner, J., Frackowiak, R., & Price, C. J. (2004). Structural plasticity in the bilingual brain. *Nature, 431,* 757.

Merzenich, M. M. (2001). Cortical plasticity contributing to child development. In J. L. McClelland & R. S. Siegler (Eds.), *Mechanisms of cognitive development: Behavioral and neural perspectives* (pp. 67–95). Mahwah, NJ: Erlbaum.

Metz, K. E. (1995). Reassessment of developmental constraints on children's science instruction. *Review of Educational Research, 65,* 93–127.

Miller, G. A. (2010). Mistreating psychology in the decades of the brain. *Perspectives on Psychological Science, 5,* 716–743.

Miller, J. G. (1997). A cultural-psychology perspective on intelligence. In R. J. Sternberg & E. L. Grigorenko (Eds.), *Intelligence, heredity, and environment* (pp. 269–302). Cambridge, England: Cambridge University Press.

Moran, S., & John-Steiner, V. (2003). Creativity in the making: Vygotsky's contemporary contribution to the dialectic of development and creativity. In R. K. Sawyer, V. John-Steiner, S. Moran, R. J. Sternberg, D. H. Feldman, J. Nakamura, & M. Csikszentmihalyi (Eds.), *Creativity and development* (pp. 61–90). Oxford, England: Oxford University Press.

Morra, S., Gobbo, C., Marini, Z., & Sheese, R. (2008). *Cognitive development: Neo-Piagetian perspectives.* New York, NY: Erlbaum.

Murphy, P. K., Wilkinson, I. A. G., & Soter, A. O. (2011). Instruction based on discussion. In R. E. Mayer & P. A. Alexander (Eds.), *Handbook of research on learning and instruction* (pp. 382–407). New York, NY: Routledge.

Nelson, C. A., Thomas, K. M., & de Haan, M. (2006). Neural bases of cognitive development. In D. Kuhn, R. Siegler (Vol. Eds.), W. Damon, & R. M. Lerner (Series Eds.), *Handbook of child psychology. Vol. 2: Cognition, perception, and language* (6th ed., pp. 3–57). New York, NY: Wiley.

Nelson, K. (1996). *Language in cognitive development: The emergence of the mediated mind.* Cambridge, England: Cambridge University Press.

Nettles, S. M., Caughy, M. O., & O'Campo, P. J. (2008). School adjustment in the early grades: Toward an integrated model of neighborhood, parental, and child processes. *Review of Educational Research, 78,* 3–32.

Newport, E. L. (1990). Maturational constraints on language learning. *Cognitive Science, 14,* 11–28.

Nieto, S. (1995). *Affirming diversity* (2nd ed.). White Plains, NY: Longman.

Nippold, M. A. (1988). The literate lexicon. In M. A. Nippold (Ed.), *Later language development: Ages nine through nineteen* (pp. 29–48). Boston, MA: Little, Brown.

Norenzayan, A., Choi, I., & Peng, K. (2007). Perception and cognition. In S. Kitayama & D. Cohen (Eds.), *Handbook of cultural psychology* (pp. 569–594). New York, NY: Guilford.

Nuemi, J.-W. (2008). Self and socialization: How do young people navigate through adolescence? In H. W. Marsh, R. G. Craven, & D. M. McInerney (Eds.), *Self-processes, learning, and enabling human potential* (pp. 305–327). Charlotte, NC: Information Age.

O'Grady, W. (1997). *Syntactic development.* Chicago, IL: University of Chicago.

Ornstein, R. (1997). *The right mind: Making sense of the hemispheres.* San Diego, CA: Harcourt Brace.

Ortony, A., Turner, T. J., & Larson-Shapiro, N. (1985). Cultural and instructional influences on figurative comprehension by inner city children. *Research in the Teaching of English, 19*(1), 25–36.

Owens, R. E., Jr. (2008). *Language development* (7th ed.). Boston, MA: Allyn & Bacon.

Padilla, A. M. (2006). Second language learning: Issues in research and teaching. In P. A. Alexander & P. H. Winne (Eds.), *Handbook of educational psychology* (2nd ed., pp. 571–591). Mahwah, NJ: Erlbaum.

Paus, T., Zijdenbos, A., Worsley, K., Collins, D. L., Blumenthal, J., Giedd, J. N., . . . Evans, A. C. (1999). Structural maturation of neural pathways in children and adolescents: In vivo study. *Science, 283,* 1908–1911.

Pellegrini, A. D. (2009). Research and policy on children's play. *Child Development Perspectives, 3,* 131–136.

Pelucchi, B., Hay, J. F., & Saffran, J. R. (2009). Statistical learning in a natural language by 8-month-old infants. *Child Development, 80,* 674–685.

Pérez, B. (1998). *Sociocultural contexts of language and literacy.* Mahwah, NJ: Erlbaum.

Perkins, D. N. (1992). *Smart schools: From training memories to educating minds.* New York, NY: Free Press/Macmillan.

Piaget, J. (1929). *The child's conception of the world.* New York, NY: Harcourt, Brace.

Piaget, J. (1952a). *The child's conception of number* (C. Gattegno & F. M. Hodgson, Trans.). London: Routledge & Kegan Paul.

Piaget, J. (1952b). *The origins of intelligence in children* (M. Cook, Trans.). New York, NY: Norton.

Piaget, J. (1959). *The language and thought of the child* (3rd ed.; M. Gabain, Trans.). London: Routledge & Kegan Paul.

Piaget, J. (1970). Piaget's theory. In P. H. Mussen (Ed.), *Carmichael's manual of psychology* (pp. 703–732). New York, NY: Wiley.

Piaget, J. (1971). The theory of stages in cognitive development. In D. R. Green (Ed.), *Measurement and Piaget* (pp. 1–11). New York, NY: McGraw-Hill.

Piaget, J. (1980). *Adaptation and intelligence: Organic selection and phenocopy* (S. Eames, Trans.). Chicago, IL: University of Chicago Press.

Pinker, S. (2007). *The stuff of thought: Language as a window into human nature.* New York, NY: Viking.

Premack, D. (2004). Is language the key to human intelligence? *Science, 303,* 318–320.

Price-Williams, D. R., Gordon, W., & Ramirez, M. (1969). Skill and conservation: A study of pottery-making children. *Developmental Psychology, 1,* 769.

Pulos, S., & Linn, M. C. (1981). Generality of the controlling variables scheme in early adolescence. *Journal of Early Adolescence, 1,* 26–37.

Radziszewska, B., & Rogoff, B. (1988). Influence of adult and peer collaborators on children's planning skills. *Developmental Psychology, 24,* 840–848.

Raikes, H., Pan, B. A., Luze, G., Tamis-LeMonda, C. S., Brooks-Gunn, J., Constantine, J., . . . Rodriguez, E. T. (2006). Mother-child bookreading in low-income families: Correlates and outcomes during the first three years of life. *Child Development, 77,* 924–953.

Rayner, K., Foorman, B. R., Perfetti, C. A., Pesetsky, D., & Seidenberg, M. S. (2001). How psychological science informs the teaching of reading. *Psychological Science in the Public Interest, 2,* 31–74.

Reich, P. A. (1986). *Language development.* Upper Saddle River, NJ: Prentice Hall.

Reyna, V. F., Chapman, S. B., Dougherty, M. R., & Confrey, J. (Eds.) (2012). *The adolescent brain: Learning, reasoning, and decision making.* Washington, DC: American Psychological Association.

Risley, T. R., & Hart, B. (2006). Promoting early language development. In N. F. Watt, C. Ayoub, R. H. Bradley, J. E. Puma, & W. A. LeBoeuf (Eds.), *The crisis in young mental health: Critical issues and effective programs: Vol. 4. Early intervention programs and policies* (pp. 83–88). Westport, CT: Praeger.

Rogoff, B. (1990). *Apprenticeship in thinking: Cognitive development in social context.* New York, NY: Oxford University Press.

Rogoff, B. (1991). Social interaction as apprenticeship in thinking: Guidance and participation in spatial planning. In L. B. Resnick, J. M. Levine, & S. D. Teasley (Eds.), *Perspectives on socially shared cognition* (pp. 349–364). Washington, DC: American Psychological Association.

Rogoff, B. (2003). *The cultural nature of human development.* Oxford, England: Oxford University Press.

Rogoff, B., Moore, L., Najafi, B., Dexter, A., Correa-Chávez, M., & Solís, J. (2007). Children's development of cultural repertoires through participation in everyday routines and practices. In J. E. Grusec & P. D. Hastings (Eds.), *Handbook of socialization: Theory and research* (pp. 490–515). New York, NY: Guilford.

Rosser, R. (1994). *Cognitive development: Psychological and biological perspectives.* Boston, MA: Allyn & Bacon.

Ruffman, T., Perner, J., Olson, D. R., & Doherty, M. (1993). Reflecting on scientific thinking: Children's understanding of the hypothesis-evidence relation. *Child Development, 64,* 1617–1636.

Saffran, J. R. (2003). Statistical language learning: Mechanisms and constraints. *Current Directions in Psychological Science, 12,* 110–114.

Sarama, J., & Clements, D. H. (2009). "Concrete" computer manipulatives in mathematics education. *Child Development Perspectives, 3,* 145–150.

Scardamalia, M., & Bereiter, C. (1985). Fostering the development of self-regulation in children's knowledge processing. In S. F. Chipman, J. W. Segal, & R. Glaser (Eds.), *Thinking and learning skills: Vol. 2. Research and open questions* (pp. 65–80). Mahwah, NJ: Erlbaum.

Schauble, L. (1990). Belief revision in children: The role of prior knowledge and strategies for generating evidence. *Journal of Experimental Child Psychology, 49,* 31–57.

Schimmoeller, M. A. (1998, April). *Influence of private speech on the writing behaviors of young children: Four case studies.* Paper presented at the annual meeting of the American Educational Research Association, San Diego, CA.

Schliemann, A. D., & Carraher, D. W. (1993). Proportional reasoning in and out of school. In P. Light & G. Butterworth (Eds.), *Context and cognition: Ways of learning and knowing* (pp. 47–73). Mahwah, NJ: Erlbaum.

Shen, H., Sabaliauskas, N., Sherpa, A., Fenton, A. A., Stelzer, A., Aoki, C., & Smith, S. S. (2010). A critical role for $\alpha 4\beta\delta$ GABA$_A$ receptors in shaping learning deficits at puberty in mice. *Science, 327*(5972), 1515–1518.

Sherman, J., & Bisanz, J. (2009). Equivalence in symbolic and nonsymbolic contexts: Benefits of solving problems with manipulatives. *Journal of Educational Psychology, 101,* 88–100.

Shweder, R. A., Goodnow, J., Hatano, G., Levine, R. A., Marcus, H., & Miller, P. (1998). The cultural psychology of development: One mind, many mentalities. In W. Damon (Editor-in-Chief) & R. M. Lerner (Vol. Ed.), *Handbook of child psychology: Vol. 1. Theoretical models of human development* (5th ed., pp. 865–937). New York, NY: Wiley.

Siegel, D. J. (2012). *The developing mind: How relationships and the brain interact to shape who we are* (2nd ed.). New York, NY: Guilford.

Siegler, R. S., & Chen, Z. (2008). Differentiation and integration: Guiding principles for analyzing cognitive change. *Developmental Science, 11,* 433–448.

Siegler, R. S., & Lin, X. (2010). Self-explanations promote children's learning. In H. S. Waters & W. Schneider (Eds.), *Metacognition, strategy use, and instruction* (pp. 85–112.). New York, NY: Guilford.

Slavin, R. E., & Cheung, A. (2005). A synthesis of research on language of reading instruction for English language learners. *Review of Educational Research, 75,* 247–284.

Smith, C. L. (2007). Bootstrapping processes in the development of students' commonsense matter theories: Using analogical mappings, thought experiments, and learning to measure to promote conceptual restructuring. *Cognition and Instruction, 25,* 337–398.

Smith, H. L. (1998). Literacy and instruction in African American communities: Shall we overcome? In B. Pérez (Ed.), *Sociocultural contexts of language and literacy* (pp. 189–222). Mahwah, NJ: Erlbaum.

Smitherman, G. (2007). The power of the rap: The Black idiom and the new Black poetry. In H. S. Alim & J. Baugh (Eds.), *Talkin Black talk: Language, education, and social change* (pp. 77–91). New York, NY: Teachers College Press.

Solórzano, R. W. (2008). High stakes testing: Issues, implications, and remedies for English language learners. *Educational Researcher, 78,* 260–329.

Spalding, K. L., Bergmann, O., Alkass, K., Bernard, S., Salehpour, M., Huttner, H. B., . . . Frisèn, J. (2013). Dynamics of hippocampal neurogenesis in adult humans. *Cell, 153,* 1219–1227.

Spelke, E. S. (2003). What makes humans smart? In D. Gentner & S. Goldin-Meadow (Eds.), *Advances in the investigation of language and thought* (pp. 277–311). Cambridge, MA: MIT Press.

Spencer, J. P., Blumberg, M. S., McMurray, B., Robinson, S. R., Samuelson, L. K., & Tomblin, J. B. (2009). Short arms and talking eggs: Why we should no longer abide the nativist–empiricist debate. *Child Development Perspectives, 3,* 79–87.

Spinath, F. M., Price, T. S., Dale, P. S., & Plomin, R. (2004). The genetic and environmental origins of language disability and ability. *Child Development, 75,* 445–454.

Stanovich, K. E. (2000). *Progress in understanding reading: Scientific foundations and new frontiers.* New York, NY: Guilford.

Steinberg, L. (2009). Should the science of adolescent brain development inform public policy? *American Psychologist, 64,* 739–750.

Stevens, G. (2004). Using census data to test critical-period hypothesis for second-language acquisition. *Psychological Science, 15,* 215–216.

Strozer, J. R. (1994). *Language acquisition after puberty.* Washington, DC: Georgetown University Press.

Tamburrini, J. (1982). Some educational implications of Piaget's theory. In S. Modgil & C. Modgil (Eds.), *Jean Piaget: Consensus and controversy* (pp. 309–325). New York, NY: Praeger.

Tanner, J. M., & Inhelder, B. (Eds.) (1960). *Discussions of child development: A consideration* of the biological, psychological, and cultural approaches to the understanding of human development and behavior: Vol. 4. The proceedings of the fourth meeting of the World Health Organization Study Group on the Psychobiological Development of the Child, Geneva, 1956. New York, NY: International Universities Press.

Tatum, B. D. (1997). "Why are all the Black kids sitting together in the cafeteria?" and other conversations about race. New York, NY: Basic Books.

Thelen, E., & Smith, L. B. (1998). Dynamic systems theories. In W. Damon (Series Ed.) & R. M. Lerner (Vol. Ed.), Handbook of child psychology: Vol. 1. Theoretical models of human development (5th ed., pp. 563–634). New York, NY: Wiley.

Thomas, M. S. C., & Johnson, M. H. (2008). New advances in understanding sensitive periods in brain development. Current Directions in Psychological Science, 17, 1–5.

Thompson, R. A., & Nelson, C. A. (2001). Developmental science and the media: Early brain development. American Psychologist, 56, 5–15.

Tong, F., Lara-Alecio, R., Irby, B., Mathes, P., & Kwok, O.-M. (2008). Accelerating early academic oral English development in transitional bilingual and structured English immersion programs. American Educational Research Journal, 45, 1011–1044.

Torres-Guzmán, M. E. (1998). Language, culture, and literacy in Puerto Rican communities. In B. Pérez (Ed.), Sociocultural contexts of language and literacy (pp. 99–122). Mahwah, NJ: Erlbaum.

Tourniaire, F., & Pulos, S. (1985). Proportional reasoning: A review of the literature. Educational Studies in Mathematics, 16, 181–204.

Trout, J. D. (2003). Biological specializations for speech: What can the animals tell us? Current Directions in Psychological Science, 12, 155–159.

Tse, L. (2001). Why don't they learn English: Separating fact from fallacy in the U.S. language debate. New York, NY: Teachers College Press.

Tyler, K. M., Uqdah, A. L., Dillihunt, M. L., Beatty-Hazelbaker, R., Connor, T., Gadson, N., . . . Stevens, R. (2008). Cultural discontinuity: Toward a quantitative investigation of a major hypothesis in education. Educational Researcher, 37, 280–297.

U.S. Department of Education. (1993). National excellence: A case for developing America's talent. Washington, DC: Office of Educational Research and Improvement.

Valdés, G., Bunch, G., Snow, C., & Lee, C. (with Matos, L.). (2005). Enhancing the development of students' language(s). In L. Darling-Hammond & J. Bransford (Eds.), Preparing teachers for a changing world: What teachers should learn and be able to do (pp. 126–168). San Francisco, CA: Jossey-Bass/Wiley.

van de Pol, J., Volman, M., & Beishuizen, J. (2010). Scaffolding in teacher–student interaction: A decade of research. Educational Psychology Review, 22, 271–296.

Van Dooren, W., De Bock, D., Hessels, A., Janssens, D., & Verschaffel, L. (2005). Not everything is proportional: Effects of age and problem type on propensities for overgeneralization. Cognition and Instruction, 23, 57–86.

van Merriënboer, J. J. G., & Sweller, J. (2005). Cognitive load theory and complex learning: Recent developments and future directions. Educational Psychology Review, 17, 147–177.

Varma, S., McCandliss, B. D., & Schwartz, D. L. (2008). Scientific and pragmatic challenges for bridging education and neuroscience. Educational Researcher, 37(3), 140–152.

Vygotsky, L. S. (1978). Mind in society: The development of higher psychological processes. Cambridge, MA: Harvard University Press.

Vygotsky, L. S. (1986). Thought and language (rev. ed; A. Kozulin, Ed. and Trans.). Cambridge, MA: MIT Press. (Original work published 1934)

Vygotsky, L. S. (1987). The collected works of L. S. Vygotsky (Vol. 3; R. W. Rieber & A. S. Carton, Eds.). New York, NY: Plenum Press.

Vygotsky, L. S. (1997). Educational psychology (R. Silverman, Trans.). Boca Raton, FL: St. Lucie Press.

Walker, E. F. (2002). Adolescent neurodevelopment and psychopathology. Current Directions in Psychological Science, 11, 24–28.

Walshaw, M., & Anthony, G. (2008). The teacher's role in classroom discourse: A review of recent research into mathematics classrooms. Review of Educational Research, 78, 516–551.

Winsler, A., Díaz, R. M., Espinosa, L., & Rodriguez, J. L. (1999). When learning a second language does not mean losing the first: Bilingual language development in low-income, Spanish-speaking children attending bilingual preschool. Child Development, 70, 349–362.

Winsler, A., & Naglieri, J. (2003). Overt and covert verbal problem-solving strategies: Developmental trends in use, awareness, and relations with task performance in children aged 5 to 17. Child Development, 74, 659–678.

Wong, B. Y. L., Hoskyn, M., Jai, D., Ellis, P., & Watson, K. (2008). The comparative efficacy of two approaches to teaching sixth graders opinion essay writing. Contemporary Educational Psychology, 33, 757–784.

Wood, D., Bruner, J. S., & Ross, G. (1976). The role of tutoring in problem-solving. Journal of Child Psychology and Psychiatry, 17, 89–100.

Wright, S. C., Taylor, D. M., & Macarthur, J. (2000). Subtractive bilingualism and the survival of the Inuit language: Heritage-versus second-language education. Journal of Educational Psychology, 92, 63–84.

Yaden, D. B., Jr., & Templeton, S. (Eds.). (1986). Metalinguistic awareness and beginning literacy: Conceptualizing what it means to read and write. Portsmouth, NH: Heinemann.

CHAPTER 3

Adalbjarnardottir, S., & Selman, R. L. (1997). "I feel I have received a new vision": An analysis of teachers' professional development as they work with students on interpersonal issues. Teaching and Teacher Education, 13, 409–428.

Ainsworth, M. D. S., Blehar, M. C., Waters, E., & Wall, S. (1978). Patterns of attachment. Hillsdale, NJ: Erlbaum.

Albert, D., Chein, J., & Steinberg, L. (2013). The teenage brain: Peer influences on adolescent decision making. Current Directions in Psychological Science, 22, 114–120.

Alemán, A. M. M., & Vartman, K. L. (2009). Online social networking on campus: Understanding what matters in student culture. New York, NY: Routledge.

Alessandri, S. M., & Lewis, M. (1993). Parental evaluation and its relation to shame and pride in young children. Sex Roles, 29, 335–343.

Allen, J. P., & Antonishak, J. (2008). Adolescent peer influences: Beyond the dark side. In M. J. Prinstein & K. A. Dodge (Eds.), Understanding peer influence in children and adolescents (pp. 141–160). New York, NY: Guilford.

Allen, J. P., Porter, M., McFarland, C., McElhaney, K. B., & Marsh, P. (2007). The relation of attachment security to adolescents' paternal and peer relationships, depression, and externalizing behavior. Child Development, 78, 1222–1239.

Allen, L., & Aber, J. L. (2006). The development of ethnic identity during adolescence. Developmental Psychology, 42, 1–10.

Altermatt, E. R. (2012). Children's achievement-related discourse with peers: Uncovering the processes of peer influence. In A. M. Ryan & G. W. Ladd (Eds.), Peer relationships and adjustment at school (pp. 109–134). Charlotte, NC: Information Age.

Altschul, I., Oyserman, D., & Bybee, D. (2006). Racial-ethnic identity in mid-adolescence: Content and change as predictors of academic achievement. Child Development, 77, 1155–1169.

Anderman, L. H., Freeman, T. M., & Mueller, C. E. (2007). The "social" side of social context: Interpersonal affiliative dimensions of students' experiences and academic dishonesty. In E. M. Anderman & T. B. Murdock (Eds.), The psychology of academic cheating (pp. 203–228). San Diego, CA: Elsevier.

Anderson, C. A., Berkowitz, L., Donnerstein, E., Huesmann, L. R., Johnson, J. D., Linz, D., . . . Wartella, E. (2003). The influence of media violence on youth. Psychological Science in the Public Interest, 4, 81–110.

Ansary, N. S., Elias, M. J., Greene, M. B., & Green, S. (2015). Guidance for schools selecting antibullying approaches: Translating evidence-based strategies to contemporary implementation realities. Educational Researcher, 44, 27–36.

Arens, A. K., Yeung, A. S., Craven, R. G., & Hasselhorn, M. (2011). The twofold multidimensionality of academic self-concept: Domain specificity and separation between competence and affect components. *Journal of Educational Psychology, 103,* 970–981.

Asher, S. R., & McDonald, K. A. (2009). The behavioral basis of acceptance, rejection, and perceived popularity. In K. H. Rubin, W. M. Bukowski, & B. Laursen (Eds.), *Handbook of peer interactions, relationships, and groups* (pp. 232–248). New York, NY: Guilford.

Asher, S. R., & Renshaw, P. D. (1981). Children without friends: Social knowledge and social skill training. In S. R. Asher & J. M. Gottman (Eds.), *The development of children's friendships* (pp. 273–296). New York, NY: Cambridge University Press.

Aunola, K., & Nurmi, J.-E. (2005). The role of parenting style in children's problem behavior. *Child Development, 76,* 1144–1159.

Bakermans-Kranenburg, M. J., van IJzendoorn, M. H., Pijlman, F. T. A., Mesman, J., & Juffer, F. (2008). Experimental evidence for differential susceptibility: Dopamine D4 receptor polymorphism (DRD4 VNTR) moderates intervention effects on toddlers' externalizing behavior in a randomized control trial. *Developmental Psychology, 44,* 293–300.

Bandura, A. (2008). Toward an agentic theory of the self. In H. W. Marsh, R. G. Craven, & D. M. McInerney (Eds.), *Self-processes, learning, and enabling human potential* (pp. 15–49). Charlotte, NC: Information Age.

Banks, J. A., & Banks, C. A. M. (Eds.). (1995). *Handbook of research on multicultural education.* New York, NY: Macmillan.

Barber, B. K., Stolz, H. E., & Olsen, J. A. (2005). Parental support, psychological control, and behavioral control: Assessing relevance across time, culture, and method. *Monographs of the Society for Research in Child Development, 70*(4; Serial No. 282).

Barron, B. (2006). Interest and self-sustained learning as catalysts of development: A learning ecology perspective. *Human Development, 49,* 193–224.

Basinger, K. S., Gibbs, J. C., & Fuller, D. (1995). Context and the measurement of moral judgment. *International Journal of Behavioral Development, 18,* 537–556.

Bates, J. E., & Pettit, G. S. (2007). Temperament, parenting, and socialization. In J. E. Grusec & P. D. Hastings (Eds.), *Handbook of socialization: Theory and research* (pp. 153–177). New York, NY: Guilford.

Batson, C. D. (1991). *The altruism question: Toward a social-psychological answer.* Hillsdale, NJ: Erlbaum.

Batson, C. D., & Thompson, E. R. (2001). Why don't moral people act morally? Motivational considerations. *Current Directions in Psychological Science, 10,* 54–57.

Baumeister, R. F., Campbell, J. D., Krueger, J. I., & Vohs, K. D. (2003). Does high self-esteem cause better performance, interpersonal success, happiness, or healthier lifestyles? *Psychological Science in the Public Interest, 4,* 1–44.

Baumeister, R. F., Smart, L., & Boden, J. M. (1996). Relation of threatened egotism to violence and aggression: The dark side of high self-esteem. *Psychological Review, 103,* 5–33.

Baumrind, D. (1989). Rearing competent children. In W. Damon (Ed.), *Child development today and tomorrow* (pp. 349–378). San Francisco, CA: Jossey-Bass.

Baumrind, D. (1991). Parenting styles and adolescent development. In R. Lerner, A. C. Petersen, & J. Brooks-Gunn (Eds.), *The encyclopedia of adolescence* (pp. 746–758). New York, NY: Garland Press.

Bellanca, J. A., & Stirling, T. (2011). *Classrooms without borders: Using Internet projects to teach communication and collaboration.* New York, NY: Teachers College Press.

Bellmore, A. (2011). Peer rejection and unpopularity: Associations with GPAs across the transition to middle school. *Journal of Educational Psychology, 103,* 282–295.

Belsky, J., & Pluess, M. (2009). The nature (and nurture?) of plasticity in early human development. *Perspectives on Psychological Science, 4,* 345–351.

Benenson, J. F., Maiese, R., Dolenszky, E., Dolensky, N., Sinclair, N., & Simpson, A. (2002). Group size regulates self-assertive versus self-deprecating responses to interpersonal competition. *Child Development, 73,* 1818–1829.

Bergin, D. A., & Cooks, H. C. (2008). High school students of color talk about accusations of "acting White." In J. U. Ogbu (Ed.), *Minority status, oppositional culture, and schooling* (pp. 145–166). New York, NY: Routledge.

Berndt, T. J. (1992). Friendship and friends' influence in adolescence. *Current Directions in Psychological Science, 1,* 156–159.

Bierman, K. L., Miller, C. L., & Stabb, S. D. (1987). Improving the social behavior and peer acceptance of rejected boys: Effect of social skill training with instructions and prohibitions. *Journal of Consulting and Clinical Psychology, 55,* 194–200.

Bierman, K. L., & Powers, C. J. (2009). Social skills training to improve peer relations. In K. H. Rubin, W. M. Bukowski, & B. Laursen (Eds.), *Handbook of peer interactions, relationships, and groups* (pp. 603–621). New York, NY: Guilford.

Bjorklund, D. F., & Green, B. L. (1992). The adaptive nature of cognitive immaturity. *American Psychologist, 47,* 46–54.

Blanton, H., & Burkley, M. (2008). Deviance regulation theory: Applications to adolescent social influence. In M. J. Prinstein & K. A. Dodge (Eds.), *Understanding peer influence in children and adolescents* (pp. 94–121). New York, NY: Guilford.

Blasi, A. (1980). Bridging moral cognition and moral action: A critical review of the literature. *Psychological Bulletin, 88,* 593–637.

Blasi, A. (1995). Moral understanding and the moral personality: The process of moral integration. In W. M. Kurtines & J. L. Gewirtz (Eds.), *Moral development: An introduction* (pp. 229–253). Boston, MA: Allyn & Bacon.

Bong, M., & Skaalvik, E. M. (2003). Academic self-concept and self-efficacy: How different are they really? *Educational Psychology Review, 15,* 1–40.

Boom, J., Brugman, D., & van der Heijden, P. G. M. (2001). Hierarchical structure of moral stages assessed by a sorting task. *Child Development, 72,* 535–548.

Bosacki, S. L. (2000). Theory of mind and self-concept in preadolescents: Links with gender and language. *Journal of Educational Psychology, 92,* 709–717.

Bouchey, H. A., & Harter, S. (2005). Reflected appraisals, academic self-perceptions, and math/science performance during early adolescence. *Journal of Educational Psychology, 97,* 673–686.

Bracken, B. (2009). Positive self-concepts. In R. Gilman, E. S. Huebner, & M. J. Furlong (Eds.), *Handbook of positive psychology in schools* (pp. 89–106). New York, NY: Routledge.

Bradley, R. H. (2010). The HOME environment. In M. H. Bornstein (Ed.), *Handbook of cultural developmental science* (pp. 505–530). New York, NY: Psychology Press.

Bradshaw, C. P., Waasdorp, T. E., & O'Brennan, L. M. (2013). A latent class approach to examining forms of peer victimization. *Journal of Educational Psychology, 105,* 839–849.

Brendgen, M., Boivin, M., Vitaro, F., Bukowski, W. M., Dionne, G., Tremblay, R. E., & Pérusse, D. (2008). Linkages between children's and their friends' social and physical aggression: Evidence for a gene-environment interaction? *Child Development, 79,* 13–29.

Brody, G. H., & Shaffer, D. R. (1982). Contributions of parents and peers to children's moral socialization. *Developmental Review, 2,* 31–75.

Brophy, J., Alleman, J., & Knighton, B. (2009). *Inside the social studies classroom.* New York, NY: Routledge.

Brown, B. B. (1990). Peer groups. In S. Feldman & G. Elliott (Eds.), *At the threshold: The developing adolescent* (pp. 171–196). Cambridge, MA: Harvard University Press.

Brown, B. B. (1999). "You're going out with *who?*" Peer group influences on adolescent romantic relationships. In W. Furman, B. B. Brown, & C. Feiring (Eds.), *The development of romantic relationships in adolescence* (pp. 291–329). Cambridge, England: Cambridge University Press.

Brown, B. B. (2011). Popularity in peer group perspective: The role of status in adolescent peer systems. In A. H. N. Cillessen, D. Schwartz, & L. Mayeux (Eds.), *Popularity in the peer system* (pp. 165–192). New York, NY: Guilford.

Brown, B. B., Bakken, J. P., Ameringer, S. W., & Mahon, S. D. (2008). A comprehensive conceptualization of the peer influence process in adolescence. In M. J. Prinstein & K. A. Dodge (Eds.), *Understanding peer influence in children and adolescents* (pp. 17–44). New York, NY: Guilford.

Brown, B. B., Eicher, S. A., & Petrie, S. (1986). The importance of peer group ("crowd") affiliation in adolescence. *Journal of Adolescence, 9,* 73–96.

Brown, L. M., Tappan, M. B., & Gilligan, C. (1995). Listening to different voices. In W. M. Kurtines & J. L. Gewirtz (Eds.), *Moral development: An introduction* (pp. 311–335). Boston, MA: Allyn & Bacon.

Brown, R. P., Osterman, L. L., & Barnes, C. D. (2009). School violence and the culture of honor. *Psychological Science, 20,* 1400–1405.

Brummelman, E., Thomaes, S., Orobio de Castro, B., Overbeek, G., & Bushman, B. J. (2014). "That's not just beautiful—That's incredibly beautiful!": The adverse impact of inflated praise on children with low self-esteem. *Psychological Science, 25,* 728–735.

Bryan, T. (1991). Social problems and learning disabilities. In B. Y. L. Wong (Ed.), *Learning about learning disabilities* (pp. 195–229). San Diego, CA: Academic Press.

Bukowski, W. M., Brendgen, M., & Vitaro, F. (2007). Peers and socialization: Effects on externalizing and internalizing problems. In J. E. Grusec & P. D. Hastings (Eds.), *Handbook of socialization: Theory and research* (pp. 355–381). New York, NY: Guilford.

Bukowski, W. M., Motzoi, C., & Meyer, F. (2009). Friendship as process, function, and outcome. In K. H. Rubin, W. M. Bukowski, & B. Laursen (Eds.), *Handbook of peer interactions, relationships, and groups* (pp. 217–231). New York, NY: Guilford.

Bukowski, W. M., Velasquez, A. M., & Brendgen, M. (2008). Variation in patterns of peer influence: Considerations of self and other. In M. J. Prinstein & K. A. Dodge (Eds.), *Understanding peer influence in children and adolescents* (pp. 125–140). New York, NY: Guilford.

Burgess, K. B., Wojslawowicz, J. C., Rubin, K. H., Rose-Krasnor, L., & Booth-LaForce, C. (2006). Social information processing and coping strategies of shy/withdrawn and aggressive children: Does friendship matter? *Child Development, 77,* 371–383.

Buston, K., & Hart, G. (2001). Heterosexism and homophobia in Scottish school education: Exploring the nature of the problem. *Journal of Adolescence, 24*(1), 95–110.

Butler, R. (2008). Evaluating competence and maintaining self-worth between early and middle childhood: Blissful ignorance or the construction of knowledge and strategies in context? In H. W. Marsh, R. G. Craven, & D. M. McInerney (Eds.), *Self-processes, learning, and enabling human potential* (pp. 193–222). Charlotte, NC: Information Age.

Byrne, B. M. (2002). Validating the measurement and structure of self-concept: Snapshots of past, present, and future research. *American Psychologist, 57,* 897–909.

Caldwell, M. S., Rudolph, K. D., Troop-Gordon, W., & Kim, D. (2004). Reciprocal influences among relational self-views, social disengagement, and peer stress during early adolescence. *Child Development, 75,* 1140–1154.

Caprara, G. V., Barbaranelli, C., Pastorelli, C., Bandura, A., & Zimbardo, P. G. (2000). Prosocial foundations of children's academic achievement. *Psychological Science, 11,* 302–306.

Caprara, G. V., Dodge, K. A., Pastorelli, C., & Zelli, A. (2007). How marginal deviations sometimes grow into serious aggression. *Child Development Perspectives, 1,* 33–39.

Card, N. A., Stucky, B. D., Sawalani, G. M., & Little T. D. (2008). Direct and indirect aggression during childhood and adolescence: A meta-analytic review of gender differences, intercorrelations, and relations to maladjustment. *Child Development, 79,* 1185–1229.

Carrasco, R. L. (1981). Expanded awareness of student performance: A case study in applied ethnographic monitoring in a bilingual classroom. In H. T. Trueba, G. P. Guthrie, & K. H. Au (Eds.), *Culture and the bilingual classroom: Studies in classroom ethnography* (pp. 153–177). Rowley, MA: Newbury House.

Carter, K., & Doyle, W. (2006). Classroom management in early childhood and elementary classrooms. In C. M. Evertson & C. S. Weinstein (Eds.), *Handbook of classroom management: Research, practice, and contemporary issues* (pp. 373–406). Mahwah, NJ: Erlbaum.

Casey, B. J., & Caudle, K. (2013). The teenage brain: Self control. *Current Directions in Psychological Science, 22,* 82–87.

Caspi, A. (1998). Personality development across the life course. In W. Damon (Series Ed.) & N. Eisenberg (Vol. Ed.), *Handbook of child psychology: Vol. 3. Social, emotional, and personality development* (5th ed., pp. 311–388). New York, NY: Wiley.

Certo, J. (2011). Social skills and leadership abilities among children in small group literature discussions. *Journal of Research in Childhood Education, 25*(1), 62–81.

Certo, J. L., Cauley, K. M., & Chafin, C. (2003). Students' perspectives on their high school experience. *Adolescence, 38,* 705–724.

Chang, L. (2003) Variable effects of children's aggression, social withdrawal, and prosocial leadership as functions of teacher beliefs and behaviors. *Child Development, 74,* 535–548.

Chang, L., Liu, H., Wen, Z., Fung, K. Y., Wang, Y., & Xu, Y. (2004). Mediating teacher liking and moderating authoritative teaching on Chinese adolescents' perceptions of antisocial and prosocial behaviors. *Journal of Educational Psychology, 96,* 369–380.

Chang, M.-L., & Davis, H. A. (2009). Understanding the role of teacher appraisals in shaping the dynamics of their relationships with students: Deconstructing teachers' judgments of disruptive behavior/students. In P. Schutz & M. Zembylas (Eds.), *Advances in teacher emotion research: The impact of teachers' lives* (pp. 95–125). New York, NY: Springer.

Chapman, J. W., Tunmer, W. E., & Prochnow, J. E. (2000). Early reading-related skills and performance, reading self-concept, and the development of academic self-concept: A longitudinal study. *Journal of Educational Psychology, 92,* 703–708.

Chen, W.-B., & Gregory, A. (2008, March). *Parental involvement in schooling: What types work for low-achieving adolescents and what does this mean for schools?* Paper presented at the annual meeting of the American Educational Research Association, New York, NY.

Chen, X., Chung, J., & Hsiao, C. (2009). Peer interactions and relationships from a cross-cultural perspective. In K. H. Rubin, W. M. Bukowski, & B. Laursen (Eds.), *Handbook of peer interactions, relationships, and groups* (pp. 432–451). New York, NY: Guilford.

Chen, X., & Wang, L. (2010). China. In M. H. Bornstein (Ed.), *Handbook of cultural developmental science* (pp. 429–444). New York, NY: Psychology Press.

Chernyak, N., & Kushnir, T. (2013). Giving preschoolers choice increases sharing behavior. *Psychological Science, 24,* 1971–1979.

Chiu, M.-S. (2012). The internal/external frame of reference model, big-fish-little-pond effect, and combined model for mathematics and science. *Journal of Educational Psychology, 104,* 87–107.

Christenson, S. L. (2004). Families with aggressive children and adolescents. In J. C. Conoley & A. P. Goldstein (Eds.), *School violence intervention* (2nd ed., pp. 359–399). New York, NY: Guilford.

Cillessen, A. H. N., & Rose, A. J. (2005). Understanding popularity in the peer system. *Current Directions in Psychological Science, 14,* 102–105.

Cillessen, A. H. N., Schwartz, D., & Mayeux, L. (Eds.) (2011). *Popularity in the peer system.* New York, NY: Guilford.

Cillessen, A. H. N., & van den Berg, Y. H. M. (2012). Popularity and school adjustment. In A. M. Ryan & G. W. Ladd (Eds.), *Peer relationships and adjustment at school* (pp. 135–164). Charlotte, NC: Information Age.

Cohen, G. L., & Garcia, J. (2008). Identity, belonging, and achievement: A model, interventions, implications. *Current Directions in Psychological Science, 17,* 365–369.

Coie, J. D., & Cillessen, A. H. N. (1993). Peer rejection: Origins and effects on children's development. *Current Directions in Psychological Science, 2,* 89–92.

Coie, J. D., & Dodge, K. A. (1998). Aggression and antisocial behavior. In W. Damon (Series Ed.) & N. Eisenberg (Vol. Ed.), *Handbook of child psychology: Vol. 3. Social, emotional, and personality development* (5th ed., pp. 779–862). New York, NY: Wiley.

Colby, A., & Kohlberg, L. (1984). Invariant sequence and internal consistency in moral judgment stages. In W. M. Kurtines & J. L. Gewirtz (Eds.), *Morality, moral behavior, and moral development* (pp. 41–51). New York, NY: Wiley.

Colby, A., Kohlberg, L., Gibbs, J., & Lieberman, M. (1983). A longitudinal study of moral judgment. *Monographs of the Society for Research in Child Development, 48*(1–2, Serial No. 200).

Cole, D. A., Maxwell, S. E., Martin, J. M., Peeke, L. G., Seroczynski, A. D., Tram, J. M., . . . Maschman, T. (2001). The development of multiple domains of child and adolescent self-concept: A cohort sequential longitudinal design. *Child Development, 72,* 1723–1746.

Cole, P. M., & Tan, P. Z. (2007). Emotion socialization from a cultural perspective. In J. E. Grusec & P. D. Hastings (Eds.), *Handbook of socialization: Theory and research* (pp. 516–542). New York, NY: Guilford.

Collins, W. A., Maccoby, E. E., Steinberg, L., Hetherington, E. M., & Bornstein, M. H. (2000). Contemporary research on parenting: The case for nature and nurture. *American Psychologist, 55,* 218–232.

Connolly, J., & McIsaac, C. (2009). Romantic relationships in adolescence. In R. M. Lerner & L. Steinberg (Eds.), *Handbook of adolescent psychology, Vol. 2. Contextual influences on adolescent development* (3rd ed., pp. 104–151). Hoboken, NJ: Wiley.

Connor, D. J., & Baglieri, S. (2009). Tipping the scales: Disabilities studies ask "How much diversity can you take?" In S. R. Steinberg (Ed.), *Diversity and multiculturalism: A reader* (pp. 341–361). New York, NY: Peter Lang.

Cook, P. J., & Ludwig, J. (2008). The burden of "acting White": Do Black adolescents disparage academic achievement? In J. U. Ogbu (Ed.), *Minority status, oppositional culture, and schooling* (pp. 275–297). New York, NY: Routledge.

Coplan, R. J., & Arbeau, K. A. (2009). Peer interactions and play in early childhood. In K. H. Rubin, W. M. Bukowski, & B. Laursen (Eds.), *Handbook of peer interactions, relationships, and groups* (pp. 143–161). New York, NY: Guilford.

Cornell, D., Gregory, A., Huang, F., & Fan, X. (2013). Perceived prevalence of teasing and bullying predicts high school dropout rates. *Journal of Educational Psychology, 105,* 138–149.

Correa-Chávez, M., Rogoff, B., & Mejía Arauz, R. (2005). Cultural patterns in attending to two events at once. *Child Development, 76,* 664–678.

Crain, W. (2005). *Theories of development: Concepts and applications* (5th ed.). Upper Saddle River, NJ: Prentice Hall/Pearson.

Creasey, G. L., Jarvis, P. A., & Berk, L. E. (1998). Play and social competence. In O. N. Saracho & B. Spodek (Eds.), *Multiple perspectives on play in early childhood education* (pp. 116–143). Albany, NY: State University of New York Press.

Crick, N. R., & Dodge, K. A. (1996). Social information-processing mechanisms in reactive and proactive aggression. *Child Development, 67,* 993–1002.

Crick, N. R., Grotpeter, J. K., & Bigbee, M. A. (2002). Relationally and physically aggressive children's intent attributions and feelings of distress for relational and instrumental peer provocation. *Child Development, 73,* 1134–1142.

Crick, N. R., Murray-Close, D., Marks, P. E. L., & Mohajeri-Nelson, N. (2009). Aggression and peer relationships in school-age children: Relational and physical aggression in group and dyadic contexts. In K. H. Rubin, W. M. Bukowski, & B. Laursen (Eds.), *Handbook of peer interactions, relationships, and groups* (pp. 287–302). New York, NY: Guilford.

Crocker, J., & Knight, K. M. (2005). Contingencies of self-worth. *Current Directions in Psychological Science, 14,* 200–203.

Crockett, L., Losoff, M., & Peterson, A. C. (1984). Perceptions of the peer group and friendship in early adolescence. *Journal of Early Adolescence, 4,* 155–181.

Crosnoe, R. (2011). *Fitting in, standing out: Navigating the social challenge of high school to get an education.* Cambridge, England: Cambridge University Press.

Cross, W. E., Jr., Strauss, L., & Fhagen-Smith, P. (1999). African American identity development across the life span: Educational implications. In R. H. Sheets & E. R. Hollins (Eds.), *Racial and ethnic identity in school practices: Aspects of human development* (pp. 29–47). Mahwah, NJ: Erlbaum.

Crosson-Tower, C. (2010). *Understanding child abuse and neglect* (8th ed.). Boston, MA: Allyn & Bacon.

Cunningham, C. E., & Cunningham, L. J. (2006). Student-mediated conflict resolution programs. In R. A. Barkley (Ed.), *Attention-deficit hyperactivity disorder: A handbook for diagnosis and treatment* (3rd ed., pp. 590–607). New York, NY: Guilford.

Damon, W. (1988). *The moral child: Nurturing children's natural moral growth.* New York, NY: Free Press.

Damon, W., & Hart, D. (1988). *Self-understanding from childhood and adolescence.* New York, NY: Cambridge University Press.

Darwich, L., Hymel, S., & Waterhouse, T. (2012). School avoidance and substance use among lesbian, gay, bisexual, and questioning youths: The impact of peer victimization and adult support. *Journal of Educational Psychology, 104,* 381–392.

Davila, J. (2008). Depressive symptoms and adolescent romance: Theory, research, and implications. *Child Development Perspectives, 2*(1), 26–31.

Davis-Kean, P. E., Huesmann, R., Jager, J., Collins, W. A., Bates, J. E., & Lansford, J. E. (2008). Changes in the relation of self-efficacy beliefs and behaviors across development. *Child Development, 79,* 1257–1269.

Davis-Kean, P. E., & Sandler, H. M. (2001). A meta-analysis of measures of self-esteem for young children: A framework for future measures. *Child Development, 72,* 887–906.

Davison, M. (2011, April). *Are you standing in my shoes? How affective and cognitive teaching sequences influence historical empathy.* Paper presented at the annual meeting of the American Educational Research Association, New Orleans, LA.

Dawson, G., & Bernier, R. (2007). Development of social brain circuitry in autism. In D. Coch, G. Dawson, & K. W. Fischer (Eds.), *Human behavior, learning, and the developing brain: Atypical development* (pp. 28–55). New York, NY: Guilford.

DeRidder, L. M. (1993). Teenage pregnancy: Etiology and educational interventions. *Educational Psychology Review, 5,* 87–107.

Deutsch, M. (1993). Educating for a peaceful world. *American Psychologist, 48,* 510–517.

DeVries, R., & Zan, B. (1996). A constructivist perspective on the role of the sociomoral atmosphere in promoting children's development. In C. T. Fosnot (Ed.), *Constructivism: Theory, perspectives, and practice* (pp. 103–119). New York, NY: Teachers College Press.

DeYoung, C. G., Hirsh, J. B., Shane, M. S., Papademetris, X., Rajeevan, N., & Gray, J. R. (2010). Testing predictions from personality neuroscience: Brain structure and the Big Five. *Psychological Science, 21,* 820–828.

Dilg, M. (2010). *Our worlds in our words: Exploring race, class, gender, and sexual orientation in multicultural classrooms.* New York, NY: Teachers College Press.

Dinh, J. E., & Lord, R. G. (2013). Current trends in moral research: What we know and where to go from here. *Current Directions in Psychological Science, 22,* 380–385.

Dishion, T. J., Piehler, T. F., & Myers, M. W. (2008). Dynamics and ecology of adolescent peer influence. In M. J. Prinstein & K. A. Dodge (Eds.), *Understanding peer influence in children and adolescents* (pp. 72–93). New York, NY: Guilford.

Dodge, K. A., Godwin, J., & The Conduct Problems Prevention Research Group. (2013). Social-information-processing patterns mediate the impact of preventive intervention on adolescent antisocial behavior. *Psychological Science, 24,* 456–465.

Dodge, K. A., Lansford, J. E., Burks, V. S., Bates, J. E., Pettit, G. S., Fontaine, R., & Price, J. M. (2003). Peer rejection and social information-processing factors in the development of aggressive behavior problems in children. *Child Development, 74,* 374–393.

Dodge, K. A., Malone, P. S., Lansford, J. E., Miller, S., Pettit, G. S., & Bates, J. E. (2009). A dynamic cascade model of the development of substance-use onset. *Monographs of the Society for Research in Child Development, 74*(3, Serial No. 294), 1–119.

Doll, B., Song, S., & Siemers, E. (2004). Classroom ecologies that support or discourage bullying. In D. L. Espelage & S. M. Swearer (Eds.), *Bullying in American schools: A social-ecological perspective on prevention and intervention* (pp. 161–183). Mahwah, NJ: Erlbaum.

Donaldson, S. K., & Westerman, M. A. (1986). Development of children's understanding of ambivalence and causal theories of emotion. *Developmental Psychology, 22,* 655–662.

Dowson, M., & McInerney, D. M. (2001). Psychological parameters of students' social and work avoidance goals: A qualitative investigation. *Journal of Educational Psychology, 93,* 35–42.

DuBois, D. L., Burk-Braxton, C., Swenson, L. P., Tevendale, H. D., & Hardesty, J. L. (2002). Race and gender influences on adjustment in early adolescence: Investigation of an integrative model. *Child Development, 73,* 1573–1592.

Dubow, E. F., Huesmann, L. R., & Greenwood, D. (2007). Media and youth socialization: Underlying processes and moderators of effects. In J. E. Grusec & P. D. Hastings (Eds.), *Handbook of socialization: Theory and research* (pp. 404–430). New York, NY: Guilford.

Dunning, D., Heath, C., & Suls, J. M. (2004). Flawed self-assessment: Implications for health, education, and the workplace. *Psychological Science in the Public Interest, 5,* 69–106.

Dweck, C. S. (2000). *Self-theories: Their role in motivation, personality, and development.* Philadelphia, PA: Psychology Press.

Eccles, J. S. (2007). Families, schools, and developing achievement-related motivations and engagement. In J. E. Grusec & P. D. Hastings (Eds.), *Handbook of socialization: Theory and research* (pp. 665–691). New York, NY: Guilford.

Eccles, J. (2009). Who am I and what am I going to do with my life? Personal and collective identities as motivators of action. *Educational Psychologist, 44,* 78–89.

Eckert, P. (1989). *Jocks and burnouts: Social categories and identity in the high school.* New York, NY: Teachers College Press.

Eisenberg, N. (1982). The development of reasoning regarding prosocial behavior. In N. Eisenberg (Ed.), *The development of prosocial behavior* (pp. 219–249). San Diego, CA: Academic Press.

Eisenberg, N. (1995). Prosocial development: A multifaceted model. In W. M. Kurtines & J. L. Gewirtz (Eds.), *Moral development: An introduction* (pp. 401–429). Boston, MA: Allyn & Bacon.

Eisenberg, N., Carlo, G., Murphy, B., & Van Court, N. (1995). Prosocial development in late adolescence: A longitudinal study. *Child Development, 66,* 1179–1197.

Eisenberg, N., & Fabes, R. A. (1998). Prosocial development. In W. Damon (Series Ed.) & N. Eisenberg (Vol. Ed.), *Handbook of child psychology: Vol. 3. Social, emotional, and personality development* (5th ed., pp. 701–778). New York, NY: Wiley.

Eisenberg, N., Martin, C. L., & Fabes, R. A. (1996). Gender development and gender effects. In D. C. Berliner & R. C. Calfee

(Eds.), *Handbook of educational psychology* (pp. 358–396). New York, NY: Macmillan.

Eisenberg, N., Spinrad, T. L., & Sadovsky, A. (2006). Empathy-related responding in children. In M. Killen & J. Smetana (Eds.), *Handbook of moral development* (pp. 517–549). Mahwah, NJ: Erlbaum.

Eisenberg, N., Zhou, Q., & Koller, S. (2001). Brazilian adolescents' prosocial moral judgment and behavior: Relations to sympathy, perspective taking, gender-role orientation, and demographic characteristics. *Child Development, 72,* 518–534.

Elkind, D. (1981). *Children and adolescents: Interpretive essays on Jean Piaget* (3rd ed.). New York, NY: Oxford University Press.

Ellenwood, S., & Ryan, K. (1991). Literature and morality: An experimental curriculum. In W. M. Kurtines & J. L. Gewirtz (Eds.), *Moral behavior and development: Vol. 3. Application.* Mahwah, NJ: Erlbaum.

Ellis, W. E., & Zarbatany, L. (2007). Peer group status as a moderator of group influence on children's deviant, aggressive, and prosocial behavior. *Child Development, 78,* 1240–1254.

Ellison, N. B., Steinfield, C., & Lampe, C. (2007). The benefits of Facebook "friends": Social capital and college students' use of online social network sites. *Journal of Computer-Mediated Communication, 12,* 1143–1168.

Elmore, K. C., & Oyserman, D. (2012). If "we" can succeed, "I" can too: Identity-based motivation and gender in the classroom. *Contemporary Educational Psychology, 37,* 176–185.

Else-Quest, N. M., Hyde, J. S., Goldsmith, H. H., & Van Hulle, C. A. (2006). Gender differences in temperament: A meta-analysis. *Psychological Bulletin, 132,* 33–72.

Epstein, J. S. (1998). Introduction: Generation X, youth culture, and identity. In J. S. Epstein (Ed.), *Youth culture: Identity in a postmodern world* (pp. 1–23). Malden, MA: Blackwell.

Erikson, E. H. (1950). *Childhood and society.* New York, NY: Norton.

Erikson, E. H. (1963). *Childhood and society* (2nd ed.). New York, NY: Norton.

Erikson, E. H. (1972). Eight ages of man. In C. S. Lavatelli & F. Stendler (Eds.), *Readings in child behavior and child development* (pp. 19–30). San Diego, CA: Harcourt Brace Jovanovich.

Espelage, D. L., Aragon, S. R., Birkett, M., & Koenig, B. W. (2008). Homophobic teasing, psychological outcomes, and sexual orientation among high school students: What influence do parents and schools have? *School Psychology Review, 37,* 202–216.

Espelage, D. L., Mebane, S. E., & Adams, R. S. (2004). Empathy, caring, and bullying: Toward an understanding of complex associations. In D. L. Espelage & S. M. Swearer (Eds.), *Bullying in American schools: A social-ecological perspective on prevention and intervention* (pp. 37–61). Mahwah, NJ: Erlbaum.

Espelage, D. L., & Swearer, S. W. (Eds.) (2004). *Bullying in American schools: A social-ecological*

perspective on prevention and intervention. Mahwah, NJ: Erlbaum.

Farver, J. A. M., & Branstetter, W. H. (1994). Preschoolers' prosocial responses to their peers' distress. *Developmental Psychology, 30,* 334–341.

Feddes, A. R., Noack, P., & Rutland, A. (2009). Direct and extended friendship effects on minority and majority children's interethnic attitudes: A longitudinal study. *Child Development, 80,* 377–390.

Feldman, A. F., & Matjasko, J. L. (2005). The role of school-based extracurricular activities in adolescent development: A comprehensive review and future directions. *Review of Educational Research, 75,* 159–210.

Figner, B., & Weber, E. U. (2011). Who takes risks when and why? Determinants of risk taking. *Current Directions in Psychological Science, 20,* 211–216.

Flanagan, C. A., & Faison, N. (2001). Youth civic development: Implications of research for social policy and programs. *Social Policy Report of the Society for Research in Child Development, 15*(1), 1–14.

Flanagan, C. A., & Tucker, C. J. (1999). Adolescents' explanations for political issues: Concordance with their views of self and society. *Developmental Psychology, 35,* 1198–1209.

Flavell, J. H., & Miller, P. H. (1998). Social cognition. In W. Damon (Series Ed.), D. Kuhn, & R. S. Siegler (Vol. Eds.), *Handbook of child psychology: Vol. 2. Cognition, perception, and language* (5th ed., pp. 851–898). New York, NY: Wiley.

Flavell, J. H., Miller, P. H., & Miller, S. A. (2002). *Cognitive development* (4th ed.). Upper Saddle River, NJ: Prentice Hall.

Fontaine, R. G., Yang, C., Dodge, K. A., Bates, J. E., & Pettit, G. S. (2008). Testing an individual systems model of response evaluation and decision (RED) and antisocial behavior across adolescence. *Child Development, 79,* 462–475.

Fox, N. A., Henderson, H. A., Rubin, K. H., Calkins, S. D., & Schmidt, L. A. (2001). Continuity and discontinuity of behavioral inhibition and exuberance: Psychophysical and behavioral influences across the first four years of life. *Child Development, 72,* 1–21.

Freedman, S. G. (1990). *Small victories: The real world of a teacher, her students, and their high school.* New York, NY: Harper & Row.

The Freedom Writers (with Gruwell, E.). (1999). *The Freedom Writers diary: How a teacher and 150 teens used writing to change themselves and the world around them.* New York, NY: Broadway Books.

Frey, K. S., Hirschstein, M. K., Edstrom, L. V., & Snell, J. L. (2009). Observed reductions in school bullying, nonbullying aggression, and destructive bystander behavior: A longitudinal evaluation. *Journal of Educational Psychology, 101,* 466–481.

Furman, W., Brown, B. B., & Feiring, C. (Eds.). (1999). *The development of romantic relationships in adolescence*. Cambridge, England: Cambridge University Press.

Furman, W., & Collins, W. A. (2009). Adolescent romantic relationships and experiences. In K. H. Rubin, W. M. Bukowski, & B. Laursen (Eds.), *Handbook of peer interactions, relationships, and groups* (pp. 341–360). New York, NY: Guilford.

Furman, W., & Simon, V. A. (2008). Homophily in adolescent romantic relationships. In M. J. Prinstein & K. A. Dodge (Eds.), *Understanding peer influence in children and adolescents* (pp. 203–224). New York, NY: Guilford.

Galambos, N. L., Barker, E. T., & Almeida, D. M. (2003). Parents *do* matter: Trajectories of change in externalizing and internalizing problems in early adolescence. *Child Development, 74*, 578–594.

Gallese, V., Gernsbacher, M. A., Heyes, C., Hickok, G., & Iacoboni, M. (2011). Mirror neuron forum. *Perspectives on Psychological Science, 6*, 369–407.

Galván, A. (2012). Risky behavior in adolescents: The role of the developing brain. In V. F. Reyna, S. B. Chapman, M. R. Dougherty, & J. Confrey (Eds.), *The adolescent brain: Learning, reasoning, and decision making* (pp. 267–289). Washington, DC: American Psychological Association.

Gardiner, H. W., & Kosmitzki, C. (2008). *Lives across cultures: Cross-cultural human development* (4th ed.). Boston, MA: Allyn & Bacon.

Gavin, L. A., & Fuhrman, W. (1989). Age differences in adolescents' perceptions of their peer groups. *Developmental Psychology, 25*, 827–834.

Gazelle, H., & Ladd, G. W. (2003). Anxious solitude and peer exclusion: A diathesis-stress model of internalizing trajectories in childhood. *Child Development, 74*, 257–278.

Gehlbach, H., Brinkworth, M. E., & Harris, A. D. (2012). Changes in teacher–student relationships. *British Journal of Educational Psychology, 82*, 690–704.

Gehlbach, H., Brown, S. W., Ioannou, A., Boyer, M. A., Hudson, N., Niv-Solomon, A., . . . Janik, L. (2008). Increasing interest in social studies: Social perspective taking and self-efficacy in stimulating simulations. *Contemporary Educational Psychology, 33*, 894–914.

Gest, S. D., Domitrovich, C. E., & Welsh, J. A. (2005). Peer academic reputation in elementary school: Associations with changes in self-concept and academic skills. *Journal of Educational Psychology, 97*, 337–346.

Gianotti, L. R. R., Knoch, D., Faber, P. L., Lehmann, D., Pascual-Marqui, R. D., Diezi, C., . . . Fehr, E. (2009). Tonic activity level in the right prefrontal cortex predicts individuals' risk taking. *Psychological Science, 20*, 33–38.

Gibbs, J. C. (1995). The cognitive developmental perspective. In W. M. Kurtines & J. L. Gewirtz (Eds.), *Moral development: An introduction* (pp. 27–48). Boston, MA: Allyn & Bacon.

Gilligan, C. F. (1982). *In a different voice.* Cambridge, MA: Harvard University Press.

Gilligan, C. F. (1985, March). Keynote address. Conference on Women and Moral Theory, Stony Brook, NY.

Gilligan, C. F. (1987). Moral orientation and moral development. In E. F. Kittay & D. T. Meyers (Eds.), *Women and moral theory* (pp. 19–33). Totowa, NJ: Rowman & Littlefield.

Gilligan, C. F., & Attanucci, J. (1988). Two moral orientations: Gender differences and similarities. *Merrill-Palmer Quarterly, 34*, 223–237.

Gnepp, J. (1989). Children's use of personal information to understand other people's feelings. In C. Saarni & P. L. Harris (Eds.), *Children's understanding of emotion* (pp. 151–180). Cambridge, England: Cambridge University Press.

Goodnow, J. J. (1992). *Parental belief systems: The psychological consequences for children.* Mahwah, NJ: Erlbaum.

Goodwin, M. H. (2006). *The hidden life of girls: Games of stance, status, and exclusion.* Malden, MA: Blackwell.

Gottman, J. M. (1986). The world of coordinated play: Same- and cross-sex friendship in young children. In J. M. Gottman & J. G. Parker (Eds.), *Conversations of friends: Speculations on affective development* (pp. 139–191). Cambridge, England: Cambridge University Press.

Graham, S., & Hudley, C. (2005). Race and ethnicity in the study of motivation and competence. In A. J. Elliot & C. S. Dweck (Eds.), *Handbook of competence and motivation* (pp. 392–413). New York, NY: Guilford Press.

Granic, I., Lobel, A., & Engels, R. C. M. E. (2014). The benefits of playing video games. *American Psychologist, 69*, 66–78.

Gray, M. R., & Steinberg, L. (1999). Unpacking authoritative parenting: Reassessing a multidimensional concept. *Journal of Marriage and the Family, 61*, 574–587.

Greenhow, C., Robelia, B., & Hughes, J. E. (2009). Web 2.0 and classroom research: What path should we take now? *Educational Researcher, 38*, 246–259.

Greeno, J. G. (2006). Learning in activity. In R. K. Sawyer (Ed.), *The Cambridge handbook of the learning sciences* (pp. 79–96). Cambridge, England: Cambridge University Press.

Greenspan, S., & Granfield, J. M. (1992). Reconsidering the construct of mental retardation: Implications of a model of social competence. *American Journal of Mental Retardation, 96*, 442–453.

Greitemeyer, T. (2011). Effects of prosocial media on social behavior: When and why does media exposure affect helping and aggression? *Current Directions in Psychological Science, 20*, 251–255.

Grimes, N. (2002). *Bronx masquerade.* New York, NY: Penguin.

Gross, E. F., Juvonen, J., & Gable, S. L. (2002). Internet use and well-being in adolescence. *Journal of Social Issues, 58*, 75–90.

Guay, F., Boivin, M., & Hodges, E. V. E. (1999). Social comparison processes and academic achievement: The dependence of the development of self-evaluations on friends' performance. *Journal of Educational Psychology, 91*, 564–568.

Guerra, N. G., Huesmann, L. R., & Spindler, A. (2003). Community violence exposure, social cognition, and aggression among urban elementary school children. *Child Development, 74*, 1561–1576.

Guerra, N. G., & Slaby, R. G. (1990). Cognitive mediators of aggression in adolescent offenders: 2. Intervention. *Developmental Psychology, 26*, 269–277.

Gummerum, M., Keller, M., Takezawa, M., & Mata, J. (2008). To give or not to give: Children's and adolescents' sharing and moral negotiations in economic decision situations. *Child Development, 79*, 562–576.

Guthrie, P. (2001). "Catching sense" and the meaning of belonging on a South Carolina sea island. In S. S. Walker (Ed.), *African roots/American cultures: Africa in the creation of the Americas* (pp. 275–283). Lanham, MD: Rowman & Littlefield.

Gutiérrez, K. D., & Rogoff, B. (2003). Cultural ways of learning: Individual traits or repertoires of practice. *Educational Researcher, 32*(5), 19–25.

Haidt, J. (2012). *The righteous mind: Why good people are divided by politics and religion.* New York, NY: Random House.

Hale-Benson, J. E. (1986). *Black children: Their roots, culture, and learning styles.* Baltimore, MD: Johns Hopkins University Press.

Halgunseth, L. C., Ispa, J. M., & Rudy, D. (2006). Parental control in Latino families: An integrated review of the literature. *Child Development, 77*, 1282–1297.

Hamlin, J. K., & Wynn, K. (2011). Young infants prefer prosocial to antisocial others. *Cognitive Development, 26*, 30–39.

Hamm, J. V., Hoffman, A., & Farmer, T. W. (2012). Peer cultures of academic effort and achievement in adolescence. In A. M. Ryan & G. W. Ladd (Eds.), *Peer relationships and adjustment at school* (pp. 219–250). Charlotte, NC: Information Age.

Hamovitch, B. (2007). Hoping for the best: "Inclusion" and stigmatization in a middle school. In S. Books (Ed.), *Invisible children in the society and its schools* (3rd ed., pp. 263–281). Mahwah, NJ: Erlbaum.

Hampson, S. E. (2008). Mechanisms by which childhood personality traits influence adult well-being. *Current Directions in Psychological Science, 17*, 264–268.

Hanish, L. D., Kochenderfer-Ladd, B., Fabes, R. A., Martin, C. L., & Denning, D. (2004). Bullying among young children: The influence of peers and teachers. In D. L. Espelage & S. M. Swearer (Eds.), *Bullying in American schools: A social-ecological perspective on prevention and intervention* (pp. 141–159). Mahwah, NJ: Erlbaum.

Harris, J. R. (1998). *The nurture assumption: Why children turn out the way they do.* New York, NY: Free Press.

Harris, M. J., & Rosenthal, R. (1985). Mediation of interpersonal expectancy effects: 31 meta-analyses. *Psychological Bulletin, 97,* 363–386.

Harris, P. L. (2006). Social cognition. In W. Damon, R. M. Lerner (Series Eds.), D. Kuhn, & R. Siegler (Vol. Eds.), *Handbook of child psychology: Vol. 2. Cognition, perception, and language* (6th ed., pp. 811–858). New York, NY: Wiley.

Hart, D. (1988). The adolescent self-concept in social context. In D. K. Lapsley & F. C. Power (Eds.), *Self, ego, and identity: Integrative approaches* (pp. 71–90). New York, NY: Springer-Verlag.

Hart, D., Atkins, R., & Fegley, S. (2003). Personality and development in childhood: A person-centered approach. *Monographs of the Society for Research in Child Development, 68*(1, Serial No. 272).

Hart, D., & Fegley, S. (1995). Prosocial behavior and caring in adolescence: Relations to self-understanding and social judgment. *Child Development, 66,* 1346–1359.

Harter, S. (1983). Children's understanding of multiple emotions: A cognitive-developmental approach. In W. F. Overton (Ed.), *The relationship between social and cognitive development* (pp. 147–194). Mahwah, NJ: Erlbaum.

Harter, S. (1999). *The construction of the self: A developmental perspective.* New York, NY: Guilford.

Harter, S., & Whitesell, N. R. (1989). Developmental changes in children's understanding of single, multiple, and blended emotion concepts. In C. Saarni & P. Harris (Eds.), *Children's understanding of emotion* (pp. 81–116). Cambridge, England: Cambridge University Press.

Harter, S., Whitesell, N. R., & Junkin, L. J. (1998). Similarities and differences in domain-specific and global self-evaluations of learning-disabled, behaviorally disordered, and normally achieving adolescents. *American Educational Research Journal, 35,* 653–680.

Harwood, R. L., Miller, J. G., & Irizarry, N. L. (1995). *Culture and attachment: Perceptions of the child in context.* New York, NY: Guilford.

Hastings, P. D., Utendale, W. T., & Sullivan, C. (2007). The socialization of prosocial development. In J. E. Grusec & P. D. Hastings (Eds.), *Handbook of socialization: Theory and research* (pp. 638–664). New York, NY: Guilford.

Hattie, J. A. C. (2009). *Visible learning: A synthesis of over 800 meta-analyses relating to achievement.* London: Routledge.

Hawley, P. H. (2014). The duality of human nature: Coercion and prosociality in youths' hierarchy ascension and social success. *Psychological Science, 23,* 433–438.

Hearold, S. (1986). A synthesis of 1,043 effects of television on social behavior. In G. Comstock (Ed.), *Public communication and behavior* (Vol. 1, pp. 65–133). New York, NY: Academic Press.

Helwig, C. C., & Jasiobedzka, U. (2001). The relation between law and morality: Children's reasoning about socially beneficial and unjust laws. *Child Development, 72,* 1382–1393.

Helwig, C. C., Zelazo, P. D., & Wilson, M. (2001). Children's judgments of psychological harm in normal and noncanonical situations. *Child Development, 72,* 66–81.

Hemmings, A. B. (2004). *Coming of age in U.S. high schools: Economic, kinship, religious, and political crosscurrents.* Mahwah, NJ: Erlbaum.

Herbert, J., & Stipek, D. (2005). The emergence of gender differences in children's perceptions of their academic competence. *Journal of Applied Developmental Psychology, 26,* 276–295.

Hewitt, J., & Scardamalia, M. (1998). Design principles for distributed knowledge building processes. *Educational Psychology Review, 10,* 75–96.

Hickey, D. J. (2011). Participation by design: Improving individual motivation by looking beyond it. In D. M. McInerney, R. A. Walker, & G. A. D. Liem (Eds.), *Sociocultural theories of learning and motivation: Looking back, looking forward* (pp. 137–161). Charlotte, NC: Information Age.

Higgins, A. (1995). Educating for justice and community: Lawrence Kohlberg's vision of moral education. In W. M. Kurtines & J. L. Gewirtz (Eds.), *Moral development: An introduction* (pp. 49–81). Boston, MA: Allyn & Bacon.

Hill, P. L., & Roberts, B. W. (2010). Propositions for the study of moral personality development. *Current Directions in Psychological Science, 19,* 380–383.

Hitlin, S., Brown, J. S., & Elder, G. H., Jr. (2006). Racial self-categorization in adolescence: Multiracial development and social pathways. *Child Development, 77,* 1298–1308.

Hobson, P. (2004). *The cradle of thought: Exploring the origins of thinking.* Oxford, England: Oxford University Press.

Hodson, G. (2011). Do ideologically intolerant people benefit from intergroup contact? *Current Directions in Psychological Science, 20,* 154–159.

Hoffman, M. L. (1975). Altruistic behavior and the parent-child relationship. *Journal of Personality and Social Psychology, 31,* 937–943.

Hoffman, M. L. (2000). *Empathy and moral development: Implications for caring and justice.* New York, NY: Cambridge University Press.

Hoglund, W. L. G. (2007). School functioning in early adolescence: Gender-linked responses to peer victimization. *Journal of Educational Psychology, 99,* 683–699.

Hollenstein, T., & Lougheed, J. P. (2013). Beyond storm and stress: Typicality, transactions, timing, and temperament to account for adolescent change. *American Psychologist, 68,* 444–454.

Hong, Y.-Y., Wan, C., No, S., & Chiu, C.-Y. (2007). Multicultural identities. In S. Kitayama & D. Cohen (Eds.), *Handbook of cultural psychology* (pp. 323–345). New York, NY: Guilford.

Honz, K., Kiewra, K. A., & Yang, Y.-S. (2010). Cheating perceptions and prevalence across academic settings. *Mid-Western Educational Researcher, 23,* 10–17.

Horne, A. M., Orpinas, P., Newman-Carlson, D., & Bartolomucci, C. L. (2004). Elementary school Bully Busters Program: Understanding why children bully and what to do about it. In D. L. Espelage & S. M. Swearer (Eds.), *Bullying in American schools: A social-ecological perspective on prevention and intervention* (pp. 297–325). Mahwah, NJ: Erlbaum.

Hudley, C., & Graham, S. (1993). An attributional intervention to reduce peer-directed aggression among African American boys. *Child Development, 64,* 124–138.

Huesmann, L. R., Moise-Titus, J., Podolski, C., & Eron, L. (2003). Longitudinal relations between children's exposure to TV violence and their aggressive and violent behavior in young adulthood: 1977–1992. *Developmental Psychology, 39,* 201–221.

Huntsinger, C. S., & Jose, P. E. (2006). A longitudinal investigation of personality and social adjustment among Chinese American and European American adolescents. *Child Development, 77,* 1309–1324.

Igoa, C. (2007). Immigrant children: Art as a second language. In S. Books (Ed.), *Invisible children in the society and its schools* (3rd ed., pp. 117–140). Mahwah, NJ: Erlbaum.

Izard, C., Fine, S., Schultz, D., Mostow, A., Ackerman, B., & Youngstrom, E. (2001). Emotion knowledge as a predictor of social behavior and academic competence in children at risk. *Psychological Science, 12,* 18–23.

Jarrett, O. S. (2002). Recess in elementary school: What does the research say? ERIC Clearinghouse on Elementary and Early Childhood Education. Retrieved from ERIC database. (ED466331)

Joët, G., Usher, E., & Bressoux, P. (2011). Sources of self-efficacy: An investigation of elementary school students in France. *Journal of Educational Psychology, 103,* 649–663.

Johnson, D. W., & Johnson, R. T. (1996). Conflict resolution and peer mediation programs in elementary and secondary schools: A review of the research. *Review of Educational Research, 66,* 459–506.

Johnson, D. W., & Johnson, R. T. (2006). Conflict resolution, peer mediation, and peacemaking. In C. M. Evertson & C. S. Weinstein (Eds.), *Handbook of classroom management: Research, practice, and contemporary issues* (pp. 803–832). Mahwah, NJ: Erlbaum.

Jones, M. H., Audley-Piotrowski, S. R., & Kiefer, S. M. (2012). Relationships among adolescents' perceptions of friends' behaviors, academic self-concept, and math performance. *Journal of Educational Psychology, 104,* 19–31.

Jordan, J. V. (2006). Relational resilience in girls. In S. Goldstein & R. B. Brooks (Eds.), *Handbook of resilience in children* (pp. 79–90). New York, NY: Springer.

Joseph, J. E., Liu, X., Jiang, Y., Lynam, D., & Kelly, T. H. (2009). Neural correlates of emotional reactivity in sensation seeking. *Psychological Science, 20,* 215–223.

Joshi, M. S., & MacLean, M. (1994). Indian and English children's understanding of the distinction between real and apparent emotion. *Child Development, 65,* 1372–1384.

Josselson, R. (1988). The embedded self: I and Thou revisited. In D. K. Lapsley & F. C. Power (Eds.), *Self, ego, and identity: Integrative approaches* (pp. 91–106). New York, NY: Springer-Verlag.

Joussemet, M., Vitaro, F., Barker, E. D., Côté, S., Nagin, D. S., Zoccolillo, M., & Tremblay, R. E. (2008). Controlling parenting and physical aggression during elementary school. *Child Development, 79,* 411–425.

Juvonen, J. (2006). Sense of belonging, social bonds, and school functioning. In P. A. Alexander & P. H. Winne (Eds.), *Handbook of educational psychology* (2nd ed., pp. 655–674). Mahwah, NJ: Erlbaum.

Juvonen, J., & Cadigan, R. J. (2002). Social determinants of public behavior of middle school youth: Perceived peer norms and need to be accepted. In F. Pajares & T. Urdan (Eds.), *Adolescence and education, Vol. 2: Academic motivation of adolescents* (pp. 277–297). Greenwich, CT: Information Age.

Juvonen, J., & Galván, A. (2008). Peer influence in involuntary social groups. In M. J. Prinstein & K. A. Dodge (Eds.), *Understanding peer influence in children and adolescents* (pp. 225–244). New York, NY: Guilford.

Juvonen, J., & Weiner, B. (1993). An attributional analysis of students' interactions: The social consequences of perceived responsibility. *Educational Psychology Review, 5,* 325–345.

Kağıtçıbaşı, Ç. (2007). *Family, self, and human development across cultures: Theory and applications* (2nd ed.). Mahwah, NJ: Erlbaum.

Kahne, J. E., & Sporte, S. E. (2008). Developing citizens: The impact of civic learning opportunities on students' commitment to civic participation. *American Educational Research Journal, 45,* 738–766.

Kaplan, A., & Flum, H. (2012). Identify formation in educational settings: A critical focus for education in the 21st century. *Contemporary Educational Psychology, 37,* 171–175.

Keogh, B. K. (2003). *Temperament in the classroom.* Baltimore, MD: Brookes.

Kidd, D. C., & Castano, E. (2013). Reading literacy fiction improves theory of mind. *Science, 342*(6156), 377–380.

Killen, M., & Smetana, J. (2008). Moral judgment and moral neuroscience: Intersections, definitions, and issues. *Child Development Perspectives, 2*(1), 1–6.

Kim, J., & Cicchetti, D. (2006). Longitudinal trajectories of self-system processes and depressive symptoms among maltreated and nonmaltreated children. *Child Development, 77,* 624–639.

Kindermann, T. A. (2007). Effects of naturally existing peer groups on changes in academic engagement in a cohort of sixth graders. *Child Development, 78,* 1186–1203.

Kindermann, T. A., McCollam, T., & Gibson, E. (1996). Peer networks and students' classroom engagement during childhood and adolescence. In J. Juvonen & K. Wentzel (Eds.), *Social motivation: Understanding children's school adjustment* (pp. 279–312). Cambridge, England: Cambridge University Press.

Kochanska, G., Aksan, N., Knaack, A., & Rhines, H. M. (2004). Maternal parenting and children's conscience: Early security as moderator. *Child Development, 75,* 1229–1242.

Kochanska, G., Gross, J. N., Lin, M.-H., & Nichols, K. E. (2002). Guilt in young children: Development, determinants, and relations with a broader system of standards. *Child Development, 73,* 461–482.

Kochanska, G., Tjebkes, T. L., & Forman, D. R. (1998). Children's emerging regulation of conduct: Restraint, compliance, and internalization from infancy to the second year. *Child Development, 69,* 1378–1389.

Kodluboy, D. W. (2004). Gang-oriented interventions. In J. C. Conoley & A. P. Goldstein (Eds.), *School violence intervention* (2nd ed., pp. 194–232). New York, NY: Guilford.

Kohlberg, L. (1976). Moral stages and moralization: The cognitive-developmental approach. In T. Lickona (Ed.), *Moral development and behavior: Theory, research, and social issues* (pp. 219–240). New York, NY: Holt, Rinehart & Winston.

Kohlberg, L. (1984). *The psychology of moral development: The nature and validity of moral stages.* San Francisco, CA: Harper & Row.

Kohlberg, L. (1986). A current statement on some theoretical issues. In S. Modgil & C. Modgil (Eds.), *Lawrence Kohlberg: Consensus and controversy* (pp. 485–546). Philadelphia, PA: Falmer Press.

Kohlberg, L., & Kramer, R. (1969). Continuities and discontinuities in childhood and adult moral development. *Human Development, 12,* 93–120.

Kowalski, R. M., & Limber, S. P. (2007). Electronic bullying among middle school students. *Journal of Adolescent Health, 41,* S22–S30.

Krebs, D. L. (2008). Morality: An evolutionary account. *Perspectives on Psychological Science, 3,* 149–172.

Krebs, D. L., & Van Hesteren, F. (1994). The development of altruism: Toward an integrative model. *Developmental Review, 14,* 103–158.

Kurtines, W. M., Berman, S. L., Ittel, A., & Williamson, S. (1995). Moral development: A co-constructivist perspective. In W. M. Kurtines & J. L. Gewirtz (Eds.), *Moral development: An introduction* (pp. 337–376). Boston, MA: Allyn & Bacon.

Ladd, G. W., Kochenderger-Ladd, B., Visconti, K. J., & Ettekal, I. (2012). Classroom peer relations and children's social and scholastic development. In A. M. Ryan & G. W. Ladd (Eds.), *Peer relationships and adjustment at school* (pp. 11–49). Charlotte, NC: Information Age.

Ladd, G. W., Kochenderfer-Ladd, B., Visconti, K. J., Ettekal, I., Sechler, C. M., & Cortes, K. I. (2014). Grade-school children's social collaborative skills: Links with partner preference and achievement. *American Educational Research Journal, 51,* 152–183.

Ladd, G. W., & Troop-Gordon, W. (2003). The role of chronic peer difficulties in the development of children's psychological adjustment problems. *Child Development, 74,* 1344–1367.

LaFontana, K. M., & Cillessen, A. H. N. (2010). Developmental changes in the priority of perceived status in childhood and adolescence. *Social Development, 19,* 130–147.

Lamborn, S. D., Mounts, N. S., Steinberg, L., & Dornbusch, S. M. (1991). Patterns of competence and adjustment among adolescents from authoritative, authoritarian, indulgent, and neglectful families. *Child Development, 62,* 1049–1065.

Lapsley, D. K. (1993). Toward an integrated theory of adolescent ego development: The "new look" at adolescent egocentrism. *American Journal of Orthopsychiatry, 63,* 562–571.

Larson, R. W., & Brown, J. R. (2007). Emotional development in adolescence: What can be learned from a high school theater program? *Child Development, 78,* 1083–1099.

Larson, R. W., Clore, G. L., & Wood, G. A. (1999). The emotions of romantic relationships: Do they wreak havoc on adolescents? In W. Furman, B. B. Brown, & C. Feiring (Eds.), *The development of romantic relationships in adolescence* (pp. 19–49). Cambridge, England: Cambridge University Press.

Laupa, M., & Turiel, E. (1995). Social domain theory. In W. M. Kurtines & J. L. Gewirtz (Eds.), *Moral development: An introduction.* Boston, MA: Allyn & Bacon.

Laursen, B., Bukowski, W. M., Aunola, K., & Nurmi, J.-E. (2007). Friendship moderates prospective associations between social isolation and adjustment problems in young children. *Child Development, 78,* 1395–1404.

Leaf, J. B., Oppenheim-Leaf, M. L., Call, N. A., Sheldon, J. B., Sherman, J. A., Taubman, M., et al. (2012). Comparing the teaching interaction procedure to social stories for people with autism. *Journal of Applied Behavior Analysis, 45,* 281–298.

Leary, M. R. (1999). Making sense of self-esteem. *Current Directions in Psychological Science, 8,* 32–35.

Leffert, J. S., Siperstein, G. N., & Millikan, E. (2000). Understanding social adaptation in children with mental retardation: A social-cognitive perspective. *Exceptional Children, 66,* 530–545.

Lenski, A., Husemann, N., Trautwein, U., & Lüdtke, O. (2010, April–May). *Academic cheating: A multidimensional point of view.* Paper presented at the annual meeting of the

American Educational Research Association, Denver, CO.

Leonard, J., & Martin, D. B. (Eds.). (2013). *The brilliance of black children in mathematics: Beyond the numbers and toward new discourse.* Charlotte, NC: Information Age.

Levitt, M. J., Guacci-Franco, N., & Levitt, J. L. (1993). Convoys of social support in childhood and early adolescence: Structure and function. *Developmental Psychology, 29,* 811–818.

Lewis, M., & Sullivan, M. W. (2005). The development of self-conscious emotions. In A. J. Elliot & C. S. Dweck (Eds.), *Handbook of competence and motivation* (pp. 185–201). New York, NY: Guilford.

Li, Y., Anderson, R. C., Nguyen-Jahiel, K., Dong, T., Archodidou, A., Kim, I.-H., . . . Miller, B. (2007). Emergent leadership in children's discussion groups. *Cognition and Instruction, 25,* 75–111.

Liem, G. A. D., Marsh, H. W., Martin, A. J., McInerney, D. M., & Yeung, A. S. (2013). The big-fish-little-pond effect and a national policy of within-school ability streaming: Alternative frames of reference. *American Educational Research Journal, 50,* 326–370.

Lippa, R. A. (2002). *Gender, nature, and nurture.* Mahwah, NJ: Erlbaum.

Liu, D., Sabbagh, M. A., Gehring, W. J., & Wellman, H. M. (2009). Neural correlates of children's theory of mind development. *Child Development, 80,* 318–326.

Lockhart, K. L., Chang, B., & Story, T. (2002). Young children's beliefs about the stability of traits: Protective optimism? *Child Development, 73,* 1408–1430.

Loose, F., Régner, I., Morin, A. J. S., & Dumas, F. (2012). Are academic discounting and devaluing double-edged swords? Their relations to global self-esteem, achievement goals, and performance among stigmatized students. *Journal of Educational Psychology, 104,* 713–725.

Luna, B., Paulsen, D. J., Padmanabhan, A., & Geier, C. (2013). The teenage brain: Cognitive control and motivation. *Current Directions in Psychological Science, 22,* 94–100.

Luyckx, K., Schwartz, S. J., Berzonsky, M. D., Soenens, B., Vansteenkiste, M., Smits, I., & Goossens, L. (2008). Capturing ruminative exploration: Extending the four dimensional model of identity formation in late adolescence. *Journal of Research in Personality, 42,* 58–82.

Mac Iver, D. J., Reuman, D. A., & Main, S. R. (1995). Social structuring of the school: Studying what is, illuminating what could be. In J. T. Spence, J. M. Darley, & D. J. Foss (Eds.), *Annual review of psychology* (Vol. 46, pp. 375–400). Palo Alto, CA: Annual Review.

Maccoby, E. E. (2002). Gender and group process: A developmental perspective. *Current Directions in Psychological Science, 11,* 54–58.

Mahoney, J. L., Cairns, B. D., & Farmer, T. W. (2003). Promoting interpersonal competence and educational success through extracurricular activity participation. *Journal of Educational Psychology, 95,* 409–418.

Maikovich, A. K., Jaffee, S. R., Odgers, C. L., & Gallop, R. (2008). Effects of family violence on psychopathology symptoms in children previously exposed to maltreatment. *Child Development, 79,* 1498–1512.

Malti, T., Gummerum, M., Keller, M., & Buchman, M. (2009). Children's moral motivation, sympathy, and prosocial behavior. *Child Development, 80,* 442–460.

Manning, M. L., & Baruth, L. G. (2009). *Multicultural education of children and adolescents* (5th ed.). Boston, MA: Allyn & Bacon/ Pearson.

Marcia, J. E. (1980). Identity in adolescence. In J. Adelson (Ed.), *Handbook of adolescent psychology* (pp. 159–187). New York, NY: Wiley.

Marcia, J. E. (1991). Identity and self-development. In R. M. Lerner, A. C. Petersen, & J. Brooks-Gunn (Eds.), *Encyclopedia of adolescence* (Vol. 1, pp. 529–533). New York, NY: Garland.

Marcus, R. F. (1980). Empathy and popularity of preschool children. *Child Study Journal, 10,* 133–145.

Margolin, G., & Gordis, E. B. (2004). Children's exposure to violence in the family and community. *Current Directions in Psychological Science, 13,* 152–155.

Markus, H. R., & Kitayama, S. (1991). Culture and the self: Implications for cognition, emotion, and motivation. *Psychological Review, 98,* 224–253.

Marsh, H. W., & Craven, R. (1997). Academic self-concept: Beyond the dustbowl. In G. D. Phye (Ed.), *Handbook of classroom assessment: Learning, achievement, and adjustment* (pp. 131–198). San Diego, CA: Academic Press.

Marsh, H. W., & O'Mara, A. J. (2008). Self-concept is as multidisciplinary as it is multidimensional: A review of theory, measurement, and practice in self-concept research. In H. W. Marsh, R. G. Craven, & D. M. McInerney (Eds.), *Self-processes, learning, and enabling human potential* (pp. 87–115). Charlotte, NC: Information Age.

Martin, A. J., & Dowson, M. (2009). Interpersonal relationships, motivation, engagement, and achievement: Yields for theory, current issues, and educational practice. *Review of Educational Research, 79,* 327–365.

Martin, A. J., Nejad, H. G., Colmar, S., & Liem, G. A. D. (2013). Adaptability: How students' responses to uncertainty and novelty predict their academic and non-academic outcomes. *Journal of Educational Psychology, 105,* 728–746.

Martinez, R. S., & Huberty, T. J. (2010). Anxiety in students with learning difficulties and learning disabilities. In J. C. Cassady (Ed.), *Anxiety in schools: The causes, consequences, and solutions for academic anxieties* (pp. 137–152). New York, NY: Peter Lang.

Matthews, G., Zeidner, M., & Roberts, R. D. (2006). Models of personality and affect for education: A review and synthesis. In P. A. Alexander & P. H. Winne (Eds.), *Handbook of educational psychology* (2nd ed., pp. 163–186). Mahwah, NJ: Erlbaum.

Maughan, A., & Cicchetti, D. (2002). Impact of child maltreatment and interadult violence on children's emotion regulation abilities and socioemotional adjustment. *Child Development, 73,* 1525–1542.

Mayer, J. D., Salovey, P., & Caruso, D. R. (2008). What is emotional intelligence and what does it predict? In P. C. Kyllonen, R. D. Roberts, & L. Stankov (Eds.), *Extending intelligence: Enhancement and new constructs* (pp. 319–348). New York, NY: Erlbaum/Taylor & Francis.

Mayer, M. J., & Furlong, M. J. (2010). How safe are our schools? *Educational Researcher, 39,* 16–26.

Mayeux, L., Houser, J. J., & Dyches, K. D. (2011). Social acceptance and popularity: Two distinct forms of peer status. In A. H. N. Cillessen, D. Schwartz, & L. Mayeux (Eds.), *Popularity in the peer system* (pp. 79–102). New York, NY: Guilford.

McDevitt, T. M., & Ormrod, J. E. (2007). *Child development and education* (3rd ed.). Upper Saddle River, NJ: Merrill/Prentice Hall.

McElhaney, K. B., Antonishak, J., & Allen, J. P. (2008). "They like me, they like me not": Popularity and adolescents' perceptions of acceptance predicting social functioning over time. *Child Development, 79,* 720–731.

McInerney, D. M., Marsh, H. W., & Craven, R. (2008). Self-processes, learning, and enabling human potential. In H. W. Marsh, R. G. Craven, & D. M. McInerney (Eds.), *Self-processes, learning, and enabling human potential* (pp. 3–11). Charlotte, NC: Information Age.

McLoyd, V. C. (1998). Socioeconomic disadvantage and child development. *American Psychologist, 53,* 185–204.

McMillan, J. H., Singh, J., & Simonetta, L. G. (1994). The tyranny of self-oriented self-esteem. *Educational Horizons, 72*(3), 141–145.

Mendoza-Denton, R., & Mischel, W. (2007). Integrating system approaches to culture and personality: The cultural cognitive-affective processing system. In S. Kitayama & D. Cohen (Eds.), *Handbook of cultural psychology* (pp. 175–195). New York, NY: Guilford.

Menon, M., Tobin, D. D., Corby, B. C., Menon, M., Hodges, E. V. E., & Perry, D. G. (2007). The developmental costs of high self-esteem for antisocial children. *Child Development, 78,* 1627–1639.

Meyer, E. J. (2009). Creating schools that value sexual diversity. In S. R. Steinberg (Ed.), *Diversity and multiculturalism: A reader* (pp. 173–192). New York, NY: Peter Lang.

Meyers, D. T. (1987). The socialized individual and individual autonomy: An intersection between philosophy and psychology. In E. F. Kittay & D. T. Meyers (Eds.), *Women and moral theory* (pp. 139–153). Totowa, NJ: Rowman & Littlefield.

Mikulincer, M., & Shaver, P. R. (2005). Attachment security, compassion, and altruism. *Current Directions in Psychological Science, 14,* 34–38.

Miller, B. C., & Benson, B. (1999). Romantic and sexual relationship development during adolescence. In W. Furman, B. B. Brown, & C. Feiring (Eds.), *The development of romantic relationships in adolescence* (pp. 99–121). Cambridge, England: Cambridge University Press.

Miller, D. T., & Prentice, D. A. (1994). The self and the collective. *Personality and Social Psychology Bulletin, 20,* 451–453.

Miller, J. G. (2007). Cultural psychology of moral development. In S. Kitayama & D. Cohen (Eds.), *Handbook of cultural psychology* (pp. 477–499). New York, NY: Guilford.

Miller, P. A., Eisenberg, N., Fabes, R. A., & Shell, R. (1996). Relations of moral reasoning and vicarious emotion to young children's prosocial behavior toward peers and adults. *Developmental Psychology, 32,* 210–219.

Moll, J., de Oliveira-Souza, R., Garrido, G. J., Bramati, I. E., Caparelli-Daquer, E. M., Paiva, M. L., . . . Grafman, J. (2007). The self as a moral agent: Linking the neural bases of social agency and moral sensitivity. *Social Neuroscience, 2,* 336–352.

Moore, S., & Rosenthal, D. (2006). *Sexuality in adolescence: Current trends.* London: Routledge.

Morelli, G. A., & Rothbaum, F. (2007). Situating the child in context: Attachment relationships and self-regulation in different cultures. In S. Kitayama & D. Cohen (Eds.), *Handbook of cultural psychology* (pp. 500–527). New York, NY: Guilford.

Narváez, D., & Rest, J. (1995). The four components of acting morally. In W. M. Kurtines & J. L. Gewirtz (Eds.), *Moral development: An introduction* (pp. 385–400). Boston, MA: Allyn & Bacon.

Nasir, N. S., McLaughlin, M. W., & Jones, A. (2009). What does it mean to be African American? Constructions of race and academic identity in an urban public high school. *American Educational Research Journal, 46,* 73–114.

Neel, R. S., Jenkins, Z. N., & Meadows, N. (1990). Social problem-solving behaviors and aggression in young children: A descriptive observational study. *Behavioral Disorders, 16,* 39–51.

Nell, V. (2002). Why young men drive dangerously: Implications for injury prevention. *Current Directions in Psychological Science, 11,* 75–79.

Newcomb, A. F., & Bagwell, C. L. (1995). Children's friendship relations: A meta-analysis review. *Psychological Bulletin, 117,* 306–347.

Newman, R. S. (2008). Adaptive and nonadaptive help seeking with peer harassment: An integrative perspective of coping and self-regulation. *Educational Psychologist, 43,* 1–15.

Nucci, L. P. (2001). *Education in the moral domain.* Cambridge, England: Cambridge University Press.

Nucci, L. P. (2006). Classroom management for moral and social development. In C. M.

Evertson & C. S. Weinstein (Eds.), *Handbook of classroom management: Research, practice, and contemporary issues* (pp. 711–731). Mahwah, NJ: Erlbaum.

Nucci, L. (2009). *Nice is not enough: Facilitating moral development.* Upper Saddle River, NJ: Merrill/Pearson.

Nucci, L. P., & Nucci, M. S. (1982). Children's social interactions in the context of moral and conventional transgressions. *Child Development, 53,* 403–412.

Nucci, L. P., & Weber, E. K. (1995). Social interactions in the home and the development of young children's conceptions of the personal. *Child Development, 66,* 1438–1452.

Nuemi, J.-W. (2008). Self and socialization: How do young people navigate through adolescence? In H. W. Marsh, R. G. Craven, & D. M. McInerney (Eds.), *Self-processes, learning, and enabling human potential* (pp. 305–327). Charlotte, NC: Information Age.

Nunner-Winkler, G. (1984). Two moralities? A critical discussion of an ethic of care and responsibility versus an ethic of rights and justice. In W. M. Kurtines & J. L. Gewirtz (Eds.), *Morality, moral behavior, and moral development* (pp. 348–361). New York, NY: Wiley.

O'Connor, M. C., & Paunonen, S. V. (2007). Big Five personality predictors of post-secondary academic performance. *Personality and Individual Differences, 43,* 971–990.

Ogbu, J. U. (2008a). Collective identity and the burden of "acting White" in Black history, community, and education. In J. U. Ogbu (Ed.), *Minority status, oppositional culture, and schooling* (pp. 29–63). New York, NY: Routledge.

Ogbu, J. U. (2008b). Multiple sources of peer pressures among African American students. In J. U. Ogbu (Ed.), *Minority status, oppositional culture, and schooling* (pp. 89–111). New York, NY: Routledge.

O'Mara, A. J., Marsh, H. W., Craven, R. G., & Debus, R. L. (2006). Do self-concept interventions make a difference? A synergistic blend of construct validation and meta-analysis. *Educational Psychologist, 41,* 181–206.

Oppenheimer, L. (1986). Development of recursive thinking: Procedural variations. *International Journal of Behavioral Development, 9,* 401–411.

Orenstein, P. (1994). *Schoolgirls: Young women, self-esteem, and the confidence gap.* New York, NY: Doubleday.

Oskamp, S. (Ed.). (2000). *Reducing prejudice and discrimination.* Mahwah, NJ: Erlbaum.

Paciello, M., Fida, R., Tramontano, C., Lupinetti, C., & Caprara, G. V. (2008). Stability and change of moral disengagement and its impact on aggression and violence in late adolescence. *Child Development, 79,* 1288–1309.

Paget, K. F., Kritt, D., & Bergemann, L. (1984). Understanding strategic interactions in television commercials: A developmental study. *Journal of Applied Developmental Psychology, 5,* 145–161.

Pajares, F. (2009). Toward a positive psychology of academic motivation: The role of self-efficacy beliefs. In R. Gilman, E. S. Huebner, & M. J. Furlong (Eds.), *Handbook of positive psychology in schools* (pp. 149–160). New York, NY: Routledge.

Parada, R. H., Craven, R. G., & Marsh, H. W. (2008). The Beyond Bullying Secondary Program: An innovative program empowering teachers to counteract bullying in schools. In H. W. Marsh, R. G. Craven, & D. M. McInerney (Eds.), *Self-processes, learning, and enabling human potential* (pp. 373–395). Charlotte, NC: Information Age.

Park, N., & Peterson, C. (2009). Strengths of character in schools. In R. Gilman, E. S. Huebner, & M. J. Furlong (Eds.), *Handbook of positive psychology in schools* (pp. 65–76). New York, NY: Routledge.

Parks, C. P. (1995). Gang behavior in the schools: Reality or myth? *Educational Psychology Review, 7,* 41–68.

Patrick, H., Anderman, L. H., & Ryan, A. M. (2002). Social motivation and the classroom social environment. In C. Midgley (Ed.), *Goals, goal structures, and patterns of adaptive learning* (pp. 85–108). Mahwah, NJ: Erlbaum.

Pearce, M. J., Jones, S. M., Schwab-Stone, M. E., & Ruchkin, V. (2003). The protective effects of religiousness and parent involvement on the development of conduct problems among youth exposed to violence. *Child Development, 74,* 1682–1696.

Pedersen, S., Vitaro, F., Barker, E. D., & Borge, A. I. H. (2007). The timing of middle-childhood peer rejection and friendship: Linking early behavior to early-adolescent adjustment. *Child Development, 78,* 1037–1051.

Pellegrini, A. D. (2002). Bullying, victimization, and sexual harassment during the transition to middle school. *Educational Psychologist, 37,* 151–163.

Pellegrini, A. D. (2011). "In the eye of the beholder": Sex bias in observations and ratings of children's aggression. *Educational Researcher, 40,* 281–286.

Pellegrini, A. D., & Archer, J. (2005). Sex differences in competitive and aggressive behavior. In B. J. Ellis & D. F. Bjorklund (Eds.), *Origins of the social mind: Evolutionary psychology and child development* (pp. 219–244). New York, NY: Guilford.

Pellegrini, A. D., & Bartini, M. (2000). A longitudinal study of bullying, victimization, and peer affiliation during the transition from primary school to middle school. *American Educational Research Journal, 37,* 699–725.

Pellegrini, A. D., & Bohn, C. M. (2005). The role of recess in children's cognitive performance and school adjustment. *Educational Researcher, 34*(1), 13–19.

Pellegrini, A. D., Roseth, C. J., Van Ryzin, M. J., & Solberg, D. W. (2011). Popularity as a form of social dominance: An evolutionary perspective. In A. H. N. Cillessen, D. Schwartz, & L. Mayeux (Eds.), *Popularity in* the peer system (pp. 123–139). New York, NY: Guilford.

Perner, J., & Wimmer, H. (1985). "John thinks that Mary thinks that . . ." Attribution of second-order beliefs by 5- to 10-year-old children. Journal of Experimental Child Psychology, 39, 437–471.

Petersen, R. D. (2004). Understanding contemporary gangs in America: An interdisciplinary approach. Upper Saddle River, NJ: Prentice Hall.

Pettit, G. S. (2004). Violent children in developmental perspective: Risk and protective factors and the mechanisms through which they (may) operate. Current Directions in Psychological Science, 13, 194–197.

Pfeifer, J. H., Brown, C. S., & Juvonen, J. (2007). Teaching tolerance in schools: Lessons learned since Brown v. Board of Education about the development and reduction of children's prejudice. Social Policy Report, 21(2), 3–13, 16–17, 20–23. Ann Arbor, MI: Society for Research in Child Development.

Phinney, J. (1990). Ethnic identity in adolescents and adults: Review of research. Psychological Bulletin, 108, 499–514.

Poulin, F., & Boivin, M. (1999). Proactive and reactive aggression and boys' friendship quality in mainstream classrooms. Journal of Emotional and Behavioral Disorders, 7, 168–177.

Powell, G. J. (1983). The psychosocial development of minority children. New York, NY: Brunner/Mazel.

Power, F. C., Higgins, A., & Kohlberg, L. (1989). Lawrence Kohlberg's approach to moral education. New York, NY: Columbia University Press.

Powers, S. I., Hauser, S. T., & Kilner, L. A. (1989). Adolescent mental health. American Psychologist, 44, 200–208.

Prinstein, M. J., & Dodge, K. A. (Eds.). (2008). Understanding peer influence in children and adolescents. New York, NY: Guilford.

Prot, S., Gentile, D. A., Anderson, C. A., Suzuki, K., Swing, E., Lim, K. M., . . . Lam, B. C. P. (2014). Long-term relations among prosocial-media use, empathy, and prosocial behavior. Psychological Science, 25, 358–368.

Raine, A. (2008). From genes to brain to antisocial behavior. Current Directions in Psychological Science, 17, 323–328.

Reimer, J., Paolitto, D. P., & Hersh, R. H. (1983). Promoting moral growth: From Piaget to Kohlberg (2nd ed.). White Plains, NY: Longman.

Rest, J., Narvaez, D., Bebeau, M., & Thoma, S. (1999). A neo-Kohlbergian approach: The DIT and schema theory. Educational Psychology Review, 11, 291–324.

Reyna, V. F., Chapman, S. B., Dougherty, M. R., & Confrey, J. (Eds.). (2012). The adolescent brain: Learning, reasoning, and decision making. Washington, DC: American Psychological Association.

Rivers, I., Chesney, T., & Coyne, I. (2011). Cyberbullying. In C. P. Monks & I. Coyne (Eds.), Bullying in different contexts (pp. 211–230). Cambridge, England: Cambridge University Press.

Rivers, I., Poteat, V. P., Noret, N., & Ashurst, N. (2009). Observing bullying at school: The mental health implications of witness status. School Psychology Quarterly, 24(4), 211–223.

Rizzolatti, G., & Sinigaglia, C. (2008). Mirrors in the brain—How our minds share actions and emotions (F. Anderson, Trans.). Oxford, England: Oxford University Press.

Robins, R. W., & Trzesniewski, K. H. (2005). Self-esteem development across the lifespan. Current Directions in Psychological Science, 14, 158–162.

Robinson, J. P., & Espelage, D. L. (2012). Bullying explains only part of LGBTQ–heterosexual risk disparities: Implications for policy and practice. Educational Researcher, 41, 309–319.

Rogoff, B. (2003). The cultural nature of human development. Oxford, England: Oxford University Press.

Rose, A. J. (2002). Co-rumination in the friendship of girls and boys. Child Development, 73, 1830–1843.

Rose, A. J., Schwartz-Mette, R. A., Smith, R. L., Asher, S. R., Swenson, L. P., Carlson, W., & Waller, E. M. (2012). How girls and boys expect disclosure about problems will make them feel: Implications for friendships. Child Development, 83, 844–863.

Ross, M., & Wang, Q. (2010). Why we remember and what we remember: Culture and autobiographical memory. Perspectives on Psychological Science, 5, 401–409.

Ross, S. W, & Horner, R. H. (2009). Bully prevention in positive behavior support. Journal of Applied Behavior Analysis, 42, 747–759.

Rothbart, M. K. (2011). Becoming who we are: Temperament and personality in development. New York, NY: Guilford.

Rothbaum, F., & Trommsdorff, G. (2007). Do roots and wings complement or oppose one another? The socialization of relatedness and autonomy in cultural context. In J. E. Grusec & P. D. Hastings (Eds.), Handbook of socialization: Theory and research (pp. 461–489). New York, NY: Guilford.

Rubin, K. H., Cheah, C., & Menzer, M. M. (2010). Peers. In M. H. Bornstein (Ed.), Handbook of cultural developmental science (pp. 223–237). New York, NY: Psychology Press.

Rudolph, K. D., Caldwell, M. S., & Conley, C. S. (2005). Need for approval and children's well-being. Child Development, 76, 309–323.

Ruffman, T., Slade, L., & Crowe, E. (2002). The relation between children's and mothers' mental state language and theory-of-mind understanding. Child Development, 73, 734–751.

Rushton, J. P. (1980). Altruism, socialization, and society. Upper Saddle River, NJ: Prentice Hall.

Ryan, A. M. (2000). Peer groups as a context for the socialization of adolescents' motivation, engagement, and achievement in school. Educational Psychologist, 35, 101–111.

Ryan, A. M. (2001). The peer group as a context for the development of young adolescent motivation and achievement. Child Development, 72, 1135–1150.

Ryan, A. M., & Shim, S. S. (2008). An exploration of young adolescents' social achievement goals and social adjustment in middle school. Journal of Educational Psychology, 100, 672–687.

Ryan, R. M., & Kuczkowski, R. (1994). The imaginary audience, self-consciousness, and public individuation in adolescence. Journal of Personality, 62, 219–237.

Salmivalli, C., & Peets, K. (2009). Bullies, victims, and bully–victim relationships in middle childhood and early adolescence. In K. H. Rubin, W. M. Bukowski, & B. Laursen (Eds.), Handbook of peer interactions, relationships, and groups (pp. 322–340). New York, NY: Guilford.

Sandstrom, M. J. (2011). The power of popularity: Influence processes in childhood and adolescence. In A. H. N. Cillessen, D. Schwartz, & L. Mayeux (Eds.), Popularity in the peer system (pp. 219–244). New York, NY: Guilford Press.

Saudino, K. J., & Plomin, R. (2007). Why are hyperactivity and academic achievement related? Child Development, 78, 972–986.

Savin-Williams, R. C. (2008). Then and now: Recruitment, definition, diversity, and positive attributes of same-sex populations. Developmental Psychology, 44, 135–138.

Schlaefli, A., Rest, J. R., & Thoma, S. J. (1985). Does moral education improve moral judgment? A meta-analysis of intervention studies using the defining issues test. Review of Educational Research, 55, 319–352.

Schofield, J. W. (1995). Improving intergroup relations among students. In J. A. Banks & C. A. M. Banks (Eds.), Handbook of research on multicultural education (pp. 635–646). New York, NY: Macmillan.

Schult, C. A. (2002). Children's understanding of the distinction between intentions and desires. Child Development, 73, 1727–1747.

Schultz, K., Buck, P., & Niesz, T. (2000). Democratizing conversations: Racialized talk in a post-desegregated middle school. American Educational Research Journal, 37, 33–65.

Schunk, D. H., & Pajares, F. (2004). Self-efficacy in education revisited: Empirical and applied evidence. In D. M. McInerney & S. Van Etten (Eds.), Big theories revisited (pp. 115–138). Greenwich, CT: Information Age.

Schwartz, D., Dodge, K. A., Coie, J. D., Hubbard, J. A., Cillessen, A. H., Lemerise, E. A., & Bateman, H. (1998). Social-cognitive and behavioral correlates of aggression and victimization in boys' play groups. Journal of Abnormal Child Psychology, 26, 431–440.

Seaton, E. K., Scottham, K. M., & Sellers, R. M. (2006). The status model of racial identity development in African American adolescents: Evidence of structure, trajectories, and well-being. Child Development, 77, 1416–1426.

Seaton, M., Marsh, H. W., & Craven, R. G. (2010). Big-fish-little-pond effect:

Generalizability and moderation—two sides of the same coin. *American Educational Research Journal, 47,* 390–433.

Selman, R. L. (1980). *The growth of interpersonal understanding.* San Diego, CA: Academic Press.

Shariff, S. (2008). *Cyber-bullying: Issues and solutions for the school, the classroom and the home.* London: Routledge.

Sheets, R. H. (1999). Human development and ethnic identity. In R. H. Sheets & E. R. Hollins (Eds.), *Racial and ethnic identity in school practices: Aspects of human development* (pp. 91–101). Mahwah, NJ: Erlbaum.

Shrum, W., & Cheek, N. H. (1987). Social structure during the school years: Onset of the degrouping process. *American Sociological Review, 52,* 218–223.

Shulman, S., Elicker, J., & Sroufe, L. A. (1994). Stages of friendship growth in preadolescence as related to attachment history. *Journal of Social and Personal Relationships, 11,* 341–361.

Simons, R. L., Whitbeck, L. B., Conger, R. D., & Conger, K. J. (1991). Parenting factors, social skills, and value commitments as precursors to school failure, involvement with deviant peers, and delinquent behavior. *Journal of Youth and Adolescence, 20,* 645–664.

Sinai, M., Kaplan, A., & Flum, H. (2012). Promoting identity exploration within the school curriculum: A design-based study in a junior high literature lesson in Israel. *Contemporary Educational Psychology, 37,* 195–205.

Singer, D. G., & Singer, J. L. (1994). Barney & Friends *as education and entertainment: Phase 3. A national study: Can preschoolers learn through exposure to Barney & Friends?* New Haven, CT: Yale University Family Television Research and Consultation Center.

Sleeter, C. E., & Grant, C. A. (1999). *Making choices for multicultural education: Five approaches to race, class, and gender* (3rd ed.). Upper Saddle River, NJ: Merrill/Prentice Hall.

Smetana, J. G. (1981). Preschool children's conceptions of moral and social rules. *Child Development, 52,* 1333–1336.

Smetana, J. G. (2005). Adolescent-parent conflict: Resistance and subversion as developmental process. In L. Nucci (Ed.), *Conflict, contradiction, and contrarian elements in moral development and education* (pp. 69–91). Mahwah, NJ: Erlbaum.

Smetana, J. G. (2006). Social cognitive domain theory: Consistencies and variations in children's moral and social judgments. In M. Killen & J. Smetana (Eds.), *Handbook of moral development* (pp. 119–154). Mahwah, NJ: Erlbaum.

Smetana, J. G., & Braeges, J. L. (1990). The development of toddlers' moral and conventional judgments. *Merrill-Palmer Quarterly, 36,* 329–346.

Smith, E. R., & Semin, G. R. (2007). Situated social cognition. *Current Directions in Psychological Science, 16,* 132–135.

Smokowski, P., Buchanan, R. L., & Bacalleo, M. L. (2009). Acculturation and adjustment in

Latino adolescents: How cultural risk factors and assets influence multiple domains of adolescent mental health. *Journal of Primary Prevention, 30,* 371–393.

Snarey, J. (1995). In a communitarian voice: The sociological expansion of Kohlbergian theory, research, and practice. In W. M. Kurtines & J. L. Gewirtz (Eds.), *Moral development: An introduction* (pp. 109–134). Boston, MA: Allyn & Bacon.

Somerville, L. H. (2013). The teenage brain: Sensitivity to social evaluation. *Current Directions in Psychological Science, 22,* 121–127.

Somerville, L. H., Jones, R. M., & Casey, B. J. (2010). A time of change: Behavioral and neural correlates of adolescent sensitivity to appetitive and aversive environmental cues. *Brain and Cognition, 72,* 124–133.

Somerville, L. H., Jones, R. M., Ruberry, E. J., Dyke, J. P., Glover, G., & Casey, B. J. (2013). The medial prefrontal cortex and the emergence of self-conscious emotion in adolescence. *Psychological Science, 24,* 1554–1562.

Spear, L. P. (2007). Brain development and adolescent behavior. In D. Coch, K. W. Fischer, & G. Dawson (Eds.), *Human behavior, learning, and the developing brain: Typical development* (pp. 362–396). New York, NY: Guilford.

Spinrad, T. L., & Eisenberg, N. (2009). Empathy, prosocial behavior, and positive development in schools. In R. Gilman, E. S. Huebner, & M. J. Furlong (Eds.), *Handbook of positive psychology in schools* (pp. 119–129). New York, NY: Routledge.

Spunt, R. P., & Lieberman, M. D. (2013). The busy social brain: Evidence for automaticity and control in the neural systems supporting social cognition and action understanding. *Psychological Science, 24,* 80–86.

Sroufe, L. A., Carlson, E., & Shulman, S. (1993). Individuals in relationships: Development from infancy through adolescence. In D. C. Funder, R. D. Parke, C. Tomlinson-Keasey, & K. Widaman (Eds.), *Studying lives through time: Personality and development* (pp. 315–342). Washington, DC: American Psychological Association.

Steinberg, L. (1996). *Beyond the classroom: Why school reform has failed and what parents need to do.* New York, NY: Touchstone.

Steinberg, L. (2009). Should the science of adolescent brain development inform public policy? *American Psychologist, 64,* 739–750.

Steinberg, L., Cauffman, E., Woolard, J., Graham, S., & Banich, M. (2009). Are adolescents less mature than adults? *American Psychologist, 64,* 583–594.

Stewart, L., & Pascual-Leone, J. (1992). Mental capacity constraints and the development of moral reasoning. *Journal of Experimental Child Psychology, 54,* 251–287.

Stice, E. (2003). Puberty and body image. In C. Hayward (Ed.), *Gender differences at puberty* (pp. 61–76). Cambridge, England: Cambridge University Press.

Stice, E., & Barrera, M., Jr. (1995). A longitudinal examination of the reciprocal relations between perceived parenting and adolescents' substance use and externalizing behaviors. *Developmental Psychology, 31,* 322–334.

Strelau, J. (2008). *Temperament as a regulator of behavior: After fifty years of research.* Clinton Corners, NY: Werner.

Sullivan, J. R., & Conoley, J. C. (2004). Academic and instructional interventions with aggressive students. In J. C. Conoley & A. P. Goldstein (Eds.), *School violence intervention* (2nd ed., pp. 235–255). New York, NY: Guilford.

Suttles, G. D. (1970). Friendship as a social institution. In G. J. McCall, M. McCall, N. K. Denzin, G. D. Scuttles, & S. Kurth (Eds.), *Social relationships* (pp. 95–135). Chicago, IL: Aldine de Gruyter.

Swearer, S. M., Espelage, D. L., Vaillancourt, T., & Hymel, S. (2010). What can be done about school bullying? Linking research to educational practice. *Educational Researcher, 39,* 38–47.

Tager-Flusberg, H. (2007). Evaluating the theory-of-mind hypothesis of autism. *Current Directions in Psychological Science, 16,* 311–315.

Tatum, B. D. (1997). *"Why are all the Black kids sitting together in the cafeteria?" and other conversations about race.* New York, NY: Basic Books.

Thapa, A., Cohen, J., Guffey, S., & Higgins-D'Alessandro, A. (2013). A review of school climate research. *Review of Educational Research, 83,* 357–385.

Thomas, A., & Chess, S. (1977). *Temperament and development.* New York, NY: Brunner/Mazel.

Thompson, M., & Grace, C. O. (with Cohen, L. J.). (2001). *Best friends, worst enemies: Understanding the social lives of children.* New York, NY: Ballantine.

Thompson, R. A., & Wyatt, J. M. (1999). Current research on child maltreatment: Implications for educators. *Educational Psychology Review, 11,* 173–201.

Thorkildsen, T. A., Golant, C. J., & Cambray-Engstrom, E. (2008). Essential solidarities for understanding Latino adolescents' moral and academic engagement. In C. Hudley & A. E. Gottfried (Eds.), *Academic motivation and the culture of school in childhood and adolescence* (pp. 73–98). New York, NY: Oxford University Press.

Tisak, M. (1993). Preschool children's judgments of moral and personal events involving physical harm and property damage. *Merrill-Palmer Quarterly, 39,* 375–390.

Trautwein, U., Gerlach, E., & Lüdtke, O. (2008). Athletic classmates, physical self-concept, and free-time physical activity: A longitudinal study of frame of reference effects. *Journal of Educational Psychology, 100,* 988–1001.

Triandis, H. C. (1995). *Individualism and collectivism.* Boulder, CO: Westview Press.

Troop-Gordon, W., & Asher, S. R. (2005). Modification in children's goals when encountering obstacles in conflict resolution. *Child Development, 76,* 568–582.

Tsethlikai, M., & Greenhoot, A. F. (2006). The influence of another's perspective on children's recall of previously misconstrued events. *Developmental Psychology, 42,* 732–745.

Tsethlikai, M., Guthrie-Fulbright, Y., & Loera, S. (2007, March). *Social perspective coordination ability and children's recall of mutual conflict.* Paper presented at the biennial meeting of the Society for Research in Child Development, Boston, MA.

Turiel, E. (1983). *The development of social knowledge: Morality and convention.* Cambridge, England: Cambridge University Press.

Turiel, E. (1998). The development of morality. In W. Damon (Series Ed.) & N. Eisenberg (Vol. Ed.), *Handbook of child psychology: Vol. 3. Social, emotional, and personality development* (5th ed., pp. 863–932). New York, NY: Wiley.

Turiel, E. (2002). *The culture of morality: Social development, context, and conflict.* Cambridge, England: Cambridge University Press.

Turnbull, A. P., Pereira, L., & Blue-Banning, M. (2000). Teachers as friendship facilitators. *Teaching Exceptional Children, 32*(5), 66–70.

Vadeboncoeur, J. A., Vellos, R. E., & Goessling, K. P. (2011). Learning as (one part) identity construction. In D. M. McInerney, R. A. Walker, & G. A. D. Liem (Eds.), *Sociocultural theories of learning and motivation: Looking back, looking forward* (pp. 223–251). Charlotte, NC: Information Age.

Valentine, J. C., DuBois, D. L., & Cooper, H. (2004). The relation between self-beliefs and academic achievement: A meta-analytic review. *Educational Psychologist, 39,* 111–133.

Valiente, C., Lemery-Chalfant, K., & Swanson, J. (2010). Prediction of kindergartners' academic achievement from their effortful control and emotionality: Evidence for direct and moderated relations. *Journal of Educational Psychology, 102,* 550–560.

Valkenburg, P. M., & Peter, J. (2009). Social consequences of the Internet for adolescents: A decade of research. *Current Directions in Psychological Science, 18,* 1–5.

van den Berg, Y. H. M., Seters, E., & Cillessen, A. H. N. (2012). Changing peer perceptions and victimization through classroom arrangements: A field experiment. *Journal of Abnormal Child Psychology, 40,* 403–412.

van Goozen, S. H. M., Fairchild, G., & Harold, G. T. (2008). The role of neurobiological deficits in childhood antisocial behavior. *Current Directions in Psychological Science, 17,* 224–228.

Vaughn, S. (1991). Social skills enhancement in students with learning disabilities. In B. Y. L. Wong (Ed.), *Learning about learning disabilities* (pp. 407–440). San Diego, CA: Academic Press.

Veenstra, R., Lindenberg, S., Huitsing, G., Sainio, M., & Salmivalli, C. (2014). The role of teachers in bullying: The relation between antibullying attitudes, efficacy, and efforts to reduce bullying. *Journal of Educational Psychology, 106,* 1135–1143.

Viding, E., & McCrory, E. J. (2012) Genetic and neurocognitive contributions to the development of psychopathy. *Development and Psychopathology, 24,* 969–983.

Vitaro, F., Boivin, M., Brendgen, M., Girard, A., & Dionne, G. (2012). Social experiences in kindergarten and academic achievement in grade 1: A monozygotic twin difference study. *Journal of Educational Psychology, 104,* 366–380.

Vitaro, F., Gendreau, P. L., Tremblay, R. E., & Oligny, P. (1998). Reactive and proactive aggression differentially predict later conduct problems. *Journal of Child Psychology and Psychiatry and Allied Disciplines, 39,* 377–385.

Wainryb, C., Brehl, B. A., & Matwin, S. (2005). Being hurt and hurting others: Children's narrative accounts and moral judgments of their own interpersonal conflicts. *Monographs of the Society for Research in Child Development, 70*(3; Serial No. 281).

Walker, J. M. T., & Hoover-Dempsey, K. V. (2006). Why research on parental involvement is important to classroom management. In C. M. Evertson & C. S. Weinstein (Eds.), *Handbook of classroom management: Research, practice, and contemporary issues* (pp. 665–684). Mahwah, NJ: Erlbaum.

Walker, L. J. (1991). Sex differences in moral reasoning. In W. M. Kurtines & J. L. Gewirtz (Eds.), *Handbook of moral behavior and development: Vol. 2. Research* (pp. 333–364). Mahwah, NJ: Erlbaum.

Walker, L. J. (1995). Sexism in Kohlberg's moral psychology? In W. M. Kurtines & J. L. Gewirtz (Eds.), *Moral development: An introduction* (pp. 83–107). Boston, MA: Allyn & Bacon.

Ward, C., Bochner, S., & Furnham, A. (2001). *The psychology of culture shock* (2nd ed.). London: Routledge.

Waterhouse, L. (2006). Multiple intelligences, the Mozart effect, and emotional intelligence: A critical review. *Educational Psychologist, 41,* 207–225.

Watkins, D. E., & Wentzel, K. R. (2008). Training boys with ADHD to work collaboratively: Social and learning outcomes. *Contemporary Educational Psychology, 33,* 625–646.

Watson, M. (2008). Developmental discipline and moral education. In L. Nucci & D. Narvaez (Eds.), *Handbook of moral and character education* (pp. 175–203). New York, NY: Routledge.

Watson, M. W., Andreas, J. B., Fischer, K. W., & Smith, K. (2005). Patterns of risk factors leading to victimization and aggression in children and adolescents. In K. A. Kendall-Tackett & S. M. Giacomoni (Eds.), *Child victimization: Maltreatment, bullying and dating violence, prevention and intervention* (pp. 12.1–12.23). Kingston, NJ: Civic Research Institute.

Webber, J., & Plotts, C. A. (2008). *Emotional and behavioral disorders: Theory and practice* (5th ed.). Boston, MA: Allyn and Bacon.

Wellman, H. M., Cross, D., & Watson, J. (2001). Meta-analysis of theory-of-mind development: The truth about false belief. *Child Development, 72,* 655–684.

Wellman, H. M., Phillips, A. T., & Rodriguez, T. (2000). Young children's understanding of perception, desire, and emotion. *Child Development, 71,* 895–912.

Wentzel, K. R. (1999). Social-motivational processes and interpersonal relationships: Implications for understanding motivation at school. *Journal of Educational Psychology, 91,* 76–97.

Wentzel, K. R. (2009). Peers and academic functioning at school. In K. H. Rubin, W. M. Bukowski, & B. Laursen (Eds.), *Handbook of peer interactions, relationships, and groups* (pp. 531–547). New York, NY: Guilford.

Wentzel, K. R., Filisetti, L., & Looney, L. (2007). Adolescent prosocial behavior: The role of self-processes and contextual cues. *Child Development, 78,* 895–910.

Wentzel, K. R., & Looney, L. (2007). Socialization in school settings. In J. E. Grusec & P. D. Hastings (Eds.), *Handbook of socialization: Theory and research* (pp. 382–403). New York, NY: Guilford.

Wentzel, K. R., & Watkins, D. E. (2011). Instruction based on peer interactions. In R. E. Mayer & P. A. Alexander (Eds.), *Handbook of research on learning and instruction* (pp. 322–343). New York, NY: Routledge.

White, R., & Cunningham, A. M. (1991). *Ryan White: My own story.* New York, NY: Signet.

Whitesell, N. R., Mitchell, C. M., Kaufman, C. E., Spicer, P., & the Voices of Indian Teens Project Team. (2006). Developmental trajectories of personal and collective self-concept among American Indian adolescents. *Child Development, 77,* 1487–1503.

Wigfield, A., Eccles, J. S., & Pintrich, P. R. (1996). Development between the ages of 11 and 25. In D. C. Berliner & R. C. Calfee (Eds.), *Handbook of educational psychology* (pp. 148–185). New York, NY: Macmillan.

Willard, N. E. (2007). *Cyberbullying and cyberthreats: Responding to the challenge of online social aggression, threats, and distress.* Champaign, IL: Research Press.

Wimmer, H., & Perner, J. (1983). Beliefs about beliefs: Representation and constraining function of wrong beliefs in young children's understanding of deception. *Cognition, 13,* 103–128.

Witmer, S. (1996). Making peace, the Navajo way. *Tribal College Journal, 8,* 24–27.

Wittmer, D. S., & Honig, A. S. (1994). Encouraging positive social development in young children. *Young Children, 49*(5), 4–12.

Woolfe, T., Want, S. C., & Siegal, M. (2002). Signposts to development: Theory of mind in deaf children. *Child Development, 73,* 768–778.

Yates, M., & Youniss, J. (1996). A developmental perspective on community service in adolescence. *Social Development, 5,* 85–111.

Yau, J., & Smetana, J. G. (2003). Conceptions of moral, social-conventional, and personal events among Chinese preschoolers in Hong Kong. *Child Development, 74,* 647–658.

Yeager, D. S., & Dweck, C. S. (2012). Mindsets that promote resilience: When students believe that personal characteristics can be developed. *Educational Psychologist, 47,* 302–314.

Yeung, R. S., & Leadbeater, B. J. (2007, March). *Peer victimization and emotional and behavioral problems in adolescence: The moderating effect of adult emotional support.* Paper presented at the biennial meeting of the Society for Research in Child Development, Boston, MA.

Yip, T., & Fuligni, A. J. (2002). Daily variation in ethnic identity, ethnic behaviors, and psychological well-being among American adolescents of Chinese descent. *Child Development, 73,* 1557–1572.

Young, L., & Saxe, R. (2009). Innocent intentions: A correlation between forgiveness for accidental harm and neural activity. *Neuropsychologia, 47,* 2065–2072.

Youniss, J., & Yates, M. (1999). Youth service and moral-civic identity: A case for everyday morality. *Educational Psychology Review, 11,* 361–376.

Yuker, H. E. (Ed.). (1988). *Attitudes toward persons with disabilities.* New York, NY: Springer.

Zahn-Waxler, C., Radke-Yarrow, M., Wagner, E., & Chapman, M. (1992). Development of concern for others. *Developmental Psychology, 28,* 126–136.

Zahn-Waxler, C., & Robinson, J. (1995). Empathy and guilt: Early origins of feelings of responsibility. In J. P. Tangney & K. W. Fischer (Eds.), *Self-conscious emotions: The psychology of shame, guilt, embarrassment, and pride* (pp. 143–173). New York, NY: Guilford.

Zeidner, M., Roberts, R. D., & Matthews, G. (2002). Can emotional intelligence be schooled? A critical review. *Educational Psychologist, 37,* 215–231.

Zelli, A., Dodge, K. A., Lochman, J. E., & Laird, R. D. (1999). The distinction between beliefs legitimizing aggression and deviant processing of social cues: Testing measurement validity and the hypothesis that biased processing mediates the effects of beliefs on aggression. *Journal of Personality and Social Psychology, 77,* 150–166.

Zimmerman, B. J., & Moylan, A. R. (2009). Self-regulation: Where metacognition and motivation intersect. In D. J. Hacker, J. Dunlosky, & A. C. Graesser (Eds.), *Handbook of metacognition in education* (pp. 299–315). New York, NY: Routledge.

CHAPTER 4

Aboud, F. E., & Yousafzai, A. K. (2015). Global health and development in early childhood. *Annual Review of Psychology, 66,* 433–457.

Adger, C. T., Wolfram, W., & Christian, D. (2007). *Dialects in schools and communities* (2nd ed.). New York, NY: Routledge.

Aikens, N. L., & Barbarin, O. (2008). Socioeconomic differences in reading trajectories: The contribution of family, neighborhood, and school contexts. *Journal of Educational Psychology, 100,* 235–251.

Alim, H. S., & Baugh, J. (Eds.). (2007). *Talkin Black talk: Language, education, and social change.* New York, NY: Teachers College Press.

Allen, J. P., & Antonishak, J. (2008). Adolescent peer influences: Beyond the dark side. In M. J. Prinstein & K. A. Dodge (Eds.), *Understanding peer influence in children and adolescents* (pp. 141–160). New York, NY: Guilford.

Allison, K. W. (1998). Stress and oppressed social category membership. In J. Swim & C. Stangor (Eds.), *Prejudice: The target's perspective* (pp. 149–170). San Diego, CA: Academic Press.

Altermatt, E. R., Jovanovic, J., & Perry, M. (1998). Bias or responsivity? Sex and achievement-level effects on teachers' classroom questioning practices. *Journal of Educational Psychology, 90,* 516–527.

American Friends of Tel Aviv University. (2015, February 26). Teacher prejudices put girls off math, science, study suggests. *ScienceDaily.* Retrieved from www.sciencedaily.com/releases/2015/02/150226110454.htm

American Psychological Association. (2012). Facing the school dropout dilemma. Washing, DC: Author. Retrieved from http://www.apa.org/pi/families/resources/school-dropout-prevention.pdf

Anderman, E. M. (2012). Adolescence. In K. R. Harris, S. Graham, T. Urdan, A. G. Bus, S. Major, & H. L. Swanson (Eds.), *APA educational psychology handbook, Vol 3: Application to learning and teaching* (pp. 43–61). Washington, DC: American Psychological Association.

Anderman, E. M., & Anderman, L. H. (2014). *Classroom motivation* (2nd ed.). Boston, MA: Pearson.

Anderson, L. W., & Pellicer, L. O. (1998). Toward an understanding of unusually successful programs for economically disadvantaged students. *Journal of Education for Students Placed at Risk, 3,* 237–263.

Aronson, J., & Steele, C. M. (2005). Stereotypes and the fragility of academic competence, motivation, and self-concept. In A. J. Elliot & C. S. Dweck (Eds.), *Handbook of competence and motivation* (pp. 436–456). New York, NY: Guilford.

Arroyo, I., Burleson, W., Tai, M., Muldner, K., & Woolf, B. P. (2013). Gender differences in the use and benefit of advanced learning technologies for mathematics. *Journal of Educational Psychology, 105*(4), 957–969.

Ashiabi, G. S., & O'Neal, K. K. (2008). A framework for understanding the association between food insecurity and children's developmental outcomes. *Child Development Perspectives, 2,* 71–77.

Atran, S., Medin, D. L., & Ross, N. O. (2005). The cultural mind: Environmental decision making and cultural modeling within and across populations. *Psychological Review, 112,* 744–776.

Attie, I., Brooks-Gunn, J., & Petersen, A. (1990). A developmental perspective on eating

disorders and eating problems. In M. Lewis & S. M. Miller (Eds.), *Handbook of developmental psychopathology* (pp. 409–420). New York, NY: Plenum Press.

Au, K. H. (1980). Participation structures in a reading lesson with Hawaiian children: Analysis of a culturally appropriate instructional event. *Anthropology and Education Quarterly, 11,* 91–115.

Auster, C. J., & Mansbach, C. S. (2012). The gender marketing of toys: An analysis of color and type of toy on the Disney store website. *Sex Roles, 67*(7–8), 375–388. doi:10.1007/s11199-012-0177-8.

Auyeung, B., Baron-Cohen, S., Ashwin, E., Knickmeyer, R., Taylor, K., Hackett, G., et al. (2009). Fetal testosterone predicts sexually differentiated childhood behavior in girls and in boys. *Psychological Science, 20,* 144–148.

Bailey, A. L., Osipova, A., & Reynolds Kelly, K. (2016). Language development. In L. Corno & E. M. Anderman (Eds.), *Handbook of educational psychology* (3rd ed.) (pp. 199–212). New York, NY: Routledge.

Balfanz, R., Herzog, L., & Mac Iver, D. J. (2007). Preventing student disengagement and keeping students on the graduation path in urban middle-grades schools: Early identification and effective interventions. *Educational Psychologist, 42*(4), 223–235.

Balfanz, R., & Legters, N. (2004). *Locating the dropout crisis: Which high schools produce the nation's dropouts? Where are they located? Who attends them?* Baltimore, MD: Center for Research on the Education of Students Placed at Risk.

Bandura, A., Barbaranelli, C., Caprara, G. V., & Pastorelli, C. (2001). Self-efficacy beliefs as shapers of children's aspirations and career trajectories. *Child Development, 72,* 187–206.

Banks, J., Cochran-Smith, M., Moll, L., Richert, A., Zeichner, K., LePage, P., et al. (with McDonald, M.). (2005). Teaching diverse learners. In L. Darling-Hammond & J. Bransford (Eds.), *Preparing teachers for a changing world: What teachers should learn and be able to do* (pp. 232–274). San Francisco, CA: Jossey-Bass/Wiley.

Banks, J. A., & Banks, C. A. M. (Eds.). (1995). *Handbook of research on multicultural education.* New York, NY: Macmillan.

Barbarin, O., Mercado, M., & Jigjidsuren, D. (2010). Development for tolerance and respect for diversity in the context of immigration. In E. L. Grigorenko & R. Takanishi (Eds.), *Immigration, diversity, and education* (pp. 276–288). New York, NY: Routledge.

Battin-Pearson, S., Newcomb, M. D., Abbott, R. D., Hill, K. G., Catalano, R. F., & Hawkins, J. D. (2000). Predictors of early high school dropout: A test of five theories. *Journal of Educational Psychology, 92,* 568–582.

Becker, B. E., & Luthar, S. S. (2002). Social-emotional factors affecting achievement outcomes among disadvantaged students: Closing the achievement gap. *Educational Psychologist, 37,* 197–214.

Belfiore, P. J., & Hornyak, R. S. (1998). Operant theory and application to self-monitoring in adolescents. In D. H. Schunk & B. J. Zimmerman (Eds.), *Self-regulated learning: From teaching to self-reflective practice* (pp. 184–202). New York, NY: Guilford.

Bem, S. L. (1981). Gender schema theory: A cognitive account of sex typing. *Psychological Review, 88,* 354–364.

Bem, S. L. (1983). Gender schema theory and its implications for child development: Raising gender-aschematic children in a gender-schematic society. *Signs: Journal of Women in Culture and Society, 8,* 598–616.

Bem, S. L. (1984). Androgyny and gender schema theory: A conceptual and empirical integration. In T. B. Sonderegger (Ed.), *Nebraska Symposium on Motivation* (Vol. 32, pp. 179–226). Lincoln: University of Nebraska Press.

Benenson, J. F., & Christakos, A. (2003) The greater fragility of females' versus males' closest same-sex friendships. *Child Development, 74,* 1123–1129.

Benenson, J. F., Maiese, R., Dolenszky, E., Dolensky, N., Sinclair, N., & Simpson, A. (2002). Group size regulates self-assertive versus self-deprecating responses to interpersonal competition. *Child Development, 73,* 1818–1829.

Berliner, D. C. (2005, April). *Ignoring the forest, blaming the trees: Our impoverished view of educational reform.* Paper presented at the annual meeting of the American Educational Research Association, Montreal, Canada.

Bigler, R. S., & Liben, L. S. (2007). Developmental intergroup theory: Explaining and reducing children's social stereotyping and prejudice. *Current Directions in Psychological Science, 16,* 162–166.

Binns, K., Steinberg, A., Amorosi, S., & Cuevas, A. M. (1997). *The Metropolitan Life survey of the American teacher 1997: Examining gender issues in public schools.* New York, NY: Louis Harris and Associates.

Bleeker, M. M., & Jacobs, J. E. (2004). Achievement in math and science: Do mothers' beliefs matter 12 years later? *Journal of Educational Psychology, 96,* 97–109.

Boling, C. J., & Evans, W. H. (2008). Reading success in the secondary classroom. *Preventing School Failure, 52*(2), 59–66.

Bornholt, L. J., Goodnow, J. J., & Cooney, G. H. (1994). Influences of gender stereotypes on adolescents' perceptions of their own achievement. *American Educational Research Journal, 31,* 675–692.

Bosacki, S. L. (2000). Theory of mind and self-concept in preadolescents: Links with gender and language. *Journal of Educational Psychology, 92,* 709–717.

Boutte, G. S., & McCormick, C. B. (1992). Authentic multicultural activities: Avoiding pseudomulticulturalism. *Childhood Education, 68,* 140–144.

Branch, C. (1999). Race and human development. In R. H. Sheets & E. R. Hollins (Eds.), *Racial and ethnic identity in school practices: Aspects of human development* (pp. 7–28). Mahwah, NJ: Erlbaum.

Branum-Martin, L., Mehta, P.D., Carlson, C.D., Francis, D. J., & Goldenberg, C. (2014). The nature of Spanish versus English language use at home. *Journal of Educational Psychology, 106* (1), 181–199.

Brayboy, B. M. J., & Searle, K. A. (2007). Thanksgiving and serial killers: Representations of American Indians in schools. In S. Books (Ed.), *Invisible children in the society and its schools* (3rd ed., pp. 173–192). Mahwah, NJ: Erlbaum.

Brody, G. H., Chen, Y.-F., Murry, V. M., Ge, X., Simons, R. L., Gibbons, F. X., et al. (2006). Perceived discrimination and the adjustment of African American youths: A five-year longitudinal analysis with contextual moderation effects. *Child Development, 77,* 1170–1189.

Brooks-Gunn, J. (2003). Do you believe in magic? What we can expect from early childhood intervention programs. *Social Policy Report of the Society for Research in Child Development, 17*(1), 3–14.

Brooks-Gunn, J., Linver, M. R., & Fauth, R. C. (2005). Children's competence and socioeconomic status in the family and neighborhood. In A. J. Elliot & C. S. Dweck (Eds.), *Handbook of competence and motivation* (pp. 414–435). New York, NY: Guilford.

Brophy, J., Alleman, J., & Knighton, B. (2009). *Inside the social studies classroom.* New York, NY: Routledge.

Bussey, K., & Bandura, A. (1992). Self-regulatory mechanisms governing gender development. *Child Development, 63,* 1236–1250.

Byrnes, J. P. (2003). Factors predictive of mathematics achievement in White, Black, and Hispanic 12th graders. *Journal of Educational Psychology, 95,* 316–326.

Cameron, L., Rutland, A., Brown, R., & Douch, R. (2006). Changing children's intergroup attitudes toward refugees: Testing different models of extended contact. *Child Development, 77,* 1208–1219.

Card, N. A., Stucky, B. D., Sawalani, G. M., & Little T. D. (2008). Direct and indirect aggression during childhood and adolescence: A meta-analytic review of gender differences, intercorrelations, and relations to maladjustment. *Child Development, 79,* 1185–1229.

Casey, B. M., Andrews, N., Schindler, H., Kersh, J. E., Samper, A., & Copley, J. (2008). The development of spatial skills through interventions involving block building activities. *Cognition and Instruction, 26,* 269–309.

Castagno, A. E., & Brayboy, B. M. J. (2008). Culturally responsive schooling for indigenous youth: A review of the literature. *Review of Educational Research, 78,* 941–993.

Castelli, L., De Dea, C., & Nesdale, D. (2008). Learning social attitudes: Children's sensitivity to the nonverbal behaviors of adult models during interracial interactions. *Personality and Social Psychology Bulletin, 34*(11), 1504–1513.

Cazden, C. B. (2001). *Classroom discourse: The language of teaching and learning* (2nd ed.). Portsmouth, NH: Heinemann.

Chapman, C., Laird, J., & KewalRamani, A. (2010). *Trends in high school dropout and completion rates in the United States: 1972–2008.* Washington, DC: National Center for Education Statistics, U.S. Department of Education.

Chen, X., Chung, J., & Hsiao, C. (2009). Peer interactions and relationships from a cross-cultural perspective. In K. H. Rubin, W. M. Bukowski, & B. Laursen (Eds.), *Handbook of peer interactions, relationships, and groups* (pp. 432–451). New York, NY: Guilford.

Chisholm, J. S. (1996). Learning "respect for everything": Navajo images of development. In C. P. Hwant, M. E. Lamb, & I. E. Sigel (Eds.), *Images of childhood* (pp. 167–183). Mahwah, NJ: Erlbaum.

Christenson, S. L., & Thurlow, M. L. (2004). School dropouts: Prevention, considerations, interventions, and challenges. *Current Directions in Psychological Science, 13,* 36–39.

Christle, C. A., Jolivette, K., & Nelson, M. (2007). School characteristics related to high school dropout rates. *Remedial and Special Education, 28*(6), 325–339. doi:10.1177/0741 9325070280060201.

Clark, R. M. (1983). *Family life and school achievement: Why poor black children succeed or fail.* Chicago, IL: University of Chicago Press.

Coe, J., Salamon, L., & Molnar, J. (1991). *Homeless children and youth.* New Brunswick, NJ: Transaction.

Cohen, A. B. (2009). Many forms of culture. *American Psychologist, 64,* 194–204.

Cole, C.M. Waldron, N., & Majd, M. (2004). Academic progress of students across inclusive and traditional settings. *Mental Retardation, 42,* 136–144.

Cole, D. A., Martin, J. M., Peeke, L. A., Seroczynski, A. D., & Fier, J. (1999). Children's over- and underestimation of academic competence: A longitudinal study of gender differences, depression, and anxiety. *Child Development, 70,* 459–473.

Cole, P. M., Tamang, B. L., & Shrestha, S. (2006). Cultural variations in the socialization of young children's anger and shame. *Child Development, 77,* 1237–1251.

Connell, N. M., Schell-Busey, N. M., Pearce, A. N., & Negro, P. (2014). Badgrlz? Exploring sex differences in cyberbullying behaviors. *Youth Violence and Juvenile Justice, 12*(3), 209–228.

Cook, T. D., Herman, M. R., Phillips, M., & Settersten, R. A., Jr. (2002). Some ways in which neighborhoods, nuclear families, friendship groups, and schools jointly affect changes in early adolescent development. *Child Development, 73,* 1283–1309.

Correa-Chávez, M., Rogoff, B., & Mejía Arauz, R. (2005). Cultural patterns in attending to two events at once. *Child Development, 76,* 664–678.

Cornell, D., Gregory, A., Huang, F., & Fan, X. (2013). Perceived prevalence of teasing and bullying predicts high school dropout rates. *Journal of Educational Psychology, 105*(1), 138–149.

Cosden, M., Morrison, G., Albanese, A. L., & Macias, S. (2001). When homework is not home work: After-school programs for homework assistance. *Educational Psychologist, 36,* 211–221.

Crago, M. B., Annahatak, B., & Ningiuruvik, L. (1993). Changing patterns of language socialization in Inuit homes. *Anthropology and Education Quarterly, 24,* 205–223.

Crick, N. R., Grotpeter, J. K., & Bigbee, M. A. (2002). Relationally and physically aggressive children's intent attributions and feelings of distress for relational and instrumental peer provocation. *Child Development, 73,* 1134–1142.

Croninger, R. G., & Valli, L. (2009). "Where is the action?" Challenges to studying the teaching of reading in elementary classrooms. *Educational Researcher, 38,* 100–108.

Crosnoe, R., & Cooper, C. E. (2010). Economically disadvantaged children's transitions into elementary school: Linking family processes, school contexts, and educational policy. *American Educational Research Journal, 47,* 258–291.

Cross, W. E., Jr., Strauss, L., & Fhagen-Smith, P. (1999). African American identity development across the life span: Educational implications. In R. H. Sheets & E. R. Hollins (Eds.), *Racial and ethnic identity in school practices: Aspects of human development* (pp. 29–47). Mahwah, NJ: Erlbaum.

Crouter, A. C., Whiteman, S. D., McHale, S. M., & Osgood, D. W. (2007). Development of gender attitude traditionality across middle childhood and adolescence. *Child Development, 78,* 911–926.

Davenport, E. C., Jr., Davison, M. L., Kuang, H., Ding, S., Kim, S., & Kwak, N. (1998). High school mathematics course-taking by gender and ethnicity. *American Educational Research Journal, 35,* 497–514.

Davila, J. (2008). Depressive symptoms and adolescent romance: Theory, research, and implications. *Child Development Perspectives, 2*(1), 26–31.

de Boer, H., Bosker, R. J., & van der Werf, M. P. C. (2010). Sustainability of teacher expectation bias effects on long-term student performance. *Journal of Educational Psychology, 102,* 168–179.

de la Fuente, J., Santiago, J., Román, A., Dumitrache, C., & Casasanto, D. (2014). When you think about it, your past is in front of you: How culture shapes spatial conceptions of time. *Psychological Science, 25*(9), 1682–1690.

Deaux, K. (1984). From individual differences to social categories: Analysis of a decade's research on gender. *American Psychologist, 39,* 105–116.

DeBose, C. E. (2007). The Ebonics phenomenon, language planning, and the hegemony of Standard English. In H. S. Alim & J. Baugh (Eds.), *Talkin Black talk: Language, education, and social change* (pp. 30–42). New York, NY: Teachers College Press.

Dekker, S., Krabbendam, L., Lee, N. C., Boschloo, A., de Groot, R., & Jolles, J. (2013). Sex differences in goal orientation in adolescents aged 10–19: The older boys adopt work-avoidant goals twice as often as girls. *Learning and Individual Differences, 26,* 196–200.

Delgado-Gaitan, C. (1994). Socializing young children in Mexican-American families: An intergenerational perspective. In P. M. Greenfield & R. R. Cocking (Eds.), *Cross-cultural roots of minority child development* (pp. 55–86). Mahwah, NJ: Erlbaum.

Deyhle, D. (2008). Navajo youth and Anglo racism: Cultural integrity and resistance. In J. U. Ogbu (Ed.), *Minority status, oppositional culture, and schooling* (pp. 433–480). New York, NY: Routledge.

Deyhle, D., & LeCompte, M. (1999). Cultural differences in child development: Navajo adolescents in middle schools. In R. H. Sheets & E. R. Hollins (Eds.), *Racial and ethnic identity in school practices: Aspects of human development* (pp. 123–139). Mahwah, NJ: Erlbaum.

Deyhle, D., & Margonis, F. (1995). Navajo mothers and daughters: Schools, jobs, and the family. *Anthropology and Education Quarterly, 26,* 135–167.

Diekman, A. B., Brown, E. R., Johnston, A. M., & Clark, E. K. (2010). Seeking congruity between goals and roles: A new look at why women opt out of science, technology, engineering, and mathematics careers. *Psychological Science, 21,* 1051–1057.

Dovidio, J. F., & Gaertner, S. L. (1999). Reducing prejudice: Combating intergroup biases. *Current Directions in Psychological Science, 8,* 101–105.

Duncan, G. J., & Magnuson, K. A. (2005). Can family socioeconomic resources account for racial and ethnic test score gaps? *The Future of Children, 15*(1), 35–54.

Dupere, V., Leventhal, T., Crosnoe, R., & Dion, E. (2010). Understanding the positive role of neighborhood socioeconomic advantage in achievement: The contribution of the home, child care, and school environments. *Developmental Psychology, 46*(5), 1227–1244.

Dweck, C. S. (2000). *Self-theories: Their role in motivation, personality, and development.* Philadelphia, PA: Psychology Press.

Eaton, W. O., & Enns, L. R. (1986). Sex differences in human motor activity level. *Psychological Bulletin, 100,* 19–28.

Eccles, J. S. (2005). Subjective task value and the Eccles et al. model of achievement-related choices. In A. J. Elliot & C. S. Dweck (Eds.), *Handbook of competence and motivation* (pp. 105–121). New York, NY: Guilford.

Eccles, J. S. (2007). Families, schools, and developing achievement-related motivations and engagement. In J. E. Grusec & P. D. Hastings (Eds.), *Handbook of socialization: Theory and research* (pp. 665–691). New York, NY: Guilford.

Eccles, J. S. (2009). Who am I and what am I going to do with my life? Personal and collective identities as motivators of action. *Educational Psychologist, 44,* 78–89.

Edwards, P. A., & Turner, J. D. (2010). Do you hear what I hear? Using the parent story approach to listen and learn from African American parents. In M. L. Dantas & P. C. Manyak (Eds.), *Home–school connections in a multicultural society: Learning from and with culturally and linguistically diverse families* (pp. 137–155). New York, NY: Routledge.

Eisenberg, N., Martin, C. L., & Fabes, R. A. (1996). Gender development and gender effects. In D. C. Berliner & R. C. Calfee (Eds.), *Handbook of educational psychology* (pp. 358–396). New York, NY: Macmillan.

Eriks-Brophy, A., & Crago, M. B. (1994). Transforming classroom discourse: An Inuit example. *Language and Education, 8*(3), 105–122.

Eustice, K. (2012, November 7). Teaching in multicultural classrooms: Tips, challenges and opportunities. *The Guardian.* Retrieved from http://www.theguardian.com/teacher-network/teacher-blog/2012/nov/07/teaching-multicutural-classroom-advice-challenges

Evans, G. W. (2004). The environment of childhood poverty. *American Psychologist, 59,* 77–92.

Evans, G. W., Gonnella, C., Marcynyszyn, L. A., Gentile, L., & Salpekar, N. (2005). The role of chaos in poverty and children's socioemotional adjustment. *Psychological Science, 16,* 560–565.

Evans, G. W., & Schamberg, M. A. (2009). Childhood poverty, chronic stress, and adult working memory. *Proceedings of the National Academy of Sciences of the United States of America, 106,* 6545–6549.

Evans-Winters, V., & Ivie, C. (2009). Lost in the shuffle: Re-calling a critical pedagogy for urban girls. In S. R. Steinberg (Ed.), *Diversity and multiculturalism: A reader* (pp. 411–421). New York, NY: Peter Lang.

Fabes, R. A., Martin, C. L., & Hanish, L. D. (2003). Young children's play qualities in same-, other-, and mixed-sex peer groups. *Child Development, 74,* 921–932.

Fairchild, H. H., & Edwards-Evans, S. (1990). African American dialects and schooling: A review. In A. M. Padilla, H. H. Fairchild, & C. M. Valadez (Eds.), *Bilingual education: Issues and strategies* (pp. 75–85). Newbury Park, CA: Sage.

Fan, W., & Wolters, C.A. (2012). School motivation and high school dropout: The mediating role of educational expectation. *British Journal of Educational Psychology, 84,* 22–39.

Farkas, G. (2008). Quantitative studies of oppositional culture: Arguments and evidence. In J. U. Ogbu (Ed.), *Minority status, oppositional culture, and schooling* (pp. 312–347). New York, NY: Routledge.

Farrell, E. (1990). *Hanging in and dropping out: Voices of at-risk high school students.* New York, NY: Teachers College Press.

Feng, J., Spence, I., & Pratt, J. (2007). Playing an action video game reduces gender differences in spatial cognition. *Psychological Science, 18,* 850–855.

Fennema, E. (1987). Sex-related differences in education: Myths, realities, and interventions. In V. Richardson-Koehler (Ed.), *Educators' handbook: A research perspective* (pp. 329–347). White Plains, NY: Longman.

Finn, J. D. (1989). Withdrawing from school. *Review of Educational Research, 59,* 117–142.

Ford, M. E. (1996). Motivational opportunities and obstacles associated with social responsibility and caring behavior in school contexts. In J. Juvonen & K. R. Wentzel (Eds.), *Social motivation: Understanding children's school adjustment* (pp. 126–153). Cambridge, England: Cambridge University Press.

Foulds, J., Wells, J. E., & Mulder, R. (2014). The association between material living standard and psychological distress: Results from a New Zealand population survey. *International Journal of Social Psychiatry, 60*(8), 766–771.

Frankland, H. C., Turnbull, A. P., Wehmeyer, M. L., & Blackmountain, L. (2004). An exploration of the self-determination construct and disability as it relates to the Diné (Navajo) culture. *Education and Training in Developmental Disabilities, 39*(3), 191–205.

Fredricks, J. A., Blumenfeld, P. C., & Paris, A. H. (2004). School engagement: Potential of the concept, state of the evidence. *Review of Educational Research, 74,* 59–109.

Freedom Writers (with Gruwell, E.) (1999). *The Freedom Writers diary: How a teacher and 150 teens used writing to change themselves and the world around them.* New York, NY: Broadway Books.

French, D. C., Jansen, E. A., & Pidada, S. (2002). United States and Indonesian children's and adolescents' reports of relational aggression by disliked peers. *Child Development, 73,* 1143–1150.

Frost, J. L., Shin, D., & Jacobs, P. J. (1998). Physical environments and children's play. In O. N. Saracho & B. Spodek (Eds.), *Multiple perspectives on play in early childhood education* (pp. 255–294). Albany: State University of New York Press.

Fuchs, L. S., Fuchs, D., Craddock, C., Hollenbeck, K. N., Hamlett, C. L., & Schatschneider, C. (2008). Effects of small-group tutoring with and without validated classroom instruction on at-risk, students' math problem solving: Are two tiers of prevention better than one? *Journal of Educational Psychology, 100,* 491–509.

Fuligni, A. J. (1998). The adjustment of children from immigrant families. *Current Directions in Psychological Science, 7,* 99–103.

Furnham, A., & Mak, T. (1999). Sex-role stereotyping in television commercials: A review and comparison of fourteen studies done on five continents over 25 years. *Sex Roles, 41,* 413–437.

Gallagher, A. M., & Kaufman, J. C. (Eds.). (2005). *Gender differences in mathematics: An integrative psychological approach.* Cambridge, England: Cambridge University Press.

Galliher, R. V., Jones, M. D., & Dahl, A. (2011). Concurrent and longitudinal effects of ethnic identity and experiences of discrimination on psychosocial adjustment of Navajo adolescents. *Developmental Psychology, 47*(2), 509–526. doi:10.1037/a0021061.

Ganley, C. M., & Vasilyeva, M. (2014). The role of anxiety and working memory in gender differences in mathematics. *Journal of Educational Psychology, 106*(1), 105–120.

García, E. E. (1994). *Understanding and meeting the challenge of student cultural diversity.* Boston, MA: Houghton Mifflin.

Garibaldi, A. M. (1992). Educating and motivating African American males to succeed. *Journal of Negro Education, 61*(1), 4–11.

Garnier, H. E., Stein, J. A., & Jacobs, J. K. (1997). The process of dropping out of high school: A 19-year perspective. *American Educational Research Journal, 34,* 395–419.

Gay, G. (2006). Connections between classroom management and culturally responsive teaching. In C. M. Evertson & C. S. Weinstein (Eds.), *Handbook of classroom management: Research, practice, and contemporary issues* (pp. 343–370). Mahwah, NJ: Erlbaum.

Gay, G. (2010). *Culturally responsive teaching: Theory, research, and practice* (2nd ed.). New York, NY: Teachers College Press.

Gerard, J. M., & Buehler, C. (2004). Cumulative environmental risk and youth maladjustment: The role of youth attributes. *Child Development, 75,* 1832–1849.

Gilliland, H. (1988). Discovering and emphasizing the positive aspects of the culture. In H. Gilliland & J. Reyhner (Eds.), *Teaching the Native American.* Dubuque, IA: Kendall/Hunt.

Godley, A., & Escher, A. (2011, April). *Bidialectical African-American students' views on code-switching in and out of school.* Paper presented at the annual meeting of the American Educational Research Association, New Orleans, LA.

Goldenberg, C. (2001). Making schools work for low-income families in the 21st century. In S. B. Neuman & D. K. Dickinson (Eds.), *Handbook of early literacy research* (pp. 211–231). New York, NY: Guilford.

Goldstein, S., & Brooks, R. B. (2006). Why study resilience? In. S. Goldstein & R. B. Brooks (Eds.), *Handbook of resilience in children* (pp. 3–15). New York, NY: Springer.

Gollnick, D. M., & Chinn, P. C. (2009). *Multicultural education in a pluralistic society*

(8th ed.). Upper Saddle River, NJ: Merrill/Pearson.

Goodnow, J. J. (2010). Culture. In M. H. Bornstein (Ed.), *Handbook of cultural developmental science* (pp. 3–19). New York, NY: Psychology Press.

Gottfried, M. A. (2014). The positive effects of classroom diversity: Exploring the relationship between English language learner classmates and socioemotional skills in early elementary children. *The Elementary School Journal, 115*(1), 22–48.

Grant, C. A., & Gomez, M. L. (2001). *Campus and classroom: Making schooling multicultural* (2nd ed.). Upper Saddle River, NJ: Merrill/Prentice Hall.

Greenfield, P. M., Trumbull, E., Keller, H., Rothstein-Fisch, C., Suzuki, L. K., & Quiroz, B. (2006). Cultural conceptions of learning and development. In P. A. Alexander & P. H. Winne (Eds.), *Handbook of educational psychology* (2nd ed., pp. 675–692). Mahwah, NJ: Erlbaum.

Greenhow, C., Robelia, B., & Hughes, J. E. (2009). Web 2.0 and classroom research: What path should we take now? *Educational Researcher, 38,* 246–259.

Griffin, S. A., Case, R., & Capodilupo, A. (1995). Teaching for understanding: The importance of the central conceptual structures in the elementary mathematics curriculum. In A. McKeough, J. Lupart, & A. Marini (Eds.), *Teaching for transfer: Fostering generalization in learning* (pp. 123–151). Mahwah, NJ: Erlbaum.

Grissmer, D. W., Williamson, S., Kirby, S. N., & Berends, M. (1998). Exploring the rapid rise in Black achievement scores in the United States (1970–1990). In U. Neisser (Ed.), *The rising curve: Long-term gains in IQ and related measures* (pp. 251–285). Washington, DC: American Psychological Association.

Gruman, D. H., Harachi, T. W., Abbott, R. D., Catalano, R. F., & Fleming, C. B. (2008). Longitudinal effects of student mobility on three dimensions of elementary school engagement. *Child Development, 79,* 1833–1852.

Grusec, J. E., & Hastings, P. D. (Eds.). (2007). *Handbook of socialization: Theory and research.* New York, NY: Guilford.

Gutiérrez, K. D., & Rogoff, B. (2003). Cultural ways of learning: Individual traits or repertoires of practice. *Educational Researcher, 32*(5), 19–25.

Halpern, D. F. (2004). A cognitive-process taxonomy for sex differences in cognitive abilities. *Current Directions in Psychological Science, 13,* 135–139.

Halpern, D. F. (2006). Assessing gender gaps in learning and academic achievement. In P. A. Alexander & P. H. Winne (Eds.), *Handbook of educational psychology* (2nd ed., pp. 635–653). Mahwah, NJ: Erlbaum.

Halpern, D. F., Benbow, C. P., Geary, D. C., Gur, R. C., Hyde, J. S., & Gernsbacher, M.

A. (2007). The science of sex differences in science and mathematics. *Psychological Science in the Public Interest, 8*(1), 1–51.

Halpern, D. F., & LaMay, M. L. (2000). The smarter sex: A critical review of sex differences in intelligence. *Educational Psychology Review, 12*, 229–246.

Hamre, B. K., & Pianta, R. C. (2005). Can instructional and emotional support in the first-grade classroom make a difference for children at risk of school failure? *Child Development, 76*, 949–967.

Hankin, B. L., Mermelstein, R., & Roesch, L. (2007). Sex differences in adolescent depression: Stress exposure and reactivity models. *Child Development, 78*, 279–295.

Harber, K. D., Gorman, J. L., Gengaro, F. P., Butisingh, S., Tsang, W., & Ouellette, R. (2012). Students' race and teachers' social support affect the positive feedback bias in public schools. *Journal of Educational Psychology, 104*(4), 1149–1161.

Hardré, P. L., & Reeve, J. (2003). A motivational model of rural students' intentions to persist in, versus drop out of, high school. *Journal of Educational Psychology, 95*, 347–356.

Hardy, M. S. (2002). Behavior-oriented approaches to reducing youth gun violence. *The Future of Children, 12*(2), 101–117.

Harris, J. R. (1995). Where is the child's environment? A group socialization theory of development. *Psychological Review, 102*, 458–489.

Harter, S. (1999). *The construction of the self: A developmental perspective.* New York, NY: Guilford.

Hattie, J. A. C. (2009). *Visible learning: A synthesis of over 800 meta-analyses relating to achievement.* London, England: Routledge.

Hawkins, F. P. L. (1997). *Journey with children: The autobiography of a teacher.* Niwot, CO: University Press of Colorado.

Hayward, C. (Ed.). (2003). *Gender differences at puberty.* Cambridge, England: Cambridge University Press.

Heath, S. B. (1982). Questioning at home and at school: A comparative study. In G. Spindler (Ed.), *The ethnography of schooling: Educational anthropology in action* (pp. 102–131). New York, NY: Holt, Rinehart & Winston.

Heath, S. B. (1983). *Ways with words: Language, life, and work in communities and classrooms.* Cambridge, England: Cambridge University Press.

Heath, S. B. (1989). Oral and literate traditions among Black Americans living in poverty. *American Psychologist, 44*, 367–373.

Hemphill, F.C., Vanneman, A., & Rhaman, T. (2011). *Achievement gaps: How Hispanic and White students in public schools perform in mathematics and reading on the National Assessment of Educational Progress.* NCES Publication 2011-459. Washington DC: National Center for Education Statistics, U.S. Department of Education.

Herbert, J., & Stipek, D. (2005). The emergence of gender differences in children's perceptions of their academic competence. *Journal of Applied Developmental Psychology, 26*, 276–295.

Herman, M. (2004). Forced to choose: Some determinants of racial identification in multiracial adolescents. *Child Development, 75*, 730–748.

Hernandez, D. J., Denton, N. A., & Macartney, S. E. (2008). Children in immigrant families: Looking to America's future. *Social Policy Report, 22*(3), 3–22.

Hill, N. E., Bush, K. R., & Roosa, M. W. (2003). Parenting and family socialization strategies and children's mental health: Low-income Mexican-American and Euro-American mothers and children. *Child Development, 74*, 189–204.

Hilliard, A. I. (1992). Behavioral style, culture, and teaching and learning. *Journal of Negro Education, 61*(3), 370–377.

Hilliard, A. I. (1995, November). *Teacher education from an African American perspective.* Paper presented at the Invitational Conference on Defining the Knowledge Base for Urban Teacher Education. Atlanta, GA.

Hines, M., Golombok, S., Rust, J., Johnston, K. J., Golding, J., & the Avon Longitudinal Study of Parents and Children Study Team. (2002). Testosterone during pregnancy and gender role behavior of preschool children: A longitudinal, population study. *Child Development, 73*, 1678–1687.

Hong, Y., Morris, M. W., Chiu, C., & Benet-Martínez, V. (2000). Multicultural minds: A dynamic constructivist approach to culture and cognition. *American Psychologist, 55*, 709–720.

Hubbs-Tait, L., Nation, J. R., Krebs, N. F., & Bellinger, D. C. (2005). Neurotoxicants, micronutrients, and social environments: Individual and combined effects on children's development. *Psychological Science in the Public Interest, 6*, 57–121.

Hughes, J. M., Bigler, R. S., & Levy, S. R. (2007). Consequences of learning about historical racism among European American and African American children. *Child Development, 78*, 1689–1705.

Huguet, P., & Régner, I. (2007). Stereotype threat among schoolgirls in quasi-ordinary classroom circumstances. *Journal of Educational Psychology, 99*, 545–560.

Hulit, L. M., & Howard, M. R. (2006). *Born to talk* (4th ed.). Boston, MA: Allyn & Bacon.

Hurley, E. A., Allen, B. A., & Boykin, A. W. (2009). Culture and the interaction of student ethnicity with reward structure in group learning. *Cognition And Instruction, 27*(2), 121–146.

Hursh, D. (2007). Assessing No Child Left Behind and the rise of neoliberal education policies. *American Educational Research Journal, 44*, 493–518.

Hyde, J. S. (2005). The gender similarities hypothesis. *American Psychologist, 60*, 581–592.

Hyde, J. S. (2007). New directions in the study of gender similarities and differences. *Current Directions in Psychological Science, 16*, 259–263.

Hyde, J. S., & Durik, A. M. (2005). Gender, competence, and motivation. In A. J. Elliot & C. S. Dweck (Eds.), *Handbook of competence and motivation* (pp. 375–391). New York, NY: Guilford.

Hyde, J. S., Lindberg, S. M., Linn, M. C., Ellis, A. B., & Williams, C. C. (2008). Gender similarities characterize math performance. *Science, 321*(5888), 494–495.

Hymel, S., Comfort, C., Schonert-Reichl, K., & McDougall, P. (1996). Academic failure and school dropout: The influence of peers. In J. Juvonen & K. R. Wentzel (Eds.), *Social motivation: Understanding children's school adjustment* (pp. 313–345). Cambridge, England: Cambridge University Press.

Igoa, C. (1995). *The inner world of the immigrant child.* Mahwah, NJ: Erlbaum.

Inglehart, M., Brown, D. R., & Vida, M. (1994). Competition, achievement, and gender: A stress theoretical analysis. In P. R. Pintrich, D. R. Brown, & C. E. Weinstein (Eds.), *Student motivation, cognition, and learning: Essays in honor of Wilbert J. McKeachie* (pp. 311–329). Mahwah, NJ: Erlbaum.

Institute of Education Sciences. (2008). *Dropout prevention.* Washington, DC: Author.

Irving, M. A., & Hudley, C. (2008). Oppositional identity and academic achievement among African American males. In J. U. Ogbu (Ed.), *Minority status, oppositional culture, and schooling* (pp. 374–394). New York, NY: Routledge.

Ivory, J. D. (2006). Still a man's game: Gender representation in online reviews of video games. *Mass Communication and Society, 9*(1), 103–114.

Janosz, M., Le Blanc, M., Boulerice, B., & Tremblay, R. E. (2000). Predicting different types of school dropouts: A typological approach with two longitudinal samples. *Journal of Educational Psychology, 92*, 171–190.

Jenlink, C. L. (1994, April). *Music: A lifeline for the self-esteem of at-risk students.* Paper presented at the annual meeting of the American Educational Research Association, New Orleans, LA.

Jiang, B. (2010). English language learners: Understanding their needs. In G. S. Goodman (Ed.), *Educational psychology reader: The art and science of how people learn* (pp. 179–194). New York, NY: Peter Lang.

Jimerson, S., Egeland, B., & Teo, A. (1999). A longitudinal study of achievement trajectories: Factors associated with change. *Journal of Educational Psychology, 91*, 116–126.

Jones, S. M., & Dindia, K. (2004). A meta-analytic perspective on sex equity in the classroom. *Review of Educational Research, 74*, 443–471.

Jovanovic, J., & King, S. S. (1998). Boys and girls in the performance-based science classroom: Who's doing the performing? *American Educational Research Journal, 35*, 477–496.

Jozefowicz, D. M., Arbreton, A. J., Eccles, J. S., Barber, B. L., & Colarossi, L. (1994, April). *Seventh grade student, parent, and teacher factors associated with later school dropout or movement into alternative educational settings.* Paper presented at the annual meeting of the American Educational Research Association, New Orleans, LA.

Kağitçibaşi, Ç. (2007). *Family, self, and human development across cultures: Theory and applications* (2nd ed.). Mahwah, NJ: Erlbaum.

Kahne, J. E., & Sporte, S. E. (2008). Developing citizens: The impact of civic learning opportunities on students' commitment to civic participation. *American Educational Research Journal, 45,* 738–766.

Keil, F. C., & Newman, G. E. (2008). Two tales of conceptual change: What changes and what remains the same. In S. Vosniadou (Ed.), *International handbook on conceptual change* (pp. 83–101). New York, NY: Routledge.

Kelly, A., & Smail, B. (1986). Sex stereotypes and attitudes to science among eleven-year-old children. *British Journal of Educational Psychology, 56,* 158–168.

Killen, M. (2007). Children's social and moral reasoning about exclusion. *Current Directions in Psychological Science, 16,* 32–36.

Kim, J. (2011). Is it bigger than hip-hop? Examining the problems and potential of hip-hop in the curriculum. In V. Kinloch (Ed.), *Urban literacies: Critical perspectives on language, learning, and community* (pp. 160–176). New York, NY: Teachers College Press.

Kim, Y., & Lim, J. H. (2013). Gendered socialization with an embodied agent: Creating a social and affable mathematics learning environment for middle-grade females. *Journal of Educational Psychology, 105*(4), 1164–1174.

Kincheloe, J. L. (2009). No short cuts in urban education: Metropedagogy and diversity. In S. R. Steinberg (Ed.), *Diversity and multiculturalism: A reader* (pp. 379–409). New York, NY: Peter Lang.

Kitayama, S., Duffy, S., & Uchida, Y. (2007). Self as cultural mode of being. In S. Kitayama & D. Cohen (Eds.), *Handbook of cultural psychology* (pp. 136–174). New York, NY: Guilford.

Koeppel, J., & Mulrooney, M. (1992). The Sister Schools Program: A way for children to learn about cultural diversity—When there isn't any in their school. *Young Children, 48*(1), 44–47.

Koger, S. M., Schettler, T., & Weiss, B. (2005). Environmental toxins and developmental disabilities: A challenge for psychologists. *American Psychologist, 60,* 243–255.

Koltko-Rivera, M. E. (2004). The psychology of worldviews. *Review of General Psychology, 8,* 3–58.

Korhonen, J., Linnanmäki, K., & Aunio, P. (2014). Learning difficulties, academic well-being and educational dropout: A person-centred approach. *Learning and Individual Differences, 31,* 1–10.

Kraus, M. W., Piff, P. K., & Keltner, D. (2011). Social class as culture: The convergence of resources and rank in the social realm. *Current Directions in Psychological Science, 20,* 246–250.

Kumar, R., Warnke, J. H., & Karabenick, S. A. (2014). Arab-American male identity

negotiations: Caught in the crossroads of ethnicity, religion, nationality and current contexts. *Social Identities: Journal for the Study of Race, Nation and Culture, 20*(1), 22–41.

Ladson-Billings, G. (1994a). *The dreamkeepers: Successful teachers of African American children.* San Francisco, CA: Jossey-Bass.

Ladson-Billings, G. (1995a). But that's just good teaching! The case for culturally relevant pedagogy. *Theory into Practice, 34,* 159–165.

LaFromboise, T., Coleman, H. L. K., & Gerton, J. (1993). Psychological impact of biculturalism: Evidence and theory. *Psychological Bulletin, 114,* 395–412.

Laird, J., Kienzl, G., DeBell, M., & Chapman, C. (2007). *Dropout rates in the United States: 2005* (Compendium Report, National Center for Education Statistics 2007-059). Washington, DC: National Center for Education Statistics.

Lareau, A. (2003). *Unequal childhoods: Class, race, and family life.* Berkeley, CA: University of California Press.

Leaper, C., & Friedman, C. K. (2007). The socialization of gender. In J. E. Grusec & P. D. Hastings (Eds.), *Handbook of socialization: Theory and research* (pp. 561–587). New York, NY: Guilford.

Lee, J.-S., & Bowen, N. K. (2006). Parent involvement, cultural capital, and the achievement gap among elementary school children. *American Educational Research Journal, 43,* 193–218.

Lee, O. (1999). Science knowledge, world views, and information sources in social and cultural contexts: Making sense after a natural disaster. *American Educational Research Journal, 36,* 187–219.

Lee, V. E., & Burkam, D. T. (2003). Dropping out of high school: The role of school organization and structure. *American Educational Research Journal, 40,* 353–393.

Leventhal, T., & Brooks-Gunn, J. (2000). The neighborhoods they live in: The effects of neighborhood residence upon child and adolescent outcomes. *Psychological Bulletin, 126,* 309–337.

Li, J. (2005). Mind or virtue: Western and Chinese beliefs about learning. *Current Directions in Psychological Science, 14,* 190–194.

Li, J., & Fischer, K. W. (2004). Thought and affect in American and Chinese learners' beliefs about learning. In D. Y. Dai & R. J. Sternberg (Eds.), *Motivation, emotion, and cognition: Integrative perspectives on intellectual functioning and development* (pp. 385–418). Mahwah, NJ: Erlbaum.

Liben, L. S., & Bigler, R. S. (2002). The developmental course of gender differentiation: Conceptualizing, measuring, and evaluating constructs and pathways. *Monographs of the Society for Research in Child Development, 67*(2, Serial No. 269).

Lindberg, S. M., Hyde, J. S., Petersen, J. L., & Linn, M. C. (2010). New trends in gender and mathematics performance: A meta-analysis. *Psychological Bulletin, 136,* 1123–1135.

Lipka, J., with Mohatt, G. V., & the Ciulistet Group. (1998). *Transforming the culture of schools: Yup'ik Eskimo examples.* Mahwah, NJ: Erlbaum.

Lipka, J., Yanez, E., Andrew-Ihrke, D., & Adam, S. (2009). A two-way process for developing effective culturally based math: Examples from math in a cultural context. In B. Greer, S. Mukhopadhyay, A. B. Powell, & S. Nelson-Barber (Eds.), *Culturally responsive mathematics education* (pp. 257–280). New York, NY: Routledge.

Lipman, P. (1995). "Bringing out the best in them": The contribution of culturally relevant teachers to educational reform. *Theory into Practice, 34,* 202–208.

Lippa, R. A. (2002). *Gender, nature, and nurture.* Mahwah, NJ: Erlbaum.

Liss, M. B. (1983). Learning gender-related skills through play. In M. B. Liss (Ed.), *Social and cognitive skills: Sex roles and children's play* (pp. 147–166). San Diego, CA: Academic Press.

Lomawaima, K. T. (1995). Educating Native Americans. In J. A. Banks & C. A. M. Banks (Eds.), *Handbook of research on multicultural education* (pp. 451–467). New York, NY: Macmillan.

Lopez, A. M. (2003). Mixed-race school-age children: A summary of census 2000 data. *Educational Researcher, 32*(6), 25–37.

Losh, S. C. (2003). On the application of social cognition and social location to creating causal explanatory structures. *Educational Research Quarterly, 26*(3), 17–33.

Lucas, K., & Sherry, J. L. (2004). Sex differences in video game play: A communication-based explanation. *Communication Research, 31,* 499–523.

Lundeberg, M., & Mohan, L. (2009). Context matters: Gender and cross-cultural differences in confidence. In D. J. Hacker, J. Dunlosky, & A. C. Graesser (Eds.), *Handbook of metacognition in education* (pp. 221–239). New York, NY: Routledge.

Luthar, S. S. (2006). Over-scheduling versus other stressors: Challenges of high socioeconomic status families. *Social Policy Report, 20*(4), 16–17. Ann Arbor, MI: Society for Research in Child Development.

Luthar, S. S., & Latendresse, S. J. (2005). Children of the affluent: Challenges to well-being. *Current Directions in Psychological Science, 14,* 49–53.

Lytton, H., & Romney, D. M. (1991). Parents' differential socialization of boys and girls: A meta-analysis. *Psychological Bulletin, 109,* 267–296.

Maccoby, E. E. (2002). Gender and group process: A developmental perspective. *Current Directions in Psychological Science, 11,* 54–58.

MacLean, D. J., Sasse, D. K., Keating, D. P., Stewart, B. E., & Miller, F. K. (1995, April). *All-girls' mathematics and science instruction in early adolescence: Longitudinal effects.* Paper presented at the annual meeting of the American Educational Research Association, San Francisco, CA.

Manning, M. L., & Baruth, L. G. (2009). *Multicultural education of children and adolescents* (5th ed.). Boston, MA: Allyn & Bacon/Pearson.

Marks, H. M. (2000). Student engagement in instructional activity: Patterns in the elementary, middle, and high school years. *American Educational Research Journal, 37,* 153–184.

Markus, H. R., & Hamedani, M. G. (2007). Sociocultural psychology: The dynamic interdependence among self systems and social systems. In S. Kitayama & D. Cohen (Eds.), *Handbook of cultural psychology* (pp. 3–39). New York, NY: Guilford.

Marsh, H. W., Martin, A. J., & Cheng, J. H. S. (2008). A multilevel perspective on gender in classroom motivation and climate: Potential benefits of male teachers for boys? *Journal of Educational Psychology, 100,* 78–95.

Martin, A. J., Liem, G. A., Mok, M., & Xu, J. (2012). Problem solving and immigrant student mathematics and science achievement: Multination findings from the Programme for International Student Assessment (PISA). *Journal of Educational Psychology, 104*(4), 1054–1073.

Martin, C. L., & Ruble, D. (2004). Children's search for gender cues: Cognitive perspectives on gender development. *Current Directions in Psychological Science, 13,* 67–70.

Masten, A. S. (2001). Ordinary magic: Resilience processes in development. *American Psychologist, 56,* 227–238.

Masten, A. S., & Coatsworth, J. D. (1998). The development of competence in favorable and unfavorable environments. *American Psychologist, 53,* 205–220.

Mathews, J. (1988). *Escalante: The best teacher in America.* New York, NY: Henry Holt.

Matthews, J. S., Ponitz, C. C., & Morrison, F. J. (2009). *Journal of Educational Psychology, 101,* 689–704.

Matute-Bianchi, M. E. (2008). Situational ethnicity and patterns of school performance among immigrant and nonimmigrant Mexican-descent students. In J. U. Ogbu (Ed.), *Minority status, oppositional culture, and schooling* (pp. 398–432). New York, NY: Routledge.

McBrien, J. L. (2005a). *Discrimination and academic motivation in adolescent refugee girls.* Unpublished doctoral dissertation, Emory University, Atlanta, GA.

McCall, R. B. (1994). Academic underachievers. *Current Directions in Psychological Science, 3,* 15–19.

McCall, R. B., & Plemons, B. W. (2001). The concept of critical periods and their implications for early childhood services. In D. B. Bailey, Jr., J. T. Bruer, F. J. Symons, & J. W. Lichtman (Eds.), *Critical thinking about critical periods* (pp. 267–287). Baltimore, MD: Brookes.

McCarthy, A., Lee, K., Itakura, S., & Muir, D. W. (2006). Cultural display rules drive eye gaze during thinking. *Journal of Cultural Psychology, 37,* 717–722.

McDevitt, T. M., & Ormrod, J. E. (2013). *Child development and education* (5th ed.). Upper Saddle River, NJ: Merrill/Prentice Hall.

McGlothlin, H., & Killen, M. (2006). Intergroup attitudes of European American children attending ethnically homogeneous schools. *Child Development, 77,* 1375–1386.

McIntyre, E. (2010). Issues in funds of knowledge teaching and research: Key concepts from a study of Appalachian families and schooling. In M. L. Dantas & P. C. Manyak (Eds.), *Home–school connections in a multicultural society: Learning from and with culturally and linguistically diverse families* (pp. 201–217). New York, NY: Routledge.

McLoyd, V. C. (1998). Socioeconomic disadvantage and child development. *American Psychologist, 53,* 185–204.

McMichael, C. (2013). Unplanned but not unwanted? Teen pregnancy and parenthood among young people with refugee backgrounds. *Journal of Youth Studies, 16*(5), 663–678.

McMillan, J. H., & Reed, D. F. (1994). At-risk students and resiliency: Factors contributing to academic success. *Clearing House, 67*(3), 137–140.

Medin, D. L. (2005, August). *Role of culture and expertise in cognition.* Invited address presented at the annual meeting of the American Psychological Association, Washington, DC.

Mehan, H. (1979). *Social organization in the classroom.* Cambridge, MA: Harvard University Press.

Mejía-Arauz, R., Rogoff, B., Dexter, A., & Najafi, B. (2007). Cultural variation in children's social organization. *Child Development, 78,* 1001–1014.

Mickelson, R.A. (1990). The attitude-achievement paradox among Black adolescents. *Sociology of Education, 63,* 44–61.

Milam, A. J., Furr-Holden, C. M., & Leaf, P. J. (2010). Perceived school and neighborhood safety, neighborhood violence and academic achievement in urban school children. *The Urban Review, 42*(5), 458–467.

Miller, L. S. (1995). *An American imperative: Accelerating minority educational advancement.* New Haven, CT: Yale University Press.

Miller, M. K., & Summers, A. (2007). Gender differences in video game characters' roles, appearances, and attire as portrayed in video game magazines. *Sex Roles, 57,* 733–742.

Miller, P. M. (2011). A critical analysis of the research on student homelessness. *Review of Educational Research, 81,* 308–337.

Miller, S. M. (2003). How literature discussion shapes thinking: ZPDs for teaching/learning habits of the heart and mind. In A. Kozulin, B. Gindis, V. S. Ageyev, & S. M. Miller (Eds.), *Vygotsky's educational theory in cultural context* (pp. 289–316). Cambridge, England: Cambridge University Press.

Milner, H. R. (2006). Classroom management in urban classrooms. In C. M. Evertson & C. S. Weinstein (Eds.), *Handbook of classroom management: Research, practice, and*

contemporary issues (pp. 491–522). Mahwah, NJ: Erlbaum.

Mizuochi, I., & Dolan, T. (1994). The problems facing Japanese children at school in England. *Cambridge Journal of Education, 24*(1), 123–134.

Mohan, E. (2009). Putting multiethnic students on the radar: A case for greater consideration of our multiethnic students. In S. R. Steinberg (Ed.), *Diversity and multiculturalism: A reader* (pp. 132–141). New York, NY: Peter Lang.

Mohatt, G., & Erickson, F. (1981). Cultural differences in teaching styles in an Odawa school: A sociolinguistic approach. In H. T. Trueba, G. P. Guthrie, & K. H. Au (Eds.), *Culture and the bilingual classroom: Studies in classroom ethnography* (pp. 105–119). Rowley, MA: Newbury House.

Moje, E. B., & Hinchman, K. (2004). Culturally responsive practices for youth literacy learning. In T. L. Jetton & J. A. Dole (Eds.), *Adolescent literacy research and practice* (pp. 321–350). New York, NY: Guilford.

Monzó, L. D. (2010). Fostering academic identities among Latino immigrant students: Contextualizing parents' roles. In M. L. Dantas & P. C. Manyak (Eds.), *Home–school connections in a multicultural society: Learning from and with culturally and linguistically diverse families* (pp. 112–130). New York, NY: Routledge.

Moore, S., & Rosenthal, D. (2006). *Sexuality in adolescence: Current trends.* London, England: Routledge.

Morales, J. R., & Guerra, N. G. (2006). Effects of multiple context and cumulative stress on urban children's adjustment in elementary school. *Child Development, 77,* 907–923.

Morelli, G. A., & Rothbaum, F. (2007). Situating the child in context: Attachment relationships and self-regulation in different cultures. In S. Kitayama & D. Cohen (Eds.), *Handbook of cultural psychology* (pp. 500–527). New York, NY: Guilford.

Mosborg, S. (2002). Speaking of history: How adolescents use their knowledge of history in reading the daily news. *Cognition and Instruction, 20,* 323–358.

Murdock, T. B. (2000). Incorporating economic context into educational psychology: Methodological and conceptual challenges. *Educational Psychologist, 35,* 113–124.

National Research Council. (2004). *Engaging schools: Fostering high school students' motivation to learn.* Washington, DC: National Academies Press.

National Science Foundation. (2007). *Women, minorities, and persons with disabilities in science and engineering: 2007.* Arlington, VA: Author. Retrieved from http://www.nsf.gov/statistics/wmpd

NCSS Task Force on Ethnic Studies Curriculum Guidelines. (1992). Curriculum guidelines for multicultural education. *Social Education, 56,* 274–294.

Nelson-Barber, S., & Estrin, E. T. (1995). Bringing Native American perspectives to mathematics and science teaching. *Theory into Practice, 34,* 174–185.

Nesdale, D., Maass, A., Durkin, K., & Griffiths, J. (2005). Group norms, threat, and children's racial prejudice. *Child Development, 76,* 652–663.

Nettles, S. M., Caughy, M. O., & O'Campo, P. J. (2008). School adjustment in the early grades: Toward an integrated model of neighborhood, parental, and child processes. *Review of Educational Research, 78,* 3–32.

Newkirk, T. (2002). *Misreading masculinity: Boys, literacy, and popular culture.* Portsmouth, NH: Heinemann.

Newmann, F. M. (1981). Reducing student alienation in high schools: Implications of theory. *Harvard Educational Review, 51,* 546–564.

Nietfeld, J. L., Shores, L. R., & Hoffmann, K. F. (2014). Self-regulation and gender within a game-based learning environment. *Journal of Educational Psychology, 106*(4), 961–973.

Noble, K. G., Tottenham, N., & Casey, B. J. (2005). Neuroscience perspectives on disparities in school readiness and cognitive achievement. *The Future of Children, 15*(1), 71–89.

Norenzayan, A., Choi, I., & Peng, K. (2007). Perception and cognition. In S. Kitayama & D. Cohen (Eds.), *Handbook of cultural psychology* (pp. 569–594). New York, NY: Guilford.

Nosek, B. A., & Smyth, F. L. (2011). Implicit social cognitions predict sex difference in math engagement and achievement. *American Educational Research Journal, 48,* 1125–1156.

Nuttall, R. L., Casey, M. B., & Pezaris, E. (2005). Spatial ability as mediator of gender differences on mathematics tests. In A. M. Gallagher & J. C. Kaufman (Eds.), *Gender differences in mathematics: An integrative psychological approach* (pp. 121–142). Cambridge, England: Cambridge University Press.

Ochs, E. (1982). Talking to children in western Samoa. *Language and Society, 11,* 77–104.

O'Donnell, D. A., Schwab-Stone, M. E., & Muyeed, A. Z. (2002). Multidimensional resilience in urban children exposed to community violence. *Child Development, 73,* 1265–1282.

Ogbu, J. U. (1999). Beyond language: Ebonics, proper English, and identity in a Black-American speech community. *American Educational Research Journal, 36,* 147–184.

Ogbu, J. U. (2003). *Black American students in an affluent suburb: A study of academic disengagement.* Mahwah, NJ: Erlbaum.

Oskamp, S. (Ed.). (2000). *Reducing prejudice and discrimination.* Mahwah, NJ: Erlbaum.

Owens, R. E., Jr. (1995). *Language disorders: A functional approach to assessment and intervention* (2nd ed.). Boston, MA: Allyn & Bacon.

Padilla, A. M. (1994). Bicultural development: A theoretical and empirical examination. In R. G. Malgady & O. Rodriguez (Eds.), *Theoretical and conceptual issues in Hispanic mental health* (pp. 20–51). Malabar, FL: Krieger.

Pahlke, E., Hyde, J. S., & Mertz, J. E. (2013). The effects of single-sex compared with coeducational schooling on mathematics and science achievement: Data from Korea. *Journal of Educational Psychology, 105*(2), 444–452.

Pajares, F. (2005). Gender differences in mathematics self-efficacy beliefs. In A. M. Gallagher & J. C. Kaufman (Eds.), *Gender differences in mathematics: An integrative psychological approach* (pp. 294–315). Cambridge, England: Cambridge University Press.

Paris, D., & Kirkland, D. E. (2011). "The consciousness of the verbal artist": Understanding vernacular literacies in digital and embodied spaces. In V. Kinloch (Ed.), *Urban literacies: Critical perspectives on language, learning, and community* (pp. 177–194). New York, NY: Teachers College Press.

Parke, R. D., Coltrane, S., Duffy, S., Buriel, R., Dennis, J., Powers, J., et al. (2004). Economic stress, parenting, and child adjustment in Mexican American and European American families. *Child Development, 75,* 1632–1656.

Passolunghi, M. C., Rueda Ferreira, T. I., & Tomasetto, C. (2014). Math–gender stereotypes and math-related beliefs in childhood and early adolescence. *Learning and Individual Differences, 34,* 70–76.

Pawlas, G. E. (1994). Homeless students at the school door. *Educational Leadership, 51*(8), 79–82.

Payne, R. K. (2005). *A framework for understanding poverty* (4th rev. ed.). Highlands, TX: aha! Process.

Pearce, R. R. (2006). Effects of cultural and social structural factors on the achievement of White and Chinese American students at school transition points. *American Educational Research Journal, 43,* 75–101.

Pedersen, E., Faucher, T. A., & Eaton, W. W. (1978). A new perspective on the effects of first-grade teachers on children's subsequent adult status. *Harvard Educational Review, 48*(1), 1–31.

Pellegrini, A. D. (2011). "In the eye of the beholder": Sex bias in observations and ratings of children's aggression. *Educational Researcher, 40,* 281–286.

Pellegrini, A. D., & Archer, J. (2005). Sex differences in competitive and aggressive behavior. In B. J. Ellis & D. F. Bjorklund (Eds.), *Origins of the social mind: Evolutionary psychology and child development* (pp. 219–244). New York, NY: Guilford.

Pellegrini, A. D., Kato, K., Blatchford, P., & Baines, E. (2002). A short-term longitudinal study of children's playground games across the first year of school: Implications for social competence and adjustment to school. *American Educational Research Journal, 39,* 991–1015.

Pfeifer, J. H., Brown, C. S., & Juvonen, J. (2007). Teaching tolerance in schools: Lessons learned since *Brown v. Board of Education* about the development and reduction of children's

prejudice. *Social Policy Report, 21*(2), 3–13, 16–17, 20–23. Ann Arbor, MI: Society for Research in Child Development.

Phelan, P., Yu, H. C., & Davidson, A. L. (1994). Navigating the psychosocial pressures of adolescence: The voices and experiences of high school youth. *American Educational Research Journal, 31,* 415–447.

Phillips, G., McNaughton, S., & MacDonald, S. (2004). Managing the mismatch: Enhancing early literacy progress for children with diverse language and cultural identities in mainstream urban schools in New Zealand. *Journal of Educational Psychology, 96,* 309–323.

Pianta, R. C. (1999). *Enhancing relationships between children and teachers.* Washington, DC: American Psychological Association.

Pianta, R. C., & Hamre, B. K. (2009). Conceptualization, measurement, and improvement of classroom processes: Standardized observation can leverage capacity. *Educational Researcher, 38,* 109–119.

Pipher, M. (1994). *Reviving Ophelia: Saving the selves of adolescent girls.* New York, NY: Putnam.

Pitner, R. O., Astor, R. A., Benbenishty, R., Haj-Yahia, M. M., & Zeira, A. (2003). The effects of group stereotypes on adolescents' reasoning about peer retribution. *Child Development, 74,* 413–425.

Polakow, V. (2007). In the shadows of the ownership society: Homeless children and their families. In S. Books (Ed.), *Invisible children in the society and its schools* (3rd ed., pp. 39–62). Mahwah, NJ: Erlbaum.

Pollack, W. S. (2006). Sustaining and reframing vulnerability and connection: Creating genuine resilience in boys and young males. In S. Goldstein & R. B. Brooks (Eds.), *Handbook of resilience in children* (pp. 65–77). New York, NY: Springer.

Ponitz, C. C., Rimm-Kaufman, S. E., Brock, L. L., & Nathanson, L. (2009). Early adjustment, gender differences, and classroom organizational climate in first grade. *Elementary School Journal, 110,* 142–162.

Quinn, P. C., & Liben, L. S. (2008). A sex difference in mental rotation in young infants. *Psychological Science, 19,* 1067–1070.

Quiroga, C. V., Janosz, M., Bisset, S., & Morin, A. J. (2013). Early adolescent depression symptoms and school dropout: Mediating processes involving self-reported academic competence and achievement. *Journal of Educational Psychology, 105*(2), 552–560.

Raikes, H., Pan, B. A., Luze, G., Tamis-LeMonda, C. S., Brooks-Gunn, J., Constantine, J., et al. (2006). Mother-child bookreading in low-income families: Correlates and outcomes during the first three years of life. *Child Development, 77,* 924–953.

Ramey, C. T., & Ramey, S. L. (1998). Early intervention and early experience. *American Psychologist, 53,* 109–120.

Rasmussen, H. N., & Lavish, L. (2014). Broad definitions of culture in the field of multicultural psychology. In J. Teramoto

Pedrotti & L. M. Edwards (Eds.), *Perspectives on the intersection of multiculturalism and positive psychology* (pp. 17–30). New York, NY: Springer Science + Business Media.

Raudenbush, S. W. (2009). The *Brown* legacy and the *O'Connor* challenge: Transforming schools in the images of children's potential. *Educational Researcher, 38,* 169–180.

Reis, S. M., McCoach, D. B., Little, C. A., Muller, L. M., & Kaniskan, R. B. (2011). The effects of differentiated instruction and enrichment pedagogy on reading achievement in five elementary schools. *American Educational Research Journal, 48,* 462–501.

Reschly, A. L., & Christenson, S. L. (2009). Parents as essential partners for fostering students' learning outcomes. In R. Gilman, E. S. Huebner, & M. J. Furlong (Eds.), *Handbook of positive psychology in schools* (pp. 257–272). New York, NY: Routledge.

Reynolds, R. E., Taylor, M. A., Steffensen, M. S., Shirey, L. L., & Anderson, R. C. (1982). Cultural schemata and reading comprehension. *Reading Research Quarterly, 17,* 353–366.

Rhodes, M., & Gelman, S. A. (2008). Categories influence predictions about individual consistency. *Child Development, 79,* 1270–1287.

Robinson, J. P., & Lubienski, S. T. (2011). The development of gender achievement gaps in mathematics and reading during elementary and middle school: Examining direct cognitive assessments and teacher ratings. *American Educational Research Journal, 48,* 268–302.

Rogoff, B. (2003). *The cultural nature of human development.* Oxford, England: Oxford University Press.

Rogoff, B. (2007, March). Cultural perspectives help us see developmental processes. In M. Gauvain & R. L. Munroe (Chairs), *Contributions of socio-historical theory and cross-cultural research to the study of child development.* Symposium conducted at the biennial meeting of the Society for Research in Child Development, Boston, MA.

Rose, A. J., & Smith, R. L. (2009). Sex differences in peer relationships. In K. H. Rubin, W. M. Bukowski, & B. Laursen (Eds.), *Handbook of peer interactions, relationships, and groups* (pp. 379–393). New York, NY: Guilford.

Rothbart, M. K. (2011). *Becoming who we are: Temperament and personality in development.* New York, NY: Guilford.

Rubie-Davies, C., Hattie, J., & Hamilton, R. (2006). Expecting the best for students: Teacher expectations and academic outcomes. *British Journal of Educational Psychology, 76,* 429–444.

Ruble, D. N., Martin, C. L., & Berenbaum, S. A. (2006). Gender development. In W. Damon & R. M. Lerner (Series Eds.) & N. Eisenberg (Vol. Ed.), *Handbook of child psychology: Vol. 3. Social, emotional, and personality development* (6th ed., pp. 858–932). Hoboken, NJ: Wiley.

Rudolph, K. D., Caldwell, M. S., & Conley, C. S. (2005). Need for approval and children's well-being. *Child Development, 76,* 309–323.

Rumberger, R. W. (1995). Dropping out of middle school: A multilevel analysis of students and schools. *American Educational Research Journal, 32,* 583–625.

Ryan, R. M., & Kuczkowski, R. (1994). The imaginary audience, self-consciousness, and public individuation in adolescence. *Journal of Personality, 62,* 219–237.

Sadker, M. P., & Sadker, D. (1994). *Failing at fairness: How our schools cheat girls.* New York, NY: Touchstone.

Sam, D. L., & Berry, J. W. (2010). Acculturation: When individuals and groups of different cultural backgrounds meet. *Perspectives on Psychological Science, 5,* 472–481.

Sanders, M. G. (1996). Action teams in action: Interviews and observations in three schools in the Baltimore School—Family—Community Partnership Program. *Journal of Education for Students Placed at Risk, 1,* 249–262.

Schoon, I. (2006). *Risk and resilience: Adaptations in changing times.* Cambridge, England: Cambridge University Press.

Schultz, K., Buck, P., & Niesz, T. (2000). Democratizing conversations: Racialized talk in a post-desegregated middle school. *American Educational Research Journal, 37,* 33–65.

Seiffge-Krenke, I., Aunola, K., & Nurmi, J.-E. (2009). Changes in stress perception and coping during adolescence: The role of situational and personal factors. *Child Development, 80,* 259–279.

Sidel, R. (1996). *Keeping women and children last: America's war on the poor.* New York, NY: Penguin.

Siegler, R. S. (2009). Improving the numerical understanding of children from low-income families. *Child Development Perspectives, 3,* 118–124.

Sigman, M., & Whaley, S. E. (1998). The role of nutrition in the development of intelligence. In U. Neisser (Ed.), *The rising curve: Long-term gains in IQ and related measures* (pp. 155–182). Washington, DC: American Psychological Association.

Sirin, S. R. (2005). Socioeconomic status and academic achievement: A meta-analytic review of research. *Review of Educational Research, 75,* 417–453.

Sirin, S. R., & Ryce, P. (2010). Cultural incongruence between teachers and families: Implications for immigrant students. In E. L. Grigorenko & R. Takanishi (Eds.), *Immigration, diversity, and education* (pp. 151–169). New York, NY: Routledge.

Skoog, T., & Stattin, H. (2014). Why and under what contextual conditions do early-maturing girls develop problem behaviors? *Child Development Perspectives, 8*(3), 158–162.

Sleeter, C. E., & Grant, C. A. (1999). *Making choices for multicultural education: Five approaches to race, class, and gender* (3rd ed.). Upper Saddle River, NJ: Merrill/Prentice Hall.

Slesnick, N., Dashora, P., Letcher, A., Erdem, G., & Serovich, J. (2009). A review of services and interventions for runaway and homeless youth: Moving forward. *Children and Youth Services Review, 31*(7), 732–742.

Slonim, M. B. (1991). *Children, culture, ethnicity: Evaluating and understanding the impact.* New York, NY: Garland.

Smeding, A., Dumas, F., Loose, F., & Régner, I. (2013). Order of administration of math and verbal tests: An ecological intervention to reduce stereotype threat on girls' math performance. *Journal of Educational Psychology, 105*(3), 850–860.

Smitherman, G. (1994). "The blacker the berry the sweeter the juice": African American student writers. In A. H. Dyson & C. Genishi (Eds.), *The need for story: Cultural diversity in classroom and community* (pp. 80–101). Urbana, IL: National Council of Teachers of English.

Smitherman, G. (1998). Black English/Ebonics: What it be like? In T. Perry & L. Delpit (Eds.), *The real Ebonics debate: Power, language, and the education of African-American children* (pp. 29–37). Boston, MA: Beacon Press.

Sonnleitner, P., Brunner, M., Keller, U., & Martin, R. (2014). Differential relations between facets of problem solving and students' immigration background. *Journal of Educational Psychology, 106*(3), 681–695.

Spears, A. K. (2007). Improvisation, semantic license, and augmentation. In H. S. Alim & J. Baugh (Eds.), *Talkin Black talk: Language, education, and social change* (pp. 100–111). New York, NY: Teachers College Press.

Spelke, E. S. (2005). Sex differences in intrinsic aptitude for mathematics and science? A critical review. *American Psychologist, 60,* 950–958.

Spencer, M. B., Dupree, D., Tinsley, B., McGee, E. O., Hall, J., Fegley, S. G., & Elmore, T. G. (2012). Resistance and resiliency in a color-conscious society: Implications for learning and teaching. In K. R. Harris, S. Graham, T. Urdan, C. B. McCormick, G. M. Sinatra, J. Sweller, ... J. Sweller (Eds.), *APA educational psychology handbook, Vol 1: Theories, constructs, and critical issues* (pp. 461–494). Washington, DC: American Psychological Association.

Spera, C. (2005). A review of the relationship among parenting practices, parenting styles, and adolescent school achievement. *Educational Psychology Review, 17,* 125–146.

Stack, C. B., & Burton, L. M. (1993). Kinscripts. *Journal of Comparative Family Studies, 24,* 157–170.

Stieff, M., Dixon, B. L., Ryu, M., Kumi, B. C., & Hegarty, M. (2014). Strategy training eliminates sex differences in spatial problem solving in a STEM domain. *Journal of Educational Psychology, 106*(2), 390–402.

Suh, S., Suh, J., & Houston, I. (2007). Predictors of categorical at-risk high school dropouts. *Journal of Counseling & Development, 85,* 196–203.

Suina, J. H., & Smolkin, L. B. (1994). From natal culture to school culture to dominant society culture: Supporting transitions for Pueblo Indian students. In P. M. Greenfield & R. R. Cocking (Eds.), *Cross-cultural roots of minority child development* (pp. 115–130). Mahwah, NJ: Erlbaum.

Tate, W. F. (1995). Returning to the root: A culturally relevant approach to mathematics pedagogy. *Theory into Practice, 34,* 166–173.

Tatum, B. D. (1997). *"Why are all the Black kids sitting together in the cafeteria?" and other conversations about race.* New York, NY: Basic Books.

Tharp, R. G. (1989). Psychocultural variables and constants: Effects on teaching and learning in schools. *American Psychologist, 44,* 349–359.

Théberge, C. L. (1994, April). *Small-group vs. whole-class discussion: Gaining the floor in science lessons.* Paper presented at the annual meeting of the American Educational Research Association, New Orleans, LA.

Theobald, P., & Herley, W. (2009). Rurality, locality, and the diversity question. In S. R. Steinberg (Ed.), *Diversity and multiculturalism: A reader* (pp. 423–434). New York, NY: Peter Lang.

Thomas, J. R., & French, K. E. (1985). Gender differences across age in motor performance: A meta-analysis. *Psychological Bulletin, 98,* 260–282.

Thompson, T. L., & Zerbinos, E. (1995). Gender roles in animated cartoons: Has the picture changed in 20 years? *Sex Roles, 32,* 651–673.

Torrance, E. P. (1995). Insights about creativity: Questioned, rejected, ridiculed, ignored. *Educational Psychology Review, 7,* 313–322.

Trawick-Smith, J. (2003). *Early childhood development: A multicultural perspective* (3rd ed.). Upper Saddle River, NJ: Merrill/Prentice Hall.

Tucker-Drob, E. M. (2013). How many pathways underlie socioeconomic differences in the development of cognition and achievement? *Learning and Individual Differences, 25,* 12–220.

Turner, E. O. (2015). Districts' responses to demographic change: Making sense of race, class, and immigration in political and organizational context. *American Educational Research Journal, 52*(1), 4–39.

Tyler, K. M., Boykin, A. W., & Walton, T. R. (2006). Cultural considerations in teachers' perceptions of student classroom behavior and achievement. *Teaching & Teacher Education: An International Journal of Research and Studies, 22*(8), 998–1005.

Tyler, K. M., Uqdah, A. L., Dillihunt, M. L., Beatty-Hazelbaker, R., Connor, T., Gadson, N., et al. (2008). Cultural discontinuity: Toward a quantitative investigation of a major hypothesis in education. *Educational Researcher, 37,* 280–297.

Ulichny, P. (1996). Cultures in conflict. *Anthropology and Education Quarterly, 27,* 331–364.

U.S. Census Bureau. (2010). *Income, poverty, and health insurance coverage in the United States: 2010.* Washington, DC: U.S. Author.

U.S. Census Bureau. (2013). *Language use in the United States: 2011.* Washington, DC: Author.

U.S. Department of Education. (2015). *Early high school dropouts: What are their characteristics?* Washington, DC: Author.

Valkenburg, P. M., & Peter, J. (2009). Social consequences of the Internet for adolescents: A decade of research. *Current Directions in Psychological Science, 18,* 1–5.

Valla, J. M., & Ceci, S. J. (2011). Can sex differences in science be tied to the long reach of prenatal hormones? Brain organization theory, digit ratio (2D/4D), and sex differences in preferences and cognition. *Perspectives in Psychological Science, 6,* 134–146.

van den Bergh, L., Denessen, E., Hornstra, L., Voeten, M., & Holland, R. W. (2010). The implicit prejudiced attitudes of teachers: Relations to teacher expectations and the ethnic achievement gap. *American Educational Research Journal, 47,* 497–527.

Vang, C. (2010). The psycho-social dimensions of multicultural education. In G. S. Goodman (Ed.), *Educational psychology reader: The art and science of how people learn* (pp. 195–208). New York, NY: Peter Lang.

Varelas, M., & Pappas, C. C. (2006). Intertextuality in read-alouds of integrated science-literacy units in urban primary classrooms: Opportunities for the development of thought and language. *Cognition and Instruction, 24,* 211–259.

Volet, S. (1999). Learning across cultures: Appropriateness of knowledge transfer. *International Journal of Educational Research, 31,* 625–643.

Vuoksimaa, E., Kaprio, J., Kremen, W. S., Hokkanen, L., Viken, R. J., Tuulio-Henriksson, A., et al. (2010). Having a male co-twin masculinizes mental rotation performance in females, *Psychological Science, 21,* 1069–1071.

Walton, G. M., & Spencer, S. J. (2009). Latent ability: Grades and test scores systematically underestimate intellectual ability of negatively stereotyped students. *Psychological Science, 20,* 1132–1139.

Ward, C., Bochner, S., & Furnham, A. (2001). *The psychology of culture shock* (2nd ed.). London: Routledge.

Weatherford, J. (1988). *Indian givers: How the Indians of the Americas transformed the world.* New York, NY: Crown.

Weichold, K., Silbereisen, R. K., & Schmitt-Rodermund, E. (2003). Short-term and long-term consequences of early versus late physical maturation in adolescents. In C. Hayward (Ed.), *Gender differences at puberty* (pp. 241–276). Cambridge, England: Cambridge University Press.

Weis, R., & Cerankosky, B. C. (2010). Effects of video-game ownership on young boys' academic and behavioral functioning: A randomized, controlled study. *Psychological Science, 21,* 463–470.

Weisgram, E. S., Bigler, R. S., & Liben, L. S. (2010). Gender, values, and occupational interests among children, adolescents, and adults. *Child Development, 81,* 778–796.

Wentzel, K. R. (2009). Peers and academic functioning at school. In K. H. Rubin, W. M. Bukowski, & B. Laursen (Eds.), *Handbook of peer interactions, relationships, and groups* (pp. 531–547). New York, NY: Guilford.

Wentzel, K. R., Battle, A., Russell, S. L., & Looney, L. B. (2010). Social supports from teachers and peers as predictors of academic and social motivation. *Contemporary Educational Psychology, 35,* 193–202.

Werner, E. E. (1995). Resilience in development. *Current Directions in Psychological Science, 4,* 81–85.

Werner, E. E. (2006). What can we learn about resilience from large-scale longitudinal studies? In S. Goldstein & R. B. Brooks (Eds.), *Handbook of resilience in children* (pp. 91–105). New York, NY: Springer.

Werner, E. E., & Smith, R. S. (2001). *Journeys from childhood to midlife: Risk, resilience, and recovery.* Ithaca, NY: Cornell University Press.

Wigfield, A., Byrnes, J. P., & Eccles, J. S. (2006). Development during early and middle adolescence. In P. A. Alexander & P. H. Winne (Eds.), *Handbook of educational psychology* (2nd ed., pp. 87–113). Mahwah, NJ: Erlbaum.

Wigfield, A., Eccles, J. S., & Pintrich, P. R. (1996). Development between the ages of 11 and 25. In D. C. Berliner & R. C. Calfee (Eds.), *Handbook of educational psychology* (pp. 148–185). New York, NY: Macmillan.

Williams, K. M. (2001a). "Frontin' it": Schooling, violence, and relationships in the 'hood. In J. N. Burstyn, G. Bender, R. Casella, H. W. Gordon, D. P. Guerra, K. V. Luschen, R. Stevens, & K. M. Williams, *Preventing violence in schools: A challenge to American democracy* (pp. 95–108). Mahwah, NJ: Erlbaum.

Wright, M. O., & Masten, A. S. (2006). Resilience processes in development: Fostering positive adaptation in the context of adversity. In S. Goldstein & R. B. Brooks (Eds.), *Handbook of resilience in children* (pp. 17–37). New York, NY: Springer.

Yu, S. L., Elder, A. D., & Urdan, T. C. (1995, April). *Motivation and cognitive strategies in students with a "good student" or "poor student" self-schema.* Paper presented at the annual meeting of the American Educational Research Association, San Francisco, CA.

Zambo, D., & Brozo, W. G. (2009). *Bright beginnings for boys: Engaging young boys in active literacy.* Newark, DE: International Reading Association.

CHAPTER 5

Accardo, P. J. (Ed.). (2008). *Capute and Accardo's neurodevelopmental disabilities in infancy and childhood: Vol. II: The spectrum of developmental disabilities* (3rd ed.). Baltimore, MD: Brookes.

Ackerman, P. L., & Lohman, D. F. (2006). Individual differences in cognitive functions. In P. A. Alexander & P. H. Winne (Eds.),

Handbook of educational psychology (2nd ed., pp. 139–161). Mahwah, NJ: Erlbaum.

Algozzine, B., Browder, D., Karvonen, M., Test, D. W., & Wood, W. M. (2001). Effects of interventions to promote self-determination for individuals with disabilities. *Review of Educational Research, 71*, 219–277.

Ambrose, D., Allen, J., & Huntley, S. B. (1994). Mentorship of the highly creative. *Roeper Review, 17*, 131–133.

American Psychiatric Association. (2000). *Diagnostic and statistical manual of mental disorders* (4th ed.). Washington, DC: Author.

American Psychiatric Association. (2013). *Diagnostic and statistical manual of mental disorders* (5th ed.). Washington, DC: Author.

Angold, A., Worthman, C., & Costello, E. J. (2003). Puberty and depression. In C. Hayward (Ed.), *Gender differences at puberty* (pp. 137–164). Cambridge, England: Cambridge University Press.

Bacon, S. (2014, October 14). Students with developmental disabilities have fun learning farming skills. *Kansas City Star*. Retrieved from http://www.kansascity.com/news/local/community/816/article2754624.html

Barkley, R. A. (2006). *Attention-deficit hyperactivity disorder: A handbook for diagnosis and treatment* (3rd ed.). New York, NY: Guilford.

Barkley, R. A. (2010). School interventions. In G. S. Goodman (Ed.), *Educational psychology reader: The art and science of how people learn* (pp. 66–74). New York, NY: Peter Lang.

Bassett, D. S., Jackson, L., Ferrell, K. A., Luckner, J., Hagerty, P. J., Bunsen, T. D., & MacIsaac, D. (1996). Multiple perspectives on inclusive education: Reflections of a university faculty. *Teacher Education and Special Education, 19*, 355–386.

Becker, M., Lüdtke, O., Trautwein, U., Köller, O., & Baumert, J. (2012). The differential effects of school tracking on psychometric intelligence: Do academic-track schools make students smarter? *Journal of Educational Psychology, 104*(3), 682–699.

Beckett, C., Maughan, B., Rutter, M., Castle, J., Colvert, E., Groothues, C., et al. (2006). Do the effects of early severe deprivation on cognition persist into early adolescence? Findings from the English and Romanian adoptees study. *Child Development, 77*, 696–711.

Beike, S. M., & Zentall, S. S. (2012). "The snake raised its head": Content novelty alters the reading performance of students at risk for reading disabilities and ADHD. *Journal of Educational Psychology, 104*(3), 529–540.

Beirne-Smith, M., Patton, J. R., & Kim, S. H. (2006). *Mental retardation: An introduction to intellectual disabilities* (7th ed.). Upper Saddle River, NJ: Merrill/Prentice Hall.

Bergeron, R., & Floyd, R. G. (2006). Broad cognitive abilities of children with mental retardation: An analysis of group and individual profiles. *American Journal of Mental Retardation, 111*, 417–432.

Beukelman, D. R., & Mirenda, P. A. (2005). *Augmentative and alternative communication: Supporting children and adults with complex communication needs* (3rd ed.). Baltimore, MD: Brookes.

Bishop, D. V. M. (2006). What causes specific language impairment in children? *Current Directions in Psychological Science, 15*, 217–221.

Blake, J. J., Lund, E. M., Zhou, Q., Kwok, O., & Benz, M. R. (2012). National prevalence rates of bully victimization among students with disabilities in the United States. *School Psychology Quarterly, 27*(4), 210–222.

Bornstein, M. H., Hahn, C.-S., Bell, C., Haynes, O. M., Slater, A., Golding, J., et al. (2006). Stability in cognition across early childhood: A developmental cascade. *Psychological Science, 17*, 151–158.

Bracken, B. A., McCallum, R. S., & Shaughnessy, M. F. (1999). An interview with Bruce A. Bracken and R. Steve McCallum, authors of the Universal Nonverbal Intelligence Test (UNIT). *North American Journal of Psychology, 1*, 277–288.

Braden, J. P. (1992). Intellectual assessment of deaf and hard-of-hearing people: A quantitative and qualitative research synthesis. *School Psychology Review, 21*, 82–94.

Bressler, S. L. (2002). Understanding cognition through large-scale cortical networks. *Current Directions in Psychological Science, 11*, 58–61.

Brody, N. (1992). *Intelligence* (2nd ed.). San Diego, CA: Academic Press.

Brody, N. (1997). Intelligence, schooling, and society. *American Psychologist, 52*, 1046–1050.

Brooks-Gunn, J., Klebanov, P. K., & Duncan, G. J. (1996). Ethnic differences in children's intelligence test scores: Role of economic deprivation, home environment, and maternal characteristics. *Child Development, 67*, 396–408.

Buchoff, T. (1990). Attention deficit disorder: Help for the classroom teacher. *Childhood Education, 67*, 86–90.

Byrnes, J. P. (2003). Factors predictive of mathematics achievement in White, Black, and Hispanic 12th graders. *Journal of Educational Psychology, 95*, 316–326.

Byrnes, J. P. (2012). How neuroscience contributes to our understanding of learning and development in typically developing and special-needs students. In K. R. Harris, S. Graham, & T. Urdan (Eds.), *APA handbook of educational psychology, Volume 1: Theories, constructs, and critical issues* (pp. 561–595). Washington, DC: American Psychological Association.

Cacioppo, J. T., Petty, R. E., Feinstein, J. A., & Jarvis, W. B. G. (1996). Dispositional differences in cognitive motivation: The life and times of individuals varying in need for cognition. *Psychological Bulletin, 119*, 197–253.

Callahan, C. M., Moon, T. R., Oh, S., Azano, A. P., & Hailey, E. P. (2015). What works in gifted education: Documenting the effects of an integrated curricular/instructional model for gifted students. *American*

Educational Research Journal, 52(1), 137–167. doi:10.3102/0002831214549448.

Campbell, F. A., & Burchinal, M. R. (2008). Early childhood interventions: The Abecedarian Project. In P. C. Kyllonen, R. D. Roberts, & L. Stankov (Eds.), *Extending intelligence: Enhancement and new constructs* (pp. 61–84). New York, NY: Erlbaum/Taylor & Francis.

Campbell, L., Campbell, B., & Dickinson, D. (1998). *Teaching and learning through multiple intelligences* (2nd ed.). Boston, MA: Allyn & Bacon.

Candler-Lotven, A., Tallent-Runnels, M. K., Olivárez, A., & Hildreth, B. (1994, April). *A comparison of learning and study strategies of gifted, average-ability, and learning-disabled ninth-grade students.* Paper presented at the annual meeting of the American Educational Research Association, New Orleans, LA.

Capron, C., & Duyme, M. (1989). Assessment of effects of socio-economic status on IQ in a full cross-fostering study. *Nature, 340*, 552–554.

Carlin, M. T., Soraci, S. A., Strawbridge, C. P., Dennis, N., Loiselle, R., & Checile, N. A. (2003). Detection of changes in naturalistic scenes: Comparison of individuals with and without mental retardation. *Journal of Mental Retardation, 108*, 181–193.

Carroll, J. B. (1993). *Human cognitive abilities: A survey of factor-analytic studies.* New York, NY: Cambridge University Press.

Carroll, J. B. (2003). The higher stratum structure of cognitive abilities: Current evidence supports g and about ten broad factors. In H. Nyborg (Ed.), *The scientific study of general intelligence* (pp. 5–21). New York, NY: Pergamon.

Casey, B. J. (2001). Disruption of inhibitory control in developmental disorders: A mechanistic model of implicated frontostriatal circuitry. In J. L. McClelland & R. S. Siegler (Eds.), *Mechanisms of cognitive development: Behavioral and neural perspectives* (pp. 327–349). Mahwah, NJ: Erlbaum.

Cassidy, S. (2004). Learning styles: An overview of theories, models, and measures. *Educational Psychology, 24*, 419–444.

Cattell, R. B. (1963). Theory of fluid and crystallized intelligence: A critical experiment. *Journal of Educational Psychology, 54*, 1–22.

Cattell, R. B. (1987). *Intelligence: Its structure, growth, and action.* Amsterdam: North-Holland.

Ceci, S. J. (2003). Cast in six ponds and you'll reel in something: Looking back on 25 years of research. *American Psychologist, 58*, 855–864.

Centers for Disease Control. (2014, March 27). CDC estimates 1 in 68 children has been identified with autism spectrum disorder. Retrieved from http://www.cdc.gov/media/releases/2014/p0327-autism-spectrum-disorder.html

Chai, Z., Vail, C. O., & Ayres, K. M. (2015). Using an iPad application to promote early literacy development in young children with disabilities. *The Journal of Special Education, 48*, 256–267.

Chall, J. S. (1996). *Stages of reading development* (2nd ed.). Fort Worth, TX: Harcourt Brace.

Chan, J. M., & O'Reilly, M. F. (2008). A Social Stories™ intervention package for students with autism in inclusive classroom settings. *Journal of Applied Behavior Analysis, 41,* 405–409.

Chang, M.-L., & Davis, H. A. (2009). Understanding the role of teacher appraisals in shaping the dynamics of their relationships with students: Deconstructing teachers' judgments of disruptive behavior/students. In P. Schutz & M. Zembylas (Eds.), *Advances in teacher emotion research: The impact of teachers' lives* (pp. 95–125). New York, NY: Springer.

Cherkassky, V. L., Kana, R. K., Keller, T. A., & Just, M. A. (2006). Functional connectivity in a baseline resting-state network in autism. *NeuroReport, 17,* 1687–1690.

Clarke, S., Dunlap, G., Foster-Johnson, L., Childs, K. E., Wilson, D., White, R., et al. (1995). Improving the conduct of students with behavioral disorders by incorporating student interests into curricular areas. *Behavioral Disorders, 20,* 221–237.

Cohen, I. L. (2007). A neural network model of autism: Implications for theory and treatment. In D. Mareschal, S. Sirois, G. Westermann, & M. H. Johnson (Eds.), *Neuroconstructivism: Vol. 2. Perspectives and prospects* (pp. 231–264). Oxford, England: Oxford University Press.

Connors, E. C., Chrastil, E. R., Sánchez, J., & Merabet, L. B. (2014). Virtual environments for the transfer of navigation skills in the blind: A comparison of directed instruction vs. video game based learning approaches. *Frontiers in Human Neuroscience, 8*(223), 1–13.

Corno, L., Cronbach, L. J., Kupermintz, H., Lohman, D. F., Mandinach, E. B., Porteus, A. W., & Talbert, J. E. (2002). *Remaking the concept of aptitude: Extending the legacy of Richard E. Snow.* Mahwah, NJ: Erlbaum.

Cornoldi, C. (2010). Metacognition, intelligence, and academic performance. In H. S. Waters & W. Schneider (Eds.), *Metacognition, strategy use, and instruction* (pp. 257–277). New York, NY: Guilford.

Coyle, T. R., Pillow, D. R., Snyder, A. C., & Kochunov, P. (2011). Processing speed mediates the development of general intelligence (g) in adolescence. *Psychological Science, 22,* 1265–1269.

Crago, M. B. (1988). *Cultural context in the communicative interaction of young Inuit children.* Unpublished doctoral dissertation, McGill University, Montreal, Canada.

Crane, M. (2010, April 19). School blends students with, without autism. *Columbus Dispatch.* Retrieved from http://www.dispatch.com/content/stories/local/2010/04/19/school-blends-students-with-without-autism.html

Crosland, K., & Dunlap, G. (2012). Effective strategies for the inclusion of children with autism in general education classrooms. *Behavior Modification, 36*(3), 251–269.

Curry, L. (1990). A critique of the research on learning styles. *Educational Leadership, 47*(2), 50–56.

Cutting, L. E., Eason, S. H., Young, K. M., & Alberstadt, A. L. (2009). Reading comprehension: Cognition and neuroimaging. In K. Pugh & P. McCardle (Eds.), *How children learn to read: Current issues and new directions in the integration of cognition, neurobiology and genetics of reading and dyslexia research and practice* (pp. 195–213). New York, NY: Psychology Press.

Dai, D. Y. (2002, April). *Effects of need for cognition and reader beliefs on the comprehension of narrative text.* Paper presented at the annual meeting of the American Educational Research Association, New Orleans, LA.

Dai, D. Y. (2010). *The nature and nurture of giftedness: A new framework for understanding gifted education.* New York, NY: Teachers College Press.

Dai, D. Y., & Sternberg, R. J. (2004). Beyond cognitivism: Toward an integrated understanding of intellectual functioning and development. In D. Y. Dai & R. J. Sternberg (Eds.), *Motivation, emotion, and cognition: Integrative perspectives on intellectual functioning and development* (pp. 3–38). Mahwah, NJ: Erlbaum.

Dalrymple, N. J. (1995). Environmental supports to develop flexibility and independence. In K. A. Quill (Ed.), *Teaching children with autism: Strategies to enhance communication and socialization* (pp. 243–264). New York, NY: Delmar.

Davies, P. T., & Woitach, M. J. (2008). Children's emotional security in the interparental relationship. *Current Directions in Psychological Science, 17,* 269–274.

Davis, O. S. P., Haworth, C. M. A., & Plomin, R. (2009). Dramatic increase in heritability of cognitive development from early to middle childhood: An 8-year longitudinal study of 8,700 pairs of twins. *Psychological Science, 20,* 1301–1308.

Dawson, M., Soulières, I., Gernsbacher, M. A., & Mottron, L. (2007). The level and nature of autistic intelligence. *Psychological Science, 18,* 657–662.

de Boer, A., Pijl, S. J., Post, W., & Minnaert, A. (2013). Peer acceptance and friendships of students with disabilities in general education: The role of child, peer, and classroom variables. *Social Development, 22*(4), 831–844.

de Jong, T. (2011). Instruction based on computer simulations. In R. E. Mayer & P. A. Alexander (Eds.), *Handbook of research on learning and instruction* (pp. 446–466). New York, NY: Routledge.

DeBacker, T. K., & Crowson, H. M. (2008). Measuring need for closure in classroom learners. *Contemporary Educational Psychology, 33,* 711–732.

DeBacker, T. K., & Crowson, H. M. (2009). The influence of need for closure on learning and teaching. *Educational Psychology Review, 21,* 303–323.

Dickens, W. T., & Flynn, J. R. (2006). Black Americans reduce the racial IQ gap: Evidence from standardization samples. *Psychological Science, 17,* 913–920.

Diliberto, J. A., & Brewer, D. (2014). Six tips for successful IEP meetings. *Teaching Exceptional Children, 47*(2), 128–135.

Dirks, J. (1982). The effect of a commercial game on children's Block Design scores on the WISC-R test. *Intelligence, 6,* 109–123.

Dodge, K. A. (2009). Mechanisms of gene–environment interaction effects in the development of conduct disorder. *Perspectives on Psychological Science, 4,* 408–414.

Duckworth, A. L., Quinn, P. D., & Tsukayama, E. (2012). What No Child Left Behind leaves behind: The roles of IQ and self-control in predicting standardized achievement test scores and report card grades. *Journal of Educational Psychology, 104*(2), 439-451.

Duckworth, A. L., & Seligman, M. E. P. (2005). Self-discipline outdoes IQ in predicting academic performance of adolescents. *Psychological Science, 16,* 939–944.

DuPaul, G. J., Ervin, R. A., Hook, C. L., & McGoey, K. E. (1998). Peer tutoring for children with attention deficit hyperactivity disorder: Effects on classroom behavior and academic performance. *Journal of Applied Behavior Analysis, 31,* 579–592.

Dyson, A. (2008). Disproportionality in special needs education in England. *Journal of Special Education, 42*(1), 36–46.

Erath, S. A., Tu, K. M., Buckhalt, J. A., & El-Sheikh, M. (2015). Associations between children's intelligence and academic achievement: The role of sleep. *Journal of Sleep Research,*

Ericsson, K. A. (2003). The acquisition of expert performance as problem solving. In J. E. Davidson & R. J. Sternberg (Eds.), *The psychology of problem solving* (pp. 31–83). Cambridge, England: Cambridge University Press.

Estell, D. B., Jones, M. H., Pearl, R., Van Acker, R., Farmer, T. W., & Rodkin, P. C. (2008). Peer groups, popularity, and social preference: Trajectories of social functioning among students with and without learning disabilities. *Journal of Learning Disabilities, 41,* 5–14.

Evans, J. J., Floyd, R. G., McGrew, K. S., & Leforgee, M. H. (2001). The relations between measures of Cattell-Horn-Carroll (CHC) cognitive abilities and reading achievement during childhood and adolescence. *School Psychology Review, 31,* 246–262.

Evertson, C. M., & Weinstein, C. S. (Eds.). (2006). *Handbook of classroom management: Research, practice, and contemporary issues.* Mahwah, NJ: Erlbaum.

Faranoe, S. V., Perlis, R. H., Doyle, A. E., Smoller, J., Goralnick, J., Holmgren, M., et al. (2005). Molecular genetics of attention-deficit/hyperactivity disorder. *Biological Psychiatry, 57,* 1313–1323.

Ferrell, K. A. (1996). Your child's development. In M. C. Holbrook (Ed.), *Children with visual impairments: A parent's guide* (pp. 73–96). Bethesda, MD: Woodbine House.

Fessler, M. A., Rosenberg, M. S., & Rosenberg, L. A. (1991). Concomitant learning disabilities and learning problems among students with behavioral/emotional disorders. *Behavioral Disorders, 16*, 97–106.

Feuerstein, R, Feuerstein, R. S., & Falik, L. H. (2010). *Beyond smarter: Mediated learning and the brain's capacity for change.* New York, NY: Teachers College Press.

Fey, M. E., Catts, H., & Larrivee, L. (1995). Preparing preschoolers for the academic and social challenges of school. In M. E. Fey, J. Windsor, & S. F. Warren (Eds.), *Language intervention: Preschool through elementary years* (pp. 3–37). Baltimore, MD: Brookes.

Fidler, D. J., Hepburn, S. L., Mankin, G., & Rogers, S. J. (2005). Praxis skills in young children with Down syndrome, other developmental disabilities, and typically developing children. *American Journal on Occupational Therapy, 59*, 129–138.

Flanagan, D. P., & Ortiz, S. O. (2001). *Essentials of cross-battery assessment.* New York, NY: Wiley.

Fletcher, J. M., Lyon, G. R., Fuchs, L. S., & Barnes, M. A. (2007). *Learning disabilities: From identification to intervention.* New York: Guilford.

Fletcher, J. M., & Vaughn, S. (2009). Response to intervention: Preventing and remediating academic difficulties. *Child Development Perspectives, 3*, 30–37.

Florence, B., Gentaz, E., Pascale, C., & Sprenger-Charolles, L. (2004). The visuo-haptic and haptic exploration of letters increases the kindergarten-children's understanding of the alphabetic principle. *Cognitive Development, 19*, 433–449.

Flum, H., & Kaplan, A. (2006). Exploratory orientation as an educational goal. *Educational Psychologist, 41*, 99–110.

Flynn, J. R. (2007). *What is intelligence? Beyond the Flynn effect.* New York, NY: Cambridge University Press.

Ford, D. Y. (2012). Gifted and talented education: History, issues, and recommendations. In K. R. Harris, S. Graham, T. Urdan, S. Graham, J. M. Royer, M. Zeidner, ... M. Zeidner (Eds.), *APA educational psychology handbook, Vol 2: Individual differences and cultural and contextual factors* (pp. 83–110). Washington, DC: American Psychological Association.

Ford, D. Y. (2014). Segregation and the underrepresentation of Blacks and Hispanics in gifted education: Social inequality and deficit paradigms. *Roeper Review: A Journal on Gifted Education, 36*(3), 143–154.

Fuchs, L. S., Compton, D. L., Fuchs, D., Paulsen, K., Bryant, J. D., & Hamlett, C. L. (2005). The prevention, identification, and cognitive determinants of math difficulty. *Journal of Educational Psychology, 97*, 493–513.

Fuchs, L. S., & Fuchs, D. (2009). On the importance of a unified model of responsiveness to intervention. *Child Development Perspectives, 3*, 41–43.

Funder, D. C. (1991). Global traits: A neo-Allportian approach to personality. *Psychological Science, 2*, 31–39.

Furnham, A. (2012). Learning styles and approaches to learning. In K. R. Harris, S. Graham, & T. Urdan (Eds.), *APA educational psychology handbook, Vol 2: Individual differences and cultural and contextual factors* (pp. 59–81). Washington, DC: American Psychological Association.

Gallese, V., Gernsbacher, M. A., Heyes, C., Hickok, G., & Iacoboni, M. (2011). Mirror neuron forum. *Perspectives on Psychological Science, 6*, 369–407.

Gardner, H. (1983). *Frames of mind: The theory of multiple intelligences.* New York, NY: Basic Books.

Gardner, H. (1999). *Intelligence reframed: Multiple intelligences for the 21st century.* New York, NY: Basic Books.

Gardner, H. (2000a). A case against spiritual intelligence. *International Journal of the Psychology of Religion, 10*(1), 27–34.

Gardner, H. (2000b). *The disciplined mind: Beyond facts and standardized tests, the K–12 education that every child deserves.* New York, NY: Penguin.

Gardner, H. (2003, April). *Multiple intelligences after twenty years.* Paper presented at the annual meeting of the American Educational Research Association, Chicago, IL.

Gardner, H. (2011). The theory of multiple intelligences. In M. A. Gernsbacher, R. W. Pew, L. M. Hough, J. R. Pomerantz, M. A. Gernsbacher, R. W. Pew, ... J. R. Pomerantz (Eds.), *Psychology and the real world: Essays illustrating fundamental contributions to society* (pp. 122–130). New York, NY, US: Worth Publishers.

Gardner, H., & Hatch, T. (1990). Multiple intelligences go to school: Educational implications of the theory of multiple intelligences. *Educational Researcher, 18*(8), 4–10.

Gathercole, S. E., Lamont, E., & Alloway, T. P. (2006). Working memory in the classroom. In S. Pickering (Ed.), *Working memory and education* (p. 219–240). New York, NY: Academic Press.

Gatzke-Kopp, L. M., & Beauchaine, T. P. (2007). Central nervous system substrates of impulsivity: Implications for the development of attention-deficit/hyperactivity disorder and conduct disorder. In D. Coch, G. Dawson, & K. W. Fischer (Eds.), *Human behavior, learning, and the developing brain: Atypical development* (pp. 239–263). New York, NY: Guilford.

Gay, G. (2006). Connections between classroom management and culturally responsive teaching. In C. M. Evertson & C. S. Weinstein (Eds.), *Handbook of classroom management: Research, practice, and contemporary issues* (pp. 343–370). Mahwah, NJ: Erlbaum.

Gearheart, B. R., Weishahn, M. W., & Gearheart, C. J. (1992). *The exceptional child in the regular classroom* (5th ed.). Upper Saddle River, NJ: Merrill/Prentice Hall.

Gernsbacher, M. A., Stevenson, J. L., Khandakar, S., & Goldsmith, H. H. (2008). Why does joint attention look atypical in autism? *Child Development Perspectives, 2*(1), 38–45.

Gladwell, M. (2006, May). *Behavior in the blink of an eye.* Presentation at the annual meeting of the Association for Psychological Science, New York, NY.

Glaser, D. (2000). Child abuse and neglect and the brain: A review. *Journal of Child Psychology and Psychiatry and Allied Disciplines, 41*, 97–116.

Goldstein, S., & Rider, R. (2006). Resilience and the disruptive disorders of childhood. In S. Goldstein & R. B. Brooks (Eds.), *Handbook of resilience in children* (pp. 203–222). New York, NY: Springer.

Goldston, D. B., Molock, S. D., Whitbeck, L. B., Murakami, J. L., Zayas, L. H., & Nagayama Hall, G. C. (2008). Cultural considerations in adolescent suicide prevention and psychosocial treatment. *American Psychologist, 63*, 14–31.

Gonsalves, B. D., & Cohen, N. J. (2010). Brain imaging, cognitive processes, and brain networks. *Perspectives on Psychological Science, 5*, 744–752.

Goswami, U. (2007). Typical reading development and developmental dyslexia across languages. In D. Coch, G. Dawson, & K. W. Fischer (Eds.), *Human behavior, learning, and the developing brain: Atypical development* (pp. 145–167). New York, NY: Guilford.

Graham, S. (2009). Giftedness in adolescence: African American gifted youth and their challenges from a motivational perspective. In F. D. Horowitz, R. F. Subotnik, & D. J. Matthews (Eds.), *The development of giftedness and talent across the life span* (pp. 109–129). Washington, DC: American Psychological Association.

Grandin, T. (1995). *Thinking in pictures and other reports of my life with autism.* New York, NY: Random House.

Grandin, T., & Johnson, C. (2005). *Animals in translation: Using the mysteries of autism to decode animal behavior.* New York, NY: Simon & Schuster.

Granello, D. H., & Granello, P. F. (2006). *Suicide: An essential guide for helping professionals and educators.* Boston, MA: Pearson.

Greenfield, P. M., Trumbull, E., Keller, H., Rothstein-Fisch, C., Suzuki, L. K., & Quiroz, B. (2006). Cultural conceptions of learning and development. In P. A. Alexander & P. H. Winne (Eds.), *Handbook of educational psychology* (2nd ed., pp. 675–692). Mahwah, NJ: Erlbaum.

Greer, D., Rowland, A. L., & Smith, S. J. (2014). Critical considerations for teaching students with disabilities in online environments. *Teaching Exceptional Children, 46*(5), 79–91.

Gregg, N. (2009). *Adolescents and adults with learning disabilities and ADHD: Assessment and accommodation.* New York, NY: Guilford.

Gresalfi, M. S. (2009). Taking up opportunities to learn: Constructing dispositions in mathematics classrooms. *Journal of the Learning Sciences, 18,* 327–369.

Grinberg, D., & McLean-Heywood, D. (1999). *Perceptions of behavioural competence in depressed and non-depressed children with behavioural difficulties.* Paper presented at the annual meeting of the American Educational Research Association, Montreal, Canada.

Griswold, K. S., & Pessar, L. F. (2000). Management of bipolar disorder. *American Family Physician, 62,* 1343–1356.

Haier, R. J. (2003). Positron emission tomography studies of intelligence: From psychometrics to neurobiology. In H. Nyborg (Ed.), *The scientific study of general intelligence* (pp. 41–52). New York, NY: Pergamon.

Hallahan, D. P., Kauffman, J. M., & Pullen, P. C. (2009). *Exceptional learners: An introduction to special education* (11th ed.). Boston, MA: Allyn & Bacon.

Hallahan, D. P., Kauffman, J. M., & Pullen, P. C. (2015). *Exceptional learners: An introduction to special education* (13th ed.). Boston, MA: Pearson.

Hallowell, E. (1996). *When you worry about the child you love.* New York, NY: Simon & Schuster.

Halpern, D. F. (1998). Teaching critical thinking for transfer across domains. *American Psychologist, 53,* 449–455.

Halpern, D. F. (2008). Is intelligence critical thinking? Why we need a new definition of intelligence. In P. C. Kyllonen, R. D. Roberts, & L. Stankov (Eds.), *Extending intelligence: Enhancement and new constructs* (pp. 349–370). New York, NY: Erlbaum/Taylor & Francis.

Halvorsen, A. T., & Sailor, W. (1990). Integration of students with severe and profound disabilities: A review of research. In R. Gaylord-Ross (Ed.), *Issues and research in special education* (Vol. 1, pp. 110–172). New York, NY: Teachers College Press.

Hamovitch, B. (2007). Hoping for the best: "Inclusion" and stigmatization in a middle school. In S. Books (Ed.), *Invisible children in the society and its schools* (3rd ed., pp. 263–281). Mahwah, NJ: Erlbaum.

Harris, C. R. (1991). Identifying and serving the gifted new immigrant. *Teaching Exceptional Children, 23*(4), 26–30.

Harris, M. (1992). *Language experience and early language development: From input to uptake.* Hove, England: Erlbaum.

Harris, P. L. (2006). Social cognition. In W. Damon, R. M. Lerner (Series Eds.), D. Kuhn, & R. Siegler (Vol. Eds.), *Handbook of child psychology: Vol. 2. Cognition, perception, and language* (6th ed., pp. 811–858). New York, NY: Wiley.

Hart, E. L., Lahey, B. B., Loeber, R., Applegate, B., & Frick, P. J. (1995). Developmental changes in attention-deficit hyperactivity disorder in boys: A four-year longitudinal study. *Journal of Abnormal Child Psychology, 23,* 729–750.

Harter, S. (1999). *The construction of the self: A developmental perspective.* New York, NY: Guilford.

Hathaway, W. L., Dooling-Litfin, J. K., & Edwards, G. (2006). Integrating the results of an evaluation: Ten clinical cases. In R. A. Barkley (Ed.), *Attention-deficit hyperactivity disorder: A handbook for diagnosis and treatment* (3rd ed., pp. 410–412). New York, NY: Guilford.

Hattie, J. A. C. (2009). *Visible learning: A synthesis of over 800 meta-analyses relating to achievement.* London, England: Routledge.

Haxby, J. V., Gobbini, M. I., Furey, M. L., Ishai, A., Schouten, J. L., & Pietrini, P. (2001). Distributed and overlapping representations of faces and objects in ventral temporal cortex. *Science, 293,* 2425–2430.

Hayward, C. (Ed.). (2003). *Gender differences at puberty.* Cambridge, England: Cambridge University Press.

Haywood, H. C., & Lidz, C. S. (2007). *Dynamic assessment in practice: Clinical and educational applications.* Cambridge, England: Cambridge University Press.

Heath, S. B. (1989). Oral and literate traditions among black Americans living in poverty. *American Psychologist, 44,* 367–373.

Heward, W. L. (2009). *Exceptional children: An introduction to special education* (9th ed.). Upper Saddle River, NJ: Merrill/Pearson Education.

Hobson, P. (2004). *The cradle of thought: Exploring the origins of thinking.* Oxford, England: Oxford University Press.

Horn, J. L. (2008). Spearman, g, expertise, and the nature of human cognitive capability. In P. C. Kyllonen, R. D. Roberts, & L. Stankov (Eds.), *Extending intelligence: Enhancement and new constructs* (pp. 185–230). New York, NY: Erlbaum/Taylor & Francis.

Hughes, F. P. (1998). Play in special populations. In O. N. Saracho & B. Spodek (Eds.), *Multiple perspectives on play in early childhood education* (pp. 171–193). Albany: State University of New York Press.

Hunt, E. (2008). Improving intelligence: What's the difference from education? In P. C. Kyllonen, R. D. Roberts, & L. Stankov (Eds.), *Extending intelligence: Enhancement and new constructs* (pp. 15–35). New York, NY: Erlbaum/Taylor & Francis.

Hunt, P., & Goetz, L. (1997). Research on inclusive educational programs, practices, and outcomes for students with severe disabilities. *Journal of Special Education, 31,* 3–29.

Hutchins, E. (1995). *Cognition in the wild.* Cambridge, MA: MIT Press.

Institute of Medicine. (2011). *Adverse effects of vaccines: Evidence and causality.* Washington, DC: National Academies.

Jacoby, R., & Glauberman, N. (Eds.). (1995). *The bell curve debate: History, documents, opinions.* New York, NY: Random House.

Job, J. M., & Klassen, R. M. (2012). Predicting performance on academic and non-academic tasks: A comparison of adolescents with and without learning disabilities. *Contemporary Educational Psychology, 37*(2), 162–169.

Johnson, W. (2010). Understanding the genetics of intelligence: Can height help? Can corn oil? *Current Perspectives in Psychological Science, 19,* 177–182.

Joseph, L. M., & Konrad, M. (2009). Teaching students with intellectual or developmental disabilities to write: A review of the literature. *Research in Developmental Disabilities, 30,* 1–19.

Jung, R. E., & Haier, R. J. (2007). The parieto-frontal integration theory (P-FIT) of intelligence: Converging neuroimaging evidence. *Behavioral and Brain Sciences, 30,* 135–154.

Kadziela-Olech, H., Cichocki, P., Chwiesko, J., Konstantynowicz, J., & Braszko, J. J. (2015). Serum matrix metalloproteinase-9 levels and severity of symptoms in boys with attention deficit hyperactivity disorder ADHD/hyperkinetic disorder HKD. *European Child & Adolescent Psychiatry, 24*(1), 55–63.

Kağitçibaşi, Ç. (2007). *Family, self, and human development across cultures: Theory and applications* (2nd ed.). Mahwah, NJ: Erlbaum.

Kalbfleisch, M. L., & Gillmarten, C. (2013). Left brain vs. right brain: Findings on visual spatial capacities and the functional neurology of giftedness. *Roeper Review: A Journal on Gifted Education, 35*(4), 265–275.

Kan, K., Wicherts, J. M., Dolan, C. V., & van der Maas, H. J. (2013). On the nature and nurture of intelligence and specific cognitive abilities: The more heritable, the more culture dependent. *Psychological Science, 24*(12), 2420–2428.

Kana, R. K., Keller, T. A., Minshew, N. J., & Just, M. A. (2007). Inhibitory control in high-functioning autism: Decreased activation and underconnectivity in inhibition networks. *Biological Psychiatry, 62,* 198–206.

Kang, M. J., Hsu, M., Krajbich, I. M., Loewenstein, G., McClure, S. M., Wang, J. T.-Y., et al. (2009). The wick in the candle of learning: Epistemic curiosity activates reward circuitry and enhances memory. *Psychological Science, 20,* 963–973.

Karama, S., Colom, R., Johnson, W., Deary, I. J., Haier, R., Waber, D. P., Lepage, C., Ganjavi, H., Jung, R., & Evans, A. C. (2011). Cortical thickness correlates of specific cognitive performance accounted for by the general factor of intelligence in healthy children aged 6 to 18. *Neuroimage, 55*(4), 1443–1453.

Kauffman, J. M., & Landrum, T. J. (2013). *Characteristics of emotional and behavioral disorders of children and youth* (9th ed.). Upper Saddle River: Merrill/Pearson.

Keogh, B. K. (2003). *Temperament in the classroom.* Baltimore, MD: Brookes.

Kercood, S., Zentall, S. S., Vinh, M., & Tom-Wright, K. (2012). Attentional cuing in math word problems for girls at-risk for ADHD and their peers in general education settings. *Contemporary Educational Psychology, 37*(2), 106–112.

Kern, L., Dunlap, G., Childs, K. E., & Clark, S. (1994). Use of a classwide self-management program to improve the behavior of students with emotional and behavioral disorders. *Education and Treatment of Children, 17,* 445–458.

King, P. M., & Kitchener, K. S. (2002). The reflective judgment model: Twenty years of research on epistemic cognition. In B. K. Hofer & P. R. Pintrich (Eds.), *Personal epistemology: The psychology of beliefs about knowledge and knowing* (pp. 37–61). Mahwah, NJ: Erlbaum.

Klingberg, A. K., Keonig, J. I., & Bilbe, G. (2002). Training of working memory in children with ADHD. *Journal of Clinical and Experimental Neuropsychology, 24,* 781–791.

Konopasek, D. E., & Forness, S. R. (2014). Issues and criteria for the effective use of psychopharmacological interventions in schooling. In H. M. Walker & F. M. Gresham (Eds.), *Handbook of evidence-based practices for students with emotional and behavioral disorders* (pp. 457–472). New York, NY: Guilford.

Kornhaber, M., Fierros, E., & Veenema, S. (2004). *Multiple intelligences: Best ideas from research and practice.* Boston, MA: Allyn & Bacon.

Kovas, Y., & Plomin, R. (2007). Learning abilities and disabilities: Generalist genes, specialist environments. *Current Directions in Psychological Science, 16,* 284–288.

Krätzig, G. P., & Arbuthnott, K. D. (2006). Perceptual learning style and learning proficiency: A test of the hypothesis. *Journal of Educational Psychology, 98,* 238–246.

Kuhn, D. (2001a). How do people know? *Psychological Science, 12,* 1–8.

Kuhn, D. (2001b). Why development does (and does not) occur: Evidence from the domain of inductive reasoning. In J. L. McClelland & R. S. Siegler (Eds.), *Mechanisms of cognitive development: Behavioral and neural perspectives* (pp. 221–249). Mahwah, NJ: Erlbaum.

Kuhn, D. (2006). Do cognitive changes accompany developments in the adolescent brain? *Perspectives on Psychological Science, 1,* 59–67.

Kuhn, D., & Franklin, S. (2006). The second decade: What develops (and how)? In W. Damon, R. M. Lerner (Series Eds.), D. Kuhn, & R. Siegler (Vol. Eds.), *Handbook of child psychology: Vol. 2. Cognition, perception, and language* (6th ed., pp. 953–993). New York, NY: Wiley.

Kulik, J. A., & Kulik, C. C. (1997). Ability grouping. In N. Colangelo & G. Davis (Eds.), *Handbook of gifted education* (2nd ed., pp. 230–242). Boston, MA: Allyn & Bacon.

Kuncel, N. R., & Hezlett, S. A. (2007). Standardized tests predict graduate students' success. *Science, 315,* 1080–1081.

Kyllonen, P. (2016). Human cognitive abilities: Their organization, development, and use. In L. Corno & E. M. Anderman (Eds.), *Handbook of educational psychology* (3rd ed., pp. 121–134). New York, NY: Routledge.

LaBlance, G. R., Steckol, K. F., & Smith, V. L. (1994). Stuttering: The role of the classroom teacher. *Teaching Exceptional Children, 26*(2), 10–12.

Laboratory of Comparative Human Cognition. (1982). Culture and intelligence. In R. J. Sternberg (Ed.), *Handbook of human intelligence* (pp. 462–719). Cambridge, England: Cambridge University Press.

Lane, K., Falk, K., & Wehby, J. (2006). Classroom management in special education classrooms and resource rooms. In C. M. Evertson & C. S. Weinstein (Eds.), *Handbook of classroom management: Research, practice, and contemporary issues* (pp. 439–460). Mahwah, NJ: Erlbaum.

Lane, K. L., Menzies, H. M., Kalberg, J. R., & Oakes, W. P. (2012). A comprehensive, integrated three-tier model to meet students' academic, behavioral, and social needs. In K. R. Harris, S. Graham, & T. Urdan (Eds.), *APA educational psychology handbook, Vol. 3: Application to learning and teaching* (pp. 551–581). Washington, DC: American Psychological Association.

Leiter, J., & Johnsen, M. C. (1997). Child maltreatment and school performance declines: An event-history analysis. *American Educational Research Journal, 34,* 563–589.

Li, J. (2004). High abilities and excellence: A cultural perspective. In L. V. Shavinina & M. Ferrari (Eds.), *Beyond knowledge: Extracognitive aspects of developing high ability* (pp. 187–208). Mahwah, NJ: Erlbaum.

Li, J., & Fischer, K. W. (2004). Thought and affect in American and Chinese learners' beliefs about learning. In D. Y. Dai & R. J. Sternberg (Eds.), *Motivation, emotion, and cognition: Integrative perspectives on intellectual functioning and development* (pp. 385–418). Mahwah, NJ: Erlbaum.

Linn, M. C., Clement, C., Pulos, S., & Sullivan, P. (1989). Scientific reasoning during adolescence: The influence of instruction in science knowledge and reasoning strategies. *Journal of Research in Science Teaching, 26,* 171–187.

Locke, J. L. (1993). *The child's path to spoken language.* Cambridge, MA: Harvard University Press.

Lord, C. E. (2010). Autism: From research to practice. *American Psychologist, 65,* 815–826.

Luckasson, R., Borthwick-Duffy, S., Buntinx, W. H. E., Coulter, D. L., Craig, E. M., Reeve, A., et al. (Eds.). (2002). *Mental retardation: Definition, classification, and systems of supports* (10th ed.). Washington, DC: American Association on Mental Retardation.

MacMaster, K., Donovan, L. A., & MacIntyre, P. D. (2002). The effects of being diagnosed with a learning disability on children's self-esteem. *Child Study Journal, 32,* 101–108.

Madden, N. A., & Slavin, R. E. (1983). Mainstreaming students with mild handicaps: Academic and social outcomes. *Review of Educational Research, 53,* 519–569.

Maglione, M. A., Das, L., Raaen, L., Smith, A., Chari, R., Newberry, S., ... Gidengil, C. (2014). Safety of vaccines used for routine immunization of U.S. children: A systematic review. *Pediatrics, 134*(2), 325–337.

Mason, L. (2003). Personal epistemologies and intentional conceptual change. In G. M. Sinatra & P. R. Pintrich (Eds.), *Intentional conceptual change* (pp. 199–236). Mahwah, NJ: Erlbaum.

Mastropieri, M. A., & Scruggs, T. E. (1992). Science for students with disabilities. *Review of Educational Research, 62,* 377–411.

Mastropieri, M. A., & Scruggs, T. E. (2007). *The inclusive classroom: Strategies for effective instruction* (3rd ed.). Upper Saddle River, NJ: Merrill/Prentice Hall.

Matthews, D. J. (2009). Developmental transitions in giftedness and talent: Childhood into adolescence. In F. D. Horowitz, R. F. Subotnik, & D. J. Matthews (Eds.), *The development of giftedness and talent across the life span* (pp. 89–107). Washington, DC: American Psychological Association.

Matthews, G., Zeidner, M., & Roberts, R. D. (2006). Models of personality and affect for education: A review and synthesis. In P. A. Alexander & P. H. Winne (Eds.), *Handbook of educational psychology* (2nd ed., pp. 163–186). Mahwah, NJ: Erlbaum.

Maughan, A., & Cicchetti, D. (2002). Impact of child maltreatment and interadult violence on children's emotion regulation abilities and socioemotional adjustment. *Child Development, 73,* 1525–1542.

Mayer, R. E. (2011b). Instruction based on visualizations. In R. E. Mayer & P. A. Alexander (Eds.), *Handbook of research on learning and instruction* (pp. 427–445). New York, NY: Routledge.

Mayer, R. E., & Massa, L. J. (2003). Three facets of visual and verbal learners: Cognitive ability, cognitive style, and learning preference. *Journal of Educational Psychology, 95,* 833–846.

McGinn, P. V., Viernstein, M. C., & Hogan, R. (1980). Fostering the intellectual development of verbally gifted adolescents. *Journal of Educational Psychology, 72,* 494–498.

McGlynn, S. M. (1998). Impaired awareness of deficits in a psychiatric context: Implications for rehabilitation. In D. J. Hacker, J. Dunlosky, & A. C. Graesser (Eds.), *Metacognition in educational theory and practice* (pp. 221–248). Mahwah, NJ: Erlbaum.

McGrew, K. S., Flanagan, D. P., Zeith, T. Z., & Vanderwood, M. (1997). Beyond *g*: The impact of *Gf–Gc* specific cognitive abilities research on the future use and interpretation of intelligence tests in the schools. *School Psychology Review, 26,* 189–210.

McLoyd, V. C. (1998). Socioeconomic disadvantage and child development. *American Psychologist, 53,* 185–204.

Mehan, H. (1979). *Social organization in the classroom.* Cambridge, MA: Harvard University Press.

Mellard, D. F., & Johnson, E. (2008). *RTI: A practitioner's guide to implementing response to intervention.* Thousand Oaks, CA: Corwin.

Meltzer, L. (Ed.) (2007). *Executive function in education: From theory to practice.* New York, NY: Guilford.

Meltzer, L., & Krishnan, K. (2007). Executive function difficulties and learning disabilities: Understandings and misunderstandings. In L. Meltzer (Ed.), *Executive function in education: From theory to practice* (pp. 77–105). New York, NY: Guilford.

Mendaglio, S. (2010). Anxiety in gifted students. In J. C. Cassady (Ed.), *Anxiety in schools: The causes, consequences, and solutions for academic anxieties* (pp. 153–173). New York, NY: Peter Lang.

Messick, S. (1994b). The matter of style: Manifestations of personality in cognition, learning, and testing. *Educational Psychologist, 29*, 121–136.

Miller, L. K. (2005). What the savant syndrome can tell us about the nature and nurture of talent. *Journal for the Education of the Gifted, 28*, 361–373.

Minami, M., & McCabe, A. (1996). Compressed collections of experiences: Some Asian American traditions. In A. McCabe (Ed.), *Chameleon readers: Some problems cultural differences in narrative structure pose for multicultural literacy programs* (pp. 72–97). New York, NY: McGraw-Hill.

Moon, S. M., Feldhusen, J. F., & Dillon, D. R. (1994). Long-term effects of an enrichment program based on the Purdue Three-Stage Model. *Gifted Child Quarterly, 38*, 38–48.

Moore, J. I., Ford, D. Y., & Milner, H. R. (2011). Recruitment is not enough: Retaining African American students in gifted education. In D. Y. Ford, T. C. Grantham, M. S. Henfield, M. T. Scott, D. A. Harmon, S. Porchèr, ... C. Price (Eds.), *Gifted and advanced Black students in school: An anthology of critical works* (pp. 295–322). Waco, TX, US: Prufrock Press.

Moreno, R. (2006). Learning in high-tech and multimedia environments. *Current Directions in Psychological Science, 15*, 63–67.

Murphy, P. K., & Mason, L. (2006). Changing knowledge and beliefs. In P. A. Alexander & P. H. Winne (Eds.), *Handbook of educational psychology* (2nd ed., pp. 305–324). Mahwah, NJ: Erlbaum.

Myles, B. S., & Simpson, R. L. (2001). Understanding the hidden curriculum: An essential social skill for children and youth with Asperger syndrome. *Intervention in School and Clinic, 36*, 279–286.

National Center for Learning Disabilities. (2014). *The state of learning disabilities.* New York, NY: Author. Retrieved from http://www.ncld.org/wp-content/uploads/2014/11/2014-State-of-LD.pdf

National Institute on Deafness and Other Communication Disorders. (2010). *Statistics on voice, speech, and language.* Retrieved from http://www.nidcd.nih.gov/health/statistics/pages/vsl.aspx

National Institute on Deafness and Other Communication Disorders. (2014). Quick

statistics. Retrieved from http://www.nidcd.nih.gov/health/statistics/pages/quick.aspx

Neisser, U. (Ed.). (1998). *The rising curve: Long-term gains in IQ and related measures.* Washington, DC: American Psychological Association.

Neisser, U., Boodoo, G., Bouchard, T. J., Boykin, A. W., Brody, N., Ceci, S. J., et al. (1996). Intelligence: Knowns and unknowns. *American Psychologist, 51*, 77–101.

Nelson, J. R., Benner, G. J., & Bohaty, J. (2014). Addressing the academic performance problems and challenges of EBD students. In H. M. Walker & F. M. Gresham (Eds.), *Handbook of evidence-based practices for students having emotional and behavioral disorders* (pp. 363–377). New York, NY: Guilford.

Nephin, D. (2014, September 15). Teen with disabilities enrolls in college program. *Washington Times.* Retrieved from http://www.washingtontimes.com/news/2014/sep/15/teen-with-disabilities-enrolls-in-college-program/?page=all

Nichols, P. D., & Mittelholtz, D. J. (1997). Constructing the concept of aptitude: Implications for the assessment of analogical reasoning. In G. D. Phye (Ed.), *Handbook of academic learning: Construction of knowledge* (pp. 128–147). San Diego, CA: Academic Press.

Nieto, S., & Bode, P. (2008). *Affirming diversity: The sociopolitical context of multicultural education* (5th ed.). Boston, MA: Allyn & Bacon.

Nigg, J. T. (2010). Attention-deficit/hyperactivity disorder: Endophenotypes, structure, and etiological pathways. *Current Directions in Psychological Science, 19*, 24–29.

Nikopoulos, C. K., & Keenan, M. (2004). Effects of video modeling on social initiations by children with autism. *Journal of Applied Behavior Analysis, 37*, 93–96.

Nisbett, R. E. (2009). *Intelligence and how to get it.* New York, NY: Norton.

Olvera, P., & Gómez-Cerrillo, L. (2014). Integrated intellectual assessment of the bilingual student. In A. B. Clinton, A. B. Clinton (Eds.), *Assessing bilingual children in context: An integrated approach* (pp. 109–135). Washington, DC: American Psychological Association.

Organization for Economic Cooperation and Development. (2015). *Neuromyth 6: The left-brain right-brain myth.* Retrieved from http://www.oecd.org/edu/ceri/neuromyth6.htm

Ormrod, J. E., & McGuire, D. J. (2007). *Case studies: Applying educational psychology* (2nd ed.). Upper Saddle River, NJ: Merrill/Prentice Hall.

Owens, R. E., Farinella, K. A., & Metz, D. E. (2015). *Introduction to communication disorders.* Boston, MA: Pearson.

Ozonoff, S., & Schetter, P. L. (2007). Executive dysfunction in autism spectrum disorders: From research to practice. In L. Meltzer (Ed.), *Executive function in education: From theory to practice* (pp. 133–160). New York, NY: Guilford.

Palincsar, A. S., & Herrenkohl, L. R. (1999). Designing collaborative contexts: Lessons

from three research programs. In A. M. O'Donnell & A. King (Eds.), *Cognitive perspectives on peer learning* (pp. 151–177). Mahwah, NJ: Erlbaum.

Park, D. C., & Huang, C.-M. (2010). Culture wires the brain: A cognitive neuroscience perspective. *Perspectives on Psychological Science, 5*, 391–400.

Parker, W. D. (1997). An empirical typology of perfectionism in academically talented children. *American Educational Research Journal, 34*, 545–562.

Patton, J. R., Blackbourn, J. M., & Fad, K. S. (1996). *Exceptional individuals in focus* (6th ed.). Upper Saddle River, NJ: Merrill/Prentice Hall.

Pea, R. D. (1993). Practices of distributed intelligence and designs for education. In G. Salomon (Ed.), *Distributed cognitions: Psychological and educational considerations* (pp. 47–87). Cambridge, England: Cambridge University Press.

Pellegrini, A. D., & Bohn, C. M. (2005). The role of recess in children's cognitive performance and school adjustment. *Educational Researcher, 34*(1), 13–19.

Pellegrini, A. D., & Horvat, M. (1995). A developmental contextualist critique of attention deficit hyperactivity disorder. *Educational Researcher, 24*(1), 13–19.

Pelphrey, K. A., & Carter, E. J. (2007). Brain mechanisms underlying social perception deficits in autism. In D. Coch, G. Dawson, & K. W. Fischer (Eds.), *Human behavior, learning, and the developing brain: Atypical development* (pp. 56–86). New York, NY: Guilford.

Perkins, D. N. (1995). *Outsmarting IQ: The emerging science of learnable intelligence.* New York, NY: Free Press.

Perkins, D. N., & Ritchhart, R. (2004). When is good thinking? In D. Y. Dai & R. J. Sternberg (Eds.), *Motivation, emotion, and cognition: Integrative perspectives on intellectual functioning and development* (pp. 351–384). Mahwah, NJ: Erlbaum.

Perkins, D. N., Tishman, S., Ritchhart, R., Donis, K., & Andrade, A. (2000). Intelligence in the wild: A dispositional view of intellectual traits. *Educational Psychology Review, 12*, 269–293.

Peter, T., & Roberts, L. W. (2010). "Bad" boys and "sad" girls? Examining internalizing and externalizing effects on parasuicides among youth. *Journal of Youth and Adolescence, 39*(5), 495–503.

Peterson, C. C. (2002). Drawing insight from pictures: The development of concepts of false drawing and false belief in children with deafness, normal hearing, and autism. *Child Development, 73*, 1442–1459.

Pfiffner, L. J., Barkley, R. A., & DuPaul, G. J. (2006). Treatment of ADHD in school settings. In R. A. Barkley, *Attention-deficit hyperactivity disorder: A handbook for diagnosis and treatment* (3rd ed., pp. 547–589). New York, NY: Guilford.

Phelps, L., McGrew, K. S., Knopik, S. N., & Ford, L. (2005). The general (g), broad, and narrow CHC stratum characteristics of the WJ III and WISC-III tests: A confirmatory cross-battery investigation. *School Psychology Quarterly, 20*, 66–88.

Piirto, J. (1999). *Talented children and adults: Their development and education* (2nd ed.). Upper Saddle River, NJ: Merrill/Prentice Hall.

Posner, M. I., & Rothbart, M. K. (2007). *Educating the human brain.* Washington, DC: American Psychological Association.

Proctor, B. (2012). Relationships between Cattell–Horn–Carroll (CHC) cognitive abilities and math achievement within a sample of college students with learning disabilities. *Journal of Learning Disabilities, 45*(3), 278–287.

Proctor, B. E., Floyd, R. G., & Shaver, R. B. (2005). Cattell-Horn-Carroll broad cognitive ability profiles of low math achievers. *Psychology in the Schools, 42*(1), 1–12.

Prout, H. T. (2009). Positive psychology and students with intellectual disabilities. In R. Gilman, E. S. Huebner, & M. J. Furlong (Eds.), *Handbook of positive psychology in schools* (pp. 371–381). New York, NY: Routledge.

Pugh, K., & McCardle, P. (Eds.) (2009). *How children learn to read: Current issues and new directions in the integration of cognition, neurobiology and genetics of reading and dyslexia research and practice.* New York, NY: Psychology Press.

Purdie, N., Hattie, J., & Carroll, A. (2002). A review of the research on interventions for attention deficit hyperactivity disorder: What works best? *Review of Educational Research, 72*, 61–99.

Quill, K. A. (1995). Visually cued instruction for children with autism and pervasive developmental disorders. *Focus on Autistic Behavior, 10*(3), 10–20.

Raine, A. (2008). From genes to brain to antisocial behavior. *Current Directions in Psychological Science, 17*, 323–328.

Raine, A., Reynolds, C., & Venables, P. H. (2002). Stimulation seeking and intelligence: A prospective longitudinal study. *Journal of Personality and Social Psychology, 82*, 663–674.

Ramey, C. T. (1992). High-risk children and IQ: Altering intergenerational patterns. *Intelligence, 16*, 239–256.

Ratey, J. J. (2001). *A user's guide to the brain: Perception, attention, and the four theaters of the brain.* New York, NY: Vintage.

Raudenbush, S. W. (1984). Magnitude of teacher expectancy effects on pupil IQ as a function of the credibility of expectancy induction: A synthesis of findings from 18 experiments. *Journal of Educational Psychology, 76*(1), 85–97.

Rhodes, B. (2008). Challenges and opportunities for intelligence augmentation. In P. C. Kyllonen, R. D. Roberts, & L. Stankov (Eds.), *Extending intelligence: Enhancement and new constructs* (pp. 395–405). New York, NY: Erlbaum/Taylor & Francis.

Ricciuti, H. N. (1993). Nutrition and mental development. *Current Directions in Psychological Science, 2*, 43–46.

Rice, M., Hadley, P. A., & Alexander, A. L. (1993). Social biases toward children with speech and language impairments: A correlative causal model of language limitations. *Applied Psycholinguistics, 14*, 445–471.

Richards, C. M., Symons, D. K., Greene, C. A., & Szuszkiewicz, T. A. (1995). The bidirectional relationship between achievement and externalizing behavior disorders. *Journal of Learning Disabilities, 28*, 8–17.

Roberts, R. D., & Lipnevich, A. A. (2012). From general intelligence to multiple intelligences: Meanings, models, and measures. In K. R. Harris, S. Graham, & T. Urdan (Eds.), *APA educational psychology handbook, Vol 2: Individual differences and cultural and contextual factors* (pp. 33–57). Washington, DC: American Psychological Association.

Rogers, K. B. (2002). Grouping the gifted and talented: Questions and answers. *Roeper Review: A Journal on Gifted Education, 24*(3), 102–107.

Rogoff, B. (2003). *The cultural nature of human development.* Oxford, England: Oxford University Press.

Rogowsky, B. A., Calhoun, B. M., & Tallal, P. (2015). Matching learning style to instructional method: Effects on comprehension. *Journal of Educational Psychology, 107*(1), 64–78.

Rohrer, D., & Pashler, H. (2012). Learning styles: Where's the evidence? *Medical Education, 46*(7), 634–635.

Rose, C. A., Espelage, D. L., Aragon, S. R., & Elliott, J. (2011). Bullying and victimization among students in special education and general education curricula. *Exceptionality Education International, 21*(2–3), 2–14.

Rowe, D. C., Jacobson, K. C., & Van den Oord, E. J. C. G. (1999). Genetic and environmental influences on vocabulary IQ: Parental education level as moderator. *Child Development, 70*, 1151–1162.

Rowe, M. B. (1978). *Teaching science as continuous inquiry.* New York, NY: McGraw-Hill.

Royer, J. M., & Randall, J. (2012). Testing accommodations for students with disabilities. In K. R. Harris, S. Graham, & T. Urdan (Eds.), *APA educational psychology handbook, Vol. 3: Application to learning and teaching* (pp. 551–581). Washington, DC: American Psychological Association.

Rueda, M. R., Rothbart, M. K., McCandliss, B. D., Saccomanno, L., & Posner, M. I. (2005). Training, maturation, and genetic influences on the development of executive attention. *Proceedings of the National Academy of Sciences, USA, 102*, 14931–14936.

Rutter, M. L. (1997). Nature-nurture integration: The example of antisocial behavior. *American Psychologist, 52*, 390–398.

Saklofske, D. H., van de Vijver, F. R., Oakland, T., Mpofu, E., & Suzuki, L. A. (2015). Intelligence and culture: History and assessment. In S. Goldstein, D. Princiotta, & J. A. Naglieri (Eds.), *Handbook of intelligence:*

Evolutionary theory, historical perspective, and current concepts (pp. 341–365). New York, NY, US: Springer Science + Business Media.

Sampson, M. B., Szabo, S., Falk-Ross, F., Foote, M. M., & Linder, P. E. (Eds.). (2007). *Multiple literacies in the 21st century: The twenty-eighth yearbook of the College Reading Association.* Logan, UT: College Reading Association.

Sands, D., & Wehmeyer, M. (2005). Teaching goal setting and decision making to students with developmental disabilities. In M. L. Wehmeyer & M. Agran (Eds.), *Mental retardation and intellectual disabilities: Teaching students using innovative and research-based strategies* (pp. 273–296). Auckland, New Zealand: Pearson Education New Zealand.

Sattler, J. M. (2001). *Assessment of children: Cognitive applications* (4th ed.). San Diego, CA: Author.

Scarr, S., & McCartney, K. (1983). How people make their own environments: A theory of genotype environment effects. *Child Development, 54*, 424–435.

Schick, B., de Villiers, P., de Villiers, J., & Hoffmeister, R. (2007). Language and theory of mind: A study of deaf children. *Child Development, 78*, 376–396.

Schirmer, B. R. (1994). *Language and literacy development in children who are deaf.* Boston, MA: Allyn & Bacon.

Schrandt, J. A., Townsend, D. B., & Poulson, C. L. (2009). Teaching empathy skills to children with autism. *Journal of Applied Behavior Analysis, 42*, 17–32.

Seeley, K. (1989). Facilitators for the gifted. In J. Feldhusen, J. VanTassel-Baska, & K. Seeley, *Excellence in educating the gifted* (pp. 279–298). Denver, CO: Love.

Shavinina, L. V., & Ferrari, M. (2004). Extracognitive facets of developing high ability: Introduction to some important issues. In L. V. Shavinina & M. Ferrari (Eds.), *Beyond knowledge: Extracognitive aspects of developing high ability* (pp. 3–13). Mahwah, NJ: Erlbaum.

Sigman, M., & Whaley, S. E. (1998). The role of nutrition in the development of intelligence. In U. Neisser & U. Neisser (Eds.), *The rising curve: Long-term gains in IQ and related measures* (pp. 155–182). Washington, DC: American Psychological Association.

Silvia, P. J. (2015). Intelligence and creativity are pretty similar after all. *Educational Psychology Review.*

Simonton, D. K. (2001). Talent development as a multidimensional, multiplicative, and dynamic process. *Current Directions in Psychological Science, 10*, 39–42.

Skowronek, J. S., Leichtman, M. D., & Pillemer, D. B. (2008). Long-term episodic memory in children with attention-deficit/hyperactivity disorder. *Learning Disabilities Research and Practice, 23*(1), 25–35.

Slavin, R. E. (1987). Ability grouping and student achievement in elementary schools: A best-evidence synthesis. *Review of Educational Research, 57*, 293–336.

Slavin, R. E. (2011). Instruction based on cooperative learning. In R. E. Mayer & P.

A. Alexander (Eds.), *Handbook of research on learning and instruction* (pp. 344–360). New York, NY: Routledge.

Smith, T. E. C., Polloway, E. A., Doughty, T. T., Patton, R. R., & Dowdy, C. A. (2016). *Teaching students with special needs in inclusive settings* (7th ed.). Boston, MA: Pearson Education.

Snider, V. E. (1990). What we know about learning styles from research in special education. *Educational Leadership, 48*(2), 53.

Snyder, J., Schrepferman, L., McEachern, A., Barner, S., Johnson, K., & Provines, J. (2008). Peer deviancy training and peer coercion: Dual processes associated with early-onset conduct problems. *Child Development, 79,* 252–268.

Soodak, L. C., & McCarthy, M. R. (2006). Classroom management in inclusive settings. In C. M. Evertson & C. S. Weinstein (Eds.), *Handbook of classroom management: Research, practice, and contemporary issues* (pp. 461–489). Mahwah, NJ: Erlbaum.

Southerland, S. A., & Sinatra, G. M. (2003). Learning about biological evolution: A special case of intentional conceptual change. In G. M. Sinatra & P. R. Pintrich (Eds.), *Intentional conceptual change* (pp. 317–345). Mahwah, NJ: Erlbaum.

Spearman, C. (1904). General intelligence, objectively determined and measured. *American Journal of Psychology, 15,* 201–293.

Spearman, C. (1927). *The abilities of man: Their nature and measurement.* New York, NY: Macmillan.

Spinath, F. M., Price, T. S., Dale, P. S., & Plomin, R. (2004). The genetic and environmental origins of language disability and ability. *Child Development, 75,* 445–454.

Stainback, S., & Stainback, W. (1992). Schools as inclusive communities. In W. Stainback & S. Stainback (Eds.), *Controversial issues confronting special education: Divergent perspectives* (pp. 29–43). Boston, MA: Allyn & Bacon.

Stanley, J. C. (1980). On educating the gifted. *Educational Researcher, 9*(3), 8–12.

Stanovich, K. (2009). *What intelligence tests miss: The psychology of rational thought.* New Haven, CT: Yale University Press.

Stanovich, K. E. (1999). *Who is rational? Studies of individual differences in reasoning.* Mahwah, NJ: Erlbaum.

Staub, D. (1998). *Delicate threads: Friendships between children with and without special needs in inclusive settings.* Bethesda, MD: Woodbine House.

Stein, J. A., & Krishnan, K. (2007). Nonverbal learning disabilities and executive function: The challenges of effective assessment and teaching. In L. Meltzer (Ed.), *Executive function in education: From theory to practice* (pp. 106–132). New York, NY: Guilford.

Steiner, H. H., & Carr, M. (2003). Cognitive development in gifted children: Toward a more precise understanding of emerging differences in intelligence. *Educational Psychology Review, 15,* 215–246.

Sternberg, R. J. (1985). *Beyond IQ: A triarchic theory of human intelligence.* Cambridge, England: Cambridge University Press.

Sternberg, R. J. (1997). The concept of intelligence and its role in lifelong learning and success. *American Psychologist, 52,* 1030–1037.

Sternberg, R. J. (1998). Teaching triarchically improves school achievement. *Journal of Educational Psychology, 90,* 374–384.

Sternberg, R. J. (2002). Raising the achievement of all students: Teaching for successful intelligence. *Educational Psychology Review, 14,* 383–393.

Sternberg, R. J. (2003). *Wisdom, intelligence, and creativity synthesized.* Cambridge, England: Cambridge University Press.

Sternberg, R. J. (2004). Culture and intelligence. *American Psychologist, 59,* 325–338.

Sternberg, R. J. (2005). Intelligence, competence, and expertise. In A. J. Elliot & C. S. Dweck (Eds.), *Handbook of competence and motivation* (pp. 15–30). New York, NY: Guilford.

Sternberg, R. J. (2007). Intelligence and culture. In S. Kitayama & D. Cohen (Eds.), *Handbook of cultural psychology* (pp. 547–568). New York, NY: Guilford.

Sternberg, R. J. (2010). *College admissions for the twenty-first century.* Cambridge, MA: Harvard University Press.

Sternberg, R. J. (2012). The triarchic theory of successful intelligence. In D. P. Flanagan & P. L. Harrison (Eds.), *Contemporary intellectual assessment: Theories, tests, and issues* (3rd ed., pp. 156–177). New York, NY: Guilford Press.

Sternberg, R. J., & Detterman, D. K. (Eds.). (1986). *What is intelligence? Contemporary views on its nature and definition.* Norwood, NJ: Ablex.

Sternberg, R. J., Forsythe, G. B., Hedlund, J., Horvath, J. A., Wagner, R. K., Williams, W. M., et al. (2000). *Practical intelligence in everyday life.* Cambridge, England: Cambridge University Press.

Sternberg, R. J., Grigorenko, E. L., & Kidd, K. K. (2005). Intelligence, race, and genetics. *American Psychologist, 60,* 46–59.

Sternberg, R. J., Jarvin, L., Birney, D. P., Naples, A., Stemler, S. E., Newman, T., & ... Grigorenko, E. L. (2014). Testing the theory of successful intelligence in teaching grade 4 language arts, mathematics, and science. *Journal of Educational Psychology, 106*(3), 881–899.

Subotnik, R. F., Olszewski-Kubilius, P., & Worrell, F. C. (2011). Rethinking giftedness and gifted education: A proposed direction forward base on psychological science. *Psychological Science in the Public Interest, 12,* 3–54.

Subotnik, R. F., Olszewski-Kubilius, P., & Worrell, F. C. (2012). A proposed direction forward for gifted education based on psychological science. *Gifted Child Quarterly, 56*(4), 176–188.

Subotnik, R. F., & Rickoff, R. (2010). Should eminence based on outstanding innovation be the goal of gifted education and talent

development? Implications for policy and research. *Learning and Individual Differences, 20*(4), 358–364.

Sullivan, A. L. (2008, March). *Examining the local context of English language learner representation in special education.* Poster presented at the annual meeting of the American Educational Research Association, New York, NY.

Sullivan, R. C. (1994). Autism: Definitions past and present. *Journal of Vocational Rehabilitation, 4,* 4–9.

Swanson, H. L. (2008). Working memory and intelligence in children: What develops? *Journal of Educational Psychology, 100,* 581–602.

Swanson, H. L. (2016). Cognition and cognitive disabilities. In L. Corno & E. Anderman (Eds.), *Handbook of Educational Psychology* (3rd ed.) (pp. 135-145). New York, NY: Routledge.

Swanson, H. L., Hoskyn, M., & Lee, C. (1999). *Interventions for students with learning disabilities: A meta-analysis of treatment outcomes.* New York, NY: Guilford.

Tager-Flusberg, H. (2007). Evaluating the theory-of-mind hypothesis of autism. *Current Directions in Psychological Science, 16,* 311–315.

Tager-Flusberg, H., & Skwerer, D. P. (2007). Williams syndrome: A model developmental syndrome for exploring brain-behavior relationships. In D. Coch, G. Dawson, & K. W. Fischer (Eds.), *Human behavior, learning, and the developing brain: Atypical development* (pp. 87–116). New York, NY: Guilford.

Tarver, J., Daley, D., & Sayal, K. (2014). Attention-deficit hyperactivity disorder (ADHD): An updated review of the essential facts. *Child: Care, Health and Development, 40*(6), 762–774.

Terry, A. W. (2008). Student voices, global echoes: Service-learning and the gifted. *Roeper Review, 30,* 45–51.

Theimann, K. S., & Goldstein, H. (2004). Effects of peer training and written text cueing on social communication of school-age children with pervasive developmental disorder. *Journal of Speech, Language, and Hearing Research, 47,* 126–144.

Tompkins, G. E., & McGee, L. M. (1986). Visually impaired and sighted children's emerging concepts about written language. In D. B. Yaden, Jr., & S. Templeton (Eds.), *Metalinguistic awareness and beginning literacy: Conceptualizing what it means to read and write* (pp. 259–275). Portsmouth, NH: Heinemann.

Torrance, E. P. (1989). A reaction to "Gifted black students: Curriculum and teaching strategies." In C. J. Maker & S. W. Schiever (Eds.), *Critical issues in gifted education: Vol. 2. Defensible programs for cultural and ethnic minorities* (pp. 270–274). Austin, TX: Pro-Ed.

Treffert, D. A., & Wallace, G. L. (2002). Islands of genius. *Scientific American, 286*(6), 76–85.

Turkheimer, E., Haley, A., Waldron, M., D'Onofrio, B., & Gottesman, I. I. (2003).

Socioeconomic status modifies heritability of IQ in young children. *Psychological Science, 14,* 623–628.

Turnbull, A. P., Pereira, L., & Blue-Banning, M. (2000). Teachers as friendship facilitators. *Teaching Exceptional Children, 32*(5), 66–70.

Turnbull, A. P., Turnbull, R., & Wehmeyer, M. L. (2010). *Exceptional lives: Special education in today's schools* (6th ed.). Upper Saddle River, NJ: Merrill.

Turner, J. C., Meyer, D. K., Cox, K. E., Logan, C., DiCintio, M., & Thomas, C. T. (1998). Creating contexts for involvement in mathematics. *Journal of Educational Psychology, 90,* 730–745.

Tuttle, D. W., & Tuttle, N. R. (1996). *Self-esteem and adjusting with blindness: The process of responding to life's demands* (2nd ed.). Springfield, IL: Charles C Thomas.

Udall, A. J. (1989). Curriculum for gifted Hispanic students. In C. J. Maker & S. W. Schiever (Eds.), *Critical issues in gifted education: Vol. 2. Defensible programs for cultural and ethnic minorities* (pp. 41–56). Austin, TX: Pro-Ed.

U.S. Department of Education. (2006). *26th annual report to Congress on the implementation of the Individuals with Disabilities Education Act, 2004.* Washington, DC: Author.

U.S. Department of Education. (2014). *Repeated reading.* Washington, DC: Author. Retrieved from http://ies.ed.gov/ncee/wwc/pdf/intervention_reports/wwc_repeatedreading_051314.pdf

U.S. Department of Education, National Center for Education Statistics. (2010). *Digest of education statistics: 2010.* Retrieved from http://nces.ed.gov/programs/digest/2010menu_tables.asp

U.S. Department of Education, Office of Special Education and Rehabilitative Services. (2000). *A guide to the individualized education program.* Washington, DC: Author.

van der Linden, W. J. (2007). A hierarchical framework for modeling speed and accuracy on test items. *Psychometrika, 72*(3), 287–308.

van IJzendoorn, M. H., & Juffer, F. (2005). Adoption is a successful natural intervention enhancing adopted children's IQ and school performance. *Current Directions in Psychological Science, 14,* 326–330.

VanSledright, B., & Limón, M. (2006). Learning and teaching social studies: A review of cognitive research in history and geography. In P. A. Alexander & P. H. Winne (Eds.), *Handbook of educational psychology* (2nd ed., pp. 545–570). Mahwah, NJ: Erlbaum.

VanTassel-Baska, J. L. (Ed.) (2008). *Alternative assessments with gifted and talented students.* Waco, TX: Prufrock Press.

Varnum, M. E. W., Grossmann, I., Kitayama, S., & Nisbett, R. E. (2010). The origin of cultural differences in cognition: The social orientation hypothesis. *Current Directions in Psychological Science, 19,* 9–13.

Waber, D. P. (2010). *Rethinking learning disabilities: Understanding children who struggle in school.* New York, NY: Guilford.

Waite, M. C., Theodoros, D. G., Russell, T. G., & Cahill, L. M. (2010). Assessment of children's literacy via an Internet-based telehealth system. *Telemedicine and E-Health, 16*(5), 564–575.

Waite, M. C., Theodoros, D. G., Russell, T. G., & Cahill, L. M. (2012). Assessing children's speech intelligibility and oral structures, and functions via an Internet-based telehealth system. *Journal of Telemedicine and Telecare, 18*(4), 198–203.

Wanzek, J., & Vaughn, S. (2007). Research-based implications from extensive early reading interventions. *School Psychology Review, 36,* 541–561.

Waterhouse, L. (2006). Multiple intelligences, the Mozart effect, and emotional intelligence: A critical review. *Educational Psychologist, 41,* 207–225.

Webber, J., & Plotts, C. A. (2008). *Emotional and behavioral disorders: Theory and practice* (5th ed.). Boston, MA: Allyn & Bacon.

Wehmeyer, M. L., Agran, M., Hughes, C., Martin, J., Mithaug, D. E., & Palmer, S. (2007). *Promoting self-determination in students with intellectual and developmental disabilities.* New York, NY: Guilford.

West, R. F., Toplak, M. E., & Stanovich, K. E. (2008). Heuristics and biases as measures of critical thinking: Associations with cognitive ability and thinking dispositions. *Journal of Educational Psychology, 100,* 930–941.

Westefeld, J. S., Bell, A., Bermingham, C., Button, C., Shaw, K., Skow, C., et al. (2010). Suicide among preadolescents: A call to action. *Journal of Loss and Trauma, 15,* 381–407.

White, R., & Cunningham, A. M. (1991). *Ryan White: My own story.* New York, NY: Signet.

Wilder, A. A., & Williams, J. P. (2001). Students with severe learning disabilities can learn higher order comprehension skills. *Journal of Educational Psychology, 93,* 268–278.

Wiles, J., & Bondi, J. (2001). *The new American middle school: Educating preadolescents in an era of change.* Upper Saddle River, NJ: Merrill/Prentice Hall.

Williams, D. (1996). *Autism: An inside-outside approach.* London, England: Jessica Kingsley.

Winner, E. (1996). The rage to master: The decisive role of talent in the visual arts. In K. A. Ericsson (Ed.), *The road to excellence: The acquisition of expert performance in the arts and sciences, sports, and games* (pp. 271–302). Mahwah, NJ: Erlbaum.

Winner, E. (2000a). Giftedness: Current theory and research. *Current Directions in Psychological Science, 9,* 153–156.

Winner, E. (2000b). The origins and ends of giftedness. *American Psychologist, 55,* 159–169.

Wood, J. W. (1998). *Adapting instruction to accommodate students in inclusive settings* (3rd ed.). Upper Saddle River, NJ: Merrill/Prentice Hall.

Wood, J. W., & Rosbe, M. (1985). Adapting the classroom lecture for the mainstreamed

student in the secondary schools. *Clearing House, 58,* 354–358.

Yeo, M., & Sawyer, S. (2005). Chronic illness and disability. *British Medical Journal, 330*(7492), 721–723.

Yeo, R. A., Gangestad, S. W., & Thoma, R. J. (2007). Developmental instability and individual variation in brain development: Implications for the origin of neurodevelopmental disorders. *Current Directions in Psychological Science, 16,* 245–249.

Zhang, L.-F., & Sternberg, R. J. (2006). *The nature of intellectual styles.* Mahwah, NJ: Erlbaum.

CHAPTER 6

Alexander, P. A., & Judy, J. E. (1988). The interaction of domain-specific and strategic knowledge in academic performance. *Review of Educational Research, 58,* 375–404.

Alexander, P. A., Kulikowich, J. M., & Schulze, S. K. (1994). How subject-matter knowledge affects recall and interest. *American Educational Research Journal, 31,* 313–337.

Alexander, P. A., Schallert, D. L., & Reynolds, R. E. (2009). What is learning anyway? A topographic perspective considered. *Educational Psychologist, 44,* 176–192.

Allen, B. A., & Boykin, A. W. (1991). The influence of contextual factors on Afro-American and Euro-American children's performance: Effects of movement opportunity and music. *International Journal of Psychology, 26,* 373–387.

Alloway, T. P., Gathercole, S. E., Kirkwood, H., & Elliott, J. (2009). The cognitive and behavioral characteristics of children with low working memory. *Child Development, 80,* 606–621.

Altmann, E. M., & Gray, W. D. (2002). Forgetting to remember: The functional relationship of decay and interference. *Psychological Science, 13,* 27–33.

Anderson, J. R. (1983). *The architecture of cognition.* Cambridge, MA: Harvard University Press.

Anderson, J. R. (2005). *Cognitive psychology and its implications* (6th ed.). New York, NY: Worth.

Anderson, J. R., Reder, L. M., & Simon, H. A. (1996). Situated learning and education. *Educational Researcher, 25*(4), 5–11.

Anderson, M. C., Ochsner, K. N., Kuhl, B., Cooper, J., Robertson, E., Gabrieli, S. W., … Gabrieli, J. D. E. (2004). Neural systems underlying the suppression of unwanted memories. *Science, 303,* 232–235.

Anderson, R. C., Reynolds, R. E., Schallert, D. L., & Goetz, E. T. (1977). Frameworks for comprehending discourse. *American Educational Research Journal, 14,* 367–381.

Andiliou, A., Ramsay, C. M., Murphy, P. K., & Fast, J. (2012). Weighing opposing positions: Examining the effects of intratextual persuasive messages on students' knowledge and beliefs. *Contemporary Educational Psychology, 37,* 113–127.

Atkins, S. M., Bunting, M. F., Bolger, D. J., & Dougherty, M. R. (2012). Training the adolescent brain: Neural plasticity and the acquisition of cognitive abilities. In V. F. Reyna, S. B. Chapman, M. R. Dougherty, & J. Confrey (Eds.), *The adolescent brain: Learning, reasoning, and decision making* (pp. 211–241). Washington, DC: American Psychological Association.

Atkinson, R. C., & Shiffrin, R. M. (1968). Human memory: A proposed system and its control processes. In K. W. Spence & J. T. Spence (Eds.), *The psychology of learning and motivation: Advances in research and theory* (Vol. 2, pp. 89–195). San Diego, CA: Academic Press.

Atkinson, R. K., Levin, J. R., Kiewra, K. A., Meyers, T., Kim, S., Atkinson, L. A., ... Hwang, Y. (1999). Matrix and mnemonic text-processing adjuncts: Comparing and combining their components. *Journal of Educational Psychology, 91,* 342–357.

Atran, S., Medin, D. L., & Ross, N. O. (2005). The cultural mind: Environmental decision making and cultural modeling within and across populations. *Psychological Review, 112,* 744–776.

Ausubel, D. P., Novak, J. D., & Hanesian, H. (1978). *Educational psychology: A cognitive view* (2nd ed.). New York, NY: Holt, Rinehart & Winston.

Baddeley, A. D. (2001). Is working memory still working? *American Psychologist, 56,* 851–864.

Baer, J., & Garrett, T. (2010). Teaching for creativity in an era of content standards and accountability. In R. A. Beghetto & J. C. Kaufman (Eds.), *Nurturing creativity in the classroom* (pp. 6–23). New York, NY: Cambridge University Press.

Bangert-Drowns, R. L., Hurley, M. M., & Wilkinson, B. (2004). The effects of school-based writing-to-learn interventions on academic achievement: A meta-analysis. *Review of Educational Research, 74,* 29–58.

Banich, M. T. (2009). Executive function: The search for an integrated account. *Current Directions in Psychological Science, 18,* 89–94.

Banks, J. A. (1991). Multicultural literacy and curriculum reform. *Educational Horizons, 69*(3), 135–140.

Barkley, R. A. (2006). *Attention-deficit hyperactivity disorder: A handbook for diagnosis and treatment* (3rd ed.). New York, NY: Guilford.

Baroody, A. J., Eiland, M. D., Purpura, D. J., & Reid, E. E. (2013). Can computer-assisted discovery learning foster first graders' fluency with the most basic addition combinations? *American Educational Research Journal, 50,* 533–573.

Barron, E., Riby, L. M., Greer, J., & Smallwood, J. (2011). Absorbed in thought: The effect of mind wandering on the processing of relevant and irrelevant events. *Psychological Science, 22,* 596–601.

Barrouillet, P., & Camos, V. (2012). As time goes by: Temporal constraints in working memory. *Current Directions in Psychological Science, 2,* 413–419.

Barsalou, L. W., Simmons, W. K., Barbey, A., & Wilson, C. D. (2003). Grounding conceptual knowledge in modality-specific systems. *Trends in Cognitive Sciences, 7,* 84–91.

Barton, A. C., Tan, E., & Rivet, A. (2008). Creating hybrid spaces for engaging school science among urban middle school girls. *American Educational Research Journal, 45,* 68–103.

Bauer, P. J. (2002). Long-term recall memory: Behavioral and neuro-developmental changes in the first 2 years of life. *Current Directions in Psychological Science, 11,* 137–141.

Bauer, P. J., DeBoer, T., & Lukowski, A. F. (2007). In the language of multiple memory systems: Defining and describing developments in long-term declarative memory. In L. M. Oakes & P. J. Bauer (Eds.), *Short- and long-term memory in infancy and early childhood: Taking the first steps toward remembering* (pp. 240–270). New York, NY: Oxford University Press.

Beardsley, P. M., Bloom, M. V., & Wise, S. B. (2012). Challenges and opportunities for teaching and designing effective K–12 evolution curricula. In K. S. Rosengren, S. K. Brem, E. M. Evans, & G. M. Sinatra (Eds.), *Evolution challenges: Integrating research and practice in teaching and learning about evolution* (pp. 287–310). Oxford, England: Oxford University Press.

Behrmann, M. (2000). The mind's eye mapped onto the brain's matter. *Current Directions in Psychological Science, 9,* 50–54.

Beilock, S. L., & Carr, T. H. (2004). From novice to expert performance: Memory, attention, and the control of complex sensorimotor skills. In A. M. Williams & N. J. Hodges (Eds.), *Skill acquisition in sport: Research, theory, and practice* (pp. 309–327). London: Routledge.

Beirne-Smith, M., Patton, J. R., & Kim, S. H. (2006). *Mental retardation: An introduction to intellectual disabilities* (7th ed.). Upper Saddle River, NJ: Merrill/Prentice Hall.

Bellezza, F. S. (1986). Mental cues and verbal reports in learning. In G. H. Bower (Ed.), *The psychology of learning and motivation: Advances in research and theory* (Vol. 20, pp. 237–273). San Diego, CA: Academic Press.

Ben-Yehudah, G., & Fiez, J. A. (2007). Development of verbal working memory. In D. Coch, K. W. Fischer, & G. Dawson (Eds.), *Human behavior, learning, and the developing brain: Typical development* (pp. 301–328). New York, NY: Guilford.

Best, J. R., & Miller, P. H. (2010). A developmental perspective on executive function. *Child Development, 81,* 1641–1660.

Best, R. M., Dockrell, J. E., & Braisby, N. (2006). Lexical acquisition in elementary science classes. *Journal of Educational Psychology, 98,* 824–838.

Bjorklund, D. F., & Coyle, T. R. (1995). Utilization deficiencies in the development of memory strategies. In F. E. Weinert & W. Schneider (Eds.), *Research on memory development: State of the art and future directions* (pp. 161–180). Mahwah, NJ: Erlbaum.

Bjorklund, D. F., & Jacobs, J. W. (1985). Associative and categorical processes in children's memory: The role of automaticity in the development of organization in free recall. *Journal of Experimental Child Psychology, 39,* 599–617.

Bjorklund, D. F., Muir-Broaddus, J. E., & Schneider, W. (1990). The role of knowledge in the development of strategies. In D. F. Bjorklund (Ed.), *Children's strategies: Contemporary views of cognitive development* (pp. 93–128). Mahwah, NJ: Erlbaum.

Bjorklund, D. F., Schneider, W., Cassel, W. S., & Ashley, E. (1994). Training and extension of a memory strategy: Evidence for utilization deficiencies in high- and low-IQ children. *Child Development, 65,* 951–965.

Booth, J. L., & Newton, K. J. (2012). Fractions: Could they really be the gatekeeper's doorman? *Contemporary Educational Psychology, 37,* 247–253.

Bower, G. H. (1994). Some relations between emotions and memory. In P. Ekman & R. J. Davidson (Eds.), *The nature of emotion: Fundamental questions* (pp. 303–305). New York, NY: Oxford University Press.

Bower, G. H., Black, J. B., & Turner, T. J. (1979). Scripts in memory for text. *Cognitive Psychology, 11,* 177–220.

Bower, G. H., & Forgas, J. P. (2001). Mood and social memory. In J. P. Forgas (Ed.), *Handbook of affect and social cognition* (pp. 95–120). Mahwah, NJ: Erlbaum.

Bower, G. H., Karlin, M. B., & Dueck, A. (1975). Comprehension and memory for pictures. *Memory and Cognition, 3,* 216–220.

Brainerd, C. J., & Reyna, V. F. (2005). *The science of false memory.* Oxford, England: Oxford University Press.

Brewer, W. F. (2008). Naive theories of observational astronomy: Review, analysis, and theoretical implications. In S. Vosniadou (Ed.), *International handbook of research on conceptual change* (pp. 155–204). New York, NY: Routledge.

Brophy, J. E. (2004). *Motivating students to learn* (2nd ed.). Mahwah, NJ: Erlbaum.

Brophy, J. E., Alleman, J., & Knighton, B. (2009). *Inside the social studies classroom.* New York: Routledge.

Bryck, R. L., & Fisher, P. A. (2012). Training the brain: Practical applications of neural plasticity from the intersection of cognitive neuroscience, developmental psychology, and prevention science. *American Psychologist, 67,* 87–100.

Bulgren, J. A., Schumaker, J. B., & Deshler, D. D. (1994). The effects of a recall enhancement routine on the test performance of secondary students with and without learning disabilities. *Learning Disabilities Research and Practice, 9,* 2–11.

Butler, A. C., Zaromb, F. M., Lyle, K. B., & Roediger, H. L., III (2009). Using popular films to enhance classroom learning: The good, the bad, and the interesting. *Psychological Science, 20,* 1161–1168.

Carlson, R., Chandler, P., & Sweller, J. (2003). Learning and understanding science instructional material. *Journal of Educational Psychology, 95,* 629–640.

Carlson, S. M., & Moses, L. J. (2001). Individual differences in inhibitory control and children's theory of mind. *Child Development, 72,* 1032–1053.

Carmichael, C. A., & Hayes, B. K. (2001). Prior knowledge and exemplar encoding in children's concept acquisition. *Child Development, 72,* 1071–1090.

Castagno, A. E., & Brayboy, B. M. J. (2008). Culturally responsive schooling for Indigenous youth: A review of the literature. *Review of Educational Research, 78,* 941–993.

Castelli, D. M., Hillman, C. H., Buck, S. M., & Erwin, H. E. (2007). Physical fitness and academic achievement in third- and fifth-grade students. *Journal of Sport & Exercise Psychology, 29,* 239–252.

Cattani, A., Clibbens, J., & Perfect, T. J. (2007). Visual memory for shapes in deaf signers and nonsigners and in hearing signers and nonsigners: Atypical lateralization and enhancement. *Neuropsychology, 21,* 114–121.

Chang, L., Mak, M. C. K., Li, T., Wu, B. P., Chen, B. B., & Hui, J. L. (2011). Cultural adaptations to environmental variability: An evolutionary account of East–West differences. *Educational Psychology Review, 23,* 99–129.

Chapman, S. B., Gamino, J. F., & Mudar, R. A. (2012). Higher order strategic gist reasoning in adolescence. In V. F. Reyna, S. B. Chapman, M. R. Dougherty, & J. Confrey (Eds.), *The adolescent brain: Learning, reasoning, and decision making* (pp. 123–151). Washington, DC: American Psychological Association.

Chein, J. M., & Schneider, W. (2012). The brain's learning and control architecture. *Current Directions in Psychological Science, 21,* 78–84.

Cherry, E. C. (1953). Some experiments on the recognition of speech, with one and with two ears. *Journal of the Acoustical Society of America, 25,* 975–979.

Chi, M. T. H. (1978). Knowledge structures and memory development. In R. S. Siegler (Ed.), *Children's thinking: What develops?* (pp. 73–96). Mahwah, NJ: Erlbaum.

Chi, M. T. H. (2008). Three types of conceptual change: Belief revision, mental model transformation, and categorical shift. In S. Vosniadou (Ed.), *International handbook on conceptual change* (pp. 61–82). New York, NY: Routledge.

Chinn, C. A., & Buckland, L. A. (2012). Model-based instruction: Fostering change in evolutionary conceptions and in epistemic practices. In K. S. Rosengren, S. K. Brem, E. M. Evans, & G. M. Sinatra (Eds.), *Evolution challenges: Integrating research and practice in teaching and learning about evolution* (pp. 211–232). Oxford, England: Oxford University Press.

Chinn, C. A., & Malhotra, B. A. (2002). Children's responses to anomalous scientific data: How is conceptual change impeded? *Journal of Educational Psychology, 94,* 327–343.

Chinn, C. A., & Samarapungavan, A. (2009). Conceptual change—Multiple routes, multiple mechanisms: A commentary on Ohlsson (2009). *Educational Psychologist, 44,* 48–57.

Cho, B.-Y. (2010, April–May). *Describing adolescents' Internet reading strategies: Bridging the knowledge of traditional and new forms of reading.* Paper presented at the annual meeting of the American Educational Research Association, Denver, CO.

Clark, B. (1997). *Growing up gifted* (5th ed.). Upper Saddle River, NJ: Merrill/Prentice Hall.

Clark, D. B. (2006). Longitudinal conceptual change in students' understanding of thermal equilibrium: An examination of the process of conceptual restructuring. *Cognition and Instruction, 24,* 467–563.

Clark, J. M., & Paivio, A. (1991). Dual coding theory and education. *Educational Psychology Review, 3,* 149–210.

Cohen, I. L. (2007). A neural network model of autism: Implications for theory and treatment. In D. Mareschal, S. Sirois, G. Westermann, & M. H. Johnson (Eds.), *Neuroconstructivism: Vol. 2. Perspectives and prospects* (pp. 231–264). Oxford, England: Oxford University Press.

Coltheart, M., Lea, C. D., & Thompson, K. (1974). In defense of iconic memory. *Quarterly Journal of Experimental Psychology, 26,* 633–641.

Cook, R. G., & Smith, J. D. (2006). Stages of abstraction and exemplar memorization in pigeon category learning. *Psychological Science, 17,* 1059–1067.

Correa-Chávez, M., Rogoff, B., & Mejía Arauz, R. (2005). Cultural patterns in attending to two events at once. *Child Development, 76,* 664–678.

Courchesne, E., Townsend, J., Akshoomoff, N. A., Saitoh, O., Yeung-Courchesne, R., Lincoln, A. J., ... Lau, L. (1994). Impairment of shifting attention in autistic and cerebellar patients. *Behavioral Neuroscience, 108,* 848–865.

Cowan, N. (1995). *Attention and memory: An integrated framework.* New York, NY: Oxford University Press.

Cowan, N. (2007). What infants can tell us about working memory development. In L. M. Oakes & P. J. Bauer (Eds.), *Short- and long-term memory in infancy and early childhood: Taking the first steps toward remembering* (pp. 126–150). New York, NY: Oxford University Press.

Cowan, N. (2010). The magical mystery four: How is working memory capacity limited, and why? *Current Directions in Psychological Science, 19,* 51–57.

Cowan, N., Saults, J. S., & Morey, C. C. (2006). Development of working memory for verbal-spatial associations. *Journal of Memory and Language, 55,* 274–289.

Craik, F. I. M. (2006). Distinctiveness and memory: Comments and a point of view. In R. R. Hunt & J. B. Worthen (Eds.) *Distinctiveness and memory* (pp. 425–442). Oxford, England: Oxford University Press.

Craik, F. I. M., & Watkins, M. J. (1973). The role of rehearsal in short-term memory. *Journal of Verbal Learning and Verbal Behavior, 12,* 598–607.

Crooks, T. J. (1988). The impact of classroom evaluation practices on students. *Review of Educational Research, 58,* 438–481.

Dahan, D. (2010). The time course of interpretation in speech comprehension. *Current Directions in Psychological Science, 19,* 121–126.

Das, J. P., Naglieri, J. A., & Kirby, J. R. (1994). *Assessment of cognitive processes.* Boston, MA: Allyn & Bacon.

Day, S. B., & Goldstone, R. L. (2012). The import of knowledge export: Connecting findings and theories of transfer of learning. *Educational Psychologist, 47,* 153–176.

De Corte, E., Greer, B., & Verschaffel, L. (1996). Mathematics teaching and learning. In D. C. Berliner & R. C. Calfee (Eds.), *Handbook of educational psychology* (pp. 491–549). New York, NY: Macmillan.

De La Paz, S., & McCutchen, D. (2011). Learning to write. In R. E. Mayer & P. A. Alexander (Eds.), *Handbook of research on learning and instruction* (pp. 32–54). New York, NY: Routledge.

DeLoache, J. S., & Todd, C. M. (1988). Young children's use of spatial categorization as a mnemonic strategy. *Journal of Experimental Child Psychology, 46,* 1–20.

Delval, J. (1994). Stages in the child's construction of social knowledge. In M. Carretero & J. F. Voss (Eds.), *Cognitive and instructional processes in history and the social sciences* (pp. 77–102). Mahwah, NJ: Erlbaum.

DeMarie, D., & López, L. M. (2014). Memory in schools. In R. Fivush & P. J. Bauer (Eds.), *Wiley handbook on the development of human memory* (Vol. 2, pp. 836–864). New York, NY: Wiley.

Dempster, F. N. (1985). Proactive interference in sentence recall: Topic-similarity effects and individual differences. *Memory and Cognition, 13,* 81–89.

Di Vesta, F. J., & Gray, S. G. (1972). Listening and notetaking. *Journal of Educational Psychology, 63,* 8–14.

Dinges, D. F., & Rogers, N. L. (2008). The future of human intelligence: Enhancing cognitive capability in a 24/7 world. In P. C. Kyllonen, R. D. Roberts, & L. Stankov (Eds.), *Extending intelligence: Enhancement and new constructs* (pp. 407–430). New York, NY: Erlbaum/Taylor & Francis.

diSessa, A. A. (1996). What do "just plain folk" know about physics? In D. R. Olson & N. Torrance (Eds.), *The handbook of education and human development: New models of learning, teaching, and schooling* (pp. 709–730). Cambridge, MA: Blackwell.

diSessa, A. A. (2006). A history of conceptual change research. In R. K. Sawyer (Ed.), *The Cambridge handbook of the learning sciences* (pp. 265–281). Cambridge, England: Cambridge University Press.

Driver, R., Asoko, H., Leach, J., Mortimer, E., & Scott, P. (1994). Constructing scientific knowledge in the classroom. *Educational Researcher, 23*(7), 5–12.

Dunlosky, J., Rawson, K. A., Marsh, E. J., Nathan, M. J., & Willingham, D. T. (2013). Improving students' learning with effective learning techniques: Promising directions from cognitive and educational psychology. *Psychological Science in the Public Interest, 14*, 4–58.

Eaton, J. F., Anderson, C. W., & Smith, E. L. (1984). Students' misconceptions interfere with science learning: Case studies of fifth-grade students. *Elementary School Journal, 84*, 365–379.

Edens, K. M., & Potter, E. F. (2001). Promoting conceptual understanding through pictorial representation. *Studies in Art Education, 42*, 214–233.

Ennis, C. D., & Chen, A. (2011). Learning motor skill in physical education. In R. E. Mayer & P. A. Alexander (Eds.), *Handbook of research on learning and instruction* (pp. 148–165). New York, NY: Routledge.

Erdelyi, M. H. (2010). The ups and downs of memory. *American Psychologist, 65*, 623–633.

Ericsson, K. A. (1996). *The road to excellence: The acquisition of expert performance in the arts and science, sports, and games.* Mahwah, NJ: Erlbaum.

Ericsson, K. A. (2003). The acquisition of expert performance as problem solving. In J. E. Davidson & R. J. Sternberg (Eds.), *The psychology of problem solving* (pp. 31–83). Cambridge, England: Cambridge University Press.

Evans, G. W., & Schamberg, M. A. (2009). Childhood poverty, chronic stress, and adult working memory. *Proceedings of the National Academy of Sciences of the United States of America, 106*, 6545–6549.

Feltz, D. L., Landers, D. M., & Becker, B. J. (1988). A revised meta-analysis of the mental practice literature on motor skill performance. In D. Druckman & J. A. Swets (Eds.), *Enhancing human performance: Issues, theories, and techniques* (pp. 1–65). Washington, DC: National Research Council.

Fernbach, P. M., Rogers, T., Fox, C. R., & Sloman, S. V. (2013). Political extremism is supported by an illusion of understanding. *Psychological Science, 24*, 939–945.

Féry, Y.-A., & Morizot, P. (2000). Kinesthetic and visual image in modeling closed motor skills: The example of the tennis serve. *Perceptual and Motor Skills, 90*, 707–722.

Finn, B., & Roediger, H. L., III. (2011). Enhancing retention through reconsolidation: Negative emotional arousal following retrieval enhances later recall. *Psychological Science, 22*, 781–786.

Fisher, A. V., Godwin, K. E., & Seltman, H. (2014). Visual environment, attention allocation, and learning in young children: When too much of a good thing may be bad. *Psychological Science, 25*, 1362–1370.

Flavell, J. H. (2000). Development of children's knowledge about the mental world. *International Journal of Behavioral Development, 24*(1), 15–23.

Flavell, J. H., Miller, P. H., & Miller, S. A. (2002). *Cognitive development* (4th ed.). Upper Saddle River, NJ: Prentice Hall.

Fletcher, J. M., Lyon, G. R., Fuchs, L. S., & Barnes, M. A. (2007). *Learning disabilities: From identification to intervention.* New York, NY: Guilford.

Foerde, K., Knowlton, B. J., & Poldrack, R. A. (2006). Modulation of competing memory systems by distraction. *Proceedings of the National Academy of Sciences, 103*, 11778–11783.

Fox, E. (2009). The role of reader characteristics in processing and learning from informational text. *Review of Educational Research, 79*, 197–261.

Frederiksen, N. (1984b). The real test bias: Influences of testing on teaching and learning. *American Psychologist, 39*, 193–202.

Fuchs, L. S., Geary, D. C., Compton, D. L., Fuchs, D., Schatschneider, C., Hamlett, C. L., . . . Changas, P. (2013). Effects of first-grade number knowledge tutoring with contrasting forms of practice. *Journal of Educational Psychology, 105*, 58–77.

Gagné, R. M. (1985). *The conditions of learning and theory of instruction* (4th ed.). New York, NY: Holt, Rinehart & Winston.

Gardner, H., Torff, B., & Hatch, T. (1996). The age of innocence reconsidered: Preserving the best of the progressive traditions in psychology and education. In D. R. Olson & N. Torrance (Eds.), *The handbook of education and human development: New models of learning, teaching, and schooling* (pp. 28–55). Cambridge, MA: Blackwell.

Gaskins, I. W., & Pressley, M. (2007). Teaching metacognitive strategies that address executive function processes within a schoolwide curriculum. In L. Meltzer (Ed.), *Executive function in education: From theory to practice* (pp. 261–286). New York, NY: Guilford.

Gathercole, S. E., & Hitch, G. J. (1993). Developmental changes in short-term memory: A revised working memory perspective. In A. F. Collins, S. E. Gathercole, M. A. Conway, & P. E. Morris (Eds.), *Theories of memory* (pp. 189–209). Hove, England: Erlbaum.

Gathercole, S. E., Lamont, E., & Alloway, T. P. (2006). Working memory in the classroom. In S. Pickering (Ed.), *Working memory and education* (pp. 219–240). New York, NY: Academic Press.

Geary, D. C. (2005). Folk knowledge and academic learning. In B. J. Ellis & D. F. Bjorklund (Eds.), *Origins of the social mind: Evolutionary psychology and child development* (pp. 493–519). New York, NY: Guilford.

Geary, D. C., Hoard, M. K., Byrd-Craven, J., Nugent, L., & Numtee, C. (2007). Cognitive mechanisms underlying achievement deficits in children with mathematical learning disability. *Child Development, 78*, 1343–1359.

Gelman, S. A. (2003). *The essential child: Origins of essentialism in everyday thought.* New York, NY: Oxford University Press.

Gelman, S. A., & Kalish, C. W. (2006). Conceptual development. In W. Damon, R. M. Lerner (Series Eds.), D. Kuhn, & R. Siegler (Vol. Eds.), *Handbook of child psychology: Vol. 2. Cognition, perception, and language* (6th ed., pp. 687–733). New York, NY: Wiley.

Giaconia, R. M. (1988). Teacher questioning and wait-time (Doctoral dissertation, Stanford University, 1988). *Dissertation Abstracts International, 49*, 462A.

Gilliland, H. (1988). Discovering and emphasizing the positive aspects of the culture. In H. Gilliland & J. Reyhner (Eds.), *Teaching the Native American.* Dubuque, IA: Kendall/Hunt.

Glanzer, M., & Nolan, S. D. (1986). Memory mechanisms in text comprehension. In G. H. Bower (Ed.), *The psychology of learning and motivation: Advances in research and theory* (Vol. 20, pp. 275–317). San Diego, CA: Academic Press.

Glynn, S. M., Yeany, R. H., & Britton, B. K. (Eds.). (1991). *The psychology of learning science.* Mahwah, NJ: Erlbaum.

Gonsalves, B. D., & Cohen, N. J. (2010). Brain imaging, cognitive processes, and brain networks. *Perspectives on Psychological Science, 5*, 744–752.

Grandin, T., & Panek, R. (2014). *The autistic brain: Helping different kinds of minds succeed.* Boston, MA: Houghton Mifflin.

Greeno, J. G., Collins, A. M., & Resnick, L. B. (1996). Cognition and learning. In D. C. Berliner & R. C. Calfee (Eds.), *Handbook of educational psychology* (pp. 15–46). New York, NY: Macmillan.

Gregg, N. (2009). *Adolescents and adults with learning disabilities and ADHD: Assessment and accommodation.* New York, NY: Guilford.

Gresalfi, M. S., & Lester, F. (2009). What's worth knowing in mathematics? In S. Tobias & T. M. Duffy (Eds.), *Constructivist instruction: Success or failure?* (pp. 264–290). New York, NY: Routledge.

Hacker, D. J., Dunlosky, J., & Graesser, A. C. (2009a). A growing sense of "agency." In D. J. Hacker, J. Dunlosky, & A. C. Graesser (Eds.), *Handbook of metacognition in education* (pp. 1–4). New York, NY: Routledge.

Halpern, D. F. (2006). Assessing gender gaps in learning and academic achievement. In P. A. Alexander & P. H. Winne (Eds.), *Handbook of educational psychology* (2nd ed., pp. 635–653). Mahwah, NJ: Erlbaum.

Halpern, D. F., & LaMay, M. L. (2000). The smarter sex: A critical review of sex differences in intelligence. *Educational Psychology Review, 12*, 229–246.

Han, X., Chen, M., Wang, F., Windrem, M., Wang, S., Shanz, S., . . . Nedergaard, M. (2013). Forebrain engraftment by human glial progenitor cells enhances synaptic plasticity and learning in adult mice. *Cell Stem Cell, 12,* 342–353.

Haskell, R. E. (2001). *Transfer of learning: Cognition, instruction, and reasoning.* San Diego, CA: Academic Press.

Hatano, G., & Inagaki, K. (1993). Desituating cognition through the construction of conceptual knowledge. In P. Light & G. Butterworth (Eds.), *Context and cognition: Ways of learning and knowing* (pp. 115–133). Mahwah, NJ: Erlbaum.

Hatano, G., & Inagaki, K. (2003). When is conceptual change intended? A cognitive-sociocultural view. In G. M. Sinatra & P. R. Pintrich (Eds.), *Intentional conceptual change* (pp. 407–427). Mahwah, NJ: Erlbaum.

Hattie, J. (2009). *Visible learning: A synthesis of over 800 meta-analyses relating to achievement.* London: Routledge.

Hattie, J., & Timperley, H. (2007). The power of feedback. *Review of Educational Research, 77,* 81–112.

Healey, M. K., Campbell, K. L., Hasher, L., & Ossher, L. (2010). Direct evidence for the role of inhibition in resolving interference in memory. *Psychological Science, 21,* 1464–1470.

Heatherton, T. F., Macrae, C. N., & Kelley, W. M. (2004). What the social brain sciences can tell us about the self. *Current Directions in Psychological Science, 13,* 190–193.

Hecht, S. A., Close, L., & Santisi, M. (2003). Sources of individual differences in fraction skills. *Journal of Experimental Child Psychology, 86,* 277–302.

Heuer, F., & Reisberg, D. (1992). Emotion, arousal, and memory for detail. In S. Christianson (Ed.), *Handbook of emotion and memory* (pp. 151–180). Hillsdale, NJ: Erlbaum.

Heward, W. L. (2009). *Exceptional children: An introduction to special education* (9th ed.). Upper Saddle River, NJ: Merrill/Pearson Education.

Horn, J. L. (2008). Spearman, *g,* expertise, and the nature of human cognitive capability. In P. C. Kyllonen, R. D. Roberts, & L. Stankov (Eds.), *Extending intelligence: Enhancement and new constructs* (pp. 185–230). New York, NY: Erlbaum/Taylor & Francis.

Huey, E. D., Krueger, F., & Grafman, J. (2006). Representations in the human prefrontal cortex. *Current Directions in Psychological Science, 15,* 167–171.

Hunt, R. R., & Worthen, J. B. (Eds.). (2006). *Distinctiveness and memory.* Oxford, England: Oxford University Press.

Hynd, C. (1998a). Conceptual change in a high school physics class. In B. Guzzetti & C. Hynd (Eds.), *Perspectives on conceptual change: Multiple ways to understand knowing and learning in a complex world* (pp. 27–36). Mahwah, NJ: Erlbaum.

Hynd, C. (1998b). Observing learning from different perspectives: What does it mean for Barry and his understanding of gravity? In B. Guzzetti & C. Hynd (Eds.), *Perspectives on conceptual change: Multiple ways to understand*

knowing and learning in a complex world (pp. 235–244). Mahwah, NJ: Erlbaum.

Hynd, C. (2003). Conceptual change in response to persuasive messages. In G. M. Sinatra & P. R. Pintrich (Eds.), *Intentional conceptual change* (pp. 291–315). Mahwah, NJ: Erlbaum.

Igoa, C. (2007). Immigrant children: Art as a second language. In S. Books (Ed.), *Invisible children in the society and its schools* (3rd ed., pp. 117–140). Mahwah, NJ: Erlbaum.

Immordino-Yang, M. H., Christodoulou, J. A., & Singh, V. (2012). Rest is not idleness: Implications of the brain's default mode for human development and education. *Perspectives on Psychological Science, 7,* 352–364.

Inagaki, K., & Hatano, G. (2006). Young children's conception of the biological world. *Current Directions in Psychological Science, 15,* 177–181.

Jegede, O. J., & Olajide, J. O. (1995). Wait-time, classroom discourse, and the influence of sociocultural factors in science teaching. *Science Education, 79,* 233–249.

Johnson, J., Im-Bolter, N., & Pascual-Leone, J. (2003). Development of mental attention in gifted and mainstream children: The role of mental capacity, inhibition, and speed of processing. *Child Development, 74,* 1594–1614.

Johnson-Glenberg, M. C. (2000). Training reading comprehension in adequate decoders/poor comprehenders: Verbal versus visual strategies. *Journal of Educational Psychology, 92,* 772–782.

Jones, M. S., Levin, M. E., Levin, J. R., & Beitzel, B. D. (2000). Can vocabulary-learning strategies and pair-learning formats be profitably combined? *Journal of Educational Psychology, 92,* 256–262.

Kail, R. V. (1990). *The development of memory in children* (3rd ed.). New York, NY: Freeman.

Kail, R. V. (2007). Longitudinal evidence that increases in processing speed and working memory enhance children's reasoning. *Psychological Science, 18,* 312–313.

Kalyuga, S. (2010). Schema acquisition and sources of cognitive load. In J. L. Plass, R. Moreno, & R. Brünken (Eds.), *Cognitive Load Theory* (pp. 48–64). Cambridge, England: Cambridge University Press.

Karpicke, J. D. (2012). Retrieval-based learning: Active retrieval promotes meaningful learning. *Current Directions in Psychological Science, 21,* 157–163.

Keil, F. C. (1986). The acquisition of natural kind and artifact terms. In W. Demopolous & A. Marras (Eds.), *Language learning and concept acquisition* (pp. 133–153). Norwood, NJ: Ablex.

Keil, F. C. (1989). *Concepts, kinds, and cognitive development.* Cambridge, MA: MIT Press.

Keil, F. C., & Newman, G. E. (2008). Two tales of conceptual change: What changes and what remains the same. In S. Vosniadou (Ed.), *International handbook on conceptual change* (pp. 83–101). New York, NY: Routledge.

Kelemen, D. (1999). Why are rocks pointy? Children's preference for teleological explanations of the natural world. *Developmental Psychology, 35,* 1440–1452.

Kelemen, D. (2004). Are children "intuitive theists"?: Reasoning about purpose and design in nature. *Psychological Science, 15,* 295–301.

Kendeou, P., & van den Broek, P. (2005). The effects of readers' misconceptions on comprehension of scientific text. *Journal of Educational Psychology, 97,* 235–245.

Kesebir, S., & Oishi, S. (2010). A spontaneous self-reference effect in memory: Why some birthdays are harder to remember than others. *Psychological Science, 21,* 1525–1531.

Kiewra, K. A. (1989). A review of note-taking: The encoding-storage paradigm and beyond. *Educational Psychology Review, 1,* 147–172.

Kiewra, K. A., DuBois, N. F., Christian, D., & McShane, A. (1988). Providing study notes: Comparison of three types of notes for review. *Journal of Educational Psychology, 80,* 595–597.

King, A. (1992). Comparison of self-questioning, summarizing, and notetaking-review as strategies for learning from lectures. *American Educational Research Journal, 29,* 303–323.

King, A. (1994). Guiding knowledge construction in the classroom: Effects of teaching children how to question and how to explain. *American Educational Research Journal, 31,* 338–368.

King, A. (1999). Discourse patterns for mediating peer learning. In A. M. O'Donnell & A. King (Eds.), *Cognitive perspectives on peer learning* (pp. 87–115). Mahwah, NJ: Erlbaum.

Kintsch, W. (2009). Learning and constructivism. In S. Tobias & T. M. Duffy (Eds.), *Constructivist instruction: Success or failure?* (pp. 223–241). New York, NY: Routledge.

Kirby, M., Maggi, S., & D'Angiulli, A. (2011). School start times and the sleep–wake cycle of adolescents: A review of critical evaluation of available evidence. *Educational Researcher, 40,* 56–61.

Kirsh, D. (2009). Problem solving and situated cognition. In P. Robbins & M. Aydede (Eds.), *The Cambridge handbook of situated cognition* (pp. 264–306). Cambridge, England: Cambridge University Press.

Kitsantas, A., Zimmerman, B. J., & Cleary, T. (2000). The role of observation and emulation in the development of athletic self-regulation. *Journal of Educational Psychology, 92,* 811–817.

Kiyonaga, A., & Egner, T. (2014). The working memory Stroop effect: When internal representations clash with external stimuli. *Psychological Science, 25,* 1619–1629.

Koob, A. (2009). *The root of thought.* Upper Saddle River, NJ: Pearson.

Kosslyn, S. M. (1985). Mental imagery ability. In R. J. Sternberg (Ed.), *Human abilities: An information-processing approach* (pp. 151–172). New York, NY: Freeman.

Kosslyn, S. M., Margolis, J. A., Barrett, A. M., Goldknopf, E. J., & Daly, P. F. (1990).

Age differences in imagery ability. *Child Development, 61,* 995–1010.

Ku, Y.-M., Chan, W.-C., Wu, Y.-C., & Chen, Y.-H. (2008, March). *Improving children's comprehension of science text: Effects of adjunct questions and notetaking.* Paper presented at the annual meeting of the American Educational Research Association, New York, NY.

Kuhn, D. (2006). Do cognitive changes accompany developments in the adolescent brain? *Perspectives on Psychological Science, 1,* 59–67.

Kunzinger, E. L., III. (1985). A short-term longitudinal study of memorial development during early grade school. *Developmental Psychology, 21,* 642–646.

LaBar, K. S., & Phelps, E. A. (1998). Arousal-mediated memory consolidation: Role of the medial temporal lobe in humans. *Psychological Science, 9,* 490–493.

Lee, V. R. (2010, April–May). *Misconstruals or more? The interactions of orbit diagrams and explanations of the seasons.* Paper presented at the annual meeting of the American Educational Research Association, Denver, CO.

Lehmann, M., & Hasselhorn, M. (2007). Variable memory strategy use in children's adaptive intratask learning behavior: Developmental changes and working memory influences in free recall. *Child Development, 78,* 1068–1082.

Leuner, B., Mendolia-Loffredo, S., Kozorovitskiy, Y., Samburg, D., Gould, E., & Shors, T. J. (2004). Learning enhances the survival of new neurons beyond the time when the hippocampus is required for memory. *Journal of Neuroscience, 24,* 7477–7481.

Levstik, L. S. (2011). Learning history. In R. E. Mayer & P. A. Alexander (Eds.), *Handbook of research on learning and instruction* (pp. 108–126). New York, NY: Routledge.

Lewandowsky, S., Ecker, U. K. H., Seifert, C. M., Schwarz, N., & Cook, J. (2012). Misinformation and its correction: Continued influence and successful debiasing. *Psychological Science in the Public Interest, 13,* 106–131.

Lien, M.-C., Ruthruff, E., & Johnston, J. C. (2006). Attentional limitations in doing two tasks at once: The search for exceptions. *Current Directions in Psychological Science, 15,* 89–93.

Limpo, T., & Alves, R. A. (2013). Modeling writing development: Contribution of transcription and self-regulation to Portuguese students' text generation quality. *Journal of Educational Psychology, 105,* 401–413.

Lin, Z., & He, S. (2012). Emergent filling in induced by motion integration reveals a high-level mechanism in filling in. *Psychological Science, 23,* 1534–1541.

Lindsey, R. V., Shroyer, J. D., Pashler, H., & Mozer, M. C. (2014). Improving students' long-term knowledge retention through personalized review. *Psychological Science, 25,* 639–647.

Linn, M. C. (2008). Teaching for conceptual change: Distinguish or extinguish ideas. In

S. Vosniadou (Ed.), *International handbook on conceptual change* (pp. 694–722). New York, NY: Routledge.

Linn, M. C., & Eylon, B.-S. (2011). *Science learning and instruction: Taking advantage of technology to promote knowledge integration.* New York, NY: Routledge.

Linnenbrink, E. A., & Pintrich, P. R. (2003). Achievement goals and intentional conceptual change. In G. M. Sinatra & P. R. Pintrich (Eds.), *Intentional conceptual change* (pp. 347–374). Mahwah, NJ: Erlbaum.

Loftus, E. F., & Loftus, G. R. (1980). On the permanence of stored information in the human brain. *American Psychologist, 35,* 409–420.

Logie, R. H. (2011). The functional organization and capacity limits of working memory. *Current Directions in Psychological Science, 20,* 240–245.

Lucariello, J., Kyratzis, A., & Nelson, K. (1992). Taxonomic knowledge: What kind and when? *Child Development, 63,* 978–998.

Lustig, C., Konkel, A., & Jacoby, L. L. (2004). Which route to recovery? Controlled retrieval and accessibility bias in retroactive interference. *Psychological Science, 15,* 729–735.

Lyon, G. R., & Krasnegor, N. A. (Eds.). (1996). *Attention, memory, and executive function.* Baltimore, MD: Brookes.

Mac Iver, D. J., Reuman, D. A., & Main, S. R. (1995). Social structuring of the school: Studying what is, illuminating what could be. In J. T. Spence, J. M. Darley, & D. J. Foss (Eds.), *Annual review of psychology* (Vol. 46, pp. 375–400). Palo Alto, CA: Annual Review.

Machiels-Bongaerts, M., Schmidt, H. G., & Boshuizen, H. P. (1993). Effects of mobilizing prior knowledge on information processing: Studies of free recall and allocation of study time. *British Journal of Psychology, 84,* 481–498.

Macnamara, B. N., Hambrick, D. Z., & Oswald, F. L. (2014). Deliberate practice and performance in music, games, sports, education, and professions: A meta-analysis. *Psychological Science, 25,* 1608–1618.

Mandler, G. (2011). From association to organization. *Current Directions in Psychological Science, 20,* 232–235.

Mandler, J. M. (2007). On the origins of the conceptual system. *American Psychologist, 62,* 741–751.

Marcus, G. (2008). *Kluge: The haphazard construction of the human mind.* Boston, MA: Houghton Mifflin.

Marley, S. C., Szabo, Z., Levin, J. R., & Glenberg, A. M. (2008, March). *Activity, observed activity, and children's recall of orally presented narrative passages.* Paper presented at the annual meeting of the American Educational Research Association, New York, NY.

Marsh, E. J. (2007). Retelling is not the same as recalling: Implications for memory. *Current Directions in Psychological Science, 16,* 16–20.

Martínez, P., Bannan-Ritland, B., Kitsantas, A., & Baek, J. Y. (2008, March). *The impact of an integrated science reading intervention on elementary children's misconceptions regarding slow geomorphological changes caused by water.* Paper presented at the annual meeting of the American Educational Research Association, New York, NY.

Mason, L. (2003). Personal epistemologies and intentional conceptual change. In G. M. Sinatra & P. R. Pintrich (Eds.), *Intentional conceptual change* (pp. 199–236). Mahwah, NJ: Erlbaum.

Masten, A. S., Herbers, J. E., Desjardins, C. D., Cutuli, J. J., McCormick, C. M., Sapienza, J. K., . . . Zelazo, P. D. (2012). Executive function skills and school success in young children experiencing homelessness. *Educational Researcher, 41,* 375–384.

Masters, J., Russell, M. K., Humez, A., Driscoll, M. J., Wing, R. E., & Nikula, J. (2010, April–May). *The impact of collaborative, scaffolded learning in K–12 schools: A meta-analysis.* Paper presented at the annual meeting of the American Educational Research Association, Denver, CO.

Mather, M., & Sutherland, M. R. (2011). Arousal-biased competition in perception and memory. *Perspectives on Psychological Science, 6,* 114–133.

Mayer, R. E. (1996). Learning strategies for making sense out of expository text: The SOI model for guiding three cognitive processes in knowledge construction. *Educational Psychology Review, 8,* 357–371.

Mayer, R. E. (2011b). Instruction based on visualizations. In R. E. Mayer & P. A. Alexander (Eds.), *Handbook of research on learning and instruction* (pp. 427–445). New York, NY: Routledge.

McClelland, J. L. (2013). Incorporating rapid neocortical learning of new schema-consistent information into complementary learning systems theory. *Journal of Experimental Psychology: General, 142,* 1190–1210.

McCrudden, M. T., & Schraw, G. (2007). Relevance and goal-focusing in text processing. *Educational Psychology Review, 19,* 113–139.

McDaniel, M. A., & Einstein, G. O. (1989). Material-appropriate processing: A contextualist approach to reading and studying strategies. *Educational Psychology Review, 1,* 113–145.

McDermott, K. B., & Naaz, F. (2014). Is recitation an effective tool for adult learners? *Journal of Applied Research in Memory and Cognition, 3,* 207–213.

McNamara, D. S., & Magliano, J. P. (2009). Self-explanation and metacognition: The dynamics of reading. In D. J. Hacker & A. C. Graesser (Eds.), *Handbook of metacognition in education* (pp. 60–81). New York, NY: Routledge.

Medin, D. L. (2005, August). *Role of culture and expertise in cognition.* Invited address presented at the annual meeting of the American Psychological Association, Washington, DC.

Meltzer, L. (Ed.) (2007). *Executive function in education: From theory to practice.* New York, NY: Guilford.

Mercer, C. D., & Pullen, P. C. (2005). *Students with learning disabilities* (6th ed.). Upper Saddle River, NJ: Merrill/Prentice Hall.

Metcalfe, L. A., Harvey, E. A., & Laws, H. B. (2013). The longitudinal relation between academic/cognitive skills and externalizing behavior problems in preschool children. *Journal of Educational Psychology, 105,* 881–894.

Middleton, M. J., & Midgley, C. (2002). Beyond motivation: Middle school students' perceptions of press for understanding in math. *Contemporary Educational Psychology, 27,* 373–391.

Miller, G. A. (1956). The magical number seven, plus or minus two: Some limits on our capacity for processing information. *Psychological Review, 63,* 81–97.

Minsky, M. (2006). *The emotion machine: Commonsense thinking, artificial intelligence, and the future of the human mind.* New York, NY: Simon & Schuster.

Minstrell, J., & Stimpson, V. (1996). A classroom environment for learning: Guiding students' reconstruction of understanding and reasoning. In L. Schauble & R. Glaser (Eds.), *Innovations in learning: New environments for education* (pp. 175–202). Mahwah, NJ: Erlbaum.

Miyake, A., & Friedman, N. P. (2012). The nature and organization of individual differences in executive functions: Four general conclusions. *Current Directions in Psychological Science, 21,* 8–14.

Mooney, C. M. (1957). Age in the development of closure ability in children. *Canadian Journal of Psychology, 11,* 219–226.

Moran, S., & Gardner, H. (2006). Extraordinary achievements: A developmental and systems analysis. In W. Damon, R. M. Lerner (Series Eds.), D. Kuhn, & R. Siegler (Vol. Eds.), *Handbook of child psychology: Vol. 2. Cognition, perception, and language* (6th ed., pp. 905–949). New York, NY: Wiley.

Moreno, R. (2006). Learning in high-tech and multimedia environments. *Current Directions in Psychological Science, 15,* 63–67.

Morris, C. D., Bransford, J. D., & Franks, J. J. (1977). Levels of processing versus transfer appropriate processing. *Journal of Verbal Learning and Verbal Behavior, 16,* 519–533.

Murphy, P. K. (2007). The eye of the beholder: The interplay of social and cognitive components in change. *Educational Psychologist, 42,* 41–53.

Murphy, P. K., & Alexander, P. A. (2008). Examining the influence of knowledge, beliefs, and motivation in conceptual change. In S. Vosniadou (Ed.), *Handbook of research on conceptual change* (pp. 583–616). New York, NY: Taylor & Francis.

Murphy, P. K., & Mason, L. (2006). Changing knowledge and beliefs. In P. A. Alexander & P. H. Winne (Eds.), *Handbook of educational psychology* (2nd ed., pp. 305–324). Mahwah, NJ: Erlbaum.

Nee, D. E., Berman, M. G., Moore, K. S., & Jonides, J. (2008). Neuroscientific evidence about the distinction between short- and long-term memory. *Current Directions in Psychological Science, 17,* 102–106.

Neisser, U. (1967). *Cognitive psychology.* New York, NY: Appleton-Century-Crofts.

Nelson, C. A., III, Thomas, K. M., & de Haan, M. (2006). Neural bases of cognitive development. In D. Kuhn, R. Siegler (Vol. Eds.), W. Damon, & R. M. Lerner (Series Eds.), *Handbook of child psychology. Vol. 2: Cognition, perception, and language* (6th ed., pp. 3–57). New York, NY: Wiley.

Nelson-Barber, S., & Estrin, E. T. (1995). Bringing Native American perspectives to mathematics and science teaching. *Theory into Practice, 34,* 174–185.

Nesbit, J. C., & Adesope, O. O. (2006). Learning with concept and knowledge maps: A meta-analysis. *Review of Educational Research, 76,* 413–448.

Newman, L. S. (1990). Intentional and unintentional memory in young children: Remembering vs. playing. *Journal of Experimental Child Psychology, 50,* 243–258.

Noble, K. G., McCandliss, B. D., & Farah, M. J. (2007). Socioeconomic gradients predict individual differences in neurocognitive abilities. *Developmental Science, 10,* 464–460.

Novak, J. D. (1998). *Learning, creating, and using knowledge: Concept maps as facilitative tools in schools and corporations.* Mahwah, NJ: Erlbaum.

Oakes, L. M., & Rakison, D. H. (2003). Issues in the early development of concepts and categories: An introduction. In D. H. Rakison & L. M. Oakes (Eds.), *Early category and concept development: Making sense of the blooming, buzzing confusion* (pp. 3–23). Oxford, England: Oxford University Press.

Oberauer, K., & Hein, L. (2012). Attention to information in working memory. *Current Directions in Psychological Science, 21,* 164–169.

Oberheim, N. A., Takano, T., Han, X., He, W., Lin, J. H. C., Wang, F., . . . Nedergaard, M. (2009). Uniquely hominid features of adult human astrocytes. *Journal of Neuroscience, 29,* 3276–3287.

Ormrod, J. E. (2016). *Human learning* (7th ed.). Upper Saddle River, NJ: Pearson.

Ornstein, P. A., Grammer, J. K., & Coffman, J. L. (2010). Teachers' "mnemonic style" and the development of skilled memory. In H. S. Waters & W. Schneider (Eds.), *Metacognition, strategy use, and instruction* (pp. 23–53). New York, NY: Guilford.

Ozgungor, S., & Guthrie, J. T. (2004). Interactions among elaborative interrogation, knowledge, and interest in the process of constructing knowledge from text. *Journal of Educational Psychology, 96,* 437–443.

Öztekin, I., Davachi, L., & McElree, B. (2010). Are representations in working memory distinct from representations in long-term memory? Neural evidence in support of a single store. *Psychological Science, 21,* 1123–1133.

Pashler, H., Rohrer, D., Cepeda, N. J., & Carpenter, S. K. (2007). Enhancing learning and retarding forgetting: Choices and consequences. *Psychonomic Bulletin & Review, 14,* 187–193.

Paxton, R. J. (1999). A deafening silence: History textbooks and the students who read them. *Review of Educational Research, 69,* 315–339.

Payne, J. D., & Kensinger, E. A. (2010). Sleep's role in the consolidation of emotional episodic memories. *Current Directions in Psychological Science, 19,* 290–295.

Pellegrini, A. D., & Bjorklund, D. F. (1997). The role of recess in children's cognitive performance. *Educational Psychologist, 32,* 35–40.

Perkins, D. N., & Ritchhart, R. (2004). When is good thinking? In D. Y. Dai & R. J. Sternberg (Eds.), *Motivation, emotion, and cognition: Integrative perspectives on intellectual functioning and development* (pp. 351–384). Mahwah, NJ: Erlbaum.

Perry, R. P. (1985). Instructor expressiveness: Implications for improving teaching. In J. G. Donald & A. M. Sullivan (Eds.), *Using research to improve teaching* (pp. 35–49). San Francisco: Jossey-Bass.

Peterson, L. R., & Peterson, M. J. (1959). Short-term retention of individual items. *Journal of Experimental Psychology, 58,* 193–198.

Pezdek, K., & Banks, W. P. (Eds.). (1996). *The recovered memory/false memory debate.* San Diego: Academic Press.

Phelps, E. A., & Sharot, T. (2008). How (and why) emotion enhances the subjective sense of recollection. *Current Directions in Psychological Science, 17,* 147–152.

Phye, G. D. (1997). Classroom assessment: A multidimensional perspective. In G. D. Phye (Ed.), *Handbook of classroom assessment: Learning, achievement, and adjustment* (pp. 33–51). San Diego, CA: Academic Press.

Piirto, J. (1999). *Talented children and adults: Their development and education* (2nd ed.). Upper Saddle River, NJ: Merrill/Prentice Hall.

Pine, K. J., & Messer, D. J. (2000). The effect of explaining another's actions on children's implicit theories of balance. *Cognition and Instruction, 18,* 35–51.

Pintrich, P. R., Marx, R. W., & Boyle, R. A. (1993). Beyond cold conceptual change: The role of motivational beliefs and classroom contextual factors in the process of conceptual change. *Review of Educational Research, 63,* 167–199.

Plass, J. L., Moreno, R., & Brünken, R. (Eds.). (2010). *Cognitive Load Theory.* Cambridge, England: Cambridge University Press.

Plumert, J. M. (1994). Flexibility in children's use of spatial and categorical organizational strategies in recall. *Developmental Psychology, 30,* 738–747.

Porat, D. A. (2004). *It's not written here, but this is what happened:* Students' cultural comprehension of textbook narratives on the Israeli-Arab conflict. *American Educational Research Journal, 41,* 963–996.

Posner, M. I., & Rothbart, M. K. (2007). *Educating the human brain.* Washington, DC: American Psychological Association.

Pressley, M. (1982). Elaboration and memory development. *Child Development, 53,* 296–309.

Pressley, M., & Hilden, K. (2006). Cognitive strategies: Production deficiencies and successful strategy instruction everywhere. In W. Damon, R. M. Lerner (Series Eds.), D. Kuhn, & R. Siegler (Vol. Eds.), *Handbook of child psychology: Vol. 2. Cognition, perception, and language* (6th ed., pp. 511–556). New York, NY: Wiley.

Pressley, M., Levin, J. R., & Delaney, H. D. (1982). The mnemonic keyword method. *Review of Educational Research, 52,* 61–91.

Pritchard, R. (1990). The effects of cultural schemata on reading processing strategies. *Reading Research Quarterly, 25,* 273–295.

Proctor, R. W., & Dutta, A. (1995). *Skill acquisition and human performance.* Thousand Oaks, CA: Sage.

Quinn, P. C. (2002). Category representation in young infants. *Current Directions in Psychological Science, 11,* 66–70.

Rabinowitz, M., & Glaser, R. (1985). Cognitive structure and process in highly competent performance. In F. D. Horowitz & M. O'Brien (Eds.), *The gifted and the talented: Developmental perspectives* (pp. 75–97). Washington, DC: American Psychological Association.

Rasch, B., & Born, J. (2008). Reactivation and consolidation of memory during sleep. *Current Directions in Psychological Science, 17,* 188–192.

Reiner, M., Slotta, J. D., Chi, M. T. H., & Resnick, L. B. (2000). Naive physics reasoning: A commitment to substance-based conceptions. *Cognition and Instruction, 18,* 1–34.

Reisberg, D., & Heuer, F. (1992). Remembering the details of emotional events. In E. Winograd & U. Neisser (Eds.), *Affect and accuracy in recall: Studies of "flashbulb" memories* (pp. 162–190). Cambridge, England: Cambridge University Press.

Resnick, L. B. (1989). Developing mathematical knowledge. *American Psychologist, 44,* 162–169.

Rittle-Johnson, B. (2006). Promoting transfer: Effects of self-explanation and direct instruction. *Child Development, 77,* 1–15.

Robinson, D. H., & Kiewra, K. A. (1995). Visual argument: Graphic organizers are superior to outlines in improving learning from text. *Journal of Educational Psychology, 87,* 455–467.

Roediger, H. L., III, & McDermott, K. B. (2000). Tricks of memory. *Current Directions in Psychological Science, 9,* 123–127.

Rogers, T. B., Kuiper, N. A., & Kirker, W. S. (1977). Self-reference and the encoding of personal information. *Journal of Personality and Social Psychology, 35,* 677–688.

Rogoff, B. (2001). *Everyday cognition: Its development in social context.* New York, NY: Replica Books.

Rogoff, B. (2003). *The cultural nature of human development.* Oxford, England: Oxford University Press.

Rogoff, B., Moore, L., Najafi, B., Dexter, A., Correa-Chávez, M., & Solís, J. (2007). Children's development of cultural repertoires through participation in everyday routines and practices. In J. E. Grusec & P. D. Hastings (Eds.), *Handbook of socialization: Theory and research* (pp. 490–515). New York, NY: Guilford.

Rohrer, D., & Pashler, H. (2010). Recent research on human learning challenges conventional instructional strategies. *Educational Researcher, 39,* 406–412.

Rosch, E. H. (1977). Human categorization. In N. Warren (Ed.), *Advances in cross-cultural psychology* (Vol. 1, pp. 1–72). San Diego, CA: Academic Press.

Roscoe, R. D., & Chi, M. T. H. (2007). Understanding tutor learning: Knowledge-building and knowledge-telling in peer tutors' explanations and questions. *Review of Educational Research, 77,* 534–574.

Rosengren, K. S., Brem, S. K., Evans, E. M., & Sinatra, G. M. (Eds.). (2012). *Evolution challenges: Integrating research and practice in teaching and learning about evolution.* Oxford, England: Oxford University Press.

Ross, B. H., & Spalding, T. L. (1994). Concepts and categories. In R. J. Sternberg (Ed.), *Handbook of perception and cognition* (Vol. 12, pp. 119–148). New York, NY: Academic Press.

Roth, K. J. (1990). Developing meaningful conceptual understanding in science. In B. F. Jones & L. Idol (Eds.), *Dimensions of thinking and cognitive instruction* (pp. 139–175). Mahwah, NJ: Erlbaum.

Roth, K. J., & Anderson, C. (1988). Promoting conceptual change learning from science textbooks. In P. Ramsden (Ed.), *Improving learning: New perspectives* (pp. 109–141). London: Kogan Page.

Rowe, M. B. (1974). Wait-time and rewards as instructional variables, their influence on language, logic, and fate control: Part one—Wait time. *Journal of Research in Science Teaching, 11,* 81–94.

Rowe, M. B. (1987). Wait-time: Slowing down may be a way of speeding up. *American Educator, 11,* 38–43, 47.

Ruchkin, D. S., Grafman, J., Cameron, K., & Berndt, R. S. (2003). Working memory retention systems: A state of activated long-term memory. *Behavioral and Brain Sciences, 26,* 709–728.

Rumelhart, D. E., & Ortony, A. (1977). The representation of knowledge in memory. In R. C. Anderson, R. J. Spiro, & W. E. Montague (Eds.), *Schooling and the acquisition of knowledge* (pp. 99–136). Mahwah, NJ: Erlbaum.

Sadoski, M., & Paivio, A. (2001). *Imagery and text: A dual coding theory of reading and writing.* Mahwah, NJ: Erlbaum.

Schacter, D. L. (1999). The seven sins of memory: Insights from psychology and neuroscience. *American Psychologist, 54,* 182–203.

Schacter, D. L. (2012). Adaptive constructive processes and the future of memory. *American Psychologist, 67,* 603–613.

Schiller, D., Monfils, M.-H., Raoi, C. M., Johnson, D. C., LeDoux, J. E., & Phelps, E. A. (2010). Preventing the return of fear in humans using reconsolidation update mechanisms. *Nature, 463*(7277), 49–53.

Schneider, W., & Pressley, M. (1989). *Memory development between 2 and 20.* New York, NY: Springer-Verlag.

Schraw, G. (2006). Knowledge: Structures and processes. In P. A. Alexander & P. H. Winne (Eds.), *Handbook of educational psychology* (2nd ed., pp. 245–263). Mahwah, NJ: Erlbaum.

Schunk, D. H. (1998). Teaching elementary students to self-regulate practice of mathematical skills with modeling. In D. H. Schunk & B. J. Zimmerman (Eds.), *Self-regulated learning: From teaching to self-reflective practice* (pp. 137–159). New York, NY: Guilford.

Schwamborn, A., Mayer, R. E., Thillmann, H., Leopold, C., & Leutner, D. (2010). Drawing as a generative activity and drawing as a prognostic activity. *Journal of Educational Psychology, 102,* 872–879.

Schwartz, D. L., & Heiser, J. (2006). Spatial representations and imagery in learning. In R. K. Sawyer (Ed.), *The Cambridge handbook of the learning sciences* (pp. 283–298). Cambridge, England: Cambridge University Press.

Seligman, M. E. P., Railton, P., Baumeister, R. F., & Sripada, C. (2013). Navigating into the future or driven by the past. *Perspectives on Psychological Science, 8,* 119–141.

Shanahan, T. (2004). Overcoming the dominance of communication: Writing to think and to learn. In T. L. Jetton & J. A. Dole (Eds.), *Adolescent literacy research and practice* (pp. 59–74). New York, NY: Guilford.

Shepard, L., Hammerness, K., Darling-Hammond, L., & Rust, F. (with Snowden, J. B., Gordon, E., Gutierrez, C., & Pacheco, A.). (2005). Assessment. In L. Darling-Hammond & J. Bransford (Eds.), *Preparing teachers for a changing world: What teachers should learn and be able to do* (pp. 275–326). San Francisco: Jossey-Bass/Wiley.

Sherman, D. K., & Cohen, G. L. (2002). Accepting threatening information: Self-affirmation and the reduction of defensive biases. *Current Directions in Psychological Science, 11,* 119–123.

Shute, V. J. (2008). Focus on formative feedback. *Review of Educational Research, 78,* 153–189.

Siegel, D. J. (2012). *The developing mind: How relationships and the brain interact to shape who we are* (2nd ed.). New York, NY: Guilford.

Sinatra, G. M., Kienhues, D., & Hofer, B. K. (2014). Addressing challenges to public understanding of science: Epistemic cognition, motivated reasoning, and conceptual change. *Educational Psychologist, 49,* 123–138.

Sinatra, G. M., & Mason, L. (2008). Beyond knowledge: Learner characteristics influencing conceptual change. In S. Vosniadou (Ed.), *International handbook on conceptual change* (pp. 560–582). New York, NY: Routledge.

Sinatra, G. M., & Pintrich, P. R. (Eds.). (2003). *Intentional conceptual change.* Mahwah, NJ: Erlbaum.

Sizer, T. R. (2004). *Horace's compromise: The dilemma of the American high school.* Boston, MA: Houghton Mifflin.

Skowronek, J. S., Leichtman, M. D., & Pillemer, D. B. (2008). Long-term episodic memory in children with attention-deficit/hyperactivity disorder. *Learning Disabilities Research and Practice, 23*(1), 25–35.

Smith, C. L. (2007). Bootstrapping processes in the development of students' commonsense matter theories: Using analogical mappings, thought experiments, and learning to measure to promote conceptual restructuring. *Cognition and Instruction, 25,* 337–398.

Sneider, C., & Pulos, S. (1983). Children's cosmographies: Understanding the earth's shape and gravity. *Science Education, 67,* 205–221.

Soemer, A., & Schwan, S. (2012). Visual mnemonics for language learning: Static pictures versus animated morphs. *Journal of Educational Psychology, 104,* 565–579.

SooHoo, S., Takemoto, K. Y., & McCullagh, P. (2004). A comparison of modeling and imagery on the performance of a motor skill. *Journal of Sport Behavior, 27,* 349–366.

Spalding, K. L., Bergmann, O., Alkass, K., Bernard, S., Salehpour, M., Huttner, H. B., . . . Frisén, J. (2013). Dynamics of hippocampal neurogenesis in adult humans. *Cell, 153,* 1219–1227.

Spires, H. A., & Donley, J. (1998). Prior knowledge activation: Inducing engagement with informational texts. *Journal of Educational Psychology, 90,* 249–260.

Squire, L. R., & Alvarez, P. (1998). Retrograde amnesia and memory consolidation: A neurobiological perspective. In L. R. Squire & S. M. Kosslyn (Eds.), *Findings and current opinion in cognitive neuroscience* (pp. 75–84). Cambridge, MA: MIT Press.

Stepans, J. (1991). Developmental patterns in students' understanding of physics concepts. In S. M. Glynn, R. H. Yeany, & B. K. Britton (Eds.), *The psychology of learning science* (pp. 89–115). Mahwah, NJ: Erlbaum.

Strike, K. A., & Posner, G. J. (1992). A revisionist theory of conceptual change. In R. A. Duschl & R. J. Hamilton (Eds.), *Philosophy of science, cognitive psychology, and educational theory and practice* (pp. 147–176). New York, NY: State University of New York Press.

Swanson, H. L., Cooney, J. B., & O'Shaughnessy, T. E. (1998). Learning disabilities and memory. In B. Y. L. Wong (Ed.), *Learning about learning disabilities* (2nd ed., pp. 107–162). San Diego, CA: Academic Press.

Sweller, J. (1988). Cognitive load during problem solving: Effects on learning. *Cognitive Science, 12,* 257–285.

Sweller, J. (2008). Human cognitive architecture. In J. M. Spector, M. D. Merrill, J. van Merriënboer, & M. P. Driscoll (Eds.), *Handbook of research on educational communications and technology* (3rd ed., pp. 369–381). New York, NY: Erlbaum.

Sweller, J. (2010). Cognitive Load Theory: Recent theoretical advances. In J. L. Plass, R. Moreno, & R. Brünken (Eds.), *Cognitive Load Theory* (pp. 29–47). Cambridge, England: Cambridge University Press.

Talmi, D., Grady, C. L., Goshen-Gottstein, Y., & Moscovitch, M. (2005). Neuroimaging the serial position curve: A test of single-store versus dual-store models. *Psychological Science, 16,* 716–723.

Tennyson, R. D., & Cocchiarella, M. J. (1986). An empirically based instructional design theory for teaching concepts. *Review of Educational Research, 56,* 40–71.

Tharp, R. G. (1989). Psychocultural variables and constants: Effects on teaching and learning in schools. *American Psychologist, 44,* 349–359.

Thompson, H., & Carr, M. (1995, April). *Brief metacognitive intervention and interest as predictors of memory for text.* Paper presented at the annual meeting of the American Educational Research Association, San Francisco, CA.

Tirosh, D., & Graeber, A. O. (1990). Evoking cognitive conflict to explore preservice teachers' thinking about division. *Journal for Research in Mathematics Education, 21,* 98–108.

Tobin, K. (1987). The role of wait time in higher cognitive level learning. *Review of Educational Research, 57,* 69–95.

Tomporowski, P. D., Davis, C. L., Miller, P. H., & Naglieri, J. A. (2008). Exercise and children's intelligence, cognition, and academic achievement. *Educational Psychology Review, 20,* 111–131.

Torney-Purta, J. (1994). Dimensions of adolescents' reasoning about political and historical issues: Ontological switches, developmental processes, and situated learning. In M. Carretero & J. F. Voss (Eds.), *Cognitive and instructional processes in history and the social sciences* (pp. 103–122). Mahwah, NJ: Erlbaum.

Trachtenberg, J. T., Chen, B. E., Knott, G. W., Feng, G., Sanes, J. R., Welker, E., & Svoboda, K. (2002). Long-term *in vivo* imaging of experience-dependent synaptic plasticity in adult cortex. *Nature, 420,* 788–794.

Tulving, E. (1983). *Elements of episodic memory.* Oxford, England: Oxford University Press.

Tulving, E., & Thomson, D. M. (1973). Encoding specificity and retrieval processes in episodic memory. *Psychological Review, 80,* 352–373.

Turnbull, A. P., Turnbull, R., & Wehmeyer, M. L. (2010). *Exceptional lives: Special education in today's schools* (6th ed.). Upper Saddle River, NJ: Merrill.

Tyler, K. M., Uqdah, A. L., Dillihunt, M. L., Beatty-Hazelbaker, R., Connor, T., Gadson, N., . . . Stevens, R. (2008). Cultural discontinuity: Toward a quantitative investigation of a major hypothesis in education. *Educational Researcher, 37,* 280–297.

Urgolites, Z. J., & Wood, J. N. (2013). Visual long-term memory stores high-fidelity representations of observed actions. *Psychological Science, 24,* 403–411.

van der Veen, J. (2012). Draw your physics homework? Art as a path to understanding in physics teaching. *American Educational Research Journal, 49,* 356–407.

van Merriënboer, J. J. G., & Kester, L. (2008). Whole-task models in education. In J. M. Spector, M. D. Merrill, J. van Merriënboer, & M. P. Driscoll (Eds.), *Handbook of research on educational communications and technology* (3rd ed., pp. 441–456). New York, NY: Erlbaum.

Van Meter, P., & Garner, J. (2005). The promise and practice of learner-generated drawing: Literature review and synthesis. *Educational Psychology Review, 17,* 285–325.

VanSledright, B., & Brophy, J. (1992). Storytelling, imagination, and fanciful elaboration in children's historical reconstructions. *American Educational Research Journal, 29,* 837–859.

Verdi, M. P., Kulhavy, R. W., Stock, W. A., Rittschof, K. A., & Johnson, J. T. (1996). Text learning using scientific diagrams: Implications for classroom use. *Contemporary Educational Psychology, 21,* 487–499.

Vosniadou, S. (Ed.). (2008). *International handbook of research on conceptual change.* New York, NY: Routledge.

Vosniadou, S., & Brewer, W. F. (1987). Theories of knowledge restructuring in development. *Review of Educational Research, 57,* 51–67.

Vosniadou, S., Vamvakoussi, X., & Skopeliti, I. (2008). The framework theory approach to the problem of conceptual change. In S. Vosniadou (Ed.), *International handbook on conceptual change* (pp. 3–34). New York, NY: Routledge.

Wang, Q., & Ross, M. (2007). Culture and memory. In S. Kitayama & D. Cohen (Eds.), *Handbook of cultural psychology* (pp. 645–667). New York, NY: Guilford.

Waters, H. S. (1982). Memory development in adolescence: Relationships between metamemory, strategy use, and performance. *Journal of Experimental Child Psychology, 33,* 183–195.

Weiss, M. R., & Klint, K. A. (1987). "Show and tell" in the gymnasium: An investigation of developmental differences in modeling and verbal rehearsal of motor skills. *Research Quarterly for Exercise and Sport, 58,* 234–241.

Wellman, H. M., & Gelman, S. A. (1998). Knowledge acquisition in foundational domains. In W. Damon (Series Ed.), D. Kuhn, & R. S. Siegler (Vol. Eds.), *Handbook of child psychology: Vol. 2. Cognition, perception, and language* (5th ed., pp. 523–573). New York, NY: Wiley.

White, J. J., & Rumsey, S. (1994). Teaching for understanding in a third-grade geography lesson. In J. Brophy (Ed.), *Advances in research on teaching: Vol. 4. Case studies of teaching and learning in social studies* (pp. 33–69). Greenwich, CT: JAI Press.

Willingham, D. B. (1999). The neural basis of motor-skill learning. *Current Directions in Psychological Science, 8,* 178–182.

Wilson, P. T., & Anderson, R. C. (1986). What they don't know will hurt them: The role of prior knowledge in comprehension. In J. Orasanu (Ed.), *Reading comprehension: From research to practice* (pp. 31–48). Mahwah, NJ: Erlbaum.

Winer, G. A., & Cottrell, J. E. (1996). Does anything leave the eye when we see? Extramission beliefs of children and adults. *Current Directions in Psychological Science, 5,* 137–142.

Winer, G. A., Cottrell, J. E., Gregg, V., Fournier, J. S., & Bica, L. A. (2002). Fundamentally misunderstanding visual perception: Adults' belief in visual emissions. *American Psychologist, 57,* 417–424.

Wingfield, A., & Byrnes, D. L. (1981). *The psychology of human memory.* San Diego, CA: Academic Press.

Winn, W. (1991). Learning from maps and diagrams. *Educational Psychology Review, 3,* 211–247.

Wiser, M., & Smith, C. L. (2008). Learning and teaching about matter in grades K–8: When should the atomic–molecular theory be introduced? In S. Vosniadou (Ed.), *International handbook on conceptual change* (pp. 205–231). New York, NY: Routledge.

Wittrock, M. C. (1974). Learning as a generative process. *Educational Psychologist, 11,* 87–95.

Wixted, J. T. (2005). A theory about why we forget what we once knew. *Current Directions in Psychological Science, 14,* 6–9.

Wood, E., Willoughby, T., Bolger, A., & Younger, J. (1993). Effectiveness of elaboration strategies for grade school children as a function of academic achievement. *Journal of Experimental Child Psychology, 56,* 240–253.

Zeelenberg, R., Wagenmakers, E.-J., & Rotteveel, M. (2006). The impact of emotion on perception: Bias or enhanced processing? *Psychological Science, 17,* 287–291.

Zhang, W., & Luck, S. J. (2009). Sudden death and gradual decay in visual working memory. *Psychological Science, 20,* 423–428.

Zimmerman, B. J., & Kitsantas, A. (1999). Acquiring writing revision skill: Shifting from process to outcome self-regulatory goals. *Journal of Educational Psychology, 91,* 241–250.

CHAPTER 7

Afflerbach, P., & Cho, B.-Y. (2010). Determining and describing reading strategies: Internet and traditional forms of reading. In H. S. Waters & W. Schneider (Eds.), *Metacognition, strategy use, and instruction* (pp. 201–225). New York, NY: Guilford.

Agarwal, P. K., D'Antonio, L., Roediger, H. L., III, McDermott, K. B., & McDaniel, M. A. (2014). Classroom-based programs of retrieval practice reduce middle school and high school students' test anxiety. *Journal of Applied Research in Memory and Cognition, 3,* 131–139.

Alexander, P. A., & the Disciplined Reading and Learning Research Laboratory. (2012). Reading into the future: Competence for the 21st century. *Educational Psychologist, 47,* 259–280.

Alexander, P. A., Graham, S., & Harris, K. R. (1998). A perspective on strategy research: Progress and prospects. *Educational Psychology Review, 10,* 129–154.

Alexander, P. A., & Judy, J. E. (1988). The interaction of domain-specific and strategic knowledge in academic performance. *Review of Educational Research, 58,* 375–404.

Amabile, T. M. (1996). *Creativity in context: Update to the social psychology of creativity.* Boulder, CO: Westview.

Amabile, T. M., & Hennessey, B. A. (1992). The motivation for creativity in children. In A. K. Boggiano & T. S. Pittman (Eds.), *Achievement and motivation: A social-developmental perspective* (pp. 54–74). Cambridge, England: Cambridge University Press.

Amsterlaw, J. (2006). Children's beliefs about everyday reasoning. *Child Development, 77,* 443–464.

Anderson, J. R., Greeno, J. G., Reder, L. M., & Simon, H. A. (2000). Perspectives on learning, thinking, and activity. *Educational Researcher, 29*(4), 11–13.

Andre, T., & Windschitl, M. (2003). Interest, epistemological belief, and intentional conceptual change. In G. M. Sinatra & P. R. Pintrich (Eds.), *Intentional conceptual change* (pp. 173–197). Mahwah, NJ: Erlbaum.

Anzai, Y. (1991). Learning and use of representations for physics expertise. In K. A. Ericsson & J. Smith (Eds.), *Toward a general theory of expertise: Prospects and limits* (pp. 64–92). Cambridge, England: Cambridge University Press.

Astington, J. W., & Pelletier, J. (1996). The language of mind: Its role in teaching and learning. In D. R. Olson & N. Torrance (Eds.), *The handbook of education and human development: New models of learning, teaching, and schooling* (pp. 593–620). Cambridge, MA: Blackwell.

Azevedo, R. (2005). Computer environments as metacognitive tools for enhancing learning. *Educational Psychologist, 40,* 193–197.

Azevedo, R., & Witherspoon, A. M. (2009). Self-regulated learning with hypermedia. In D. J. Hacker, J. Dunlosky, & A. C. Graesser (Eds.), *Handbook of metacognition in education* (pp. 319–339). New York, NY: Routledge.

Baer, J., & Garrett, T. (2010). Teaching for creativity in an era of content standards and accountability. In R. A. Beghetto & J. C. Kaufman (Eds.), *Nurturing creativity in the classroom* (pp. 6–23). New York, NY: Cambridge University Press.

Baird, B., Smallwood, J., Mrazek, M. D., Kam, J. W. Y., Franklin, M. S., & Schooler, J. W. (2012). Inspired by distraction: Mind wandering facilitates creative incubation. *Psychological Science, 23,* 1117–1122.

Baker, L., & Brown, A. L. (1984). Metacognitive skills of reading. In D. Pearson (Ed.), *Handbook of reading research* (pp. 353–394). White Plains, NY: Longman.

Bangert-Drowns, R. L., Hurley, M. M., & Wilkinson, B. (2004). The effects of school-based writing-to-learn interventions on academic achievement: A meta-analysis. *Review of Educational Research, 74,* 29–58.

Barnett, J. E. (2001, April). *Study strategies and preparing for exams: A survey of middle and high school students.* Paper presented at the annual meeting of the American Educational Research Association, Seattle, WA.

Barnett, J. E., Di Vesta, F. J., & Rogozinski, J. T. (1981). What is learned in note taking? *Journal of Educational Psychology, 73,* 181–192.

Barnett, S. M., & Ceci, S. J. (2002). When and where do we apply what we learn? A taxonomy of far transfer. *Psychological Bulletin, 128,* 612–637.

Barron, B. (2000). Problem solving in video-based microworlds: Collaborative and individual outcomes of high-achieving sixth-grade students. *Journal of Educational Psychology, 92,* 391–398.

Bassok, M. (2003). Analogical transfer in problem solving. In J. E. Davidson & R. J. Sternberg (Eds.), *The psychology of problem solving* (pp. 343–369). Cambridge, England: Cambridge University Press.

Beal, C. R., Arroyo, I., Cohen, P. R., & Woolf, B. P. (2010). Evaluation of AnimalWatch: An intelligent tutoring system for arithmetic and fractions. *Journal of Interactive Online Learning, 9,* 64–77.

Beghetto, R. A., & Kaufman, J. C. (2010). Broadening conceptions of creativity in the classroom. In R. A. Beghetto & J. C. Kaufman (Eds.), *Nurturing creativity in the classroom* (pp. 191–205). New York, NY: Cambridge University Press.

Beirne-Smith, M., Patton, J. R., & Kim, S. H. (2006). *Mental retardation: An introduction to intellectual disabilities* (7th ed.). Upper Saddle River, NJ: Merrill/Prentice Hall.

Belland, B. R. (2011). Distributed cognition as a lens to understand the effects of scaffolds: The role of transfer of responsibility. *Educational Psychology Review, 23,* 577–600.

Bendixen, L. D., & Feucht, F. C. (Eds.). (2010). *Personal epistemology in the classroom: Theory, research, and implications for practice.* Cambridge, England: Cambridge University Press.

Bermejo, V. (1996). Cardinality development and counting. *Developmental Psychology, 32,* 263–268.

Berthold, K., & Renkl, A. (2009). Instructional aids to support a conceptual understanding of multiple representations. *Journal of Educational Psychology, 101,* 70–87.

Beyer, B. K. (1985). Critical thinking: What is it? *Social Education, 49,* 270–276.

Bol, L., Hacker, D. J., Walck, C. C., & Nunnery, J. A. (2012). The effects of individual or group guidelines on the calibration accuracy and achievement of high school biology students. *Contemporary Educational Psychology, 37,* 280–287.

Bonney, C. R., & Sternberg, R. J. (2011). Learning to think critically. In R. E. Mayer & P. A. Alexander (Eds.), *Handbook of research on learning and instruction* (pp. 166–196). New York, NY: Routledge.

Boyle, J. R. (2011). Strategic note-taking for inclusive middle school science classrooms. *Remedial and Special Education, 34,* 78–90.

Bransford, J. D., & Schwartz, D. L. (1999). Rethinking transfer: A simple proposal with multiple implications. In A. Iran-Nejad & P. D. Pearson (Eds.), *Review of research in education* (Vol. 24, pp. 61–100). Washington, DC: American Educational Research Association.

Brenner, M. E., Mayer, R. E., Moseley, B., Brar, T., Durán, R., Reed, B. S., & Webb, D. (1997). Learning by understanding: The role of multiple representations in learning algebra. *American Educational Research Journal, 34,* 663–689.

Brooks, L. W., & Dansereau, D. F. (1987). Transfer of information: An instructional perspective. In S. M. Cormier & J. D. Hagman (Eds.), *Transfer of learning: Contemporary research and applications* (pp. 121–150). San Diego, CA: Academic Press.

Brown, A. L., Campione, J., & Day, J. (1981). Learning to learn: On training students to learn from texts. *Educational Researcher, 10*(2), 14–21.

Brownell, M. T., Mellard, D. F., & Deshler, D. D. (1993). Differences in the learning and transfer performance between students with learning disabilities and other low-achieving students on problem-solving tasks. *Learning Disabilities Quarterly, 16,* 138–156.

Buehl, M. M., & Alexander, P. A. (2006). Examining the dual nature of epistemological beliefs. *International Journal of Educational Research, 45,* 28–42.

Bugg, J. M., & McDaniel, M. A. (2012). Selective benefits of question self-generation and answering for remembering expository text. *Journal of Educational Psychology, 104,* 922–931.

Bulgren, J. A., Marquis, J. G., Lenz, B. K., Deshler, D. D., & Schumaker, J. B. (2011). The effectiveness of a question-exploration routine for enhancing the content learning of secondary students. *Journal of Educational Psychology, 103,* 578–593.

Butler, D. L., & Winne, P. H. (1995). Feedback and self-regulated learning: A theoretical synthesis. *Review of Educational Research, 65,* 245–281.

Campione, J. C., Brown, A. L., & Bryant, N. R. (1985). Individual differences in learning and memory. In R. J. Sternberg (Ed.), *Human abilities: An information-processing approach* (pp. 103–126). New York, NY: Freeman.

Carr, M. (2010). The importance of metacognition for conceptual change and strategy use in mathematics. In H. S. Waters & W. Schneider (Eds.), *Metacognition, strategy use, and instruction* (pp. 176–197). New York, NY: Guilford.

Carr, M., & Biddlecomb, B. (1998). Metacognition in mathematics from a constructivist perspective. In D. J. Hacker, J. Dunlosky, & A. C. Graesser (Eds.), *Metacognition in educational theory and practice* (pp. 69–91). Mahwah, NJ: Erlbaum.

Chandler, M. J., Hallett, D., & Sokol, B. W. (2002). Competing claims about competing knowledge claims. In B. K. Hofer & P. R. Pintrich (Eds.), *Personal epistemology: The psychology of beliefs about knowledge and knowing* (pp. 145–168). Mahwah, NJ: Erlbaum.

Chein, J. M., & Schneider, W. (2012). The brain's learning and control architecture. *Current Directions in Psychological Science, 21,* 78–84.

Chen, Z. (1999). Schema induction in children's analogical problem solving. *Journal of Educational Psychology, 91,* 703–715.

Chinn, C. A., Anderson, R. C., & Waggoner, M. A. (2001). Patterns of discourse in two kinds of literature discussion. *Reading Research Quarterly, 36,* 378–411.

Chinn, C. A., & Buckland, L. A. (2012). Model-based instruction: Fostering change in evolutionary conceptions and in epistemic practices. In K. S. Rosengren, S. K. Brem, E. M. Evans, & G. M. Sinatra (Eds.), *Evolution challenges: Integrating research and practice in teaching and learning about evolution* (pp. 211–232). Oxford, England: Oxford University Press.

Clark, B. (1997). *Growing up gifted* (5th ed.). Upper Saddle River, NJ: Merrill/Prentice Hall.

Clark, R. E., & Blake, S. B. (1997). Designing training for novel problem-solving transfer. In R. D. Tennyson, F. Schott, N. M. Seel, & S. Dijkstra (Eds.), *Instructional design: International perspectives. Vol. 1: Theory, research, and models* (pp. 183–214). Mahwah, NJ: Erlbaum.

Cognition and Technology Group at Vanderbilt. (1990). Anchored instruction and its relationship to situated cognition. *Educational Researcher, 19*(6), 2–10.

Cognition and Technology Group at Vanderbilt. (1996). Looking at technology in context: A framework for understanding technology and education research. In D. C. Berliner & R. C. Calfee (Eds.), *Handbook of educational psychology* (pp. 807–840). New York, NY: Macmillan.

Collins, A., Brown, J. S., & Newman, S. E. (1989). Cognitive apprenticeship: Teaching the crafts of reading, writing, and mathematics. In L. B. Resnick (Ed.), *Knowing, learning, and instruction: Essays in honor of Robert Glaser* (pp. 453–494). Mahwah, NJ: Erlbaum.

Cornoldi, C. (2010). Metacognition, intelligence, and academic performance. In H. S. Waters & W. Schneider (Eds.), *Metacognition, strategy use, and instruction* (pp. 257–277). New York, NY: Guilford.

Cox, B. D. (1997). The rediscovery of the active learner in adaptive contexts: A developmental-historical analysis of transfer of training. *Educational Psychologist, 32,* 41–55.

Csikszentmihalyi, M. (1996). *Creativity: Flow and the psychology of discovery and invention.* New York, NY: HarperCollins.

Dahlin, B., & Watkins, D. (2000). The role of repetition in the processes of memorizing and understanding: A comparison of the views of Western and Chinese secondary students in Hong Kong. *British Journal of Educational Psychology, 70,* 65–84.

Dai, D. Y. (2010). *The nature and nurture of giftedness: A new framework for understanding gifted education.* New York, NY: Teachers College Press.

Davidson, J. E., & Sternberg, R. J. (1998). Smart problem solving: How metacognition helps. In D. J. Hacker, J. Dunlosky, & A. C. Graesser (Eds.), *Metacognition in educational theory and practice* (pp. 47–68). Mahwah, NJ: Erlbaum.

Davidson, J. E., & Sternberg, R. J. (Eds.). (2003). *The psychology of problem solving.* Cambridge, England: Cambridge University Press.

Day, S. B., & Goldstone, R. L. (2012). The import of knowledge export: Connecting findings and theories of transfer of learning. *Educational Psychologist, 47,* 153–176.

De Corte, E. (2003). Transfer as the productive use of acquired knowledge, skills, and motivations. *Current Directions in Psychological Science, 12,* 142–146.

De Corte, E., Op't Eynde, P., Depaepe, F., & Verschaffel, L. (2010). The reflexive relation between students' mathematics-related beliefs and the mathematics classroom culture. In L. D. Bendixen & F. C. Feucht (Eds.), *Personal epistemology in the classroom: Theory, research, and implications for practice* (pp. 292–327). Cambridge, England: Cambridge University Press.

De La Paz, S., & Felton, M. K. (2010). Reading and writing from multiple source documents in history: Effects of strategy instruction with low to average high school writers. *Contemporary Educational Psychology, 35,* 174–192.

Dee-Lucas, D., & Larkin, J. H. (1991). Equations in scientific proofs: Effects on comprehension. *American Educational Research Journal, 28,* 661–682.

Derry, S. J., Levin, J. R., Osana, H. P., & Jones, M. S. (1998). Developing middle school students' statistical reasoning abilities through simulation gaming. In S. P. Lajoie (Ed.), *Reflections on statistics: Learning, teaching, and assessment in grades K–12* (pp. 175–195). Mahwah, NJ: Erlbaum.

Dole, J. A., Duffy, G. G., Roehler, L. R., & Pearson, P. D. (1991). Moving from the old to the new: Research on reading comprehension instruction. *Review of Educational Research, 61,* 239–264.

Dominowski, R. L. (1998). Verbalization and problem solving. In D. J. Hacker, J. Dunlosky, & A. C. Graesser (Eds.), *Metacognition in educational theory and practice* (pp. 25–45). Mahwah, NJ: Erlbaum.

Duncker, K. (1945). On problem solving. *Psychological Monographs, 58*(Whole No. 270).

Dunlosky, J., Rawson, K. A., Marsh, E. J., Nathan, M. J., & Willingham, D. T. (2013). Improving students' learning with effective learning techniques: Promising directions from cognitive and educational psychology. *Psychological Science in the Public Interest, 14,* 4–58.

Dunning, D., Heath, C., & Suls, J. M. (2004). Flawed self-assessment: Implications for health, education, and the workplace. *Psychological Science in the Public Interest, 5,* 69–106.

DuPaul, G. J., & Eckert, T. L. (1994). The effects of social skills curricula: Now you see them, now you don't. *School Psychology Quarterly, 9,* 113–132.

Eason, S. H., Goldberg, L. F., Young, K. M., Geist, M. C., & Cutting, L. E. (2012). Reader–text interactions: How differential text and question types influence cognitive skills needed for reading comprehension. *Journal of Educational Psychology, 104,* 515–528.

Edmonds, M. S., Vaughn, S., Wexler, J., Reutebuch, C., Cable, A., Tackett, K. K., & Schnakenberg, J. W. (2009). A synthesis of reading interventions and effects of reading comprehension outcomes for older struggling students. *Review of Educational Research, 79,* 262–300.

Eigsti, I.-M., Zayas, V., Mischel, W., Shoda, Y., Ayduk, O., Dadlani, M. B., . . . Casey, B. J. (2006). Predicting cognitive control from preschool to late adolescence and young adulthood. *Psychological Science, 17,* 478–484.

Elder, A. D. (2002). Characterizing fifth grade students' epistemological beliefs in science. In B. K. Hofer & P. R. Pintrich (Eds.), *Personal epistemology: The psychology of beliefs about knowledge and knowing* (pp. 347–363). Mahwah, NJ: Erlbaum.

Ellis, E. S., & Friend, P. (1991). Adolescents with learning disabilities. In B. Y. L. Wong (Ed.), *Learning about learning disabilities* (pp. 505–561). San Diego, CA: Academic Press.

Ellis, N. R. (Ed.). (1979). *Handbook of mental deficiency: Psychological theory and research.* Mahwah, NJ: Erlbaum.

Emmer, E. T. (1994, April). *Teacher emotions and classroom management.* Paper presented at the annual meeting of the American Educational Research Association, New Orleans, LA.

Engle, R. A., Lam, D. P., Meyer, X. S., & Nix, S. E. (2012). How does expansive framing promote transfer? Several proposed explanations and a research agenda for investigating them. *Educational Psychologist, 47,* 215–231.

Ennis, R. H. (1996). *Critical thinking.* Upper Saddle River, NJ: Prentice Hall.

Esquivel, G. B. (1995). Teacher behaviors that foster creativity. *Educational Psychology Review, 7,* 185–202.

Fairweather, E., & Cramond, B. (2010). Infusing creative and critical thinking into the curriculum together. In R. A. Beghetto & J. C. Kaufman (Eds.), *Nurturing creativity in the classroom* (pp. 113–141). New York, NY: Cambridge University Press.

Feldhusen, J. F., & Treffinger, D. J. (1980). *Creative thinking and problem solving in gifted education.* Dubuque, IA: Kendall/Hunt.

Flavell, J. H., Friedrichs, A. G., & Hoyt, J. D. (1970). Developmental changes in memorization processes. *Cognitive Psychology, 1,* 324–340.

Flavell, J. H., Miller, P. H., & Miller, S. A. (2002). *Cognitive development* (4th ed.). Upper Saddle River, NJ: Prentice Hall.

Fonseca, B. A., & Chi, M. T. H. (2011). Instruction based on self-explanation. In R. E. Mayer & P. A. Alexander (Eds.), *Handbook of research on learning and instruction* (pp. 296–321). New York, NY: Routledge.

Frederiksen, N. (1984a). Implications of cognitive theory for instruction in problem-solving. *Review of Educational Research, 54,* 363–407.

Fuchs, L. S., Fuchs, D., Prentice, K., Burch, M., Hamlett, C. L., Owen, R., . . . Jancek, D. (2003). Explicitly teaching for transfer: Effects on third-grade students' mathematical problem solving. *Journal of Educational Psychology, 95,* 295–305.

Gijbels, D., Dochy, F., Van den Bossche, P., & Segers, M. (2005). Effects of problem-based learning: A meta-analysis from the angle of assessment. *Review of Educational Research, 75,* 27–61.

Ginsburg, H. P., Cannon, J., Eisenband, J., & Pappas, S. (2006). Mathematical thinking and learning. In K. McCartney & D. Phillips (Eds.), *Blackwell handbook of early childhood development* (pp. 208–229). Malden, MA: Blackwell.

Glogger, I., Schwonke, R., Holzäpfel, L., Nückles, M., & Renkl, A. (2012). Learning strategies assessed by journal writing: Prediction of learning outcomes by quantity, quality, and combinations of learning strategies. *Journal of Educational Psychology, 104,* 452–468.

Glover, J. A., Ronning, R. R., & Reynolds, C. R. (Eds.). (1989). *Handbook of creativity.* New York, NY: Plenum.

Goldstein, S., & Rider, R. (2006). Resilience and the disruptive disorders of childhood. In S. Goldstein & R. B. Brooks (Eds.), *Handbook of resilience in children* (pp. 203–222). New York, NY: Springer.

Goldstone, R. L., & Day, S. B. (2012). Introduction to "new conceptualizations of transfer of learning." *Educational Psychologist, 47,* 149–152.

Graesser, A. C., McNamara, D. S., & VanLehn, K. (2005). Scaffolding deep comprehension strategies through Point&Query, AutoTutor, and iSTART. *Educational Psychologist, 40,* 225–234.

Graham, S., & Harris, K. R. (1996). Addressing problems in attention, memory, and executive functioning. In G. R. Lyon & N. A. Krasnegor (Eds.), *Attention, memory, and executive function* (pp. 349–365). Baltimore, MD: Brookes.

Gray, W. D., & Orasanu, J. M. (1987). Transfer of cognitive skills. In S. M. Cormier & J. D. Hagman (Eds.), *Transfer of learning: Contemporary research and applications* (pp. 184–215). San Diego, CA: Academic Press.

Greene, J. A., Hutchinson, L. A., Costa, L.-J., & Crompton, H. (2012). Investigating how college students' task definitions and plans relate to self-regulated learning processing and understanding of a complex science topic. *Contemporary Educational Psychology, 37,* 307–320.

Gregg, N. (2009). *Adolescents and adults with learning disabilities and ADHD: Assessment and accommodation.* New York, NY: Guilford.

Gresalfi, M. S., & Lester, F. (2009). What's worth knowing in mathematics? In S. Tobias & T. M. Duffy (Eds.), *Constructivist instruction: Success or failure?* (pp. 264–290). New York, NY: Routledge.

Grodzinsky, G. M., & Diamond, R. (1992). Frontal lobe functioning in boys with attention-deficit hyperactivity disorder. *Developmental Neuropsychology, 8,* 427–445.

Hacker, D. J., Bol, L., Horgan, D. D., & Rakow, E. A. (2000). Test prediction and performance in a classroom context. *Journal of Educational Psychology, 92,* 160–170.

Hacker, D. J., Dunlosky, J., & Graesser, A. C. (Eds.). (2009b). *Handbook of metacognition in education.* New York, NY: Routledge.

Haller, E. P., Child, D. A., & Walberg, H. J. (1988). Can comprehension be taught? A quantitative synthesis of "metacognitive" studies. *Educational Researcher, 17*(9), 5–8.

Halpern, D. F. (1997). *Critical thinking across the curriculum: A brief edition of thought and knowledge.* Mahwah, NJ: Erlbaum.

Halpern, D. F. (1998). Teaching critical thinking for transfer across domains. *American Psychologist, 53,* 449–455.

Halpern, D. F. (2008). Is intelligence critical thinking? Why we need a new definition of intelligence. In P. C. Kyllonen, R. D. Roberts, & L. Stankov (Eds.), *Extending intelligence: Enhancement and new constructs* (pp. 349–370). New York, NY: Erlbaum/Taylor & Francis.

Hamman, D., Berthelot, J., Saia, J., & Crowley, E. (2000). Teachers' coaching of learning and its relation to students' strategic learning. *Journal of Educational Psychology, 92,* 342–348.

Harris, K. R. (1982). Cognitive-behavior modification: Application with exceptional students. *Focus on Exceptional Children, 15,* 1–16.

Harris, R. J. (1977). Comprehension of pragmatic implications in advertising. *Journal of Applied Psychology, 62,* 603–608.

Haskell, R. E. (2001). *Transfer of learning: Cognition, instruction, and reasoning.* San Diego, CA: Academic Press.

Hatano, G., & Inagaki, K. (2003). When is conceptual change intended? A cognitive-sociocultural view. In G. M. Sinatra & P. R. Pintrich (Eds.), *Intentional conceptual change* (pp. 407–427). Mahwah, NJ: Erlbaum.

Hatano, G., & Oura, Y. (2003). Commentary: Reconceptualizing school learning using insight from expertise research. *Educational Researcher, 32*(8), 26–29.

Hattie, J. (2009). *Visible learning: A synthesis of over 800 meta-analyses relating to achievement.* London: Routledge.

Hattie, J., Biggs, J., & Purdie, N. (1996). Effects of learning skills interventions on student learning: A meta-analysis. *Review of Educational Research, 66,* 99–136.

Hennessey, B. A. (2010). Intrinsic motivation and creativity in the classroom: Have we come full circle? In R. A. Beghetto & J. C. Kaufman (Eds.), *Nurturing creativity in the classroom* (pp. 329–361). New York, NY: Cambridge University Press.

Hennessey, B. A., & Amabile, T. M. (1987). *Creativity and learning.* Washington, DC: National Education Association.

Heward, W. L. (2009). *Exceptional children: An introduction to special education* (9th ed.). Upper Saddle River, NJ: Merrill/Pearson Education.

Hewitt, J., Brett, C., Scardamalia, M., Frecker, K., & Webb, J. (1995, April). Supporting knowledge building through the synthesis of CSILE, FCL, & Jasper. In M. Lamon (Chair), *Schools for thought: Transforming classrooms into learning communities.* Symposium conducted at the annual meeting of the American Educational Research Association, San Francisco, CA.

Heyman, G. D. (2008). Children's critical thinking when learning from others. *Current Directions in Psychological Science, 17,* 344–347.

Hidi, S., & Anderson, V. (1986). Producing written summaries: Task demands, cognitive operations, and implications for instruction. *Review of Educational Research, 86,* 473–493.

Hmelo-Silver, C. E. (2004). Problem-based learning: What and how do students learn? *Educational Psychology Review, 16,* 235–266.

Hofer, B. K., & Pintrich, P. R. (1997). The development of epistemological theories: Beliefs about knowledge and knowing and their relation to learning. *Review of Educational Research, 67,* 88–140.

Hofer, B. K., & Pintrich, P. R. (Eds.). (2002). *Personal epistemology: The psychology of beliefs about knowledge and knowing.* Mahwah, NJ: Erlbaum.

Hoffman, B., & Nadelson, L. (2010). Motivational engagement and video gaming: A mixed methods study. *Educational Technology Research and Development, 58,* 245–270.

Houtz, J. C. (1990). Environments that support creative thinking. In C. Hedley, J. Houtz, & A. Baratta (Eds.), *Cognition, curriculum, and literacy* (pp. 61–76). Norwood, NJ: Ablex.

Hung, W., Jonassen, D. H., & Liu, R. (2008). Problem-based learning. In J. M. Spector, M. D. Merrill, J. van Merriënboer, & M. P. Driscoll (Eds.), *Handbook of research on educational communications and technology* (3rd ed., pp. 485–506). New York, NY: Erlbaum.

James, W. (1890). *The principles of psychology.* New York, NY: Holt.

Johanning, D. I., D'Agostino, J. V., Steele, D. F., & Shumow, L. (1999, April). *Student writing, post-writing group collaboration, and learning in pre-algebra.* Paper presented at the annual meeting of the American Educational Research Association, Montreal, Canada.

Kağitçibaşi, Ç. (2007). *Family, self, and human development across cultures: Theory and applications* (2nd ed.). Mahwah, NJ: Erlbaum.

Kahl, B., & Woloshyn, V. E. (1994). Using elaborative interrogation to facilitate acquisition of factual information in cooperative learning settings: One good strategy deserves another. *Applied Cognitive Psychology, 8,* 465–478.

Kalyuga, S. (2010). Schema acquisition and sources of cognitive load. In J. L. Plass, R. Moreno, & R. Brünken (Eds.), *Cognitive Load Theory* (pp. 48–64). Cambridge, England: Cambridge University Press.

Kalyuga, S., Renkl, A., & Pass, F. (2010). Facilitating flexible problem solving: A cognitive load perspective. *Educational Psychology Review, 22,* 175–186.

Kapur, M., & Bielaczyc, K. (2012). Designing for productive failure. *The Journal of the Learning Sciences, 21,* 45–83.

Kardash, C. A. M., & Amlund, J. T. (1991). Self-reported learning strategies and learning from expository text. *Contemporary Educational Psychology, 16,* 117–138.

Kardash, C. A. M., & Howell, K. L. (2000). Effects of epistemological beliefs and topic-specific beliefs on undergraduates' cognitive and strategic processing of dual-positional text. *Journal of Educational Psychology, 92,* 524–535.

Kardash, C. A. M., & Scholes, R. J. (1996). Effects of preexisting beliefs, epistemological beliefs, and need for cognition on interpretation of controversial issues. *Journal of Educational Psychology, 88,* 260–271.

Karl, S. R., & Varma, S. (2010, April–May). *The conflict between decimal numbers and whole numbers.* Paper presented at the annual meeting of the American Educational Research Association, Denver, CO.

Kaufman, J. C., & Beghetto, R. A. (2009). Creativity in the schools: A rapidly developing area of positive psychology. In R. Gilman, E. S. Huebner, & M. J. Furlong (Eds.), *Handbook of positive psychology in schools* (pp. 175–188). New York, NY: Routledge.

Kercood, S., Zentall, S. S., Vinh, M., & Tom-Wright, K. (2012). Attentional cueing in math word problems for girls at-risk for ADHD and the peers in general education settings. *Contemporary Educational Psychology, 37,* 106–112.

Kiewra, K. A. (1985). Investigating notetaking and review: A depth of processing alternative. *Educational Psychologist, 20,* 23–32.

Kiewra, K. A. (1989). A review of note-taking: The encoding-storage paradigm and beyond. *Educational Psychology Review, 1,* 147–172.

Kiewra, K. A., Benton, S. L., & Lewis, L. B. (1987). Qualitative aspects of notetaking and their relationship with information-processing ability and academic achievement. *Journal of Instructional Psychology, 14*(3), 110–117.

King, A. (1992). Comparison of self-questioning, summarizing, and notetaking-review as strategies for learning from lectures. *American Educational Research Journal, 29,* 303–323.

King, A. (1999). Discourse patterns for mediating peer learning. In A. M. O'Donnell & A. King (Eds.), *Cognitive perspectives on peer learning* (pp. 87–115). Mahwah, NJ: Erlbaum.

King, A., Staffieri, A., & Adelgais, A. (1998). Mutual peer tutoring: Effects of structuring tutorial interaction to scaffold peer learning. *Journal of Educational Psychology, 90,* 134–152.

King, P. M., & Kitchener, K. S. (2002). The reflective judgment model: Twenty years of research on epistemic cognition. In B. K. Hofer & P. R. Pintrich (Eds.), *Personal epistemology: The psychology of beliefs about knowledge and knowing* (pp. 37–61). Mahwah, NJ: Erlbaum.

Kirschner, P. A., & van Merriënboer, J. J. G. (2013). Do learners really know best? Urban legends in education. *Educational Psychologist, 48,* 169–183.

Kirsh, D. (2009). Problem solving and situated cognition. In P. Robbins & M. Aydede (Eds.), *The Cambridge handbook of situated cognition* (pp. 264–306). Cambridge, England: Cambridge University Press.

Klein, P. D. (1999). Reopening inquiry into cognitive processes in writing-to-learn. *Educational Psychology Review, 11,* 203–270.

Koedinger, K., Aleven, V., Roll, I., & Baker, R. (2009). *In vivo* experiments on whether supporting metacognition in intelligent tutoring systems yields robust learning. In D. J. Hacker, J. Dunlosky, & A. C. Graesser (Eds.), *Handbook of metacognition in education* (pp. 383–412). New York, NY: Routledge.

Kramarski, B., & Mevarech, Z. R. (2003). Enhancing mathematical reasoning in the classroom: The effects of cooperative learning and metacognitive training. *American Educational Research Journal, 40,* 281–310.

Ku, Y.-M., Chan, W.-C., Wu, Y.-C., & Chen, Y.-H. (2008, March). *Improving children's comprehension of science text: Effects of adjunct questions and notetaking.* Paper presented at the annual meeting of the American Educational Research Association, New York, NY.

Kucan, L., & Beck, I. L. (1997). Thinking aloud and reading comprehension research: Inquiry, instruction, and social interaction. *Review of Educational Research, 67,* 271–299.

Kuhn, D. (2001a). How do people know? *Psychological Science, 12,* 1–8.

Kuhn, D. (2009). The importance of learning about knowing: Creating a foundation for development of intellectual values. *Child Development Perspectives, 3,* 112–117.

Kuhn, D. (2015). Thinking together and alone. *Educational Researcher, 44,* 46–53.

Kuhn, D., & Crowell, A. (2011). Dialogic argumentation as a vehicle for developing young adolescents' thinking. *Psychological Science, 22,* 545–552.

Kuhn, D., Daniels, S., & Krishnan, A. (2003, April). *Epistemology and intellectual values as core metacognitive constructs.* Paper presented at the annual meeting of the American Educational Research Association, Chicago, IL.

Kuhn, D., & Dean, D., Jr. (2005). Is developing scientific thinking all about learning to control variables? *Psychological Science, 16,* 866–870.

Kuhn, D., & Franklin, S. (2006). The second decade: What develops (and how)? In W. Damon, R. M. Lerner (Series Eds.), D. Kuhn, & R. Siegler (Vol. Eds.), *Handbook of child psychology: Vol. 2. Cognition, perception, and language* (6th ed., pp. 953–993). New York, NY: Wiley.

Kuhn, D., Garcia-Mila, M., Zohar, A., & Andersen, C. (1995). Strategies of knowledge acquisition. *Monographs of the Society for Research in Child Development, 60* (Whole No. 245).

Kuhn, D., & Park, S.-H. (2005). Epistemological understanding and the development of intellectual values. *International Journal of Educational Research, 43,* 111–124.

Kuhn, D., & Weinstock, M. (2002). What is epistemological thinking and why does it matter? In B. K. Hofer & P. R. Pintrich (Eds.), *Personal epistemology: The psychology of beliefs about knowledge and knowing* (pp. 121–144). Mahwah, NJ: Erlbaum.

Lee, J., & Shute, V. J. (2010). Personal and social-contextual factors in K–12 academic performance: An integrative perspective on student learning. *Educational Psychologist, 45,* 185–202.

Lee, K., Ng, E. L., & Ng, S. F. (2009). The contributions of working memory and executive function to problem representation and solution generation in algebraic word problems. *Journal of Educational Psychology, 101,* 373–387.

Leelawong, K., & Biswas, G. (2008). Designing learning by teachable agents: The Betty's Brain system. *International Journal of Artificial Intelligence, 18*(3), 181–208.

Leu, D. J., O'Byrne, W. I., Zawilinski, L., McVerry, J. G., & Everett-Cacopardo, H. (2009). Expanding the new literacies conversation. *Educational Researcher, 38,* 264–269.

Leung, A. K., Maddux, W. W. Galinsky, A. D., & Chiu, C. (2008). Multicultural experience enhances creativity: The when and how. *American Psychologist, 63,* 169–181.

Levstik, L. S. (2011). Learning history. In R. E. Mayer & P. A. Alexander (Eds.), *Handbook of research on learning and instruction* (pp. 108–126). New York, NY: Routledge.

Li, J. (2005). Mind or virtue: Western and Chinese beliefs about learning. *Current Directions in Psychological Science, 14,* 190–194.

Linn, M. C. (2008). Teaching for conceptual change: Distinguish or extinguish ideas. In S. Vosniadou (Ed.), *International handbook on conceptual change* (pp. 694–722). New York, NY: Routledge.

Linn, M. C., Clement, C., Pulos, S., & Sullivan, P. (1989). Scientific reasoning during adolescence: The influence of instruction in science knowledge and reasoning strategies.

Journal of Research in Science Teaching, 26, 171–187.

Lodico, M. G., Ghatala, E. S., Levin, J. R., Pressley, M., & Bell, J. A. (1983). The effects of strategy monitoring training on children's selection of effective memory strategies. *Journal of Experimental Child Psychology, 35,* 273–277.

Loranger, A. L. (1994). The study strategies of successful and unsuccessful high school students. *Journal of Reading Behavior, 26,* 347–360.

Losh, S. C. (2003). On the application of social cognition and social location to creating causal explanatory structures. *Educational Research Quarterly, 26*(3), 17–33.

Lovett, S. B., & Flavell, J. H. (1990). Understanding and remembering: Children's knowledge about the differential effects of strategy and task variables on comprehension and memorization. *Child Development, 61,* 1842–1858.

Lubart, T. I., & Mouchiroud, C. (2003). Creativity: A source of difficulty in problem solving. In J. E. Davidson & R. J. Sternberg (Eds.), *The psychology of problem solving* (pp. 127–148). Cambridge, England: Cambridge University Press.

Luchins, A. S. (1942). Mechanization in problem solving: The effect of Einstellung. *Psychological Monographs, 54* (Whole No. 248).

Maker, C. J. (1993). Creativity, intelligence, and problem solving: A definition and design for cross-cultural research and measurement related to giftedness. *Gifted Education International, 9*(2), 68–77.

Manning, F. H., Lawless, K. A., Goldman, S. R., & Braasch, J. L. G. (2011, April). *Evaluating the usefulness of multiple sources with respect to an inquiry question: Middle school students' analysis and ranking of Internet search results.* Paper presented at the annual meeting of the American Educational Research Association, New Orleans, LA.

Marcus, G. (2008). *Kluge: The haphazard construction of the human mind.* Boston, MA: Houghton Mifflin.

Mason, L. (2010). Beliefs about knowledge and revision of knowledge: On the importance of epistemic beliefs for intentional conceptual change in elementary and middle school students. In L. D. Bendixen & F. C. Feucht (Eds.), *Personal epistemology in the classroom: Theory, research, and implications for practice* (pp. 258–291). Cambridge, England: Cambridge University Press.

Mason, L., Gava, M., & Boldrin, A. (2008). On warm conceptual change: The interplay of text, epistemological beliefs, and topic interest. *Journal of Educational Psychology, 100,* 291–309.

Mastropieri, M. A., & Scruggs, T. E. (2007). *The inclusive classroom: Strategies for effective instruction* (3rd ed.). Upper Saddle River, NJ: Merrill/Prentice Hall.

Mayer, R. E. (1985). Implications of cognitive psychology for instruction in mathematical problem solving. In E. A. Silver (Ed.),

Teaching and learning mathematical problem solving: Multiple research perspectives (pp. 123–138). Mahwah, NJ: Erlbaum.

Mayer, R. E. (1992). *Thinking, problem solving, cognition* (2nd ed.). New York, NY: Freeman.

Mayer, R. E. (2010b). Merlin C. Wittrock's enduring contributions to the science of learning. *Educational Psychologist, 45,* 46–50.

Mayer, R. E., & Wittrock, M. C. (1996). Problem-solving transfer. In D. C. Berliner & R. C. Calfee (Eds.), *Handbook of educational psychology* (pp. 47–62). New York, NY: Macmillan.

Mayer, R. E., & Wittrock, M. C. (2006). Problem solving. In P. A. Alexander & P. H. Winne (Eds.), *Handbook of educational psychology* (2nd ed., pp. 287–303). Mahwah, NJ: Erlbaum.

Mayfield, K. H., & Chase, P. N. (2002). The effects of cumulative practice on mathematics problem solving. *Journal of Applied Behavior Analysis, 35,* 105–123.

McCrudden, M. T., & Schraw, G. (2007). Relevance and goal-focusing in text processing. *Educational Psychology Review, 19,* 113–139.

McGlynn, S. M. (1998). Impaired awareness of deficits in a psychiatric context: Implications for rehabilitation. In D. J. Hacker, J. Dunlosky, & A. C. Graesser (Eds.), *Metacognition in educational theory and practice* (pp. 221–248). Mahwah, NJ: Erlbaum.

McGovern, M. L., Davis, A., & Ogbu, J. U. (2008). The Minority Achievement Committee: Students leading students to greater success in school. In J. U. Ogbu (Ed.), *Minority status, oppositional culture, and schooling* (pp. 560–573). New York, NY: Routledge.

McKeown, M. G., & Beck, I. L. (2009). The role of metacognition in understanding and supporting reading comprehension. In D. J. Hacker, J. Dunlosky, & A. C. Graesser (Eds.), *Handbook of metacognition in education* (pp. 7–25). New York, NY: Routledge.

McNamara, D. S., & Magliano, J. P. (2009). Self-explanation and metacognition: The dynamics of reading. In D. J. Hacker, J. Dunlosky, & A. C. Graesser (Eds.), *Handbook of metacognition in education* (pp. 60–81). New York, NY: Routledge.

Meichenbaum, D. (1977). *Cognitive-behavior modification: An integrative approach.* New York, NY: Plenum.

Meltzer, L. (Ed.) (2007). *Executive function in education: From theory to practice.* New York, NY: Guilford.

Meltzer, L., Pollica, L. S., & Barzillai, M. (2007). Executive function in the classroom: Embedding strategy instruction into daily teaching practices. In L. Meltzer (Ed.), *Executive function in education: From theory to practice* (pp. 165–193). New York, NY: Guilford.

Mendaglio, S. (2010). Anxiety in gifted students. In J. C. Cassady (Ed.), *Anxiety in schools: The causes, consequences, and solutions for academic anxieties* (pp. 153–173). New York, NY: Peter Lang.

Mercer, C. D., & Pullen, P. C. (2005). *Students with learning disabilities* (6th ed.). Upper Saddle River, NJ: Merrill/Prentice Hall.

Metzger, M. J., Flanagin, A. J., & Zwarun, L. (2003). College student Web use, perceptions of information credibility, and verification behavior. *Computers and Education, 41,* 271–290.

Minsky, M. (2006). *The emotion machine: Commonsense thinking, artificial intelligence, and the future of the human mind.* New York, NY: Simon & Schuster.

Monte-Sano, C. (2008). Qualities of historical writing instruction: A comparative case study of two teachers' practices. *American Educational Research Journal, 45,* 1045–1079.

Moon, J. (2008). *Critical thinking: An exploration of theory and practice.* London: Routledge.

Morelli, G. A., & Rothbaum, F. (2007). Situating the child in context: Attachment relationships and self-regulation in different cultures. In S. Kitayama & D. Cohen (Eds.), *Handbook of cultural psychology* (pp. 500–527). New York, NY: Guilford Press.

Moreno, R., & Park, B. (2010). Cognitive Load Theory: Historical development and relation to other theories. In J. L. Plass, R. Moreno, & R. Brünken (Eds.), *Cognitive Load Theory* (pp. 9–28). Cambridge, England: Cambridge University Press.

Mueller, P. A., & Oppenheimer, D. M. (2014). The pen is mightier than the keyboard: Advantages of longhand over laptop note taking. *Psychological Science, 25,* 1159–1168.

Muis, K. R. (2007). The role of epistemic beliefs in self-regulated learning. *Educational Psychologist, 42,* 173–190.

Muis, K. R., Bendixen, L. D., & Haerle, F. C. (2006). Domain-generality and domain-specificity in personal epistemology research: Philosophical and empirical reflections in the development of a theoretical framework. *Educational Psychology Review, 18,* 3–54.

Muis, K. R., & Duffy, M. C. (2013). Epistemic climate and epistemic change: Instruction designed to change students' beliefs and learning strategies and improve achievement. *Journal of Educational Psychology, 105,* 213–225.

Muis, K. R., & Franco, G. M. (2009). Epistemic beliefs: Setting the standards for self-regulated learning. *Contemporary Educational Psychology, 34,* 306–318.

Nathan, M. J. (2012). Rethinking formalisms in formal education. *Educational Psychologist, 47,* 125–148.

Ni, Y., & Zhou, Y.-D. (2005). Teaching and learning fraction and rational numbers: The origins and implications of whole number bias. *Educational Psychologist, 40,* 27–52.

Niederhauser, D. S. (2008). Educational hypertext. In J. M. Spector, M. D. Merrill, J. van Merriënboer, & M. P. Driscoll (Eds.), *Handbook of research on educational communications and technology* (3rd ed., pp. 199–210). New York, NY: Erlbaum.

Nokes, J. D., & Dole, J. A. (2004). Helping adolescent readers through explicit strategy instruction. In T. L. Jetton & J. A. Dole (Eds.), *Adolescent literacy research and practice* (pp. 162–182). New York, NY: Guilford.

Nolen, S. B. (1996). Why study? How reasons for learning influence strategy selection. *Educational Psychology Review, 8,* 335–355.

Nussbaum, E. M. (2008). Collaborative discourse, argumentation, and learning: Preface and literature review. *Contemporary Educational Psychology, 33,* 345–359.

Nussbaum, E. M., & Edwards, O. V. (2011). Critical questions and argument stratagems: A framework for enhancing and analyzing students' reasoning practices. *Journal of the Learning Sciences, 20,* 443–488.

Ornstein, P. A., Grammer, J. K., & Coffman, J. L. (2010). Teachers' "mnemonic style" and the development of skilled memory. In H. S. Waters & W. Schneider (Eds.), *Metacognition, strategy use, and instruction* (pp. 23–53). New York, NY: Guilford.

O'Sullivan, J. T., & Joy, R. M. (1994). If at first you don't succeed: Children's metacognition about reading problems. *Contemporary Educational Psychology, 19,* 118–127.

Palmer, D. J., & Goetz, E. T. (1988). Selection and use of study strategies: The role of the studier's beliefs about self and strategies. In C. E. Weinstein, E. T. Goetz, & P. A. Alexander (Eds.), *Learning and study strategies: Issues in assessment, instruction, and evaluation* (pp. 41–61). San Diego, CA: Academic Press.

Paris, S. G., & Paris, A. H. (2001). Classroom applications of research on self-regulated learning. *Educational Psychologist, 36,* 89–101.

Paris, S. G., & Winograd, P. (1990). How metacognition can promote academic learning and instruction. In B. F. Jones & L. Idol (Eds.), *Dimensions of thinking and cognitive instruction* (pp. 15–52). Mahwah, NJ: Erlbaum.

Paxton, R. J. (1999). A deafening silence: History textbooks and the students who read them. *Review of Educational Research, 69,* 315–339.

Pea, R. D. (1987). Socializing the knowledge transfer problem. *International Journal of Educational Research, 11,* 639–663.

Perkins, D. N. (1990). The nature and nurture of creativity. In B. F. Jones & L. Idol (Eds.), *Dimensions of thinking and cognitive instruction* (pp. 415–441). Mahwah, NJ: Erlbaum.

Perkins, D. N. (1995). *Outsmarting IQ: The emerging science of learnable intelligence.* New York, NY: Free Press.

Perkins, D. N., & Salomon, G. (1989). Are cognitive skills context-bound? *Educational Researcher, 18*(1), 16–25.

Perkins, D. N., & Salomon, G. (2012). Knowledge to go: A motivational and dispositional view of transfer. *Educational Psychologist, 47,* 248–258.

Perkins, D. N., & Simmons, R. (1988). Patterns of misunderstanding: An integrative model for science, math, and programming. *Review of Educational Research, 58,* 303–326.

Piirto, J. (1999). *Talented children and adults: Their development and education* (2nd ed.). Upper Saddle River, NJ: Merrill/Prentice Hall.

Pillow, B. H. (2002). Children's and adults' evaluation of the certainty of deductive inferences, inductive inferences, and guesses. *Child Development, 73,* 779–792.

Polya, G. (1957). *How to solve it.* Garden City, NY: Doubleday.

Posner, M. I., & Rothbart, M. K. (2007). *Educating the human brain.* Washington, DC: American Psychological Association.

Prawat, R. S. (1989). Promoting access to knowledge, strategy, and disposition in students: A research synthesis. *Review of Educational Research, 59,* 1–41.

Pressley, M., with McCormick, C. B. (1995). *Advanced educational psychology for educators, researchers, and policymakers.* New York, NY: HarperCollins.

Pressley, M., Borkowski, J. G., & Schneider, W. (1987). Cognitive strategies: Good strategy users coordinate metacognition and knowledge. In R. Vasta & G. Whitehurst (Eds.), *Annals of child development* (Vol. 5, pp. 80–129). New York, NY: JAI.

Pressley, M., Harris, K. R., & Marks, M. B. (1992). But good strategy instructors are constructivists! *Educational Psychology Review, 4,* 3–31.

Pressley, M., & Hilden, K. (2006). Cognitive strategies: Production deficiencies and successful strategy instruction everywhere. In W. Damon, R. M. Lerner (Series Eds.), D. Kuhn, & R. Siegler (Vol. Eds.), *Handbook of child psychology: Vol. 2. Cognition, perception, and language* (6th ed., pp. 511–556). New York, NY: Wiley.

Pressley, M., Yokoi, L., van Meter, P., Van Etten, S., & Freebern, G. (1997). Some of the reasons why preparing for exams is so hard: What can be done to make it easier? *Educational Psychology Review, 9,* 1–38.

Pugh, K. J., & Bergin, D. A. (2005). The effect of schooling on students' out-of-school experience. *Educational Researcher, 34*(9), 15–23.

Pugh, K. J., & Bergin, D. A. (2006). Motivational influences on transfer. *Educational Psychologist, 41,* 147–160.

Pulos, S., & Linn, M. C. (1981). Generality of the controlling variables scheme in early adolescence. *Journal of Early Adolescence, 1,* 26–37.

Qian, G., & Pan, J. (2002). A comparison of epistemological beliefs and learning from science text between American and Chinese high school students. In B. K. Hofer & P. R. Pintrich (Eds.), *Personal epistemology: The psychology of beliefs about knowledge and knowing* (pp. 365–385). Mahwah, NJ: Erlbaum.

Quintana, C., Zhang, M., & Krajcik, J. (2005). A framework for supporting metacognitive aspects of online inquiry through software-based scaffolding. *Educational Psychologist, 40,* 235–244.

Renkl, A. (2011). Instruction based on examples. In R. E. Mayer & P. A. Alexander (Eds.), *Handbook of research on learning and instruction* (pp. 272–295). New York, NY: Routledge.

Renkl, A., Mandl, H., & Gruber, H. (1996). Inert knowledge: Analyses and remedies. *Educational Psychologist, 31,* 115–121.

Reynolds, R. E., & Shirey, L. L. (1988). The role of attention in studying and learning. In C. E. Weinstein, E. T. Goetz, & P. A. Alexander (Eds.), *Learning and study strategies: Issues in assessment, instruction, and evaluation* (pp. 77–100). San Diego, CA: Academic Press.

Reznitskaya, A., & Gregory, M. (2013). Student thought and classroom language: Examining the mechanisms of change in dialogic teaching. *Educational Psychologist, 48,* 114–133.

Ripple, R. E. (1989). Ordinary creativity. *Contemporary Educational Psychology, 14,* 189–202.

Rittle-Johnson, B. (2006). Promoting transfer: Effects of self-explanation and direct instruction. *Child Development, 77,* 1–15.

Rittle-Johnson, B., & Star, J. R. (2009). Compared with what? The effects of different comparisons on conceptual knowledge and procedural flexibility for equation solving. *Journal of Educational Psychology, 101,* 529–544.

Roditi, B. N., & Steinberg, J. (2007). The strategy math classroom: Executive function processes and mathematics learning. In L. Meltzer (Ed.), *Executive function in education: From theory to practice* (pp. 237–260). New York, NY: Guilford.

Rohrer, D., & Pashler, H. (2010). Recent research on human learning challenges conventional instructional strategies. *Educational Researcher, 39,* 406–412.

Rosenshine, B., Meister, C., & Chapman, S. (1996). Teaching students to generate questions: A review of the intervention studies. *Review of Educational Research, 66,* 181–221.

Rule, D. C., & Bendixen, L. D. (2010). The integrative model of personal epistemology development: Theoretical underpinnings and implications for education. In L. D. Bendixen & F. C. Feucht (Eds.), *Personal epistemology in the classroom: Theory, research, and implications for practice* (pp. 94–123). Cambridge, England: Cambridge University Press.

Runco, M. A. (2004). Creativity as an extracognitive phenomenon. In L. V. Shavinina & M. Ferrari (Eds.), *Beyond knowledge: Extracognitive aspects of developing high ability* (pp. 17–25). Mahwah, NJ: Erlbaum.

Runco, M. A., & Chand, I. (1995). Cognition and creativity. *Educational Psychology Review, 7,* 243–267.

Russ, S. W. (1993). *Affect and creativity: The role of affect and play in the creative process.* Mahwah, NJ: Erlbaum.

Saljo, R., & Wyndhamn, J. (1992). Solving everyday problems in the formal setting: An empirical study of the school as context for thought. In S. Chaiklin & J. Lave (Eds.), *Understanding practice* (pp. 327–342). New York, NY: Cambridge University Press.

Sandoval, W. A., Sodian, B., Koerber, S., & Wong, J. (2014). Developing children's early competencies to engage with science. *Educational Psychologist, 49,* 139–152.

Sawyer, R. K. (2003). Emergence in creativity and development. In R. K. Sawyer, V. John-Steiner, S. Moran, R. J. Sternberg, D. H. Feldman, J. Nakamura, & M. Csikszentmihalyi, *Creativity and development* (pp. 12–60). Oxford, England: Oxford University Press.

Schmidt, R. A., & Bjork, R. A. (1992). New conceptualizations of practice: Common principles in three paradigms suggest new concepts for training. *Psychological Science, 3,* 207–217.

Schneider, W. (2010). Metacognition and memory development in childhood and adolescence. In H. S. Waters & W. Schneider (Eds.), *Metacognition, strategy use, and instruction* (pp. 54–81). New York, NY: Guilford.

Schommer, M. (1990). Effects of beliefs about the nature of knowledge on comprehension. *Journal of Educational Psychology, 82,* 498–504.

Schommer, M. (1994a). An emerging conceptualization of epistemological beliefs and their role in learning. In R. Garner & P. A. Alexander (Eds.), *Beliefs about text and instruction with text* (pp. 25–40). Mahwah, NJ: Erlbaum.

Schommer, M. (1994b). Synthesizing epistemological belief research: Tentative understandings and provocative confusions. *Educational Psychology Review, 6,* 293–319.

Schommer, M. (1997). The development of epistemological beliefs among secondary students: A longitudinal study. *Journal of Educational Psychology, 89,* 37–40.

Schommer, M., Calvert, C., Gariglietti, G., & Bajaj, A. (1997). The development of epistemological beliefs among secondary students: A longitudinal study. *Journal of Educational Psychology, 89,* 37–40.

Schommer-Aikins, M. (2002). An evolving theoretical framework for an epistemological belief system. In B. K. Hofer & P. R. Pintrich (Eds.), *Personal epistemology: The psychology of beliefs about knowledge and knowing* (pp. 103–118). Mahwah, NJ: Erlbaum.

Schommer-Aikins, M., & Easter, M. (2008). Epistemological beliefs' contributions to study strategies of Asian Americans and European Americans. *Journal of Educational Psychology, 100,* 920–929.

Schraw, G., McCrudden, M. T., Lehman, S., & Hoffman, B. (2011). An overview of thinking skills. In G. Schraw & D. R. Robinson (Eds.), *Assessment of higher order thinking skills* (pp. 19–45). Charlotte, NC: Information Age.

Schraw, G., Wade, S. E., & Kardash, C. A. M. (1993). Interactive effects of text-based and task-based importance on learning from text. *Journal of Educational Psychology, 85,* 652–661.

Schwartz, D. L., Bransford, J. D., & Sears, D. (2005). Efficiency and innovation in transfer. In J. P. Mestre (Ed.), *Transfer of learning from a modern multidisciplinary perspective* (pp. 1–51). Greenwich, CT: Information Age.

Schwartz, D. L., Chase, C. C., & Bransford, J. D. (2012). Resisting overzealous transfer: Coordinating previously successful routines with needs for new learning. *Educational Psychologist, 47,* 204–214.

Schwartz, D. L., Lindgren, R., & Lewis, S. (2009). Constructivism in an age of non-constructivist assessments. In S. Tobias & T. M. Duffy (Eds.), *Constructivist instruction: Success or failure?* (pp. 34–61). New York, NY: Routledge.

Scruggs, T. E., & Mastropieri, M. A. (1992). Classroom applications of mnemonic instruction: Acquisition, maintenance, and generalization. *Exceptional Children, 58,* 219–229.

Segedy, J. R., Kinnebrew, J. S., & Biswas, G. (2013). The effect of contextualized conversational feedback in a complex open-ended learning environment. *Educational Technology Research and Development, 61*(1), 71–89.

Shanahan, T. (2004). Overcoming the dominance of communication: Writing to think and to learn. In T. L. Jetton & J. A. Dole (Eds.), *Adolescent literacy research and practice* (pp. 59–74). New York, NY: Guilford.

Sherman, J., & Bisanz, J. (2009). Equivalence in symbolic and nonsymbolic contexts: Benefits of solving problems with manipulatives. *Journal of Educational Psychology, 101,* 88–100.

Short, E. J., Schatschneider, C. W., & Friebert, S. E. (1993). Relationship between memory and metamemory performance: A comparison of specific and general strategy knowledge. *Journal of Educational Psychology, 85,* 412–423.

Siegler, R. S. (2002). Microgenetic studies of self-explanations. In N. Granott & J. Parziale (Eds.), *Microdevelopment: Transition processes in development and learning* (pp. 31–58). New York, NY: Cambridge University Press.

Siegler, R. S., & Jenkins, E. (1989). *How children discover new strategies.* Hillsdale, NJ: Erlbaum.

Simonton, D. K. (2000). Creativity: Cognitive, personal, developmental, and social aspects. *American Psychologist, 55,* 151–158.

Simonton, D. K. (2004). Exceptional creativity and chance: Creative thought as a stochastic combinatorial process. In L. V. Shavinina & M. Ferrari (Eds.), *Beyond knowledge: Extracognitive aspects of developing high ability* (pp. 39–72). Mahwah, NJ: Erlbaum.

Simonton, D. K. (2011). Creativity and discovery as blind variation: Campbell's (1960) BVSR model after the half-century mark. *Review of General Psychology, 15,* 158–174.

Sinatra, G. M., Kienhues, D., & Hofer, B. K. (2014). Addressing challenges to public understanding of science: Epistemic cognition, motivated reasoning, and conceptual change. *Educational Psychologist, 49,* 123–138.

Sinatra, G. M., & Pintrich, P. R. (Eds.). (2003). *Intentional conceptual change.* Mahwah, NJ: Erlbaum.

Slife, B. R., Weiss, J., & Bell, T. (1985). Separability of metacognition and cognition: Problem solving in learning disabled and regular students. *Journal of Educational Psychology, 77,* 437–445.

Son, L. K., & Schwartz, B. L. (2002). The relation between metacognitive monitoring and control. In T. J. Perfect & B. L. Schwartz (Eds.), *Applied metacognition* (pp. 15–38). Cambridge, England: Cambridge University Press.

Spörer, N., & Brunstein, J. C. (2009). Fostering the reading comprehension of secondary school students through peer-assisted learning: Effects on strategy knowledge, strategy use, and task performance. *Contemporary Educational Psychology, 34,* 289–297.

Squire, K. (2011). *Video games and learning: Teaching and participatory culture in the digital age.* New York, NY: Teachers College Press.

Stahl, S. A., & Shanahan, C. (2004). Learning to think like a historian: Disciplinary knowledge through critical analysis of multiple documents. In T. L. Jetton & J. A. Dole (Eds.), *Adolescent literacy research and practice* (pp. 94–115). New York, NY: Guilford.

Stanley, J. C. (1980). On educating the gifted. *Educational Researcher, 9*(3), 8–12.

Starr, E. J., & Lovett, S. B. (2000). The ability to distinguish between comprehension and memory: Failing to succeed. *Journal of Educational Psychology, 92,* 761–771.

Sternberg, R. J. (2010). Teaching for creativity. In R. A. Beghetto & J. C. Kaufman (Eds.), *Nurturing creativity in the classroom* (pp. 394–414). New York, NY: Cambridge University Press.

Stone, N. J. (2000). Exploring the relationship between calibration and self-regulated learning. *Educational Psychology Review, 12,* 437–475.

Swanson, H. L. (1993). An information processing analysis of learning disabled children's problem solving. *American Educational Research Journal, 30,* 861–893.

Swanson, H. L., Jerman, O., & Zheng, X. (2008). Growth in working memory and mathematical problem solving in children at risk and not at risk for serious math difficulties. *Journal of Educational Psychology, 100,* 343–379.

Sweller, J. (1994). Cognitive load theory, learning difficulty, and instructional design. *Learning and Instruction, 4,* 295–312.

Sweller, J. (2009). Cognitive bases of human creativity. *Educational Psychology Review, 21,* 11–19.

Thomas, J. W. (1993a). Expectations and effort: Course demands, students' study practices, and academic achievement. In T. M. Tomlinson (Ed.), *Motivating students to learn: Overcoming barriers to high achievement* (pp. 139–176). Berkeley, CA: McCutchan.

Thomas, J. W. (1993b). Promoting independent learning in the middle grades: The role of instructional support practices. *Elementary School Journal, 93,* 575–591.

Thorndike, E. L. (1924). Mental discipline in high school studies. *Journal of Educational Psychology, 15,* 1–22, 83–98.

Tobias, S., Fletcher, J. D., Dai, D. Y., & Wind, A. P. (2011). Review of research on computer games. In S. Tobias & J. D. Fletcher (Eds.), *Computer games and instruction* (pp. 127–221). Charlotte, NC: Information Age.

Torrance, E. P. (1970). *Encouraging creativity in the classroom.* Dubuque, IA: Wm. C. Brown.

Torrance, E. P. (1989). A reaction to "Gifted Black Students: Curriculum and Teaching Strategies." In C. J. Maker & S. W. Schiever (Eds.), *Critical issues in gifted education: Vol. 2. Defensible programs for cultural and ethnic minorities* (pp. 270–274). Austin, TX: Pro-Ed.

Turnbull, A. P., Turnbull, R., & Wehmeyer, M. L. (2010). *Exceptional lives: Special education in today's schools* (6th ed.). Upper Saddle River, NJ: Merrill.

Turner, J. C. (1995). The influence of classroom contexts on young children's motivation for literacy. *Reading Research Quarterly, 30,* 410–441.

Turner, J. C., Meyer, D. K., Cox, K. E., Logan, C., DiCintio, M., & Thomas, C. T. (1998). Creating contexts for involvement in mathematics. *Journal of Educational Psychology, 90,* 730–745.

Tweed, R. G., & Lehman, D. R. (2002). Learning considered within a cultural context. *American Psychologist, 57,* 89–99.

Tyler, K. M., Uqdah, A. L., Dillihunt, M. L., Beatty-Hazelbaker, R., Connor, T., Gadson, N., . . . Stevens, R. (2008). Cultural discontinuity: Toward a quantitative investigation of a major hypothesis in education. *Educational Researcher, 37,* 280–297.

Van Meter, P., Yokoi, L., & Pressley, M. (1994). College students' theory of notetaking derived from their perceptions of notetaking. *Journal of Educational Psychology, 86,* 323–338.

VanLehn, K. (2011). The relative effectiveness of human tutoring, intelligent tutoring systems, and other tutoring systems. *Educational Psychologist, 46,* 197–221.

VanSledright, B., & Limón, M. (2006). Learning and teaching social studies: A review of cognitive research in history and geography. In P. A. Alexander & P. H. Winne (Eds.), *Handbook of educational psychology* (2nd ed., pp. 545–570). Mahwah, NJ: Erlbaum.

Vaughn, S., Klingner, J. K., Swanson, E. A., Boardman, A. G., Roberts, G., Mohammed, S. S., & Stillman-Spisak, S. J. (2011). Efficacy of collaborative strategic reading with middle school students. *American Educational Research Journal, 48,* 938–964.

Veenman, M. V. J. (2011). Learning to self-monitor and self-regulate. In R. E. Mayer & P. A. Alexander (Eds.), *Handbook of research on learning and instruction* (pp. 197–218). New York, NY: Routledge.

Volet, S. (1999). Learning across cultures: Appropriateness of knowledge transfer. *International Journal of Educational Research, 31,* 625–643.

Vye, N. J., Schwartz, D. L., Bransford, J. D., Barron, B. J., Zech, L., & The Cognition and Technology Group at Vanderbilt. (1998). SMART environments that support monitoring, reflection, and revision. In D. J. Hacker, J. Dunlosky, & A. C. Graesser (Eds.), *Metacognition in educational theory and practice* (pp. 305–346). Mahwah, NJ: Erlbaum.

Vygotsky, L. S. (1978). *Mind in society: The development of higher psychological processes.* Cambridge, MA: Harvard University Press.

Waber, D. P. (2010). *Rethinking learning disabilities: Understanding children who struggle in school.* New York, NY: Guilford.

Wade-Stein, D., & Kintsch, E. (2004). Summary Street: Interactive computer support for writing. *Cognition and Instruction, 22,* 333–362.

Wagner, J. F. (2010). A transfer-in-pieces consideration of the perception of structure in the transfer of learning. *Journal of the Learning Sciences, 19,* 443–479.

Walker, C. M., Wartenberg, T. E., & Winner, E. (2013). Engagement in philosophical dialogue facilitates children's reasoning about subjectivity. *Developmental Psychology, 49,* 1338–1347.

Walkington, C., Sherman, M., & Petrosino, A. (2012). "Playing the game" of story problems: Coordinated situation-based reasoning with algebraic representation. *Journal of Mathematical Behavior, 31,* 174–195.

Ward, W., Cole, R., Bolaños, D., Buchenroth-Martin, C., Svirsky, E., & Weston, T. (2013). My Science Tutor: A conversational multimedia virtual tutor. *Journal of Educational Psychology, 105,* 1115–1125.

Waters, H. S., & Kunnmann, T. W. (2010). Metacognition and strategy discovery in early childhood. In H. S. Waters & W. Schneider (Eds.), *Metacognition, strategy use, and instruction* (pp. 3–22). New York, NY: Guilford.

Weinstein, C. E., Goetz, E. T., & Alexander, P. A. (Eds.). (1988). *Learning and study strategies: Issues in assessment, instruction, and evaluation.* San Diego, CA: Academic Press.

Weinstein, C. E., & Hume, L. M. (1998). *Study strategies for lifelong learning.* Washington, DC: American Psychological Association.

Weisberg, R. W. (1993). *Creativity: Beyond the myth of genius.* New York, NY: Freeman.

Weissberg, R. P. (1985). Designing effective social problem-solving programs for the classroom. In B. H. Schneider, K. H. Rubin, & J. E. Ledingham (Eds.), *Children's peer relations: Issues in assessment and intervention* (pp. 225–242). New York, NY: Springer-Verlag.

Wellman, H. M. (1985). The child's theory of mind: The development of conceptions of cognition. In S. R. Yussen (Ed.), *The growth of reflection in children* (pp. 169–206). San Diego, CA: Academic Press.

Wellman, H. M. (1990). *The child's theory of mind.* Cambridge, MA: MIT Press.

Wentzel, K. R. (2009). Peers and academic functioning at school. In K. H. Rubin, W.

M. Bukowski, & B. Laursen (Eds.), *Handbook of peer interactions, relationships, and groups* (pp. 531–547). New York, NY: Guilford.

Wentzel, K. R., & Watkins, D. E. (2011). Instruction based on peer interactions. In R. E. Mayer & P. A. Alexander (Eds.), *Handbook of research on learning and instruction* (pp. 322–343). New York, NY: Routledge.

White, B. Y., & Frederiksen, J. (2005). A theoretical framework and approach for fostering metacognitive development. *Educational Psychologist, 40,* 211–223.

Wiley, J., Goldman, S. R., Graesser, A. C., Sanchez, C. A., Ash, I. K., & Hemmerich, J. A. (2009). Source evaluation, comprehension, and learning in Internet science inquiry tasks. *American Educational Research Journal, 46,* 1060–1106.

Williams, J. P., Stafford, K. B., Lauer, K. D., Hall, K. M., & Pollini, S. (2009). Embedding reading comprehension training in content-area instruction. *Journal of Educational Psychology, 101,* 1–20.

Wong, B. Y. L. (1985). Self-questioning instructional research: A review. *Review of Educational Research, 55,* 227–268.

Wong, B. Y. L. (Ed.). (1991). *Learning about learning disabilities.* San Diego, CA: Academic Press.

Wood, E., Willoughby, T., McDermott, C., Motz, M., Kaspar, V., & Ducharme, M. J. (1999). Developmental differences in study behavior. *Journal of Educational Psychology, 91,* 527–536.

Yang, F.-Y., & Tsai, C.-Ch. (2010). An epistemic framework for scientific reasoning in informal contexts. In L. D. Bendixen & F. C. Feucht (Eds.), *Personal epistemology in the classroom: Theory, research, and implications for practice* (pp. 124–162). Cambridge, England: Cambridge University Press.

Zhong, C.-B., Dijksterhuis, A., & Galinsky, A. D. (2008). The merits of unconscious thought in creativity. *Psychological Science, 19,* 912–918.

Zimmerman, B. J., & Moylan, A. R. (2009). Self-regulation: Where metacognition and motivation intersect. In D. J. Hacker, J. Dunlosky, & A. C. Graesser (Eds.), *Handbook of metacognition in education* (pp. 299–315). New York, NY: Routledge.

CHAPTER 8

Afflerbach, P., & Cho, B.-Y. (2010). Determining and describing reading strategies: Internet and traditional forms of reading. In H. S. Waters & W. Schneider (Eds.), *Metacognition, strategy use, and instruction* (pp. 201–225). New York, NY: Guilford.

Afflerbach, P, VanSledright, B., & Dromsky, A. (2003, April). *Reading and thinking like historians: Investigating a 4th grade performance assessment.* Paper presented at the annual meeting of the American Educational Research Association, Chicago, IL.

Alexander, P. A., & the Disciplined Reading and Learning Research Laboratory. (2012). Reading into the future: Competence for the 21st century. *Educational Psychologist, 47,* 259–280.

Alfassi, M. (2004). Reading to learn: Effects of combined strategy instruction on high school students. *Journal of Educational Research, 97,* 171–184.

Alibali, M. W., Spencer, R. C., Knox, L., & Kita, S. (2011). Spontaneous gestures influence strategy choices in problem solving. *Psychological Science, 22,* 1138–1144.

Anderson, L. W., & Pellicer, L. O. (1998). Toward an understanding of unusually successful programs for economically disadvantaged students. *Journal of Education for Students Placed at Risk, 3,* 237–263.

Andriessen, J. (2006). Arguing to learn. In R. K. Sawyer (Ed.), *The Cambridge handbook of the learning sciences* (pp. 443–459). Cambridge, England: Cambridge University Press.

Anthony, J. L., & Francis, D. J. (2005). Development of phonological awareness. *Current Directions in Psychological Science, 14,* 255–259.

Arnesen, T., Elstad, E., Christophersen, K.-A., & Vavik, L. (2014, April). *What significance does students' access to Internet in school have for their perseverance in academic work? An empirical analysis based on Nordic students.* Poster presented at the annual meeting of the American Educational Research Association, Philadelphia, PA.

Atran, S., Medin, D. L., & Ross, N. O. (2005). The cultural mind: Environmental decision making and cultural modeling within and across populations. *Psychological Review, 112,* 744–776.

Banks, J., Cochran-Smith, M., Moll, L., Richert, A., Zeichner, K., LePage, P., . . . Duffy, H. (with McDonald, M.). (2005). Teaching diverse learners. In L. Darling-Hammond & J. Bransford (Eds.), *Preparing teachers for a changing world: What teachers should learn and be able to do* (pp. 232–274). San Francisco, CA: Jossey-Bass/Wiley.

Barab, S. A., & Dodge, T. (2008). Strategies for designing embodied curriculum. In J. M. Spector, M. D. Merrill, J. van Merriënboer, & M. P. Driscoll (Eds.), *Handbook of research on educational communications and technology* (3rd ed., pp. 97–110). New York, NY: Erlbaum.

Barchfeld, P., Sodian, B., Thoermer, C., & Bullock, M. (2005, April). *The development of experiment generation abilities from primary school to late adolescence.* Poster presented at the biennial meeting of the Society for Research in Child Development, Atlanta, GA.

Barnett, M. (2005, April). *Engaging inner city students in learning through designing remote operated vehicles.* Paper presented at the annual meeting of the American Educational Research Association, Montreal, Canada.

Baroody, A. J., Eiland, M. D., Purpura, D. J., & Reid, E. E. (2013). Can computer-assisted discovery learning foster first graders' fluency with the most basic addition combinations? *American Educational Research Journal, 50,* 533–573.

Bartlett, F. C. (1932). *Remembering: A study in experimental and social psychology.* Cambridge, England: Cambridge University Press.

Barton, K. C., & Levstik, L. S. (1996). "Back when God was around and everything": Elementary children's understanding of historical time. *American Educational Research Journal, 33,* 419–454.

Bassett, D. S., Jackson, L., Ferrell, K. A., Luckner, J., Hagerty, P. J., Bunsen, T. D., & MacIsaac, D. (1996). Multiple perspectives on inclusive education: Reflections of a university faculty. *Teacher Education and Special Education, 19,* 355–386.

Beck, I. L., McKeown, M. G., Sinatra, G. M., & Loxterman, J. A. (1991). Revising social studies text from a text-processing perspective: Evidence of improved comprehensibility. *Reading Research Quarterly, 26,* 251–276.

Beike, S. M., & Zentall, S. S. (2012). "The snake raised its head": Content novelty alters the reading performance of students at risk for reading disabilities and ADHD. *Journal of Educational Psychology, 104,* 529–540.

Bellanca, J. A., & Stirling, T. (2011). *Classrooms without borders: Using Internet projects to teach communication and collaboration.* New York, NY: Teachers College Press.

Bendixen, L. D., & Rule, D. C. (2004). An integrative approach to personal epistemology: A guiding model. *Educational Psychologist, 39,* 69–80.

Benton, S. L. (1997). Psychological foundations of elementary writing instruction. In G. D. Phye (Ed.), *Handbook of academic learning: Construction of knowledge* (pp. 235–264). San Diego, CA: Academic Press.

Bereiter, C., & Scardamalia, M. (1987). *The psychology of written composition.* Hillsdale, NJ: Erlbaum.

Bereiter, C., & Scardamalia, M. (2006). Education for the Knowledge Age: Design-centered models of teaching and instruction. In P. A. Alexander & P. H. Winne (Eds.), *Handbook of educational psychology* (2nd ed., pp. 695–713). Mahwah, NJ: Erlbaum.

Berkin, C., Crocco, M., & Winslow, B. (2009). *Clio in the classroom: A guide to teaching U.S. women's history.* New York, NY: Oxford University Press.

Bermejo, V. (1996). Cardinality development and counting. *Developmental Psychology, 32,* 263–268.

Berninger, V. W., Fuller, F., & Whitaker, D. (1996). A process model of writing development across the life span. *Educational Psychology Review, 8,* 193–218.

Berti, A. E., Toneatti, L., & Rosati, V. (2010). Children's conceptions about the origin of species: A study of Italian children's conceptions with and without instruction. *Journal of the Learning Sciences, 19,* 506–538.

Bielaczyc, K., & Collins, A. (2006). Fostering knowledge-creating communities. In A. M. O'Donnell, C. E. Hmelo-Silver, & G. Erkens (Eds.), *Collaborative learning, reasoning, and technology* (pp. 37–60). Mahwah, NJ: Erlbaum.

Bochenhauer, M. H. (1990, April). *Connections: Geographic education and the National Geographic Society.* Paper presented at the annual meeting of the American Educational Research Association, Boston, MA.

Booth, J. L., & Newton, K. J. (2012). Fractions: Could they really be the gatekeeper's doorman? *Contemporary Educational Psychology, 37,* 247–253.

Boscardin, C. K., Muthén, B., Francis, D. J., & Baker, E. L. (2008). Early identification of reading difficulties using heterogeneous developmental trajectories. *Journal of Educational Psychology, 100,* 192–208.

Botelho, M. J., Cohen, S. L., Leoni, L., Chow, P., & Sastri, P. (2010). Respecting children's cultural and linguistic knowledge. In M. L. Dantas & P. C. Manyak (Eds.), *Home–school connections in a multicultural society: Learning from and with culturally and linguistically diverse families* (pp. 237–256). New York, NY: Routledge.

Boxerman, J. Z. (2009, April). *Students' understanding of erosion.* Paper presented at the annual meeting of the American Educational Research Association, San Diego, CA.

Bråten, I., Britt, M. A., Strømsø, H. I., & Rouet, J.-F. (2011). The role of epistemic beliefs in the comprehension of multiple expository texts: Toward an integrated model. *Educational Psychologist, 46,* 48–70.

Brayboy, B. M. J., & Searle, K. A. (2007). Thanksgiving and serial killers: Representations of American Indians in schools. In S. Books (Ed.), *Invisible children in the society and its schools* (3rd ed., pp. 173–192). Mahwah, NJ: Erlbaum.

Britton, B. K., Stimson, M., Stennett, B., & Gülgöz, S. (1998). Learning from instructional text: Test of an individual differences model. *Journal of Educational Psychology, 90,* 476–491.

Bromme, R., Kienhues, D., & Porsch, T. (2010). Who knows what and who can we believe? Epistemological beliefs are beliefs about knowledge (mostly) to be attained from others. In L. D. Bendixen & F. C. Feucht (Eds.), *Personal epistemology in the classroom: Theory, research, and implications for practice* (pp. 163–193). Cambridge, England: Cambridge University Press.

Bronfenbrenner, U. (2005). *Making human beings human: Bioecological perspectives on human development.* Thousand Oaks, CA: Sage.

Brophy, J. E., & Alleman, J. (1996). *Powerful social studies for elementary students.* Fort Worth, TX: Harcourt, Brace.

Brophy, J., Alleman, J., & Knighton, B. (2009). *Inside the social studies classroom.* New York, NY: Routledge.

Brown, A. L., & Campione, J. C. (1994). Guided discovery in a community of learners. In K. McGilly (Ed.), *Classroom lessons: Integrating cognitive theory and classroom practice* (pp. 229–270). Cambridge, MA: MIT Press.

Brown, A. L., & Campione, J. C. (1996). Psychological theory and the design of innovative learning environments: On procedures, principles, and systems. In L. Schauble & R. Glaser (Eds.), *Innovations in learning: New environments for education* (pp. 289–325). Mahwah, NJ: Erlbaum.

Brown, D. E., & Clement, J. (1989). Overcoming misconceptions via analogical reasoning: Abstract transfer versus explanatory model construction. *Instructional Science, 18,* 237–262.

Bullock, M., & Ziegler, A. (1999). Scientific reasoning: Developmental and individual differences. In F. E. Weinert & W. Schneider (Eds.), *Individual development from 3 to 12: Findings from the Munich longitudinal study.* New York, NY: Cambridge University Press.

Byrnes, J. P. (1996). *Cognitive development and learning in instructional contexts.* Boston, MA: Allyn & Bacon.

Cain, K., Oakhill, J., & Bryant, P. (2004). Children's reading comprehension ability: Concurrent prediction by working memory, verbal ability, and component skills. *Journal of Educational Psychology, 96,* 31–42.

Campione, J. C., Shapiro, A. M., & Brown, A. L. (1995). Forms of transfer in a community of learners: Flexible learning and understanding. In A. McKeough, J. Lupart, & A. Marini (Eds.), *Teaching for transfer: Fostering generalization in learning* (pp. 35–68). Mahwah, NJ: Erlbaum.

Carbonneau, K. J., Marley, S. C., & Selig, J. P. (2013). A meta-analysis of the efficacy of teaching mathematics with concrete manipulatives. *Journal of Educational Psychology, 105,* 380–400.

Carr, M. (2010). The importance of metacognition for conceptual change and strategy use in mathematics. In H. S. Waters & W. Schneider (Eds.), *Metacognition, strategy use, and instruction* (pp. 176–197). New York, NY: Guilford.

Carr, N. (2011). *The shallows: What the Internet is doing to our brains.* New York, NY: W. W. Norton.

Case, R., & Okamoto, Y., in collaboration with Griffin, S., McKeough, A., Bleiker, C., Henderson, B., & Stephenson, K. M. (1996). The role of central conceptual structures in the development of children's thought. *Monographs of the Society for Research in Child Development, 61*(1, Serial No. 246).

Certo, J. (2011). Social skills and leadership abilities among children in small group literature discussions. *Journal of Research in Childhood Education, 25*(1), 62–81.

Chall, J. S. (1996). *Stages of reading development* (2nd ed.). Fort Worth, TX: Harcourt Brace.

Chinn, C. A. (2006). Learning to argue. In A. M. O'Donnell, C. E. Hmelo-Silver, & G. Erkens (Eds.), *Collaborative learning, reasoning, and technology* (pp. 355–383). Mahwah, NJ: Erlbaum.

Chinn, C. A., & Buckland, L. A. (2012). Model-based instruction: Fostering change in evolutionary conceptions and in epistemic practices. In K. S. Rosengren, S. K. Brem, E. M. Evans, & G. M. Sinatra (Eds.), *Evolution challenges: Integrating research and practice in teaching and learning about evolution* (pp. 211–232). Oxford, England: Oxford University Press.

Christenson, S. L., & Thurlow, M. L. (2004). School dropouts: Prevention, considerations, interventions, and challenges. *Current Directions in Psychological Science, 13,* 36–39.

Claessens, A., Engel, M., & Curran, F. C. (2014). Academic content, student learning, and persistence of preschool effects. *American Educational Research Journal, 51,* 403–434.

Clark, D. B. (2006). Longitudinal conceptual change in students' understanding of thermal equilibrium: An examination of the process of conceptual restructuring. *Cognition and Instruction, 24,* 467–563.

Clark, R. E., Yates, K., Early, S., & Moulton, K. (2009). An analysis of the failure of electronic media and discovery-based learning: Evidence for the performance benefits of guided training methods. In K. H. Silber & R. Foshay (Eds.), *Handbook of training and improving workplace performance: Vol. 1. Instructional design and training delivery* (pp. 263–297). New York, NY: Wiley.

Clarke, B., Gersten, R., & Newman-Gonchar, R. (2010). RTI in mathematics: Beginnings of a knowledge base. In T. A. Glover & S. Vaughn (Eds.), *The promise of response to intervention: Evaluating current science and practice* (pp. 187–203). New York, NY: Guilford.

Clarke, L. K. (1988). Invented versus traditional spelling in first graders' writings: Effects on learning to spell and read. *Research in the Teaching of English, 22,* 281–309.

Clement, J. (1982). Algebra word problem solutions: Thought processes underlying a common misconception. *Journal for Research in Mathematics Education, 13,* 16–30.

Clement, J. (2008). The role of explanatory models in teaching for conceptual change. In S. Vosniadou (Ed.), *International handbook on conceptual change* (pp. 417–452). New York, NY: Routledge.

Cognition and Technology Group at Vanderbilt. (1993). Anchored instruction and situated cognition revisited. *Educational Technology, 33*(3), 52–70.

Cole, M., & Hatano, G. (2007). Cultural-historical activity theory: Integrating phylogeny, cultural history, and ontogenesis in cultural psychology. In S. Kitayama & D. Cohen (Eds.), *Handbook of cultural psychology* (pp. 109–135). New York, NY: Guilford.

Collins, A. (2006). Cognitive apprenticeship. In R. K. Sawyer (Ed.), *The Cambridge handbook of the learning sciences* (pp. 47–60). Cambridge, England: Cambridge University Press.

Collins, A., Hawkins, J., & Carver, S. M. (1991). A cognitive apprenticeship for disadvantaged students. In B. Means, C. Chelemer, & M. S. Knapp (Eds.), *Teaching advanced skills to at-risk students* (pp. 216–243). San Francisco, CA: Jossey-Bass.

Connor, C. M., Morrison, F. J., Fishman, B., Crowe, E. C., Al Otaiba, S., & Schatschneider,

C. (2013). A longitudinal cluster-randomized controlled study on the accumulating effects of individualized literacy instruction on students' reading from first through third grade. *Psychological Science, 24,* 1408–1419.

Cromley, J. G., & Azevedo, R. (2007). Testing and refining the direct and inferential mediation model of reading comprehension. *Journal of Educational Psychology, 99,* 311–325.

Cummins, J. (2007). Pedagogies for the poor? Realigning reading instruction for low-income students with scientifically based reading research. *Educational Researcher, 36,* 564–572.

Curtis, M. E. (2004). Adolescents who struggle with word identification: Research and practice. In T. L. Jetton & J. A. Dole (Eds.), *Adolescent literacy research and practice* (pp. 119–134). New York, NY: Guilford.

Davis, J. H. (2008). *Why our schools need the arts.* New York, NY: Teachers College Press.

Davison, M. (2011, April). *Are you standing in my shoes? How affective and cognitive teaching sequences influence historical empathy.* Paper presented at the annual meeting of the American Educational Research Association, New Orleans, LA.

De Corte, E., Greer, B., & Verschaffel, L. (1996). Mathematics teaching and learning. In D. C. Berliner & R. C. Calfee (Eds.), *Handbook of educational psychology* (pp. 491–549). New York, NY: Macmillan.

De Corte, E., Op't Eynde, P., Depaepe, F., & Verschaffel, L. (2010). The reflexive relation between students' mathematics-related beliefs and the mathematics classroom culture. In L. D. Bendixen & F. C. Feucht (Eds.), *Personal epistemology in the classroom: Theory, research, and implications for practice* (pp. 292–327). Cambridge, England: Cambridge University Press.

De La Paz, S. (2005). Effects of historical reasoning instruction and writing strategy mastery in culturally and academically diverse middle school classrooms. *Journal of Educational Psychology, 97,* 139–156.

De La Paz, S., & McCutchen, D. (2011). Learning to write. In R. E. Mayer & P. A. Alexander (Eds.), *Handbook of research on learning and instruction* (pp. 32–54). New York, NY: Routledge.

Dehaene, S. (2007). A few steps toward a science of mental life. *Mind, Brain, and Education, 1*(1), 28–47.

Dennen, V. P., & Burner, K. J. (2008). The cognitive apprenticeship model in educational practice. In J. M. Spector, M. D. Merrill, J. van Merriënboer, & M. P. Driscoll (Eds.), *Handbook of research on educational communications and technology* (3rd ed., pp. 425–439). New York, NY: Erlbaum.

Driver, R. (1995). Constructivist approaches to science teaching. In L. P. Steffe & J. Gale (Eds.), *Constructivism in education.* Hillsdale, NJ: Erlbaum.

Eberbach, C., & Crowley, K. (2009). From everyday to scientific observation: How children learn to observe the biologist's world. *Review of Educational Research, 79,* 39–68.

Edelson, D. C., & Reiser, B. J. (2006). Making authentic practices accessible to learners. In R. K. Sawyer (Ed.), *The Cambridge handbook of the learning sciences* (pp. 335–354). Cambridge, England: Cambridge University Press.

Edwards, A. R., Esmonde, I., & Wagner, J. F. (2011). Learning mathematics. In R. E. Mayer & P. A. Alexander (Eds.), *Handbook of research on learning and instruction* (pp. 55–77). New York, NY: Routledge.

Egbert, J. (2009). *Supporting learning with technology: Essentials of classroom practice.* Upper Saddle River, NJ: Pearson/Merrill Prentice Hall.

Ehri, L. C. (1998). Word reading by sight and by analogy in beginning readers. In C. Hulme & R. M. Joshi (Eds.), *Reading and spelling: Development and disorders* (pp. 87–111). Mahwah, NJ: Erlbaum.

Ehri, L. C., Dreyer, L. G., Flugman, B., & Gross, A. (2007). Reading Rescue: An effective tutoring intervention model for language-minority students who are struggling readers in first grade. *American Educational Research Journal, 44,* 414–448.

Ehri, L. C., Nunes, S. R., Stahl, S. A., & Willows, D. M. (2001). Systematic phonics instruction helps students learn to read: Evidence from the National Reading Panel's meta-analysis. *Review of Educational Research, 71,* 393–447.

Elbro, C., & Petersen, D. K. (2004). Long-term effects of phoneme awareness and letter sound training: An intervention study with children at risk for dyslexia. *Journal of Educational Psychology, 96,* 660–670.

Engle, R. A. (2006). Framing interactions to foster generative learning: A situative explanation of transfer in a community of learners. *Journal of the Learning Sciences, 15,* 451–498.

Engle, R. A., & Conant, F. R. (2002). Guiding principles for fostering productive disciplinary engagement: Explaining an emergent argument in a community of learners classroom. *Cognition and Instruction, 20,* 399–483.

Enyedy, N. (2005). Inventing mapping: Creating cultural forms to solve collective problems. *Cognition and Instruction, 23,* 427–466.

Epstein, T. (2000). Adolescents' perspectives on racial diversity in U.S. history: Case studies from an urban classroom. *American Educational Research Journal, 37,* 185–214.

Epstein, T., & Shiller, J. (2009). Race, gender, and the teaching and learning of national history. In W. Parker (Ed.), *Social studies today: Research and practice* (pp. 95–104). New York, NY: Routledge.

Evans, E. M., Rosengren, K. S., Lane, J. D., & Price, K. L. S. (2012). Encountering counterintuitive ideas: Constructing a developmental learning progression for evolution understanding. In K. S. Rosengren, S. K. Brem, E. M. Evans, & G. M. Sinatra (Eds.), *Evolution challenges: Integrating research and practice in teaching and learning about evolution* (pp. 174–199). Oxford, England: Oxford University Press.

Feinberg, M., & Willer, R. (2011). Apocalypse soon? Dire messages reduce belief in global warming by contradicting just-world beliefs. *Psychological Science, 22,* 34–38.

Felton, R. H. (1998). The development of reading skills in poor readers: Educational implications. In C. Hulme & R. M. Joshi (Eds.), *Reading and spelling: Development and disorders* (pp. 219–233). Mahwah, NJ: Erlbaum.

Ferretti, R. P., Lewis, W. E., & Andrews-Weckerly, S. (2009). Do goals affect the structure of students' argumentative writing strategies? *Journal of Educational Psychology, 101,* 577–589.

Ferretti, R. P., MacArthur, C. A., & Dowdy, N. S. (2000). The effects of an elaborated goal on the persuasive writing of students with learning disabilities and their normally achieving peers. *Journal of Educational Psychology, 92,* 694–702.

Fitzgerald, J. (1992). Variant views about good thinking during composing: Focus on revision. In M. Pressley, K. R. Harris, & J. T. Guthrie (Eds.), *Promoting academic competence and literacy in school* (pp. 337–358). San Diego, CA: Academic Press.

Forbes, M. L., Ormrod, J. E., Bernardi, J. D., Taylor, S. L., & Jackson, D. L. (1999, April). *Children's conceptions of space, as reflected in maps of their hometown.* Paper presented at the annual meeting of the American Educational Research Association, Montreal, Canada.

Fox, E., & Alexander, P. A. (2011). Learning to read. In R. E. Mayer & P. A. Alexander (Eds.), *Handbook of research on learning and instruction* (pp. 7–31). New York, NY: Routledge.

Fuchs, D., Fuchs, L. S., Mathes, P. G., & Simmons, D. C. (1997). Peer-assisted learning strategies: Making classrooms more responsive to diversity. *American Educational Research Journal, 34,* 174–206.

Fuchs, L. S., Fuchs, D., Craddock, C., Hollenbeck, K. N., Hamlett, C. L., & Schatschneider, C. (2008). Effects of small-group tutoring with and without validated classroom instruction on at-risk, students' math problem solving: Are two tiers of prevention better than one? *Journal of Educational Psychology, 100,* 491–509.

Fuchs, L. S., Fuchs, D., Prentice, K., Burch, M., Hamlett, C. L., Owen, R., . . . Jancek, D. (2003). Explicitly teaching for transfer: Effects on third-grade students' mathematical problem solving. *Journal of Educational Psychology, 95,* 295–305.

Furnham, A. (2003). Belief in a just world: Research progress over the past decade. *Personality and Individual Differences, 34,* 795–817.

Furtak, E. M., Seidel, T., Iverson, H., & Briggs, D. C. (2012). Experimental and quasi-experimental studies of inquiry-based science teaching: A meta-analysis. *Review of Educational Research, 82,* 300–329.

Gallistel, C. R., & Gelman, R. (1992). Preverbal and verbal counting and computation. *Cognition, 44*, 43–74.

Garner, R. (1998). Epilogue: Choosing to learn or not-learn in school. *Educational Psychology Review, 10*, 227–237.

Gaskins, I. W., Satlow, E., & Pressley, M. (2007). Executive control of reading comprehension in the elementary school. In L. Meltzer (Ed.), *Executive function in education: From theory to practice* (pp. 194–215). New York, NY: Guilford.

Gauvain, M., & Munroe, R. L. (2009). Contributions of societal modernity to cognitive development: A comparison of four cultures. *Child Development, 80*, 1628–1642.

Geary, D. C. (2006). Development of mathematical understanding. In W. Damon, R. M. Lerner (Series Eds.), D. Kuhn, & R. Siegler (Vol. Eds.), *Handbook of child psychology: Vol. 1. Cognition, perception, and language* (6th ed., pp. 777–810). New York, NY: Wiley.

Geary, D. C., Hoard, M. K., Nugent, L., & Bailey, D. H. (2012). Mathematical cognition deficits in children with learning disabilities and persistent low achievement: A five-year prospective study. *Journal of Educational Psychology, 104*, 206–223.

Gifford, R. (2011). The dragons of inaction: Psychological barriers that limit climate change mitigation and adaptation. *American Psychologist, 66*, 290–302.

Gijbels, D., Dochy, F., Van den Bossche, P., & Segers, M. (2005). Effects of problem-based learning: A meta-analysis from the angle of assessment. *Review of Educational Research, 75*, 27–61.

Gil, L., Bråten, I., Vidal-Abarca, E., & Strømsø, H. I. (2010). Summary versus argument tasks when working with multiple documents: Which is better for whom? *Contemporary Educational Psychology, 35*, 157–173.

Ginsburg, H. P., Cannon, J., Eisenband, J., & Pappas, S. (2006). Mathematical thinking and learning. In K. McCartney & D. Phillips (Eds.), *Blackwell handbook of early childhood development* (pp. 208–229). Malden, MA: Blackwell.

Göbel, S. M., Watson, S. E., Lervåg, A., & Hulme, C. (2014). Children's arithmetic development: It is number knowledge, not the approximate number sense, that counts. *Psychological Science, 25*, 789–798.

Goldberg, R. F., & Thompson-Schill, S. L. (2009). Developmental "roots" in mature biological knowledge. *Psychological Science, 20*, 480–487.

Goldin-Meadow, S., & Beilock, S. L. (2010). Action's influence on thought: The case of gesture. *Perspectives on Psychological Science, 5*, 664–674.

Goswami, U. (2007). Typical reading development and developmental dyslexia across languages. In D. Coch, G. Dawson, & K. W. Fischer (Eds.), *Human behavior, learning, and the developing brain: Atypical development* (pp. 145–167). New York, NY: Guilford.

Gottfried, A. W., Schlackman, J., Gottfried, A. E., & Boutin-Martinez, A. S. (2015). Parental provision of early literacy environment as related to reading and educational outcomes across the academic lifespan. *Parenting: Science and Practice, 15*, 24–38.

Graesser, A. C., McNamara, D. S., & VanLehn, K. (2005). Scaffolding deep comprehension strategies through Point&Query, AutoTutor, and iSTART. *Educational Psychologist, 40*, 225–234.

Graham, S. (2006). Writing. In P. A. Alexander & P. H. Winne (Eds.), *Handbook of educational psychology* (2nd ed., pp. 457–478). Mahwah, NJ: Erlbaum.

Graham, S., Harris, K. R., & Olinghouse, N. (2007). Addressing executive function problems in writing: An example from the self-regulated strategy development model. In L. Meltzer (Ed.), *Executive function in education: From theory to practice* (pp. 216–236). New York, NY: Guilford.

Graham, S., McKeown, D., Kiuhara, S., & Harris, K. R. (2012). A meta-analysis of writing instruction for students in the elementary grades. *Journal of Educational Psychology, 104*, 879–896.

Graham, S., & Perin, D. (2007). A meta-analysis of writing instruction for adolescent students. *Journal of Educational Psychology, 99*, 445–476.

Greeno, J. G., Collins, A. M., & Resnick, L. B. (1996). Cognition and learning. In D. C. Berliner & R. C. Calfee (Eds.), *Handbook of educational psychology* (pp. 15–46). New York, NY: Macmillan.

Gregg, M., & Leinhardt, G. (1994a, April). *Constructing geography.* Paper presented at the annual meeting of the American Educational Research Association, New Orleans, LA.

Gregg, M., & Leinhardt, G. (1994b). Mapping out geography: An example of epistemology and education. *Review of Educational Research, 64*, 311–361.

Gregg, N. (2009). *Adolescents and adults with learning disabilities and ADHD: Assessment and accommodation.* New York, NY: Guilford.

Griffin, S., & Case, R. (1996). Evaluating the breadth and depth of training effects when central conceptual structures are taught. In R. Case & Y. Okamoto (Eds.), The role of central structures in the development of children's thought. *Monographs of the Society for Research in Child Development, 61*(Serial No. 246, Nos. 1–2).

Guthrie, J. T., Wigfield, A., Barbosa, P., Perencevich, K. C., Taboada, A., Davis, M. H., . . . Tonks, S. (2004). Increasing reading comprehension and engagement through concept-oriented reading instruction. *Journal of Educational Psychology, 96*, 403–423.

Hacker, D. J., & Bol, L. (2004). Metacognitive theory: Considering the social-cognitive influences. In D. M. McNerney & S. Van Etten (Eds.), *Big theories revisited* (pp. 275–297). Greenwich, CT: Information Age.

Hacker, D. J., Dunlosky, J., & Graesser, A. C. (Eds.) (2009b). *Handbook of metacognition in education.* New York, NY: Routledge.

Hacker, D. J., Keener, M. C., & Kircher, J. C. (2009). Writing is applied metacognition. In D. J. Hacker, J. Dunlosky, & A. C. Graesser (Eds.), *Handbook of metacognition in education* (pp. 154–172). New York, NY: Routledge.

Halford, G. S., & Andrews, G. (2006). Reasoning and problem solving. In R. W. Damon, M. Lerner (Series Eds.), D. Kuhn, & R. Siegler (Vol. Eds.), *Handbook of child psychology: Vol. 2. Cognition, perception, and language* (6th ed., pp. 557–608). New York, NY: Wiley.

Hallenbeck, M. J. (1996). The cognitive strategy in writing: Welcome relief for adolescents with learning disabilities. *Learning Disabilities Research and Practice, 11*, 107–119.

Harris, K. R., Santangelo, T., & Graham, S. (2010). Metacognition and strategies instruction in writing. In H. S. Waters & W. Schneider (Eds.), *Metacognition, strategy use, and instruction* (pp. 226–256). New York, NY: Guilford.

Hartley, K., & Bendixen, L. D. (2001). Educational research in the Internet age: Examining the role of individual characteristics. *Educational Researcher, 30*(9), 22–26.

Hatano, G., & Inagaki, K. (2003). When is conceptual change intended? A cognitive-sociocultural view. In G. M. Sinatra & P. R. Pintrich (Eds.), *Intentional conceptual change* (pp. 407–427). Mahwah, NJ: Erlbaum.

Hecht, S. A., & Vagi, K. J. (2010). Sources of group and individual differences in emerging fraction skills. *Journal of Educational Psychology, 102*, 843–859.

Hemphill, L., & Snow, C. (1996). Language and literacy development: Discontinuities and differences. In D. R. Olson & N. Torrance (Eds.), *The handbook of education and human development: New models of learning, teaching, and schooling* (pp. 170–201). Cambridge, MA: Blackwell.

Herbert, J., & Stipek, D. (2005). The emergence of gender differences in children's perceptions of their academic competence. *Journal of Applied Developmental Psychology, 26*, 276–295.

Hewitt, J., Brett, C., Scardamalia, M., Frecker, K., & Webb, J. (1995, April). Supporting knowledge building through the synthesis of CSILE, FCL, and Jasper. In M. Lamon (Chair), *Schools for thought: Transforming classrooms into learning communities.* Symposium conducted at the annual meeting of the American Educational Research Association, San Francisco, CA.

Hewitt, J., & Scardamalia, M. (1998). Design principles for distributed knowledge building processes. *Educational Psychology Review, 10*, 75–96.

Hiebert, E. H., & Fisher, C. W. (1992). The tasks of school literacy: Trends and issues. In J. Brophy (Ed.), *Advances in research on teaching: Vol. 3. Planning and managing learning tasks and activities* (pp. 191–223). Greenwich, CT: JAI.

Hiebert, E. H., & Raphael, T. E. (1996). Psychological perspectives on literacy and extensions to educational practice. In D. C. Berliner & R. C. Calfee (Eds.), *Handbook of educational psychology* (pp. 550–602). New York, NY: Macmillan.

Hiebert, J., Carpenter, T. P., Fennema, E., Fuson, K., Human, P., Murray, H., . . . Wearne, D. (1996). Problem solving as a basis for reform in curriculum and instruction: The case of mathematics. *Educational Researcher, 25*(4), 12–21.

Hmelo-Silver, C. E. (2004). Problem-based learning: What and how do students learn? *Educational Psychology Review, 16,* 235–266.

Hmelo-Silver, C. E. (2006). Design principles for scaffolding technology-based inquiry. In A. M. O'Donnell, C. E. Hmelo-SIlver, & G. Erkens (Eds.), *Collaborative learning, reasoning, and technology* (pp. 147–170). Mahwah, NJ: Erlbaum.

Hmelo-Silver, C. E., Duncan, R. G., & Chinn, C. A. (2007). Scaffolding and achievement in problem-based and inquiry learning: A response to Kirschner, Sweller, and Clark (2006). *Educational Psychologist, 42,* 99–107.

Hogan, K., Nastasi, B. K., & Pressley, M. (2000). Discourse patterns and collaborative scientific reasoning in peer and teacher-guided discussions. *Cognition and Instruction, 17,* 379–432.

Hughes, J. M., Bigler, R. S., & Levy, S. R. (2007). Consequences of learning about historical racism among European American and African American children. *Child Development, 78,* 1689–1705.

Hulme, C., Bowyer-Crane, C., Carroll, J. M., Duff, F. J., & Snowling, M. J. (2012). The causal role of phoneme awareness and letter–sound knowledge in learning to read: Combining intervention studies with mediation analyses. *Psychological Science, 23,* 572–577.

Hulme, C., & Joshi, R. M. (Eds.). (1998). *Reading and spelling: Development and disorders.* Mahwah, NJ: Erlbaum.

Hung, W., Jonassen, D. H., & Liu, R. (2008). Problem-based learning. In J. M. Spector, M. D. Merrill, J. van Merriënboer, & M. P. Driscoll (Eds.), *Handbook of research on educational communications and technology* (3rd ed., pp. 485–506). New York, NY: Erlbaum.

Hynd, C. (1998b). Observing learning from different perspectives: What does it mean for Barry and his understanding of gravity? In B. Guzzetti & C. Hynd (Eds.), *Perspectives on conceptual change: Multiple ways to understand knowing and learning in a complex world* (pp. 235–244). Mahwah, NJ: Erlbaum.

Inglis, A., & Biemiller, A. (1997, March). *Fostering self-direction in mathematics: A cross-age tutoring program that enhances math problem solving.* Paper presented at the annual meeting of the American Educational Research Association, Chicago, IL.

Ito, M., Baumer, S., Bittanti, M., Boyd, D., Cody, R., Herr-Stephenson, B., . . . Tripp, L. (2009). *Hanging out, messing around, geeking out: Living and learning with new media.* Cambridge, MA: MIT Press.

Jacoby, K. (2008). *Shadows at dawn: A borderlands massacre and the violence of history.* New York, NY: Penguin.

Janzen, J. (2008). Teaching English language learners in the content areas. *Review of Educational Research, 78,* 1010–1038.

Jetton, T. L., & Dole, J. A. (Eds.). (2004). *Adolescent literacy research and practice.* New York, NY: Guilford.

Johnson, D. W., & Johnson, R. T. (2009b). Energizing learning: The instructional power of conflict. *Educational Researcher, 38,* 37–51.

Juel, C. (1998). What kind of one-on-one tutoring helps a poor reader? In C. Hulme & R. M. Joshi (Eds.), *Reading and spelling: Development and disorders* (pp. 449–471). Mahwah, NJ: Erlbaum.

Katzir, T., & Paré-Blagoev, J. (2006). Applying cognitive neuroscience research to education: The case of literacy. *Educational Psychologist, 41,* 53–74.

Keil, F. C., & Newman, G. E. (2008). Two tales of conceptual change: What changes and what remains the same. In S. Vosniadou (Ed.), *International handbook on conceptual change* (pp. 83–101). New York, NY: Routledge.

Kellogg, R. T. (1994). *The psychology of writing.* New York, NY: Oxford University Press.

Kester, L., Paas, F., & van Merriënboer, J. J. G. (2010). Instructional control of cognitive load in the design of complex learning environments. In J. L. Plass, R. Moreno, & R. Brünken (Eds.), *Cognitive Load Theory* (pp. 109–130). Cambridge, England: Cambridge University Press.

Kincheloe, J. L. (2009). No short cuts in urban education: Metropedagogy and diversity. In S. R. Steinberg (Ed.), *Diversity and multiculturalism: A reader* (pp. 379–409). New York, NY: Peter Lang.

King, A. (1999). Discourse patterns for mediating peer learning. In A. M. O'Donnell & A. King (Eds.), *Cognitive perspectives on peer learning* (pp. 87–115). Mahwah, NJ: Erlbaum.

Kintsch, W. (2009). Learning and constructivism. In S. Tobias & T. M. Duffy (Eds.), *Constructivist instruction: Success or failure?* (pp. 223–241). New York, NY: Routledge.

Kirsh, D. (2009). Problem solving and situated cognition. In P. Robbins & M. Aydede (Eds.), *The Cambridge handbook of situated cognition* (pp. 264–306). Cambridge, England: Cambridge University Press.

Kitayama, S. (2002). Culture and basic psychological processes—Toward a system view of culture: Comment on Oyserman et al. (2002). *Psychological Bulletin, 128,* 89–96.

Klauda, S. L., & Guthrie, J. T. (2008). Relationships of three components of reading fluency to reading comprehension. *Journal of Educational Psychology, 100,* 310–321.

Klingner, J. K., & Vaughn, S. (2004). Strategies for struggling second-language readers. In T. L. Jetton & J. A. Dole (Eds.), *Adolescent literacy research and practice* (pp. 183–209). New York, NY: Guilford.

Knapp, N. F. (1995, April). *Tom and Joshua: Two at-risk readers at home and at school.* Paper presented at the annual meeting of the American Educational Research Association, San Francisco, CA.

Koltko-Rivera, M. E. (2004). The psychology of worldviews. *Review of General Psychology, 8,* 3–58.

Kornhaber, M., Fierros, E., & Veenema, S. (2004). *Multiple intelligences: Best ideas from research and practice.* Boston, MA: Allyn & Bacon.

Koslowski, B. (2012). Scientific reasoning: Explanation, confirmation bias and scientific practice. In G. Feist & M. Gorman (Eds.), *Handbook of the psychology of science and technology* (pp. 151–192). Dordrecht, The Netherlands: Springer.

Krajcik, J. S., & Blumenfeld, P. C. (2006). Project-based learning. In R. K. Sawyer (Ed.), *The Cambridge handbook of the learning sciences* (pp. 317–333). Cambridge, England: Cambridge University Press.

Kuhn, D. (2009). The importance of learning about knowing: Creating a foundation for development of intellectual values. *Child Development Perspectives, 3,* 112–117.

Kuhn, D. (2015). Thinking together and alone. *Educational Researcher, 44,* 46–53.

Kuhn, D., & Crowell, A. (2011). Dialogic argumentation as a vehicle for developing young adolescents' thinking. *Psychological Science, 22,* 545–552.

Kuhn, D., & Dean, D., Jr. (2005). Is developing scientific thinking all about learning to control variables? *Psychological Science, 16,* 866–870.

Kuhn, D., & Franklin, S. (2006). The second decade: What develops (and how)? In W. Damon, R. M. Lerner (Series Eds.), D. Kuhn, & R. Siegler (Vol. Eds.), *Handbook of child psychology: Vol. 2. Cognition, perception, and language* (6th ed., pp. 953–993). New York, NY: Wiley.

Kuhn, D., & Pearsall, S. (2000). Developmental origins of scientific thinking. *Journal of Cognition and Development, 1,* 113–129.

Ladson-Billings, G. (1995b). Toward a theory of culturally relevant pedagogy. *American Educational Research Journal, 32,* 465–491.

Lampert, M., Rittenhouse, P., & Crumbaugh, C. (1996). Agreeing to disagree: Developing sociable mathematical discourse. In D. R. Olson & N. Torrance (Eds.), *The handbook of education and human development: New models of learning, teaching, and schooling* (pp. 731–764). Cambridge, MA: Blackwell.

Langer, J. A. (2011). *Envisioning knowledge: Building literacy in the academic disciplines.* New York, NY: Teachers College Press.

Larkin, S. (2008, March). *The development of metacognition within the context of learning to write.* Paper presented at the annual meeting of the American Educational Research Association, New York, NY.

Lave, J. (1991). Situating learning in communities of practice. In L. B. Resnick, J. M. Levine, & S. D. Teasley (Eds.), *Perspectives on socially shared cognition* (pp. 63–82). Washington, DC: American Psychological Association.

Lave, J., & Wenger, E. (1991). *Situated learning: Legitimate peripheral participation.* Cambridge, England: Cambridge University Press.

Leaper, C., & Friedman, C. K. (2007). The socialization of gender. In J. E. Grusec & P. D. Hastings (Eds.), *Handbook of socialization: Theory and research* (pp. 561–587). New York, NY: Guilford.

Lee, P., & Ashby, R. (2001). Empathy, perspective taking, and rational understanding. In O. L. Davis, E. A. Yeager, & S. J. Foster (Eds.), *Historical empathy and perspective taking in the social studies* (pp. 21–50). Lanham, MD: Rowman & Littlefield.

Lehrer, R., & Schauble, L. (2006). Cultivating model-based reasoning in science education. In R. K. Sawyer (Ed.), *The Cambridge handbook of the learning sciences* (pp. 371–387). Cambridge, England: Cambridge University Press.

Leinhardt, G., Beck, I. L., & Stainton, C. (Eds.). (1994). *Teaching and learning in history.* Hillsdale, NJ: Erlbaum.

Leon, T. M. (2008, March). *Middle school readers comprehending, analyzing, and evaluating persuasive text.* Paper presented at the annual meeting of the American Educational Research Association, New York, NY.

Leu, D. J., O'Byrne, W. I., Zawilinski, L., McVerry, J. G., & Everett-Cacopardo, H. (2009). Expanding the new literacies conversation. *Educational Researcher, 38,* 264–269.

Levstik, L. S. (2011). Learning history. In R. E. Mayer & P. A. Alexander (Eds.), *Handbook of research on learning and instruction* (pp. 108–126). New York, NY: Routledge.

Lewandowsky, S., Oberauer, K., & Gignac, G. E. (2013). NASA faked the moon landing— Therefore, (climate) science is a hoax: An anatomy of the motivated rejection of science. *Psychological Science, 24,* 622–633.

Li, Y., Anderson, R. C., Nguyen-Jahiel, K., Dong, T., Archodidou, A., Kim, I.-H., . . . Miller, B. (2007). Emergent leadership in children's discussion groups. *Cognition and Instruction, 25,* 75–111.

Liben, L. S., & Downs, R. M. (1989a). Educating with maps: Part I, the place of maps. *Teaching Thinking and Problem Solving, 11*(1), 6–9.

Liben, L. S., & Downs, R. M. (1989b). Understanding maps as symbols: The development of map concepts in children. In H. W. Reese (Ed.), *Advances in child development and behavior* (Vol. 22, pp. 145–201). San Diego, CA: Harcourt Brace Jovanovich.

Liben, L. S., & Myers, L. J. (2007). Developmental changes in children's understanding of maps: What, when, and how? In J. M. Plumert & J. P. Spencer (Eds.), *The emerging spatial mind* (pp. 193–218). New York, NY: Oxford University Press.

Limpo, T., & Alves, R. A. (2013). Modeling writing development: Contribution of transcription and self-regulation to Portuguese students' text generation quality. *Journal of Educational Psychology, 105,* 401–413.

Linn, M. C., & Eylon, B.-S. (2011). *Science learning and instruction: Taking advantage of technology to promote knowledge integration.* New York, NY: Routledge.

Linn, M. C., Songer, N. B., & Eylon, B.-S. (1996). Shifts and convergences in science learning and instruction. In D. C. Berliner & R. C. Calfee (Eds.), *Handbook of educational psychology* (pp. 438–490). New York, NY: Macmillan.

Lipson, M. Y. (1983). The influence of religious affiliation on children's memory for text information. *Reading Research Quarterly, 18,* 448–457.

Lorch, R. F., Lorch, E. P., Freer, B. D., Dunlap, E. E., Hodell, E. C., & Calderhead, W. J. (2014). Using valid and invalid experimental designs to teach the control of variables strategy in higher and lower achieving classrooms. *Journal of Educational Psychology, 106,* 18–35.

Losh, S. C. (2003). On the application of social cognition and social location to creating causal explanatory structures. *Educational Research Quarterly, 26*(3), 17–33.

Ma, W., Adesope, O. O., Nesbit, J. C., & Liu, Q. (2014). Intelligent tutoring systems and learning outcomes: A meta-analysis. *Journal of Educational Psychology, 106,* 901–918.

MacDonald, S., Uesiliana, K., & Hayne, H. (2000). Cross-cultural and gender differences in childhood amnesia. *Memory, 8,* 365–376.

Manning, F. H., Lawless, K. A., Goldman, S. R., & Braasch, J. L. G. (2011, April). *Evaluating the usefulness of multiple sources with respect to an inquiry question: Middle school students' analysis and ranking of Internet search results.* Paper presented at the annual meeting of the American Educational Research Association, New Orleans, LA.

Marks, H. M. (2000). Student engagement in instructional activity: Patterns in the elementary, middle, and high school years. *American Educational Research Journal, 37,* 153–184.

Martínez, P., Bannan-Ritland, B., Kitsantas, A., & Baek, J. Y. (2008, March). *The impact of an integrated science reading intervention on elementary children's misconceptions regarding slow geomorphological changes caused by water.* Paper presented at the annual meeting of the American Educational Research Association, New York, NY.

Mason, L. (2003). Personal epistemologies and intentional conceptual change. In G. M. Sinatra & P. R. Pintrich (Eds.), *Intentional conceptual change* (pp. 199–236). Mahwah, NJ: Erlbaum.

Mastropieri, M. A., & Scruggs, T. E. (1992). Science for students with disabilities. *Review of Educational Research, 62,* 377–411.

Mastropieri, M. A., & Scruggs, T. E. (2000). *The inclusive classroom: Strategies for effective instruction.* Upper Saddle River, NJ: Merrill/Prentice Hall.

Matthews, L. E., Jones, S. M., & Parker, Y. A. (2013). Advancing a framework for culturally relevant, cognitively demanding mathematics tasks. In J. Leonard & D. B. Martin (Eds.), *The brilliance of black children in mathematics: Beyond the numbers and toward new discourse* (pp. 123–150). Charlotte, NC: Information Age.

Mayer, R. E. (1982). Memory for algebra story problems. *Journal of Educational Psychology, 74,* 199–216.

Mayer, R. E. (1999). *The promise of educational psychology: Learning in the content areas.* Upper Saddle River, NJ: Merrill/Prentice Hall.

Mayer, R. E. (2008). Applying the science of learning: Evidence-based principles for the design of multimedia instruction. *American Psychologist, 63,* 760–769.

McCrink, K., & Wynn, K. (2007). Ratio abstraction by 6-month-old infants. *Psychological Science, 18,* 740–745.

McCutchen, D. (1996). A capacity theory of writing: Working memory in composition. *Educational Psychology Review, 8,* 299–325.

McDevitt, M., & Chaffee, S. H. (1998). Second chance political socialization: "Trickle-up" effects of children on parents. In T. J. Johnson, C. E. Hays, & S. P. Hays (Eds.), *Engaging the public: How government and the media can reinvigorate American democracy* (pp. 57–66). Lanhan, MD: Rowman & Littlefield.

McLane, J. B., & McNamee, G. D. (1990). *Early literacy.* Cambridge, MA: Harvard University Press.

Medin, D. L. (2005, August). *Role of culture and expertise in cognition.* Invited address presented at the annual meeting of the American Psychological Association, Washington, DC.

Meltzer, L. (Ed.) (2007). *Executive function in education: From theory to practice.* New York, NY: Guilford.

Mergendoller, J. R., Markham, T., Ravitz, J., & Larmer, J. (2006). Pervasive management of project based learning: Teachers as guides and facilitators. In C. M. Evertson & C. S. Weinstein (Eds.), *Handbook of classroom management: Research, practice, and contemporary issues* (pp. 583–615). Mahwah, NJ: Erlbaum.

Metz, K. E. (2004). Children's understanding of scientific inquiry: Their conceptualizations of uncertainty in investigations of their own design. *Cognition and Instruction, 22,* 219–290.

Metz, K. E. (2011). Disentangling robust developmental constraints from the instructionally mutable: Young children's epistemic reasoning about a study of their own design. *Journal of the Learning Sciences, 20,* 50–110.

Monte-Sano, C. (2008). Qualities of historical writing instruction: A comparative case study of two teachers' practices. *American Educational Research Journal, 45,* 1045–1079.

Morra, S., Gobbo, C., Marini, Z., & Sheese, R. (2008). *Cognitive development: Neo-Piagetian perspectives.* New York, NY: Erlbaum.

Mosborg, S. (2002). Speaking of history: How adolescents use their knowledge of history in reading the daily news. *Cognition and Instruction, 20,* 323–358.

Muis, K. R. (2004). Personal epistemology and mathematics: A critical review and synthesis of research. *Review of Educational Research, 74,* 317–377.

Mullen, M. K., & Yi, S. (1995). The cultural context of talk about the past: Implications for the development of autobiographical memory. *Cognitive Development, 10,* 407–419.

Murphy, P. K., & Mason, L. (2006). Changing knowledge and beliefs. In P. A. Alexander & P. H. Winne (Eds.), *Handbook of educational psychology* (2nd ed., pp. 305–324). Mahwah, NJ: Erlbaum.

Murphy, P. K., Wilkinson, I. A. G., & Soter, A. O. (2011). Instruction based on discussion. In R. E. Mayer & P. A. Alexander (Eds.), *Handbook of research on learning and instruction* (pp. 382–407). New York, NY: Routledge.

Myers, L. J., & Liben, L. S. (2008). The role of intentionality and iconicity in children's developing comprehension and production of cartographic symbols. *Child Development, 79,* 668–684.

Nagy, W., Berninger, V. W., & Abbott, R. D. (2006). Contributions of morphology beyond phonology to literacy outcomes of upper elementary and middle-school students. *Journal of Educational Psychology, 98,* 134–147.

Nagy, W., Berninger, V., Abbott, R., Vaughan, K., & Vermeulen, K. (2003). Relationship of morphology and other language skills to literacy skills in at-risk second-grade readers and at-risk fourth-grade writers. *Journal of Educational Psychology, 95,* 730–742.

National Council for the Social Studies (NCSS). (1994). *Expectations of excellence: Curriculum standards for social studies.* Washington, DC: Author.

National Geographic Education Project. (1994). *Geography for life: National geography standards.* Washington, DC: National Geographic Research and Education, National Geographical Society.

Newmann, F. M., & Wehlage, G. G. (1993). Five standards of authentic instruction. *Educational Leadership, 50*(7), 8–12.

Nokes, J. D., Dole, J. A., & Hacker, D. J. (2007). Teaching high school students to use heuristics while reading historical texts. *Journal of Educational Psychology, 99,* 492–504.

Nolen, S. B. (2011). Motivation, engagement, and identity: Opening a conversation. In D. M. McInerney, R. A. Walker, & G. A. D. Liem (Eds.), *Sociocultural theories of learning and motivation: Looking back, looking forward* (pp. 109–135). Charlotte, NC: Information Age.

Norton, E. S., Kovelman, I., & Pettito, L.-A. (2007). Are there separate neural systems for spelling? New insights into the role of rules and memory in spelling from functional magnetic resonance imaging. *Mind, Brain, and Behavior, 1*(1), 48–59.

Nussbaum, E. M. (2008). Collaborative discourse, argumentation, and learning: Preface and literature review. *Contemporary Educational Psychology, 33,* 345–359.

Olsen, D. G. (1995). "Less" can be "more" in the promotion of thinking. *Social Education, 59*(3), 130-134.

Ormrod, J. E., Jackson, D. L., Kirby, B., Davis, J., & Benson, C. (1999, April). *Cognitive development as reflected in children's conceptions of early American history.* Paper presented at the annual meeting of the American Educational Research Association, Montreal, Canada.

Owens, R. E., Jr. (2008). *Language development* (7th ed.). Boston, MA: Allyn & Bacon.

Page-Voth, V., & Graham, S. (1999). Effects of goal setting and strategy use on the writing performance and self-efficacy of students with writing and learning problems. *Journal of Educational Psychology, 91,* 230–240.

Palincsar, A. S., & Brown, A. L. (1984). Reciprocal teaching of comprehension-fostering and comprehension-monitoring activities. *Cognition and Instruction, 1,* 117–175.

Paris, S. G., & Turner, J. C. (1994). Situated motivation. In P. R. Pintrich, D. R. Brown, & C. E. Weinstein (Eds.), *Student motivation, cognition, and learning: Essays in honor of Wilbert J. McKeachie* (pp. 213–238). Mahwah, NJ: Erlbaum.

Park, D. C., & Huang, C.-M. (2010). Culture wires the brain: A cognitive neuroscience perspective. *Perspectives on Psychological Science, 5,* 391–400.

Patrick, H., Mantzicopoulos, Y., & Samarapungavan, A. (2009). Motivation for learning science in kindergarten: Is there a gender gap and does integrated inquiry and literacy instruction make a difference? *Journal of Research in Science Teaching, 46,* 166–191.

Paxton, R. J. (1999). A deafening silence: History textbooks and the students who read them. *Review of Educational Research, 69,* 315–339.

Pea, R. D. (1993). Practices of distributed intelligence and designs for education. In G. Salomon (Ed.), *Distributed cognitions: Psychological and educational considerations* (pp. 47–87). Cambridge, England: Cambridge University Press.

Pearson, P. D., Hansen, J., & Gordon, C. (1979). The effect of background knowledge on young children's comprehension of explicit and implicit information. *Journal of Reading Behavior, 11,* 201–209.

Peck, C. L., & Herriot, L. (2015). Teachers' beliefs about social studies. In H. Fives & M. G. Gill (Eds.), *International handbook of research on teachers' beliefs* (pp. 387–402). New York, NY: Routledge.

Piaget, J. (1929). *The child's conception of the world.* New York, NY: Harcourt, Brace.

Pickens, J. (2006, Winter). "Poop study" engages primary students. *Volunteer Monitor* (National Newsletter of Volunteer Watershed Monitoring), *18*(1), 13, 21.

Piirto, J. (1999). *Talented children and adults: Their development and education* (2nd ed.). Upper Saddle River, NJ: Merrill/Prentice Hall.

Plass, J. L., Kalyuga, S., & Leutner, D. (2010). Individual differences and Cognitive Load Theory. In J. L. Plass, R. Moreno, & R. Brünken (Eds.), *Cognitive Load Theory* (pp. 65–87). Cambridge, England: Cambridge University Press.

Plumert, J. M., & Spencer, J. P. (Eds.). (2007). *The emerging spatial mind.* Oxford, England: Oxford University Press.

Porat, D. A. (2004). *It's not written here, but this is what happened:* Students' cultural comprehension of textbook narratives on the Israeli-Arab conflict. *American Educational Research Journal, 41,* 963–996.

Posner, M. I., & Rothbart, M. K. (2007). *Educating the human brain.* Washington, DC: American Psychological Association.

Pressley, M., & Harris, K. R. (2006). Cognitive strategies instruction: From basic research to classroom instruction. In P. A. Alexander & P. H. Winne (Eds.), *Handbook of educational psychology* (2nd ed., pp. 265–286). Mahwah, NJ: Erlbaum.

Purcell-Gates, V., McIntyre, E., & Freppon, P. A. (1995). Learning written storybook language in school: A comparison of low-SES children in skills-based and whole language classrooms. *American Educational Research Journal, 32,* 659–685.

Quinlan, T. (2004). Speech recognition technology and students with writing difficulties: Improving fluency. *Journal of Educational Psychology, 96,* 337–346.

Ramani, G. B., Siegler, R. S., & Hitti, A. (2012). Taking it to the classroom: Number board games as a small group learning activity. *Journal of Educational Psychology, 104,* 661–672.

Rayner, K., Foorman, B. R., Perfetti, C. A., Pesetsky, D., & Seidenberg, M. S. (2001). How psychological science informs the teaching of reading. *Psychological Science in the Public Interest, 2,* 31–74.

Reis, S. M., McCoach, D. B., Little, C. A., Muller, L. M., & Kaniskan, R. B. (2011). The effects of differentiated instruction and enrichment pedagogy on reading achievement in five elementary schools. *American Educational Research Journal, 48,* 462–501.

Renkl, A., & Atkinson, R. K. (2010). Learning from worked-out examples and problem solving. In J. L. Plass, R. Moreno, & R. Brünken (Eds.), *Cognitive Load Theory* (pp. 91–108). Cambridge, England: Cambridge University Press.

Reynolds, R. E., Taylor, M. A., Steffensen, M. S., Shirey, L. L., & Anderson, R. C. (1982). Cultural schemata and reading comprehension. *Reading Research Quarterly, 17,* 353–366.

Reznitskaya, A., & Gregory, M. (2013). Student thought and classroom language: Examining the mechanisms of change in dialogic teaching. *Educational Psychologist, 48,* 114–133.

Richland, L. E., Stigler, J. W., & Holyoak, K. J. (2012). Teaching the conceptual structure of mathematics. *Educational Psychologist, 47,* 189–203.

Rittle-Johnson, B. (2006). Promoting transfer: Effects of self-explanation and direct instruction. *Child Development, 77,* 1–15.

Rittle-Johnson, B., Siegler, R. S., & Alibali, M. W. (2001). Developing conceptual understanding and procedural skill in mathematics: An iterative process. *Journal of Educational Psychology, 93,* 346–362.

Rittle-Johnson, B., & Star, J. R. (2009). Compared with what? The effects of different comparisons on conceptual knowledge and procedural flexibility for equation solving. *Journal of Educational Psychology, 101,* 529–544.

Rivers, I., Chesney, T., & Coyne, I. (2011). Cyberbullying. In C. P. Monks & I. Coyne (Eds.), *Bullying in different contexts* (pp. 211–230). Cambridge, England: Cambridge University Press.

Roberts, T. A., & Meiring, A. (2006). Teaching phonics in the context of children's literature or spelling: Influences on first-grade reading, spelling, and writing and fifth-grade comprehension. *Journal of Educational Psychology, 98,* 690–713.

Roditi, B. N., & Steinberg, J. (2007). The strategy math classroom: Executive function processes and mathematics learning. In L. Meltzer (Ed.), *Executive function in education: From theory to practice* (pp. 237–260). New York, NY: Guilford.

Rogoff, B. (1990). *Apprenticeship in thinking: Cognitive development in social context.* New York, NY: Oxford University Press.

Rogoff, B. (1994, April). *Developing understanding of the idea of communities of learners.* Paper presented at the annual meeting of the American Educational Research Association, New Orleans, LA.

Rogoff, B. (2003). *The cultural nature of human development.* Oxford, England: Oxford University Press.

Rogoff, B., Matusov, E., & White, C. (1996). Models of teaching and learning: Participation in a community of learners. In D. R. Olson & N. Torrance (Eds.), *The handbook of education and human development: New models of learning, teaching, and schooling* (pp. 388–414). Cambridge, MA: Blackwell.

Rohrer, D., & Pashler, H. (2010). Recent research on human learning challenges conventional instructional strategies. *Educational Researcher, 39,* 406–412.

Roth, W.-M. (2011). Object/motives and emotion: A cultural-historical activity theoretic approach to motivation in learning and work. In D. M. McInerney, R. A. Walker, & G. A. D. Liem (Eds.), *Sociocultural theories of learning and motivation: Looking back, looking forward* (pp. 43–63). Charlotte, NC: Information Age.

Rothstein-Fisch, C., & Trumbull, E. (2008). *Managing diverse classrooms: How to build on students' strengths.* Alexandria, VA: Association for Supervision and Curriculum Development.

Sacks, C. H., & Mergendoller, J. R. (1997). The relationship between teachers' theoretical orientation toward reading and student outcomes in kindergarten children with different initial reading abilities. *American Educational Research Journal, 34,* 721–739.

Salend, S. J., & Hofstetter, E. (1996). Adapting a problem-solving approach to teaching mathematics to students with mild disabilities. *Intervention in School and Clinic, 31*(4), 209–217.

Salomon, G. (1993). No distribution without individuals' cognition: A dynamic interactional view. In G. Salomon (Ed.), *Distributed cognitions: Psychological and educational considerations* (pp. 111–138). Cambridge, England: Cambridge University Press.

Sampson, M. B., Szabo, S., Falk-Ross, F., Foote, M. M., & Linder, P. E. (Eds.). (2007). *Multiple literacies in the 21st century: The twenty-eighth yearbook of the College Reading Association.* Logan, UT: College Reading Association.

Sandoval, W. A., Sodian, B., Koerber, S., & Wong, J. (2014). Developing children's early competencies to engage with science. *Educational Psychologist, 49,* 139–152.

Sarama, J., & Clements, D. H. (2009). "Concrete" computer manipulatives in mathematics education. *Child Development Perspectives, 3,* 145–150.

Sawyer, R. K., & Greeno, J. G. (2009). Situativity and learning. In P. Robbins & M. Aydede (Eds.), *The Cambridge handbook of situated cognition* (pp. 347–367). Cambridge, England: Cambridge University Press.

Saxe, G. B., & Esmonde, I. (2005). Studying cognition in flux: A historical treatment of *fu* in the shifting structure of Oksapmin mathematics. *Mind, Culture, and Activity, 12,* 171–225.

Scardamalia, M., & Bereiter, C. (1986). Research on written composition. In M. C. Wittrock (Ed.), *Handbook of research on teaching* (3rd ed., pp. 778–803). New York, NY: Macmillan.

Scardamalia, M., & Bereiter, C. (2006). Knowledge building: Theory, pedagogy, and technology. In R. K. Sawyer (Ed.), *The Cambridge handbook of the learning sciences* (pp. 97–115). Cambridge, England: Cambridge University Press.

Schoenfeld, A. H. (1988). When good teaching leads to bad results: The disasters of "well-taught" mathematics courses. *Educational Psychologist, 23,* 145–166.

Schoenfeld, A. H. (1992). Learning to think mathematically: Problem solving, metacognition, and sense making in mathematics. In D. A. Grouws (Ed.), *Handbook of research on mathematics teaching and learning* (pp. 334–370). New York, NY: Macmillan.

Schwarz, B. B., Neuman, Y., & Biezuner, S. (2000). Two wrongs may make a right . . . if they argue together! *Cognition and Instruction, 18,* 461–494.

Segal, A., Tversky, B., & Black, J. (2014). Conceptually congruent actions can promote thought. *Journal of Applied Research in Memory and Cognition, 3,* 124–130.

Serpell, R., Baker, L., & Sonnenschein, S. (2005). *Becoming literate in the city: The Baltimore Early Childhood Project.* Cambridge, England: Cambridge University Press.

Shanahan, C. (2004). Teaching science through literacy. In T. L. Jetton & J. A. Dole (Eds.), *Adolescent literacy research and practice* (pp. 75–93). New York, NY: Guilford.

Shanahan, T., & Tierney, R. J. (1990). Reading–writing connections: The relations among three perspectives. In J. Zutell & S. McCormick (Eds.), *Literacy theory and research: Analyses from multiple paradigms. Thirty-ninth yearbook of the National Reading Conference* (pp. 13–34). Chicago, IL: National Reading Conference.

Share, D. L. (1995). Phonological recoding and self-teaching: Sine qua non of reading acquisition. *Cognition, 55,* 151–218.

Shayne, R. K., Fogel, V. A., Miltenberger, R. G., & Koehler, S. (2012). The effects of exergaming on physical activity in a third-grade physical education class. *Journal of Applied Behavior Analysis, 45,* 211–215.

Shaywitz, S. E., Mody, M., & Shaywitz, B. A. (2006). Neural mechanisms in dyslexia. *Current Directions in Psychological Science, 15,* 278–281.

Siegler, R. S. (1989). Mechanisms of cognitive growth. *Annual Review of Psychology, 40,* 353–379.

Siegler, R. S., Duncan, G. J., Davis-Kean, P. E., Duckworth, K., Claessens, A., Engel, M., . . . Chen, M. (2012). Early predictors of high school mathematics achievement. *Psychological Science, 23,* 691–697.

Siegler, R. S., & Jenkins, E. (1989). *How children discover new strategies.* Hillsdale, NJ: Erlbaum.

Sinatra, G. M., & Pintrich, P. R. (Eds.). (2003). *Intentional conceptual change.* Mahwah, NJ: Erlbaum.

Singer, J., Marx, R. W., Krajcik, J., & Chambers, J. C. (2000). Constructing extended inquiry projects: Curriculum materials for science education reform. *Educational Psychologist, 35,* 165–178.

Sitko, B. M. (1998). Knowing how to write: Metacognition and writing instruction. In D. J. Hacker, J. Dunlosky, & A. C. Graesser (Eds.), *Metacognition in educational theory and practice* (pp. 93–115). Mahwah, NJ: Erlbaum.

Slavin, R. E., Lake, C., Chambers, B., Cheung, A., & Davis, S. (2009). Effective reading programs for the elementary grades: A best-evidence synthesis. *Review of Educational Research, 79,* 1391–1466.

Smith, C. L. (2007). Bootstrapping processes in the development of students' commonsense matter theories: Using analogical mappings, thought experiments, and learning to measure to promote conceptual restructuring. *Cognition and Instruction, 25,* 337–398.

Smith, E. R., & Conrey, F. R. (2009). The social context of cognition. In P. Robbins & M. Aydede (Eds.), *The Cambridge handbook of situated cognition* (pp. 454–466). Cambridge, England: Cambridge University Press.

Snir, J., Smith, C. L., & Raz, G. (2003). Linking phenomena with competing underlying models: A software tool for introducing students to the particulate model of matter. *Science Education, 87,* 794–830.

Snowling, M. J., Gallagher, A., & Frith, U. (2003). Family risk of dyslexia is continuous: Individual differences in the precursors of reading skill. *Child Development, 74,* 358–373.

Southerland, S. A., & Sinatra, G. M. (2003). Learning about biological evolution: A special case of intentional conceptual change. In G. M. Sinatra & P. R. Pintrich (Eds.), *Intentional conceptual change* (pp. 317–345). Mahwah, NJ: Erlbaum.

Spiro, R. J., & DeSchryver, M. (2009). Constructivism: When it's the wrong idea and when it's the only idea. In S. Tobias & T. M. Duffy (Eds.), *Constructivist instruction: Success or failure?* (pp. 106–123). New York, NY: Routledge.

Spivey, N. N. (1997). *The constructivist metaphor: Reading, writing, and the making of meaning.* San Diego, CA: Academic Press.

Spörer, N., & Brunstein, J. C. (2009). Fostering the reading comprehension of secondary school students through peer-assisted learning: Effects on strategy knowledge, strategy use, and task performance. *Contemporary Educational Psychology, 34,* 289–297.

Spunt, R. P., Falk, E. B., & Lieberman, M. D. (2010). Dissociable neural systems support retrieval of *how* and *why* action knowledge. *Psychological Science, 21,* 1593–1598.

Squire, K. (2011). *Video games and learning: Teaching and participatory culture in the digital age.* New York, NY: Teachers College Press.

Stahl, G., Koschmann, T., & Suthers, D. D. (2006). Computer-supported collaborative learning. In R. K. Sawyer (Ed.), *The Cambridge handbook of the learning sciences* (pp. 409–425). Cambridge, England: Cambridge University Press.

Stahl, S. A., & Miller, P. D. (1989). Whole language and language experience approaches for beginning reading: A quantitative research synthesis. *Review of Educational Research, 59,* 87–116.

Stahl, S. A., & Shanahan, C. (2004). Learning to think like a historian: Disciplinary knowledge through critical analysis of multiple documents. In T. L. Jetton & J. A. Dole (Eds.), *Adolescent literacy research and practice* (pp. 94–115). New York, NY: Guilford.

Stanovich, K. E. (2000). *Progress in understanding reading: Scientific foundations and new frontiers.* New York, NY: Guilford.

Steenbergen-Hu, S., & Cooper, H. (2013). A meta-analysis of the effectiveness of intelligent tutoring systems on K–12 students' mathematical learning. *Journal of Educational Psychology, 105,* 970–987.

Steffensen, M. S., Joag-Dev, C., & Anderson, R. C. (1979). A cross-cultural perspective on reading comprehension. *Reading Research Quarterly, 15,* 10–29.

Stuebing, K. K., Barth, A. E., Cirino, P. T., Francis, D. J., & Fletcher, J. M. (2008). A response to recent reanalyses of the National Reading Panel Report: Effects of systematic phonics instruction are practically significant. *Journal of Educational Psychology, 100,* 123–134.

Swanson, H. L. (2006). Cross-sectional and incremental changes in working memory and mathematical problem solving. *Journal of Educational Psychology, 98,* 265–281.

Swanson, H. L., Cooney, J. B., & O'Shaughnessy, T. E. (1998). Learning disabilities and memory. In B. Y. L. Wong (Ed.), *Learning about learning disabilities* (2nd ed., pp. 107–162). San Diego, CA: Academic Press.

Swanson, H. L., & O'Connor, R. (2009). The role of working memory and fluency practice on the reading comprehension of students who are dysfluent readers. *Journal of Learning Disabilities, 42,* 548–575.

Sweller, J., Kirschner, P. A., & Clark, R. E. (2007). Why minimally guided teaching techniques do not work: A reply to commentaries. *Educational Psychologist, 42,* 115–121.

Tate, W. F. (1995). Returning to the root: A culturally relevant approach to mathematics pedagogy. *Theory into Practice, 34,* 166–173.

Thanukos, A., & Scotchmoor, J. (2012). Making connections: Evolution and the nature and process of science. In K. S. Rosengren, S. K. Brem, E. M. Evans, & G. M. Sinatra (Eds.), *Evolution challenges: Integrating research and practice in teaching and learning about evolution* (pp. 410–427). Oxford, England: Oxford University Press.

Thapa, A., Cohen, J., Guffey, S., & Higgins-D'Alessandro, A. (2013). A review of school climate research. *Review of Educational Research, 83,* 357–385.

Thompson, M., & Grace, C. O. (with Cohen, L. J.). (2001). *Best friends, worst enemies: Understanding the social lives of children.* New York, NY: Ballantine.

Tobias, S., & Fletcher, J. D. (2012). Reflections on "A review of trends in serious gaming." *Review of Educational Research, 82,* 233–237.

Tompkins, G. E., & McGee, L. M. (1986). Visually impaired and sighted children's emerging concepts about written language. In D. B. Yaden, Jr., & S. Templeton (Eds.), *Metalinguistic awareness and beginning literacy: Conceptualizing what it means to read and write* (pp. 259–275). Portsmouth, NH: Heinemann.

Tourniaire, F., & Pulos, S. (1985). Proportional reasoning: A review of the literature. *Educational Studies in Mathematics, 16,* 181–204.

Trawick-Smith, J. (2003). *Early childhood development: A multicultural perspective* (3rd ed.). Upper Saddle River, NJ: Merrill/Prentice Hall.

Turkanis, C. G. (2001). Creating curriculum with children. In B. Rogoff, C. G. Turkanis, & L. Bartlett (Eds.), *Learning together: Children and adults in a school community* (pp. 91–102). New York, NY: Oxford University Press.

Turnbull, A. P., Turnbull, R., & Wehmeyer, M. L. (2010). *Exceptional lives: Special education in today's schools* (6th ed.). Upper Saddle River, NJ: Merrill.

Turner, J. C. (1995). The influence of classroom contexts on young children's motivation for literacy. *Reading Research Quarterly, 30,* 410–441.

Vadasy, P. F., Sanders, E. A., & Peyton, J. A. (2006). Code-oriented instruction for kindergarten students at risk for reading difficulties: A randomized field trial with paraeducator implementers. *Journal of Educational Psychology, 98,* 508–528.

Valkenburg, P. M., & Peter, J. (2009). Social consequences of the Internet for adolescents: A decade of research. *Current Directions in Psychological Science, 18,* 1–5.

van den Broek, P., Lynch, J. S., Naslund, J., Ievers-Landis, C. E., & Verduin, K. (2003). The development of comprehension of main ideas in narratives: Evidence from the selection of titles. *Journal of Educational Psychology, 95,* 707–718.

van Drie, J., van Boxtel, C., & van der Linden, J. (2006). Historical reasoning in a computer-supported collaborative learning environment. In A. M. O'Donnell, C. E. Hmelo-SIlver, & G. Erkens (Eds.), *Collaborative learning, reasoning, and technology* (pp. 265–296). Mahwah, NJ: Erlbaum.

VanLehn, K. (2011). The relative effectiveness of human tutoring, intelligent tutoring systems, and other tutoring systems. *Educational Psychologist, 46,* 197–221.

VanSledright, B., & Limón, M. (2006). Learning and teaching social studies: A review of cognitive research in history and geography. In P. A. Alexander & P. H. Winne (Eds.), *Handbook of educational psychology* (2nd ed., pp. 545–570). Mahwah, NJ: Erlbaum.

Verhallen, M. J. A. J., Bus, A. G., & de Jong, M. T. (2006). The promise of multimedia stories for kindergarten children at risk. *Journal of Educational Psychology, 98,* 410–419.

Vidal-Abarca, E., Martínez, G., & Gilabert, R. (2000). Two procedures to improve instructional text: Effects on memory and learning. *Journal of Educational Psychology, 92,* 1–10.

Vosniadou, S. (Ed.) (2008). *International handbook of research on conceptual change.* New York, NY: Routledge.

Vygotsky, L. S. (1978). *Mind in society: The development of higher psychological processes.* Cambridge, MA: Harvard University Press.

Vygotsky, L. S. (1986). *Thought and language* (rev. ed; A. Kozulin, Ed. and Trans.). Cambridge, MA: MIT Press. (Original work published 1934)

Walshaw, M., & Anthony, G. (2008). The teacher's role in classroom discourse: A review of recent research into mathematics classrooms. *Review of Educational Research, 78,* 516–551.

Wang, Q., & Ross, M. (2007). Culture and memory. In S. Kitayama & D. Cohen (Eds.), *Handbook of cultural psychology* (pp. 645–667). New York, NY: Guilford.

Ward, W., Cole, R., Bolaños, D., Buchenroth-Martin, C., Svirsky, E., & Weston, T. (2013). My Science Tutor: A conversational multimedia virtual tutor. *Journal of Educational Psychology, 105,* 1115–1125.

Warschauer, M. (2011). *Learning in the cloud: How (and why) to transform schools with digital media.* New York, NY: Teachers College Press.

Wasley, P. A., Hampel, R. L., & Clark, R. W. (1997). *Kids and school reform.* San Francisco, CA: Jossey-Bass.

Webb, N. M., & Farivar, S. (1994). Promoting helping behavior in cooperative small groups in middle school mathematics. *American Educational Research Journal, 31,* 369–395.

Wells, G. (2011). Motive and motivation in learning to teach. In D. M. McInerney, R. A. Walker, & G. A. D. Liem (Eds.), *Sociocultural theories of learning and motivation: Looking back, looking forward* (pp. 87–107). Charlotte, NC: Information Age.

Wenger, E. (1998). *Communities of practice: Learning, meaning, and identity.* Cambridge, England: Cambridge University Press.

Wentzel, K. R., & Watkins, D. E. (2011). Instruction based on peer interactions. In R. E. Mayer & P. A. Alexander (Eds.), *Handbook of research on learning and instruction* (pp. 322–343). New York, NY: Routledge.

White, B., Frederiksen, J., & Collins, A. (2009). The interplay of scientific inquiry and metacognition: More than a marriage of convenience. In D. J. Hacker, J. Dunlosky, & A. C. Graesser (Eds.), *Handbook of metacognition in education* (pp. 175–205). New York, NY: Routledge.

White, T., & Pea, R. (2011). Distributed by design: On the promises and pitfalls of collaborative learning with multiple representations. *Journal of the Learning Sciences, 20,* 489–547.

Wigfield, A., Byrnes, J. P., & Eccles, J. S. (2006). Development during early and middle adolescence. In P. A. Alexander & P. H. Winne (Eds.), *Handbook of educational psychology* (2nd ed., pp. 87–113). Mahwah, NJ: Erlbaum.

Wiley, J., Goldman, S. R., Graesser, A. C., Sanchez, C. A., Ash, I. K., & Hemmerich, J. A. (2009). Source evaluation, comprehension, and learning in Internet science inquiry tasks. *American Educational Research Journal, 46,* 1060–1106.

Williams, J. P., Stafford, K. B., Lauer, K. D., Hall, K. M., & Pollini, S. (2009). Embedding reading comprehension training in content-area instruction. *Journal of Educational Psychology, 101,* 1–20.

Wilson, A. J., & Dehaene, S. (2007). Number sense and developmental dyscalculia. In D. Coch, G. Dawson, & K. W. Fischer (Eds.),

Human behavior, learning, and the developing brain: Atypical development (pp. 212–238). New York, NY: Guilford.

Wimmer, H., Landerl, K., & Frith, U. (1999). Learning to read German: Normal and impaired acquisition. In M. Harris & G. Hatano (Eds.), *Learning to read and write: A cross-linguistic perspective* (pp. 34–50). Cambridge, England: Cambridge University Press.

Wirkala, C., & Kuhn, D. (2011). Problem-based learning in K–12 education: Is it effective and how does it achieve its effects? *American Educational Research Journal, 48,* 1157–1186.

Wiser, M., & Smith, C. L. (2008). Learning and teaching about matter in grades K–8: When should the atomic–molecular theory be introduced? In S. Vosniadou (Ed.), *International handbook on conceptual change* (pp. 205–231). New York, NY: Routledge.

Wolfe, M. B. W., & Goldman, S. R. (2005). Relations between adolescents' text processing and reasoning. *Cognition and Instruction, 23,* 467–502.

Wood, D. K., Frank, A. R., & Wacker, D. P. (1998). Teaching multiplication facts to students with learning disabilities. *Journal of Applied Behavior Analysis, 31,* 323–338.

Wouters, P., van Nimwegen, C., van Oostendorp, H., & van der Spek, E. D. (2013). A meta-analysis of the cognitive and motivational effects of serious games. *Journal of Educational Psychology, 105,* 249–265.

Yeager, E. A., Foster, S. J., Maley, S. D., Anderson, T., Morris, J. W., III, & Davis, O. L., Jr. (1997, March). *The role of empathy in the development of historical understanding.* Paper presented at the annual meeting of the American Educational Research Association, Chicago, IL.

Zaragoza, J. M., & Fraser, B. J. (2008, March). *Learning environments and attitudes among elementary-school students in traditional environmental science and field-study classrooms.* Paper presented at the annual meeting of the American Educational Research Association, New York, NY.

Zhang, J., Scardamalia, M., Reeve, R., & Messina, R. (2009). Designs for collective cognitive responsibility in knowledge-building communities. *Journal of the Learning Sciences, 18*(1), 7–44.

Zohar, A., & Aharon-Kraversky, S. (2005). Exploring the effects of cognitive conflict and direct teaching for students of different academic levels. *Journal of Research in Science Teaching, 42,* 829–855.

Zusho, A., & Clayton, K. (2011). Culturalizing achievement goal theory and research. *Educational Psychologist, 46,* 239–260.

CHAPTER 9

Alberto, P. A., & Troutman, A. C. (2013). *Applied behavior analysis for teachers* (9th ed.). Upper Saddle River, NJ: Merrill/Pearson.

American Psychological Association Zero Tolerance Task Force. (2008). Are zero

tolerance policies effective in the schools? An evidentiary review and recommendations. *American Psychologist, 63,* 852–862.

Anderman, E. M., & Anderman, L. H. (2010). *Classroom motivation.* Upper Saddle River, NJ: Pearson.

Anderman, E. M., & Mueller, C. E. (2010). Middle school transitions and adolescent development. In J. Meece & J. Eccles (Eds.), *Handbook of research on schools, schooling, and human development* (pp. 198–215). Mahwah, NJ: Erlbaum.

Anderman, L. H., Patrick, H., Hruda, L. Z., & Linnenbrink, E. A. (2002). Observing classroom goal structures to clarify and expand goal theory. In C. Midgley (Ed.), *Goals, goal structures, and patterns of adaptive learning* (pp. 243–278). Mahwah, NJ: Erlbaum.

Appel, J. B., & Peterson, N. J. (1965). Punishment: Effects of shock intensity on response suppression. *Psychological Reports, 16,* 721–730.

Ardoin, S. P., Martens, B. K., & Wolfe, L. A. (1999). Using high-probability instructional sequences with fading to increase student compliance during transitions. *Journal of Applied Behavior Analysis, 32,* 339–351.

Atance, C. M. (2008). Future thinking in young children. *Current Directions in Psychological Science, 17,* 295–298.

Austin, J. L, & Soeda, J. M. (2008). Fixed-time teacher attention to decrease off-task behaviors of typically developing third graders. *Journal of Applied Behavior Analysis, 41,* 279–283.

Azrin, N. H. (1960). Effects of punishment intensity during variable-interval reinforcement. *Journal of the Experimental Analysis of Behavior, 3,* 123–142.

Azrin, N. H., Vinas, V., & Ehle, C. T. (2007). Physical activity as reinforcement for classroom calmness of ADHD children: A preliminary study. *Child and Family Behavior Therapy, 29,* 1–8.

Ballenger, C. (1992). Because you like us: The language of control. *Harvard Educational Review, 62,* 199–208.

Bangert-Drowns, R. L., Kulik, C. C., Kulik, J. A., & Morgan, M. (1991). The instructional effect of feedback in test-like events. *Review of Educational Research, 61,* 213–238.

Barbetta, P. M. (1990). GOALS: A group-oriented adapted levels system for children with behavior disorders. *Academic Therapy, 25,* 645–656.

Barbetta, P. M., Heward, W. L., Bradley, D. M., & Miller, A. D. (1994). Effects of immediate and delayed error correction on the acquisition and maintenance of sight words by students with developmental disabilities. *Journal of Applied Behavior Analysis, 27,* 177–178.

Barrish, H. H., Saunders, M., & Wolf, M. M. (1969). Good behavior game: Effects of individual contingencies for group consequences on disruptive behavior in a classroom. *Journal of Applied Behavior Analysis, 2,* 119–124.

Bay-Hinitz, A. K., Peterson, R. F., & Quilitch, H. R. (1994). Cooperative games: A way to modify aggressive and cooperative behaviors in young children. *Journal of Applied Behavior Analysis, 27,* 435–446.

Beaulieu, L., Hanley, G. P., & Roberson, A. A. (2013). Effects of peer mediation on preschools' compliance and compliance precursors. *Journal of Applied Behavior Analysis, 46,* 555–567.

Beirne-Smith, M., Patton, J. R., & Kim, S. H. (2006). *Mental retardation: An introduction to intellectual disabilities* (7th ed.). Upper Saddle River, NJ: Merrill/Prentice Hall.

Belfiore, P. J., Lee, D. L., Vargas, A. U., & Skinner, C. H. (1997). Effects of high-preference single-digit mathematics problem completion on multiple-digit mathematics problem performance. *Journal of Applied Behavior Analysis, 30,* 327–330.

Bembenutty, H., & Karabenick, S. A. (2004). Inherent association between academic delay of gratification, future time perspective, and self-regulated learning. *Educational Psychology Review, 16,* 35–57.

Berg, W. K., Wacker, D. P., Cigrand, K., Merkle, S., Wade J., Henry, K., & Wang, Y.-C. (2007). Comparing functional analysis and paired-choice assessment results in classroom settings. *Journal of Applied Behavior Analysis, 40,* 545–552.

Binder, L. M., Dixon, M. R., & Ghezzi, P. M. (2000). A procedure to teach self-control to children with attention deficit hyperactivity disorder. *Journal of Applied Behavior Analysis, 33,* 233–237.

Boyanton, D. (2010). Behaviorism and its effect upon learning in the schools. In G. S. Goodman (Ed.), *Educational psychology reader: The art and science of how people learn* (pp. 49–65). New York, NY: Peter Lang.

Bradshaw, C. P., Mitchell, M. M., & Leaf, P. J. (2010). Examining the effects of schoolwide behavioral interventions and supports on student outcomes. *Journal of Positive Behavior Interventions, 12*(3), 133–148.

Brendgen, M., Wanner, G., Vitaro, F., Bukowski, W. M., & Tremblay, R. E. (2007). Verbal abuse by the teacher during childhood and academic, behavioral, and emotional adjustment in young adulthood. *Journal of Educational Psychology, 99,* 26–38.

Brown, W. H., Fox, J. J., & Brady, M. P. (1987). Effects of spatial density on 3- and 4-year-old children's socially directed behavior during freeplay: An investigation of a setting factor. *Education and Treatment of Children, 10,* 247–258.

Buchoff, T. (1990). Attention deficit disorder: Help for the classroom teacher. *Childhood Education, 67,* 86–90.

Burnett, P. (2001). Elementary students' preferences for teacher praise. *Journal of Classroom Interaction, 36,* 16–23.

Butler, D. L., & Winne, P. H. (1995). Feedback and self-regulated learning: A theoretical synthesis. *Review of Educational Research, 65,* 245–281.

Cameron, J. (2001). Negative effects of reward on intrinsic motivation—A limited phenomenon: Comment on Deci, Koestner, and Ryan (2001). *Review of Educational Research, 71,* 29–42.

Cammilleri, A. P., Tiger, J. H., & Hanley, G. P. (2008). Developing stimulus control of young children's requests to teachers: Classwide applications of multiple schedules. *Journal of Applied Behavior Analysis, 41,* 299–303.

Carey, R. G., & Bucher, B. (1983). Positive practice overcorrection: The effects of duration of positive practice on acquisition and response reduction. *Journal of Applied Behavior Analysis, 16,* 101–109.

Christenson, S. L., & Thurlow, M. L. (2004). School dropouts: Prevention, considerations, interventions, and challenges. *Current Directions in Psychological Science, 13,* 36–39.

Cizek, G. J. (2003). *Detecting and preventing classroom cheating: Promoting integrity in assessment.* Thousand Oaks, CA: Corwin.

Conyers, C., Miltenberger, R., Maki, A., Barenz, R., Jurgens, M., Sailer, A., . . . Kopp, B. (2004). A comparison of response cost and differential reinforcement of other behavior to reduce disruptive behavior in a preschool classroom. *Journal of Applied Behavior Analysis, 37,* 411–415.

Cooper, H. (1989). Synthesis of research on homework. *Educational Leadership, 47*(3), 85–91.

Cooper, J. O., Heron, T. E., & Heward, W. L. (2007). *Applied behavior analysis* (2nd ed.). Upper Saddle River, NJ: Pearson/Merrill/Prentice Hall.

Corno, L. (1996). Homework is a complicated thing. *Educational Researcher, 25*(8), 27–30.

Covington, M. V. (1992). *Making the grade: A self-worth perspective on motivation and school reform.* Cambridge, England: Cambridge University Press.

Craft, M. A., Alberg, S. R., & Heward, W. L. (1998). Teaching elementary students with developmental disabilities to recruit teacher attention in a general education classroom: Effects on teacher praise and academic productivity. *Journal of Applied Behavior Analysis, 31,* 399–415.

Crone, D. A., & Horner, R. H. (2003). *Building positive behavior support systems in schools: Functional behavioral assessment.* New York, NY: Guilford.

Cuskelly, M., Zhang, A., & Hayes, A. (2003). A mental age-matched comparison study of delay of gratification in children with Down syndrome. *International Journal of Disability, Development and Education, 50,* 239–251.

Deci, E. L., Koestner, R., & Ryan, R. M. (2001). Extrinsic rewards and intrinsic motivation in education: Reconsidered once again. *Review of Educational Research, 71,* 1–27.

Deci, E. L., & Moller, A. C. (2005). The concept of competence: A starting place for understanding intrinsic motivation and self-determined extrinsic motivation. In A. J. Elliot & C. S. Dweck (Eds.), *Handbook of competence and motivation* (pp. 579–597). New York, NY: Guilford.

Deci, E. L., & Ryan, R. M. (1985). *Intrinsic motivation and self-determination in human behavior.* New York, NY: Plenum.

DeVault, G., Krug, C., & Fake, S. (1996, September). Why does Samantha act that way: Positive behavioral support leads to successful inclusion. *Exceptional Parent,* 43–47.

Donaldson, J. M., Vollmer, T. R., Krous, T., Downs, S., & Berard, K. P. (2011). An evaluation of the good behavior game in kindergarten classrooms. *Journal of Applied Behavior Analysis, 44,* 605–609.

Doyle, W. (1990). Classroom management techniques. In O. C. Moles (Ed.), *Student discipline strategies: Research and practice* (pp. 113–127). Albany, NY: State University of New York Press.

Dreikurs, R. (1998). *Maintaining sanity in the classroom: Classroom management techniques* (2nd ed.). Bristol, PA: Hemisphere.

Ebbinghaus, H. (1913). *Memory: A contribution to experimental psychology* (H. A. Ruger & C. E. Bussenius, Trans.). New York, NY: Teachers College, Columbia University. (Original work published 1885)

Eber, L. (2002). Wraparound and positive behavioral interventions and supports in the schools. *Journal of Emotional and Behavioral Disorders, 10,* 171–180.

Elliott, S. N., & Busse, R. T. (1991). Social skills assessment and intervention with children and adolescents. *School Psychology International, 12,* 63–83.

Ellis, E. S., & Friend, P. (1991). Adolescents with learning disabilities. In B. Y. L. Wong (Ed.), *Learning about learning disabilities* (pp. 505–561). San Diego, CA: Academic Press.

Ellis, J., Fitzsimmons, S., & Small-McGinley, J. (2010). Encouraging the discouraged: Students' views for elementary classrooms. In G. S. Goodman (Ed.), *Educational psychology reader: The art and science of how people learn* (pp. 251–272). New York, NY: Peter Lang.

Evertson, C. M., & Weinstein, C. S. (Eds.). (2006). *Handbook of classroom management: Research, practice, and contemporary issues.* Mahwah, NJ: Erlbaum.

Feltz, D. L., Chase, M. A., Moritz, S. E., & Sullivan, P. J. (1999). A conceptual model of coaching efficacy: Preliminary investigation and instrument development. *Journal of Educational Psychology, 91,* 765–776.

Ferster, C. B., & Skinner, B. F. (1957). *Schedules of reinforcement.* Englewood Cliffs, NJ: Prentice Hall.

Fisher, W. W., Rodriguez, N. M., & Owen, T. M. (2013). Functional assessment and treatment of perseverative speech about restricted topics in an adolescent with Asperger syndrome. *Journal of Applied Behavior Analysis, 46,* 307–311.

Flower, A., McKenna, J. W., Bunuan, R. L., Muething, C. S., & Vega, R., Jr. (2014). Effects of the Good Behavior Game on challenging behaviors in school settings. *Review of Educational Research, 84,* 546–571.

Fowler, S. A., & Baer, D. M. (1981). "Do I have to be good all day?" The timing of delayed reinforcement as a factor in generalization. *Journal of Applied Behavior Analysis, 14,* 13–24.

Freeland, J. T., & Noell, G. H. (1999). Maintaining accurate math responses in elementary school students: The effects of delayed intermittent reinforcement and programming common stimuli. *Journal of Applied Behavior Analysis, 32,* 211–215.

Frost, J. L., Shin, D., & Jacobs, P. J. (1998). Physical environments and children's play. In O. N. Saracho & B. Spodek (Eds.), *Multiple perspectives on play in early childhood education* (pp. 255–294). Albany, NY: State University of New York Press.

Fuller, M. L. (2001). Multicultural concerns and classroom management. In C. A. Grant & M. L. Gomez, *Campus and classroom: Making schooling multicultural* (2nd ed., pp. 109–134). Upper Saddle River, NJ: Merrill/Prentice Hall.

Galton, F. (1880). Statistics of mental imagery. *Mind, 5,* 301–318.

Geckeler, A. S., Libby, M. E., Graff, R. B., & Ahearn, W. H. (2000). Effects of reinforcer choice measured in single-operant and concurrent-schedule procedures. *Journal of Applied Behavior Analysis, 33,* 347–351.

Goldstein, S., & Rider, R. (2006). Resilience and the disruptive disorders of childhood. In S. Goldstein & R. B. Brooks (Eds.), *Handbook of resilience in children* (pp. 203–222). New York, NY: Springer.

Gootman, M. E. (1998). Effective in-house suspension. *Educational Leadership, 56*(1), 39–41.

Grauvogel-MacAleese, A. N., & Wallace, M. D. (2010). Use of peer-mediated intervention in children with attention deficit hyperactivity disorder. *Journal of Applied Behavior Analysis, 43,* 547–551.

Green, L., Fry, A. F., & Myerson, J. (1994). Discounting of delayed rewards: A life-span comparison. *Psychological Science, 5,* 33–36.

Greer, B. D., Neidert, P. L., Dozier, C. L., Payne, S. W., Zonneveld, K. L. M., & Harper, A. M. (2013). Functional analysis and treatment of problem behavior in early education classes. *Journal of Applied Behavior Analysis, 46,* 289–295.

Gregory, A., Skiba, R. J., & Noguera, P. A. (2010). The achievement gap and the discipline gap: Two sides of the same coin? *Educational Researcher, 39,* 59–68.

Hall, R. V., Axelrod, S., Foundopoulos, M., Shellman, J., Campbell, R. A., & Cranston, S. S. (1971). The effective use of punishment to modify behavior in the classroom. *Educational Technology, 11*(4), 24–26.

Haring, N. G., & Liberty, K. A. (1990). Matching strategies with performance in facilitating generalization. *Focus on Exceptional Children, 22*(8), 1–16.

Harlow, H. F., & Zimmerman, R. R. (1959). Affectional responses in the infant monkey. *Science, 130,* 421–432.

Harrison, A. M., & Pyles, D. A. (2013). The effects of verbal instruction and shaping to improve tackling by high school football players. *Journal of Applied Behavior Analysis, 46,* 518–522.

Hattie, J., & Gan, M. (2011). Instruction based on feedback. In R. E. Mayer & P. A. Alexander (Eds.), *Handbook of research on learning and instruction* (pp. 249–271). New York, NY: Routledge.

Hattie, J., & Timperley, H. (2007). The power of feedback. *Review of Educational Research, 77,* 81–112.

Hausman, N. L., Ingvarsson, E. T., & Kahng, S. W. (2014). A comparison of reinforcement schedules to increase independent responding in individuals with intellectual disabilities. *Journal of Applied Behavior Analysis, 47,* 155–159.

Heck, A., Collins, J., & Peterson, L. (2001). Decreasing children's risk taking on the playground. *Journal of Applied Behavior Analysis, 34,* 349–352.

Heward, W. L. (2009). *Exceptional children: An introduction to special education* (9th ed.). Upper Saddle River, NJ: Merrill/Pearson Education.

Hidi, S., & Harackiewicz, J. M. (2000). Motivating the academically unmotivated: A critical issue for the 21st century. *Review of Educational Research, 70,* 151–179.

Hine, P., & Fraser, B. J. (2002, April). *Combining qualitative and quantitative methods in a study of Australian students' transition from elementary to high school.* Paper presented at the annual meeting of the American Educational Research Association, New Orleans, LA.

Hobson, P. (2004). *The cradle of thought: Exploring the origins of thinking.* Oxford, England: Oxford University Press.

Hoerger, M. L., & Mace, F. C. (2006). A computerized test of self-control predicts classroom behavior. *Journal of Applied Behavior Analysis, 39,* 147–159.

Hoffman, M. L. (1975). Altruistic behavior and the parent-child relationship. *Journal of Personality and Social Psychology, 31,* 937–943.

Hoffman, M. L. (2000). *Empathy and moral development: Implications for caring and justice.* New York, NY: Cambridge University Press.

Homme, L. E., deBaca, P. C., Devine, J. V., Steinhorst, R., & Rickert, E. J. (1963). Use of the Premack principle in controlling the behavior of nursery school children. *Journal of the Experimental Analysis of Behavior, 6,* 544.

Huff, J. A. (1988). Personalized behavior modification: An in-school suspension program that teaches students how to change. *School Counselor, 35,* 210–214.

Hyman, I., Kay, B., Tabori, A., Weber, M., Mahon, M., & Cohen, I. (2006). Bullying: Theory, research, and interventions. In C. M. Evertson & C. S. Weinstein (Eds.), *Handbook of classroom management: Research, practice, and contemporary issues* (pp. 855–884). Mahwah, NJ: Erlbaum.

Igoa, C. (1995). *The inner world of the immigrant child.* Mahwah, NJ: Erlbaum.

Ihlo, T., & Nantais, M. (2010). Evidence-based interventions within a multi-tier framework for positive behavioral supports. In T. A. Glover & S. Vaughn (Eds.), *The promise of response to intervention: Evaluating current science and practice* (pp. 239–266). New York, NY: Guilford.

James, W. (1890). *The principles of psychology.* New York, NY: Holt.

Jiang, B. (2010). English language learners: Understanding their needs. In G. S. Goodman (Ed.), *Educational psychology reader: The art and science of how people learn* (pp. 179–194). New York, NY: Peter Lang.

Johnson, B. M., Miltenberger, R. G., Knudson, P., Emego-Helm, K., Kelso, P., Jostad, C., & Langley, L. (2006). A preliminary evaluation of two behavioral skills training procedures for teaching abduction-prevention skills to schoolchildren. *Journal of Applied Behavior Analysis, 39,* 25–34.

Johnson, D. W., & Johnson, R. T. (1987). *Learning together and alone: Cooperative, competitive, and individualistic learning* (2nd ed.). Englewood Cliffs, NJ: Prentice Hall.

Jones, M. C. (1924). The elimination of children's fears. *Journal of Experimental Psychology, 7,* 382–390.

Kehle, T. J., Bray, M. A., Theodore, L. A., Jenson, W. R., & Clark, E. (2000). A multi-component intervention designed to reduce disruptive classroom behavior. *Psychology in the Schools, 37,* 475–481.

Kellam, S. G., Rebok, G. W., Ialongo, N., & Mayer, L. S. (1994). The course and malleability of aggressive behavior from early first grade into middle school: Results of a developmental epidemiology-based preventive trial. *Journal of Child Psychology and Psychiatry and Allied Disciplines, 35,* 259–281.

Kelley, M. L., & Carper, L. B. (1988). Home-based reinforcement procedures. In J. C. Witt, S. N. Elliott, & F. M. Gresham (Eds.), *Handbook of behavior therapy in education* (pp. 419–438). New York, NY: Plenum.

Kitayama, S., Duffy, S., & Uchida, Y. (2007). Self as cultural mode of being. In S. Kitayama & D. Cohen (Eds.), *Handbook of cultural psychology* (pp. 136–174). New York, NY: Guilford.

Krumboltz, J. D., & Krumboltz, H. B. (1972). *Changing children's behavior.* Upper Saddle River, NJ: Prentice Hall.

Kulik, J. A., & Kulik, C. C. (1988). Timing of feedback and verbal learning. *Review of Educational Research, 58,* 79–97.

Landau, S., & McAninch, C. (1993). Young children with attention deficits. *Young Children, 48*(4), 49–58.

Landrum, T. J., & Kauffman, J. M. (2006). Behavioral approaches to classroom management. In C. M. Evertson & C. S. Weinstein (Eds.), *Handbook of classroom management: Research, practice, and contemporary issues* (pp. 47–71). Mahwah, NJ: Erlbaum.

Lane, K., Falk, K., & Wehby, J. (2006). Classroom management in special education classrooms and resource rooms. In C. M. Evertson & C. S. Weinstein (Eds.), *Handbook of classroom management: Research, practice, and contemporary issues* (pp. 439–460). Mahwah, NJ: Erlbaum.

Lane, K. L., Menzies, H. M., Bruhn, A. L., & Crnobori, M. (2011). *Managing challenging behaviors in schools: Research-based strategies that work.* New York, NY: Guilford.

Lannie, A. L., & Martens, B. K. (2004). Effects of task difficulty and type of contingency on students' allocation of responding to math worksheets. *Journal of Applied Behavior Analysis, 37,* 53–65.

Lejuez, C. W., Schaal, D. W., & O'Donnell, J. (1998). Behavioral pharmacology and the treatment of substance abuse. In J. J. Plaud & G. H. Eifert (Eds.), *From behavior theory to behavior therapy* (pp. 116–135). Boston, MA: Allyn & Bacon.

Lepper, M. R., & Hodell, M. (1989). Intrinsic motivation in the classroom. In C. Ames & R. Ames (Eds.), *Research on motivation in education: Vol. 3. Goals and cognitions* (pp. 73–105). San Diego, CA: Academic Press.

Lerman, D. C., & Iwata, B. A. (1995). Prevalence of the extinction burst and its attenuation during treatment. *Journal of Applied Behavior Analysis, 28,* 93–94.

Lerman, D. C., & Vorndran, C. M. (2002). On the status of knowledge for using punishment: Implications for treating behavior disorders. *Journal of Applied Behavior Analysis, 35,* 431–464.

Lewis, T. J., Newcomer, L. L., Trussell, R., & Richter, M. (2006). Schoolwide positive behavior support: Building systems to develop and maintain appropriate social behavior. In C. M. Evertson & C. S. Weinstein (Eds.), *Handbook of classroom management: Research, practice, and contemporary issues* (pp. 833–854). Mahwah, NJ: Erlbaum.

Lovitt, T. C., Guppy, T. E., & Blattner, J. E. (1969). The use of free-time contingency with fourth graders to increase spelling accuracy. *Behaviour Research and Therapy, 7,* 151–156.

Mace, F. C., Hock, M. L., Lalli, J. S., West, B. J., Belfiore, P., Pinter, E., & Brown, D. K. (1988). Behavioral momentum in the treatment of noncompliance. *Journal of Applied Behavior Analysis, 21,* 123–141.

Martin, S. S., Brady, M. P., & Williams, R. E. (1991). Effects of toys on the social behavior of preschool children in integrated and nonintegrated groups: Investigation of a setting event. *Journal of Early Intervention, 15,* 153–161.

Maxmell, D., Jarrett, O. S., & Dickerson, C. (1998, April). *Are we forgetting the children's needs? Recess through the children's eyes.* Paper presented at the annual meeting of the American Educational Research Association, San Diego, CA.

McCaslin, M., & Good, T. L. (1996). The informal curriculum. In D. C. Berliner & R. C. Calfee (Eds.), *Handbook of educational psychology* (pp. 622–670). New York, NY: Macmillan.

McClowry, S. G. (1998). The science and art of using temperament as the basis for intervention. *School Psychology Review, 27,* 551–563.

McComas, J. J., Thompson, A., & Johnson, L. (2003). The effects of presession attention on problem behavior maintained by different reinforcers. *Journal of Applied Behavior Analysis, 36,* 297–307.

McGill, P. (1999). Establishing operations: Implications for the assessment, treatment, and prevention of problem behavior. *Journal of Applied Behavior Analysis, 32,* 393–418.

McGinnis, M. A., Houchins-Juárez, N., McDaniel, J. L., & Kennedy, C. H. (2010). Abolishing and establishing operation analyses of social attention as positive reinforcement for problem behavior. *Journal of Applied Behavior Analysis, 43,* 119–123.

Mercer, C. D., & Pullen, P. C. (2005). *Students with learning disabilities* (6th ed.). Upper Saddle River, NJ: Merrill/Prentice Hall.

Meyer, K. A. (1999). Functional analysis and treatment of problem behavior exhibited by elementary school children. *Journal of Applied Behavior Analysis, 32,* 229–232.

Michael, J. (2000). Implications and refinements of the establishing operation concept. *Journal of Applied Behavior Analysis, 33,* 401–410.

Miller, R. R., & Barnet, R. C. (1993). The role of time in elementary associations. *Current Directions in Psychological Science, 2,* 106–111.

Mineka, S., & Zinbarg, R. (2006). A contemporary learning theory perspective on the etiology of anxiety disorders: It's not what you thought it was. *American Psychologist, 61,* 10–26.

Moles, O. C. (Ed.). (1990). *Student discipline strategies: Research and practice.* Albany, NY: State University of New York Press.

Mueller, M. M., Nkosi, A., & Hine, J. F. (2011). Functional analysis in public schools: A summary of 90 functional analyses. *Journal of Applied Behavior Analysis, 44,* 807–818.

Murphy, E. S., McSweeney, F. K., Smith, R. G., & McComas, J. J. (2003). Dynamic changes in reinforcer effectiveness: Theoretical, methodological, and practical implications for applied research. *Journal of Applied Behavior Analysis, 36,* 421–438.

Narciss, S. (2008). Feedback strategies for interactive learning tasks. In J. M. Spector, M. D. Merrill, J. van Merriënboer, & M. P. Driscoll (Eds.), *Handbook of research on educational communications and technology* (3rd ed., pp. 125–143). New York, NY: Erlbaum.

Neef, N. A., Marckel, J., Ferreri, S. J., Bicard, D. F., Endo, S., Aman, M. G., . . . Armstrong, N. (2005). Behavioral assessment of impulsivity: A comparison of children with and without attention deficit hyperactivity disorder. *Journal of Applied Behavior Analysis, 38,* 23–37.

Newquist, M. H., Dozier, C. L., & Neidert, P. L. (2012). A comparison of the effects of brief rules, a timer, and preferred toys on self-control. *Journal of Applied Behavior Analysis, 45,* 497–509.

Nichols, J. D., Ludwin, W. G., & Iadicola, P. (1999). A darker shade of gray: A year-end analysis of discipline and suspension data. *Equity and Excellence in Education, 32*(1), 43–55.

Northup, J., Broussard, C., Jones, K., George, T., Vollmer, T. R., & Herring, M. (1995). The differential effects of teachers and peer attention on the disruptive classroom behavior of three children with a diagnosis of attention deficit hyperactivity disorder. *Journal of Applied Behavior Analysis, 28,* 227–228.

Nucci, L. P. (2001). *Education in the moral domain.* Cambridge, England: Cambridge University Press.

Osher, D., Bear, G. G., Sprague, J. R., & Doyle, W. (2010). How can we improve school discipline? *Educational Researcher, 39,* 48–58.

Parke, R. D. (1974). Rules, roles, and resistance to deviation: Explorations in punishment, discipline, and self-control. In A. Pick (Ed.), *Minnesota Symposia on Child Psychology* (Vol. 8, pp. 111–144). Minneapolis, MN: University of Minnesota Press.

Patton, J. R., Blackbourn, J. M., & Fad, K. S. (1996). *Exceptional individuals in focus* (6th ed.). Upper Saddle River, NJ: Merrill/Prentice Hall.

Pavlov, I. P. (1927). *Conditioned reflexes* (G. V. Anrep, Trans.). London, England: Oxford University Press.

Payne, S. W., & Dozier, C. L. (2013). Positive reinforcement as treatment for problem behavior maintained by negative reinforcement. *Journal of Applied Behavior Analysis, 46,* 699–703.

Pellegrini, A. D., & Bohn, C. M. (2005). The role of recess in children's cognitive performance and school adjustment. *Educational Researcher, 34*(1), 13–19.

Pellegrini, A. D., Huberty, P. D., & Jones, I. (1995). The effects of recess timing on children's playground and classroom behaviors. *American Educational Research Journal, 32,* 845–864.

Perry, D. G., & Perry, L. C. (1983). Social learning, causal attribution, and moral internalization. In J. Bisanz, G. L. Bisanz, & R. Kail (Eds.), *Learning in children: Progress in cognitive development research* (pp. 105–136). New York, NY: Springer-Verlag.

Pfiffner, L. J., Barkley, R. A., & DuPaul, G. J. (2006). Treatment of ADHD in school settings. In R. A. Barkley, *Attention-deficit hyperactivity disorder: A handbook for diagnosis and treatment* (3rd ed., pp. 547–589). New York, NY: Guilford.

Pfiffner, L. J., & O'Leary, S. G. (1993). School-based psychological treatments. In J. L. Matson (Ed.), *Handbook of hyperactivity in children* (pp. 234–255). Boston, MA: Allyn & Bacon.

Pfiffner, L. J., Rosen, L. A., & O'Leary, S. G. (1985). The efficacy of an all-positive approach to classroom management. *Journal of Applied Behavior Analysis, 18,* 257–261.

Phillips, E. L., Phillips, E. A., Fixsen, D. L., & Wolf, M. M. (1971). Achievement place: Modification of the behaviors of predelinquent boys within a token economy. *Journal of Applied Behavior Analysis, 4,* 45–59.

Piersel, W. C. (1987). Basic skills education. In C. A. Maher & S. G. Forman (Eds.), *A behavioral approach to education of children and youth* (pp. 39–74). Mahwah, NJ: Erlbaum.

Pigott, H. E., Fantuzzo, J. W., & Clement, P. W. (1986). The effects of reciprocal peer tutoring and group contingencies on the academic performance of elementary school children. *Journal of Applied Behavior Analysis, 19,* 93–98.

Piirto, J. (1999). *Talented children and adults: Their development and education* (2nd ed.). Upper Saddle River, NJ: Merrill/Prentice Hall.

Pintrich, P. R., & Schunk, D. H. (2002). *Motivation in education: Theory, research, and applications* (2nd ed.). Upper Saddle River, NJ: Merrill/Prentice Hall.

Pipkin, C. S. P., & Vollmer, T. R. (2009). Applied implications of reinforcement history effects. *Journal of Applied Behavior Analysis, 42,* 83–103.

Pipkin, C. S., Vollmer, T. R., & Sloman, K. N. (2010). Effects of treatment integrity failures during differential reinforcement of alternative behavior: A translational model. *Journal of Applied Behavior Analysis, 43,* 47–70.

Powers, M. D., & Crowel, R. L. (1985). The educative effects of positive practice overcorrection: Acquisition, generalization, and maintenance. *School Psychology Review, 14,* 360–372.

Premack, D. (1959). Toward empirical behavior laws: I. Positive reinforcement. *Psychological Review, 66,* 219–233.

Premack, D. (1963). Rate differential reinforcement in monkey manipulation. *Journal of Experimental Analysis of Behavior, 6,* 81–89.

Pressley, M., with McCormick, C. B. (1995). *Advanced educational psychology for educators, researchers, and policymakers.* New York, NY: HarperCollins.

Rachlin, H. (1991). *Introduction to modern behaviorism* (3rd ed.). New York, NY: Freeman.

Reeve, J. (2006). Extrinsic rewards and inner motivation. In C. M. Evertson & C. S. Weinstein (Eds.), *Handbook of classroom management: Research, practice, and contemporary issues* (pp. 645–664.). Mahwah, NJ: Erlbaum.

Rescorla, R. A. (1967). Pavlovian conditioning and its proper control procedures. *Psychological Review, 74,* 71–80.

Rescorla, R. A. (1988). Pavlovian conditioning: It's not what you think it is. *American Psychologist, 43,* 151–160.

Ricciardi, J. N., Luiselli, J. K., & Camare, M. (2006). Shaping approach responses as intervention for specific phobia in a child

with autism. *Journal of Applied Behavior Analysis, 39,* 445–448.

Rimm, D. C., & Masters, J. C. (1974). *Behavior therapy: Techniques and empirical findings.* San Diego, CA: Academic Press.

Rispoli, M., O'Reilly, M., Lang, R., Machalicek, W., Davis, T., Lancioni, G., & Sigafoos, J. (2011). Effects of motivating operations on problem and academic behavior in classrooms. *Journal of Applied Behavior Analysis, 44,* 187–192.

Robinson, S. L., & Griesemer, S. M. R. (2006). Helping individual students with problem behavior. In C. M. Evertson & C. S. Weinstein (Eds.), *Handbook of classroom management: Research, practice, and contemporary issues* (pp. 787–802). Mahwah, NJ: Erlbaum.

Rodriguez, N. M., Thompson, R. H., & Baynham, T. Y. (2010). Assessment of the relative effects of attention and escape on noncompliance. *Journal of Applied Behavior Analysis, 43,* 143–147.

Rortvedt, A. K., & Miltenberger, R. G. (1994). Analysis of a high-probability instructional sequence and time-out in the treatment of child noncompliance. *Journal of Applied Behavior Analysis, 27,* 327–330.

Rotenberg, K. J., & Mayer, E. V. (1990). Delay of gratification in Native and White children: A cross-cultural comparison. *International Journal of Behavioral Development, 13,* 23–30.

Rothbart, M. K. (2011). *Becoming who we are: Temperament and personality in development.* New York, NY: Guilford.

Ruef, M. B., Higgins, C., Glaeser, B., & Patnode, M. (1998). Positive behavioral support: Strategies for teachers. *Intervention in School and Clinic, 34*(1), 21–32.

Sanders, M. G. (1996). Action teams in action: Interviews and observations in three schools in the Baltimore School–Family–Community Partnership Program. *Journal of Education for Students Placed at Risk, 1,* 249–262.

Schunk, D. H., & Pajares, F. (2005). Competence perceptions and academic functioning. In A. J. Elliot & C. S. Dweck (Eds.), *Handbook of competence and motivation* (pp. 85–104). New York, NY: Guilford.

Shabani, D. B., Katz, R. C., Wilder, D. A., Beauchamp, K., Taylor, C. R., & Fischer, K. J. (2002). Increasing social initiations in children with autism: Effects of a tactile prompt. *Journal of Applied Behavior Analysis, 35,* 79–83.

Shoda, Y., Mischel, W., & Peake, P. K. (1990). Predicting adolescent cognitive and self-regulatory competencies from preschool delay of gratification: Identifying diagnostic conditions. *Developmental Psychology, 26,* 978–986.

Shute, V. J. (2008). Focus on formative feedback. *Review of Educational Research, 78,* 153–189.

Skinner, B. F. (1938). *The behavior of organisms: An experimental analysis.* Englewood Cliffs, NJ: Prentice Hall.

Skinner, B. F. (1953). *Science and human behavior.* New York, NY: Macmillan.

Skinner, B. F. (1954). The science of learning and the art of teaching. *Harvard Educational Review, 24,* 86–97.

Skinner, B. F. (1968). *The technology of teaching.* New York, NY: Appleton-Century-Crofts.

Skinner, B. F., & Epstein, R. (1982). *Skinner for the classroom.* Champaign, IL: Research Press.

Slavin, R. E. (1983). When does cooperative learning increase student achievement? *Psychological Bulletin, 94,* 429–445.

Sran, S. K., & Borrero, J. C. (2010). Assessing the value of choice in a token system. *Journal of Applied Behavior Analysis, 43,* 553–557.

Steinberg, L., Graham, S., O'Brien, L., Woolard, J., Cauffman, E., & Banich, M. (2009). Age differences in future orientation and delay discounting. *Child Development, 80,* 28–44.

Stokes, J. V., Luiselli, J. K., & Reed, D. D. (2010). A behavioral intervention for teaching tackling skills to high school football athletes. *Journal of Applied Behavior Analysis, 43,* 509–512.

Stokes, J. V., Luiselli, J. K., Reed, D. D., & Fleming, R. K. (2010). Behavioral coaching to improve offensive line pass-blocking skills of high school football athletes. *Journal of Applied Behavior Analysis, 43,* 463–472.

Sullivan, J. S. (1989). Planning, implementing, and maintaining an effective in-school suspension program. *Clearing House, 62,* 409–410.

Taylor, J. C., & Romanczyk, R. G. (1994). Generating hypotheses about the function of student problem behavior by observing teacher behavior. *Journal of Applied Behavior Analysis, 27,* 251–265.

Tiger, J. H., Hanley, G. P., & Hernandez, E. (2006). An evaluation of the value of choice with preschool children. *Journal of Applied Behavior Analysis, 39,* 1–16.

Tunstall, P., & Gipps, C. (1996). Teacher feedback to young children in formative assessment: A typology. *British Educational Research Journal, 22,* 389–404.

Turnbull, A. P., Turnbull, R., & Wehmeyer, M. L. (2010). *Exceptional lives: Special education in today's schools* (6th ed.). Upper Saddle River, NJ: Merrill.

Ulke-Kurcuoglu, B., & Kircaali-Iftar, G. (2010). A comparison of the effects of providing activity and material choice to children with autism spectrum disorders. *Journal of Applied Behavior Analysis, 43,* 717–721.

Urdan, T., & Mestas, M. (2006). The goals behind performance goals. *Journal of Educational Psychology, 98,* 354–365.

Van Camp, C. M., Lerman, D. C., Kelley, M. E., Roane, H. S., Contrucci, S. A., & Vorndran, C. M. (2000). Further analysis of idiosyncratic antecedent influences during the assessment and treatment of problem behavior. *Journal of Applied Behavior Analysis, 33,* 207–221.

Van Houten, R., Nau, P., MacKenzie-Keating, S., Sameoto, D., & Colavecchia, B. (1982). An analysis of some variables influencing the effectiveness of reprimands. *Journal of Applied Behavior Analysis, 15,* 65–83.

Vollmer, T. R., & Hackenberg, T. D. (2001). Reinforcement contingencies and social reinforcement: Some reciprocal relations between basic and applied research. *Journal of Applied Behavior Analysis, 34,* 241–253.

Wang, M.-T., & Holcombe, R. (2010). Adolescents' perceptions of school environment, engagement, and academic achievement in middle school. *American Educational Research Journal, 47,* 633–662.

Warren, J. S., Bohanon-Edmonson, H. M., Turnbull, A. P., Sailor, W., Wickham, D., Griggs, P., & Beech, S. E. (2006). School-wide positive behavior support: Addressing behavior problems that impeded student learning. *Educational Psychology Review, 18,* 187–198.

Watson, J. B., & Rayner, R. (1920). Conditioned emotional reactions. *Journal of Experimental Psychology, 3,* 1–14.

Wheeler, J. J., & Richey, D. D. (2014). *Behavior management: Principles and practice of positive behavioral supports* (3rd ed.). Upper Saddle River, NJ: Pearson.

White, A. G., & Bailey, J. S. (1990). Reducing disruptive behaviors of elementary physical education students with sit and watch. *Journal of Applied Behavior Analysis, 23,* 353–359.

Wilkinson, L. A. (2003). Using behavioral consultation to reduce challenging behavior in the classroom. *Preventing School Failure, 47,* 100–105.

Wolpe, J., & Plaud, J. J. (1997). Pavlov's contributions to behavior therapy: The obvious and the not so obvious. *American Psychologist, 52,* 966–972.

Zambo, D., & Brem, S. K. (2004). Emotion and cognition in students who struggle to read: New insights and ideas. *Reading Psychology, 25,* 1–16.

CHAPTER 10

Abrami, P. C., Venkatesh, V., Meyer, E. J., & Wade, C. A. (2013). Using electronic portfolios to foster literacy and self-regulated learning skills in elementary students. *Journal of Educational Psychology, 105*(4), 1188–1209.

Aikins, J. W., & Litwack, S. D. (2011). Prosocial skills, social competence, and popularity. In A. H. N. Cillessen, D. Schwartz, & L. Mayeux (Eds.), *Popularity in the peer system* (pp. 140–162). New York, NY: Guilford.

Anderman, L. H., & Klassen, R. M. (2016). *Teacher cognition and affect in the classroom.* In L. Corno & E. M. Anderman (Eds.), *Handbook of educational psychology* (Vol. 3, pp. 402–414). Mahwah, NJ: Lawrence Erlbaum.

Anderson, C. A., Berkowitz, L., Donnerstein, E., Huesmann, L. R., Johnson, J. D., Linz, D., et al. (2003). The influence of media violence on youth. *Psychological Science in the Public Interest, 4,* 81–110.

Anderson, D. R. (2003). The Children's Television Act: A public policy that benefits children. *Applied Developmental Psychology, 24,* 337–340.

Anderson, L. H. (1999). *Speak.* New York, NY: Puffin Books.

Anderson, R. C., Nguyen-Jahiel, K., McNurlen, B., Archodidou, A., Kim, S.-Y., Reznitskaya, A., et al. (2001). The snowball phenomenon: Spread of ways of talking and ways of thinking across groups of children. *Cognition and Instruction, 19,* 1–46.

Arbib, M. (Ed.). (2005). *Action to language via the mirror neuron system.* New York, NY: Cambridge University Press.

Asaro-Saddler, K., & Bak, N. (2014). Persuasive writing and self-regulation training for writers with autism spectrum disorders. *Journal of Special Education, 48*(2), 92–105.

Assor, A., & Connell, J. P. (1992). The validity of students' self-reports as measures of performance affecting self-appraisals. In D. H. Schunk & J. L. Meece (Eds.), *Student perceptions in the classroom* (pp. 25–46). Mahwah, NJ: Erlbaum.

Bandura, A. (1965). Influence of models' reinforcement contingencies on the acquisition of imitative responses. *Journal of Personality and Social Psychology, 1,* 589–595.

Bandura, A. (1977). *Social learning theory.* Upper Saddle River, NJ: Prentice Hall.

Bandura, A. (1982). Self-efficacy mechanism in human agency. *American Psychologist, 37,* 122–147.

Bandura, A. (1986). *Social foundations of thought and action: A social cognitive theory.* Upper Saddle River, NJ: Prentice Hall.

Bandura, A. (1989). Human agency in social cognitive theory. *American Psychologist, 44,* 1175–1184.

Bandura, A. (1997). *Self-efficacy: The exercise of control.* New York, NY: Freeman.

Bandura, A. (2000). Exercise of human agency through collective efficacy. *Current Directions in Psychological Science, 9,* 75–78.

Bandura, A. (2008). Toward an agentic theory of the self. In H. W. Marsh, R. G. Craven, & D. M. McInerney (Eds.), *Self-processes, learning, and enabling human potential* (pp. 15–49). Charlotte, NC: Information Age.

Bandura, A., Barbaranelli, C., Caprara, G. V., & Pastorelli, C. (2001). Self-efficacy beliefs as shapers of children's aspirations and career trajectories. *Child Development, 72,* 187–206.

Bandura, A., Ross, D., & Ross, S. A. (1961). Transmission of aggression through imitation of aggressive models. *Journal of Abnormal and Social Psychology, 63,* 575–582.

Bandura, A., Ross, D., & Ross, S. A. (1963). Imitation of film-mediated aggressive models. *Journal of Abnormal and Social Psychology, 66,* 3–11.

Bates, J. E., & Pettit, G. S. (2007). Temperament, parenting, and socialization. In J. E. Grusec & P. D. Hastings (Eds.), *Handbook of socialization: Theory and research* (pp. 153–177). New York, NY: Guilford.

Bear, P., Torgerson, C., & Dubois-Gerchak, K. (2010). A positive procedure to increase compliance in the general education classroom for a student with serious emotional disorders. In G. S. Goodman (Ed.), *Educational psychology*

reader: The art and science of how people learn (pp. 75–87). New York, NY: Peter Lang.

Beaulieu, L., Hanley, G. P., & Roberson, A. A. (2013). Effects of peer mediation on preschoolers' compliance and compliance precursors. *Journal of Applied Behavior Analysis, 46*(3), 555–567.

Beirne-Smith, M., Patton, J. R., & Kim, S. H. (2006). *Mental retardation: An introduction to intellectual disabilities* (7th ed.). Upper Saddle River, NJ: Merrill/Prentice Hall.

Belfiore, P. J., & Hornyak, R. S. (1998). Operant theory and application to self-monitoring in adolescents. In D. H. Schunk & B. J. Zimmerman (Eds.), *Self-regulated learning: From teaching to self-reflective practice* (pp. 184–202). New York, NY: Guilford.

Berardi-Coletta, B., Buyer, L. S., Dominowski, R. L., & Rellinger, E. A. (1995). Metacognition and problem solving: A process-oriented approach. *Journal of Experimental Psychology: Learning, Memory, and Cognition, 21,* 205–223.

Berger. J.-L., & Karabenick, S. A. (2010, April–May). *Changes and reciprocal causation of expectancy–value and learning strategy use in math over one term of high school.* Paper presented at the annual meeting of the American Educational Research Association, Denver, CO.

Biemiller, A., Shany, M., Inglis, A., & Meichenbaum, D. (1998). Factors influencing children's acquisition and demonstration of self-regulation on academic tasks. In D. H. Schunk & B. J. Zimmerman (Eds.), *Self-regulated learning: From teaching to self-reflective practice* (pp. 203–224). New York, NY: Guilford.

Blair, C., & Razza, R. P. (2007). Relating effortful control, executive function, and false belief understanding to emerging math and literacy ability in kindergarten. *Child Development, 78,* 647–663.

Blanchard, F. A., Lilly, T., & Vaughn, L. A. (1991). Reducing the expression of racial prejudice. *Psychological Science, 2,* 101–105.

Bong, M., & Skaalvik, E. M. (2003). Academic self-concept and self-efficacy: How different are they really? *Educational Psychology Review, 15,* 1–40.

Boyer, E., Miltenberger, R. G., Batsche, C., & Fogel, V. (2009). Video modeling by experts with video feedback to enhance gymnastics skills. *Journal of Applied Behavior Analysis, 42,* 855–860.

Braaksma, M. A. H., Rijlaarsdam, G., & van den Bergh, H. (2002). Observational learning and the effects of model-observer similarity. *Journal of Educational Psychology, 94,* 405–415.

Braun, L. J. (1998). *The cat who saw stars.* New York, NY: G. P. Putnam's Sons.

Bronson, M. B. (2000). *Self-regulation in early childhood: Nature and nurture.* New York, NY: Guilford.

Brunstein, J. C., & Glaser, C. (2011). Testing a path-analytic mediation model of how self-regulated writing strategies improve fourth graders' composition skills: A randomized controlled trial. *Journal of Educational Psychology, 103*(4), 922–938.

Bryan, J. H. (1975). Children's cooperation and helping behaviors. In E. M. Hetherington (Ed.), *Review of child development research* (Vol. 5, pp. 127–181). Chicago, IL: University of Chicago Press.

Buckley, M., & Saarni, C. (2009). Emotion regulation: Implications for positive youth development. In R. Gilman, E. S. Huebner, & M. J. Furlong (Eds.), *Handbook of positive psychology in schools* (pp. 107–118). New York, NY: Routledge.

Bushman, B. J., & Anderson, C. A. (2001). Media violence and the American public: Scientific facts versus media misinformation. *American Psychologist, 56*, 477–489.

Butler, D. L., & Schnellert, L. (2015). Success for students with learning disabilities: What does self-regulation have to do with it? In T. Cleary & T. Cleary (Eds.), *Self-regulated learning interventions with at-risk youth: Enhancing adaptability, performance, and well-being* (pp. 89–111). Washington, DC: American Psychological Association.

Butler, D. L., & Winne, P. H. (1995). Feedback and self-regulated learning: A theoretical synthesis. *Review of Educational Research, 65*, 245–281.

Butler, R. (1990). The effects of mastery and competitive conditions on self-assessment at different ages. *Child Development, 61*, 201–210.

Butler, R. (1998a). Age trends in the use of social and temporal comparison for self-evaluation: Examination of a novel developmental hypothesis. *Child Development, 69*, 1054–1073.

Butler, R. (1998b). Determinants of help seeking: Relations between perceived reasons for classroom help-avoidance and help-seeking behaviors in an experimental context. *Journal of Educational Psychology, 90*, 630–644.

Butler, R. (2005). Competence assessment, competence, and motivation between early and middle childhood. In A. J. Elliot & C. S. Dweck (Eds.), *Handbook of competence and motivation* (pp. 202–221). New York, NY: Guilford.

Carnagey, N. L., Anderson, C. A., & Bartholow, B. D. (2007). Media violence and social neuroscience: New questions and new opportunities. *Current Directions in Psychological Science, 16*, 178–182.

Carter, K., & Doyle, W. (2006). Classroom management in early childhood and elementary classrooms. In C. M. Evertson & C. S. Weinstein (Eds.), *Handbook of classroom management: Research, practice, and contemporary issues* (pp. 373–406). Mahwah, NJ: Erlbaum.

Carver, C. S., & Scheier, M. F. (1990). Origins and functions of positive and negative affect: A control-process view. *Psychological Review, 97*, 19–35.

Casella, R. (2001a). The cultural foundations of peer mediation: Beyond a behaviorist model of urban school conflict. In J. N. Burstyn, G. Bender, R. Casella, H. W. Gordon, D. P. Guerra, K. V. Luschen, … K. M. Williams (Eds.), *Preventing violence in schools: A challenge to American democracy* (pp. 159–179). Mahwah, NJ: Erlbaum.

Casey, W. M., & Burton, R. V. (1982). Training children to be consistently honest through verbal self-instructions. *Child Development, 53*, 911–919.

Castagno, A. E., & Brayboy, B. M. J. (2008). Culturally responsive schooling for Indigenous youth: A review of the literature. *Review of Educational Research, 78*, 941–993.

Chen, J., & Morris, D. (2008, March). *Sources of science self-efficacy beliefs among high school students in different tracking levels.* Paper presented at the annual meeting of the American Educational Research Association, New York, NY.

Chen, P. P. (2003). Exploring the accuracy and predictability of the self-efficacy beliefs of seventh-grade mathematics students. *Learning and Individual Differences, 14*, 79–92.

Chen, X., & Wang, L. (2010). China. In M. H. Bornstein (Ed.), *Handbook of cultural developmental science* (pp. 429–444). New York, NY: Psychology Press.

Coch, D., Dawson, G., & Fischer, K. W. (Eds.). (2007). *Human behavior, learning, and the developing brain: Atypical development.* New York, NY: Guilford.

Cohen, R. L. (1989). Memory for action events: The power of enactment. *Educational Psychology Review, 1*, 57–80.

Cole, D. A., Martin, J. M., Peeke, L. A., Seroczynski, A. D., & Fier, J. (1999). Children's over- and underestimation of academic competence: A longitudinal study of gender differences, depression, and anxiety. *Child Development, 70*, 459–473.

Cole, P. M., Tamang, B. L., & Shrestha, S. (2006). Cultural variations in the socialization of young children's anger and shame. *Child Development, 77*, 1237–1251.

Cooney, C. (1997). *Wanted.* New York, NY: Scholastic.

Cooper, J. O., Heron, T. E., & Heward, W. L. (2007). *Applied behavior analysis* (2nd ed.). Upper Saddle River, NJ: Pearson/Merrill/Prentice Hall.

Corno, L., Cronbach, L. J., Kupermintz, H., Lohman, D. F., Mandinach, E. B., Porteus, A. W., & Talbert, J. E. (2002). *Remaking the concept of aptitude: Extending the legacy of Richard E. Snow.* Mahwah, NJ: Erlbaum.

Corno, L., & Mandinach, E. B. (2004). What we have learned about student engagement in the past twenty years. In D. M. McInerney & S. Van Etten (Eds.), *Big theories revisited* (pp. 299–328). Greenwich, CT: Information Age.

Cosden, M., Morrison, G., Albanese, A. L., & Macias, S. (2001). When homework is not home work: After-school programs for homework assistance. *Educational Psychologist, 36*, 211–221.

Covington, M. V. (1992). *Making the grade: A self-worth perspective on motivation and school reform.*

Cambridge, England: Cambridge University Press.

Cunningham, C. E., & Cunningham, L. J. (2006). Student-mediated conflict resolution programs. In R. A. Barkley, *Attention-deficit hyperactivity disorder: A handbook for diagnosis and treatment* (3rd ed., pp. 590–607). New York, NY: Guilford.

Damon, W. (1988). *The moral child: Nurturing children's natural moral growth.* New York, NY: Free Press.

Dapretto, M., Davies, M. S., Pfeifer, J. H., Scott, A. A., Sigman, M., Bookheimer, S. Y., et al. (2006). Understanding emotions in others: Mirror neuron dysfunction in children with autism spectrum disorders. *Nature Neuroscience, 9*(1), 28–30.

Deci, E. L., & Ryan, R. M. (1985). *Intrinsic motivation and self-determination in human behavior.* New York, NY: Plenum.

Deci, E. L., & Ryan, R. M. (1992). The initiation and regulation of intrinsically motivated learning and achievement. In A. K. Boggiano & T. S. Pittman (Eds.), *Achievement and motivation: A social-developmental perspective* (pp. 9–36). Cambridge, England: Cambridge University Press.

Desoete, A., Roeyers, H., & De Clercq, A. (2003). Can offline metacognition enhance mathematical problem solving? *Journal of Educational Psychology, 95*, 188–200.

Deutsch, M. (1993). Educating for a peaceful world. *American Psychologist, 48*, 510–517.

Dijkstra, P., Kuyper, H., van der Werf, G., Buunk, A. P., & van der Zee, Y. G. (2008). Social comparison in the classroom: A review. *Review of Educational Research, 78*, 828–879.

Duckworth, A. L., & Seligman, M. E. P. (2005). Self-discipline outdoes IQ in predicting academic performance of adolescents. *Psychological Science, 16*, 939–944.

Dunning, D., Heath, C., & Suls, J. M. (2004). Flawed self-assessment: Implications for health, education, and the workplace. *Psychological Science in the Public Interest, 5*, 69–106.

DuPaul, G., & Hoff, K. (1998). Reducing disruptive behavior in general education classrooms: The use of self-management strategies. *School Psychology Review, 27*, 290–304.

Dweck, C. S. (2000). *Self-theories: Their role in motivation, personality, and development.* Philadelphia: Psychology Press.

Ebesutani, C., Kim, E., & Young, J. (2014). The role of violence exposure and negative affect in understanding child and adolescent aggression. *Child Psychiatry and Human Development, 45*(6), 736–745.

Eccles, J. S., Wigfield, A., & Schiefele, U. (1998). Motivation to succeed. In W. Damon (Series Ed.) & N. Eisenberg (Vol. Ed.), *Handbook of child psychology: Vol. 3. Social, emotional, and personality development* (5th ed., pp. 1017–1095). New York, NY: Wiley.

Eilam, B. (2001). Primary strategies for promoting homework performance. *American Educational Research Journal, 38*, 691–725.

Eisenberg, N., Vaughan, J., & Hofer, C. (2009). Temperament, self-regulation, and peer social competence. In K. H. Rubin, W. M. Bukowski, & B. Laursen (Eds.), *Handbook of peer interactions, relationships, and groups* (pp. 473–489). New York, NY: Guilford.

Elliott, R., & Vasta, R. (1970). The modeling of sharing: Effects associated with vicarious reinforcement, symbolization, age, and generalization. *Journal of Experimental Child Psychology, 10*, 8–15.

Elliott, S. N., & Busse, R. T. (1991). Social skills assessment and intervention with children and adolescents. *School Psychology International, 12*, 63–83.

Ellis, E. S., & Friend, P. (1991). Adolescents with learning disabilities. In B. Y. L. Wong (Ed.), *Learning about learning disabilities* (pp. 505–561). San Diego, CA: Academic Press.

Falco, L. D. (2008, March). *Improving middle school students' self-beliefs for learning mathematics: A Skill Builders intervention follow-up.* Paper presented at the annual meeting of the American Educational Research Association, New York, NY.

Fast, L. A., Lewis, J. L., Bryant, M. J., Bocian, K. A., Cardullo, R. A., Rettig, M., & Hammond, K. A. (2010). Does math self-efficacy mediate the effect of the perceived classroom environment on standardized math test performance? *Journal of Educational Psychology, 102*(3), 729–740.

Féry, Y.-A., & Morizot, P. (2000). Kinesthetic and visual image in modeling closed motor skills: The example of the tennis serve. *Perceptual and Motor Skills, 90*, 707–722.

Fitzsimmons, G. M., & Finkel, E. J. (2010). Interpersonal influences on self-regulation. *Current Directions in Psychological Science, 19*, 101–105.

Fletcher, J. M., Lyon, G. R., Fuchs, L. S., & Barnes, M. A. (2007). *Learning disabilities: From identification to intervention.* New York, NY: Guilford.

Fletcher, K. L., & Cassady, J. C. (2010). Overcoming academic anxieties: Promoting effective coping and self-regulation strategies. In J. C. Cassady (Ed.), *Anxiety in schools: The causes, consequences, and solutions for academic anxieties* (pp. 177–200). New York, NY: Peter Lang.

Ford, M. E. (1992). *Motivating humans: Goals, emotions, and personal agency beliefs.* Newbury Park, CA: Sage.

Försterling, F., & Morgenstern, M. (2002). Accuracy of self-assessment and task performance: Does it pay to know the truth? *Journal of Educational Psychology, 94*, 576–585.

Friedel, J. M., Cortina, K. S., Turner, J. C., & Midgley, C. (2010). Changes in efficacy beliefs in mathematics across the transition to middle school: Examining the effects of perceived teacher and parent goal emphases. *Journal of Educational Psychology, 102*(1), 102–114.

Friedlander, L. J., Connolly, J. A., Pepler, D. J., & Craig, W. M. (2013). Extensiveness and persistence of aggressive media exposure as longitudinal risk factors for teen dating violence. *Psychology of Violence, 3*(4), 310–322.

Fries, S., Dietz, F., & Schmid, S. (2008). Motivational interference in learning: The impact of leisure alternatives on subsequent self-regulation. *Contemporary Educational Psychology, 33*, 119–133.

Gallese, V., Gernsbacher, M. A., Heyes, C., Hickok, G., & Iacoboni, M. (2011). Mirror neuron forum. *Perspectives on Psychological Science, 6*, 369–407.

Geiger, K. B., LeBlanc, L. A., Dillon, C. M., & Bates, S. L. (2010). An evaluation of preference for video George and in vivo modeling. *Journal of Applied Behavior Analysis, 43*, 279–283.

Gerst, M. S. (1971). Symbolic coding processes in observational learning. *Journal of Personality and Social Psychology, 19*, 7–17.

Gladding, S. T., & Villalba, J. (2014). Imitation, impersonation, and transformation: Using male role models in films to promote maturity. *Journal of Counseling & Development, 92*(1), 114–121.

Goddard, R. D. (2001). Collective efficacy: A neglected construct in the study of schools and student achievement. *Journal of Educational Psychology, 93*, 467–476.

Goddard, R. D., Hoy, W. K., & Woolfolk Hoy, A. (2000). Collective teacher efficacy: Its meaning, measure, and impact on student achievement. *American Educational Research Journal, 37*, 479–507.

Grace, D. M., David, B. J., & Ryan, M. K. (2008). Investigating preschoolers' categorical thinking about gender through imitation, attention, and the use of self-categories. *Child Development, 79*, 1928–1941.

Graham, S., & Golen, S. (1991). Motivational influences on cognition: Task involvement, ego involvement, and depth of information processing. *Journal of Educational Psychology, 83*, 187–194.

Graham, S., & Harris, K. R. (1996). Addressing problems in attention, memory, and executive functioning. In G. R. Lyon & N. A. Krasnegor (Eds.), *Attention, memory, and executive function* (pp. 349–365). Baltimore, MD: Brookes.

Greene, J. A., & Azevedo, R. (2009). A macro-level analysis of SRL processes and their relations to the acquisition of a sophisticated mental model of a complex system. *Contemporary Educational Psychology, 34*, 18–29.

Guerra, N. G., Huesmann, L. R., & Spindler, A. (2003). Community violence exposure, social cognition, and aggression among urban elementary school children. *Child Development, 74*, 1561–1576.

Guskey, T. R. (1988). Teacher efficacy, self-concept, and attitudes toward the implementation of instructional innovation. *Teaching and Teacher Education, 4*, 63–69.

Hampson, S. E. (2008). Mechanisms by which childhood personality traits influence adult well-being. *Current Directions in Psychological Science, 17*, 264–268.

Harnishfeger, K. K. (1995). The development of cognitive inhibition: Theories, definitions, and research evidence. In F. N. Dempster & C. J. Brainerd (Eds.), *Interference and inhibition in cognition* (pp. 175–204). San Diego, CA: Academic Press.

Harris, K. R. (1982). Cognitive-behavior modification: Application with exceptional students. *Focus on Exceptional Children, 15*, 1–16.

Harris, K. R. (1986). Self-monitoring of attentional behavior versus self-monitoring of productivity: Effects of on-task behavior and academic response rate among learning disabled children. *Journal of Applied Behavior Analysis, 19*, 417–423.

Harris, K. R., Graham, S., Brindle, M., & Sandmel, K. (2009). Metacognition and children's writing. In D. J. Hacker, J. Dunlosky, & A. C. Graesser (Eds.), *Handbook of metacognition in education* (pp. 131–153). New York, NY: Routledge.

Harris, P. L., & Want, S. (2005). On learning what not to do: The emergence of selective imitation in tool use by young children. In S. Hurley & N. Chater (Eds.), *Perspectives on imitation: From neuroscience to social science: Vol. 2. Imitation, human development, and culture* (pp. 149–162). Cambridge, MA: MIT Press.

Harter, S. (1999). *The construction of the self: A developmental perspective.* New York, NY: Guilford.

Hatzigeorgiadis, A., Zourbanos, N., Galanis, E., & Theodorakis, Y. (2011). Self-talk and sports performance: A meta-analysis. *Perspectives on Psychological Science, 6*, 348–356.

Hawkins, F. P. L. (1997). *Journey with children: The autobiography of a teacher.* Niwot, CO: University Press of Colorado.

Hayes, S. C., Rosenfarb, I., Wulfert, E., Munt, E. D., Korn, Z., & Zettle, R. D. (1985). Self-reinforcement effects: An artifact of social standard setting? *Journal of Applied Behavior Analysis, 18*, 201–214.

Hickey, D. J. (2011). Participation by design: Improving individual motivation by looking beyond it. In D. M. McInerney, R. A. Walker, & G. A. D. Liem (Eds.), *Sociocultural theories of learning and motivation: Looking back, looking forward* (pp. 137–161). Charlotte, NC: Information Age.

Hitchcock, C., Dowrick, P. W., & Prater, M. A. (2003). Video self-modeling interventions in school-based settings: A review. *Remedial and Special Education, 24*, 36–46.

Hofer, M. (2010). Adolescents' development of individual interests: A product of multiple goal regulation? *Educational Psychologist, 45*, 149–166.

Hunter, S., Hurley, R. A., & Taber, K. H. (2013). A look inside the mirror neuron system. *Journal of Neuropsychiatry and Clinical Neurosciences, 25*(3), 170–175.

Jiang, F., & Guo, B. (2002). From personal efficacy to collective efficacy: The new development of Bandura's theory of self-efficacy. *Psychological Science* [China], *25*(1), 114–115.

Joët, G., Usher, E. L., & Bressoux, P. (2011). Sources of self-efficacy: An investigation of elementary school students in France. *Journal of Educational Psychology, 103*(3), 649–663.

Johnson, D. W., & Johnson, R. T. (1996). Conflict resolution and peer mediation programs in elementary and secondary schools: A review of the research. *Review of Educational Research, 66,* 459–506.

Johnson, D. W., & Johnson, R. T. (2006). Conflict resolution, peer mediation, and peacemaking. In C. M. Evertson & C. S. Weinstein (Eds.), *Handbook of classroom management: Research, practice, and contemporary issues* (pp. 803–832). Mahwah, NJ: Erlbaum.

Johnson, D. W., & Johnson, R. T. (2009a). An educational psychology success story: Social interdependence theory and cooperative learning. *Educational Researcher, 38,* 365–379.

Johnson, D. W., Johnson, R., Dudley, B., Ward, M., & Magnuson, D. (1995). The impact of peer mediation training on the management of school and home conflicts. *American Educational Research Journal, 32,* 829–844.

Jones, M. H., Estell, D. B., & Alexander, J. M. (2008). Friends, classmates, and self-regulated learning: Discussions with peers inside and outside the classroom. *Metacognition Learning, 3,* 1–15.

Jones, S. S. (2007). Imitation in infancy: The development of mimicry. *Psychological Science, 18,* 593–599.

Jordan, A. B. (2003). Children remember prosocial program lessons but how much are they learning? *Applied Developmental Psychology, 24,* 341–345.

Kehle, T. J., Clark, E., Jenson, W. R., & Wampold, B. (1986). Effectiveness of the self-modeling procedure with behaviorally disturbed elementary age children. *School Psychology Review, 15,* 289–295.

Kitsantas, A., Dabbagh, N., Hiller, S. E., & Mandell, B. (2015). Learning technologies as supportive contexts for promoting college student self-regulated learning. In T. Cleary & T. Cleary (Eds.), *Self-regulated learning interventions with at-risk youth: Enhancing adaptability, performance, and well-being* (pp. 277–294). Washington, DC: American Psychological Association.

Kitsantas, A., Zimmerman, B. J., & Cleary, T. (2000). The role of observation and emulation in the development of athletic self-regulation. *Journal of Educational Psychology, 92,* 811–817.

Klassen, R. (2002). Writing in early adolescence: A review of the role of self-efficacy beliefs. *Educational Psychology Review, 14,* 173–203.

Klassen, R. M., & Chiu, M. M. (2010). Effects on teachers' self-efficacy and job satisfaction: Teacher gender, years of experience, and job stress. *Journal of Educational Psychology, 102*(3), 741–756.

Klassen, R. M., & Tze, V. M. C. (2014). Teachers' self-efficacy, personality, and teaching effectiveness: A meta-analysis. *Educational Research Review, 12,* 59–76.

Klassen, R. M., & Usher, E. L. (2010). Self-efficacy in educational settings: Recent research and emerging directions. In S. Karabenick & T. C. Urdan (Eds.), *Advances in motivation and achievement: Vol. 16A. The decade ahead: Theoretical perspectives on motivation and achievement* (pp. 1–33). Bingley, England: Emerald Group Publishing.

Kochanska, G., Gross, J. N., Lin, M.-H., & Nichols, K. E. (2002). Guilt in young children: Development, determinants, and relations with a broader system of standards. *Child Development, 73,* 461–482.

Krebs, D. L. (2008). Morality: An evolutionary account. *Perspectives on Psychological Science, 3,* 149–172.

Kuhl, J. (1985). Volitional mediators of cognition-behavior consistency: Self-regulatory processes and actions versus state orientation. In J. Kuhl & J. Beckmann (Eds.), *Action control: From cognition to behavior* (pp. 101–128). Berlin, Germany: Springer-Verlag.

Larson, R. W., & Brown, J. R. (2007). Emotional development in adolescence: What can be learned from a high school theater program? *Child Development, 78,* 1083–1099.

Leaper, C., & Friedman, C. K. (2007). The socialization of gender. In J. E. Grusec & P. D. Hastings (Eds.), *Handbook of socialization: Theory and research* (pp. 561–587). New York, NY: Guilford.

Lee, J., & Shute, V. J. (2010). Personal and social-contextual factors in K–12 academic performance: An integrative perspective on student learning. *Educational Psychologist, 45,* 185–202.

Lee, W., Lee, M. J., & Bong, M. (2014). Testing interest and self-efficacy as predictors of academic self-regulation and achievement. *Contemporary Educational Psychology, 39*(2), 86–99.

Lenroot, R. K., Gogtay, N., Greenstein, D. K., Wells, E. M., Wallace, G. L., Clasen, L. S., et al. (2007). Sexual dimorphism of brain development trajectories during childhood and adolescence. *NeuroImage, 36,* 1065–1073.

Lewis, M. D., & Stieben, J. (2004). Emotion regulation in the brain: Conceptual issues and directions for developmental research. *Child Development, 75,* 371–376.

Liem, A. D., Lau, S., & Nie, Y. (2008). The role of self-efficacy, task value, and achievement goals in predicting learning strategies, task disengagement, peer relationship, and achievement outcome. *Contemporary Educational Psychology, 33,* 486–512.

Liew, J., McTigue, E. M., Barrois, L., & Hughes, J. N. (2008). Adaptive and effortful control and academic self-efficacy beliefs on literacy and math achievement: A longitudinal study on 1st through 3rd graders. *Early Childhood Research Quarterly, 23,* 515–526.

Locke, E. A., & Latham, G. P. (1990). *A theory of goal setting and task performance.* Upper Saddle River, NJ: Prentice Hall.

Lodewyk, K. R., & Winne, P. H. (2005). Relations among the structure of learning tasks, achievement, and changes in self-efficacy in secondary students. *Journal of Educational Psychology, 97,* 3–12.

Lowry, R., Sleet, D., Duncan, C., Powell, K., & Kolbe, L. (1995). Adolescents at risk for violence. *Educational Psychology Review, 7,* 7–39.

Mace, F. C., Belfiore, P. J., & Shea, M. C. (1989). Operant theory and research on self-regulation. In B. J. Zimmerman & D. H. Schunk (Eds.), *Self-regulated learning and academic achievement: Theory, research, and practice* (pp. 27–50). New York, NY: Springer-Verlag.

Marchand, G., & Skinner, E. A. (2007). Motivational dynamics of children's academic help-seeking and concealment. *Journal of Educational Psychology, 99,* 65–82.

Marsh, H. W., Xu, M., & Martin, A. J. (2012). Self-concept: A synergy of theory, method, and application. In K. R. Harris, S. Graham, T. Urdan, C. B. McCormick, G. M. Sinatra, J. Sweller, ... J. Sweller (Eds.), *APA educational psychology handbook, Vol 1: Theories, constructs, and critical issues* (pp. 427–458). Washington, DC: American Psychological Association.

Martin, C. L., & Ruble, D. (2004). Children's search for gender cues: Cognitive perspectives on gender development. *Current Directions in Psychological Science, 13,* 67–70.

Mathews, J. (1988). *Escalante: The best teacher in America.* New York, NY: Henry Holt.

Matthews, J. S., Ponitz, C. C., & Morrison, F. J. (2009). Early gender differences in self-regulation and academic achievement. *Journal of Educational Psychology, 101,* 689–704.

Mayer, R. E. (2011b). Instruction based on visualizations. In R. E. Mayer & P. A. Alexander (Eds.), *Handbook of research on learning and instruction* (pp. 427–445). New York, NY: Routledge.

McCaslin, M., & Good, T. L. (1996). The informal curriculum. In D. C. Berliner & R. C. Calfee (Eds.), *Handbook of educational psychology* (pp. 622–670). New York, NY: Macmillan.

McCaslin, M., & Hickey, D. T. (2001). Self-regulated learning and academic achievement: A Vygotskian view. In B. Zimmerman & D. Schunk (Eds.), *Self-regulated learning and academic achievement: Theory, research, and practice* (2nd ed., pp. 227–252). Mahwah, NJ: Erlbaum.

McDaniel, L. (1997). *For better, for worse, forever.* New York, NY: Bantam.

McMillan, J. H. (2010). The practical implications of educational aims and contexts for formative assessment. In H. L. Andrade & G. J. Cizek (Eds.), *Handbook of formative assessment* (pp. 41–58). New York, NY: Routledge.

Mega, C., Ronconi, L., & De Beni, R. (2014). What makes a good student? How emotions, self-regulated learning, and motivation contribute to academic achievement. *Journal of Educational Psychology, 106*(1), 121–131.

Meichenbaum, D. (1977). *Cognitive-behavior modification: An integrative approach.* New York, NY: Plenum.

Meichenbaum, D. (1985). Teaching thinking: A cognitive-behavioral perspective. In S. F. Chipman, J. W. Segal, & R. Glaser (Eds.), *Thinking and learning skills: Vol. 2. Research and open questions* (pp. 407–426). Mahwah, NJ: Erlbaum.

Meichenbaum, D., & Goodman, J. (1971). Training impulsive children to talk to themselves: A means of developing self-control. *Journal of Abnormal Psychology, 77,* 115–126.

Meltzer, L. (Ed.). (2007). *Executive function in education: From theory to practice.* New York, NY: Guilford.

Meltzer, L., Pollica, L. S., & Barzillai, M. (2007). Executive function in the classroom: Embedding strategy instruction into daily teaching practices. In L. Meltzer (Ed.), *Executive function in education: From theory to practice* (pp. 165–193). New York, NY: Guilford.

Meltzoff, A. N. (2005). Imitation and other minds: The "like me" hypothesis. In S. Hurley & N. Chater (Eds.), *Perspectives on imitation: From neuroscience to social science* (pp. 55–77). Cambridge, MA: MIT Press.

Menéndez, R. (Director). (1988). *Stand and deliver* [Motion picture]. United States: Warner Studios.

Menesini, E., Codecasa, E., Benelli, B., & Cowie, H. (2003). Enhancing children's responsibility to take action against bullying: Evaluation of a befriending intervention in Italian middle schools. *Aggressive Behavior, 29*(1), 10–14.

Mercer, C. D., & Pullen, P. C. (2005). *Students with learning disabilities* (6th ed.). Upper Saddle River, NJ: Merrill/Prentice Hall.

Middleton, M., & Abrams, E. (2004, April). *The effect of pre-service teachers' sense of efficacy on their self-reflective practice.* Paper presented at the Annual Meeting of the American Educational Research Association, San Diego, CA.

Miller, C., Doering, A., & Scharber, C. (2010). No such thing as failure, only feedback: Designing innovative opportunities for e-assessment and technology-mediated feedback. *Journal of Interactive Learning Research, 21*(2), 197–224.

Miller, R. B., & Brickman, S. J. (2004). A model of future-oriented motivation and self-regulation. *Educational Psychology Review, 16,* 9–33.

Miller, S. D., Heafner, T., Massey, D., & Strahan, D. B. (2003, April). *Students' reactions to teachers' attempts to create the necessary conditions to promote the acquisition of self-regulation skills.* Paper presented at the annual meeting of the American Educational Research Association, Chicago, IL.

Mineka, S., & Zinbarg, R. (2006). A contemporary learning theory perspective on the etiology of anxiety disorders: It's not what you thought it was. *American Psychologist, 61,* 10–26.

Mitchem, K. J., & Young, K. R. (2001). Adapting self-management programs for classwide use. *Remedial and Special Education, 22*(2), 75–88.

Moore, S., & Rosenthal, D. (2006). *Sexuality in adolescence: Current trends.* London, England: Routledge.

Morelli, G. A., & Rothbaum, F. (2007). Situating the child in context: Attachment relationships and self-regulation in different cultures. In S. Kitayama & D. Cohen (Eds.), *Handbook of cultural psychology* (pp. 500–527). New York, NY: Guilford.

Moreno, R. (2006). Learning in high-tech and multimedia environments. *Current Directions in Psychological Science, 15,* 63–67.

Narciss, S. (2008). Feedback strategies for interactive learning tasks. In J. M. Spector, M. D. Merrill, J. van Merriënboer, & M. P. Driscoll (Eds.), *Handbook of research on educational communications and technology* (3rd ed., pp. 125–143). New York, NY: Erlbaum.

Nelson, J. R., Smith, D. J., Young, R. K., & Dodd, J. M. (1991). A review of self-management outcome research conducted with students who exhibit behavioral disorders. *Behavioral Disorders, 16,* 169–179.

Newman, R. S. (2008). Adaptive and nonadaptive help seeking with peer harassment: An integrative perspective of coping and self-regulation. *Educational Psychologist, 43,* 1–15.

Nielsen, M., & Tomaselli, K. (2010). Overimitation in Kalahari bushman children and the origins of human cultural cognition. *Psychological Science, 21,* 729–736.

Nikopoulos, C. K., & Keenan, M. (2004). Effects of video modeling on social initiations by children with autism. *Journal of Applied Behavior Analysis, 37,* 93–96.

Nolen, S. B. (1996). Why study? How reasons for learning influence strategy selection. *Educational Psychology Review, 8,* 335–355.

Nucci, L. P. (2001). *Education in the moral domain.* Cambridge, England: Cambridge University Press.

Obama, B. H. (2004). *Dreams from my father: A story of race and inheritance* (rev. ed.). New York, NY: Three Rivers Press.

Pajares, F. (2009). Toward a positive psychology of academic motivation: The role of self-efficacy beliefs. In R. Gilman, E. S. Huebner, & M. J. Furlong (Eds.), *Handbook of positive psychology in schools* (pp. 149–160). New York, NY: Routledge.

Pang, V. O. (1995). Asian Pacific American students: A diverse and complex population. In J. A. Banks & C. A. M. Banks (Eds.), *Handbook of research on multicultural education* (pp. 412–424). New York, NY: Macmillan.

Paris, S. G., & Ayres, L. R. (1994). *Becoming reflective students and teachers with portfolios and authentic assessment.* Washington, DC: American Psychological Association.

Paris, S. G., & Paris, A. H. (2001). Classroom applications of research on self-regulated learning. *Educational Psychologist, 36,* 89–101.

Pea, R. D. (1993). Practices of distributed intelligence and designs for education. In G. Salomon (Ed.), *Distributed cognitions: Psychological and educational considerations* (pp. 47–87). Cambridge, England: Cambridge University Press.

Pekrun, R. (2006). The control-value theory of achievement emotions: Assumptions, corollaries, and implications for educational research and practice. *Educational Psychology Review, 18,* 315–341.

Perry, N. E. (1998). Young children's self-regulated learning and contexts that support it. *Journal of Educational Psychology, 90,* 715–729.

Perry, N. E., VandeKamp, K. O., Mercer, L. K., & Nordby, C. J. (2002). Investigating teacher-student interactions that foster self-regulated learning. *Educational Psychologist, 37,* 5–15.

Pietsch, J., Walker, R., & Chapman, E. (2003). The relationship among self-concept, self-efficacy, and performance in mathematics during secondary school. *Journal of Educational Psychology, 95,* 589–603.

Piirto, J. (1999). *Talented children and adults: Their development and education* (2nd ed.). Upper Saddle River, NJ: Merrill/Prentice Hall.

Plante, I., & O'Keefe, P. A. (2010, April–May). *The relation among achievement goals and expectancy-value variables in predicting grades and career intentions.* Paper presented at the annual meeting of the American Educational Research Association, Denver, CO.

Plavnick, J. B., Ferreri, S. J., & Maupin, A. N. (2010). The effects of self-monitoring on the procedural integrity of a behavioral intervention for young children with developmental disabilities. *Journal of Applied Behavior Analysis, 43,* 315–320.

Poche, C., Yoder, P., & Miltenberger, R. (1988). Teaching self-protection to children using television techniques. *Journal of Applied Behavior Analysis, 21,* 253–261.

Posner, M. I., & Rothbart, M. K. (2007). *Educating the human brain.* Washington, DC: American Psychological Association.

Powers, L. E., Sowers, J. A., & Stevens, T. (1995). An exploratory, randomized study of the impact of mentoring on the self-efficacy and community-based knowledge of adolescents with severe physical challenges. *Journal of Rehabilitation, 61*(1), 33–41.

Prater, M. A., Carter, N., Hitchcock, C., & Dowrick, P. (2011). Video self-monitoring to improve academic performance: A literature review. *Psychology in the Schools, 49*(1), 71–81.

Raver, C. C. (2014). Children's emotion regulation in classroom settings. In S. H. Landry, C. L. Cooper, S. H. Landry, & C. L. Cooper (Eds.), *Wellbeing in children and families* (Vol. I, pp. 37–53). New York, NY: Wiley-Blackwell.

Reid, R., Trout, A. L., & Schartz, M. (2005). Self-regulation interventions for children with attention deficit/hyperactivity disorder. *Exceptional Children, 71,* 361–377.

Richards, J. M. (2004). The cognitive consequences of concealing feelings. *Current Directions in Psychological Science, 13,* 131–134.

Rosenthal, T. L., Alford, G. S., & Rasp, L. M. (1972). Concept attainment, generalization, and retention through observation and verbal coding. *Journal of Experimental Child Psychology, 13,* 183–194.

Rosenthal, T. L., & Bandura, A. (1978). Psychological modeling: Theory and practice. In S. L. Garfield & A. E. Begia (Eds.), *Handbook of psychotherapy and behavior change: An empirical analysis* (2nd ed., pp. 621–658). New York, NY: Wiley.

Rosenthal, T. L., & Zimmerman, B. J. (1978). *Social learning and cognition.* San Diego, CA: Academic Press.

Rothbart, M. K. (2011). *Becoming who we are: Temperament and personality in development.* New York, NY: Guilford.

Rothbart, M. K., Sheese, B. E., & Posner, M. I. (2007). Executive attention and effortful control: Linking temperament, brain networks, and genes. *Child Development Perspectives, 1,* 2–7.

Rushton, J. P. (1980). *Altruism, socialization, and society.* Upper Saddle River, NJ: Prentice Hall.

Sands, D. J., & Wehmeyer, M. L. (Eds.). (1996). *Self-determination across the life span: Independence and choice for people with disabilities.* Baltimore, MD: Brookes.

Sasso, G. M., & Rude, H. A. (1987). Unprogrammed effects of training high-status peers to interact with severely handicapped children. *Journal of Applied Behavior Analysis, 20,* 35–44.

Schneider, W. (2010). Metacognition and memory development in childhood and adolescence. In H. S. Waters & W. Schneider (Eds.), *Metacognition, strategy use, and instruction* (pp. 54–81). New York, NY: Guilford.

Schraw, G., & Moshman, D. (1995). Metacognitive theories. *Educational Psychology Review, 7,* 351–371.

Schumaker, J. B., & Hazel, J. S. (1984). Social skill assessment and training for the learning disabled: Who's on first and what's on second? (Pt. 1). *Journal of Learning Disabilities, 17,* 422–431.

Schunk, D. H. (1983). Developing children's self-efficacy and skills: The roles of social comparative information and goal setting. *Contemporary Educational Psychology, 8,* 76–86.

Schunk, D. H. (1984). Enhancing self-efficacy and achievement through rewards and goals: Motivational and informational effects. *Journal of Educational Research, 78*(1), 29–34.

Schunk, D. H. (1987). Peer models and children's behavioral change. *Review of Educational Research, 57,* 149–174.

Schunk, D. H. (1989a). Self-efficacy and achievement behaviors. *Educational Psychology Review, 1,* 173–208.

Schunk, D. H. (1989b). Self-efficacy and cognitive skill learning. In C. Ames & R. Ames (Eds.), *Research on motivation in education: Vol. 3. Goals and cognitions* (pp. 13–44). San Diego, CA: Academic Press.

Schunk, D. H. (1989c). Social cognitive theory and self-regulated learning. In B. J.

Zimmerman & D. H. Schunk (Eds.), *Self-regulated learning and academic achievement: Theory, research, and practice* (pp. 83–110). New York, NY: Springer-Verlag.

Schunk, D. H. (1998). Teaching elementary students to self-regulate practice of mathematical skills with modeling. In D. H. Schunk & B. J. Zimmerman (Eds.), *Self-regulated learning: From teaching to self-reflective practice* (pp. 137–159). New York, NY: Guilford.

Schunk, D. H., & Hanson, A. R. (1985). Peer models: Influence on children's self-efficacy and achievement. *Journal of Educational Psychology, 77,* 313–322.

Schunk, D. H., Hanson, A. R., & Cox, P. D. (1987). Peer-model attributes and children's achievement behaviors. *Journal of Educational Psychology, 79,* 54–61.

Schunk, D. H., & Pajares, F. (2004). Self-efficacy in education revisited: Empirical and applied evidence. In D. M. McInerney & S. Van Etten (Eds.), *Big theories revisited* (pp. 115–138). Greenwich, CT: Information Age.

Schunk, D. H., & Pajares, F. (2005). Competence perceptions and academic functioning. In A. J. Elliot & C. S. Dweck (Eds.), *Handbook of competence and motivation* (pp. 85–104). New York, NY: Guilford.

Schunk, D. H., & Swartz, C. W. (1993). Goals and progress feedback: Effects on self-efficacy and writing achievement. *Contemporary Educational Psychology, 18,* 337–354.

Schunk, D. H., & Zimmerman, B. J. (1997). Social origins of self-regulatory competence. *Educational Psychologist, 32,* 195–208.

Shih, S.-S., & Alexander, J. M. (2000). Interacting effects of goal setting and self- or other-referenced feedback on children's development of self-efficacy and cognitive skill within the Taiwanese classroom. *Journal of Educational Psychology, 92,* 536–543.

Shute, V. J. (2008). Focus on formative feedback. *Review of Educational Research, 78,* 153–189.

Silk, J. S., Steinberg, L., & Morris, A. S. (2003). Adolescents' emotion regulation in daily life: Links to depressive symptoms and problem behavior. *Child Development, 74,* 1869–1880.

Sinatra, G. M., & Mason, L. (2008). Beyond knowledge: Learner characteristics influencing conceptual change. In S. Vosniadou (Ed.), *International handbook on conceptual change* (pp. 560–582). New York, NY: Routledge.

Skaalvik, E. M., & Skaalvik, S. (2008). Teacher self-efficacy: Conceptual analysis and relations with teacher burnout and perceived school context. In H. W. Marsh, R. G. Craven, & D. M. McInerney (Eds.), *Self-processes, learning, and enabling human potential* (pp. 223–247). Charlotte, NC: Information Age.

Slavin, R. E. (2011). Instruction based on cooperative learning. In R. E. Mayer & P. A. Alexander (Eds.), *Handbook of research on learning and instruction* (pp. 344–360). New York, NY: Routledge.

Smith, D. J., Young, K. R., West, R. P., Morgan, R. P., & Rhode, G. (1988). Reducing the

disruptive behavior of junior high school students: A classroom self-management procedure. *Behavioral Disorders, 13,* 231–239.

Smith, K. A., Shepley, S. B., Alexander, J. L., Davis, A., & Ayres, K. M. (2015). Self-instruction using mobile technology to learn functional skills. *Research in Autism Spectrum Disorders, 11,* 93–100.

Sørlie, M-A., & Torsheim, T. (2011). Multilevel analysis of the relationship between teacher collective efficacy and problem behaviour in school. *School Effectiveness and School Improvement: An International Journal of Research, Policy and Practice, 22,* 175–191.

Spaulding, C. L. (1992). *Motivation in the classroom.* New York, NY: McGraw-Hill.

Steinberg, L. (2009). Should the science of adolescent brain development inform public policy? *American Psychologist, 64,* 739–750.

Stevenson, H. C., & Fantuzzo, J. W. (1986). The generality and social validity of a competency-based self-control training intervention for underachieving students. *Journal of Applied Behavior Analysis, 19,* 269–272.

Stipek, D. J. (1996). Motivation and instruction. In D. C. Berliner & R. C. Calfee (Eds.), *Handbook of educational psychology* (pp. 85–113). New York, NY: Macmillan.

Stoeber, J., Schneider, N., Hussain, R., & Matthews, K. (2014). Perfectionism and negative affect after repeated failure: Anxiety, depression, and anger. *Journal of Individual Differences, 35*(2), 87–94.

Stright, A. D., Neitzel, C., Sears, K. G., & Hoke-Sinex, L. (2001). Instruction begins in the home: Relations between parental instruction and children's self-regulation in the classroom. *Journal of Educational Psychology, 93,* 456–466.

Suina, J. H., & Smolkin, L. B. (1994). From natal culture to school culture to dominant society culture: Supporting transitions for Pueblo Indian students. In P. M. Greenfield & R. R. Cocking (Eds.), *Cross-cultural roots of minority child development* (pp. 115–130). Mahwah, NJ: Erlbaum.

Sullivan, J. R., & Conoley, J. C. (2004). Academic and instructional interventions with aggressive students. In J. C. Conoley & A. P. Goldstein (Eds.), *School violence intervention* (2nd ed., pp. 235–255). New York, NY: Guilford.

Sweeny, K., Carroll, P. J., & Shepperd, J. A. (2006). Is optimism always best? Future outlooks and preparedness. *Current Directions in Psychological Science, 15,* 302–306.

Thomas, J. W. (1993b). Promoting independent learning in the middle grades: The role of instructional support practices. *Elementary School Journal, 93,* 575–591.

Trautwein, U., Lüdtke, O., Kastens, C., & Köller, O. (2006). Effort on homework in grades 5–9: Development, motivational antecedents, and the association with effort on classwork. *Child Development, 77,* 1094–1111.

Trommsdorff, G. (2009). Culture and development of self-regulation. *Social and Personality Psychology Compass, 3*(5), 687–701.

Tschannen-Moran, M., Woolfolk Hoy, A., & Hoy, W. K. (1998). Teacher efficacy: Its meaning and measure. *Review of Educational Research*, 68, 202–248.

Turnbull, A. P., Turnbull, R., & Wehmeyer, M. L. (2010). *Exceptional lives: Special education in today's schools* (6th ed.). Upper Saddle River, NJ: Merrill.

Usher, E. L. (2009). Sources of middle school students' self-efficacy in mathematics: A qualitative investigation. *American Educational Research Journal*, 46, 275–314.

Usher, E. L., & Pajares, F. (2008). Sources of self-efficacy in school: Critical review of the literature and future directions. *Review of Educational Research*, 78, 751–796.

Usher, E. L., & Pajares, F. (2009). Sources of self-efficacy in mathematics: A validation study. *Contemporary Educational Psychology*, 34, 89–101.

Valentine, J. C., DuBois, D. L., & Cooper, H. (2004). The relation between self-beliefs and academic achievement: A meta-analytic review. *Educational Psychologist*, 39, 111–133.

Valiente, C., Lemery-Calfant, K., Swanson, J., & Reiser, M. (2008). Prediction of children's academic competence from their effortful control, relationships, and classroom participation. *Journal of Educational Psychology*, 100, 67–77.

van den Broek, P., Lorch, R. F., Jr., Linderholm, T., & Gustafson, M. (2001). The effects of readers' goals on inference generation and memory for texts. *Memory and Cognition*, 29, 1081–1087.

Veenstra, R., Lindenberg, S., Huitsing, G., Sainio, M., & Salmivalli, C. (2014). The role of teachers in bullying: The relation between antibullying attitudes, efficacy, and efforts to reduce bullying. *Journal of Educational Psychology*, 106(4), 1135–1143.

Velanova, K., Wheeler, M. E., & Luna, B. (2008). Maturational changes in anterior cingulate and frontoparietal recruitment support the development of error processing and inhibitory control. *Cerebral Cortex*, 18, 2505–2522.

Vintere, P., Hemmes, N. S., Brown, B. L., & Poulson, C. L. (2004). Gross-motor skill acquisition by preschool dance students under self-instruction procedures. *Journal of Applied Behavior Analysis*, 37, 305–322.

Volet, S., Vaura, M., & Salonen, P. (2009). Self- and social regulation in learning contexts: An integrative perspective. *Educational Psychologist*, 44, 215–226.

Vye, N. J., Schwartz, D. L., Bransford, J. D., Barron, B. J., Zech, L., & The Cognition and Technology Group at Vanderbilt. (1998). SMART environments that support monitoring, reflection, and revision. In D. J. Hacker, J. Dunlosky, & A. C. Graesser (Eds.), *Metacognition in educational theory and practice* (pp. 305–346). Mahwah, NJ: Erlbaum.

Vygotsky, L. S. (1986). *Thought and language* (rev. ed; A. Kozulin, Ed. and Trans.). Cambridge,

MA: MIT Press. (Original work published 1934)

Walker, E., Shapiro, D., Esterberg, M., & Trotman, H. (2010). Neurodevelopment and schizophrenia: Broadening the focus. *Current Directions in Psychological Science*, 19, 204–208.

Wang, J., & Lin, E. (2005). Comparative studies on U.S. and Chinese mathematics learning and the implications for standards-based mathematics teaching reform. *Educational Researcher*, 34(5), 3–13.

Wang, M.-T., & Holcombe, R. (2010). Adolescents' perceptions of school environment, engagement, and academic achievement in middle school. *American Educational Research Journal*, 47, 633–662.

Ware, H., & Kitsantas, A. (2007). Teacher and collective efficacy beliefs as predictors of professional commitment. *Journal of Educational Research*, 100, 303–310.

Webber, J., & Plotts, C. A. (2008). *Emotional and behavioral disorders: Theory and practice* (5th ed.). Boston, MA: Allyn & Bacon.

Webber, J., Scheuermann, B., McCall, C., & Coleman, M. (1993). Research on self-monitoring as a behavior management technique in special education classrooms: A descriptive review. *Remedial and Special Education*, 14(2), 38–56.

Wehmeyer, M. L., Agran, M., Hughes, C., Martin, J., Mithaug, D. E., & Palmer, S. (2007). *Promoting self-determination in students with intellectual and developmental disabilities.* New York, NY: Guilford.

Weissberg, R. P. (1985). Designing effective social problem-solving programs for the classroom. In B. H. Schneider, K. H. Rubin, & J. E. Ledingham (Eds.), *Children's peer relations: Issues in assessment and intervention* (pp. 225–242). New York, NY: Springer-Verlag.

Wigfield, A., & Wagner, A. L. (2005). Competence, motivation, and identity development during adolescence. In A. J. Elliot & C. S. Dweck (Eds.), *Handbook of competence and motivation* (pp. 222–239). New York, NY: Guilford.

Williams, K. M. (2001b). What derails peer mediation? In J. N. Burstyn, G. Bender, R. Casella, H. W. Gordon, D. P. Guerra, K. V. Luschen, R. Stevens, & K. M. Williams, *Preventing violence in schools: A challenge to American democracy* (pp. 199–208). Mahwah, NJ: Erlbaum.

Williams, T., & Williams, K. (2010). Self-efficacy and performance in mathematics: Reciprocal determinism in 33 nations. *Journal of Educational Psychology*, 102, 453–456.

Wilson, B. L., & Corbett, H. D. (2001). *Listening to urban kids: School reform and the teachers they want.* Albany, NY: State University of New York Press.

Winne, P. H. (1995). Inherent details in self-regulated learning. *Educational Psychologist*, 30, 173–187.

Winne, P. H., & Hadwin, A. F. (1998). Studying as self-regulated learning. In D. J. Hacker,

J. Dunlosky, & A. C. Graesser (Eds.), *Metacognition in educational theory and practice* (pp. 277–304). Mahwah, NJ: Erlbaum.

Winters, F. I., Greene, J. A., & Costich, C. M. (2008). Self-regulation of learning within computer-based learning environments: A critical analysis. *Educational Psychology Review*, 20, 429–444.

Wisner Fries, A. B., & Pollak, S. D. (2007). Emotion processing and the developing brain. In D. Coch, K. W. Fischer, & G. Dawson (Eds.), *Human behavior, learning, and the developing brain: Typical development* (pp. 329–361). New York, NY: Guilford.

Wolters, C. A. (1998). Self-regulated learning and college students' regulation of motivation. *Journal of Educational Psychology*, 90, 224–235.

Wolters, C. A. (2003). Regulation of motivation: Evaluating an underemphasized aspect of self-regulated learning. *Educational Psychologist*, 38, 189–205.

Wolters, C. A., & Rosenthal, H. (2000). The relation between students' motivational beliefs and their use of motivational regulation strategies. *International Journal of Educational Research*, 33, 801–820.

Wong, B. Y. L., Hoskyn, M., Jai, D., Ellis, P., & Watson, K. (2008). The comparative efficacy of two approaches to teaching sixth graders opinion essay writing. *Contemporary Educational Psychology*, 33, 757–784.

Yell, M. L., Robinson, T. R., & Drasgow, E. (2001). Cognitive behavior modification. In T. J. Zirpoli & K. J. Melloy, *Behavior management: Applications for teachers* (3rd ed., pp. 200–246). Upper Saddle River, NJ: Merrill/Prentice Hall.

Zeldin, A. L., & Pajares, F. (2000). Against the odds: Self-efficacy beliefs of women in mathematical, scientific, and technological careers. *American Educational Research Journal*, 37, 215–246.

Ziegler, S. G. (1987). Effects of stimulus cueing on the acquisition of groundstrokes by beginning tennis players. *Journal of Applied Behavior Analysis*, 20, 405–411.

Zimmerman, B. J. (1998). Developing self-fulfilling cycles of academic regulation: An analysis of exemplary instructional models. In D. H. Schunk & B. J. Zimmerman (Eds.), *Self-regulated learning: From teaching to self-reflective practice* (pp. 1–19). New York, NY: Guilford.

Zimmerman, B. J. (2004). Sociocultural influence and students' development of academic self-regulation: A social-cognitive perspective. In D. M. McInerney & S. Van Etten (Eds.), *Big theories revisited* (pp. 139–164). Greenwich, CT: Information Age.

Zimmerman, B. J. (2013). From cognitive modeling to self-regulation: A social cognitive career path. *Educational Psychologist*, 48(3), 135–147.

Zimmerman, B. J., & Campillo, M. (2003). Motivating self-regulated problem solvers. In J. E. Davidson & R. J. Sternberg (Eds.), *The psychology of problem solving* (pp. 233–262).

Cambridge, England: Cambridge University Press.

Zimmerman, B. J., & Kitsantas, A. (2005). The hidden dimension of personal competence: Self-regulated learning and practice. In A. J. Elliot & C. S. Dweck (Eds.), *Handbook of competence and motivation* (pp. 509–526). New York, NY: Guilford.

Zimmerman, B. J., & Labuhn, A. S. (2012). Self-regulation of learning: Process approaches to personal development. In K. R. Harris, S. Graham, T. Urdan, C. B. McCormick, G. M. Sinatra, J. Sweller, ... J. Sweller (Eds.), *APA educational psychology handbook, Vol 1: Theories, constructs, and critical issues* (pp. 399–425). Washington, DC: American Psychological Association.

Zimmerman, B. J., & Moylan, A. R. (2009). Self-regulation: Where metacognition and motivation intersect. In D. J. Hacker, J. Dunlosky, & A. C. Graesser (Eds.), *Handbook of metacognition in education* (pp. 299–315). New York, NY: Routledge.

Zimmerman, B. J., & Risemberg, R. (1997). Self-regulatory dimensions of academic learning and motivation. In G. D. Phye (Ed.), *Handbook of academic learning: Construction of knowledge* (pp. 106–125). San Diego, CA: Academic Press.

Zusho, A., & Barnett, P. A. (2011). Personal and contextual determinants of ethnically diverse female high school students' patterns of academic help seeking and help avoidance in English and mathematics. *Contemporary Educational Psychology, 36*, 152–164.

CHAPTER 11

Ablard, K. E., & Lipschultz, R. E. (1998). Self-regulated learning in high-achieving students: Relations to advanced reasoning, achievement goals, and gender. *Journal of Educational Psychology, 90*, 94–101.

Adam, J., Shirako, A., & Maddux, W. W. (2010). Cultural variance in the interpersonal effects of anger in negotiations. *Psychological Science, 21*, 882–889.

Adolphs, R., & Damasio, A. R. (2001). The interaction of affect and cognition: A neurobiological perspective. In J. P. Forgas (Ed.), *Handbook of affect and social cognition* (pp. 27–49). Mahwah, NJ: Erlbaum.

Ahmed, W., van der Werf, G., Kuyper, H., & Minnaert, A. (2013). Emotions, self-regulated learning, and achievement in mathematics: A growth curve analysis. *Journal of Educational Psychology, 105*(1), 150–161.

Ainley, M. (2006). Connecting with learning: Motivation, affect, and cognition in interest processes. *Educational Psychology Review, 18*, 391–405.

Ainley, M., & Ainley, J. (2011). Student engagement with science in early adolescence: The contribution of enjoyment to students' continuing interest in learning about science. *Contemporary Educational Psychology, 36*, 4–12.

Alexander, E. S. (2008). *How to hope: A model of the thoughts, feelings, and behaviors involved in transcending challenge and uncertainty.* Saarbrücken, Germany: VDM Verlag.

Alexander, J. M., Johnson, K. E., Leibham, M. E., & Kelley, K. (2008). The development of conceptual interests in young children. *Cognitive Development, 23*, 324–334.

Alexander, P. A., Kulikowich, J. M., & Schulze, S. K. (1994). How subject-matter knowledge affects recall and interest. *American Educational Research Journal, 31*, 313–337.

Alim, H. S. (2007). "The Whig party don't exist in my hood": Knowledge, reality, and education in the hip hop nation. In H. S. Alim & J. Baugh (Eds.), *Talkin Black talk: Language, education, and social change* (pp. 15–29). New York, NY: Teachers College Press.

Amabile, T. M., & Hennessey, B. A. (1992). The motivation for creativity in children. In A. K. Boggiano & T. S. Pittman (Eds.), *Achievement and motivation: A social-developmental perspective* (pp. 54–74). Cambridge, England: Cambridge University Press.

Ames, C. (1992). Classrooms: Goals, structures, and student motivation. *Journal of Educational Psychology, 84*, 261–271.

Anderman, E. M. (1998). The middle school experience: Effects on the math and science achievement of adolescents with LD. *Journal Of Learning Disabilities, 31*(2), 128–138.

Anderman, E. M. (2002). School effects on psychological outcomes during adolescence. *Journal of Educational Psychology, 94*(4), 795–809.

Anderman, E. M., & Dawson, H. (2011). Learning with motivation. In R. E. Mayer & P. A. Alexander (Eds.), *Handbook of research on learning and instruction* (pp. 219–241). New York, NY: Routledge.

Anderman, E. M., Griesinger, T., & Westerfield, G. (1998). Motivation and cheating during early adolescence. *Journal of Educational Psychology, 90*, 84–93.

Anderman, E. M., & Maehr, M. L. (1994). Motivation and schooling in the middle grades. *Review of Educational Research, 64*, 287–309.

Anderman, E. M., & Mueller, C. E. (2010). Middle school transitions and adolescent development. In J. Meece & J. Eccles (Eds.), *Handbook of research on schools, schooling, and human development* (pp. 198–215). Mahwah, NJ: Erlbaum.

Anderman, E. M., Noar, S., Zimmerman, R. S., & Donohew, L. (2004). The need for sensation as a prerequisite for motivation to engage in academic tasks. In M. L. Maehr & P. Pintrich (Eds.), *Advances in motivation and achievement: Motivating students, improving schools: The legacy of Carol Midgley* (Vol. 13, pp. 1–26). Greenwich, CT: JAI Press.

Anderman, L. H., & Anderman, E. M. (2009). Oriented towards mastery: Promoting positive motivational goals for students. In R. Gilman, E. S. Huebner, & M. J. Furlong (Eds.), *Handbook of positive psychology in schools* (pp. 161–173). New York, NY: Routledge.

Anderman, L. H., Andrzejewski, C. E., & Allen, J. (2011). How do teachers support students' motivation and learning in their classrooms? *Teachers College Record, 113*, 969–1003.

Anderman, L. H., & Freeman, T. (2004). Students' sense of belonging in school. In M. L. Maehr & P. R. Pintrich (Eds.), *Advances in motivation and achievement, Vol. 13. Motivating students, improving schools: The legacy of Carol Midgley.* Oxford, UK: Elsevier.

Anderman, L. H., Patrick, H., Hruda, L. Z., & Linnenbrink, E. A. (2002). Observing classroom goal structures to clarify and expand goal theory. In C. Midgley (Ed.), *Goals, goal structures, and patterns of adaptive learning* (pp. 243–278). Mahwah, NJ: Erlbaum.

Anderson, L. W., & Pellicer, L. O. (1998). Toward an understanding of unusually successful programs for economically disadvantaged students. *Journal of Education for Students Placed at Risk, 3*, 237–263.

Andre, T., & Windschitl, M. (2003). Interest, epistemological belief, and intentional conceptual change. In G. M. Sinatra & P. R. Pintrich (Eds.), *Intentional conceptual change* (pp. 173–197). Mahwah, NJ: Erlbaum.

Archambault, I., Eccles, J. S., & Vida, M. N. (2010). Ability self-concepts and subjective value in literacy: Joint trajectories from grades 1 through 12. *Journal of Educational Psychology, 102*, 804–816.

Arnett, J. J. (1999). Adolescent storm and stress, reconsidered. *American Psychologist, 54*, 317–326.

Aronson, J., & Steele, C. M. (2005). Stereotypes and the fragility of academic competence, motivation, and self-concept. In A. J. Elliot & C. S. Dweck (Eds.), *Handbook of competence and motivation* (pp. 436–456). New York, NY: Guilford.

Ashcraft, M. H. (2002). Math anxiety: Personal, educational, and cognitive consequences. *Current Directions in Psychological Science, 11*, 181–184.

Ashiabi, G. S., & O'Neal, K. K. (2008). A framework for understanding the association between food insecurity and children's developmental outcomes. *Child Development Perspectives, 2*, 71–77.

Assor, A., Vansteenkiste, M., & Kaplan, A. (2009). Identified versus introjected approach and introjected avoidance motivations in school and in sports: The limited benefits of self-worth strivings. *Journal of Educational Psychology, 101*, 482–497.

Babad, E. (1993). Teachers' differential behavior. *Educational Psychology Review, 5*, 347–376.

Bao, X., & Lam, S. (2008). Who makes the choice? Rethinking the role of autonomy and relatedness in Chinese children's motivation. *Child Development, 79*, 269–283.

Barab, S. A., Gresalfi, M., & Ingram-Goble, A. (2010). Transformational play: Using games to position person, content, and context. *Educational Researcher, 39*, 525–536.

Barron, B. (2006). Interest and self-sustained learning as catalysts of development: A learning ecologies perspective. *Human Development, 49,* 193–224.

Bartlett, M., Rudolph, K. D., Flynn, M., Abaied, J., & Koerber, C. (2007, March). *Need for approval as a moderator of children's responses to victimization.* Paper presented at the biennial meeting of the Society for Research in Child Development, Boston, MA.

Battistich, V., Solomon, D., Kim, D., Watson, M., & Schaps, E. (1995). Schools as communities, poverty levels of student populations, and students' attitudes, motives, and performance: A multilevel analysis. *American Educational Research Journal, 32,* 627–658.

Becker, B. E., & Luthar, S. S. (2002). Social-emotional factors affecting achievement outcomes among disadvantaged students: Closing the achievement gap. *Educational Psychologist, 37,* 197–214.

Becker, M., McElvany, N., & Kortenbruck, M. (2010). Intrinsic and extrinsic reading motivation as predictors of reading literacy: A longitudinal study. *Journal of Educational Psychology, 102,* 773–785.

Beilock, S. L. (2008). Math performance in stressful situations. *Current Directions in Psychological Science, 17,* 339–343.

Beirne-Smith, M., Patton, J. R., & Kim, S. H. (2006). *Mental retardation: An introduction to intellectual disabilities* (7th ed.). Upper Saddle River, NJ: Merrill/Prentice Hall.

Ben-Zeev, T., Carrasquillo, C. M., Ching, A. M. L., Kliengklom, T. J., McDonald, K. L., Newhall, D. C., et al. (2005). "Math is hard!" (Barbie™, 1994): Responses of threat vs. challenge-mediated arousal to stereotypes alleging intellectual inferiority. In A. M. Gallagher & J. C. Kaufman (Eds.), *Gender differences in mathematics: An integrative psychological approach* (pp. 189–206). Cambridge, England: Cambridge University Press.

Benes, F. M. (2007). Corticolimbic circuitry and psychopathology: Development of the corticolimbic system. In D. Coch, G. Dawson, & K. W. Fischer (Eds.), *Human behavior, learning, and the developing brain: Atypical development* (pp. 331–361). New York, NY: Guilford.

Benita, M., Roth, G., & Deci, E. L. (2014). When are mastery goals more adaptive? It depends on experiences of autonomy support and autonomy. *Journal of Educational Psychology, 106*(1), 258–267.

Benner, A. D., & Graham, S. (2009). The transition to high school as a developmental process among multiethnic urban youth. *Child Development, 80,* 356–376.

Bergin, D. A., & Cooks, H. C. (2008). High school students of color talk about accusations of "acting White." In J. U. Ogbu (Ed.), *Minority status, oppositional culture, and schooling* (pp. 145–166). New York, NY: Routledge.

Berlyne, D. E. (1960). *Conflict, arousal, and curiosity.* New York, NY: McGraw-Hill.

Blackwell, L. S., Trzesniewski, K. H., & Dweck, C. S. (2007). Implicit theories of

intelligence predict achievement across an adolescent transition: A longitudinal study and an intervention. *Child Development, 78,* 246–263.

Bleske-Rechek, A., Lubinski, D., & Benbow, C. P. (2004). Meeting the educational needs of special populations: Advanced Placement's role in developing exceptional human capital. *Psychological Science, 15,* 217–224.

Blumenfeld, P. C., Kempler, T. M., & Krajcik, J. S. (2006). Motivation and cognitive engagement in learning environments. In R. K. Sawyer (Ed.), *The Cambridge handbook of the learning sciences* (pp. 475–488). Cambridge, England: Cambridge University Press.

Boggiano, A. K., & Pittman, T. S. (Eds.). (1992). *Achievement and motivation: A social-developmental perspective.* Cambridge, England: Cambridge University Press.

Boman, P., Furlong, M. J. Shochet, I., Lilles, E., & Jones, C. (2009). Optimism and the school context. In R. Gilman, E. S. Huebner, & M. J. Furlong (Eds.), *Handbook of positive psychology in schools* (pp. 51–64). New York, NY: Routledge.

Bong, M. (2009). Age-related differences in achievement goal differentiation. *Journal of Educational Psychology, 101,* 879–896.

Botelho, M. J., Cohen, S. L., Leoni, L., Chow, P., & Sastri, P. (2010). Respecting children's cultural and linguistic knowledge. In M. L. Dantas & P. C. Manyak (Eds.), *Home–school connections in a multicultural society: Learning from and with culturally and linguistically diverse families* (pp. 237–256). New York, NY: Routledge.

Bower, G. H. (1994). Some relations between emotions and memory. In P. Ekman & R. J. Davidson (Eds.), *The nature of emotion: Fundamental questions* (pp. 303–305). New York, NY: Oxford University Press.

Bower, G. H., & Forgas, J. P. (2001). Mood and social memory. In J. P. Forgas (Ed.), *Handbook of affect and social cognition* (pp. 95–120). Mahwah, NJ: Erlbaum.

Boyatzis, R. E. (1973). Affiliation motivation. In D. C. McClelland & R. S. Steele (Eds.), *Human motivation: A book of readings* (pp. 252–276). Morristown, NJ: General Learning Press.

Brody, G. H., Chen, Y.-F., Murry, V. M., Ge, X., Simons, R. L., Gibbons, F. X., et al. (2006). Perceived discrimination and the adjustment of African American youths: A five-year longitudinal analysis with contextual moderation effects. *Child Development, 77,* 1170–1189.

Brophy, J. E. (1986). *On motivating students* (Occasional Paper No. 101). East Lansing, MI: Michigan State University, Institute for Research on Teaching.

Brophy, J. E. (2004). *Motivating students to learn* (2nd ed.). Mahwah, NJ: Erlbaum.

Brophy, J. E. (2006). Observational research on generic aspects of classroom teaching. In P. A. Alexander & P. H. Winne (Eds.), *Handbook of educational psychology* (2nd ed., pp. 755–780). Mahwah, NJ: Erlbaum.

Brophy, J. E. (2008). Developing students' appreciation for what is taught in school. *Educational Psychologist, 43,* 132–141.

Brophy, J. E., Alleman, J., & Knighton, B. (2009). *Inside the social studies classroom.* New York, NY: Routledge.

Brown, B. B. (1993). School culture, social politics, and the academic motivation of U.S. students. In T. M. Tomlinson (Ed.), *Motivating students to learn: Overcoming barriers to high achievement* (pp. 63–98). Berkeley, CA: McCutchan.

Buehl, M. M., & Alexander, P. A. (2001). Beliefs about academic knowledge. *Educational Psychology Review, 13,* 385–418.

Burhans, K. K., & Dweck, C. S. (1995). Helplessness in early childhood: The role of contingent worth. *Child Development, 66,* 1719–1738.

Butler, R. (1994). Teacher communication and student interpretations: Effects of teacher responses to failing students on attributional inferences in two age groups. *British Journal of Educational Psychology, 64,* 277–294.

Cacioppo, J. T., Petty, R. E., Feinstein, J. A., & Jarvis, W. B. G. (1996). Dispositional differences in cognitive motivation: The life and times of individuals varying in need for cognition. *Psychological Bulletin, 119,* 197–253.

Cameron, J. (2001). Negative effects of reward on intrinsic motivation—a limited phenomenon: Comment on Deci, Koestner, and Ryan (2001). *Review of Educational Research, 71,* 29–42.

Cameron, J., & Pierce, W. D. (1994). Reinforcement, reward, and intrinsic motivation: A meta-analysis. *Review of Educational Research, 64,* 363–423.

Camras, L. A., Chen, Y., Bakeman, R., Norris, K., & Cain, T. R. (2006). Culture, ethnicity, and children's facial expressions: A study of European American, Mainland Chinese, Chinese American, and adopted Chinese girls. *Emotion, 6,* 103–114.

Carrasco, R. L. (1981). Expanded awareness of student performance: A case study in applied ethnographic monitoring in a bilingual classroom. In H. T. Trueba, G. P. Guthrie, & K. H. Au (Eds.), *Culture and the bilingual classroom: Studies in classroom ethnography* (pp. 153–177). Rowley, MA: Newbury House.

Carter, R., Williams, S., & Silverman, W. K. (2008). Cognitive and emotional facets of test anxiety in African American school children. *Cognition and Emotion, 22,* 539–551.

Carver, C. S., & Scheier, M. F. (1990). Origins and functions of positive and negative affect: A control-process view. *Psychological Review, 97,* 19–35.

Cassady, J. C. (2004). The influence of cognitive test anxiety across the learning-testing cycle. *Learning and Instruction, 14,* 569–592.

Cassady, J. C. (Ed.) (2010a). *Anxiety in schools: The causes, consequences, and solutions for academic anxieties.* New York, NY: Peter Lang.

Cassidy, J., Ziv, Y., Mehta, T. G., & Feeney, B. C. (2003). Feedback seeking in children and adolescents: Associations with self-perceptions, attachment representations, and depression. *Child Development, 74*, 612–628.

Certo, J. L., Cauley, K. M., & Chafin, C. (2003). Students' perspectives on their high school experience. *Adolescence, 38*, 705–724.

Chabrán, M. (2003). Listening to talk from and about students on accountability. In M. Carnoy, R. Elmore, & L. S. Siskin (Eds.), *The new accountability: High schools and high-stakes testing* (pp. 129–145). New York, NY: RoutledgeFalmer.

Chang, M.-L., & Davis, H. A. (2009). Understanding the role of teacher appraisals in shaping the dynamics of their relationships with students: Deconstructing teachers' judgments of disruptive behavior/students. In P. Schutz & M. Zembylas (Eds.), *Advances in teacher emotion research: The impact of teachers' lives* (pp. 95–125). New York, NY: Springer.

Chen, J. A., & Pajares, F. (2010). Implicit theories of ability of grade 6 science students: Relation to epistemological beliefs and academic motivation and achievement in science. *Contemporary Educational Psychology, 35*, 75–87.

Chinn, C. A. (2006). Learning to argue. In A. M. O'Donnell, C. E. Hmelo-Silver, & G. Erkens (Eds.), *Collaborative learning, reasoning, and technology* (pp. 355–383). Mahwah, NJ: Erlbaum.

Chiu, C.-Y., & Hong, Y.-Y. (2005). Cultural competence: Dynamic processes. In A. J. Elliot & C. S. Dweck (Eds.), *Handbook of competence and motivation* (pp. 489–505). New York, NY: Guilford.

Christenson, S. L., & Thurlow, M. L. (2004). School dropouts: Prevention, considerations, interventions, and challenges. *Current Directions in Psychological Science, 13*, 36–39.

Ciani, K. D., Middleton, M. J., Summers, J. J., & Sheldon, K. M. (2010). Buffering against performance classroom goal structures: The importance of autonomy support and classroom community. *Contemporary Educational Psychology, 35*, 88–99.

Cizek, G. J. (2003). *Detecting and preventing classroom cheating: Promoting integrity in assessment.* Thousand Oaks, CA: Corwin.

Clark, B. (1997). *Growing up gifted* (5th ed.). Upper Saddle River, NJ: Merrill/Prentice Hall.

Cleveland, M. J., Gibbons, F. X., Gerrard, M., Pomery, E. A., & Brody, G. H. (2005). The impact of parenting on risk cognitions and risk behavior: A study of mediation and moderation in a panel of African American adolescents. *Child Development, 76*, 900–916.

Clifford, M. M. (1990). Students need challenge, not easy success. *Educational Leadership, 48*(1), 22–26.

Clore, G. L., Gasper, K., & Garvin, E. (2001). Affect as information. In J. P. Forgas (Ed.), *Handbook of affect and social cognition* (pp. 121–144). Mahwah, NJ: Erlbaum.

Coddington, C. S., & Guthrie, J. T. (2008, March). *Intrinsic and avoidance motivation for school reading.* Paper presented at the annual meeting of the American Educational Research Association, New York, NY.

Cohen, G. L., & Garcia, J. (2008). Identity, belonging, and achievement: A model, interventions, implications. *Current Directions in Psychological Science, 17*, 365–369.

Cohen, G. L., Garcia, J., Purdie-Vaughns, V., Apfel, N., & Brzustoski, P. (2009). Recursive processes in self-affirmation: Intervening to close the minority achievement gap. *Science, 324*(5925), 400–403.

Cole, P. M., Bruschi, C. J., & Tamang, B. L. (2002). Cultural differences in children's emotional reactions to difficult situations. *Child Development, 73*, 983–996.

Cole, P. M., Tamang, B. L., & Shrestha, S. (2006). Cultural variations in the socialization of young children's anger and shame. *Child Development, 77*, 1237–1251.

Cole, P. M., & Tan, P. Z. (2007). Emotion socialization from a cultural perspective. In J. E. Grusec & P. D. Hastings (Eds.), *Handbook of socialization: Theory and research* (pp. 516–542). New York, NY: Guilford.

Collins, A., & Halverson, R. (2009). *Rethinking education in the age of technology: The digital revolution and schooling in America.* New York, NY: Teachers College Press.

Combs, A. W., Richards, A. C., & Richards, F. (1976). *Perceptual psychology: A humanistic approach to the study of persons.* New York, NY: Harper & Row.

Conley, A. M. (2012). Patterns of motivation beliefs: Combining achievement goal and expectancy-value perspectives. *Journal of Educational Psychology, 104*(1), 32–47.

Connell, J. P., & Wellborn, J. G. (1991). Competence, autonomy, and relatedness: A motivational analysis of self-system processes. In M. R. Gunnar & L. A. Sroufe (Eds.), *Self processes and development: The Minnesota Symposia on Child Psychology* (Vol. 23, pp. 43–77). Mahwah, NJ: Erlbaum.

Cook, P. J., & Ludwig, J. (2008). The burden of "acting White": Do Black adolescents disparage academic achievement? In J. U. Ogbu (Ed.), *Minority status, oppositional culture, and schooling* (pp. 275–297). New York, NY: Routledge.

Corpus, J. H., McClintic-Gilbert, M. S., & Hayenga, A. O. (2009). Within-year changes in children's intrinsic and extrinsic motivational orientations: Contextual predictors and academic outcomes. *Contemporary Educational Psychology, 34*, 154–166.

Corpus, J. H., Tomlinson, T. D., & Stanton, P. R. (2004, April). *Does social-comparison praise undermine children's intrinsic motivation?* Paper presented at the American Educational Research Association, San Diego, CA.

Costa, P. T., Jr., & McCrae, R. R. (1992). Trait psychology comes of age. In T. B. Sondereger (Ed.), *Nebraska Symposium on Motivation:*

Psychology and aging (pp. 169–204). Lincoln, NE: University of Nebraska Press.

Covington, M. V. (1987). Achievement motivation, self-attributions, and the exceptional learner. In J. D. Day & J. G. Borkowski (Eds.), *Intelligence and exceptionality.* Norwood, NJ: Ablex.

Covington, M. V. (1992). *Making the grade: A self-worth perspective on motivation and school reform.* Cambridge, England: Cambridge University Press.

Covington, M. V. (2000). Intrinsic versus extrinsic motivation in schools: A reconciliation. *Current Directions in Psychological Science, 9*, 22–25.

Covington, M. V., & Müeller, K. J. (2001). Intrinsic versus extrinsic motivation: An approach/avoidance reformulation. *Educational Psychology Review, 13*, 157–176.

Csikszentmihalyi, M. (1990). *Flow: The psychology of optimal experience.* New York, NY: HarperPerennial.

Csikszentmihalyi, M. (1996). *Creativity: Flow and the psychology of discovery and invention.* New York, NY: HarperCollins.

Csikszentmihalyi, M., Abuhamdeh, S., & Nakamura, J. (2005). Flow. In A. J. Elliot & C. S. Dweck (Eds.), *Handbook of competence and motivation* (pp. 598–608). New York, NY: Guilford.

Csikszentmihalyi, M., & Nakamura, J. (1989). The dynamics of intrinsic motivation: A study of adolescents. In C. Ames & R. Ames (Eds.), *Research on motivation in education: Vol. 3. Goals and cognitions* (pp. 45–71). San Diego, CA: Academic Press.

Curtis, K. A. (1992). Altering beliefs about the importance of strategy: An attributional intervention. *Journal of Applied Social Psychology, 22*, 953–972.

Curtis, K. A., & Graham, S. (1991, April). *Altering beliefs about the importance of strategy: An attributional intervention.* Paper presented at the annual meeting of the American Educational Research Association, Chicago, IL.

Dai, D. Y. (2010). *The nature and nurture of giftedness: A new framework for understanding gifted education.* New York, NY: Teachers College Press.

d'Ailly, H. (2003). Children's autonomy and perceived control in learning: A model of motivation and achievement in Taiwan. *Journal of Educational Psychology, 95*, 84–96.

Damasio, A. R. (1994). *Descartes' error: Emotion, reason, and the human brain.* New York, NY: Avon Books.

Danner, F. (2011, April). *School belonging and trajectories of depressive symptoms across adolescence and young adulthood.* Paper presented at the annual meeting of the American Educational Research Association, New Orleans, LA.

Darnon, C., Dompnier, B., Gilliéron, O., & Butera, F. (2010). The interplay of mastery and performance goals in social comparison: A multiple-goal perspective. *Journal Of Educational Psychology, 102*(1), 212–222.

Daschmann, E. C., Nett, U. E., Wimmer, B. M., Goetz, T., & Stupnisky, R. H. (2010,

April–May). *Students' and teachers' perspectives on the antecedents of boredom: An interview study.* Paper presented at the annual meeting of the American Educational Research Association, Denver, CO.

Davies, P. G., & Spencer, S. J. (2005). The gender-gap artifact: Women's underperformance in quantitative domains through the lens of stereotype threat. In A. M. Gallagher & J. C. Kaufman (Eds.), *Gender differences in mathematics: An integrative psychological approach* (pp. 172–188). Cambridge, England: Cambridge University Press.

Davis, H. A. (2003). Conceptualizing the role and influence of student-teacher relationships on children's social and cognitive development. *Educational Psychologist, 38,* 207–234.

Davis, L. E., Ajzen, I., Saunders, J., & Williams, T. (2002). The decision of African American students to complete high school: An application of the theory of planned behavior. *Journal of Educational Psychology, 94,* 810–819.

Dawson, G., & Bernier, R. (2007). Development of social brain circuitry in autism. In D. Coch, G. Dawson, & K. W. Fischer (Eds.), *Human behavior, learning, and the developing brain: Atypical development* (pp. 28–55). New York, NY: Guilford.

de Boer, H., Bosker, R. J., & van der Werf, M. P. C. (2010). Sustainability of teacher expectation bias effects on long-term student performance. *Journal of Educational Psychology, 102,* 168–179.

deCharms, R. (1972). Personal causation training in the schools. *Journal of Applied Social Psychology, 2,* 95–113.

Deci, E. L. (1992). The relation of interest to the motivation of behavior: A self-determination theory perspective. In K. A. Renninger, S. Hidi, & A. Krapp (Eds.), *The role of interest in learning and development* (pp. 43–70). Mahwah, NJ: Erlbaum.

Deci, E. L., Koestner, R., & Ryan, R. M. (2001). Extrinsic rewards and intrinsic motivation in education: Reconsidered once again. *Review of Educational Research, 71,* 1–27.

Deci, E. L., & Moller, A. C. (2005). The concept of competence: A starting place for understanding intrinsic motivation and self-determined extrinsic motivation. In A. J. Elliot & C. S. Dweck (Eds.), *Handbook of competence and motivation* (pp. 579–597). New York, NY: Guilford.

Deci, E. L., & Ryan, R. M. (1985). *Intrinsic motivation and self-determination in human behavior.* New York, NY: Plenum Press.

Deci, E. L., & Ryan, R. M. (1992). The initiation and regulation of intrinsically motivated learning and achievement. In A. K. Boggiano & T. S. Pittman (Eds.), *Achievement and motivation: A social-developmental perspective* (pp. 9–36). Cambridge, England: Cambridge University Press.

Deci, E. L., & Ryan, R. M. (1995). Human autonomy: The basis for true self-esteem. In M. H. Kernis (Ed.), *Efficacy, agency, and self-esteem* (pp. 31–49). New York, NY: Plenum Press.

Deyhle, D., & LeCompte, M. (1999). Cultural differences in child development: Navajo adolescents in middle schools. In R. H. Sheets & E. R. Hollins (Eds.), *Racial and ethnic identity in school practices: Aspects of human development* (pp. 123–139). Mahwah, NJ: Erlbaum.

Diekman, A. B., Brown, E. R., Johnston, A. M., & Clark, E. K. (2010). Seeking congruity between goals and roles: A new look at why women opt out of science, technology, engineering, and mathematics careers. *Psychological Science, 21,* 1051–1057.

Dien, T. (1998). Language and literacy in Vietnamese American communities. In B. Pérez (Ed.), *Sociocultural contexts of language and literacy* (pp. 23–54). Mahwah, NJ: Erlbaum.

Dijkstra, P., Kuyper, H., van der Werf, G., Buunk, A. P., & van der Zee, Y. G. (2008). Social comparison in the classroom: A review. *Review of Educational Research, 78,* 828–879.

Dodge, K. A., Asher, S. R., & Parkhurst, J. T. (1989). Social life as a goal-coordination task. In C. Ames & R. Ames (Eds.), *Research on motivation in education: Vol. 3. Goals and cognitions* (pp. 107–138). San Diego, CA: Academic Press.

Dotterer, A. M., McHale, S. M., & Crouter, A. C. (2009). The development and correlates of academic interests from childhood through adolescence. *Journal of Educational Psychology, 101,* 509–519.

Dowson, M., & McInerney, D. M. (2001). Psychological parameters of students' social and work avoidance goals: A qualitative investigation. *Journal of Educational Psychology, 93,* 35–42.

Doyle, W. (1986a). Classroom organization and management. In M. C. Wittrock (Ed.), *Handbook of research on teaching* (3rd ed., pp. 392–431). New York, NY: Macmillan.

DuBois, D. L., Burk-Braxton, C., Swenson, L. P., Tevendale, H. D., & Hardesty, J. L. (2002). Race and gender influences on adjustment in early adolescence: Investigation of an integrative model. *Child Development, 73,* 1573–1592.

Dunlap, G., dePerczel, M., Clarke, S., Wilson, D., Wright, S., White, R., et al. (1994). Choice making to promote adaptive behavior for students with emotional and behavioral challenges. *Journal of Applied Behavior Analysis, 27,* 505–518.

Durik, A. M., & Harackiewicz, J. M. (2007). Different strokes for different folks: How individual interest moderates the effects of situational factors on task interest. *Journal of Educational Psychology, 99,* 597–610.

Durik, A., M., Vida, M., & Eccles, J. S. (2006). Task values and ability beliefs as predictors of high school literacy choices: A developmental analysis. *Journal of Educational Psychology, 98,* 382–393.

Dweck, C. S. (1986). Motivational processes affecting learning. *American Psychologist, 41,* 1040–1048.

Dweck, C. S. (2000). *Self-theories: Their role in motivation, personality, and development.* Philadelphia: Psychology Press.

Dweck, C. S. (2009). Foreword. In F. D. Horowitz, R. F. Subotnik, & D. J. Matthews (Eds.), *The development of giftedness and talent across the life span* (pp. xi–xiv). Washington, DC: American Psychological Association.

Dweck, C. S., & Elliott, E. S. (1983). Achievement motivation. In E. M. Hetherington (Ed.), *Handbook of child psychology: Vol. 4. Socialization, personality, and social development* (4th ed., pp. 643–691). New York, NY: Wiley.

Dweck, C. S., & Leggett, E. L. (1988). A social-cognitive approach to motivation and personality. *Psychological Review, 95,* 256–273.

Dweck, C. S., Mangels, J. A., & Good, C. (2004). Motivational effects on attention, cognition, and performance. In D. Y. Dai & R. J. Sternberg (Eds.), *Motivation, emotion, and cognition: Integrative perspectives on intellectual functioning and development* (pp. 41–55). Mahwah, NJ: Erlbaum.

Dweck, C. S., & Molden, D. C. (2005). Self-theories: Their impact on competence motivation and acquisition. In A. J. Elliot & C. S. Dweck (Eds.), *Handbook of competence and motivation* (pp. 122–140). New York, NY: Guilford.

Eccles, J. (2009). Who am I and what am I going to do with my life? Personal and collective identities as motivators of action. *Educational Psychologist, 44,* 78–89.

Eccles, J. S. (2005). Subjective task value and the Eccles et al. model of achievement-related choices. In A. J. Elliot & C. S. Dweck (Eds.), *Handbook of competence and motivation* (pp. 105–121). New York, NY: Guilford.

Eccles, J. S. (2007). Families, schools, and developing achievement-related motivations and engagement. In J. E. Grusec & P. D. Hastings (Eds.), *Handbook of socialization: Theory and research* (pp. 665–691). New York, NY: Guilford.

Eccles, J. S., & Midgley, C. (1989). Stage-environment fit: Developmentally appropriate classrooms for young adolescents. In C. Ames & R. Ames (Eds.), *Research on motivation in education: Vol. 3. Goals and cognition* (pp. 139–186). San Diego, CA: Academic Press.

Eccles, J. S., Wigfield, A., & Schiefele, U. (1998). Motivation to succeed. In W. Damon (Series Ed.) & N. Eisenberg (Vol. Ed.), *Handbook of child psychology: Vol. 3. Social, emotional, and personality development* (5th ed., pp. 1017–1095). New York, NY: Wiley.

Eccles (Parsons), J. S., Adler, T. F., Futterman, R., Goff, S. B., Kaczala, C. M., Meece, J. L., et al. (1983). Expectancies, values, and academic behaviors. In J. T. Spence (Ed.), *Achievement and achievement motivation* (pp. 75–146). San Francisco, CA: Freeman.

Efklides, A. (2011). Interactions of metacognition with motivation and affect in self-regulated learning: The MASRL model. *Educational Psychologist, 46,* 6–25.

Eid, M., & Diener, E. (2001). Norms for experiencing emotions in different cultures: Inter- and intranational differences. *Journal of Personality and Social Psychology, 81*, 869–885.

Eisenberg, N., Martin, C. L., & Fabes, R. A. (1996). Gender development and gender effects. In D. C. Berliner & R. C. Calfee (Eds.), *Handbook of educational psychology* (pp. 358–396). New York, NY: Macmillan.

Elkind, D. (1981). *Children and adolescents: Interpretive essays on Jean Piaget* (3rd ed.). New York, NY: Oxford University Press.

Elliot, A. J., & Dweck, C. S. (Eds.). (2005). *Handbook of competence and motivation.* New York, NY: Guilford.

Elliot, A. J., & McGregor, H. A. (2001). A 2 × 2 achievement goal framework. *Journal of Personality And Social Psychology, 80*(3), 501–519.

Elliot, A. J., Murayama, K., & Pekrun, R. (2011). A 3 × 2 achievement goal model. *Journal of Educational Psychology, 103*, 632–648.

Elmore, K. C., & Oyserman, D. (2012). If "we" can succeed, "I" can too: Identity-based motivation and gender in the classroom. *Contemporary Educational Psychology, 37*(3), 176–185.

Epstein, J. L. (1989). Family structures and student motivation. In R. E. Ames & C. Ames (Eds.), *Research on motivation in education: Vol. 3. Goals and cognitions* (pp. 259–295). New York, NY: Academic Press.

Estrada, M., Woodcock, A., Hernandez, P. R., & Schultz, P. (2011). Toward a model of social influence that explains minority student integration into the scientific community. *Journal of Educational Psychology, 103*(1), 206–222.

Evans, G. W., Gonnella, C., Marcynyszyn, L. A., Gentile, L., & Salpekar, N. (2005). The role of chaos in poverty and children's socioemotional adjustment. *Psychological Science, 16*, 560–565.

Eysenck, M. W. (1992). *Anxiety: The cognitive perspective.* Hove, England: Erlbaum.

Fairweather, E., & Cramond, B. (2010). Infusing creative and critical thinking into the curriculum together. In R. A. Beghetto & J. C. Kaufman (Eds.), *Nurturing creativity in the classroom* (pp. 113–141). New York, NY: Cambridge University Press.

Feather, N. T. (1982). *Expectations and actions: Expectancy-value models in psychology.* Mahwah, NJ: Erlbaum.

Fisher, P. H., Dobbs-Oates, J., Doctoroff, G. L., & Arnold, D. H. (2012). Early math interest and the development of math skills. *Journal of Educational Psychology, 104*(3), 673–681. doi:10.1037/a0027756.

Fiske, A. P., & Fiske, S. T. (2007). Social relationships in our species and cultures. In S. Kitayama & D. Cohen (Eds.), *Handbook of cultural psychology* (pp. 283–306). New York, NY: Guilford.

Fletcher, K. L., & Cassady, J. C. (2010). Overcoming academic anxieties: Promoting effective coping and self-regulation strategies.

In J. C. Cassady (Ed.), *Anxiety in schools: The causes, consequences, and solutions for academic anxieties* (pp. 177–200). New York, NY: Peter Lang.

Ford, M. E. (1992). *Motivating humans: Goals, emotions, and personal agency beliefs.* Newbury Park, CA: Sage.

Ford, M. E., & Smith, P. R. (2007). Thriving with social purpose: An integrative approach to the development of optimal human functioning. *Educational Psychologist, 42*, 153–171.

Försterling, F., & Morgenstern, M. (2002). Accuracy of self-assessment and task performance: Does it pay to know the truth? *Journal of Educational Psychology, 94*, 576–585.

Foster-Johnson, L., Ferro, J., & Dunlap, G. (1994). Preferred curriculum activities and reduced problem behaviors in students with intellectual disabilities. *Journal of Applied Behavior Analysis, 27*, 493–504.

Fowler, J. W., & Peterson, P. L. (1981). Increasing reading persistence and altering attributional style of learned helpless children. *Journal of Educational Psychology, 73*, 251–260.

Fredricks, J. A., Blumenfeld, P. C., & Paris, A. H. (2004). School engagement: Potential of the concept, state of the evidence. *Review of Educational Research, 74*, 59–109.

Fredrickson, B. (2009). *Positivity: Groundbreaking research reveals how to embrace the hidden strength of positive emotions, overcome negativity, and thrive.* New York, NY: Crown.

Freeman, K. E., Gutman, L. M., & Midgley, C. (2002). Can achievement goal theory enhance our understanding of the motivation and performance of African American young adolescents? In C. Midgley (Ed.), *Goals, goal structures, and patterns of adaptive learning* (pp. 175–204). Mahwah, NJ: Erlbaum.

Frydenberg, E., & Lewis, R. (2000). Teaching coping to adolescents: When and to whom? *American Educational Research Journal, 37*, 727–745.

Fuligni, A. J., & Hardway, C. (2004). Preparing diverse adolescents for the transition to adulthood. *The Future of Children, 14*(2), 99–119.

Furrer, C., & Skinner, E. (2003). Sense of relatedness as a factor in children's academic engagement and performance. *Journal of Educational Psychology, 95*, 148–162.

Gabriele, A. J. (2007). The influence of achievement goals on the constructive activity of low achievers during collaborative problem solving. *British Journal of Educational Psychology, 77*, 1221–141.

Gabriele, A. J., & Boody, R. M. (2001, April). *The influence of achievement goals on the constructive activity of low achievers during collaborative problem solving.* Paper presented at the annual meeting of the American Educational Research Association, Seattle, WA.

Gallini, J. (2000, April). *An investigation of self-regulation developments in early adolescence: A comparison between non-at-risk and at-risk students.* Paper presented at the annual

meeting of the American Educational Research Association, New Orleans, LA.

Ganley, C. M., & Vasilyeva, M. (2014). The role of anxiety and working memory in gender differences in mathematics. *Journal of Educational Psychology, 106*(1), 105–120.

García, E. E. (1992). "Hispanic" children: Theoretical, empirical, and related policy issues. *Educational Psychology Review, 4*, 69–93.

Garner, R. (1998). Epilogue: Choosing to learn or not-learn in school. *Educational Psychology Review, 10*, 227–237.

Garner, R., Brown, R., Sanders, S., & Menke, D. J. (1992). "Seductive details" and learning from text. In K. A. Renninger, S. Hidi, & A. Krapp (Eds.), *The role of interest in learning and development* (pp. 239–254). Mahwah, NJ: Erlbaum.

Gaskill, P. J. (2001, April). *Differential effects of reinforcement feedback and attributional feedback on second-graders' self-efficacy.* Paper presented at the annual meeting of the American Educational Research Association, Seattle, WA.

Gay, G. (2010). *Culturally responsive teaching: Theory, research, and practice* (2nd ed.). New York, NY: Teachers College Press.

Gentry, M., Gable, R. K., & Rizza, M. G. (2002). Students' perceptions of classroom activities: Are there grade-level and gender differences? *Journal of Educational Psychology, 94*, 539–544.

Gillen-O'Neel, C., & Fuligni, A. (2013). A longitudinal study of school belonging and academic motivation across high school. *Child Development, 84*(2), 678–692.

Gniewosz, B., & Noack, P. (2012). What you see is what you get: The role of early adolescents' perceptions in the intergenerational transmission of academic values. *Contemporary Educational Psychology, 37*(1), 70–79.

Goetz, T., Frenzel, A. C., Hall, N. C., & Pekrun, R. (2008). Antecedents of academic emotions: Testing the internal/external frame of reference model for academic enjoyment. *Contemporary Educational Psychology, 33*, 9–33.

Goldenberg, C. (1992). The limits of expectations: A case for case knowledge about teacher expectancy effects. *American Educational Research Journal, 29*, 517–544.

Goldstein, S., & Rider, R. (2006). Resilience and the disruptive disorders of childhood. In S. Goldstein & R. B. Brooks (Eds.), *Handbook of resilience in children* (pp. 203–222). New York, NY: Springer.

Good, C., Aronson, J., & Inzlicht, M. (2003). Improving adolescents' standardized test performance: An intervention to reduce the effects of stereotype threat. *Journal of Applied Developmental Psychology, 24*, 645–662.

Good, T. L., & Brophy, J. E. (1994). *Looking in classrooms* (6th ed.). New York, NY: HarperCollins.

Good, T. L., & Nichols, S. L. (2001). Expectancy effects in the classroom: A special focus on improving the reading performance of minority students in first-grade classrooms. *Educational Psychologist, 36*, 113–126.

Gottfried, A. E., Fleming, J. S., & Gottfried, A. W. (2001). Continuity of academic intrinsic motivation from childhood through late adolescence: A longitudinal study. *Journal of Educational Psychology, 93,* 3–13.

Graham, S. (1989). Motivation in Afro-Americans. In G. L. Berry & J. K. Asamen (Eds.), *Black students: Psychosocial issues and academic achievement* (pp. 40–68). Newbury Park, CA: Sage.

Graham, S. (1990). Communicating low ability in the classroom: Bad things good teachers sometimes do. In S. Graham & V. S. Folkes (Eds.), *Attribution theory: Applications to achievement, mental health, and interpersonal conflict* (pp. 17–36). Mahwah, NJ: Erlbaum.

Graham, S. (1991). A review of attribution theory in achievement contexts. *Educational Psychology Review, 3,* 5–39.

Graham, S., & Weiner, B. (1996). Theories and principles of motivation. In D. C. Berliner & R. C. Calfee (Eds.), *Handbook of educational psychology* (pp. 63–84). New York, NY: Macmillan.

Greenspan, D. A., Solomon, B., & Gardner, H. (2004). The development of talent in different domains. In L. V. Shavinina & M. Ferrari (Eds.), *Beyond knowledge: Extracognitive aspects of developing high ability* (pp. 119–135). Mahwah, NJ: Erlbaum.

Hagtvet, K. A., & Johnsen, T. B. (Eds.). (1992). *Advances in test anxiety research* (Vol. 7). Amsterdam: Swets & Zeitlinger.

Hamre, B. K., & Pianta, R. C. (2005). Can instructional and emotional support in the first-grade classroom make a difference for children at risk of school failure? *Child Development, 76,* 949–967.

Hardré, P. L., Crowson, H. M., DeBacker, T. K., & White, D. (2007). Predicting the motivation of rural high school students. *Journal of Experimental Education, 75,* 247–269.

Hardré, P. L., & Reeve, J. (2003). A motivational model of rural students' intentions to persist in, versus drop out of, high school. *Journal of Educational Psychology, 95,* 347–356.

Hareli, S., & Weiner, B. (2002). Social emotions and personality inferences: A scaffold for a new direction in the study of achievement motivation. *Educational Psychologist, 37,* 183–193.

Harmon-Jones, E. (2001). The role of affect in cognitive-dissonance processes. In J. P. Forgas (Ed.), *Handbook of affect and social cognition* (pp. 237–255). Mahwah, NJ: Erlbaum.

Harter, S. (1990). Causes, correlates, and the functional role of global self-worth: A life-span perspective. In R. J. Sternberg & J. Kolligian, Jr. (Eds.), *Competence considered* (pp. 67–97). New Haven, CT: Yale University Press.

Harter, S. (1992). The relationship between perceived competence, affect, and motivational orientation within the classroom: Processes and patterns of change. In A. K. Boggiano & T. S. Pittman (Eds.), *Achievement and motivation: A social-developmental perspective* (pp. 77–114). Cambridge, England: Cambridge University Press.

Harter, S. (1999). *The construction of the self: A developmental perspective.* New York, NY: Guilford.

Hattie, J. (2008). Processes of integrating, developing, and processing self information. In H. W. Marsh, R. G. Craven, & D. M. McInerney (Eds.), *Self-processes, learning, and enabling human potential* (pp. 51–85). Charlotte, NC: Information Age.

Hattie, J., & Gan, M. (2011). Instruction based on feedback. In R. E. Mayer & P. A. Alexander (Eds.), *Handbook of research on learning and instruction* (pp. 249–271). New York, NY: Routledge.

Hattie, J., & Timperley, H. (2007). The power of feedback. *Review of Educational Research, 77,* 81–112.

Hattie, J. A. C. (2009). *Visible learning: A synthesis of over 800 meta-analyses relating to achievement.* London, England: Routledge.

Hawley, C. A., (2005). Saint or sinner? Teacher perceptions of a child with traumatic brain injury. *Pediatric Rehabilitation, 8,* 117–129.

Hay, I., Ashman, A. F., van Kraayenoord, C. E., & Stewart, A. L. (1999). Identification of self-verification in the formation of children's academic self-concept. *Journal of Educational Psychology, 91,* 225–229.

Heine, S. J. (2007). Culture and motivation: What motivates people to act in the ways that they do? In S. Kitayama & D. Cohen (Eds.), *Handbook of cultural psychology* (pp. 714–733). New York, NY: Guilford.

Hemmings, A. B. (2004). *Coming of age in U.S. high schools: Economic, kinship, religious, and political crosscurrents.* Mahwah, NJ: Erlbaum.

Hennessey, B. A. (1995). Social, environmental, and developmental issues and creativity. *Educational Psychology Review, 7,* 163–183.

Heron, W. (1957). The pathology of boredom. *Scientific American, 196*(1), 52–56.

Hess, R. D., & Azuma, M. (1991). Cultural support for learning: Contrasts between Japan and the United States. *Educational Researcher, 29*(9), 2–8.

Heuer, F., & Reisberg, D. (1992). Emotion, arousal, and memory for detail. In S. Christianson (Ed.), *Handbook of emotion and memory* (pp. 151–180). Hillsdale, NJ: Erlbaum.

Heward, W. L. (2009). *Exceptional children: An introduction to special education* (9th ed.). Upper Saddle River, NJ: Merrill/Pearson Education.

Hickey, D. J. (2011). Participation by design: Improving individual motivation by looking beyond it. In D. M. McInerney, R. A. Walker, & G. A. D. Liem (Eds.), *Sociocultural theories of learning and motivation: Looking back, looking forward* (pp. 137–161). Charlotte, NC: Information Age.

Hidi, S., & Harackiewicz, J. M. (2000). Motivating the academically unmotivated: A critical issue for the 21st century. *Review of Educational Research, 70,* 151–179.

Hidi, S., & Renninger, K. A. (2006). The four-phase model of interest development. *Educational Psychologist, 41,* 111–127.

Hidi, S., Renninger, K. A., & Krapp, A. (2004). Interest, a motivational variable that combines affecting and cognitive functioning. In D. Y. Dai & R. J. Sternberg (Eds.), *Motivation, emotion, and cognition: Integrative perspectives on intellectual functioning and development* (pp. 89–115). Mahwah, NJ: Erlbaum.

Hidi, S., Weiss, J., Berndorff, D., & Nolan, J. (1998). The role of gender, instruction, and a cooperative learning technique in science education across formal and informal settings. In L. Hoffman, A. Krapp, K. Renninger, & J. Baumert (Eds.), *Interest and learning: Proceedings of the Seeon Conference on Interest and Gender* (pp. 215–227). Kiel, Germany: IPN.

Hill, K. T., & Sarason, S. B. (1966). The relation of test anxiety and defensiveness to test and school performance over the elementary school years: A further longitudinal study. *Monographs for the Society of Research in Child Development, 31*(2, Serial No. 104).

Hine, P., & Fraser, B. J. (2002, April). *Combining qualitative and quantitative methods in a study of Australian students' transition from elementary to high school.* Paper presented at the annual meeting of the American Educational Research Association, New Orleans, LA.

Hinkley, J. W., McInerney, D. M., & Marsh, H. W. (2001, April). *The multi-faceted structure of school achievement motivation: A case for social goals.* Paper presented at the annual meeting of the American Educational Research Association, Seattle, WA.

Hinnant, J. B., O'Brien, M., & Ghazarian, S. R. (2009). The longitudinal relations of teacher expectations to achievement in the early school years. *Journal of Educational Psychology, 101,* 662–670.

Hofer, M. (2010). Adolescents' development of individual interests: A product of multiple goal regulation? *Educational Psychologist, 45,* 149–166.

Hom, A., & Battistich, V. (1995, April). *Students' sense of school community as a factor in reducing drug use and delinquency.* Paper presented at the annual meeting of the American Educational Research Association, San Francisco, CA.

Hong, E., O'Neil, H. F., & Feldon, D. (2005). Gender effects on mathematics achievement: Mediating role of state and trait self-regulation. In A. M. Gallagher & J. C. Kaufman (Eds.), *Gender differences in mathematics: An integrative psychological approach* (pp. 264–293). Cambridge, England: Cambridge University Press.

Hong, Y., Chiu, C., & Dweck, C. S. (1995). Implicit theories of intelligence: Reconsidering the role of confidence in achievement motivation. In M. H. Kernis (Ed.), *Efficacy, agency, and self-esteem* (pp. 197–216). New York, NY: Plenum Press.

Hsee, C. K., Yang, A. X., & Wang, L. (2010). Idleness aversion and the need for justifiable busyness. *Psychological Science, 21,* 926–930.

Huberty, T. J. (2008). Best practices in school-based interventions for anxiety and depression. In A. Thomas & J. Grimes (Eds.), *Best practices in school psychology–V* (pp. 1473–1486). Bethesda, MD: National Association of School Psychologists.

Hufton, N., Elliott, J., & Illushin, L. (2002). Achievement motivation across cultures: Some puzzles and their implications for future research. *New Directions for Child and Adolescent Development, 96,* 65–85.

Huguet, P., & Régner, I. (2007). Stereotype threat among schoolgirls in quasi-ordinary classroom circumstances. *Journal of Educational Psychology, 99,* 545–560.

Hulleman, C. S., Godes, O., Hendricks, B. L., & Harackiewicz, J. M. (2010). Enhancing interest and performance with a utility value intervention. *Journal of Educational Psychology, 102,* 880–895.

Hynd, C. (2003). Conceptual change in response to persuasive messages. In G. M. Sinatra & P. R. Pintrich (Eds.), *Intentional conceptual change* (pp. 291–315). Mahwah, NJ: Erlbaum.

Igoa, C. (1995). *The inner world of the immigrant child.* Mahwah, NJ: Erlbaum.

Ito, M., Baumer, S., Bittanti, M., Boyd, D., Cody, R., Herr-Stephenson, B., et al. (2009). *Hanging out, messing around, geeking out: Living and learning with new media.* Cambridge, MA: MIT Press.

Iyengar, S. S., & Lepper, M. R. (1999). Rethinking the value of choice: A cultural perspective on intrinsic motivation. *Journal of Personality and Social Psychology, 76,* 349–366.

Izard, C. (2007). Basic emotions, natural kinds, emotion schemas, and a new paradigm. *Perspectives on Psychological Science, 2,* 260–280.

Jacobs, J. E., Davis-Kean, P., Bleeker, M., Eccles, J. S., & Malanchuk, O. (2005). "I can, but I don't want to": The impact of parents, interests, and activities on gender differences in math. In A. M. Gallagher & J. C. Kaufman (Eds.), *Gender differences in mathematics: An integrative psychological approach* (pp. 246–263). Cambridge, England: Cambridge University Press.

Jacobs, J. E., Lanza, S., Osgood, D. W., Eccles, J. S., & Wigfield, A. (2002). Changes in children's self-competence and values: Gender and domain differences across grades one through twelve. *Child Development, 73,* 509–527.

Jacobsen, B., Lowery, B., & DuCette, J. (1986). Attributions of learning disabled children. *Journal of Educational Psychology, 78,* 59–64.

Jagacinski, C. M., & Nicholls, J. G. (1984). Conceptions of ability and related affects in task involvement and ego involvement. *Journal of Educational Psychology, 76,* 909–919.

Jagacinski, C. M., & Nicholls, J. G. (1987). Competence and affect in task involvement and ego involvement: The impact of social comparison information. *Journal of Educational Psychology, 79,* 107–114.

Jain, S., & Dowson, M. (2009). Mathematics anxiety as a function of multidimensional self-regulation and self-efficacy. *Contemporary Educational Psychology, 34,* 240–249.

Jang, H., Reeve, J., & Deci, E. L. (2010). Engaging students in learning activities: It is not autonomy support or structure but autonomy support and structure. *Journal of Educational Psychology, 102,* 588–600.

Johnson, D. W., & Johnson, R. T. (2009a). An educational psychology success story: Social interdependence theory and cooperative learning. *Educational Researcher, 38,* 365–379.

Jussim, L., Eccles, J., & Madon, S. (1996). Social perception, social stereotypes, and teacher expectations: Accuracy and the quest for the powerful self-fulfilling prophecy. In M. P. Zanna (Ed.), *Advances in experimental social psychology* (Vol. 28, pp. 281–388). New York, NY: Academic Press.

Juvonen, J. (2000). The social functions of attributional face-saving tactics among early adolescents. *Educational Psychology Review, 12,* 15–32.

Juvonen, J. (2006). Sense of belonging, social bonds, and school functioning. In P. A. Alexander & P. H. Winne (Eds.), *Handbook of educational psychology* (2nd ed., pp. 655–674). Mahwah, NJ: Erlbaum.

Kagan, J. (2010). Emotions and temperament. In M. H. Bornstein (Ed.), *Handbook of cultural developmental science* (pp. 175–194). New York, NY: Psychology Press.

Kağitçibaşi, Ç. (2007). *Family, self, and human development across cultures: Theory and applications* (2nd ed.). Mahwah, NJ: Erlbaum.

Kaplan, A., & Midgley, C. (1999). The relationship between perceptions of the classroom goal structure and early adolescents' affect in school: The mediating role of coping strategies. *Learning and Individual Differences, 11,* 187–212.

Kenrick, D. T., Griskevicius, V., Neuberg, S. L., & Schaller, M. (2010). Renovating the pyramid of needs: Contemporary extensions built upon ancient foundations. *Perspectives on Psychological Science, 5,* 292–314.

Kerns, L. L., & Lieberman, A. B. (1993). *Helping your depressed child.* Rocklin, CA: Prima.

Kesebir, S., Graham, J., & Oishi, S. (2010). A theory of human needs should be human-centered, not animal-centered: Commentary on Kenrick et al. (2010). *Perspectives on Psychological Science, 5,* 315–319.

Keys, T. D., Conley, A. M., Duncan, G. J., & Domina, T. (2012). The role of goal orientations for adolescent mathematics achievement. *Contemporary Educational Psychology, 37*(1), 47–54.

Kiefer, S. M., & Ellerbrock, C. R. (2011, April). *Social goals: Relations with academic beliefs and school identification during early adolescence.* Paper presented at the annual meeting of the American Educational Research Association, New Orleans, LA.

Kim, H. S., Sherman, D. K., & Taylor, S. E. (2008). Culture and social support. *American Psychologist, 63,* 518–526.

Kim, S., Lee, M., Chung, Y., & Bong, M. (2010). Comparison of brain activation during norm-referenced versus criterion-referenced feedback: The role of perceived competence and performance-approach goals. *Contemporary Educational Psychology, 35*(2), 141–152.

King, N. J., & Ollendick, T. H. (1989). Children's anxiety and phobic disorders in school settings: Classification, assessment, and intervention issues. *Review of Educational Research, 59,* 431–470.

King, R. B., & McInerney, D. M. (2014). The work avoidance goal construct: Examining its structure, antecedents, and consequences. *Contemporary Educational Psychology, 39*(1), 42–58.

Knapp, M. S., Turnbull, B. J., & Shields, P. M. (1990). New directions for educating the children of poverty. *Educational Leadership, 48*(1), 4–9.

Knowlton, D. (1995). Managing children with oppositional behavior. *Beyond Behavior, 6*(3), 5–10.

Koestner, R., Ryan, R. M., Bernieri, F., & Holt, K. (1984). Setting limits in children's behavior: The differential effects of controlling versus informational styles on intrinsic motivation and creativity. *Journal of Personality, 52,* 233–248.

Kuhbandner, C., Spitzer, B., & Pekrun, R. (2011). Read-out of emotional information from iconic memory: The longevity of threatening stimuli. *Psychological Science, 22,* 695–700.

Kuhl, J., & Kraska, K. (1989). Self-regulation and metamotivation: Computational mechanisms, development, and assessment. In R. Kanfer, P. L. Ackerman, & R. Cudeck (Eds.), *Abilities, motivation, and methodology: The Minnesota Symposium on Learning and Individual Differences* (pp. 343–374). Mahwah, NJ: Erlbaum.

Kuhn, D., & Park, S.-H. (2005). Epistemological understanding and the development of intellectual values. *International Journal of Educational Research, 43,* 111–124.

Kuklinski, M. R., & Weinstein, R. S. (2001). Classroom and developmental differences in a path model of teacher expectancy effects. *Child Development, 72,* 1554–1578.

Kumar, R., Gheen, M. H., & Kaplan, A. (2002). Goal structures in the learning environment and students' disaffection from learning and schooling. In C. Midgley (Ed.), *Goals, goal structures, and patterns of adaptive learning* (pp. 143–173). Mahwah, NJ: Erlbaum.

Kunter, M., Frenzel, A., Nagy, G., Baumert, J., & Pekrun, R. (2011). Teacher enthusiasm: Dimensionality and context specificity. *Contemporary Educational Psychology, 36,* 289–301.

La Guardia, J. G., (2009). Developing who I am: A self-determination theory approach to the establishment of healthy identities. *Educational Psychologist, 44,* 90–104.

Labouvie-Vief, G., & González, M. M. (2004). Dynamic integration: Affect optimization and differentiation in development. In D. Y. Dai & R. J. Sternberg (Eds.), *Motivation, emotion, and cognition: Integrative perspectives on intellectual functioning and development* (pp. 237–272). Mahwah, NJ: Erlbaum.

Ladd, G. W., & Dinella, L. M. (2009). Continuity and change in early school engagement: Predictive of children's achievement trajectories from first to eighth grade? *Journal of Educational Psychology, 101*, 190–206.

LaFontana, K. M., & Cillessen, A. H. N. (2010). Developmental changes in the priority of perceived status in childhood and adolescence. *Social Development, 19*, 130–147.

Lan, W. Y., Repman, J., Bradley, L., & Weller, H. (1994, April). *Immediate and lasting effects of criterion and payoff on academic risk taking.* Paper presented at the annual meeting of the American Educational Research Association, New Orleans, LA.

Landers, D. M. (2007). The arousal–performance relationship revisited. In D. Smith (Ed.), *Essential readings in sport and exercise psychology* (pp. 211–218). Champaign, IL: Human Kinetics.

Langer, E. J. (1997). *The power of mindful learning.* Reading, MA: Addison-Wesley.

Langer, J. A. (2000). Excellence in English in middle and high school: How teachers' professional lives support student achievement. *American Educational Research Journal, 37*, 397–439.

Lapan, R. T., Tucker, B., Kim, S.-K., & Kosciulek, J. F. (2003). Preparing rural adolescents for post-high school transitions. *Journal of Counseling and Development, 81*, 329–342.

Lapsley, D. K. (1993). Toward an integrated theory of adolescent ego development: The "new look" at adolescent egocentrism. *American Journal of Orthopsychiatry, 63*, 562–571.

Larson, R. W. (2000). Toward a psychology of positive youth development. *American Psychologist, 55*, 170–183.

Larson, R. W., & Brown, J. R. (2007). Emotional development in adolescence: What can be learned from a high school theater program? *Child Development, 78*, 1083–1099.

Larson, R. W., Moneta, G., Richards, M. H., & Wilson, S. (2002). Continuity, stability, and change in daily emotional experience across adolescence. *Child Development, 73*, 1151–1165.

Lau, S., & Nie, Y. (2008). Interplay between personal goals and classroom goal structures in predicting student outcomes: A multilevel analysis of person-context interactions. *Journal of Educational Psychology, 100*, 15–29.

Lawlor, M. S., & Schonert-Reichl, L. A. (2008, March). *The benefits of being good during early adolescence: Altruism, happiness, and the mediating role of relatedness.* Paper presented at the annual meeting of the American Educational Research Association, New York, NY.

Lazarus, R. S. (1991). *Emotion and adaptation.* New York, NY: Oxford University Press.

Leaper, C., & Friedman, C. K. (2007). The socialization of gender. In J. E. Grusec & P. D. Hastings (Eds.), *Handbook of socialization: Theory and research* (pp. 561–587). New York, NY: Guilford.

Lee, J., & Shute, V. J. (2010). Personal and social-contextual factors in K–12 academic performance: An integrative perspective on student learning. *Educational Psychologist, 45*, 185–202.

Lee, J. Q., McInerney, D. M., Liem, G. A. D., & Ortiga, Y. P. (2010). The relationship between future goals and achievement goal orientations: An intrinsic–extrinsic motivation perspective. *Contemporary Educational Psychology, 35*, 264–279.

Lee, W., Lee, M. J., & Bong, M. (2014). Testing interest and self-efficacy as predictors of academic self-regulation and achievement. *Contemporary Educational Psychology, 39(2)*, 86–99.

Lepper, M. R., Corpus, J. H., & Iyengar, S. S. (2005). Intrinsic and extrinsic motivational orientations in the classroom: Age differences and academic correlates. *Journal of Educational Psychology, 97*, 184–196.

Lepper, M. R., & Hodell, M. (1989). Intrinsic motivation in the classroom. In C. Ames & R. Ames (Eds.), *Research on motivation in education: Vol. 3. Goals and cognitions* (pp. 73–105). San Diego, CA: Academic Press.

Levy-Tossman, I., Kaplan, A., & Assor, A. (2007). Academic goal orientations, multiple goal profiles, and friendship intimacy among early adolescents. *Contemporary Educational Psychology, 32*, 231–252.

Lewis, M., & Sullivan, M. W. (2005). The development of self-conscious emotions. In A. J. Elliot & C. S. Dweck (Eds.), *Handbook of competence and motivation* (pp. 185–201). New York, NY: Guilford.

Li, J. (2005). Mind or virtue: Western and Chinese beliefs about learning. *Current Directions in Psychological Science, 14*, 190–194.

Li, J. (2006). Self in learning: Chinese adolescents' goals and sense of agency. *Child Development, 77*, 482–501.

Li, J., & Fischer, K. W. (2004). Thought and affect in American and Chinese learners' beliefs about learning. In D. Y. Dai & R. J. Sternberg (Eds.), *Motivation, emotion, and cognition: Integrative perspectives on intellectual functioning and development* (pp. 385–418). Mahwah, NJ: Erlbaum.

Liem, A. D., Lau, S., & Nie, Y. (2008). The role of self-efficacy, task value, and achievement goals in predicting learning strategies, task disengagement, peer relationship, and achievement outcome. *Contemporary Educational Psychology, 33*, 486–512.

Lillard, A. S. (1997). Other folks' theories of mind and behavior. *Psychological Science, 8*, 268–274.

Linnenbrink, E. A. (2005). The dilemma of performance-approach goals: The use of multiple goal contexts to promote students' motivation and learning. *Journal of Educational Psychology, 97*, 197–213.

Linnenbrink, E. A., & Pintrich, P. R. (2002). Achievement goal theory and affect: An asymmetrical bidirectional model. *Educational Psychologist, 37*, 69–78.

Linnenbrink, E. A., & Pintrich, P. R. (2003). Achievement goals and intentional conceptual change. In G. M. Sinatra & P. R. Pintrich (Eds.), *Intentional conceptual change* (pp. 347–374). Mahwah, NJ: Erlbaum.

Linnenbrink, E. A., & Pintrich, P. R. (2004). Role of affect in cognitive processing in academic contexts. In D. Y. Dai & R. J. Sternberg (Eds.), *Motivation, emotion, and cognition: Integrative perspectives on intellectual functioning and development* (pp. 57–87). Mahwah, NJ: Erlbaum.

Lippa, R. A. (2002). *Gender, nature, and nurture.* Mahwah, NJ: Erlbaum.

Locke, E. A., & Latham, G. P. (2006). New directions in goal-setting theory. *Current Directions in Psychological Science, 15*, 265–268.

Lockhart, K. L., Chang, B., & Story, T. (2002). Young children's beliefs about the stability of traits: Protective optimism? *Child Development, 73*, 1408–1430.

Lopez, S. J., Rose, S., Robinson, C., Marques, S. C., & Pais-Ribeiro, J. (2009). Measuring and promoting hope in schoolchildren. In R. Gilman, E. S. Huebner, & M. J. Furlong (Eds.), *Handbook of positive psychology in schools* (pp. 37–50). New York, NY: Routledge.

Luo, W., Paris, S. G., Hogan, D., & Luo, Z. (2011). Do performance goals promote learning? A pattern analysis of Singapore students' achievement goals. *Contemporary Educational Psychology, 36*, 165–176.

Mac Iver, D. J., Stipek, D. J., & Daniels, D. H. (1991). Explaining within-semester changes in student effort in junior high school and senior high school courses. *Journal of Educational Psychology, 83*, 201–211.

Maehr, M. L., & Anderman, E. M. (1993). Reinventing schools for early adolescents: Emphasizing task goals. *Elementary School Journal, 93*, 593–610.

Maehr, M. L., & McInerney, D. M. (2004). Motivation as personal investment. In D. M. McInerney & S. Van Etten (Eds.), *Big theories revisited* (pp. 61–90). Greenwich, CT: Information Age.

Mangels, J. (2004, May). *The influence of intelligence beliefs on attention and learning: A neurophysiological approach.* Invited address presented at the annual meeting of the American Psychological Society, Chicago, IL.

Marachi, R., Friedel, J., & Midgley, C. (2001, April). *"I sometimes annoy my teacher during math": Relations between student perceptions of the teacher and disruptive behavior in the classroom.* Paper presented at the annual meeting of the American Educational Research Association, Seattle, WA.

Marcia, J. E. (1980). Identity in adolescence. In J. Adelson (Ed.), *Handbook of adolescent psychology* (pp. 159–187). New York, NY: Wiley.

Marcus, G. (2008). *Kluge: The haphazard construction of the human mind.* Boston, MA: Houghton Mifflin.

Marks, H. M. (2000). Student engagement in instructional activity: Patterns in the elementary, middle, and high school years. *American Educational Research Journal, 37,* 153–184.

Marsh, H. W., Martin, A. J., & Cheng, J. H. S. (2008). A multilevel perspective on gender in classroom motivation and climate: Potential benefits of male teachers for boys? *Journal of Educational Psychology, 100,* 78–95.

Martinez, R. S., & Huberty, T. J. (2010). Anxiety in students with learning difficulties and learning disabilities. In J. C. Cassady (Ed.), *Anxiety in schools: The causes, consequences, and solutions for academic anxieties* (pp. 137–152). New York, NY: Peter Lang.

Maslow, A. H. (1943). A theory of human motivation. *Psychological Review, 50,* 514–539.

Maslow, A. H. (1973). Theory of human motivation. In R. J. Lowry (Ed.), *Dominance, self-esteem, self-actualization: Germinal papers of A. H. Maslow.* Monterey, CA: Brooks-Cole.

Maslow, A. H. (1987). *Motivation and personality* (3rd ed.). New York, NY: Harper & Row.

Mason, L., Gava, M., & Boldrin, A. (2008). On warm conceptual change: The interplay of text, epistemological beliefs, and topic interest. *Journal of Educational Psychology, 100,* 291–309.

Masten, A. S. (2001). Ordinary magic: Resilience processes in development. *American Psychologist, 56,* 227–238.

Matthews, G., Zeidner, M., & Roberts, R. D. (2006). Models of personality and affect for education: A review and synthesis. In P. A. Alexander & P. H. Winne (Eds.), *Handbook of educational psychology* (2nd ed., pp. 163–186). Mahwah, NJ: Erlbaum.

McCall, R. B. (1994). Academic underachievers. *Current Directions in Psychological Science, 3,* 15–19.

McCaslin, M., & Good, T. L. (1996). The informal curriculum. In D. C. Berliner & R. C. Calfee (Eds.), *Handbook of educational psychology* (pp. 622–670). New York, NY: Macmillan.

McClure, J., Meyer, L. H., Garisch, J., Fischer, R., Weir, K. F., & Walkey, F. H. (2011). Students' attributions for their best and worst marks: Do they relate to achievement? *Contemporary Educational Psychology, 36,* 71–81.

McDaniel, M. A., Waddill, P. J., Finstad, K., & Bourg, T. (2000). The effects of text-based interest on attention and recall. *Journal of Educational Psychology, 92,* 492–502.

McGregor, H. A., & Elliot, A. J. (2002). Achievement goals as predictors of achievement-relevant processes prior to task engagement. *Journal of Educational Psychology, 94,* 381–395.

McKown, C., & Weinstein, R. S. (2003). The development and consequences of stereotype consciousness in middle childhood. *Child Development, 74,* 498–515.

McLoyd, V. C. (1998). Socioeconomic disadvantage and child development. *American Psychologist, 53,* 185–204.

Meece, J. L. (1994). The role of motivation in self-regulated learning. In D. H. Schunk & B. J. Zimmerman (Eds.), *Self-regulation of learning and performance: Issues and educational applications* (pp. 25–44). Mahwah, NJ: Erlbaum.

Mellers, B. A., & McGraw, A. P. (2001). Anticipated emotions as guides to choice. *Current Directions in Psychological Science, 10,* 210–214.

Mendaglio, S. (2010). Anxiety in gifted students. In J. C. Cassady (Ed.), *Anxiety in schools: The causes, consequences, and solutions for academic anxieties* (pp. 153–173). New York, NY: Peter Lang.

Mercer, C. D., & Pullen, P. C. (2005). *Students with learning disabilities* (6th ed.). Upper Saddle River, NJ: Merrill/Prentice Hall.

Mesquita, B., & Leu, J. (2007). The cultural psychology of emotion. In S. Kitayama & D. Cohen (Eds.), *Handbook of cultural psychology* (pp. 734–759). New York, NY: Guilford.

Meyer, D. K., & Turner, J. C. (2002). Discovering emotion in classroom motivation research. *Educational Psychologist, 37,* 107–114.

Meyer, D. K., & Turner, J. C. (2006). Re-conceptualizing emotion and motivation to learn in classroom contexts. *Educational Psychology Review, 18,* 377–390.

Mezulis, M. H., Abramson, L. Y., Hyde, J. S., & Hankin, B. L. (2004). Is there a universal positivity bias in attributions? A meta-analytic review of individual, developmental, and cultural differences in the self-serving attributional bias. *Psychological Bulletin, 130,* 711–747.

Middleton, M. J., & Midgley, C. (1997). Avoiding the demonstration of lack of ability: An under-explored aspect of goal theory. *Journal of Educational Psychology, 89,* 710–718.

Middleton, M. J., & Midgley, C. (2002). Beyond motivation: Middle school students' perceptions of press for understanding in math. *Contemporary Educational Psychology, 27,* 373–391.

Midgley, C. (1993). Motivation and middle level schools. In M. Maehr & P. R. Pintrich (Eds.), *Advances in motivation and achievement* (Vol. 8, pp. 217–274). Greenwich, CT: JAI Press.

Midgley, C. (Ed.). (2002). *Goals, goal structures, and patterns of adaptive learning.* Mahwah, NJ: Erlbaum.

Midgley, C., Kaplan, A., & Middleton, M. (2001). Performance-approach goals: Good for what, for whom, under what circumstances, and at what cost? *Journal of Educational Psychology, 93,* 77–86.

Midgley, C., Middleton, M. J., Gheen, M. H., & Kumar, R. (2002). Stage-environment fit revisited: A goal theory approach to examining school transitions. In C. Midgley (Ed.), *Goals, goal structures, and patterns of adaptive learning* (pp. 109–142). Mahwah, NJ: Erlbaum.

Miller, R. B., & Brickman, S. J. (2004). A model of future-oriented motivation and self-regulation. *Educational Psychology Review, 16,* 9–33.

Milner, H. R. (2006). Classroom management in urban classrooms. In C. M. Evertson & C. S. Weinstein (Eds.), *Handbook of classroom management: Research, practice, and contemporary issues* (pp. 491–522). Mahwah, NJ: Erlbaum.

Minsky, M. (2006). *The emotion machine: Commonsense thinking, artificial intelligence, and the future of the human mind.* New York, NY: Simon & Schuster.

Miranda, A., Villaescusa, M. I., & Vidal-Abarca, E. (1997). Is attribution retraining necessary? Use of self-regulation procedures for enhancing the reading comprehension strategies of students with learning disabilities. *Journal of Learning Disabilities, 30,* 503–512.

Mitchell, M. (1993). Situational interest: Its multifaceted structure in the secondary school mathematics classroom. *Journal of Educational Psychology, 85,* 424–436.

Morales, J. R., & Guerra, N. G. (2006). Effects of multiple context and cumulative stress on urban children's adjustment in elementary school. *Child Development, 77,* 907–923.

Morelli, G. A., & Rothbaum, F. (2007). Situating the child in context: Attachment relationships and self-regulation in different cultures. In S. Kitayama & D. Cohen (Eds.), *Handbook of cultural psychology* (pp. 500–527). New York, NY: Guilford.

Mouratidis, A., Vansteenkiste, M., Lens, W., Michou, A., & Soenens, B. (2013). Within-person configurations and temporal relations of personal and perceived parent-promoted aspirations to school correlates among adolescents. *Journal of Educational Psychology, 105*(3), 895–910.

Murayama, K., Elliot, A. J., & Yamagata, S. (2011). Separation of performance-approach and performance-avoidance achievement goals: A broader analysis. *Journal of Educational Psychology, 103,* 238–256.

Murdock, T. B. (1999). The social context of risk: Status and motivational predictors of alienation in middle school. *Journal of Educational Psychology, 91,* 62–75.

Murphy, P. K., & Alexander, P. A. (2000). A motivated exploration of motivation terminology. *Contemporary Educational Psychology, 25,* 3–53.

Nagengast, B., Marsh, H. W., Scalas, L. F., Xu, M. K., Hau, K.-T., & Trautwein, U. (2011). Who took the "x" out of expectancy–value theory? A psychological mystery, a substantive–methodological synergy, and a cross-national generalization. *Psychological Science, 22,* 1058–1066.

Nett, U. E., Goetz, T., & Hall, N. C. (2011). Coping with boredom in school: An experience sampling perspective. *Contemporary Educational Psychology, 36,* 49–59.

Newman, R. S., & Schwager, M. T. (1995). Students' help seeking during problem solving: Effects of grade, goal, and prior achievement. *American Educational Research Journal, 32,* 352–376.

Nicholls, J. G. (1978). The development of the concepts of effort and ability, perception of academic attainment, and the understanding that difficult tasks require more ability. *Child Development, 49(3),* 800–814.

Nicholls, J. G. (1990). What is ability and why are we mindful of it? A developmental perspective. In R. J. Sternberg & J. Kolligian (Eds.), *Competence considered* (pp. 11–40). New Haven, CT: Yale University Press.

Nisbett, R. E. (2009). *Intelligence and how to get it.* New York, NY: Norton.

Nolen, S. B. (1996). Why study? How reasons for learning influence strategy selection. *Educational Psychology Review, 8,* 335–355.

Nolen, S. B. (2007). Young children's motivation to read and write: Development in social contexts. *Cognition and Instruction, 25,* 219–270.

Nolen, S. B. (2011). Motivation, engagement, and identity: Opening a conversation. In D. M. McInerney, R. A. Walker, & G. A. D. Liem (Eds.), *Sociocultural theories of learning and motivation: Looking back, looking forward* (pp. 109–135). Charlotte, NC: Information Age.

Oakes, J., & Guiton, G. (1995). Matchmaking: The dynamics of high school tracking decisions. *American Educational Research Journal, 32,* 3–33.

Ogbu, J. U. (2003). *Black American students in an affluent suburb: A study of academic disengagement.* Mahwah, NJ: Erlbaum.

Ogbu, J. U. (2008b). Multiple sources of peer pressures among African American students. In J. U. Ogbu (Ed.), *Minority status, oppositional culture, and schooling* (pp. 89–111). New York, NY: Routledge.

Osborne, J. W., & Simmons, C. M. (2002, April). *Girls, math, stereotype threat, and anxiety: Physiological evidence.* Paper presented at the annual meeting of the American Educational Research Association, New Orleans, LA.

Osborne, J. W., Tillman, D., & Holland, A. (2010). Stereotype threat and anxiety for disadvantaged minorities and women. In J. C. Cassady (Ed.), *Anxiety in schools: The causes, consequences, and solutions for academic anxieties* (pp. 119–136). New York, NY: Peter Lang.

Osterman, K. F. (2000). Students' need for belonging in the school community. *Review of Educational Research, 70,* 323–367.

Otis, N., Grouzet, F. M. E., & Pelletier, L. G. (2005). Latent motivational change in an academic setting: A 3-year longitudinal study. *Journal of Educational Psychology, 97,* 170–183.

Oyserman, D. (2008). Possible selves: Identity-based motivation and school success. In H. W. Marsh, R. G. Craven, & D. M. McInerney (Eds.), *Self-processes, learning, and enabling human potential* (pp. 269–288). Charlotte, NC: Information Age.

Page-Voth, V., & Graham, S. (1999). Effects of goal setting and strategy use on the writing

performance and self-efficacy of students with writing and learning problems. *Journal of Educational Psychology, 91,* 230–240.

Pajares, F. (2009). Toward a positive psychology of academic motivation: The role of self-efficacy beliefs. In R. Gilman, E. S. Huebner, & M. J. Furlong (Eds.), *Handbook of positive psychology in schools* (pp. 149–160). New York, NY: Routledge.

Paley, V. G. (1984). *Boys and girls: Superheroes in the doll corner.* Chicago, IL: University of Chicago Press.

Palmer, D. J., & Goetz, E. T. (1988). Selection and use of study strategies: The role of the studier's beliefs about self and strategies. In C. E. Weinstein, E. T. Goetz, & P. A. Alexander (Eds.), *Learning and study strategies: Issues in assessment, instruction, and evaluation* (pp. 41–61). San Diego, CA: Academic Press.

Pang, V. O. (1995). Asian Pacific American students: A diverse and complex population. In J. A. Banks & C. A. M. Banks (Eds.), *Handbook of research on multicultural education* (pp. 412–424). New York, NY: Macmillan.

Paris, S. G., & Cunningham, A. E. (1996). Children becoming students. In D. C. Berliner & R. C. Calfee (Eds.), *Handbook of educational psychology* (pp. 117–147). New York, NY: Macmillan.

Paris, S. G., & Turner, J. C. (1994). Situated motivation. In P. R. Pintrich, D. R. Brown, & C. E. Weinstein (Eds.), *Student motivation, cognition, and learning: Essays in honor of Wilbert J. McKeachie* (pp. 213–238). Mahwah, NJ: Erlbaum.

Patall, E. A. (2013). Constructing motivation through choice, interest, and interestingness. *Journal of Educational Psychology, 105(2),* 522–534.

Patall, E. A., Cooper, H., & Wynn, S. R. (2010). The effectiveness and relative importance of choice in the classroom. *Journal of Educational Psychology, 102,* 896–915.

Patrick, H. (1997). Social self-regulation: Exploring the relations between children's social relationships, academic self-regulation, and school performance. *Educational Psychologist, 32,* 209–220.

Patrick, H., Anderman, L. H., & Ryan, A. M. (2002). Social motivation and the classroom social environment. In C. Midgley (Ed.), *Goals, goal structures, and patterns of adaptive learning* (pp. 85–108). Mahwah, NJ: Erlbaum.

Patrick, H., Ryan, A. M., Anderman, L. H., Middleton, M. J., Linnenbrink, L., Hruda, L. Z., et al. (1997). *Observing Patterns of Adaptive Learning (OPAL): A scheme for classroom observations.* Ann Arbor, MI: The University of Michigan.

Patrick, H., Ryan, A. M., & Kaplan, A. M. (2007). Early adolescents' perceptions of the classroom social environment, motivational beliefs, and engagement. *Journal of Educational Psychology, 99,* 83–98.

Patton, J. R., Blackbourn, J. M., & Fad, K. S. (1996). *Exceptional individuals in focus* (6th ed.). Upper Saddle River, NJ: Merrill/Prentice Hall.

Payne, R. K. (2005). *A framework for understanding poverty* (4th rev. ed.). Highlands, TX: aha! Process, Inc.

Pekrun, R. (2006). The control-value theory of achievement emotions: Assumptions, corollaries, and implications for educational research and practice. *Educational Psychology Review, 18,* 315–341.

Pekrun, R., Elliot, A. J., & Maier, M. A. (2009). Achievement goals and achievement emotions: Testing a model of their joint relations with academic performance. *Journal of Educational Psychology, 101,* 115–135.

Pekrun, R., Goetz, T., Daniels, L. M., Stupnisky, R. H., & Perry, R. P. (2010). Boredom in achievement settings: Exploring control–value antecedents and performance outcomes of a neglected emotion. *Journal of Educational Psychology, 102,* 531–549.

Pekrun, R., Goetz, T., Titz, W., & Perry, R. P. (2002). Academic emotions in students' self-regulated learning and achievement: A program of qualitative and quantitative research. *Educational Psychologist, 37,* 91–105.

Pekrun, R., Hall, N. C., Goetz, T., & Perry, R. P. (2014). Boredom and academic achievement: Testing a model of reciprocal causation. *Journal of Educational Psychology, 106(3),* 696–710.

Pellegrini, A. D., & Long, J. D. (2004). Part of the solution and part of the problem: The role of peers in bullying, dominance, and victimization during the transition from primary school through secondary school. In D. L. Espelage & S. M. Swearer (Eds.), *Bullying in American schools: A social-ecological perspective on prevention and intervention* (pp. 107–117). Mahwah, NJ: Erlbaum.

Perry, N. E., Turner, J. C., & Meyer, D. K. (2006). Classrooms as contexts for motivating learning. In P. A. Alexander & P. H. Winne (Eds.), *Handbook of educational psychology* (2nd ed., pp. 327–348). Mahwah, NJ: Erlbaum.

Perry, N. E., & Winne, P. H. (2004). Motivational messages from home and school: How do they influence young children's engagement in learning? In D. M. McInerney & S. Van Etten (Eds.), *Big theories revisited* (pp. 199–222). Greenwich, CT: Information Age.

Peterson, C. (1990). Explanatory style in the classroom and on the playing field. In S. Graham & V. S. Folkes (Eds.), *Attribution theory: Applications to achievement, mental health, and interpersonal conflict* (pp. 53–75). Mahwah, NJ: Erlbaum.

Peterson, C. (2006). *A primer in positive psychology.* New York, NY: Oxford University Press.

Peterson, C., Maier, S., & Seligman, M. (1993). *Learned helplessness: A theory for the age of personal control.* New York, NY: Oxford University Press.

Peterson, C., & Park, N. (2010). What happened to self-actualization? Commentary on Kenrick et al. (2010). *Perspectives on Psychological Science, 5,* 320–322.

Phalet, K., Andriessen, I., & Lens, W. (2004). How future goals enhance motivation and learning in multicultural classrooms. *Educational Psychology Review, 16,* 59–89.

Phelan, P., Yu, H. C., & Davidson, A. L. (1994). Navigating the psychosocial pressures of adolescence: The voices and experiences of high school youth. *American Educational Research Journal, 31,* 415–447.

Phelps, E. A., & Sharot, T. (2008). How (and why) emotion enhances the subjective sense of recollection. *Current Directions in Psychological Science, 17,* 147–152.

Pianta, R. C. (1999). *Enhancing relationships between children and teachers.* Washington, DC: American Psychological Association.

Pianta, R. C., & Hamre, B. K. (2009). Conceptualization, measurement, and improvement of classroom processes: Standardized observation can leverage capacity. *Educational Researcher, 38,* 109–119.

Piirto, J. (1999). *Talented children and adults: Their development and education* (2nd ed.). Upper Saddle River, NJ: Merrill/Prentice Hall.

Pintrich, P. R. (2003). Motivation and classroom learning. In W. M. Reynolds, G. E. Miller (Vol. Eds.), & I. B. Weiner (Editor-in-Chief), *Handbook of psychology: Vol. 7. Educational psychology* (pp. 103–122). New York, NY: Wiley.

Pintrich, P. R., & Schrauben, B. (1992). Students' motivational beliefs and their cognitive engagement in academic tasks. In D. Schunk & J. Meece (Eds.), *Students' perceptions in the classroom: Causes and consequences* (pp. 149–183). Mahwah, NJ: Erlbaum.

Plante, I., de la Sablonnière, R., Aronson, J. M., & Théorêt, M. (2013). Gender stereotype endorsement and achievement-related outcomes: The role of competence beliefs and task values. *Contemporary Educational Psychology, 38*(3), 225–235.

Plante, I., & O'Keefe, P. A. (2010, April–May). *The relation among achievement goals and expectancy-value variables in predicting grades and career intentions.* Paper presented at the annual meeting of the American Educational Research Association, Denver, CO.

Pomerantz, E. M., Altermatt, E. R., & Saxon, J. L. (2002). Making the grade but feeling distressed: Gender differences in academic performance and internal distress. *Journal of Educational Psychology, 94,* 396–404.

Pomerantz, E. M., & Saxon, J. L. (2001). Conceptions of ability as stable and self-evaluative processes: A longitudinal examination. *Child Development, 72,* 152–173.

Pool, J., Dittrich, C., & Pool, K. (2011). Arts integration in teacher preparation: Teaching the teachers. *Journal for Learning Through the Arts, 7*(1). Retrieved from http://escholarship.org/uc/item/65g5z7wp

Poortvliet, P. M., & Darnon, C. (2010). Toward a more social understanding of achievement goals: The interpersonal effects of mastery and performance goals. *Current Directions in Psychological Science, 19,* 324–328.

Posner, M. I., & Rothbart, M. K. (2007). *Educating the human brain.* Washington, DC: American Psychological Association.

Powell, S., & Nelson, B. (1997). Effects of choosing academic assignments on a student with attention deficit hyperactivity disorder. *Journal of Applied Behavior Analysis, 30,* 181–183.

Pressley, M., Borkowski, J. G., & Schneider, W. (1987). Cognitive strategies: Good strategy users coordinate metacognition and knowledge. In R. Vasta & G. Whitehurst (Eds.), *Annals of child development* (Vol. 5, pp. 80–129). New York, NY: JAI Press.

Prout, H. T. (2009). Positive psychology and students with intellectual disabilities. In R. Gilman, E. S. Huebner, & M. J. Furlong (Eds.), *Handbook of positive psychology in schools* (pp. 371–381). New York, NY: Routledge.

Pugh, K. J., & Bergin, D. A. (2006). Motivational influences on transfer. *Educational Psychologist, 41,* 147–160.

Pulfrey, C., Buchs, C., & Butera, F. (2011). Why grades engender performance-avoidance goals: The mediating role of autonomous motivation. *Journal of Educational Psychology, 103*(3), 683–700.

Qian, G., & Pan, J. (2002). A comparison of epistemological beliefs and learning from science text between American and Chinese high school students. In B. K. Hofer & P. R. Pintrich (Eds.), *Personal epistemology: The psychology of beliefs about knowledge and knowing* (pp. 365–385). Mahwah, NJ: Erlbaum.

Qin, L., Pomerantz, E. M., & Wang, Q. (2009). Are gains in decision-making autonomy during early adolescence beneficial for emotional functioning? The case of the United States and China. *Child Development, 80,* 1705–1721.

Radel, R., Sarrazin, P., Legrain, P., & Wild, T. C. (2010). Social contagion of motivation between teacher and student: Analyzing underlying processes. *Journal of Educational Psychology, 102,* 577–587.

Ratelle, C. F., Guay, F., Vallerand, R. J., Larose, S., & Senécal, C. (2007). Autonomous, controlled, and amotivated types of academic motivation: A person-oriented analysis. *Journal of Educational Psychology, 99,* 734–746.

Rawsthorne, L. J., & Elliot, A. J. (1999). Achievement goals and intrinsic motivation: A meta-analytic review. *Personality and Social Psychology Review, 3,* 326–344.

Ready, D. D., & Wright, D. L. (2011). Accuracy and inaccuracy in teachers' perceptions of young children's cognitive abilities: The role of child background and classroom context. *American Educational Research Journal, 48,* 335–360.

Reed, J. H., Schallert, D. L., Beth, A. D., & Woodruff, A. L. (2004). Motivated reader, engaged writer: The role of motivation in the literate acts of adolescents. In T. L. Jetton & J. A. Dole (Eds.), *Adolescent literacy research and practice* (pp. 251–282). New York, NY: Guilford.

Reeve, J. (2006). Extrinsic rewards and inner motivation. In C. M. Evertson & C. S. Weinstein (Eds.), *Handbook of classroom management: Research, practice, and contemporary issues* (pp. 645–664). Mahwah, NJ: Erlbaum.

Reeve, J. (2009). Why teachers adopt a controlling motivating style toward students and how they can become more autonomy supportive. *Educational Psychologist, 44,* 159–175.

Reeve, J., Bolt, E., & Cai, Y. (1999). Autonomy-supportive teachers: How they teach and motivate students. *Journal of Educational Psychology, 91,* 537–548.

Reeve, J., Deci, E. L., & Ryan, R. M. (2004). Self-determination theory: A dialectical framework for understanding sociocultural influences on student motivation. In D. M. McInerney & S. Van Etten (Eds.), *Big theories revisited* (pp. 31–60). Greenwich, CT: Information Age.

Régner, I., Escribe, C., & Dupeyrat, C. (2007). Evidence of social comparison in mastery goals in natural academic settings. *Journal of Educational Psychology, 99,* 575–583.

Renninger, K. A. (2009). Interest and identity development in instruction: An inductive model. *Educational Psychologist, 44,* 105–118.

Renninger, K. A., Hidi, S., & Krapp, A. (Eds.). (1992). *The role of interest in learning and development.* Mahwah, NJ: Erlbaum.

Reyna, C. (2000). Lazy, dumb, or industrious: When stereotypes convey attribution information in the classroom. *Educational Psychology Review, 12,* 85–110.

Reyna, C., & Weiner, B. (2001). Justice and utility in the classroom: An attributional analysis of the goals of teachers' punishment and intervention strategies. *Journal of Educational Psychology, 93,* 309–319.

Reyna, V. F., & Farley, F. (2006). Risk and rationality in adolescent decision making: Implications for theory, practice, and public policy. *Psychological Science in the Public Interest, 7*(1), 1–44.

Rhodewalt, F., & Vohs, K. D. (2005). Defensive strategies, motivation, and the self: A self-regulatory process view. In A. J. Elliot & C. S. Dweck (Eds.), *Handbook of competence and motivation* (pp. 548–565). New York, NY: Guilford.

Riggs, J. M. (1992). Self-handicapping and achievement. In A. K. Boggiano & T. S. Pittman (Eds.), *Achievement and motivation: A social-developmental perspective* (pp. 244–267). Cambridge, England: Cambridge University Press.

Roberts, G. C., Treasure, D. C., & Kavussanu, M. (1997). Motivation in physical activity contexts: An achievement goal perspective. *Advances in Motivation and Achievement, 10,* 413–447.

Robertson, J. S. (2000). Is attribution training a worthwhile classroom intervention for K–12 students with learning difficulties? *Educational Psychology Review, 12,* 111–134.

Robinson, J. P., & Lubienski, S. T. (2011). The development of gender achievement gaps in mathematics and reading during elementary and middle school: Examining direct cognitive assessments and teacher ratings. *American Educational Research Journal, 48,* 268–302.

Roderick, M., & Camburn, E. (1999). Risk and recovery from course failure in the early years of high school. *American Educational Research Journal, 36,* 303–343.

Roeser, R. W., Marachi, R., & Gehlbach, H. (2002). A goal theory perspective on teachers' professional identities and the contexts of teaching. In C. Midgley (Ed.), *Goals, goal structures, and patterns of adaptive learning* (pp. 205–241). Mahwah, NJ: Erlbaum.

Rogoff, B. (2003). *The cultural nature of human development.* Oxford, England: Oxford University Press.

Roorda, D. L., Koomen, H. M. Y., Spilt, J. L., & Oort, F. J. (2011). The influence of affective teacher–student relationships on students' school engagement and achievement: A meta-analytic approach. *Review of Educational Research, 81,* 493–529.

Rose, A. J. (2002). Co-rumination in the friendship of girls and boys. *Child Development, 73,* 1830–1843.

Rose, S. C., & Thornburg, K. R. (1984). Mastery motivation and need for approval in young children: Effects of age, sex, and reinforcement condition. *Educational Research Quarterly, 9*(1), 34–42.

Rosenthal, R. (1994). Interpersonal expectancy effects: A 30-year perspective. *Current Directions in Psychological Science, 3,* 176–179.

Rosenthal, R. (2002). Covert communication in classrooms, clinics, courtrooms, and cubicles. *American Psychologist, 57,* 839–849.

Rosenthal, R., & Jacobson, L. (1968). *Pygmalion in the classroom: Teacher expectation and pupils' intellectual development.* New York, NY: Holt, Rinehart & Winston.

Roth, W.-M. (2011). Object/motives and emotion: A cultural-historical activity theoretic approach to motivation in learning and work. In D. M. McInerney, R. A. Walker, & G. A. D. Liem (Eds.), *Sociocultural theories of learning and motivation: Looking back, looking forward* (pp. 43–63). Charlotte, NC: Information Age.

Rubie-Davies, C., Hattie, J., & Hamilton, R. (2006). Expecting the best for students: Teacher expectations and academic outcomes. *British Journal of Educational Psychology, 76,* 429–444.

Rudolph, K. D., Caldwell, M. S., & Conley, C. S. (2005). Need for approval and children's well-being. *Child Development, 76,* 309–323.

Rudolph, K. D., Lambert, S. F., Clark, A. G., & Kurlakowsky, K. D. (2001). Negotiating the transition to middle school: The role of self-regulatory processes. *Child Development, 72,* 929–946.

Rueda, R., & Moll, L. C. (1994). A sociocultural perspective on motivation. In H. F. O'Neil, Jr., & M. Drillings (Eds.), *Motivation: Theory and research* (pp. 117–137). Mahwah, NJ: Erlbaum.

Ryan, A. M., & Patrick, H. (2001). The classroom social environment and changes in adolescents' motivation and engagement

during middle school. *American Educational Research Journal, 38,* 437–460.

Ryan, A. M., Pintrich, P. R., & Midgley, C. (2001). Avoiding seeking help in the classroom: Who and why? *Educational Psychology Review, 13,* 93–114.

Ryan, A. M., & Shim, S. S. (2012). Changes in help seeking from peers during early adolescence: Associations with changes in achievement and perceptions of teachers. *Journal of Educational Psychology, 104*(4), 1122–1134.

Ryan, K. E., & Ryan, A. M. (2005). Psychological processes underlying stereotype threat and standardized math test performance. *Educational Psychologist, 40,* 53–63.

Ryan, K. E., Ryan, A. M., Arbuthnot, K., & Samuels, M. (2007). Students' motivation for standardized math exams: Insights from students. *Educational Researcher, 36*(1), 5–13.

Ryan, R. M., Connell, J. P., & Grolnick, W. S. (1992). When achievement is *not* intrinsically motivated: A theory of internalization and self-regulation in school. In A. K. Boggiano & T. S. Pittman (Eds.), *Achievement and motivation: A social-developmental perspective* (pp. 167–188). Cambridge, England: Cambridge University Press.

Ryan, R. M., & Deci, E. L. (2000). Self-determination theory and the facilitation of intrinsic motivation, social development, and well-being. *American Psychologist, 55,* 68–78.

Ryan, R. M., Mims, V., & Koestner, R. (1983). Relation of reward contingency and interpersonal context to intrinsic motivation: A review and test using cognitive evaluation theory. *Journal of Personality and Social Psychology, 45,* 736–750.

Sadker, M. P., & Sadker, D. (1994). *Failing at fairness: How our schools cheat girls.* New York, NY: Touchstone.

Sanchez, B., Colon, Y., & Esparza, P. (2005). The role of sense of school belonging and gender in the academic adjustment of Latino adolescents. *Journal of Youth and Adolescence, 34*(6), 619–628.

Sapolsky, R. (2005). Stress and cognition. In M. Gazzaniga (Ed.), *The cognitive neurosciences* (3rd, ed, pp. 1031–1042). Cambridge, MA: MIT Press.

Sarason, I. G. (Ed.). (1980). *Test anxiety: Theory, research, and applications.* Mahwah, NJ: Erlbaum.

Savani, K., Markus, H. R., Naidu, N. V. R., Kumar, S., & Berlia, N. (2010). What counts as a choice? U.S. Americans are more likely than Indians to construe actions as choices. *Psychological Science, 21,* 391–398.

Schiefele, U. (1991). Interest, learning, and motivation. *Educational Psychologist, 26,* 299–323.

Schmidt, A. C., Hanley, G. P., & Layer, S. A. (2009). A further analysis of the value of choice: Controlling for illusory discriminative stimuli and evaluating the effects of less preferred items. *Journal of Applied Behavior Analysis, 42,* 711–716.

Schraw, G., Flowerday, T., & Lehman, S. (2001). Increasing situational interest in the classroom. *Educational Psychology Review, 13,* 211–224.

Schraw, G., & Lehman, S. (2001). Situational interest: A review of the literature and directions for future research. *Educational Psychology Review, 13,* 23–52.

Schultz, G. F., & Switzky, H. N. (1990). The development of intrinsic motivation in students with learning problems: Suggestions for more effective instructional practice. *Preventing School Failure, 34*(2), 14–20.

Schunk, D. H. (1990, April). *Socialization and the development of self-regulated learning: The role of attributions.* Paper presented at the annual meeting of the American Educational Research Association, Boston, MA.

Schunk, D. H., & Pajares, F. (2004). Self-efficacy in education revisited: Empirical and applied evidence. In D. M. McInerney & S. Van Etten (Eds.), *Big theories revisited* (pp. 115–138). Greenwich, CT: Information Age.

Schunk, D. H., & Pajares, F. (2005). Competence perceptions and academic functioning. In A. J. Elliot & C. S. Dweck (Eds.), *Handbook of competence and motivation* (pp. 85–104). New York, NY: Guilford.

Schutz, P. A. (1994). Goals as the transactive point between motivation and cognition. In P. R. Pintrich, D. R. Brown, & C. E. Weinstein (Eds.), *Student motivation, cognition, and learning: Essays in honor of Wilbert J. McKeachie* (pp. 113–133). Mahwah, NJ: Erlbaum.

Sedikides, C., & Gregg, A. P. (2008). Self-enhancement: Food for thought. *Perspectives on Psychological Science, 3,* 102–116.

Seiffge-Krenke, I., Aunola, K., & Nurmi, J.-E. (2009). Changes in stress perception and coping during adolescence: The role of situational and personal factors. *Child Development, 80,* 259–279.

Seligman, M. E. P. (1975). *Helplessness: On depression, development, and death.* San Francisco, CA: Freeman.

Seligman, M. E. P. (1991). *Learned optimism.* New York, NY: Knopf.

Senko, C., Hulleman, C. S., & Harackiewicz, J. M. (2011). Achievement goal theory at the crossroads: Old controversies, current challenges, and new directions. *Educational Psychologist, 46,* 26–47.

Shavinina, L. V., & Ferrari, M. (2004). Extracognitive facets of developing high ability: Introduction to some important issues. In L. V. Shavinina & M. Ferrari (Eds.), *Beyond knowledge: Extracognitive aspects of developing high ability* (pp. 3–13). Mahwah, NJ: Erlbaum.

Shepperd, J. A., & McNulty, J. K. (2002). The affective consequences of expected and unexpected outcomes. *Psychological Science, 13,* 85–88.

Shernoff, D. J., & Csikszentmihalyi, M. (2009). Flow in schools: Cultivating engaged learners and optimal learning environments. In R. Gilman, E. S. Huebner, & M. J. Furlong

(Eds.), *Handbook of positive psychology in schools* (pp. 131–145). New York, NY: Routledge.

Shernoff, D. J., Csikszentmihalyi, M., Schneider, B., & Shernoff, E. S. (2003). Student engagement in high school classrooms from the perspective of flow theory. *School Psychology Quarterly, 18*(2), 158–176.

Shernoff, D. J., & Hoogstra, L. A. (2001). Continuing motivation beyond the high school classroom. In M. Michaelson & J. Nakamura (Eds.), *Supportive frameworks for youth engagement* (pp. 73–87). San Francisco, CA: Jossey-Bass.

Shernoff, D. J., Knauth, S., & Makris, E. (2000). The quality of classroom experiences. In M. Csikszentmihalyi & B. Schneider, *Becoming adult: How teenagers prepare for the world of work* (pp. 141–164). New York, NY: Basic Books.

Shernoff, D. J., Schneider, B., & Csikszentmihalyi, M. (2001, April). *An assessment of multiple influences on student engagement in high school classrooms.* Paper presented at the annual meeting of the American Educational Research Association, Seattle, WA.

Shim, S. S., & Ryan, A. M. (2006, April). *The nature and the consequences of changes in achievement goals during early adolescence.* Paper presented at the annual meeting of the American Educational Research Association, San Francisco, CA.

Shim, S. S., Ryan, A. M., & Anderson, C. J. (2008). Achievement goals and achievement during early adolescence: Examining time-varying predictor and outcome variables in growth-curve analysis. *Journal of Educational Psychology, 100*, 655–671.

Shute, V. J. (2008). Focus on formative feedback. *Review of Educational Research, 78*, 153–189.

Sideridis, G. D. (2005). Goal orientation, academic achievement, and depression: Evidence in favor of a revised goal theory framework. *Journal of Educational Psychology, 97*, 366–375.

Sideridis, G. D. (2008). The regulation of affect, anxiety, and stressful arousal from adopting mastery-avoidance goal orientations. *Stress and Health, 24*(1), 55–69.

Sinatra, G. M., Kardash, C. M., Taasoobshirazi, G., & Lombardi, D. (2012). Promoting attitude change and expressed willingness to take action toward climate change in college students. *Instructional Science, 40*(1), 1–17.

Sinatra, G. M., & Mason, L. (2008). Beyond knowledge: Learner characteristics influencing conceptual change. In S. Vosniadou (Ed.), *International handbook on conceptual change* (pp. 560–582). New York, NY: Routledge.

Sins, P. H. M., van Joolingen, W. R., Savelsbergh, E. R., & van Hout-Wolters, B. (2008). Motivation and performance within a collaborative computer-based modeling task: Relations between students' achievement goal orientation, self-efficacy, cognitive processing, and achievement. *Contemporary Educational Psychology, 33*, 58–77.

Sirin, S. R., & Ryce, P. (2010). Cultural incongruence between teachers and families: Implications for immigrant students. In E. L. Grigorenko & R. Takanishi (Eds.),

Immigration, diversity, and education (pp. 151–169). New York, NY: Routledge.

Skaalvik, E. (1997). Self-enhancing and self-defeating ego orientation: Relations with task avoidance orientation, achievement, self-perceptions, and anxiety. *Journal of Educational Psychology, 89*, 71–81.

Skaalvik, E. M., & Skaalvik, S. (2008). Teacher self-efficacy: Conceptual analysis and relations with teacher burnout and perceived school context. In H. W. Marsh, R. G. Craven, & D. M. McInerney (Eds.), *Self-processes, learning, and enabling human potential* (pp. 223–247). Charlotte, NC: Information Age.

Skinner, E., Furrer, C., Marchand, G., & Kindermann, T. (2008). Engagement and disaffection in the classroom: Part of a larger motivational dynamic? *Journal of Educational Psychology, 100*, 765–781.

Smith, J. L. (2004). Understanding the process of stereotype threat: A review of mediational variables and new performance goal directions. *Educational Psychology Review, 16*, 177–206.

Snow, R. E., Corno, L., & Jackson, D., III (1996). Individual differences in affective and conative functions. In D. C. Berliner & R. C. Calfee (Eds.), *Handbook of educational psychology* (pp. 243–310). New York, NY: Macmillan.

Spaulding, C. L. (1992). *Motivation in the classroom.* New York, NY: McGraw-Hill.

Spear, L. P. (2000). Neurobehavioral changes in adolescence. *Current Directions in Psychological Science, 9*, 111–114.

Spera, C. (2005). A review of the relationship among parenting practices, parenting styles, and adolescent school achievement. *Educational Psychology Review, 17*, 125–146.

Stefanou, C. R., Perencevich, K. C., DiCintio, M., & Turner, J. C. (2004). Supporting autonomy in the classroom: Ways teachers encourage student decision making and ownership. *Educational Psychologist, 39*, 97–110.

Steinberg, L. (1996). *Beyond the classroom: Why school reform has failed and what parents need to do.* New York, NY: Touchstone.

Steuer, G., & Dresel, M. (2011, April). *Dealing with errors in mathematics classrooms: The relevance of error climate and personal achievement motivation.* Paper presented at the annual meeting of the American Educational Research Association, New Orleans, LA.

Stevenson, H. W., Chen, C., & Uttal, D. H. (1990). Beliefs and achievement: A study of black, white, and Hispanic children. *Child Development, 61*, 508–523.

Stipek, D. J. (1984). Sex differences in children's attributions for success and failure on math and spelling tests. *Sex Roles, 11*, 969–981.

Stipek, D. J. (1993). *Motivation to learn: From theory to practice* (2nd ed.). Boston, MA: Allyn & Bacon.

Stipek, D. J. (1996). Motivation and instruction. In D. C. Berliner & R. C. Calfee (Eds.), *Handbook of educational psychology* (pp. 85–113). New York, NY: Macmillan.

Stodolsky, S. S., Salk, S., & Glaessner, B. (1991). Student views about learning math and social

studies. *American Educational Research Journal, 28*, 89–116.

Strain, A. C., Azevedo, R., & D'Mello, S. K. (2013). Using a false biofeedback methodology to explore relationships between learners' affect, metacognition, and performance. *Contemporary Educational Psychology, 38*(1), 22–39.

Stupnisky, R. H., Stewart, T. L., Daniels, L. M., & Perry, R. P. (2011). When do students ask why? Examining the precursors and outcomes of causal search among first-year college students. *Contemporary Educational Psychology, 36*, 201–211.

Suskind, R. (1998). *A hope in the unseen: An American odyssey from the inner city to the Ivy League.* New York, NY: Broadway Books.

Swan, K., Mitrani, M., Guerrero, F., Cheung, M., & Schoener, J. (1990, April). *Perceived locus of control and computer-based instruction.* Paper presented at the annual meeting of the American Educational Research Association, Boston, MA.

Tamir, M. (2009). What do people want to feel and why? Pleasure and utility in emotion regulation. *Current Directions in Psychological Science, 18*, 101–105.

Tamis-Lemonda, C. S., & McFadden, K. E. (2010). The United States of America. In M. H. Bornstein (Ed.), *Handbook of cultural developmental science* (pp. 299–322). New York, NY: Psychology Press.

Tanaka, A., & Murayama, K. (2014). Within-person analyses of situational interest and boredom: Interactions between task-specific perceptions and achievement goals. *Journal of Educational Psychology, 106*(4), 1122–1134.

Taylor, G., Jungert, T., Mageau, G. A., Schattke, K., Dedic, H., Rosenfield, S., & Koestner, R. (2014). A self-determination theory approach to predicting school achievement over time: The unique role of intrinsic motivation. *Contemporary Educational Psychology, 39*(4), 342–358.

Thomas, R. M. (2005). *High-stakes testing: Coping with collateral damage.* Mahwah, NJ: Erlbaum.

Thomas, S., & Oldfather, P. (1997). Intrinsic motivations, literacy, and assessment practices: "That's my grade. That's me." *Educational Psychologist, 32*, 107–123.

Thorkildsen, T. A., Golant, C. J., & Cambray-Engstrom, E. (2008). Essential solidarities for understanding Latino adolescents' moral and academic engagement. In C. Hudley & A. E. Gottfried (Eds.), *Academic motivation and the culture of school in childhood and adolescence* (pp. 73–98). New York, NY: Oxford University Press.

Timm, P., & Borman, K. (1997). The soup pot don't stretch that far no more: Intergenerational patterns of school leaving in an urban Appalachian neighborhood. In M. Sellter & L. Weis (Eds.), *Beyond black and white: New faces and voices in U.S. schools.* Albany, NY: State University of New York Press.

Tobias, S. (1994). Interest, prior knowledge, and learning. *Review of Educational Research, 64*, 37–54.

Tollefson, N. (2000). Classroom applications of cognitive theories of motivation. *Educational Psychology Review, 12*, 63–83.

Tomback, R. M., Williams, A. Y., & Wentzel, K. R. (2005, April). *Young adolescents' concerns about the transition to high school.* Poster presented at the annual meeting of the American Educational Research Association, Montreal, Canada.

Townsend, T. (2008, March). *Supporting students who struggle to learn: A community approach to development.* Paper presented at the annual meeting of the American Educational Research Association, New York, NY.

Tryon, G. S. (1980). The measurement and treatment of anxiety. *Review of Educational Research, 50*, 343–372.

Tsai, J. L. (2007). Ideal affect: Cultural causes and behavioral consequences. *Perspectives on Psychological Science, 2*, 242–259.

Tsai, Y.-M., Kunter, M., Lüdtke, O., Trautwein, U., & Ryan, R. M. (2008). What makes lessons interesting? The role of situational and individual factors in three school subjects. *Journal of Educational Psychology, 100*, 460–472.

Tucker, V. G., & Anderman, L. H. (1999, April). *Cycles of learning: Demonstrating the interplay between motivation, self-regulation, and cognition.* Paper presented at the annual meeting of the American Educational Research Association, Montreal, Canada.

Tuominen-Soini, H., Salmela-Aro, K., & Niemivirta, M. (2011). Stability and change in achievement goal orientations: A person-centered approach. *Contemporary Educational Psychology, 36*, 82–100.

Turnbull, A. P., Turnbull, R., & Wehmeyer, M. L. (2010). *Exceptional lives: Special education in today's schools* (6th ed.). Upper Saddle River, NJ: Merrill.

Turner, J. C., Meyer, D. K., Cox, K. E., Logan, C., DiCintio, M., & Thomas, C. T. (1998). Creating contexts for involvement in mathematics. *Journal of Educational Psychology, 90*, 730–745.

Turner, J. C., & Patrick, H. (2008). How does motivation develop and why does it change? Reframing motivation research. *Educational Psychologist, 43*, 119–131.

Turner, J. C., Thorpe, P. K., & Meyer, D. K. (1998). Students' reports of motivation and negative affect: A theoretical and empirical analysis. *Journal of Educational Psychology, 90*, 758–771.

Turner, J. C., Warzon, K. B., & Christensen, A. (2011). Motivating mathematics learning: Changes in teachers' practices and beliefs during a nine-month collaboration. *American Educational Research Journal, 48*, 718–762.

Ulke-Kurcuoglu, B., & Kircaali-Iftar, G. (2010). A comparison of the effects of providing activity and material choice to children with autism spectrum disorders. *Journal of Applied Behavior Analysis, 43*, 717–721.

Urdan, T. (2004). Predictors of academic self-handicapping and achievement: Examining achievement goals, classroom goal structures, and culture. *Journal of Educational Psychology, 96*, 251–264.

Urdan, T. C., & Maehr, M. L. (1995). Beyond a two-goal theory of motivation and achievement: A case for social goals. *Review of Educational Research, 65*, 213–243.

Urdan, T. C., & Midgley, C. (2001). Academic self-handicapping: What we know, what more there is to learn. *Educational Psychology Review, 13*, 115–138.

Urdan, T. C., Midgley, C., & Anderman, E. M. (1998). The role of classroom goal structure in students' use of self-handicapping strategies. *American Educational Research Journal, 35*, 101–122.

Urdan, T. C., Ryan, A. M., Anderman, E. M., & Gheen, M. H. (2002). Goals, goal structures, and avoidance behaviors. In C. Midgley (Ed.), *Goals, goal structures, and patterns of adaptive learning* (pp. 55–83). Mahwah, NJ: Erlbaum.

Valente, N. (2001). *"Who cares about school?" A student responds to learning.* Unpublished paper, University of New Hampshire, Durham.

Valkenburg, P. M., & Peter, J. (2009). Social consequences of the Internet for adolescents: A decade of research. *Current Directions in Psychological Science, 18*, 1–5.

van den Bergh, L., Denessen, E., Hornstra, L., Voeten, M., & Holland, R. W. (2010). The implicit prejudiced attitudes of teachers: Relations to teacher expectations and the ethnic achievement gap. *American Educational Research Journal, 47*, 497–527.

van Laar, C. (2000). The paradox of low academic achievement but high self-esteem in African American students: An attributional account. *Educational Psychology Review, 12*, 33–61.

Vansteenkiste, M., Lens, W., & Deci, E. L. (2006). Intrinsic versus extrinsic goal contents in self-determination theory: Another look at the quality of academic motivation. *Educational Psychologist, 41*, 19–31.

Vermeer, H. J., Boekaerts, M., & Seegers, G. (2000). Motivational and gender differences: Sixth-grade students' mathematical problem-solving behavior. *Journal of Educational Psychology, 92*, 308–315.

Vukovic, R. K., Kieffer, M. J., Bailey, S. P., & Harari, R. R. (2013). Mathematics anxiety in young children: Concurrent and longitudinal associations with mathematical performance. *Contemporary Educational Psychology, 38*(1), 1–10. doi:10.1016/j.cedpsych.2012.09.001.

Walls, T. A., & Little, T. D. (2005). Relations among personal agency, motivation, and school adjustment in early adolescence. *Journal of Educational Psychology, 97*, 23–31.

Walton, G. M., & Cohen, G. L. (2007). A question of belonging: Race, social fit, and achievement. *Journal of Personality and Social Psychology, 92*, 82–96.

Walton, G. M., & Spencer, S. J. (2009). Latent ability: Grades and test scores systematically underestimate intellectual ability of negatively stereotyped students. *Psychological Science, 20*, 1132–1139.

Wang, M.-T., & Holcombe, R. (2010). Adolescents' perceptions of school environment, engagement, and academic achievement in middle school. *American Educational Research Journal, 47*, 633–662.

Wehmeyer, M. L., Agran, M., Hughes, C., Martin, J., Mithaug, D. E., & Palmer, S. (2007). *Promoting self-determination in students with intellectual and developmental disabilities.* New York, NY: Guilford.

Weiner, B. (1984). Principles for a theory of student motivation and their application within an attributional framework. In R. Ames & C. Ames (Eds.), *Research on motivation in education: Vol. 1. Student motivation* (pp. 15–38). San Diego, CA: Academic Press.

Weiner, B. (1986). *An attributional theory of motivation and emotion.* New York, NY: Springer-Verlag.

Weiner, B. (2000). Intrapersonal and interpersonal theories of motivation from an attributional perspective. *Educational Psychology Review, 12*, 1–14.

Weiner, B. (2004). Attribution theory revisited: Transforming cultural plurality into theoretical unity. In D. M. McInerney & S. Van Etten (Eds.), *Big theories revisited* (pp. 13–29). Greenwich, CT: Information Age.

Weiner, B. (2005). Motivation from an attribution perspective and the social psychology of perceived competence. In A. J. Elliot & C. S. Dweck (Eds.), *Handbook of competence and motivation* (pp. 73–84). New York, NY: Guilford.

Weinstein, C. E., Hagen, A. S., & Meyer, D. K. (1991, April). *Work smart . . . not hard: The effects of combining instruction in using strategies, goal using, and executive control on attributions and academic performance.* Paper presented at the annual meeting of the American Educational Research Association, Chicago, IL.

Weinstein, R. S. (2002). *Reaching higher: The power of expectations in schooling.* Cambridge, MA: Harvard University Press.

Weinstein, R. S., Madison, S. M., & Kuklinski, M. R. (1995). Raising expectations in schooling: Obstacles and opportunities for change. *American Educational Research Journal, 32*, 121–159.

Weisgram, E. S., Bigler, R. S., & Liben, L. S. (2010). Gender, values, and occupational interests among children, adolescents, and adults. *Child Development, 81*, 778–796.

Wells, G. (2011). Motive and motivation in learning to teach. In D. M. McInerney, R. A. Walker, & G. A. D. Liem (Eds.), *Sociocultural theories of learning and motivation: Looking back, looking forward* (pp. 87–107). Charlotte, NC: Information Age.

Wentzel, K. R. (1997). Student motivation in middle school: The role of perceived pedagogical caring. *Journal of Educational Psychology, 89*(3), 411–419.

Wentzel, K. R. (1999). Social-motivational processes and interpersonal relationships: Implications for understanding motivation at school. *Journal of Educational Psychology, 91*, 76–97.

Wentzel, K. R., Filisetti, L., & Looney, L. (2007). Adolescent prosocial behavior: The role of self-processes and contextual cues. *Child Development, 78*, 895–910.

Wentzel, K. R., & Wigfield, A. (1998). Academic and social motivational influences on students' academic performance. *Educational Psychology Review, 10*, 155–175.

White, R. (1959). Motivation reconsidered: The concept of competence. *Psychological Review, 66*, 297–333.

Wigfield, A. (1994). Expectancy-value theory of achievement motivation: A developmental perspective. *Educational Psychology Review, 6*, 49–78.

Wigfield, A., Byrnes, J. P., & Eccles, J. S. (2006). Development during early and middle adolescence. In P. A. Alexander & P. H. Winne (Eds.), *Handbook of educational psychology* (2nd ed., pp. 87–113). Mahwah, NJ: Erlbaum.

Wigfield, A., & Eccles, J. (1992). The development of achievement task values: A theoretical analysis. *Developmental Review, 12*, 265–310.

Wigfield, A., & Eccles, J. (2000). Expectancy-value theory of achievement motivation. *Contemporary Educational Psychology, 25*, 68–81.

Wigfield, A., Eccles, J. S., Mac Iver, D., Reuman, D., & Midgley, C. (1991). Transitions at early adolescence: Changes in children's domain-specific self-perceptions and general self-esteem across the transition to junior high school. *Developmental Psychology, 27*, 552–565.

Wigfield, A., & Karpathian, M. (1991). Who am I and what can I do? Children's self-concepts and motivation in achievement situations. *Educational Psychologist, 26*(3–4), 233–261.

Wigfield, A., Tonks, S., & Eccles, J. S. (2004). Expectancy value theory in cross-cultural perspective. In D. M. McInerney & S. Van Etten (Eds.), *Big theories revisited* (pp. 165–198). Greenwich, CT: Information Age.

Wijnia, L., Loyens, S. M., Derous, E., & Schmidt, H. G. (2014). Do students' topic interest and tutors' instructional style matter in problem-based learning? *Journal of Educational Psychology, 106*(4), 919–933.

Wiles, J., & Bondi, J. (2001). *The new American middle school: Educating preadolescents in an era of change.* Upper Saddle River, NJ: Merrill/Prentice Hall.

Williams, K. M. (2001a). "Frontin' it": Schooling, violence, and relationships in the 'hood. In J. N. Burstyn, G. Bender, R. Casella, H. W. Gordon, D. P. Guerra, K. V. Luschen, R. Stevens, & K. M. Williams, *Preventing violence in schools: A challenge to American democracy* (pp. 95–108). Mahwah, NJ: Erlbaum.

Wilson, B. L., & Corbett, H. D. (2001). *Listening to urban kids: School reform and the teachers they want.* Albany, NY: State University of New York Press.

Wilson, T. D., & Gilbert, D. T. (2008). Explaining away: A model of affective adaptation. *Perspectives on Psychological Science, 3*, 370–386.

Winner, E. (1997). Exceptionally high intelligence and schooling. *American Psychologist, 52*, 1070–1081.

Winner, E. (2000a). Giftedness: Current theory and research. *Current Directions in Psychological Science, 9*, 153–156.

Winner, E. (2000b). The origins and ends of giftedness. *American Psychologist, 55*, 159–169.

Wlodkowski, R. J. (1978). *Motivation and teaching: A practical guide.* Washington, DC: National Education Association.

Wlodkowski, R. J., & Ginsberg, M. B. (1995). *Diversity and motivation: Culturally responsive teaching.* San Francisco, CA: Jossey-Bass.

Wolters, C. A. (2003). Regulation of motivation: Evaluating an underemphasized aspect of self-regulated learning. *Educational Psychologist, 38*, 189–205.

Wolters, C. A. (2004). Advancing achievement goal theory: Using goal structures and goal orientations to predict students' motivation, cognition, and achievement. *Journal of Educational Psychology, 96*, 236–250.

Wong, B. Y. L. (Ed.). (1991). *Learning about learning disabilities.* San Diego, CA: Academic Press.

Wu, X., Anderson, R. C., Nguyen-Jahiel, K., & Miller, B. (2013). Enhancing motivation and engagement through collaborative discussion. *Journal of Educational Psychology, 105*(3), 622–632.

Yeager, D. S., Bundick, M. J., & Johnson, R. (2012). The role of future work goal motives in adolescent identity development: A longitudinal mixed-methods investigation. *Contemporary Educational Psychology, 37*(3), 206–217.

Yeager, D. S., & Walton, G. M. (2011). Social-psychological interventions in education: They're not magic. *Review of Educational Research, 81*, 267–301.

Yerkes, R. M., & Dodson, J. D. (1908). The relation of strength of stimulus to rapidity of habit-formation. *Journal of Comparative Neurology of Psychology, 18*, 459–482.

Yeung, A. S., Lau, S., & Nie, Y. (2011). Primary and secondary students' motivation in learning English: Grade and gender differences. *Contemporary Educational Psychology, 36*(3), 246–256.

Youniss, J., & Yates, M. (1999). Youth service and moral-civic identity: A case for everyday morality. *Educational Psychology Review, 11*, 361–376.

Zahorik, J. A. (1994, April). *Making things interesting.* Paper presented at the annual meeting of the American Educational Research Association, New Orleans, LA.

Zajonc, R. B. (1980). Feeling and thinking: Preferences need no inferences. *American Psychologist, 35*, 151–175.

Zeelenberg, R., Wagenmakers, E.-J., & Rotteveel, M. (2006). The impact of emotion on perception: Bias or enhanced processing? *Psychological Science, 17*, 287–291.

Zeidner, M. (1998). *Test anxiety: The state of the art.* New York, NY: Plenum Press.

Zeidner, M., & Matthews, G. (2005). Evaluation anxiety: Current theory and research. In A. J. Elliot & C. S. Dweck (Eds.), *Handbook of competence and motivation* (pp. 141–163). New York, NY: Guilford.

Ziegert, D. I., Kistner, J. A., Castro, R., & Robertson, B. (2001). Longitudinal study of young children's responses to challenging achievement situations. *Child Development, 72*, 609–624.

Zimmerman, B. J. (1998). Developing self-fulfilling cycles of academic regulation: An analysis of exemplary instructional models. In D. H. Schunk & B. J. Zimmerman (Eds.), *Self-regulated learning: From teaching to self-reflective practice* (pp. 1–19). New York, NY: Guilford.

Zimmerman, B. J., Bandura, A., & Martinez-Pons, M. (1992). Self-motivation for academic attainment: The role of self-efficacy beliefs and personal goal setting. *American Educational Research Journal, 29*, 663–676.

Zohar, A., & Aharon-Kraversky, S. (2005). Exploring the effects of cognitive conflict and direct teaching for students of different academic levels. *Journal of Research in Science Teaching, 42*, 829–855.

CHAPTER 12

Afflerbach, P., & Cho, B.-Y. (2010). Determining and describing reading strategies: Internet and traditional forms of reading. In H. S. Waters & W. Schneider (Eds.), *Metacognition, strategy use, and instruction* (pp. 201–225). New York, NY: Guilford.

Airasian, P. W. (1994). *Classroom assessment* (2nd ed.). New York, NY: McGraw-Hill.

Alfassi, M. (2004). Reading to learn: Effects of combined strategy instruction on high school students. *Journal of Educational Research, 97*, 171–184.

Alfieri, L., Brooks, P. J., Aldrich, N. J., & Tenenbaum, H. R. (2011). Does discovery-based instruction enhance learning? *Journal of Educational Psychology, 103*, 1–18.

Alleman, J., & Brophy, J. (1998). Strategic learning opportunities during out-of-school hours. *Social Studies and the Young Learner, 10*(4), 10–13.

Alleman, J., Knighton, B., Botwinski, B., Brophy, J., Ley, R., & Middlestead, S. (2010). *Homework done right: Powerful learning in real-life situations.* Thousand Oaks, CA: Corwin.

Anderson, J. R., Reder, L. M., & Simon, H. A. (1996). Situated learning and education. *Educational Researcher, 25*(4), 5–11.

Anderson, L. W., & Krathwohl, D. R. (Eds.). (2001). *A taxonomy for learning, teaching, and assessing: A revision of Bloom's taxonomy of educational objectives.* New York, NY: Longman.

Anderson, R. C., Nguyen-Jahiel, K., McNurlen, B., Archodidou, A., Kim, S.-Y., Reznitskaya, A., . . . Gilbert, L. (2001). The snowball phenomenon: Spread of ways of talking and ways of thinking across groups of children. *Cognition and Instruction, 19*, 1–46.

Applebee, A. N., Langer, J. A., Nystrand, M., & Gamoran, A. (2003). Discussion-based approaches to developing understanding: Classroom instruction and student performance in middle and high school English. *American Educational Research Journal, 40,* 685–730.

Arlin, M. (1984). Time, equality, and mastery learning. *Review of Educational Research, 54,* 65–86.

Aronson, E., & Patnoe, S. (1997). *The jigsaw classroom: Building cooperation in the classroom* (2nd ed.). New York, NY: Longman.

Aulls, M. W. (1998). Contributions of classroom discourse to what content students learn during curriculum enactment. *Journal of Educational Psychology, 90,* 56–69.

Ausubel, D. P., Novak, J. D., & Hanesian, H. (1978). *Educational psychology: A cognitive view* (2nd ed.). New York, NY: Holt, Rinehart & Winston.

Azevedo, R., & Witherspoon, A. M. (2009). Self-regulated learning with hypermedia. In D. J. Hacker, J. Dunlosky, & A. C. Graesser (Eds.), *Handbook of metacognition in education* (pp. 319–339). New York, NY: Routledge.

Barab, S. A., Gresalfi, M., & Arici, A. (2009). Why educators should care about games. *Teaching for the 21st Century, 67*(1), 76–80.

Barab, S. A., Gresalfi, M., & Ingram-Goble, A. (2010). Transformational play: Using games to position person, content, and context. *Educational Researcher, 39,* 525–536.

Baroody, A. J., Eiland, M. D., Purpura, D. J., & Reid, E. E. (2013). Can computer-assisted discovery learning foster first graders' fluency with the most basic addition combinations? *American Educational Research Journal, 50,* 533–573.

Battistich, V., Solomon, D., Kim, D., Watson, M., & Schaps, E. (1995). Schools as communities, poverty levels of student populations, and students' attitudes, motives, and performance: A multilevel analysis. *American Educational Research Journal, 32,* 627–658.

Beal, C. R., Arroyo, I., Cohen, P. R., & Woolf, B. P. (2010). Evaluation of AnimalWatch: An intelligent tutoring system for arithmetic and fractions. *Journal of Interactive Online Learning, 9,* 64–77.

Beck, I. L., & McKeown, M. G. (1994). Outcomes of history instruction: Paste-up accounts. In M. Carretero & J. F. Voss (Eds.), *Cognitive and instructional processes in history and the social sciences* (pp. 237–256). Mahwah, NJ: Erlbaum.

Beck, I. L., & McKeown, M. G. (2001). Inviting students into the pursuit of meaning. *Educational Psychology Review, 13,* 225–241.

Belfiore, P. J., & Hornyak, R. S. (1998). Operant theory and application to self-monitoring in adolescents. In D. H. Schunk & B. J. Zimmerman (Eds.), *Self-regulated learning: From teaching to self-reflective practice* (pp. 184–202). New York, NY: Guilford.

Bell, P., & Linn, M. C. (2002). Beliefs about science: How does science instruction contribute? In B. K. Hofer & P. R. Pintrich

(Eds.), *Personal epistemology: The psychology of beliefs about knowledge and knowing* (pp. 321–346). Mahwah, NJ: Erlbaum.

Bellanca, J. A., & Stirling, T. (2011). *Classrooms without borders: Using Internet projects to teach communication and collaboration.* New York, NY: Teachers College Press.

Bereiter, C., & Scardamalia, M. (2006). Education for the Knowledge Age: Design-centered models of teaching and instruction. In P. A. Alexander & P. H. Winne (Eds.), *Handbook of educational psychology* (2nd ed., pp. 695–713). Mahwah, NJ: Erlbaum.

Berger, R. (2003). *An ethic of excellence: Building a culture of craftsmanship with students.* Portsmouth, NH: Heinemann.

Biemiller, A., Shany, M., Inglis, A., & Meichenbaum, D. (1998). Factors influencing children's acquisition and demonstration of self-regulation on academic tasks. In D. H. Schunk & B. J. Zimmerman (Eds.), *Self-regulated learning: From teaching to self-reflective practice* (pp. 203–224). New York, NY: Guilford.

Block, J. H. (1980). Promoting excellence through mastery learning. *Theory into Practice, 19,* 66–74.

Bloom, B. S. (1981). *All our children learning.* New York, NY: McGraw-Hill.

Blumenfeld, P. C., Kempler, T. M., & Krajcik, J. S. (2006). Motivation and cognitive engagement in learning environments. In R. K. Sawyer (Ed.), *The Cambridge handbook of the learning sciences* (pp. 475–488). Cambridge, England: Cambridge University Press.

Boxerman, J. Z. (2009, April). *Students' understanding of erosion.* Paper presented at the annual meeting of the American Educational Research Association, San Diego, CA.

Bransford, J., Vye, N., Stevens, R., Kuhl, P., Schwartz, D., Bell, P., . . . Sabelli, N. (2006). Learning theories and education: Toward a decade of synergy. In P. A. Alexander & P. H. Winne (Eds.), *Handbook of educational psychology* (2nd ed., pp. 209–244). Mahwah, NJ: Erlbaum.

Brophy, J. (2006). Observational research on generic aspects of classroom teaching. In P. A. Alexander & P. H. Winne (Eds.), *Handbook of educational psychology* (2nd ed., pp. 755–780). Mahwah, NJ: Erlbaum.

Brophy, J. (2008). Developing students' appreciation for what is taught in school. *Educational Psychologist, 43,* 132–141.

Brophy, J., Alleman, J., & Knighton, B. (2009). *Inside the social studies classroom.* New York, NY: Routledge.

Brown, A. L., & Palincsar, A. S. (1987). Reciprocal teaching of comprehension strategies: A natural history of one program for enhancing learning. In J. Borkowski & J. D. Day (Eds.), *Cognition in special education: Comparative approaches to retardation, learning disabilities, and giftedness* (pp. 81–132). Norwood, NJ: Ablex.

Brown, A. L., & Reeve, R. A. (1987). Bandwidths of competence: The role of supportive contexts in learning and development. In L. S.

Liben (Ed.), *Development and learning: Conflict or congruence?* (pp. 173–223). Mahwah, NJ: Erlbaum.

Brown, M. C., McNeil, N. M., & Glenberg, A. M. (2009). Using concreteness in education: Real problems, potential solutions. *Child Development Perspectives, 3,* 160–164.

Bruner, J. S. (1966). *Toward a theory of instruction.* Cambridge, MA: Harvard University Press.

Bruning, R. H., Schraw, G. J., & Ronning, R. R. (1995). *Cognitive psychology and instruction* (2nd ed.). Upper Saddle River, NJ: Merrill/Prentice Hall.

Bryan, T., Burstein, K., & Bryan, J. (2001). Students with learning disabilities: Homework problems and promising practices. *Educational Psychologist, 36,* 167–180.

Bulgren, J. A., Deshler, D. D., Schumaker, J. B., & Lenz, B. K. (2000). The use and effectiveness of analogical instruction in diverse secondary content classrooms. *Journal of Educational Psychology, 92,* 426–441.

Calderhead, J. (1996). Teachers: Beliefs and knowledge. In D. C. Berliner & R. C. Calfee (Eds.), *Handbook of educational psychology* (pp. 709–725). New York, NY: Macmillan.

Calfee, R., Dunlap, K., & Wat, A. (1994). Authentic discussion of texts in middle grade schooling: An analytic-narrative approach. *Journal of Reading, 37,* 546–556.

Carney, R. N., & Levin, J. R. (2002). Pictorial illustrations *still* improve students' learning from text. *Educational Psychology Review, 14,* 5–26.

Carnine, D. (1989). Teaching complex content to learning disabled students: The role of technology. *Exceptional Children, 55,* 524–533.

Carr-Chellman, A. (2012, May). Why boys, why games? *Leading and Learning with Technology,* 12–26.

Castagno, A. E., & Brayboy, B. M. J. (2008). Culturally responsive schooling for Indigenous youth: A review of the literature. *Review of Educational Research, 78,* 941–993.

Certo, J. (2011). Social skills and leadership abilities among children in small group literature discussions. *Journal of Research in Childhood Education, 25*(1), 62–81.

Chiu, M. M. (2008). Effects of argumentation on group micro-creativity: Statistical discourse analyses of algebra students' collaborative problem solving. *Contemporary Educational Psychology, 33,* 382–402.

Clark, A.-M., Anderson, R. C., Kuo, L., Kim, I., Archodidou, A., & Nguyen-Jahiel, K. (2003). Collaborative reasoning: Expanding ways for children to talk and think in school. *Educational Psychology Review, 15,* 181–198.

Clark, R. E., Feldon, D. F., van Merriënboer, J. J. G., Yates, K. A., & Early, S. (2008). Cognitive task analysis. In J. M. Spector, M. D. Merrill, J. van Merriënboer, & M. P. Driscoll (Eds.), *Handbook of research on educational communications and technology* (3rd ed., pp. 577–593). New York, NY: Erlbaum.

Clement, J. (2008). The role of explanatory models in teaching for conceptual change.

In S. Vosniadou (Ed.), *International handbook of research on conceptual change* (pp. 417–452). New York, NY: Routledge.

Cobb, P., & Yackel, E. (1996). Constructivist, emergent, and sociocultural perspectives in the context of developmental research. *Educational Psychologist, 31,* 175–190.

Cohen, E. G. (1994). Restructuring the classroom: Conditions for productive small groups. *Review of Educational Research, 64,* 1–35.

Cohen, E. G., Lockheed, M. E., & Lohman, M. R. (1976). The Center for Interracial Cooperation: A field experiment. *Sociology of Education, 59,* 47–58.

Cohen, E. G., & Lotan, R. A. (1995). Producing equal-status interaction in the heterogeneous classroom. *American Educational Research Journal, 32,* 99–120.

Cole, N. S. (1990). Conceptions of educational achievement. *Educational Researcher, 19*(3), 2–7.

Connolly, F. W., & Eisenberg, T. E. (1990). The feedback classroom: Teaching's silent friend. *T.H.E. Journal, 17*(5), 75–77.

Connor, D. F. (2006). Stimulants. In R. A. Barkley, *Attention-deficit hyperactivity disorder: A handbook for diagnosis and treatment* (3rd ed., pp. 608–647). New York, NY: Guilford.

Cooper, H. (1989). Synthesis of research on homework. *Educational Leadership, 47*(3), 85–91.

Cooper, H., Robinson, J. C., & Patall, E. A. (2006). Does homework improve academic achievement? A synthesis of research, 1987–2003. *Review of Educational Research, 76,* 1–62.

Cooper, H., & Valentine, J. C. (2001). Using research to answer practical questions about homework. *Educational Psychologist, 36,* 143–153.

Corkill, A. J. (1992). Advance organizers: Facilitators of recall. *Educational Psychology Review, 4,* 33–67.

Corno, L. (1996). Homework is a complicated thing. *Educational Researcher, 25*(8), 27–30.

Corno, L. (2008). On teaching adaptively. *Educational Psychologist, 43,* 161–173.

Corno, L., & Snow, R. E. (1986). Adapting teaching to individual differences among learners. In M. C. Wittrock (Ed.), *Handbook of research on teaching* (3rd ed., pp. 605–629). New York, NY: Macmillan.

Cosden, M., Morrison, G., Albanese, A. L., & Macias, S. (2001). When homework is not home work: After-school programs for homework assistance. *Educational Psychologist, 36,* 211–221.

Crook, C. (1995). On resourcing a concern for collaboration within peer interactions. *Cognition and Instruction, 13,* 541–547.

Cushing, L. S., & Kennedy, C. H. (1997). Academic effects of providing peer support in general education classrooms on students without disabilities. *Journal of Applied Behavior Analysis, 30,* 139–151.

Dansereau, D. F. (1988). Cooperative learning strategies. In C. E. Weinstein, E. T. Goetz, & P. A. Alexander (Eds.), *Learning and study strategies: Issues in assessment, instruction, and evaluation* (pp. 103–120). San Diego, CA: Academic Press.

Dansereau, D. F. (1995). Derived structural schemas and the transfer of knowledge. In A. McKeough, J. Lupart, & A. Marini (Eds.), *Teaching for transfer: Fostering generalization in learning* (pp. 93–122). Mahwah, NJ: Erlbaum.

de Jong, T. (2011). Instruction based on computer simulations. In R. E. Mayer & P. A. Alexander (Eds.), *Handbook of research on learning and instruction* (pp. 446–466). New York, NY: Routledge.

de Jong, T., & van Joolingen, W. R. (1998). Scientific discovery learning with computer simulations of conceptual domains. *Review of Educational Research, 68,* 179–201.

Dettmers, S., Trautwein, U., Lüdtke, O., Goetz, T., Frenzel, A. C., & Pekrun, R. (2011). Students' emotions during homework in mathematics: Testing a theoretical model of antecedents and achievement outcomes. *Contemporary Educational Psychology, 36,* 25–35.

Dettmers, S., Trautwein, U., Lüktke, O., Kunter, M., & Baumert, J. (2010). Homework works if homework quality is high: Using multilevel modeling to predict the development of achievement in mathematics. *Journal of Educational Psychology, 102,* 467–482.

Deutsch, M. (1993). Educating for a peaceful world. *American Psychologist, 48,* 510–517.

Doyle, W. (1983). Academic work. *Review of Educational Research, 53,* 159–199.

Dumont, H., Trautwein, U., Lüdtke, O., Neumann, M., Niggli, A., & Schnyder, I. (2012). Does parental homework involvement mediate the relationship between family background and educational outcomes? *Contemporary Educational Psychology, 37,* 55–69.

DuNann, D. G., & Weber, S. J. (1976). Short- and long-term effects of contingency managed instruction on low, medium, and high GPA students. *Journal of Applied Behavior Analysis, 9,* 375–376.

DuPaul, G. J., Ervin, R. A., Hook, C. L., & McGoey, K. E. (1998). Peer tutoring for children with attention deficit hyperactivity disorder: Effects on classroom behavior and academic performance. *Journal of Applied Behavior Analysis, 31,* 579–592.

Dymond, S. K., Renzaglia, A., & Chun, E. (2007). Elements of effective high school service learning programs that include students with and without disabilities. *Remedial and Special Education, 28*(4), 227–243.

Eccles, J. S. (2007). Families, schools, and developing achievement-related motivations and engagement. In J. E. Grusec & P. D. Hastings (Eds.), *Handbook of socialization: Theory and research* (pp. 665–691). New York, NY: Guilford.

Edelson, D. C., & Reiser, B. J. (2006). Making authentic practices accessible to learners. In R. K. Sawyer (Ed.), *The Cambridge handbook of the learning sciences* (pp. 335–354). Cambridge, England: Cambridge University Press.

Edmonds, M. S., Vaughn, S., Wexler, J., Reutebuch, C., Cable, A., Tackett, K. K., & Schnakenberg, J. W. (2009). A synthesis of reading interventions and effects of reading comprehension outcomes for older struggling students. *Review of Educational Research, 79,* 262–300.

Egbert, J. (2009). *Supporting learning with technology: Essentials of classroom practice.* Upper Saddle River, NJ: Pearson/Merrill/Prentice Hall.

Eilam, B. (2001). Primary strategies for promoting homework performance. *American Educational Research Journal, 38,* 691–725.

Esmonde, I. (2009). Ideas and identities: Supporting equity in cooperative mathematics learning. *Review of Educational Research, 79,* 1008–1043.

Fantuzzo, J. W., King, J., & Heller, L. R. (1992). Effects of reciprocal peer tutoring on mathematics and school adjustment: A component analysis. *Journal of Educational Psychology, 84,* 331–339.

Fennema, E. (1987). Sex-related differences in education: Myths, realities, and interventions. In V. Richardson-Koehler (Ed.), *Educators' handbook: A research perspective* (pp. 329–347). White Plains, NY: Longman.

Ferguson, E. L., & Hegarty, M. (1995). Learning with real machines or diagrams: Application of knowledge to real-world problems. *Cognition and Instruction, 13,* 129–160.

Ferguson, R. (1998). Can schools narrow the Black-White test score gap? In C. Jencks & M. Phillips (Eds.), *The Black-White test score gap* (pp. 318–374). Washington, DC: Brookings Institute.

Fiedler, E. D., Lange, R. E., & Winebrenner, S. (1993). In search of reality: Unraveling the myths about tracking, ability grouping and the gifted. *Roeper Review, 16*(1), 4–7.

Finn, J. D., Pannozzo, G. M., & Achilles, C. M. (2003). The "why's" of class size: Student behavior in small classes. *Review of Educational Research, 73,* 321–368.

Fletcher, J. M., Lyon, G. R., Fuchs, L. S., & Barnes, M. A. (2007). *Learning disabilities: From identification to intervention.* New York, NY: Guilford.

Fox, P. W., & LeCount, J. (1991, April). *When more is less: Faculty misestimation of student learning.* Paper presented at the annual meeting of the American Educational Research Association, Chicago, IL.

Frederiksen, N. (1984a). Implications of cognitive theory for instruction in problem-solving. *Review of Educational Research, 54,* 363–407.

Fries, S., Dietz, F., & Schmid, S. (2008). Motivational interference in learning: The impact of leisure alternatives on subsequent self-regulation. *Contemporary Educational Psychology, 33,* 119–133.

Fuchs, D., Fuchs, L. S., Mathes, P. G., & Simmons, D. C. (1997). Peer-assisted learning strategies: Making classrooms more responsive to diversity. *American Educational Research Journal, 34,* 174–206.

Fuchs, L. S., Compton, D. L., Fuchs, D., Paulsen, K., Bryant, J. D., & Hamlett, C. L. (2005). The prevention, identification, and cognitive determinants of math difficulty. *Journal of Educational Psychology, 97,* 493–513.

Fuchs, L. S., Fuchs, D., Karns, K., Hamlett, C. L., Dutka, S., & Katzaroff, M. (1996). The relation between student ability and the quality and effectiveness of explanations. *American Educational Research Journal, 33,* 631–664.

Fueyo, V., & Bushell, D., Jr. (1998). Using number line procedures and peer tutoring to improve the mathematics computation of low-performing first graders. *Journal of Applied Behavior Analysis, 31,* 417–430.

Furtak, E. M., Seidel, T., Iverson, H., & Briggs, D. C. (2012). Experimental and quasi-experimental studies of inquiry-based science teaching: A meta-analysis. *Review of Educational Research, 82,* 300–329.

Garbe, G., & Guy, D. (2006, Summer). No homework left behind. *Educational Leadership* [Online issue]. Retrieved February 23, 2009, from http://www.ascd.org/publications/educational_leadership/summer06/vol63/num09/toc.aspx

García, E. E. (1994). *Understanding and meeting the challenge of student cultural diversity.* Boston, MA: Houghton Mifflin.

García, E. E. (1995). Educating Mexican American students: Past treatment and recent developments in theory, research, policy, and practice. In J. A. Banks & C. A. M. Banks (Eds.), *Handbook of research on multicultural education* (pp. 372–387). New York, NY: Macmillan.

Gayford, C. (1992). Patterns of group behavior in open-ended problem solving in science classes of 15-year-old students in England. *International Journal of Science Education, 14,* 41–49.

Gehlbach, H., Brown, S. W., Ioannou, A., Boyer, M. A., Hudson, N., Niv-Solomon, A., . . . Janik, L. (2008). Increasing interest in social studies: Social perspective taking and self-efficacy in stimulating stimulations. *Contemporary Educational Psychology, 33,* 894–914.

Gillies, R. M. (2003). The behaviors, interactions, and perceptions of junior high school students during small-group learning. *Journal of Educational Psychology, 95,* 137–147.

Gillies, R. M., & Ashman, A. D. (1998). Behavior and interactions of children in cooperative groups in lower and middle elementary grades. *Journal of Educational Psychology, 90,* 746–757.

Ginsburg-Block, M. D., Rohrbeck, C. A., & Fantuzzo, J. W. (2006). A meta-analytic review of social, self-concept, and behavioral outcomes of peer-assisted learning. *Journal of Educational Psychology, 98,* 732–749.

Glass, A. L., & Sinha, N. (2013). Multiple-choice questioning is an efficient instructional methodology that may be widely implemented in academic courses to improve exam performance. *Current Directions in Psychological Science, 22,* 471–477.

Good, T. L., McCaslin, M. M., & Reys, B. J. (1992). Investigating work groups to promote problem solving in mathematics. In J. Brophy (Ed.), *Advances in research on teaching: Vol. 3. Planning and managing learning tasks and activities* (pp. 115–160). Greenwich, CT: JAI.

Graesser, A. C., D'Mello, S., & Cade, W. (2011). Instruction based on tutoring. In R. E. Mayer & P. A. Alexander (Eds.), *Handbook of research on learning and instruction* (pp. 408–426). New York, NY: Routledge.

Graesser, A. C., McNamara, D. S., & VanLehn, K. (2005). Scaffolding deep comprehension strategies through Point&Query, AutoTutor, and iSTART. *Educational Psychologist, 40,* 225–234.

Greenwood, C. R., Carta, J. J., & Hall, R. V. (1988). The use of peer tutoring strategies in classroom management and educational instruction. *School Psychology Review, 17,* 258–275.

Griffin, M. M., & Griffin, B. W. (1994, April). *Some can get there from here: Situated learning, cognitive style, and map skills.* Paper presented at the annual meeting of the American Educational Research Association, New Orleans, LA.

Gronlund, N. E., & Brookhart, S. M. (2009). *Writing instructional objectives* (8th ed.). Upper Saddle River, NJ: Merrill/Pearson.

Guinee, K. (2003, April). *Comparison of second-graders' narrative stories written using paper-and-pencil and a multimedia computer-based writing tool.* Paper presented at the annual meeting of the American Educational Research Association, Chicago, IL.

Guskey, T. R. (1985). *Implementing mastery learning.* Belmont, CA: Wadsworth.

Guskey, T. R. (2010). Formative assessment: The contributions of Benjamin S. Bloom. In H. L. Andrade & G. J. Cizek (Eds.), *Handbook of formative assessment* (pp. 106–124). New York, NY: Routledge.

Hacker, D. J., & Tenent, A. (2002). Implementing reciprocal teaching in the classroom: Overcoming obstacles and making modifications. *Journal of Educational Psychology, 94,* 699–718.

Hadjioannou, X. (2007). Bringing the background to the foreground: What do classroom environments that support authentic discussions look like? *American Educational Research Journal, 44,* 370–399.

Hardy, I., Jonen, A., Möller, K., & Stern, E. (2006). Effects of instructional support within constructivist learning environments for elementary school students' understanding of "floating and sinking." *Journal of Educational Psychology, 98,* 307–326.

Hartley, J., & Trueman, M. (1982). The effects of summaries on the recall of information from prose: Five experimental studies. *Human Learning, 1,* 63–82.

Hatano, G., & Inagaki, K. (1991). Sharing cognition through collective comprehension activity. In L. B. Resnick, J. M. Levine, & S. D. Teasley (Eds.), *Perspectives on socially shared cognition* (pp. 331–348). Washington, DC: American Psychological Association.

Hatano, G., & Inagaki, K. (1993). Desituating cognition through the construction of conceptual knowledge. In P. Light & G. Butterworth (Eds.), *Context and cognition: Ways of learning and knowing* (pp. 115–133). Mahwah, NJ: Erlbaum.

Hatano, G., & Inagaki, K. (2003). When is conceptual change intended? A cognitive-sociocultural view. In G. M. Sinatra & P. R. Pintrich (Eds.), *Intentional conceptual change* (pp. 407–427). Mahwah, NJ: Erlbaum.

Hattie, J. A. C. (2009). *Visible learning: A synthesis of over 800 meta-analyses relating to achievement.* London: Routledge.

Hattie, J. A. C., & Gan, M. (2011). Instruction based on feedback. In R. E. Mayer & P. A. Alexander (Eds.), *Handbook of research on learning and instruction* (pp. 249–271). New York, NY: Routledge.

Herrenkohl, L. R., & Guerra, M. R. (1998). Participant structures, scientific discourse, and student engagement in fourth grade. *Cognition and Instruction, 16,* 431–473.

Heward, W. L. (2009). *Exceptional children: An introduction to special education* (9th ed.). Upper Saddle River, NJ: Merrill/Pearson Education.

Hewitt, J., & Scardamalia, M. (1996, April). *Design principles for the support of distributed processes.* Paper presented at the annual meeting of the American Educational Research Association, New York, NY.

Hewitt, J., & Scardamalia, M. (1998). Design principles for distributed knowledge building processes. *Educational Psychology Review, 10,* 75–96.

Hirsch, E. D., Jr. (1996). *The schools we need and why we don't have them.* New York, NY: Doubleday.

Hmelo-Silver, C. E. (2006). Design principles for scaffolding technology-based inquiry. In A. M. O'Donnell, C. E. Hmelo-Silver, & G. Erkens (Eds.), *Collaborative learning, reasoning, and technology* (pp. 147–170). Mahwah, NJ: Erlbaum.

Hogan, D. M., & Tudge, J. R. H. (1999). Implications of Vygotsky's theory for peer learning. In A. M. O'Donnell & A. King (Eds.), *Cognitive perspectives on peer learning* (pp. 39–65). Mahwah, NJ: Erlbaum.

Hogan, K., Nastasi, B. K., & Pressley, M. (2000). Discourse patterns and collaborative scientific reasoning in peer and teacher-guided discussions. *Cognition and Instruction, 17,* 379–432.

Igoa, C. (1995). *The inner world of the immigrant child.* Mahwah, NJ: Erlbaum.

Inglis, A., & Biemiller, A. (1997, March). *Fostering self-direction in mathematics: A cross-age tutoring program that enhances math problem solving.* Paper presented at the annual meeting of the American Educational Research Association, Chicago, IL.

Iran-Nejad, A., & Stewart, W. (2010). Understanding as an educational objective: From seeking and playing with taxonomies to discovering and reflecting on revelations. *Research in the Schools, 17,* 64–76.

Jadallah, M., Anderson, R. C., Nguyen-Jahiel, K., Miller, B. W., Kim, I.-H., Kuo, L.-J., . . . Wu, X. (2011). Influence of a teacher's scaffolding moves during child-led small-group discussions. *American Educational Research Journal, 48,* 194–230.

Johnson, D. W., & Johnson, R. T. (1991). *Learning together and alone: Cooperative, competitive, and individualistic learning* (3rd ed.). Upper Saddle River, NJ: Prentice Hall.

Johnson, D. W., & Johnson, R. T. (2009a). An educational psychology success story: Social interdependence theory and cooperative learning. *Educational Researcher, 38,* 365–379.

Johnson, D. W., & Johnson, R. T. (2009b). Energizing learning: The instructional power of conflict. *Educational Researcher, 38,* 37–51.

Johnson-Glenberg, M. C. (2000). Training reading comprehension in adequate decoders/poor comprehenders: Verbal versus visual strategies. *Journal of Educational Psychology, 92,* 772–782.

Jonassen, D. H., Hannum, W. H., & Tessmer, M. (1989). *Handbook of task analysis procedures.* New York, NY: Praeger.

Kanar, A. M., & Bell, B. S. (2013). Guiding learners through technology-based instruction: The effects of adaptive guidance design and individual differences on learning over time. *Journal of Educational Psychology, 105,* 1067–1081.

Karich, A. C., Burns, M. K., & Maki, K. E. (2014). Updated meta-analysis of learner control within educational technology. *Review of Educational Research, 84,* 392–410.

Karpov, Y. V. (2003). Vygotsky's doctrine of scientific concepts: Its role for contemporary education. In A. Kozulin, B. Gindis, V. S. Ageyev, & S. M. Miller (Eds.), *Vygotsky's educational theory in cultural context* (pp. 65–82). Cambridge, England: Cambridge University Press.

King, A. (1997). ASK to THINK—TEL WHY®©: A model of transactive peer tutoring for scaffolding higher level complex learning. *Educational Psychologist, 32,* 221–235.

King, A. (1999). Discourse patterns for mediating peer learning. In A. M. O'Donnell & A. King (Eds.), *Cognitive perspectives on peer learning* (pp. 87–115). Mahwah, NJ: Erlbaum.

King, A., Staffieri, A., & Adelgais, A. (1998). Mutual peer tutoring: Effects of structuring tutorial interaction to scaffold peer learning. *Journal of Educational Psychology, 90,* 134–152.

Kirschner, F., Paas, F., & Kirschner, P. A. (2009). A cognitive load approach to collaborative learning: United brains for complex tasks. *Educational Psychology Review, 21,* 31–42.

Kirschner, P. A., Sweller, J., & Clark, R. E. (2006). Why minimal guidance during instruction does not work: An analysis of the failure of constructivist, discovery, problem-based, experiential, and inquiry-based teaching. *Educational Psychologist, 41,* 75–86.

Kirschner, P. A., & van Merriënboer, J. J. G. (2013). Do learners really know best? Urban legends in education. *Educational Psychologist, 48,* 169–183.

Klahr, D. (2009). "To everything there is a season, and a time to every purpose under the heavens": What about direct instruction? In S. Tobias & T. M. Duffy (Eds.), *Constructivist instruction: Success or failure?* (pp. 291–310). New York, NY: Routledge.

Koedinger, K., Aleven, V., Roll, I., & Baker, R. (2009). *In vivo* experiments on whether supporting metacognition in intelligent tutoring systems yields robust learning. In D. J. Hacker, J. Dunlosky, & A. C. Graesser (Eds.), *Handbook of metacognition in education* (pp. 383–412). New York, NY: Routledge.

Konstantopoulos, S., & Chung, V. (2011). The persistence of teacher effects in elementary grades. *American Educational Research Journal, 48,* 361–386.

Kreijns, K., Kirschner, P. A., & Vermeulen, M. (2013). Social aspects of CSCL environments: A research framework. *Educational Psychologist, 48,* 229–242.

Ku, Y.-M., Chan, W.-C., Wu, Y.-C., & Chen, Y.-H. (2008, March). *Improving children's comprehension of science text: Effects of adjunct questions and notetaking.* Paper presented at the annual meeting of the American Educational Research Association, New York, NY.

Kuhn, D. (2015). Thinking together and alone. *Educational Researcher, 44,* 46–53.

Kuhn, D., & Crowell, A. (2011). Dialogic argumentation as a vehicle for developing young adolescents' thinking. *Psychological Science, 22,* 545–552.

Kuhn, D., & Pease, M. (2008). What needs to develop in the development of inquiry skills? *Cognition and Instruction, 26,* 512–599.

Kuhn, D., & Pease, M. (2010). The dual components of developing strategy use: Production and inhibition. In H. S. Waters & W. Schneider (Eds.), *Metacognition, strategy use, and instruction* (pp. 135–159). New York, NY: Guilford.

Kuhn, D., Shaw, V., & Felton, M. (1997). Effects of dyadic interaction on argumentative reasoning. *Cognition and Instruction, 15,* 287–315.

Kulik, C. C., Kulik, J. A., & Bangert-Drowns, R. L. (1990). Effectiveness of mastery learning programs: A meta-analysis. *Review of Educational Research, 60,* 265–299.

Ladd, G. W., Kochenderfer-Ladd, B., Visconti, K. J., Ettekal, I., Sechler, C. M., & Cortes, K. I. (2014). Grade-school children's social collaborative skills: Links with partner preference and achievement. *American Educational Research Journal, 51,* 152–183.

Lambert, M. C., Cartledge, G., Heward, W. L., & Lo, Y.-Y. (2006). Effects of response cards on disruptive behavior and academic responding during math lessons by fourth-grade urban students. *Journal of Positive Behavioral Interventions, 8,* 88–99.

Lamon, M., Chan, C., Scardamalia, M., Burtis, P. J., & Brett, C. (1993, April). *Beliefs about learning and constructive processes in reading: Effects of a computer supported intentional learning environment (CSILE).* Paper presented at the annual meeting of the American Educational Research Association, Atlanta, GA.

Lampert, M., Rittenhouse, P., & Crumbaugh, C. (1996). Agreeing to disagree: Developing sociable mathematical discourse. In D. R. Olson & N. Torrance (Eds.), *The handbook of education and human development: New models of learning, teaching, and schooling* (pp. 731–764). Cambridge, MA: Blackwell.

Leach, J. T., & Scott, P. H. (2008). Teaching for conceptual understanding: An approach drawing on individual and sociocultural perspectives. In S. Vosniadou (Ed.), *International handbook on conceptual change* (pp. 647–675). New York, NY: Routledge.

Lee-Pearce, M. L., Plowman, T. S., & Touchstone, D. (1998). Starbase-Atlantis, a school without walls: A comparative study of an innovative science program for at-risk urban elementary students. *Journal of Education for Students Placed at Risk, 3,* 223–235.

Lepper, M. R., Aspinwall, L. G., Mumme, D. L., & Chabay, R. W. (1990). Self-perception and social perception processes in tutoring: Subtle social control strategies of expert tutors. In J. M. Olson & M. P. Zanna (Eds.), *Self-inference processes: The Ontario Symposium* (pp. 217–238). Mahwah, NJ: Erlbaum.

Leu, D. J., O'Byrne, W. I., Zawilinski, L., McVerry, J. G., & Everett-Cacopardo, H. (2009). Expanding the new literacies conversation. *Educational Researcher, 38,* 264–269.

Levin, J. R., & Mayer, R. E. (1993). Understanding illustrations in text. In B. K. Britton, A. Woodward, & M. Binkley (Eds.), *Learning from textbooks: Theory and practice* (pp. 95–113). Mahwah, NJ: Erlbaum.

Levstik, L. S. (2011). Learning history. In R. E. Mayer & P. A. Alexander (Eds.), *Handbook of research on learning and instruction* (pp. 108–126). New York, NY: Routledge.

Levy, I., Kaplan, A., & Patrick, H. (2000, April). *Early adolescents' achievement goals, intergroup processes, and attitudes towards collaboration.* Paper presented at the annual meeting of the American Educational Research Association, New Orleans, LA.

Linn, M. C. (2008). Teaching for conceptual change: Distinguish or extinguish ideas. In S. Vosniadou (Ed.), *International handbook on conceptual change* (pp. 694–722). New York, NY: Routledge.

Linn, M. C., & Eylon, B.-S. (2011). *Science learning and instruction: Taking advantage of technology to promote knowledge integration.* New York, NY: Routledge.

Lorch, R. F., Jr., Lorch, E. P., Calderhead, W. J., Dunlap, E. E., Hodell, E. C., & Freer, B. D. (2010). Learning the control of variables strategy in higher and lower achieving classrooms: Contributions of explicit instruction and experimentation. *Journal of Educational Psychology, 102,* 90–101.

Lorch, R. F., Jr., Lorch, E. P., & Inman, W. E. (1993). Effects of signaling topic structure on text recall. *Journal of Educational Psychology, 85,* 281–290.

Lotan, R. A. (2006). Managing groupwork in heterogeneous classrooms. In C. M. Evertson & C. S. Weinstein (Eds.), *Handbook of classroom management: Research, practice, and contemporary issues* (pp. 525–539). Mahwah, NJ: Erlbaum.

Lou, Y., Abrami, P. C., & d'Apollonia, S. (2001). Small group and individual learning with technology: A meta-analysis. *Review of Educational Research, 71,* 449–521.

Lou, Y., Abrami, P. C., Spence, J. C., Poulsen, C., Chambers, B., & d'Apollonia, S. (1996). Within-class grouping: A meta-analysis. *Review of Educational Research, 66,* 423–458.

Mac Iver, D. J., Reuman, D. A., & Main, S. R. (1995). Social structuring of the school: Studying what is, illuminating what could be. In J. T. Spence, J. M. Darley, & D. J. Foss (Eds.), *Annual review of psychology* (Vol. 46, pp. 375–400). Palo Alto, CA: Annual Review.

MacLean, D. J., Sasse, D. K., Keating, D. P., Stewart, B. E., & Miller, F. K. (1995, April). *All-girls' mathematics and science instruction in early adolescence: Longitudinal effects.* Paper presented at the annual meeting of the American Educational Research Association, San Francisco, CA.

Marzano, R. J., & Kendall, J. S. (2007). *The new taxonomy of educational objectives* (2nd ed.). Thousand Oaks, CA: Corwin.

Mathes, P. G., Torgesen, J. K., & Allor, J. H. (2001). The effects of peer-assisted literacy strategies for first-grade readers with and without additional computer-assisted instruction. *American Educational Research Journal, 38,* 371–410.

Mayer, R. E. (2004). Should there be a three-strikes rule against pure discovery learning? *American Psychologist, 59,* 14–19.

Mayer, R. E. (2010a). Fostering scientific reasoning with multimedia instruction. In H. S. Waters & W. Schneider (Eds.), *Metacognition, strategy use, and instruction* (pp. 160–175). New York, NY: Guilford.

Mayer, R. E. (2011a). *Applying the science of learning.* Boston, MA: Allyn & Bacon.

Mayer, R. E., & Gallini, J. (1990). When is an illustration worth ten thousand words? *Journal of Educational Psychology, 82,* 715–726.

McAshan, H. H. (1979). *Competency-based education and behavioral objectives.* Englewood Cliffs, NJ: Educational Technology.

McDaniel, M. A., & Einstein, G. O. (1989). Material-appropriate processing: A contextualist approach to reading and studying strategies. *Educational Psychology Review, 1,* 113–145.

McDevitt, M., & Chaffee, S. H. (1998). Second chance political socialization: "Trickle-up" effects of children on parents. In T. J.

Johnson, C. E. Hays, & S. P. Hays (Eds.), *Engaging the public: How government and the media can reinvigorate American democracy* (pp. 57–66). Lanhan, MD: Rowman & Littlefield.

McGee, L. M. (1992). An exploration of meaning construction in first graders' grand conversations. In C. K. Kinzer & D. J. Leu (Eds.), *Literacy research, theory, and practice: Views from many perspectives* (pp. 177–186). Chicago: National Reading Conference.

Meirick, P. C., & Wackman, D. B. (2004). Kids Voting and political knowledge: Narrowing gaps, informing votes. *Social Science Quarterly, 85,* 1161–1177.

Mercer, C. D., & Pullen, P. C. (2005). *Students with learning disabilities* (6th ed.). Upper Saddle River, NJ: Merrill/Prentice Hall.

Mergendoller, J. R., Markham, T., Ravitz, J., & Larmer, J. (2006). Pervasive management of project based learning: Teachers as guides and facilitators. In C. M. Evertson & C. S. Weinstein (Eds.), *Handbook of classroom management: Research, practice, and contemporary issues* (pp. 583–615). Mahwah, NJ: Erlbaum.

Merrill, P. F., Hammons, K., Vincent, B. R., Reynolds, P. L., Christensen, L., & Tolman, M. N. (1996). *Computers in education* (3rd ed.). Boston, MA: Allyn & Bacon.

Miller, M. D., Linn, R. L., & Gronlund, N. E. (2009). *Measurement and assessment in teaching* (10th ed.). Upper Saddle River, NJ: Merrill/Pearson.

Minstrell, J., & Stimpson, V. (1996). A classroom environment for learning: Guiding students' reconstruction of understanding and reasoning. In L. Schauble & R. Glaser (Eds.), *Innovations in learning: New environments for education* (pp. 175–202). Mahwah, NJ: Erlbaum.

Moje, E. B., & Shepardson, D. P. (1998). Social interactions and children's changing understanding of electric circuits: Exploring unequal power relations in "peer"-learning groups. In B. Guzzetti & C. Hynd (Eds.), *Perspectives on conceptual change: Multiple ways to understand knowing and learning in a complex world* (pp. 225–234). Mahwah, NJ: Erlbaum.

Monte-Sano, C. (2008). Qualities of historical writing instruction: A comparative case study of two teachers' practices. *American Educational Research Journal, 45,* 1045–1079.

Moreno, R. (2006). Learning in high-tech and multimedia environments. *Current Directions in Psychological Science, 15,* 63–67.

Moreno, R., & Park, B. (2010). Cognitive Load Theory: Historical development and relation to other theories. In J. L. Plass, R. Moreno, & R. Brünken (Eds.), *Cognitive Load Theory* (pp. 9–28). Cambridge, England: Cambridge University Press.

Morgan, D. P., & Jenson, W. R. (1988). *Teaching behaviorally disordered students: Preferred practices.* Upper Saddle River, NJ: Merrill/Prentice Hall.

Munro, D. W., & Stephenson, J. (2009). The effects of response cards on student and teacher behavior during vocabulary

instruction. *Journal of Applied Behavior Analysis, 42,* 795–800.

Murphy, P. K., Wilkinson, I. A. G., & Soter, A. O. (2011). Instruction based on discussion. In R. E. Mayer & P. A. Alexander (Eds.), *Handbook of research on learning and instruction* (pp. 382–407). New York, NY: Routledge.

Murphy, P. K., Wilkinson, I. A. G., Soter, A. O., Hennessey, M. N., & Alexander, J. F. (2009). Examining the effects of classroom discussion on students' comprehension of text: A meta-analysis. *Journal of Educational Psychology, 101,* 740–764.

Narciss, S. (2008). Feedback strategies for interactive learning tasks. In J. M. Spector, M. D. Merrill, J. van Merriënboer, & M. P. Driscoll (Eds.), *Handbook of research on educational communications and technology* (3rd ed., pp. 125–143). New York, NY: Erlbaum.

Newby, T. J., Ertmer, P. A., & Stepich, D. A. (1994, April). *Instructional analogies and the learning of concepts.* Paper presented at the annual meeting of the American Educational Research Association, New Orleans, LA.

Niederhauser, D. S. (2008). Educational hypertext. In J. M. Spector, M. D. Merrill, J. van Merriënboer, & M. P. Driscoll (Eds.), *Handbook of research on educational communications and technology* (3rd ed., pp. 199–210). New York, NY: Erlbaum.

Nixon, A. S. (2005, April). *Moral reasoning in the digital age: How students, teachers, and parents judge appropriate computer uses.* Paper presented at the annual meeting of the American Educational Research Association, Montreal, Canada.

Nolen, S. B. (2011). Motivation, engagement, and identity: Opening a conversation. In D. M. McInerney, R. A. Walker, & G. A. D. Liem (Eds.), *Sociocultural theories of learning and motivation: Looking back, looking forward* (pp. 109–135). Charlotte, NC: Information Age.

Nussbaum, E. M. (2008). Collaborative discourse, argumentation, and learning: Preface and literature review. *Contemporary Educational Psychology, 33,* 345–359.

O'Donnell, A. M. (1999). Structuring dyadic interaction through scripted cooperation. In A. M. O'Donnell & A. King (Eds.), *Cognitive perspectives on peer learning* (pp. 179–196). Mahwah, NJ: Erlbaum.

O'Donnell, A. M. (2006). The role of peers and group learning. In P. A. Alexander & P. H. Winne (Eds.), *Handbook of educational psychology* (2nd ed., pp. 781–802). Mahwah, NJ: Erlbaum.

O'Donnell, A. M., & O'Kelly, J. (1994). Learning from peers: Beyond the rhetoric of positive results. *Educational Psychology Review, 6,* 321–349.

Onosko, J. J. (1996). Exploring issues with students despite the barriers. *Social Education, 60*(1), 22–27.

Palincsar, A. S., & Brown, A. L. (1984). Reciprocal teaching of comprehension-fostering and comprehension-monitoring activities. *Cognition and Instruction, 1,* 117–175.

Palincsar, A. S., & Brown, A. L. (1989). Classroom dialogues to promote self-regulated comprehension. In J. Brophy (Ed.), *Advances in research on teaching* (Vol. 1, pp. 35–71). Greenwich, CT: JAI.

Palincsar, A. S., & Herrenkohl, L. R. (1999). Designing collaborative contexts: Lessons from three research programs. In A. M. O'Donnell & A. King (Eds.), *Cognitive perspectives on peer learning* (pp. 151–177). Mahwah, NJ: Erlbaum.

Palmer, E. L. (1965). Accelerating the child's cognitive attainments through the inducement of cognitive conflict: An interpretation of the Piagetian position. *Journal of Research in Science Teaching, 3,* 324.

Patall, E. A., Cooper, H., & Wynn, S. R. (2010). The effectiveness and relative importance of choice in the classroom. *Journal of Educational Psychology, 102,* 896–915.

Pea, R. D., & Maldonado, H. (2006). WILD for learning: Interacting through new computing devices anytime, anywhere. In R. K. Sawyer (Ed.), *The Cambridge handbook of the learning sciences* (pp. 427–441). Cambridge, England: Cambridge University Press.

Pellegrino, J. W., Chudowsky, N., & Glaser, R. (Eds.), (2001). *Knowing what students know: The science and design of educational assessment.* Washington DC: National Academy Press.

Pfeifer, J. H., Brown, C. S., & Juvonen, J. (2007). Teaching tolerance in schools: Lessons learned since *Brown v. Board of Education* about the development and reduction of children's prejudice. *Social Policy Report, 21*(2), 3–13, 16–17, 20–23. Ann Arbor, MI: Society for Research in Child Development.

Pianta, R. C., Barnett, W. S., Burchinal, M., & Thornburg, K. R. (2009). The effects of preschool education: What we know, how public policy is or is not aligned with the evidence base, and what we need to know. *Psychological Science in the Public Interest, 10,* 49–88.

Pianta, R. C., & Hamre, B. K. (2009). Conceptualization, measurement, and improvement of classroom processes: Standardized observation can leverage capacity. *Educational Researcher, 38,* 109–119.

Piirto, J. (1999). *Talented children and adults: Their development and education* (2nd ed.). Upper Saddle River, NJ: Merrill/Prentice Hall.

Pittman, K., & Beth-Halachmy, S. (1997, March). *The role of prior knowledge in analogy use.* Paper presented at the annual meeting of the American Educational Research Association, Chicago, IL.

Plass, J. L., Kalyuga, S., & Leutner, D. (2010). Individual differences and Cognitive Load Theory. In J. L. Plass, R. Moreno, & R. Brünken (Eds.), *Cognitive Load Theory* (pp. 65–87). Cambridge, England: Cambridge University Press.

Popham, W. J. (2014). *Classroom assessment: What teachers need to know* (7th ed.). Upper Saddle River, NJ: Pearson.

Portes, P. R. (1996). Ethnicity and culture in educational psychology. In D. C. Berliner &

R. C. Calfee (Eds.), *Handbook of educational psychology* (pp. 331–357). New York, NY: Macmillan.

Pugh, K. J., Schmidt, K., & Russell, C. (2010, May). *Fostering transformative experiences in science: A design-based study.* Paper presented at the annual meeting of the American Educational Research Association, Denver, CO.

Qin, Z., Johnson, D. W., & Johnson, R. T. (1995). Cooperative versus competitive efforts and problem solving. *Review of Educational Research, 65,* 129–143.

Quintana, C., Zhang, M., & Krajcik, J. (2005). A framework for supporting metacognitive aspects of online inquiry through software-based scaffolding. *Educational Psychologist, 40,* 235–244.

Redfield, D. L., & Rousseau, E. W. (1981). A meta-analysis of experimental research on teacher questioning behavior. *Review of Educational Research, 51,* 237–245.

Reeve, J. (2009). Why teachers adopt a controlling motivating style toward students and how they can become more autonomy supportive. *Educational Psychologist, 44,* 159–175.

Reinking, D., & Leu, D. J. (Chairs). (2008, March). *Understanding Internet reading comprehension and its development among adolescents at risk of dropping out of school.* Poster session presented at the annual meeting of the American Educational Research Association, New York, NY.

Reynolds, R. E., & Shirey, L. L. (1988). The role of attention in studying and learning. In C. E. Weinstein, E. T. Goetz, & P. A. Alexander (Eds.), *Learning and study strategies: Issues in assessment, instruction, and evaluation* (pp. 77–100). San Diego, CA: Academic Press.

Reznitskaya, A., & Gregory, M. (2013). Student thought and classroom language: Examining the mechanisms of change in dialogic teaching. *Educational Psychologist, 48,* 114–133.

Rittle-Johnson, B. (2006). Promoting transfer: Effects of self-explanation and direct instruction. *Child Development, 77,* 1–15.

Robinson, A. (1991). Cooperation or exploitation? The argument against cooperative learning for talented students. *Journal for the Education of the Gifted, 14,* 9–27.

Robinson, D. R., Schofield, J. W., & Steers-Wentzell, K. L. (2005). Peer and cross-age tutoring in math: Outcomes and their design implications. *Educational Psychology Review, 17,* 327–362.

Roscoe, R. D., & Chi, M. T. H. (2007). Understanding tutor learning: Knowledge-building and knowledge-telling in peer tutors' explanations and questions. *Review of Educational Research, 77,* 534–574.

Rosenshine, B. (2009). The empirical support for direct instruction. In S. Tobias & T. M. Duffy (Eds.), *Constructivist instruction: Success or failure?* (pp. 201–220). New York, NY: Routledge.

Rosenshine, B., & Meister, C. (1994). Reciprocal teaching: A review of the research. *Review of Educational Research, 64,* 479–530.

Rosenshine, B., & Stevens, R. (1986). Teaching functions. In M. C. Wittrock (Ed.), *Handbook of research on teaching* (3rd ed., pp. 376–391). New York, NY: Macmillan.

Rowe, M. B. (1987). Wait-time: Slowing down may be a way of speeding up. *American Educator, 11,* 38–43, 47.

Ruef, M. B., Higgins, C., Glaeser, B., & Patnode, M. (1998). Positive behavioral support: Strategies for teachers. *Intervention in School and Clinic, 34*(1), 21–32.

Sadoski, M., & Paivio, A. (2001). *Imagery and text: A dual coding theory of reading and writing.* Mahwah, NJ: Erlbaum.

Sarama, J., & Clements, D. H. (2009). "Concrete" computer manipulatives in mathematics education. *Child Development Perspectives, 3,* 145–150.

Sawyer, R. K. (2006). Introduction: The new science of learning. In R. K. Sawyer (Ed.), *The Cambridge handbook of the learning sciences* (pp. 1–16). Cambridge, England: Cambridge University Press.

Scardamalia, M., & Bereiter, C. (2006). Knowledge building: Theory, pedagogy, and technology. In R. K. Sawyer (Ed.), *The Cambridge handbook of the learning sciences* (pp. 97–115). Cambridge, England: Cambridge University Press.

Scevak, J. J., Moore, P. J., & Kirby, J. R. (1993). Training students to use maps to increase text recall. *Contemporary Educational Psychology, 18,* 401–413.

Schiffman, G., Tobin, D., & Buchanan, B. (1984). Microcomputer instruction for the learning disabled. *Annual Review of Learning Disabilities, 2,* 134–136.

Schofield, J. W. (2006). Internet use in schools: Promise and problems. In R. K. Sawyer (Ed.), *The Cambridge handbook of the learning sciences* (pp. 521–534). Cambridge, England: Cambridge University Press.

Schwartz, D. L., & Martin, T. (2004). Inventing to prepare for future learning: The hidden efficiency of encouraging original student production in statistics instruction. *Cognition and Instruction, 22,* 129–184.

Shuell, T. J. (1996). Teaching and learning in a classroom context. In D. C. Berliner & R. C. Calfee (Eds.), *Handbook of educational psychology* (pp. 726–764). New York, NY: Macmillan.

Sinatra, G. M., & Mason, L. (2008). Beyond knowledge: Learner characteristics influencing conceptual change. In S. Vosniadou (Ed.), *International handbook on conceptual change* (pp. 560–582). New York, NY: Routledge.

Sitko, B. M. (1998). Knowing how to write: Metacognition and writing instruction. In D. J. Hacker, J. Dunlosky, & A. C. Graesser (Eds.), *Metacognition in educational theory and practice* (pp. 93–115). Mahwah, NJ: Erlbaum.

Skinner, B. F. (1968). *The technology of teaching.* New York, NY: Appleton-Century-Crofts.

Slater, W. H. (2004). Teaching English from a literacy perspective: The goal of high literacy for all students. In T. L. Jetton & J. A. Dole

(Eds.), *Adolescent literacy research and practice* (pp. 40–58). New York, NY: Guilford.

Slavin, R. E. (2011). Instruction based on cooperative learning. In R. E. Mayer & P. A. Alexander (Eds.), *Handbook of research on learning and instruction* (pp. 344–360). New York, NY: Routledge.

Slavin, R. E., Hurley, E. A., & Chamberlain, A. (2003). Cooperative learning and achievement: Theory and research. In W. Reynolds & G. Miller (Eds.), *Handbook of psychology: Vol. 7. Educational psychology* (pp. 177–198). New York, NY: Wiley.

Slavin, R. E., & Lake, C. (2008). Effective programs in elementary mathematics: A best-evidence synthesis. *Review of Educational Research, 78,* 427–515.

Small, M. Y., Lovett, S. B., & Scher, M. S. (1993). Pictures facilitate children's recall of unillustrated expository prose. *Journal of Educational Psychology, 85,* 520–528.

Smith, C. L. (2007). Bootstrapping processes in the development of students' commonsense matter theories: Using analogical mappings, thought experiments, and learning to measure to promote conceptual restructuring. *Cognition and Instruction, 25,* 337–398.

Snir, J., Smith, C. L., & Raz, G. (2003). Linking phenomena with competing underlying models: A software tool for introducing students to the particulate model of matter. *Science Education, 87,* 794–830.

Spicker, H. H. (1992). Identifying and enriching: Rural gifted children. *Educational Horizons, 70*(2), 60–65.

Spiro, R. J., & DeSchryver, M. (2009). Constructivism: When it's the wrong idea and when it's the only idea. In S. Tobias & T. M. Duffy (Eds.), *Constructivist instruction: Success or failure?* (pp. 106–123). New York, NY: Routledge.

Spörer, N., & Brunstein, J. C. (2009). Fostering the reading comprehension of secondary school students through peer-assisted learning: Effects on strategy knowledge, strategy use, and task performance. *Contemporary Educational Psychology, 34,* 289–297.

Squire, K. (2011). *Video games and learning: Teaching and participatory culture in the digital age.* New York, NY: Teachers College Press.

Stacey, K. (1992). Mathematical problem solving in groups: Are two heads better than one? *Journal of Mathematical Behavior, 11,* 261–275.

Staples, M. (2007). Supporting whole-class collaborative inquiry in a secondary mathematics classroom. *Cognition and Instruction, 25,* 161–217.

Steenbergen-Hu, S., & Cooper, H. (2013). A meta-analysis of the effectiveness of intelligent tutoring systems on K–12 students' mathematical learning. *Journal of Educational Psychology, 105,* 970–987.

Stein, J. A., & Krishnan, K. (2007). Nonverbal learning disabilities and executive function: The challenges of effective assessment and teaching. In L. Meltzer (Ed.), *Executive*

function in education: From theory to practice (pp. 106–132). New York, NY: Guilford.

Sternberg, R. J., & Horvath, J. A. (1995). A prototype view of expert teaching. *Educational Researcher, 24*(6), 9–17.

Stevens, R. J., & Slavin, R. E. (1995). The cooperative elementary school: Effects of students' achievement, attitudes, and social relations. *American Educational Research Journal, 32,* 321–351.

Stokes, J. V., Luiselli, J. K., & Reed, D. D. (2010). A behavioral intervention for teaching tackling skills to high school football athletes. *Journal of Applied Behavior Analysis, 43,* 509–512.

Sullivan, J. R., & Conoley, J. C. (2004). Academic and instructional interventions with aggressive students. In J. C. Conoley & A. P. Goldstein (Eds.), *School violence intervention* (2nd ed., pp. 235–255). New York, NY: Guilford.

Swan, K., Mitrani, M., Guerrero, F., Cheung, M., & Schoener, J. (1990, April). *Perceived locus of control and computer-based instruction.* Paper presented at the annual meeting of the American Educational Research Association, Boston, MA.

Sweller, J. (2010). Cognitive Load Theory: Recent theoretical advances. In J. L. Plass, R. Moreno, & R. Brünken (Eds.), *Cognitive Load Theory* (pp. 29–47). Cambridge, England: Cambridge University Press.

Tamin, R. M., Bernard, R. M., Borokhovski, E., Abrami, P. C., & Schmid, R. F. (2011). What forty years of research says about the impact of technology on learning: A second-order meta-analysis and validation study. *Review of Educational Research, 81,* 4–28.

Tarver, S. G. (1992). Direct Instruction. In W. Stainback & S. Stainback (Eds.), *Controversial issues confronting special education* (pp. 143–165). Boston, MA: Allyn & Bacon.

Tharp, R. G. (1989). Psychocultural variables and constants: Effects on teaching and learning in schools. *American Psychologist, 44,* 349–359.

Théberge, C. L. (1994, April). *Small-group vs. whole-class discussion: Gaining the floor in science lessons.* Paper presented at the annual meeting of the American Educational Research Association, New Orleans, LA.

Tobias, S, & Fletcher, J. D. (Eds.). (2011). *Computer games and instruction.* Charlotte, NC: Information Age.

Tomlinson, C. A., & McTighe, J. (2006). *Integrating Differentiated Instruction and Understanding by Design.* Alexandria, VA: Association for Supervision and Curriculum Development.

Trautwein, U., Lüdtke, O., Kastens, C., & Köller, O. (2006). Effort on homework in grades 5–9: Development, motivational antecedents, and the association with effort on classwork. *Child Development, 77,* 1094–1111.

Trautwein, U., Niggli, A., Schnyder, I., & Lüdtke, O. (2009). Between-teacher differences in homework assignments and the development of students' homework effort, homework emotions, and achievement.

Journal of Educational Psychology, 101, 176–189.

Turnbull, A. P., Turnbull, R., & Wehmeyer, M. L. (2010). *Exceptional lives: Special education in today's schools* (6th ed.). Upper Saddle River, NJ: Merrill.

van Garderen, D. (2004). Reciprocal teaching as a comprehension strategy for understanding mathematical word problems. *Reading and Writing Quarterly, 20,* 225–229.

van Merriënboer, J. J. G., & Kester, L. (2008). Whole-task models in education. In J. M. Spector, M. D. Merrill, J. van Merriënboer, & M. P. Driscoll (Eds.), *Handbook of research on educational communications and technology* (3rd ed., pp. 441–456). New York, NY: Erlbaum.

van Merriënboer, J. J. G., Kirschner, P. A., & Kester, L. (2003). Taking the load off a learner's mind: Instructional design for complex learning. *Educational Psychologist, 38,* 5–13.

Vaughn, S., Klingner, J. K., Swanson, E. A., Boardman, A. G., Roberts, G., Mohammed, S. S., & Stillman-Spisak, S. J. (2011). Efficacy of collaborative strategic reading with middle school students. *American Educational Research Journal, 48,* 938–964.

Verdi, M. P., & Kulhavy, R. W. (2002). Learning with maps and texts: An overview. *Educational Psychology Review, 14,* 27–46.

Wade, S. E. (1992). How interest affects learning from text. In K. A. Renninger, S. Hidi, & A. Krapp (Eds.), *The role of interest in learning and development* (pp. 255–277). Mahwah, NJ: Erlbaum.

Wade-Stein, D., & Kintsch, E. (2004). Summary Street: Interactive computer support for writing. *Cognition and Instruction, 22,* 333–362.

Walshaw, M., & Anthony, G. (2008). The teacher's role in classroom discourse: A review of recent research into mathematics classrooms. *Review of Educational Research, 78,* 516–551.

Ward, W., Cole, R., Bolaños, D., Buchenroth-Martin, C., Svirsky, E., & Weston, T. (2013). My Science Tutor: A conversational multimedia virtual tutor. *Journal of Educational Psychology, 105,* 1115–1125.

Warschauer, M. (2011). *Learning in the cloud: How (and why) to transform schools with digital media.* New York, NY: Teachers College Press.

Wasley, P. A., Hampel, R. L., & Clark, R. W. (1997). *Kids and school reform.* San Francisco, CA: Jossey-Bass.

Watkins, C. L. (1997). *Project Follow Through: A case study of contingencies influencing instructional practices of the educational establishment.* Cambridge, MA: Cambridge Center for Behavioral Studies.

Webb, N. M. (1989). Peer interaction and learning in small groups. *International Journal of Educational Research, 13,* 21–39.

Webb, N. M., & Farivar, S. (1999). Developing productive group interaction in middle school mathematics. In A. M. O'Donnell & A. King (Eds.), *Cognitive perspectives on peer learning* (pp. 117–149). Mahwah, NJ: Erlbaum.

Webb, N. M., Franke, M. L., Ing, M., Chan, A., De, T., Freund, D., & Battey, D. (2008). The role of teacher instructional practices in student collaboration. *Contemporary Educational Psychology, 33,* 360–381.

Webb, N. M., & Mastergeorge, A. M. (2003). The development of students' helping behavior and learning in peer-directed small groups. *Cognition and Instruction, 21,* 361–428.

Webb, N. M., Nemer, K. M., Chizhik, A. W., & Sugrue, B. (1998). Equity issues in collaborative group assessment: Group composition and performance. *American Educational Research Journal, 35,* 607–651.

Webb, N. M., Nemer, K. M., & Zuniga, S. (2002). Short circuits or superconductors? Effects of group composition on high-achieving students' science assessment performance. *American Educational Research Journal, 39,* 943–989.

Webb, N. M., & Palincsar, A. S. (1996). Group processes in the classroom. In D. C. Berliner & R. C. Calfee (Eds.), *Handbook of educational psychology* (pp. 841–873). New York, NY: Macmillan.

Weinert, F. E., & Helmke, A. (1995). Learning from wise Mother Nature or Big Brother Instructor: The wrong choice as seen from an educational perspective. *Educational Psychologist, 30,* 135–142.

Wentzel, K. R. (2009). Peers and academic functioning at school. In K. H. Rubin, W. M. Bukowski, & B. Laursen (Eds.), *Handbook of peer interactions, relationships, and groups* (pp. 531–547). New York, NY: Guilford.

White, B. Y., & Frederiksen, J. R. (1998). Inquiry, modeling, and metacognition: Making science accessible to all students. *Cognition and Instruction, 16,* 3–118.

White, B. Y., & Frederiksen, J. R. (2005). A theoretical framework and approach for fostering metacognitive development. *Educational Psychologist, 40,* 211–223.

White, B. Y., Frederiksen, J., & Collins, A. (2009). The interplay of scientific inquiry and metacognition: More than a marriage of convenience. In D. J. Hacker, J. Dunlosky, & A. C. Graesser (Eds.), *Handbook of metacognition in education* (pp. 175–205). New York, NY: Routledge.

White, J. R., & McVeigh, J. (2010, April–May). Paper presented at the annual meeting of the American Educational Research Association, New Orleans, LA.

Wiggins, G., & McTighe, J. (2005). *Understanding by Design* (expanded 2nd ed.). Alexandria, VA: Association for Supervision and Curriculum Development.

Wiggins, G., & McTighe, J. (2011). *The Understanding by Design guide to creating high-quality units.* Alexandria, VA: Association for Supervision and Curriculum Development.

Williams, S. M. (2010, April–May). *The impact of collaborative, scaffolded learning in K–12 schools: A meta-analysis.* Paper presented at the annual meeting of the American Educational Research Association, Denver, CO.

Wilson, P. T., & Anderson, R. C. (1986). What they don't know will hurt them: The role of prior knowledge in comprehension. In J. Orasanu (Ed.), *Reading comprehension: From research to practice* (pp. 31–48). Mahwah, NJ: Erlbaum.

Winn, W. (1991). Learning from maps and diagrams. *Educational Psychology Review, 3,* 211–247.

Winters, F. I., Greene, J. A., & Costich, C. M. (2008). Self-regulation of learning within computer-based learning environments: A critical analysis. *Educational Psychology Review, 20,* 429–444.

Wise, A. F., & O'Neill, K. (2009). Beyond more versus less: A reframing of the debate on instructional guidance. In S. Tobias & T. M. Duffy (Eds.), *Constructivist instruction: Success or failure?* (pp. 82–105). New York, NY: Routledge.

Wittwer, J., & Renkl, A. (2008). Why instructional explanations often do not work: A framework for understanding the effectiveness of instructional explanations. *Educational Psychologist, 43,* 49–64.

Wixson, K. K. (1984). Level of importance of post-questions and children's learning from text. *American Educational Research Journal, 21,* 419–433.

Wood, J. W., & Rosbe, M. (1985). Adapting the classroom lecture for the mainstreamed student in the secondary schools. *Clearing House, 58,* 354–358.

Wu, X., Anderson, R. C., Nguyen-Jahiel, K., & Miller, B. (2013). Enhancing motivation and engagement through collaborative discussion. *Journal of Educational Psychology, 105,* 622–632.

Xu, J. (2008). Models of secondary school students' interest in homework: A multilevel analysis. *American Educational Research Journal, 45,* 1180–1205.

Zimmerman, B. J. (1998). Developing self-fulfilling cycles of academic regulation: An analysis of exemplary instructional models. In D. H. Schunk & B. J. Zimmerman (Eds.), *Self-regulated learning: From teaching to self-reflective practice* (pp. 1–19). New York, NY: Guilford.

Zimmerman, B. J., & Didenedetto, M. K. (2008). Mastery learning and assessment: Implications for students and teachers in an era of high-stakes testing. *Psychology in the Schools, 45,* 206–216.

Zook, K. B. (1991). Effects of analogical processes on learning and misrepresentation. *Educational Psychology Review, 3,* 41–72.

CHAPTER 13

Abelev, M. S. (2009). Advancing out of poverty: Social class worldview and its relation to resilience. *Journal of Adolescent Research, 24*(1), 114–141.

Adger, C. T., Wolfram, W., & Christian, D. (2007). *Dialects in schools and communities* (2nd ed.). New York, NY: Routledge.

Ahn, H. J., & Rodkin, P. C. (2014). Classroom-level predictors of the social status of aggression: Friendship centralization, friendship density, teacher–student attunement, and gender. *Journal of Educational Psychology, 106*(4), 1144–1155.

Allday, R. A., Bush, M., Ticknor, N., & Walker, L. (2011). Using teacher greetings to increase speed to task engagement. *Journal of Applied Behavior Analysis, 44,* 393–396.

Allday, R. A., & Pakurar, K. (2007). Effects of teacher greetings on student on-task behavior. *Journal of Applied Behavior Analysis, 40,* 317–320.

Ames, C. (1984). Competitive, cooperative, and individualistic goal structures: A cognitive-motivational analysis. In R. Ames & C. Ames (Eds.), *Research on motivation in education: Vol. 1. Student motivation* (pp. 177–207). San Diego, CA: Academic Press.

Anderman, E. M. (2002). School effects on psychological outcomes during adolescence. *Journal of Educational Psychology, 94,* 795–809.

Anderman, E. M., Lane, D. R., Zimmerman, R., Cupp, P. K., & Phebus, V. (2009). Comparing the efficacy of permanent classroom teachers to temporary health educators for pregnancy and HIV prevention instruction. *Health Promotion Practice, 10*(4), 597–605.

Anderman, L. H., Andrzejewski, C. E., & Allen, J. (2011). How do teachers support students' motivation and learning in their classrooms? *Teachers College Record, 113* (5), 969–1003.

Anderman, L. H., & Freeman, T. (2004). Students' sense of belonging in school. In M. L. Maehr & P. R. Pintrich (Eds.), *Advances in motivation and achievement, Vol. 13. Motivating students, improving schools: The legacy of Carol Midgley.* Oxford, UK: Elsevier.

Anderman, L. H., Patrick, H., Hruda, L. Z., & Linnenbrink, E. A. (2002). Observing classroom goal structures to clarify and expand goal theory. In C. Midgley (Ed.), *Goals, goal structures, and patterns of adaptive learning* (pp. 243–278). Mahwah, NJ: Erlbaum.

Astor, R. A., Meyer, H. A., & Behre, W. J. (1999). Unowned places and times: Maps and interviews about violence in high schools. *American Educational Research Journal, 36,* 3–42.

Babad, E. (1995). The "teacher's pet phenomenon," students' perceptions of teachers' differential behavior, and students' morale. *Journal of Educational Psychology, 87,* 361–374.

Babad, E., Avni-Babad, D., & Rosenthal, R. (2003). Teachers' brief nonverbal behaviors in defined instructional situations can predict students' evaluations. *Journal of Educational Psychology, 95,* 553–562.

Baker, J. (1999). Teacher-student interaction in urban at-risk classrooms: Differential behavior, relationship quality, and student satisfaction with school. *Elementary School Journal, 100,* 57–70.

Bandura, A. (1986). *Social foundations of thought and action: A social cognitive theory.* Upper Saddle River, NJ: Prentice Hall.

Barkley, R. A. (2006). *Attention-deficit hyperactivity disorder: A handbook for diagnosis and treatment* (3rd ed.). New York, NY: Guilford.

Battistich, V., Solomon, D., Kim, D., Watson, M., & Schaps, E. (1995). Schools as communities, poverty levels of student populations, and students' attitudes, motives, and performance: A multilevel analysis. *American Educational Research Journal, 32*, 627–658.

Battistich, V., Solomon, D., Watson, M., & Schaps, E. (1997). Caring school communities. *Educational Psychologist, 32*, 137–151.

Becker, B. E., & Luthar, S. S. (2002). Social-emotional factors affecting achievement outcomes among disadvantaged students: Closing the achievement gap. *Educational Psychologist, 37*, 197–214.

Beirne-Smith, M., Patton, J. R., & Kim, S. H. (2006). *Mental retardation: An introduction to intellectual disabilities* (7th ed.). Upper Saddle River, NJ: Merrill/Prentice Hall.

Bender, G. (2001). Resisting dominance? The study of a marginalized masculinity and its construction within high school walls. In J. N. Burstyn, G. Bender, R. Casella, H. W. Gordon, D. P. Guerra, K. V. Luschen, R. Stevens, & K. M. Williams, *Preventing violence in schools: A challenge to American democracy* (pp. 61–77). Mahwah, NJ: Erlbaum.

Blanton, H., & Burkley, M. (2008). Deviance regulation theory: Applications to adolescent social influence. In M. J. Prinstein & K. A. Dodge (Eds.), *Understanding peer influence in children and adolescents* (pp. 94–121). New York, NY: Guilford.

Blugental, D. B., Lyon, J. E., Lin, E. K., McGrath, E. P., & Bimbela, A. (1999). Children "tune out" to the ambiguous communication style of powerless adults. *Child Development, 70*, 214–230.

Bornstein, M. H., & Cote, L. R. (2010). Immigration and acculturation. In M. H. Bornstein (Ed.), *Handbook of cultural developmental science* (pp. 531–552). New York, NY: Psychology Press.

Borum, R., Cornell, D. G., Modzeleski, W., & Jimerson, S. R. (2010). What can be done about school shootings? A review of the evidence. *Educational Researcher, 39*, 27–37.

Brophy, J. (2008). Developing students' appreciation for what is taught in school. *Educational Psychologist, 43*, 132–141.

Brophy, J. E. (2006). Observational research on generic aspects of classroom teaching. In P. A. Alexander & P. H. Winne (Eds.), *Handbook of educational psychology* (2nd ed., pp. 755–780). Mahwah, NJ: Erlbaum.

Brown, R. P., Osterman, L. L., & Barnes, C. D. (2009). School violence and the culture of honor. *Psychological Science, 20*, 1400–1405.

Buchoff, T. (1990). Attention deficit disorder: Help for the classroom teacher. *Childhood Education, 67*, 86–90.

Bulotsky-Shearer, R. J., Dominguez, X., & Bell, E. R. (2012). Preschool classroom behavioral context and school readiness outcomes for low-income children: A multilevel examination of child-and classroom-level

influences. *Journal of Educational Psychology, 104*(2), 421–438.

Burstyn, J. N., & Stevens, R. (2001). Involving the whole school in violence prevention. In J. N. Burstyn, G. Bender, R. Casella, H. W. Gordon, D. P. Guerra, K. V. Luschen, R. Stevens, & K. M. Williams, *Preventing violence in schools: A challenge to American democracy* (pp. 139–158). Mahwah, NJ: Erlbaum.

Campbell, D. E. (1996). *Choosing democracy: A practical guide to multicultural education.* Upper Saddle River, NJ: Merrill/Prentice Hall.

Carbrera, N. J., Shannon, J. D., West, J., & Brooks-Gunn, J. (2006). Parental interactions with Latino infants: Variation by country of origin and English proficiency. *Child Development, 77*, 1190–1207.

Carini, P. F., & Himley, M., (with Christine, C., Espinosa, C., & Fournier, J.). (2010). *Jenny's story: Taking the long view of the child.* New York, NY: Teachers College Press.

Carr, A. A. (1997, March). *The participation "race": Kentucky's site based decision teams.* Paper presented at the annual meeting of the American Educational Research Association, Chicago, IL.

Carter, K., & Doyle, W. (2006). Classroom management in early childhood and elementary classrooms. In C. M. Evertson & C. S. Weinstein (Eds.), *Handbook of classroom management: Research, practice, and contemporary issues* (pp. 373–406). Mahwah, NJ: Erlbaum.

Casella, R. (2001b). What is violent about "school violence"? The nature of violence in a city high school. In J. N. Burstyn, G. Bender, R. Casella, H. W. Gordon, D. P. Guerra, K. V. Luschen, R. Stevens, & K. M. Williams, *Preventing violence in schools: A challenge to American democracy* (pp. 15–46). Mahwah, NJ: Erlbaum.

Cassady, J. C. (Ed.). (2010a). *Anxiety in schools: The causes, consequences, and solutions for academic anxieties.* New York, NY: Peter Lang.

Castagno, A. E., & Brayboy, B. M. J. (2008). Culturally responsive schooling for Indigenous youth: A review of the literature. *Review of Educational Research, 78*, 941–993.

Cazden, C. B. (2001). *Classroom discourse: The language of teaching and learning* (2nd ed.). Portsmouth, NH: Heinemann.

Centers for Disease Control. (2015). *Understanding school violence: Fact sheet 2015.* Retrived from http://www.cdc.gov/violenceprevention/pdf/school_violence_fact_sheet-a.pdf

Certo, J., Cauley, K. M., & Chafin, C. (2002, April). *Students' perspectives on their high school experience.* Paper presented at the annual meeting of the American Educational Research Association, New Orleans, LA.

Certo, J. L., Cauley, K. M., & Chafin, C. (2003). Students' perspectives on their high school experience. *Adolescence, 38*, 705–724.

Chang, M.-L., & Davis, H. A. (2009). Understanding the role of teacher appraisals in shaping the dynamics of their relationships with students: Deconstructing

teachers' judgments of disruptive behavior/students. In P. Schutz & M. Zembylas (Eds.), *Advances in teacher emotion research: The impact of teachers' lives* (pp. 95–125). New York, NY: Springer.

Chester, M. D., & Beaudin, B. Q. (1996). Efficacy beliefs of newly hired teachers in urban schools. *American Educational Research Journal, 33*, 233–257.

Christenson, S. L., & Sheridan, S. M. (2001). *Schools and families: Creating essential connections for learning.* New York, NY: Guilford.

Ciani, K. D., Middleton, M. J., Summers, J. J., & Sheldon, K. M. (2010). Buffering against performance classroom goal structures: The importance of autonomy support and classroom community. *Contemporary Educational Psychology, 35*, 88–99.

Cizek, G. J. (2003). *Detecting and preventing classroom cheating: Promoting integrity in assessment.* Thousand Oaks, CA: Corwin.

Clark, B. (1997). *Growing up gifted* (5th ed.). Upper Saddle River, NJ: Merrill/Prentice Hall.

Cohen, G. L., & Garcia, J. (2008). Identity, belonging, and achievement: A model, interventions, implications. *Current Directions in Psychological Science, 17*, 365–369.

Coie, J. D., & Dodge, K. A. (1998). Aggression and antisocial behavior. In W. Damon (Series Ed.) & N. Eisenberg (Vol. Ed.), *Handbook of child psychology: Vol. 3. Social, emotional, and personality development* (5th ed., pp. 779–862). New York, NY: Wiley.

Colvin, G., Ainge, D., & Nelson, R. (1997). How to defuse defiance, threats, challenges, confrontations. *Teaching Exceptional Children, 29*(6), 47–51.

Connor, C. M., Spencer, M., Day, S. L., Giuliani, S., Ingebrand, S. W., McLean, L., & Morrison, F. J. (2014). Capturing the complexity: Content, type, and amount of instruction and quality of the classroom learning environment synergistically predict third graders' vocabulary and reading comprehension outcomes. *Journal of Educational Psychology, 106*(3), 762–778.

Crone, D. A., Horner, R. H., & Hawken, L. S. (2004). *Responding to problem behavior in schools: The behavior education program.* New York, NY: Guilford.

Dai, D. Y. (2010). *The nature and nurture of giftedness: A new framework for understanding gifted education.* New York, NY: Teachers College Press.

Dantas, M. L., & Manyak, P. C. (Eds.) (2010). *Home–school connections in a multicultural society: Learning from and with culturally and linguistically diverse families.* New York, NY: Routledge.

Davis, C., & Yang, A. (2005). *Parents and teachers working together.* Turners Falls, MA: Northeast Foundation for Children.

Davis, G. A., & Thomas, M. A. (1989). *Effective schools and effective teachers.* Boston, MA: Allyn & Bacon.

Davis, H. A. (2003). Conceptualizing the role and influence of student-teacher relationships on children's social and cognitive development. *Educational Psychologist, 38,* 207–234.

Deci, E. L. (1992). The relation of interest to the motivation of behavior: A self-determination theory perspective. In K. A. Renninger, S. Hidi, & A. Krapp (Eds.), *The role of interest in learning and development* (pp. 43–70). Mahwah, NJ: Erlbaum.

Dempster, F. N., & Corkill, A. J. (1999). Interference and inhibition in cognition and behavior: Unifying themes for educational psychology. *Educational Psychology Review, 11,* 1–88.

DeVoe, J. F., Peter, K., Noonan, M., Snyder, T. D., & Baum, K. (2005). *Indicators of school crime and safety: 2005* (NCES 2006–001/NCJ 210697). Washington, DC: U.S. Departments of Education and Justice. Retrieved from http://ojp.usdoj.gov/bjs/abstract/iscs05.htm

Deyhle, D., & LeCompte, M. (1999). Cultural differences in child development: Navajo adolescents in middle schools. In R. H. Sheets & E. R. Hollins (Eds.), *Racial and ethnic identity in school practices: Aspects of human development* (pp. 123–139). Mahwah, NJ: Erlbaum.

Diamond, S. C. (1991). What to do when you can't do anything: Working with disturbed adolescents. *Clearing House, 64,* 232–234.

Dicke, T., Parker, P. D., Marsh, H. W., Kunter, M., Schmeck, A., & Leutner, D. (2014). Self-efficacy in classroom management, classroom disturbances, and emotional exhaustion: A moderated mediation analysis of teacher candidates. *Journal of Educational Psychology, 106*(2), 569–583.

Dien, T. (1998). Language and literacy in Vietnamese American communities. In B. Pérez (Ed.), *Sociocultural contexts of language and literacy* (pp. 23–54). Mahwah, NJ: Erlbaum.

Dishion, T. J., Piehler, T. F., & Myers, M. W. (2008). Dynamics and ecology of adolescent peer influence. In M. J. Prinstein & K. A. Dodge (Eds.), *Understanding peer influence in children and adolescents* (pp. 72–93). New York, NY: Guilford.

Dodge, K. A., Lansford, J. E., Burks, V. S., Bates, J. E., Pettit, G. S., Fontaine, R., et al. (2003). Peer rejection and social information-processing factors in the development of aggressive behavior problems in children. *Child Development, 74,* 374–393.

Doyle, W. (1983). Academic work. *Review of Educational Research, 53,* 159–199.

Doyle, W. (1984). How order is achieved in classrooms: An interim report. *Journal of Curriculum Studies, 16,* 259–277.

Doyle, W. (1986a). Classroom organization and management. In M. C. Wittrock (Ed.), *Handbook of research on teaching* (3rd ed., pp. 392–431). New York, NY: Macmillan.

Doyle, W. (1990). Classroom management techniques. In O. C. Moles (Ed.), *Student discipline strategies: Research and practice* (pp. 113–127). Albany, NY: State University of New York Press.

Doyle, W. (2006). Ecological approaches to classroom management. In C. M. Evertson &

C. S. Weinstein (Eds.), *Handbook of classroom management: Research, practice, and contemporary issues* (pp. 97–125). Mahwah, NJ: Erlbaum.

Dreikurs, R. (1998). *Maintaining sanity in the classroom: Classroom management techniques* (2nd ed.). Bristol, PA: Hemisphere.

Dumont, H., Trautwein, U., Lüdtke, O., Neumann, M., Niggli, A., & Schnyder, I. (2012). Does parental homework involvement mediate the relationship between family background and educational outcomes? *Contemporary Educational Psychology, 37*(1), 55–69.

Dumont, H., Trautwein, U., Nagy, G., & Nagengast, B. (2014). Quality of parental homework involvement: Predictors and reciprocal relations with academic functioning in the reading domain. *Journal of Educational Psychology, 106*(1), 144–161.

Dwyer, K., & Osher, D. (2000). *Safeguarding our children: An action guide.* Washington, DC: U.S. Departments of Education and Justice, American Institutes for Research. Retrieved from http://www.ed.gov/pubs/edpubs.html

Dwyer, K., Osher, D., & Warger, C. (1998). *Early warning, timely response: A guide to safe schools.* Washington, DC: U.S. Department of Education. Retrieved from http://www.ed.gov/offices/OSERS/OSEP/earlywrn.html

Eaton, W. O., & Enns, L. R. (1986). Sex differences in human motor activity level. *Psychological Bulletin, 100,* 19–28.

Ellis, J., Fitzsimmons, S., & Small-McGinley, J. (2010). Encouraging the discouraged: Students' views for elementary classrooms. In G. S. Goodman (Ed.), *Educational psychology reader: The art and science of how people learn* (pp. 251–272). New York, NY: Peter Lang.

Emmer, E. T., & Evertson, C. M. (1981). Synthesis of research on classroom management. *Educational Leadership, 38*(4), 342–347.

Emmer, E. T., & Evertson, C. M. (2009). *Classroom management for middle and high school teachers* (8th ed.). Upper Saddle River, NJ: Pearson.

Emmer, E. T., & Gerwels, M. C. (2006). Classroom management in middle and high school classrooms. In C. M. Evertson & C. S. Weinstein (Eds.), *Handbook of classroom management: Research, practice, and contemporary issues* (pp. 407–437). Mahwah, NJ: Erlbaum.

Emmer, E. T., & Stough, L. M. (2001). Classroom management: A critical part of educational psychology, with implications for teacher education. *Educational Psychologist, 36,* 103–112.

Epstein, J. L. (1996). Perspectives and previews on research and policy for school, family, and community partnerships. In A. Booth & J. F. Dunn (Eds.), *Family-school links: How do they affect educational outcomes?* (pp. 209–246). Mahwah, NJ: Erlbaum.

Espelage, D., Anderman, E. M., Brown, V. E., Jones, A., Lane, K. L., McMahon, S. D., Reddy, L.A., & Reynolds, C. R. (2013). Understanding and preventing violence

directed against teachers: Recommendations for a national research, practice, and policy agenda. *American Psychologist, 68*(2), 75–87.

Espelage, D. L., Holt, M. K., & Henkel, R. R. (2003). Examination of peer-group contextual effects on aggression during early adolescence. *Child Development, 74,* 205–220.

Espinoza, G., & Juvonen, J. (2011). Perceptions of the school social context across the transition to middle school: Heightened sensitivity among Latino students? *Journal of Educational Psychology, 103,* 749–758.

Estrada, J. J., Gilreath, T. D., Astor, R. A., & Benbenishty, R. (2014). Gang membership, school violence, and the mediating effects of risk and protective behaviors in California high schools. *Journal of School Violence, 13*(2), 228–251.

Evertson, C. M., & Emmer, E. T. (1982). Effective management at the beginning of the year in junior high classes. *Journal of Educational Psychology, 74,* 485–498.

Evertson, C. M., & Emmer, E. T. (2009). *Classroom management for elementary teachers* (8th ed.). Upper Saddle River, NJ: Pearson.

Evertson, C. M., & Weinstein, C. S. (Eds.). (2006). *Handbook of classroom management: Research, practice, and contemporary issues.* Mahwah, NJ: Erlbaum.

Filax, G. (2007). Queer in/visibility: The case of Ellen, Michel, and Oscar. In S. Books (Ed.), *Invisible children in the society and its schools* (3rd ed., pp. 213–234). Mahwah, NJ: Erlbaum.

Finders, M., & Lewis, C. (1994). Why some parents don't come to school. *Educational Leadership, 51*(8), 50–54.

Fingerhut, L. A., & Christoffel, K. K. (2002). Firearm-related death and injury among children and adolescents. *The Future of Children, 12*(2), 25–37.

Finkelhor, D., & Ormrod, R. (2000, December). *Juvenile victims of property crimes.* Washington, DC: U.S. Department of Justice, Office of Justice Programs, Office of Juvenile Justice and Delinquency Prevention.

Flanagan, C. A., Cumsille, P., Gill, S., & Gallay, L. S. (2007). School and community climates and civic commitments: Patterns for ethnic minority and majority students. *Journal of Educational Psychology, 99,* 421–431.

Fletcher, K. L., & Cassady, J. C. (2010). Overcoming academic anxieties: Promoting effective coping and self-regulation strategies. In J. C. Cassady (Ed.), *Anxiety in schools: The causes, consequences, and solutions for academic anxieties* (pp. 177–200). New York, NY: Peter Lang.

Forman, S. G., & Barakat, N. M. (2011). Cognitive-behavioral therapy in the schools: Bringing research to practice through effective implementation. *Psychology in the Schools, 48,* 283–296.

Fosnot, C. T. (1996). Constructivism: A psychological theory of learning. In C. T. Fosnot (Ed.), *Constructivism: Theory, perspectives, and practice* (p. 833). New York, NY: Teachers College Press.

Fuller, M. L. (2001). Multicultural concerns and classroom management. In C. A. Grant & M. L. Gomez, *Campus and classroom: Making schooling multicultural* (2nd ed., pp. 109–134). Upper Saddle River, NJ: Merrill/Prentice Hall.

Garbarino, J., Bradshaw, C. P., & Vorrasi, J. A. (2002). Mitigating the effects of gun violence on children and youth. *The Future of Children, 12*(2), 73–85.

García, E. E. (1995). Educating Mexican American students: Past treatment and recent developments in theory, research, policy, and practice. In J. A. Banks & C. A. M. Banks (Eds.), *Handbook of research on multicultural education* (pp. 372–387). New York, NY: Macmillan.

Gebo, E., & Sullivan, C. J. (2014). A statewide comparison of gang and non-gang youth in public high schools. *Youth Violence and Juvenile Justice, 12*(3), 191–208.

Gettinger, M. (1988). Methods of proactive classroom management. *School Psychology Review, 17*, 227–242.

Gettinger, M., & Kohler, K. M. (2006). Process-outcome approaches to classroom management and effective teaching. In C. M. Evertson & C. S. Weinstein (Eds.), *Handbook of classroom management: Research, practice, and contemporary issues* (pp. 73–95). Mahwah, NJ: Erlbaum.

Glasser, W. (1969). *Schools without failure.* New York, NY: Harper & Row.

Goddard, R. D., Hoy, W. K., & Woolfolk Hoy, A. (2000). Collective teacher efficacy: Its meaning, measure, and impact on student achievement. *American Educational Research Journal, 37*, 479–507.

Goldstein, L. S., & Lake, V. E. (2000). "Love, love, and more love for children": Exploring preservice teachers' understanding of caring. *Teaching and Teacher Education, 16*, 861–872.

Granger, D. A., Whalen, C. K., Henker, B., & Cantwell, C. (1996). ADHD boys' behavior during structured classroom social activities: Effects of social demands, teacher proximity, and methylphenidate. *Journal of Attention Disorders, 1*(1), 16–30.

Green, C. L., Walker, J. M. T., Hoover-Dempsey, K. V., & Sandler, H. M. (2007). Parents' motivation for involvement in children's education: An empirical test of a theoretical model of parental involvement. *Journal of Educational Psychology, 99*, 532–544.

Greenberg, M. T., Weissberg, R. P., O'Brien, M. U., Zins, J. E., Fredericks, L., Resnik, H., et al. (2003). Enhancing school-based prevention and youth development through coordinated social, emotional, and academic learning. *American Psychologist, 58*, 466–474.

Gregg, N. (2009). *Adolescents and adults with learning disabilities and ADHD: Assessment and accommodation.* New York, NY: Guilford.

Gregory, A., Cornell, D., Fan, X., Sheras, P., Shih, T. H., & Huang, F. (2010). Authoritative school discipline: High school practices associated with lower bullying and victimization. *Journal of Educational Psychology, 102*(2), 483–496.

Gut, J., Reimann, G., & Grob, A. (2013). A contextualized view on long-term predictors of academic performance. *Journal of Educational Psychology, 105*(2), 436–443.

Hamovitch, B. (2007). Hoping for the best: "Inclusion" and stigmatization in a middle school. In S. Books (Ed.), *Invisible children in the society and its schools* (3rd ed., pp. 263–281). Mahwah, NJ: Erlbaum.

Hamre, B. K., & Pianta, R. C. (2005). Can instructional and emotional support in the first-grade classroom make a difference for children at risk of school failure? *Child Development, 76*, 949–967.

Hanley, G. P., Tiger, J. H., Ingvarsson, E. T., & Cammilleri, A. P. (2009). Influencing preschoolers' free-play activity preferences: An evaluation of satiation and embedded reinforcement. *Journal of Applied Behavior Analysis, 42*, 33–41.

Hattie, J., & Gan, M. (2011). Instruction based on feedback. In R. E. Mayer & P. A. Alexander (Eds.), *Handbook of research on learning and instruction* (pp. 249–271). New York, NY: Routledge.

Henley, M. (2010). *Classroom management: A proactive approach* (2nd ed.). Columbus, OH: Merrill/Pearson.

Heward, W. L. (2009). *Exceptional children: An introduction to special education* (9th ed.). Upper Saddle River, NJ: Merrill/Pearson Education.

Hidalgo, N. M., Siu, S., Bright, J. A., Swap, S. M., & Epstein, J. L. (1995). Research on families, schools, and communities: A multicultural perspective. In J. A. Banks & C. A. M. Banks (Eds.), *Handbook of research on multicultural education* (pp. 498–524). New York, NY: Macmillan.

Hiebert, E. H., & Raphael, T. E. (1996). Psychological perspectives on literacy and extensions to educational practice. In D. C. Berliner & R. C. Calfee (Eds.), *Handbook of educational psychology* (pp. 550–602). New York, NY: Macmillan.

Hill, N. E., & Taylor, L. C. (2004). Parental school involvement and children's academic achievement: Pragmatics and issues. *Current Directions in Psychological Science, 13*, 161–164.

Hindman, A. H., & Morrison, F. J. (2011). Family involvement and educator outreach in head start: Nature, extent, and contributions to early literacy skills. *The Elementary School Journal, 111*(3), 359–386.

Hochweber, J., Hosenfeld, I., & Klieme, E. (2014). Classroom composition, classroom management, and the relationship between student attributes and grades. *Journal of Educational Psychology, 106*(1), 289–300.

Hogan, T., Rabinowitz, M., & Craven, J. A., III. (2003). Representation in teaching: Inferences from research of expert and novice teachers. *Educational Psychologist, 38*, 235–247.

Hom, A., & Battistich, V. (1995, April). *Students' sense of school community as a factor in reducing drug use and delinquency.* Paper presented at the annual meeting of the American Educational Research Association, San Francisco, CA.

Hong, S., & Ho, H.-Z. (2005). Direct and indirect longitudinal effects of parental involvement on student achievement: Second-order latent growth modeling across ethnic groups. *Journal of Educational Psychology, 97*, 32–42.

Houts, R. M., Caspi, A., Pianta, R. C., Arseneault, L., & Moffitt, T. E. (2010). The challenging pupil in the classroom: The effect of the child on the teacher. *Psychological Science, 21*, 1802–1810.

Howell, J. C., & Lynch, J. P. (2000, August). *Youth gangs in schools. Juvenile Justice Bulletin* (OJJDP Publication NCJ-183015). Washington, DC: U.S. Department of Justice, Office of Juvenile Justice and Delinquency Prevention.

Hughes, J. N. (2011). Longitudinal effects of teacher and student perceptions of teacher-student relationship qualities on academic adjustment. *Elementary School Journal, 112*(1), 38–60.

Hughes, J. N., Luo, W., Kwok, O.-M., & Loyd, L. K. (2008). Teacher-student support, effortful engagement, and achievement: A 3-year longitudinal study. *Journal of Educational Psychology, 100*, 1–14.

Hughes, J. N., Wu, J. Y., Kwok, O. M., Villarreal, V., & Johnson, A. Y. (2012). Indirect effects of child reports of teacher–student relationship on achievement. *Journal of Educational Psychology, 104*(2), 350–365.

Hyman, I., Kay, B., Tabori, A., Weber, M., Mahon, M., & Cohen, I. (2006). Bullying: Theory, research, and interventions. In C. M. Evertson & C. S. Weinstein (Eds.), *Handbook of classroom management: Research, practice, and contemporary issues* (pp. 855–884). Mahwah, NJ: Erlbaum.

Igoa, C. (1995). *The inner world of the immigrant child.* Mahwah, NJ: Erlbaum.

Ihlo, T., & Nantais, M. (2010). Evidence-based interventions within a multi-tier framework for positive behavioral supports. In T. A. Glover & S. Vaughn (Eds.), *The promise of response to intervention: Evaluating current science and practice* (pp. 239–266). New York, NY: Guilford.

Iruka, I. U., Winn, D. M. C., Kingsley, S. J., & Orthodoxou, Y. J. (2011). Links between parent-teacher relationships and kindergartners' social skills: Do child ethnicity and family income matter? *Elementary School Journal, 111*(3), 387–408.

Jang, H., Reeve, J., & Deci, E. L. (2010). Engaging students in learning activities: It is not autonomy support or structure but autonomy support and structure. *Journal of Educational Psychology, 102*, 588–600.

Johnson, W., McGue, M., & Iacono, W. G. (2005). Disruptive behavior and school grades: Genetic and environmental relations in 11-year-olds. *Journal of Educational Psychology, 97*, 391–405.

Jones, V. (1996). Classroom management. In J. Sikula, T. J. Buttery, & E. Guyton (Eds.), *Handbook of research on teacher education* (2nd ed., pp. 503–521). New York, NY: Macmillan.

Juvonen, J. (2006). Sense of belonging, social bonds, and school functioning. In P. A. Alexander & P. H. Winne (Eds.), *Handbook of educational psychology* (2nd ed., pp. 655–674). Mahwah, NJ: Erlbaum.

Kağıtçıbaşı, Ç. (2007). *Family, self, and human development across cultures: Theory and applications* (2nd ed.). Mahwah, NJ: Erlbaum.

Keller, H. R., & Tapasak, R. C. (2004). Classroom-based approaches. In J. C. Conoley & A. P. Goldstein (Eds.), *School violence intervention* (2nd ed., pp. 103–130). New York, NY: Guilford.

Keogh, B. K. (2003). *Temperament in the classroom.* Baltimore, MD: Brookes.

Kim, D., Solomon, D., & Roberts, W. (1995, April). *Classroom practices that enhance students' sense of community.* Paper presented at the annual meeting of the American Educational Research Association, San Francisco.

Kincheloe, J. L. (2009). No short cuts in urban education: Metropedagogy and diversity. In S. R. Steinberg (Ed.), *Diversity and multiculturalism: A reader* (pp. 379–409). New York, NY: Peter Lang.

Klassen, R. M., Perry, N. E., & Frenzel, A. C. (2012). Teachers' relatedness with students: An underemphasized component of teachers' basic psychological needs. *Journal of Educational Psychology, 104*(1), 150–165.

Klein, J., & Cornell, D. (2010). Is the link between large high schools and student victimization an illusion? *Journal of Educational Psychology, 102*(4), 933–946.

Kodluboy, D. W. (2004). Gang-oriented interventions. In J. C. Conoley & A. P. Goldstein (Eds.), *School violence intervention* (2nd ed., pp. 194–232). New York, NY: Guilford.

Koegel, L. K., Koegel, R. L., & Dunlap, G. (Eds.). (1996). *Positive behavioral support: Including people with difficult behavior in the community.* Baltimore, MD: Brookes.

Koestner, R., Ryan, R. M., Bernieri, F., & Holt, K. (1984). Setting limits in children's behavior: The differential effects of controlling versus informational styles on intrinsic motivation and creativity. *Journal of Personality, 52*, 233–248.

Kounin, J. S. (1970). *Discipline and group management in classrooms.* New York, NY: Holt, Rinehart & Winston.

Kumar, R., Gheen, M. H., & Kaplan, A. (2002). Goal structures in the learning environment and students' disaffection from learning and schooling. In C. Midgley (Ed.), *Goals, goal structures, and patterns of adaptive learning* (pp. 143–173). Mahwah, NJ: Erlbaum.

Ladd, G. W., Herald-Brown, S. L., & Reiser, M. (2008). Does chronic classroom peer rejection predict the development of children's classroom participation during the grade school years? *Child Development, 79*, 1001–1015.

Ladson-Billings, G. (1994a). *The dreamkeepers: Successful teachers of African American children.* San Francisco, CA: Jossey-Bass.

Lam, S. F., Chow-Yeung, K., Wong, B. P., Lau, K. K., & Tse, S. I. (2013). Involving parents in paired reading with preschoolers: Results from a randomized controlled trial. *Contemporary Educational Psychology, 38*(2), 126–135.

Lane, K., Falk, K., & Wehby, J. (2006). Classroom management in special education classrooms and resource rooms. In C. M. Evertson & C. S. Weinstein (Eds.), *Handbook of classroom management: Research, practice, and contemporary issues* (pp. 439–460). Mahwah, NJ: Erlbaum.

Lane, K. L., Kalberg, J. R., & Menzies, H. M. (2009). *Developing schoolwide programs to prevent and manage problem behaviors: A step-by-step approach.* New York, NY: Guilford.

Lane, K. L., Menzies, H. M., Bruhn, A. L., & Crnobori, M. (2011). *Managing challenging behaviors in schools: Research-based strategies that work.* New York, NY: Guilford.

Langer, J. A. (2000). Excellence in English in middle and high school: How teachers' professional lives support student achievement. *American Educational Research Journal, 37*, 397–439.

Learning First Alliance. (2001). *Every child learning: Safe and supportive schools.* Washington, DC: Association for Supervision and Curriculum Development.

Lee, J., & Shute, V. J. (2010). Personal and social-contextual factors in K–12 academic performance: An integrative perspective on student learning. *Educational Psychologist, 45*, 185–202.

Lee, J.-S., & Bowen, N. K. (2006). Parent involvement, cultural capital, and the achievement gap among elementary school children. *American Educational Research Journal, 43*, 193–218.

Lee, V. E., & Burkam, D. T. (2003). Dropping out of high school: The role of school organization and structure. *American Educational Research Journal, 40*, 353–393.

Levine, D. U., & Lezotte, L. W. (1995). Effective schools research. In J. A. Banks & C. A. M. Banks (Eds.), *Handbook of research on multicultural education* (pp. 525–547). New York, NY: Macmillan.

Lewis, T. J., Newcomer, L. L., Trussell, R., & Richter, M. (2006). Schoolwide positive behavior support: Building systems to develop and maintain appropriate social behavior. In C. M. Evertson & C. S. Weinstein (Eds.), *Handbook of classroom management: Research, practice, and contemporary issues* (pp. 833–854). Mahwah, NJ: Erlbaum.

Lickona, T. (1991). Moral development in the elementary school classroom. In W. M. Kurtines & J. L. Gewirtz (Eds.), *Moral behavior and development: Vol. 3. Application* (pp. 143–161). Mahwah, NJ: Erlbaum.

Lipka, J. (1994). Schools failing minority teachers. *Educational Foundations, 8*, 57–80.

López, G. R. (2001). Redefining parental involvement: Lessons from high-performing migrant-impacted schools. *American Educational Research Journal, 38*, 253–288.

Mac Iver, D. J., Reuman, D. A., & Main, S. R. (1995). Social structuring of the school: Studying what is, illuminating what could be. In J. T. Spence, J. M. Darley, & D. J. Foss (Eds.), *Annual review of psychology* (Vol. 46, pp. 375–400). Palo Alto, CA: Annual Review, Inc.

Marachi, R., Friedel, J., & Midgley, C. (2001, April). *"I sometimes annoy my teacher during math": Relations between student perceptions of the teacher and disruptive behavior in the classroom.* Paper presented at the annual meeting of the American Educational Research Association, Seattle, WA.

Marsh, S. (2015, January 27). Five top reasons people become teachers—and why they quit. *The Guardian.* Retrieved from http://www.theguardian.com/teacher-network/2015/jan/27/five-top-reasons-teachers-join-and-quit

Masten, A. S. (2001). Ordinary magic: Resilience processes in development. *American Psychologist, 56*, 227–238.

Mayer, M. J., & Furlong, M. J. (2010). How safe are our schools? *Educational Researcher, 39*, 16–26.

McCarty, T. L., & Watahomigie, L. J. (1998). Language and literacy in American Indian and Alaska Native communities. In B. Pérez (Ed.), *Sociocultural contexts of language and literacy* (pp. 69–98). Mahwah, NJ: Erlbaum.

McCormick, M. P., Cappella, E., O'Connor, E. E., & McClowry, S. G. (2013). Parent involvement, emotional support, and behavior problems. *Elementary School Journal, 114*(2), 277–300.

McIntyre, E. (2010). Issues in funds of knowledge teaching and research: Key concepts from a study of Appalachian families and schooling. In M. L. Dantas & P. C. Manyak (Eds.), *Home–school connections in a multicultural society: Learning from and with culturally and linguistically diverse families* (pp. 201–217). New York, NY: Routledge.

Meehan, B. T., Hughes, J. N., & Cavell, T. A. (2003). Teacher-student relationships as compensatory resources for aggressive children. *Child Development, 74*, 1145–1157.

Mehan, H. (1979). *Social organization in the classroom.* Cambridge, MA: Harvard University Press.

Mendaglio, S. (2010). Anxiety in gifted students. In J. C. Cassady (Ed.), *Anxiety in schools: The causes, consequences, and solutions for academic anxieties* (pp. 153–173). New York, NY: Peter Lang.

Mercer, C. D., & Pullen, P. C. (2005). *Students with learning disabilities* (6th ed.). Upper Saddle River, NJ: Merrill/Prentice Hall.

Miles, S. B., & Stipek, D. (2006). Contemporaneous and longitudinal associations between social behavior and literacy achievement in a sample of low-income elementary school children. *Child Development, 77*, 103–117.

Miller, A. (2006). Contexts and attributions for difficult behavior in English classrooms. In C. M. Evertson & C. S. Weinstein (Eds.),

Handbook of classroom management: Research, practice, and contemporary issues (pp. 1093–1120). Mahwah, NJ: Erlbaum.

Miller, M. D., Linn, R. L., & Gronlund, N. E. (2009). *Measurement and assessment in teaching* (10th ed.). Upper Saddle River, NJ: Merrill/Pearson.

Milner, H. R. (2006). Classroom management in urban classrooms. In C. M. Evertson & C. S. Weinstein (Eds.), *Handbook of classroom management: Research, practice, and contemporary issues* (pp. 491–522). Mahwah, NJ: Erlbaum.

Minami, M., & Ovando, C. J. (1995). Language issues in multicultural contexts. In J. A. Banks & C. A. M. Banks (Eds.), *Handbook of research on multicultural education* (pp. 427–444). New York, NY: Macmillan.

Monti, J. D., Pomerantz, E. M., & Roisman, G. I. (2014). Can parents' involvement in children's education offset the effects of early insensitivity on academic functioning? *Journal of Educational Psychology, 106*(3), 859–869.

Moore, J. W., & Edwards, R. P. (2003). An analysis of aversive stimuli in classroom demand contexts. *Journal of Applied Behavior Analysis, 36,* 339–348.

Morgan, D. P., & Jenson, W. R. (1988). *Teaching behaviorally disordered students: Preferred practices.* Upper Saddle River, NJ: Merrill/Prentice Hall.

Morrison, G. M., Furlong, M. J., D'Incau, B., & Morrison, R. L. (2004). The safe school: Integrating the school reform agenda to prevent disruption and violence at school. In J. C. Conoley & A. P. Goldstein (Eds.), *School violence intervention* (2nd ed., pp. 256–296). New York, NY: Guilford.

Munn, P., Johnstone, M., & Chalmers, V. (1990, April). *How do teachers talk about maintaining effective discipline in their classrooms?* Paper presented at the annual meeting of the American Educational Research Association, Boston, MA.

Murdock, T. B., Hale, N. M., & Weber, M. J. (2001). Predictors of cheating among early adolescents: Academic and social motivations. *Contemporary Educational Psychology, 26,* 96–115.

Narciss, S. (2008). Feedback strategies for interactive learning tasks. In J. M. Spector, M. D. Merrill, J. van Merriënboer, & M. P. Driscoll (Eds.), *Handbook of research on educational communications and technology* (3rd ed., pp. 125–143). New York, NY: Erlbaum.

National Center for Education Statistics. (2007, September). *Crime, violence, discipline, and safety in U.S. public schools: Findings from the School Survey on Crime and Safety, 2005–06.* Washington: U.S. Department of Education.

Newkirk, T. (2002). *Misreading masculinity: Boys, literacy, and popular culture.* Portsmouth, NH: Heinemann.

Nichols, J. D. (April, 2004). *Empowerment and relationships: A classroom model to enhance student motivation.* Paper presented at the American Educational Research Association, San Diego, CA.

Nucci, L. P. (2006). Classroom management for moral and social development. In C. M. Evertson & C. S. Weinstein (Eds.), *Handbook of classroom management: Research, practice, and contemporary issues* (pp. 711–731). Mahwah, NJ: Erlbaum.

Nucci, L. (2009). *Nice is not enough: Facilitating moral development.* Upper Saddle River, NJ: Merrill/Pearson.

O'Conner, E., & McCartney, K. (2007). Examining teacher-child relationships and achievement as part of an ecological model of development. *American Educational Research Journal, 48,* 120–162.

O'Connor, E. E., Dearing, E., & Collins, B. A. (2011). Teacher–child relationship and behavior problem trajectories in elementary school. *American Educational Research Journal, 48,* 120–162.

Ogbu, J. U. (2003). *Black American students in an affluent suburb: A study of academic disengagement.* Mahwah, NJ: Erlbaum.

Osher, D., Bear, G. G., Sprague, J. R., & Doyle, W. (2010). How can we improve school discipline? *Educational Researcher, 39,* 48–58.

Osterman, K. F. (2000). Students' need for belonging in the school community. *Review of Educational Research, 70,* 323–367.

O'Toole, M. E. (2000). *The school shooter: A threat assessment perspective.* Quantico, VA: Federal Bureau of Investigation. Retrieved from http://www.fbi.gov/publications/school/school2.pdf

Pakarinen, E., Aunola, K., Kiuru, N., Lerkkanen, M. K., Poikkeus, A. M., Siekkinen, M., & Nurmi, J. E. (2014). The cross-lagged associations between classroom interactions and children's achievement behaviors. *Contemporary Educational Psychology, 39*(3), 248–261.

Patall, E. A., Cooper, H., & Robinson, J. C. (2008). Parent involvement in homework: A research synthesis. *Review of Educational Research, 78,* 1039–1101.

Patall, E. A., Cooper, H., & Wynn, S. R. (2010). The effectiveness and relative importance of choice in the classroom. *Journal of Educational Psychology, 102,* 896–915.

Patrick, H., Kaplan, A., & Ryan, A. M. (2011). Positive classroom motivational environments: Convergence between mastery goal structure and classroom social climate. *Journal of Educational Psychology, 103,* 367–382.

Patrick, H., & Pintrich, P. R. (2001). Conceptual change in teachers' intuitive conceptions of learning, motivation, and instruction: The role of motivational and epistemological beliefs. In B. Torff & R. J. Sternberg (Eds.), *Understanding and teaching the intuitive mind: Student and teacher learning* (pp. 117–143). Mahwah, NJ: Erlbaum.

Patrick, H., Ryan, A. M., & Kaplan, A. M. (2007). Early adolescents' perceptions of the classroom social environment, motivational beliefs, and engagement. *Journal of Educational Psychology, 99,* 83–98.

Patton, J. R., Blackbourn, J. M., & Fad, K. S. (1996). *Exceptional individuals in focus* (6th ed.). Upper Saddle River, NJ: Merrill/Prentice Hall.

Payne, R. K. (2005). *A framework for understanding poverty* (4th rev. ed.). Highlands, TX: aha! Process, Inc.

Peguero, A. A., & Bracy, N. L. (2014). School order, justice, and education: Climate, discipline practices, and dropping out. *Journal of Research on Adolescence,*

Pekrun, R., Goetz, T., Daniels, L. M., Stupnisky, R. H., & Perry, R. P. (2010). Boredom in achievement settings: Exploring control–value antecedents and performance outcomes of a neglected emotion. *Journal of Educational Psychology, 102,* 531–549.

Pellegrini, A. D. (2002). Bullying, victimization, and sexual harassment during the transition to middle school. *Educational Psychologist, 37,* 151–163.

Pellegrini, A. D., & Horvat, M. (1995). A developmental contextualist critique of attention deficit hyperactivity disorder. *Educational Researcher, 24*(1), 13–19.

Peter, F., & Dalbert, C. (2010). Do my teachers treat me justly? Implications of students' justice experience for class climate experience. *Contemporary Educational Psychology, 35,* 297–305.

Petras, H., Masyn, K. E., Buckley, J. A., Ialongo, N. S., & Kellam, S. (2011). Who is most at risk for school removal? A multilevel discrete-time survival analysis of individual-and context-level influences. *Journal of Educational Psychology, 103*(1), 223–237.

Pfiffner, L. J., Barkley, R. A., & DuPaul, G. J. (2006). Treatment of ADHD in school settings. In R. A. Barkley (Ed.), *Attention-deficit hyperactivity disorder: A handbook for diagnosis and treatment* (3rd ed., pp. 547–589). New York, NY: Guilford.

Pianta, R. C. (1999). *Enhancing relationships between children and teachers.* Washington, DC: American Psychological Association.

Pianta, R. C. (2006). Classroom management and relationships between children and teachers: Implications for research and practice. In C. M. Evertson & C. S. Weinstein (Eds.), Handbook of classroom management: Research, practice, and contemporary issues (pp. 685–709). Mahwah, NJ: Erlbaum.

Platts, J., & Williamson, Y. (2000). The use of cognitive-behavioural therapy for counseling in schools. In N. Barwick (Ed.), *Clinical counseling in schools* (pp. 96–107). New York, NY: Routledge.

Polakow, V. (2007). In the shadows of the ownership society: Homeless children and their families. In S. Books (Ed.), *Invisible children in the society and its schools* (3rd ed., pp. 39–62). Mahwah, NJ: Erlbaum.

Polloway, E. A., & Patton, J. R. (1993). *Strategies for teaching learners with special needs* (5th ed.). Upper Saddle River, NJ: Merrill/Prentice Hall.

Poteat, V. P., O'Dwyer, L. M., & Mereish, E. H. (2012). Changes in how students use and are called homophobic epithets over time: Patterns predicted by gender, bullying, and victimization status. *Journal of Educational Psychology, 104*(2), 393–406.

Power, F. C., Higgins, A., & Kohlberg, L. (1989). *Lawrence Kohlberg's approach to moral education.* New York, NY: Columbia University Press.

Pugh, K. J., Linnenbrink-Garcia, L., Koskey, K. L., Stewart, V. C., & Manzey, C. (2010). Motivation, learning, and transformative experience: A study of deep engagement in science. *Science Education, 94*, 1–28.

Reese, L., Jensen, B., & Ramirez, D. (2014). Emotionally supportive classroom contexts for young Latino children in rural California. *Elementary School Journal, 114*(4), 501–526.

Reeve, J. (2009). Why teachers adopt a controlling motivating style toward students and how they can become more autonomy supportive. *Educational Psychologist, 44*, 159–175.

Reschly, A. L., & Christenson, S. L. (2009). Parents as essential partners for fostering students' learning outcomes. In R. Gilman, E. S. Huebner, & M. J. Furlong (Eds.), *Handbook of positive psychology in schools* (pp. 257–272). New York, NY: Routledge.

Robers, S., Kemp, J., Rathbun, A., Morgan, R. E., & Snyder, T. D. (2014). *Indicators of school crime and safety: 2013.* Washington, DC: National Center for Education Statistics and Bureau of Justice Statistics.

Robers, S., Zhang, J., Truman, J., & Snyder, T. D. (2012). *Indicators of school crime and safety: 2011.* Washington, DC: National Center for Education Statistics and Bureau of Justice Statistics.

Robinson, D. R., Schofield, J. W., & Steers-Wentzell, K. L. (2005). Peer and cross-age tutoring in math: Outcomes and their design implications. *Educational Psychology Review, 17*, 327–362.

Robinson, S. L., & Griesemer, S. M. R. (2006). Helping individual students with problem behavior. In C. M. Evertson & C. S. Weinstein (Eds.), *Handbook of classroom management: Research, practice, and contemporary issues* (pp. 787–802). Mahwah, NJ: Erlbaum.

Rogers, C. R. (1983). *Freedom to learn for the 80's.* Upper Saddle River, NJ: Merrill/Prentice Hall.

Roorda, D. L., Koomen, H. M. Y., Spilt, J. L., & Oort, F. J. (2011). The influence of affective teacher–student relationships on students' school engagement and achievement: A meta-analytic approach. *Review of Educational Research, 81*, 493–529.

Ross, S. W, & Horner, R. H. (2009). Bully prevention in positive behavior support. *Journal of Applied Behavior Analysis, 42*, 747–759.

Rothbart, M. K. (2011). *Becoming who we are: Temperament and personality in development.* New York, NY: Guilford.

Rozalski, M. E., & Yell, M. L. (2004). Law and school safety. In J. C. Conoley & A. P. Goldstein (Eds.), *School violence intervention* (2nd ed., pp. 507–523). New York, NY: Guilford.

Rudman, M. K. (1993). Multicultural children's literature: The search for universals. In M. K. Rudman (Ed.), *Children's literature: Resource for the classroom* (2nd ed., pp. 113–145). Norwood, MA: Christopher-Gordon.

Ryan, A. M., & Patrick, H. (2001). The classroom social environment and changes in adolescents' motivation and engagement during middle school. *American Educational Research Journal, 38*, 437–460.

Sabers, D. S., Cushing, K. S., & Berliner, D. C. (1991). Differences among teachers in a task characterized by simultaneity, multidimensionality, and immediacy. *American Educational Research Journal, 28*, 63–88.

Salend, S. J., & Taylor, L. (1993). Working with families: A cross-cultural perspective. *Remedial and Special Education, 14*(5), 25–32, 39.

Sanders, M. G. (1996). Action teams in action: Interviews and observations in three schools in the Baltimore School–Family–Community Partnership Program. *Journal of Education for Students Placed at Risk, 1*, 249–262.

Sapolsky, R. (2005). Stress and cognition. In M. Gazzaniga (Ed.), *The cognitive neurosciences* 3rd ed., pp. 1031–1042). Cambridge, MA: MIT Press.

Sapon-Shevin, M., Dobbelaere, A., Corrigan, C., Goodman, K., & Mastin, M. (1998). Everyone here can play. *Educational Leadership, 56*(1), 42–45.

Scott, J., & Bushell, D. (1974). The length of teacher contacts and students' off-task behavior. *Journal of Applied Behavior Analysis, 7*, 39–44.

Scruggs, T. E., & Mastropieri, M. A. (1994). Successful mainstreaming in elementary science classes: A qualitative study of three reputational cases. *American Educational Research Journal, 31*, 785–811.

Serpell, R., Baker, L., & Sonnenschein, S. (2005). *Becoming literate in the city: The Baltimore Early Childhood Project.* Cambridge, England: Cambridge University Press.

Silberman, M. L., & Wheelan, S. A. (1980). *How to discipline without feeling guilty: Assertive relationships with children.* Champaign, IL: Research Press.

Silverberg, R. P. (2003, April). *Developing relational space: Teachers who came to understand themselves and their students as learners.* Paper presented at the annual meeting of the American Educational Research Association, Chicago, IL.

Smith, A. K. (2009). *The art of possibility: Creating more successful learners.* Malibu, CA: Center for Collaborative Action Research, Pepperdine University. Retrieved from http://cadres. pepperdine.edu/ccar/projects.school.html

Snoeyink, R. (2010). Using video self-analysis to improve "withitness" of student teachers. *Journal of Computing in Teacher Education, 26*(3), 101–110.

Sørlie, M., & Torsheim, T. (2011). Multilevel analysis of the relationship between teacher collective efficacy and problem behaviour in school. *School Effectiveness and School Improvement, 22*(2), 175–191.

Spaulding, C. L. (1992). *Motivation in the classroom.* New York, NY: McGraw-Hill.

Spera, C. (2005). A review of the relationship among parenting practices, parenting styles, and adolescent school achievement. *Educational Psychology Review, 17*, 125–146.

Stack, C. B., & Burton, L. M. (1993). Kinscripts. *Journal of Comparative Family Studies, 24*, 157–170.

Stiggins, R. J., & Chappuis, J. (2012). *An introduction to student-involved assessment FOR learning* (6th ed.). Boston, MA: Pearson Assessment Training Institute.

Stipek, D., & Miles, S. (2008). Effects of aggression on achievement: Does conflict with the teacher make it worse? *Child Development, 79*, 1721–1735.

Stipek, D. J. (1996). Motivation and instruction. In D. C. Berliner & R. C. Calfee (Eds.), *Handbook of educational psychology* (pp. 85–113). New York, NY: Macmillan.

Stodolsky, S. S., Salk, S., & Glaessner, B. (1991). Student views about learning math and social studies. *American Educational Research Journal, 28*, 89–116.

Striepling-Goldstein, S. H. (2004). The low-aggression classroom: A teacher's view. In J. C. Conoley & A. P. Goldstein (Eds.), *School violence intervention* (2nd ed., pp. 23–53). New York, NY: Guilford.

Strother, D. B. (Ed.). (1991). *Learning to fail: Case studies of students at risk.* Bloomington, IN: Phi Delta Kappa, Maynard R. Bemis Center for Evaluation, Development, and Research.

Sullivan-DeCarlo, C., DeFalco, K., & Roberts, V. (1998). Helping students avoid risky behavior. *Educational Leadership, 56*(1), 80–82.

Sutherland, K. S., & Morgan, P. L. (2003). Implications of transactional processes in classrooms for students with emotional/behavioral disorders. *Preventing School Failure, 48*(6), 32–45.

Sutton, R. E., & Wheatley, K. F. (2003). Teachers' emotions and teaching: A review of the literature and directions for future research. *Educational Psychology Review, 15*, 327–358.

Swanson, H. L., O'Connor, J. E., & Cooney, J. B. (1990). An information processing analysis of expert and novice teachers' problem solving. *American Educational Research Journal, 27*, 533–556.

Swearer, S. M., Espelage, D. L., Vaillancourt, T., & Hymel, S. (2010). What can be done about school bullying? Linking research to educational practice. *Educational Researcher, 39*, 38–47.

Syvertsen, A. K., Flanagan, C. A., & Stout, M. D. (2009). Code of silence: Students' perceptions of school climate and willingness to intervene in a peer's dangerous plan. *Journal of Educational Psychology, 101*, 219–232.

Tamis-Lemonda, C. S., & McFadden, K. E. (2010). The United States of America. In M. H. Bornstein (Ed.), *Handbook of cultural developmental science* (pp. 299–322). New York, NY: Psychology Press.

Troop-Gordon, W., & Ladd, G. W. (2005). Trajectories of peer victimization and perceptions of the self and schoolmates: Precursors to internalizing and externalizing problems. *Child Development*, 76, 1072–1091.

Turnbull, A. P., Pereira, L., & Blue-Banning, M. (2000). Teachers as friendship facilitators. *Teaching Exceptional Children*, 32(5), 66–70.

Turnbull, A. P., Turnbull, R., & Wehmeyer, M. L. (2010). *Exceptional lives: Special education in today's schools* (6th ed.). Upper Saddle River, NJ: Merrill.

Tutwiler, S. W. (2007). How schools fail African American boys. In S. Books (Ed.), *Invisible children in the society and its schools* (3rd ed., pp. 141–156). Mahwah, NJ: Erlbaum.

Tyler, K. M., Uqdah, A. L., Dillihunt, M. L., Beatty-Hazelbaker, R., Connor, T., Gadson, N., et al. (2008). Cultural discontinuity: Toward a quantitative investigation of a major hypothesis in education. *Educational Researcher*, 37, 280–297.

U.S. Department of Education. (2014). *The condition of education 2014*. NCES Document 2014-083. Washington, DC: National Center for Education Statistics.

U.S. Secret Service National Threat Assessment Center, in collaboration with the U.S. Department of Education. (2000, October). *Safe school initiative: An interim report on the prevention of targeted violence in schools*. Washington, DC: Author.

Veenman, S. (1984). Perceived problems of beginning teachers. *Review of Educational Research*, 54, 143–178.

Vitaro, F., Boivin, M., Brendgen, M., Girard, A., & Dionne, G. (2012). Social experiences in kindergarten and academic achievement in grade 1: A monozygotic twin difference study. *Journal of Educational Psychology*, 104(2), 366–380.

Vitaro, F., Brendgen, M., Larose, S., & Tremblay, R. E. (2005). Kindergarten disruptive behaviors, protective factors, and educational achievement by early adulthood. *Journal of Educational Psychology*, 97, 617–629.

Waasdorp, T. E., Bradshaw, C. P., & Duong, J. (2011). The link between parents' perceptions of the school and their responses to school bullying: Variation by child characteristics and the forms of victimization. *Journal of Educational Psychology*, 103(2), 324–335.

Walker, H. M., Horner, R. H., Sugai, G., Bullis, M., Sprague, J. R., Bricker, D., et al. (1996). Integrated approaches to preventing antisocial behavior patterns among school-age children and youth. *Journal of Emotional and Behavioral Disorders*, 4, 194–209.

Walker, J. M., Ice, C. L., Hoover-Dempsey, K. V., & Sandler, H. M. (2011). Latino parents' motivations for involvement in their children's schooling: An exploratory study. *The Elementary School Journal*, 111(3), 409–429.

Walker, J. M. T., & Hoover-Dempsey, K. V. (2006). Why research on parental involvement is important to classroom management. In C. M. Evertson & C. S. Weinstein (Eds.), *Handbook of classroom management: Research, practice, and contemporary issues* (pp. 665–684). Mahwah, NJ: Erlbaum.

Wang, M.-T., & Holcombe, R. (2010). Adolescents' perceptions of school environment, engagement, and academic achievement in middle school. *American Educational Research Journal*, 47, 633–662.

Warren, J. S., Bohanon-Edmonson, H. M., Turnbull, A. P., Sailor, W., Wickham, D., Griggs, P., et al. (2006). School-wide positive behavior support: Addressing behavior problems that impeded student learning. *Educational Psychology Review*, 18, 187–198.

Watson, M. (2008). Developmental discipline and moral education. In L. Nucci & D. Narvaez (Eds.), *Handbook of moral and character education* (pp. 175–203). New York, NY: Routledge.

Watson, M., & Battistich, V. (2006). Building and sustaining caring communities. In C. M. Evertson & C. S. Weinstein (Eds.), *Handbook of classroom management: Research, practice, and contemporary issues* (pp. 253–279). Mahwah, NJ: Erlbaum.

Watson, M. W., Andreas, J. B., Fischer, K. W., & Smith, K. (2005). Patterns of risk factors leading to victimization and aggression in children and adolescents. In K. A. Kendall-Tackett & S. M. Giacomoni (Eds.), *Child Victimization: Maltreatment, bullying and dating violence, prevention and intervention* (pp. 12.1–12.23). Kingston, NJ: Civic Research Institute.

Weinert, F. E., & Helmke, A. (1995). Learning from wise Mother Nature or Big Brother Instructor: The wrong choice as seen from an educational perspective. *Educational Psychologist*, 30, 135–142.

Wentzel, K. R., Battle, A., Russell, S. L., & Looney, L. B. (2010). Social supports from teachers and peers as predictors of academic and social motivation. *Contemporary Educational Psychology*, 35, 193–202.

Wentzel, K. R., Donlan, A. E., Morrison, D. A., Russell, S. L., & Baker, S. A. (2009, April). *Adolescent non-compliance: A social ecological perspective*. Paper presented at the annual meeting of the American Educational Research Association, San Diego, CA.

Williams, K. D. (2001). *Ostracism: The power of silence*. New York, NY: Guilford.

Williams, K. M. (2001a). "Frontin' it": Schooling, violence, and relationships in the 'hood. In J. N. Burstyn, G. Bender, R. Casella, H. W. Gordon, D. P. Guerra, K. V. Luschen, R. Stevens, & K. M. Williams, *Preventing violence in schools: A challenge to American democracy* (pp. 95–108). Mahwah, NJ: Erlbaum.

Winner, E. (1997). Exceptionally high intelligence and schooling. *American Psychologist*, 52, 1070–1081.

Woolfolk, A. E., & Brooks, D. M. (1985). The influence of teachers' nonverbal behaviors on students' perceptions and performances. *Elementary School Journal*, 85, 513–528.

Woolfolk Hoy, A., Davis, H., & Pape, S. J. (2006). Teacher knowledge and beliefs. In P. A. Alexander & P. H. Winne (Eds.), *Handbook of educational psychology* (2nd ed., pp. 715–737). Mahwah, NJ: Erlbaum.

Woolfolk Hoy, A., & Weinstein, C. S. (2006). Student and teacher perspectives on classroom management. In C. M. Evertson & C. S. Weinstein (Eds.), *Handbook of classroom management: Research, practice, and contemporary issues* (pp. 181–219). Mahwah, NJ: Erlbaum.

Wynne, E. A. (1990). Improving pupil discipline and character. In O. C. Moles (Ed.), *Student discipline strategies: Research and practice* (pp. 167–190). Albany, NY: State University of New York Press.

Zambo, D., & Brem, S. K. (2004). Emotion and cognition in students who struggle to read: New insights and ideas. *Reading Psychology*, 25, 1–16.

CHAPTER 14

Agarwal, P. K., D'Antonio, L., Roediger, H. L., III, McDermott, K. B., & McDaniel, M. A. (2014). Classroom-based programs of retrieval practice reduce middle school and high school students' test anxiety. *Journal of Applied Research in Memory and Cognition, 3*, 131–139.

Alleman, J., & Brophy, J. (1997). Elementary social studies: Instruments, activities, and standards. In G. D. Phye (Ed.), *Handbook of classroom assessment: Learning, achievement, and adjustment* (pp. 321–357). San Diego, CA: Academic Press.

Anderman, E. M., & Dawson, H. (2011). Learning with motivation. In R. E. Mayer & P. A. Alexander (Eds.), *Handbook of research on learning and instruction* (pp. 219–241). New York, NY: Routledge.

Anderman, L. H., Freeman, T. M., & Mueller, C. E. (2007). The "social" side of social context: Interpersonal affiliative dimensions of students' experiences and academic dishonesty. In E. M. Anderman & T. B. Murdock (Eds.), *The psychology of academic cheating* (pp. 203–228). San Diego, CA: Elsevier.

Andrade, H. L. (2010). Students as the definitive source of formative assessment: Academic self-assessment and the self-regulation of learning. In H. L. Andrade & G. J. Cizek (Eds.), *Handbook of formative assessment* (pp. 90–105). New York, NY: Routledge.

Andrade, H. L., & Cizek, G. J. (Eds.). (2010). *Handbook of formative assessment*. New York, NY: Routledge.

Arter, J. A., & Chappuis, J. (2006). *Creating and recognizing quality rubrics*. Boston, MA: Pearson.

Barkley, R. A. (2006). *Attention-deficit hyperactivity disorder: A handbook for diagnosis and treatment* (3rd ed.). New York, NY: Guilford.

Baxter, G. P., Elder, A. D., & Glaser, R. (1996). Knowledge-based cognition and performance assessment in the science classroom. *Educational Psychologist, 31*, 133–140.

Beirne-Smith, M., Patton, J. R., & Kim, S. H. (2006). *Mental retardation: An introduction to intellectual disabilities* (7th ed.). Upper Saddle River, NJ: Merrill/Prentice Hall.

Black, P., & Wiliam, D. (1998). Assessment and classroom learning. *Assessment in Education, 5*(1), 7–74.

Boschee, F., & Baron, M. A. (1993). *Outcome-based education: Developing programs through strategic planning.* Lancaster, PA: Technomic.

Brophy, J. E. (1986). *On motivating students* (Occasional Paper No. 101). East Lansing, MI: Michigan State University, Institute for Research on Teaching.

Brophy, J. E. (2004). *Motivating students to learn* (2nd ed.). Mahwah, NJ: Erlbaum.

Brown, A. L., & Campione, J. C. (1996). Psychological theory and the design of innovative learning environments: On procedures, principles, and systems. In L. Schauble & R. Glaser (Eds.), *Innovations in learning: New environments for education* (pp. 289–325). Mahwah, NJ: Erlbaum.

Carbonneau, K. J., & Selig, J. P. (2011, April). *Teacher judgments of student mathematics achievement: The moderating role of student-teacher conflict.* Paper presented at the annual meeting of the American Educational Research Association, New Orleans, LA.

Carey, L. M. (1994). *Measuring and evaluating school learning* (2nd ed.). Boston, MA: Allyn & Bacon.

Carpenter, S. K. (2012). Testing enhances the transfer of learning. *Current Directions in Psychological Science, 21,* 279–283.

Carter, R., Williams, S., & Silverman, W. K. (2008). Cognitive and emotional facets of test anxiety in African American school children. *Cognition and Emotion, 22,* 539–551.

Cassady, J. C. (2010b). Test anxiety: Contemporary theories and implications for learning. In J. C. Cassady (Ed.), *Anxiety in schools: The causes, consequences, and solutions for academic anxieties* (pp. 7–26). New York, NY: Peter Lang.

Castagno, A. E., & Brayboy, B. M. J. (2008). Culturally responsive schooling for Indigenous youth: A review of the literature. *Review of Educational Research, 78,* 941–993.

Chappuis, J. (2009). *Seven strategies of assessment for learning.* Boston, MA: Pearson Assessment Training Institute.

Cheng, L. R. (1987). *Assessing Asian language performance.* Rockville, MD: Aspen.

Cizek, G. J. (2003). *Detecting and preventing classroom cheating: Promoting integrity in assessment.* Thousand Oaks, CA: Corwin.

Clifford, M. M. (1990). Students need challenge, not easy success. *Educational Leadership, 48*(1), 22–26.

Corliss, S. B., & Linn, M. C. (2011). Assessing learning from inquiry science instruction. In G. Schraw & D. R. Robinson (Eds.), *Assessment of higher order thinking skills* (pp. 219–243). Charlotte, NC: Information Age.

Crehan, K. D. (2001). An investigation of the validity of scores on locally developed performance measures in a school assessment

program. *Educational and Psychological Measurement, 61,* 841–848.

Crooks, T. J. (1988). The impact of classroom evaluation practices on students. *Review of Educational Research, 58,* 438–481.

Danner, F. (2008, March). *The effects of perceptions of classroom assessment practices and academic press on classroom mastery goals and high school students' self-reported cheating.* Paper presented at the annual meeting of the American Educational Research Association, New York, NY.

Darley, J. M., & Gross, P. H. (1983). A hypothesis-confirming bias in labeling effects. *Journal of Personality and Social Psychology, 44,* 20–33.

Darling-Hammond, L., Ancess, J., & Falk, B. (1995). *Authentic assessment in action: Studies of schools and students at work.* New York, NY: Teachers College Press.

Delandshere, G., & Petrosky, A. R. (1998). Assessment of complex performances: Limitations of key measurement assumptions. *Educational Researcher, 27*(2), 14–24.

Dempster, F. N. (1991). Synthesis of research on reviews and tests. *Educational Leadership, 48*(7), 71–76.

DiMartino, J., & Castaneda, A. (2007). Assessing applied skills. *Educational Leadership, 64,* 38–42.

diSessa, A. A. (2007). An interactional analysis of clinical interviewing. *Cognition and Instruction, 25,* 523–565.

Dunlosky, J., Rawson, K. A., Marsh, E. J., Nathan, M. J., & Willingham, D. T. (2013). Improving students' learning with effective learning techniques: Promising directions from cognitive and educational psychology. *Psychological Science in the Public Interest, 14,* 4–58.

D'Ydewalle, G., Swerts, A., & De Corte, E. (1983). Study time and test performance as a function of test expectations. *Contemporary Educational Psychology, 8*(1), 55–67.

Evans, E. D., & Craig, D. (1990). Teacher and student perceptions of academic cheating in middle and senior high schools. *Journal of Educational Research, 84*(1), 44–52.

Feuerstein, R., Feuerstein, R. S., & Falik, L. H. (2010). *Beyond smarter: Mediated learning and the brain's capacity for change.* New York, NY: Teachers College Press.

Foos, P. W., & Fisher, R. P. (1988). Using tests as learning opportunities. *Journal of Educational Psychology, 80,* 179–183.

Ford, D. Y., & Harris, J. J. (1992). The American achievement ideology and achievement differentials among preadolescent gifted and nongifted African American males and females. *The Journal of Negro Education, 61*(1), 45–64.

Frederiksen, J. R., & Collins, A. (1989). A systems approach to educational testing. *Educational Researcher, 18*(9), 27–32.

Frederiksen, N. (1984b). The real test bias: Influences of testing on teaching and learning. *American Psychologist, 39,* 193–202.

Fuchs, L. S., Compton, D. L., Fuchs, D., Hollenbeck, K. N., Craddock, C. F., &

Hamlett, C. L. (2008). Dynamic assessment of algebraic learning in predicting third graders' development of mathematical problem solving. *Journal of Educational Psychology, 100,* 829–850.

Gaudry, E., & Bradshaw, G. D. (1971). The differential effect of anxiety on performance in progressive and terminal school examinations. In E. Gaudry & C. D. Spielberger (Eds.), *Anxiety and educational achievement.* Sydney, Australia: Wiley.

Geiger, M. A. (1997). An examination of the relationship between answer changing, testwiseness and examination performance. *Journal of Experimental Education, 66,* 49–60.

Glover, J. A. (1989). The "testing" phenomenon: Not gone but nearly forgotten. *Journal of Educational Psychology, 81,* 392–399.

Glover, T. A., & Vaughn, S. (Eds.). (2010). *The promise of response to intervention: Evaluating current science and practice.* New York, NY: Guilford.

Grant, C. A., & Gomez, M. L. (2001). *Campus and classroom: Making schooling multicultural* (2nd ed.). Upper Saddle River, NJ: Merrill/Prentice Hall.

Gregg, N. (2009). *Adolescents and adults with learning disabilities and ADHD: Assessment and accommodation.* New York, NY: Guilford.

Grolnick, W. S., & Ryan, R. M. (1987). Autonomy in children's learning: An experimental and individual difference investigation. *Journal of Personality and Social Psychology, 52,* 890–898.

Gronlund, N. E., & Waugh, C. K. (2009). *Assessment of student achievement* (9th ed.). Upper Saddle River, NJ: Merrill/Pearson.

Haertel, E. (2013). How is testing supposed to improve schooling? *Measurement: Interdisciplinary Research and Perspectives, 11*(1–2), 1–18.

Hamers, J. H. M., & Ruijssenaars, A. J. J. M. (1997). Assessing classroom learning potential. In G. D. Phye (Ed.), *Handbook of academic learning: Construction of knowledge* (pp. 550–571). San Diego, CA: Academic Press.

Hamp-Lyons, L. (1992). Holistic writing assessment for LEP students. In *Focus on evaluation and measurement* (Vol. 2, pp. 317–369). Washington, DC: U.S. Department of Education.

Hattie, J., & Gan, M. (2011). Instruction based on feedback. In R. E. Mayer & P. A. Alexander (Eds.), *Handbook of research on learning and instruction* (pp. 249–271). New York, NY: Routledge.

Hay, P. J. (2008). (Mis)appropriations of criteria and standards-referenced assessment in a performance-based subject. *Assessment in Education: Principles, Policy, and Practice, 15,* 153–168.

Haywood, H. C., & Lidz, C. S. (2007). *Dynamic assessment in practice: Clinical and educational applications.* Cambridge, England: Cambridge University Press.

Hiebert, E. H., Valencia, S. W., & Afflerbach, P. P. (1994). Definitions and perspectives. In S.

W. Valencia, E. H. Hiebert, & P. P. Afflerbach (Eds.), *Authentic reading assessment: Practices and possibilities* (pp. 6–25). Newark, DE: International Reading Association.

Hill, K. T. (1984). Debilitating motivation and testing: A major educational problem, possible solutions, and policy applications. In R. Ames & C. Ames (Eds.), *Research on motivation in education: Vol. 1. Student motivation* (pp. 245–274). San Diego, CA: Academic Press.

Hill, K. T., & Wigfield, A. (1984). Test anxiety: A major educational problem and what can be done about it. *Elementary School Journal, 85,* 105–126.

Hong, E., Sas, M., & Sas, J. C. (2006). Test-taking strategies of high and low mathematics achievers. *Journal of Educational Research, 99,* 144–155.

Hoover, J. J. (2009). *RTI assessment essentials for struggling learners.* Thousand Oaks, CA: Corwin.

Hughes, G. B. (2010). Formative assessment practices that maximize learning for students at risk. In H. L. Andrade & G. J. Cizek (Eds.), *Handbook of formative assessment* (pp. 212–232). New York, NY: Routledge.

Johnson, R. L., Penny, J. A., & Gordon, B. (2009). *Assessing performance: Designing, scoring, and validating performance tasks.* New York, NY: Guilford.

Khattri, N., & Sweet, D. (1996). Assessment reform: Promises and challenges. In M. B. Kane & R. Mitchell (Eds.), *Implementing performance assessment: Promises, problems, and challenges* (pp. 1–21). Mahwah, NJ: Erlbaum.

Klassen, S. (2006). Contextual assessment in science education: Background, issues, and policy. *Science Education, 90,* 820–851.

Lenski, A., Husemann, N., Trautwein, U., & Lüdtke, O. (2010, April–May). *Academic cheating: A multidimensional point of view.* Paper presented at the annual meeting of the American Educational Research Association, Denver, CO.

Lester, F. K., Jr., Lambdin, D. V., & Preston, R. V. (1997). A new vision of the nature and purposes of assessment in the mathematics classroom. In G. D. Phye (Ed.), *Handbook of classroom assessment: Learning, achievement, and adjustment* (pp. 287–319). San Diego, CA: Academic Press.

Li, J., & Fischer, K. W. (2004). Thought and affect in American and Chinese learners' beliefs about learning. In D. Y. Dai & R. J. Sternberg (Eds.), *Motivation, emotion, and cognition: Integrative perspectives on intellectual functioning and development* (pp. 385–418). Mahwah, NJ: Erlbaum.

Linn, R. L. (1994). Performance assessment: Policy promises and technical measurement standards. *Educational Researcher, 23*(9), 4–14.

Lovett, B. J. (2010). Extended time testing accommodations for students with disabilities: Answers to five fundamental questions. *Review of Educational Research, 80,* 611–638.

Mac Iver, D. J., Reuman, D. A., & Main, S. R. (1995). Social structuring of the school:

Studying what is, illuminating what could be. In J. T. Spence, J. M. Darley, & D. J. Foss (Eds.), *Annual review of psychology* (Vol. 46, pp. 375–400). Palo Alto, CA: Annual Review.

Maehr, M. L., & Anderman, E. M. (1993). Reinventing schools for early adolescents: Emphasizing task goals. *Elementary School Journal, 93,* 593–610.

Magnusson, S. J., Boyle, R. A., & Templin, M. (1994, April). *Conceptual development: Re-examining knowledge construction in science.* Paper presented at the annual meeting of the American Educational Research Association, New Orleans, LA.

McDaniel, M. A., Agarwal, P. K., Huelser, B. J., McDermott, K. B., & Roediger, H. L., III. (2011). Test-enhanced learning in a middle school science classroom: The effects of quiz frequency and placement. *Journal of Educational Psychology, 103,* 399–414.

McMillan, J. H. (2010). The practical implications of educational aims and contexts for formative assessment. In H. L. Andrade & G. J. Cizek (Eds.), *Handbook of formative assessment* (pp. 41–58). New York, NY: Routledge.

Mellard, D. F., & Johnson, E. (2008). *RTI: A practitioner's guide to implementing response to intervention.* Thousand Oaks, CA: Corwin.

Mercer, C. D., & Pullen, P. C. (2005). *Students with learning disabilities* (6th ed.). Upper Saddle River, NJ: Merrill/Prentice Hall.

Messick, S. (1994a). The interplay of evidence and consequences in the validation of performance assessments. *Educational Researcher, 23*(2), 13–23.

Meyer, L. H., Weir, K. F., McClure, J., & Walkey, F. (2008, March). *The relationship of motivation orientations to future achievement in secondary school.* Paper presented at the annual meeting of the American Educational Research Association, New York, NY.

Miller, M. D., Linn, R. L., & Gronlund, N. E. (2009). *Measurement and assessment in teaching* (10th ed.). Upper Saddle River, NJ: Merrill/Pearson.

Millman, J., Bishop, C. H., & Ebel, R. (1965). An analysis of test-wiseness. *Educational and Psychological Measurement, 25,* 707–726.

Morgan, D. P., & Jenson, W. R. (1988). *Teaching behaviorally disordered students: Preferred practices.* Upper Saddle River, NJ: Merrill/Prentice Hall.

Murdock, T. B., Miller, A., & Kohlhardt, J. (2004). Effects of classroom context variables on high school students' judgments of the acceptability and likelihood of cheating. *Journal of Educational Psychology, 96,* 765–777.

Newmann, F. M. (1997). Authentic assessment in social studies: Standards and examples. In G. D. Phye (Ed.), *Handbook of classroom assessment: Learning, achievement, and adjustment* (pp. 360–380). San Diego, CA: Academic Press.

Nitko, A. J., & Brookhart, S. M. (2011). *Educational assessment of students* (6th ed.). Boston, MA: Pearson/Allyn & Bacon.

O'Connor, K. (2011). *A repair kit for grading: 15 fixes for broken grades* (2nd ed.). Boston, MA: Pearson Assessment Training Institute.

Panadero, E., & Jonsson, A. (2013). The use of scoring rubrics for formative assessment purposes revisited: A review. *Educational Research Review, 9,* 129–144.

Paris, S. G., & Ayres, L. R. (1994). *Becoming reflective students and teachers with portfolios and authentic assessment.* Washington, DC: American Psychological Association.

Paris, S. G., & Paris, A. H. (2001). Classroom applications of research on self-regulated learning. *Educational Psychologist, 36,* 89–101.

Paris, S. G., & Turner, J. C. (1994). Situated motivation. In P. R. Pintrich, D. R. Brown, & C. E. Weinstein (Eds.), *Student motivation, cognition, and learning: Essays in honor of Wilbert J. McKeachie* (pp. 213–238). Mahwah, NJ: Erlbaum.

Parkes, J. (2001). The role of transfer in the variability of performance assessment scores. *Educational Assessment, 7,* 143–164.

Petersen, G. A., Sudweeks, R. R., & Baird, J. H. (1990, April). *Test-wise responses of third-, fifth-, and sixth-grade students to clued and unclued multiple-choice science items.* Paper presented at the annual meeting of the American Educational Research Association, Boston, MA.

Piirto, J. (1999). *Talented children and adults: Their development and education* (2nd ed.). Upper Saddle River, NJ: Merrill/Prentice Hall.

Popham, W. J. (2006). *Assessment for educational leaders.* Boston, MA: Pearson/Allyn and Bacon.

Popham, W. J. (2014). *Classroom assessment: What teachers need to know* (7th ed.). Upper Saddle River, NJ: Pearson.

Putwain, D. W. (2007). Test anxiety in UK schoolchildren: Prevalence and demographic patterns. *British Journal of Educational Psychology, 77,* 579–593.

Quellmalz, E., & Hoskyn, J. (1997). Classroom assessment of reading strategies. In G. D. Phye (Ed.), *Handbook of classroom assessment: Learning, achievement, and adjustment* (pp. 103–130). San Diego, CA: Academic Press.

Ready, D. D., & Wright, D. L. (2011). Accuracy and inaccuracy in teachers' perceptions of young children's cognitive abilities: The role of child background and classroom context. *American Educational Research Journal, 48,* 335–360.

Reeve, J., Deci, E. L., & Ryan, R. M. (2004). Self-determination theory: A dialectical framework for understanding sociocultural influences on student motivation. In D. M. McInerney & S. Van Etten (Eds.), *Big theories revisited* (pp. 31–60). Greenwich, CT: Information Age.

Ritts, V., Patterson, M. L., & Tubbs, M. E. (1992). Expectations, impressions, and judgments of physically attractive students: A review. *Review of Educational Research, 62,* 413–426.

Robinson, J. P., & Lubienski, S. T. (2011). The development of gender achievement gaps in mathematics and reading during elementary and middle school: Examining direct cognitive assessments and teacher ratings. *American Educational Research Journal, 48,* 268–302.

Roediger, H. L., III, & Karpicke, J. D. (2006). The power of testing memory: Basic research and implications for educational practice. *Perspectives on Psychological Science, 1,* 181–210.

Rogoff, B. (2003). *The cultural nature of human development.* Oxford, England: Oxford University Press.

Rohrer, D., & Pashler, H. (2010). Recent research on human learning challenges conventional instructional strategies. *Educational Researcher, 39,* 406–412.

Russell, M. K. (2010). Technology-aided formative assessment of learning: New developments and applications. In H. L. Andrade & G. J. Cizek (Eds.), *Handbook of formative assessment* (pp. 125–138). New York, NY: Routledge.

Sax, G. (2010). *Principles of educational and psychological measurement and evaluation* (4th ed.). Belmont, CA: Wadsworth.

Scarcella, R. (1990). *Teaching language-minority students in the multicultural classroom.* Upper Saddle River, NJ: Prentice Hall.

Scruggs, T. E., & Lifson, S. A. (1985). Current conceptions of test-wiseness: Myths and realities. *School Psychology Review, 14,* 339–350.

Seethaler, P. M. Fuchs, L. S., Fuchs, D., & Compton, D. L. (2012). Predicting first graders' development of calculation versus word-problem performance: The role of dynamic assessment. *Journal of Educational Psychology, 104,* 224–234.

Shepard, L. (2000). The role of assessment in a learning culture. *Educational Researcher, 29*(7), 4–14.

Shepard, L., Hammerness, K., Darling-Hammond, L., & Rust, F. (with Snowden, J. B., Gordon, E., Gutierrez, C., & Pacheco, A.). (2005). Assessment. In L. Darling-Hammond & J. Bransford (Eds.), *Preparing teachers for a changing world: What teachers should learn and be able to do* (pp. 275–326). San Francisco: Jossey-Bass/Wiley.

Shernoff, D. (2013). *Optimal learning environments to promote student engagement.* New York, NY: Springer.

Shriner, J. G., & Spicuzza, R. J. (1995). Procedural considerations in the assessment of students at risk for school failure. *Preventing School Failure, 39*(2), 33–38.

Sieber, J. E., Kameya, L. I., & Paulson, F. L. (1970). Effect of memory support on the problem-solving ability of test-anxious children. *Journal of Educational Psychology, 61,* 159–168.

Sireci, S. G., Scarpati, S. E., & Li, S. (2005). Test accommodations for students with disabilities: An analysis of the interaction hypothesis. *Review of Educational Research, 75,* 457–490.

Spaulding, C. L. (1992). *Motivation in the classroom.* New York, NY: McGraw-Hill.

Stein, J. A., & Krishnan, K. (2007). Nonverbal learning disabilities and executive function: The challenges of effective assessment and teaching. In L. Meltzer (Ed.), *Executive function in education: From theory to practice* (pp. 106–132). New York, NY: Guilford.

Stiggins, R. J., & Chappuis, J. (2012). *An introduction to student-involved assessment FOR learning* (6th ed.). Boston, MA: Pearson Assessment Training Institute.

Stipek, D. J. (1993). *Motivation to learn: From theory to practice* (2nd ed.). Boston, MA: Allyn & Bacon.

Stokes, J. V., Luiselli, J. K., Reed, D. D., & Fleming, R. K. (2010). Behavioral coaching to improve offensive line pass-blocking skills of high school football athletes. *Journal of Applied Behavior Analysis, 43,* 463–472.

Stupnisky, R. H., Stewart, T. L., Daniels, L. M., & Perry, R. P. (2011). When do students ask why? Examining the precursors and outcomes of causal search among first-year college students. *Contemporary Educational Psychology, 36,* 201–211.

Szpunar, K. K., Jing, H. G., & Schacter, D. L. (2014). Overcoming overconfidence in learning from video-recorded lectures: Implications of interpolated testing for online education. *Journal of Applied Research in Memory and Cognition, 3,* 161–164.

Turnbull, A. P., Turnbull, R., & Wehmeyer, M. L. (2010). *Exceptional lives: Special education in today's schools* (6th ed.). Upper Saddle River, NJ: Merrill.

Turner, J. C., Meyer, D. K., Cox, K. E., Logan, C., DiCintio, M., & Thomas, C. T. (1998). Creating contexts for involvement in mathematics. *Journal of Educational Psychology, 90,* 730–745.

Tzuriel, D. (2000). Dynamic assessment of young children: Educational and intervention perspectives. *Educational Psychology Review, 12,* 385–435.

Usher, E. L. (2009). Sources of middle school students' self-efficacy in mathematics: A qualitative investigation. *American Educational Research Journal, 46,* 275–314.

Valdés, G., Bunch, G., Snow, C., & Lee, C. (with Matos, L.). (2005). Enhancing the development of students' language(s). In L. Darling-Hammond & J. Bransford (Eds.), *Preparing teachers for a changing world: What teachers should learn and be able to do* (pp. 126–168). San Francisco, CA: Jossey-Bass/Wiley.

van den Bergh, L., Denessen, E., Hornstra, L., Voeten, M., & Holland, R. W. (2010). The implicit prejudiced attitudes of teachers: Relations to teacher expectations and the ethnic achievement gap. *American Educational Research Journal, 47,* 497–527.

van Kraayenoord, C. E., & Paris, S. G. (1997). Australian students' self-appraisal of their work samples and academic progress. *Elementary School Journal, 97,* 523–537.

Warren, G. (1979). Essay versus multiple-choice tests. *Journal of Research in Science Teaching, 16,* 563–567.

Warschauer, M. (2011). *Learning in the cloud: How (and why) to transform schools with digital media.* New York, NY: Teachers College Press.

Wentzel, K. R. (2009). Peers and academic functioning at school. In K. H. Rubin, W. M. Bukowski, & B. Laursen (Eds.), *Handbook of peer interactions, relationships, and groups* (pp. 531–547). New York, NY: Guilford.

Whitaker Sena, J. D., Lowe, P. A., & Lee, S. W. (2007). Significant predictors of test anxiety among students with and without learning disabilities. *Journal of Learning Disabilities, 40,* 360–376.

Wiggins, G. (1992). Creating tests worth taking. *Educational Leadership, 49*(8), 26–33.

Wiggins, G., & McTighe, J. (2007). *Schooling by design.* Alexandria, VA: Association of Supervision and Curriculum Development.

Wiley, D. E., & Haertel, E. H. (1996). Extended assessment tasks: Purposes, definitions, scoring, and accuracy. In M. B. Kane & R. Mitchell (Eds.), *Implementing performance assessment: Promises, problems, and challenges* (pp. 61–89). Mahwah, NJ: Erlbaum.

Wiliam, D. (2011). *Embedded formative assessment.* Bloomington, IN: Solution Tree.

Zeidner, M., & Matthews, G. (2005). Evaluation anxiety: Current theory and research. In A. J. Elliot & C. S. Dweck (Eds.), *Handbook of competence and motivation* (pp. 141–163). New York, NY: Guilford Press.

CHAPTER 15

Adger, C. T., Wolfram, W., & Christian, D. (2007). *Dialects in schools and communities* (2nd ed.). New York, NY: Routledge.

Airasian, P. W. (1994). *Classroom assessment* (2nd ed.). New York, NY: McGraw-Hill.

American Educational Research Association, American Psychological Association, & National Council on Measurement in Education. (1999). *Standards for Educational and Psychological Testing* (2nd ed.). Washington, DC: American Educational Research Association.

American Statistical Association (2014). *ASA statement on using value-added models for educational assessment.* Alexandria, VA: Author. Retrieved from https://www.amstat.org/policy/pdfs/ASA_VAM_Statement.pdf

Ames, C. (1984). Competitive, cooperative, and individualistic goal structures: A cognitive-motivational analysis. In R. Ames & C. Ames (Eds.), *Research on motivation in education: Vol. 1. Student motivation* (pp. 177–207). San Diego, CA: Academic Press.

Anderman, E. M., Gimbert, B., O'Connell, A., & Riegel, L. (2015). Approaches to academic growth assessment. *British Journal of Educational Psychology, 85,* 138–153. Advance online publication. doi: 10.1111/bjep.12053.

Anderman, E. M., Griesinger, T., & Westerfield, G. (1998). Motivation and cheating during early adolescence. *Journal of Educational Psychology, 90,* 84–93.

Aronson, J., & Steele, C. M. (2005). Stereotypes and the fragility of academic competence, motivation, and self-concept. In A. J. Elliot & C. S. Dweck (Eds.), *Handbook of competence and motivation* (pp. 436–456). New York, NY: Guilford.

Arter, J. A., & Spandel, V. (1992). Using portfolios of student work in instruction and assessment. *Educational Measurement: Issues and Practice, 11*(1), 36–44.

Au, W. (2007). High-stakes testing and curricular control: A qualitative metasynthesis. *Educational Researcher, 36*(5), 258–267.

Baker, E. L. (2007). The end(s) of testing. *Educational Researcher, 36*, 309–317.

Balfanz, R., Legters, N., West, T. C., & Weber, L. M. (2007). Are NCLB's measures, incentives, and improvement strategies the right ones for the nation's low-performing high schools? *American Educational Research Journal, 44*, 559–593.

Ballou, D., Sanders, W., & Wright, P. (2004). Controlling for student background in value-added assessment of teachers. *Journal of Educational and Behavioral Statistics, 29*, 37–65.

Banta, T. W. (Ed.). (2003). *Portfolio assessment: Uses, cases, scoring, and impact*. San Francisco, CA: Jossey-Bass.

Barkley, R. A. (2006). *Attention-deficit hyperactivity disorder: A handbook for diagnosis and treatment* (3rd ed.). New York, NY: Guilford.

Beirne-Smith, M., Patton, J. R., & Kim, S. H. (2006). *Mental retardation: An introduction to intellectual disabilities* (7th ed.). Upper Saddle River, NJ: Merrill/Prentice Hall.

Bleeker, M. M., & Jacobs, J. E. (2004). Achievement in math and science: Do mothers' beliefs matter 12 years later? *Journal of Educational Psychology, 96*, 97–109.

Boykin, A. W. (1994). Harvesting talent and culture: African-American children and educational reform. In R. J. Rossi (Ed.), *Schools and students at risk: Context and framework for positive change* (pp. 116–138). New York, NY: Teachers College Press.

Bracken, B. A., & Walker, K. C. (1997). The utility of intelligence tests for preschool children. In D. P. Flanagan, J. L. Genshaft, & P. L. Harrison (Eds.), *Contemporary intellectual assessment: Theories, tests, and issues* (pp. 484–502). New York, NY: Guilford.

Brookhart, S. M. (2004). *Grading*. Upper Saddle River, NJ: Merrill/Prentice Hall.

Brophy, J. E. (2004). *Motivating students to learn* (2nd ed.). Mahwah, NJ: Erlbaum.

Brown, A. B., & Clift, J. W. (2010). The unequal effect of adequate yearly progress: Evidence from school visits. *American Educational Research Journal, 47*, 774–798.

Brown, R. T., Reynolds, C. R., & Whitaker, J. S. (1999). Bias in mental testing since *Bias in Mental Testing*. *School Psychology Quarterly, 14*, 208–238.

Buck, G., Kostin, I., & Morgan, R. (2002). *Examining the relationship of content to gender-based performance differences in advanced placement exams* (Research Report No. 2002-12). New York, NY: The College Board.

Carbonneau, K. J., & Selig, J. P. (2011, April). *Teacher judgments of student mathematics achievement: The moderating role of student-teacher conflict*. Paper presented at the annual meeting of the American Educational Research Association, New Orleans, LA.

Carhill, A., Suárez-Orozco, C., & Páez, M. (2008). Explaining English language proficiency among adolescent immigrant students. *American Educational Research Journal, 45*, 1045–1079.

Carter, R., Williams, S., & Silverman, W. K. (2008). Cognitive and emotional facets of test anxiety in African American school children. *Cognition and Emotion, 22*, 539–551.

Carver, S. M. (2006). Assessing for deep understanding. In R. K. Sawyer (Ed.), *The Cambridge handbook of the learning sciences* (pp. 205–221). Cambridge, England: Cambridge University Press.

Chabrán, M. (2003). Listening to talk from and about students on accountability. In M. Carnoy, R. Elmore, & L. S. Siskin (Eds.), *The new accountability: High schools and high-stakes testing* (pp. 129–145). New York, NY: RoutledgeFalmer.

Cizek, G. J. (2003). *Detecting and preventing classroom cheating: Promoting integrity in assessment*. Thousand Oaks, CA: Corwin.

Cummins, J. (2008). BICS and CALP: Empirical and theoretical status of the distinction. In B. Street & N. H. Hornberger (Eds.), *Encyclopedia of language and education* (2nd ed., Vol. 2, pp. 71–83). New York, NY: Springer.

Dai, D. Y. (2010). *The nature and nurture of giftedness: A new framework for understanding gifted education*. New York, NY: Teachers College Press.

Darling-Hammond, L., Ancess, J., & Falk, B. (1995). *Authentic assessment in action: Studies of schools and students at work*. New York, NY: Teachers College Press.

Dempster, F. N., & Corkill, A. J. (1999). Interference and inhibition in cognition and behavior: Unifying themes for educational psychology. *Educational Psychology Review, 11*, 1–88.

DiMartino, J. (2007, April 25). Accountability, or mastery? *Education Week, 26*(34), 36, 44.

DiMartino, J., & Castaneda, A. (2007). Assessing applied skills. *Educational Leadership, 64*, 38–42.

Dixon, L. Q., Zhao, J., Shin, J.-Y., Wu, S., Su, J.-H., Burgess-Brigham, R., . . . Snow, C. (2012). What we know about second language acquisition: A synthesis from four perspectives. *Review of Educational Research, 82*, 5–60.

Duckworth, A. L., & Seligman, M. E. P. (2005). Self-discipline outdoes IQ in predicting academic performance of adolescents. *Psychological Science, 16*, 939–944.

Duncan, G. J., Dowsett, C. J., Claessens, A., Magnuson, K., Huston, A. C., Klevanov, P., . . . Japel, C. (2007). School readiness and later achievement. *Developmental Psychology, 43*, 1428–1446.

Durost, W. N. (1961). How to tell parents about standardized test results. *Test Service Notebook* (No. 26). New York, NY: Harcourt, Brace, & World.

Farran, D. C. (2001). Critical periods and early intervention. In D. B. Bailey, Jr., J. T. Bruer, F. J. Symons, & J. W. Lichtman (Eds.), *Critical thinking about critical periods* (pp. 233–266). Baltimore, MD: Brookes.

Feuerstein, R, Feuerstein, R. S., & Falik, L. H. (2010). *Beyond smarter: Mediated learning and the brain's capacity for change*. New York, NY: Teachers College Press.

Finn, A. S., Kraft, M. A., West, M. R., Leonard, J. A., Bish, C. E., Martin, R. E., . . . Gabrieli, J. D. E. (2014). Cognitive skills, student achievement tests, and schools. *Psychological Science, 25*, 736–744.

Finnigan, K. S., & Gross, B. (2007). Do accountability policy sanctions influence teacher motivation? Lessons from Chicago's low-performing schools. *American Educational Research Journal, 44*, 594–629.

Ford, D. Y., & Harris, J. J. (1992). The American achievement ideology and achievement differentials among preadolescent gifted and nongifted African American males and females. *The Journal of Negro Education, 61*(1), 45–64.

Forte, E. (2010). Examining the assumptions underlying the NCLB federal accountability policy on school improvement. *Journal of Educational Psychology, 102*, 76–88.

Frisbie, D. A., & Waltman, K. K. (1992). Developing a personal grading plan. *Educational Measurement: Issues and Practice, 11*(3), 35–42. Reprinted in K. M. Cauley, F. Linder, & J. H. McMillan (Eds.), (1994), *Educational psychology 94/95*. Guilford, CT: Dushkin.

Garcia, E. E. (2005, April). *Any test in English is a test of English: Implications for high stakes testing*. Paper presented at the annual meeting of the American Educational Research Association, Montreal, Canada.

García, G. E., & Pearson, P. D. (1994). Assessment and diversity. In L. Darling-Hammond (Ed.), *Review of research in education* (Vol. 20, pp. 337–391). Washington, DC: American Educational Research Association.

Gilpin, L. (1968). *The enduring Navaho*. Austin, TX: University of Texas Press.

Good, C., Aronson, J., & Inzlicht, M. (2003). Improving adolescents' standardized test performance: An intervention to reduce the effects of stereotype threat. *Journal of Applied Developmental Psychology, 24*, 645–662.

Gottfried, A. E., Fleming, J. S., & Gottfried, A. W. (1994). Role of parental motivational practices in children's academic intrinsic motivation and achievement. *Journal of Educational Psychology, 86*, 104–113.

Graham, S., & Golen, S. (1991). Motivational influences on cognition: Task involvement, ego involvement, and depth of information processing. *Journal of Educational Psychology, 83*, 187–194.

Gregg, N. (2009). *Adolescents and adults with learning disabilities and ADHD: Assessment and accommodation.* New York, NY: Guilford.

Haertel, E., & Linn, R. (1996). Comparability. In G. Phillips (Ed.), *Technical issues in large-scale performance assessment* (pp. 59–78). Washington, DC: National Center for Education Statistics.

Halpern, D. F., Benbow, C. P., Geary, D. C., Gur, R. C., Hyde, J. S., & Gernsbacher, M. A. (2007). The science of sex differences in science and mathematics. *Psychological Science in the Public Interest, 8*(1), 1–51.

Haywood, H. C., & Lidz, C. S. (2007). *Dynamic assessment in practice: Clinical and educational applications.* Cambridge, England: Cambridge University Press.

Heath, S. B. (1989). Oral and literate traditions among black Americans living in poverty. *American Psychologist, 44,* 367–373.

Ho, A. D. (2008). The problem with "proficiency": Limitations of statistics and policy under No Child Left Behind. *Educational Researcher, 37,* 351–360.

Holme, J. J., Richards, M. P., Jimerson, J. B., & Cohen, R. W. (2010). Assessing the effects of high school exit examinations. *Review of Educational Research, 80,* 476–526.

Humphry, S. M., & Heldsinger, S. A. (2014). Common structural design features of rubrics can represent a threat to validity. *Educational Researcher, 43,* 253–263.

Hursh, D. (2007). Assessing No Child Left Behind and the rise of neoliberal education policies. *American Educational Research Journal, 44,* 493–518.

Jennings, J. L., & Bearak, J. M. (2014). "Teaching to the test" in the NCLB era: How test predictability affects our understanding of student performance. *Educational Researcher, 43,* 381–389.

Johnson, R. L., Penny, J. A., & Gordon, B. (2009). *Assessing performance: Designing, scoring, and validating performance tasks.* New York, NY: Guilford.

Johnson, R. S., Mims-Cox, J. S., & Doyle-Nichols, A. (2006). *Developing portfolios in education: A guide to reflection, inquiry, and assessment.* Thousand Oaks, CA: Sage.

Jones, M. G., Jones, B. D., & Hargrove, T. Y. (2003). *The unintended consequences of high-stakes testing.* Lanham, MD: Rowman & Littlefield.

Kieffer, M. J., Lesaux, N. K., Rivera, M., & Francis, D. J. (2009). Accommodations for English language learners taking large-scale assessments: A meta-analysis on effectiveness and validity. *Review of Educational Research, 79,* 1168–1201.

Kuhn, D. (2001). How do people know? *Psychological Science, 12,* 1–8.

Kumar, R., Gheen, M. H., & Kaplan, A. (2002). Goal structures in the learning environment and students' disaffection from learning and schooling. In C. Midgley (Ed.), *Goals, goal structures, and patterns of adaptive learning* (pp. 143–173). Mahwah, NJ: Erlbaum.

La Guardia, J. G., (2009). Developing who I am: A self-determination theory approach to the establishment of healthy identities. *Educational Psychologist, 44,* 90–104.

La Paro, K. M., & Pianta, R. C. (2000). Predicting children's competence in the early school years: A meta-analytic review. *Review of Educational Research, 70,* 443–484.

Lester, F. K., Jr., Lambdin, D. V., & Preston, R. V. (1997). A new vision of the nature and purposes of assessment in the mathematics classroom. In G. D. Phye (Ed.), *Handbook of classroom assessment: Learning, achievement, and adjustment* (pp. 287–319). San Diego, CA: Academic Press.

Leu, D. J., O'Byrne, W. I., Zawilinski, L., McVerry, J. G., & Everett-Cacopardo, H. (2009). Expanding the new literacies conversation. *Educational Researcher, 38,* 264–269.

Lidz, C. S. (1991). Issues in the assessment of preschool children. In B. A. Bracken (Ed.), *The psychoeducational assessment of preschool children* (2nd ed., pp. 18–31). Boston, MA: Allyn & Bacon.

Mastropieri, M. A., & Scruggs, T. E. (2007). *The inclusive classroom: Strategies for effective instruction* (3rd ed.). Upper Saddle River, NJ: Merrill/Prentice Hall.

McCaffrey, D. F., Lockwood, J. R., Koretz, D. M., & Hamilton, L. S. (2003). *Evaluating value-added models for teacher accountability.* Santa Monica, CA: RAND Corporation. Retrieved from http://www.rand.org/content/dam/rand/pubs/monographs/2004/RAND_MG158.pdf

Mercer, C. D., & Pullen, P. C. (2005). *Students with learning disabilities* (6th ed.). Upper Saddle River, NJ: Merrill/Prentice Hall.

Messick, S. (1983). Assessment of children. In W. Kessen (Ed.), *Handbook of child psychology* (Vol. 1, pp. 477–526). New York, NY: Wiley.

Meyer, M. S. (2000). The ability-achievement discrepancy: Does it contribute to an understanding of learning disabilities? *Educational Psychology Review, 12,* 315–337.

Miller, M. D., Linn, R. L., & Gronlund, N. E. (2009). *Measurement and assessment in teaching* (10th ed.). Upper Saddle River, NJ: Merrill/Pearson.

Mintrop, H., & Sunderman, G. L. (2009). Predictable failure of federal sanctions-driven accountability for school improvement—And why we may retain it anyway. *Educational Researcher, 38,* 353–364.

Nez, C., with Avila, J. S. (2011). *Code talker.* New York, NY: Berkley.

Nichols, P. D., & Mittelholtz, D. J. (1997). Constructing the concept of aptitude: Implications for the assessment of analogical reasoning. In G. D. Phye (Ed.), *Handbook of academic learning: Construction of knowledge* (pp. 128–147). San Diego, CA: Academic Press.

Nitko, A. J., & Brookhart, S. M. (2011). *Educational assessment of students* (6th ed.). Boston, MA: Pearson/Allyn & Bacon.

O'Connor, K. (2011). *A repair kit for grading: 15 fixes for broken grades* (2nd ed.). Boston, MA: Pearson Assessment Training Institute.

Osborne, J. W., Tillman, D., & Holland, A. (2010). Stereotype threat and anxiety for disadvantaged minorities and women. In J. C. Cassady (Ed.), *Anxiety in schools: The causes, consequences, and solutions for academic anxieties* (pp. 119–136). New York, NY: Peter Lang.

Padilla, A. M. (2006). Second language learning: Issues in research and teaching. In P. A. Alexander & P. H. Winne (Eds.), *Handbook of educational psychology* (2nd ed., pp. 571–591). Mahwah, NJ: Erlbaum.

Padilla-Walker, L. M. (2006). The impact of daily extra credit quizzes on exam performance. *Teaching of Psychology, 33,* 236–239.

Paris, S. G., Lawton, T. A., Turner, J. C., & Roth, J. L. (1991). A developmental perspective on standardized achievement testing. *Educational Researcher, 20*(5), 12–20, 40.

Parker, W. D. (1997). An empirical typology of perfectionism in academically talented children. *American Educational Research Journal, 34,* 545–562.

Pattison, E., Grodsky, E., & Muller, C. (2013). Is the sky falling? Grade inflation and the signaling power of grades. *Educational Researcher, 42,* 259–265.

Paulson, F. L., Paulson, P. R., & Meyer, C. A. (1991). What makes a portfolio a portfolio? *Educational Leadership, 49*(5), 60–63.

Perkins, D., Tishman, S., Ritchhart, R., Donis, K., & Andrade, A. (2000). Intelligence in the wild: A dispositional view of intellectual traits. *Educational Psychology Review, 12,* 269–293.

Petersen, G. A., Sudweeks, R. R., & Baird, J. H. (1990, April). *Test-wise responses of third-, fifth-, and sixth-grade students to clued and unclued multiple-choice science items.* Paper presented at the annual meeting of the American Educational Research Association, Boston, MA.

Phillips, B. N., Pitcher, G. D., Worsham, M. E., & Miller, S. C. (1980). Test anxiety and the school environment. In I. G. Sarason (Ed.), *Test anxiety: Theory, research, and applications.* Mahwah, NJ: Erlbaum.

Piirto, J. (1999). *Talented children and adults: Their development and education* (2nd ed.). Upper Saddle River, NJ: Merrill/Prentice Hall.

Pitoniak, M. J., & Royer, J. M. (2001). Testing accommodations for examinees with disabilities: A review of psychometric, legal, and social policy issues. *Review of Educational Research, 71,* 53–104.

Plank, S. B., & Condliffe, B. F. (2013). Pressures of the season: An examination of classroom quality and high-stakes accountability. *American Educational Research Journal, 50,* 1152–1182.

Plunk, A. D., Tate, W. F., Bierut, L. J., & Grucza, R. A. (2014). Intended and unintended effects of state-mandated high school science and mathematics course graduation requirements on educational attainment. *Educational Researcher, 43,* 230–241.

Polikoff, M. S., McEachin, A. J., Wrabel, S. L., & Duque, M. (2014). The waive of the future? School accountability in the waiver era. *Educational Researcher, 43,* 45–54.

Popham, W. J. (2014). *Classroom assessment: What teachers need to know* (7th ed.). Upper Saddle River, NJ: Pearson.

Porter, A. C., & Polikoff, M. S. (2007). NCLB: State interpretations, early effects, and suggestions for reauthorization. *Social Policy Report, 21*(4) (Society for Research in Child Development).

Pulfrey, C., Buchs, C., & Butera, F. (2011). Why grades engender performance-avoidance goals: The mediating role of autonomous motivation. *Journal of Educational Psychology, 103,* 683–700.

Putwain, D. W. (2007). Test anxiety in UK schoolchildren: Prevalence and demographic patterns. *British Journal of Educational Psychology, 77,* 579–593.

Quellmalz, E. S., Davenport, J. L., Timms, M. J., DeBoer, G. E., Jordan, K. A., Huang, C.-W., & Buckley, B. C. (2013). Next-generation environments for assessing and promoting complex science learning. *Journal of Educational Psychology, 105,* 1100–1114.

Reddy, Y. M., & Andrade, H. (2010). A review of rubric use in higher education. *Assessment and Evaluation in Higher Education, 35,* 435–448.

Ricks, J. H. (1959). On telling parents about test results. *Test Service Bulletin* (No. 59). New York, NY: Psychological Corporation.

Robinson, J. P. (2010). The effects of test translation on young English learners' mathematics performance. *Educational Researcher, 39,* 582–590.

Robinson, J. P., & Lubienski, S. T. (2011). The development of gender achievement gaps in mathematics and reading during elementary and middle school: Examining direct cognitive assessments and teacher ratings. *American Educational Research Journal, 48,* 268–302.

Rogoff, B. (2003). *The cultural nature of human development.* Oxford, England: Oxford University Press.

Ryan, R. M., & Brown, K. W. (2005). Legislating competence: High-stakes testing policies and their relations with psychological theories and research. In A. J. Elliot & C. S. Dweck (Eds.), *Handbook of competence and motivation* (pp. 354–372). New York, NY: Guilford.

Sanders, C. E. (1997). Assessment during the preschool years. In G. D. Phye (Ed.), *Handbook of classroom assessment: Learning, achievement, and adjustment* (pp. 227–264). San Diego, CA: Academic Press.

Sarason, I. G. (Ed.). (1980). *Test anxiety: Theory, research, and applications.* Mahwah, NJ: Erlbaum.

Sattler, J. M. (2001). *Assessment of children: Cognitive applications* (4th ed.). San Diego, CA: Author.

Sax, G. (2010). *Principles of educational and psychological measurement and evaluation* (4th ed.). Belmont, CA: Wadsworth.

Scruggs, T. E., & Lifson, S. A. (1985). Current conceptions of test-wiseness: Myths and realities. *School Psychology Review, 14,* 339–350.

Shepard, L., Hammerness, K., Darling-Hammond, L., & Rust, F. (with Snowden, J. B., Gordon, E., Gutierrez, C., & Pacheco, A.). (2005). Assessment. In L. Darling-Hammond & J. Bransford (Eds.), *Preparing teachers for a changing world: What teachers should learn and be able to do* (pp. 275–326). San Francisco, CA: Jossey-Bass/Wiley.

Shih, S.-S., & Alexander, J. M. (2000). Interacting effects of goal setting and self- or other-referenced feedback on children's development of self-efficacy and cognitive skill within the Taiwanese classroom. *Journal of Educational Psychology, 92,* 536–543.

Siskin, L. S. (2003). When an irresistible force meets an immovable object: Core lessons about high schools and accountability. In M. Carnoy, R. Elmore, & L. S. Siskin (Eds.), *The new accountability: High schools and high-stakes testing* (pp. 175–194). New York, NY: RoutledgeFalmer.

Smith, J. L. (2004). Understanding the process of stereotype threat: A review of mediational variables and new performance goal directions. *Educational Psychology Review, 16,* 177–206.

Solórzano, R. W. (2008). High stakes testing: Issues, implications, and remedies for English language learners. *Educational Researcher, 78,* 260–329.

Spandel, V. (1997). Reflections on portfolios. In G. D. Phye (Ed.), *Handbook of academic learning: Construction of knowledge* (pp. 573–591). San Diego, CA: Academic Press.

Stein, J. A., & Krishnan, K. (2007). Nonverbal learning disabilities and executive function: The challenges of effective assessment and teaching. In L. Meltzer (Ed.), *Executive function in education: From theory to practice* (pp. 106–132). New York, NY: Guilford.

Sternberg, R. J. (2002). Raising the achievement of all students: Teaching for successful intelligence. *Educational Psychology Review, 14,* 383–393.

Stiggins, R. J., & Chappuis, J. (2012). *An introduction to student-involved assessment FOR learning* (6th ed.). Boston, MA: Pearson Assessment Training Institute.

Stipek, D. J. (1996). Motivation and instruction. In D. C. Berliner & R. C. Calfee (Eds.), *Handbook of educational psychology* (pp. 85–113). New York, NY: Macmillan.

Stipek, D. J. (2002). At what age should children enter kindergarten? A question for policy makers and parents. *Social Policy Report of the Society for Research in Child Development, 16*(2), 3–16.

Stringfield, S. C., & Yakimowski-Srebnick, M. E. (2005). Promise, progress, problems, and paradoxes of three phases of accountability: A longitudinal case study of the Baltimore City Public Schools. *American Educational Research Journal, 42,* 43–75.

Südkamp, A., Kaiser, J., & Möller, J. (2012). Accuracy of teachers' judgments of students' academic achievement: A meta-analysis. *Journal of Educational Psychology, 104,* 743–762.

Thomas, R. M. (2005). *High-stakes testing: Coping with collateral damage.* Mahwah, NJ: Erlbaum.

Thomas, S., & Oldfather, P. (1997). Intrinsic motivations, literacy, and assessment practices: "That's my grade. That's me." *Educational Psychologist, 32,* 107–123.

Turnbull, A. P., Turnbull, R., & Wehmeyer, M. L. (2010). *Exceptional lives: Special education in today's schools* (6th ed.). Upper Saddle River, NJ: Merrill.

Turner, J. C., Meyer, D. K., Cox, K. E., Logan, C., DiCintio, M., & Thomas, C. T. (1998). Creating contexts for involvement in mathematics. *Journal of Educational Psychology, 90,* 730–745.

Tyler, K. M., Uqdah, A. L., Dillihunt, M. L., Beatty-Hazelbaker, R., Connor, T., Gadson, N., . . . Stevens, R. (2008). Cultural discontinuity: Toward a quantitative investigation of a major hypothesis in education. *Educational Researcher, 37,* 280–297.

Valla, J. M., & Ceci, S. J. (2011). Can sex differences in science be tied to the long reach of prenatal hormones? Brain organization theory, digit ratio (2D/4D), and sex differences in preferences and cognition. *Perspectives in Psychological Science, 6,* 134–146.

Valli, L., & Buese, D. (2007). The changing roles of teachers in an era of high-stakes accountability. *American Educational Research Journal, 44,* 519–558.

Venn, J. J. (2000). *Assessing students with special needs* (2nd ed.). Upper Saddle River, NJ: Merrill/Prentice Hall.

Vucko, S., & Hadwin, A. (April, 2004). *Going beyond* I like it *in a portfolio context: Scaffolding the development of six grade-two students' reflections.* Paper presented at the American Educational Research Association, San Diego, CA.

Walton, G. M., & Spencer, S. J. (2009). Latent ability: Grades and test scores systematically underestimate intellectual ability of negatively stereotyped students. *Psychological Science, 20,* 1132–1139.

Wang, M.-T., & Holcombe, R. (2010). Adolescents' perceptions of school environment, engagement, and academic achievement in middle school. *American Educational Research Journal, 47,* 633–662.

Whitaker Sena, J. D., Lowe, P. A., & Lee, S. W. (2007). Significant predictors of test anxiety among students with and without learning disabilities. *Journal of Learning Disabilities, 40,* 360–376.

Wodtke, K. H., Harper, F., & Schommer, M. (1989). How standardized is school testing? An exploratory observational study of standardized group testing in kindergarten. *Educational Evaluation and Policy Analysis, 11,* 223–235.

Wright, W. E. (2006). A catch–22 for language learners. *Educational Leadership*, 64(3), 22–27.

Zwick, R., & Sklar, J. C. (2005). Predicting college grades and degree completion using high school grades and SAT scores: The role of student ethnicity and first language. *American Educational Research Journal*, 42, 439–464.

APPENDIX A

Gottfried, A. E., Fleming, J. S., & Gottfried, A. W. (2001). Continuity of academic intrinsic motivation from childhood through late adolescence: A longitudinal study. *Journal of Educational Psychology, 93,* 3–13.

Janos, P. M., & Robinson, N. M. (1985). Psychosocial development in intellectually gifted children. In F. D. Horowitz & M. O'Brien (Eds.), *The gifted and talented: Developmental perspectives* (pp. 149–196). Washington, DC: American Psychological Association.

Marsh, H. W., Gerlach, E., Trautwein, U., Lüdtke, O., & Brettschneider, W.-D. (2007). Longitudinal study of preadolescent sport self-concept and performance: Reciprocal effects and causal ordering. *Child Development, 78,* 1640–1656.

McGrew, K. S., Flanagan, D. P., Zeith, T. Z., & Vanderwood, M. (1997). Beyond *g:* The impact of *Gf–Gc* specific cognitive abilities research on the future use and interpretation of intelligence tests in the schools. *School Psychology Review, 26,* 189–210.

Name Index

Abaied, J., 384
Abbott, R. D., 120, 267, 269
Abelev, M. S., 473
Aber, J. L., 69
Ablard, K. E., 381
Aboud, F. E., 120
Abrami, P. C., 341, 416, 443
Abrams, E., 339
Abramson, Y. L., 378
Abuhamdeh, S., 362
Accardo, P. J., 149
Achilles, C. M., 445
Ackerman, P. L., 131, 138
Adalbjarnardottir, S., 76
Adam, I., 406
Adam, S., 108
Adams, R. S., 79
Adelgais, A., 222, 447
Adesope, O. O., 51, 187, 263
Adger, C. T., 50, 100, 102, 103,
    104, 111, 472, 570
Adolphs, R., 398
Afflerbach, P., 223, 242, 269,
    274, 283, 432, 528
Agarwal, P. K., 216, 506, 533
Aharon-Kraversky, S., 279, 400
Ahearn, W. H., 306
Ahmed, W., 400
Ahn, H. J., 473
Aikens, N. L., 120
Aikins, J. W., 342
Ainge, D., 483
Ainley, J., 367
Ainley, M., 367, 368
Ainsworth, M. D. S., 58
Airasian, P. W., 426, 551
Aitchison, J., 50
Ajzen, I., 379
Aksan, N., 59
Albanese, A. L., 125, 350, 429
Alberg, S. R., 298
Alberstadt, A. L., 147
Albert, D., 71
Alberto, P. A., 302, 311
Aldrich, N. J., 439
Alemán, A. M. M., 66
Alessandri, S. M., 88
Aleven, V., 223, 433
Alexander, A. L., 150
Alexander, E. S., 383
Alexander, J. F., 436
Alexander, J. L., 343
Alexander, J. M., 337, 341,
    368, 389, 550
Alexander, P. A., 182, 191, 198,
    216, 220, 221, 222, 223,
    229, 267, 274, 368, 381,
    383, 391, 400
Alfassi, M., 272, 438
Alfieri, L., 439
Alford, G. S., 332
Algozzine, B., 166
Alibali, M. W., 250, 274
Alim, H. S., 102, 369
Allday, R. A., 460
Alleman, J., 108, 184, 253,
    283, 368, 415, 428,
    429, 527
Allen, B. A., 109, 195
Allen, J., 164, 374, 397, 460
Allen, J. P., 59, 67, 70, 74, 125
Allen, L., 69

Allison, K. W., 110
Allor, J. H., 446
Alloway, T. P., 146, 206, 207
Almeida, D. M., 70
Altermatt, E. R., 70
Altermatt, E. R., 114, 117,
    406
Altmann, E. M., 204
Altschul, I., 69
Alvarez, P., 181
Alves, R. A., 202, 268
Amabile, T. M., 237, 238, 239,
    239, 371
Ambrose, D., 164
American Educational Research
    Association, 240
American Educational Research
    Association, American
    Psychological Association,
    & National Council
    on Measurement in
    Education, 571
American Friends of Tel Aviv
    University, 117
American Psychiatric
    Association, 145, 149,
    155
American Psychological
    Association, 119, 123
American Psychological
    Association Zero
    Tolerance Task Force, 303
American Statistical
    Association, 568
Ameringer, S. W., 70
Ames, C., 367, 465, 550
Amlund, J. T., 216, 217
Amorosi, S., 116
Amsterlaw, J., 241
Ancess, J., 526, 555
Anderman, E. M., 105, 116,
    125, 300, 304, 363, 365,
    370, 373, 381, 382, 390,
    396, 397, 401, 404,
    405, 460, 463, 502, 548,
    566, 568
Anderman, L. H., 69, 105, 125,
    300, 304, 339, 359, 374,
    379, 381, 384, 396, 397,
    460, 463, 523
Andersen, C., 216, 219
Andersen, J., 26
Anderson, C., 196, 199
Anderson, C. A., 77, 329
Anderson, C. J., 381
Anderson, D. R., 330
Anderson, J. R., 181, 182,
    185, 186, 189, 191, 202,
    227, 427
Anderson, L. W., 125, 261,
    419, 421
Anderson, M. C., 201
Anderson, R. C., 45, 100, 191,
    192, 242, 258, 330, 368,
    425, 434, 436
Anderson, V., 217
Andiliou, A ., 197
Andrade, A., 139, 558
Andrade, H., 543
Andrade, H. L., 503, 504,
    506, 507
Andre, T., 216, 221, 367

Andreas, J. B., 77, 493
Andrew-Ihrke, D., 108
Andrews, G., 35, 275
Andrews-Weckerly, S., 272
Andriessen, I., 388
Andriessen, J., 45, 254
Andrzejewski, C. E., 374, 397,
    460
Angold, A., 153
Annahatak, B., 103
Ansary, N. S., 82
Anthony, G., 256, 435, 450
Anthony, J. L., 267, 269
Antonishak, J., 67, 70, 74, 125
Anzai, Y., 233
Apfel, N., 367
Appel, J. B., 313
Apperly, I. A., 35
Applebee, A. N., 434, 435
Applegate, B., 149
Aragon, S. R., 73
Arbeau, K. A., 42, 80
Arbib, M., 328
Arbreton, A. J., 124
Arbuthnot, K., 386
Arbuthnott, K. D., 5, 139
Archambault, I., 367, 389
Archer, J., 79, 114
Ardoin, S. P., 311
Arens, A. K., 62
Arici, A., 441
Arlin, M., 451
Arnesen, T., 265
Arnett, J. J., 403
Arnold, D. H., 367
Aronson, E., 444
Aronson, J., 110, 376, 387,
    406, 570
Arroyo, I., 117, 236, 433
Arseneault, L., 462
Arter, J. A., 505, 554, 555
Asaro-Saddler, K., 351
Ash, D., 44
Ashby, R., 280
Ashcraft, M. H., 401, 403
Asher, S. R., 73, 74, 78, 385,
    490
Ashiabi, G. S., 120, 407
Ashley, E., 190
Ashman, A. D., 444
Ashman, A. F., 369
Ashurst, N., 78
Asoko, H., 197
Aspinwall, L. G., 446
Assor, A., 335, 376, 381
Astington, J. W., 216
Astor, R. A., 110, 490, 492
Atance, C. M., 299, 300
Atkins, R., 60
Atkins, S. M., 174, 178
Atkinson, R. C., 176
Atkinson, R. K., 187, 189,
    195, 276
Atran, S., 106, 206, 259
Attanucci, J., 88
Attie, I., 117
Au, K. H., 104, 109
Au, W., 566
Audley-Piotrowski, S. R., 70
Aulls, M. W., 426, 436
Aunio, P., 123
Aunola, K., 59, 70, 116, 403

Auster, C. J., 117
Austin, J. L., 312
Ausubel, D. P., 193, 424, 449
Auyeung, B., 115
Avni-Babad, D., 467
Ayres, K. M., 166, 343
Ayres, L. R., 344, 507
Azano, A. P., 164
Azevedo, R., 222, 223, 267,
    273, 346, 405, 416,
    432, 433
Azrin, N. H., 297, 313
Azuma, M., 388

Babad, E., 393, 467
Bacalleo, M. L., 69
Bacon, S., 159
Baddeley, A. D., 178, 181
Baek, J. Y., 196, 265
Baer, D. M., 300, 301
Baer, J., 192, 238
Baglieri, S., 81
Bagwell, C. L., 71
Bailey, A. L., 102
Bailey, C., 207
Bailey, D. H., 284
Bailey, J. S., 303
Baines, D., 114
Baird, D., 234
Baird, J. H., 532, 561
Bajaj, A., 220
Bak, N., 351
Bakeman, R., 406
Baker, E. L., 267, 568
Baker, J., 467
Baker, L., 218, 267, 479
Baker, R., 223, 433
Baker, S. A., 462
Bakermans-Kranenebrug,
    M. J., 59
Bakken, J. P., 70
Balfanz, R., 123, 124, 566
Ballenger, C., 319
Ballou, D., 566, 568
Bandura, A., 66, 83, 115,
    116, 324, 325, 328,
    329, 330, 331, 333,
    334, 335, 336, 337,
    338, 339, 340, 342,
    345, 351, 352, 366,
    467
Bangert-Drowns, R. L., 186,
    216, 298, 431
Banich, M., 67, 178
Banks, C. A. M., 64, 105
Banks, J., 107, 259
Banks, J. A., 64, 105, 206
Banks, W. P., 201
Bannan-Ritland, B., 196, 265
Banta, T. W., 555
Bao, X., 374, 375
Barab, S. A., 5, 260, 369, 441
Barakat, M. M., 486
Barbaranelli, C., 83, 115, 334
Barbarin, O., 111, 120
Barber, B. K., 59
Barber, B. L., 124
Barbetta, P. M., 318
Barbey, A., 182
Barchfeld, P., 278
Barker, E. D., 73
Barker, E. T., 70

Barkley, R. A., 129, 149, 150,
    207, 303, 473, 474,
    537, 572
Barnes, C. D., 78, 490
Barnes, M. A., 148, 207, 351,
    452
Barnet, R. C., 292
Barnett, J. E., 214, 216, 222
Barnett, M., 261
Barnett, P. A., 346
Barnett, S. M., 227, 229
Barnett, W. S., 42, 416
Baron, M. A., 528
Baroody, A. J., 189, 191, 193,
    274, 440
Barrera, M., Jr., 59
Barrett, A. M., 190
Barrish, H. H., 307
Barrois, L., 349
Barron, B., 70, 234, 367, 368,
    373
Barron, E., 177
Barrouillet, P., 179
Barsalou, L. W., 182
Barth, A. E., 269
Bartholow, B. D., 329
Bartini, M., 78
Bartlett, F. C., 257, 258
Bartolomucci, C. L., 78
Barton, A. C., 195
Barton, K. C., 280, 281
Baruth, L. G., 60
Barzillai, M., 216, 217
Basinger, K. S., 71
Bassett, D. S., 144, 161, 285
Bassok, M., 228
Bastian, K. C., 14
Bates, J. E., 60, 76, 349
Bates, S. L., 329
Batsche, C., 329
Batson, 91, 83, 87
Batson, C. D., 87
Battin-Pearson, S., 124
Battistich, V., 363, 390, 450,
    463, 475
Battle, A., 114, 461
Bauer, P. J., 181, 204
Baugh, J., 102
Baum, K., 490
Baumeister, R. F., 63, 77, 205
Baumert, J., 15, 136, 368, 429
Baumrind, D., 59
Baxter, G. P., 526, 528
Bay-Hinitz, A. K., 310
Baynham, T. Y., 295
Beal, C. R., 236, 433
Bearak, J. M., 566
Beardsley, P. M., 198
Beauchaine, T. P., 149, 154
Beaudin, B. Q., 475
Beaulieu, L., 306, 348
Bebeau, M., 87
Bebko, J. M., 35
Beck, I. L., 218, 222, 268, 280,
    425, 436
Beck, S. R., 35
Becker, B. E., 119, 124, 391,
    407, 473
Becker, B. J., 190
Becker, M., 136, 362

Subject Index